Planning and Implementing Resource Discovery Tools in Academic Libraries

Mary Pagliero Popp
Indiana University, USA

Diane Dallis
Indiana University, USA

A volume in the Advances in Library and Information Science (ALIS) Book Series

Managing Director:	Lindsay Johnston
Senior Editorial Director:	Heather A. Probst
Book Production Manager:	Sean Woznicki
Development Manager:	Joel Gamon
Development Editor:	Hannah Abelbeck
Assistant Acquisitions Editor:	Kayla Wolfe
Typesetter:	Milan Vracarich, Jr.
Cover Design:	Nick Newcomer

Published in the United States of America by
Information Science Reference (an imprint of IGI Global)
701 E. Chocolate Avenue
Hershey PA 17033
Tel: 717-533-8845
Fax: 717-533-8661
E-mail: cust@igi-global.com
Web site: http://www.igi-global.com

Library of Congress Cataloging-in-Publication Data

Planning and implementing resource discovery tools in academic libraries / Mary Pagliero Popp and Diane Dallis, editors.
      pages cm
   Summary: "This book addresses the many new resource discovery tools and products in existence as well as their potential uses and applications"--Provided by publisher.
   Includes bibliographical references and index.
   ISBN 978-1-4666-1821-3 (hardcover) -- ISBN 978-1-4666-1822-0 (ebook) (print) -- ISBN 978-1-4666-1823-7 (print & perpetual access) (print) 1. Online library catalogs. 2. Federated searching. 3. Library web sites. 4. Library catalogs and users. 5. Information behavior. 6. Academic libraries--United States--Case studies. 7. Academic libraries--Canada--Case studies. I. Popp, Mary Pagliero, 1949- II. Dallis, Diane, 1971-
   Z699.35.C38P58 2012
   025.5'24--dc23
                              2012003667

This book is published in the IGI Global book series Advances in Library and Information Science (ALIS) Book Series (ISSN: 2326-4136; eISSN: 2326-4144)

British Cataloguing in Publication Data
A Cataloguing in Publication record for this book is available from the British Library.

Advances in Library and Information Science (ALIS) Book Series

ISSN: 2326-4136
EISSN: 2326-4144

MISSION

The **Advances in Library and Information Science (ALIS)** book series is comprised of high quality, research-oriented publications on the continuing developments and trends affecting the public, school, and academic fields, as well as specialized libraries and librarians globally. These discussions on professional and organizational considerations in library and information resource development and management assist in showcasing the latest methodologies and tools in the field.

The ALIS book series aims to expand the body of library science literature by covering a wide range of topics affecting the profession and field at large. The series also seeks to provide readers with an essential resource for uncovering the latest research in library and information science management, development, and technologies.

COVERAGE

- Academic libraries in the digital age
- Blogging in libraries
- Cataloging and classification
- Collection development
- Community outreach
- Digital literacy
- Ethical practices in libraries
- Green libraries
- Librarian education
- Mobile library services
- Remote access technologies
- University libraries in developing countries

IGI Global is currently accepting manuscripts for publication within this series. To submit a proposal for a volume in this series, please contact our Acquisition Editors at Acquisitions@igi-global.com or visit: http://www.igi-global.com/publish/.

The Advances in Library and Information Science (ALIS) Book Series (ISSN 2326-4136) is published by IGI Global, 701 E. Chocolate Avenue, Hershey, PA 17033-1240, USA, www.igi-global.com. This series is composed of titles available for purchase individually; each title is edited to be contextually exclusive from any other title within the series. For pricing and ordering information please visit http://www.igi-global.com/book-series/advances-library-information-science-alis/73002. Postmaster: Send all address changes to above address. Copyright © 2012 IGI Global. All rights, including translation in other languages reserved by the publisher. No part of this series may be reproduced or used in any form or by any means – graphics, electronic, or mechanical, including photocopying, recording, taping, or information and retrieval systems – without written permission from the publisher, except for non commercial, educational use, including classroom teaching purposes. The views expressed in this series are those of the authors, but not necessarily of IGI Global.

Titles in this Series

For a list of additional titles in this series, please visit: www.igi-global.com

Recent Developments in the Design, Construction, and Evaluation of Digital Libraries Case Studies
Colleen Cool (Graduate School of Library and Information Studies, Queens College, USA) and Kwong Bor Ng
(Queens College, CUNY, USA)
Information Science Reference • copyright 2013 • 275pp • H/C (ISBN: 9781466629912) • US $175.00 (our price)

Design, Development, and Management of Resources for Digital Library Services
Tariq Ashraf (University of Delhi, India) and Puja Anand Gulati (University of Delhi, India)
Information Science Reference • copyright 2013 • 438pp • H/C (ISBN: 9781466625006) • US $175.00 (our price)

Public Law Librarianship Objectives, Challenges, and Solutions
Laurie Selwyn (Law Librarian [Ret.], USA) and Virginia Eldridge (Grayson County, Texas Law Library, USA)
Information Science Reference • copyright 2013 • 341pp • H/C (ISBN: 9781466621848) • US $175.00 (our price)

Library Collection Development for Professional Programs Trends and Best Practices
Sara Holder (McGill University, Canada)
Information Science Reference • copyright 2013 • 504pp • H/C (ISBN: 9781466618978) • US $175.00 (our price)

Library Automation and OPAC 2.0 Information Access and Services in the 2.0 Landscape
Jesus Tramullas (University of Zaragoza, Spain) and Piedad Garrido (University of Zaragoza, Spain)
Information Science Reference • copyright 2013 • 409pp • H/C (ISBN: 9781466619128) • US $175.00 (our price)

Planning and Implementing Resource Discovery Tools in Academic Libraries
Mary Pagliero Popp (Indiana University, USA) and Diane Dallis (Indiana University, USA)
Information Science Reference • copyright 2012 • 342pp • H/C (ISBN: 9781466618213) • US $175.00 (our price)

Remote Access Technologies for Library Collections Tools for Library Users and Managers
Diane M. Fulkerson (University of South Florida Polytechnic Library, USA)
Information Science Reference • copyright 2012 • 232pp • H/C (ISBN: 9781466602342) • US $175.00 (our price)

Partnerships and Collaborations in Public Library Communities Resources and Solutions
Karen Ellis (Taylor Public Library, USA)
Information Science Reference • copyright 2012 • 254pp • H/C (ISBN: 9781613503874) • US $175.00 (our price)

E-Reference Context and Discoverability in Libraries Issues and Concepts
Sue Polanka (Wright State University, USA)
Information Science Reference • copyright 2012 • 294pp • H/C (ISBN: 9781613503089) • US $175.00 (our price)

www.igi-global.com

701 E. Chocolate Ave., Hershey, PA 17033
Order online at www.igi-global.com or call 717-533-8845 x100
To place a standing order for titles released in this series, contact: cust@igi-global.com
Mon-Fri 8:00 am - 5:00 pm (est) or fax 24 hours a day 717-533-8661

Editorial Advisory Board

Table of Contents

Section 1
Framework for Discovery

Section 2
Selecting a Discovery Tool

Section 3
The User Experience Part One: User Behavior and Expectations

Section 5
Implementation

Section 6
Discovery in the Wild: Representative Examples of Discovery Tools in Use

Section 7
Critique of Discovery

Foreword

The time is ripe for a thorough discussion of resource discovery tools in the academic library environment; and not merely an offering of practical advice on selection and implementation, but also a critical analysis of why such tools have gained importance in the marketplace, their affordances, and their limitations. Framing this discussion are two critical shifts in how academic libraries view the information discovery landscape, both driven by recent trends in user behavior and design practice, as well as the continuing development of the discovery tool market itself.

A move from the disjointed world of Online Public Access Catalogs (OPACs) and native database interfaces to the discovery layer represents a significant shift in focus from the primacy of content and its providers to that of the user and the needs of scholars. Changes in the expectations users bring to the discovery experience, brought on by faster, more satisfying interactions with mass market search engines (think Google) and the consumer Web (think Amazon), extend academic libraries' attention past content provision to ensuring that resources are easily discoverable and accessible within an increasingly networked scholarly life. This shift from content-centeredness to user-centeredness is abetted by the rise of user-centered design and usability assessment, which push academic libraries toward more flexible discovery environments featuring more agile architectures and continual cycles of innovation, testing, and improvement.

In the networked world, academic libraries must expand their conceptions of information discovery beyond the development and implementation of local tools by exposing their data to search engines and providing functional paths to local resources from the open Web, where scholars increasingly live, work, and initiate the discovery process. This shift in focus from local tools to the exposure of underlying data is amplified by a move by many academic libraries to decouple back-end inventory and data systems from end-user interfaces, in concept if not in practice. While functionality and cost remain major concerns, the quality of the data underlying a discovery platform has emerged as a key purchasing consideration. The emergence of flexible, open source front-end platforms (think Blacklight) fuels the schism between interface and infrastructure, leading many academic libraries to question long-standing vendor relationships and historical patterns of platform lock-in.

So, if discovery is now centered on the user and enabling data, how does an academic library work through the process of selecting, implementing, and assessing a resource discovery system? How does a library sort through the alternatives to find the best match for its distinctive operating environment, be it at a research university, a community college, or on a liberal arts campus? *Planning and Implementing Discovery Tools in Academic Libraries* is an important attempt to provide guidance for navigating these waters, delivering practical advice on selecting and implementing a discovery tool, as well as critical discussions of current offerings and the potential value implementing a discovery system might bring to an academic library and its users.

Damon E. Jaggars
Columbia University, United States

Damon E. Jaggars *is the Associate University Librarian for Collections & Services at the Columbia University Libraries, which includes administrative responsibility for the collections and services for fifteen library facilities as well as system-wide organizational assessment, communications, marketing, and access services functions. His research has focused on service quality assessment and emerging service models for research and teaching support, including a recently published study on the potential of the research library to positively affect retention and completion for humanities doctoral students. Prior to coming to Columbia, Damon served as Associate Director for User Services at the University of Texas at Austin Libraries.*

Preface

The old saying, "the times they are a-changing" certainly applies to academic libraries, librarians, and the users they serve. Changes in technology and responses to technology, search engines, social networking, and new habits have made an impact on the ways users connect to information.

Despite the large, recent changes in technology, some of these attitudes and habits are not new. The need for library instruction in locating appropriate sources for information has been acknowledged for hundreds of years (Lorenzen, 2001), beginning in Germany in the 17th to 19th centuries. What is new, however, is the fact that users now have far more choice in sources of information. The results of the two recent OCLC studies of information resource use (DeRosa, et al., 2005; 2010) indicate that nearly all users begin their searches with commercial search engines.

Connaway, Dickey, & Radford (2011) enjoin librarians to create or purchase systems that work similarly to Web search engines, because they are perceived as being both easy to use and convenient. They note that,

In order to entice people to use libraries and to change their perceptions of libraries, the library experience needs to become more like that available on the Web (e.g., Google, Amazon.com, and iTunes) and to be embedded in individual workflows. The Web environment is familiar to users, therefore, they are comfortable and confident in making the choice to search for information there. (p. 187)

They go on to say that "information seekers will readily sacrifice content for convenience. Convenience is thus one of the primary criteria used for making choices during the information seeking process" (p. 188).

The recent ERIAL (Ethnographic Research in Illinois Academic Libraries) study, a 5 institution ethnographic research study of undergraduates' search behavior in five Illinois academic libraries, supports the importance of modeling the library search experience on familiar Web sources and provides additional data. Librarians at Illinois Wesleyan University studied the way their students did research. In their description of the results, they note that "Google's simplicity and single search box seems to have created the expectation among students of a specific search experience in the library" (Asher & Duke, 2012, p. 72). The authors continue, "in comparison with the ease of the Google search experience, the various and fragmented catalogs, databases, and interfaces contained on a typical academic library's Web site are extremely complex." Their research showed that search is "a significant weakness" (p. 73) leading to anxiety and confusion; students experienced difficulties in selecting databases and creating effective searches. These results were also found in studies conducted at other ERIAL participating libraries. Asher and Duke posit that students' lack of understanding about effective ways to do library research "could possibly be viewed as a reasonable response to their successful experiences in utilizing the Internet to fulfill their information seeking needs, with little need to understand or investigate how search engines actually work" (p. 84).

As the authors in these chapters attest, resource discovery products, sometimes called Web-scale discovery, were developed to meet the needs of users for a simple search and the desires of librarians to present scholarly research in ways appropriate for today's user. There has always been a desire to identify good sources to be used by undergraduates, but focus groups of faculty and graduate students at Indiana University a few years ago stunned the librarians leading the discussions by the lack of knowledge exhibited, even by senior faculty members, of appropriate information resources in their fields. Resource discovery products have something for everyone.

RESOURCE DISCOVERY: WHAT IT IS NOW AND WHERE IT IS GOING?

Jason Vaughan has written widely about Web-scale resource discovery tools. He has defined resource discovery tools as having the following characteristics (Vaughan, 2011; 2012):

- Content harvested from locally hosted and remote repositories (including the library catalog) and added to a central index.
- Content from publishers and aggregators that is pre-indexed into the central index. This material includes journal articles, e-books, reports, and similar materials, both purchased and licensed.
- A Google-like search box providing a familiar search experience, along with advanced search tools.
- Fast and ranked (by relevancy, but also by other options) search results.
- The ability to use faceted navigation to narrow search results.

The Indiana University Bloomington Libraries have had experience with two resource discovery tools, WorldCat Local and EBSCO Discovery Services. We would expand Vaughan's brief mention of the topic of delivery to focus more specifically on ease of delivery. A Web-scale discovery service provides information on where to find print resources, direct links to freely available Web-based content, and immediate access to the full-text of subscription content available to library users, such as articles and e-books, through an Open URL link resolver.

Where do Next Generation Catalogs fit into this setting? In their general form, these catalogs do not fit into the definition of a resource discovery tool, because they only include the library catalog and, perhaps, locally created information sources. However, beginning in 2011 and continuing into 2012, new catalogs are being made available that combine an open source next generation catalog side-by-side with a resource discovery tool. This new development will be important to follow and will provide an alternative resource discovery experience. Three examples of such catalog/discovery tool combinations are:

- The VuFind catalog at Villanova University that has also incorporated Summon (https://library.villanova.edu/Find/Search/Home);
- The Blacklight catalog at the University of Virginia, combining the catalog and Primo Central. (http://search.lib.virginia.edu/)'

- The Columbia University information system (CLIO Beta) combining a Blacklight catalog with Summon (as of this writing, available at http://cliobeta.columbia.edu/).

In an article published in March 2012, Marshall Breeding challenges librarians and vendors to envision the future of discovery systems. His priorities include identifying ways to add content not yet available in discovery systems, continued work on relevancy algorithms, moving toward use of the discovery system as a Web site replacement for libraries, increasing social networking opportunities and, perhaps most intriguing, collection browsing (Breeding, 2012).

AN OVERVIEW OF THE CONTENT OF THIS BOOK

Planning and Implementing Resource Discovery Tools in Academic Libraries contains 7 sections, beginning with an overview of the issues and ending with a critique of the discovery tool.

Framework for Discovery sets the stage. It includes a literature review on information seeking among academic users, a review of the precursor to discovery tools, federated search, that reflects on the knowledge gained from that experience and the ways it informs selection of discovery tools, providing insights from the University of Florida, and an overview of the many issues surrounding planning, implementation, use, and maintenance of discovery tools.

In **Selecting a Discovery Tool**, the section begins with a description of a framework for evaluating discovery tools with a focus on involving library staff and other stakeholders used at the University of Nevada Las Vegas. Librarians from the University of South Florida describe the results of interviews with librarians from fifteen academic institutions who had selected a discovery service; librarians from Pennsylvania State University elucidate the Request for Proposal (RFP) process; and an article from Colorado State University, a medium-sized library, shares criteria for evaluation of discovery tools in a smaller setting. Librarians from the University of Chicago discuss the technical, functional, and usability layers that are important in evaluation of a tool.

Several libraries share their knowledge of user behavior in **The User Experience Part One: User Behavior and Expectations**. The section begins with a discussion of the role of serendipity in the research process and ways that discovery tools can support serendipity. Librarians from the University of Illinois discuss the results of their extensive transaction log analysis of the ways users search their Gateway. The University of Minnesota's research as part of a phased approach to discovery is explained, and its conclusions about discovery tools are presented. In a chapter about the methods used at the University of Michigan, the authors discuss persona analysis, surveys that included usability tests and guerilla usability. The last chapter in the section analyzes search results of actual user searches in both Google Scholar and Summon.

Researchers at the University of Baltimore begin the next section, **The User Experience Part Two: User Testing and User-Centered Design in Implementing Discovery Solutions**, discussing their tests of EBSCO Discovery Services, Primo from ExLibris, and Serials Solutions Summon in which they identified tasks that worked well for test participants and those that did not. Librarians at the University of Manitoba share the results of their user studies that showed Summon did make a difference in users' success. Librarians at Southern Illinois University Edwardsville talk about their work to make their Web site more effective through ongoing redesign and testing rather than purchase of a discovery tool. The section concludes with a description of user testing at the University of Southern California showing that users were more successful in completing basic research tasks after implementation of a discovery tool.

A variety of implementation issues is discussed in the **Implementation** section, including resource selection and configuration of the public interface with examples from Drake University; the development of an in-house discovery tool at the University of New Mexico; and lessons learned from a situation in which selection and implementation of a discovery tool were accomplished within a short window of time at the North Carolina Agricultural and Technical State University. Authors representing several universities share their work in embedding the discovery tool within such environments as a learning management system and an enterprise portal. Two chapters provide insight into discovery in a consortial environment; one discusses selection and implementation of a discovery tool in a 5-library consortium, while a second group of authors discuss reasons for library staff resistance to discovery tools gleaned from their research. Librarians from James Madison University provide tips for supporting organizational buy-in of the discovery tool through addressing specific staff concerns, providing training, and monitoring and assessing the discovery product's performance. A case study in marketing a new discovery system at American University, a study showing the impact of a discovery tool on collection use at the University of Texas at San Antonio, and research about the impact of discovery tools on cataloging maintenance and authority control round out the section.

Discovery in the Wild allows librarians from the U. S. and Europe to share their experiences in selecting and implementing a discovery product. Products discussed include EBSCO Discovery Service, Encore Synergy, Primo and Primo Central, Summon, and WorldCat Local.

Concluding the book is a section that offers a **Critique of Resource Discovery**. Chapters address the problems of next generation search tools and the challenges and opportunities of the metadata environment in the context of discovery tools. The last chapter in this section evaluates discovery tools in light of the needs of researchers in music.

CONCLUSION

This book had several goals:

- Propose a working definition of "resource discovery" that can be used in professional discussions about resource discovery products.
- Identify user behaviors based on empirical research that lead to a need for "resource discovery."
- Identify best practices for selecting a discovery tool.
- Identify best practices for setting up a discovery tool and making it available to users. Locate and share usability test results for resource discovery and related tools and their implementation into library products and services.
- Present representative examples of the implementation of discovery tools (based on the working definition) in libraries, particularly in academic settings. Give readers information about how the decision to implement was made, key decision points in setting up the discovery tool, presentation to users, user reactions, and the creation of tools in which the resource discovery tool can be incorporated into the places where users learn and do their research.
- Identify areas of concern in use of a resource discovery tool and suggest future enhancements.
- Provide an overview of the literature of discovery tools.

We believe that our colleagues who wrote the various chapters in this work have succeeded well in meeting these goals. We hope that you find their ideas and experiences helpful.

Diane Dallis
Indiana University, USA

Mary Pagliero Popp
Indiana University, USA

REFERENCES

Asher, A. D., & Duke, L. M. (2012). Searching for answers: Student research behavior at Illinois Wesleyan University . In Asher, A. D., & Duke, L. M. (Eds.), *College libraries and student culture: What we now know* (pp. 71–85). Chicago, IL: American Library Association.

Breeding, M. (2012). Looking forward to the next generation of discovery services. *Computers in Libraries, 32*(2), 28–21.

Connaway, L. S., Dickey, T. J., & Radford, M. L. (2011). "If it is too inconvenient I'm not going after it:" Convenience as a critical factor in information-seeking behaviors. *Library & Information Science Research, 33*(3), 179–190. doi:doi:10.1016/j.lisr.2010.12.002

De Rosa, C., Cantrell, J., Carlson, M., Gallagher, P., Hawk, J., & Sturtz, C. ...Olszewski, L. (2010). *Perceptions of libraries, 2010: Context and community.* Dublin, OH: OCLC. Retrieved from http://www.oclc.org/reports/2010perceptions.htm

De Rosa, C., Cantrell, J., Cellentani, D., Hawk, J., Jenkins, L., & Wilson, A. (2005). *Perceptions of libraries and information resources. A report to the OCLC membership.* Dublin, OH: OCLC Online Computer Library Center. Retrieved from http://www.oclc.org/reports/pdfs/Percept_all.pdf

Lorenzen, M. (2001). A brief history of library instruction in the United States of America. *Illinois Libraries, 83*(2), 8–18.

Vaughan, J. (2011). Web scale discovery what and why? *Library Technology Reports, 47*(1), 5–11.

Vaughan, J. (2012). Investigations into library Web-scale discovery services. *Information Technology and Libraries, 32*(1), 32–82.

Acknowledgment

The editors wish to acknowledge the individuals and organizations whose help and participation made the completion of this book possible.

Special thanks to the Editorial Advisory Board (EAB) members who spent many hours thoughtfully reviewing and providing feedback on numerous proposals and chapters. The EAB members were heavily consulted and insured the integrity and quality of this publication. The members include Kristine Brancolini, David Dahl, Courtney Greene, Sigrid Kelsey, Alesia McManus, Shane Nackerud, Billie Peterson-Lugo, Ken Varnum, and Scott Walter.

The editors are especially appreciative of the work of the graduate student Manuscript Assistants, Marissa Ellerman and Rachael Cohen who assisted greatly with preparation of the manuscript and final editing. Marissa and Rachael re-energized the editors in the last months of work and brought new perspective and enthusiasm to the topic. The quality of their work and their commitment to the project are worthy of special recognition.

The Indiana University Librarians Association (InULA) is thanked for their support in the form of a generous grant that funded the Manuscript Assistants salary. The editors are grateful for the support of their colleagues.

The editors wish to recognize the generous support of Indiana University Bloomington Libraries Administration and the Librarian Support Grant selection committee for the grant funding that also helped to fund the Manuscript Assistants.

The editors express their deepest gratitude for the understanding and support of Courtney Greene and Carolyn Walters, the editors' supervisors whose patience and flexibility enabled the completion of this book.

Finally, the editors share their sincerest gratitude for the kindness, generosity, and understanding of their families Johnny Popp, Garett Montanez, and James Dallis Montanez.

Diane Dallis
Indiana University, USA

Mary Pagliero Popp
Indiana University, USA

Section 1
Framework for Discovery

Chapter 1
Understanding Information Seeking Behavior of Faculty and Students:
A Review of the Literature

Nancy Falciani-White
Wheaton College, USA

ABSTRACT

This chapter reviews significant information seeking literature, focusing on general models that can provide a framework for those not familiar with the research in that area. It then explores models and characteristics that are unique to academic users, specifically undergraduate students, graduate students, and faculty members, highlighting similarities and differences among these groups of users. Changes to information seeking that have resulted from technological advances are also examined. The chapter concludes with a look at resource discovery tools in light of what is known about the information seeking behaviors of academic users, and recommendations are provided for those considering adoption of resource discovery tools.

DOI: 10.4018/978-1-4666-1821-3.ch001

INTRODUCTION

The design of systems and interfaces is a complicated matter that must take myriad details into consideration. One of those details is how users interact with the system or interface, and there is an entire field of study, that of human computer interactions, that deals with just this issue. The interaction between user and system impacts both sides of the equation, as it influences how the system or interface is designed, but also has significant influence on the success of those using the system. Use studies comprise one of the most significant bodies of research in librarianship (Krikelas, 1983), but one that has focused on the user's experience of the system (as opposed to focusing on the system itself) only since the 1970s (Case, 2008).

From the users' perspective, both Ellis (1989) and Kuhlthau (2004) agree that if the system with which a user interacts operates in a way that runs contrary to that user's process of seeking information, that user will encounter difficulty in finding the information needed to satisfy his or her information need. Borgman (1986, 1996) acknowledges the complexity of satisfying user needs by stating that "[o]n any given system, people will search in different ways, with different levels of success and satisfaction" (p. 393). She nevertheless suggests that it is not possible to design a system that functions well unless we first understand how people search, and that this has historically been the most significant flaw of library catalogs.

Web-based resource discovery tools represent the latest attempt to overlay the traditional approach to library resources with a user-friendly, streamlined, aggregated access point that would allow users to discover resources they might not have identified using traditional tools. How well these tools serve users depends, however, upon how well they integrate with the ways in which these users already search for information.

Information seeking has been studied from the perspectives of psychology, education, marketing, information science, library science, medicine, and others. Due to its immense size, it is not possible to address all the literature on information seeking in a single chapter, even when focusing on those publications specific to libraries and library-related interfaces (Case, 2008; Dervin & Nilan, 1986; Krikelas, 1983; Wilson, 1981, 1997). This chapter will instead strive to present a brief review of significant empirical and theoretical literature on this topic. The chapter will begin with a general introduction and some basic models, and then proceed to examine more specific behaviors exhibited by academic users, specifically undergraduate students, graduate students, and faculty members, by examining literature unique to those populations. It will explore and compare some proposed models of the information seeking process, and will look at possible changes to information seeking that have come about as a result of the Internet, Web 2.0 and social networking tools, and other technological advances. This chapter will conclude with a look at the implications of these information seeking behaviors on the adoption of resource discovery tools.

ESTABLISHING A CONTEXT FOR INFORMATION SEEKING

Information seeking behaviors are a subset of the broader category of information behaviors comprising "complex combination[s] of different biologically primary abilities such as language, information processing, decision-making, etc. that are found in all humans" (Spink, 2010, p. 46). Information seeking behaviors specifically are those steps and processes that lead an individual to information. Typically, information seeking begins when an individual recognizes a need or gap that needs to be satisfied (Kuhlthau, 2004; Wilson, 1981). Krikelas (1983) refers to this need as an unacceptable level of uncertainty in relation to a task or situation in one's personal or work-related life (p. 6). The behaviors performed to satisfy that need, or alleviate the uncertainty, continue until the need is perceived as satisfied by the individual (Brown, 1991; Krikelas, 1983). Needs in this sense could be cognitive (thinking), affective (feelings), or physiological (physical; Brown, 1991; Kuhlthau, 2004; Wilson, 1981, 1997), and those needs are in turn influenced by the context, or environment, in which they occur (Brown, 1991; Krikelas, 1983). Spink (2010) suggests that these information behaviors are driven by an innate instinct that all humans possess, but that these instincts are influenced by environmental, cultural, and developmental factors.

Fundamental to an understanding of information seeking is an understanding of relevance, precision, and recall. While entire literature reviews can and have been written on these topics (Saracevic, 1975, 2007a, 2007b; Schamber, Eisenberg, & Nilan, 1990), the purpose of their inclusion in the present review is to introduce them as concepts within the information seeking context. Relevance, considered a core concern in the field of information science (Froehlich, 1994; Schamber, 1994; Saracevic, 2007a) is difficult to define, and thus a somewhat controversial topic in the literature (Cooper & Chen, 2001; Froehlich, 1994; Schamber, 1994). Within the context of information seeking, relevance is the extent to which the results of a search match the search criteria (Berry & Browne, 2005; Froehlich, 1994; Saracevic, 2007a). Kent, Berry, Leuhrs, and Perry (1955) introduced the notions of "recall" (p. 95) and "pertinency" (p. 99; later renamed "precision;" Borgman, Moghdam, & Corbett, 1984, p. 134), which could be used to measure the extent to which search results are relevant. Precision is the percentage of a set of search results that are actually determined to be relevant to the information seeker's need, while recall is the percentage of all possible relevant results that were retrieved by a particular set of search criteria (Berry & Browne, 2005; Schamber, 1994).

Relevance be can determined by a system (relevance ranking), which typically applies an algorithm to the search results, utilizing the number of search words that appear in a result, as well as their frequencies and proximities, among other criteria (Clarke, Cormack, & Tudhope, 2000; Lu, Kim, & Wilbur, 2009; Saracevic, 2007a). But relevance is also subjective, in that it can only truly be determined by the person doing the information seeking. These are called "relevance judgments" or "user criteria" (e.g., topicality, pertinence, system constraints, etc.) for evaluating search results (Froehlich, 1994, p. 124; Schamber et al., 1990, p. 773). Saracevic and Kantor (1988a) suggest the impact that these relevance judgments or user criteria can have on search results, finding that information seekers who had well-defined questions were more likely to return relevant results than those information seekers who had less well-defined questions (p. 182).

Related to relevance judgments and user criteria in that they exert external influence on the process an individual undertakes to fulfill an information need, a number of factors influence the way in which the process is approached and carried out. Savolainen (2006) called them "contextual factors" or "indicators" (p. 110). Two significant factors are time and convenience.

Savolainen (2006) identified three ways in which time impacts information seeking. First, time functions as part of the context of information seeking, meaning that time is inherently part of the information seeking process and its associated behaviors. Second, time functions as an influence on access to sources of information (e.g., time constraints can restrict access to resources, such as those only available through interlibrary loan services). Third, time functions as a change agent in the information seeking process itself, in that time constraints influence the order in which sources are consulted and thus later directions taken in the information search. Connaway, Dickey & Radford (2011) identify time as a component of convenience, and Twait (2005) identifies time as one of the criteria that students use in selecting sources. The issue of time permeates the review done by Connaway & Dickey (2010) entitled *The Digital Information Seeker*, and influences when or how information seeking ends (Prabha, Connaway, Olszewski, & Jenkins, 2007).

Convenience is another significant influence on the information seeking process. Connaway et al. (2011) identified convenience as the choice of an information source, satisfaction and ease of use of the source, and the time constraints of the information seeking process. If a convenient source is more likely to be selected for use than a less convenient source, it can impact where an individual goes for information (the Internet vs. a research database; an online journal vs. a print journal), how long an individual stays in the various stages of the information seeking process, and potentially the overall results of their information seeking endeavor. Convenience is a consideration among undergraduate students, graduate students, and faculty, and across age groups; it is of greatest concern among graduate students (Connaway et al., 2011). Biddix, Chung & Park (2011) identify efficiency as a higher priority among students than credibility of the sources supplying their information, while Twait (2005) identified convenience as one of several criteria students use in selecting sources. Lombardo and Condic (2001) found that undergraduates favored more conveniently available sources, but did so because of confusion surrounding the process of research and ways of accessing other sources. Twelve studies reviewed by Connaway & Dickey (2010) also found convenience to be an important factor influencing information seeking behaviors.

Information seeking behaviors are often thought to be developmental in nature (Brown, 1991; Kuhlthau, 1988b; Solomon, 2002), which suggests that they usually improve over time. While this chapter will look at the behaviors of users according to their academic identifiers (i.e., undergraduate students, graduate students, faculty) because outreach and services to academic users

are frequently organized according to those terms, it should be noted that it may be more appropriate to consider these users in terms of their experience with information seeking processes: novice, experienced, and expert. Thus it is possible for an undergraduate to be an experienced searcher and well-developed in his or her approach to information, just as it is possible for a faculty member, usually considered an expert searcher, to have a less well-developed approach to information seeking processes. One of the significant differences between novice and expert searchers is in the area of subject knowledge, which can influence search terms chosen and overall searching strategies and have a marked influence on information seeking success (Hsieh-Yee, 1993; Pennanen & Vakkari, 2003). Yet there is overlap in the ways in which these divergent groups seek information, and the author will try to draw the reader's attention to these similarities when they occur.

General Models of Information Seeking Behavior

The models of information seeking presented here are not specific to any single context, and so can be applied in a variety of environments. Some serve the academic environment very well, and can be considered as additions to the specific models outlined below.

Saracevic (1987; Saracevic, Kantor, Chamis, & Trivison, 1988; Saracevic & Kantor, 1988a, 1988b) conducted an extensive study that explored the factors influencing the success of information seeking. Of significant interest were the user (problem, internal knowledge state, intent, and public knowledge estimate), the question (structure and classification), the searcher (language ability, logical ability, learning style, and search experience), the search (question analysis, search strategy, and search procedures), and the items retrieved (distribution and analysis). While not a single overarching model of the process information seekers go through, the study nevertheless identifies various components involved in the process and the extent to which they contribute to its overall success.

The Berrypicking model (Bates, 1989) suggests that users most frequently demonstrate an evolving search pattern, rather than a single query that retrieves a set of results that perfectly satisfies that user's information need. Information seekers who search in this way have an initial conceptualization of their information need and perform a search for information based on that conceptualization, which returns a set of results. The user gathers information from this initial set of results, and may identify some resources, and then on the basis of that information refine the information need and search terms. This subsequent search results in a new set of resources from which the user obtains information and additional resources that once again inform the information need. The information seeker is thus "berrypicking," gathering information a piece at a time while the information need and search criteria continue to evolve.

Wilson (1999; Wilson, Ford, Ellis, Foster, & Spink, 2002) identifies the information seeking process as a series of problem-solving behaviors intended to solve the "problem" of the initial information need. In solving this problem, the information seeker progresses through four stages: Problem Identification (What kind of problem do I have?), Problem Definition (Exactly what is the nature of my problem?), Problem Resolution (How do I find the answer to my problem?), and potentially Problem Solution (This is the answer to the problem, or This is how we're going to deal with the problem; Wilson 1999). The initial state of problem identification introduces a high level of uncertainty for the information seeker, and progression through the four stages leads from uncertainty to an increasing level of certainty, which culminates in the solution of the problem. Each stage could involve multiple attempts to find information to satisfy the information need, but the person will remain at each stage until the level of uncertainty is reduced enough to allow progression to the next stage.

INFORMATION SEEKING AND RETRIEVAL AMONG ACADEMIC USERS

Undergraduate Students

What makes the information seeking that undergraduate students engage in unique? Why might a model of information seeking devised from interactions with undergraduates possibly not be applicable to other information seekers? Undergraduate students engage in information-seeking behaviors predominantly to satisfy academic needs such as writing papers, preparing for class discussions, or preparing for tests and exams (Baro, Onyenania & Osaheni, 2010; Kakai, Ikoja-Odongo, & Kigongo-Bukenya, 2004). The search for information to satisfy personal needs or sports interests is much less prevalent, although this can vary depending on whether the undergraduate student in question is a traditional student or a "mature," or non-traditional, student (Baro et al., 2010; Given, 2002).

In searching to satisfy these academic needs, however, it is important to note that undergraduate students typically "do not think in terms of an information-seeking strategy, but rather in terms of a coping strategy" (Leckie, 1996, p. 202). There is a certain amount of anxiety involved in the process (Kuhlthau, 1985, 1988a, 2004; Mellon, 1986), and this results in students' trying to conduct research in a way that is as painless as possible. This interest in convenience manifests in students' conducting research as quickly as they are able, using resources with which they are already familiar (regardless of whether they are the best resources for the project), and hesitant to interact with professors or librarians for assistance (Given, 2002; Leckie, 1996; Lee, 2008; Valentine, 1993). The principle of least effort, which is explored in a variety of literature and is found to apply to most researchers, even those who are can be considered experts, supports these findings (Mann, 1993).

When exploring models of information seeking and retrieval among undergraduate users, one of the most well-known models is the Information Search Process (ISP) developed by Carol Kuhlthau (1985, 1988a,

2004). The ISP model explores not just the actions that a user performs when looking for information, but also looks at the affective (feelings) and cognitive (thought) stages through which a user goes. Kuhlthau's initial research was done to determine the process used by high school seniors (1985, 1988a), but the process has been studied among undergraduates and determined to be applicable (Fister, 1992; Kuhlthau, 1988b, 2004; Swain, 1996). Kuhlthau also conducted a longitudinal study to trace the behaviors of students initially studied as high school seniors, once they completed four years of undergraduate education (1988b, 2004).

The Information Search Process comprises six stages: initiation, selection, exploration, formulation, collection and presentation. During these six stages, students move from ambiguity to specificity or focus in their cognitive engagement, while their physical actions move from an exploratory search for relevant information that might help them decide on a topic and begin seeking a focus, to the documentation of information and a continued search for information that was more pertinent to their focused topic (Kuhlthau, 1985, 1988a, 2004). They are essentially moving through the process of reducing uncertainty, as outlined by Wilson (1999) above. Swain (1996) experienced that Kuhlthau's six stages were not always followed in order, and also identified that social interactions played a significant role in a number of the stages. This impact of social interactions, especially engagement with peers, on the information seeking process has also been born out in the research of Valentine (1993) and Given (2002).

Whitmire (2003) identified a relationship between undergraduate students' stage of epistemological belief (their belief in the nature of knowledge) and their information seeking behaviors. Those exhibiting higher epistemological beliefs were more likely to use a variety of search strategies, accept and integrate opinions or viewpoints that were counter to their thesis, and engage in more advanced information seeking strategies overall. This emphasizes the developmental nature of information seeking, since epistemological belief typically develops as individuals mature (Whitmire, 2003).

Faculty Members

As expert information seekers, faculty members bring a number of strengths to bear on the seeking process. They are experts in their disciplines, so they are very familiar with the authors involved in key areas of research as well as the language used to describe those areas of research. In addition to these specific strengths, faculty members also bring simple experience to their information seeking. They have done research in a variety of contexts and have developed a process of information seeking that works well for them.

In an extensive study of social scientists, Ellis (1989) identified six behaviors characteristic of information searching: starting, chaining, browsing, differentiating, monitoring, and extracting. *Starting* incorporates all activities involved in beginning a search for information (e.g., reading reviews and review articles, exploratory searches in library catalogs and indexes, etc.), while *chaining* refers to the process of tracking citations either backward (searching out resources cited in a consulted work) or forward (searching out resources that reference a consulted work). *Browsing* refers to semi-directed searches for material of interest among shelves of books in a library or in a journal table of contents, for example. *Differentiating* utilizes differences between sources as a means of determining how appropriate each source is for the project at hand, and *monitoring* involves faculty maintaining an awareness of developments in their field by monitoring particular sources. Finally, *extracting* involves a faculty member systematically examining a specific source, such as a journal or a publisher's catalog, to identify material of interest (Ellis, 1989, p. 178). These behaviors represent an iterative process, and Ellis himself hesitated to define the relationships that existed among the behaviors (1989).

Starting is similar to the Initiation and Selection stages demonstrated by undergraduate searchers in Kuhlthau's model (1985, 1988a, 1988b, 2004), though the faculty members' experience with their subject matter suggests that a somewhat different approach is understandable. Ellis's model has been applied to researchers in the humanities (Buchanan, Cunningham, Blandford, Rimer, & Warwick, 2005; Ellis, 1993; Ge, 2010), and the sciences (Ellis, 1993) and it has been repeated among social scientists (Ge, 2010; Shen, 2007). With all three groups it has been found to be applicable, despite research that suggests that information seeking behaviors differ among disciplines (Whitmire, 2002; Leckie, 1996). It could be that the model Ellis proposes is broad enough to encompass the general behaviors that all expert researchers exhibit.

Ellis's (1989) model has been updated by Meho and Tibbo (2003) who propose a new, though related, model comprising the behaviors starting, chaining, browsing, differentiating, monitoring, extracting, accessing, networking, verifying, and information managing grouped into four interrelated stages: searching, accessing, processing, and ending, which like Ellis's behaviors, are iterative. The additional accessing, networking, verifying, and information managing characteristics grew out of the then-current technological environment.

Ge (2010) also proposed an update to Ellis's (1989) model, suggesting the addition of a preparation and planning characteristic and an information management characteristic, though the focus of the article was on how electronic information resources influenced the information seeking process.

The literature frequently identifies the need to browse (Ellis, 1989, 1993; Meho & Tibbo, 2003; Stone, 1982; Watson-Boone, 1994), especially among humanities scholars, as is the need for primary documents (Stone, 1982; Watson-Boone, 1994). Ge (2010) also identified the need to browse, but the scholars studied indicated that they now tended to browse on the Internet more than they did in the library in the traditional sense defined by Ellis (1989). Other frequently reinforced information seeking behaviors among faculty are informal contacts with colleagues and tracking references, termed chaining by Ellis (Ellis, 1989, 1993; Ge, 2010; Niu et al., 2010; Shen, 2007; Watson-Boone, 1994). Ge (2010) and Shen (2010) also highlighted evaluating sources (differentiating as defined by Ellis) as common practices among faculty in their studies.

Recent research examining the information seeking behaviors of faculty members has frequently been conducted in light of technological changes that have occurred since the rise of the Internet and the development of a number of tools that impact the way in which information is sought (Buchanan et al., 2005; Ge, 2010; Niu et al., 2010; Shen, 2007). These changes will be discussed in greater depth later in this chapter.

Graduate Students

The review of the research that examines the information seeking behaviors of graduate students as a unique population follows that of both undergraduate students and faculty because many behaviors are shared with those two groups (Barrett, 2005).

Often more experienced at searching than undergraduates, graduate students have usually moved past the anxiety that frequently characterizes undergraduates (Barrett, 2005), although this can vary depending on the nature of the experiences they have had and the new situation in which they find themselves (Fleming-May & Yuro, 2009). Graduate students are also much more likely than undergraduates to self-identify as scholars-in-training (Barrett, 2005; Delgadillo & Lynch, 1999; Fleming-May & Yuro, 2009). Factors that influence information seeking behaviors include perceived ability, search experience, computer and Web experience, and frequency of use of electronic sources (Korobili, Malliari, & Zapounidou, 2011; Malliari, Korobili, & Zapounidou, 2011). Graduate students are more likely to visit the physical library than are undergraduate students, and are more likely to use journal articles and conference proceedings as sources (Fleming-May & Yuro, 2009). Graduate students from outside of the United States demonstrate somewhat different information behaviors than do their American counterparts (e.g., students from outside the United States are more likely to find information in library books and use the library catalog than are students in the United States, but are more likely to be begin a search through a Web search engine), although the fundamental information seeking behaviors are quite similar (Fleming-May & Yuro, 2009; Liao, Finn, & Lu, 2007).

There is not an extensive collection of literature that examines the information seeking behaviors of graduate students specifically (Barrett, 2005; Fleming-May & Yuro, 2009). Based upon the literature reviewed here, however, graduate students could be said to fall along a continuum which features undergraduate (novice) information seekers at one extreme and faculty (expert) information seekers at the other.

There was a significant disparity in the literature as to where studies located graduate students along the continuum. While those studied by Barrett (2005) and Fleming-May and Yuro (2009) exhibited more expert behaviors such as chaining, a focus on primary resources, and attending conferences and consulting with colleagues to gain information, the majority of those studied by Korobili et al. (2011) demonstrated a "low to medium level of information-seeking skills"

(p. 161). Delgadillo and Lynch (1999) studied graduate students who had completed their first, third and fourth years of study and found that those who had completed their third and fourth years of study were more sophisticated in their research processes, suggesting that the longer a graduate student remains in a program of study, the further along the continuum the student moves toward becoming an expert information seeker (Fleming-May & Yuro, 2009).

INFORMATION SEEKING IN A DIGITAL ENVIRONMENT

It is important to include a section on information seeking in the digital environment in this review, simply because so much information seeking now takes place within its confines—it has become common for information searches to begin with a search engine (Biddix et al., 2011; De Rosa et al., 2005).

Borgman (1986) explores four variables that come into play when searching in an automated environment: the searcher (the person interacting with the system), the system itself (e.g., a catalog or database), the search process (how a search is actually conducted--search terms, search structure, etc.), and the search results. The way in which the searcher interacts with the other three variables is at the heart of information seeking research. Borgman (1986) goes on to identify two types of knowledge that must be employed when seeking information in that environment: mechanical knowledge and conceptual knowledge. Mechanical knowledge is demonstrated by an understanding of how to structure a search, navigate the system, and select search terms, while conceptual knowledge comprises how to narrow or broaden a search, how to select certain databases as potential starting points in a search, etc. Both types of knowledge can serve either as facilitators in searching, or as barriers. Borgman (1986) acknowledges that personality, frequency of searching, and experience in doing searches can also influence the "searcher" variable.

Bates (1989) suggested that as content moved to an online environment, the search environment encountered by those seeking information would become more complex, both in the types and formats of resources available and the ways information seekers interact with those resources. Knight and Spink (2008, p. 224) identify six ways in which Web search engines differ from more traditional online library search environments:

1. *Open architecture* – resulting in no enforceable quality standards regarding the accuracy or quality of content.
2. *Open classification and meta-tagging system* – resulting in Web pages failing to be indexed appropriately by search engines.
3. *Highly dynamic use of the hypertext* – favoring browsing over query - making in many instances.
4. *Dynamic/fluid content structure* – resulting in pages being "moved" within directories of a given Website, and frequent 404 errors (where pages no longer exist as formerly known URLs).
5. *Partial representation* – at any one time a Search Engine can literally only provide a "snap-shot" of the Internet at one given time in history. Servers that are offline or networks that have temporarily been interrupted cannot be "indexed" by a crawling search engine (Sullivan 2002).
6. *Sheer volume* – the sheer size of the Internet means that the snap-shot a search engine takes of the Internet at any one time is likely to represent less than 30% of the known Web.

Research done on searching in the Web environment has shown that most Web queries are short (Clarke et al., 2000; Jansen & Spink, 2006; Spink, Wolfram, Jansen, Saracevic, 2001), involve little query reformulation (Spink et al, 2001; Spink, Jansen, & Ozmultu, 2000), and are constructed simply,

rarely utilizing advanced search techniques (Spink et al., 2001). A query is defined as a set of terms (a word or some other unbroken alphanumeric combination) intended to answer an information need (Spink et al., 2001). Typically, despite the large number of search results returned, less than twenty-nine percent of users view more than the first page of results and only about one third look beyond the second page (Jansen & Spink, 2003, 2006; Spink et al., 2001). Information seekers on the Web typically view an average of eight Web documents (Web pages relevant to their query), though the majority in fact view no more than five in the course of their session (Jansen & Spink, 2003; Spink et al. 2001).

Bawden and Robinson (2009) have identified a number of pathologies that they associate with this more complex environment, including information overload, information avoidance, information anxiety and library anxiety. Perhaps one of the most common issues encountered in the current digital environment is information overload. Discussed in the literature of numerous disciplines, information overload occurs when there is so much potentially useful information available to an individual that it becomes difficult for that individual to select which information sources would be most likely to satisfy the information need (Bawden & Robinson, 2009; Edmunds & Morris, 2000; Savolainen, 2006, 2007). Information overload is certainly not a new idea, as Bawden & Robinson (2009) suggest, citing the Biblical book of Ecclesiastes, the Smithsonian Institute in 1852 and the Royal Society's Scientific Information Conference in 1948. However it began to be recognized as a widespread problem in the 1990s, exacerbated by the Internet and development of the World Wide Web (Bawden & Robinson, 2009; Edmunds & Morris, 2000; Nazim, 2008; Savolainen, 2007).

The related issue of information anxiety can be caused by an overabundance of information or a paucity of information, a lack of understanding either of the information environment in which one is functioning, or confusion related to the content itself (Bawden & Robinson, 2009).

One of the ways in which individuals cope with information overload is to adopt satisficing as a way of ending their search for information. Although the concept of satisficing is prevalent in a number of disciplines, including philosophy and sociology, within the context of library and information science, satisficing occurs when individuals determine how much information is "good enough" to satisfy their information need, rather than trying to evaluate or interact with *all* of the available information on their topic (Agosto, 2002; Bawden & Robinson, 2009; Prabha et al., 2007; Warwick, Rimmer, Blandford, Gow, & Buchanan, 2009; Zach, 2005). Agosto (2002), in a study of high school girls researching on the Internet, takes the broad notion of "good enough" to greater specificity, identifying two specific behaviors. Reduction is the satisficing behavior of limiting to a small subset of the information that could possibly be used to inform the information search (e.g., through revisiting familiar and previously successful information sources). Termination is the way in which the information seeking process concludes (e.g., due to time constraints and the discovery of information repetition; Agosto, 2002). Termination behaviors are similar to the "stopping rules" defined by Kraft and Lee (1979), which identified satiation, disgust, and a combination of the two as the three reasons why individuals stop searching for information.

Another method of dealing with information overload is the incorporation of "push" technologies, which enable an individual to have information automatically delivered to them, in a variety of formats, according to pre-defined criteria such as a topic, set of keywords, journal title (Savolainen, 2006, 2007).

Extensive research that has been done on searchers in the online environment suggests that there have been changes in cognitive approach (from a linear search pattern to a non-linear pattern; Cromley & Azevedo, 2009; Kim, 2001; Yang,

2005). Foster (2006) suggests that non-linearity manifests itself at all levels of human information behavior, and is not necessarily a recent development specific to the digital environment. Rather it is possible that this online environment, with its social media and constant interconnectivity, is simply another technological tool (similar to online databases or catalogs, email, Google, RSS feeds, bibliographic management tools) that acts as an external force on the information seeking process, rather than actually changing it from within. The adoption, rejection, and use of these tools are explored in numerous studies (Buchanan et al., 2005; Ge, 2010; Nicholas, Clark, Rowlands, & Jamali, 2009; Niu et al., 2010; Shen, 2007).

Changes to the information seeking process itself seem to be minimal. Nicholas et al. (2009) explored the use of electronic journals among researchers in the United Kingdom and discovered that researchers exhibited both chaining and browsing behaviors in that environment. In a subsequent article, faculty members highlighted the importance of the "cited by" feature available in Google Scholar as well as the references searching available through Web of Science, both tools that facilitate chaining (Nicholas, Williams, Rowland, & Jamali, 2010).

Whitmire (2004) examined the process through which students evaluate the information they find on the Internet and suggests a complex evaluation process dependent upon epistemological development is utilized. Concerns over the quality of resources encountered online and the evaluation of those sources, a component of Ellis's (1989, 1993) differentiating behavior, is also a concern among faculty (Niu et al., 2010). Meho and Tibbo (2003) identified accessing information as an information seeking behavior that has come to have more significance in the digital environment, and Meho and Tibbo (2003) and Ge (2010) both proposed the addition of information *management* to Ellis's information seeking characteristics, citing the need to organize the information being obtained now in multiple formats (though whether this can actually be considered part of the information seeking process remains in question). The increased need for information management may be a result of the sense of information overload prevalent in the current digital environment.

Speed is also an important factor—those who regularly search using Google or another search engine are accustomed to retrieving results almost instantly (Boyd et al, 2006; Connaway et al., 2011; Nazim, 2008; Niu et al, 2010; Savolainen, 2006; Way, 2010)--as was ease of navigation and ease of use (Nicholas et al., 2010). Hepworth (2007) identifies individuals who use and interact with information in the ways stated above as "information consumers," and notes the growing desire for personalization and the ability to tailor a technological product to personal needs and interests. Ultimately, information environments are being asked to mirror the "experience of the world where people interact face-to-face or with physical information products" (Hepworth, 2007, p. 36-37). These preferences, while not specifically information seeking behaviors, can impact the choice of search tools and can help to explain why those tools are utilized in the ways that they are.

Information Seeking and Web-Based Resource Discovery Tools

It has become increasingly necessary to accommodate the changes in information seeking behaviors and characteristics outlined above. Whereas "[t]he user once built workflows around the library systems and services...now, increasingly, the library must build its services around user workflows" (Connaway et al., 2011, p. 179). Web-based resource discovery tools represent one of the ways in which the library is trying to accommodate those user workflows.

Because the development and implementation of Web-based resource discovery tools is so recent, there is little published literature that deals with information seeking in this context, or even with the tools themselves (Way, 2010). The majority of literature found that could be considered relevant to the discovery environment deals with information seeking using federated search tools. Although not identical in function or design, both federated searching and discovery tools are built upon the concept of metasearching, the ability to search multiple resources simultaneously (Breeding, 2005). Thus federated searching could be viewed as an early attempt at resource discovery services (Vaughan, 2011). Such literature has been used to provide insight into discovery tools by other authors (Way, 2010), and will serve the same function in this review.

Resource discovery is accomplished when users are able to find materials they want in a format they can use (Chapman, 2007). According to Vaughan (2011), Web-based resource discovery services are tools which provide content, discovery, delivery, and flexibility by searching large amounts of pre-harvested and indexed material within a single simple, seamless (to the end user) interface. Some examples of current Web-based resource discovery tools available or in development include the eXtensible Catalog (Bowen, 2008), OCLC WorldCat®1 Local (Shadle, 2009), Serials Solutions®2 Summon™3 (Vaughan & ALA TechSource, 2011), and EBSCO Discovery Services™4 (Vaughan & ALA TechSource, 2011) among others. They are intended to facilitate the discovery of useful resources across databases, platforms, and interfaces (Vaughan, 2011; Way, 2010). The ability to pre-harvest and index data is one of the significant differences between these discovery tools and federated searching tools. Federated search tools conduct searches across multiple databases simultaneously, but initiate the search and collect the data only when it is requested by the user. Pre-harvesting and indexing allow resource discovery tools to return results more quickly because the data is already aggregated. This also allows results to be ranked by relevancy, something that federated search tools were never able to manage (Boyd et al, 2006; Medeiros, 2009). In light of users' propensity to only view the first page of Web results and a limited number of documents (Jansen & Spink, 2003; Spink et al., 2001), the availability of relevance ranking within Web-based resource discovery tools is a significant usability consideration.

In addition to relevance ranking, resource discovery tools also typically employ faceted searching. Facets allow users to refine their searches according to suggestions associated with the metadata within the results already returned. Some examples of possible facets include narrowing a search by format (e.g., video, music, and microfilm), language, and publication date. Called "guided navigation" by Olson (2007, p. 552), this process relieves information seekers of the necessity of having a clearly defined idea of what they are want to find at the outset of their search, instead allowing them to begin with a keyword search and then narrow their idea to greater specificity (Tunkelang, 2009). It is often thought to be most useful for broader searches often associated with less experienced information seekers (Olson, 2007).

Studies of user interactions with federated searching suggest that users like the single Google-like search box provided by many federated search interfaces, as well as freedom from having to select among myriad unique databases (Boyd et al, 2006; Gibson, Goddard, & Gordon, 2009). Speed is also an important factor (Boyd et al, 2006; Way, 2010), as is subject groupings of results and a friendly interface (Gibson et al., 2009). These studies are supported by broader research into information seeking behaviors more generally, which agree that students want convenience (Biddix et al., 2011; Connaway et al., 2011; Connaway & Dickey, 2010; Lee, 2008; Mann, 1993; Twait, 2005) and are confused by having to select from multiple databases, citing "a mismatch between students' inadequate knowledge of information sources and the complex structure imposed by the library" (Lee, 2008, p. 217). This frustration is something that faculty share, though likely for different reasons (Niu et al., 2010).

In a 2004 study comparing university students' use and perceptions of a Web search engine with a Web-based library catalog, Fast and Campbell discovered that while students admired the organization of the library catalog, they didn't understand it and preferred to search the Web despite its inherent clutter. In addition, students trusted documents found in the library catalog, but believed they were capable of accurately evaluating the less reliable documents available through a Web search. Ultimately, a Web search was preferred to a library search because the Web search was perceived as easier. Students were more confident in their interactions with the search engine, as opposed to the seeming complexity of the library catalog. The Web search also appeared to return more immediately, easily accessible results (Fast & Campbell, 2004).

Work at North Carolina State University with the Endeca catalog (Antelman, Lynema, & Pace, 2006) revealed more relevant results located through the discovery tool than through their traditional catalog, and raised questions as to how these types of tools would impact authority searching. Olson's (2007) study with Ph.D. students at the University of Chicago, which evaluated the resource discovery tool AquaBrowser[5], found that of twelve students observed, nine found new material related to their research. Thomas and Buck (2010) identified both strengths and weaknesses in their user testing comparing their local and consortial catalogs with WorldCat Local. For example, users had a more difficult time locating a book by title in WorldCat Local than in the local and consortial catalog because of the merging of books and article formats (Thomas & Buck, 2010). These studies provide a reminder that as promising as these tools are, they are not a panacea.

FUTURE RESEARCH DIRECTIONS

Web-based resource discovery tools can potentially serve the information seeking needs of a variety of information seekers. It seems that they would almost certainly serve undergraduate students, particularly in the early "exploratory" stages of their information seeking process (Kuhlthau, 1985, 1988a, 1988b, 2004), but whether they would so adequately meet the needs of faculty members, the expert searchers explored here, may depend on features available in the individual systems.

Faculty have expressed interest in a single resource that would allow them to search many resources simultaneously (Broadbent, 1986; Niu et al., 2010), and Nicholas et al. (2010) cite the broader contextualization of research as one of the reasons faculty like to use Google and Google Scholar™[6] as information seeking tools. Yet the studies conducted by Ellis (1989, 1993), Meho & Tibbo (2003), Ge (2010), Watson-Boone (1994) and others suggest that behaviors such as chaining, browsing, and monitoring, which often do not function well in an aggregated environment, are integral to the way in which these users research. How does the system facilitate browsing? Do RSS feeds or other technologies allow faculty members to monitor new material being published in their discipline? Can citation searches be conducted? How well these tools can address these behaviors that are integral to the ways in which faculty approach research may well dictate whether or not these tools are ever able to serve more than the novice information seeker. Although somewhat dated, both Bates (1989) and Ellis (1989) provide recommendations for the design of systems that would take information seeking behaviors into account. It would also be interesting to note whether, and to what extent, marketing of resource discovery tools and their more social features might increase their use, particularly among the "information consumers" identified by Hepworth (2007).

It is clear from the literature that confusion continues to surround the organization and use of library catalogs (Fast & Campbell, 2004) as well as the research process itself (Lombardo & Condic, 2001). What role can information literacy or library research skills education play in supporting academic research, particularly among more novice researchers (Biddix et al., 2011; Nazim, 2008)? While it is unlikely that instruction of this type would address all expectations that users bring to Web-based library resources, it could help those engaged in information seeking to understand the process better including ways to maximize the efficiency and effectiveness of their information seeking endeavors.

While a significant body of literature exists that addresses the information seeking behaviors of academic users in a variety of contexts, Web-based resource discovery tools are new enough that little literature exists that addresses them and their use. Studies exploring the information seeking behaviors of academic users utilizing these tools would be an obvious augmentation to the existing research. Are Web-based resource discovery interfaces simply new tools that are used in partnership with existing behaviors, or do academic users adopt new information seeking strategies when interacting with these tools? Do the existing models hold up in this new search environment? Do these tools adequately serve the more advanced information seeking needs of faculty members? How much instruction do users need to use these tools effectively? Do facets work and are they used? Is the inclusion of so much data comfortable (like Google) or overwhelming? Is academic research any better because of the relevancy ranking in these tools? Do users actually interact with the refinement and narrowing functions included? How does the ability to narrow results to scholarly materials help undergraduates? Do users pick the resource discovery tools for their research or do they stick to the tried and true (Google and Google Scholar™)? These are just some of the areas that would benefit from additional exploration.

CONCLUSION

Kuhlthau (2004) provides a fitting reminder as libraries move forward with these tools:

[W]e each enter the [information seeking] process with a system of personal constructs built on past experience. Learning in libraries involves a vigorous process of using information in which the learner is actively engaged in seeking meaning from the information he or she gathers as a search progresses. The topic or problem changes and emerges in a series of stages or levels of understanding, which are dependent upon not only the information he or she encounters but also the individual's perspective, background, and knowledge. Therefore, the user uniquely creates each search within the framework of his or her personal constructs related to the problem at hand and to his or her larger worldview...The user's personal perspective determines what he or she selects to learn along the way; that perspective directs the search through personal choice of relevance. (p. 7)

Research still needs to be done both on Web-based resource discovery tools generally and on their compatibility with what is understood about information seeking behaviors of academic users. Nevertheless, the literature suggests that while it is impossible for any system to meet the needs of every user, with some possible augmentation these tools are a positive step toward meeting the diverse needs of academic users.

REFERENCES

Agosto, D. E. (2002). Bounded rationality and satisficing in young people's Web-based decision making. *Journal of the American Society for Information Science and Technology, 53*(1), 16–27. doi:10.1002/asi.10024

Antelman, K., Lynema, E., & Pace, A. K. (2006). Toward a twenty-first century library catalog. *Information Technology & Libraries, 25*(3), 128–139.

Baro, E. E., Onyenania, G. O., & Osaheni, O. (2010). Information seeking behaviour of undergraduate students in the humanities in three universities in Nigeria. *South African Journal of Library & Information Science, 76*(2), 109–117.

Barrett, A. (2005). The information-seeking habits of graduate student researchers in the humanities. *Journal of Academic Librarianship, 31*(4), 324–331. doi:10.1016/j.acalib.2005.04.005

Bates, M. J. (1989). The design of browsing and berrypicking techniques for the online search interface. *Online Review, 13*(5), 407–424. doi:10.1108/eb024320

Bawden, D., & Robinson, L. (2009). The dark side of information: Overload, anxiety and other paradoxes and pathologies. *Journal of Information Science, 35*(2), 180–191. doi:10.1177/0165551508095781

Berry, M. W., & Browne, M. (2005). *Understanding search engines: Mathematical modeling and text retrieval*. Philadelphia, PA: SIAM, Society for Industrial and Applied Mathematics. doi:10.1137/1.9780898718164

Biddix, J. P., Chung, C. J., & Park, H. W. (2011). Convenience or credibility? A study of college student online research behaviors. *The Internet and Higher Education, 14*(3), 175–182. doi:10.1016/j.iheduc.2011.01.003

Borgman, C. L. (1986). Why are online catalogs hard to use? Lessons learned from information-retrieval studies. *Journal of the American Society for Information Science American Society for Information Science, 37*(6), 387–400.

Borgman, C. L. (1996). Why are online catalogs still hard to use? *Journal of the American Society for Information Science American Society for Information Science, 47*(7), 493–503. doi:10.1002/(SICI)1097-4571(199607)47:7<493::AID-ASI3>3.0.CO;2-P

Borgman, C. L., Moghdam, D., & Corbett, P. K. (1984). *Effective online searching: A basic text.* New York, NY: M. Dekker.

Bowen, J. (2008). Metadata to support next-generation library resource discovery: Lessons from the eXtensible catalog, phase 1. *Information Technology & Libraries, 27*(2), 5–19.

Boyd, J., Hampton, M., Morrison, P., Pugh, P., Cervone, F., & Scherlen, A. (2006). The one-box challenge: Providing a federated search that benefits the research process. *Serials Review, 32*(4), 247–254. doi:10.1016/j.serrev.2006.08.005

Breeding, M. (2005). Plotting a new course for metasearch. *Computers in Libraries, 25*(2), 27–29.

Broadbent, E. (1986). A study of humanities faculty library information seeking behavior. *Cataloging & Classification Quarterly, 6,* 23–37. doi:10.1300/J104v06n03_03

Brown, M. E. (1991). A general model of information-seeking behavior. Proceedings of the 54th ASIS Annual Meeting, 28, (pp. 9-14).

Buchanan, G., Cunningham, S. J., Blandford, A., Rimmer, J., & Warwick, C. (2005). Information seeking by humanities scholars. *Lecture Notes in Computer Science, 3652,* 218–229. doi:10.1007/11551362_20

Case, D. O. (2008). *Looking for information: A survey of research on information seeking, needs, and behavior.* Bingley, U.K: Emerald.

Chapman, A. (2007). Resource discovery: Catalogs, cataloging, and the user. *Library Trends, 55*(4), 917–931.

Clarke, C. L. A., Cormack, G. V., & Tudhope, E. A. (2000). Relevance ranking for one to three term queries. *Information Processing & Management, 36*(2), 291–311. doi:10.1016/S0306-4573(99)00017-5

Connaway, L. S., & Dickey, T. J. (2010). *The digital information seeker: Report of findings from selected OCLC, RIN and JISC user behaviour projects.* London, UK: HEFCE on behalf of the JISC.

Connaway, L. S., Dickey, T. J., & Radford, M. L. (2011). "If it is too inconvenient, I'm not going after it": Convenience as a critical factor in information-seeking behaviors. *Library & Information Science Research, 33*(3), 179–190. doi:10.1016/j.lisr.2010.12.002

Cooper, M. D., & Chen, H. (2001). Predicting the relevance of a library catalog search. *Journal of the American Society for Information Science and Technology, 52*(10), 813–827. doi:10.1002/asi.1140

Cromley, J. G., & Azevedo, R. (2009). Locating information within extended hypermedia. *Educational Technology Research and Development, 57*(3), 287–313. doi:10.1007/s11423-008-9106-5

De Rosa, C., Cantrell, J., Cellentani, D., Hawk, J., Jenkins, L., & Wilson, A. (2005). *Perceptions of libraries and information resources. A report to the OCLC membership.* Dublin, OH: OCLC Online Computer Library Center. Retrieved from http://www.oclc.org/reports/pdfs/Percept_all.pdf

Delgadillo, R., & Lynch, B. P. (1999). Future historians: Their quest for information. *College & Research Libraries, 60*(3), 245–259.

Dervin, B., & Nilan, M. (1986). Information needs and uses. *Annual Review of Information Science & Technology, 21*, 3–33.

Edmunds, A., & Morris, A. (2000). The problem of information overload in business organizations: A review of the literature. *International Journal of Information Management, 20*(1), 17–28. doi:10.1016/S0268-4012(99)00051-1

Ellis, D. (1989). A behavioural approach to information retrieval system design. *The Journal of Documentation, 45*(3), 171–212. doi:10.1108/eb026843

Ellis, D. (1993). Modeling the information-seeking patterns of academic researchers: A grounded theory approach. *The Library Quarterly, 63*(4), 469–486. doi:10.1086/602622

Fast, K. V., & Campbell, D. G. (2004). "I still like Google": University student perceptions of searching OPACs and the Web. *Proceedings of the 67th ASIS&T Annual Meeting, 41*, (pp. 138-146).

Fister, B. (1992). The research processes of undergraduate students. *Journal of Academic Librarianship, 18*(3), 163–169.

Fleming-May, R., & Yuro, L. (2009). From student to scholar: The academic library and social sciences PhD students' transformation. portal . *Libraries and the Academy, 9*(2), 199–221. doi:10.1353/pla.0.0040

Foster, A. (2006). A non-linear perspective on information seeking. In A. Spink & C. Cole (Eds.), *New directions in human information behavior* (155-170). Dordrecht, The Netherlands: Springer.

Froehlich, T. J. (1994). Relevance reconsidered—Towards an agenda for the 21st century: Introduction to special topic issue on relevance research. *Journal of the American Society for Information Science American Society for Information Science, 45*(3), 124–134. doi:10.1002/(SICI)1097-4571(199404)45:3<124::AID-ASI2>3.0.CO;2-8

Ge, X. (2010). Information-seeking behavior in the digital age: A multidisciplinary study of academic researchers. *College & Research Libraries, 71*(5), 435–455.

Gibson, I., Goddard, L., & Gordon, S. (2009). One box to search them all: Implementing federated search at an academic library. *Library Hi Tech, 27*(1), 118–133. doi:10.1108/07378830910942973

Given, L. M. (2002). The academic and the everyday: Investigating the overlap in mature undergraduates' information-seeking behaviors. *Library & Information Science Research, 24*(1), 17–29. doi:10.1016/S0740-8188(01)00102-5

Hepworth, M. (2007). Knowledge of information behaviour and its relevance to the design of people-centred information products and services. *The Journal of Documentation, 63*(1), 33–56. doi:10.1108/00220410710723876

Hsieh-Yee, I. (1993). Effects of search experience and subject knowledge on the search tactics of novice and experienced searchers. *Journal of the American Society for Information Science American Society for Information Science, 44*(3), 161–174. doi:10.1002/(SICI)1097-4571(199304)44:3<161::AID-ASI5>3.0.CO;2-8

Jansen, B. J., & Spink, A. (2003). An analysis of Web documents retrieved and viewed. In *Proceedings of the 4th International Conference on Internet Computing*, Las Vegas, Nevada, 23-26 June (pp. 65-69).

Jansen, B. J., & Spink, A. (2006). How are we searching the World Wide Web? A comparison of nine search engine transaction logs. *Information Processing & Management, 42*, 248–263. doi:10.1016/j.ipm.2004.10.007

Kakai, M., Ikoja-Odongo, R., & Kigongo-Bukenya, I. M. N. (2004). A study of the information-seeking behavior of undergraduate students of Makerere University, Uganda. *World Libraries, 14*(1), 14–26.

Kent, A., Berry, M., Leuhrs, F. U., & Perry, J. W. (1955). Machine literature searching VIII. Operational criteria for designing information retrieval systems. *American Documentation, 6*(2), 93–101. doi:10.1002/asi.5090060209

Kim, K. (2001). Information seeking on the Web: Effects of user and task variables. *Library & Information Science Research, 23*(3), 233–255. doi:10.1016/S0740-8188(01)00081-0

Knight, S. A., & Spink, A. (2008). Toward a Web search information behavior model . In Spink, A., & Zimmer, M. (Eds.), *Web search: Multidisciplinary perspectives* (pp. 209–234). Berlin, Germany: Springer. doi:10.1007/978-3-540-75829-7_12

Korobili, S., Malliari, A., & Zapounidou, S. (2011). Factors that influence information-seeking behavior: The case of Greek graduate students. *Journal of Academic Librarianship, 37*(2), 155–165. doi:10.1016/j.acalib.2011.02.008

Kraft, D., & Lee, T. (1979). Stopping rules and their effect on expected search length. *Information Processing & Management, 15*(1), 47–58. doi:10.1016/0306-4573(79)90007-4

Krikelas, J. (1983). Information-seeking behavior: Patterns and concepts. *Drexel Library Quarterly, 19*(2), 5–20.

Kuhlthau, C. C. (1985). A process approach to library skills instruction. *School Library Media Quarterly, 13*(1), 35–40.

Kuhlthau, C. C. (1988a). Developing a model of the library search process: Cognitive and affective aspects. *Research Quarterly, 28*(2), 232–242.

Kuhlthau, C. C. (1988b). Perceptions of the information search process in libraries: A study of changes from high school through college. *Information Processing & Management, 24*(4), 419–427. doi:10.1016/0306-4573(88)90045-3

Kuhlthau, C. C. (2004). *Seeking meaning: A process approach to library and information services* (2nd ed.). Westport, CT: Libraries Unlimited.

Leckie, G. J. (1996). Desperately seeking citations: Uncovering faculty assumptions about the undergraduate research process. *Journal of Academic Librarianship, 22*(3), 201–208. doi:10.1016/S0099-1333(96)90059-2

Lee, H. (2008). Information structures and undergraduate students. *Journal of Academic Librarianship, 34*(3), 211–219. doi:10.1016/j.acalib.2008.03.004

Liao, Y., Finn, M., & Lu, J. (2007). Information-seeking behavior of international graduate students vs. American graduate students: A user study at Virginia Tech 2005. *College & Research Libraries, 68*(1), 5–25.

Lombardo, S. V., & Condic, K. S. (2001). Convenience or content: A study of undergraduate periodical use. *RSR. Reference Services Review, 29*(4), 327–337. doi:10.1108/EUM0000000006494

Lu, Z., Kim, W., & Wilbur, W. J. (2009). Evaluating relevance ranking strategies for MEDLINE retrieval. *Journal of the American Medical Informatics Association, 16*(1), 32–36. doi:10.1197/jamia.M2935

Malliari, A., Korobili, S., & Zapounidou, S. (2011). Exploring the information seeking behavior of Greek graduate students: A case study set in the University of Macedonia. *The International Information & Library Review, 43*(2), 79–91. doi:10.1016/j.iilr.2011.04.006

Mann, T. (1993). *Library research models: A guide to classification, cataloging, and computers.* New York, NY: Oxford University Press.

Medeiros, N. (2009). Researching the research process: Information-seeking behavior, Summon, and Google Books. *OCLC Systems & Services, 25*(3), 153–155. doi:10.1108/10650750910982520

Meho, L. I., & Tibbo, H. R. (2003). Modeling the information-seeking behavior of social scientists: Ellis's study revisited. *Journal of the American Society for Information Science and Technology, 54*(6), 570–587. doi:10.1002/asi.10244

Mellon, C. A. (1986). Library anxiety: A grounded theory and its development. *College & Research Libraries, 47*(2), 160–165.

Nazim, M. (2008). Information searching behavior in the Internet age: A users' study of Aligarh Muslim University. *The International Information & Library Review, 40*(1), 73–81. doi:10.1016/j.iilr.2007.11.001

Nicholas, D., Clark, D., Rowlands, I., & Jamali, H. R. (2009). Online use and information seeking behaviour: Institutional and subject comparisons of UK researchers. *Journal of Information Science, 35*(6), 660–676. doi:10.1177/0165551509338341

Nicholas, D., Williams, P., Rowlands, I., & Jamali, H. R. (2010). Researchers' e-journal use and information seeking behaviour. *Journal of Information Science, 36*(4), 494–516. doi:10.1177/0165551510371883

Niu, X., Hemminger, B. M., Lown, C., Adams, S., Brown, C., & Level, A. (2010). National study of information seeking behavior of academic researchers in the United States. *Journal of the American Society for Information Science and Technology, 61*(5), 869–890. doi:10.1002/asi.21307

Olson, T. A. (2007). Utility of a faceted catalog for scholarly research. *Library Hi Tech, 25*(4), 550–561. doi:10.1108/07378830710840509

Pennanen, M., & Vakkari, P. (2003). Students' conceptual structure, search process, and outcome while preparing a research proposal: A longitudinal case study. *Journal of the American Society for Information Science and Technology, 54*(8), 759–770. doi:10.1002/asi.10273

Prabha, C., Connaway, L. S., Olszewski, L., & Jenkins, L. R. (2007). What is enough? Satisficing information needs. *The Journal of Documentation, 63*(1), 74–89. doi:10.1108/00220410710723894

Saracevic, T. (1975). Relevance: A review of and a framework for the thinking on the notion in information science. *Journal of the American Society for Information Science American Society for Information Science, 26*(6), 321–343. doi:10.1002/asi.4630260604

Saracevic, T. (1987). Experiments on the cognitive aspects of information seeking and information retrieving (NSF Research Project IST-850 5411). Cleveland, OH: Case Western Reserve University.

Saracevic, T. (2007a). Relevance: A review of the literature and a framework for thinking on the notion in information science. Part II: Nature and manifestations of relevance. *Journal of the American Society for Information Science and Technology, 58*(13), 1915–1933. doi:10.1002/asi.20682

Saracevic, T. (2007b). Relevance: A review of the literature and a framework for thinking on the notion in information science. Part III: Behavior and effects of relevance. *Journal of the American Society for Information Science and Technology*, *58*(13), 2126–2144. doi:10.1002/asi.20681

Saracevic, T., & Kantor, P. (1988a). A study of information seeking and retrieving, II: Users, questions, and effectiveness. Journal of the American Society for Information Science, 39(3), 177-196. doi: 0.1002/(SICI)1097-4571(198805)39:3<177::AID-ASI3>3.0.CO;2-F

Saracevic, T., & Kantor, P. (1988b). A study of information seeking and retrieving, III: Searchers, searches, and overlap. *Journal of the American Society for Information Science American Society for Information Science*, *39*(3), 197–216. doi:10.1002/(SICI)1097-4571(198805)39:3<197::AID-ASI4>3.0.CO;2-A

Saracevic, T., Kantor, P., Chamis, A. Y., & Trivison, D. (1988). A study of information seeking and retrieving, I: Background and methodology. *Journal of the American Society for Information Science American Society for Information Science*, *39*(3), 161–176. doi:10.1002/(SICI)1097-4571(198805)39:3<161::AID-ASI2>3.0.CO;2-0

Savolainen, R. (2006). Time as a context of information seeking. *Library & Information Science Research*, *28*(1), 110–127. doi:10.1016/j.lisr.2005.11.001

Savolainen, R. (2007). Filtering and withdrawing: Strategies for coping with information overload in everyday contexts. *Journal of Information Science*, *33*(5), 611–621. doi:10.1177/0165551506077418

Schamber, L. (1994). Relevance and information behavior. *Annual Review of Information Science & Technology*, *29*, 3–48.

Schamber, L., Eisenberg, M. B., & Nilan, M. S. (1990). A re-examination of relevance: Toward a dynamic, situational definition. *Information Processing & Management*, *26*(6), 755–776. doi:10.1016/0306-4573(90)90050-C

Shadle, S. (2009). Electronic resources in a next-generation catalog: The case of Worldcat Local. *Journal of Electronic Resources Librarianship*, *21*(3/4), 192–199. doi:10.1080/19411260903446006

Shen, Y. (2007). Information seeking in academic research: A study of the Sociology faculty at the University of Wisconsin-Madison. *Information Technology and Libraries*, *26*(1), 4–13.

Solomon, P. (2002). Discovering information in context. *Annual Review of Information Science & Technology*, *36*(1), 229–264. doi:10.1002/aris.1440360106

Spink, A. (2010). *Information behavior: An evolutionary instinct*. Berlin, Germany: Springer.

Spink, A., Jansen, B. J., & Ozmultu, H. C. (2000). Use of query reformulation and relevance feedback by Excite users. *Internet Research: Electronic Networking Applications and Policy*, *10*(4), 317–328. doi:10.1108/10662240010342621

Spink, A., Wolfram, D., Jansen, B. J., & Saracevic, T. (2001). Searching the Web: The public and their queries. *Journal of the American Society for Information Science and Technology*, *52*(3), 226–234. doi:10.1002/1097-4571(2000)9999:9999<::AID-ASI1591>3.0.CO;2-R

Stone, S. (1982). Humanities scholars: Information needs and uses. *The Journal of Documentation*, *38*(4), 292–313. doi:10.1108/eb026734

Swain, D. E. (1996). Information search process model: How freshmen begin research. Proceedings of the ASIS Annual Meeting, 33, (pp. 95-99).

Thomas, B., & Buck, S. (2010). OCLC's WorldCat Local versus III's WebPAC: Which interface is better at supporting common user tasks? *Library Hi Tech, 28*(4), 648–671. doi:10.1108/07378831011096295

Tunkelang, D. (2009). *Faceted search*. San Rafael, CA: Morgan & Claypool Publishers.

Twait, M. (2005). Undergraduate students' source selection criteria: A qualitative study. *Journal of Academic Librarianship, 31*(6), 567–573. doi:10.1016/j.acalib.2005.08.008

Valentine, B. (1993). Undergraduate research behavior: Using focus groups to generate theory. *Journal of Academic Librarianship, 19*(5), 300–304. doi:10.1016/0099-1333(93)90026-2

Vaughan, J. (2011). Web scale discovery: What and why? *Library Technology Reports, 47*(1), 5–11.

Vaughan, J., & ALA TechSource. (2011). *Web scale discovery services*. Chicago, IL: ALA TechSource.

Warwick, C., Rimmer, J., Blandford, A., Gow, J., & Buchanan, G. (2009). Cognitive economy and satisficing in information seeking: A longitudinal study of undergraduate information behavior. *Journal of the American Society for Information Science and Technology, 60*(12), 2402–2415. doi:10.1002/asi.21179

Watson-Boone, R. (1994). The information needs and habits of humanities scholars. *Research Quarterly, 34*(2), 203–216.

Way, D. (2010). The impact of Web-scale discovery on the use of a library collection. *Serials Review, 36*(4), 214–220. doi:10.1016/j.serrev.2010.07.002

Whitmire, E. (2002). Disciplinary differences in undergraduates' information-seeking behavior. *Journal of the American Society for Information Science and Technology, 53*(8), 631–638. doi:10.1002/asi.10123

Whitmire, E. (2003). Epistemological beliefs and the information-seeking behavior of undergraduates. *Library & Information Science Research, 25*(2), 127–142. doi:10.1016/S0740-8188(03)00003-3

Whitmire, E. (2004). The relationship between undergraduates' epistemological beliefs, reflective judgment, and their information-seeking behavior. *Information Processing & Management, 40*(1), 97–111. doi:10.1016/S0306-4573(02)00099-7

Wilson, T. D. (1981). On user studies and information needs. *The Journal of Documentation, 37*(1), 3–15. doi:10.1108/eb026702

Wilson, T. D. (1997). Information behaviour: An interdisciplinary perspective. *Information Processing & Management, 33*(4), 551–572. doi:10.1016/S0306-4573(97)00028-9

Wilson, T. D. (1999). Exploring models of information behaviour: The 'uncertainty' project. *Information Processing & Management, 35*(6), 839–849. doi:10.1016/S0306-4573(99)00029-1

Wilson, T. D., Ford, N., Ellis, D., Foster, A., & Spink, A. (2002). Information seeking and mediated search, Part 2: Uncertainty and its correlates. *Journal of the American Society for Information Science and Technology, 53*(9), 704–715. doi:10.1002/asi.10082

Yang, K. (2005). Information retrieval on the web. *Annual Review of Information Science & Technology, 39*, 33–80. doi:10.1002/aris.1440390109

Zach, L. (2005). When is "enough" enough? Modeling the information-seeking and stopping behavior of senior arts administrators. *Journal of the American Society for Information Science and Technology, 56*(1), 23–35. doi:10.1002/asi.20092

KEY TERMS AND DEFINITIONS

Berrypicking: An evolving process of information seeking in which the user identifies useful information in the midst of a search which in turn informs the search and narrows the focus of the information need (see Bates, 1989).

Chaining: A process of tracking references both forward and backward from an initial source (see Ellis, 1989).

Differentiating: A process of evaluating resources based on criteria such as topic, perspective, date, quality, etc. (see Ellis, 1989).

Epistemological Development: A process of understanding and constructing knowledge. This is usually a component of an individual's natural maturation (see Whitmire, 2003, 2004).

Exploration: A process of identifying information on a broad topic of interest to determine the extent of available resources and potential areas of focus (see Kuhlthau, 1985, 1988a, 1988b, 2004).

Extracting: A process of reviewing information sources and highlighting or consolidating information of relevance to the information need (see Ellis, 1989).

Information Seeking: The mental, physical, and emotional components involved in identifying an information need and identifying and locating information that will satisfy that need.

Initiation: The beginning of a research project or information seeking activity, usually an assignment (for students), proposal acceptance (for faculty), etc. (see Kuhlthau, 1985, 1988a, 1988b, 2004).

Monitoring: A process of keeping up with print, electronic, or interpersonal resources in an area of interest by various means (e.g., conference attendance, browsing the tables of contents of journals, etc.; see Ellis, 1989).

Precision: The percentage of a set of search results that are actually determined to be relevant to the information seeker's need (see Berry & Brown, 2005; Schamber, 1994).

Recall: The percentage of all possible relevant results that were retrieved by a particular set of search criteria (see Berry & Brownee, 2005; Schamber, 1994).

Relevance/Relevancy: The extent to which the results of a search match the search criteria (see Berry & Browne, 2005; Froehlich, 1994; Saracevic, 2007a).

Satisficing: Combines the notions of "satisfying" and "sufficing"—having found "good enough" sources to satisfy an information need (see Prabha et al., 2007).

ENDNOTES

[1] Worldcat is a registered trademark of OCLC.
[2] Serials Solution is a registered trademark of Serials Solutions
[3] Summons is owned by ProQuest LLC
[4] EBSCO Discovery Service is owned by EBSCO Publishing Industries
[5] AquaBrowser is a registered trademark of Serials Solutions
[6] Google Scholar is owned by Google, Inc.

Chapter 2
From Metasearching to Discovery:
The University of Florida Experience

LeiLani Freund
University of Florida, USA

Christian Poehlmann
University at Albany, State University of New York, USA

Colleen Seale
University of Florida, USA

ABSTRACT

Many academic libraries implemented a metasearch or federated search platform as a way to expand the amount of relevant information available to library users. While the metasearch concept seemed to hold great promise, it failed to live up to expectations and users failed to embrace the technology. Nevertheless, the single search box proved to be popular with search engine users, and metasearch would prove to be a forerunner to more evolved discovery solutions. In this chapter, the authors describe experiences with a metasearch product, usability testing, and how that experience shaped decision-making for the chosen discovery solution platform. The available discovery services are explored, and the process for selection at the University of Florida Libraries is described along with the plans for future evaluation of the implemented service.

INTRODUCTION

The George A. Smathers Libraries of the University of Florida (UF) form the largest information resource system in the state. The Libraries consist of nine physically separate campus libraries. Eight are in the system known as the George A. Smathers Libraries and one (the Legal Information Center) is attached to its respective administrative unit. The University of Florida Libraries are also part of a broader state system. While maintaining a separate library catalog, UF's library catalog is also part of a shared catalog and integrated library management system among the other ten State

DOI: 10.4018/978-1-4666-1821-3.ch002

University System (SUS) libraries in Florida operated by the Florida Center for Library Automation (FCLA). FCLA was established in 1984 by the Florida State legislature to automate and integrate the library catalogs of the State University Library System. UF's online public access catalog (OPAC) began with NOTIS-based software acquired in 1980. Later this software was adopted by the SUS. In 2004, the SUS libraries began migration to Aleph®1, the Ex Libris™2 integrated library management system. In 2007, Endeca^SM3 was added as a catalog search engine overlay and the new public catalog interface for UF and the SUS. Later in 2010, open source software, Solr Lucene, replaced Endeca^SM as the catalog search engine.

While the library catalog or OPAC evolved and access to government documents, digital collections and e-journals, books and other materials vastly improved, integrated access to databases and full-text content lagged behind. Like many other academic libraries, the University of Florida George A. Smathers Libraries' first step on the path to discovery involved the implementation of a metasearch or federated search platform. In this chapter, the authors will describe experiences with a metasearch product, the implementation and product evaluation process through user feedback and usability testing and how it shaped later decision-making for a more evolved discovery solution. The chapter concludes with a discussion of plans for a new discovery product.

DEFINITION, HISTORY, AND OVERVIEW OF METASEARCHING

A metasearch (now often used interchangeably with parallel search, federated search, broadcast search, cross-database search or search portal) is a search simultaneously conducted across several bibliographic and full-text databases, platforms, vendors, sources and protocols using a single search interface. The search results may be returned in various ways (listed by database or in a merged list; sorted by relevancy, date, or other attributes; de-duplicated or not) but always in a consistent format.

How did metasearching evolve? As Judy Luther stated in a *Library Journal* article published in 2003, "Metasearch isn't a new concept. Dialog in the 1970s and subsequently SilverPlatter executed a single search simultaneously across multiple bibliographic databases" (Luther, 2003, p. 37). The mid to late 1990s saw not only the introduction of Google (named search engine of choice in the Top 100 Web Sites for 1998 by *PC Magazine*), but also Web metacrawlers or metasearch engines such as Dogpile, WebCrawler and Metacrawler that could execute a single search query across multiple search engines to retrieve search results.

Soon after, a similar concept for libraries in the form of a library portal began appearing in the marketplace and in the literature. Library portals offered a single interface for access to a number of resources which might include the local library catalog, other library catalogs, the Internet and/or Web sites, and various other resources. In 2000, Jerry Campbell delivered a white paper at an Association of Research Libraries (ARL) membership meeting, subsequently published as a report, on the concept of a scholars' portal. "To begin with, *scholars portal* would provide a number of highly desirable gateway functions. These might include an explanatory guide to information.coms as well as cross-platform access to commercial databases" (Campbell, 2000, para. 18). In 2002, the ARL Scholars Portal Working Group issued a final report on key features needed for a "super discovery tool." "This tool needs to search, aggregate, integrate, and deliver licensed and openly available digital content across a broad range of subject fields and from multiple institutions" (ARL, 2002, para. 6). The critical core features included: "First, the ability to query two distinct streams of electronic resources and databases: "universal stream" of unrestricted resources (Web pages and searchable databases) from Web sites targeted for quality and academic relevance, and "local stream" of information, access to which is restricted to local users by license or other agreement. Second, the ability to map a search against different types of metadata" (ARL, 2002, para. 8).

Library metasearch tools were also in development. Among the earliest, the California Digital Library launched its SearchLight tool in January 2000. Searchlight allowed "users to simultaneously search online catalogs, indexes, e-journals, electronic texts, reference resources, and more" (California Digital Library, 2005, para. 1). In October 2000, the National Library of Medicine (NLM) released the NLM Gateway allowing users to search a number of its databases. In 2003, the National Information Standards Organization (NISO) established a Metasearch Initiative to address issues and industry standards including interoperability, standardized search protocols and usage statistics, authentication, etc. In an effort to provide the one-stop search option, metasearch initiatives were undertaken by both public and academic libraries. Some of the key players and products in the metasearch environment at that time included: Auto-Graphics (Agent®[4]), BiblioMondo (ZonePro), Endeavor (ENCompass), Ex Libris™ (MetaLib®[5]), Fretwell-Downing (ZPORTAL™[6]), Gaylord (Polaris®[7] PowerPAC™[8]), Innovative Interfaces, Inc. (Millennium Access Plus), MuseGlobal (MuseSearch), Sirsi (iBistro), VTLS™[9] (Chameleon iPortal), OCLC (SiteSearch™[10]), and WebFeat®[11] (Knowledge Prism).

LITERATURE REVIEW

Along with the discussion of initial metasearch product selection and implementation, numerous articles have been published in the professional literature on usability testing and user reactions to metasearch products. Generally, the main goals of a metasearch implementation were to respond to a perceived user need, to raise awareness of the library's investment in underutilized electronic resources, to streamline research for the user by creating a one-stop search of multiple databases in one simultaneous, effective search, to reduce the burden of learning different databases and their search interfaces, and to provide a simple search interface. The perceived advantages for users included in addition to those listed above, a simple, easy to navigate interface, and time savings. Problems discussed from the library perspective and/or the user perspective included significant staff investment, navigation problems, subject categorization, limited search options, the display and formatting of results (lack of relevancy ranking, lack of enough information to determine usefulness of resource), slowness, user authentication, authorization, ability to merge results and remove duplicates, incomplete coverage and incompatibility of some subscription databases with the metasearch product, and hosting issues among others. The following articles are representative examples of the many published studies on usability testing and user feedback of various metasearch tools.

Boston College implemented MetaQuest™[12] with the first release of MetaLib® in 2001 and in 2003, in preparation for the next release, conducted a series of user studies and resource usability studies. The studies revealed that users "preferred to redo a search completely and ignored tool-based navigation options in favor of browser-based navigation options" (Tallent, 2004, p. 70). The Quick Search function was found to be the most popular enhancement due to "its simplicity and the user's desire to start searching immediately" (Tallent, 2004, p. 74). Although students admitted that their database usage was limited, "they would broaden their choices if they could do the searches simultaneously" (Tallent, 2004, p. 74). The studies also showed that students preferred complete citations in the search results (more information up front) and appreciated linking to full-text (Tallent 2004).

As part of a sabbatical project conducted in 2003-2004, Susan Elliot's white paper, *MetaSearch and Usability*, describes a broad investigation of metasearch tools with a focus on usability and an in-depth analysis of three of the leading tools, Endeavor's ENCompass, Ex Libris™' MetaLib®, and MuseGlobal's MuseSearch. Five areas of usability-related problems found generally affecting all metasearch tools included navigation, adherence to Web and graphical user interface conventions, choice of resources and search options, feedback regarding search progress, and results display (Elliot 2004).

In an article by Frank Cervone at Northwestern University, one of the issues identified through usability testing was the problem of selecting a predefined subject area before running a search which the author suggested "could be a major impediment to effective use of a federated search product" (Cervone, 2005, p. 12). Further, Cervone noted that "research indicates that searching by 'subject' categories does not work well for many user communities because they need to be able to select databases across disciplines" (Cervone, 2005, p.12). In the MetaLib® product, if a specific group of databases is not selected, the Quick Search system default is to run the search in a group of broad interdisciplinary databases. Comments from users indicated that this type of search was very successful and provides a good place to start their research (Cervone 2005).

At the University of Maryland, another academic library with a MetaLib® implementation, Wrubel and Schmidt conducted observation-based formal usability testing of the Quick Search and Cross Search screens. Problems encountered during the testing included interface workflow, navigation problems (use of browser's back button), issues with subject categorization, difficulty determining relevancy and format of search results, and a slower search process among others. Conclusions from the study included that, "students perceived metasearch to be a useful tool," however, "students expect to search metasearch interfaces the same way they search Internet search engines, but the underlying technology does not yet make this possible" (Wrubel & Schmidt, 2007, p. 302).

While not strictly a study on usability testing, Gail Herrera at the University of Mississippi Libraries has written about the libraries' experiences with the federated search product, Innovative Interfaces' MetaFind, which was made available to users in March 2003. This product was chosen because it tied into an established digital initiative partnership with the vendor. Feedback received from a LibQUAL+®[13] survey conducted in 2003 indicated users wanted more personal control than the library was providing (i.e. easy to use access tools that allow finding things on one's own, and making information easily accessible for independent use). After the implementation of MetaFind along with other changes, the libraries did receive notably improved scores in this category in a follow-up survey conducted in 2005 (Herrara 2007).

In 2005, Ponsford and vanDuinkerken at Texas A & M University conducted usability testing of their federated search product, Search Now (Ex Libris™' MetaLib® version 3). As explained in the article, round one of the testing was conducted for assessment purposes, to determine major problem areas with the metasearch tool, then to make appropriate changes. The test administered to nearly 50 volunteers (including faculty, staff and students) covered use of both the federated search and the resource discovery features (finding specific titles) and included additional questions on the overall experience using the product and recommendations for changes. From feedback received in the initial testing, the look of both the search and navigation tabs was changed. The second or validation round was conducted to determine if those changes were successful and if other issues needed to be addressed. The study showed that the volunteers generally found the search feature "easy to use and likable" (Ponsford, 2007, p. 176). Some of the suggestions gathered through the study included adding the ability to search by source, also by more than one category or QuickSet at a time, to limit by format, year, and by scholarly publications (Ponsford & vanDuinkerken, 2007).

The Research Libraries Group (RLG) conducted a survey of metasearch expectations and implementation experiences among its members in 2005. Although implementation wasn't complete for all surveyed at the time, the survey found that enthusiasm about metasearch was very high but the level of satisfaction was low (RLG 2005).

More recently, at Sam Houston State University an assessment of students' use and satisfaction with the library's implementation of a WebFeat® federated search product was conducted six months after the beta version was released in Aug. 2007. Data was gathered via an online survey to which students were invited to participate by a randomly distributed email invitation. Results of the analysis of 475 responses showed that although the product (called E-Z Search) was used frequently during the first year of implementation, it received weak levels of satisfaction (35%). The authors, Abe Korah and Erin Cassidy, speculated that use might be due to its prominent placement on the library's Web page, one-search box simplicity and bright color. Use was also more likely by undergraduates than graduate students. Other findings were that students who were frequent Internet users were not predisposed to prefer E-Z Search and that more experienced users demonstrated a stronger preference for individual databases rather than the federated search. The authors concluded that satisfaction with the federated search product could increase by "improving the precision, relevancy and ranking of the results, as well as the readability of the display" (Korah & Cassidy, 2010, p. 331).

The usability studies of the various metasearch products summarized above provide a laundry list of problems and issues that future search products need to address to be considered successful. Navigation issues are the most common theme in the literature on both discovery and federated search products. While many users desire a very Google-like search experience, some desire greater control over either the databases or subjects searched. Ultimately, for discovery to overcome the shortcomings of federated search, the interface needs to have a simple search box as the default with the ability to quickly and easily switch to a more sophisticated interface if desired, as well as immediate and relevant search results.

CASE STUDY: METASEARCHING SERVICES AT UF

Examining the MetaLib® Product

The staff of the University of Florida George A. Smathers Libraries began looking at metasearch engines in 2005. Because Ex Libris™ (Aleph®) was the integrated library management system in use since 2004 at the UF Libraries and several of the other state universities in Florida, it was logical to start with MetaLib®, the Ex Libris™ Library Portal search tool. UF Libraries staff members were introduced to MetaLib® during the summer of 2005 in several public services forums. The team responsible for evaluation of the product encouraged librarians from all areas to begin testing MetaLib® during the fall 2005 semester, in advance of trying to make a decision on a beta test or going public with the new product.

MetaLib® provides a single interface and portal to a wide variety of information sources including citation databases, full-text databases and e-journals, and library catalogs. It also provides links to the native database interface; this is particularly crucial for resources not available as a cross-searchable database in MetaLib®. The MetaLib® portal has five main modules, each providing a number of options. "QuickSearch" provides a Google-like interface with a simple or advanced option to cross search pre-selected, fixed sets of databases chosen by the institution to best suit local users. "Find Database" allows users to search for databases by title or keyword or browse discipline-specific subject lists created by the local librarians. "Find e-Journal" allows users to search the library's list of journals such as the ExLibris™/SFX® or Serials Solutions® list.

The "MetaSearch" function is the centerpiece of the product, providing the full cross-database search functionality in MetaLib®. MySpace™[14] is the personalization feature, allowing set-up of search queries and email alerts, configuration of preferences, and creation of citation or journal lists.

Librarian Reactions and Issues

Initial reaction to the MetaLib® features was not encouraging despite the often expressed desire on the part of reference librarians to have the ability to search across database and catalog holdings. Most of the comments came from public services librarians, but a small core group of technical services staff well-versed in the nuances of searching the library catalog and databases provided invaluable feedback as well. The primary issues of concern from the librarians were unintuitive navigation and unclear terminology. In addition, some of the inherent features of cross-database searching were very unfamiliar to the library staff. These included the lack of immediacy of the search and what seemed like slow returns as well as the need to understand the ranking algorithm and tweak it. With the help of the Florida Center for Library Automation (FCLA), the organization that provides Information Technology (IT) support as well as purchasing and access to selected information resources for all the public universities in Florida, some customization of the more unintuitive features was achieved. However, library staff members from all divisions and branches were still concerned that MetaLib® would be very confusing to patrons. Some librarians questioned whether users would be able to understand the overall purpose of the search tool, let alone be able to navigate its features. Concerns were also raised about the difficulty of administering and maintaining the product.

In January 2006, a UF Libraries MetaLib® Pilot Implementation Group was formed to address staff concerns and begin usability testing. According to an article later written by members of the Implementation Group, they were "troubled by inconsistent icons and terminology, personalization features that were difficult to understand and use, and the confusing and unpredictable manner in which MetaLib® retrieved, ranked, and displayed results" (Ochoa et al, 2007, p. 51). The MySpace™ functions were also specifically identified as being particularly difficult for even experienced users to understand. Several other institutions in the Florida state university system were also interested in MetaLib® and one institution, the University of South Florida, had already done user testing. Initial usability study data was shared across the universities and statewide planning began in earnest to conduct training sessions and learn more about administering the MetaLib® product.

Usability Testing

In the spring semester of 2006 the Implementation Group at the University of Florida conducted local task-based usability tests with six undergraduate students, five graduate students, and four non-library faculty researchers. Because of time constraints, the Implementation Group kept the sample of users relatively small. Some of the participants were personal contacts of the task force members. Others were recruited via announcements on undergraduate and graduate listservs and some of the students were library student assistants. The participants were chosen to cover a broad range of academic disciplines and represented varying levels of expertise with library use and computers.

The first part of the usability testing was an introduction to MetaLib® and about five minutes of exploration followed by some questions that gathered first impressions. The scenario-based part of the testing consisted of twelve tasks in five focus areas: finding databases; searching (within the MetaLib® portal); finding e-journals; displaying, sorting, and navigating results; and using MySpace™. The task force used Camtasia Studio

3.0 to capture cursor movements, navigation, and verbal responses. After the task-based testing, the participants answered a post-test questionnaire and received an invitation to participate in a follow-up pizza lunch and focus group that would take place two weeks later. These recorded focus groups were small, consisting of only one to four participants and a task force member.

Usability Results: What Was Learned?

The usability tests and results are described in detail in the Ochoa et al. (2007) article, "confirming expectations that students and scholars would find many features of the MetaLib® system difficult to understand and use" (p. 60). Based on these results, more changes were made to the interface to improve usability but issues remained that would drive later efforts by librarians to explore further innovations in library search tools and eventually seek out a Web-based discovery product. The MetaLib® usability testing issues and recommendations included:

Work on Terminology and "Help" Screens

Participants had difficulty with jargon and suggested more user-friendly terminology. For example, the "MetaSearch" label was changed locally to "CrossSearch" in the hope of being more descriptive to UF users. Many test users confessed to being totally lost in the navigation system. As a result, some of the implementation group members began work on an in-house, contextual "help" system. The contextual help provided some explanation of terms and directions to users, but librarians were certain that few students would read it. Comments from test participants had made it clear they were looking for ease of use and transparency. The complex, tabbed look of the product was unavoidable to obtain full functionality of all the features and

thus unlikely to fulfill the desire for transparency and a "Google-like" look and feel.

Icons vs. Text

The MetaLib® icons were confusing to the test users. Replacing icons with text is difficult in MetaLib®, prompting the addition of text legends at the top of the results page. Again, the legends may have helped the users who were truly motivated to use the product, but for the more casual user would simply clutter the interface and discourage use.

Finding e-Journals

Over 75% of the test users successfully located their assigned e-journal title and only had difficulty finding coverage dates. This problem was later resolved when the Libraries subscribed to the Serials Solutions® link resolver, but because the Serials Solutions® product was from a different vendor than the ExLibris™ federated search engine, two knowledge bases (KB) had to be maintained. Each time a journal title was added, changed, or removed, back-end work had to occur in both products. The search for a less labor-intensive solution would be ongoing.

Find Databases by Subject

Few of the test participants ever found this function, but when users did find it, they had to click-through a confusing number of tabs and selection boxes to get to the database lists. Eight-five percent of the test subjects were unable to find a database containing a specific subject keyword. The task force submitted to Ex Libris™ and FCLA several suggestions for navigation improvements and one task force member made it her mission to help the subject selectors create short lists of preferred cross-searchable databases in each subject area. Despite a lot of work to create useful subject lists, the navigation within this function remains too complex for most users who seem to prefer and be more aware of the popular and readily accessible subject guides (LibGuides) later developed by the subject librarians. Although the MetaLib® "Find Databases" function to this date still serves as a database locator of sorts, it is rarely updated and remains confusing to the users. The search for an alternative remained in the minds of those who would later look critically at discovery tool features to determine the availability of database location functions and ease of linkage to the native database from within the discovery interface.

Metasearch and MySpace™

Both of these modules were deemed unusable by the users and the task force. Those who found MetaSearch and managed to understand what it meant were still hopelessly confused by the navigation. No one understood why some databases were available for cross searching and some were not. More than one test user expressed dislike of being directed out of the metasearch function to a different database where the search had to be repeated. Others found the subject-specific lists of databases to be of no use for interdisciplinary search topics. If no personal lists have been saved, users of MySpace™ face an almost blank screen and have no idea what to do next. Test users indicated that they would likely give up when using these modules unless clear instructions could be produced. Even some of the members of the Implementation Group could not locate email and citation export functions in these modules. The task force recommended holding both of these functions back during beta testing. The decision was subsequently made not to hold back these functions so central to the purpose of a federated search tool, but the fact remained that the users were mystified by the task of finding the right database lists to cross search. Although appreciation of the functionality of cross searching was expressed by the test users, ease of use had not been accomplished by the federated search product.

Search Results

The test users had great difficulty interpreting the search results as they waited for the searching to complete and pondered what "retrieved" or "searching" might mean as MetaLib® queried the databases separately. In a recent article written by Brian Kenney (2011) at the Sydney Jones Library of the University of Liverpool, a colleague likened watching metasearch engine results display to "watching paint dry" (p. 25). UF users would concur. They were perplexed by what was happening and commented on the need for instantaneous, relevant results, even if they were only partial results. Although the advantage of federated searching lies in the real-time search results that are as up-to-date as the underlying databases, the lure of a faster response and one immediate list of displayed results would beckon to users and librarians alike.

MetaLib®: Success or Failure?

Beta testing commenced in the summer of 2006 and despite remaining problems, the MetaLib® product became a part of the repertoire of resource navigation tools for the University of Florida community. Acknowledging the difficulty of the MySpace™ and MetaSearch functions, librarians felt that holding back a large part of the functionality of this search tool was unwise. Although the vendor and FCLA experts were very responsive and great strides were made to improve usability, there were simply too many issues to make the metasearch engine a popular tool among librarians or users. The graduate students who worked one-on-one with librarians and teaching faculty with long-term projects were the two main groups of users. Due to the steep learning curve and the often slow display of search results, MetaLib® was really never adopted by librarian instructors in the the 50-minute information literacy classes that were part of the UF Writing Program for freshmen, the largest component of the Smathers

Libraries' library instruction program. A major issue for the administrators of this tool has remained the labor intensive nature of making changes to the underlying knowledge base as well as to features such as the subject-specific lists of cross-searchable databases. As discussed, although a huge effort was undertaken by the subject specialists to create these lists of "favorite" databases, years later, many of those lists remain the same, never updated to include new databases because the subject approach to the metasearch function is so rarely used.

As new metasearch products developed and older ones improved, it was clear that many of the problems are simply inherent in the nature of these tools. As users became more accustomed to Google and Google-like search engines with their simplified search box and ranked results, the metasearch tools looked more and more outdated. Although MetaLib® has remained a part of the services offered at the University of Florida, it has been used by fewer rather than more students as the years have passed. The combination of the many problems discussed above gradually led to its failure as a viable search option. Clearly, librarians and users at the University of Florida were ready for a service that could provide more discoverability.

FROM METASEARCHING TO DISCOVERY

The Environment

As the search for an alternative or improvement to MetaLib® began, librarians at the University of Florida were aware that research, especially by students, started outside not just the library building, but the library as gateway. This mirrored a global trend. In its landmark 2003 Environmental Scan, OCLC (De Rosa et al, 2005) identified three trends that defined the twenty-first century information consumer. They are: self-sufficiency; satisfaction; seamlessness. Information consumers are self-sufficient. They are uninterested in mediated information seeking. They are satisfied with what they find. In many cases, it doesn't matter to the information consumer that he or she could achieve better results from a series of searches in proprietary databases. If one search in a search engine (primarily Google) results in a set of results that is good enough, then the information consumer prefers this solution. This leads to the third trend – seamlessness. One self-performed search in an interface that provides a "good enough" set of results is far preferable to a series of searches across multiple platforms, perhaps guided or taught by an intermediary, that provide a better set of results.

In another OCLC study, this one conducted in 2010 to survey library perceptions, not a single survey respondent of any age or group began their information search on a library Web site, preferring search engines like Google and Yahoo. However, about 30% of the surveyed college students eventually used library databases and about 58% found their way to the library Web site. The 30% figure held steady between the earlier 2005 survey and the 2010 survey. Forty-three percent indicated that information from library sources is more trustworthy than from search engines. The study concludes that "College students feel that search engines trump libraries for speed, convenience, reliability and ease of use. Libraries trump search engines for trustworthiness and accuracy" (De Rosa et al., 2010, p. 54). Although the trusted image of the librarian or library was untarnished, users valued convenience and ease of discovery more. This trend was clearly demonstrated by the MetaLib® usability testing in Florida and at other institutions. If the navigation and special features like MySpace™ were too complex and took too long to figure out, users were likely to give up very quickly.

Librarians are well aware, through decades of trying, that ultimately it is impossible to change user behavior on a large scale. Users can be taught to be more information literate in the sense of discrimination among information resources. But if one service provides quick results that are good enough, there is nothing librarians can do to keep this tide from rolling in. However, around 2008, commercially viable Web-scale discovery services began to appear that allowed librarians to meet the information needs of users on their own terms. If the librarians couldn't bring the users to the library (databases), then the librarians would bring the library (databases) to the users.

In light of this, in early 2011 the University of Florida Libraries decided to embark on the implementation of a Web-scale discovery service. Two librarians secured an internal grant for a one-year pilot project funded through student technology fees. All University of Florida students pay a yearly technology fee, and these funds are distributed via a grant application process approved by a student committee that is overseen by the University of Florida Chief Information Officer. The timeframe was short, but the UF Libraries now had an opportunity to introduce a new service that could completely change the way the academic user started his or her research.

Discovery Selection Process

As part of the selection process, a library task force (the grant recipients, the electronic resource coordinator, a metadata specialist and cataloging librarian, and interested public services librarians) was appointed and a number of vendors were contacted and invited to campus to demonstrate their discovery services. EBSCO representatives visited the campus on several occasions and set up a trial for the University of Florida. Serials Solutions® representatives also visited campus several times; however the Summon™ product was not available as a trial specific to UF. This was not a significant issue since the open nature of the product allowed testing using the installations at a number of other Association of Research Libraries (ARL) institutions. SWETS visited UF to demonstrate their

discovery service, but the task force members viewed the SWETS product as a federated search system, and thus not really a viable alternative to include in the discovery discussion. Mango+ is a locally developed interface that can "sit over" any of a number of discovery services, including Primo Central®[15], Summon™, and EBSCO Discovery™. The Florida Center for Library Automation (FCLA) Mango+ interface was evaluated simultaneously with the underlying Ex Libris™ discovery service, Primo Central®. Two of the selection task force members attended a Webinar on WorldCat® Local. For reference and referral during the selection process a LibGuide was also compiled at: http://guides.uflib.ufl.edu/content.php?pid=209947&search_terms=discovery. Key articles on discovery services are listed in the guide as well as links to a comparison chart of discovery platforms.

Testing and User Feedback

A usability study of these platforms was done by the selection task force. The task force created a number of searches to run on each platform and compare results, including look and feel. One of the important variables the task force wished to measure was the currency or timeliness of the results. In order to accomplish this, the test searches focused on current events. The four test searches were: *Afghan War Troop Withdrawal; Great Financial Crisis; Tax Expenditures (date limit of 2011); and Kindleberger.* These searches were run, and the results were compared for currency and relevancy. Also, the look and feel of the interfaces were compared. The ease of filtering, sorting, and lack of duplicates were considered important factors. Also considered important was the response time. All platforms had a very quick response time, particularly in comparison to MetaLib®.

Due to the short timeframe available to make a decision, no formal user groups were formed to evaluate the platforms. The previously mentioned

Figure 1.

The most appealing/intuitive interface is? Please tell us why in the comments section of this question.	
Answer Options	**Response Percent**
Serials Solutions Summon	60.0%
Ebsco Discovery	30.0%
WorldCat Local	10.0%
Mango+	0.0%
Swetswise Discovery	0.0%

LibGuide, with links to the various platforms and suggested searches, was disseminated to University of Florida Libraries faculty and staff with a survey designed to elicit their opinions on the services. (See Appendix 1 for the questionnaire.)

Survey results indicated that over half of the Summon™, WorldCat® Local, and EBSCO users agreed or strongly agreed with the statement "I can find articles from the top journals in my subject area." Both Summon™ and EBSCO Discovery Service™ performed well in the relevancy criterion. The other discovery services under consideration did not fare as well.

Overall, task force members and the library staff and users surveyed preferred Summon™ both in terms of the underlying information as well as the interface. Users were asked to rank the discovery services interface from 1(best) – 5 (worst). Summon™ was a clear favorite in this category with 60% of survey respondents preferring it to all other discovery services. EBSCO Discovery Service ™ was a clear second with 30% of users selecting it as the preferred platform. Mango+ and Swetswise were the least favorite, with users being neutral at best and no users selected either as the preferred discovery service. WorldCat® Local was generally viewed less favorably than EBSCO or Summon™, although 1% ranked it best or second best. Users, by a wide margin, preferred the Summon™ interface over all others (see Figure 1).

Comparison of Federation and Discovery Products

Discovery architecture is significantly different from federated search architecture. Federated search products search live databases, while discovery services search databases of pre-indexed metadata and text. The strength of federated search is that it searches databases in real-time, and the search results are as up-to-date as the databases being searched. Discovery services need to secure and index the underlying metadata before it can be returned in search results. Securing the metadata can be a major undertaking. At the time of the University of Florida discovery service selection process (Spring 2011) the leading Web-scale discovery services also had business ties to content providers. This led to the situation where some database metadata was available to one discovery service but not the other. To address this problem, discovery services generally go directly to the source journals themselves to secure content. When unable to directly secure this content, EBSCO and Serials Solutions® take widely different approaches.

The EBSCO Discovery Service™ is ultimately a hybrid comprised of a discovery layer (pre-indexed metadata) and a federated search service that searches databases that are not pre-indexed. This results in a somewhat unusual user experience. Results for the pre-indexed metadata are returned almost instantly while the federated search continues to run in the background. The disadvantage of this federated search is the time to return results. Even in the robust federated search function of the EBSCO product, results are trickling in while users are reviewing the immediate results returned by the discovery function. A user used to the immediate results of Google will find the EBSCO experience radically different if the user selects an Integrated Search resource. The interface is more complex, and the results list changes as the federation completes. Given the negative feedback from librarians and students regarding slow and confusing results displays in MetaLib®, it was felt that this similar experience in EBSCO would be a major drawback.

Local files, such as catalogs and institutional repositories can also be indexed in both EBSCO Discovery Service™ and Summon™. For catalogs, a one-time MARC export must be made. Institutional repositories can be harvested through the Open Archives Initiative (OAI). Customers can then designate their own databases to be "private" (visible only to their own instance) or "public" (visible to all instances).

By default, Summon™ is searchable by all users, on or off campus, without authentication to the campus network. Thus, non-UF affiliated users could still search the library catalog as well as other databases without logging in to the campus network. Authentication would be required to retrieve full-text, but non-UF users could get citations and abstracts when available. EBSCO can be set to allow guest access, but this suppresses information in records as well as full-text. A notation appears onscreen that information from a database is available, but that the user must authenticate to the campus network to view the citation, abstract, and full-text. In guest mode, authentication is not required to view catalog records.

To access full-text an OpenURL resolver is always required. UF subscribes to the Serials Solutions® 360Link link resolver and Electronic Resources Management system. Since Summon™ is a Serials Solutions® product, it is administered within the Serials Solutions® Client Center. Met-

aLib® is used as UF's federated search solution. This requires the maintenance of two knowledge bases (KB). Each time an electronic resource is added, changed, or removed, changes must be made in each KB. If a URL changes, Serials Solutions® will handle the change in 360Link, but the URL must be manually changed in MetaLib®. This also doubles the time when troubleshooting any federated search. Updating Summon™ is a much more efficient workflow, greatly simplifying troubleshooting and eliminating the need to maintain two knowledge bases.

Cost and Sustainability

Although, first year costs will be paid with the technology fee funding grant, cost and sustainability are major inhibitors of Web-scale discovery implementation. Most of the services reviewed cost in the mid to high five figures per year of subscription. Multi-year licenses served to somewhat mitigate the high-cost, but it still proved a high barrier, even for the University of Florida where the materials budget had fared fairly well in recent years. While there was little room for an additional bibliographic utility in the budget as is, one idea under consideration is to impose a small surcharge on each budget line to fund the service in the future should it live up to expectations.

Selection Decision

In late June 2011, the committee met to review and recommend the Serials Solutions® Summon™ Web-scale discovery service for implementation at the University of Florida Libraries. The task force selected Summon™ as the more appropriate product for the University of Florida for a number of reasons that include: its single index; superior user interface; relevance ranking; accessibility; unified knowledgebase; autosuggest; peer-reviewed content verified by Ulrich's™; and one-click access to full-text.

EVALUATION OF DISCOVERY AND FUTURE RESEARCH DIRECTIONS

During this first year of implementation, the Smathers Libraries' task force along with other public services librarians will do a thorough review of the Summon™ capabilities and acceptance by end users. Metrics may be difficult to establish. It is known that the implementation of any Web-scale discovery service, or any federated search product for that matter, will distort usage statistics. Federated search will distort search sessions by searching all databases, or all within a subject subset, even if the user ultimately does not retrieve any articles from the searched database. Discovery will distort search sessions in the opposite direction since the metadata is pre-indexed and searched outside of the native interface.

Summon's™ Client Center provides detailed usage statistics including number of visits, searches, average number of searches per visit, etc. Google Analytics™[16] was also recently added to complement this usage data. The Libraries plan to purchase an additional product, Serial Solutions® 360 Counter, which will provide a better measure of what is being used in terms of library content.

Summon™ does not attempt to return results for resources which it does not index. This results in a simpler interface, and a very quick final list of results. Users are prompted to search un-indexed databases in the native interface through the Database Recommender feature. This could be a major handicap, since it is unclear at this juncture how many users will actually take the time to conduct a second search; it may be unlikely except in the case of faculty or graduate students conducting long-term research. This is an area the task force members anticipate exploring in depth during the post-implementation evaluation period.

As the 2006 federated search testing demonstrated, few methods provide the wealth of information gained from actually conversing with users, and focus groups provide the framework for a detailed conversation. This provides an oppor-

tunity to evaluate needs and results qualitatively. The task force members feel the best way to assess the usability of the discovery service will be to survey the end users and conduct focus groups. Currently, a link labeled "Feedback," just under the search box takes users to an online survey. (See Appendix 2.) Unfortunately, the response rate to this Web survey has been very small. For this reason, the Libraries are planning a more directed survey in a classroom setting accompanied by food as compensation. As a first step in the assessment process, an initial survey will combine questions about the users' usual means of starting research with a hands-on exercise that asks them to conduct a typical search in Summon, followed by their impressions of its usability. The outcome of this first exercise will likely determine the direction of further testing, whether in survey form or directly observable usability testing similar to what was done for MetaLib®. The survey results along with the combined data from Serials Solutions® and Google Analytics™ on the actual length and content of searches should give the UF librarians a good picture of how searchers are actually using the discovery service and at least an early impression of how successful or unsuccessful it is as a research tool.

CONCLUSION

Web-scale discovery services will continue to proliferate in coming years. Unless the producers of federated search solutions find a way to rapidly increase the response time, discovery will sound the death knell for federation. Hybrid solutions, because of their complicated interface, will continue to run in second place because they fail to deliver what our users want, when they want it, and how they want it. Google has created the expectation from users that usable search results will come from a simple search in a plain interface. Libraries that choose a more traditional approach may continue to lose the interest of their patrons who will increasingly obtain information from outside the library. UF Libraries are hopeful that a Web-scale discovery solution will vastly improve access to library resources and hold the interest of the academic community.

REFERENCES

ARL Scholars Portal Working Group. (2002). *ARL scholars portal working group final report.* Washington, DC: Association of Research Libraries. Retrieved from http://www.arl.org/resources/pubs/portals/report-may-2002.shtml

California Digital Library. (August 25, 2005). *SearchLight: Lights out!* Retrieved from http://www.cdlib.org/cdlinfo/2005/08/25/searchlight-lights-out/

Campbell, J. D. (2000). The case for creating a scholars portal to the web: A white paper. *ARL: A Bimonthly Report on Research Library Issues and Actions from ARL, CNI, and SPARC*, 211. Retrieved from http://www.arl.org/resources/pubs/portals/case-whitepaper.shtml

Cervone, F. (2005). What we've learned from doing usability testing on openURL resolvers and federated search engines. *Computers in Libraries*, *25*(9), 10–14.

De Rosa, C., Cantrell, J., Carlson, M., Gallagher, P., Hawk, J., & Sturtz, C. … Olszewski, L. (2010). *Perceptions of libraries, 2010: Context and community.* Dublin, OH: OCLC. Retrieved from http://www.oclc.org/reports/2010perceptions.htm

De Rosa, C., Cantrell, J., Cellentani, D., Hawk, J., Jenkins, L., & Wilson, A. (2005). *Perceptions of libraries and information resources. A report to the OCLC membership.* Dublin, Ohio: OCLC Online Computer Library Center. Retrieved from http://www.oclc.org/reports/pdfs/Percept_all.pdf

Elliot, S. A. (2004). *Metasearch and usability: Towards a seamless interface to library resources.* White paper, Consortium Library, University of Alaska Anchorage. Retrieved from http:www.lib.uaa.alaska.edu/tundra/msuse1.pdf

Google Timeline. (n.d.). *Website.* Retrieved from http://www.google.com/corporate/timeline/#1997

Herrera, G. (2007). MetaSearching and beyond: Implementation experiences and advice from an academic library. *Information Technology and Libraries*, *26*(2), 44–52.

Kenney, B. (2011). Liverpool's discovery. *Library Journal*, *136*(3), 24–27.

Korah, A., & Cassidy, E. (2010). Students and federated searching: A survey of use and satisfaction. *Reference and User Services Quarterly*, *49*(4), 325–332.

Luther, J. (2003). Trumping Google? Metasearching's promise. *Library Journal*, *128*(16), 36–39.

Magazine, P. C. (1999). *Top 100 websites.* Retrieved from http://web.archive.org/web/19990508042436/www.zdnet.com/pcmag/special/web100/search2.html

NISO (National Information Standards Organization). (n.d.). *NISO metasearch initiative.* Retrieved from http://www.niso.org/workrooms/mi/#background

Ochoa, M., Jesano, R., Nemmers, J., Newsom, C., O'Brien, M., & Victor, P. (2007). Testing the federated searching waters. *Journal of Web Librarianship*, *1*(3), 47–66. doi:10.1300/J502v01n03_04

Ponsford, B., & vanDuinkerken, W. (2007). User expectations in the time of Google: Usability testing of federated searching. *Internet Reference Services Quarterly*, *12*(1/2), 159–178. doi:10.1300/J136v12n01_08

Research Libraries Group. (2005). *Metasearch survey among RLG members.* Retrieved from http://www.oclc.org/research/activities/past/rlg/metasearch.htm

Tallent, E. (2004). Metasearching in Boston College libraries – A case study of user reactions. *New Library World, 105*(1), 69–75. doi:10.1108/03074800410515282

U.S. National Library of Medicine. (March 15, 2010). *NLM gateway fact sheet.* Retrieved from http://www.nlm.nih.gov/pubs/factsheets/gateway.html

Wrubel, L., & Schmidt, K. (2007). Usability testing of a metasearch interface: A case study. *College & Research Libraries, 68*(4), 292–311.

ADDITIONAL READING

Armstrong, A. (2009). Student perceptions of federated searching vs single database searching. *RSR. Reference Services Review, 37*(3), 291–303. doi:10.1108/00907320910982785

Avery, S., Ward, D., & Hinchliffe, L. (2007). Planning and implementing a federated searching system: An examination of the crucial roles of technical, functional, and usability testing. *Internet Reference Services Quarterly, 12*(1/2), 179–194. doi:10.1300/J136v12n01_09

Baer, W. (2004). Federated searching: Friend or foe? *College & Research Libraries News, 65*(9), 518–519.

Boss, R. W. (2002). How to plan and implement a library portal. *Library Technology Reports, 38*(6), 1–61.

Boss, S. C., & Nelson, M. L. (2005). Federated search tools: The next step in the quest for one-stop-shopping. *The Reference Librarian, 44*(91/92), 139–160. doi:10.1300/J120v44n91_10

Breeding, M. (2005). Plotting a new course for metasearch. *Computers in Libraries, 25*(2), 27–29.

Breeding, M. (2011). Discovering Harry Pottery Barn. *Computers in Libraries, 31*(2), 21–23.

Campbell, J. (2001). The case for creating a scholars portal to the Web: A white paper. *Portal (Baltimore, Md.), 1*(1), 15–21. doi:doi:10.1353/pla.2001.0002

Caswell, J., & Wynstra, J. (2010). Improving the search experience: Federated search and the library gateway. *Library Hi Tech, 28*(3), 391–401. doi:10.1108/07378831011076648

Chaffin, N., Cullen, K., & Jaramillo, G. R. (2005). Cross-database searching: The implementation of MetaLib. *Technical Services Quarterly, 22*(4), 39–53. doi:10.1300/J124v22n04_03

Christenson, H., & Tennant, R. (2005). *Integrating information resources: Principles, technologies, and approaches.* Oakland, CA: California Digital Library. Retrieved from http://www.cdlib.org/inside/projects/metasearch/nsdl/nsdl_report2.pdf

Cox, C. N. (2007). *Federated search: Solution or setback for online library services.* Binghamton, NY: Haworth Information Press.

Fei, X. (2009). Implementation of a federated search system: Resource accessibility issues. *Serials Review, 35*(4), 235–241. doi:10.1016/j.serrev.2009.08.019

Freund, L., Nemmers, J., & Ochoa, M. (2007). Metasearching: An annotated bibliography. *Internet Reference Services Quarterly, 12*(3/4), 411–430. doi:10.1300/J136v12n03_11

Frost, W. (2004). Do we want or need metasearching? *Library Journal, 129*(6), 68.

Fryer, D. (2004). Federated search engines. *Online, 28*(2), 16–19.

Gibson, I., Goddard, L., & Gordon, S. (2009). One box to search them all: Implementing federated search at an academic library. *Library Hi Tech, 27*(1), 118–133. doi:10.1108/07378830910942973

Goodwin, S., & Gola, C. (2008). Preparing staff for federated searching: A community of practice approach. *Internet Reference Services Quarterly, 13*(2/3), 245–259. doi:10.1080/10875300802103908

Hane, P. (2003). The truth about federated searching. *Information Today, 20*(9), 24.

Helfer, D., & Wakimoto, J. (2005). Metasearching: The good, the bad, and the ugly of making It work in your library. *Searcher, 13*(2), 40–41.

Jackson, M. (2002). The advent of portals. *Library Journal, 127*(15), 36–39.

Jackson, M. (2002). The ARL scholars portal initiative. *Journal of Library Administration, 36*(3), 81–91. doi:10.1300/J111v36n03_08

Jacsó, P. (2004). Thoughts about federated searching. *Information Today, 21*(9), 17–20.

James, D., Garrett, M., & Krevit, L. (2009). Discovering discovery tools: Evaluating vendors and implementing Web 2.0 environments. *Library Hi Tech, 27*(2), 268–276. doi:10.1108/07378830910968218

Lockwood, C., & MacDonald, P. (2007). Implementation of a federated search system in the academic library: Lessons learned. *Internet Reference Services Quarterly, 12*(1/2), 73–91. doi:10.1300/J136v12n01_04

Luther, J., & Kelly, M. (2011). The next generation of discovery. *Library Journal, 136*(5), 66–71.

Lynch, C. (1997). Building the infrastructure of resource sharing: Union catalogs, distributed search, and cross-database linkage. *Library Trends, 45*(3), 448–461.

Madison, O., & Hyland-Carver, M. (2005). Issues in planning for portal implementation: Perfection not required. *Journal of Library Administration, 43*(1/2), 113–134. doi:10.1300/J111v43n01_08

Moen, W., Oguz, F., & McClure, C. (2004). The challenges of nonstandardized vendor usage data in a statewide metasearch environment: The Library of Texas experience. *The Library Quarterly, 74*(4), 403–422. doi:10.1086/427412

Newton, V., & Silberger, K. (2007). Simplifying complexity through a single federated search box. *Online, 31*(4), 19–21.

Notess, G. (2011). Deciphering discovery. *Online, 35*(1), 45–47.

Ruddock, B., & Hartley, D. (2010). How UK academic libraries choose metasearch systems. *Aslib Proceedings: New Information Perspectives, 62*(1), 85–105. doi:doi:10.1108/00012531011015226

Sadeh, T. (2004). The challenge of metasearching. *New Library World, 105*(3/4), 104–112. doi:10.1108/03074800410526721

Scherlen, A. (2006). The one-box challenge: Providing a federated search that benefits the research process. *Serials Review, 32*(4), 247–254. doi:10.1016/j.serrev.2006.08.005

Tang, R., Hsieh-Yee, I., & Zhang, S. (2007). User perceptions of MetaLib combined search: An investigation of how users make sense of federated searching. *Internet Reference Services Quarterly, 12*(1/2), 211–236. doi:10.1300/J136v12n01_11

Tennant, R. (2001). Cross-database search: One-stop shopping. *Library Journal (1976), 126*(17), 29-30.

Tennant, R. (2003). The right solution: Federated search tools. *Library Journal, 128*(11), 28–30.

Tennant, R. (2005). Is metasearching dead? *Library Journal, 130*(12), 28.

Webster, P. (2004). Metasearching in an academic environment. *Online, 28*(2), 20–23.

Williams, S. C., Bonnell, A., & Stoffel, B. (2009). Student feedback on federated search use, satisfaction, and Web presence: Qualitative findings of focus groups. *Reference and User Services Quarterly, 49*(2), 131–139.

KEY TERMS AND DEFINITIONS

Federated Search/Metasearch: A search simultaneously conducted across several bibliographic and full-text databases, platforms, vendors, sources and protocols using a single search interface. The search results may be returned in various ways listed by database or in a merged list; sorted by relevancy, date, or other attributes; de-duplicated or not but always in a consistent format.

Knowledge Base (KB): A database that contains information such as descriptive metadata, institutional availability, licensing information, etc. about electronic resources to facilitate linkage to external systems.

Library Portal: A system or gateway that sits between the user and the electronic library resources or databases being used; the starting point for finding information and streamlining access to resources.

Link Resolver: The software that combines information about user permissions and licensing with OpenURL data to access a full-text resource through a link.

MARC Export: The process of creating a batch file of bibliographic and holdings information to export or upload.

Metacrawler: A metasearch engine that executes a single search query across multiple search engines to retrieve search results.

Metadata: Data elements that describe objects or information resources to facilitate discovery.

Open Archives Initiative: A project to build a framework or standard protocols for digital archives, repositories, or archival holdings (journals) that allows automatic harvesting or sharing of metadata.

OpenURL: A standardized form of a URL (uniform resource locator) that links metadata and other unique identifiers (bibliographic information) for a specific resource to services (such as the full-text in PDF or HTML format) for that resource.

Peer-Reviewed Journal: A journal publication that uses a panel of qualified individuals in the relevant field of study to review and determine the suitability of papers submitted to the journal for publication.

Relevant: In relation to results returned from search engine queries, expected or compatible with the search terms entered in the search query.

Usability Testing: Testing a product by some means of direct observation of how real users interact with the system or product being evaluated.

Web-Scale Discovery (Service): A product or service which searches across databases of pre-harvested, pre-indexed metadata and text (including library catalogs, digital repositories, full-text resources, etc.) to return ranked results in a user-friendly format providing a "Google-like" search experience.

ENDNOTES

[1] Aleph is a registered trademark of Ex Libris Ltd.

[2] Ex Libris is a trademark of Ex Libris Ltd.

[3] Endeca is a service mark of Oracle Corporation and its affiliates.

[4] AGent is a registered trademark of Auto-Graphics.

[5] MetaLib is a registered trademark of Ex Libris Ltd.

[6] ZPORTAL is a registered trademark of OCLC.

[7]   Polaris a registered trademark of Polaris Library Systems.

[8]   Power Pac is a trademark of Polaris Library Systems.

[9]   VTLS is a trademark of VTLS, Inc.

[10] SiteSearch is a trademark of OCLC.

[11] WebFeat is a registered trademark of Serials Solutions.

[12] MetaQuest is a trademark of MetaQuest, Inc.

[13] LIBQUAL+ is a registered trademark of the Association of Research Libraries.

[14] MySpace is a trademark of MySpace, LLC.

[15] Primo Central is owned by Ex Libris Ltd. or its affiliates.

[16] Google Analytics is a trademark of Google, Inc.

APPENDIX 1: SURVEY ON WEBSCALE DISCOVERY AT UF

Available at: http://www.surveymonkey.com/s.aspx?sm=MWbyRXQm4NQA2UiKPFzaftQarhRL6S%2fR2Jus3j3tKaw%3d

This is a short survey (10 Questions) to get your views on the web scale discovery services under evaluation at UF.

1. What is your primary role at UF?

○ Library Administration

○ Librarian

○ Staff

○ Graduate Student/Post Doc

○ Undergraduate Student

Other (please specify)

[   ]

2. My subject expertise is in:

○ 1. Social Sciences

○ 2. Humanities

○ 3. Health Sciences

○ 4. Physical Sciences

Other (please specify)

[   ]

3. I can easily narrow down my search results by clicking on different links (such as year or subject).

	Strongly Disagree	Disagree	Neutral	Agree	Strongly Agree
Ebsco Discovery	○	○	○	○	○
Mango+	○	○	○	○	○
Serials Solutions Summon	○	○	○	○	○
Swetswise Discovery	○	○	○	○	○
WorldCat Local	○	○	○	○	○

Comments

4. I can get to the full-text of an article in one mouse click.

	Rarely	Sometimes	Frequently
Ebsco Discovery	○	○	○
Mango+	○	○	○
Serials Solutions Summon	○	○	○
Swetswise Discovery	○	○	○
WorldCat Local	○	○	○

Comments

5. I can limit my search so I only get articles from scholarly (peer reviewed) journals.

	Strongly Disagree	Disagree	Neutral	Agree	Strongly Agree
Ebsco Discovery	○	○	○	○	○
Mango+	○	○	○	○	○
Serials Solutions Summon	○	○	○	○	○
Swetswise Discovery	○	○	○	○	○
WorldCat Local	○	○	○	○	○

Comments

6. I can find articles from the top journals in my subject area.

	Strongly Disagree	Disagree	Neutral	Agree	Strongly Agree	N/A
Ebsco Discovery	○	○	○	○	○	○
Mango+	○	○	○	○	○	○
Serials Solutions Summon	○	○	○	○	○	○
Swetswise Discovery	○	○	○	○	○	○
WorldCat Local	○	○	○	○	○	○

Comments

7. I can easily save and share citations of articles I find.

	Strongly Disagree	Disagree	Neutral	Agree	Strongly Agree
Ebsco Discovery	○	○	○	○	○
Mango+	○	○	○	○	○
Serials Solutions Summon	○	○	○	○	○
Swetswise Discovery	○	○	○	○	○
WorldCat Local	○	○	○	○	○

Other (please specify)

8. The most appealing/intuitive interface is? Please tell us why in the comments section of this question.

○ Ebsco Discovery

○ Mango+

○ Serials Solutions Summon

○ Swetswise Discovery

○ WorldCat Local

Comments

9. Please rank the discovery services you have used.

	Worst (5)	4	3	2	Best (1)	N/A
Ebsco Discovery	○	○	○	○	○	○
Mango+	○	○	○	○	○	○
Serials Solutions Summon	○	○	○	○	○	○
Swetswise Discovery	○	○	○	○	○	○
WorldCat Local	○	○	○	○	○	○

10. Are there any other comments about any of the services you would like to make?

APPENDIX 2: UF ONESEARCH SURVEY

Available at: http://www.surveymonkey.com/s/uf_onesearch

UF OneSearch

1. Overall, are you satisfied with your experience using OneSearch, neither satisfied or dissatisfied with it, or dissatisfied with it?

○ Extremely satisfied
○ Moderately satisfied
○ Slightly satisfied
○ Neither satisfied nor dissatisfied
○ Slightly dissatisfied
○ Moderately dissatisfied
○ Extremely dissatisfied

2. How likely are you to recommend our service to people you know ?

○ Extremely likely
○ Very likely
○ Moderately likely
○ Slightly likely
○ Not at all likely

3. Are there any comments or suggestions that you would like to make about OneSearch?

4. Which of the following categories best describes your status at UF?

○ Undergraduate
○ Graduate Student
○ Visiting Scholar/Researcher
○ Faculty
○ Administrator
○ Staff
○ Unaffiliated

5. Please tell us which college you are affiliated with.

○ Agricultural & Life Sciences
○ Business Administration
○ Dentistry
○ Design, Construction & Planning
○ Education
○ Engineering
○ Fine Arts

○ Health & Human Performance
○ Journalism & Communications
○ Law
○ Liberal Arts & Sciences
○ Libraries
○ Medicine
○ Nursing

○ Pharmacy
○ Public Health & Health Professions
○ Veterinary Medicine
○ Other
○ Unaffiliated

6. If you would like a response to your feedback, please supply your email address below.

Name: [_____]
Email Address: [_____]

[Done]

Chapter 3
Details, Details, Details:
Issues in Planning for, Implementing, and Using Resource Discovery Tools

David P. Brennan
Pennsylvania State University, Milton S. Hershey Medical Center, USA

ABSTRACT

This chapter presents a high-level, non-system-specific discussion of issues surrounding the planning, implementation, use, and maintenance of discovery tools. The purpose of this chapter is to facilitate discussion as the library prepares to evaluate discovery tools and prepare for their implementation. In some ways, these issues are not markedly different from any library system implementation and can be understood on the basis of existing project management literature; however, there are issues specific to discovery tools and their integration with existing library systems and workflows that should be considered. Additional post-implementation issues specific to discovery tools are also presented.

INTRODUCTION

This book is intended to assist administrators and librarians in their planning and implementation processes. Many of the concepts in this chapter have been touched upon elsewhere throughout the book; however the intent is not to repeat, but to place some of the issues surrounding the plan-

ning, implementation, and use of discovery tools in a larger context in order to provide a basis for discussion as the library prepares to enter the world of resource discovery. None of what is discussed here is vendor- or system-specific, but is intended to generate questions that planners and systems personnel can ask of vendors and developers as the selection and implementation process moves forward. Much of what is presented here can also be a part of any Request for Proposal (RFP) to

DOI: 10.4018/978-1-4666-1821-3.ch003

vendors – if the library has specific needs relative to implementing a discovery tool, making sure they are in the RFP is vital. (Caswell, 2007) In complex projects such as this, it is easy to miss details that become important later on; "action items" are flagged in this chapter that can serve as reminders of these details. Note that the terms "discovery system(s)" and "discovery tool(s)" are used interchangeably throughout. As noted in the literature review, the terminology used to describe these types of products varies widely. There are topics that are out of the scope of this chapter's focus, such as optional ERM (Electronic Resource Management) modules that available with some discovery systems. These additional features, if important to the library, should be included in the vendor evaluation process.

BACKGROUND AND LITERATURE REVIEW

The purpose of a discovery tool is to aggregate and expose content from a variety of existing resources. This makes it an adjunct to other resources, not a replacement; without external databases and internal datasets there would be nothing to "discover." The reasons for a library to consider implementing a discovery tool can be compelling. The sheer number of data sources currently available to most libraries is overwhelming to the user, and discovery tools are a means of addressing that confusion (Vaughan, 2011a). In the print environment, access to resources was relatively proscribed by the tools available – the printed (and then the online) catalog. The environment has transitioned to where:

... information resources are relatively abundant, and user attention is relatively scarce. Users have many resources available to them, and may not spend a very long time on any one. Many finding tools are available side by side on the network, and large consolidated resources have appeared in the

form of search engines. Even within the library, there are now several finding tools available ... The user is crowded with opportunity. No single resource is the sole focus of a user's attention. In fact, the network is now the focus of a user's attention, and the available 'collection' is a very much larger resource than the local catalogued collection. The user wishes to 'discover' and use much more than is in the local catalogued collection. (Dempsey, 2006, p. 1)

Like Z39.50 before it, however, a discovery tool cannot entirely take the place of discipline-specific search tools (East, 2003; Fagan, 2011). Think about the user's needs – for some specialized libraries, a discovery tool may not provide much utility beyond core, dedicated, subject-specific databases and Web-based resources (Luther, 2011; Dartmouth, 2009). Native search interfaces in specialized databases take advantage of controlled vocabulary and indexing that are not a part of the data harvesting done by a discovery tool.

Do you need a discovery tool? Are existing data sources for your users well-defined and well-known to them? Are they sufficient to meet your users' needs?

As a relatively young technology, discovery systems and capabilities are evolving at a rapid pace. In addition, the equally rapid changes in the marketplace mean that vendors change licenses frequently – what impact this will have on discovery systems in the long term is unknown (Breeding, 2011). Feedback on actual use and real world experience with discovery systems is somewhat sparse. Internal and unpublished reports, blogs, and library Web site FAQs often provide information that cannot be easily found in the published scholarly literature (e.g. Queens University, 2010; Tarulli, 2009).

Locating relevant citations can be a challenge. Searches done using *Library, Information Science & Technology Abstracts* and the *Library Literature*

& Information Science Index show widely varied indexing, using terms such as "discovery tools", "resource discovery" and "discovery service" along with more traditional (and less useful) indexing terms such as "information retrieval" and "electronic information resources". Vendors also use different terminology to describe their products, including such terms as "discovery layer", "discovery platform", "Web-scale discovery" and even "eDiscovery". Without clear indexing, producing a comprehensive list of the available and relevant literature would be problematic, although a five-year literature review in *Library, Information Science & Technology Abstracts* and the *Library Literature & Information Science Index* using the terms "discovery tool*" OR "discovery system" OR "discovery layer" OR "discovery platform" OR "Web-scale discovery" and limited to scholarly peer-reviewed journals resulted in 93 hits. These were evaluated for relevance (i.e. the major focus being the evaluation of discovery systems either in general or product-specific) – 32 met this criterion, with a notable drop-off in relevance prior to 2008. 15 of those were directly related to a specific product. An additional method is to search for citations using a product name such as "Summon™[1]" (Serials Solutions[®2]) or "WorldCat Local[®3]". These typically produce case reports of the implementation of a specific product at a particular library and can be useful, especially if the library doing the report is similar in scope to one's own library.

DETAILS, DETAILS, DETAILS

What Will Follow

The remainder of this chapter will focus on a variety of topics related to the planning and implementation of discovery systems. These will be grouped into the following general areas:

- Organizational concerns: strategic planning and alignment;
- The overall purpose of a discovery tool and defining the resources to be "discovered";
- Financial issues: up-front and ongoing costs;
- Interoperability and technical support issues: library and institutional systems;
- Setup and configuration: internal development and vendor-provided solutions;
- Data integrity, interface design, and customizing for usability;
- Rolling out the system: marketing it to your users;
- Life with a discovery tool: long-term administration, statistics, staffing, and workflows.

Organizational Concerns: Strategic Planning and Alignment

Planning and implementing a discovery tool is, from a project perspective, no different than any other system-related rollout, although the scope and intersection with other systems and constituencies is much wider. The constituencies involved in this type of project can also be wide-ranging, including local Information Technology staff (IT), vendors (of both the discovery tool and other data sources), the institution as a whole, students, faculty, and library staff. Each of these groups will interact with the planning and implementation process in different ways. Library project planning in general is supported in the literature and there are several citations provided in the list of additional readings. (e.g. Cervone, 2010; Feeney, 2011; Massis, 2010). Project planning concerns will be highlighted in each of the following sections of the chapter. Examples related to the evaluation of specific discovery tool products are represented elsewhere in this book.

Given the scope of a discovery tool in the service portfolio of the library, it is important to see that it aligns with the library and institutional strategic plans. A significant amount of time and resources will be invested in a discovery tool across the library organization (and other units such as IT), so as with any other library service or project, having the implementation of a discovery tool integrated into library and institutional strategic plans will help provide a larger framework to achieve buy-in from all of the units involved (Shumaker 2009; Stoffle, 2011).

Does your project plan align with the library and institutional strategic plans?

The Overall Purpose of a Discovery Tool and Defining the Resources to be "Discovered"

In concept, a discovery tool is supposed to make *all* of the resources available to the library "discoverable". What *are* all of the resources? This question is at the heart of the planning process. What does the library want its users to be able to find (Tallent, 2010)? Take an inventory of every data set available to the library, internal and external, vendor- and library-created. In general, this includes all of the content to which the library subscribes – bibliographic databases and content aggregation resources – as well as internally-maintained data sets such as the library catalog, special collections, and archives. The list should include the type of platform on which each data set runs; this can be compared to the list of databases and platforms that can be indexed by any particular discovery tool. An excellent and thorough example of this type of resource examination has been done by the University of Minnesota Libraries (Hanson, 2010). Indexing and discoverability of local resources such as the library's Web site, other institutional Web sites, locally created digital resources (such as GIS spatial data created by a department at the University), and resources such as Libguides™4 using discovery tools is an issue that does not appear to have been examined in the literature, being somewhat ceded to Google and

site search tools. If the intent of a discovery tool is to point a user to relevant information, and it is to be promoted as the single, best point of entry for the user, it would seem that these resources could be deemed relevant. For example, suppose a user searches on copyright. The Web page or Libguide™ on copyright that the reference staff spent a great deal of time to create has as much place in a search result as any other resource, and would have local relevance as well.

After creating the list--prioritize, prioritize, prioritize. It is unlikely that every resource will be available via the discovery tool, at least not immediately; lower-priority datasets can be worked on after the initial implementation. Which resources absolutely *must* be included? Again, one size does not fit all; there is no right or wrong answer. Each library and institution has to consider these issues when thinking about what they want to make "discoverable" and how. At the heart of this question is expected use and target audience, hence the need to prioritize.

What datasets do you want your users to "discover"? Include both internal and external resources. What are the highest priorities for your users?

Financial Issues: Up-Front and Ongoing Costs

With any acquisition of a library system, whether an ILS or a discovery tool, financial considerations drive product choices, and there are both up-front and continuing costs. Up-front, the product must be acquired and implemented. In the acquisition phase, financial questions often pose the choice between a commercial vs. an open-source solution. As with an ILS, the choice of an open-source discovery tool is often a tempting one, but those libraries considering it need to keep in mind that there are underlying development costs (deVoe, 2007). Open-source products by their nature have no "vendor" as such, and thus no fixed support channel, relying on the user community for development. If the organization has sufficient development expertise in-house, this may not be an issue. For commercial products, both vendor support and internal staff costs to operate and maintain the tool must be considered in the project plan and budget.

These costs intersect each of the remaining topics presented in this chapter, as each will require either acquisition funding or staff/development funding. These intersections will be mentioned in context within each section.

Briefly these intersections are:

- Interoperability and technical support issues: library and institutional systems – this will require staff time to interact with the discovery system vendor and institutional IT staff to resolve issues related to proxy access, identity management etc.
- Setup and configuration: internal development and vendor-provided solutions – this requires internal staff working with the discovery system vendor to arrange for initial data harvesting and functional testing.
- Data integrity, interface design, and customizing for usability – this requires staff time to evaluate and make changes to data loads and field mapping, modify the interface for usability and correct any functional issues after the data harvest is completed
- Rolling out the system: marketing it to users – this requires effort on the part of the library PR staff to make users aware of the new system; front-line staff will also have to prepare training materials
- Life with a discovery tool: long-term administration, statistics, staffing, and workflows – this integrates the discovery tool into the rest of the library's operations. Additional staff time will be needed to maintain the system.

Does the library's budget support both the initial acquisition and ongoing operating costs of the discovery tool, including any consulting costs? Does it support the staff time necessary to develop and maintain the tool?

Interoperability and Technical Support Issues: Library and Institutional Systems

A discovery tool must interoperate with a number of different library systems. These include those from which the data is to be harvested, authentication/identity management systems, and link resolvers. If the discovery tool under consideration does not work with the library's existing link resolver, does the vendor either have its own resolver (and is it bundled with the discovery tool?) or does it support another link resolver? If the link resolver needs to be replaced, this is another project issue involving data vendors and internal staff that will be put in place prior to implementation of the discovery tool. For example, the implementation of Serials Solutions Summon™ at Penn State also included the replacement of the SFX®[5] link resolver with Serials Solutions 360 Link, in part to resolve issues with SFX® at the Hershey campus, which is on a separate network.

Discovery tools by their nature are public-facing, and generally open, but once a user tries to access a subscribed resource, the proxy and authentication components come into play, and, particularly in consortial and multi-campus settings, these components need to work smoothly across all locations. Consultation with IT will be important to resolve any authentication and identity management issues, either internally or with proxied remote access. The complexity of disparate networks, varying subscriptions among libraries under the same organizational umbrella and issues revolving around identity management all play a significant role in the implementation of a discovery tool. Depending on the product under consideration, there may have to be multiple instances of a table or interface to accommodate these organizational structures.

Consider the interaction between the discovery tool and authentication/proxy systems at your institution.

Setup and Configuration: Internal Development and Vendor-Provided Solutions

Initial configuration and the assistance a vendor can provide is a major issue in any system implementation. Loads from commercial databases for which the vendor has license agreements should certainly be routine. However, this poses some potential issues as the marketplace matures. As the industry consolidates and companies increasingly provide both discovery tool and database products, there will naturally be competitive pressure. How well a discovery tool vendor can integrate access to a competitor's database product may turn out to be an interesting question (Breeding, 2011).

The ease with which additional resources can be added and removed is part of this equation, and investigation of the administrative modules of any discovery tool is warranted. If the back end is not easy to use, life with a particular discovery tool may not be pleasant for the library staff. It is likely that major publisher's packages are part of any commercial discovery tool. If a number of the local platforms that the library intends to harvest via OAI are not available, this may be a weakness in a particular product. If the library is satisfied generally with a particular product, the vendor's development process may be an avenue for investigation to see how long it will be until they can support a particular local platform. From a budgetary perspective, questions to ask include:

- How much of this configuration is included in the initial cost, and are there limits to the services provided before additional fees are charged?

- If the library requires vendor support for customization, how much of that can be provided during the initial support period when it is most needed?
- What level of local technical support is required?

Answers to these questions will provide a good idea of how much staff time will be dedicated to the configuration and, if not new staff, how this work is to be integrated with their existing responsibilities. The willingness and ability of a vendor to provide configuration services and training to library staff is an important part a successful implementation.

Investigate not only a product's features but the vendor's documentation, tools and services.

DATA INTEGRITY, INTERFACE DESIGN, AND CUSTOMIZING FOR USABILITY

The discussion of configuration and implementation issues above are somewhat generic – the choices made can be said to apply to any number of systems such as an ILS or content management system. Some issues, however, are more specific to discovery tools. These include data integrity between systems and the ability to customize specific features of the discovery tool.

Data Integrity

There are decisions to be made about data in existing systems that will impact the functionality of the discovery tool. These include:

- variations in mapping for facets such as material type, date, language, content provider
- the quality of underlying records harvested by the discovery tool

- availability data for physical items
- refresh of data from all sources
- de-duplication of electronic resources

"Faceted searching", also termed "faceted browsing" or "faceted navigation" – the ability to apply filters such as language, date range, and material type to a list of search results – is a common feature of discovery tools and some ILS products. Records harvested from the ILS must have fields and terms mapped to their corresponding fields and terms in the discovery system. As an example, if the library has material types for CD, DVD, video, etc., but the facet term in the discovery tool is "Audiovisual Materials"- these disparate types will need to be mapped to the discovery tool terminology when the data is loaded. It may be important to the library to keep the distinction in types – for example an archive that maintains both lantern slides and 35mm slides – as the result list may not reflect the actual media format. Material types are not static. Does the discovery tool vendor support changing these after the fact (and at what cost) if the library changes material type designations or a new material type is needed? The same applies to other facets such as date and language limits; each of these may require mapping and customization. There may also be specialized facets, not included in the default configuration of the discovery tool, that are important to the user; an example might be scripture references for religious studies material or molecular formulae that are in a specific database. Questions to ask include:

- How customizable are the facet terms used in the discovery system?
- Can the list of facets be expanded, terms removed, list reordered if desired?

Facets are not static – can they be manipulated to reflect changing needs?

The issue of mapping points to the quality of the underlying cataloging in the ILS. The discovery tool can only present what it is given. If there are significant errors in the data from the ILS, such as items never removed as a result of an inventory, these will be reflected in the discovery tool result set. Many libraries have also shadowed records of various types that are not displayed to the public; these records need to be excluded from results in the discovery tool. These issues apply equally to any locally-created data sets that will be a part of the resources crawled by the discovery tool; but it is likely the ILS will be the largest single source of local data to be reviewed.

Availability/location data for physical items is also important in the interface between the discovery tool and the ILS. This also applies to any custom databases the library may want to include in the discovery tool, such as an archive system – where an artifact is physically located is a vital piece of data. Particularly with multiple sites and campuses, does the discovery tool adequately reflect the actual location and availability of physical materials? Is there a delay in harvesting or is the data real-time?

How does the discovery tool retrieve and display availability data for physical items?

Related to availability data is the basic question of record maintenance. No data set is static, especially not the ILS, where records are added and deleted on a daily basis. How does the discovery tool handle updating from all of the data sources it crawls?

Commercial products that the discovery tool indexes are updated automatically; for local resources, there may be labor involved in this process. Does the library have to prepare data files from local systems to update the discovery tool? This presents a workflow issue that will have to be addressed.

How often does a discovery tool refresh data from local sources and what work is required to enable this refresh?

Deduplication of multiple records (often called deduping) can be issue in the result list from a discovery tool. Since the discovery tool crawls across many sources, it is not uncommon to have the same title available in multiple database packages. This problem has been present since the use of Z39.50 allowed for searches across multiple data sources (Turner, 2004). Questions to ask here include:

- How does a particular discovery tool present links to the same materials from different sources?
- If a single citation is available from three sources, does this result in three entries in the result set, or one entry with multiple links?
- Is this behavior customizable, and to what degree?

Duplication is not necessarily a bad thing, but the way it is presented to the user can be either confusing or not, depending on the interface. For example, displaying the same citation three different times in a result set will be confusing, while having a single entry of the citation with the same three source entries underneath would be less so. How confusing the user interface is to the end-user and what can be done to make the presentation of the result list more effective leads into the next section.

How is deduping of resources handled in the discovery system? Is this customizable?

Interface Design and Customizing for Usability

Interface design and the ability to customize it to suit local needs should be part of the product evaluation process (Vaughan, 2011b). Many libraries do very little customization either by choice or due to lack of staffing (Luther, 2011). Design evaluation metrics are available from a number of sources (e.g. Hearst, 2009). Assuming that customization is desired, questions to ask include:

- What options are available to customize and brand the user interface?
- Are APIs and documentation available to add and change functionality as desired?

Leading into the discussion of marketing, a key area of customization is branding; the library may want the discovery tool to have a similar "look and feel" to other resources. Both open-source and commercial product customization require an investment in staff time and expertise, both of which might be in short supply.

Can the user interface be customized and branded to suit local needs?

Rolling out the System: Marketing it to Users

As the discovery tool becomes a reality, it needs to be marketed and promoted. The library marketing team can leverage their existing networks and strategies to promote this new resource to both users and front-line staff. As with any other tool, user education is necessary to demonstrate its most effective use versus a specialized tool to meet a specific information need. Promotional and educational materials in electronic and print form will need to be developed and produced. What training materials are available from the vendor and can they be easily customized? Specialized libraries or libraries that serve graduate and research populations benefit from being able to customize the training materials to meet their users' information searching needs rather than using generic examples focused on undergraduates. The library's Web design staff will also be involved through this process to allow for search boxes, links to documentation and help, and other resources. Again, the discovery tool does not replace existing resources, but the extent to which the tool will be highlighted at a particular location is a decision to be made based on its utility to the user population (Luther, 2011).

Include a marketing strategy in your project plan.

Life with a Discovery Tool: Statistics, Staffing, and Workflows

Several issues remain to consider as a part of "life with a discovery tool": statistical reporting, the organizational support needed for maintenance of the discovery tool, and further tailoring of the tool to meet local needs based on user feedback.

Every library collects reams of statistics on every aspect of operation, for various reasons ranging from internal operational requirements to accreditation reports. The addition of a discovery tool adds to the statistical pool – the library will be able to report on the usage of the system itself, but what capabilities will it have to aggregate statistics of resources accessed through it? Does the discovery tool incorporate a statistics module and is it COUNTER-compliant? The potential exists for the same access to be counted and reported multiple times and in multiple locations. It will thus be important in the planning process to investigate what is recorded and where in order to not artificially duplicate and inflate usage.

What changes will be made in harvesting resource usage statistics?

Staff time, particularly of those staff supporting the ILS and internal data resources will be an ongoing need beyond the implementation phase of the discovery tool. This need will have to be defined and included in job descriptions and work plans. As each set of systems matures, there will be further integration issues. Patches and fixes to

one system may adversely impact the discovery tool and vice-versa. In the same way that data is not static, systems themselves are not static. For example, in addition to keeping their respective systems operational, staff must also deal with how they interact with the new discovery tool. The discovery tool presents a different set of problems in that it is an aggregation of all of the other data sources provided by the library, in effect itself relying on all of the others to function. In practice, it is likely that updates to one system will have effects on the discovery tool. For commercial products, it is incumbent upon the discovery tool vendor to make sure that data harvesting and indexing is working properly, and the vendor must work with data providers in the event of problems. For locally hosted library systems, the system administrator will have to work with both the discovery tool vendor and the vendor of the hosted product to resolve data harvesting issues in the event of a problem.

In the project plan, consider the changes a discovery tool will make to workflows and system maintenance.

Finally, as a living system, the discovery tool will require changes as it is used. As part of the regular evaluation of library resources, the library will receive feedback on this resource, both good and bad, and will need to respond to that feedback with additional customization as time goes on.

FUTURE RESEARCH DIRECTIONS

The body of research on discovery tools is growing as these products are integrated into the service offerings of a variety of libraries. Research and evaluation of systems after they have been in operation is going to be most useful to those libraries in the planning and implementation phase, as they can provide valuable insight into real-world issues related to discovery tools (e.g. Dartmouth, 2009; Gross & Sheridan, 2011).

There is significant potential for future research as these systems mature, particularly in the area of exposing locally-developed datasets. Other issues that will be fruitful topics for research include: implementation issues experienced by libraries, ways usage statistics are developed and analyzed, the impact of the discovery tool on circulation and interlibrary loan, the impact of changes to link resolvers and authentication methods on the discovery tool, and user acceptance.

CONCLUSION

Discovery tools can be an important part of a library's service offerings. Each library will have different priorities and user needs to consider, and any particular system may or may not meet those needs. Hopefully, the issues raised in this chapter will facilitate discussion among administrators and librarians as they plan and implement a discovery system. As with any large systems project, careful planning and the elimination of artificial timetables and unrealistic expectations make the difference between a successful and a mediocre implementation.

REFERENCES

Breeding, M. (2011). *Building comprehensive resource discovery platforms*. Retrieved December 9, 2011, from http://www.alatechsource.org/blog/2011/03/building-comprehensive-resource-discovery-platforms.html

Caswell, J. V., & Wynstra, J. (2007). Developing the right RFP for selecting your federated search product: Lessons learned and tips from recent experience. *Internet Reference Services Quarterly, 12*(1/2), 49–71. doi:10.1300/J136v12n01_03

Dartmouth College Library. (2009). *An evaluation of serials solutions summon as a discovery service for the Dartmouth College Library*. Retrieved December 9, 2011, from http://www.dartmouth.edu/~library/admin/docs/Summon_Report.pdf

Dempsey, L. (2006). The library catalogue in the new discovery environment: Some thoughts. *Ariadne, 48*, 1.

deVoe, K. (2007). Innovations affecting us—Open source in the library: An alternative to the commercial ILS? *Against The Grain, 19*(2), 88-89.

East, J. (2003). Z39.50 and personal bibliographic software. *Library Hi Tech Journal, 21*(1), 34–43. doi:10.1108/07378830310467382

Fagan, J. (2011). Federated search is dead-And good riddance! *Journal of Web Librarianship, 5*(2), 77–79. doi:10.1080/19322909.2011.573533

Gross, J., & Sheridan, L. (2011). Web scale discovery: The user experience. *New Library World, 112*(5), 236–247. doi:10.1108/03074801111136275

Hearst, M. (2009). *Search user interfaces*. Cambridge, UK: Cambridge University Press.

Luther, J., & Kelly, M. C. (2011). The next generation of discovery. *Library Journal, 136*(5), 66–71.

Queens University. Kingston, Ontario, Canada. (2010). *Summon frequently asked questions*. Retrieved December 9, 2011, from http://library.queensu.ca/summon/faq

Shumaker, D., & Strand, J. (2009). Changing your game through alignment. *Information Outlook, 13*(7), 41–44.

Stoffle, C. J., & Cuillier, C. (2011). From surviving to thriving. *Journal of Library Administration, 51*(1), 130–155. doi:10.1080/01930826.2011.531645

Tallent, E. (2010). Where are we going? Are we there yet? *Internet Reference Services Quarterly, 15*(1), 3–10. doi:10.1080/10875300903543770

Tarulli, L. (2009). *Choosing a discovery tool* [Blog post]. Retrieved December 9, 2011, from http://laureltarulli.wordpress.com/2009/02/05/choosing-a-discovery-tool/

Turner, S. (2004). Resource integration in the library: Link-Resolvers and federated searching. *Mississippi Libraries, 68*(3), 63–66.

Vaughan, J. (2011a). Web scale discovery what and why? *Library Technology Reports, 47*(1), 5–11.

Vaughan, J. (2011b). Questions to consider. *Library Technology Reports, 47*(1), 54–59.

ADDITIONAL READING

Allison, D. (2010). Information portals: The next generation catalog. *Journal of Web Librarianship, 4*(4), 375–389. doi:10.1080/19322909.2010.507972

Barba, S., & Perrin, J. (2010). Great expectations: How digital project planning fosters collaboration between academic libraries and external entities. *Unabashed Librarian, 155*, 18–22.

Blythe, K. (2008). A faceted catalogue aids doctoral-level searchers. *Evidence Based Library & Information Practice, 3*(3), 80–82.

Breeding, M. (2009). *Open source discovery interfaces gain momentum.* Retrieved from http://www.alatechsource.org/sln/april-2009

Breeding, M. (2010). The state of the art in library discovery 2010. *Computers in Libraries, 30*(1), 31–34.

Cervone, H. (2011). Overcoming resistance to change in digital library projects. *OCLC Systems & Services, 27*(2), 95–98. doi:10.1108/10650751111135391

Cervone, H. F. (2010). Managing digital libraries: The view from 30,000 feet: Using cost benefit analysis to justify digital library projects. *OCLC Systems & Services, 26*(2), 76–79. doi:10.1108/10650751011048443

Collins, M., & Rathemacher, A. J. (2010). Open forum: The future of library systems. *The Serials Librarian, 58*(1-4), 167–173. doi:10.1080/03615261003625703

Dempsey, L. (2008). Reconfiguring the library systems environment. *Portal: Libraries and the Academy, 8*(2), 111–120. doi:10.1353/pla.2008.0016

Dempsey, L. (2011). *There is more to discovery than you think...*[Blog post]. Retrieved December 9, 2011, from http://orweblog.oclc.org/archives/002153.html

Feeney, M., & Sult, L. (2011). Project management in practice: Implementing a process to ensure accountability and success. *Journal of Library Administration, 51*(7/8), 744–763. doi:10.1080/01930826.2011.601273

Hanson, C., Hessel, H., Barneson, J., Boudewyns, D., Fransen, J., & Friedman-Shedlov, L. ... Traill, S. (2009). *Discoverability phase 2 final report* (pp. 1-76). University of Minnesota Libraries. Retrieved from http://purl.umn.edu/99734

Hargraves, I. (2007). Controversies of information discovery. *Knowledge, Technology & Policy, 20*(2), 83–90. doi:10.1007/s12130-007-9017-5

Hill, J. S. (2008). Is it worth it? Management issues related to database quality. *Cataloging & Classification Quarterly, 46*(1), 5–26. doi:10.1080/01639370802182885

Ho, B., Kelley, K., & Garrison, S. (2009). Implementing VuFind as an alternative to Voyager's WebVoyage interface: One library's experience. *Library Hi Tech, 27*(1), 82–92. doi:10.1108/07378830910942946

James, D., Garrett, M., & Krevit, L. (2009). Discovering discovery tools evaluating vendors and implementing Web 2.0 environments. *Library Hi Tech, 27*(2), 268–276. doi:10.1108/07378830910968218

Massis, B. E. (2010). Project management in the library. *New Library World, 111*(11), 526–529. doi:10.1108/03074801011094895

Shneiderman, B. (2002). Inventing discovery tools: Combining information visualization with data mining. *Information Visualization, 1*(1), 5–12.

Sridhar, V., Nath, D., & Malik, A. (2009). Analysis of user involvement and participation on the quality of IS planning projects: An exploratory study. *Journal of Organizational and End User Computing, 21*(3), 80–98. doi:10.4018/joeuc.2009070105

Templin, P. (2011). Unrealistic expectations. *Industrial Engineer: IE, 43*(11), 28–28.

Wakimoto, J. C., Walker, D. S., & Dabbour, K. S. (2006). The myths and realities of SFX in academic libraries. *Journal of Academic Librarianship, 32*(2), 127–136. doi:10.1016/j.acalib.2005.12.008

Williams, S. C., & Foster, A. K. (2011). Promise fulfilled? An EBSCO discovery service usability study. *Journal of Web Librarianship, 5*(3), 179–198. doi:10.1080/19322909.2011.597590

Yang, S. Q., & Wagner, K. (2010). Evaluating and comparing discovery tools: How close are we towards next generation catalog? *Library Hi Tech, 28*(4), 690–709. doi:10.1108/07378831011096312

Zeigen, L., & Crum, J. (2009). Library catalogs and other discovery tools. *OLA Quarterly, 15*(1), 1.

KEY TERMS AND DEFINITIONS

API: Application programming interface – a specification intended to be used as an interface by software components to communicate with each other. APIs are commonly used to design interfaces for interacting with systems, for example to show real-time status of an item (data from the online catalog) in the result list of a discovery system.

COUNTER Compliant: COUNTER (Counting Online Usage of Networked Electronic Resources) is an international initiative serving librarians, publishers and intermediaries by setting standards that facilitate the recording and reporting of online usage statistics. (http://www.projectcounter.org/documents/COUNTER_compliance_stepwise_guide.pdf)

Data Integrity: The reliability and correctness of data; in moving information from one system to another, insuring that translation and mapping do not alter the original data.

De-Duplication / Deduping: A means to streamline the display of identical materials from multiple sources, i.e. a single display of a title followed by sources rather than a separate entry for each title/source.

Discovery Tool/System: A service to aggregate access to a wide variety of a library's resources, both internal and external. It provides a single point to search across multiple databases.

ERM: Electronic Resource Management (ERM) systems are software used to manage digital subscriptions in libraries, allowing libraries to pull together license agreements, information about vendors, subscription data, and similar information.

Facets and "Faceted Searching": Attributes of a resource. These may include material types, language, location, date, etc. "Facets" are commonly used to refine a search. Facets are "mapped" from a source system to a discovery system.

Hosting: A vendor service whereby a given system is physically maintained on a server outside of the library or institution.

Identity Management: A means by which users can be authenticated as having permission to access a given network. Seamless authentication across multiple systems is the goal of identity management.

ILS: Integrated Library System – the traditional online library catalog and the systems (such as acquisitions, cataloging, circulation, serials) that support it.

Link Resolver: A software package that connects citations in one database to the full-text document in another database (e.g. SFX® or LinkSource®)

Mapping: A means to translate information from a data field in a source to a field in a target. For example, a "map" could be from an online catalog record field for "Library" to a discovery system field for "Location"

Material Type: A definition of the format of an item such as a book, CD, online resource, or serial.

OAI: Open Archives Initiative (http://www.openarchives.org) is an effort to enhance access to e-print archives as a means of increasing the availability of scholarly communication.

Proxy/Proxied Remote Access: A means to allow users to connect to library resources when off-campus. A proxy server accepts a request from a user, authenticates the user, then passes the request to the supplier, making it appear to the supplier that the request was made from an on-site user.

RFP: Request for Proposal; a document sent to potential vendors that outlines system requirements.

Z39.50: Z39.50 is a protocol for searching and retrieving information from remote computer databases. It is often incorporated into integrated library systems and personal bibliographic reference software such as EndNote® or RefWorks®. Searches for interlibrary loan are often implemented with Z39.50 queries.

ENDNOTES

[1]   Summon is owned by ProQuest LLC
[2]   Serials Solutions is a registered trademark of Serials Solutions
[3]   WorldCat is a registered trademark of OCLC
[4]   LibGuides is owned by Springshare LLC
[5]   SFX Link Resolver is a registered trademark of ExLibris

Section 2
Selecting a Discovery Tool

Billie Peterson-Lugo
Baylor University, United States

OVERVIEW

With the recent introduction of web scale discovery services, librarians may finally have a tool that eliminates silos and enables the discovery of the larger corpus of a library's resources. However, entrée to this new world comes with some challenges. As Jason Vaughn succinctly states in this book (and others echo), "Selection of a web scale discovery service is, quite simply, a big deal!" Because of the significant costs – both direct and indirect – the process of selecting the best web scale discovery service is akin to that used to select an integrated library system (ILS). Library administrators appoint a committee; committee members develop lists of criteria and "test drive" the systems in other libraries; vendors demonstrate their products; committee members obtain feedback from library staff and perhaps library users, as well as "references" from other libraries. In the end, all of the data is evaluated, synthesized, and fed into a final recommendation – resulting in a decision.

However, web scale discovery services are significantly different than integrated library systems and come with their own unique complexities. Traditionally, an ILS is – integrated. It is a tidy package with acquisition, cataloging, circulation, and serials modules that interact with each other and display pertinent information to the end user. A web scale discovery service, on the other hand, incorporates a vast number of local and proprietary information silos; they must be able to ingest existing local databases – the online catalog, the institutional repository, the digital repository, etc. – and then assimilate the locally-generated content with the vendor's database structure and content; they must integrate with existing technology, such as the library's open URL function, the library's circulation system, and local authentication practices; and in the end, they must provide the ability to both search broadly and hone in quickly on specific research needs. For many librarians, this type of system and understanding its functionality is unlike anything they have encountered before. Now, add to this list the fact that web scale discovery services are evolving very quickly, which impacts the decision-making timeline.

The following five chapters provide a menu of pragmatic techniques – requests for proposals, evaluation grids, best practices, surveys, test implementations – that should guide those who are just now beginning this process. Additionally, despite the disparate approaches taken for the selection of a web scale discovery service, these chapters share common themes:

- Build a multi-faceted team of library and IT staff for the selection process;
- Educate library staff – before, during, and after the final selection is made;
- Be clear on the issues a web scale discovery service will address;
- Create lists of "requirements" and "desirables" expected in the system;
- Set a framework for the evaluation process;
- Set a reasonable time frame for the process;
- Understand that there are both direct (monetary) and indirect (staff support) costs for both the implementation and maintenance of a web scale discovery service.

Every library is different – their goals; their technology and staff structures; their users' needs; their financial resources. No one selection process described in the following chapters may exactly fit your library's environment, but ideally the content in this section will provide a sufficient number of ideas so that you can feel comfortable designing an evaluation and selection process that will meet the needs of your library.

Chapter 4
Evaluating and Selecting a Library Web-Scale Discovery Service

Jason Vaughan
University of Nevada- Las Vegas, USA

ABSTRACT

Selecting a major new discovery service for students and researchers is an important undertaking. Web-scale discovery has implications for library staff and the work they do. More importantly, Web-scale discovery offers promise in simplifying the research process for library users and steering them toward selected and often scholarly content owned or licensed by the host library. Given such broad implications, prospective customers should carefully evaluate options to meet their goal of finding the best potential match for their library. This chapter provides a frame for such an evaluation, based in part on the evaluation process used at the University of Nevada, Las Vegas Libraries. It highlights the important internal and external steps library staff may wish to consider as they evaluate these discovery services for their local environment. By involving a wide range of stakeholders and conducting thorough research, libraries are in the best position to make an informed and confident decision.

DOI: 10.4018/978-1-4666-1821-3.ch004

INTRODUCTION

In the context of this chapter, a library Web-scale discovery service is a service which builds a central, searchable index containing a large portion of a library's locally hosted and remotely licensed content, and which provides a search and retrieval interface to search this index. The selection, implementation, and care of a Web-scale discovery service is not a casual undertaking. Subscription-based in nature, discovery service products carry a significant ongoing cost, and in some cases, a separate initial purchase/setup cost. Despite vendor promises to the contrary, library staff will be involved in a series of implementation steps that will likely last several months at absolute minimum. On an ongoing basis, some number of staff will be dedicated to the nurturing of this service. This could involve:

- web designers hoping to refine the interface themselves or suggest to the vendor tweaks to consider for a future release;
- catalogers and metadata experts who may clean up local record deficiencies exposed by the discovery service;
- staff reporting broken links;
- staff monitoring vendor developments, such as the availability of major new content sets the vendor incorporates into the index, and working to effectively communicate such updates to colleagues.

For those working frontline service desks, staff will be involved in:

- answering users' questions about the service (e.g. "What does this search?");
- some level of instruction, including leading students to other library databases and resources;
- detecting the skill level of researchers, such as novice or advanced, and acknowledging that Web-scale discovery may be

more suited to some user groups or users in particular disciplines;
- working with their Web designer colleagues and usability specialists to try and ensure the library's overall portal to information--the library's Web site--is well designed and perhaps self-sufficient to the greatest degree possible

In sum, there are significant costs associated with library Web-scale discovery. However, it is important not to fixate on these costs, real as they are. Today's students, faculty, and other researchers should be the most important focus, and for them, Web-scale discovery holds major promise. A single service that can search a vast amount, likely the majority of the library's content assets, is a significant step forward for discovery, with the impact augmented even more as this content is presented in a clean search and discovery interface offering features and functionality expected by today's researchers.

BACKGROUND

An established body of literature exists related to evaluation and selection of federated search systems, a technology that could most closely be considered the precursor to modern day Web-scale discovery services. Similarly, a growing body of literature is emerging related to modern day Web-scale discovery services, the direct focus of this monograph. Regarding the former, federated search technologies, *Internet Reference Services Quarterly* devoted volume year 2007 to the topic of federated search, simultaneously co-published in the 2007 monograph *Federated Search: Solution or Setback for Online Library Services* (Cox, 2007). Of particular note in this monograph are a chapter on developing requests for proposals (RFPs) by Casell and Wynstra (2007) and an annotated bibliography from Freund, et al. (2007).

Boock, et al. describe the selection (and subsequent implementation and assessment) of a federated search tool at Oregon State University (2006). Boss (2002) provides extensive request for proposal specifications related to portal products (similar to federated search), as well as model instructions for an RFP. Boss and Nelson (2005) reviewed four federated search products, and provide a list of representative questions libraries should consider in their evaluations as well as a comparison matrix. Christenson and Tennant discuss metasearch software and integration principles, as well as integrated search needs assessment conducted at the California Digital Library (2005). Gibson, et al. (2009) describe the steps taken by most institutions evaluating federated search tools, including formation of a committee, specifications development, and product trials, and talk about features of federated search that are also relevant to more modern Web-scale discovery services, such as speed, relevancy, and faceting. Marshall, et al. (2006) mention several considerations related to evaluation of federated search, and describe features which could be considered desirable for any discovery platform, including modern Web-scale discovery services which later evolved.

Apart from federated search literature, a growing body of literature is emerging related to modern day Web-scale discovery services. A large amount of literature exists talking about why Web-scale discovery is important; much of this literature involves survey work of end-users, their searching habits, and expectations. Such information is useful background and can help develop criteria for any entity wishing to undertake a needs assessment and marketplace review. Examples include research conducted or commissioned by OCLC (De Rosa, C., Cantrell, J., Hawk, J., & Wilson, A., 2006; Calhoun, K., Cantrell, J., Gallagher, P., Hawk, H., & Cellentani, D., 2009), Ithaka (Schonfeld et al. 2010), the University of California Libraries (2005), and the Library of Congress (Bates, 2003, and

Calhoun, 2006). Various academic libraries have published reports detailing their investigations related to their own evaluations of these services for their academic environment. These include Oregon State University (Boock,et. al. 2009), the University of Arizona (Allgood, 2010), the University of Michigan (Bhatnagar et al., 2010), the University of Minnesota (Hanson, et al., 2009, 2010), the University of Wisconsin (Detinger, et al., 2008), and the University of Nevada-Las Vegas (Vaughan, 2011; Vaughan, 2012). Vaughan and Hanken (2011) hosted an online workshop, part three of which focuses on a framework for evaluating Web-scale discovery services. Several published articles compare established Web-scale discovery services across a variety of parameters (Rowe, 2010, 2011). Vaughan (2011) provides a detailed question list to consider asking vendors during a library's evaluation phase. Similarly, much press information exists on the discovery service vendor Web sites, as well as interviews with representatives from these vendors, describing their services and what they feel elevates their particular product above competitors (Brunning, 2010).

THE EVALUATION PROCESS

Given such potential impact, libraries should spend some effort in researching such services, giving themselves some confidence that their selection is sound. Perhaps only selection of an integrated library system (ILS) is more of a "big deal;" with an ILS, there would be no question that library decision-makers would do their homework and, hopefully, involve multiple stakeholders. The same principles should apply when evaluating Web-scale discovery services. A library could choose to take an "easy route" by just selecting a service marketed by the same vendor whose ILS is used by the library. Apart from this, presuming a library wishes to conduct a careful evaluation, selection of a Web-scale discovery service can involve extensive internal and external steps. This chapter seeks to outline some of the general steps--a possible recipe--libraries may wish to consider in their own evaluation and selection. Prior to this journey, some things should be acknowledged and accepted. Change is inevitable, and Web-scale discovery services are evolving rapidly. New vendors are entering the marketplace, content indexed by these services is growing exponentially, and the features and functionality offered by the interfaces are tweaked often. Web-scale discovery does not follow the slow traditional ILS development cycle. If the evaluation process stretches to a year, or perhaps even half that time, things will appear a bit different than they did at the beginning. Regardless of the rapid pace of development, the services are maturing. Vendors are now beyond their initial releases, and the adoption base among libraries for all of the major services is great enough that discovery has emerged from the "early adopter" phase. Such growing stability can help in the evaluation phase--salespeople are more familiar with the services they are trying to sell, the library literature discussing such services is starting to emerge, and there are plenty of other adopters to speak to.

The remainder of this chapter seeks to highlight several key internal and external steps a library should consider during an evaluation and selection journey. It should be noted from the outset that the author writes from the perspective of a medium sized academic institution, the University of Nevada, Las Vegas, with the following characteristics:

- doctoral degree granting institution;
- student full time equivalent of approximately 20,000 students, 3,000 of which are graduate students;
- slightly over 100 fulltime library staff;
- library materials budget of $6.3 million;
- nearly 1.7 million held volumes, and distinguished special collections;
- subscriptions to 27,000 electronic journals.

While the following information can be used as a template of general steps, such steps may need to be adapted based on local library criteria. For example, libraries seeking a discovery solution for implementation in a shared consortial environment will have a series of additional questions and considerations.

Establishing an Evaluation Team

As they would with an ILS investigation, libraries will likely choose to establish a functional team of library experts--representative stakeholders--to lead the evaluation, selection, and recommendation for purchase. A wide swath of the library staff should have a vested interest, regardless of where they sit in the hierarchy, regardless of functional department where they reside. Frontline staff interacting with end users, and back of the house staff focused on activities such as processing, maintenance, and troubleshooting, should both have a solid presence on the evaluation team. Such a team may be charged with executing a comprehensive set of evaluative activities comprised of internal and external steps, and with handing over a final deliverable--a recommendation to purchase a particular service, or a recommendation to "wait and see," if an option permitted by library administration. Published examples of discovery related charges exist. At the University of Nevada, Las Vegas (UNLV), it was noted in their Discovery Task Force charge, "Informed through various efforts and research at the local and broader levels, and as expressed in the Libraries 2010/12 strategic plan, the UNLV Libraries have the desire to enable and maximize the discovery of library resources for our users . . . as such, the Discovery Task Force advises Libraries Administration on a solution that appears to best meet the goal of enabling and maximizing the discovery of library resources." (Vaughan, 2012, p.53). At the University of Minnesota Libraries, the charter of the Discoverability Exploratory Subgroup noted it was "focused on the library user and will recommend ways to make relevant resources more visible and easier to find, particularly within the user's workflow" and that it would "develop a set of principles related to discovery to help guide the Libraries' strategic decisions about the selection, development, and support of relevant tools and services" (Hanson, et al., 2009, pA-1). The charge of their libraries' Discoverability Phase 2 Group included objectives such as "Present a high-level vision for our new discovery environment," and "identify relevant characteristics in the user communities we serve as regards to Discovery and Delivery, conducting additional research as needed" (Hanson, et al., 2010, p.8). At the University of Michigan Libraries, the charge noted that the group was to "undertake a comparison of Search Tools, Google Scholar[1]™, and Summon[2]™ to explore the possibility of offering an alternative to Search Tools as the primary gateway for finding journal articles" (Varnum, et al., 2010, p.16). Charters and charges for Web-scale discovery evaluation groups need not differ from charges for other library working groups. They should contain a membership roster, guiding principles, a list of objectives/deliverables with a target delivery date(s), and clarity concerning to whom the group/committee / task force reports.

Framing the Evaluation Model

Against what criteria set is the library evaluating discovery services? Some required and/or desired attributes are perhaps enumerated in the evaluation group's charge, or perhaps this is an initial focus for the evaluation group. Luther and Kelly outline four evaluative areas. These include: content (e.g. "scope and depth of content being indexed"); search (e.g. "quality of results, including relevance ranking"); fit (e.g. "compatibility with existing software and content"); and cost (e.g. "justification in light of libraries' goals and objectives") (Luther, et al., 2011, p.67). At the UNLV Libraries, staff evaluated these new services against three general areas: content covered

in the central discovery service index, the end user out of the box interface, and the ability for local library staff to customize and enhance the interface (Vaughan, 2012). Arizona State created a criteria set that included considerations such as "implementation time," "comprehensive content coverage," and "privileged local content in search results (show local content first)" (Allgood, 2010, p.8). A team at the University of Minnesota Libraries recommended eight principles to follow when evaluating discovery technologies, such as "Users draw little distinction between discovery and delivery; systems, data, and information objects should be optimized for fulfillment" (Hanson, et al., 2009, p.24). Other institutions have formulated discovery principles, some within a larger strategic planning framework. These include the University of Wisconsin, Madison Libraries (Detinger, et al., 2008), the University of California Libraries (2005), and the University of Nevada, Las Vegas Libraries (2009). Evaluating the myriad aspects of Web-scale discovery services is complex enough; a library evaluation team should have a frame of reference for what they are evaluating, or risk losing focus.

Staff Education and Information Sharing

Despite the maturation of Web-scale discovery services for libraries, they are still quite new, with the majority of services entering general release in 2010. Despite the growing adoption rate, many librarians may possess only a general knowledge of these services, and some have never heard of them. Given the potential impact of such a service, if a laudable goal is to involve many library stakeholders in the evaluative journey, efforts toward staff education should be an initial consideration and focus. Indeed, the evaluation team may have some members who themselves need to establish a more solid footing on what Web-scale discovery entails. Once this is secure, other stakeholders can be involved. Establishing a means of easy communication and information sharing, such as an internal staff Web site, wiki, or blog, can help serve as a focal point for colleagues to visit and learn, on their own time, at their own initiative. The Web site should not be stagnant, as changes occur rapidly in the Web-scale discovery space. Information provided could include:

- representative, introductory articles from the growing body of library literature;
- links to existing implementations of the services under consideration, acknowledging that results may be limited given an unaffiliated "visitor" status, and that the collections searched are not the evaluation library's own and may not include all item types or underlying host systems like those found at the library conducting their investigations;
- basic documents such as the evaluation group's charge, meeting minutes, and anticipated timeline;
- announcements and links to Webinars and online workshops focused on Web-scale discovery;
- discovery service changes, updates, and press releases;
- additional opportunities, such as vendor meetings and round tables at library conferences.

Apart from a Web site, the evaluation group could augment staff education efforts by providing an open, scheduled venue for their colleagues to attend. Such a venue could include watching an archived Web-scale discovery Webinar together, visiting sample implementations together, and, perhaps most importantly, having time for an open question and answer session. Later, such venues could include updates on the group's work, and, toward the end, final vetting of what the group has recommended.

Staff Feedback

Educating staff is a great first step geared to interest and involve a wide range of internal stakeholders in the evaluation process. Deeper engagement of staff entails efforts to solicit, gather, analyze, and respond to feedback from staff. As mentioned, hosting open question and answer sessions is one method, involving members from the evaluation team, as they are hopefully the local experts on the topic. In addition, discovery service vendors themselves could respond to questions. Internal staff surveys provide an anonymous feedback mechanism which staff can complete on their own time, at their own convenience. UNLV employed two staff surveys during its discovery service evaluations. The first was at an early stage when staff awareness of Web-scale discovery was low, and asked questions related to the concept of Web-scale discovery in general, with no mention of particular named services. The second was provided after their knowledge had increased, closer to the recommendation stage, and in response to particular services which were in general release. The University of Michigan Libraries surveyed their broad university community, gathering nearly a thousand responses in the process. They noted, "The goal of the user survey was to help us prioritize the feature set we were using to rank various discovery tools so we could best reflect the preferences of our users in making a recommendation." (Varnum, et al., 2010, pp 5-6). They identified a dozen typical user behaviors associated with search and working with search results, and asked users to rate the importance of each feature on a five point scale.

If warranted, multiple staff surveys could be employed. One could be tailored to collections and content, and distributed to staff in collection development, reference, and faculty liaison areas. Another could focus on the user interface, satisfaction with sample searches and relevancy, etc., and be distributed to a wider cross section of stakeholders. A different approach may be to have the surveys open to all library staff, trusting that self-selectors will respond according to their area of expertise. An initial survey could try and sense what colleagues feel are the important attributes, or even "must haves" with whatever discovery service may be selected (e.g. "please rank on a 1-10 scale how vital it is that a discovery service accommodate records from these local repositories: ILS, digital collections management system, institutional repository, electronic reserves)." A later survey, administered after ample time to test drive existing discovery service implementations from early adopters, and perhaps after having hosted onsite vendor visits and associated question and answer sessions, could gather specific targeted feedback on each discovery service under serious consideration (e.g. "Students using service [x] have useful and adequate actions they can perform against a returned record set, such as e-mail, print, export to a bibliographic citation program, save in a list: strongly agree, agree, neutral, disagree, strongly disagree)." Survey questions can be of various types, such as 'rank on a scale,' multiple choice, or yes/no. Answers to these question types are easy to aggregate to gather trends across a large number of responses. However, equally important, perhaps more important, is to offer questions with open ended, or free text, responses. This will entail some level of manual summation and detection of common patterns, praise, and/or concerns. This offers a way for staff to express opinions and share thoughts that other predetermined questions and answers cannot precisely gather. It also allows staff to express their opinions in a neutral, anonymous environment. Once survey results are analyzed, they may help inform information gaps or the need to pursue more information from the vendor on a particular topic. In the interest of transparency, survey results could be shared with staff once aggregated, and there should be an attempt to research and ultimately answer any questions or concerns raised with the open end response questions.

Discovery Service Vendor Dialog

Throughout the evaluation, there will be extensive discussions with the various vendors whose services are under consideration. Such dialog can take the form of detailed question lists sent to the vendor, an official request for proposal (RFP), through teleconferences and on-site demonstrations and discussion, and by attending meetings and presentations at library conferences. Perhaps the best initial way to gather initial, but substantive information is to send each vendor a detailed question list on evaluation criteria important to the library; this can take the form of a categorized question list or administered as an official RFP. What topics could be covered? As an example and as noted above, UNLV chose to focus on content, the end user interface, and library flexibility with customizing features and functionality of the service. More specifically, the UNLV evaluation team (Vaughan, 2012, p.44) categorized questions into nine focused areas, sending the questions to, and receiving responses from, the major discovery service vendors:

- Background information; e.g. *When did product development begin?*
- Local Systems Coverage and Integration; e.g. *With what metadata schemas does your discovery service work--MARC, Dublin core, etc.*
- Remotely licensed publisher/aggregator content; e.g. *Here are some major publishers whose access to content this library licenses. Have you forged agreements with these publishers or does your discovery service otherwise index these items?*
- Records Maintenance and Rights Management; e.g. *How is your system initialized with the correct set of rights management information when a new library customer subscribes to your service?*
- Seamlessness and interoperability with existing content repositories; e.g. *For ILS re-*

cords related to physical holdings, is item status information provided directly within the discovery service results list?

- Usability philosophy; e.g. *Describe how your product incorporates published, established best practices in terms of a customer focused, usable interface.*
- Local "look and feel" customization options controllable by the library; e.g. *Which of the following can the library control: color scheme, logo/branding, facet categories and placement, etc.?*
- User experience: presentation, search functionality, and what the user can do with results; e.g. *At what point does a user leave the context and confines of the discovery interface and enter the interface of a different system, whether remote or local?*
- Administrative interface; e.g. *Describe in detail the statistics reporting capabilities offered by your system.*

Other institutions may choose to issue an RFP; such steps are discussed in another chapter in this book. Regardless of method employed, detailed dialog with the vendors is a necessary step in any evaluation scenario. Be prepared to administer multiple question lists at different stages of the evaluation process. For example, onsite vendor demonstrations, new features unveiled at a semi-annual library conference, or feedback from early adopters can all spur additional vendor questions. For each question, consolidating all vendor answers underneath the original question and coding responses by vendor can facilitate the evaluation process by enabling easier comparisons among the services.

Onsite Demonstrations

Onsite demonstrations are a critical step in a library's evaluation process. These offer a chance for library staff to question vendors on any aspect of the discovery service, and engage further with the discovery service evaluation process. Technical and Web design staff can ask questions about interface features and customization options, and support staff can view the administrative interface they would be using to help maintain the service for their library. Vendors can be questioned about what they feel elevates their service above their competitors, and highlight differentiators. To make the most of onsite demonstrations, consider scheduling vendor visits in close proximity to each other--even in as short a time span as a couple of weeks or a month. This can maintain library staff engagement, keep details fresh in the mind, and make it easier to compare features and functionality across the various services.

Content Overlap Analysis

Ultimately, content indexed and available for end user discovery is one of the most important considerations in the evaluation of a discovery tool. Vendors early to market have enjoyed claims of having the largest centralized indexes. As the market matures, most major services now claim huge centralized indexes which, on an annualized basis, can grow by millions and millions of items. Still, it is prudent to conduct a detailed content overlap analysis to see matches between indexed items and content licensed by the library. In a similar vein, it is important to acknowledge locally hosted content, and grasp what amount of this content the discovery service vendor can ingest and place into the central index. For local content, several repositories will likely jump to mind as important to include in the central index:

- MARC bibliographic records from the ILS catalog
- Dublin Core or other records from a digital collection management system
- Records from an institutional repository
- Records in locally developed and hosted database, with varying schema

The scope of local collections desired for inclusion will in part depend on whether a library is considering an individual installation or a consortial implementation. Unique, locally developed and hosted databases may exist for specialized collections not yet or ever intended to be MARC cataloged into an ILS, or input into another major local repository, one whose data and record structures are familiar to discovery vendors. For these unique databases, three options exist:

- catalog and input the records into an existing major local system which the database vendor recognizes and has ingestors for;
- work with the vendor on other options to port the information into the centralized index (creation of custom ingestors; output in a comma delimited file that can be understood on the receiving end, perhaps for a consultation cost);
- elect not to have the content in the centralized index.

When one speaks of a "collection overlap analysis," it usually refers to remotely hosted publisher/aggregator content licensed by the library, and indeed, such content should be compared against content centrally indexed by the discovery vendor. As noted by Allgood, "Electronic serial coverage is tricky to calculate" (2010, p16). A central requirement in conducting an overlap analysis is a unique key of some sort, the logical choice being an ISSN. Titles, dates of coverage, and ISSNs can usually be extracted from some local knowledge base in use at the library, such as an electronic resource management system or a link resolver knowledge base. Providing this to the vendor is the easy part; the more difficult part is for the vendor to precisely match the library's licensed content with centrally indexed items. Some vendors may be able to do this; others, at time of writing, find this challenging. Some vendors market their discovery services from a database perspective ("the discovery service includes content from these databases"), while others are more precise, by providing a precise title list of journals/newspapers indexed. The latter approach is more desirable, as it provides more granular information, and an aggregated database containing content from multiple journal sources is, in a sense, a rather arbitrary and artificial construct. Some vendors provide lists of indexed journal or database titles on their public Web sites; for others, such information is available upon request during the evaluation process. Vendors may be able to indicate what percentage of a library's journal/newspaper holdings are indexed to the article level in the discovery service. For other vendors, the prospective library may need to come up with an arbitrary "most important journal list," based on factors which could include objective criteria such as usage statistics and subjective criteria such as a determination that particular titles are core for their institution's curriculum. Such variations in content overlap analysis techniques are noted by both Arizona State University (Allgood, 2010) and UNLV (Vaughan, 2012). Apart from licensed remote content, it is also important to understand what open access repository information is included in the central index, such as materials from the HathiTrust, the Directory of Open Access Journals, and arXiv e-prints.

Early Adopter Feedback

Vendor press and marketing materials and conversations with vendors will provide a wealth of information on the history, capabilities, and future directions of each Web-scale discovery service under review. Vendors should, and do, genuinely respect a library conducting thorough evaluations of not only their own but their competitors' products, and acknowledge that their service may not be the one ultimately selected. They also are aware of features and functionality that their service offers, and which they think-- accurately or inaccurately--their competitors' services do not. However, an even more unbiased assessment can be derived from speaking with early adopters of the various Web-scale discovery services. As noted, multiple early adopters exist for each major service, and at least some of these adopters have had the service in place in their public environments for several years. They have had time to assess the service from multiple angles, including the perspectives of the end user, library staff, and the vendor's support and responsiveness.

Early Adopter Feedback: End User Perspective

Some early adopters have already conducted their own usability testing with local users, and may have sensed important patterns or areas for future improvement, perhaps improving things themselves or suggesting tweaks to the vendors. Early adopters may have a sense of similar or varying satisfaction levels among different user groups, such as undergraduates, graduates, faculty, and/or the broader community. For example, certain graduate students and faculty in particular disciplines may be happier with the content coverage than those in other disciplines. Potential questions to ask early adopters are numerous, such as:

- *Have oddities, issues, or difficulties arisen with the interface or search results (e.g. known item searching)*
- *Do you find challenges exist with users being aware of (and using) other important library resources after the launch of the Web-scale discovery service--such as other discipline specific databases?*
- *Is there an interface feature or functionality your users have expressed confusion with, or a feature absent that they'd like to see?*
- *Have instructional materials/sessions/outreach efforts been updated to incorporate the Web-scale discovery service, and if so, have any insights been gathered from end user questions?*

Early Adopter Feedback: Library Staff Perspective

Questions related to the library staff perspective could include topics such as the success of the public launch in terms of what went right and what did not. They could address the satisfaction with and adoption of the service by reference and instruction staff, and address back of the house activities associated with maintaining the service. Over the course of a year, early adopters have likely gained experience and insights with questions/issues such as:

- *Have a majority of librarians "switched" to using the discovery service as a first stop in their efforts to assist users? Have some remained devoted to the ILS catalog, and if so, do you have insights about why?*
- *Did you incorporate the Web-scale discovery service as the default search box on your Web site, and was this successful in retrospect? What efforts did you undertake to market your service and what would you recommend?*
- *Have difficulties arisen with trying to get particular, unique local collections into the centralized index?*
- *Have the automatic local record updating processes (adds/deletes/changes) worked smoothly over time?*
- *Have metadata mapping issues/limitations occurred? Has there been a need for "dumbing down" metadata from various systems (to fit the underlying discovery system schema; if so, did this have any negative ramifications?*
- *Have unanticipated interoperability difficulties arisen between different systems in use (e.g. the local ILS, the rights management knowledgebase and/or link resolver in use, the digital collections management system, etc.)?*

- *Have any workflows been altered with technical services staff responsibilities? What new activities have started? Have any activities ceased?*

Early Adopter Feedback: Vendor Support Structure

Finally, insights can be gathered on the post-implementation support structures and responsiveness of the vendors. Questions along these lines of investigation could include:

- *Did the vendor promise a particular feature or functionality which it has yet to deliver?*
- *Have you been satisfied with the continued addition of new content and the update cycle for the centralized index?*
- *Have you had to report issues to the vendor, and if so, were these one-time issues or has anything systemic developed? How satisfied have you been with the vendor responsiveness, and do appropriate support structures seem to be in place?*

Gathering answers to questions such as these will not necessarily make or break a strong preference for a particular service, unless early multiple adopters of the same service all report unhappiness. Still, such feedback can highlight important concepts that may not have been considered simply because the library conducting the evaluation has no firsthand experience with implementing, launching, and living with a discovery service for an extended period. There may not be the need to contact early adopters for every service; it is perhaps left to the end of the evaluation process to add ancillary information for services which have been shortlisted for continued consideration. It is important to acknowledge that an early adopter's institution, mission, and capabilities may vary somewhat from the evaluation library's environment, in terms of undergraduate versus graduate

focus, the number of staff on hand that can develop an interface and conduct usability testing, and other factors. However, remembering that a new Web-scale discovery service could become a library's default search tool, and acknowledging that the relationship could be long term, it is important not to skip a conversation with early adopters prior to making a final recommendation. Examples of other questions related to discovery and conversations with early adopters can be found from the University of Minnesota Libraries (Hanson, et al., 2009), and the UNLV Libraries (Vaughan, 2012).

Features Comparison / Rating Matrix

During the evaluation, it is likely the team will review feature comparison matrices created by others, or create a matrix themselves, befitting their local environment, and to ensure that the comparison is current–as mentioned, Web-scale discovery services are changing rapidly. Comparison matrices can be important, both by merit of listing important, significant, or desired features and functionality, and comparing products across these parameters. Related to the precursor technology of federated search, Dorner and Curtis (2004) conducted a detailed survey of ten federated search/portal interface products against seventy-nine features clustered into eight broad categories such as searching, customization, and software platforms supported. Oregon State University created an initial comparison matrix across four products, with factors categorized under "search and retrieval," "content" and "added features" (Boock, et al, 2009) and, later, a second matrix comparing two products (Boock, et al, 2009). UNLV created a comparison matrix across five services with the categories of "content," "end user interface features," "library staff customization capabilities," and "fundamentals" (e.g. "Implementations exist in which records have been harvested from digital collections and institutional repositories"). Michigan also notes the creation of a review/ranking matrix (Varnum, et al., 2010). Published literature also exists comparing various products, including works from Rowe (2010, 2011) and Brubaker, et al. (2011). Similar to a comparison/rating matrix, an evaluation team could also create a broad pros/cons list for each service, based on some of the same functional areas as above. The pros/cons list might offer a few more details than a "yes/no/somewhat" comparison matrix.

Vendor Quotes

Pricing for Web-scale discovery services is an important factor influencing a library's final decision. As noted, each major discovery service is offered as a subscription service, with content continually added and capabilities improved. Each vendor hosts and maintains its growing centralized index in the cloud, as well as the associated Web application search interface. A few vendors offer the option for the local library to host the search interface if desired, and this decision may influence the annual subscription price. Other pricing factors vary by vendor, and can include the amount of local library content (ILS bibliographic records, digital collection objects, etc.) included in the central index, the parent university's degree granting status, and the university's FTE student count, or, for other library types, the size of their user community. As mentioned, some services may also have an additional one-time set up or implementation fee. Vendors may offer multi-year, consortial, or "purchase by this date" discounts.

Further Steps to Consider

Steps outlined above are typical steps any systematic evaluation effort will likely entail. However, there are other steps to consider, depending on the local institutional environment and with how much effort–and how long an evaluation process–the local library is comfortable. Following are a few examples of additional evaluation steps that may be

considered. These include pre-selection usability testing, feedback from outside stakeholders, the vendor offering to install a test implementation scoped to the library's local and remotely hosted content, and the vendor allowing the library to review implementation and content mapping documents.

It may be possible, albeit somewhat challenging, to conduct usability testing of various services prior to actual selection, implementation, and launch. Oregon State University Libraries asked their usability group to conduct testing on their local libraries' catalog and the Web-scale discovery service implemented at the University of Washington (Boock, et al., 2009). Their usability testing included undergraduate and graduate students, library staff, and instructors and faculty. While it is technically possible to conduct usability testing with local users using existing implementations in service elsewhere, it would be difficult to gather substantive information attuned to the evaluating library's local environment. Users would be searching other institutional collections and not their own; authentication barriers may exist; and existing implementations may have a design or feature set implemented which the local library might do differently. While few would disagree that usability testing is prudent after a local launch of a discovery service, usability testing before the fact can be tricky and has caveats that must be acknowledged up-front. Some published research on discovery service usability testing is available for review from, for example, Dartmouth College (DeFelice, et al., 2009).

At time of writing, the major market for library Web-scale discovery services are academic libraries, with their rich and varied sets of locally hosted and remotely licensed content. Some or most academic institutions likely have a faculty senate, faculty library advisory board, student advisory board, or some other advising group which may offer feedback on a major new service which the library wishes to introduce. Choosing to engage and seek feedback from such groups can be a double edged sword; it is laudable to involve such individuals as future stakeholders who will be using a service ultimately selected, but at the same time, librarians have the best insights into the collective whole of locally and remotely licensed content, as well as expertise of how students search for information, based on years of observation, reference assistance, and instruction and information literacy efforts.

Some vendors may offer to scope the evaluating library's collection and implement a temporary fully functional instance of the discovery service they market for some set period of time, even up to a year, for testing and evaluation purposes. If a library were seriously considering that vendor's service, this would give the library the single best opportunity to evaluate the platform. The library would learn about the steps required to map and ingest local content into the centralized index. If the library chose and was allowed to launch the service as a pilot project for their public environment, they would have the opportunity to gauge student and faculty feedback to the service with no financial obligation; such feedback could extend to conducting actual usability testing. This step perhaps represents the extreme of an evaluative process. It would require effort, perhaps significant effort, on the part of library staff and the vendor to proceed through an evaluation implementation. It would expose the public and the librarians supporting them to a new discovery interface, which, ultimately, may not be selected as the best fit by the library conducting the evaluation. However, it is mentioned here as another possible, but detailed and lengthy, evaluation step to consider.

Upon request, and perhaps subject to confidentially disclosures, some vendors may be willing to share the actual implementation processes and procedures with a library that is investigating but not yet committed to their discovery service. Such documents would likely include a timeline for implementation, a list of vendor team individuals and their associated responsibilities with whom a library would be working, detailed mapping

templates to map content housed in disparate local repositories to the underlying discovery service schema, and required scripting or update routines to ensure changes to local records are updated and reflected in the central discovery service index. The vendor may also provide a management/configuration guide which illustrates how to tweak attributes of the interface, configure and understand statistics, etc. Taken as a collective whole, this set of information would provide significant insights into the discovery service, such as, for example, what things can be changed at the mapping, label, or overall interface levels. Such materials could provide some sense of how easy and rapid, or not, an implementation would be, as well as which things could be tweaked post implementation. These materials could also shed light on vendor support structures in place.

FUTURE RESEARCH DIRECTIONS

Future research directions related to Web-scale discovery include avenues focused on content, interface development, and adoption rate. Regarding content, it is currently challenging to precisely understand what material is indexed and included within the pre-aggregated central indexes associated with Web-scale discovery services. Such confusion hinders a full adequate comparison between the various services. To this end, a NISO Open Discovery Initiative working group was formed in late 2011, comprised of members representing publishers/information providers, system vendors, and libraries. As noted in the press announcement (NISO, 2011), "it is often not clear which resources are available, which are indexed in full text or by citations only, or both, and whether the metadata derives from aggregated databases or directly through the full-text." One general outcome of the group is to help develop standards and best practices to help fill this information gap. It will be interesting to monitor the outcomes of this group and other efforts that may develop to better understand what content is indexed and included in these services. Another content related research direction includes further studies of how Web-scale discovery services may change traditional resource use, such as a potential decrease in the use of traditional abstracting and indexing databases, due to the same or similar content being indexed and searchable in Web-scale discovery services. Doug Way (2010) performed some initial research in this area based on data from Grand Valley State University. Another area of research involves end user interface development, whether provided as an update or new release from the service vendor, or by library technical staff taking advantage of the open API based nature of many of these discovery services. Web-scale discovery services are constantly evolving with new features and functionality. Finally, future research could look at the anticipated growing library adoption rate of such services as they mature, and what generalized effect, if any, a growing install base has on the search habits of end users. For example, as noted above, changes may be observed in use of abstracting and indexing databases; another change may be a decrease in use of the library's traditional online public access catalog.

CONCLUSION

As evidenced above, there is any number of comprehensive steps involved in a library's evaluation of Web-scale discovery services suited to the local environment. Internally focused steps entail, most importantly, seeking to engage a broad array of library staff in the evaluation and selection process. Such engagement may evolve from educational efforts at the beginning, to constructing surveys, hosting question and answer sessions, and providing a venue for final vetting of a selection. Externally focused steps include extensive work gathering information from discovery service vendors, whether through question lists, an official RFP, teleconferences, and meetings at library conferences. It also involves a thorough review of vendor press releases and other information material, as well as a review of the emerging body of library literature authored by colleagues who have already completed their evaluative journeys. Despite the steps involved and potentially extensive time dedicated toward an evaluation, the rewards are promising. An easy-to-use interface, presenting search results pulled from a huge base of the library's local and remotely hosted content is something of which students, faculty, and even some librarians have long dreamed.

REFERENCES

Allgood, T. (2010, October). *Library one search: implementing Web-scale discovery in an academic research library.* Paper presented at the Library and Information Technology National Forum, Atlanta, GA. Retrieved from http://connect.ala.org/files/90278/library_one_search_lita2010_pdf_12610.pdf

Bates, M. (2003). *Task force recommendation 2.3 research and design review: Improving user access to library catalog and portal information, final report, version 3* (pp. 1-58). Retrieved from http://www.loc.gov/catdir/bibcontrol/2.3BatesReport6-03.doc.pdf

Bhatnagar, G., Dennis, S., Duque, G., Henry, S., MacEachern, M., Teasley, S., & Varnum, K. (2010). *University of Michigan Library Article Discovery Working Group final report.* University of Michigan Library. 1-15. Retrieved from http://www.lib.umich.edu/files/adwg/final-report.pdf

Boock, M., Buck, S., Chadwell, F., Nichols, J., & Reese, T. (2009). *Discovery services task force recommendation to university librarian* (pp. 1-8). Retrieved from http://ir.library.oregonstate.edu/xmlui/bitstream/handle/1957/13817/discovery%20search%20task%20force%20recommendations%20-%20redacted%20version.pdf

Boock, M., Chadwell, F., & Reese, T. (2009). *WorldCat local task force report to LAMP* (pp. 1-15). Retrieved from http://ir.library.oregon-state.edu/xmlui/bitstream/handle/1957/11167/WorldCat%20local%20task%20force%20re-port_cost%20redacted.pdf;jsessionid=4C7ED6F788688C5C307B9C2601B2C4BB?sequence=1

Boss, R. (2002). *Library technology reports: How to plan and implement a library portal.* Chicago, IL: American Library Association.

Brubaker, N., & Leach-Murray, S. (2011). Shapes in the cloud: Finding the right discovery layer. *Online, 35*(2), 20–26.

Brunning, D., & Machovec, G. (2010). An interview with Nancy Dushkin, VP discovery and delivery solutions at Ex Libris, regarding Primo Central. *The Charleston Advisor, 12*(2), 58–59. doi:10.5260/chara.12.2.58

Brunning, D., & Machovec, G. (2010). An interview with Sam Brooks and Michael Gorrell on the EBSCOhost integrated search and EBSCO Discovery Service. *The Charleston Advisor, 11*(3), 62–65.

Brunning, D., & Machovec, G. (2010). Interview about Summon with Jane Burke, vice president of Serials Solutions. *The Charleston Advisor, 11*(4), 60–62.

Calhoun, K. (2006). *The changing nature of the catalog and its integration with other discovery tools: final report* (pp. 1-52). Retrieved from http://www.loc.gov/catdir/calhoun-report-final.pdf

Calhoun, K., Cantrell, J., Gallagher, P., Hawk, H., & Cellentani, D. (2009). *Online catalogs: What users and librarians want* (pp. 1-59). Dublin, OH: OCLC Online Computer Library Center, Inc. Retrieved from http://www.oclc.org/reports/onlinecatalogs/fullreport.pdf

Caswell, J., & Wynstra, J. (2007). Developing the right RFP for selecting your federated search product: Lessons learned and tips from recent experience . In Cox, C. (Ed.), *Federated search: Solution or setback for online library services* (pp. 49–71). Binghamton, NY: The Haworth Information Press. doi:10.1300/J136v12n01_03

Christenson, H., & Tennant, R. (2005). *Integrating information resources: Principles, technologies, and approaches* (pp. 1-16). Retrieved from http://www.cdlib.org/inside/projects/metasearch/nsdl/nsdl_report2.pdf

Cox, C. (2007). *Federated search: Solution or setback for online library services.* Binghamton, NY: The Haworth Information Press.

De Rosa, C., Cantrell, J., Hawk, J., & Wilson, A. (2006). *College students' perceptions of libraries and information resources* (pp. 1-100). Dublin, OH: OCLC Online Computer Library Center, Inc. Retrieved from http://www.oclc.org/reports/pdfs/studentperceptions.pdf

DeFelice, B., Kortfelt, J., et al. (2009). *An evaluation of serial solutions summon as a discovery service for the Dartmouth College Library.* Retrieved from http://www.dartmouth.edu/~library/admin/docs/Summon_Report.pdf

Detinger, S., Keclik, K., Barclay, A., Bruns, T., Larson, E., Quattrucci, A., et al. (2008). *Resource discovery exploratory task force final report.* Retrieved from http://staff.library.wisc.edu/rdetf/RDETF-final-report.pdf

Dorner, D., & Curtis, A. (2004). A comparative review of the common user interface products. *Library Hi Tech, 22*(2), 182–197. doi:10.1108/07378830410543502

Gibson, I., Goddard, L., & Gordon, S. (2009). One box to search them all: Implementing federated search at an academic library. *Library Hi Tech, 27*(1), 118–133. doi:10.1108/07378830910942973

Hanson, C., Hessel, H., Barneson, J., Boudewyns, D., Fransen, J., & Friedman-Shedlov, L. ... Traill, S. (2009). *Discoverability phase 1 final report.* University of Minnesota Libraries. Retrieved from http://purl.umn.edu/48258

Hanson, C., Hessel, H., Barneson, J., Boudewyns, D., Fransen, J., & Friedman-Shedlov, L. ... Traill, S. (2009). *Discoverability phase 2 final report.* University of Minnesota Libraries. Retrieved from http://purl.umn.edu/99734

Luther, J., & Kelly, M. (2011). The next generation of discovery. *Library Journal, 136*(35), 67–71.

Marshall, P., Herman, S., & Rajan, S. (2006). In search of more meaningful search. *Serials Review, 32*(3), 172–180. doi:10.1016/j.serrev.2006.06.001

National Information Standards Organization. (2011). *NISO launches new open discovery initiative to develop standards and recommended practices for library discovery services based on indexed search.* Retrieved from http://www.niso.org/news/pr/view?item_key=21d5364c586575fd5d4dd408f17c5dc062b1ef5f

Rowe, R. (2010). Web-scale discovery: A review of Summon, EBSCO Discovery Service, and WorldCat local. *The Charleston Advisor, 12*(1), 5–10. doi:10.5260/chara.12.1.5

Rowe, R. (2011). Encore Synergy, Primo Central: Web-scale discovery: A review of two products on the market. *The Charleston Advisor, 12*(4), 11–15. doi:10.5260/chara.12.4.11

Schonfeld, R., & Housewright, R. (2010). *Faculty survey 2009: Key strategic insights for libraries, publishers, and societies* (pp. 1-35). Retrieved from http://www.ithaka.org/ithaka-s-r/research/faculty-surveys-2000–2009/Faculty%20Study%202009.pdf

University of California Libraries Bibliographic Services Task Force. (2005). *Rethinking how we provide bibliographic services for the University of California: Final report.* University of California Libraries. Retrieved from http://libraries.universityofcalifornia.edu/sopag/BSTF/Final.pdf

University of Nevada Las Vegas University Libraries. (2009). *UNLV libraries strategic plan 2009-2011.* Retrieved from http://library.nevada.edu/about/strategic_plan09-11.pdf

Vaughan, J. (2011). *Library technology reports: LibraryWeb scale discovery services.* Chicago, IL: American Library Association.

Vaughan, J. (2012). Investigations into library Web-scale discovery services. *Information Technology and Libraries, 31*(1), 32–82. doi:10.6017/ital.v31i1.1916

Vaughan, J., & Hanken, T. (2011). *Evaluating and implementing Web-scale discovery services in your library.* Retrieved from http://www.alatechsource.org/blog/2011/07/continuing-the-conversation-evaluating-and-implementing-web-scale-discovery-services--0

Way, D. (2010). The impact of Web-scale discovery on the use of a library collection. *Serials Review, 36*(4), 214–220. doi:10.1016/j.serrev.2010.07.002

ADDITIONAL READING

Atkins, S. (2004). Projecting success: Effective project management in academic libraries. *25th International Association of Scientific and Technological University Libraries Proceedings.* Retrieved from http://www.iatul.org/doclibrary/public/Conf_Proceedings/2004/Stephanie20Atkins.pdf

Breeding, M. (2011). *Library technology guides: Key resources in the field of library automation.* Retrieved from http://www.librarytechnology.org/

Charleston Advisor. (n.d.). Retrieved from http://www.charlestonco.com

Covey, D. (2002). *Usage and usability assessment: Library practices and concerns*. Washington, DC: Digital Library Federation. Retrieved from http://www.clir.org/pubs/reports/pub105/pub105.pdf

Cox, C. (2007). *Federated search: solution or setback for online library services*. Binghamton, NY: The Haworth Information Press.

Ex Libris Group, Ltd. (2011). *Ex Libris Primo Central*. Retrieved from http://www.exlibrisgroup.com/category/PrimoCentral

Fagan, J., & Keach, J. (2009). *Web project management for academic libraries*. Oxford, UK: Chandos Publishing. doi:10.1533/9781780630199

Frame, J. (2003). *Managing projects in organizations: How to make the best use of time, techniques, and people*. San Francisco, CA: Jossey-Bass.

Industries, E. B. S. C. O. Inc. (2011). *EBSCO discovery service*. Retrieved from http://www.ebscohost.com/discovery

Innovative Interfaces, Inc. (2011). *Innovative Interfaces Encore Synergy*. Retrieved from http://encoreforlibraries.com/products/#es

Nielsen, J. (n.d.). *useit.com: Jakob Nielsen's website*. Retrieved from http://www.useit.com

Online Computer Library Center. (2011). *OCLC WorldCat Local*. Retrieved from http://www.oclc.org/worldcatlocal/

ProQuest. LLC. (2011). *Serials solutions summon*. Retrieved from http://www.serialssolutions.com/discovery/summon/

Rubin, J., & Chisnell, D. (2008). *Handbook of usability testing: How to plan, design, and conduct effective tests*. Hoboken, NJ: Wiley Publishing, Inc.

Tay, A. (n.d.). *Unified resource discovery comparison: Articles on discovery*. Retrieved April 8, 2012 from https://sites.google.com/site/urd2comparison/articles-on-discovery

University of Michigan University Library Usability Group. (2010). *Usability in the library*. Retrieved November 29, 2011, from http://www.lib.umich.edu/usability-library

Vaughan, J., & Hanken, T. (2011). *Continuing the conversation: Evaluating and implementing Web-scale discovery services in your library (part 2)*. Retrieved from http://www.alatechsource.org/blog/2011/07/continuing-the-conversation-evaluating-and-implementing-web-scale-discovery-services--0

Webber, D., & Peters, A. (2010). *Integrated library systems: Planning, selecting, and implementing*. Santa Barbara, CA: Libraries Unlimited.

KEY TERMS AND DEFINITIONS

Centralized Index: The majority of major Web-scale discovery services create an aggregated centralized index, hosted in the cloud, which contains a combination of both local library content and remotely hosted content licensed or purchased by the library. This index also often contains open access content.

Cloud: A common name for remotely hosted storage area that can contain files, records, and other information. Cloud services may be free or available for a fee; paid services often provide additional functions or space. Discovery service vendors provide access to resources remotely "in the cloud" to libraries.

Comparison Matrix: A method of comparing items with particular attributes or characteristics. A matrix is often set up in a tabular format, with the items being compared along one axis, and the attributes/characteristics along the other axis.

Content Overlap Analysis: A comparison of content held/licensed by the local library, and what portion of this content can be, or is, indexed in the discovery service's central index, and thus available for search and retrieval.

Integrated Library System (ILS): An enterprise system typically used to manage daily library operations such as acquisitions, item description, serials control, circulation, and a public catalog interface for discovery and access to materials.

Library Web-Scale Discovery Service: In the context of this chapter, a service which builds a central, searchable index containing a large portion of a library's locally hosted and remotely licensed content, and which provides a search and retrieval interface to search this index.

Locally Hosted Information: Items (full text, digital objects, etc.) or bibliographic records cataloged, hosted, and searchable within a local information repository housed and under the control of the local library.

Metadata: Descriptive data which describes an object. Such description may include elements such as title, author, creation date, and description of content.

Remotely Licensed Information: Licensed/subscribed content hosted on a networked system housed outside of the subscribing institution. This often includes publisher or aggregator content to which the library subscribes, but which is hosted natively by the publisher, aggregator, or another 3rd party service.

Request for Proposal (RFP): An often structured, early formal step associated with the procurement of a product and/or service. An invitation is provided for potential product/service suppliers to submit a proposal in response to the invitation, in the hopes of being selected to provide the requested product/service, often determined by a bidding process and formal review of all submitted proposals.

Rights Management: Configuration activities and/or settings undertaken to ensure that licensed publisher resources are accessible only to individuals licensed to view/download such resources (e.g. such as staff and students affiliated with an institution which has paid for and licensed access to such materials).

ENDNOTES

[1]   Google Scholar is owned by Google Inc.

[2]   Summon is owned by ProQuest LLC

Chapter 5
Best Practices for Selecting the Best Fit

Monica Metz-Wiseman
University of South Florida, USA

Melanie Griffin
University of South Florida, USA

Carol Ann Borchert
University of South Florida, USA

Deborah Henry
University of South Florida St. Petersburg, USA

ABSTRACT

The authors of this chapter interviewed librarians from fifteen academic institutions who participated in a selection process for a discovery service. The pool of academic institutions engaged in the interviews represented universities and colleges of varying sizes in order to capture a variety of approaches to selection. Institutions were further chosen based on their use of a defined selection process that resulted in a recommendation and implementation of a discovery service. These interviews informed the identification of best practices and challenges faced in the selection process. The methodology and a summary of the interviews are described. The challenge of pursuing best practices is also discussed.

INTRODUCTION

The proliferation of resources that support research, teaching, and creative work understandably confuses and overwhelms the academic library user community. These resources can include licensed and open-access content, digitized materials, bibliographic tools, link resolvers and institutional repositories. Even an "expert" researcher encounters difficulty navigating a growing number of resources, interfaces, and search options that can be offered by the academic library. Google has created an expectation of a simple search process that libraries are now attempting to replicate. While next generation catalogs and federated search engines served as the first step in improving the user experience, the locus of attention for academic libraries now rests on

DOI: 10.4018/978-1-4666-1821-3.ch005

commercially developed or open source discovery services. Discovery services strive to integrate as much content as possible through a single search to arrive at the Google-like experience. As these tools multiply and develop, the selection process is increasingly complex and time-consuming, yet remains critical. In the selection process, what are the best practices that play a role in a successful implementation of a discovery service?

BACKGROUND

The literature on discovery services is emerging. As recently as 2007, researchers spoke of next-generation catalogs, which added new facets and search capabilities to the existing materials in the catalog. Prior to next-generation catalogs, federated search engines aimed to facilitate student research. Librarians from Paul Smith's College in New York described their experience selecting a faceted open-source backup to their catalog called Fac-Back-OPAC (Beccaria & Scott, 2007). *Serials Review* published a column that brought together five different libraries that evaluated different federated search products in an attempt to provide a single search box for their patrons (Boyd et al., 2006). Each discussed reasons for implementing these products, what criteria they used, what problem(s) they were trying to solve, and benefits and limitations. Marcin and Morris addressed the inclusion of federated search capability in the catalog as a desired characteristic in their article discussing the evaluation and selection process for a next-generation catalog (2008). At the 2010 NASIG Annual Conference, Collins moderated a session on open source library systems and next generation catalogs. In summarizing the session, Collins noted that "[m]any of the same themes were repeated, specifically...enhanced discovery tools that facilitate searching and integrate the catalog with other data streams including federated search results, article databases, and institutional repository contents" (Collins, 2011, p.172). Dempsey

discussed discovery versus location of information, how commercial resources offering a unified discovery experience changed user expectations in searching for library resources, and the need for discovery tools to create a better user experience (2006). Breeding, in his introduction to the 2007 *Library Technology Reports* examining next generation catalogs, described the desired features of a next-generation catalog and called for a move to combine the searching for books and articles into a single search, rather than just adding new search capabilities to the existing catalog. In his article, "In Search of a Really Next-Generation Catalog," Singer declared, "it is time to shed the trappings of the card catalog and reconfigure our assets to work with the Web instead of around it" (Singer, 2008, p.142).

As noted by Dempsey and Breeding, discovery services added a new dimension to next generation catalogs by pulling journal articles and other materials into a single search, rather than having patrons muddle through fragmented resources to perform a complete search of the literature. In 2005, the University of California Bibliographic Services Task Force observed that:

Users who are accustomed to Google expect to enter one search and retrieve information pulled together from across the information space and presented in a single ranked list. They want more than the ability to search multiple catalogs or multiple A&I databases simultaneously. They expect to search the full range of tools cited above or subsets the user wishes to select. (2005, p.19)

Their report described a number of desired features in such a system, including direct access to content, recommender features, customization, search strategies in the event of a failed search, and FRBRized search results. The Task Force also outlined principles to guide the redesign of their services to rethink their system architecture and focus more on services and less on the systems themselves. In his 2010 article, Breeding succinctly defined the functionality of a unified discovery tool: "[a] great discovery interface should operate in a mostly self-explanatory way, allowing users to concentrate on selecting and evaluating the resources returned rather than struggling through the search tools that the library provides" (2010, p.34). Calhoun discussed the need for "revitalizing the catalog" in her 2006 report to the Library of Congress but predicted that "[t]he catalog will evolve toward full integration with other discovery tools and with the larger scholarly information universe" (p.16).

There is scant literature, however, that discusses best practices for selecting a discovery service in depth. Most of the materials that do are located in the grey literature of library reports and, as a result, are institution-specific. *An Evaluation of Serials Solutions Summon as a Discovery Service for the Dartmouth College Library*, for example, reported on Dartmouth's decision to "accept...an invitation from ProQuest®1 to work with them" on the creation of Summon™2 (Dartmouth College Library, 2009, p. 2), a selection process that is not extensible to other libraries. While other library reports such as the Oregon State University task force report (Boock et al., 2009) and the University of Wisconsin Madison's *Resource Discovery Exploratory Task Force Final Report* (2008) described the processes used in selecting a tool, the focus tended to be on the recommendation rather than the process of reaching the recommendation. The *University of Michigan Article Discovery Working Group Final Report* (2010) was slightly different, focusing on explaining the researcher persona-based method used to evaluate discovery services, but it did not provide specifics on which tools to examine or determining which criteria were important in a Web-scale discovery service. The exception to literature focusing exclusively on local practice rule was Jason Vaughn's *Library Technology Reports*, "Web Scale Discovery Services" (2011). In particular, Chapter Seven, "Questions to Consider," included questions to ask when evaluating discovery services, including

specific sections on background questions, local library resources, indexed content, open-access content, relevancy ranking, authentication, and the user interface.

Methodology to Determine Best Practices

Given the dearth of literature outlining best practices for selecting a discovery service, this chapter establishes a framework for a selection process. The authors contacted thirty-one academic librarians requesting their participation in an interview to summarize their selection of a discovery tool using a defined process. A defined process is an ad-hoc group or standing committee that engages in the evaluation of discovery services resulting in a recommendation for implementation. These interviews provide the foundation for best practices in the selection process of a discovery service (see Appendix A: Interview Protocol).

Selection of Participating Libraries

The authors selected fifteen participating libraries based on two criteria: participation in a defined selection process and the size of the institution. The authors defined "small" institutions as fewer than 10,000 FTE, "medium" between 10,000 and 20,000 FTE, and "large" as over 20,000 FTE. Interviewees for this study were librarians at institutions that satisfied the sizing band requirement and engaged in a defined discovery tool process (see Table 1).

Process Used

Those institutions that agreed to participate in the study were assured that their responses would be aggregated with no attribution of quotes or identification of specific institutions beyond the summarized results. Questions were sent by email in advance of the interview. For over half of the interviews, two or more librarians representing

Table 1. Institutions of librarians interviewed

Institution	Size
Claremont College	small
Indiana University Southeast	small
Midwestern State University	small
Western Carolina University	small
Williamette University/ORBIS	small
American University	medium
Illinois State University	medium
University of Miami	medium
University of North Carolina – Greensboro	medium
Washington University in St. Louis	medium
East Carolina University	large
Pennsylvania State University	large
Texas A&M University	large
University of Iowa	large
University of Michigan	large

an institution participated in the interview. Each interview conducted from May through June 2011 began with a request for the interviewees to provide an overview of the discovery selection process.

Librarians representing sixteen institutions where no defined selection process took place for a discovery tool were not interviewed or included in the study. They represented institutions where one of the following scenarios applied:

- The library was an early adopter for a discovery service when there were no other or very limited options, rendering a selection process unnecessary.
- The library was a beta site for a particular product with no selection process.
- The dean or director decided which discovery service the library would purchase.

Summary of Interviews

Need for Discovery Service

Experience with or active engagement in the review of next generation catalogs or federated search products often resulted in the search for a discovery service. As the market for discovery services matured, librarians began to realize that these tools were the next logical step to improve access for the user community by integrating multiple catalogs and databases. Existing teams or committees could then redirect efforts from a focus on the catalog and federated searching to discovery services. The interviewees included beta testers and developers of discovery services who concentrated on the development and improvement of emerging products. Most institutions sought a short range solution, often for two to three years, and anticipated that they would continue to observe and track open source and commercial discovery services after implementing the selected tool. Efforts by library consortia to review discovery services also led institutions to launch a selection committee. Institutions connected to consortia that engaged in the analysis, recommendations, and selections for discovery services indicated the benefit of this work, citing it as a means to facilitate lending and borrowing within the consortia, realize lower costs, encourage collaboration, and reduce redundancy of effort. Another reason for launching a team to select a discovery service was an institutional culture of early emerging technology adoption. The user community provided the final impetus to examine discovery services. LIBQUAL®[3] feedback related to federated searching prompted a look at discovery services as a means to add article content through the online catalog.

Selection Committees

The composition of the selection committees varied in size from four to twenty individuals. With the exception of one institution, the selection committee included a broad representation of the areas within an academic library such as public services, information technology (IT), collections, scholarly publishing, and technical services. Institutions with multiple campuses, medical programs, or law schools included representation from their respective libraries on the selection group. Committees either tackled the review as an entire group or split into smaller groups that focused on one aspect of the selection process. Smaller groups might conduct usability testing, develop a Request for Proposals (RFP), analyze content or examine the technical underpinnings of the discovery service and report back to the larger group.

Evaluation Process

The review process itself highlighted both commonalities and unique approaches. Most groups engaged in a literature review; developed weighted criteria or metrics; created surveys for the library staff for evaluation purposes; engaged users through focus groups, usability testing, and interviews; invited vendors on-site for presentations; spoke to other libraries about their implementation of a particular product or tool; and researched discovery services during conferences. The selection groups were evenly split on setting up a trial or "guerilla testing" discovery services using a production system at another college or university. Some unique approaches included developing a process that was totally user-centered, creating a task force comprised entirely of public service librarians, calling for a vote early in the process to ensure buy-in from public services staff on whether to proceed with a discovery service, and using personas (undergraduate, graduate, faculty) to guide the process. In some cases, representa-

tives from one university or school traveled to another for a site visit to discuss implementation and satisfaction with a particular discovery service.

Challenges and Solutions

Although some of the libraries interviewed faced unique challenges because of their organizational structure, technical issues, commitments to partners, or other conditions, several common challenges emerged. While identifying the challenges, the interviewees often discussed those difficulties in terms of the solutions they found (see Table 2).

Staff Buy-in and Training

More than half of the interviewees (53%, 8 of 15) stated concern over obtaining consensus from the majority of staff members, particularly those expected to promote and teach the discovery service during instruction sessions and from service desks. This study's data indicated that large and medium sized institutions encountered this challenge more often (60%, 3 of 5). Giving staff the opportunity to weigh in during the selection process ensured that they understood the need for and the benefit of the tool. Reaction to the new product varied; some staff readily accepted the discovery service while in other environments reviewing teams met with some resistance. Some staff required assurance that the new product would complement rather than replace specific databases and existing search tools already heavily used and favored by library users. Good or bad experiences with vendor products in the past sometimes resulted in bias towards or against that vendor. Small, medium, and large libraries encountered the challenge of providing adequate training opportunities for staff. As technical and search skill levels varied, training had to be addressed. If the impetus for the discovery service project did not come from the administration, the reviewing team had the challenge of presenting and justifying any recommendations to the organization's leadership.

Table 2. Challenges (listed in order of times cited by respondents)

Challenge	Total number of respondents	%	Large	Medium	Small
Buy-in & staff training	8	53% (8 of 15)	60% (3 of 5)	60% (3 of 5)	40% (2 of 5)
Product availability & testing environment	7	47% (7 of 15)	40% (2 of 5)	60% (3 of 5)	40% (2 of 5)
Deadlines & project timeline	7	47% (7 of 15)	40% (2 of 5)	40% (2 of 5)	60% (3 of 5)
Team management	6	40% (6 of 15)	60% (3 of 5)	40% (2 of 5)	20% (1 of 5)
Technology issues	6	40% (6 of 15)	20% (1 of 5)	40% (2 of 5)	60% (3 of 5)
Critical ranking & relevancy	3	20% (3 of 15)	40% (2 of 5)	0	20% (1 of 5)
Vendor verification	2	13% (2 of 15)	20% (1 of 5)	20% (1 of 5)	0
Marketing	1	7% (1 of 15)	0	20% (1 of 5)	0

Total number of institutions = 15; Large = 5; Medium = 5, Small = 5
Percentages rounded up or down (< or > .5)

Product Availability and Testing Environment

The lack of products from which to choose presented another shared challenge (47%, 7 of 15). Institutions that started investigating early in the development of discovery services found few open-source or commercial options available. Advertised products were in the early stages of development. Few to no organizations were in a position to share practical experience. Interviewees expressed their concern over the risks associated with reviewing, testing, and selecting products still under development and changing rapidly. Although extensive discussions with vendors were recommended, at some point participants believed that the institution must make the best decision possible based on the current state of available products.

While interviewees preferred conducting tests with the institution's own records, several had to manage testing using another organization's site and records. A few comments indicated that receiving feedback in a timely manner from the staff members doing the testing was a challenge.

Sometimes staff struggled to think like a library user rather than a library professional. Several interviewees recommended site visits to include vendor presentations with an open forum for questions and selection committee visits to other customers of a specific discovery service. Usability testing after implementation provided the vendor with suggestions to improve the product and help the library decide whether to continue using the tool.

Project Timeline

Several interviewees identified meeting deadlines during the project as a challenge (47%, 7 of 15). Responses from small libraries (60%, 3 of 5) indicated they may have had a more difficult time with this than the larger organizations (40%, 2 of 5). With large workloads and so many details to manage, reviewers strongly recommended that a longer and/or more flexible timeline would benefit the investigative review and selection process. Organizations requiring formal RFPs faced an additional burden within a short time frame.

Team Management

Overall, forty percent (6 of 15) of the participants in this study identified issues related to managing a large and diverse review team, consisting of members from different departments, institutional partners, and/or multiple campuses. Some interviewees stressed the need to continually encourage team members to share feedback while keeping other members from dominating the process. Responses from large institutions reflected that team management required more attention (60%, 3 of 5) than in the smaller organizations (medium 40%, 2 of 5, and small 20%, 1 of 5). Positive suggestions to keep members on track and engaged included clear goals, good communication, regular or frequent meetings, collaborative work space, and valuing different perspectives from team members.

Technology

Interviewees faced institution-mandated and/or consortia technical demands (40%, 6 of 15). The discovery service had to be compatible with a library's existing technologies, often resulting in little or no flexibility. Some products were removed immediately from consideration if this was an issue. Participant responses suggest an inverse relationship between the size of institution and technology concerns. Also, some libraries reported implementing and/or integrating more than one new system at the same time as the discovery service.

Other Identified Challenges

Although cited by fewer participants, other challenges included ranking the features and facets of the discovery service and assigning weight to these features (3 comments). In some cases, reviewers ranked too many criteria as highly desirable. Participants mentioned issues with establishing relevancy priorities when ranking results and determining what resources the organization wanted to promote (for instance, by having them appear higher in the results list). Sometimes complicated relationships with vendors were noted, as was the need to verify information provided by vendors (2 comments). Checking customer references to verify product claims was an important part of the process. Lastly, one institution named marketing the new tool a challenge.

Best Practices

Having addressed the characteristics of the selection process, the challenges faced and proposed solutions, what might be considered best practices in the selection process for a discovery service? The interviewees identified the following:

User Needs

- Engage the user through usability testing, focus groups, three-minute surveys, online surveys, interviews, and observation to ensure that the discovery service meets the needs of the various user groups.
- Develop personas complete with a suite of user-focused needs specific to the university to provide a clearer path to a discovery service that best works for that university. Usability testing can then provide validation to this process.

Setting Criteria

- Develop weighted criteria early in the process to focus efforts, narrow the field of possibilities, and fulfill requirements of the RFP process. Excel spreadsheets and surveys assist in organizing weighted or clustered criteria.
- Complete an environmental scan of institutional needs such as interoperability with existing tools such as link resolvers, user needs, pricing, and consortia require-

ments early on to streamline and focus the process.

Library Engagement

- Preserve institutional memory by transitioning next-generation catalog and federated searching working groups to discovery services. This leads to reduced learning curves, builds on expertise, and generally helps smooth the way to a valued discovery service.
- Engage library staff, particularly public service librarians, through presentations, meetings, surveys, and the selection process in order to lead to consensus on selection, promotion, and integration of the discovery service into existing services of the academic library.
- Ensure broad representation from across the library on the selection team to fashion a multi-faceted review of the discovery service.

Vendors

- Solicit vendor presentations and visits to focus on specific questions and areas to provide the necessary background, details, and insight into future directions for the vendor and product.
- Obtain written responses from vendors to form a set of responses that can be referenced at any point.
- Schedule vendor presentations after the review team has had an opportunity to work with the tool to encourage more in-depth and relevant questions and comments.

Testing

- Beta testing and trials, although time-consuming and labor-intensive, allow universities to test access independently with their records and collections. When this is not possible, guerrilla testing is beneficial.
- Parallel testing of existing tools (MetaLib[4], Aquabrowser[5], Google Scholar[6], etc.) with discovery services allows for a more accurate, complete, and realistic comparison.
- Apply previous searches by users against discovery services to provide context and supply a test with a higher degree of accuracy.

Consultation Outside the University

- Check references to obtain a candid assessment of an institution's satisfaction with a discovery product.
- Work within a consortium, where there is commonality of interest and direction, to facilitate interlibrary loan, provide a common interface to the user community, and reduce duplication of effort and costs to implement.
- Participate in site visits to other colleges or universities, which can lead to candid and valuable insights with a product or tool.

One of the more daunting challenges associated with evaluating and selecting a discovery service is the relative newness of the available services and the rapid rate at which they continue to evolve. There is a very real possibility that, if the selection process is lengthy, the available products might look and function very differently at the end of the process. Many of the institutions interviewed for this chapter indicated that their selection process would be recursive and that a decision ought to be revisited to take the market's evolution into account. At the same time, the criteria used to select a discovery service ought to be adapted, suggesting the continued need for assessing the selection practices detailed above.

FUTURE RESEARCH DIRECTIONS

As discovery services continue to develop, there is limited published research on best practices for selecting a discovery service, particularly for doing so in a consortia environment. This study highlights some of the options available to consortia members, including implementing dependently with or independently from the consortia, but the best practices defined here do not extensively explore the topic. A related avenue for future research is balancing the collective buying power of the consortia with the needs of individual member institutions.

As many of the case studies documented in this chapter indicate, the selection process often includes limited time for usability testing. As more libraries implement discovery services, there will be opportunities to focus on users and incorporate their feedback into our understanding of both the positive aspects of and limitations to these tools. To further understanding of discovery tools, research questions could address the following:

- Does the positive acceptance of a discovery service vary with user types—undergraduates, graduate students, or faculty?
- How does a library gauge success with a discovery tool?
- Can users, ranging from undergraduates to faculty, find what they need, or does a discovery service simply provide a more authoritative starting point for research?
- What is the impact of teaching faculty's perception of the discovery service on their students' use of the selected tool?
- What impact will discovery services have on users who have been trained to use specific resources?

Once available, the results of usability testing could be coupled with the technological assessments often conducted by libraries in the initial selection process to provide a holistic paradigm for selecting the best fit.

CONCLUSION

The librarians interviewed for this chapter led or participated in a discovery services selection process at their institutions. The interviewees revealed the process and rationale used in arriving at a short list of products, what worked particularly well within the selection process, and challenges faced. The best practices identified help to create a plan for academic libraries with designs to select a discovery service. The selection practices described by those who had recommended and implemented a discovery service within this study can then be adapted or imitated in order to arrive at a best fit for a discovery service for an academic institution. While this road map could aid in selecting the most appropriate product, this is but one aspect of the broader process that includes implementation, continued engagement with the user community, and ongoing assessment and evaluation as discovery services emerge and evolve. These are all areas that deserve attention in the quest for a successful implementation of discovery services.

ACKNOWLEDGMENT

The authors would like to express thanks and appreciation to the librarians interviewed and the institutions they represent for participating in this study.

REFERENCES

Beccaria, M., & Scott, D. (2007). Fac-back-OPAC: An open source interface to your library system. *Computers in Libraries*, *27*(9), 6–56.

Bhatnagar, G., Dennis, S., Duque, G., Henry, S., MacEachern, M., Teasley, S., & Varnum, K. (2010). *University of Michigan Article Discovery Working Group final report*. Retrieved from http://www.lib.umich.edu/files/adwg/final-report.pdf

Boock, M., Buck, S., Chadwell, F., Nichols, J., & Reese, T. (2009). *Discovery services task force recommendation to university librarian*. Retrieved from http://hdl.handle.net/1957/13817

Boyd, J., Hampton, M., Morrison, P., Pugh, P., & Cervone, F. (2006). The one-box challenge: Providing a federated search that benefits the research process. *Serials Review, 32*(4), 247–254. doi:10.1016/j.serrev.2006.08.005

Breeding, M. (2007). Introduction. *Library Technology Reports, 43*(4), 5–14.

Breeding, M. (2010). The state of the art in library discovery 2010. *Computers in Libraries, 30*(1), 31–34.

Calhoun, K. (2006). *The changing nature of the catalog and its integration with other discovery tools*. Retrieved from http://www.loc.gov/catdir/calhoun-report-final.pdf

Collins, M., & Rathemacher, A. J. (2010). Open forum: The future of library systems. *The Serials Librarian, 58*(1-4), 167–173. doi:10.1080/03615261003625703

Dartmouth College Library. (2009). *An evaluation of Serials Solutions Summon as a discovery service for the Dartmouth College Library*. Retrieved May 19, 2011, from http://www.dartmouth.edu/~library/admin/docs/Summon_Report.pdf

Dempsey, L. (2006). The library catalogue in the new discovery environment: Some thoughts. *Ariadne, 48*. Retrieved May 24, 2011, from http://www.ariadne.ac.uk/issue48/dempsey/

Dentinger, S., Keclik, K., Barclay, A., Bruns, T., Larson, E., Quattrucci, K., et al. (2008). *Resource discovery exploratory task force final report*. Retrieved May 24, 2011, from http://staff.library.wisc.edu/rdetf/RDETF-final-report.pdf

Marcin, S., & Morris, P. (2008). OPAC: The next generation. *Computers in Libraries, 28*(5), 6–64. doi:doi:10.1108/07378831111138170

Singer, R. (2008). In search of a really "next generation" catalog. *Journal of Electronic Resources Librarianship, 20*(3), 139–142. doi:10.1080/19411260802412752

University of California Libraries Bibliographic Services Task Force. (2005). *Rethinking how we provide bibliographic services for the University of California: Final report*. University of California Libraries. Retrieved from http://libraries.universityofcalifornia.edu/sopag/BSTF/Final.pdf

ADDITIONAL READING

Antelman, K., Lynema, E., & Pace, A. (2006). Toward a twenty-first century library catalog. *Information Technology and Libraries, 25*(3), 128–138.

Arnold, S. E. (2011). Data fusion, discovery, and the next big thing in research. *Information Today, 28*(4), 20–21.

Bowen, J. (2008). Metadata to support next-generation library resource discovery: Lessons from the eXtensible catalog, phase 1. *Information Technology & Libraries, 27*(2), 5–19.

Byrum, J., Jr. (2005). *Recommendations for urgently needed improvement of OPAC and the role of the National Bibliographic Agency in achieving it*. Paper presented at the World Library and Information Congress, 71st IFLA General Conference and Council, Oslo, Norway. Retrieved December 1, 2011 from http://archive.ifla.org/IV/ifla71/papers/124e-Byrum.pdf

Coffman, S. (1999). Building Earth's largest library: Driving into the future. *Searcher, 7*(3), 34–37.

Colyar, N. (2005). The process of selecting federated search and link resolver products. *Law & Liberty, 68*(2), 13–14.

Custer, M. (2011). *Our road to Summon: ECU Libraries* [PowerPoint slides]. Retrieved May 24, 2011, from http://www.google.com/url?sa=t&rct=j&q=&esrc=s&frm=1&source=web&cd=1&cts=1331408223507&ved=0CCMQFjAA&url=http%3A%2F%2Fwww.aserl.org%2Fwp-content%2Fuploads%2F2011%2F07%2FSummon_ECU.ppt&ei=VK1bT4n4JqXr0QG3yL3BDw&usg=AFQjCNH20wdkAdeeGQm0RDTXPgPwJlmaew&sig2=OrVkmPJLPHp_l222s1akbg

Emanuel, J. (2011). Usability of the VuFind next-generation online catalog. *Information Technology & Libraries, 30*(1), 44–52.

Garrison, S., Boston, G., & Bair, S. (2011, April). *Taming lightning in more than one bottle: Implementing a local next-generation catalog versus a hosted Web-scale discovery service*. Paper presented at the Meeting of the Association of College and Research Libraries, Philadelphia, PA. Retrieved June 15, 2011, from http://www.aip.cz/download/20110523_Summon_article_WMU_Garrison.pdf

Hawkins, D. T. (2011). *Web scale information discovery: The opportunity, the reality, the future—An NFAIS symposium*. The Conference Circuit. Retrieved December 2, 2011, from http://www.theconferencecircuit.com/2011/10/04/web-scale-information-discovery-the-opportunity-the-reality-the-future-an-nfais-symposium/

James, D., Garrett, M., & Krevit, L. (2009). Discovering discovery tools: Evaluating vendors and implementing Web 2.0 environments. *Library Hi Tech, 27*(2), 268–276. doi:10.1108/07378830910968218

Luther, J., & Kelly, M. C. (2011). The next generation of discovery. *Library Journal, 136*(5), 66-71. Retrieved December 2, 2011 from http://www.libraryjournal.com/lj/articlereview/889893-457/the_next_generation_of_discovery.html.csp

Mann, T. (2005). Research at risk. *Library Journal, 130*(12), 38–40.

Mann, T. (2008). A critical review. [Review of the article The changing nature of the catalog and its integration with other discovery tools]. *Journal of Library Metadata, 8*(2), 169–197. doi:10.1080/10911360802087374

Pace, A. (2004). Dismantling integrated library systems. *Library Journal, 129*(2), 34–36.

Raschke, G., & Boyer, J. (2011). *Summon and resource discovery at the NCSU libraries* [PowerPoint slides]. Retrieved May 24, 2011, from www.aserl.org/wp-content/uploads/2011/07/Summon_NCSU.ppt

Safley, E., Montgomery, D., & Gardner, S. (2011). Oasis or quicksand: Implementing a catalog discovery layer to maximize access to electronic resources. *The Serials Librarian, 60*(1-4), 164–168. doi:10.1080/0361526X.2011.556028

Tam, W., Cox, A., & Bussey, A. (2009). Student user preferences for features of next-generation OPACs. *Program: Electronic Library and Information Systems, 43*(4), 349–374. doi:10.1108/00330330910998020

Tennant, R. (2005). Is metasearching dead? *Library Journal, 130*(12), 28.

Vaughan, J. (2011). Questions to consider. *Library Technology Reports, 47*(1), 54–59.

Vaughan, J. (2011). For more information. *Library Technology Reports, 47*(1), 60–61.

Vaughan, J. (2011). Investigations into library Web scale discovery services. *Information Technology and Libraries, 125*(1), 669-678. Retrieved May 20, 2011, from http://www.ala.org/lita/ital/sites/ala.org.lita.ital/files/content/prepub/vaughan2011.pdf

Ward, J., Mofjeld, P., & Shadle, S. (2008). World-Cat Local at the University of Washington libraries. *Library Technology Reports, 44*(6), 4–41.

Yang, S. Q., & Wagner, K. (2010). Evaluating and comparing discovery tools: How close are we towards next generation catalog? *Library Hi Tech, 28*(4), 690–709. doi:10.1108/07378831011096312

Yee, M. (2005). FRBRization: A method for turning online public finding lists into online public catalogs. *Information Technology and Libraries, 24*(3), 77–95.

Young, J. (2005, May 20). 100 colleges sign up with Google to speed access to library resources. *The Chronicle of Higher Education, 51*(37), A30.

KEY TERMS AND DEFINITIONS

Discovery Services: Web-based and mobile-friendly initiatives or products that strive to integrate content, including books, journal articles, images, multimedia, and more, through a single search

Defined Selection Process: An ad-hoc group or standing committee that engages in evaluation that results in a recommendation

FRBRized Search Results: Search results organized by the Functional Requirements for Bibliographic Records (FRBR) hierarchical system, which brings related works together to facilitate retrieval

FTE: Full-Time Equivalent; a measure of student enrollment

Guerrilla Testing: Low cost testing of another institution's instance of a discovery service

LibQUAL: Survey instrument developed by Texas A&M University Libraries and the Association of Research Libraries that measures user perceptions of service quality

Next Generation Catalog: A catalog with added features, including facets, do you mean...?, and social networking; often an overlay to the existing catalog; typically does not include article content

Personas: Fictional identities representing various user groups (undergraduates, graduates, faculty), based on very specific data collected about real people

RFP: Request for Proposal; a formal process to request information about product features and costs that is required under certain conditions often dictated by institutional or state mandates

Unified Discovery Experience: A research process by which the user is able to search all library resources in a single comprehensive search, regardless of format or location, via a single tool, such as a discovery service

ENDNOTES

[1]   ProQuest is a registered trademark of ProQuest LLC

[2]   Summon is a trademark of ProQuest LLC.

[3]   LIBQUAL is a registered trademark of Association of Research Libraries.

[4]   MetaLib is a registered trademark of Ex Libris Ltd.

[5]   AquaBrowser is a registered trademark of Serials Solutions.

[6]   Google Scholar is a trademark of Google, Inc.

APPENDIX: INTERVIEW PROTOCOL

- The authors contacted thirty-one academic librarians by telephone or email to create a group comprised of librarians who had engaged in a defined selection process for a discovery service at varying sized institutions.
- Libraries at these institutions had either implemented or were in the process of implementing a discovery service as identified by a review of library Web sites, vendor information, or conference presentations.
- Institutions that had not engaged in a defined selection process were not interviewed or included in this study.
- Librarians who participated in the study met two criteria: 1) the institution they represented had engaged in a defined selection process and 2) met a specific sizing band using the Carnegie Classification of Institutions of Higher Education.
- All interview responses appear in the aggregate with no attribution of quotes or identification of specific institutions beyond the summarized results, including the identification of the specific discovery service selected.
- Participating librarians were asked in a telephone interview to provide an overview of the selection process and then answer the following questions received in advance of the telephone call:
  1. How did you decide on what discovery tools to evaluate?
  2. What do you consider to be the most effective elements that your group employed in the selection process for a discovery tool?
  3. What challenges did you face and how did you overcome them in the selection process?
- At least two of the authors were present on each call and recorded notes for each of the interviews. The authors shared interview notes on Google Docs for review and analysis.
- The series of interviews was conducted from May through June 2011.

Chapter 6
Criteria to Consider when Evaluating Web-based Discovery Tools

Amy Hoseth
Colorado State University, USA

ABSTRACT

As libraries re-think their collections, emphasizing online access and building digital resource collections that are growing at an exponential pace, Web-based discovery tools are under consideration by many academic libraries. These tools enable users to easily and quickly search across a broad range of pre-harvested, indexed content, including materials from databases, library catalogs and local collections. In 2010, the Colorado State University (CSU) Libraries conducted an extensive review of four Web-scale discovery services (EBSCO Discovery Service™[1]; Primo Central™[2] from ExLibris™[3]; Summon™[4] from Serials Solutions®[5]; and WorldCat®[6] Local) in order to recommend one for purchase. Based on that experience, this chapter suggests five key criteria to consider when evaluating and selecting Web-based discovery tools.

INTRODUCTION

Once upon a time, academic libraries held a virtual monopoly on scholarly research: resources were widely disseminated in a variety of print publications and users had to rely on the expertise of skilled librarians to help them navigate the complicated research landscape. However, today that landscape is dramatically different. The Internet has not only provided reasonable alternatives to library resources in the form of search engines such as Google Scholar™[7], but has also reshaped user expectations regarding online search and discovery.

DOI: 10.4018/978-1-4666-1821-3.ch006

In order to meet users' high expectations and simplify access to a vast and complicated sea of information, many academic libraries are exploring and purchasing Web-scale discovery tools. These tools, which "[search] across a vast range of pre-harvested and indexed content quickly and seamlessly" (Vaughan, 2011b, p. 6) allow users to easily search and retrieve traditional library catalog content; article-level database content; and items from local digital collections—all from one simple search box that can be easily integrated into a library's home page and search screens.

In 2010 the Colorado State University Libraries conducted an extensive review of four Web-scale discovery services in order to recommend one for purchase. Based on that experience, this chapter suggests five key criteria to consider when evaluating and selecting Web-based discovery tools and shares information learned through CSU's search process that may be useful to other institutions undertaking similar reviews.

WEB-SCALE DISCOVERY

Web-scale discovery is clearly "one of the most significant breakthroughs in library automation in recent decades" (Breeding, 2010, p. 34), but since these tools are so new to the marketplace, limited research has been published on their selection, implementation, use and impact. WorldCat® Local, from OCLC, premiered at the University of Washington in 2007. Summon™, from Serials Solutions®, debuted in 2009. The EBSCO Discovery Service™ and Ex Libris' Primo Central™ both launched in 2010.

While each Web-scale discovery tool has its own unique features, they can be united by a common definition. In general, "Web-scale discovery services for libraries are those services capable of searching quickly and seamlessly across a vast range of local and remote pre-harvested and indexed content, providing relevancy-ranked results in an intuitive interface." (Vaughan, 2011a, p. 32)

These tools offer a single Google-like search box; functions such as faceting that allow users to easily manipulate sets of results; and flexibility so that they work well regardless of the underlying library systems.

LITERATURE REVIEW

Due to the fact that Web-scale discovery tools are still relatively new, the published literature on their selection, implementation, use, and impact remains thin. In particular, few articles exist to guide libraries through the process of evaluating and selecting a Web-scale discovery tool. This gap is problematic for academic libraries seeking current information before they make a long-term and often costly investment for their institution. However, early research is beginning to appear. The most recent literature on the topic includes in-depth reviews of the technology along with use and impact studies from several libraries that were among the first to adopt the services.

The need for new, user-friendly library search interfaces has been discussed in the library literature for some time. Marshall Breeding (2010) heralded the coming of new discovery platforms "that aim to manage access through a single index to all library content to the same extent that search engines address content on the Web" (p. 34), and Jeff Wisniewski (2010) encouraged librarians to "[take] a serious look" at the newly launched Web-scale systems that seemed ready to fulfill the "'one search box to rule them all' quest" that librarians have long desired. (p. 55) Most recently, a study from OCLC (2011) took an in-depth look at the prospects for "single search" within libraries, archives and museums (LAMs) regardless of how resources within those institutions might be siloed.

Several broad summaries and reviews of these new tools have now been published. By far the most comprehensive work is an issue of *Library Technology Reports* written by Jason Vaughan.

Vaughan provides an overview of Web-scale discovery, an in-depth exploration of each of the four leading tools (EBSCO Discovery Service™, Primo Central™, Summon™ and WorldCat® Local), as well as a discussion about differentiators between the services. (Vaughan, 2011b) An initial review of Summon™, EBSCO Discovery Service™, and WorldCat® Local was published in *The Charleston Advisor* in mid-2010, including information about pricing options and contracts (Rowe, 2010), while a second review included similar information about Primo Central™. (Rowe, 2011)

Some notable research has emerged from those libraries that were early adopters or beta partners for Web-scale discovery tools. Doug Way of Michigan's Grand Valley State University published an article on the impact of Web-scale discovery on the library's collection. (2010) Key outcomes from their implementation of Summon™ included a decrease in the use of abstracting and indexing (A&I) databases and an increase in the use of full-text sources. Way noted that "the results of this study suggest that [Web-scale discovery tools have] the potential to radically change how users interact with and discover… library collections." (p. 219) At Oregon State University a member of their Summon™ implementation team wrote about their modification of Summon™'s out-of-the-box user interface to improve the overall user experience. (Klein, 2010) The Dartmouth College Library also published a detailed report evaluating its experience with Summon™ as a discovery service (DeFelice, et al., 2009), and two librarians from an Australian university have published on a series of usability studies conducted there. (Gross & Sheridan, 2011)

WorldCat® Local has arguably been the subject of the most published coverage. WorldCat® Local was developed through a partnership between the University of Washington (UW) Libraries and OCLC, and since it was first launched in 2007 the team at UW Libraries has published extensively on the tool. Most notably their implementation team produced a special issue of *Library Technology Reports* that discussed everything from planning and implementation to usage and impact. (Ward, Shadle, & Mofield, 2008) Since then they have published follow-up research that examines the impact of WorldCat® Local implementation on inter-library loan (Deardorff & Nance, 2009) and the appearance of electronic resources within the tool. (Shadle, 2009) OCLC has conducted and published its own usability studies of WorldCat® Local, which are posted on its Web site. (OCLC, 2009, 2010) OCLC also regularly hosts Web sessions, podcasts, and presentations by libraries that are using WorldCat® Local, many of which are posted to the OCLC Web site.

Finally, beyond the published literature, many institutions have posted informal articles, conference presentations, and Web sites with additional details about local implementations of Web-scale discovery tools. And in July of 2011, ALA TechSource hosted a two-part Webinar on Web-scale discovery, in which both libraries that have implemented a specific tool, and libraries that are considering implementation, held an open discussion about their experiences and questions online. (Vaughan & Hanken, 2011c, 2011d) Additional research is sure to be published as Web-scale discovery expands into more libraries and its longer-term impact on both collections and users is explored.

ABOUT THE CSU LIBRARIES

Colorado State University is a land-grant institution located in Fort Collins, Colorado, at the base of the Rocky Mountains. The university has more than 25,000 students and offers over 150 programs of study in eight colleges. The CSU Libraries includes both Morgan Library on the main campus and a smaller library at the College of Veterinary Medicine and Biomedical Sciences. The libraries' holdings include more than two million books, bound journals, and government documents, as well as access to hundreds of thousands of electronic resources.

In 2009 the university president created the Library/IT Task Force to evaluate the Libraries' current structure, policies, and strategies. One of the task force's key recommendations was that the library should "[pursue] strategies to provide easier, more [user friendly] access to the multitude of disparate materials available through the CSU Libraries." (Colorado State University Libraries, 2009) While the library had recently implemented VuFind to overlay the existing catalog interface, no formal evaluation of the newly available Web-scale discovery tools had yet been conducted. Library administrators and staff were interested in determining whether a Web-scale discovery tool could help to meet the library's growing needs.

Therefore, in response to the task force report, the library dean created the Discovery Tools Committee. Committee members were charged with exploring the Web-scale discovery tools currently available and recommending a plan and a budget for moving forward. In particular, library administration hoped that Web-scale discovery would provide easier and more comprehensive searching capabilities to faculty and advanced researchers. The six-person Discovery Tools Committee included representatives from the libraries' technology services unit, metadata, collections and contracts, college liaisons, and access services.

When the committee was formed in late 2009, a number of new and emerging Web-scale discovery tools were already available or soon to be released. Ultimately the committee reviewed the four products that were seen as "major players" in the discovery market at the time: EBSCO Discovery Service™, Primo Central™, Summon™ and WorldCat® Local. The committee issued Requests for Information (RFIs) to each vendor; invited vendors to campus to present information about their products; and attended conferences and meetings to gather additional information. An executive report and final recommendation

was submitted by the committee to the library dean in June 2010.

KEY CRITERIA

As the CSU Libraries' Discovery Tools Committee began its work, one of its first challenges was to identify key criteria that could be used to assess and evaluate each product. These decision points allowed committee members to gather useful and synonymous information about each product while allowing for comparisons across the various vendors and their tools. At the committee's first official meeting, the group reviewed a brief, early version of a comparison matrix that had been drafted by the committee chair. This first, rough document contained 23 points of comparison (ranging from cost to resource coverage to integration with the library's link resolver) and was based on a matrix that had been created and used for the acquisition of an earlier technology product. Over time, this matrix was expanded and refined based on the work of the committee and consultations with both vendors and other libraries. While the final decision matrix was quite detailed, the entire document can be effectively distilled into five key criteria: (1) the overall goal or purpose behind a library's acquisition of a Web-scale discovery tool; (2) cost; (3) coverage and/or content; (4) usability; and (5) technology issues. (See Table 1 for a summary.)

Criterion 1: Goal/Purpose

One question that requires careful consideration before the purchase of a Web-scale discovery tool is "What will the Web-scale resource allow users to accomplish?" Today's discovery tools are best-known for their ability to allow searching across a broad range of resource types without many of the limitations of traditional federated search. However, they may also act as next-generation OPACs, streamlining and improving access to

Table 1. Summary of key criteria

Summary of Key Criteria
Criteria 1: Goal/purpose • What will the Web-scale resource allow users to accomplish? • What is the purpose of this tool for your library? • How will the tool work with existing library resources? • Who are your users, and what kind of tool do they need?
Criteria 2: Cost • What are the total costs associated with each product? • Is consortial pricing/purchase an option? • How will the implementation of Web-scale discovery affect other subscriptions (for example, specific databases or federated search products)? • Consider the costs of local staffing and support
Criteria 3: Coverage/content • What existing resources are covered by the Web-scale tool? • How does the tool manage handoffs to native databases/resources? • What resources are not indexed/included, and how will users access them?
Criteria 4: Usability • Need to conduct both formal and informal testing; consult resources for information on the science of usability • "Test drive" implementations at other libraries • Elements to study include the user interface, faceting, relevancy ranking, search options, customization options, and more
Criteria 5: Technology issues • How much local support is required for the Web-scale tool to run smoothly? • How well will the tool integrate with existing library applications (including your ILS, knowledge base, institutional repository, etc.) • Consider the API: is it customizable? Is it robust? • Is the Web-scale discovery system mobile-friendly? Does it effectively serve users with disabilities?

locally held collections. As one researcher noted, "Web scale discovery can justly be described as being two products in one: It is both a next-generation OPAC and federated search system (on steroids). (Wisniewski, 2010, p. 57) Depending on the needs of a specific library, certain products may be preferable to others. Carefully considering the library's goals beforehand will help to frame your product research: What will the ideal tool do for your library? How will it help your users? At the CSU Libraries, a cross-departmental team had already implemented a local installation of VuFind in 2009. Therefore, looking at how Web-scale discovery tools incorporated or supplanted the existing OPAC was an important consideration.

Another critical question to consider is who will be using the product—who are your users and what are their needs? Web-scale discovery tools return results from mixed sources (monographs, serials, local archival collections, etc.), which is different from the results generated by traditional search tools. For some users this provides a huge improvement to the search experience. For others it may be a new form of information overload. Considering your clientele is an important step in determining which product will best suit your library.

Vaughan, in his review of Web-scale discovery services, noted:

Established faculty instructors (and librarians) may be used to the existing ILS, have their favorite topical databases, and enjoy browsing the table of contents of favorite journals. This competes with freshmen undergraduates, who, as research shows, want quick, relevant information from the first tool they search. (2011b, p. 52)

The CSU Libraries' discovery tool committee found that, based on information from both its own review of these tools and reviews from other institutions, Web-scale discovery tools appeared best for general or interdisciplinary searching. Experienced or discipline-specific researchers seemed most likely to continue using native database interfaces for more tailored and customized searches.

Because these Web-scale tools are so new, relatively few studies of their impact on discovery and use exist. However, the experiences of other libraries will be an important consideration as more institutions consider the implementation of a Web-scale discovery tool. Early research has identified several potential impacts from Web-scale discovery, including a decrease in the use of abstracting and indexing (A&I) databases and an increase in the use of full-text sources after an implementation of Summon™ (Way, 2010), and a significant increase in inter-library loan (ILL) requests after the implementation of WorldCat® Local. (Deardorff & Nance, 2009)

Criterion 2: Cost

Another key criterion in the selection of a Web-scale discovery tool is cost. As one author noted, "Web-scale discovery is far from inexpensive." (Wisniewski, 2010, p. 57) Libraries should carefully evaluate the costs associated with each product, in addition to the overall pros and cons of each, in order to make accurate comparisons across tools.

As is the case for many other library products, pricing for Web-scale discovery tools is highly variable and differs from product to product and from library to library. While the size of the institution (FTE) and/or the number of users appear to be the main criteria used to set prices, vendors may also consider other factors such as the level of features and content purchased (for some products) or the type of library (public or academic, for example). Most products charge an annual subscription fee along with one-time set-up or implementation fees. Two recent reviews of Web-scale discovery tools have included pricing details (Rowe, 2010, 2011), although individual

libraries will need to work closely with vendors to gather current pricing information.

At the CSU Libraries it was helpful to chart anticipated costs over a five-year period, including setup and annual fees as well as longer-range costs. For some products, the committee mapped out several different pricing structures based on different services or configurations. Reviewing prices over the long-term enabled more clear comparisons between products. Some tools have higher setup fees but lower annual fees, while others are the reverse. Looking at the total cost for each product over a set period of time helped to provide a clearer picture.

A related piece of those anticipated costs, although difficult to pinpoint, is how the implementation of a Web-scale discovery tool may impact current subscriptions. For example, would it be possible to cancel A&I databases? Could you discontinue an existing federated search product? Would you have to add another knowledge base? Most of the libraries that the committee consulted in 2010 had not yet made cancellation decisions based on their implementation of Web-scale discovery; however, such additions or removals would obviously have an impact on the library's overall financial picture.

Other considerations should also come into play when libraries are considering the purchase of Web-based discovery tools. First, libraries may wish to consider whether there is an option for consortial pricing or participation. Vendors may be willing to give price breaks or other benefits to groups of libraries who purchase Web-based tools as a group, and consortia may benefit from having multiple institutions using the same product.

Second, it is important to realize that the costs of local staffing and support are not insignificant and may impact the overall cost of adding a Web-scale discovery tool to the library's resources. For example, the Web-scale discovery tool may require the purchasing library to prepare local catalog data for inclusion, a task that will require both time and effort. The purchase may also require changes to the library Web site—from relatively simple modifications such as making room for the tool on a home page, to more complicated fixes such as those requiring API development in order for the resource and the Web site to work well together.

As one author noted, "All vendors offer completely hosted versions of their discovery service—providing the hardware, maintaining backups, and hosting the interface and centralized index. Such a scenario relieves local staff from maintaining hardware and performing backups." (Vaughan, 2011b, p. 50) Conversely, while hosting the hardware locally may provide additional options for flexibility and customization, there are costs associated with that as well. For example, if a library decides to customize the interface, significant Web and IT support will be required to create and maintain the updated design. Ultimately, libraries will need to consider staffing and support costs in addition to vendor pricing.

Criterion 3: Coverage/Content

The coverage and content provided by a Web-scale discovery tool is critical, and is a feature that should be carefully considered by libraries—although it can be difficult to pinpoint exactly what that coverage is. As Vaughan noted, "As far as content scope goes, the overall volume of content natively indexed by each service remains a differentiator, but the difference is rapidly shrinking" as vendors aggressively pursue and make deals with publishers in order to expand their universe of content. (2011b, p. 49) Indeed, given the shifting nature of these deals and the ongoing development of Web-based discovery, the specific content accessible through any one discovery tool is likely to remain a moving target.

Both Rowe's recent reviews of Web-scale products (2010, 2011) and Vaughan's overview of the marketplace (2011b) are excellent resources for libraries that wish to gain both an understanding of how each product incorporates and standard-

izes content, and insight into overall coverage. Currently, Web-scale discovery tools are offered by both content providers (such as EBSCO) and third-party vendors (such as Serials Solutions®). Libraries may wish to consider whether they are substantially invested in a particular vendor or publisher when evaluating Web-scale tools, and pay particular attention to how each tool handles content from that source.

At the CSU Libraries, content was an important consideration as the committee reviewed Web-scale discovery tools. One key member of the cross-departmental committee was the serials librarian, who provided detailed holdings and subscription information to each vendor so that the vendors could run overlap studies. These studies helped to provide a clearer picture of coverage and identify areas of particular weakness or strength. Several products had very high overlap with CSU's existing collections, although overlap—like coverage—is a moving target. For any library that is considering the purchase of a Web-scale discovery tool, overlap studies provide important information and should be diligently pursued.

Studying the coverage provided by Web-scale discovery tools also highlighted a potential shift in how libraries and librarians view their digital collections. Rather than providing specific, quantifiable data on exactly what a library owns or has access to, Web-scale discovery opens up the possibility that patrons who use these tools may actually be searching a universe of content that is more extensive than the full body of content delineated by a library's contracts, agreements and local holdings. In the world of Web-scale discovery, identifying exactly what a user is searching when they use these tools becomes a new and challenging task.

Regardless of how well a tool's content mirrors a library's existing collection, there still appears to be a role for native databases and their sophisticated search interfaces. Indeed, some Web-scale discovery tools highlight specific databases or collections within a set of search results and may include direct links that make it easy for users to shift from the Web-scale discovery tool directly into a native database. Libraries should research how each Web scale discovery tool manages such handoffs. And there remains the possibility that for some resources not all of their content will be available through Web-scale discovery. Libraries should consider how users will access any unincorporated resources.

Criterion 4: Usability

Yet another key criterion that the CSU Libraries identified in its consideration of Web-scale discovery tools is usability. As Marshall Breeding noted, "A great discovery interface should operate in a mostly self-explanatory way, allowing users to concentrate on selecting and evaluating the resources returned rather than struggling through the search tools that the library provides." (2010, p. 34) This concept is central to the purpose of Web-scale discovery: not only to provide access to a wide range of resources, but to make them easily searchable via a simple interface. In this way, "[Web-scale discovery] finally gets us to a true single search, which is what users have long assumed we were providing and have been disappointed to find out we weren't." (Wisniewski, 2010, p. 57)

Usability is a science, and many articles have been written over the years about both Web usability in general and its measurement in relation to specific Web-based library services. Usability has been broadly defined as "a quality attribute that assesses how easy user interfaces are to use," incorporating such factors as learnability (how easily users can accomplish tasks the first time they use the tool); efficiency; memorability; errors; and overall satisfaction. (Nielsen, 2003) Usability can be studied in numerous ways, ranging from survyes and focus grops to user testing and field studies.

In order to explore the usability of Web-scale discovery tools, the CSU Libraries committee spent time reviewing actual implementations of Web-scale discovery tools at other libraries. In order to thoroughly explore the tools and develop a good feel for the pros and cons of each, the committee divided into two sub-groups, with each subgroup studying two of the four available products intensively in order to more thoroughly review all documentation and sample instances. When possible, libraries may wish to "test-drive" trial implementations locally. While vendors have conducted (and continue to conduct) their own in-house usability studies, and some early adopters have done their own internal studies, each library should conduct its own careful analysis of the various features and general "look and feel" of each Web-scale discovery tool. Libraries should also explore how well, or whether, the tool meets the needs of users with disabilities.

The CSU discovery tool committee carefully researched the user interfaces of each Web-scale discovery tool—both the search screen on the front end and the results set that users see after they have run a search. In terms of searching, the committee looked closely at faceting and search options such as advanced search. The ease and flexibility of search interface customizations were also considered for each product. Specifically, the committee examined whether the search interface was customizable and whether limits could be set—before or after the search—to narrow in on specific resources.

On the results page, the committee considered the extent to which a library could customize the appearance of the results page for each search tool. The team also carefully studied how each discovery tool handled relevancy ranking and facets, two critical elements of all online searching. While most of the tools had a similar look and feel to their out-of-the-box results pages, subtle differences existed for each. Some discovery tools allow libraries to build their own user interface, which requires a certain amount of local support on the part of the purchasing library. A number of institutions have published articles on their own experience with this kind of customization, including the University of Washington Libraries (Shadle, 2009), Dartmouth College (DeFelice, et al., 2009) and the Oregon State University Libraries (Klein, 2010).

Criterion 5: Technology Issues

Issues related to technology are yet another important criterion for libraries to consider when evaluating Web-based discovery tools. Libraries should carefully consider how much local support is needed to make the product work well. While most of these tools offer "plug-and-play" options, some amount of local customization may be needed or desired before it is presented to users. Libraries with more information technology (IT) support will obviously find it easier to implement such changes. On the flip side, querying vendors on their tech support and product updates is equally important. Each vendor has different methods for communicating with libraries and making upgrades; understanding how customer support works in this environment is key.

At the CSU Libraries, an important consideration was how well these Web-scale discovery tools would integrate with existing library applications. As Vaughan notes, "A critical step for any library considering a Web scale discovery service is to ask the vendor detailed questions about integration with the underlying ILS." (2011b, p. 50) The CSU Libraries had recently implemented VuFind; therefore the committee was interested in whether other institutions using these Web-scale tools were also using VuFind. In addition, the committee was concerned about the level of integration between Web-scale tools and the knowledge base; would the use of a certain Web-scale tool require multiple knowledge bases, or just one? Using more than one knowledge base would require additional local support.

Other technology issues that libraries may wish to consider when reviewing Web-scale discovery tools include:

- API options – is the API robust enough to meet your requirements? And to what extent can it be customized?
- How mobile-friendly is a particular tool? Does the vendor have a mobile interface? Can you test it?
- How does the tool handle any content that is not integrated into its interface? What "helps" will the vendor provide (or will the library need to create) in order to steer users towards additional content?

The number of technological issues that could arise with the implementation of any Web-scale discovery tool is potentially vast, and far exceeds this author's ability to list them all here. At CSU, the discovery tool committee was headed by a member of the IT staff, and several of the committee members were well-versed with the library's various systems. Their knowledge and insight was critical to the committee's overall success.

Further Considerations

The experience of the CSU Libraries in reviewing and evaluating Web-scale discovery tools not only identified the five key criteria outlined above, but also highlighted a number of practical recommendations that may be valuable to libraries conducting similar reviews. First, as mentioned above, involving individuals from across the library (including IT staff) in the overall analysis was extremely helpful to the evaluation process. The committee felt that the small cross-departmental team worked well.

Conducting a thorough, methodical review of each available product was another important step. The CSU Libraries' discovery tool committee drafted a lengthy RFI that was provided to each vendor; every vendor, without fail, responded with a thorough and detailed response. The committee followed up on the RFIs with visits from vendor representatives and attendance at conferences and events where committee members had the opportunity to ask additional questions. Conducting usability testing on the tools themselves, as mentioned earlier, is another important consideration.

Contacting other institutions that are already using these products was enormously helpful to the committee's work; fortunately, that body of institutions is growing. The institutions to which the committee spoke were very helpful in sharing candid thoughts about their experiences implementing Web-scale discovery; their views on how the tools are shaping user experiences at their libraries; and the challenges that they had experienced along the way. While few institutions have been using these products for long, the experience of those contacted by the committee was extremely helpful.

After six months of careful study and review, the CSU Libraries' Discovery Tools Committee issued its final report. The committee identified one Web-scale product in particular as the one that was most likely to meet the library's needs. However, due to a number of factors—including concerns about cost and integration with existing resources—the library decided not to purchase a Web-scale product at that time. The criteria outlined above were not only useful in evaluating each Web-scale discovery product, but were also helpful when framing the final report and presenting assessments of each of the products reviewed. The CSU Libraries remain open to the idea of purchasing a Web-scale discovery tool at a later date, and continue to monitor the market closely.

DIRECTIONS FOR FUTURE RESEARCH

Just as Web-scale discovery is in its infancy, so, too, is the body of literature on the topic. The relatively small scope of research related to Web-scale discovery, its implementation, and its impact on both library procedures and user behavior is certain to grow as more libraries adopt and implement these tools. In the short term,

published reports from libraries on their own use and implementation of Web-scale discovery would be useful additions to the literature. Over time, significant research on how Web-scale discovery tools impact the use of existing library resources and services, such as A&I databases and interlibrary loan, will be invaluable. Also important will be research related to how library users perceive and manipulate these new tools, from undergraduates to graduate and faculty users, as well as usability studies. Library faculty and staff perceptions of Web-scale discovery will also make for interesting research, both in terms of how they implement them to help users and how they teach the products to others. In short, given the youth of Web-scale discovery, nearly all areas of these tools' implementation, use, and outcomes offer opportunities for additional research.

CONCLUSION

As a growing number of institutions consider the implementation of Web-scale discovery tools at their libraries, the need for comparable, quantifiable comparisons across and between products will continue to grow. In this chapter, the author has shared five key criteria that were used to analyze currently available Web-scale tools: (1) the overall goal or purpose behind a library's acquisition of a Web-scale discovery tool; (2) cost; (3) coverage and/or content; (4) usability; and (5) technology issues. As these tools continue to mature and are deployed at an increasing number of libraries, other criteria may develop that will be equally important for evaluators to consider.

Ultimately, each library will need to make its own determination about which product best suits its users and local environment. As Vaughan notes in the introduction to *Library Technology Reports*, "Each library considering a serious marketplace review [of Web-scale discovery tools] should thoroughly do its homework." (2011b, p. 11) By sharing the key criteria that were used by the CSU

Libraries in its 2010 evaluation of four leading Web-scale discovery tools (WorldCat® Local, Summon™, EBSCO Discovery Service™; and Primo Central™), the author hopes to give other libraries a starting point from which to begin their own research, and therefore make their homework that much easier.

REFERENCES

Breeding, M. (2010). The state of the art in library discovery 2010. *Computers in Libraries, 30*(1), 31–34.

Colorado State University Libraries. (2009). *Library/IT task force final report*. Retrieved from http://lib.colostate.edu/images/about/goals/it/LibraryTFreportFINAL.docx

Deardorff, T., & Nance, H. (2009). WorldCat Local implementation: The impact on interlibrary loan. *Interlending & Document Supply, 37*(4), 177–180. doi:10.1108/02641610911006265

DeFelice, B., Kortfelt, J., Mead, J., Mounts, M., Pawlek, C., & Seaman, D. . . . Wheelock, C. (2009). *An evaluation of Serials Solutions Summon as a discovery service for the Dartmouth College Library*. Retrieved from http://www.dartmouth.edu/~library/admin/docs/Summon_Report.pdf

Gross, J., & Sheridan, L. (2011). Web scale discovery: The user experience. *New Library World, 112*(5/6), 236–247. doi:10.1108/03074801111136275

Klein, M. (2010). Hacking Summon. *Code4Lib Journal, 11*, 11-18.

Nielsen, J. (2003). *Usability 101: Introduction to usability*. Retrieved from www.useit.com/alertbox/20030825.html

OCLC. (2009). *Some findings from WorldCat Local usability tests prepared for ALA Annual, July 2009*. Retrieved from http://www.oclc.org/worldcatlocal/about/213941usf_some_findings_about_worldcat_local.pdf

OCLC. (2010). *Findings from WorldCat Local usability tests*. Retrieved from http://www.oclc.org/worldcatlocal/about/213941usf_some_findings_about_worldcat_local_2011.pdf

Prescott, L., & Erway, R. (2011). *Single search: The quest for the holy grail. OCLC research*. Retrieved from http://www.oclc.org/research/publications/library/2011/2011-17.pdf

Rowe, R. (2010). Web-scale discovery: A review of Summon, EBSCO Discovery Service, and WorldCat Local. *The Charleston Advisor, 12*(1), 5–10. doi:10.5260/chara.12.1.5

Rowe, R. (2011). Encore Synergy and Primo Central: Web-scale discovery: A review of two products on the market. *The Charleston Advisor, 12*(4), 11–15. doi:10.5260/chara.12.4.11

Shadle, S. (2009). Electronic resources in a next-generation catalog: The case of WorldCat Local. *Journal of Electronic Resources Librarianship, 21*(3/4), 192–199. doi:10.1080/19411260903446006

Vaughan, J. (2011a). Web-scale discovery. *American Libraries, 42*(1), 32.

Vaughan, J. (2011b). Web scale discovery services. *Library Technology Reports, 47*(1).

Vaughan, V., & Hanken, T. (2011c) *Continuing the conversation: Evaluating and implementing web-scale discovery services in your library* [PowerPoint Presentation]. Retrieved from http://www.alatechsource.org/blog/2011/07/continuing-the-conversation-evaluating-and-implementing-web-scale-discovery-services-in.

Vaughan, V., & Hanken, T. (2011d) *Continuing the conversation: Evaluating and implementing Web-scale discovery services in your library (Part 2)* [PowerPoint Presentation]. Retrieved from http://www.alatechsource.org/blog/2011/07/continuing-the-conversation-evaluating-and-implementing-web-scale-discovery-services--0

Ward, J. L., Shadle, S., & Mofield, P. (2008). WorldCat Local impact summary at the University of Washington. *Library Technology Reports, 44*(6), 41.

Way, D. (2010). The impact of Web-scale discovery on the use of a library collection. *Serials Review, 36*(4), 214–220. doi:10.1016/j.serrev.2010.07.002

Wisniewski, J. (2010). Web scale discovery: The future's so bright, I gotta wear shades. *Online, 34*(4), 55–58.

ADDITIONAL READING

Association of College and Research Libraries, Research Planning and Review Committee. (2011). *Environmental scan 2010.* Retrieved from http://www.ala.org/acrl/sites/ala.org.acrl/files/content/publications/whitepapers/EnvironmentalScan201.pdf

Chen, Y., Germain, C., & Rorissa, A. (2011). Defining usability: How library practice differs from published research. *portal . Libraries and the Academy, 11*(2), 599–628. doi:10.1353/pla.2011.0020

Connaway, L., Dickey, T., & Radford, M. (2011). "If it is too inconvenient, I'm not going after it": Convenience as a critical factor in information-seeking behaviors. *Library & Information Science Research, 33,* 179–190. doi:10.1016/j.lisr.2010.12.002

De Rosa, C., Cantrell, J., Carlson, M., Gallagher, P., Hawk, J., Sturtz, C., & Gauder, B..... Olszewski, L. (2010). *Perceptions of libraries, 2010: Context and community.* Retrieved from http://www.oclc.org/US/EN/reports/2010perceptions/2010perceptions_all.pdf

De Rosa, C., Dempsey, L., & Wilson, A. (2003). *The 2003 OCLC environmental scan: Pattern recognition.* Retrieved from http://www.oclc.org/US/EN/reports/escan/

Diedrichs, C. (2009). Discovery and delivery: Making it work for users. *The Serials Librarian, 56*(1-4), 79–93. doi:10.1080/03615260802679127

Dixon, L., Duncan, C., Fagan, J., Mandernach, M., & Warlick, S. E. (2010). Finding articles and journals via Google Scholar, journal portals, and link resolvers: Usability study results. *Reference and User Services Quarterly, 50*(2), 170–181.

Jansen, B., & Spink, A. (2006). How are we searching the World Wide Web? A comparison of nine search engine transaction logs. *Information Processing & Management, 42*(1), 248–263. doi:10.1016/j.ipm.2004.10.007

Krug, S. (2005). *Don't make me think: A common sense approach to Web usability.* Indianapolis, IN: New Riders Press.

OCLC. (2005). *Perceptions of libraries and information resources.* Retrieved from http://www.oclc.org/US/EN/reports/pdfs/Percept_all.pdf

OCLC. (2011). *Libraries at Webscale: A discussion document.* Retrieved from http://www.oclc.org/US/EN/reports/webscale/libraries-at-webscale.pdf

Powers, A. (2006). To buy or not to buy? Evaluating databases and making sound purchase decisions. *The Charleston Advisor, 7*(4), 48–50.

Salter, A. A. (2003). How to evaluate and purchase an ILS. *Library Technology Reports, 39*(3), 11–26.

Schonfeld, R., & Housewright, R. (2010). *Ithaka S&R faculty survey 2009: Key strategic insights for libraries, publishers, and societies.* Retrieved from http://www.ithaka.org/ithaka-s-r/research/faculty-surveys-2000-2009/Faculty%20Study%202009.pdf

Spink, A., & Cole, C. (2006). Human information behavior: Integrating diverse approaches and information use. *Journal of the American Society for Information Science and Technology, 57*(1), 25–35. doi:10.1002/asi.20249

Timpson, H., & Sansom, G. (2011). A student perspective on e-resource discovery: Has the Google factor changed publisher platform searching forever? *The Serials Librarian, 61*(2), 253–266. doi:10.1080/0361526X.2011.592115

KEY TERMS AND DEFINITIONS

A&I Databases (Abstracting and Indexing Databases): Databases that contain bibliographic citations and abstracts, but not full-text documents.

API (Application Programming Interface): A set of rules and specifications that facilitates interactions between different software programs. In the context of Web-scale discovery, some Web-scale discovery tools offer APIs that libraries can customize to facilitate the interactions between the tool and existing library resources, such as the library Web site or catalog.

Facets: Defined, mutually exclusive, and collectively exhaustive aspects, properties, or characteristics of a subject that allow for classification and searching. For example, books may be classified using an author facet, a date facet, a subject facet, etc.

Federated Search: An information retrieval technology that simultaneously searches multiple resources (such as databases). A user makes a single query, which is then run in numerous different search engines. Federated search products search the native interface; Web-scale discovery products search a combined index of resources that includes content from native products.

Integrated Library System (ILS): An automated resource planning system for libraries, which allows them to track and manage functions such as acquisitions, cataloging, circulation, and the online public access catalog (OPAC).

Knowledge Base: In libraries, a database that contains information about a library's electronic content and holdings. Different library products may have their own knowledge base.

Online Public Access Catalog (OPAC): An online bibliography of a library collection, available to the public.

Overlap Study: Research that compares two sources of data, in order to identify items that are available in each source. For example, a library may conduct an overlap study between two databases to identify which resources are indexed in both databases, and which resources are unique to one database or the other.

Relevancy Ranking: The ordering of retrieved records by a database or search engine so that the most relevant results appear first. A variety of indicators (such as date or frequency) and/or algorithms are used to determine relevancy.

Request for Information (RFI): A request, generally made during a project planning or research phase, where a potential customer asks a vendor for more information about a product.

Usability: The ease-of-use and "learnability" of an object. In short, how easy it is to use something. Usability is measured according to specific methods and tools. For example, to study the usability of a Web site, researchers may conduct surveys, interviews, or focus groups to gather feedback from individuals on their use of the site.

Web-Scale Discovery Tools: "Web-scale discovery services for libraries are those services capable of searching quickly and seamlessly across a vast range of local and remote pre-harvested and indexed content, providing relevancy-ranked results in an intuitive interface." (Vaughan, 2011b)

ENDNOTES

[1]   EBSCO Discovery Service is owned by EBSCO Publishing Industries

[2] Primo Central is owned by Ex Libris Ltd. or its affiliates.

[3] ExLibris is a trademark of Ex Libris Ltd.

[4] Summon is owned by ProQuest LLC

[5] Serials Solution is a registered trademark of Serials Solutions

[6] Worldcat is a registered trademark of OCLC.

[7] Google Scholar is a trademark of Google, Inc.

Chapter 7
Thinking Inside the Grid:
Selecting a Discovery System through the RFP Process

Dace Freivalds
Pennsylvania State University Libraries, USA

Binky Lush
Pennsylvania State University Libraries, USA

ABSTRACT

Many libraries are in the process of purchasing and implementing Web-scale discovery systems. In order to ensure that the selected system meets the needs of the institution's users, a thorough and careful evaluation of potential systems is critical. Using the Penn State University Libraries' selection process as an example, this chapter describes the use of a formal Request for Proposal (RFP) process to evaluate Web-scale discovery systems impartially and objectively. While the RFP was mandated at Penn State, the methodology presented here can serve as a model for selecting a discovery system even when a library is not required to use an RFP. The chapter provides sample evaluation grids, scoring schemes, team guidelines, reference check questions, and other tools that can be used during the selection process to ensure a thorough and complete evaluation.

INTRODUCTION

Selecting a single tool to make the vast resources of a large academic library more discoverable can be a daunting task. Typically, the library will look for a system that will improve access

to and discovery of its online catalog and other local and remote resources such as digitized collections, licensed databases, scholarly content at the article level, and library Web pages. Ideally, the system will provide access to the full breadth of the library's content through a single search box and offer more accommodating search types with innovative uses of faceted searching, word

DOI: 10.4018/978-1-4666-1821-3.ch007

stemming, spelling variants, translations, results visualization, and intuitive methods for refining result sets. The system should be so straightforward that students will choose to use it over Google as their starting point for research, yet sophisticated enough to refine the results to scholarly journals or full-text online. Comparing the content, features and functionality of the Web-scale discovery systems currently in the marketplace in order to select one that meets local needs and priorities as well as budget requirements can be difficult. A systematic, step-by-step process of identifying features that are absolutely necessary and those that are desirable, but not essential, makes the potentially difficult task of choosing a Web-scale discovery system easier. This chapter describes a structured approach to selecting a discovery system, and, using the Pennsylvania State University (Penn State) Libraries' RFP process as an example, highlights the specific steps an institution can take in developing a careful and thorough evaluation process.

LITERATURE REVIEW

While library literature contains a growing body of work on Web-scale discovery systems, there is limited professional library literature that specifically addresses the use of a structured, methodological process, much less a Request for Proposal (RFP), to evaluate and select a discovery system. Luther and Kelly (2011) identify content, search, fit and cost as factors to consider when selecting a discovery system while Vaughan (2011) breaks down the list of questions to consider when contemplating the purchase of a discovery system into seven sections: General and Background Questions, Local Library Resources, Publisher and Aggregator Agreements and Indexed Content, Open-Access Content, Relevancy Ranking, Authentication and Rights Management, and User Interface. Boock, Buck, Chadwell, Nichols and Reese (2009) and Brubaker, Leach-Murray

and Parker (2011), in describing their processes for finding the right discovery layer, compare the features of various discovery systems. Rowe (2010) reviews three products (Serials Solutions®[1] Summon™[2], EBSCO Discovery Services™[3], and OCLC WorldCat®[4] Local) and provides comparative review scores for them, while the University of Michigan's Article Discovery Group (2010) created "a list of concrete features and tasks that could serve as a basis for the comparison and evaluation of article discovery tools" which then became the criteria used to evaluate individual tools (Bhatnagar et al., 2010, p. 5).

Library literature does, however, contain numerous articles on the use of an RFP or a structured, evaluative process for selecting other library information services such as a federated search product (Caswell & Wynstra, 2007), serials vendor (Westfall, 2011) and library management system (Calvert & Read, 2006). The value of including input from end users, including faculty and students, in developing an RFP and in evaluating the competing products is described by Ryan (2004). Valuable information on the RFP process can also be obtained from more general articles from the information science field that describe the standard steps involved in the process (Peters, 2011; Clegg and Montgomery, 2006) and review the pros and cons of the process (Schachter, 2003; Schrage, 1996; Wisniewski, 2009).

There is no consensus on the value of using an RFP for selecting an IT service. Schrage (1996) states that "The RFP is a sorry, anachronistic relic that persists more as a function of government practice and organizational inertia than any demonstrable value over time" (p. 45). Wisniewski (2009), in offering selection tips for a next-generation OPAC and in the interest of selecting and implementing the system in a timely manner, implores "Please, no RFP. If you're in an environment where its use is mandated then so be it, but if not, I urge you to spend your time elsewhere" (p. 56). On the other hand, the Gartner Research Group has found that a properly crafted and executed RFP process will increase the likelihood of selecting the right service provider by 40% (Karamouzis & Longwood, 2007). Schachter (2003) indicates that while the RFP process has a reputation for being a cumbersome process, "its usefulness is that it causes you to be very clear in your own mind as to what you require for the project, system, or service that you are outsourcing" (p. 10). Clegg and Montgomery (2006) state that "Using a structured RFP will help you focus on your key requirements, show suppliers you mean business, and indicate to your stakeholders that you understand the intricacies of sourcing complex enterprise-wide products" (p. 33). Other advantages of RFPs over simple negotiations with vendors are that they "create a level playing field, with measurable criteria for evaluating suppliers' offerings", and especially critical given current budget situations, "suppliers' pricing proposals are revealed in advance of negotiations." (Clegg & Montgomery, 2006, p. 24).

BACKGROUND

The Pennsylvania State University Libraries are comprised of 14 libraries at University Park and libraries at 23 other campuses throughout the Commonwealth of Pennsylvania including the Dickinson School of Law, the Milton S. Hershey Medical Center, and the Penn State affiliated Pennsylvania College of Technology. The University Libraries serve 87,100 students as well as faculty, staff, alumni and community patrons state and worldwide, and are ranked among the top-ten North American research libraries based on the 2009-2010 Association of Research Libraries (ARL) Library Investment Index Rankings (Association of Research Libraries, 2011). Penn State uses the SirsiDynix®5 Symphony®6 integrated library system (ILS) and e-library interface with digital collections hosted in ContentDM®7, Olive, and DPubs. The Libraries' resources total more than five million volumes increasing at the rate

of 103,000 volumes per year. In addition to its collections of 109,000 current serials, 430,000 maps, 3.5 million microforms, 127,000 film and video materials, and more than 125,000 e-books, the Libraries have 1.7 million digitized items.

With a rapidly increasing digital collection hosted on a variety of platforms, vast physical collections in many locations and a sizeable amount of subscription content, the University Libraries needed a system that would provide an effective search across all collections to improve discovery of the extensive, but dispersed, resources. The Libraries sought to provide a next generation interface as a single starting point for its users in searching multiple local collections and licensed resources with a usable interface and intuitive methods for refining results to easily drill down to the most relevant items.

PRELIMINARY INVESTIGATION

The investigation into these next generation catalog interfaces began in early 2008 when a Libraries group was charged with exploring options for a front-end interface for access to the catalog and other local and remote resources. The products were many and varied, and the team's initial investigation included a survey of the entire interface landscape. At that time, "discovery" only included the catalog and local collections; Web-scale discovery was not yet a part of the equation.

The Next Generation Public Interface Team identified a list of fifteen open source and commercial solutions worth investigating. Each member of the group researched and reported on one or more of these products as a preliminary means of identifying options and features that were of interest in a next generation interface.

The team developed an initial list of features that the Libraries' faculty and staff felt were required or considered highly desirable in a new interface. The group sent a survey to the University Libraries faculty and staff to determine which features were most important to them, and to solicit other suggestions for features not identified in the initial investigation. The survey asked the respondents to rate the importance of each feature, sought suggestions for additional features and asked what impact a next generation interface might have on the roles faculty and staff play in the Libraries. From these responses, as well as the group's discussions and readings, many of which are included in the additional reading section at the end of this chapter, they developed an Interface Features Grid to compare products and to identify criteria for determining which products merited further investigation (Appendix A). The group was able to identify four vendors whose interfaces met the list of initial requirements and invited them to Penn State to demonstrate their systems. The purpose of these demonstrations was two-fold: to allow the faculty and staff to see the features of next generation interfaces and to provide an opportunity to ask questions of the vendors.

The team developed a second set of surveys to gather feedback from faculty and staff who attended the product demonstrations. After seeing the next generation interfaces in action, the Libraries' faculty and staff had a better understanding of the systems and were able to provide more effective feedback on which features would be most important to the Penn State University Libraries' users. A comprehensive requirements list and a vision of the Libraries' optimal interface were starting to take shape.

In addition to functionality, the usability of these next generation interfaces was of utmost concern to the Libraries, and the team conducted a third survey to gather Libraries' student employee perceptions of the usability of current implementations of three of these systems at other institutions. (One interface did not yet have a live implementation). The students provided feedback on what they liked and disliked about each system and how intuitive each was to use.

The group used the student usability survey results combined with the Libraries' faculty/staff

feedback on the vendor demonstrations to update the Interface Features Grid and record perceptions to assist them in making an initial recommendation to the Libraries' administration. The group narrowed the field down to two finalists, comparable in search functionality, integrated indexing, user and social features, interface customization, integrated library system (ILS) integration, and enhancement features.

At that time, the first Web-scale discovery product was announced, and the team realized that in order to make the Libraries' resources more accessible and discoverable, the scope of its investigation should extend beyond simply a new interface to a full Web-scale discovery system. With endorsement from the Libraries' administration, the team moved forward, utilizing their background investigative work and Interface Features Grid to develop the requirements and the selection criteria to evaluate viable options and recommend a Web-scale discovery system for the Penn State University Libraries via the Request for Proposal (RFP) process.

THE RFP PROCESS

Investigating and evaluating potential systems involves a thorough understanding of the institution's requirements, clearly communicating those requirements to vendors, and finally, determining how well each system meets those requirements. Since Penn State was required to use a Request for Proposal, this evaluation was done through the RFP process.

The RFP process consists of articulating and documenting requirements, writing the RFP, evaluating the proposals received in response to the RFP, conducting vendor visits and demonstrations, performing reference checks, and making the final recommendation. Following this process step by step helped the Penn State University Libraries clearly define exactly what they required in a

Discovery System and allowed for a systematic and thorough evaluation of the options.

Defining Requirements

An effective evaluation of any system begins with determining user needs and defining a set of requirements both mandatory and desirable. The practice of completing a needs assessment and the background work necessary to determine these requirements in itself ensures that the organization has a very clear idea of what it is looking for in a system, and provides the means by which it can evaluate the options impartially and objectively.

The Penn State University Libraries' requirements for a discovery system evolved from the original next-generation catalog Interface Features List. As the team learned more about interfaces, and later, Web-scale discovery systems, it refined the initial list into a solid inventory of requirements that served as the framework for the RFP.

The requirements were divided into four sections that could be reviewed independently: Functional, Usability, Administrative, and Technical. The requirements were marked as mandatory or desirable, or where appropriate, were presented as an open-ended question. The Libraries wanted to determine not only whether the proposed system met each requirement, but encouraged each vendor to expand upon the answer to include areas beyond the requirement for which a system had additional capabilities.

Functional Requirements included the discovery features, how the system worked, and how well it integrated with existing Libraries systems:

1. *Collection Integration* covered indexing and integrating multiple collections and collection types and data formats.
2. *RSS/Saved Searches/List* and *Persistent Links* included support of user-created lists, searches, RSS feeds of new book lists and persistent links to a single record.

3. *Holdings information* requirements specifically asked about real time availability, shelf location and circulation information for items in our Libraries' catalog.
4. *Extended Content* covered the system's ability to support book covers, tables of contents, reviews and ratings, etc.
5. *Search, Advanced Search, Faceted Search* and *Call Number Browse* asked whether the system supported general search functionality (such as Boolean operators) as well as faceted searching, the ability to refine a set of search results, a robust advanced search functionality and the ability to view items in the same call number range.
6. *Suggestions (Did you mean?)* included questions about popular items related to the search, suggested search terms, and support of multiple language search.
7. *Relevancy Ranking* asked about the system's search algorithm and whether it was configurable.
8. *Results* included requirements such as the ability for administrators to set a default sort while permitting the user to perform other types, limitations on the sorting and the use of icons that display in the results.
9. *Mobile Optimization* covered the system's support for mobile browsers.
10. *SMS* asked whether patrons could text themselves record information directly from the system.
11. *Export/Print* posed questions about the system's ability to export to citation software such as EndNote, RefWorks and Zotero in multiple formats, print results or email results.
12. *Portability* included questions about embedding the search in other places or platforms, such as the Course Management system or Libraries Research Guides.

Usability Requirements were centered on the user interface itself, accessibility of the system, look and feel and the system's ease of use:

1. *Internationalization* covered questions about multiple language and Unicode support.
2. *Accessibility* ensured that the system would meet the required ADA (Americans with Disabilities Act) and Section 508 Accessibility Requirements.
3. *Personalization* asked about Web 2.0 support including personalized customer views as well as tagging, ratings and reviews.
4. *Look and Feel* posed questions about the flexibility of the interface and the possible customizations.
5. *User Helps and Documentation* asked about the availability and the ability to customize user helps.

Administrative Requirements included questions about the management and control of the system:

1. *Customization* asked about the extent of configuration and customization that could be done by the library.
2. *Administration* covered questions about support for multiple administrators, multiple roles, tools for access control, and individual logins for multiple administrators.
3. *Administrative* passwords specified that administrative passwords should not be shared.

Technical Requirements focused on security, maintenance, browser support, system monitoring and reporting in the following areas:

1. The *System* section asked about the system's integration with a variety of Integrated Library Systems, transaction auditing, support for custom APIs and ODBC (Open Database Connectivity), user-friendly error

messages and the vendor's demonstrated commitment to development of software that supports the academic community.
2. *Browser Support* asked for a current list of supported browsers.
3. *Security* and *System Authentication and Authorization* included mandatory security requirements based on Penn State University policy for authorization and authentication.
4. *Monitoring and Reporting* asked about the tools available for monitoring and reporting, logs, metrics, auditing and benchmarking.
5. *System Maintenance and Technical Support* covered documentation, levels of technical support, maintenance, upgrades and the developer community.

Writing the RFP

An effectively written RFP provides clear proposal instructions, including the format in which the proposal must be submitted, how the evaluation decision will be made, how the bidders may submit their questions, as well as the selection criteria and timeline for the RFP evaluation process. The RFP must supply background information about the organization sending it out, including objectives and general terms and conditions. The most critical portion of the RFP is the requirements section as it is here that the desired system is truly defined. It is imperative that the RFP be clearly written and effectively organized to successfully communicate the organization's system needs and the desired outcome of the RFP process.

While many Libraries' faculty and staff contributed to defining the requirements for the discovery system, a small group of four individuals was charged to prepare the draft of the RFP. To ensure consistent language and format throughout the Requirements sections of the RFP, one individual was appointed to do the actual writing with the rest of the group serving as reviewers. The writing group was also responsible for identifying and providing contact information for the vendors to whom the RFP would be sent. The group worked closely with the University's Strategic Purchasing Manager who supplied the template for the RFP, proposal instructions, Penn State Information, General Terms and Conditions, Security Level Agreements, and a form for pricing information, and was ultimately responsible for finalizing and submitting the RFP on the Libraries' behalf.

Evaluating the Proposals

A predefined process for systematically assessing each proposal is key to a successful evaluation process. Having a set of guidelines and systems in place before the evaluations begin ensures fair and consistent appraisals of each proposal, system and vendor and an informed final decision.

Once the RFP was issued, the University Libraries appointed an RFP Evaluation Group which was responsible for evaluating the proposals and recommending the vendor whose proposal was most responsive to the discovery system project needs within the Libraries' available resources. Rejection of all proposals was an acceptable outcome if the group determined that no vendor met the requirements. The RFP Evaluation Group consisted of 17 faculty and staff from across the Libraries. Representatives from public, access and technical services joined forces with campus librarians, archivists, business office personnel and information technology (IT) specialists to evaluate the systems based on vendor proposals (pre- and post-demonstration), libraries-wide feedback, qualitative analysis and vendor-provided references.

Before meeting with the Evaluation Group, the two co-chairs reviewed proposal evaluation instructions received from University Purchasing as well as general RFP evaluation guidelines (Axia Consulting, 2010) and used that information to document rules for the group (Appendix B). Since many members of the group had worked closely with the systems and vendors during the initial investigation of next-generation interfaces, it was

important to remind the group that the proposals were to be evaluated solely on responses to the criteria listed in the RFP and not on any previous discussions or interactions with the vendors. In order to take into consideration the importance of the various criteria, the co-chairs developed a scoring scheme that used a combined weighting and scoring method. The weight was multiplied by the score to calculate points for each requirement. The weighting scheme was based on a 1 to 5 range, to give greater emphasis to the essential and desirable requirements. The range was broken down as follows: 1 = Nice to have, 3 = Desirable, 5 = Essential. The scoring scheme was a 0 to 4 range broken down as follows: 0 = Not met, 1 = Barely met, 2 = Partially met, 3 = Fully Met, 4 = Exceeded.

Once the scoring was established, the group's co-chairs created an evaluation grid broken into the four requirements sections - Functional, Usability, Administrative, and Technical (Appendix C). Each requirement in the subsections of the four requirement categories was marked as mandatory (m) or desirable (d), or where appropriate, was presented as an open-ended question (desc). The grid was pre-populated with weights based on whether each requirement was essential or desirable and with formulas to calculate points for each requirement category. Since the maximum possible points per requirement section varied greatly, total points for each section of the RFP would be calculated as a percentage of total possible points for each section to normalize the scoring. Once these materials were completed, the co-chairs were ready to meet with the Evaluation Group.

The RFP Evaluation Group co-chairs held an initial meeting at which they distributed and discussed specific evaluation guidelines, scoring guidelines, the scoring schemes, an evaluation timeline, the evaluation grid and the vendor proposals. The preparation of these materials ahead of time enabled the group members to focus on the evaluation task and not concern themselves with the process.

The second meeting of the RFP Evaluation Group took place one month later. Group members had spent the month reviewing the proposals and evaluating and scoring them based on evaluation and scoring guidelines. Completed individual evaluation grids were compiled into a single grid for each vendor, showing each team member's score for each requirement on a single line for easy comparison. The group spent one hour per vendor, comparing scores for each requirement in the RFP. Where the scoring was similar, the scores were averaged without discussion. In the case of vastly different scores, the group discussed and clarified the requirement and either came to a group consensus or if no consensus could be reached, took the average of the scores. Scores for each section were totaled and the vendors were ranked by score. Based on this scoring, the group was able to easily identify three vendors to bring to campus for demonstrations and further discussions.

Setting up Vendor Visits and System Demonstrations

The next step in evaluating the vendors and products is to invite the top candidates for meetings with stakeholders and an open product demonstration. Though the responses to the RFPs are an important part of the evaluation, seeing the system put through its paces, and meeting the vendors face to face provides a less quantitative, though no less important, evaluation criterion.

The three vendors that the Penn State University Libraries invited to campus followed an identical full-day schedule beginning with breakfast with the RFP Evaluation Group co-chairs and a member of the Next Generation Interface Team, followed by a demonstration and question and answer period for all Libraries faculty and staff. Meetings with the RFP Evaluation Group, Libraries' Administration, and the Libraries' Information Technology and Infrastructure departments made up the rest of the agenda. The meetings were an

excellent opportunity to follow up on questions for each vendor after the initial evaluation, and to clarify and acquire more detail and a better understanding of each system.

All participants in the meetings and attendees of the demonstrations were asked to complete a short survey on each system (Appendix D). After all of the vendor visits were completed, Libraries faculty and staff were surveyed again and asked to rank the three vendor products in order of best fit for the Libraries. The results of both surveys were tabulated, and shared with the RFP Evaluation Group for discussion at its final meeting.

Checking References

There is no substitute in the RFP process for talking with others who actually use and have implemented a product that is being evaluated. Conversations with actual users can bring to light some as of yet undiscovered positives and negatives that need to be considered as part of the selection process.

In their proposals, each vendor provided a list of institutions at which their system was implemented. The group selected Libraries that were similar in student population and collection size, and set up phone interviews with the person(s) involved in the implementation. These reference calls were made after the vendor visits and prior to the final evaluation meeting. The same set of questions was asked of each institution (Appendix E). The reference checks were a critical component of the evaluation, and enabled the group to gather valuable, qualitative information on each vendor and system that was not readily discernible from the proposals or the demonstrations.

Making the Final Decision and Recommendation

After careful review and evaluation of proposal, vendors, products and demonstrations, the process, if done well, should make clear the one product that best fits the selection criteria.

The Penn State University Libraries' RFP Evaluation Group met one last time for a final evaluation of the three candidates. Prior to the meeting, group members completed and uploaded their post-demonstration evaluation grids so that all of the scores could be reviewed together. The responses to outstanding questions from the RFPs, clarification of points from their proposals and a better knowledge of each of the products after the demonstrations, allowed the members to update their pre-demonstration scoring to reflect this new understanding. The group went through the evaluation grids line by line again and the consensus was much greater this time. Following the guidelines and evaluation grid established for this RFP evaluation as well as the results of the vendor surveys and the responses to the reference calls, the group successfully rated the proposed systems and was able to clearly identify the discovery system that best fit the needs of the Penn State University Libraries.

The structure provided by the detailed requirements, the RFP process and the evaluation grid allowed the evaluation group to confidently recommend a discovery system and to provide data to back up that recommendation. A brief narrative and summary evaluation forms for the three finalists were included in the final recommendation report presented to the Libraries' administration. The summary evaluation included a final ranking (e.g., winning bid, alternate bid, etc.), pre- and post-visit scores, qualitative evaluation comments, Libraries' faculty and staff feedback scores, comments from references, and a price summary (Appendix F). Libraries' administration found the completed summary forms for each vendor particularly useful as they contained all pertinent information in an easy to scan format.

LESSONS LEARNED

Processes can always be improved, but there were some aspects of the RFP process described in the previous sections that definitely enhanced the effort.

Planning and preparation are vital to the success of a structured evaluation and selection process. Penn State University Libraries Discovery System RFP Evaluation Group meetings were easy and relatively painless because of the planning and preparation done prior to the evaluation process. Defining the guidelines for evaluation and scoring prior to the first meeting with the entire group gave a purpose and focus to the group as the course of action was already defined. Laying out and sticking to a strict agenda for each of the all-day evaluation meetings kept the group on task, as did defining real deliverables as outcomes for each of the two meetings. Group members appreciated the respect for their time, and were able to give their best and full attention to potentially tedious meetings. The right mix of group members provided a range of perspectives that allowed assessment of proposal responses from multiple viewpoints, and ultimately enabled the group to make the best decision for the institution.

Hindsight is 20/20, however, and there are a number of ways that the evaluation and selection process could have been made easier and more efficient.

The evaluation and scoring schemes should have been defined before writing the list of requirements and RFP. Assigning weights to requirements while writing those requirements would have made the development of the scoring grid more manageable and efficient.

Guidelines for scoring "not applicable" responses should have been determined ahead of time. Without firm guidelines, some members of the Penn State RFP Evaluation Group assigned a score of "0" (or "not met") to "not applicable" responses while others left that part of the grid blank resulting in inconsistent and unfair scoring.

In addition, certain individuals on the Penn State group did not feel qualified to respond to every question. For example, a public services librarian was not comfortable evaluating a response on system authentication, authorization and security. Ultimately the group chose to average those responses based on the number of people who did respond, rather than assigning a "0" to the unanswered question.

Stakeholders, including librarians and library staff, should have been educated on the system or service that was being procured prior to vendor visits. At Penn State, many of the members of the RFP Evaluation Group had also been involved in the Next Generation Interface Team and knew discovery systems inside and out. Others attending vendor demonstrations were not as well versed in the concept of discovery systems, and as librarians and staff began to ask questions after the vendor demonstrations, it became clear that a better job of educating the constituency should have been done prior to the vendor visits. If the audience had come with a better understanding of these products, the question and answer time might have covered some more advanced topics or focused on some of the specific features that made each system unique.

FUTURE RESEARCH DIRECTIONS

Implementation of a Web-scale discovery system is a new, and significant, expense for libraries. Funds are limited and must be used wisely. This chapter describes and promotes the use of a structured selection and evaluation process for procuring a discovery system. Such a process can be time-consuming and require considerable library staff as well as vendor resources, and going forward, a review of the structured evaluation and selection process should be conducted to determine its cost-effectiveness. Would the same decision have been reached without the formal process, and did the competitive nature of the process result in better pricing? Increasingly, it appears that more and more libraries are becoming early adopters or development partners with vendors in order to both contribute to the strategic direction of a product and to receive financial incentives. Is the structured process described here a viable option for institutions evaluating whether or not to become an early adopter or development partner for discovery systems? While the financial incentives of becoming a development partner or early adopter can be attractive, what process can be used to ensure an objective evaluation of the vendor's offering?

CONCLUSION

A Web-scale discovery system is a significant investment for many libraries. A careful and thorough evaluation process will go a long way towards ensuring that the selected system meets the library's local needs, priorities and budget requirements. The evaluation process can be a formal RFP, as was mandated at Penn State, or a less formal, but no less structured comparison of features, functionality, content and pricing that will enable the selection team to determine whether and how well the products meet stated requirements.

Whether conducted as part of a RFP or less formally, the steps of the structured process described in this chapter can be time-consuming and require considerable staff resources. The process does, however, offer many advantages. In fact, at Penn State, one vendor originally questioned the need to select the Web-scale discovery system via the RFP process, but later complimented the process and the thorough evaluation of its system. The RFP process forced the Penn State team to clearly identify the purpose and scope of the project, and to articulate requirements and reach consensus on which ones were mandatory. Following guidelines established by the team leads, the group was able to quickly eliminate products that did not meet mandatory requirements, and focus on viable options. The process ensured that vendors would respond point by point to the stated requirements, and that the group objectively and impartially evaluated products based on written responses from the vendors rather than on statements made by vendors during earlier visits, phone calls, meetings, etc. In addition, it identified the deliverables to which Penn State could hold the vendor of the chosen system. This, as was discovered during the implementation phase, was critical in making sure the selected system met the specific needs of the Penn State University Libraries. The pricing proposals supplied as part of the RFP responses enabled the group to do side-by side comparisons of projected costs over multiple years. In Penn State's case, the pricing proposals showed considerable range, which required a careful analysis of exactly what was being offered by each vendor, but ultimately led to a better understanding of the proposals.

Given the budgetary situation in which many libraries find themselves today and the huge expense of purchasing a Web-scale discovery system, a structured process for evaluation and selection can help ensure that funds are used wisely. Whether or not it is done as part of a RFP process or less formally, the structure provided by the process will enable those charged with the selection to confidently recommend a discovery system and provide data to back up that recommendation.

REFERENCES

Axia Consulting. (2010). *RFP scoring guidelines, 15 key guidelines for scoring IT software proposals / RFP's*. Retrieved from http://www.axia-consulting.co.uk/html/rfp_scoring_guidelines.html

Bhatnagar, G., Dennis, S., Duque, G., Henry, S., MacEachern, M., Teasley, S., & Varnum, K. (2010). *University of Michigan Article Discovery Working Group final report*. Retrieved from http://www.lib.umich.edu/files/adwg/final-report.pdf

Boock, M., & Buck, S. Chadwell, F. Nichols, J., & Reese, T. (2009). *Discovery services task force recommendation to University Librarian*. Retrieved from http://ir.library.oregonstate.edu/xmlui/bitstream/handle/1957/13817/discovery search task force recommendations – redacted version.pdf

Brubaker, N., Leach-Murray, S., & Parker, S. (2011). Shapes in the cloud. *Online, 35*(2), 20–26.

Calvert, P., & Read, M. (2006). RFPs: A necessary evil or indispensable tool? *The Electronic Library, 24*(5), 649–661. doi:10.1108/02640470610707259

Caswell, J., & Wynstra, J. (2007). Developing the right RFP for selecting your federated search product: Lessons learned and tips from recent experience. *Internet Reference Services Quarterly, 12*(1-2), 49–71. doi:10.1300/J136v12n01_03

Clegg, H., & Montgomery, S. (2006). How to write an RFP for information products. *Information Outlook, 10*(6), 23–31.

Karamouzis, F., & Longwood, J. (2007). *Guidelines of an RFP process for standardized IT service provider selections*. Gartner Research Group.

Kyrillidou, M. (2011). *Library investment index 2002-03 through 2009-10*. Retrieved from http://www.arl.org/bm~doc/index10.xls

Luther, J., & Kelly, M. (2011). The next generation of discovery. *Library Journal, 136*(5), 66–71.

Peters, C. (2011). *An overview of the RFP process for nonprofits and libraries*. Retrieved from http://www.techsoup.org/learningcenter/techplan/page5507.cfm

Rowe, R. (2010). Web-scale discovery: A review of Summon, EBSCO Discovery Service, and WorldCat Local. *The Charleston Advisor, 12*(1), 5–10. doi:10.5260/chara.12.1.5

Ryan, T. (2004). Turning patrons into partners when choosing an integrated library system. *Computers in Libraries, 24*(3), 6–56.

Schachter, D. (2004). How to manage the RFP process. *Information Outlook, 8*(11), 10–12.

Schrage, M. (1996). RFPs: May they rest in peace. *Computerworld, 30*(14), 37.

Vaughan, J. (2011). Questions to consider. *Library Technology Reports, 47*(1), 54–59.

Westfall, M. (2011). Using a request for proposal (RFP) to select a serials vendor: The University of Tennessee experience. *Serials Review, 37*(2), 87–92. doi:10.1016/j.serrev.2011.01.005

Wisniewski, J. (2009). Next-gen OPACs: No time like the present. *Online, 33*(5), 54–57.

ADDITIONAL READING

Allison, D. (2010). Information portals: The next generation catalog. *Journal of Web Librarianship, 4*(4), 375–389. doi:10.1080/19322909.2010.507972

Breeding, M. (2007). Next generation catalogs. *Library Technology Reports, 43*(4).

Breeding, M. (2010). The state of the art in library discovery 2010. *Computers in Libraries, 30*(1), 31–34.

Breeding, M. (2011). *Advances in library discovery services: The state of the art in 2011* [PowerPoint Presentation]. Internet Librarian 2011. Retrieved from http://www.librarytechnology.org/ltg-displaytext.pl?RC=16196

Breeding, M. (2011). Library discovery services: From the ground to the cloud . In Corrado, E., & Mouliason, H. (Eds.), *Getting started with cloud computing* (pp. 71–86). New York, NY: Neal-Schuman Publishers, Inc.

Carlin, A., & Donalan, R. (2007). A sheep in wolf's clothing: Discovery tools and the OPAC. *The Reference Librarian, 48*(2), 67–71. doi:10.1300/J120v48n02_10

Cohn, J. M., & Kelsey, A. L. (2010). *The complete library technology planner: A guidebook with sample technology plans and RFPs on CD-ROM.* New York, NY: Neal-Schuman Publishers.

Dahl, M. (2009). The evolution of library discovery systems in the Web environment. *OLA Quarterly, 15*(1), 5–9.

Dentinger, S., Keclik, K., Barclay, A., Bruns, T., Larson, E., & Quatrucci, A. … Walker, N. (2008). *Resource discovery exploratory task force final report.* Retrieved from http://staff.library.wisc.edu/rdetf/RDETF-final-report.pdf

Emanuel, J. (2011). Usability of the VuFind next-generation online catalog. *Information Technology and Libraries, 30*(1), 44–52.

Fowler, M. (2004). How to bring sanity to insane RFP's. *AIIM E-Doc Magazine, 18*(2), 44–48.

Greene, T. (2003, March 19). RFP strategy. *New World (New Orleans, La.), 20,* 49.

Kern, M., & Emanuel, J. (2009). Next generation catalogs: What do they do and why should we care? *Reference and User Services Quarterly, 49*(2), 117–120.

Nagy, A. (2011). Defining the next-generation catalog. *False . Library Technology Reports, 47*(7), 11–15.

Sadeh, T. (2007). Time for a change: New approaches for a new generation of library users. *New Library World, 108*(7/8), 307–316. doi:10.1108/03074800710763608

Sadeh, T. (2008). User experience in the library: A case study. *New Library World, 109*(1/2), 7–24. doi:10.1108/03074800810845976

Sierra, T., Ryan, J., & Wust, M. (2007). Beyond OPAC 2.0: Library catalog as versatile discovery platform. *The Code4Lib Journal, 1.* Retrieved from http://journal.code4lib.org/articles/10

Singer, R. (2008). In search of a really "next generation" catalog. *Journal of Electronic Resources Librarianship*, *20*(3), 139–142. doi:10.1080/19411260802412752

Vaughan, J. (2011). Dispatches from the field: Web-scale discovery. *American Libraries*, *42*(1/2), 32.

Vaughan, J. (2011). Library Web-scale discovery services. *Library Technology Reports*, *47*(1).

Waller, N. (2003). The model RFP. *Library Technology Reports*, *39*(4), 20–30.

Waller, N. (2003). New model and nontraditional RFPs. *Library Technology Reports*, *39*(4), 42–47.

Waller, N. (2003). Writing the RFP. *Library Technology Reports*, *39*(4), 31–41.

Way, D. (2010). The impact of Web-scale discovery on the use of a library collection. *Scholarly Publications*, Paper 9. http://scholarworks.gvsu.edu/library_sp/9

Wisniewski, J. (2010). Web-scale discovery: The future's so bright, I gotta wear shades. *Online*, *34*(4), 55–58.

Yang, S. Q., & Wagner, K. (2010). Evaluating and comparing discovery tools: How close are we towards next generation catalog? *Library Hi Tech*, *28*(4), 690–709. doi:10.1108/07378831011096312

KEY TERMS AND DEFINITIONS

Application Programming Interface (API): A defined set of instructions or guidelines that allows programmatic access to one system's data or functions by other systems.

Next-Generation Interface: A user interface that typically sits on top of a library's online catalog and provides improved access to the library's collections. Most next generation interfaces include enhanced searching with features like facets, multiple sort options, relevancy ranking, and enriched content as well as tagging and reviews by users.

Open Database Connectivity (ODBC): A standard for accessing different database systems. ODBC makes it possible to access any data from any application, regardless of which database management system (DBMS) is handling the data.

Request for Proposal (RFP): A request sent to vendors for a proposed solution, pricing and implementation timeline that meets a defined set of requirements for a service or product. Often used as a means of competitively evaluating complex services or products.

Web-scale Discovery System: A library system that allows searching across all of the libraries' content from a single interface. This content may include the entire catalog and local collections as well as content from subscription journals and databases. These services harvest and pre-index the local and subscription content into a large centralized index for fast search results.

ENDNOTES

1. Serials Solution is a registered trademark of Serials Solutions
2. Summon is owned by ProQuest LLC
3. EBSCO Discovery Service is owned by EBSCO Publishing Industries
4. Worldcat is a registered trademark of OCLC
5. SirsiDynix is a registered trademark of SirsiDynix Corporation.
6. Symphony is a registered trademark of SirsiDynix Corporation.
7. ContentDM is a registered trademark of OCLC

APPENDIX A

Interface Features Grid

Features (Most important to least important)	Vendor 1	Vendor 2	Vendor 3	Vendor 4
Single sign on				
Relevancy Ranking Algorithm				
Faceted Search				
Did You Mean?				
Unicode compliant				
Supports FRBR				
Integrated federated search				
Enriched content				
User-generated lists				
Mobile platforms				
Suggest popular items				
User reviews, rating and tagging				
Additional Features (suggested by Faculty/Staff)				
Sort				
Library/location limits				
Search widget				
Material type locations				
SMS notification				
Integration of collections				
Export to Endnote/Refworks				
Advanced Search interface				
Real time holdings information				
Purchase options				
Saved searches				
Accessibility				
Admin				
Implementation				
Developer Community				

APPENDIX B

RFP Evaluation Guidelines

University Libraries Discovery System RFP Evaluation Group Guidelines
General Guidelines:
1. Group members may not communicate directly with vendors. All contact with vendors must be through XXXXX, Strategic Purchasing Manager, Penn State University Purchasing Services. If a vendor contacts an RFP Evaluation Group member, that member must refer the vendor to Purchasing. 2. Group members should perform as fair an evaluation as possible of all proposals and set aside any prejudices. Previous knowledge of a vendor should not be used in evaluating the proposals. 3. If additional information or clarification is needed from a vendor, the group will request it through Purchasing. 4. All RFP Evaluation Group members should maintain confidentiality. Preliminary conclusions or results should not be communicated outside of the evaluation group. 5. All RFP Evaluation Group members must keep all internal workings of the group confidential until the group has completed its work and its report, and all bidders have been officially notified of the selection.
Scoring Guidelines:

1. The objective of our evaluation is to ensure consistent and unbiased scoring, remove individual scoring subjectivity, and achieve a consensus score for each proposal and items within it.
2. Proposals must be evaluated solely on the criteria listed in the RFP. Only materials presented in the written proposals and vendor demonstrations can be considered in the evaluation.
3. RFP Evaluation Group members should not consider prior experience with the product in scoring the proposals.
4. Each group member should evaluate and score the proposals individually following the steps below:
    a. Step 1: Review all proposals. Take notes and prepare questions for discussion. Do not score at this point.
    b. Step 2: Determine whether the proposal is within the scope of the project described and required in the RFP. If it is not, notify the group.
    c. Step 3: Score the proposals using the RFP Evaluation Grid.
5. Once individual scoring has been completed, the group will meet to discuss and compare its individual findings.
6. Vendors whose proposals do not meet the mandatory requirements as stated in the RFP will be eliminated.
7. During group discussions, each member may change his/her initial individual scoring. Final scores will be totaled for the group as a whole.
8. The group will strive to reach consensus. Be prepared to compromise and adjust your initial scores if there are compelling reasons. If consensus cannot be reached, scores will be averaged.
9. Only scores from group members will be used to determine which vendors should be short-listed and invited for on-site visits. No one from outside the RFP Evaluation Group will be allowed any input at this stage.

APPENDIX C

RFP Evaluation Grid

Notes:
• In the grid below, m=mandatory, d=desirable, desc = a response that requires a more involved description on the part of the vendor.
• The section below is an excerpt from a larger grid.

Penn State University Libraries Discovery System RFP Evaluation
Vendor: XYZ Software Company **Reviewer:** Reviewer#1

	Requirement	m,d,desc	Weight	Score (0-4)	Points (Weight x Score)	Notes
5	**Functional Requirements**					
5.1	**Collection Integration**					
1	Integrate/index/search multiple collections and collection types	m	5			
2	Search one collection or multiple collections at once	d	3			
3	Specific files excluded from indexing	desc	1			
4	Data formats	desc	5			
5	Data harvesting description	desc	5			
6	Collections included in initial installation	desc	5			
7	Ability for in-house integration, cost of integrating collection	desc	3			
8	Timeliness of indexing	desc	5			
5.2	**RSS/Saved Search/Lists**					
1	Support for RSS/Atom feeds	m	5			
2	Saved search - lists and individual records	m	5			
3	Support for user-created lists	d	1			
5.3	**Holdings Information**					
1	Display of real-time holdings information	m	5			

APPENDIX D

Library Feedback Survey Questions

University Libraries Post Vendor Visit and Demonstration Survey Questions
1. Please rate your overall impression of Product X . [1(lowest) - 5 (highest)]
2. Please comment on your overall impression of Product X.
3. What did you like most about Product X?
4. Please list the features of Product X that you feel would be most valuable to the Penn State University Libraries or that you would like to see implemented.
5. What additional functionality would you like to see?
6. Are there questions about this interface that weren't answered during the demo? If so, please list below.
7. Would Product X be a good fit for the Penn State University Libraries? Check the best answer:
a. Yes.
b. Perhaps, with some tweaking.
c. Maybe, need more information.
d. Not for my purposes.
e. No.
8. Was there anything about Product X that you disliked? Please comment.

APPENDIX E

Discovery System Reference Check Questions

Pennsylvania State University Libraries Discovery System Reference Check Questions
Vendor:
Product:
Institution:
Contact Information:
System Implementation and Support Questions

1. Administrative Interface
    a. How easy/difficult is the admin interface to configure and use?
    b. Who configures the interface? IT staff or library staff?
    c. What skill set is required?
2. Implementation
    a. Were you assigned a single point of contact/project manager for the implementation?
    b. How much of the implementation was done in-house? How much done by vendor?
    c. Was the system implemented in the agreed upon time frame? If not, what prevented you from meeting the deadline?
    d. Did you have any critical tech issues/show stoppers during implementation?
    e. How easy is it to integrate various/multiple collections?
    f. How much sys admin time did it take to integrate?
    g. Are there any outstanding/unresolved implementation issues?
    h. Were you satisfied with the implementation support offered by the vendor?
3. Library Implementation Team
    a. How large was your product implementation team? Which areas of the library did they represent?
    b. What would you do differently if you could re-do the implementation?
    c. Was the system implemented in the agreed upon time frame? If not, what prevented you from meeting the deadline?
4. System Maintenance
    a. How many sys admin people do you have working on regular maintenance of this product?
    b. How much time does he/she/they spend on sys admin (hours/week)?
    c. Are non-IT staff involved in the regular maintenance of this product? If yes, please describe their responsibilities.
5. Development
    a. Have you done any development/enhancements?
    b. If so, have you found the software open/transparent in terms of development?
    c. How helpful is the user group/dev community?
6. Support
    a. Are you satisfied with the tech support offered by vendor?
    b. How quickly are questions answered/issues resolved?
7. Is there any advice/warning you would give someone about to implement this product?
    a. Would you purchase this product again?
    b. Would you purchase another product from this vendor?

Public Services Questions

1. Has your institution done any formal/informal usability studies on this product/system?
    a. If so, what were your general impressions of user reaction to the product (both negative and positive)?
    b. What were the particular features your patrons like/dislike about this product?
2. Involvement
    a. How were the public services units of your library involved in the implementation?
    b. What were some of the challenges that you encountered?
3. Features
    a. What are the features that you and your colleagues most like about this product?
    b. What are the features that you and your colleagues wish the vendor would have included?
4. Impact on Service
    a. Describe the negative/positive impacts that implementation of this product have had on reference services and bibliographic instruction.

continued on following page

Technical Services Questions

1. Involvement
    a. How was the technical services unit (cataloging/acquisitions/serials) of your library involved in the implementation?
    b. What were some of the challenges that you encountered?
2. Impact on Process/Staffing
    a. Have departmental workflows, the approach to cataloging standards and practice, or any other aspect of cataloging changed, for the better or for worse, as a result of having a new public interface?
    b. Has it had an impact on your staffing levels?
    c. Are you noticing any difference in the kinds of maintenance or enhancement requests that you receive, either from patrons or from colleagues in other departments, as a result of display issues, relevancy ranking, faceted searching, or other features of the way catalog records display in the new interface?

APPENDIX F

Discovery System Vendor Summary Form

Penn State University Libraries' Discovery System RFP Summary Vendor: Product: XXXXX		
Conclusion		
_ This is the winning bid _ This is the alternate bid _ This bid is rejected		
Evaluations of Vendor Proposals		
Criteria	**Pre-Visit**	**Post-Visit**
Section 1		
Functional, Usability, Administrative Requirements and Questions	60%	70%
Section 2		
Technical Requirements and Questions	77%	75%
Total	68.5%	73%
Qualitative Evaluations by RFP Evaluation Group, Post-Visit		
Positive comments included ..... The biggest concern (**negative**) appeared to be.....		

Libraries Feedback Based on Vendor Demo			
Ranking	**1st**	**2nd**	**3rd**
XXXXX	95%	5%	0%

References
Institution: A **Positive** comments about XXXXX include the fact that in all cases implementation timeline was met … **Negatives** included the challenges of satisfactorily mapping …

5 Year Cost Summary						
Product (hosted)	**Year 1**	**Year 2**	**Year 3**	**Year 4**	**Year 5**	**5 Year Total**
Subscription (annual)						
Implementation (one-time)						
Total						

Chapter 8
Designing an Evaluation Process for Resource Discovery Tools

David Bietila
University of Chicago, USA

Tod Olson
University of Chicago, USA

ABSTRACT

This chapter discusses a process that can be used by libraries to evaluate the current generation of resource discovery tools. The process considers a three-tiered approach to the application, considering technical, functional, and usability layers. Because the current generation of discovery tools is very flexible, the process discussed uses an initial pass of evaluation to gain insight into the abilities of the tool and how users approach it. This leads to a further evaluative iteration, mainly at the usability level, where the user observations from the first iteration are used to inform more refined use cases.

INTRODUCTION

In recent years, the environment in which the evaluation of library search tools takes place has undergone relentless transformation. These tools require enormous resources to license and maintain, and they occupy a central role in allowing traversal of library resources. This makes it crucial to establish evaluation processes that enable libraries to anticipate how well this evolving set of tools will serve the needs of the library and its patrons.

DOI: 10.4018/978-1-4666-1821-3.ch008

Initial generations of digital search tools hewed closely to the designs of then familiar print tools, such as the card catalog and print index. However, the latest generation of tools has diverged notably from this design paradigm, and begun to behave more like truly digital tools, allowing access to heterogeneous sets of data, and providing flexibility of content coverage and presentation. Apart from the search tools themselves, library users have changed, and now hold significantly higher expectations for search tools, influenced by the availability of quick and ubiquitous Internet search engines. Furthermore, users now have the option to eschew library search tools in favor of commercial competitors, such as Google Scholar™[1]. Library staff must curate an increasingly diverse set of digital resources, but cannot assume the users' enthusiasm and attention for yet another tool without clear demonstrations of its value. It is certain that libraries need a means of effectively evaluating and selecting the current generation of library search tools, but it is unclear how processes must shift to best meet current demands.

This chapter details the University of Chicago Library's attempt to develop an evaluation method capable of addressing these new demands. It examines the literature related to the evaluation of current resource discovery tools and their immediate predecessors, metasearch tools, and shows how the Library's background with metasearching influenced the current evaluation. This chapter presents exposition on the circumstances of University of Chicago Library's particular evaluation project, including the software under evaluation, and the need that Library staff thought it might address. It covers the initial evaluation plan itself, and some of the assumptions and results of this plan. Finally, the chapter details the shortcomings of the initial evaluation plan, and describes what the project team needed to revise in light of both the nature of the technology under examination and the Library's organizational needs.

In the course of the evaluation, the process shifted from a relatively straightforward, linear approach to a more complex, iterative one. Two factors drove the need to shift the evaluation process. First, there was the need to address the complexity of the search tool. Many aspects of its behavior were not immediately transparent, especially regarding its handling of metadata drawn from disparate sources in irregular formats. Second, the flexibility of this generation of search tool made it difficult to establish a model use case. The Library was interested primarily in improving article search, but since it was possible to search journal databases, the online catalog, and archival and digital collections with the tool under consideration, it was not obvious what users would want to do with it, and for what use cases and user constituencies it should be optimized. Similarly, the fact that the product could be configured to include a variable set of data sources raised the challenge of conducting an effective evaluation. Since a variety of data sources could potentially be included or omitted, the evaluation team had to decide on a particular configuration to evaluate before the bulk of the testing could occur.

The authors hope that the experience of developing this process will be of some value to other libraries.

BACKGROUND AND LITERATURE REVIEW

The University of Chicago is a research and educational institution with over 5,000 undergraduates; 10,000 graduate, professional, and other students; and 2,200 faculty and other academic personnel. The University is well-known for intensive research activity in diverse areas such as economics, law, medicine, sociology, the physical sciences, and a number of other fields. The University of Chicago Library serves the needs of University researchers and students; it is a single administrative unit with a physical presence in six buildings. In addition to a physical collection of some 8.5 million items, the Library maintains access to over 57,000 individual e-journal titles and over a million e-books.

The Chicago Search Experience

Our approach to the evaluation of research discovery tools was a direct outgrowth of previous experience with a federated search tool. Similarly, while there is currently only scant literature on evaluating current resource discovery tools, the literature on federated search evaluation shares many of the same concerns. Federated searching arrived in libraries in the early 2000s, and many in the profession greeted it with enthusiasm, seeing the potential of easing the work of patrons seeking resources scattered across many search interfaces. Opponents, quick to emerge, upheld the superiority of vendors' native interfaces and asserted that federated searching was too easy and would lead to the dumbing-down of scholars. Finally, some pointed out measurable flaws, such problems with duplicate results, ranking of records from different systems, and, in broadcast search systems in particular, the slow response time to a search when the system has to wait for several remote search engines to return results. Tennant (2003) and Baer (2004) are representative examples of this discussion.

Internal discussion in the University of Chicago Library around this time mirrored discussions in the broader library community, expressing the same concerns and opportunities. The Library formed a working group to evaluate existing federated search tools. This group determined that federated searching was not a replacement for native search interfaces for core researchers. However, the group was persuaded by the potential to help users survey a number of databases in their area of research and identify the ones most likely to be productive in their research, and even to direct them to the databases' native interfaces. One internal critic became a supporter of a federated search after encountering real research situations where aggregated searches, due to their broader coverage, would return relevant and important results that were not included in the more specialized databases. (F. Conaway, personal communication, August 27, 2004)

Based on that evaluation, the Library implemented a federated search system in 2004. The goal had been to provide a single search box that would encompass many of the key article databases, as well as subject-oriented metasearches. The chosen system relied on broadcast searching, the dominant strategy at the time, where the application searches a set of databases in parallel and merges the results for presentation to the user.

Unfortunately, the broadcast proved to be slow, unreliable, and capable of missing important search results. Two LibQUAL+®[2] surveys indicated that, despite having extensive subscriptions, there was relatively high dissatisfaction related to the Library's collection of e-journals. (Cook et al, 2004; Cook et al., 2007; Tatarka 2007) More recent survey data shows a fairly high level of satisfaction with the collections *per se*, but comments showed dissatisfaction with the ways of searching and accessing articles. (Tatarka, Larsen, Olson, Schilt & Twiss-Brooks 2010; "Survey 2010 comments" 2010) The broadcast search system itself it does not seem to have been well-adopted. Librarians attribute this to an awkward user interface and the relatively slow and unreliable responses from the individual databases. This situation is echoed by Wrubel and Schmidt (2007), who found that while students recognized the same broadcast search tool as useful, usability testing found low success rates.

The Library has made efforts to improve the user interface of its broadcast search. Discouragingly, Casewell, et al. (2010) report on efforts to improve the user experience of the same search tool. After outlining much effort and many changes, they reveal that they eventually scrapped the vendor's user interface in favor of an open-source user interface layered over the product's Web API. This is neither encouraging, nor does it address underlying concerns about the speed and reliability of broadcast search.

A system using an aggregate index seems the best way to address the problems of broadcast searching, and several such products have emerged in recent years. By developing a well-considered evaluation model for the current generation of discovery tools upon which to base its evaluation process, the Library aims to identify potential technical stumbling blocks and other barriers to user adoption.

The Library's experience with the implementation of a faceted browse catalog also influenced this evaluation. A faceted catalog was desired both to allow a new way to navigate millions of bibliographic records, and to address ongoing issues that users were having with browse and keyword search in the traditional catalog., such as the lack of relevance ranking and using articles in title browse. Using a demo instance of the AquaBrowser®[3] product, the library conducted a user study to determine what, if any, measureable benefits if offered. While the study was qualitative, a number of subjects, when using the demo installation, found materials related to their dissertation topics, but which they had not discovered in the Library's traditional catalog(Olson, 2007). AquaBrowser® was implemented as an alternative to the traditional catalog, and while greeted enthusiastically by a number of users, there were also a number of complaints, some of unexpected intensity. Responses to the word cloud were polarized, and it was eventually hidden by default. While many users appreciated the results ranking, there were complaints about ranking of exact title or author matches; the ranking was significantly improved as a result. Despite technical improvements that mitigated some of the criticisms, reactions to this faceted catalog remain polarized, and both enthusiasts and detractors remain vocal.

The above experiences encouraged the evaluation team to spend more time on the recent resource discovery tool evaluation, and to work to increase the engagement of user and staff stakeholders during the process. The goal of the team was to gain greater confidence that all major issues would be found and resolved to ensure a positive reception of the product.

Evaluation Models

Attempts to evaluate federated searching products appear in the literature shortly after competing products appeared in the marketplace. Several studies focus on comparing competing products. Dorner and Curtis (2004) evaluated eleven such systems by asking vendors to respond to a survey. The survey identified 79 evaluation criteria, clas-

sified into eight broader categories: (1) searching; (2) user interaction; (3) customization; (4) authentication; (5) design; (6) database communication protocols; (7) after sale support; and (8) software platforms supported. The vendors responded whether individual features are supported. Tables of results are presented, organized by category, and include percent of criteria supported.

Boss and Nelson (2005) provide evaluations of four products. They arranged for access to demo or production implementations of each product and evaluated each product directly. Each product evaluation is organized into four areas: "Basic Design and Searching Capabilities," "Managing Search Results", "User Customization," and "Administration, Configuration, and Maintenance". The authors use these categories to frame their evaluations; they do not, however, directly compare the products.

Rowe (2010) offers a comparative review of three products, Summon™[4], EBSCO Discovery Service™[5], and WorldCat®[6] Local using twenty four items under the broad categories of content, user interface/searchability, pricing, and contract options. Each category is rated on a scale of up to four stars, and a composite score is given for each product. In this review, the three products seem fairly well-matched overall, as the composite scores vary by only half a star. However, the process of assigning ratings in the different categories is unclear.

One promising evaluation model involves a three-layer testing framework targeting the technical, functional, and usability level of a discovery system. (Avery, et al., 2007) These layers provide a way of segregating aspects of testing, which can be useful in both ensuring completeness and distributing responsibilities; it is reminiscent of how an RFP might be organized. This framework provides the basis for evaluation planning at the University of Chicago. In practice, the boundaries between layers are not always sharply defined, and some aspects of a discovery system may cut across layers. It is useful to remember that this framework is not intended as a rigorous taxonomy, but rather is intended to frame a system evaluation. The framework itself and some extensions will be discussed in more detail below.

INITIAL EVALUATION PROCESS

University of Chicago Library arranged a trial of the EBSCO Discovery Service™ product in December of 2010. The trial was to last for one year, and the vendor would configure the product to include the Library's catalog, and all compatible electronic resources. The vendor stipulated that this not be solely an internal trial, but that the Library should make the product available to our for their evaluation. Because of the public nature of this evaluation, the Library invested significantly more time and resources into it than it might for a typical product trial. The public trial was more similar to a product launch. The evaluation team worked with the Library's graphic designer to brand the product with a name ("ArticlesPlus"), logo, and other visual customizations. Configuration options were examined in detail and superfluous search options removed. There was a campaign to increase awareness of the ArticlesPlus trial among students and faculty, using Web news posts, print posters and flyers, and mentioning the tool in correspondence with faculty and in instruction sessions. The public trial made the project more resource intensive, but also focused attention on the product, and gave a clearer idea of how the tool would behave in a production environment.

The Library's technology management committee formed a project team responsible for oversight of the trial and product evaluation, selecting team members that would both represent stakeholder groups and include relevant technology staff. The group appointed had six members, equally representing public services, technical services, and technology and systems staff, with the Library's Web Program Director convening the group. The varied composition of this group enabled it to act as a proxy for diverse interests and approaches within the Library, with the aim of encouraging buy-in for the group's ultimate appraisal.

The initial evaluation plan applied the Avery-Ward-Hinchliffe model and was to assess technical, functional, and interface elements of the EBSCO Discovery Service™. The division of responsibilities for the project team thus followed conceptual structure: coordinating the functional evaluation, usability testing, and liaising with the vendor regarding technical issues. Additional roles were publicizing the product to library users and staff, and providing oversight regarding integration of the product with other library tools and data.

The primary use case initially assumed for the evaluation of this product was article searching by novice users. Previously, usability testing had suggested that article searching presented a significant challenge to patrons; failure rates were high. An internal library study concluded that searchers tended to take a "trial and error" approach due to the difficulty of identifying a productive path. While many experienced researchers have acquired familiarity with the article databases of their field, the current environment was unforgiving for the novice, and that was the primary use case the Library sought to address with this product.

Despite hope that this new search tool might improve the article searching experience for users, there was some hesitance from staff, based on disappointing experiences with the broadcast search tool and the faceted catalog that the Library had implemented in the previous decade. The Library had already tried addressing the article searching problem with a broadcast search application. These two experiences made clear the importance of the evaluation process, as an opportunity to identify potentially critical technical issues, and to ensure that the concerns of relevant constituencies were addressed. To avert the same problems, the project team sought to frame the tool effectively for library staff, demonstrate responsiveness to their concerns to build goodwill, and to identify and resolve key user concerns before widespread exposure to a general audience. Following the launch of the public trial, the team strove to maintain effective communication with users.

Technical Evaluation

The technical evaluation focused on the ability to incorporate local metadata, and the ability to integrate with the existing Web site and other applications. In this case the product was a hosted system, so much of the technical testing that would frequently be part of an evaluation project was unnecessary. There was no need for evaluation of hardware requirements and software dependencies, or capacity and indexing performance, or for analysis of the scope of ongoing maintenance required. While assessment of search responsiveness and server downtime were considered, these were ultimately deemed unnecessary barring negative feedback from staff or users on these items.

The technical evaluation assessed the constraints that this particular hosted system imposed. One can assume that a hosted system will offer less flexibility than a locally configured one, but the degree and nature of the constraints may not be immediately apparent. Testing here was guided largely by user feedback gathered during interface evaluation, which directly informed a set of recommended changes to language and layout of the interface. This provided a realistic, evidence-base test of the tool's configurability. For example, it was easy to suppress facets which were of limited use to the intended population, like 'Age' and 'Gender', and to relabel ambiguous facets like 'Source Type' and 'Subject: Major Heading' to 'Format' and 'Medical Subject', respectively. While there were limits to the supported configuration and customization, the software did allow for at least incremental improvements to the interface in nearly all problem areas.

The technical evaluation also addressed the application's capacity for interoperability and integration with other systems. This was comprised of assessment of both the handling of inputs and outputs by the tool. The ability to accept inputs was tested by loading a variety of disparate formats and sources including MARC data, finding aids in the EAD format, and OAI harvesting of digital library collections, support for citations from many article databases and licensed electronic resources. Assessment of outputs involved examination of support for open protocols and the provision of APIs to allow for manipulation of search results.

Table 1 provides a sample technical evaluation checklist, which considers both the features of the software product and its support requirements, and should help the evaluator determine whether the technology is a good match for the environment.

Functional Evaluation

Functional testing aimed to evaluate the core search mechanics of the product. For this portion of the project, the evaluation team collaborated with a standing library committee dedicated to software testing. The library committee was able to test basic search functions, such as support for Boolean searches, phrase searching, and fielded searching. The evaluation team itself examined the pre- and post-search refinements, the logic by which these options were displayed, and also the ranking of results to determine the extent to which it matched user expectations, both in cases like exact title and author searches and in more general searches.

The evaluation coordinators drafted a checklist to structure the evaluation of the tool's many functional elements. This allowed for systematic investigation of essential functionality. In most cases, this investigation was conducted through the approaches of exploring the interface or conducting test searches to establish the presence or absence of a given feature, and consulting documentation or vendor support staff. In this checklist, functional concerns were organized into six major areas.

Table 1. Technical evaluation checklist with sample requirements

Technical Feature	Important Issues
Hardware requirements	• Affects cost of ownership • Backup or development server may be desired • Hosted applications require no local hardware purchase • Tradeoff between cost and local control of environment
Operating system requirements	• Staff must be able to support the OS, keep up with patches, security, system monitoring • Overhead is different depending on a familiar OS vs. unfamiliar; bringing in a new OS will place additional demands on staff
Indexing performance and capacity	• Indexing may affect search performance, or require a dedicated indexing host if at a large scale • Complete re-index vs. incremental updates • Issues of scale with respect to the data (records or full text) and the number of simultaneous users
Search responsiveness	• Do the users perceive a performance problem?
Server downtime requirements	• Users increasingly expect 24 by 7 uptime • Locally-hosted systems may require some maintenance window
Ongoing maintenance requirements	• Regular backups • Frequency of software updates • Staff time required for software updates • Data management issues, e.g. regular imports
Staff skills required for ongoing operations and maintenance	• OS administration skills • Any required programming or scripting skills • Familiarity with application operation and configuration
Configuration options and customization	• Visual customization and branding • Display of data fields, labels • Choice of data types and sources to include in indexes
Support for importing local data, supported data formats	• Can key local collections or data sources of local significance be added? • Supported data formats (MARC, Dublin Core, etc.)

Integration APIs and output formats	• Possible to integrate with other applications:
	   o incorporate results into other systems
	   o launch searches into the discovery tool
	• Are the APIs well-documented? Do they conform to existing standards?
	• Ensure support for needed formats, e.g. XML APIs, SRU, RSS feeds, etc.

Browser requirements	• Must work equally well with all major Web browsers • Does not require JavaScript to be turned on

Throughout the evaluation the vendor liaison continuously relayed questions and problems to the vendor. The need to communicate clearly to the vendor forced the group to come to consensus regarding the specifics of any problem and exactly what it hoped to accomplish with a given change. Communications with the vendor illustrated the problems with specific, reproducible examples, and gave priority to concrete problems experienced by users, rather than vague or theoretical problems from librarians. The group assigned a high, medium, or low priority to each outstanding enhancement request and technical issue. Prioritization led the group to focus on what truly would help make better use of the product, and to move beyond a general list of dissatisfactions toward a well-articulated plan.

Interface Evaluation

The third area of evaluation focused on the interface provided for the tool, and whether the presentation would be conducive to the anticipated use cases. This was ascertained primarily through task-based usability testing. Student subjects worked through a series of representative research tasks

Table 2. Functional evaluation checklist

Functional Area	Specific Features

Content	• handling of content types, data formats, and metadata formats
	• coverage
	    o the range of particular article databases and electronic resources included in the index
	• stop words
	• language support
	    o non-english searching
	    o storage and display of non-english data
	    o support for unicode-encoded text.

Search	• advanced (or fielded) searching • Boolean searching • nested searching • wildcards and truncations.
Query expansion	• search suggestions • related or synonymous search terms • spelling suggestions • optional federated search features.
Results	• search performance • sorting options • deduping of results • support for export to citation management tools • search refinements • faceted browsing of results • relevance ranking
Record management	• saving searches and records • adding tags or personal content • annotation or manipulation of saved content.

Administration	• logging features
	    o search logs
	    o download logs
	• administrative interface and configuration options

using the tool, and each session was recorded for analysis. While some staff argued that usability testing was unnecessary because of testing done on the vendor side, this testing yielded an ample amount of useful feedback.

The evaluation group conducted two rounds of usability testing, the first round with a group of five student staff and the second with a group of eight non-staff students, mixed evenly between graduate and undergraduate participants. Using student staff may bias results to a degree, but the evaluation group deemed this sample of convenience adequate for an initial pass, given that the second round of testing would be more rigorous. These sample sizes hew to commonly accepted usability testing dictum that the researcher encoun-

ters diminishing returns in terms of the number of problems identified when going beyond a sample size of five participants (Nielsen, 2000). Student staff participants were allowed to earn their normal hourly wage for participating, and non-staff participants were offered gift cards worth $10 for approximately one hour of time.

The interface testing had three objectives:

1. Identify areas of the interface which were unclear or confusing.
2. Determine whether users could identify and use particular features of the search tool in cases where those features would be beneficial.

Table 3. Example interface evaluation tasks

Task	Type of Use	Features Targeted
Can you locate full text of the following article? Mary L. Dudziak, "Desegregation as a Cold War Imperative," 41 Stanford Law Review 61 (1988)	Known item search – full citation provided, Ability to locate full text	Simple Searching, Link Resolver
Your professor recommended an article for your paper, but you did not get the full citation. You remember that the author's last name was Molloy and the topic of the article is Asperger Syndrome. Can you track down this article?	Known item search – partial citation provided	Searching (possibly fielded), Limiters
You are writing a paper on the origins of language for a philosophy course. How might you find sources on the topic written in the discipline of philosophy, rather than linguistics or biology?	Subject search	Fielded or Boolean Searching, Subject limiters
You are working to prepare a summary of developments in the field of astronomy. Can you locate five articles on astronomy that were published in *Nature* in 2010?	Narrowing results	Use of limiters (pre- or post search)
Can you locate three reviews of the book *Imagined Communities* by Benedict Anderson?	Location of related materials (reviews)	Format limiters, Links to reviews on full records
Can you find the name of the journal in which the article "Basal **cell** carcinoma: **cell** of origin, cancer stem **cell** hypothesis and stem **cell** markers." appeared? Can you find the title of the article by J. Verne that appeared in the same issue?	Navigation of journal-level metadata	Issue trees, Journal title limiter

3. Determine whether users could succeed at typical article searching tasks using this search tool.

Tasks created for the study had to work at multiple levels to address these objectives concurrently. While all tasks provided the possibility of identifying problems with the interface itself (Objective 1, above), individual tasks targeted particular features (Objective 2), or common types of article searching needs (Objective 3). Some baseline article searching questions were included from previous studies, to provide some basis for comparison with previous evaluations. Most of the tasks had many possible solutions, but could benefit from use of a particular feature or features of the search tool. Tasks were not intended to force or guide participants to the use of specific features. Instead, each task had many possible solutions, and provided a potential opportunity to use various features.

The initial round of testing was conducted prior to the public trial of the tool, in order to identify the most prominent potential problems

for users and address them prior to more widespread exposure. Based on findings from the initial round of testing, some search limits and refinements which were found to have limited applicability were removed and the labels of others were changed to clarify their function. Though many subjects were looking for it, the Advanced Search was very difficult to find. Several general user search behaviors were observed with the product. For example, no user browsed beyond the first page of results (despite frequently encountering results sets in the millions), and no users consulted help features when attempting to learn to use the product. These observations led the evaluation team to recognize an elevated need for well developed relevance ranking, and for a clear interface that would be learnable through use, rather than through documentation.

The evaluation group conducted two rounds of usability testing, as usability literature suggests that significant usability issues can continue to be uncovered across multiple testing iterations. As long as enhancements are made after each round, progressive improvement of an interface can be accomplished. The tasks used for testing remain largely constant between iterations, so that the positive or negative impact of customizations on task outcomes can be determined. The second round of testing found the success rate for tasks to be quite high, but continued to uncover usability issues. For example, it was discovered that full text searching was enabled by default, even in cases where this was inappropriate or misleading (such as journal title searches). Another issue discovered was that users had difficulty exporting citations, due to a confusing label for this function on the full record page.

The team also solicited open comments from users during the public trial, in order to gauge general user interest and engagement with the tool. The interface was customized to include a prominent link in the header for user feedback, allowing passive collection of user feedback over the course of the evaluation. Over forty comments were submitted, and this feedback was over-whelmingly positive, supporting the premise that a different metasearch tool would improve article searching. One graduate student commented "This method of searching for journal articles is vastly superior to anything currently offered on the library Web site." Another claimed "This search engine produced far better results for my topic than google scholar™ or JSTOR®[7], etc. The ease of retrieval is a huge plus." This direct feedback helped to allay concerns of any potential negative reception of the search tool. If needed, further feedback from underrepresented user groups may be collected with targeted interviews.

Critique of Initial Evaluation

The initial evaluation plan, while generating ample useful information regarding the product, proved inadequate in answering four key questions about the product. First was the question of defining the anticipated use case. The evaluation needed to cover a significantly more complex set of use cases than just the novice article searcher.

Secondly, relevance ranking of results proved difficult to evaluate without a specific use case in mind. The third question was that of coverage. Ascertaining what resources could or should be included in this index was more complex than anticipated. In several instances, while it was technically feasible to include a resource in the index, including that resource was detrimental or distracting for users. For example, newspapers were found to be particularly distracting during testing, as was some digital content harvested from institutional collections via OAI. Consideration had to be devoted to decisions about what resources ought to make the cut for inclusion. Finally, there was the question of placement. What was the best way to integrate this application into the existing Web site and research tools? Could it be confusing to offer yet another means of accessing catalog data? Each of these questions necessitated revision of the initial evaluation plan, which will be detailed item by item.

A linear evaluation, proceeding from a fixed use case through each data-gathering step in turn, would be insufficient. An iterative model was needed, in which the team alternated between working on definition of use cases for the product and testing to gather more data about the capabilities and user interaction with the product. The more that was learned about what the product could do, the better the team could articulate how researchers might use the product and how the Library might best position it for students and researchers.. This in turn led to the development of more focused testing scenarios, which yielded more informative data. The major revelation was that, as resource discovery tools become increasingly flexible and expansive in their capabilities, defining a primary use case for benchmarking or structuring an evaluation becomes a more elusive proposition. Determining the use case(s) became a project objective in its own right, and required significant exploration and consensus-building.

There was not a single assumed use case built in to the product. Some libraries have evaluated

Table 4. Evaluation rubric for subject research

---

1. Core Databases
      a. List the most important core databases (up to five) that you would recommend to graduate students for research in your subject area.
      b. For each, indicate database name, whether the database is included in ArticlesPlus, and any notes or special considerations for this database.
2. Test Searches
      a. Please design two or three research topics that would be typical for a graduate student in your subject area. (These should include a broad search, a more focused search, and a search representative of something unique about research in this field.)
      b. Perform each search in ArticlesPlus, and then in your core databases for comparison.
      c. For each search, please describe the topic, search terms used, refinements or limits applied, and any comments regarding the search outcome.
3. Questions
      a. How would you rate the ArticlesPlus results (especially the first 25) for your searches?
      b. How did the results compare to your core databases?
      c. How did the results compare to more general tools like JSTOR or Google Scholar?
      d. In what kinds of cases would you recommend ArticlesPlus to graduate students in this subject area? If none, what changes would you like to see?
      e. Did you find the inclusion of catalog records to be an advantage or drawback? Are there any other resources that it would be particularly useful to include or remove?
      f. Please share any further comments that you have on ArticlesPlus.

---

our chosen tool as their primary catalog interface. This evaluation initially considered it primarily for novice searching of articles and online resources. However, library staff were very interested in use cases for more seasoned searchers. These users might be searching outside of their fields, or researching interdisciplinary topics for which there was no clear best database. Other staff suggested that the tool might be helpful even to experts conducting research in their own discipline.

To offer a complete assessment of the product, the evaluation expanded to consider each of these use cases. Library subject specialists were engaged to evaluate the tool's utility for each specific area. In order to gather comparable results from approximately twenty subject specialists evaluating close to forty subject areas, the evaluation group developed a rubric evaluation form to help structure this testing. The form prompted subject specialists to identify key databases and representative searches for their disciplines. Subject specialists would perform a set of representative searches and judge the results (and the relevance of the results) in comparison with the results in more focused databases, as well as in comparison with more general tools like JSTOR® or Google

Scholar™. Subject specialists were able to appraise where the absence of key resources made the tool less useful, and were able to pinpoint what resources would suffer the most due to aggregation in a central index.

This approach proved very helpful in addressing many problematic elements with the initial evaluation. The form streamlined the functional evaluation process down to a minimal number of steps (still assessing coverage, relevance, and comparison with similar tools), and allowed subject specialists to quickly iterate the evaluation process within the contexts of a variety of research areas. From the responses collected using this form, the evaluation team was able to identify patterns in search behavior across many different use cases. Across all subject areas, the tool was most frequently commended as excellent for interdisciplinary research, and generally as a starting point for research. The quality of results was deemed to be highest in the context of interdisciplinary fields such as history and sexuality studies. There were respectable ratings from the perspective of science, social science, and law research, while the tool was perceived as weaker for humanities research due to the absence, at that time, of key databases, like MLA.

The results collected through the evaluation form also contributed greatly to the assessment of the tool's coverage. While a large portion of the Library's licensed databases and electronic resources were indexed in this search tool, depth of coverage could vary by source. Some indexed materials were in included only in a "foundation index" specific to the product, rather than replicating the contents of one of the other database subscriptions. The team could not independently determine the contents of this "foundation index", but had to enlist the vendor to produce a report detailing its contents. The richness of metadata varied substantially, with some contents much more fully described than others. The availability of metadata affected the discoverability of included resources, and no comprehensive method exists for determining the level of metadata supplied for each source. Because of all of the variables involved, performing a comprehensive assessment of coverage of this metasearch tool, or comparing the coverage of multiple tools with any level of specificity remains problematic. Despite requests to the vendor, reporting options were inadequate to permit a comprehensive analysis of coverage.

The subject evaluation forms provided a more effective means of identifying content gaps. Subject specialists were asked to enumerate key databases and electronic resources for each field, and whether they were included in ArticlesPlus. By looking at the aggregate responses, the evaluation group was able to see the database content that was most frequently identified as both important and missing from ArticlesPlus across subject areas. Web of Science®[8], Lexis/Nexis®[9] Academic, and MLA were the resources most frequently indicated as essential, but not yet included in the tool's coverage (All have since been added.). While not a comprehensive assessment of coverage, this approach allowed the evaluation team to identify the highest priority gaps in coverage, and to work with the vendor to target those for future inclusion.

After determining what *could* be included in the index, there was the issue of what *should* be included. The assessment had to determine whether there were resources which could, by their inclusion, impede key use cases. The greatest concern was for the catalog records: would their inclusion clutter results lists and impede article searching, or allow for serendipitous discoveries? Again, this was an issue that resulted from the complexity of the tool, and its capacity for being optimized for many types of tasks. And in actual testing, the catalog records were not found to impede article searching. Other databases were clearly less useful in aggregation, such as indexes which covered specific musical compositions.

FUTURE RESEARCH DIRECTIONS

Creating an appropriate evaluation process is key to selecting and implementing a discovery tool that meets the needs of students, faculty and staff as well as the needs of the library's internal users. The current literature about discovery tool selection contains many good suggestions. The literature could be expanded to address the effectiveness of iterative evaluation methods, the applicability of results from peer libraries, and guidance on determining the scope of collections to be included in a discovery tool.

It is also important for libraries to tailor their evaluation to local needs. Given the flexibility and scope of current discovery tools, the understanding of these needs and how they might be met is likely to change and deepen during the evaluation. There is a need to develop agile, iterative methods for evaluating such flexible tools. As such methods are developed, it will be interesting to consider whether these methods should be applied to a broader spectrum of applications.

Iterative evaluation can be resource intensive, and libraries must determine what resources are appropriate to devote to evaluation. With this in mind, it may be possible to consider more lightweight approaches, or to identify areas where a peer institution's experiences might apply locally.

An area that has not been covered well in the literature is how these tools fit into user research behavior (e.g. do users stay within the discovery tool, or use it as a springboard to more specialized tools) and best practices for positioning the tool within a library's online offerings. To assist libraries as they plan for implementation, and to complement the user behavior data, decision points about the kinds of resources to be included in the discovery tool are needed. As more libraries implement discovery tools, this data will become accessible and present opportunities for research.

CONCLUSION

This consideration of evaluation methods is an early step in what is likely to be an ongoing process of refinement. The characteristics which make the current generation of resource discovery tools difficult to evaluate are likely to become only more pronounced in the future. As digital tools available to libraries gain additional flexibility, both in terms of the configuration of their search behaviors, and in their capacity to encompass heterogeneous resources, libraries will face more complex evaluations. Libraries must be prepare to shift to iterative approaches for evaluation, to continually refine assumptions about user needs while concurrently evaluating a product's capabilities.

REFERENCES

Avery, S., Ward, D., & Hinchliffe, L. J. (2007). Planning and implementing a federated searching system: An examination of the crucial roles of technical, functional, and usability testing. *Internet Reference Services Quarterly, 12*(1), 179–194. doi:10.1300/J136v12n01_09

Baer, W. (2004). Federated searching: Friend of foe? *College & Research Libraries News, 65*(9), 518–519.

Boss, S. C., & Nelson, M. L. (2005). Federated search tools: The next step in the quest for one-stop-shopping. *The Reference Librarian, 44*(91/92), 139–160. doi:10.1300/J120v44n91_10

Caswell, J. V., & Wynstra, J. D. (2010). Improving the search experience: Federated search and the library gateway. *Library Hi Tech, 28*(3), 391–401. doi:10.1108/07378831011076648

Cook, C., Heath, F., & Thompson, B. MaShana, D., Kyrillidou, M., & Webster, D. (2007). *LibQUAL+®️ 2007 survey: University of Chicago Library*. Washington, DC: Association of Research Libraries. Retrieved from http://www.lib.uchicago.edu/e/surveys/2007/UofCLibQUAL2007DataNotebook.pdf

Cook, C., Heath, F., Thompson, B., Askew, C., Hoseth, A., Kyrillidou, M., & Sousa, J. …Webster, D. (2004). *LibQUAL+ spring 2004 survey: University of Chicago Library*. Washington, DC: Association of Research Libraries.

Dorner, D. G., & Curtis, A. (2004). A comparative review of common user interface products. *Library Hi Tech, 22*(2), 182–197. doi:10.1108/07378830410543502

Nielsen, J. (2000). *Why you only need to test with 5 users*. Retrieved from http://www.useit.com/alertbox/20000319.html

Olson, T. A. (2007). Utility of a faceted catalog for scholarly research. *Library Hi Tech, 25*(4), 550–561. doi:10.1108/07378830710840509

Rowe, R. (2010). Web-scale discovery: A review of Summon, EBSCO Discovery Service, and WorldCat Local. *The Charleston Advisor, 12*(1), 5–10. doi:10.5260/chara.12.1.5

Tatarka, A. (2007). *LibQUAL+ survey 2007 results*. Retrieved from http://www.lib.uchicago.edu/e/surveys/2007/UofCLQSummary.pdf

Tatarka, A., Larsen, D., Olson, T., Schilt, M., & Twiss-Brooks, A. (2010). *Library survey 2010: Graduate and professional students*. Retrieved from http://www.lib.uchicago.edu/e/surveys/2010/Lbrary%20Survey%202010%20Full%20Report.pdf

Tennant, R. (2003). The right solution: Federated search tools. *Library Journal, 128*(11), 28–30.

University of Chicago Library. (2010). *Survey 2010 comments: E-resources*. Retrieved from http://www.lib.uchicago.edu/e/surveys/2010/comments/2010eresources.html

Wrubel, L., & Schmidt, K. (2007). Usability testing of a metasearch interface: A case study. *College & Research Libraries, 68*(4), 292–311.

ADDITIONAL READING

Borlund, P. (2003). The IIR evaluation model: A framework for evaluation of interactive information retrieval systems. *Information Research, 8*(3). Retrieved from http://informationr.net/ir/8-3/paper152.html

Cox, C. N. (Ed.). (2007). *Federated search: Solution or setback for online library services*. Binghamton, NY: Haworth Information Press.

Dumas, J. S., & Redish, J. C. (1999). *A practical guide to usability testing* (rev. ed.). Portland, OR: Intellect Books.

Gwizdka, J., & Lopatovska, I. (2009). The role of subjective factors in the information search process. *Journal of the American Society for Information Science and Technology, 60*(12), 2452–2464. doi:10.1002/asi.21183

Makri, S., Blandford, A., & Cox, A. L. (2008). Using information behaviours to evaluate the functionality and usability of electronic resources: From Ellis's model to resource evaluation. *Journal of the American Society for Information Science and Technology, 59*(14), 2244–2267. doi:10.1002/asi.20927

Nielsen, J. (1999). *Designing Web usability*. Indianapolis, IN: New Riders.

Rubin, J., & Chisnell, D. (2008). *Handbook of usability testing: How to plan, design, and conduct effective tests* (2nd ed.). Indianapolis, IN: Wiley.

Shneiderman, B. (2006). *Research-based Web design & usability guidelines*. Washington, DC: U.S. Government Printing Office.

Su, L. T. (1992). Evaluation measures for interactive information retrieval. *Information Processing & Management, 28*(4), 503–516. doi:10.1016/0306-4573(92)90007-M

Tenopir, C. (1980). Evaluation of library retrieval software. In *Communicating Information, Proceedings of the 43rd American Society for Information Science Annual Meeting*, Anaheim, CA, October 5-10, 1980, (pp. 64-67).

U.S. Department of Health and Human Services. (n.d.). *Usability.gov*. Retrieved from http://usability.gov/

Yang, S. Q., & Wagner, K. (2010). Evaluating and comparing discovery tools: How close are we towards next generation catalog? *Library Hi Tech, 28*(4), 690–709. doi:10.1108/07378831011096312

KEY TERMS AND DEFINITIONS

Aggregate Index: A search system where the records from many databases are merged into a single, larger database for the purpose of providing a single place to search for a wide variety of resources.

Application Programming Interface (API): A mechanism for software components to interact with each other. In a Web API,,the components interact via HTTP, and one component often asks the other to complete an action, perhaps a search, and return the results in a structured format.

Broadcast Search: A search mechanism where a user's search terms are sent to different databases and the results from the different databases are merged for presentation to the user. The term is used to emphasize the dependence on multiple database servers; these systems are subject to slow responses from the remote databases.

Deduping: The process of merging or removing duplicates when there is more than one record for an article or other resource.

Federated Search: A cross-database search, synonymous with broadcast search.

Metadata: Discrete units of information about articles or other resources represented in the metasearch database(s). Typical metadata elements include title, author, format, journal title, volume and issue number, pages, subject headings, keywords, and summary. Actual metadata elements and values vary across different providers.

Metasearch: A system that can perform a single search across a number of disparate resources, such as different article databases, catalog and digital library resources, regardless of how the search is implemented; includes both broadcast or federated search and aggregate index.

Use Case: The purpose, task or scenario under which a user approaches a resource discovery system.

ENDNOTES

[1] Google Scholar is a trademark of Google, Inc.

[2] LibQUAL+ is a registered trademark of the Association of Research Libraries.

[3] AquaBrowser is a registered trademark of Serials Solutions

[4] Summon is owned by ProQuest LLC

[5] EBSCO Discovery Service is owned by EBSCO Publishing Industries

[6] Worldcat is a registered trademark of OCLC

[7] JSTOR is a registered trademark of ITHAKA

[8] Web of Science is a registered trademark of Thomson Reuters.

[9] LexisNexis is a registered trademark of LexisNexis, a division of Reed Elsevier Inc.

Section 3
The User Experience Part One:
User Behavior and Expectations

Ken Varnum
University of Michigan, USA

OVERVIEW

Almost everything libraries choose to offer to their patrons is based on an implicit or explicit understanding of user needs and a desire to meet, or exceed, those needs. These understandings of user behavior are too often implicit, particularly in emerging technologies such as Web-scale resource discovery. This is such a new area for most libraries that knowing how to research user needs in this area, interpret the results, and implement solutions to match can seem daunting. The chapters in this section of the book help define processes that can lead to improved explicit understandings of user expectations, needs, and results.

This section starts with a chapter that helps us develop an understanding of the basic need that resource discovery tools seek to fulfill. In "Resource Discovery Tools: Supporting Serendipity," Tammera Race explores the concept of serendipity in resource discovery tools. After developing a definition of "serendipity," Ms. Race reviews specific serendipity-enhancing features in resource discovery tools to explore which are most likely to enhance serendipity.

The next chapter, "User Search Activities within an Academic Library Gateway: Implications for Web-scale Discovery Systems," by William Mischo, Mary Schlembach, Joshua Bishoff, and Elizabeth German, continues the user-driven model and explores the effect a discovery environment has on the user's searching activity. What kinds of searches to users do in a discovery environment, and how do these searches differ from traditional searches? What do users do with the search results – where do they click, and what kinds of resources do they pick? This thorough study of user behavior, based on an analysis of thousands of individual queries and following user actions, provides information that will strengthen any library's resource discovery implementation effort.

In "Setting a Direction for Discovery: A Phased Approach," Janet Fransen, Lara Friedman-Shedlov, Nicole Theis-Mahon, Stacie Traill, and Deborah Boudewyns describe a four-year effort at the University of Minnesota to carefully define what discoverability means for their library and campus, develop a vision and best practices for discovery, and, in the latest phase, to define an RFP for a unified discovery platform. Through their work, the Minnesota librarians have defined the need for exposing local content as well as more traditional catalog data, defined personas that fit the Minnesota user community, and outlined a Software as a Service model for providing a unified discovery environment.

The following chapter, "Developing a User-Centered Article Discovery Environment" by Suzanne Chapman, Scott Dennis, Kathleen Folger, and Ken Varnum, describes a review of discovery tools from a user-centric perspective. This chapter outlines a process for determining local user needs, reviewing products, and making a selection that focuses on the specific user communities a library might serve.

The final chapter in this section, "Replicating Top Users' Searches in Summon and Google Scholar," by David Noe, analyzes result quality through a comparison of search results from his institute's implementation of Summon and from Google Scholar to determine which tool, if either, is the better "one-stop shop" for research. This comparison is valuable to almost any library trying to decide whether to use a free product (Google Scholar) or invest in a commercial service (such as Summon).

These five chapters provide a solid grounding for reviewing, implementing, and measuring the success of a discovery system.

Chapter 9
Resource Discovery Tools:
Supporting Serendipity

Tammera M. Race
Western Kentucky University, USA

ABSTRACT

Serendipity, the accidental discovery of something useful, plays an important role in discovery and the acquisition of new knowledge. The process and role of serendipity varies across disciplines. As library collections have become increasingly digital faculty lament the loss of serendipity of browsing library stacks. Resource discovery tools may have features that support serendipity as part of information seeking. A comparison of four commercial Web-scale discovery tools, Online Computer Library Center (OCLC) WorldCat® Local[1], Serials Solution[2]® Summon[3]™, ExLibris[4]® Primo Central[5]™, and EBSCO Discovery Services (EDS)[6]™, links product features to characteristics that support serendipitous discovery. However, having such features is only part of the equation. Educators need to include serendipity in discussions about the research process. Future research opportunities include determining whether serendipity can be encouraged, evaluating its occurrence in the web scale environment, and studying serendipity in relation to research instruction.

INTRODUCTION

What is serendipity? A common thread of all discussions is the perception that accident creates an opportunity. Observation and research show that serendipity plays a role in discovery across many disciplines, and may be a manifestation and/or a trait of creative research. Although these serendipitous discoveries can be significant in original thinking and advancement in different fields, serendipity is both lauded and condemned as a research strategy. Serendipity is also difficult to quantify. However, studies of user behavior positively support the role of serendipitous

DOI: 10.4018/978-1-4666-1821-3.ch009

discovery as part of the research process. If we recognize that serendipity plays an important role, then we should ask how resource discovery tools can foster meaningful serendipitous discovery. Do some tools promote a discovery environment that encourages the searcher to be creative, to be open to accidental discovery?

The mission of this chapter is to explore whether some characteristics of commercial web scale discovery products may enhance opportunities for meaningful serendipitous discovery. To this end, this chapter will:

- Present comments in the literature relating to serendipity and discovery
- Discuss recent and current studies in searching behavior that recognize serendipity in the search process
- Using published articles and promotional materials, compare four commercial web scale discovery products with respect to features that support serendipity
- Suggest opportunities for research and evaluation of resource discovery tools with respect to users, search behaviors, and serendipity.

A FIELD DESCRIPTION OF SERENDIPITY

"Serendipity [noun]: the occurrence and development of events by chance in a happy or beneficial way" (Stevenson, 2010). Merton and Barber (2004) describe Horace Walpole's creation of the word "serendipity." Key to Walpole's coinage of the term was accident, "sagacity" (Merton & Barber, 2004, p.2), and discovery of something useful that was previously unsought. Since 1754 when Walpole coined the term, serendipity has proven difficult to define and quantify. However, researchers know serendipity when they encounter it (McBirnie, 2008). Based on author accounts of

historic discoveries, information seeking strategies, and their own experiences, serendipity is:

- Accidental, random, unpredictable (McBirnie, 2008; Hoeflich, 2007; Hoffman, 2005)
- Elusive (McBirnie, 2008; Foster and Ford, 2003)
- Positive, exciting, fulfilling (McBirnie, 2008; Hoelfich, 2007; Hoffman, 2005)
- A rare, but regular, occurrence (McBirnie, 2008).

In her studies of information seeking behavior, McBirnie (2008) notes that serendipity can be an active occurrence (a "happening upon"; p.607) or a passive occurrence (a "happening"; p.607).-

"Serendipity is fundamental to all science, especially the most creative and important" (Friedel, 2001, p. 37). In their literature review, Foster and Ford (2003) demonstrate that serendipity is fundamental not only to scientific research, but to social sciences and humanities research, and artistic endeavors. Accidental discovery presents new information that changes perspective and courses of action (Johnson, 2010; Guha, 2009; McBirnie, 2008). Studies of information seeking behavior document that serendipity stimulates creativity by illustrating new connections, connections that were not consciously anticipated by the researcher. Foster and Ford (2003) note that serendipitous discovery is especially important across different disciplines. Erdelez (1999) also describes serendipity as leading to opportunities for "cross-pollination" (Erdelez, 1999, p.4) of concepts. Accidental discovery in information seeking supports creative thinking by fostering novel connections and frameworks (Nutefall & Ryder, 2010). Researchers tend to discount serendipity because it is not viewed as a formal search strategy (Erdelez, 1999; Liestman, 1992). However, recent studies emphasize that accidental discovery of information is a key piece of information research (Erdelez & Makri, 2011).

"Serendipity is a form of chance. It is a chance event with a positive outcome" (Lightman, 2006, p.33). Certain factors nurture serendipity. Chief among these is chance, or luck (McBirnie, 2008; Hannan, 2006). Gest (1997) attributes serendipity to the hard work and persistence of the researcher. Similarly, many authors describe serendipity as dependent on the researcher's state of mind. These individual characteristics include:

- A sense of curiosity or wonder (Hoffman, 2005; Gest, 1997)
- A prepared mind (sagacity), knowledgeable enough to recognize opportunity (Rubin, Burkell, Quan-Haase, 2011; Hoeflich, 2007; Lightman, 2006; Hoffman, 2005; Gest, 1997)
- An open, flexible mind (McBirnie, 2008; Hoelfich, 2007; Hannan, 2006; Lightman, 2006; Hoffman, 2005)
- An observant mind (Rubin, Burkell, Quan-Haase, 2011; Lightman, 2006).

Serendipity in information seeking combines chance, perceptions, and process (McBirnie, 2008). Without the proper mix, serendipitous discovery and the creative breakthroughs that it supports, will not occur.

Serendipity and Scholarship

Serendipity plays an important role in the research process in at least four major ways. For students, the concept of serendipity demonstrates that the process of discovery has a personal component. Serendipitous occurrences are partially dependent on what experience and prior knowledge an individual brings to the table, and how they determine relevance (Beale, 2007; Steinerova, 2007; Cosign and Bothma, 2006; Campos and deFigueiredo, 2001; Kennedy, Cole, and Carter, 1999). Awareness of the possibility of serendipity emphasizes personal exploration, helping the student take ownership of the research. This ownership gener-

ates the energy critical to creating a final, original product (Kennedy, Cole, Carter, 1999).

Another aspect of serendipitous discovery that is important to both novice and accomplished researchers is the positive reinforcement gained from accidental discovery. Serendipity can energize the search by overcoming negative feelings generated by failed searches and providing stimulus for continuing the process (Erdelez, 1999). In addition, researchers may become more confident, bolstered by useful information gained accidentally and unexpectedly (Erdelez, 1999).

Serendipity is key to creative scholarship. Nutefall and Ryder (2010) note that "serendipity is a method of research that many academics have incorporated into their own information seeking behavior" (p. 232). In their 2003 study, Foster and Ford found that serendipity "emerged as an important aspect of how researchers encounter information and generate new ideas" (p. 337). Serendipity can help new ways of looking at issues and problems, and novel connections between fields of knowledge (Foster & Ford, 2003; Erdelez, 1999). Accidental information discovery may also act to confirm a particular research path or concept (Foster & Ford, 2003).

Finally, for information literacy educators, awareness of the role of serendipity is important to the research interview process. George (2005) declares that "the entire information seeking endeavor is a grand, messy process of inquiry and education, which may be uncontrollable, unpredictable, and quite possibly serendipitous" (p. 384). She encourages reference librarians to embrace large sets of search results as a key part of the undergraduate research process, rather than attempting to prematurely narrow a topic.

Research on Serendipitous Information Discovery

Research on serendipitous information discovery focuses on user perceptions and search processes, including the systems that support such processes.

For example, many authors note the link between browsability of print resources and serendipity (Nutefall & Ryder, 2010; Johnson, 2010; Hoeflich, 2007; Gup, 1997; Liestman, 1992). The following examples illustrate how aspects of information retrieval tools can support serendipitous discovery.

Browsable systems are often described in conjunction with serendipity. O'Connor (1988) discusses "creative browsing" (p. 203) as a means of uncovering new knowledge and making unique connections. In contemplating a system that supports creative browsing, O'Connor notes, "The person seeking at the frontiers of knowledge may well require a system or environment which is not anchored to existing knowledge and relationships" (p. 205). Such a system could encourage serendipity in a number of ways. Rapid retrieval of a large number of results provides options (key to creative browsing), and allows the user to narrow the search as needed. In order to evaluate the options, there should be ways to study the attributes of the results. Transparency of document structure can help indicate selection points, and classification can help with navigation. O'Connor also describes the value of communicating with other users, by incorporating commentary and user profiles. O'Connor's vision is one of a "connections system" (p. 210) that supports creativity.

Rice (1988) describes the discovery potential of browsing Online Public Access Catalogs (OPACs). Maximizing access via many points is one way to promote discovery, including serendipitous discovery. OPACs offer many different ways to find information, thus providing more discovery opportunities than print resources. Rice (1988) also discusses browsable search indexes and similar article citation retrieval as encouraging serendipitous discovery.

Ford, O'Hara, and Whiklo (2009) translate the browsability of print resources to electronic resources. Using Library of Congress class numbers as filing points and vendor book covers, the authors created an electronic reference bookshelf.

In addition, they included tagging by users, another avenue to create discovery opportunities.

Kennedy, Cole, and Carter (1999) recognize the value of large pools of results to exploration. In their study of undergraduates, the authors stress that a state of prefocus is necessary in order for students to understand the context of an issue, and to take ownership of a topic. During this state of prefocus, students benefit from broad searches, which they can gradually narrow as they move to becoming more focused. Kennedy, Cole, and Carter identify a need for better presentation of large citation lists to facilitate exploration.

Other researchers have looked at serendipity in relation to research on the Web. Campos and deFigueiredo (2001) created Max, a web browsing agent, designed to provide the user with "unexpected information" (p.162) as a jumpstart to creativity. Recognizing that serendipitous information discovery is very personal, Campos and deFigueiredo programmed Max to search based on user profiles. Using randomly selected words from these profiles, Max wandered the Web, looking for previously undiscovered information that might be of interest. Early results showed that Max could find unexpected information that changed research directions or stimulated different interests. These preliminary results support the idea of "programming for serendipity" (Campos & deFigueiredo, 2001, p. 163).

Toms (2002) focused on Web research in facilitating serendipitous information retrieval. In her study, users were provided with ten news articles, generated in response to an information request. This list included articles that were similar to and different from the initial information request. Participants described valuable accidental information encounters stimulated by the suggested articles. The results of Toms' research also indicate that serendipitous discovery can be evoked by system design.

Interactive Information Retrieval Studies

Interactive information retrieval studies look at personalizing the search experience, offering support for the subjective aspects searching. Beale (2007) created two systems that apply interactive information retrieval and facilitate personalized discovery in order to create "a more serendipitous environment" (p. 433). The Haiku system presents raw data visually, by linked data relationships. Users can comfortably explore while the system keeps and displays a history of the navigations. The second system, Mitsikeru, supports Internet browsing. Using word frequencies found on the pages visited, Mitsikeru builds a master table for each browsing session. The system maximizes the user's options by presenting all of the search results for evaluation, but the most relevant results are coded differently. Both systems support interaction between the user and the ambient intelligence of the system.

Cosign and Bothma (2006) describe the need for interactive information retrieval to support the subjective aspects of relevance. Standard information retrieval systems typically determine relevance by algorithms or topical relations. However, users determine relevance on cognitive, situational and socio-cognitive levels. Of these, cognitive relevance, the relation between the knowledge state of the user and the information being evaluated, is most related to serendipitous information discovery. Cognitive relevance describes the prepared mind necessary for serendipity to occur. Because cognitive relevance will change throughout the search process, system supports need to be dynamic and responsive to changes in determining relevance.

Tools that allow researchers to broaden and narrow searches, and work back and forth (recursively) as they create their search process promote discovery, including accidental discovery (Nutefall and Ryder, 2010; Steinerova, 2007; Kennedy, Cole and Carter, 1999). In a study of doctoral students, Steinerova (2007) begins with the assumption that relevance assessments are specific personal experiences, not results of algorithms. In addition, this study demonstrates that discovery experiences vary with each individual. The author describes the specific potential characteristics of the electronic environment that can support subjective relevance judgments. These characteristics include: flexibility in navigation and interaction, opportunities to present information visually, collective processing of information, and tools for backtracking to support non-linear searches. In order to support individualized experiences, Steinerova recommends that information retrieval systems focus less on locating information and more on providing "features of ranking, relating, and recommending" (Steinerova, 2007, p. 50).

Stevenson, Tuohy, and Norrish (2008) describe an example of enhancing resource discovery using the hypertextuality of digital resources. In designing a delivery framework consisting of a metadata repository implemented using ISO Topic Map technology, the authors created a system that mimics the browsability, the "structured serendipity" (Stevenson et al., 2008, p.1) of print collections. The topic map, using data harvested from texts in a digital resource collection, generates a graph of interconnections between people, places, and texts. These interconnections are displayed as hyperlinks, a browsable framework for navigation. This framework is dynamic, flexible, and supports non-linear exploration. All of these characteristics encourage accidental knowledge discovery.

Serendipity and Resource Discovery

Liestman (1992) cites Swanson's (1986) description of information retrieval as "a creative trial-an-error process, ...a vital span in the bridge" between conscious experience and information resources" (p. 108). Liestman continues that "serendipity is a component of this linkage" (p.525). The physical arrangement of books has been described as facilitating browsing, supporting serendipitous discovery (Johnson, 2010). McBirnie (2008) adds that serendipitous discovery is not limited to browsing, but can occur while seeking specific information as well. Toms (2000) concludes that digital libraries must provide opportunities for "serendipitous interactions" (Toms, 2000, p.3). Browsing physical collections is just one of the possible manifestations of serendipitous interaction offered by information resources. Resource discovery tools can offer other possibilities.

Based on the research examples discussed above (Research on Serendipitous Information Discovery and Interactive Information Retrieval Studies), it is possible to describe resource discovery tools which could foster serendipitous discovery. Such systems would provide many options with maximized access to resources. This access would be balanced with classification and structures that help to build connections yet minimize restrictions to exploration. Opportunities to make connections would be supported by ways to narrow large sets of results, suggestions for additional potential sources, tools for backtracking, and visual representations. Ideally these features would support interactions between the user and the system. In addition, recognizing that informal environments support serendipitous discovery, there would be ways to collaborate and communicate with other users.

TOOLS FOR SERENDIPITY

Comparing Characteristics of Web Scale Discovery Tools

"To discover something is to uncover that which is not in view" (Friedel, 2001, p. 37). Commercial web scale discovery products evolved to solve the problem of how to provide rapid access to large bodies of information across various formats and collections in the simplest way possible. The pragmatic approach has been to preaggreate multiple types of content, to index these collections, and to

develop algorithms to determine relevance rankings. Each product differs as to indexing methods, algorithm components, and collection scope, but basically solves the overarching problem in very similar ways.

Given their predetermined structure, how well can these tools support the subjective aspects of searching, including those which foster serendipitous discovery? McBirnie (2008) notes that users describe serendipity as occurring in informal environments, more so than when using highly controlled systems. Yuan and Belkin (2010) point out that standard information retrieval systems emphasize support for specific searching rather than strategies that are more cognitive, affective, and situational. They describe interactive information retrieval as key to supporting the subjective aspects, not just the algorithmic aspects of searching.

A sample of current commercial web scale discovery tools shows that while such tools have yet to achieve the level of interactive information retrieval described by Yuan and Belkin (2010), these tools do have features that can support serendipitous discovery. Table 1 summarizes these features for OCLC WorldCat® Local, Serials Solution Summon™, ExLibris Primo Central™, and EBSCO Discovery Services (EDS)™. The list of tool features that support serendipity is a compilation of features described in reviews of the literature (see Research on Serendipitous Information Discovery and Interactive Information Retrieval Studies in this chapter). The table summarizes those characteristics that encourage accidental discovery. Published literature about each product, vendor web sites, and working examples were used to determine the presence or absence of these characteristics at the time of writing this chapter.

Maximizing Access

The goal of web scale discovery tools is to traverse barriers between information silos. In that

Table 1. Summary of web-scale discovery tool features that support serendipity

Tool Features that Support Serendipity*	OCLC WorldCat Local	Serials Solution Summon	ExLibris Primo Central	EBSCO Discovery Services
Access maximized	+	+	+	+
Metadata included in indexing	-	+	+	+
Browsability	+	+	+	+
Faceted browsing	+	+	+	+
Interactive browsing support	-	+	-	+
Suggests other resources	-	+	+	-
Hypertext links	-	+	+	+
Searches across full text	-	+	+	+
Stores searches for later sessions	+	-	+	+
Supports strategy change (i.e. "bread crumbs trail")	+	-	+	+
Supports changes in search scope	+	+	+	+
Visualization of results (graphic representation)	-	-	-	+
Social networking tools (includes option to share information via social and/or bookmarking sites)	+	-	+	+
Supports user input (i.e. tagging, reviews, suggestions)	+	-	+	-
OCLC WorldCat Local® (Vaughan, 2011; Rowe, 2010; Yang & Wagner, 2010) Website: www.oclc.org/us/en/worldcatlocal/defauly.htm Example: http://www.lib.washington.edu/				
Serials Solution Summon (Vaughan, 2011; Bhatnagar et al., 2010; Rowe, 2010; Yang & Wagner, 2010; Hadro, 2009) Website: www.serialssolutions.com/summon Example: www.library.drexel.edu				
ExLibris Primo Central (Vaughan, 2011; Yang & Wagner, 2010; Breeding, 2007) Website: www.exlibrisgroup.com/category/PrimoCentral Example: http://search.library.northwestern.edu				
EBSCO Discovery Services (Vaughan, 2011; Rower, 2010) Website: www.ebscohost.com/discovery Example: http://www.lib.jmu.edu				
*+ = present, - = absent				

sense, they maximize access by indexing and providing access to bodies of information across disciplines, locations, formats, and publishers. This information includes resources of all types, such as journal articles, books, book chapters, and open access resources. However, boundaries do exist, and each vendor/library relationship defines the applicable boundaries i.e. which collections are included. Similarly, each tool maximizes information access points, but not necessarily by the same method. WorldCat® Localsearches are built on information collected from MARC record fields. Summon™, Primo Central™, and EDS ™ searches are built on information collected from metadata and full text. Each vendor has different ways of developing and collecting the metadata. Each tool has access limitations, but the options for discovery are maximized in many ways.

Creative Connections: Browsability, Facets, Interactive Browsing

Classification and structure can provide opportunities that foster accidental discovery and encourage creative connections. All four tools support browsing, and include enriched content such as book covers. As noted by Ford, O'Hara, and Whiklo (2009), including such enriched content can approximate the types of cues important to browsing in the physical environment. In addition, all four products support faceted browsing. Summon™ and EDS™ take faceted browsing one step further, allowing users to manipulate choices within the same facet or subject category. Support for interactive browsing is an effective feature for interpreting large data sets.

Creative Connections: Recommendations, Hypertext Links, Full Text Searches, Saved Searches

Other opportunities to make connections include the database recommender function when browsing with Summon, and the hyperlinked suggested searches offered by Primo Central™. WorldCat® Local, Primo Central™, and EDS™ allow searches to be saved between sessions. In Summon™, searches can be exported to be saved elsewhere.

Exploration: Adjusting Scope, Changing Strategy

All four tools support changes in the search scope, providing ways to broaden or narrow a search. WorldCat® Local, Primo Central™, and EDS™ also support changes in search strategy with a "bread crumbs trail" located on the search page. EDS™ includes a "search history" button to help with recursive searching. Such features encourage exploration and flexibility in searching.

Interpreting Large Result Sets: Graphic Representation

EDS™ is the only one of the four tools that has a significant visual component. The EDS™ Visual Search presents search results in blocks or columns. Results can be grouped according to subject or publication name, sorted by date or relevance, or filtered by date. The block view supports interactive search mapping. Although this feature is readily available, it is up to the library system administrator to decide if it is activated, and whether the block or column view is presented. Large result sets can facilitate serendipitous discovery, and tools that graphically represent results can be helpful to interpretation.

Social Networking Tools and User Input

Informal information sharing environments support serendipitous discovery. All four of these tools include some means of collaborating and communicating. WorldCat® Local and Primo Central™ provide for user contributions such as tagging or reviews. WorldCat®, Primo Central™, and EDS™ users can share information via social and/or bookmarking sites. Summon™ is the most limited; Summon™ allows users to e-mail items but it is not integrated with social networking sites.

Features Summary

The primary mission of commercial web scale discovery tools is to reduce the number of less relevant results retrieved, while maximizing the number of most relevant results, according to proprietary algorithms to ensure precision. However, there are other design aspects that are more critical to supporting serendipity. Large result sets can stimulate accidental information discovery. More emphasis on designing features to help users interpret large result sets, such as interactive browsing support and graphic representation of results, would better support serendipity. In addition, resource discovery tools can become more serendipity-friendly by building social networking tools into their products and including opportunities for informal information sharing. By being aware of the importance of serendipity and its link to certain features, web scale tool designers can consider a holistic approach, one that values precision but recognizes that the creative process often requires something less precise.

Solutions and Recommendations

Based on the features of WorldCat® Local, Summon™, Primo Central™, and EDS™, web scale discovery tools have potential to encourage serendipitous discovery. There are options to support recursive searches, creative browsing, and communication and collaboration. When features such as the EDS™ Visual Search are made available, discovery tools are even better suited for serendipity.

Designing appropriate tool features helps to support the process part of serendipity. Librarians and other educators have a role in supporting the perception part of serendipity. Although web scale discovery tools possess features that can encourage serendipitous discovery, the implied message of the single search box is that the research process consists of defining one magic query. For students beginning their academic career, a discovery tool search box may resemble a short answer test rather than a gateway to creative exploration.

Kennedy, Cole, and Carter (1999) emphasize the need for researchers to take the time to review large sets of results. Anderson (2010) describes the importance of being in a state of ambiguity in order to be creative. Teaching students to be aware of serendipity as part of the research process (Nutefall & Ryder, 2010; McBirnie, 2008) demonstrates the reality of research: it is time-consuming, recursive, and a personal experience.

FUTURE RESEARCH DIRECTIONS

Web scale discovery tools offer many opportunities for learning more about serendipity and information discovery. Some authors have asked whether serendipity can be encouraged (Liestman, 1992), and proposed that information "encountering" be evaluated in different information retrieval environments (Erdelez, 1999; p.1). Pursuing these questions in the context of current tools would help to guide future design, especially in relation to interactive information retrieval. For example, asking "super-encounterers" (Erdelez, 1999) to describe their serendipitous discoveries while using different web-scale discovery tools would demonstrate how existing features support serendipity, and offer guidance for improving. More recently, McCay-Peet and Toms (2011) identify core elements that support serendipity in digital environments. Asking users to evaluate web scale discovery tools according to these elements would help quantify whether certain tools are more serendipity-friendly.

Opportunities also exist in examining the role and impact of research instruction on accidental discovery in the web scale discovery environment. In addition, documenting how researchers at different stages of their "learning life" (Bent, Gannon-Leary, Webb, 2007) view and take advantage of serendipitous discovery could inform research instruction methods and discovery tools design.

CONCLUSION

WorldCat® Local, Summon™, Primo Central™, and EDS™ Web-scale tools facilitate access across boundaries and provide many access points. By doing so, these web scale discovery tools provide many options for serendipitous discovery. In addition, each tool includes specific features, such as faceted browsing and user supplied tags that can encourage serendipity. Future designs could better serve serendipity by providing ways to interpret large sets of results, such as features that help to visualize connections. Additionally, incorporating more interactive features would support the subjective aspects of determining relevance, a key component of serendipity.

Tool design is just part of creating a search environment favorable to serendipity. Educators need to articulate and demonstrate that research is a process, not a query. Describing serendipity as a valid and important part of research depicts research more realistically, as a dynamic process. If researchers approach information seeking as an issue of rapid problem resolution, rather than one of exploration, then system characteristics that support serendipity will fall short of their potential to inspire creative discovery.

REFERENCES

Anderson, T. D. (2010). Kickstarting creativity: Supporting the productive faces of uncertainty in information practice. *Information Research, 15*(4). Retrieved from http://www.eric.ed.gov/PDFS/EJ912765.pdf

Beale, J. (2008). The weaknesses of full-text searching. *Journal of Academic Librarianship, 34*(5), 438–444. doi:10.1016/j.acalib.2008.06.007

Beale, R. (2007). Supporting serendipity: Using ambient intelligence to augment user exploration for data mining and web browsing. *International Journal of Human-Computer Studies, 65*(5), 421–433. doi:10.1016/j.ijhcs.2006.11.012

Bent, M., Gannon-Leary, P., & Webb, J. (2007). Information literacy in a researcher's learning life: The seven ages of research. *New Review of Information Networking, 13*(2), 81–99. doi:10.1080/13614570801899983

Bhatnagar, G., Dennis, S., Duque, G., Henry, S., MacEachern, M., Teasley, S., & Varum, K. (2010). *Article discovery working group final report.* University of Michigan Library. Retrieved from http://www.lib.umich.edu/files/adwg/final-report.pdf

Björneborn, L. (2008). Serendipity dimensions and users' information behavior in the physical library interface. *Information Research, 13*(4). Retrieved from http://InformationR.net/ir/13-4/paper370.html

Breeding, M. (2007). Primo. *Library Technology Reports, 43*(4), 28–32.

Campos, J., & de Figueiredo, A. D. (2001). Searching the unsearchable: Inducing serendipitous insights. In R. Weber & C. Gresse (Eds.), *Proceedings of the Workshop Program at the Fourth International Conference on Case-Based Reasoning, ICCBR 2001, Technical Note AIC-01-003* (pp. 159-164). Washington, DC: Naval Research Laboratory, Navy Center for Applied Research in Artificial Intelligence.

Cosijn, E. E., & Bothma, T. T. (2006). Contexts of relevance for information retrieval system design. *South African Journal of Library and Information Science, 72*(1), 27–34.

Erdelez, S. (1999). Information encountering: It's more than just bumping into information. *Bulletin of the American Society for Information Science, 25*(3). Retrieved from http://www.asis.org/Bulletin/Feb-99/erdelez.html

Erdelez, S., & Makri, S. (2011). Introduction to the thematic issue on opportunistic discovery of information. *Information Research, 16*(3). Retrieved from http://informationr.net/ir/16-3/odiintro.html

Ford, L., O'Hara, L. H., & Whiklo, J. (2009). Shelflessness as a virtue: Preserving serendipity in an electronic reference collection. *Journal of Electronic Resources Librarianship, 21*(3/4), 251–262. doi:10.1080/19411260903466558

Foster, A., & Ford, N. (2003). Serendipity and information seeking: An empirical study. *The Journal of Documentation, 59*(3), 321–340. doi:10.1108/00220410310472518

Friedel, R. (2001). Serendipity is no accident. *The Kenyon Review, 23*(2), 36–46.

George, J. (2005). Socratic inquiry and the pedagogy of reference: Serendipity in information seeking. In *ACRL Twelfth National Conference: Currents and convergence: Navigating the rivers of change* (pp. 380-387). Chicago, IL: American Library Association. Retrieved from http://www.ala.org/ala/mgrps/divs/acrl/conferences/pdf/george05.pdf

Gest, H. (1997). Serendipity in scientific discovery: A closer look. *Perspectives in Biology and Medicine, 41*(1), 21–28.

Guha, M. (2009). Serendipity versus the superorganism. *Journal of Mental Health (Abingdon, England), 18*(4), 277–279. doi:10.1080/09638230903078669

Gup, T. (1997, November 21). The end of serendipity. *The Chronicle of Higher Education, 44*(13), A52.

Hannan, P. J. (2006). *Serendipity, luck and wisdom in research.* Lincoln, NE: iUniverse, Inc.

Hoeflich, M. H. (2007). Serendipity in the stacks, fortuity in the archives. *Law Library Journal, 99*(4), 813–827.

Hoffman, R. (2005). Serendipity, the grace of discovery. *Innovation (Abingdon), 5*(2), 68–69.

Johnson, I. M. (2010). Supporting serendipity? *Information Development, 26*(3), 202–203. doi:10.1177/0266666910376211

Kennedy, L., Cole, C., & Carter, S. (1999). The false focus in inline searching: The particular case of undergraduates seeking information for course assignments in the Humanities and Social Sciences. *Reference and User Services Quarterly, 38*(3), 267–273.

Liestman, D. (1992). Chance in the midst of design: approaches to library research serendipity. *Research Quarterly, 31*(4), 524–532.

Lightman, A. (2006). Wheels of fortune. *Science & Spirit, 17*(3), 28–33. doi:10.3200/SSPT.17.3.28-33

McBirnie, A. (2008). Seeking serendipity: The paradox of control. *Aslib Proceedings: New Information Perspectives, 60*(6), 600–618. doi:doi:10.1108/00012530810924294

McCay-Peet, L., & Toms, E. (2011). Measuring the dimensions of serendipity in digital environments. *Information Research, 16*(3), 1-6. Retrieved from http://www.eric.ed.gov/PDFS/EJ946482.pdf

Merton, R. K., & Barber, E. (2004). *The travels and adventures of serendipity: A study in sociological semantics and the sociology of science.* Princeton, NJ: Princeton University Press.

Nutefall, J., & Ryder, P. M. (2010). The serendipitous research process. *Journal of Academic Librarianship, 36*(3), 228–234. doi:10.1016/j.acalib.2010.03.005

O'Connor, B. (1988). Fostering creativity: Enhancing the browsing environment. *International Journal of Information Management, 8*(3), 203–210. doi:10.1016/0268-4012(88)90063-1

Rice, J. (1988). Serendipity and holism: The beauty of OPACs. *Library Journal, 113*(3), 138–141.

Rowe, R. (2010). Web-Scale discovery: A review of Summon, EBSCO Discovery Service, and WorldCat Local. *The Charleston Advisor, 12*(1), 5–10. doi:10.5260/chara.12.1.5

Rubin, V. L., Burkell, J., & Quan-Haase, A. (2011). Facets of serendipity in everyday chance encounters: A grounded theory approach to blog analysis. *Information Research, 16*(3). Retrieved from http://informationr.net/ir/16-3/paper488.html

Steinrová, J. (2007). Relevance assessment for digital libraries. *Mousaion, 25*(2), 37–57.

Stevenson, A. (Ed.). (2010). *Serendipity. Oxford Dictionary of English*. Oxford Reference Online.

Stevenson, A., Tuohy, C., & Norrish, J. (2008). Ambient findability and structured serendipity: Enhanced resources discovery for full text collections. *IATUL Proceedings, 2008*, 1–10.

Swanson, D. R. (1986). Undiscovered public knowledge. *The Library Quarterly, 56*(2), 103–118. doi:10.1086/601720

Toms, E. G. (2000). Serendipitous information retrieval. *Proceedings of the First DELOS Network of Excellence Workshop on Information Seeking, Searching and Querying in Digital Libraries* (pp. 11-12). Sophia Antipolis, France: European Research Consortium for Informatics and Mathematics.

Vaughan, J. (2011). Ebsco Discovery services. *Library Technology Reports, 47*(1), 30–38.

Vaughan, J. (2011). Ex Libris Primo Central. *Library Technology Reports, 47*(1), 39–47.

Vaughan, J. (2011). OCLC WorldCat Local. *Library Technology Reports, 47*(1), 12–21.

Vaughan, J. (2011). Serials Solutions Summon. *Library Technology Reports, 47*(1), 22–29.

Yang, S. Q., & Wagner, K. (2010). Evaluating and comparing discovery tools: How close are we towards the next generation catalog? *Library Hi Tech, 28*(4), 690–709. doi:10.1108/07378831011096312

Yuan, X., & Belkin, N. (2010). Evaluating an integrated system supporting multiple information-seeking strategies. *Journal of the American Society for Information Science and Technology, 61*(10), 1987–2010. doi:10.1002/asi.21352

ADDITIONAL READING

Bawden, D. (1986). Information systems and the stimulation of creativity. *Journal of Information Science, 12*(5), 203–216. doi:10.1177/016555158601200501

Buckland, M. K. (2007). The digital difference in reference collections. *Journal of Library Administration, 46*(2), 87–100. doi:10.1300/J111v46n02_07

Fischer, M. M., & Fröhlich, J. (2001). *Knowledge, complexity and innovation systems*. Berlin, Germany: Springer-Verlag.

Ford, N. (1999). Information retrieval and creativity: Towards support for the original thinker. *The Journal of Documentation, 55*(5), 528–542. doi:10.1108/EUM0000000007156

Green, D. (2004). *The serendipity machine: A voyage of discovery through the unexpected world of computers*. Crows Nest, Australia: Allen & Unwin.

Hagel, J. III, Brown, J. S., & Davison, L. (2010). *The power of pull: How small moves, smartly made, can set big things in motion*. New York, NY: Basic Books.

Koch, J. (2001). Hardwiring serendip: Give chance its due. *College & Research Libraries News, 62*(7), 731–732.

Macdonald, S. (1998). *Information for innovation: Managing change from an information perspective*. New York, NY: Oxford University Press.

Maglaughlin, K. L., & Sonnenwalk, D. H. (2002). User perspective on relevance criteria: A comparison among relevant, partially relevant, and not-relevant judgments. *Journal of the American Society for Information Science and Technology*, *53*(5), 327–342. doi:10.1002/asi.10049

Newman, M. W., et al. (2002). Designing for serendipity: Supporting end-user configuration of ubiquitous computing environments. In *Proceedings of the Symposium on Designing Interactive Systems*, (pp. 147-156). London, UK: Association for Computing Machinery (ACM).

Shneiderman, B. (2002). Inventing discovery tools: Combining information visualization with data mining. *Information Visualization*, *1*(1), 5–12.

Spink, A., & Cole, C. (2006). *New directions in human information behavior*. Dordrecht, The Netherlands: Springer. doi:10.1007/1-4020-3670-1

Sternberg, R. J., & Davidson, J. E. (Eds.). (1995). *The nature of insight*. Cambridge, MA: The MIT Press.

White, R. W., & Roth, R. A. (2009). *Exploratory search: Beyond the query-response paradigm*. San Rafael, CA: Morgan & Claypool Publishers.

Williamson, K. (1998). Discovered by chance: The role of incidental information acquisition in an ecological model of information use. *Library & Information Science Research*, *20*(1), 23–40. doi:10.1016/S0740-8188(98)90004-4

Xie, H. (2000). Shifts of interactive intentions and information-seeking strategies in interactive information retrieval. *Journal of the American Society for Information Science American Society for Information Science*, *51*(2), 841–857. doi:10.1002/(SICI)1097-4571(2000)51:9<841::AID-ASI70>3.0.CO;2-0

KEY TERMS AND DEFINITIONS

Browsability: Browsing is the art of looking for needed information when one has not yet completely characterized the information needed. Browsability describes an information resource with regards to the ease of browsing. For example, a browsable resource provides enough clues to determine whether an information item may satisfy the need.

Discovery Systems: As used in this chapter, a discovery system describes a tool designed to search across large and diverse collections via a default option of a single search box.

Faceted Browsing: Faceted browsing describes a discovery system feature which groups results according to categories (i.e. subject, author, format, publishing date).

Information Encountering: Information encountering describes an occurrence of unplanned information acquisition.

Interactive Information Retrieval: Interactive information retrieval describes a dynamic system that can modify retrieval in response to the actions of the user and/or user input.

Relevance/Cognitive Relevance: Relevance describes how well an information item matches an information need. Cognitive relevance describes the personal, subjective aspect of determining relevance. As an individual gains new knowledge, information may be determined to be more or less relevant depending on the modified cognitive state.

Serendipitous Information Retrieval: Serendipitous information retrieval describes the accidental retrieval of needed information. The accident aspect may be due to a number of factors, including: finding information in an unexpected location, discovering information that was unknown to exist, developing a spontaneous information need in response to novel information.

Topic Map: A topic map is a way to graphically depict key concepts and their relationships to one another.

ENDNOTES

1   Worldcat is a registered trademark of OCLC

2   Serials Solution is a registered trademark of Serials Solutions

3   Summons is owned by ProQuest LLC

4   ExLibris is a registered trademark of ExLibris LTD.

5   Primo Central is owned by Ex Libris Ltd. or its affiliates.

6   EBSCO Discovery Service is owned by EBSCO Publishing Industries

Chapter 10

User Search Activities within an Academic Library Gateway:
Implications for Web-scale Discovery Systems

William H. Mischo
University of Illinois at Urbana-Champaign, USA

Mary C. Schlembach
University of Illinois at Urbana-Champaign, USA

Joshua Bishoff
University of Illinois at Urbana-Champaign, USA

Elizabeth M. German
University of Houston, USA

ABSTRACT

Academic libraries are transitioning from access systems based on federated, broadcast search technologies to Web-scale discovery systems with central, aggregated indexes. It is important to understand user information seeking behaviors, but knowledge of user searching patterns in online catalogs is incomplete and contradictory. The University of Illinois at Urbana-Champaign Library has been collecting custom transaction log data from a main gateway built around the Easy Search (ES) federated search system. ES provides contextual search assistance suggestions that facilitate search reformulation and performs added title and phrase searches. An analysis of the transaction logs has revealed information on user search characteristics and search assistance usage. These findings show the importance of known-item searching, including journal, book, and article title searches. The Illinois team has been working with Web-scale discovery system vendors on a hybrid approach that incorporates search assistance and recommender elements with Web-scale aggregation and blended result displays.

DOI: 10.4018/978-1-4666-1821-3.ch010

INTRODUCTION

Search and discovery services offered by research libraries are currently at a crossroads. During the last decade, library gateway search services embraced federated search as a complementary service for local and consortial online public access catalogs (OPACs) (Williams, et al., 2009; Tallent, 2010; Alling & Naismith, 2007). In the last two years, the federated search approach has been superseded by the introduction of Web-scale discovery systems or next-generation catalogs (Ballard, 2011; Rowe, 2010; Williams & Foster, 2011; Fagan, 2011; Vaughan, 2011; Wisniewski, 2010). For retrieval purposes, the Web-scale discovery systems employ aggregated central indexes with heterogeneous metadata and content as opposed to the broadcast search approach employed by federated search systems. However, Web-scale systems can include a broadcast search component.

As libraries enter this transition paradigm, it is important to better understand user search behaviors and practices. In particular, models for user searching within the OPAC environment are incomplete and occasionally contradictory. While there is a great deal of research on end-user searching in both Web search engines and online catalog environments, there is a clear need for an evidence-based analysis of user search behaviors in multidimensional retrieval environments such as those offered by Web-scale discovery systems (Markey, 2007b; Tallent 2010; Lindahl, 2007; Hanson et al., 2009). The search behavior issues are detailed in the literature review below.

The University of Illinois at Urbana-Champaign (UIUC) Library has been gathering detailed data on user search behaviors within its main interface gateway. In the fall of 2007, the Library deployed a redesigned main gateway site featuring a single-entry search box that provides integrated access to the distributed information landscape (see Figure 1). The gateway was built over a locally developed federated search system, called Easy Search, which provides access to the journal literature, online catalog records, publisher e-book result matches, Web search engines, e-resource A-to-Z lists, and other targets. The Easy Search (ES) software suite functions as a discovery and recommender system, presenting users with a range of result links that provide entry into the native mode interfaces of designated targets at the point of completed search.

One of the major foci of the Illinois project work has been to identify and characterize user search behaviors within an academic library gateway. With the support of an IMLS National Leadership Grant and an NSF National Science Digital Library (NSDL) grant[1], the Illinois team has been gathering data from custom Easy Search (ES) transaction logs built and populated to provide comprehensive information about user search activities and user selected target (click-through) actions. The custom transaction logs capture and record all user entered search terms, any system generated search assistance suggestions or display prompts, and all subsequent user follow-on actions.

Using the data gathered from these custom logs, the ES team has introduced and tested a number of key search assistance functions designed to guide users in search strategy modification and reformulation and in the selection of relevant information resources. These Search assistance mechanisms offer users suggestive prompts, guided and adaptive help, reformulation suggestions, and added links and facets all within the context of their specific search. The search results display screen with a number of system search suggestions is shown in Figure 2.

The Illinois system provides what several authors have described as a just-in-time search assistance environment using strategic help and collaborative coaching techniques (Brajnik, Mizzaro, & Tesso, 2002; Antell & Huang, 2008; Graham, 2004). Evidence suggests that successful automated assistance systems need to offer context-specific assistance at those points in the

Figure 1. The Illinois gateway initial page

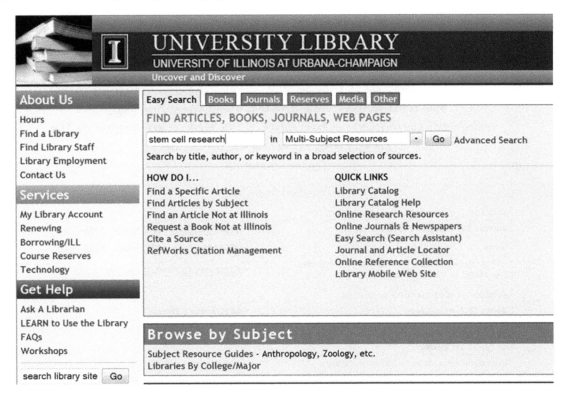

search process that provide maximum benefit to the user (Griffiths and Brophy, 2005; Ruthven, 2008; Jansen 2006b; Moukdad & Large, 2001).

The value of contextual online search assistance has been demonstrated in several research and test systems (Jansen, 2005; Kriewel & Fuhr, 2007; Brajnik, Mizzaro, & Tesso, 2002; Topi & Lucas, 2005a) but has not been applied in a large operational environment. This project has focused on identifying valuable assistance features through the user log analysis; testing the search assistance techniques by observing their application and use in the transaction logs and by conducting user interviews; and responding to user actions and feedback.

Since the introduction of the gateway in 2007, the project has gathered and stored some 11 million user search and click-through actions, including 1.54 million searches performed from the gateway from July 2010 to August 2011. This chapter will

provide a detailed analysis of user search activities over a sample of 1,394,838 gateway searches within the Illinois gateway during the Fall 2010 and Spring 2011 semesters.

The focus of this paper will be on the findings of the Illinois gateway transaction log analysis and the implications for the design, implementation, and use of Web-scale discovery systems. A better understanding of academic library user search behaviors will inform the design and evolution of Web-scale discovery systems and the manner in which they are deployed within academic library gateways. We are already seeing a variety of approaches in the way libraries utilize and offer their Web-scale systems. A number of academic libraries are using their Web-scale discovery systems as targets in Easy Search-like results displays.

Figure 2. Search results page for a keyword search on "stem cell research"

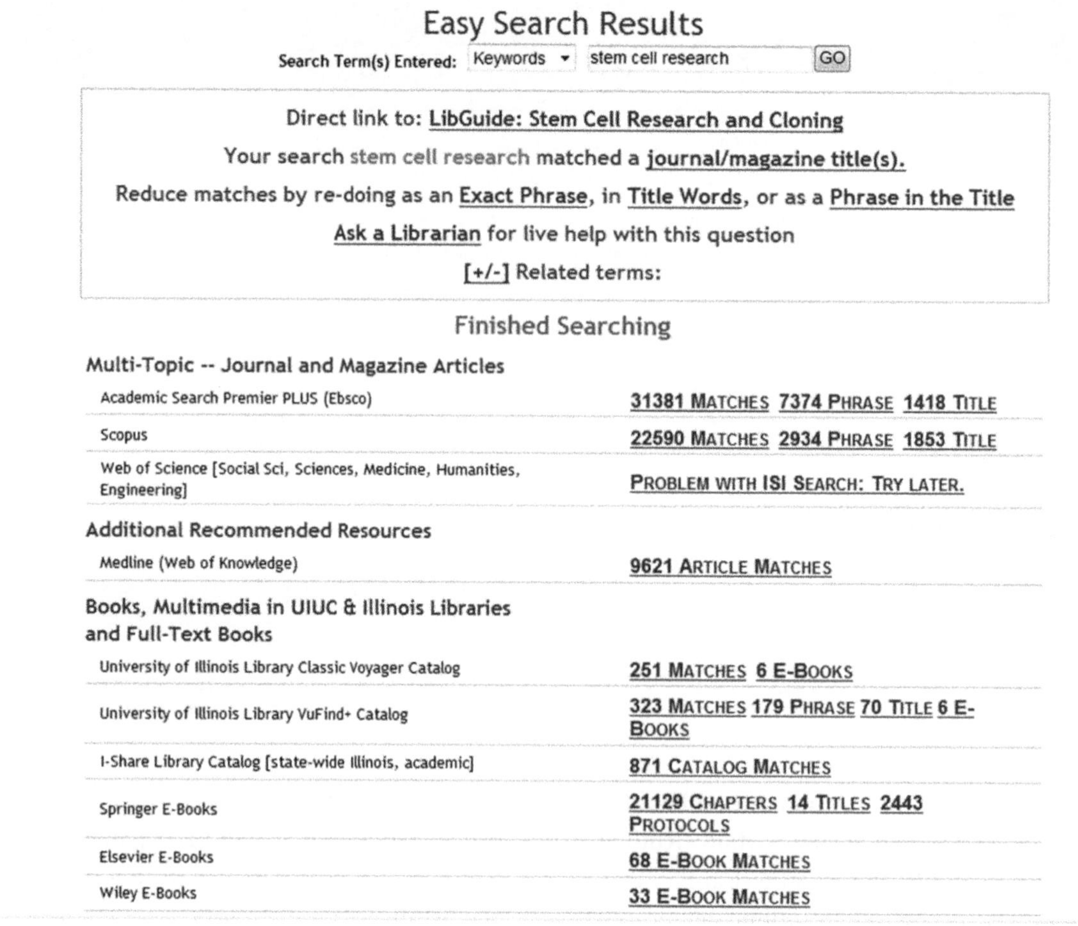

Easy Search Results

Search Term(s) Entered: Keywords ▾ stem cell research   GO

Direct link to: **LibGuide: Stem Cell Research and Cloning**
Your search stem cell research matched a **journal/magazine title(s).**
Reduce matches by re-doing as an **Exact Phrase**, in **Title Words**, or as a **Phrase in the Title**
Ask a Librarian for live help with this question
[+/-] Related terms:

Finished Searching

Multi-Topic -- Journal and Magazine Articles

Academic Search Premier PLUS (Ebsco)	**31381 MATCHES 7374 PHRASE 1418 TITLE**
Scopus	**22590 MATCHES 2934 PHRASE 1853 TITLE**
Web of Science [Social Sci, Sciences, Medicine, Humanities, Engineering]	**PROBLEM WITH ISI SEARCH: TRY LATER.**

Additional Recommended Resources

Medline (Web of Knowledge)	**9621 ARTICLE MATCHES**

Books, Multimedia in UIUC & Illinois Libraries and Full-Text Books

University of Illinois Library Classic Voyager Catalog	**251 MATCHES 6 E-BOOKS**
University of Illinois Library VuFind+ Catalog	**323 MATCHES 179 PHRASE 70 TITLE 6 E-BOOKS**
I-Share Library Catalog [state-wide Illinois, academic]	**871 CATALOG MATCHES**
Springer E-Books	**21129 CHAPTERS 14 TITLES 2443 PROTOCOLS**
Elsevier E-Books	**68 E-BOOK MATCHES**
Wiley E-Books	**33 E-BOOK MATCHES**

University of Illinois Library

The University of Illinois at Urbana-Champaign Library serves a user population of almost 43,000 students, more than 3,000 faculty, and some 8,000 staff. The Library holds more than 12 million volumes across more than 30 departmental libraries. Among the Library's most notable collections are its holdings in eastern European history, literature, science, engineering, maps, and mathematics. The Library has over 80,000 serial subscriptions across all disciplines.

The Illinois Library currently utilizes two OPACs: Endeavor's traditional Voyager®[2] catalog and a campus and statewide implementation of VuFind. Voyager® searching covers all the campus libraries and has search capabilities not found in VuFind, such as call number searching. Both systems are included in the results display for Easy Search.

LITERATURE REVIEW ON USER SEARCH BEHAVIORS

Overview

In order to place the Illinois transaction log results in the proper context, it is important to examine the rich literature devoted to understanding and modeling user information seeking behaviors. Markey (2007a) reviewed 25 years of published research findings on end-user searching, summarizing the results of 32 transaction log studies, including 26 that looked at internet search engines, 5 that studied library OPACs, and one of an Abstracting & Indexing (A&I) service. A number of more current studies have also been published.

Markey noted that, at that time, many OPAC studies dated back a decade or more and that it was important to conduct updated transaction log analyses of Web-based OPACs (Markey, 2007a). She identified several overarching user search characteristics that spanned all types of search systems, including that: users entered a small number of terms per query (reporting that the shortest mean number of terms per query—between one and two terms--came from OPACs); and that most of the examined studies reported somewhere between 2 and 4 queries per session. She also formulated a series of axioms about search behaviors and actions. These include:

- Less than 15% of queries contain the Boolean AND operator;
- Less than 3% of queries contain the OR operator;
- Less than 2% of queries contain the Boolean NOT operator;
- Less than 20% of queries contain the Boolean operators;
- End-users use Boolean syntax from other systems, such as – (minus sign) before a word (Google Boolean NOT);
- Less than 15% of queries enclose quotes around bound phrases;
- Truncation occurs in less than 5% of queries;
- Users do not use or incorrectly use advanced search features.

The more recent OPAC studies reinforce the Markey findings on query characteristics. A 2009 transaction log study of the North Carolina State University Endeca catalog found users entering an average of 2.51 terms per query with a median of two requests per session (Lown & Hemminger, 2009). A 2006 transaction log analysis of the Nanyang Technological University in Singapore showed an average of 2.86 terms per query (Lau & Goh, 2006). Moulaison (2008) found that the average terms per query were 2.6 in the OPAC of The College of New Jersey.

Web Search Engine Studies

The research on usage and search patterns within Web search engines has revealed (as noted above) that users of these systems typically perform searches with an average of 2.4 terms per query in a simple syntax, engage in short search sessions of a little over 2 queries per session, do not utilize advanced search features such as Boolean operators or limit operations, and typically view only a few of the results (Markey, 2007a; Topi and Lucas, 2005b; Jansen & Spink, 2006; Ozmutlu, Spink, & Ozmutlu, 2004).

OPAC Search Typologies

The OPAC transaction log studies have had more varied results and have generated some conflicting information. There has been a great deal of OPAC transaction log work dedicated to identifying and measuring the types of searches (subject, title, author) being conducted by users. The prevalence of subject search was emphasized in the early Council on Library Resources (CLIR) studies on OPACs (Mathews & Lawrence, 1984). Larson (1991) reported a longitudinal decline in subject searching and a concomitant rise in title keyword (known-item) searches in the University of California OPAC system (MELVYL).

Other studies also appear to dispute the subject search dominance. Villen-Rueda, Senso, and de Moya-Anegon (2007) analyzed the breakdown between author, title and subject searching in various OPAC studies and showed that subject search varied between 26% and 83% over eight studies. Their study showed a 14% subject searching rate. Cooper (2001) also conducted a longitudinal study of MELVYL data and found that the default power search (author, title, keyword) was used in 40% of the searches, while subject searching accounted for 27% of the total usage.

In an examination of OPAC transaction logs and system implanted questionnaires, Malliari and Kyriaki-Manessi (2007) found that 69% of the searches were what they termed "known-item" searches--defined as title or author searches-- and subject search constituted only 23% of the searches. Antell & Huang (2008) found that key-word searches were employed fourteen times as often–64.8% to 4.6%-- as subject search. Other studies have looked specifically at known-item searches. An early OPAC study at the University of North Carolina found that 64% of the participants conducted known-item searches (Wildemuth & O'Neill, 1995) and a recent survey at the University of Minnesota showed a 50% known-item search rate (Hanson et al., 2011).

The single most confounding element in these OPAC search type analyses is that it appears that the most critical factor in determining the most prevalent type of user search is the system default search parameters (Moulaison, 2008; Malliari & Kyriaki-Manessi, 2007; Lau & Goh, 2006; Cooper, 2001; Mi & Weng, 2008; Antell & Huang, 2008; Liu, 2010). Liu conducted a side-by-side comparative study of two Ex Libris Voyager® implementations which differed only in their default search type and concluded that "users seem to use the default search no matter which kind of search option is provided" (Liu, 2010, p. 12). Knievel, Wakimoto, and Holladay (2009) examined changes in catalog usage after the redesign of the OPAC interface at the University of Colorado and found that "patrons do not necessarily take the time to change their search types away from the default of keyword, even when they are looking for known items" (Knievel, Wakimoto, & Holladay, 2009, p.453).

Mi and Weng (2008), in a survey of Association of Research Libraries (ARL) library OPAC search features, found that 66% have OPACs that offer keyword as the search default. However, even OPAC keyword searches differ in their implementation in that some multiword keyword searches default to a phrase search unless an explicit Boolean operator is entered and some default to a Boolean AND search.

It is important to note that the earliest OPAC studies showed that a percentage of title and key-word searches are in fact topical searches and that a percentage of keyword searches are known-item searches (Mathews & Lawrence, 1984).

OPAC General Search Characteristics

It is very clear that users have varying needs and expectations when they approach and use a library search and discovery system. From the onset of OPAC studies, users have indicated that they expected journal articles to be present in the OPAC (Novotny, 2004; Jung, Herlocker, Webster, Mellinger, & Frumkin 2008; Griffiths & Brophy, 2005). Yu and Young (2004), in a three year study, found an increase in the frequency of searches that would have been more successful in resources other than the library catalog.

One of the most frequently observed phenomena connected with online information retrieval, particularly within the OPAC environment, has been the tendency to retrieve either too few or too many matches in response to a user search argument (Markey, 2007a; Novotny, 2004; Roe, 1999; Brajnik, Mizzaro, & Tesso, 2002; Graham, 2004). These studies, and others, often focus on the high percentage of zero-result matches in subject searches. Many search assistance functions, including the search assistance mechanisms introduced into the Illinois gateway, are designed to address the "too-few, too-many" problem.

Library gateways have evolved from containers emphasizing OPAC search and e-resource links to multi-function single entry search box systems that provide integrated access to distributed information resources. The challenge is to incorporate reference librarian expertise into the user search workflow (Tallent, 2010; Brajnik, Mizzaro, & Tesso, 2002; Lindahl, 2007).

A&I Service Searches

In a study analyzing the query logs of two abstracting & indexing (A&I) Services, the average number of terms per query was higher–3.16 for PsycINFO and 3.42 for two ABC-Clio history databases (Yi, Beheshti, Cole, Leide, & Large, 2006). An analysis of a typical day's log for PubMed found that the median number of terms per query was 3 and that 62% of the search sessions were comprised of one search term (Herskovic, Tanaka, Hersh, & Bernstam, 2007).

General Interface and Retrieval Issues

There is both anecdotal and user survey evidence that users prefer a single-entry Google-type search box (Lucas & Topi, 2005; Fei, 2009; Boyd, Hampton, Morrison, Pugh, & Cervone, 2006; Gibson, Goddard, & Gordon, 2009). At the 2007 Joint Conference on Digital Libraries, Daniel Russell, Research Scientist at Google, commented in a presentation that the average time spent by a Google user at the Advanced Search screen was 1 second (Russell, 2007).

It is also clear that Help modules are not used (Novotny, 2004; Jansen, Booth, & Spink, 2009; Cooper, 2001; Mi & Weng, 2008). While teaching and information literacy programs play an important role in academic libraries, Antell and Huang (2008) point out that "the information literate student is hard to find" (p. 73). O'Connor and Lundstrom (2011), summarizing the research on the information seeking behaviors of college students, write that the majority of students do not practice the information use strategies that librarians prescribe. For these reasons, Antell and Huang (2008) suggest the use of just-in-time online search assistance mechanisms such as those utilized in the Illinois Easy Search suite.

There is also a growing body of research that shows that users of Web-based information retrieval systems have difficulties with formulating and modifying search query syntax (Jansen, Spink, & Saracevic, 2000; Lucas & Topi, 2005). There is a consensus that the problem needs to be addressed at the query formulation stage and that the introduction of search features that respond to user search behaviors needs to be emphasized (Griffiths & Brophy 2005, Moukdad & Large 2001).

At present, there is little data or metrics on user searching conducted within integrated systems offering access to a range of target types. Data-driven evaluations of searching behaviors in Web-scale discovery systems are just beginning to appear. Williams & Foster (2011) reported on the implementation of an EBSCO Discovery Service™[3] (EDS) system, noting that EDS solved some of the problems present in federated search systems but some issues persisted. Some Web-scale system implementations are being used for journal literature searching only (sometimes with newspaper results disabled) with monographic results being exposed under separate OPAC search displays.

ILLINOIS GATEWAY SEARCH ASSISTANCE MECHANISMS

The search assistance functions deployed in this project are built on a multi-year transaction log analysis and are designed to address the user search behavior issues and concerns identified in the literature. The Illinois team has built a contextual and adaptive search assistance system that provides search modification suggestions and, in some cases, performs additional phrase and title searches to accommodate perceived user information needs.

The Easy Search transaction log data has provided the Illinois team with a window into system use and the ability to gauge user reactions to search assistance mechanisms. These search assistance mechanisms are designed to unobtrusively intervene within the individual user's search, providing context-specific and adaptive assistance and suggestions.

A number of search assistance functions have been operational within Easy Search for several years. These include:

- Stopword and punctuation removal; adding explicit Boolean AND operators to the user search string for those target systems where the default multiword search is an exact phrase search.
- Spelling Suggestions: a "do you mean" function with a specific link.
- Author redo prompts: keyword or title searches that look like they could be author names elicit a system question and action link "Do you want to redo this as an Author Search?"
- Prompts to limit searches that retrieve a large number of matches to bound phrase, title word, or title phrase searches.
- Direct link suggestions for frequent searches, searches where the user may want to be redirected to a different site (e.g. "Facebook", "biology library"), or searches that match LibGuides topics.
- Providing a link to E-Journal title matches for searches that match on a journal title or abbreviation.
- Rearranging search results so that e-resource A to Z results appear at the top of the display for searches that contain a "journal type" word ("journal", "magazine", "annual").
- Providing a link to an article citation resolver for searches that look like a specific article citation.

- Searches of non-selected or more focused "dark" targets (i.e. Medline, ProQuest). These background search results only appear if the comprehensive targets do not yield any or few results.

In the last year, the UIUC Libraries have introduced several new search assistance functions into the Easy Search family. These include:

- A [+-] pull down list of Related Terms from Bing is displayed;
- A pull-down preview list of the first 10 results matches for selected database;
- For several of the search targets, when multiword user-entered search terms are entered, additional title and phrase search results and links are provided. This is designed to provide enhanced access to the frequent "known-item" searches that we see in the transaction logs;
- The ability to perform a "pass-through" or command language search that overrides the ES search argument processing routines;
- Providing a live link to the Ask-a-Librarian service on the Easy Search results page. ES passes the Instant Messaging (IM) reference operator with the current search, the immediate previous search, and a link to the user's current search results to allow the operator to recreate the user's search results;
- Links inserted on the catalog display lines to e-book titles retrieved from the catalog; and
- Added searches of recommended targets using the user's search argument to query the WorldCat Application Programming Interface (API) for LC classification code information.

Figure 2 shows a number of these search assistance mechanisms.

Figure 3. Custom transaction log example

previoussearch	searchstring	searc...	catid	suggest
NULL	kwj. g. march:	899	gateway gen, opac, web	Author Redo ACSE reduce matches inspdark ...
kwj. g. march:	fromauthclick: h.march: fnj.: mig.:	900	gateway gen, opac, web	inspdark abidark

The transaction logs record all the instances where these search assistance mechanisms are suggested to the user. They also show all user actions taken in response to the search assistance functions.

ANALYSIS OF ILLINOIS GATEWAY LOGS

Transaction log analysis is a commonly-used methodology for examining the characteristics of user-system interactions and patterns. As a tool, it can inform system design by providing details regarding user action (Jansen 2006a; Peters, 1993). It is, however, not as useful for understanding user motives and determining user satisfaction. In addition, as Peters (1993) has noted, to glean some types of detailed information it is often necessary to go beyond algorithmic software analysis techniques and "hand-inspect" and re-do searches from samples of the log entries.

Rather than relying on an analysis of standard system Web logs, the Easy Search team designed and constructed custom transaction logs with all search and click-through actions written into a dynamic relational database. This database contains two tables, one containing search information and the other the target click-through information. The search table contains separate entries for: the Web site referring page; the user's IP address; the system generated session ID; the user's previous search; the user search argument or the search generated by the user execution of a specific search suggestion; the type of search being performed; the system-generated search suggestions; the user agent which records Web browser and operating system used by the client; a link key to the click-through table; and the date and time. The click-through table contains the date and time; a 3-letter code for the target that was clicked; and the link key with the search table. Figure 3 shows two lines from the search table transaction log for: (1) a keyword search for "j. g. march" that includes the search assistance prompt to the user to redo the search as an author search; and (2) the user carrying out the author search suggestion by clicking on the suggestive prompt.

The log analysis is conducted by executing various SQL (Structured Query Language) commands against the transaction log database and collecting these search results.

This log analysis will focus on gateway transaction logs gathered during the Fall 2010 and Spring 2011 semesters of the academic year at Illinois. The analysis was conducted over a set of 1,394,838 gateway searches, eliminating all searches performed by developers and testers. During this time period users also selected and clicked on specific search targets 1,293,614 times. Targets that the user then selected and went to (click-throughs) are recorded in the transaction logs and the user is then subsequently redirected to the specific content target.

Search Starting Points

The Library Gateway site, in addition to providing the single-entry search box, also provides an advanced fielded search option with keyword, title, and author search and allows users to pick and choose information resource targets by subject and type. The advanced search option is used very infrequently and accounts for only 3.41% of all the searches in the sample time period.

In addition to the overarching Easy Search tab, the Gateway provides a tab for a "Books" search and under a "Journals" tab for "Journals by Title" and "Journal Articles by Topic" searches. Table 1 shows the breakdown of search starting points for the 1,392,407 searches in this study. The majority of the searches–65.9%--are from either the single entry search boxes on the default Easy Search tab or on a departmental library site.

In addition, 39.26% of all searches are follow-on searches performed from the pull-down search menu on the Easy Search results page. 20.06% of these follow-on searches are title searches; 9.48% are Author pull-down searches; the rest are keyword searches.

These numbers support the literature by showing that a large percentage of searches–here (from above) almost 66% of searches--are default keyword searches, but it also shows some willingness to go to facet-like tabs for subset searches.

On-Campus vs. Off-Campus Use

Using a strict IP address breakdown, 45.2% of the usage of the gateway came from on-campus addresses. However, subtracting the Virtual Private Network (VPN) address space usage brings the on-campus number down to 43.65%. This still includes all wireless and remote desktop usage. So, at least 56.35% of the gateway use is from off-campus patrons. The University of Minnesota Discoverability Phase I Final Report indicated that 65% of the information requests coming into their library systems came from off-campus (Hanson et al., 2009).

Known-Item Searching

During the course of this project, several meta-analyses of user searches appearing in the logs were performed in an attempt to better characterize user search needs and intent. Categorizing the types of

Table 1. Search starting points

Search Starting Points:	Percentage of All Searches:
Easy Search tab (default)	51.6%
Departmental Library Site Search	14.3%
Journal Title Tab	12.8%
Books Tab	12.6%
Journal Article Tab	5.1%
Advanced Search Tab	3.41%

user searches can provide insight into interface design, the presentation of system features, and needed search assistance functions.

In 2007, a random sample of 3,100 user searches was analyzed in detail, with project staff re-doing user-entered Easy Search searches. This analysis showed that 49.4% of the searches were for "known-items" – specific journal/book titles, journal articles, works by specific authors, etc.

A second focused analysis was carried out in 2011, reconstructing and checking click-throughs on 8,474 searches and 3,505 search sessions. This analysis showed that 51.2% of the searches were for specific or known items as above and that known-item searches were conducted in 54.8% of the studied search sessions.

The two detailed search analyses are summarized in Table 2.

Note the increase in specific journal article searches. This is at least partially due to users entering 'cut and paste citations' into Easy Search. The known-item search percentages compared in our study were determined by direct examination and analysis of transaction log data, although clearly we do not know exactly what each user was thinking. The numbers for known-item searching were derived by direct examination of the transaction logs and redoing user searches. The numbers for known item searching in the literature are derived primarily by counting the total number of title and author searches, rather than actually redoing the searches.

Table 2. Known-item search analysis

	2007 Study	2011 Study
Total Number of Searches Examined	3,100	8,474
Overall % of Known-Item Searches	49.4%	51.2% of Searches 54.8% of Sessions
Author/Title Searches	7.4%	6.04%
Author Searches	28.9%	16.9%
Book/Monographic Title	40.5%	33.6%
Index/Abstract Title	6.8%	4.2%
Specific Journal Article Search	5.7%	26.9%
Specific Journal Title Search	11.8%	12.4%

The complementary facts that some 66% of all searches are default keyword searches and that 51% of all searches are actually known item searches reinforces the need for automated and adaptive system assistance within the search process in order to provide users with suggestions and custom links as they navigate through the search process.

SEARCH CHARACTERISTICS

Queries per Session

From the sample of 1,394,838 searches in the period studied, there were 637,375 search sessions for an average of 2.19 searches per session. Excluding the journal title searches (which tended to be single specific searches), there were 522,094 sessions averaging 2.35 searches per session. A session is defined as a series of user actions (searches and click-throughs) from the same workstation in which there is less than a 20 minute pause between actions. If there are user actions from the same workstation after a 20 minute pause, a new session is established.

In 51.95% of the 522,094 sessions, users entered only a single search term. However, if a specific type of two action search, in which a user entered a search term and then clicked on a title or phrase link facet, are removed as single search sessions, then we find that 44.03% of all searches were single query sessions.

In the 48.05% of the search sessions where users performed two or more searches, 26.04% of these sessions included 3 or more search actions, 16.02% contained 4 or more search terms, and 10.56% included 5 or more searches. The multiple query search sessions reported here are higher than in many reported studies. A recent large-scale search engine study reported that 72% of all search sessions were comprised of single searches (Jansen et al., 2009).

Terms per Query

An analysis was done over 942,027 search queries to determine the average number of words entered per query. This search argument subset included all original queries and reformulations, but did not include follow-up or repeat limit to phrase or title searches, author re-do searches, or suggested spell change searches. In this sample, the average number of terms per query was 4.33. The longest query was 276 words. There were a total of 4,077,152 words used in these searches. Table 3 details the numbers and frequencies of search terms employed per user query. Interestingly, there were about the same number of searches

Table 3. Terms per query (an average 4.33 words per query)

Number of Words in User Search Query	Frequency of Occurrence
1	102,028
2	212,072
3	219,466
4	127,875
5	77,126
6	47,315
7	32,038
8	24,464
>8 words	99,643
Average	4.33 words per query

containing 9 words or more as there were single word searches.

There is evidence that over the last several years the number of terms per query entered into the Illinois gateway has grown. An earlier analysis of a sample of 841,444 searches carried out in 2007-2008 showed an average of 3.577 words per query. A later analysis of 268,454 searches in 2008-2009 revealed an average of 3.76 terms per query.

One clear phenomenon contributing to the increasing number is the observed increase of user's copying and pasting citations and references of journal article titles from e-bibliographies and course management systems into the Easy Search system. This is evident in the transaction logs from the growth in the average terms per query and multiword search arguments that appear with the first letter of each significant word capitalized or a complete article/book citation.

Boolean Searches

The project team performed an analysis of the use of Boolean operators and similar connecting terms. The team found that commas were often used as Boolean AND operators. Also, some work was done using prepositions as boundary words in deriving exact multiword phrases. The total search percentages shown in Table 4 are all within the boundaries identified by Markey.

Actual Boolean operators appear in a very small number of searches, although some users employed commas as Boolean AND operators. In addition, users enter forced phrase searches (using quotes) and truncation symbols very infrequently. This is consistent with earlier studies showing infrequent use of explicit Boolean or adjacency operators and advanced limit functions. The search assistance functions serve to transparently introduce users to some advanced search functionalities.

Search Assistance Usage

As detailed above, the Easy Search system employs a wide variety of search assistance techniques. These include direct suggested actions, multiple search reformulation options, added contextual result links for title or phrase limit searches, Ask-a-Librarian synchronous chat assistance, query expansion suggestions, and changing the order of result displays to present what the system regards as the most relevant targets. These contextual and adaptive search assistance mechanisms recognize multiword search terms as potentially known-item searches and author-like search patterns.

In 38.6% of all the searches and 54.8% of all search sessions, the system made an explicit search assistance suggestion to the user (not including the Ask-a-Librarian chat service and related terms display). The breakdown is detailed in Table 5.

Table 6 shows the frequencies in which search assistance suggestions were taken up (clicked on) by users These percentages are given for the number of times each suggestion type was presented to users and for the frequency of use within multi-search sessions. Note that a user click on a search suggestion constitutes a second search in the transaction logs.

Table 4. Easy search observations compared to Markey 2007a axioms

Characteristics of User Searches	Percentage of all Searches
Boolean Operators ("and", "or", "not") entered	13.03%
AND operator searches (the vast majority of ANDs appear as conjunctions in known titles)	12.76%
AND operator in all caps	0.41%
OR operator-- lower and upper case entered	0.22%
NOT operator-- lower and upper case	0.13%
Commas entered	6.03%
Parentheses entered	0.88%
Quotes (single and double) entered	3.95%
Prepositions entered	27.26%
"+" sign entered	0.42%
Truncation symbol(*) entered	0.12%

Table 5. Search assistance suggestions made by easy search within search sessions

Search Assistance Suggestions made by System	Percentage of all sessions
Reduce results to exact phrase/title words	36.43%
Matching Journal Title found	17.79%
Spelling change suggested	12.61%
Redo as Author search suggested	7.69%
Direct Match/frequent search result found	6.09%
Citation entered – go to linker module	4.11%

Table 6. Utilization of search assistance suggestions by users

Search Assistance Suggestions Employed by Users	Percentage of Times Each Type Was Used When Suggested	Percentage of Multi-Query Sessions where SA was used
Spell change suggestions clicked	29.04%	7.86%
Direct link clicked	57.56%	6.58%
Journal Title match click	21.41%	6.95%
Limit to Phrase/Title or clicked on title results	28.38%	15.76%
Author Redo Offer clicked	7.95%	1.36%
Ask-a-Librarian clicked	0.14%	0.29%
Complete citation passed to linker module	2.4%	0.25%

Several of the search assistance mechanisms are heavily used, including the spell change suggestions, the direct links to frequently used searches and LibGuides, the journal title match links, the article phrase and title links, and the author search prompts.

The logs revealed that users also tended to click on the result display e-journal A to Z list links rather than the presented journal title match links. So, altogether, users went to journal title matches 21.41% of the time they were presented, constituting 6.86% of all search sessions, It is clear that users are entering journal titles and then clicking through at a high frequency into a journal matching title link or into the A to Z e-journal list. Combined with the 115,281 sessions where users chose the "Journals by Title" search tab, we are witnessing a very large number of journal title searches. Our study shows that the close interaction that Easy Search employs with the A to Z and e-resource knowledgebases is critically important.

In addition, the exact phrase/title words added links shown in the results displays for the combined EBSCO databases search, Scopus searches, and the local online catalog searches have proven very popular. These added article and book title links (limited as they are to only a few targets) are clicked on in 7.35% of all searches and 11.54% of all search sessions.

Unfortunately, Web-scale systems are not necessarily set up to perform ranked customized searches for matching journal titles and are presently not displaying facets links for article or book title and phrase matches.

Users clicked on one of the basic search assistance suggestions in 19.96% of search sessions comprised of more than one search action. In addition, users reformulated their searches by switching the type of search in the results pull-down menu (for example, from a keyword search to a title search) in 23.49% of the search sessions comprised of more than one search.

The Ask-a-Librarian synchronous links were clicked on in only 0.29% of all the search sessions but many searches were performed during times when the service was not available and, during those times, the link is not provided.

In aggregate, the study looked at the total usage of the variety of search assistance mechanisms, which include the search modification suggestions, the reformulation options, the facet display title and phrase matches, the Ask-a-Librarian link, the query expansion offerings, and the custom journal match displays. User response to the search assistance functions has been very positive. **In this analysis of 522,094 main gateway search sessions, users employed search assistance mechanisms in 32.45% of all search sessions. In 57.98% of the search sessions involving more than one query, the user clicked on or utilized one of the offered search suggestions, reformulation options, or relevant resource recommendations.** These search assistance mechanisms serve to transparently and seamlessly provide users with the advanced search functionality that studies show users are not employing at high frequencies.

Selected Content Click-throughs

User click-throughs to content targets are recorded in a separate table in the logs. Table 7 shows selected raw frequencies of click-throughs. There were a total of 1,293,614 click-throughs in the sample.

The overall percentage breakdown of the clickt-hroughs to the 65 targets by type of target is shown in Table 8.

Access to both the journal literature and the monographic literature is important to users. Electronic book searches, in addition to being performed against specific publishers, Google books, and HathiTrust, are done in the VuFind OPAC and the results links are placed behind the Voyager® and VuFind matches. In total, click-throughs into all the e-book content targets totaled 9.31% of all result target clicks and took place in 11.36% of all search sessions.

DISCUSSION AND CONCLUSION

A review of the literature on user search behaviors within OPACs reveals some contradictory data on the percentages of the type of searches (subject, title, author) being conducted by users. These studies show that the most critical factor in determining the most prevalent type of user search is the system default search parameters. It is clear that all types of searches are being performed within the default search parameters. Indeed, there is a clear need for evidence-based studies of user search behaviors in library gateway environments that provide access to heterogeneous resources.

In this context, the authors of this chapter conducted a detailed transaction log analysis of data gathered from user searching within the Illinois Easy Search gateway. Several of the user search characteristics, as gleaned from the Illinois transaction logs, differ from what is reported in the literature on end-user searching behaviors in search engines and OPACs. Users of the Illinois gateway enter an average of 4.33 terms per search query, which is higher than the 2 to 3 terms typically reported in Web search engine, OPAC, and A & I Services studies. There was approximately the same number of searches with 9 words or more as there were single word searches. In addition, 48.05% of the search sessions contain more than one search term or a combination of multiple search terms and adapted search assistance actions. This is also higher than most published averages. The percentage of known-item or specific title/author

searches exceeds 51% of the search queries and known-item searches are performed in almost 55% of the search sessions.

This study confirmed the dominance of user default searching by showing that almost 66% of searches are single entry search box searches from the default screen. However, we do see users willing to employ facet-like tabs for subset

Table 7. Highest database content click-throughs totals

Resource	Total Click-throughs
EBSCO Combined Database Search	346,027
UI Voyager® Catalog	184,015
UI VuFind Catalog	147,445
Scopus	117,041
ISI Web of Knowledge	80,891
InfoTrac	65,649
Statewide VuFind Catalog	51,409
Google Books	33,303
Springer E-books	29,243
E-Resource A-Z List	28,918
Compendex	22,650
Background Target Searches	19,294
Elsevier E-books	17.062
Wiley E-books	16,655
ABI Inform	14,967
INSPEC	13,772
Google Scholar	11,065
Newspaper Source	10.158
HathiTrust	8,320

Table 8. Click-throughs by type of target

Resource	Percentage
A&I service/periodical indexes	47.25%
All books	33.9% (OPACS 29.7%, E-books 9.31%)
Journal/Database Titles	17.41%
Web search engines	0.71%
Newspapers and news sites	0.83%
Reference titles	0.35%

searches. The complementary facts that some 66% of searches in our study are default keyword searches and that 51% of all searches are actually known item searches reinforces the need for automated and adaptive system assistance in the search process in order to facilitate both title word and author searching.

The Easy Search system provides users with unobtrusive search assistance suggestions, intervening in the search process with search modification suggestions and custom links to information content targets. The Illinois contextual search assistance suggestions and mechanisms are well-accepted by users, with 32.45% of all search sessions and 58% of the sessions that exhibit more than a single search query finding users employing one or more of various search assistance operations. Several of the search assistance mechanisms are heavily used, including the spell change suggestions, the direct links to frequent searches and LibGuides, the journal title match links, the article phrase and title links, and the author search prompts. The search assistance mechanisms serve to transparently and seamlessly provide users with the advanced search functionality that studies show users are not employing very often.

The logs revealed that users are entering complete or partial journal titles and then clicking through at a high frequency into a presented journal matching title link or into the A to Z e-journal list results. Users click on the presented journal title link 21.41% of the time that they are suggested and in over 6.86% of all search sessions. In addition, the journal title search option tab constitutes over 12% of the searches within the gateway. This study shows the importance of the close interaction that Easy Search employs with the A to Z and e-resource knowledgebases. .

The exact phrase/title words added links shown in the results displays for the combined EBSCO databases search, Scopus searches, and the local online catalog searches have proven very popular. The added article and book title links (limited as

they are to only a few targets) are clicked on in 7.35% of all searches and 11.54% of all search sessions. The added title and phrase search links serve as an example of a facet-like feature that provides convenient limiting links for users. There is some evidence that facet links in OPACs are being used (Ballard, 2011). In the North Carolina State University catalog, 34% of the search sessions contain a facet limit operation (Lown & Hemminger, 2009).

The large number of cut and paste citations entered into the search box contributes to the increase in known-item journal article searches and the increasing average number of terms per query. Likewise, the extensive use of the search assistance functions contributes to the higher number of multi-query or multi-action searches.

In terms of click-throughs to results targets, journal index click-throughs account for over 56% of the user target selections with OPAC (30%) and all monographic access clicks (39%) also being heavily utilized as targets by users.

It is also interesting to note that click-throughs on publisher e-book matches is high and growing. In total, click-throughs into all the e-book content targets totaled 9.31% of all result target clicks and took place in 11.36% of all search sessions. It goes without saying that e-resource access to journal articles and books is paramount to users in all disciplines and at all academic levels.

While the Illinois gateway targets do not directly include the Libraries' digital content access system records (although the institutional repository is one of the targets), together the journal article literature and monographic target click-throughs account for 80.66% of the target click-throughs. It is encouraging that the journal and monographic content is exactly what is being emphasized in today's Web-scale discovery systems. But, the efficacy of presenting users with an integrated and blended display of monographic records, journal articles, newspaper articles, dissertations, and report literature has not been clearly demonstrated. Several research libraries have abandoned the blended display approach for an Easy Search-like separate discovery targets display (Rochkind, 2011). From the Illinois gateway study data, it is clear that academic library search and discovery systems must accommodate both known-item searching and limiting operations. And, we have shown that academic library users will embrace hybrid content discovery systems that provide access to distributed information resources and targets.

Employing contextual and adaptive search assistance mechanisms that recognize multiword search terms as potentially known-item title searches and/or author-type searches can assist in facilitated user retrieval. However, Web-scale systems are not typically set up to perform and present customized searches for matching journal titles and are presently not displaying facets links for journal title matches or for article or book title and phrase matches.

The Illinois gateway team has been working with Web-scale discovery system vendors on the incorporation of search assistance and recommender system elements into their aggregation and blended result displays. This hybrid approach – with contextual search assistance elements and Web-scale aggregation functions – could provide users with an optimum search and discovery environment. The adoption of search assistance technologies into the Web-scale framework should result in enhanced user search formulation and modification capabilities and custom search navigation functionality. This is being tested.

FUTURE RESEARCH DIRECTIONS

There are several key research and implementation issues facing libraries with regard to Web-scale discovery system deployment. Some of these are presentation and display issues and some are access and discovery issues.

The Illinois study also showed that journal article literature and monographic target click-throughs together account for 80.66% of the user click-throughs. The fact that 19.35% of all user click-throughs are directed to resources outside of the OPAC and journal article targets--including journal or database title links, full-text Web resources, discipline and publisher repositories, and national digitization repositories--shows that there is a high percentage of user needs that may best be directed to information resources outside of the typical Web-scale system targets. How these other information targets can be integrated with the Web-scale system resources is a question that needs to be addressed. At the same time the effectiveness of Web-scale system blended results displays--where users are presented with a single integrated results display of monographic records, journal articles, newspaper articles, dissertations, local digital content, institutional repository content, etc.--needs to be studied. Several research libraries have abandoned the blended display approach for a compartmentalized Easy Search–like display. It may be that some hybrid approach is best.

The transaction log research reported in this study revealed that title searching and results display--of journal titles, article titles, and book titles--is being heavily employed by users. Adding additional title and phrase search links, as the Illinois project did, to results displays provides a popular and convenient mechanism for limiting searches to title matches. However, Web-scale discovery systems do not conveniently allow users to identify and retrieve title matches. Journal name, article title, and book titles do not typically appear as facet links. In the typical Web-scale system default keyword search mode, retrieval of title matches is at the mercy of the Web-scale system's relevancy ranking and exact matches may be buried within long lists of results. Equally problematic is the fact that Web-scale systems will return long lists of result matches from keyword or full-text matches that do not include the specific title result the user is seeking because the item is not indexed in the system. These issues need to be addressed in future Web-scale system research.

The Illinois study also clearly showed the value of contextual search assistance mechanisms in improving the user search experience. These techniques can be of benefit in a Web-scale environment and may improve search navigation and assist with the needed resource integration.

REFERENCES

Antell, K., & Huang, J. (2008). Subject searching success: Transaction logs, patron perceptions, and implications for library instruction. *Reference and User Services Quarterly, 48*(1), 68–76.

Ballard, T. (2011). Comparison of user search behaviors with classic online catalogs and discovery platforms. *The Charleston Advisor, 12*(3), 65–66. doi:10.5260/chara.12.3.65

Boyd, J., Hampton, M., Morrison, P., Pugh, P., & Cervone, F. (2006). The one-box challenge: Providing a federated search that benefits the research process. *Serials Review, 32*(4), 247–254. doi:10.1016/j.serrev.2006.08.005

Brajnik, G., Mizzaro, S., Tasso, C., & Venuti, F. (2002). Strategic help in user interfaces for information retrieval. *Journal of the American Society for Information Science and Technology, 53*(5), 343–358. doi:10.1002/asi.10035

Cooper, M. D. (2001). Usage pattern of a Web-based library catalog. *Journal of the American Society for Information Science and Technology, 52*(2), 137–148. doi:10.1002/1097-4571(2000)9999:9999<::AID-ASI1547>3.0.CO;2-E

Fagan, J. C. (2011). Federated search is dead--And good riddance. *Journal of Web Librarianship, 5*(2), 77–79. doi:10.1080/19322909.2011.573533

Fei, X. (2009). Implementation of a federated search system: Resource accessibility issues. *Serials Review, 35*(4), 235–241. doi:10.1016/j.serrev.2009.08.019

Gibson, I., Goddard, L., & Gordon, S. (2009). One box to search them all: Implementing federated search at an academic library. *Library Hi Tech, 27*(1), 118–133. doi:10.1108/07378830910942973

Graham, R. Y. (2004). Subject no-hits searches in an academic library online catalog: An exploration of two potential ameliorations. *College & Research Libraries, 65*(1), 36–54.

Griffiths, J. R., & Brophy, P. (2005). Student searching behavior and the Web: Use of academic resources and Google. *Library Trends, 53*(4), 539–554.

Hanson, C., Hessel, H., Barneson, J., Boudewyns, D., Fransen, J., & Friedman-Shedlov, L. … Traill, S. (2009). Discoverability phase 1 final report. University of Minnesota Libraries. Retrieved from http://purl.umn.edu/48258

Hanson, C., Hessel, H., Barneson, J., Boudewyns, D., Fransen, J., & Friedman-Shedlov, L. … Traill, S. (2009). *Discoverability phase 2 final report.* University of Minnesota Libraries. Retrieved from http://purl.umn.edu/99734

Herskovic, J. R., Tanaka, L. Y., Hersh, W., & Bernstam, E. (2007). A day in the life of PubMed: Analysis of a typical day's query log. *Journal of the American Medical Informatics Association, 14*(2), 212–220. doi:10.1197/jamia.M2191

Jansen, B. J. (2005). Seeking and implementing automated assistance during the search process. *Information Processing & Management, 41*, 909–928. doi:10.1016/j.ipm.2004.04.017

Jansen, B. J. (2006a). Search log analysis: What it is, what's been done, how to do it. *Library & Information Science Research, 28*, 407–432. doi:10.1016/j.lisr.2006.06.005

Jansen, B. J. (2006b). Using temporal patterns of interactions to design effective automated searching assistance. *Communications of the ACM, 49*(4), 72-73-74.

Jansen, B. J., Booth, D. L., & Spink, A. (2009). Patterns of query reformulation during Web searching. *Journal of the American Society for Information Science and Technology, 60*(7), 1358–1371. doi:10.1002/asi.21071

Jansen, B. J., & Spink, A. (2006). How are we searching the World Wide Web? A comparison of nine search engine transaction logs. *Information Processing & Management, 42*(1), 248–263. doi:10.1016/j.ipm.2004.10.007

Jansen, B. J., Spink, A., & Saracevic, T. (2000). Real life, real users, and real needs: A study and analysis of user queries on the Web. *Information Processing & Management, 36*(2), 207–227. doi:10.1016/S0306-4573(99)00056-4

Jung, S., Herlocker, J. L., Webster, J., Mellinger, M., & Frumkin, J. (2008). LibraryFind: System design and usability testing of academic metasearch system. *Journal of the American Society for Information Science and Technology, 59*(3), 375–389. doi:10.1002/asi.20749

Knievel, J. E., Wakimoto, J. C., & Holladay, S. (2009). Does interface design influence catalog use? A case study. *College & Research Libraries, 70*(5), 446–458.

Kriewel, S., & Fuhr, N. (2007). Adaptive search suggestions for digital libraries. *Lecture Notes in Computer Science, 4822*, 220–229. doi:10.1007/978-3-540-77094-7_31

Larson, R. R. (1991). The decline of subject searching: Long-term trends and patterns of index use in an online catalog. *Journal of the American Society for Information Science and Technology, 42*(3), 197–215. doi:10.1002/(SICI)1097-4571(199104)42:3<197::AID-ASI6>3.0.CO;2-T

Lau, E. P., & Goh, D. H. (2006). In search of query patterns: A case study of a university OPAC. *Information Processing & Management, 42*(5), 1316–1329. doi:10.1016/j.ipm.2006.02.003

Lindahl, D. (2007). Metasearch in the users' context. *Serials Librarian, 51*(3/4), 215-216-234.

Liu, W. (2010). Remote users' OPAC searching habits: A comparative case study through Web transaction log analysis. *Kentucky Libraries, 74*(3), 6–13.

Lown, C., & Hemminger, B. (2009). Extracting user interaction information from the transaction logs of a faceted navigation OPAC. *The Code4Lib Journal, 7*, 1-1.

Lucas, W., & Topi, H. (2005). Learning and training to search. In A. Spink, & C. Cole (Eds.), *New directions in cognitive information retrieval* (pp. 209-210-226). Netherlands: Springer.

Malliari, A., & Kyriaki-Manessi, D. (2007). Users' behaviour patterns in academic libraries' OPACs: A multivariate statistical analysis. *New Library World, 108*(3/4), 107–122. doi:10.1108/03074800710735311

Markey, K. (2007a). Twenty-five years of end-user searching, part 1: Research findings. *Journal of the American Society for Information Science and Technology, 58*(8), 1071–1081. doi:10.1002/asi.20462

Markey, K. (2007b). Twenty-five years of end-user searching, part 2: Future research directions. *Journal of the American Society for Information Science and Technology, 58*(8), 1123–1130. doi:10.1002/asi.20601

Matthews, J. R., & Lawrence, G. S. (1984). Further analysis of the CLR online catalog project. *Information Technology and Libraries, 3*, 354–376.

Mi, J., & Weng, C. (2008). Revitalizing the library OPAC: Interface, searching, and display challenges. *Information Technology and Libraries, 27*(1), 5–19.

Moukdad, H., & Large, A. (2001). Users' perceptions of the Web as revealed by transaction log analysis. *Online Information Review, 25*(6), 349–359. doi:10.1108/EUM0000000006534

Moulaison, H. (2008). OPAC queries at a medium-sized academic library: A transaction log analysis. *Library Resources & Technical Services, 52*(4), 230–237.

Novotny, E. (2004). I don't think I click: A protocol analysis study of use of a library online catalog in the internet age. *College & Research Libraries, 65*(6), 525–537.

O'Connor, L., & Lundstrom, K. (2011). The impact of social marketing strategies on the information seeking behaviors of college students. *Reference and User Services Quarterly, 50*(40351), 352–365.

Ozmutlu, S., Spink, A., & Ozmutlu, H. C. (2004). A day in the life of Web searching: An exploratory study. *Information Processing & Management, 40*(2), 319–345. doi:10.1016/S0306-4573(03)00044-X

Peters, T. A. (1993). The history and development of transaction log analysis. *Library Hi Tech, 11*(2), 41–66. doi:10.1108/eb047884

Rochkind, J. (2011). *Article search, and catalog search.* Bibliographic Wilderness Blog. [Web log comment]. Retrieved from http://bibwild. wordpress.com/2011/08/08/article-search-and-catalog-search/#comment-9644

Roe, S. (1999). Online subject access. *Journal of Internet Cataloging, 2*(1), 69–78. doi:10.1300/J141v02n01_07

Russell, D. M. (2007). *Keynote address: What are they thinking? Searching for the mind of the searcher.* Vancouver, Canada: Joint Conference on Digital Libraries.

Ruthven, I. (2008). Interactive information retrieval. *Annual Review of Information Science & Technology, 42*, 43–91. doi:10.1002/aris.2008.1440420109

Tallent, E. (2010). Where are we going? Are we there yet? *Internet Reference Services Quarterly, 15*(1), 3–10. doi:10.1080/10875300903543770

Topi, H., & Lucas, W. (2005a). Mix and match: Combining terms and operators for successful Web searches. *Information Processing & Management, 41*, 801–817. doi:10.1016/j.ipm.2004.03.007

Topi, H., & Lucas, W. (2005b). Searching the Web: Operator assistance required. *Information Processing & Management, 41*(2), 383–403. doi:10.1016/S0306-4573(02)00092-4

Villen-Rueda, L., Senso, J. A., & de Moya-Anegon, F. (2007). The use of OPAC in a large academic library: A transactional log analysis study of subject searching. *Journal of Academic Librarianship, 33*(3), 327–337. doi:10.1016/j.acalib.2007.01.018

Wildemuth, B. M., & O'Neill, A. L. (1995). The "known" in known-item searches: Empirical support for user-centered design. *College & Research Libraries, 56*(3), 265–281.

Williams, S. C., Bonnell, A., & Stoffel, B. (2009). Student feedback on federated search use, satisfaction, and Web presence: Qualitative findings of focus groups. *Reference and User Services Quarterly, 49*(2), 131–139.

Williams, S. C., & Foster, A. K. (2011). Promise fulfilled? An EBSCO discovery service usability study. *Journal of Web Librarianship, 5*(3), 179-180-198. doi: 10.1080/19322909.2011.597590

Yi, K., Beheshti, J., Cole, C., Leide, J. E., & Large, A. (2006). User search behavior of domain-specific information retrieval systems: An analysis of the query logs from PsycINFO and ABC-clio's historical abstracts/America: History and life. *Journal of the American Society for Information Science and Technology, 57*(9), 1208–1220. doi:10.1002/asi.20401

Yu, H., & Young, M. (2004). The impact of Web search engines on subject searching in OPAC. *Information Technology and Libraries*, *23*(4), 168–180.

KEY TERMS AND DEFINITIONS

Adaptive Search Assistance: A system controlled process that adapts to the user's changing needs over the course of the search by presenting users with a series of suggestions to modify, limit, or expand the search depending on specific needs.

Bound Phrase: A multi-word user search term that is searched as a specific phrase with individual words immediately adjacent to each other in the term word order.

Contextual Search Assistance: A series of system-controlled mechanisms that present the user with search assistance suggestions appropriate for the specific search context or situation.

Library Gateway: One or more overarching library Web pages presenting the user with search functionality and links to information resources; usually the library top-level page.

LibGuides: Library developed pathfinders and content sharing sites that utilize the Springshare hosted software platform and content management software.

Search Query Syntax: The format and structure of user-entered search terms.

Transaction Log: A database or file system for capturing and storing user search terms, system responses, and metadata describing every search performed by users.

Web-Scale Systems: Hosted search and discovery systems that feature blended displays of heterogeneous information resources, facet limit mechanisms, and integration with local content management systems.

ENDNOTES

[1] The work reported here was supported by the National Science Foundation grant NSF DUE 07-34992 and Institute for Museum and Library Services grant IMLS LG-06-07-0023-07.

[2] Voyager is a registered trademark of Ex Libris Ltd.

[3] EBSCO Discovery Service is owned by EBSCO Publishing Industries

Chapter 11
Setting a Direction for Discovery:
A Phased Approach

Janet Fransen
University of Minnesota, USA

Lara Friedman-Shedlov
University of Minnesota, USA

Nicole Theis-Mahon
University of Minnesota, USA

Stacie Traill
University of Minnesota, USA

Deborah Boudewyns
University of Minnesota, USA

ABSTRACT

While many other academic libraries are currently or have recently faced the challenge of setting a new direction for their discovery platforms, the University of Minnesota is perhaps unique in its phased approach to the process. In the spring of 2011, the University of Minnesota Libraries appointed a Discoverability task force to identify a Web-scale discovery solution, the third phase in the Discoverability research process. Discoverability 3 Task Force members are now synthesizing the work of two previous phases and other relevant internal and external analyses to develop requirements and selection criteria for the solution. Some of these requirements and criteria are standard for any large-scale system implementation. Others were derived from the findings of the previous two phases of the Discoverability project. The authors discuss the Libraries' phased approach to developing a vision for discovery and selecting a solution that puts the Libraries on a path to fulfilling that vision.

DOI: 10.4018/978-1-4666-1821-3.ch011

INTRODUCTION

As library users become more and more comfortable with each new innovation in the Web-based world, libraries have found themselves struggling to provide an experience that seems as effortless as Google yet directs users to resources owned or licensed by the library. The path to the perfect search tool is further complicated by the range of needs an academic library must meet. If users are to rely on a single search tool, that tool must provide a balance of ease of use and breadth/depth of results that is appropriate for:

- The freshman who needs five credible sources he or she can read, understand, and synthesize.
- The upperclassman who is capable of reading and synthesizing academic work, but still may want to find articles and books from popular sources to provide context for a topic.
- The graduate student who must find and review any and all literature related to his or her topic.
- The researcher who needs to know about new publications in his or her field, but also understand the basics of other disciplines as interdisciplinary work grows.

University of Minnesota Libraries has approached this challenge by charging successive groups with exploring aspects of user expectations and needs, inventorying data sources both within and external to the Libraries, developing a vision for an ideal discovery tool and, finally, issuing a request for proposal (RFP) for the Libraries' next discovery platform. The groups have each operated under the umbrella term "Discoverability," and each has built on the work of the previous Discoverability groups.

In this chapter, members of the three Discoverability groups describe what they found in each phase of this approach and how theoretical discussions and explorations of the current state of the art in discovery led to a series of requirements for the Libraries' next discovery solution.

BACKGROUND

The University of Minnesota is a large public research university, with a flagship campus located in the Twin Cities of Minneapolis and St. Paul, and four coordinate campuses across Minnesota. About 52,000 of the 69,000 enrolled students are on the Twin Cities campus. The University community includes over 4,000 faculty members among its 25,000 employees. The University offers Bachelor's, Master's, and Doctoral degrees in a wide variety of majors, with strong programs across disciplines.

A core value of the University of Minnesota Libraries is offering appropriate services and tools to meet the Libraries' diverse user population's needs. Over the last decade, Libraries staff members have expressed that value through projects such as:

- The Undergraduate Virtual Library, a library-novice-friendly portal for key resources, implemented in 2004 as part of a University-wide focus on undergraduate learning and retention (Prescott & Veldof, 2010).
- The Multi-dimensional Framework for Academic Support project, which analyzed user behavior and resulted in numerous initiatives to create a more productive research support environment (University of Minnesota Libraries, 2006).
- The myLibrary service, a site within the University's institutional portal with content customized according to the user's *affinity*: their role, college, department, and degree program (Hanson, Nackerud, & Jensen, 2008).

In mid-2008, the Libraries began promoting Ex Libris's™¹ Primo®² product, locally branded as MNCAT Plus, as the default search interface for the catalog. Although this early discovery layer was a step forward for undergraduates seeking a friendlier face than the librarian- and researcher-oriented Ex Libris™ Aleph®³ OPAC, more experienced researchers often found it frustrating. Clearly, it would—and will—take some time to design and implement a single discovery tool that serves all users well.

Although library roles and user needs are evolving quickly, the Libraries administration felt it was safe to assume that the Libraries will be connecting people to the information they need for many years to come. With that in mind, the time was right to launch a long-term project to determine how libraries, users, and the technology environment are evolving and what those changes mean for library-mediated discovery.

LITERATURE REVIEW

Each of the first two phases of the Discoverability project involved extensive literature reviews. Interested readers can find bibliographies in the groups' final reports (Hanson, et al., 2009 and Hanson, et al., 2011). Many resources used in those studies are included in the Additional Readings at the end of this chapter.

The Discoverability reports are part of a large volume of literature written between 2008 and 2011 that focuses or touches upon subjects such as the evolving meaning of the library collection and role of the catalog, information-seeking behavior, and user preferences. The discovery product landscape also changed dramatically, spurring librarians to consider just how to evaluate products in light of their own institution's needs.

The shift to online content and collections in libraries presents a new opportunity and challenge for discoverability in libraries. Today's library collections consist of print and non-print items,

as well as data and a variety of other information formats. Pradhan, Trivedi, and Arora (2011) discuss how Web-scale discovery allows users to search, refine, and discover all content comprising the library's collections seamlessly and cohesively. Although not entirely perfect, discovery tools allow users to perform a broadcast search across information sources and refine their search as needed. However, as Chew (2010) mentioned, these new tools are using MARC in new ways to produce a contextualized and faceted discovery environment for the user.

At the same time, libraries must contend with the fact that users' information needs and seeking behaviors cannot be generalized to one set of user requirements. Connaway, Dickey, and Radford (2011) use several research methods to show the importance of convenience as a factor in information seeking, but concede that its importance relative to other factors and even its definition depend on the user's situation. Fisher and Julien (2009) review the extensive research over the last few years on the role of context, as well as the "human factor:" academic role and discipline, occupational group, or people in everyday settings.

As discovery tools evolve, generalized assumptions ("They want it to work like Google") are becoming more nuanced. In a recent Library Journal Reviews post, librarians from four institutions discussed their experiences with the newly-adopted discovery tools. Amanda Clay Powers of Mississippi State University praises EBSCO Discovery Service™⁴ for solving common problems for both lower-level undergraduates and advanced researchers. At the same time, Powers notes that students such as upper-level undergraduates still have more success with subject-specific databases (Discovering What Works, 2011).

A small but growing body of literature evaluates the next generation discovery tools that have been adopted by other libraries facing the same set of challenges. Most of these articles focus on the selection process (Cai, Dou and Jiang, 2011; Brubaker, Leach-Murray, and Parker, 2011; Becher and Schmidt, 2011). Missing from the literature are thorough studies or evaluations of the tools once deployed; while many go into significant detail on the features and concerns regarding the discovery tools as well as the criteria used to make a decision on which to adopt, there is as yet little research on how the latest Web-scale tools perform "in the wild." Yang and Wegner's (2010) article notably relies strictly on real-life examples and demonstrations rather than vendor claims, but the study was limited to verifying the presence of specific features, rather than a thorough evaluation of their performance and/or usability. A few such studies (e.g. Emmanuel, 2011) are now available for the "next generation" catalogs that began appearing in the mid- to late-2000s, but the next wave of innovation represented by Web-scale discovery tools is still too new to have been the subject of this type of investigation. As Marshall Breeding notes in "State of the Art in Library Discovery" (2010), adoption cycles are sluggish, despite the wealth of new tools that are now available, so relatively few institutions have much experience with any of them.

PHASE 1: SURVEYING THE LANDSCAPE AND GATHERING DATA

In 2008, the Libraries convened the Discoverability Exploratory group to explore discovery behavior and corresponding tools or systems that might make relevant resources more visible and easier to find. The group's investigation involved identifying trends about user search and discovery behavior, gathering and analyzing systems data, and determining if the trends identified in the current literature aligned with that of the local data collected on user behavior at the University of Minnesota.

Trends

To identify user behavior drawn from user studies, the group compiled and analyzed available literature (as of December 2008) describing user discovery activity. The literature review included case studies such as the task force report on resource discovery from the University of Wisconsin and usability testing by the University of Washington, the EDUCAUSE study of undergraduate use of technology, and the 2008 Horizon Report. The group also consulted articles written by leading practitioners such as Peter Brantley, Lorcan Dempsey, Derek Law, and Clifford Lynch. For a complete list of articles used for the trend review, consult the suggested reading section at the end of this chapter.

A number of common themes emerged from the group's study and discussion of these articles and studies. The group consolidated these themes into five major trends:

1. Users discover relevant resources outside traditional library systems
2. Users expect discovery and delivery to coincide
3. Users increasingly rely on portable Internet-capable devices
4. Discovery increasingly happens through recommending
5. Users increasingly rely on nontraditional information objects (Hanson et al., 2009)

Although none of the individual trends identified were surprising, even in 2008, as a group the trends made a compelling case for rethinking the Libraries' discovery systems and priorities. The trends raised questions about how much, given the degree to which users rely on Google and other outside portals, the Libraries should invest in developing a search interface without a very specific or specialized audience in mind.

The trends also highlighted the importance of making local resources discoverable in those

Table 1. The group investigated any likely data source in an effort to prove or disprove the trends

Question	Data Sources investigated	Findings
How much are the Libraries' current discovery tools used? Has that number increased or decreased over time?	Statistics from the OPAC (Aleph®) and current discovery tool (Primo®)	Statistics show that users searched the catalog through either interface more often than any other library resource. However, comparisons over time proved impossible due to changes in how searches were counted.
	OpenURL link resolver (SFX®5) source and target logs	The OpenURL link resolver moves users from discovery to delivery, and the "Find It" page that presents the options for fulfillment is the most-viewed page on the Libraries website. However, logs show that users can and do discover articles through tools not controlled by the Libraries. Google Scholar™6 is the most striking example: Requests to the link resolver from Google Scholar™ have climbed steadily since its release in late 2004.
	Individual database statistics (five of the top ten most-used databases were sampled)	Not useful for answering this question due to the number of ways a user might come in contact with a database, including through proxy links, federated search, OpenURL resolver, or directly from a bookmark.
	Server logs for Archives and Special Collections finding aids	Although finding aid statistics didn't provide evidence of more or less use of library discovery tools, the statistics did underscore the fact that users approach finding aids from a very different perspective than other library web pages. Users of the main site viewed an average of four pages per visit, while finding aid users viewed an average of almost twelve pages. Twenty-five percent of finding aid users spent more than fifteen minutes per visit viewing content.
	Server logs for repositories hosted by the Libraries	Statistics for all three repositories hosted by the Libraries showed extensive traffic directed to individual items through search engines.
The Libraries currently expose the catalog to users throughout the state through a discovery layer called the MnLINK Gateway. Do users discover the Libraries' resources through that tool?	Statistics from the OPAC on how many searches were done via the Z39.50 protocol	Users of the MnLINK Gateway search University Libraries content by default, whether they intend to or not. In addition, the MnLINK Gateway "polls" multiple times for one search. Therefore, even though the top-ranked method of searching the catalog during the time period investigated was the Z39.50 protocol, the group could not conclude that users intended to search the Libraries catalog more often through that interface than any other.
What percentage of visits to the Libraries' Web site comes from mobile devices? Is that percentage increasing over time?	Server logs	Unfortunately, the Web statistics program in use during the period studied did not differentiate operating systems or devices used to access sites, so no data could be analyzed to find evidence of the trend.
Are external Web sites (such as Google or Wikipedia) driving people to the Libraries' Web site, resources on the Libraries' servers?	Server logs for pages within each of the Libraries' subdomains.	Users rarely viewed pages beyond the domain and subdomain home pages. However, a few secondary pages accounted for a disproportionate number of visits. Users were directed to those pages largely through Google searches, and occasionally from Wikipedia pages or other academic institutions' sites.

outside systems. This suggests that perhaps the library would do best to focus its resources less on search (at least on general search) and more on delivery and fulfillment.

Data to Support Trends

Identifying the most prominent trends in the literature is helpful in framing a discussion, but

eventually that discussion will always come back to the individual institution: Can one really assume that trends identified by one author or institution are valid for users at the University of Minnesota? In the spirit of evidence-based decision making, the first Discoverability group sought evidence of the trends in the Libraries' own operations and systems by formulating specific questions. Table 1 outlines a few examples.

As Table 1 illustrates, some of the questions could be addressed by data from multiple systems, but others were unlikely to be answered by any of local data. Although the group found strong anecdotal evidence of the five trends, it was difficult to support the trends' validity armed only with the local statistics and data.

Statistics offered some description of user behavior, but provided little insight into user intent. The complications encountered with the data, or lack thereof, indicated that the Libraries would benefit from closer attention to tools and processes related to efficient and ongoing data collection. Therefore, when the group synthesized the identified trends into a set of guiding principles for future investigations, the following principle was written to address the data problem. The principle reads:

In order to remain responsive, relevant, and useful to our users, we must aggressively measure and analyze user behavior through local system statistics. These efforts will complement our ongoing assessments utilizing focus groups, usability studies, and reviews of applicable literature.

Most of the other guiding principles identified by this first Discoverability group relate directly to the end user:

- Users draw little distinction between discovery and delivery; systems, data, and information objects should be optimized for fulfillment.
- In order to remain agile and responsive in a rapidly changing information environment, our systems and data structures should provide us with the greatest possible flexibility for frequent iteration and reuse by ourselves and others.
- In order to best facilitate our users' discovery of relevant information, we should strive to be end-user device/platform agnostic.

- Discovery should be organized around users rather than collections or systems. This organization should be based on realistic, evidence-based models of our users and their research tasks.
- Users are successfully discovering relevant resources through non-library systems. We need to ensure that items in our collections and licensed resources are discoverable in non-library environments.
- Users rely on system-and peer-generated recommendations to discover relevant resources. We should capture the data necessary to provide targeted suggestions to users and defer to network-level systems where critical mass already exists.

PHASE 2: DEVELOPING A VISION AND BEST PRACTICES

Grounded with the set of guiding principles, the Libraries were poised to launch a new phase of work. Two objectives in the Discoverability Phase 2 charge came directly from the guiding principles:

- Because users are successfully discovering relevant resources through non-library systems, the group was asked to inventory and analyze the internal and external data sources to which the Libraries provide access.
- Because discovery should be organized around users rather than collections or systems, the group was asked to identify and understand the user groups the discovery interface would be serving.

The sponsors assumed the next phase of the Discoverability process would result in a recommendation for the Libraries' next discovery environment. Therefore, the charge included that the group:

- Develop a vision for a future discovery environment based on the findings of Phase 1.
- Investigate and summarize how selected peer institutions have redefined and redesigned their discovery environments.

Exposing Local Data through the Discovery System

Web statistics collected during Phase 1 alerted the Libraries to the number of people finding locally produced data sources through search engines and external aggregations. However, in many cases a user would need to know that a data source existed in order to find it from within the Libraries' Web sites. In an ideal discovery environment, these local data sources should be ingested and searchable.

In addition to the library catalog, local data sources include discipline-specific repositories, digitized collections, and applications that extract and adapt catalog data for a particular purpose or audience. In many cases, these local data sources have been created over the course of years in different systems, and intended for a variety of uses. Some of the sources adhere to established metadata standards, while others rely on various homegrown metadata schemas. Some sources include digital objects and metadata describing those objects, while others include only metadata surrogates for physical and digital items. Some data sources are updated and used regularly, while others have outlived the need that initially spurred their creation.

During Phase 2, the group worked to document these many local data sources and their defining characteristics. Once defined, the group considered which characteristics made a particular data source a candidate for inclusion in the future discovery environment.

One important characteristic is the uniqueness of the data in each source. When a source does not contain objects or metadata unique to the local institution, the institution must evaluate the cost/benefit of incorporating that source into a discovery environment. A local database that largely duplicates catalog data in a non-standard metadata schema is probably not worth the time and effort required to translate it into a form ingestible by a discovery tool. On the other hand, a local database that includes both unique digitized objects and metadata for those objects may be well worth the effort to prepare it for inclusion, even if the relative cost of doing so is greater.

Uniqueness is not the sole consideration: Larger databases with non-unique content that adhere to nationally or internationally accepted metadata standards and that exist in systems with extensive capabilities for data export (such as the local catalog) typically require less effort—or at least less new effort—to expose their content. Using a "grid of exclusivity," an analyst can plot the uniqueness of a resource against the degree to which sources may be shared with external sources. The grid, shown in Figure 1, reveals the data sources with the highest exclusivity and the lowest degree of current sharing. For these sources, the effort to expose the data will have a greater benefit.

A discussion of how to expose worthwhile locally-created data leads inevitably to the question of where that data should be exposed. To begin to answer that question, the group created a list of external data aggregations with existing known value to users and their salient characteristics. Table 2 lists some types of external aggregators identified by the group.

Each type of aggregation requires a slightly different analysis to determine whether an institution should include its metadata and/or digital objects. Several factors to consider for each aggregator include:

- **Ease of access.** Is the aggregator's content freely accessible, or is authentication required?
- **Coverage.** Does the aggregator contain most of the content that users might rea-

Figure 1. The grid of exclusivity was useful in determining which data sources were most worth ingesting for the discovery layer

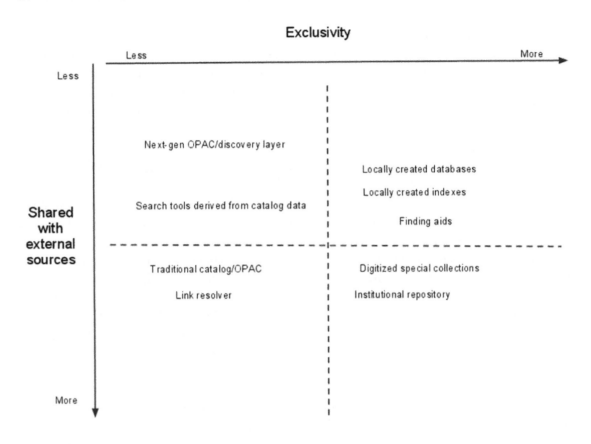

Table 2. Types of external aggregators investigated by the Phase 2 group

Aggregation Type	Examples
General metadata aggregations	WorldCat®, Google Scholar™, OAIster®[7], Primo Central™, Google
General data object aggregations	HathiTrust, Wikipedia, Internet Archive, Flickr®[8] Commons
Disciplinary aggregations	AgEcon Search, ArXiv, Earth Prints
Form aggregations	Digital Dissertations, MERLOT (learning objects), ArtSTOR, ArchiveGrid[SM9]
Topical aggregations	Minnesota Reflections (state-wide repository for cultural heritage organizations), Ethic-Share (collaboration tool for the study of ethics)

sonably expect, or are there substantial gaps in coverage?

- **Ease of contribution.** Can metadata and/or resources be contributed automatically via a protocol like OAI/PMH, or is more active effort required of contributors?

- **Standardization requirements for metadata and file formats.** Does the aggregator accept a variety of formats and standards, or must contributions adhere to a particular set of standards?

- **Cost.** Are there costs to contribute metadata or resources, and/or to search and retrieve them?
- **Rights management.** Are there use limitations imposed by the aggregator on resources it contains? Are legal rights to content managed responsibly?
- **Commitment to preservation.** Is the aggregator committed to preserving resources contributed to it?
- **Maintenance.** Does the aggregator devote effort to maintaining currency and accuracy for its data? Are contributors able to maintain and correct their contributions?
- **Local impact and interest.** Does the aggregator serve the needs of any particular local interest groups? How will increased exposure of local data impact demand on institutional resources?

Among these, standardization is perhaps the most important practical concern in analyzing the readiness of local data sources for broader exposure. This factor determines how easy it will be for any future discovery layer to ingest and expose the data. For example, metadata created according to a locally developed scheme, or metadata created according an inconsistently applied scheme, may pose difficulties for ingestion by external aggregations. While organizational capacity to create robust metadata may be limited, libraries should strive to create readily interoperable metadata whenever possible.

By making an inventory of internal data sources and external aggregations, the Libraries gained a more complete and nuanced picture of expectations for interactions among the discovery layer and other systems.

User Communities

The discovery layer connects users to the information they need. With a clear sense of both traditional library collections and more ad hoc data sources in mind, members of the Phase 2 group turned their focus to the user communities served by that data environment.

The group determined that people at the University of Minnesota rarely have information needs or information seeking behaviors that differ from their counterparts at other large research universities. In late 2009, the Libraries surveyed users of the catalog (MNCAT Classic) and the discovery layer (MNCAT Plus) and found striking differences in the degree of satisfaction and primary reasons for using each tool based on the user's college affiliation or status (Chew, 2010). Both the survey results and anecdotal evidence led the group to conclude that Libraries users' needs and behaviors are distinct from each other based on factors like discipline (arts, engineering, health sciences, etc.) and status (undergraduate, graduate student, faculty, etc.). To ensure that a cross-section of users is considered, as decisions regarding discovery are made, the group developed a set of user personas. The personas are very specific, but fictional, users.

Personas are most effective when the set is small; many software applications are written with a single user persona in mind. The group sought to maximize the number of users represented while minimizing the number of personas future decision-makers must synthesize and accommodate. After casting a broad net based on affiliation, role, discipline, and major, the group trimmed the set of personas to those for whom significant literature or first-hand knowledge existed, and who were distinct from other personas in a meaningful way. Table 3 shows the final set of sixteen personas.

The sixteen personas are based on a combination of recent literature on information seeking behavior for specific groups and input from subject specialists at the University of Minnesota. The complete personas, available on a University of Minnesota Web site, include photos and paragraphs written from the individual's perspective, as shown in Figure 2.

Table 3. Sixteen personas in four categories act as a cross-section of libraries users

Affiliates	Non-Affiliates	Health Sciences	Other Disciplines
Undergraduates Graduate Students Faculty	High School Students Engineering Professionals Commercial Users Archives Users	Clinicians Professional Students Researchers/Fellows	Arts and Humanities Visual Arts Engineering Law Physical/Life Sciences Social Sciences

Figure 2. Each persona includes a photo and paragraph written from the individual's perspective (University of Minnesota, 2010)

Affiliate Users
Undergraduates
Graduate Students
Faculty

Non-affiliate Users
High School Students
Engineering Professionals
Commercial Users
Archives Users

Health Science Disciplines
Clinicians
Professional Students - Health Sciences
Researchers/Fellows - Health Sciences

Other Disciplines
Arts and Humanities
Visual Arts
Engineering
Law
Physical/Life Sciences
Social Sciences

Edit sidebar

Graduate Students

Now that I'm a graduate student, I spend a lot of time doing the same things that faculty do - practice, I suppose. Certainly my research is much more in depth than it used to be, or that my students do in my classes. I'm so busy that I have to fit my research into any gaps I can find - it's hard to sit down and really get organized. I've heard other people mention databases that they use from the library, but I don't know how they ever found them. There are so many choices from the library and, like I said, I'm working around lots of other responsiblities so I end up getting frustrated. It would be great if I could search lots of databases at once. That way I could really make the most of the citations I'm working from. It would also help me when my research spreads into other disciplinary areas or focuses on data I'm not familiar with. What I really need to do get my research published and published in the right place and I'd love it if there were some easy tool from the library to help me with that.

From the literature

- More interested in numeric data than other groups (Desktracker stats)
- Often work from/need help with citations (Desktracker stats)
- Identify themselves more closely with academic researchers than undergraduates (Hampton-Reeves et al., 2009)
- Often lack basic research skills and work by trial and error. Largely unaware of many library services offered (University of Minnesota Libraries, 2006)

From our colleagues

Kate Peterson, Information Literacy librarian

- Graduate students are often overwhelmed by the availability of information/discovery and don't know when to stop (or how to be systematic) and thus want tools that can, for example, search multiple databases together or the 'one library search' idea, at least as a way to improve efficiency. This is mostly a social sciences and interdisciplinary challenge.
- This point from the Life Sciences profile is also relevant to many other graduate students: "Work is increasingly collaborative. Obstacles include different vocabularies, not knowing core journals, and not knowing where to publish (Marcus, Ball, Delserone, Hribar, & Loftus, 2007)

References

Hampton-Reeves, S., Mashiter, C., Westaway, J., Lumsden, P., Day, H., & Hewertson, H. (2009). Students' use of research content in teaching and learning. *Report for the Joint Information Systems Council.*

University of Minnesota Libraries. (2006). A multi-dimensional framework for academic support. Minneapolis: University of Minnesota. Retrieved from http://purl.umn.edu/5540

The Libraries' Vision for Discovery

The inventory of internal data sources, analysis of types of external aggregators, and development of user personas were all tools intended to be used by the next Discoverability group, which would be charged with recommending a specific product as the Libraries' next default discovery layer. In addition to these three practical tools, the Phase 2 group developed a high-level vision for discovery built upon the work and research from Phase 1, and the problems with having a decentralized discovery environment. The vision further synthesized the research assembled on user needs (including work from Phase 1) and local collection imperatives and opportunities. In developing and articulating the vision, the group was directed to ignore the limitations of products currently available.

The Libraries' Vision for discovery identifies seven key concepts. The seven concepts are:

1. Scopes, customized according to the user's community, past usage, and preferences.
2. Integrated metadata layer, which makes a broad range of resources available to the discovery layer.
3. Attention to processes and best practices needed to expose internal data to external systems.
4. Expand on discovery and delivery options through external data aggregations.
5. Object manipulation and personal curation, to facilitate delivery and to build on the concept of literature searching as an ongoing process in research.
6. Make use of systems that facilitate data-driven decision making.
7. Ongoing review and evolution of the discovery environment.

Below is a brief description of each of the concepts and the imposing factors, which informed the vision.

Local data sources are available in vast numbers of disparate sources, and present users with a complex, jumbled environment. If users want to be comprehensive in their searching, they need to pull information from different data sources, but may not be aware of all the existing sources.

Scopes provide a means for the discovery layer to present relevant resources and information based on a user's community affiliation. The scopes could be predetermined based on a set of characteristics associated with a user affiliation and a set of resources selected for that affiliation by a librarian, or they could be dynamic in nature and created or enhanced by the users themselves. Libraries are already using scopes as a means to organize sets of resources for specific users or user communities. For example, a library may present a set of resources for undergraduates or may list resource sets by specific discipline. The idea of scopes presented in the Phase 2 report expands this concept since it is dynamic and allows a mechanism for the user to create or enhance the set.

An integrated metadata layer would provide the backbone for the scopes. The integrated layer would allow disparate data sources to be presented in a single interface which could then be scoped. Users would see a consistent search interface and work in an environment that offers preselected data sources and provides the opportunity for users to select their own data sources.

The exploration of user communities and their needs suggests there is a strong desire for personalization in the search environment. The concept of personalization and object interaction is rooted in Web 2.0 and not new to library users. Users have come to expect that search algorithms will adapt to their behavior, and that users have the ability to manipulate and repurpose discovered items for themselves. Tools for personalization are interactive and offer opportunities for Libraries' staff to create new access points and enhance the discovery process for users.

As in Phase 1, the Phase 2 group emphasized the Libraries' need to make data-driven decisions. Systems and their functionality need to be reviewed and revised to meet the changing information needs and information seeking methods of library users. The process of reviewing functionality and seeking out improved tools should be fluid and continuous.

These key concepts provide the foundation for future exploration into discovery, and a framework for identifying and possibly choosing a discovery tool for the Libraries.

PHASE 3: DEFINING REQUIREMENTS

During the initial phases of the Discoverability process, the groups had the luxury of combining the observable with the intangible or aspirational. The Discoverability Phase 1 group gathered institutional data, but also explored trends in user behavior. Data only rarely confirmed the trends, but the group did not consider the trends any less valid because they weren't measurable by existing methods. The Discoverability Phase 2 group inventoried existing internal data sources and characterized external data sources, but also proposed a vision for a discovery layer that would meet the needs of diverse users. This vision, with its concepts of scope and an integrated metadata layer, describes an ideal beyond the capabilities of the tools currently on the market.

The group that convened for Phase 3 of the Discoverability process, in process as of this writing, has no such luxury. While the previous two groups were exploratory, the Discoverability Phase 3 group is a task force: The group is charged with conducting a request for proposal (RFP) process that will lead to the recommendation of a unified discovery environment for the University of Minnesota. The task force must reconcile the vision for an ideal discovery system with the reality of the current marketplace.

Outside Factors to Consider

If a discovery tool existed in a vacuum, the RFP process would be straight-forward. The task force could simply transform the previous group's vision into a list of requirements, issue the RFP, and wait for the responses to roll in. Unfortunately, the tool and the process are subject to many outside factors:

- The information technology environment at the institution
- The library information ecosystem, both present and anticipated future
- The current state of the art

The Information Technology Environment

After spending more than two years exploring the information seeking/discovery landscape, selecting a new discovery tool is the next logical step. At the same time, the current economic climate is quite different from that of mid-2008. Although the Libraries strive to continuously improve the user experience, it seems as though the timing could be better. Like academic institutions everywhere, the University of Minnesota and its Libraries are under increasing pressure to cut costs while maintaining service levels. However, the information technology of the Libraries relies upon the University's Office of Information Technology (OIT). OIT owns the server on which the current discovery system resides, and that server has reached the end of its life. OIT prefers not to host the next generation discovery system at all; the new discovery layer must run under a Software as a Service (SaaS) delivery model.

The SaaS requirement means that the known options are automatically narrowed. Although it is possible that a new or unknown candidate will appear once the RFP has been issued, at this writing the group assumes that the possible choices for a Web-scale hosted discovery tool are:

Figure 3. University libraries ecosystem as of Summer 2011, with year of implementation

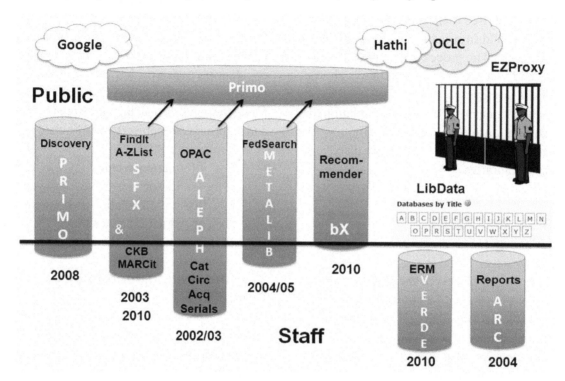

- EBSCO Discovery Service™
- Hosted Primo® with Primo Central™[10]
- Summon™[11]
- WorldCat®[12] Local

The University's purchasing department has experience with SaaS RFPs, which simplifies the process of developing the RFP. A number of requirements are boilerplate so they can be directly copied to the RFP for a discovery system.

The Library Ecosystem

A discovery tool is the lens through which the user sees the library's physical and virtual collections. It is also the user's gateway to actually getting the items they need. Library staff members see the whole picture: the discovery tool is just one part of and must fit within the elaborate library ecosystem. In the course of responding to an increasingly digital information universe, systems and pieces of software were grafted, overlaid, or linked to the core ILS. Figure 3 sketches the various systems and tools that make up the University of Minnesota Libraries discovery environment as of summer 2011.

The current Libraries ecosystem includes numerous public-facing services: the OPAC, federated search services, recommender services, FindIt (open linking from citations to full-text), and the A to Z list of available databases. Each service is provided by a separate tool, each was acquired at a different time and integrated with the Aleph® ILS, and each has its own back-end functions for staff. Further tools are needed by staff for electronic resource management (ERM) and generating reports. Additional discovery and delivery services are provided by Primo® and through LibData course pages. The increasing number of cloud-based resources, such as Google and HathiTrust, adds to the complexity, as does the need for authentication, which is handled by EZProxy®[13].

As of summer 2013, the Libraries will be adopting Ex Libris's™ new unified resource management tool, Alma. Alma will replace the tools filling all of the functions on the staff side of the diagram, but it does not perform all of the functions those tools fill on the public side. Regardless of what the Libraries choose as a discovery layer, the functions of these systems still need to be fulfilled and the discovery system will need to integrate with both the current suite of tools and with Alma.

The State of the Art

At the most fundamental level, the biggest challenge to selecting a discovery solution is the current state of the art. Web-scale discovery remains a relatively immature market, and the available systems that work within information technology environment and library ecosystem fall short of the Discoverability Phase 2 group's vision. Current systems are capable of meeting certain needs, such as integrating data from disparate sources and filtering search results on multiple criteria. But based on information gathered from preliminary testing, marketing material, and resources such as the ALA Library Technology Report "Web Scale Discovery Services" (Vaughan, 2011a), other aspects of the vision do not appear to be achievable at this time.

Scopes, as described in the Vision, are still some time away. Most systems allow the user to save a search, but are not set up to create a profile, either by the Libraries based on pre-established user groups or by the user based on past usage or stated preferences. There is little evidence that systems can handle metadata at the level of granularity that would allow the group's vision of scopes to be realized. And while the ways in which users can interact with resources they discover continue to expand, many of the functions envisioned, such as the ability to annotate or to create and share ad-hoc collections remain theoretical.

The vision is farther-reaching than the current market supports. The RFP development process, then, requires that the task force choose which aspects of the vision are most important and should be included in the RFP, whether any product is known to meet the requirement or not. The task force must also consider what questions to ask the vendors about how their products behave.

Defining and Prioritizing RFP Requirements

The group drafted initial RFP requirements based on the Libraries' vision for discovery, the known constraints of the University and Libraries environment, additional feedback from Libraries staff, and market research. The considerations outlined above made the already laborious process of compiling and refining these requirements for publication in the RFP even more lengthy and complex. In particular, the need for the system to work with the Libraries' current ILS as well the new back-end system that will be up and running in 2013 (which will be very different in terms of its functions and architecture) considerably complicated the list of requirements. The group was also concerned that the requirements anticipate the issues raised by many of the earliest adopters of Web-scale discovery services.

Key areas of the RFP include the following:

- The basic concept of "Web-scale" discovery suggested many questions about how desired outcomes would be achieved. The system will have its own massive index of article and repository content that will be integrated with local resources, providing a single search across the catalog, print and e-journals and articles, special collections and the collections of peer institutions. Related RFP requirements include questions about the types of metadata that would be ingested and indexed, how the coverage of journals and databases indexed in the discovery tool would compare to Libraries subscriptions, and how variations in the types and formats of metadata in various sources would be accommodated in the tool.

- The group is aware that the market increasingly includes tools that have been created by companies that have traditionally been in the aggregation and publishing business. Concerns have been raised about potential bias in the content and presentation of the search results. The RFP thus includes requirements to describe how indexing and relevance rankings ensure high quality and unbiased results regardless of the source of the metadata and any relationships with publishers.

- While the move to a hosted tool frees the University from many system maintenance tasks, it also potentially limits the Libraries' ability to customize the tool. A number of RFP questions concern the availability of robust APIs that will allow customers to access and extend the system's capabilities. For example, the Libraries may wish to provide specialized searches that access user account information, or supply permanent URLS for resources and sets of resources.

- The group remains committed to finding a tool that is appropriate not only for novice users, but for experienced users of library tools. Related RFP requirements include questions about how users can identify peer-reviewed material and what types of shortcuts are provided for power users. Also relevant to this point are a number of questions about how a searcher knows which databases are included in a particular search and whether and how the user is referred to specific, relevant databases for additional searching. In addition, the RFP

requests descriptions of any usability testing that the vendor has conducted.

- A concern that was raised repeatedly by Libraries staff and is echoed in the reports of early adopters of Web-scale discovery systems focuses on the ability to conduct reliable known-item searches. Early adopters note that the discovery service has not replaced the catalog, which continues to be an important tool for finding specific titles. Once the Libraries transition to Alma in 2013, users will no longer have the luxury of falling back on an OPAC should the discovery layer fail. Therefore, any discovery layer the Libraries adopt must address this challenge.

- As a large research institution with 14 separate library buildings and many specialized collections, University of Minnesota Libraries staff strongly desire the ability to search within specific collections, in addition to the ability to apply facets after a search. Related requirements ask about the ability to limit or pre-construct searches in various ways.

- The Libraries collections encompass material in over 300 languages, including over 155,000 in Chinese, Japanese, and Korean. The new discovery system must handle searching and indexing in multiple languages. Requirements outlined in the RFP ask about UTF-8 compliance, Unicode, and CJK (Chinese/Japanese/Korean) and other vernaculars, as well as normalization of searching to accommodate both use and non-use of accents and diacritics.

- The success of initiatives to improve access and discovery in the Libraries depends on the ability to analyze data from Libraries systems. The first Discoverability group uncovered the need for data and statistics that are not currently available. The RFP therefore includes detailed questions about the types and quality of statistics and reporting available from the discovery layer.

CONCLUSION

As the group readies the RFP for release and begins the process of finally selecting a discovery system from among the available options, its biggest challenge will be managing expectations about what is actually possible. For example, based on the architecture of existing Web-scale discovery systems, alphabetical browsing--a feature identified as highly desirable for locating known items--may not be available in any system. However, if a system can in other ways effectively overcome the obstacles to known item searches, it is perhaps a feature we could sacrifice.

More problematic is the Discoverability 2 group's vision of "scopes." Scopes attempt to address the needs of specific audiences, including faculty and graduate students who need to search comprehensively within a particular discipline. Yet early adopters report that while the new Web-scale systems they have adopted are effective for discovery across disciplines, they are less effective once research is focused in-depth on a specific discipline (Vaughan, 2011b). Scopes, as envisioned in Discoverability 2, may not be a feature in any currently available system. The group may instead look for configuration options and APIs that would facilitate developing something like scopes for targeted audiences in the near future.

Given the probable trade-offs and gaps between what was envisioned and what is actually available, one might well question the value of a process as lengthy and detailed as this. The phased approached has enabled Libraries staff to anticipate and more fully consider future challenges and changes for library search and discovery as well as information technology in general. These include the increasing de-coupling of "back-end" staff-facing systems from the discovery layer and the move to "the cloud." The life cycle of systems is shorter than it once was, and all libraries will need to be more nimble; data need to be more portable and transformable. While the Libraries may or may not identify a system that embodies the full vision, the multi-phase process undertaken over the past three years will continue to serve the institution well. Having articulated the ideal, the University of Minnesota is in a better position to shape the future development of systems, and is better prepared to address their short-comings in the meantime.

ACKNOWLEDGMENT

The authors gratefully acknowledge the work of all three Discoverability groups, and particularly Cody Hanson, Heather Hessel, and Chiat Naun Chew, who each filled chair or co-chair roles during the Discoverability process.

REFERENCES

Becher, M., & Schmidt, K. (2011). Taking discovery systems for a test drive. *Journal of Web Librarianship*, 5(3), 199–219. doi:10.1080/1932 2909.2011.583134

Breeding, M. (2010). State of the art in library discovery 2010. *Computers in Libraries,* January-February. Retrieved from http://www.librarytechnology.org/ltg-displaytext.pl?RC=14574

Brubaker, N., Leach-Murray, S., & Parker, S. (2011). Shapes in the cloud: Finding the right discovery layer. *Online*, 35(2), 20–26.

Chew, C. (2010). Next generation OPACs: A cataloging viewpoint. *Cataloging & Classification Quarterly*, 48(4), 330–342. doi:10.1080/01639370903437709

Chew, C., Fransen, J., Gangl, S., Hendrickson, L., Hessel, H., Mastel, K., Nelsen, A. ... Peterson, J. (2010). *MNCAT Plus and MNCAT Classic survey: Results and analysis.* Retrieved from http://purl.umn.edu/92473

Connaway, L. S., Dickey, T. J., & Radford, M. L. (2011). "If it is too inconvenient I'm not going after it:" Convenience as a critical factor in information-seeking behaviors. *Library & Information Science Research, 33*(3), 179–190. doi:10.1016/j.lisr.2010.12.002

Emanuel, J. (2011). Usability of the VuFind next-generation online catalog. *Information Technology and Libraries, 30*(1), 44–52.

Fisher, K. E., & Julien, H. (2009). Information behavior. *Annual Review of Information Science & Technology, 43*(1), 1–73. doi:10.1002/aris.2009.1440430114

Hanson, C., Hessel, H., Barneson, J., Boudewyns, D., Fransen, J., Friedman-Shedlov, L. ... Traill, S. (2009). *Discoverability phase 1 final report.* University of Minnesota Libraries. Retrieved from http://purl.umn.edu/48258

Hanson, C., Hessel, H., Barneson, J., Boudewyns, D., Fransen, J., Friedman-Shedlov, L. ... West, A. (2011). *Discoverability phase 2 final report.* University of Minnesota Libraries. Retrieved from http://purl.umn.edu/99734

Hanson, C., Nackerud, S., & Jensen, K. (2008). Affinity strings: Enterprise data for resource recommendations. *Code4Lib,* (5). Retrieved from http://journal.code4lib.org/articles/501

Library Journal Reviews. (2011, December 7). *Discovering what works: Librarians compare discovery interface experiences.* Retrieved from http://reviews.libraryjournal.com/2011/12/reference/discovering-what-works-librarians-compare-discovery-interface-experiences/

Pradhan, D. R., Trivedi, K., & Arora, J. (2011). *Searching online resources in new discovery environment: A state- of-the-art review.* Retrieved from http://ir.inflibnet.ac.in/dxml/bitstream/handle/1944/1623/14.pdf?sequence=1

Prescott, M., & Veldof, J. (2010). A process approach to defining services for undergraduates. *portal: Libraries and the Academy, 10*(1), 29–56. doi:10.1353/pla.0.0085

University of Minnesota Libraries. (2006). *A multi-dimensional framework for academic support: Final report.* University of Minnesota Libraries. Retrieved from http://purl.umn.edu/5540

University of Minnesota Libraries. (2010). *Library user communities.* University of Minnesota Libraries. Retrieved from http://purl.umn.edu/99734

Vaughan, J. (2011a). Investigations into library Web-scale discovery services. *Articles (Libraries), Paper 44.* Retrieved from http://digitalcommons.library.unlv.edu/lib_articles/44

Vaughan, J. (2011b). Web scale discovery services. *Library Technology Reports, 47*(1).

Yang, S. Q., & Wagner, K. (2010). Evaluating and comparing discovery tools: How close are we towards next generation catalog? *Library Hi Tech, 28*(4), 690–709. doi:10.1108/07378831011096312

ADDITIONAL READING

Anderson, J. Q., & Rainie, L. (2008). *The future of the Internet III.* Retrieved from http://pewinternet.org/Reports/2008/The-Future-of-the-Internet-III.aspx

Bhatnagar, G., Dennis, S., Duque, G., Henry, S., MacEachern, M., Teasley, S., & Varnum, K. (2010). *University of Michigan article discovery working group final report.* Retrieved June 16, 2011, from http://www.lib.umich.edu/files/adwg/final-report.pdf

Bowen, J. (2008). Metadata to support next-generation library resource discovery: Lessons from the eXtensible catalog, phase 1. *Information Technology & Libraries, 27*(2), 5–19.

Brantley, P. (2008). Architectures for collaboration: Roles and expectation for digital libraries. *EDUCAUSE Review, 43*(2), 30–38.

Cai, H., Dou, T., & Jiang, A. (2011). Effective approaches to the evaluation and selection of a discovery tool. In Xing, C., Crestani, F., & Rauber, A. (Eds.), *Digital libraries: For cultural heritage, knowledge dissemination, and future creation* (pp. 347–356). Berlin, Germany: Springer. doi:10.1007/978-3-642-24826-9_43

DeFelice, B., Kortfelt, J., Mead, T., Mounts, M., Pawlek, C., Seaman, D. … Wheelock, C. (2009). *An evaluation of Serials Solutions Summon as a discovery service for the Dartmouth College Library.* Retrieved May 19, 2011, from http://www.dartmouth.edu/~library/admin/docs/Summon_Report.pdf

Dempsey, L. (2006). The library catalogue in the new discovery environment: Some thoughts. *Ariadne, 48*. Retrieved from http://www.ariadne.ac.uk/issue48/dempsey/

Dentinger, S., Keclik, K., Barclay, A., Bruns, T., Larson, E., Quatrucci, A. … Walker, N. (2008). *Resource discovery exploratory task force final report.* Retrieved from http://staff.library.wisc.edu/rdetf/RDETF-final-report.pdf

DeRosa, C., Cantrell, J., Hawk, J., & Wilson, A. (2006). *College students' perceptions of libraries and information resources: A report to the OCLC membership.* Retrieved from http://www.oclc.org/reports/pdfs/studentperceptions.pdf

Inger, S., & Gardner, T. (2008). *How readers navigate to scholarly content: Comparing the changing user behaviour between 2005 and 2008 and its impact on publisher Web site design and function.* Retrieved from http://www.sic.ox14.com/howreadersnavigatetoscholarlycontent.pdf

Johnson, L., Smith, R., Willis, H., Levine, A., & Haywood, K. (2011). *2011 Horizon report.* Austin, TX: The New Media Consortium. Retrieved from http://wp.nmc.org/horizon2011/

Kroski, E. (2008). On the move with the mobile Web: Libraries and mobile technologies. *Library Technology Reports, 44*(5).

Law, D. (2007). Beyond the hybrid library: Libraries in a Web 2.0 world . In Earnshaw, R., & Vince, J. (Eds.), *Digital convergence: Libraries of the future* (pp. 107–118). London, UK: Springer. doi:10.1007/978-1-84628-903-3_9

Marcus, C., Ball, S., Delserone, L., Hribar, A., & Loftus, W. (2007). *Understanding research behaviors, information resources, and service needs of scientists and graduate students: A study by the University of Minnesota Libraries.* Retrieved from http://conservancy.umn.edu/bitstream/5546/1/Sciences_Assessment_Report_Final.pdf

Maron, N. L., & Smith, K. K. (2008). *Current models of digital scholarly communication: Results of an investigation conducted by Ithaka for the Association of Research Libraries.* Retrieved from http://www.arl.org/bm~doc/current-models-report.pdf

Nackerud, S., & Scaletta, K. (2008). Blogging in the academy. *New Directions for Student Services,* (124): 71–87. doi:10.1002/ss.296

Prabha, C., Connaway, L. S., Olszewski, L., & Jenkins, L. R. (2007). What is enough? Satisficing information needs. *The Journal of Documentation, 63*(1), 74–89. doi:10.1108/00220410710723894

Research Information Network. (2008). *Discovering physical objects: Meeting researchers' needs.* Retrieved from http://www.rin.ac.uk/our-work/using-and-accessing-information-resources/discovering-physical-objects-meeting-researchers-

Research Information Network. (2009). *E-journals: Their use, value, and impact: Final report*. Retrieved from http://www.rin.ac.uk/our-work/communicating-and-disseminating-research/e-journals-their-use-value-and-impact

Rowlands, I., Nicholas, D., Williams, P., Huntington, P., Fieldhouse, M., & Gunter, B. (2008). The Google generation: The information behaviour of the researcher of the future. *Aslib Proceedings*, *60*(4), 290–310. doi:10.1108/00012530810887953

Schonfeld, R., & Housewright, R. (2010). *Ithaka S&R faculty survey 2009: Key strategic insights for libraries, publishers, and societies*. Retrieved from http://www.ithaka.org/ithaka-s-r/research/faculty-surveys-2000-2009/Faculty%20Study%202009.pdf

Shadle, S. (2008). The local catalog is dead! Long live the local catalog! *Serials Review*, *34*(2), 85–87. doi:10.1016/j.serrev.2008.03.004

Smith, S. D., Salaway, G., & Caruso, J. B. (2009). *The ECAR study of undergraduate students and information technology, 2009*. Retrieved from http://www.educause.edu/Resources/TheE-CARStudyofUndergraduateStu/187215

Smithsonian Institution. (2010). *Information technology plan*. Retrieved from http://www.si.edu/content/ocio/pdfs/SITP.pdf

University of California Libraries Bibliographic Services Task Force. (2005). *Rethinking how we provide bibliographic services for the University of California*. Retrieved from http://libraries.universityofcalifornia.edu/sopag/BSTF/Final.pdf

Walker, J. D., & Jorn, L. (2007). *Net generation students at the University of Minnesota, Twin Cities*. Retrieved from http://www.oit.umn.edu/prod/groups/oit/@pub/@oit/@web/@evaluation-research/documents/asset/oit_asset_149639.pdf

Ward, J. L., Shadle, S., & Mofjeld, P. (2008). WorldCat Local at the University of Washington libraries. *Library Technology Reports*, *44*(6), 4–41.

KEY TERMS AND DEFINITIONS

Data Object/Digital Object: A resource described as a data or digital object may be at varying levels of granularity, including: citation information, database entries/information, e-journal articles, digitized images, online finding aids, etc. Digital objects may be "born digital" but can also be digitized versions of physical objects.

Discovery and Delivery: The process of finding information about a resource or the existence of an item and obtaining it. Discovery refers to accessing the item digitally or finding a physical location for physical items. Users are now expecting the discovery and delivery to occur together which includes the act of access online content or requesting an item.

Discovery Layer: Interface used for discovery that allows metadata from disparate sources to be presented in a single discovery interface. The discovery layer allows end-users to work within a consistent interface regardless of the source the originating metadata.

Environment: The suite of tools and services presented to users for discovery and access to relevant information resources. The environment may include a library catalog, link resolver, Web sites, licensed resources and/or homegrown databases.

Local Data Sources: Local data sources are data contained or systems managed at a local level. Examples include: the ILS (Integrated Library Systems) for a specific library or consortium or local databases created for specific collections or sub-collections.

Metadata: Structured data that describes content such as a digital object or a data object, as well as, a description for physical items/content. It may describe the characteristics of a particular resource or object as well.

Metadata Layer: A central index that includes metadata and full-text content, aggregated and made available as a unified searchable index. This central index includes data from multiple sources which may include the ILS, institutional repositories, aggregated collections from publishers or other sources.

Metadata Schema: A system used for the cataloging or structuring descriptive records. The schema defines specific elements and organizes then according to specific rules. Examples of metadata schema include: Dublin Core, Encoded Archival Description (EAD), Anglo-American Cataloging Rules (AACR2), etc.

Next Generation OPAC: An online public access catalog that provides a single search box that produces search results in a unified interface. Next Generations OPACs often incorporate Web 2.0 features such as spell check, facets, and relevancy rankings; along with enrichment features such as: tags, reviews, cover images, etc.

Personas: Set of very specific fictional users, describing knowledge, attitudes, habits, and similar information, used to determine how a product or software will serve a user type, population, or other demographic. Personas are often created to determine the needs, preferences, etc. of potential users.

Personal Curation: Refers to the ability to access, manipulate, and/or organize a digital object and interact it with it by adding personalized data such as tags, annotations, combining it with other objects to create a collection, or manipulating it for the user's own needs.

Scopes: The action of filtering, grouping, or organizing a set of resources in the discovery environment for searching or browsing, based on the tasks associated with various user communities. In effect, scopes are user-centered information silos.

User Communities: The diverse user population that libraries serve including: affiliates, non-affiliates, users of locally-managed interfaces (e.g., website, catalog), users of remote systems (e.g., WorldCat, Google Scholar), communities defined by discipline, geography, task, institutional role (e.g. faculty, staff, undergraduate, graduate student).

ENDNOTES

[1]   Ex Libris is a trademark of Ex Libris Ltd.

[2]   Primo is a registered trademark of Ex Libris Ltd.

[3]   Aleph is a registered trademark of Ex Libris Ltd.

[4]   EBSCO Discovery Service is a trademark of EBSCO Publishing.

[5]   SFX is a registered trademark of Ex Libris Ltd.

[6]   Google Scholar is a trademark of Google, Inc.

[7]   OAIster is a registered trademark of OCLC.

[8]   Flikr is a registered trademark of Yahoo! Inc.

[9]   ArchiveGrid is a service mark of OCLC.

[10] Primo Central is owned by Ex Libris Ltd. or its affiliates.

[11] Summons is owned by ProQuest LLC

[12] Worldcat is a registered trademark of OCLC.

[13] EZproxy is a registered trademark of OCLC.

Chapter 12
Developing a User-Centered Article Discovery Environment

Suzanne Chapman
University of Michigan, USA

Scott Dennis
University of Michigan, USA

Kathleen Folger
University of Michigan, USA

Ken Varnum
University of Michigan, USA

ABSTRACT

This chapter discusses the user-focused research conducted at the University of Michigan Library to help make decisions about selecting and implementing a Web-scale article discovery service. A combination of methods—persona analysis, comparative evaluations, surveys, and guerrilla usability tests—were applied to bring a user-centered approach to the article discovery service decision-making process. After the selection of the Serials Solutions®1 Summon™2 service and developing a custom interface to this resource using the Summon™ API, a follow-up user survey was conducted and search log data were analyzed to gauge the impact of the Library's decisions on users' research habits and their perceptions of the library. Users reported a high rate of satisfaction with the new article discovery service and, as a result, reported being more likely to use library online resources again.

INTRODUCTION

The University of Michigan is a Carnegie "Research I" institution with almost 42,000 students in eighteen undergraduate and graduate schools. The University of Michigan University Library is one of the top ten in the world with approximately 8.5 million volumes in its collection. The University Library has long been a leader in digitization and preservation efforts, including being in the original group of partners for the Google Books™3 scanning project and, later, creating the nucleus of the HathiTrust.

DOI: 10.4018/978-1-4666-1821-3.ch012

Serving such a breadth of content to an extremely diverse group of scholars is one of the library's main challenges, one that was not being met by a loose confederation of departmental and library Web sites maintained by local operations of the University Library in individual schools. Before the redesign effort that culminated in a tightly integrated single Web site in 2009, the library had approximately two dozen largely independent Web sites representing physical library locations and departments across the campus. Where the previous sites had been focused at particular groups of users (from the medical campus, the undergraduate college, the school of music, etc.), the new site was intended to provide a universal starting point for research to all patrons, without them needing to know where to launch their research.

In addition to completely redesigning its Web site using the Drupal open source content management system, the library also implemented VuFind, an open source search engine developed at Villanova University, as the front end to its library catalog.[4] With so much discussion and work on issues of findability and discovery in library systems, it was inevitable that the library's article discovery environment would come under scrutiny. At the time, the library was using Ex Libris's[TM5] MetaLib[®6] federated search software, locally branded as "Search Tools Quick Search," for article discovery. There was general dissatisfaction with the service, as expressed through user reports to public service librarians that patrons were turning to Google and Google Scholar[TM7] instead. An initial internal discussion about replacing the MetaLib[®] federated search service with Google Scholar™ was refocused when commercial Web-scale discovery products first became available on the market in 2009.

The idea of "Web-scale discovery" has been a hot topic in libraries ever since Marshall Breeding (2005), reacting to the debut of the Google Scholar™ search engine in November 2004, suggested that libraries should pursue a "centralized search" approach "on the scale of the Web"

(pp. 27-28) to develop new discovery tools for library-provided electronic resources—a single, comprehensive, large-scale index for all the journals, newspaper articles, and other content the library makes available online. Would such a tool meet the needs of users better than free Web search engines like Google Scholar™? Could one of these new products provide the desired article discovery capability? To answer these questions, library administration charged the Article Discovery Working Group (ADWG) with investigating the tools and services then available.

This group decided to bring a user-centered approach to the article discovery service decision-making process.[8] It conducted its research in three phases. During the investigation phase, the group set out to determine what students and faculty expected from an article discovery tool. Given these expectations, the group evaluated and sought feedback on a proposed selection. To do this, personas were developed to create archetypical users against whose hypothetical expectations real-world tools could be evaluated. Using these personas, the group conducted a comparative evaluation of discovery tools, a survey of the user community, and undertook a "guerrilla" usability evaluation of the leading tool. During the implementation phase, a satisfaction and usability survey accompanied the launch of the new tool based on the Summon™ service from Serials Solutions®. And finally, during the post-implementation phase, the library validated its decision by conducting a follow-up survey and usage statistic analysis to measure change in use and evaluate whether or not users' expectations were being met.

BACKGROUND

Potential library users do not often think of the library as the starting point for research. A 2010 survey by the OCLC Online Computer Library Center asked information consumers where they were most likely to start their search for information. Eighty-four percent of all users, and eighty-three percent of college students, reported beginning their search with an Internet search engine. Not a single survey respondent reported beginning their search on a library web site (De Rosa et al., 2011). Even among faculty, the library as a starting point for research has shown a decline since the advent of Internet search engines. A series of large-scale surveys of faculty conducted by Ithaka S+R has shown a decrease in the number of faculty who report using either the physical library building or the online library catalog as their starting point for research. Instead, they are increasingly turning to "network-level" electronic resources, including general purpose search engines (Schonfeld & Housewright, 2010).

Selection and Use of Discovery Systems

The rise of discovery tools such as Google Scholar™, Summon™, EBSCO Discovery Service™, Primo® Central, and others, has led to some research into the effects of these new tools on users and libraries. The University of Nevada, Las Vegas described their selection process, deeply focused on library staff needs and vendors (Vaughn, 2011). OCLC published a detailed report on librarian needs in a catalog which explored the specific needs of librarians. The report found, in part, that "the end user's experience of the delivery of wanted items is as important, if not more important, than his or her discovery experience" (Calhoun et al., 2009, p. 7). This finding—that the ends can justify (or at least excuse) the means—is a common thread across discovery platforms, whether defined broadly (all library resources) or narrowly ("just" the catalog or full-text online materials).

Published studies on the effects of having implemented a discovery environment have focused on seemingly more easily measured features such as full-text downloads and searches. An early study at Grand Valley State University focuses on the use of library resources in the year after that library launched Summon™. Way (2010) found that Summon™ was "increasing access to the library's resources" (p. 219). Another study at the Edith Cowan University Library in Perth, Australia focused on the user's understanding of the quality of the results returned from that library's Summon™ implementation (Gross & Sheridan, 2011).

User-Centered Research Methods

Given the fast pace of software development, it has become increasingly important to employ user-centered research methods that are streamlined in order to devote more time and resources to design, implementation, and iteration. Techniques such as personas, guerrilla usability testing, and unmoderated usability testing surveys are tools that require fewer resources, in both time and money, than formal usability testing.

The concept of personas was chiefly popularized by Cooper (1999) as simply "a precise description of our user and what he wishes to accomplish" (p. 123). Despite the fact that personas are a relatively new user-centered design technique, it is now a well-established method for "providing an emotional bridge between team members and end users" (Guenther, 2006, p. 50). Within the last few years, libraries have begun using personas to support interface design and development as well as strategic decision-making. The University of Colorado at Boulder Libraries employed personas to help understand the needs and goals of institutional repository users (Maness, Miaskiewicz, & Sumner, 2008); the Johns Hopkins University Libraries employed them to guide a discovery tool selection (Uzelac, Conaway, & Palmer, 2008); the University of Washington Libraries, to support their Web site design (U. W. Libraries, n.d.); the University of Minnesota Libraries, "to reflect the diversity of the Libraries' user communities" (Hanson, et al., 2011, p. 5); the

Cornell University Library, to determine how the library should "present itself and the information landscape to its users" (Koltay & Tancheva, 2010, p. 173); and the HathiTrust, to help developers, policy makers, user experience designers and researchers, and reference and instruction librarians "learn more about HathiTrust users, discover how we can better suit their needs, and identify areas in which to do more in-depth research" (Mishra, 2011, p. 2).

Guerrilla usability testing plays a vital role in the streamlined development process by providing a way to engage users and get quick and immediate feedback. Although not as thorough as formal usability tests, guerrilla tests still provide insight about potentially serious problems that may not be obvious to the developers. The North Carolina State University Libraries employed guerrilla testing with success to determine whether a tabbed search box effectively conveyed their search options (Teague-Rector, Ballard, & Pauley, 2011), and the University of Michigan University Library uses the method extensively to test interface labels, functionality, and design.[9] Additionally, unmoderated usability testing mechanisms have emerged in the last few years to combine the ease of a survey with the ability to track users' success at accomplishing certain tasks. This technique is "uniquely suited for collecting qualitative and quantitative data about attitudes and behaviors" (Albert, Tullis, & Tedesco, 2010, p. 5). However, unlike guerrilla usability, unmoderated testing does not involve any direct contact or conversation with the users, but does put the user in the context of the task via interactions with the live Web site or static images (Bolt & Tulathimutte, 2010).

INVESTIGATION

Persona Analysis

The first stage of the Article Discovery Working Group's (ADWG) research into user expectations was the development of personas to help model the needs and expectations of potential users of article discovery tools. The personas that were developed for this study were based significantly on work done at other institutions, particularly Johns Hopkins University (Uzelac, et al., 2008; Uzelac, 2009). The Johns Hopkins University user study was done to create data-driven personas to guide their own discovery tool selection and implementation. Interviews with seventy-eight Johns Hopkins University affiliates were completed in the spring of 2008; this group of users was reduced to six personas: the Data Cruncher, the Guide, the Browser, the Simplicity Seeker, the Complex Searcher, and the Advice Seeker (Uzelac, et al., 2008).

For the ADWG's work these personas were slightly adapted to fit particular types of users on the University of Michigan's Ann Arbor campus. After analyzing the data and grouping common behaviors, goals, and context of interviewees, the research team redefined the Johns Hopkins personas as follows:

Joan, Staff Researcher in the Applied Physics Lab
Donald, Associate Professor in the Business School
Candace, Graduate Student in Musicology
Ryan, Undergraduate Student in Political Science
Anthony, Professor in Biomedical Engineering
Asha, Undergraduate Student in English

It is important to note that even though the personas are distributed amongst academic demographics, a persona does not represent that demographic. Rather, a persona represents common goals, needs and behavior patterns that can be found across demographics. For example, Asha does not represent all undergraduate students in the humanities, although "her" needs and expectations typify many of those students.

The next step was to model how each of these personas might approach article-level research. The regular discovery tasks that they were performing, the goals and attitudes driving these tasks, and the requirements of a discovery tool that would support these goals and tasks were all described. These goals and needs were grouped together with those expressed by other personas. Thus, the common goals and needs were identified, including:

Use the most relevant and useful content
Save time
Ensure use of quality content from reputable sources
Use reliable, trustworthy and familiar sources

Different personas often expressed different needs to fulfill a common goal. For example, to find and use the most relevant and useful articles, Joan needs recommendations and reviews from colleagues and other scientists; whereas Anthony needs advanced search features such as limiters, filters, fielded searching and classification schema. Understanding the various needs of different users in accomplishing similar goals laid the foundation for the group to make data-driven decisions on what features to consider in comparing discovery tools.

Comparative Evaluation

The persona analysis led to the development of a set of features that individuals who are seeking articles through a library tool would find important. This feature set was used as the scorecard against which three different article discovery tools were measured: the University of Michigan University Library's existing implementation of Ex Libris's™ MetaLib® federated search engine; the Google Scholar™ search engine; and Serials Solutions® Summon™ service. (Summon™ was selected at this stage because it was the only fully operational library Web-scale discovery service available at the time of the investigation.)

To increase the evaluative utility of the user personas, the group distilled the goals implicit in the personas into a list of concrete features and tasks that could serve as a basis for the comparison and evaluation of the article discovery tools. This process generated a list of forty-four features and tasks, which became the criteria used to evaluate the individual tools (see Table 1, Table 2, and Table 3). To start the evaluation process, each group member formulated and ran identical searches in the tools to determine whether the features were present and the tasks could be completed. The resulting data was compiled in a lengthy spreadsheet with a row for each criterion and a column for each tool. Features were grouped into conceptual families to put similar and related functionalities together. When there were disagreements among members of the group about how to interpret the available data, the group discussed the relative strengths and weaknesses of a feature until a consensus was reached.

The completion of this process resulted in a list of features desired by users and a summary of which tools could meet the priorities. The conclusion from this analysis indicated that Summon™ would be the best choice to meet most user needs. However, before the group formally recommended that the library take on a significant investment of resources, it was decided to validate that conclusion with further testing.

Preliminary Survey

The next step was to conduct a campus survey to ask the community which of the features that varied significantly among the three identified alternatives they felt were the most important in an article discovery environment. The survey was distributed via links on the library home page and email sent to faculty and graduate students by subject specialist librarians. The survey ran for approximately ten days in Fall 2009 and received a total 974 responses from graduate students (50%), faculty or staff (30%), undergraduates (18%), other university-affiliated persons (1%), and unaffiliated persons (<1%).

Table 1. Comparison of Summon™, MetaLib®, and Google Scholar™ by persona-generated functionality

Functionality	Description	Evaluation
Scholarly Results		
Top databases & journals for subject areas are included	What is the coverage of the tool compared to the library's total online holdings?	Summon™, MetaLib yes; Google Scholar unclear
Quantify or compare number of scholarly sources obtained with the same search	Of the library's peer-reviewed / scholarly journal content, what portion is included?	Quantity OK; quality hard to judge or limit to (can limit to 'scholarly' in some cases in all three tools)
Peer-reviewed articles filter	Can search results be limited (before or after the search) to only peer-reviewed materials?	Summon™
Is the tool biased toward certain fields or not good for other fields?	Is the content in the service focused on humanities, social sciences, or sciences, to the detriment of the other categories?	No difference
Communicate Research		
Email results	Can a search result set, or selection therefrom, be emailed to someone?	Summon™
RSS feed for specific search	Are search results available in RSS so that a search alert service could be effected?	Summon™
Text citation(s) to mobile device	Can citations be texted (SMS) to a mobile device?	Easier in Summon™, but not built in
Save results/citation (e.g. to "my shelf")	Is there a way to save items once they are found, for future use?	Summon™ / MetaLib
Export in variety of formats, including RefWorks & EndNote®	Can citations be exported to common bibliographic management tools?	Easier in MetaLib and Summon™
Mobile Technology		
Can be used on high-end mobile device with full browser (ready now, could be done, etc...)	How ready is the system for tablet computers?	Yes for all three
Can be used on low-end mobile device without full browser (ready now, could be done, etc...)	How ready is the system for smart phones?	Google Scholar
Good format and interface for mobile devices	How compatible, overall, with mobile devices?	Google Scholar
iPhone, Palm, Android, etc. app capability: 'I want an app for this'	Is there an "app" version for iPhone/Android phones?	Summon™ will have one
Other Characteristics		
Cost	What range is the subscription cost?	Google Scholar is free; Cost of MetaLib and Summon™ is considerable
Available now	Is it something that could be purchased and turned on today?	All three

The survey asked users to rate the importance of all twelve features on a five-point Likert scale ranging from "Not at all important" to "Very Important." (See Appendix A for the complete survey instrument.) In Figure 1 the results are summarized graphically, with preferences of each user group sorted by the overall average importance rating. The graph reveals general agreement on discovery tool feature preferences between the three major user groups. (For additional survey results, see Bhatnagar, et al., 2010.)

Guerrilla Usability Test

Based on the findings of the persona process and the preliminary survey, there was confidence that Summon™ was the best tool on the market at that time. Before committing the resources to license the product, library administration asked that the actual product be tested with faculty and students. A brief "guerrilla usability test" was conducted, consisting of impromptu interactions with volunteer participants. Guerrilla tests are designed to be brief, narrowly focused sessions with little or no overhead. Library staff went to various library locations (near reference desks

Table 2. Comparison of Summon™, MetaLib®, and Google Scholar™ by persona-generated functionality: technology/customizability

Functionality	Description	Evaluation
Technology/Customizability		
Authentication ability	Can user log in with a campus authentication service and be recognized as a library user?	No difference
Can be integrated into the front page of library/navigation bar	Can the tool be embedded in the library's web site?	Summon™ best, then MetaLib
Full text provided immediately in results—or direct link to PDF of full text with no additional database navigation	To what extent do citations link directly to full text (or do users need to do further searches in a publisher's or aggregator's site?)	All via proxy/citation linker
Can we customize to provide something like "tip of the day" for searching?	Is the user interface customizable for short-term needs?	Summon™ best, then MetaLib
Can results list be made into a static URL?	Can a user bookmark the search results page and get back to the same search again?	Summon™
Static URL for article? (URL in the location bar)	Do individual citations have permanent URLs for sharing or future reference?	No difference
Appealing, intuitive interface	Is the service easy and satisfying to use?	Summon™ best, then Google Scholar
Can we integrate local tagging system?	Can locally developed bookmarking or tagging systems be integrated into the service?	Summon™
Can we integrate tools to indicate "Library Approved" journals/databases?	Is there a way for librarian subject specialists to indicate that certain journals are more authoritative than others?	Summon™
Compare the time each tool takes to do the same exact search	Which service has the fastest response time?	Summon™ and Google Scholar much faster than MetaLib
Provide access to delivery services (links in results/records to request forms)	Can articles not in the University Library's collection be easily requested through the existing document delivery service?	No difference
Easy access to tutorials—either built in help/tutorial or link to library-created guides	Are help pages adequate and easily accessible?	No difference
Meets basic accessibility standards	Is the site accessible to visually impaired users?	No difference

or library entrances), approached passers-by and asked if they had a few minutes to test a potential new service. (See Appendix B for the script used in this test.)

In this manner, a total twenty-four evaluations were conducted with undergraduate students (10), graduate students (5), faculty (5), library staff (2), and other university-affiliated persons (2). The goal of this evaluation was to gain insight into the likelihood that the University community would use the Summon™ product if it were offered. Dartmouth College's Summon™ implementation was selected as the test platform because, although it is a smaller institution than the University of Michigan, Dartmouth provides a similar undergraduate education as well as graduate programs in business, engineering, and medicine. Despite Dartmouth's smaller size, its journal collections are at least similar in breadth to the University of Michigan's.

Participants were asked to conduct a search on a topic with which they were familiar and to peruse the results. They were then asked several questions focused on the quality and comprehensiveness of the results for their purposes and the effectiveness of the interface. The overwhelming majority of participants (20 out of 24), when asked if results were useful, said "yes." Of the remaining responses, two said "maybe" and two said "no." Both of the "no" responses were from researchers at the medical campus who expressed a strong preference for PubMed as their article research tool. One said, "It's useful, but I'm un-

Table 3. Comparison of Summon™, MetaLib®, and Google Scholar™ by persona-generated functionality: facets/information discovery

Functionality	Description	Evaluation
Facets/Information Discovery		
Subject searching & facets	Can searches be narrowed using subject headings or keywords?	Summon™ best, then MetaLib
Suggest related topics/subtopics	Does the system suggest additional subject headings or keywords?	Summon™ best, then MetaLib
Suggest articles related to the one displayed	Does the system provide a "similar to this one" function at the citation level?	No difference
Year of publication facet	Can results be limited by year or range of years?	Summon™ best, then MetaLib
Citation tracing—track articles cited in and cited by	Does "cited by" data appear in search results?	Google Scholar
View an article's citations/notes	Are the references used in an article included in the search results?	Not in native interface for any
Narrow down results based on material type—books, chapters, articles	Can search results be narrowed by kind of item?	Summon™ best, then MetaLib
Limit by availability—physical copies in library or electronic only	Can search results be narrowed to items currently available for checkout or online?	Summon™
Open Access filter	Can results be narrowed to only open access publications?	Not in native interface for any
Search variety of databases at once	Does a single search retrieve results from multiple traditional citation databases?	Yes, but none present 'databases' as coherent whole
Restrict searching to specific database(s) or journal(s), have a facet/filter	Can a search in the system be targeted to one or more traditional citation databases or specific journals?	MetaLib
Variety of search fields (advanced searching option?)—title, author, journal, volume, issue, page number, conference name, etc.	Is there an advanced search capability that permits searching limited to particular metadata fields?	Summon™ best, then MetaLib
Search variety of materials—images, scholarly articles, opinion pieces, newspaper articles, encyclopedias, conference proceedings, patents, etc.	Does the service include a range of content types?	Summon™ best, then MetaLib & Google Scholar
Incorporates web-searching with article searching (non-journal information that's credible; like doing a site:gov or site:edu search in Google, open access journals, government web sites, associations, etc.)	Is there non-article, non-book content?	MetaLib: Not at all Summon™, Google Scholar: Limited
Auto-complete/auto-suggestion search queries (i.e., like Google)	Can the system intuit probable search queries after a certain number of user keystrokes?	No difference
Did you mean (i.e., spell check)	Does the system suggest alternate or correct spellings of words?	Google Scholar does this; Summon™ could

likely to switch from PubMed" (Dennis, Duque, MacEachern, Samuel, & Varnum, 2010, p. 3).

Participants were also asked what other tools they used for article search. Tools mentioned ranged from databases provided by the library (JSTOR®[10], the library catalog, ProQuest®[11], etc.) to freely available resources such as Google Scholar™ and PubMed. The majority of respondents (78%) said that the results they found through Summon™ were better than the results they found using their usual tool. Especially noteworthy was the fact that each of the seven participants who cited Google Scholar™ as a regular starting point

for their research felt that Summon™ provided better results. (For additional survey results, see Dennis, et al., 2010.)

IMPLEMENTATION

The results of the guerrilla test convinced library administrators to move forward with Summon™. The University Library then embarked on a rapid, three-month implementation schedule, starting with signing a contract in July 2010 and ending with launching the new service in September 2010.

Figure 1. Discovery tool feature preferences by user group

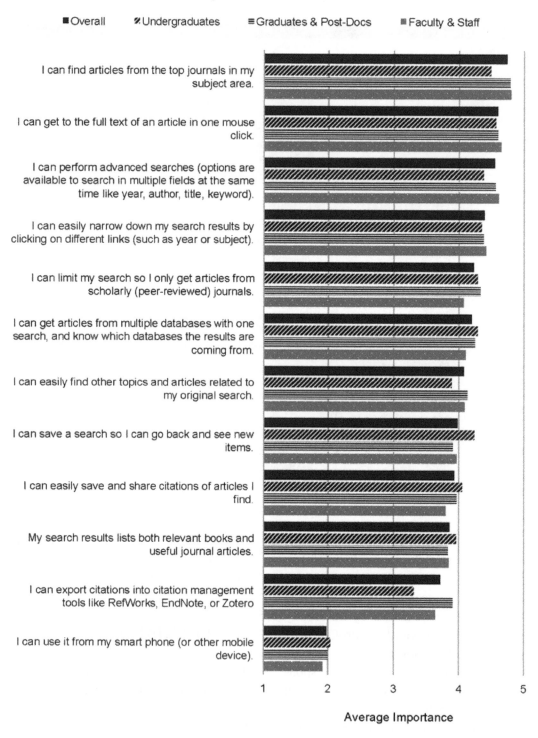

Figure 2. Screenshot of ArticlesPlus interface embedded into library website

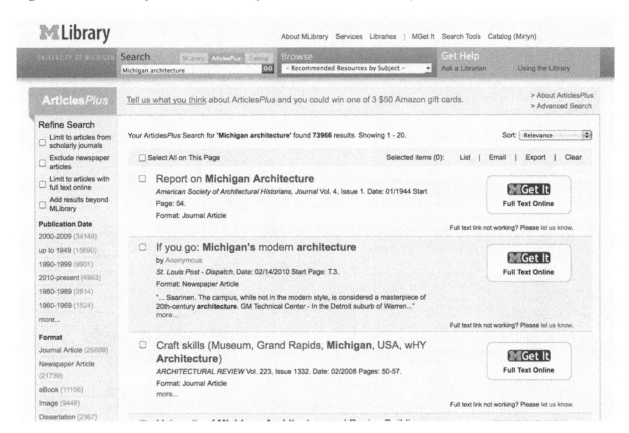

Local Customization

While the Google-like appearance of the Summon™ out-of-the-box user interface was satisfactory, the University Library opted to build its own interface to the article discovery tool using the library's content management system, Drupal. The "Article Discovery" module harnessed the search power of the Summon™ API but presented search results within the context of the library Web site (see Figure 2).[12] The Web site, which had been recently redesigned, already included an article search capability driven by MetaLib®. The previous tool was underutilized (receiving only a few hundred uses per day, compared to several thousand in each of the catalog and the rest of the library's Web content). The Article Discovery module offered the same user functionality yet took advantage of the scope and speed of the Summon™ service. Additionally, keeping the discovery process in the library context allowed the library to brand the resource clearly as a service of the library in a way that would permit migration to a different article discovery service in the future, without requiring re-branding of the service. There was also a desire for a more descriptive name for the tool than "Summon," to better convey its purpose to campus users.

The name that was ultimately selected was "Articles*Plus*," replacing the former MetaLib®-driven "Articles" search tab on the library Web site's banner. This name change reflected the Summon™ service's inclusion of more than articles as well as the anticipated improved performance and functionality.

Figure 3. Sample heat map in response to question, "Where would you click to go directly to this article?"

Launch Survey

When it was launched in late September 2010, Articles*Plus* included a link to a user satisfaction and usability evaluation survey (see Appendix C for the survey instrument). The survey was designed to gather feedback specifically about Articles*Plus*, so it was made available only from a link at the top of the new Articles*Plus* interface (see Figure 2). The survey ran from September 27 to October 31, 2010, resulting in a convenience sample of 194 responses (not all questions were required so some respondents didn't answer every question). On completion of the survey, the respondents were given the opportunity to enter a prize drawing by submitting their contact information via a form that was disconnected from the survey to ensure participant anonymity. Three respondents were selected at random to be the winners of $50 Amazon.com gift certificates. The Qualtrics™[13] survey software was selected for two reasons: first, because it was available at no charge to the Libraries through a campus license; and second, because it allowed both standard survey questions (e.g., demographics, satisfaction ratings) and task-based usability questions that recorded clicks on a screenshot of the interface with the responses compiled and presented as a heat map (see Figure 3 for an example).

It should be noted that in the early days of the survey, problems with linking to the full text of articles via the library's new OpenURL link re-

Table 4. Launch survey questions and success rates (n = 194)

Question	Success rate
Where would you click to start a new search in this page?	91%
Where would you click to get results for items not owned by the University of Michigan Library on this page?	63%
Where would you lick to go directly to this article?	72%
Where would you click to show just items that have full text available?	82%
Where would you click to go to the Advanced Articles*Plus* search page?	94%
Where would you click to find more information about the first item in the list?	91%

solver service (which was launched in conjunction with Articles*Plus*) were identified and mostly resolved. Many of the respondents mentioned these issues as being troublesome and ranked the service accordingly. Even so, results of the survey were very positive. When asked to rate Articles*Plus* on a five-point Likert scale, 79% (178 out of 187) chose either "I liked it" or "I liked it a lot." The remaining respondents chose "It was okay" (16%), "I did not like it" (4%), or "I did not like it one bit!" (1%). When asked if they got the search results they expected, users responded primarily positively: 59 respondents expressed their general satisfaction, 18 reported problems with linking to the articles or frustrations with not getting full-text access to all articles, and 24 expressed a variety of positive and negative reactions to a particular part of the interface. Some example responses:

"Yes. It gave me access to many journals all at once instead of looking in each one individually"

"I got more than expected. It is so much faster and easier to find and access the articles needed. Great!"

"Yes, though I was surprised how many results did not have links to the full text."

"It pulled up several article [sic] that did not have anything to do with the topic I was searching for."

"Holy crap, where has this been all my life?"

For the task-based usability section, users were asked six questions about where they would click to accomplish a stated goal. The questions were designed to assess the success of particular design decisions that had been heavily debated during the implementation process. Most of the questions were designed with a primary target or two in mind, which were used to evaluate "success." However, many of the tasks could still be accomplished via a secondary, possibly less direct, route. The results (summarized in Table 4) confirmed the decisions the Libraries made during the design process. (For the complete Articles*Plus* launch survey report with full-color heat maps, see Chapman, 2011.)

POST-IMPLEMENTATION

Six months after its implementation, library administration wanted to measure, more formally, the effect the Summon™ service has had on users' research habits and their perceptions of the library. To gauge the impact of Summon™ on users' perception of the utility of article discovery through the library's Web site, and in relation to other existing resources with similar functionality, data was collected and analyzed from two sources: another, more detailed Web-based survey of library users, and usage data for some of the library's largest article discovery databases.

Table 5. Six-month follow-up survey[16]

	Articles*Plus* (Summon™)	Google Scholar™	Search Tools Quick Search (MetaLib®)	Other Resources
	n=484	*n=585*	*n=435*	*n=466*
Used First All or Most of the Time	36%	37%	27%	47%
Very or Somewhat Satisfied	74%	75%	56%	85%
Have recommended it to others	41%	62%	22%	26%

Follow-up Survey

The six-month follow-up survey was designed to reveal how users viewed their own experience with online article discovery tools, and how those experiences affected preferences and perceptions for future searches. Users were asked specifically about the new Summon™ service (Articles*Plus*), Google Scholar™, the older MetaLib® federated search service (Search Tools Quick Search), which still remained available until Summer 2011, and any other resources they used to search for articles (which they were asked to name). Questions were included to gauge recentness and frequency of search resource use, satisfaction with quality of search experience, and comparison of resource features, including some open-ended questions designed to elicit more detail about the respondents' experiences with these resources. In the same manner as the launch survey, respondents were recruited with a prize drawing incentive at point-of-use on the library Web site—specifically on the Articles*Plus* (Summon™), Search Tools Quick Search (MetaLib®), and Undergraduate Library Web pages—and by email from subject specialist librarians to faculty and graduate students in academic departments. The survey ran for three weeks in the spring of 2011 and received a total of 773 survey responses from undergraduates (35%), graduate students or post-doctoral fellows (48%), faculty or staff (15%), other university-affiliated persons (2%), and unaffiliated persons (<1%)[24].

Most survey respondents had experience with Google Scholar™ (81%), Summon™ (67%), other article discovery resources (65%), and MetaLib® (61%). Only 1% of respondents reported no experience with any of these tools. Respondents named a total of thirty different other article discovery resources they used; the most frequently named were JSTOR®, PubMed, ProQuest®, PsycINFO®[14], and Web of Science®[15]. To facilitate comparisons, respondents were asked for each tool they used about how often they chose to use that tool first before trying other resources, how they rated the quality of their search experience with the tool on a satisfaction scale, and whether they had recommended it to colleagues and friends. Respondents reported starting their research and ranking their satisfaction with Google Scholar™ and the Summon™ service at comparable rates (see Table 5). However, they recommend Google Scholar™ to others more often than Summon™ by a significant margin (for unknown reasons that warrant further investigation).

Given how rarely users in the current information environment start their research on a library Web site (De Rosa et al., 2011, p.32), it was interesting to note that after only six months, a full 36% of respondents were choosing to start their research with Articles*Plus* all or most of the time, and 41% of respondents had already recommended it to someone else.

To give the library more information about how users interacted with and rated the services, the follow-up survey gave respondents the opportunity to indicate which service they preferred to use when performing specific tasks, and asked them to write in their own words why they did or didn't recommend resources. Respondents' preferences varied according to the type of task motivating their search process.

When searching for journals, respondents prefer Google Scholar™ and the Summon™ service (Articles*Plus),* followed by the MetaLib® federated search service (Search Tools Quick Search):

"ArticlesPlus is very accurate and often finds obscure journal articles I was not aware of. I enjoy using it immensely, but the ease of Google Scholar™ is often the deciding factor (I use Chrome, so I can just type into the URL bar). All other things being equal though, ArticlesPlus is winning me over."

"Google Scholar™ ranks results according to how many other people used that work in their own work, which is a great way to start weeding through a large search. Search Tools is hard to navigate, sometimes refuses to bring you back to your results list (toggling through individual results instead), you have to know whether what you want would be considered humanities or social sciences (which is often hard! especially for those of us in joint degree programs)."

Three tasks followed the same preference pattern where the Summon™ service (Articles*Plus)* was the top choice, followed by Google Scholar™ and then the MetaLib® federated search service (Search Tools Quick Search):

Getting to full-text view of articles online:

"This service [ArticlesPlus] is amazing. It found every one of 7 or so articles in one search by title and an author, and then correctly led me to a full text version each time, even for law journal articles."

"I find it harder to get full-text versions of articles from Google Scholar™."

Conducting advanced searches:

"Google Scholar™ is nice but too general. ArticlesPlus is a quick way to finding the information I need in the format I need it in. I have found more relevant articles using ArticlesPlus."

Limiting a search to scholarly, peer-reviewed journals:

"I really like the addition of ArticlesPlus to the MLibrary Web site. It really came in handy when writing a research summary when I needed to find scholarly articles."

"ArticlesPlus was recommended because it is so easy and only spits out reliable sources."

But when finding other topics and articles related to the search target, more respondents preferred Google Scholar™ to the Summon™ and MetaLib® services:

"I feel like Google Scholar™ brings up a lot more options when you're not quite sure what you're looking for. So, I usually use Google Scholar™ to see what I might want to look at, and then (because I often do this on my laptop) I login to the library and search with the specific titles I found on Google Scholar™. I'm not happy with this system because it's a lot of effort, but it's also more effective I think."

Perhaps the most compelling evidence the follow-up survey provided that the Summon™ service was meeting—and in some cases even exceeding—our library users' expectations for article discovery came from responses to the final question on the survey, which asked users who had tried Articles*Plus* if their experience using it made them likely to use library online resources again.

Table 6. Usage of four popular article discovery resources before and after Summon™ implementation[19, 20]

Winter:	JSTOR®			LexisNexis® Academic			ProQuest®			SciVerse Scopus®		
	2010	2011	Change	2010	2011	Change	2010	2011	Change	2010	2011	Change
Searches: Regular:	122,302	100,699	- 18%	73,943	308,478	+ 317%	424,738	455,794	+ 7%	31,967	34,742	+ 9%
Federated:	n/a	n/a	n/a	n/a	n/a	n/a	144,654	77,248	- 47%	73,631	39,112	- 47%
Sessions: Regular:	119,990	130,910	+ 9%	70,544	107,538	+ 52%	138,402	107,538	- 22%	11,940	15,755	+ 32%
Federated:	n/a	n/a	n/a	n/a	n/a	n/a	147,453	77,128	- 48%	n/a	n/a	n/a
Full-Text Retrievals:	224,305	207,195	- 8%	64,626	320,614	+ 396%	165,331	175,318	+ 6%	n/a	n/a	n/a

More than three-quarters of respondents (76%) either agreed or strongly agreed, and only 4% disagreed. This result confirmed more definitively the trend already apparent in comments users had submitted over the previous six months (separate from any surveys or prize incentives) through the feedback link in the Articles*Plus* interface, three-quarters of which were overwhelmingly positive. One example (a staff favorite):

"I adore ArticlesPlus. If it were a man I would date him. Expand this service any way you can. Thank you!!!"

Usage Analysis

In addition to the analysis of data from the follow-up survey, usage data for selected major article discovery resources from the Winter Terms before and after Summon™ implementation (January – April 2010 and 2011) were analyzed to explore the effect the availability of the Summon™ service might have had on usage of other resources. The winter semesters before and after Articles*Plus* was launched (Winter 2010, Winter 2011) were selected to control for variances in usage caused by the academic calendar. Available usage data was gathered from the MetaLib® federated search engine (Search Tools Quick Search), which remained available after the Libraries implemented the new Summon™ service (Articles*Plus*),[17] and from four of the library's major licensed databases named by users as preferred resources in the follow-up survey:

- JSTOR® – a major source of scholarly full text articles
- LexisNexis® Academic – a major source of popular press full text articles
- ProQuest® – both an index and a full text source, for both popular and scholarly articles
- SciVerse Scopus®[18] – a major index without full text included, and, unlike the other three, a particularly useful resource for researchers in the Health Sciences and Engineering fields

A summary of the available usage data gathered for these four databases appears in Table 6.

The findings of this analysis confirmed that, after the introduction of the Summon™ service, use of the MetaLib® federated search engine decreased significantly (by 47%), as reflected in the identical decreases in federated searches of both ProQuest® and SciVerse Scopus®. At the same time, regular searches of both databases increased, indicating that the decrease in use via the federated search tool is not attributable to decrease in demand for the databases' content.[21] Additionally, and similarly to what other institutions that have implemented Summon™ have reported (Way, 2010), there was a significant increase in usage of online full text resources. The number of full text articles retrieved from Lexis-Nexis® Academic nearly quadrupled from Winter 2010 to Winter 2011. The increase in retrieval of full text articles from ProQuest® was a less dramatic, but still significant, 6%.[22]

The exception was JSTOR®, which was used less in Winter 2011 than in Winter 2010—direct searches of it declined 18%, while retrieval of full text articles from it declined 8%. This reflects more of a decline of usage of JSTOR® for article discovery than a decline in demand for the full text it contains.[23] As one user said through the "tell us what you think of it" feedback link in the Articles*Plus* interface:

"I LOVE IT. This is so much more straightforward and useful than using JSTOR or Hathi Digital Trust [sic] on their own, and makes it really easy to find what I'm looking for. Thank you so much for implementing this incredibly necessary and useful feature - I hope it sticks around!"

CONCLUSION

By taking a data-driven, user-centered approach at each stage of the development process, from investigation to implementation and beyond, the University of Michigan University Library was able to select and launch a powerful new research tool that its users find valuable, that they recommend to peers, and that increases use of the library's online resources. The findings presented here demonstrate that a tool which combines the power of Web-scale discovery with the high-quality content licensed by university libraries can satisfy academic users of all kinds—faculty, graduate and undergraduate students alike—as much or more than Google Scholar™.

REFERENCES

Albert, B., Tullis, T., & Tedesco, D. (2010). *Beyond the usability lab: Conducting large-scale online user experience studies*. Amsterdam, The Netherlands: Morgan Kaufmann/Elsevier.

Allee, N., Dennis, S., Teasley, S., & Varnum, K. (2011). University of Michigan Library Summon™ Benefit Analysis Group final report. Unpublished manuscript.

Bhatnagar, G., Dennis, S., Duque, G., Henry, S., MacEachern, M., Teasley, S., & Varnum, K. (2010). *University of Michigan Library Article Discovery Working Group Final report*. Retrieved from http://www.lib.umich.edu/files/adwg/final-report.pdf

Bolt, N., & Tulathimutte, T. (2010). *Remote research: Real users, real time, real research*. Brooklyn, NY: Rosenfeld Media.

Breeding, M. (2005). Plotting a new course for metasearch. *Computers in Libraries, 25*(2), 27–29.

Calhoun, K., Cantrell, J., Gallagher, P., Hawk, J., & Cellentani, D. (2009). *Online catalogs: What users and librarians want*. Retrieved from http://www.oclc.org/reports/onlinecatalogs/fullreport.pdf

Chapman, S. (2011). *Articles*Plus *launch survey report*. Retrieved from http://www.lib.umich.edu/usability-report/articlesplus-launch-survey

Connaway, L. S. (2007). Mountains, valleys, and pathways: Serials users' needs and steps to meet them; Part I: Identifying serials users' needs: Preliminary analysis of focus group and semi-structured interviews at colleges and universities. *The Serials Librarian, 52*(1-2), 223–236. doi:10.1300/J123v52n01_18

Cooper, A. (1999). *The inmates are running the asylum*. Indianapolis, IN: Sams.

De Rosa, C., Cantrell, J., Carlson, M., Gallagher, P., Hawk, J., Sturtz, C., Cellentani, D., …Olszewski, L. (2011). *Perceptions of libraries, 2010: Content and community: A report to the OCLC membership.* Retrieved from http://www.oclc.org/reports/2010perceptions/2010perceptions_all.pdf

Dennis, S., Duque, G., MacEachern, M., Samuel, S., & Varnum, K. (2010). *University of Michigan Library Article Discovery Working Group supplementary report.* Retrieved from http://www.lib.umich.edu/files/adwg/ supplemental-report.pdf

Gross, J., & Sheridan, L. (2011). Web scale discovery: The user experience. *New Library World, 112*(5/6), 236–247. doi:10.1108/03074801111136275

Guenther, K. (2006). Developing personas to understand user needs. *Online, 30*(5), 49–51.

Hanson, C., Hessel, H., Boudewyns, D., Fransen, J., Friedman-Shedlov, L., Hearn, S., …West, A. (2011). *Discoverability phase 2 final report.* Retrieved from http://purl.umn.edu/99734

Koltay, Z., & Tancheva, K. (2010). Personas and a user-centered visioning process. *Performance Measurement and Metrics, 11*(2), 172–183. doi:10.1108/14678041011064089

Krug, S. (2010). *Rocket surgery made easy: The do-it-yourself guide to finding and fixing usability problems.* Berkeley, CA: New Riders.

Maness, J., Miaskiewicz, T., & Sumner, T. (2008). Using personas to understand the needs and goals of institutional repository users. *D-Lib Magazine, 14*(9/10). doi:10.1045/september2008-maness

Mishra, S. (2011). *The making of the HathiTrust personas.* Retrieved from http://www.hathitrust.org/documents/HathiTrust_Personas_Report.pdf

Schonfeld, R. C., & Housewright, R. (2010). *Faculty survey 2009: Key strategic insights for libraries, publishers, and societies.* Retrieved from http://www.ithaka.org/ithaka-s-r /research/faculty-surveys-2000-2009 /Faculty Study 2009.pdf

Teague-Rector, S., Ballard, A., & Pauley, S. K. (2011). The North Carolina State University libraries search experience: Usability testing tabbed search interfaces for academic libraries. *Journal of Web Librarianship, 5*(2), 80–95. doi:10.1080/19322909.2011.568822

U. W. Libraries (n.d.). *Personas development.* Retrieved from http://kwhitenton.com/ libraries_personas /index.html

Uzelac, E. (2009). *Creating data-driven personas to aid selection and implementation of a next-generation discovery interface.* Poster presented at the Fourteenth National Conference of the Association of College & Research Libraries, Seattle, WA. Retrieved from http://bit.ly/2waVux

Uzelac, E., Conaway, A., & Palmer, L. A. (2008). *Using data-driven personas to guide discovery tool selection and implementation.* Paper presented to the Post-Horizon Working Group at the Sheridan Libraries, Johns Hopkins University, Baltimore, MD. Retrieved July 24, 2011, from https://wiki.library.jhu.edu/download/attachments/30752/UNAPersonasCompressed.pdf

Vaughan, J. (2011). Investigations into library Web scale discovery services. *Information Technology and Libraries, 31*(1), 32-82.

Way, D. (2010). The impact of Web-scale discovery on the use of a library collection. *Serials Review, 36*(4), 214–220. doi:10.1016/j.serrev.2010.07.002

ADDITIONAL READING

Ballard, T., & Blaine, A. (2011). User search-limiting behavior in online catalogs: Comparing classic catalog use to search behavior in next-generation catalogs. *New Library World, 112*(5/6), 261–273. doi:10.1108/03074801111136293

Bowles, C., & Box, J. (2011). *Undercover user experience: Learn how to do great UX work with tiny budgets, no time, and limited support.* Berkeley, CA: New Riders.

Brubaker, N., Leach-Murray, S., & Parker, S. (2011). Shapes in the cloud: Finding the right discovery layer. *Online, 35*(2), 20–26.

Choros, K., & Muskala, M. (2009). Block map technique for the evaluation of a website. *Lecture Notes in Computer Science, 5796*, 743–751. doi:10.1007/978-3-642-04441-0_65

Dempsey, L. (2007, September 16). *Discovery happens elsewhere* [Web log message]. Retrieved from http://orweblog.oclc.org/ archives/001430.html

Fowler, F. (1995). Applied Social Research Methods Series: *Vol. 38. Improving survey questions: Design and evaluation.* Thousand Oaks, CA: Sage.

Hanson, C., Hessel, H., Barneson, J., Boudewyns, D., Fransen, J., Friedman-Shedlov, L., … Traill, S. (2009). *Discoverability phase 1 final report.* Retrieved from http://purl.umn.edu/48258

Kenney, B. (2011, February 11). Liverpool's discovery: A university library applies a new search tool to improve the user experience. *Library Journal, 136*(3), 24–27. Retrieved from http://www.libraryjournal.com/lj/home /888965-264/ liverpools_ discovery.html.csp

Krug, S. (2005). *Don't make me think! A common sense approach to Web usability* (2nd ed.). Berkeley, CA: New Riders.

Kuniavsky, M. (2003). *Observing the user experience: A practitioner's guide to user research.* San Francisco, CA: Morgan Kaufmann.

Luther, J., & Kelly, M. C. (2011, March 15). The next generation of discovery: The stage is set for a simpler search for users, but choosing a product is much more complex. *Library Journal, 136*(5), 66–71. Retrieved from http://www.libraryjournal. com /lj/home/ 889250-264/the_next_generation _of_discovery.html.csp

Medeiros, N. (2009). Researching the research process: Information-seeking behavior, Summon, and Google Books. *OCLC Systems & Services, 25*(3), 153–155. doi:10.1108/10650750910982520

Nielsen, J. (1994). *Guerrilla HCI: Using discount usability engineering to penetrate the intimidation barrier.* Retrieved from http://www.useit.com/ papers/ guerrilla_hci.html

Quesenbery, W., & Brooks, K. (2010). *Storytelling for user experience: Crafting stories for better design.* Brooklyn, NY: Rosenfeld Media.

Rowe, R. (2010). Web-scale discovery: A review of Summon, EBSCO Discovery Service, and WorldCat Local. *Charleston Advisor, 12*(1), 5–10. doi:10.5260/chara.12.1.5

Rubin, J. (1994). *Handbook of usability testing.* New York, NY: Wiley.

KEY TERMS AND DEFINITIONS

API: Application Program Interface, a way for one computer application to request and get data back from another in a machine-readable way. APIs allow computers to exchange defined sets of data without exposing the entire database to outside use.

Convenience Sample: A sample that is gathered from an audience at hand without seeking a truly random or representative group of respondents.

Guerrilla Usability: Often called low-budget usability, a quick user interaction involving one or two questions aimed to answer a specific research question. A guerrilla usability test rarely takes more than ten minutes of a participant's time, often less.

OpenURL: A Uniform Resource Locator that encodes the citation for a journal, book, or other item, in a standard way (specified by ANSI/NISO Standard Z39.88) to enable linking to the location of the full text of the item. OpenURLs are parsed by "Link Resolvers" (products like Serials Solutions® 360 Link or Ex Libris™ SFX®) that match a citation with the full text option preferred by a particular library.

Persona: An archetypical user based on an amalgamation of real-world users and traits.

ENDNOTES

1 Serials Solutions is a registered trademark of Serials Solutions

2 Summon is owned by ProQuest LLC

3 Google Books is a trademark of Google, Inc.

4 The University of Michigan University Library's website is publicly available at http://www.lib.umich.edu and its Mirlyn library catalog is at http://mirlyn.lib.umich.edu

5 ExLibris is a trademark of Ex Libris Ltd.

6 MetaLib is a registered trademark of Ex Libris Ltd.

7 Google Scholar is owned by Google, Inc.

8 Several current and former staff at the University of Michigan Libraries in addition to the authors contributed to the research and committee reports on which this article is based, including Judy Ahronheim, Nancy Allee, Gaurav Bhatnagar, Gabriel Duque, Sara Samuel, Mark MacEachern, and Stephanie Teasley. The authors gratefully acknowledge the assistance of these colleagues.

9 For examples, see the "Guerrilla Test Usability Reports" page of the University of Michigan University Library website: http://www.lib.umich.edu/usability-library/usability-reports/Guerrilla%20Test

10 JSTOR is a registered trademark of ITHAKA.

11 ProQuest® is a registered trademark of ProQuest LLC.

12 The Drupal Article Discovery module is available for installation at http://drupal.org/sandbox/bertrama/1119778 and requires a Summon™ API key, Drupal 6, PHP version 5.x, and a copy of the Summon™ API library for PHP to operate. The module provides a configuration page, a search results page, and blocks for displaying a search box and a facet box. The public interface of the University of Michigan's Articles*Plus* service utilizing this module is available at http://www.lib.umich.edu/articlesplus

13 Qualtrics is a trademark of Qualtrics, Inc.

14 PsycINFO is a registered trademark of the American Psychological Association.

15 Web of Science is a registered trademark of Thomson Reuters.

16 The follow-up survey was dynamically constructed: questions about a resource appeared only if respondents indicated they had used it; comparison questions appeared only if respondents indicated they had used more than one resource; and respondents were free to skip questions, and to select more than one resource on comparison questions. Hence the total number of responses varied for each question, and cumulative response percentages for a question may exceed 100%.

17 After considering the findings in the reports on which this article is based, library administration has since decided to terminate the University of Michigan's subscription to the MetaLib® service and rely on the Summon™ service instead to provide broad, interdisciplinary article discovery for University of Michigan library users.

18 SciVerse Scopus is a registered trademark of Elsevier.

19 Percentages in Table 6 are rounded to the nearest whole percentage point. JSTOR® and LexisNexis® Academic do not provide a way to distinguish searches and sessions initiated via a federated search service like MetaLib from those initiated via the database's native interface; hence all searches and sessions from these two databases are counted as regular. SciVerse Scopus® provides a way to distinguish between regular and federated searches, but not sessions, and contains no full text; hence all sessions from it are counted as regular, and direct full text retrievals are not available from it.

20 The increase in the number of JSTOR® sessions while searches and full text retrievals declined is likely caused by changes JSTOR® made between Winter 2010 and Winter 2011 that allow users to link to JSTOR® article citations from results lists in freely acces-

sible search engines like Google Scholar, regardless of whether the users' institutions subscribe to the JSTOR® collections providing the full text of the articles. Thus since late 2010, users in search of the full text of an article found via a search engine may be led into JSTOR®, but not permitted to retrieve the full text of it there; if they give up, or click on an OpenURL link in JSTOR® leading to the full text in another database, they have initiated a JSTOR® session without conducting a search or retrieving any full text from within JSTOR®. In Winter 2011, the University of Michigan did not subscribe to four of the nine available JSTOR® Arts & Sciences multi-disciplinary journals archive collections, so this was a common experience for our users.

[21] The increase in regular searches of SciVerse Scopus® is particularly notable; unlike ProQuest®, it is not itself a source of full text, so none of the increase in its regular use can be attributed to it being merely the target for full text retrieval via an OpenURL link from another discovery tool like Summon™ where most of the user's discovery process actually took place.

[22] The difference in magnitude between these increases in full text retrievals is likely caused in part by the different way OpenURL links to full text articles are handled by these databases: OpenURL links to articles in LexisNexis® Academic lead directly to the full text, while in ProQuest® they lead to display of a citation of the article that includes a link to the full text—if after reaching the citation, the user fails to click on the full text link, the article is never retrieved. It is likely that some users clicking on an OpenURL link in the expectation of retrieving full text who arrive at a citation display fail to persist and click a second time to reach the full text. Likewise, the large difference in how regular sessions changed is likely caused at least in part by whether the use of an OpenURL link to reach the full text of an article does (as in LexisNexis® Academic) or does not (as in ProQuest®) register as part of a session. The fact that in ProQuest® regular sessions declined by 22%, while full text retrievals increased, suggests that to a significant extent, use of the Summon™ service displaced use of the native ProQuest® interface to discover articles available in full text in ProQuest® (which were retrieved via OpenURL links leading from Summon™ to the full text in ProQuest®).

[23] Because there is considerable overlap between the full text journal back-files available in JSTOR® and the full text journal content available in other databases and publisher packages licensed by the library (such as Periodicals Archive Online, SciVerse ScienceDirect®, SpringerLink, Wiley Online Library, etc.), it is possible that the 8% decline in retrieval of full text articles from JSTOR® represents not any true decline in use of those articles, but only a switch to accessing the full text of them in other databases instead. When using JSTOR® to discover articles, the full text will most likely be retrieved from JSTOR®; but when using the Summon™ service for discovery, the full text for many of the same articles could be retrieved from other databases, especially if the OpenURL link resolver used to link from Summon™ to the full text is configured to prioritize retrieval from other databases above retrieval from JSTOR® (as is done to some extent at University of Michigan).

[24] Material in this section is based on, and the survey instrument reproduced as Appendix 3 is drawn from, an unpublished internal study at the University of Michigan Library, Summon™ Benefit Analysis Group Final Report (Allee, Dennis, Teasley, & Varnum, 2011).

APPENDIX A: INITIAL SURVEY

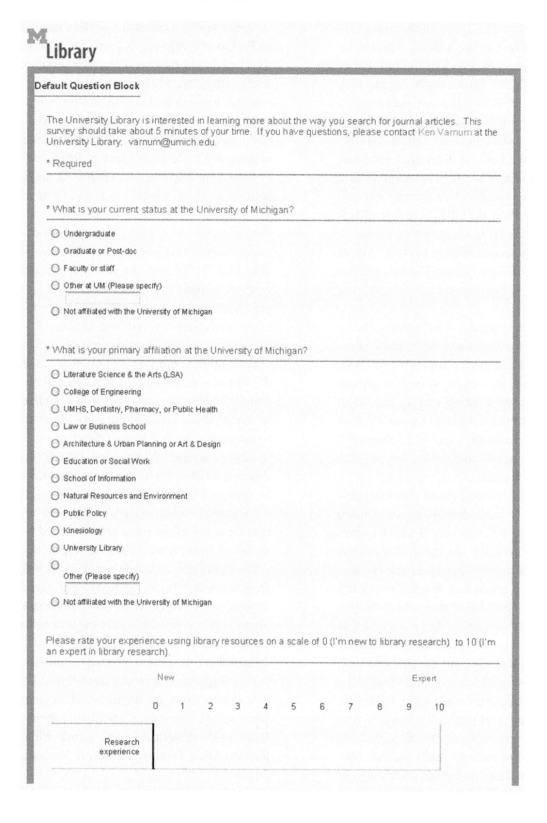

What online resources do you most frequently use to find journal articles?

Imagine you are starting a new research project and need to find journal articles. Rate the importance of the following features for finding articles.

	Not at all important	A little important	Neutral	Important	Very Important	I don't know what this is
I can find articles from the top journals in my subject area.	○	○	○	○	○	☐
I can perform advanced searches (options are available to search in multiple fields at the same time like year, author, title, keyword).	○	○	○	○	○	☐
My search results lists both relevant books and useful journal articles.	○	○	○	○	○	☐
I can limit my search so I only get articles from scholarly (peer-reviewed) journals.	○	○	○	○	○	☐
I can get articles from multiple databases with one search, and know which databases the results are coming from.	○	○	○	○	○	☐
I can easily find other topics and articles related to my original search.	○	○	○	○	○	☐
I can easily narrow down my search results by clicking on different links (such as year or subject).	○	○	○	○	○	☐

Imagine you are looking at a list of search results related to your new research project. Rate the importance of the following features for using your search results.

	Not at all important	A little important	Neutral	Important	Very Important	I don't know what this is
I can get to the full text of an article in one mouse click.	○	○	○	○	○	☐
I can save a search so I can go back and see new items.	○	○	○	○	○	☐
I can use it from my smart phone (or other	○	○	○	○	○	☐

mobile device).							
I can easily save and share citations of articles I find.	○	○	○	○	○		☐
I can export citations into citation management tools like RefWorks, EndNote, or Zotero	○	○	○	○	○		☐

Do you have any other comments or suggestions about what is important to you in an article search tool?

APPENDIX B: GUERRILLA TEST SCRIPT

Article Discovery Working Group Supplemental Report

Appendix: Interview Script

SOLICITATION

Hi, I'm ____, a librarian here. We're investigating tools to improve searching on our web site. Do you have about ten minutes to give it a test in exchange for 5 Blue Bucks?

No → Thanks anyway

Yes → Great! Please have a seat.

INTRODUCTION

This tool is not available at U-M, but other institutions have added it to their sites. We're going to use the version at Dartmouth College. Please keep in mind that the specific journals and books that Dartmouth College owns may not be the same as those that you would have access to here, if this tool were purchased.

First, some basic questions:

What is your role at the University (i.e., undergrad, grad, researcher, faculty, staff)?

What is your affiliation (school or department)?

I'd like you to think about something you might search the library for (for example, the topic of a recent or current assignment). Now, I'd like you to try that search on this site and look for some materials that might interest you.

Note what they searched:

Take a look at the results and describe to me what you've found.

Let user play around a bit, if they seem inclined. Remind them that they may not be able to reach the full text for some items.

Article Discovery Working Group Supplemental Report

Note what they searched and what they do – do they use or mention the facet? Sort? Did they click any titles? You might have to probe with questions like:

- *If you were a Dartmouth student/faculty, would all of these items be available to you online?*
- *What all kinds of items did this find?*

Did you notice the column on the left?

  Yes – what did you think about them?

  No – What do you think it's for?

Do the results seem useful?

Have you searched for articles before today?

  No – ok, thanks

  Yes –

  a.) Where do you usually search for articles?
  If needed, prompt with examples (Search Tools, Google Scholar, ProQuest, PubMed, etc.)

  b.) How does this tool compare with the one you usually use?

Any other questions or comments?

WRAP-UP
Thank you for your time. Here are your Blue Bucks.

APPENDIX C: FOLLOW-UP SURVEY

Introduction

M Library

The University Library is interested in your feedback on the online tools we offer to help you find articles. Your responses to this survey will help us provide you with quality article discovery resources for research, teaching and learning.

In appreciation of your time and effort, you will be given the option of entering into a drawing for a $50 gift card by providing your name and email address on a separate form at the completion of the survey.

The survey takes approximately 10 minutes to complete. Responses are completely confidential, and there will be no links between survey responses and the gift card form. Please contact article-discovery-survey@umich.edu with any questions or comments about this survey.

Thank you.
Summon Benefit Analysis Working Group
University Library
article-discovery-survey@umich.edu

Demographics

What is your current status at the University of Michigan (UM)?

○ Undergraduate

○ Graduate or Post-doc

○ Faculty

○ Staff

○ Other at UM (please specify):

○ Not affiliated with the University of Michigan

What is your primary affiliation at UM?

○ Architecture & Urban Planning

○ Art & Design

○ Business

○ Dentistry

○ Education

○ Engineering

○ Information, School of

○ Kinesiology

○ Law

○ Literature Science & the Arts (LSA)

○ Medicine

○ Music, Theatre & Dance

○ Natural Resources and Environment

○ Nursing

○ Pharmacy

○ Public Health

○ Public Policy

○ Rackham School of Graduate Studies

○ Social Work

Qualtrics Survey Software

11/21/11 3:14 PM

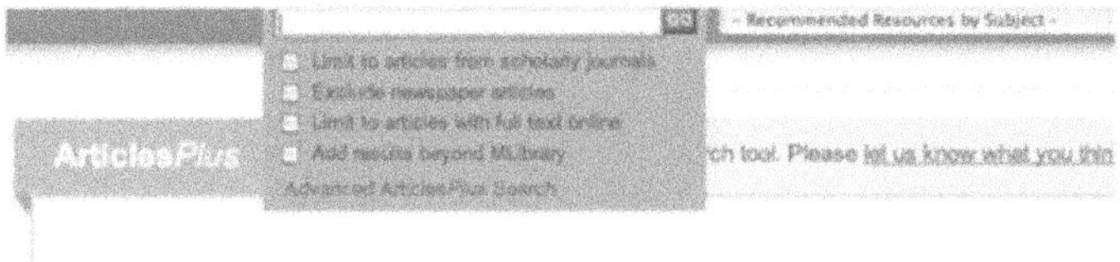

When was the last time you used ArticlesPlus?

○ Today

○ This week

○ Last week

○ This month

○ More than a month ago

How often do you use ArticlesPlus first before you try other similar resources?

○ All of the time

○ Most of the time

○ Sometimes

○ Rarely

○ No longer use

Rate the quality of your search experience using ArticlesPlus.

○ Very satisfied

○ Somewhat satisfied

○ Neither satisfied nor dissatisfied

○ Somewhat dissatisfied

○ Very dissatisfied

More about Google Scholar

Please answer the following question based on Google Scholar. A sample Google Scholar screen is shown below:

When was the last time you used Google Scholar?

○ Today

○ This week

○ Last week

○ This month

○ More than a month ago

○ More than a month ago

How often do you use Google Scholar first before you try other similar resources?

○ All of the time

○ Most of the time

○ Sometimes

○ Rarely

○ No longer use

Rate the quality of your search experience using Google Scholar.

○ Very satisfied

○ Somewhat satisfied

○ Neither satisfied nor dissatisfied

○ Somewhat dissatisfied

○ Very dissatisfied

Have you ever noticed the "Availability at Umichigan" links (illustrated below)?

[CITATION] A functional analysis of jaw mechanics in the dinosaur Triceratops
JH Ostrom - 1964 - Peabody Museum of Natural History
Cited by 37 - Related articles - Availability at UMichigan - Library Search

○ Yes

○ No

○ Not sure

More about Search Tools Quick Search

Please answer the following question based on Search Tools Quick Search. A sample Search Tools Quick Search screen is shown below:

When was the last time you used Search Tools Quick Search?

○ Today

○ This week

○ Last week

○ This month

○ More than a month ago

How often do you use Search Tools Quick Search first before you try other similar resources?

○ All of the time

○ Most of the time

○ Sometimes

○ Rarely

○ No longer use

Rate the quality of your search experience using Search Tools Quick Search.

○ Very satisfied

○ Somewhat satisfied

○ Neither satisfied nor dissatisfied

○ Somewhat dissatisfied

○ Very dissatisfied

More about Other Choice

When was the last time you used ${q://QID4/ChoiceTextEntryValue/4}?

○ Today

○ This week

○ Last week

○ This month

○ More than a month ago

How often do you use ${q://QID4/ChoiceTextEntryValue/4} first before you try other similar resources?

○ All of the time

○ Most of the time

○ Sometimes

○ Rarely

○ No longer use

Rate the quality of your search experience using ${q://QID4/ChoiceTextEntryValue/4}.

○ Very satisfied

○ Somewhat satisfied

○ Neither satisfied nor dissatisfied

○ Somewhat dissatisfied

○ Very dissatisfied

Universal Questions

Some people use multiple resources depending on their search interests and information needs. Based on your experience to date, please indicate which resource you **prefer to use** when answering the following questions. Please select only one in each row.

	ArticlesPlus	Google Scholar	Search Tools Quick Search	I don't do this
Searching for journal articles	☐	☐	☐	☐
Searching for a specific journal citation	☐	☐	☐	☐

Getting to full-text view	☐	☐	☐	☐
Doing advanced searches	☐	☐	☐	☐
Saving search results	☐	☐	☐	☐
Sharing search results	☐	☐	☐	☐
Limiting my search to scholarly, peer-reviewed journals	☐	☐	☐	☐
Finding other topics and articles related to my search	☐	☐	☐	☐
Expecting the search results to match my information need	☐	☐	☐	☐

I have recommended the following resource(s) to colleagues and friends (select all that apply):

☐ ArticlesPlus

☐ Google Scholar

☐ Search Tools Quick Search

☐ Other (please specify)

Please tell us why you recommended, or why you didn't, the above resources:

My experience using ArticlesPlus resources makes me likely to use library online resources again (select one):

○ Strongly agree

○ Agree

○ Neither agree nor disagree

○ Disagree

○ Strongly disagree

Thank you for completing this survey. If you wish to be entered in the drawing for one of five $50 Amazon.com gift certificates, click the next button below. You will not be entered in the drawing unless you click the next arrows. (Note that only active faculty, staff, researchers, and students at the University of Michigan Ann Arbor campus are eligible to enter and win.)

Chapter 13
Replicating Top Users' Searches in Summon and Google Scholar

David Earl Noe
Rollins College, USA

ABSTRACT

This chapter discusses the results of a review of the first 25 results for some of the most common searches in one college's instance of Summon™1 and the results for the same searches in Google Scholar™2. The results of the searches were provided to a panel of three librarians who did not know from which discovery service the results came. The chapter treats each search and its results as case studies and discusses both quantitative and qualitative evaluations. The study finds that neither search tool can provide reliable results for a simple search without further refinement of the search.

INTRODUCTION

The concept of resource discovery does indeed have many meanings. The various products that fit into the new, evolving class of discovery layers function differently from one another. This chapter details the results of one library's study of search results from two such unified resource discovery tools: Summon™ and Google Scholar™. This method can be used to review other unified re-

source discovery tools as librarians explore their options in this arena.

Librarians at Rollins College have encountered students saying, "I can find everything on Google Scholar™." In a recent LibQUAL®3 survey, more than one student noted that Google Scholar™ was less overwhelming than Summon™. There is one instance of a student suggesting in an instruction evaluation that the library instruction was not necessary: "I do not need to be shown how to Google the library." We cannot know exactly what the student meant by this, but it is reasonable to assume that it was a reference to the Summon™

DOI: 10.4018/978-1-4666-1821-3.ch013

basic search on the library home page and its Google-like interface. What we do know from these interactions is that this and subsequent generations of students coming to college will expect a one-stop-shopping resource discovery layer using simple searches to find information.

Faced with student expectations, increasing costs of subscription content, and tightening budgets, libraries have some tough choices to make: implement a commercial resource discovery tool, make do with free products like Google Scholar™ or WorldCat®4 Local Quick Start, or continue with the existing combination of multi-disciplinary and discipline specific databases to which the library already subscribes. Can users get the precise results they need with the simple searches they actually perform in these discovery services?

BACKGROUND

First released in mid-2009, Summon™ is a discovery tool built by Serials Solutions®5. It integrates well with the ERM (Electronic Resource Management) software and link resolver in their 360 Suite. Serials Solutions® ingests content into a unified index from databases, publishers, open access sources, and library catalogs and other local records. All subscribers share the same data set. When a search is performed, access rights and holdings are checked against access specified in an ERM, but a patron may choose to search beyond the respective library's collections. When last checked, Summon™ returned over two hundred twenty seven million items in a blank search. Not long ago, the number was twice this, but Serials Solutions® recently merged e-book titles with print books, which could account for this seeming decrease.

According to Google,

Google Scholar™ provides a simple way to broadly search for scholarly literature. From one place, you can search across many disciplines *and sources: articles, theses, books, abstracts and court opinions, from academic publishers, professional societies, online repositories, universities and other Web sites. Google Scholar™ helps you find relevant work across the world of scholarly research (Google, 2011, "What is Google Scholar?").*

Google Scholar™ (GS™) has met a mixed reception from the librarian community. It has some advanced search features, but it provides no interface for narrowing a set of results. Users can set preferences such as language, libraries with which to link, showing citation export options in results. It is free, but Google is quite secretive about the coverage of Google Scholar (GS™). The library does not know exactly what it is not paying for.

Rollins is a master's level university in Winter Park, Florida. In 2011, the college had a little over three thousand students, about three quarters of whom were undergraduates, and two hundred eight full-time faculty. The college is served by the Olin Library, which provides access to over three hundred thousand volumes, about 50,000 serial titles (print and electronic), and over one hundred databases.

Summon™ was selected by the Olin Library in the summer of 2009. Olin was using a federated search engine, but slow response, a clunky feel, complexity in choosing databases, difficulty with authentication, and ineffective use by students led to a lack of buy-in from the librarians. A focus on full text articles, the ability to refine and limit with faceted searching, ability to expand beyond Rollins, a clean interface, searching before authenticating, and integration with the Serials Solutions® 360 Suite were the primary factors leading to the selection of Summon™ .

LITERATURE REVIEW

Many of Rollins' incoming freshmen were born the year the Mosaic Web browser was released. They were five years old when Google went live. As DeRosa, et al. (2010) point out, though college students consider libraries more trustworthy and more accurate, 93% of college students use commercial search engines more often than other resources to find content online, and 75% of those do so first. Research by Connaway, Dickey, and Radford (2011, p. 187) would suggest this comes from a desire, if not a need, for convenience. They write, "Librarians need to adapt or seek to purchase services and systems that are designed to replicate the Web environment so that the systems are perceived as convenient and easy to use." Indeed, that is what libraries had hoped federated searches would do. Jansen, Zhang, and Schultz (2009) demonstrate that brand of a search engine has a "dramatic effect on a user's evaluation of system results" (p. 1592). Libraries have a reliable and trustworthy branding. Marshall, Herman, and Rjan (2006) write "For now at least, federated search provides a way for librarians to reclaim the community that Google snapped up" (p. 180). Warren (2007, p. 268) concludes "federated searching is still a long way from delivering the hoped for seamless cross-database access to the scholarly literature." Korah and Cassidy (2010) demonstrate that students will use federated search tools if they are placed prominently in the library Web page, but they are generally not satisfied with the results.

Seeking other options for unified discovery, many academic libraries began linking to Google Scholar™ and adding GS™ search boxes to their pages. Hartman and Mullen note that between 2005 and 2007, the percentage of ARL libraries including GS™ in their alphabetical lists of databases rose from 24% to 68% (2008). They also point out that twelve percent of ARL libraries include a link to Google Scholar™ on their home page. By 2008, 73% of research institutions and 33% of Master's institutions used GS™ with a link resolver to allow access to content licensed by the library (Neuhaus, Neuhaus, and Asher, 2008). Neuhaus et al. also show that GS™ on average is featured on over 40 Web pages at research institution library Web sites. An early study of GS™ by Neuhaus, Neuhaus, Asher, and Wrede (2006) suggests that GS™ is a good tool for searching scientific and medical literature but not for humanities, social sciences, education, or business; however, if an institution is resource poor, it can be a boon. Haya, Nygren, and Widmark (2007) showed that students have greater success searching in GS™ than in the Metalib federated search, but the authors suggested that neither is appropriate for a "front line" search tool. Mayr and Walter (2007) found that although GS™ is a useful supplement to abstracting and indexing databases, because of its lack of complete indexing of open access journals, lack of transparency, and questionable "up-to-dateness," it is not an ample scientific database. Jasco (2008) enumerates among the GS's™ advantages improved journal coverage (over previous iterations), the addition of Google Books™[6] to search results, geographic and language coverage, the addition of digital repositories, and the size of the database. He includes among the disadvantages innumeracy caused by inconsistent behavior of the software and problems distinguishing authors' names. It does not treat Boolean operators in the way one would expect. Jascó also notes oddities in result counts when minor changes are made to searches. Jacso (2009) writes that "Google's algorithms create phantom authors for millions of papers" (p. 26). He also reports that its citation count information is grossly overinflated. Walters (2009) finds that "a searcher who is unwilling to search multiple databases or to adopt a sophisticated search strategy is likely to achieve better than average recall and precision by using Google Scholar™" (p. 16). Howland, Wright, Boughan, and Roberts (2009) write in the results of their study that the average scholarliness score for citations found in GS™

but not in licensed databases was 17.6% higher; however, the score was higher for items found in both databases than the score of those found only in one or the other (p. 231).

Web-scale discovery, discovery service, unified discovery layer—these are just a few terms used to describe databases that index large numbers of publications and utilize a link resolver to provide access to the results. As these are relatively new tools, there is a dearth of research on the subject. ODLIS (the *Online Dictionary for Library and Information Science*) still has no definition for any of these terms.

Bhatnagar, et al. (2009) surveyed over 900 users at the University of Michigan on the subject of article discovery. At the time, Serials Solutions®' Summon™ was the only product on the market that met all of their top users' top five stated needs:

1. I can find articles from the top journals in my subject area.
2. I can get to the full text of an article in one mouse click.
3. I can perform advanced searches (options are available to search in multiple fields at the same time like year, author, title, keyword).
4. I can easily narrow down my search results by clicking on different links (such as year or subject).
5. I can limit my search so I only get articles from scholarly (peer-reviewed) journals (p. 12).

Interestingly, one stop shopping is not one of the top results, and including books in the results is the third to last. Bhatnagar, et al. do not ask respondents to address speed, which is a main concern with federated search. An early user assessment survey at Dartmouth, which was a beta test site for Summon™, found that 85% of undergraduate respondents would, if Summon™ were made available, find it important or very important to their research (Braunstein, et al., 2009, p. 5). After a redesign of the library Web

site at Edith Cowan University intended to make the Summon™ search box more apparent, Gross and Sheridan (2010) performed a small study of five users. The subjects were asked to find four resources on the library Web site. They found that subjects chose Summon™ for searches 80% of the time (p. 244). Howard and Wiebrands (2011) report that though Edith Cowan "students and academic staff have overwhelmingly responded positively to [Summon™], this was not the case with ECU librarians" (p. 9).

METHODOLOGY

Most search tool studies either evaluate results of searches created by librarians, test searches for known sets of results, or study patrons using the interface. Though librarians are great at evaluating sources, their search strategies do not reflect the way the normal user approaches a search. Testing for known items does not address user behavior, either. Observing users can tell a researcher a great deal about how they search or what they select, but it gets away from evaluating the quality of the results. Instead, at Rollins the desire was to evaluate results from some of the most common searches as case studies.

It is necessary to evaluate search results from Summon™ and GS™ using both quantitative and qualitative methods. Some data from search results can be quantified easily: number of results, duplication, whether or not a journal is scholarly, etc.; however, judging relevance and overall quality requires critical thought. The nature of each search impacts what is relevant to a search. These elements are best evaluated by experienced reference librarians.

Serials Solutions® offers usage reports that include top searches in its Summon™ Administration Console. These searches are most representative of how students use these interfaces. These searches can be sorted by number of visits (as opposed to total number of searches, which

Table 1. Top searches in Summon™ since 9/1/2009 used in study

Rank	Summon Queries	Searches	Visits
2	venice and diplomacy	384	312
5	global warming	144	49
8	harry potter	88	33
13	John Dewey inquiry	29	26
17	database design	24	21
18	richard florida	70	21
20	Kuleshov Effect	45	21
25	gone with the wind	51	18
27	linguistics branding	19	17
30	art education	29	16

counts refined searches). Searches that are obvious librarian test searches and single word searches are excluded (Table 1). These top searches were replicated in Summon™ and GS™ in May 2011.

Searches were replicated verbatim and without quotes. Newspaper articles were excluded for searches in Summon™, and results were expanded outside Olin's collection. Patents and legal documents were not included in GS™ searches. Citation and abstract information (if available) of the top twenty five results from these popular searches were recorded in tables. Citations of the search results were presented in the order they occurred in the retrieved set and given to a panel of experienced reference librarians who evaluated each set of searches. Three librarians were asked to serve on the panel. All three hold an MLS and second master's degree (one in a natural science, one in a social science, and one in the humanities). Two are women. One is a Latina. All three are ambivalent about discovery tools: they like the idea but are not convinced that they work well in practice.

Because preconceptions of a search tool may influence a user's evaluation of the results as suggested by Jansen and Schultz (2009), results were presented so the panel members were not privy to whether the results came from Summon™ or Google Scholar™. Results were presented to the panel in 20 tables (Appendix B) with eight col-

umns: rank, citation, abstract (if available), type of source (scholarly or not, book, dissertation, etc.), and blank fields for currency, reliability, relevance, and notes. Journals were assigned ahead of the study as scholarly or not scholarly according to information in Ulrich's™[7]. The Likert scale (1-5).

The librarian panel was interviewed beforehand regarding currency, reliability, and relevance and shown a few example result lists. Currency is relative to the topic. Something written 10 years ago in the biochemistry field might already be dated. Something written in the humanities could be considered useful indefinitely. The panel members all felt that reliability would be based on the publishing credentials. Without knowing the intent of the searcher, relevance is the most difficult to determine. The panel members said they would try to consider multiple possibilities. The panel met together to collectively evaluate all 500 results for 12 hours divided over two days.

This study is meant to test the resources being used by patrons and to analyze the results users see. This study is not meant to be a head-to-head competition between these two tools.

RESULTS

First, to get a broad sense of the data, the results for the currency, reliability, and relevance in both

Figure 1. Averages scores for top 10 searches

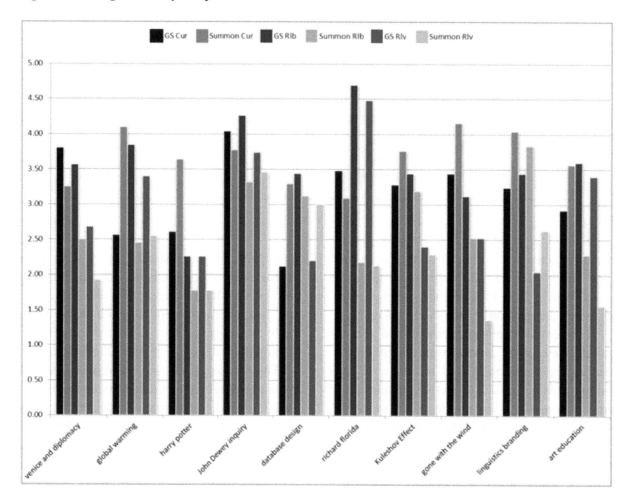

tools was averaged and compared (Figure 1). At a glance GS™ results received fair grades from the library panel. Indeed, if users accept the first few records presented by a discovery service with no further refinement, GS™ would seem to perform better. Research does suggest that the percentage of users who only view the first page of search engine results increased significantly between the late 1990's and early 2000's (Jansen, Spink, 2006). If a user does choose to not accept the first results at face value and refine a search using faceted searching, Summon™ gains a distinct advantage. In Google Scholar™, a user will have to construct a more sophisticated search to obtain better results.

Overall, the librarian panel graded Summon™ currency 0.52 higher over Google Scholar™, the closest margin (Figure 1). In reliability GS™ scores 0.85 higher than Summon™. Google suggests GS™ is limited to scholarly materials, yet it included thirty-three results graded below 3 by the librarian panel. GS™ scores 0.65 over Summon™ on relevance. Again, with faceted searching a user can quickly refine results to find the resources most appropriate to a topic.

Venice and Diplomacy

The results that receive higher marks in relevance deal with politics and diplomacy in Renaissance

Table 2. Librarian panel evaluation averages

	GS Cur	Summon Cur	GS Rlb	Summon Rlb	GS Rlv	Summon Rlv	Avg Diff
venice and diplomacy	3.80	3.25	3.56	2.50	2.68	1.92	0.79
global warming	2.56	4.10	3.84	2.45	3.40	2.55	1.26
harry potter	2.61	3.64	2.26	1.77	2.26	1.77	0.67
John Dewey inquiry	4.04	3.77	4.26	3.32	3.74	3.45	0.50
database design	2.12	3.29	3.44	3.12	2.20	3.00	0.77
richard florida	3.48	3.09	4.70	2.17	4.48	2.13	1.75
Kuleshov Effect	3.28	3.76	3.44	3.19	2.40	2.29	0.28
gone with the wind	3.44	4.16	3.12	2.52	2.52	1.36	0.83
linguistics branding	3.24	4.04	3.44	3.83	2.04	2.63	0.59
art education	2.92	3.56	3.60	2.28	3.40	1.56	1.27
mean	3.15	3.67	3.57	2.72	2.91	2.27	0.67
median	3.26	3.70	3.50	2.51	2.60	2.21	

Venice or more generally Renaissance Italy. The librarian panel gave lower grades to works in GS™ covering the Ottoman Empire, public life in Venice, contemporary diplomacy issues, environmental policy, intellectual property issues, and a book of Jacobean letters. Summon™ results that received low marks dealt with contemporary British politics, art, current papal diplomacy, mortgage finance tools as anti-communist carrots, and the FUS Foreign Service. Considering that the 10th result in Summon™ is the first useful resource, this would not be a good set of results for an undergraduate student; however, narrowing with facets will improve precision. Google Scholar's™ results were better, but they contained many book chapters. Delivery of these resources to the student might be slower.

Global Warming

Global warming is an academic topic covered by all types of non-academic press and media. This presents an interesting example for looking at a simple search intended to deal with a topic that is both broad in scope and on which there has been heavy publishing. This poses a particular problem for Summon™. Because Summon cannot limit articles to scholarly publications without excluding books, the results contain many more non-academic titles. Most of the GS™ results were articles in scholarly journals covering the science and politics of global warming, but many were quite dated. Currency was the weakest point of this set of results from GS™, but it is the only area in which the librarians graded results lower than Summon™ for this search. It was the second worst average currency for GS™ in the study. Most of the first 10 results scored below 2. GS™ performed much better on reliability and relevance. This was the third highest reliability average for Google Scholar™, but this did not correlate with currency. Global warming tied as the third most relevant average in Google Scholar™. The results in Summon™ were graded highly for currency, but reliability and relevance were troubling.

Harry Potter

Searches that deal with information in the mainstream media can be much more difficult without filters limiting to scholarly material. This being said, Google claims "Google Scholar™ provides a simple way to broadly search for scholarly literature" (Google, 2011), yet it returns many non-scholarly results. Though Google is often credited with having the most sophisticated search algorithms, GS™ does not handle this search for a popular fictional character terribly well. The currency of the GS™ results is poor except for the citations for books in the Harry Potter series. Those that were full text records were questionable. Dubious editing and optical character recognition software impact reliability. The results in Summon™ were fairly current having the second highest average of currency in Summon™ for the study, but Summon™ scores somewhat lower on reliability and relevance. When using this search string without limiting to scholarly materials, this is predictable. Books of critical work on Harry Potter were the only results that the panel graded highly.

John Dewey Inquiry

This was the first search of a strictly academic context from which intent can be somewhat easily inferred. It is doubtful that today's students' use of online search tools and subsequently discovered information would qualify as bona fide inquiry. This was also the only search with more than two words that were not an article, conjunction, or preposition. With these factors in mind, it is not too surprising that these were some of the highest scores for Summon™ in all three categories. Yet they were still lower than Google Scholar™. Though many of the results are somewhat old in the results, this is highest currency grade GS™ receives. Many results were works by Dewey. Most of the remaining results were articles on Dewey from refereed journals. The librarian panel noted this was "a reasonable list overall." This is one of the more positive evaluations they gave to any set in the study. Summon's™ results were quite different from GS™. None were penned by Dewey. These results included some of the older records returned by Summon™ in this study, but this does

not matter as much with such a topic. The librarian panel noted of the Summon™ results that it was a "dissertation-heavy list... limits its usefulness for the average undergraduate research paper."

Database Design

Database design was certainly an appropriate topic for this study. Publications should be fairly recent, and those from mainstream media should not show up here. The search suggests a general information need. Summon™ functions well here, but nether tool demonstrates exceptional performance. Core concepts of database design have not changed too much of the last few decades, but the tools used for to implement a database are changing regularly. Currency is thus somewhat important but is not absolutely critical for this topic. The librarians had a hard time judging currency for these results in GS™. Many were older and were esoteric, theoretical works. Many others were textbooks. They considered the sources moderately reliable and relevant, though. Summon™ returned more current records, but the reliability scores were mediocre. They were largely specific to particular database management systems or languages. With eight duplicate records in the results, the average scores are a less reliable indicator.

Richard Florida

The name of popular urban studies writer Richard Florida makes for a good search in GS™ and a bad one for Summon™. Google's relevance ranking shows a seemingly semantic understanding of the relationship between the words Richard and Florida. Most of the results were by Richard Florida or by others regarding his work. Summon™ did not do so well with this search. The results averaged a difference of 1.75, which has the highest in the study and close to double the study's average. The GS™ results might have been given better numbers for relevance, but Richard Florida's co-authorship of some of the results was somewhat obscured by the citations and lack of access at Olin Library. Otherwise the grading quite accurately reflects that someone searching for work by Richard Florida in GS™ will find them. This was the lowest currency average for Summon™ in the study and the second worst score for Summon™ reliability. Many results scored below 3 in all areas.

Kuleshov Effect

The Kuleshov Effect is a film editing montage effect demonstrated in the early 20th century by Russian filmmaker Lev Kuleshov. Kuleshov demonstrated that showing a montage of alternating positive and negative images can impact the emotional state the audience imposes on a character shown in between. All results in GS™ dealt specifically with the Kuleshov effect or were scientific works authored or co-authored by someone with the name Kuleshov.

The combination of Kuleshov and effect in GS™ did not limit results to the filmmaker or works on editing theory, but currency and reliability were reasonable. Those that were not about film were about effects on results of scientific experiments co-authored by scientists named Kuleshov. Summon's™ performance was quite similar. With an average difference of 0.28, this was the lowest average in the study. The articles that were not related to Kuleshov the filmmaker were authored by someone else with the name Kuleshov and were largely scientific.

Gone with the Wind

The search string, gone with the wind, posed a significant challenge for both of these tools, but Summon™ fared somewhat worse. The title of Margaret Mitchell's book has been widely appropriated for creative, ostensibly humorous naming of other works. The records that were not Mitchell's book or did not deal directly with this work covered a wide range of topics: rental law in California, the violent interaction between galaxies, wind power, turbo-charged motorcycles, improving fuel economy of semi tractors, dish cleaning systems for caterers, astronomy, finance, and sailing, and labor talks at Delta Airlines (whose headquarters are in Atlanta, interestingly). All but one of the GS™ results include the phrase, but less than half related to the work Gone with the Wind. This was the second lowest reliability score for Google Scholar™. Similar to Google Scholar™, all Summon™ results had the phase "gone with the wind" in the title. Though this was Summon's™ highest average currency score, relevance was very low; in fact, at 1.36 this was the lowest average score of both tools for any area in the study.

Linguistics Branding

This would seem an unlikely top search, but this is an area of research of a couple of members of Rollins' faculty in the International Business program. The top GS™ results tended to relate to linguistics. Few dealt with branding, but the six that did were published in the last decade. Currency and reliability scores in GS™ were close to average, but this was the second lowest relevance score. Summon™ performed better than GS™. All of the top results were from the last decade. Most were from marketing and business journals and related more to marketing and branding than linguistics. This is the only search in which Summon™ scores higher than GS™ in all three categories, yet a 2.63 average for relevance is not remarkable.

Art Education

Art education is the only search string is this study that is a common program of study at colleges. The librarian panel interpreted the search to mean broadly the teaching of art to students. One might expect to find general works regarding education like textbooks or other introductory materials, but this was not the case. Most GS™ results related to art education. Many of these were from the journal *Art Education*. With more than half of the result being 20 years old or more, currency was Google Scholar™'s biggest problem, but the librarians considered these results reliable and relevant. Currency was not a problem for Summon™, but with the second lowest score in the study reliability was a problem.. All top results had the phrase art education in the title, but very few were useful. Three of the results were LibGuides from other universities. One was a 1983 curriculum for elementary school art education from a county's board of education.

Discussion

Considering the lack of sophistication of the queries, it is no great surprise that these tools performed as poorly as they did in this this study. What was surprising was that GS™ performed as well as it did. It scored an average reliability of 3.75. Summon™ scored 0.85 points lower on average and only scored higher than GS™ on one search, linguistics branding. Summon™ only outscored GS™ in relevance on two searches.

Summon™ and GS™ offer adequate results for some more esoteric, academic searches. GS™ usually preforms better for searches with more popular contexts. Yet GS™ has some inconstancies with popular names. The search algorithm gets that Richard Florida is a person and ranks work by and about this individual before results about or by people named Richard regarding the state of Florida. Conversely, GS™ returns for a Harry Potter searcg non-scholarly works, questionable full-text versions of Rowling's novels, and scholarly works covering sundry topics by authors named Harry Potter. GS™ provides a more complete picture than Summon™. With Summon's™ faceted searching, however, results can be narrowed down much more easily than in Google Scholar™. In particular, the scholarly limiter makes a significant difference in results. Still,

neither provides a panacea for semantic searching, generating superior results from simple searches.

FUTURE RESEARCH DIRECTIONS

Librarians know that patrons are using these interfaces and will continue to do so at an increasing rate. More information is needed about how they use these types of interfaces. When available, will students narrow their results with faceted searching? More importantly, will they use it effectively? Will they spend time refining their results when facets are available than when they are not available? A larger study including more of the discovery services now emerging should be performed with more search strings and more librarian evaluators. Another question worth asking is how does the implementation of a discovery service impact usage of GS™ on a college campus? How much would promotion of a new discovery tool change patron use of Google Scholar™?

CONCLUSION

Users will have to apply more sophisticated search strategies than the simple searches used in this study to find the kind of precision retrieval needed for academic work. Topics from the mainstream prove highly problematic. Naturally, the more information there is published on a topic that is not of use for scholarly work, the more of such materials will be returned in a set of results. It has to be excluded somehow. To get greater precision in Google Scholar™, the user must develop significantly more complex searches.

Google Scholar™ has a definite advantage over Summon™ in relevance ranking over Summon™; but that is not enough to make it a one stop index for scholarly materials. GS™ narrowly produced better than average results as found by Walters (2009). GS™ does not offer faceted searching to narrow results. Many citations do not have links to documents or resolver links. The researcher cannot know what titles are actually indexed. It is a powerful tool, nevertheless.. Google Scholar™ would be an excellent supplement to any library's databases. GS™ would be a significant resource to those libraries for which discovery services are cost prohibitive.

Faceted searching distinguishes Summon™ from GS™. A slightly more ambitious researcher can gain better precision by selecting and eliminating records using various criteria available to the left of the search results. Without faceting, a user must develop a sophisticated search strategy that takes into consideration controlled vocabularies, synonyms, and terms to exclude. Then the search terms must be synthesized into a string of Boolean logic. With faceting, the possibilities that can be considered are offered graphically. The patron selecting facets uses Boolean logic without being aware of doing so. As these tools continue to be improved and datasets become larger, valuable and scarce library instruction time can be devoted less to searching strategies and more to information fluency.

There is no semantic search available yet. For now, human users will have to create searches based on the understanding of parts of speech and relationships between words. In particular, understanding idiomatic language will be a hurdle for search tools for a while. In the meantime, a terse search string will seldom produce a set of precise results in any discovery service. Librarians must either teach complex search strategies based on controlled vocabularies and Boolean logic or provide such graphical search tools as faceted searching.

"I do not need to be shown how to Google the library" says the freshman undergraduate student. Indeed, students do need instruction on how to effectively search available sets of data with a variety of search tools. There is not yet a one stop search tool, nor is there is one on the horizon. As the major content providers continue

to consolidate into fewer and larger companies and compete with one another for market share of not only content licenses but also resource discovery tools to access that information, the sharing of full text content and metadata for indexing will remain limited. If patrons use only one search tool with such simple queries and do not narrow the results by query or faceting, then they will be looking at results much like those in this study.

ACKNOWLEDGMENT

I would like to thank my colleagues Susan Montgomery, Cynthia Snyder, and Bill Svitavsky of the Olin Library at Rollins College for their time and efforts providing objective evaluations of the results. Without their work, this study would not have been possible.

REFERENCES

Bhatnagar, G., Dennis, S., Duque, G., Henry, S., MacEachern, M., Teasley, S., & Varnum, K. (2009). *University of Michigan Library Article Discovery Working Group final report.* Retrieved from http://www.lib.umich.edu/files/adwg/final-report.pdf

Braunstein, L., Cocklin, J., DeFelice, B., Hall, L., Holt, J., & Lowenstein, N. …Wheelock, C. (2009). *An evaluation of Serials Solutions Summon as a discovery service for the Dartmouth College Library.* Retrieved from http://www.dartmouth.edu/~library/admin /docs/Summon_Report.pdf

Connaway, L. S., Dickey, T. J., & Radford, M. L. (2011). "If it is too inconvenient I'm not going after it:" Convenience as a critical factor in information-seeking behaviors. *Library & Information Science Research, 33*(3), 179–190. doi:10.1016/j.lisr.2010.12.002

De Rosa, C., Cantrell, J., Carlson, M., Gallagher, P., Hawk, J., & Sturtz, C. ...Olszewski, L. (2010). *Perceptions of libraries, 2010: Context and community.* Dublin, OH: OCLC. Retrieved from http://www.oclc.org/reports/ 2010perceptions.htm

Google. (2011). *About Google Scholar.* Retrieved from http://www.scolar.google.com/intl/en/scholar/about.html

Gross, L., & Sheridan, L. (2011). Web scale discovery: The user experience. *New Library World, 112*(5/6), 236–247. doi:10.1108/03074801111136275

Hartman, K. A., & Mullen, L. B. (2008). Google scholar and academic libraries: An update. *New Library World, 109*(5/6), 211–222. doi:10.1108/03074800810873560

Haya, G., Nygren, E., & Widmark, W. (2007). Metalib and Google Scholar: A user study. *Online Information Review, 31*(3), 365–371. doi:10.1108/14684520710764122

Howard, D., & Wiebrands, C. (2011). *Culture shock: Librarians' response to Web scale search.* Paper presented at the 2011 ALIA Information Online Conference, Sydney, N.S.W. Retrieved from http://ro.ecu.edu.au/cgi/viewcontent.cgi?article=7208&context=ecuworks

Howland, J. L., Wright, T. C., Boughan, R. A., & Roberts, B. C. (2009). How scholarly is Google Scholar? A comparison to library databases. *College & Research Libraries, 70*(3), 227–234.

Jacsó, P. (2008). Google Scholar revisited. *Online Information Review, 32*(1), 102–114. doi:10.1108/14684520810866010

Jacsó, P. (2009). Google Scholar's ghost authors. *Library Journal, 134*(18), 26–27.

Jansen, B., & Spink, A. (2006). How are we searching the World Wide Web? A comparison of nine search engine transaction logs. *Information Processing & Management, 42*(1), 248–263. doi:10.1016/j.ipm.2004.10.007

Jansen, B., Zhang, M., & Schultz, C. (2009). Brand and its effect on user perception of search engine performance. *Journal of the American Society for Information Science and Technology, 60*(8), 1572–1595. doi:10.1002/asi.21081

Korah, A., & Cassidy, E. D. (2010). Students and federated searching: A survey of use and satisfaction. *Reference and User Services Quarterly, 49*(4), 325–332.

Marshall, P., Herman, S., & Rajan, S. (2006). In search of more meaningful search. *Serials Review, 32*(3), 172–180. doi:10.1016/j.serrev.2006.06.001

Mayr, P., & Walter, A. (2007). An exploratory study of Google Scholar. *Online Information Review, 31*(6), 814–830. doi:10.1108/14684520710841784

Neuhaus, C., Neuhaus, E., & Asher, A. (2008). Google scholar goes to school: The presence of Google scholar on college and university Web sites. *Journal of Academic Librarianship, 34*(1), 39–51. doi:10.1016/j.acalib.2007.11.009

Neuhaus, C., Neuhaus, E., Asher, A., & Wrede, C. (2006). The depth and breadth of Google scholar: An empirical study. *Portal: Libraries and the Academy, 6*(2), 127–141. doi:10.1353/pla.2006.0026

Walters, W. H. (2009). Google scholar search performance: Comparative recall and precision. *Portal: Libraries and the Academy, 9*(1), 5–24. doi:10.1353/pla.0.0034

Warren, D. (2007). Lost in translation: The reality of federated searching. *Australian Academic & Research Libraries, 38*(4), 258–269.

ADDITIONAL READING

Arendt, J. (2008). Imperfect tools: Google Scholar vs. traditional commercial library databases. *Against the Grain, 20*(2), 26-30.

Bar-Ilan, J., Keenoy, K., Levene, M., & Yaari, E. (2009). Presentation bias is significant in determining user preference for search results-A user study. *Journal of the American Society for Information Science and Technology, 60*(1), 135–149. doi:10.1002/asi.20941

Beall, J. (2010). How Google uses metadata to improve search results. *The Serials Librarian, 59*(1), 40–53. doi:10.1080/03615260903524222

Beel, J., Gipp, B., & Eilde, E. (2010). Academic search engine optimization. *Journal of Scholarly Publishing, 41*(2), 176–190. doi:10.3138/jsp.41.2.176

Brophy, J., & Bawden, D. (2005). Is Google enough? Comparison of an internet search engine with academic library resources. *Aslib Proceedings: New Information Perspectives, 57*(6), 498–512. doi:doi:10.1108/00012530510634235

Chen, X. (2006). MetaLib, WebFeat, and Google: The strengths and weaknesses of federated search engines compared with Google. *Online Information Review, 30*(4), 413–427. doi:10.1108/14684520610686300

Clewley, N., Chen, S. Y., & Liu, X. (2010). Cognitive styles and search engine preferences field dependence/independence vs. holism/serialism. *The Journal of Documentation, 66*(4), 585–603. doi:10.1108/00220411011052966

Fagan, J. C. (2006). Usability testing of a large, multidisciplinary library database: Basic search and visual search. *Information Technology and Libraries, 25*(3), 140–150.

Ford, N., Eaglestone, B., Madden, A., & Whittle, M. (2009). Web searching by the "general public": An individual differences perspective. *The Journal of Documentation, 65*(4), 632–667. doi:10.1108/00220410910970285

Gibson, I., Goddard, L., & Gordon, S. (2009). One box to search them all: Implementing federated search at an academic library. *Library Hi Tech, 27*(1), 118–133. doi:10.1108/07378830910942973

Giglierano, J. (2008). Attitudes of OhioLINK librarians toward Google scholar. *Journal of Library Administration, 47*(1-2), 101–113. doi:10.1080/01930820802110951

Granka, L. A. (2010). The politics of search: A decade retrospective. *The Information Society, 26*(5), 364–374. doi:10.1080/01972243.2010.511560

Haines, L. L., Light, J., O'Malley, D., & Delwiche, F. A. (2010). Information-seeking behavior of basic science researchers: Implications for library services. *Journal of the Medical Library Association, 98*(1), 73–81. doi:10.3163/1536-5050.98.1.019

Jacsó, P. (2010). Metadata mega mess in Google Scholar. *Online Information Review, 34*(1), 175–191. doi:10.1108/14684521011024191

Joint, N. (2008). Federated search engines and the development of library systems. *Library Review, 57*(9), 653–659. doi:10.1108/00242530810911770

King, D. (2008). Many libraries have gone to federated searching to win users back from Google, is it working? *Journal of Electronic Resources Librarianship, 20*(4), 213–227. doi:10.1080/19411260802554520

Lampert, L. D., & Dabbour, K. S. (2007). Librarian perspectives on teaching metasearch and federated search technologies. *Internet Reference Services Quarterly, 12*(3), 253–278. doi:10.1300/J136v12n03_02

Mayr, P., & Walter, A. (2008). Studying journal coverage in Google scholar. *Journal of Library Administration, 47*(1), 81–99. doi:10.1080/01930820802110894

Medeiros, N. (2009). Researching the research process: Information-seeking behavior, Summon, and Google books: Information-seeking behavior, Summon, and Google books. *OCLC Systems & Services, 25*(3), 153–155. doi:10.1108/10650750910982520

Quint, B. (2008). Changes at Google Scholar: A conversation with Anurag Acharya. *Journal of Library Administration, 47*(1), 77–79. doi:10.1080/01930820802110910

Robbins, S., & McCain, C. (2007). Federated searching: Instruction and promotion on ARL libraries' Web sites. *Internet Reference Services Quarterly, 12*(3), 279–296. doi:10.1300/J136v12n03_03

Robinson, M. L., & Wusteman, J. (2007). Putting Google Scholar to the test: A preliminary study. *Program: Electronic Library & Information Systems, 41*(1), 71–80. doi:10.1108/00330330710724908

Rowe, R. (2010). Web-scale discovery: A review of Summon, EBSCO Discovery Service, and WorldCat Local. *The Charleston Advisor, 12*(1), 5–10. doi:10.5260/chara.12.1.5

Sampath Kumar, B. T., & Pavithra, S. M. (2010). Evaluating the searching capabilities of search engines and metasearch engines: A comparative study. *Annals of Library & Information Studies, 57*(2), 87–97.

Shadle, S. (2009). Electronic resources in a next-generation catalog: The case of WorldCat Local. *Journal of Electronic Resources Librarianship, 21*(3), 192–199. doi:10.1080/19411260903446006

Shimer, P. (2009). Unified vs. federated: Which has the proven track record for managing information? *Information Management Journal, 43*(6), 34–38.

Shultz, M. (2007). Comparing test searches in PubMed and Google Scholar. *Journal of the Medical Library Association, 95*(4), 442–445. doi:10.3163/1536-5050.95.4.442

Tann, C., & Sanderson, M. (2009). Are Web-based informational queries changing? *Journal of the American Society for Information Science and Technology, 60*(6), 1290–1293. doi:10.1002/asi.21053

Vaughan, J. (2011). Serials Solutions Summon. *Library Technology Reports, 47*(1), 22–29.

Vaughan, J. (2011). Web scale discovery what and why? *Library Technology Reports, 47*(1), 5–11.

Vine, R. (2006). Google Scholar. *Journal of the Medical Library Association, 94*(1), 97–99.

Walters, W. H. (2007). Google Scholar coverage of a multidisciplinary field. *Information Processing & Management, 43*(4), 1121–1132. doi:10.1016/j.ipm.2006.08.006

Williams, S. C., Bonnell, A., & Stoffel, B. (2009). Student feedback on federated search use, satisfaction, and Web presence: Qualitative findings of focus groups. *Reference and User Services Quarterly, 49*(2), 131–139.

Wolfram, D., Wang, P., & Zhang, J. (2009). Identifying Web search session patterns using cluster analysis: A comparison of three search environments. *Journal of the American Society for Information Science and Technology, 60*(5), 896–910. doi:10.1002/asi.21034

KEY TERMS AND DEFINITIONS

Currency: The degree to which a record reflects the available work on a topic, which varies depending on the topic area. Scientific information may be outdated in a few years, but work in the humanities might be useful indefinitely.

Discovery Service: A unified index of records across multiple disciples and publishers that can be searched to find a list of ranked results matching the search terms and links out to available sources of for that record when selected.

Google Scholar™: A free, interdisciplinary search interface from Google that indexes the full text of scholarly literature, patents, and legal literature.

Record: A document created or received by a person or a corporate body in any format. A record in the context of library materials is usually a description of an item.

Relevance: The degree to which retrieved information is applicable to the searcher's topic, which is subjective.

Reliability: The degree to which the content of a record can be trusted based on the credentials of the author and/or the publisher, the kind of content included, whether assertions are supported, and consistency of measures.

Serials Solutions®: A division of ProQuest that produces electronic resource access and management services including Summon™.

Summon™: A hosted discovery service from Serials Solutions released in 2009 that attempts to provides access to all content found in library collections and mimics popular Web searching interfaces.

ENDNOTES

[1]   Summon is a trademark of ProQuest LLC.

[2]   Google Scholar is a trademark of Google, Inc.

[3]   LIBQUAL is a registered trademark of Association of Research Libraries.

[4]   WorldCat is a registered trademark of OCLC.

[5]   Serials Solutions is a registered trademark of Serials Solutions.

[6]   Google Books is a trademark of Google, Inc.

[7]   Ulrich's is a trademark of ProQuest LLC.

APPENDIX A

Result Details

A series of searches was completed in Google Scholar (GS) ™ and the discovery service from Summon™. Below, are the results of a review of the first 25 results for some of the most common searches in one college's instance of Summon™ and the results for the same searches in Google Scholar™.

1. (Venice and Diplomacy)

Table A-1. Librarian panel evaluation of (Venice and diplomacy)

Score	GS Currency	Summon Currency	GS Reliability	Summon Reliability	GS Relevance	Summon Relevance
1	1	2	1	5	8	12
2	2	5	5	9	3	7
3	5	9	5	6	7	2
4	10	1	7	1	3	1
5	7	7	7	3	4	2
Average	3.8	3.25	3.56	2.5	2.68	1.92

Venice and diplomacy returned about 21,000 results in Google Scholar™. Seventeen of the results were book chapters. Twelve of the books were from university presses. The last five records were book reviews from scholarly journals. The librarians found these helpful but doubt that the average undergraduate student would find them valuable. GS™ returned no duplicate results.

Summon™ returned a little under 5,000. With such a lower number of results, one might expect those from Summon™ might be more refined; however, the librarian panel's results do not indicate this. Nine of the Summon™ results were articles from non-scholarly periodicals. There were five book reviews beginning with the seventh record. The 10th record was the first the librarians found useful. Two of the results were early Twentieth Century periodicals one of which was the first result. Of the 10 results from scholarly journals, the 5 that were not book reviews were considered current and reliable but not highly relevant. One was a Web site and one was a radio talk show transcript. Summon™ results included only one duplicate record. The librarians noted that the first useful result was the 10th.

Seventeen records of a reasonably high value or better is a promising selection; however, relevance goes down after the fifth record. Reliability is not a problem until the 19th result, which was given a 1. The librarians noted that the lack of sufficient publication information led to the low score. Using the regular Google interface, an abstract for the citation was later found. The abstract mentions Venice only in the context diplomatic ties kept with of several principalities by the Šubići. The relatively current book reviews at the end of the results score low on reliability and relevance. The average relevance for the top five records was 4.4. After the fifth result, relevance becomes a problem. The sixth record received a 2. Eight records are graded 1 by the librarians beginning with the eighth result. After the sixth result, there is little correlation between the three aspects with only a couple exceptions.

Summon™, which was presented first, fared worse. The first records to score greater than a 1 in all areas were the 10th and the 11th, which received a 5 in all three areas. The only other records to score over 2 in all areas were the 21st and the 24th. The currency of the results is somewhat better than the other two areas. When the search was performed later in Summon™ limiting to scholarly publications, 11 results dealt with Venetian and Italian diplomacy during the renaissance. Most were a from 2007 and later.

2. (Global Warming)

The search returned about 822,000 records in GS™. Most of the results were articles in scholarly journals. Fourteen of the results dealt with climate and the chemistry of global warming. Six of the results covered a range of ecological issues. Four dealt with the economics of global warming. Only one was a general work, which was published in 1994. A 2009 Cambridge UP edition of this work was the first record in the Summon™ results. Though many of the results were academic materials covering the science and politics of global warming, many were dated. Ten of the records were published between the years 1992 and 2001. Eight were published between 1986 and 2000. Within the top 10 results, excepting the 1st record, the most reliable were the least current. Seven of the publications were from *Nature*. Two were from *Science*. The publication dates for those ranged from 1986 to 2006.

Table A-2. Librarian panel evaluation of (global warming)

Score	GS Currency	Summon Currency	GS Reliability	Summon Reliability	GS Relevance	Summon Relevance
1	5	0	0	7	0	7
2	8	0	2	3	2	3
3	5	3	7	4	12	5
4	7	12	9	6	10	2
5	0	5	7	0	1	3
Average	2.56	4.1	3.84	2.45	3.4	2.55

Summon™ gave 282,995 results for global warming. Sixteen results were books. The first result is included in the Rollins College library collection and was the only book from a university press (with the exception of its duplication). Seven books were from other academic publishers. Three were general reference materials on global warming. Two of these were duplicated. One record was a twenty four page teachers' guide on the topic. Only two records were from scholarly journals. One was an editorial from the *British Journal of General Practice*, which was the 12th result. The other record was a book review from *Science and Children*. Seven were from non-scholarly periodicals. One article was from *Australasian Science* regarding the Kyoto Protocol. Two were from children's multicultural magazines, of which one was a poem. Three results were letters to the editor of the *Nelson Mail*, a newspaper from New Zealand. The 24th record was an article from *Circle Track*, an auto racing magazine.

Currency was the weakest point of this set of results from Google Scholar, but it is the only area in which the librarians graded results lower than Summon™ for this search. It was the second worst average currency for GS™ in the study. Of the first 10 results, only 3 scored higher than 2. GS™ performed much better on reliability and relevance. This was the third best reliability average for Google Scholar. Again, in the first 10 records reliability did not correlate with currency. Global warming tied as the third most relevant average in Google Scholar. The one record given a 5 was an earlier edition of the first result in the Summon™ results.

The results in Summon™ were graded highly for currency. Reliability and relevance were troubling. Summon™ starts well with the first two records. The highest reliability score given was 4 of which there were only six. When performing the search again in Summon™ limiting to Scholarly Publications, the list returned only scholarly journals; however, one title was included twelve times, and another title was include five times.

3. (Harry Potter)

GS™ returned 54,200 results for Harry Potter. Eight records were books from the Harry Potter series. Three of these were full text copies posted with highly suspect copyright at best. Surprisingly, only two of the results were book reviews of Harry Potter books. Two records were elementary education material themed after Harry Potter books. Eight of the results were works authored or co-authored by scholars named Harry Potter. Of these one was from the 1993, three ranged from 1980 to 1989, and three from 1975 to 1978. One was published in the *Journal of Clinical Investigation* in 1945. Though these are bad results, they are not the worst. Included in the results was a word puzzle, an advertisement for a contest to win advance screening tickets, and a grade school book report.

Table A-3. Librarian panel evaluation of (Harry Potter)

Score	GS Currency	Summon Currency	GS Reliability	Summon Reliability	GS Relevance	Summon Relevance
1	9	0	13	14	13	17
2	4	1	3	2	3	0
3	3	8	1	3	1	1
4	1	11	0	3	0	1
5	6	2	6	0	6	3
Average	2.60	3.2	2.26	1.56	2.26	1.56

When trying to search GS™ for authors named Harry Potter, 457 results were found, largely books from the Harry Potter Series or items relating to it. This sounds much like what Jacso (2009) describes.

Summon™ returned 47,538 results for this search. The first Summon™ result was a comic from a book review of the title How Fiction Works that references Harry Potter. This definitely did not impress the librarian panel, who wrote, "We're appalled that this is the first result. It's a cartoon with a bad Harry Potter gag." Nine of the first 13 results were news transcripts. Only three records were from a scholarly journal. Both were letters to the editor of *Headache*: one was regarding Harry Potter's headaches, one was a response by another neurologist, and the last was a response from Harry Potter. This is quite funny, but not terribly useful for academic work. Only three books towards the end of the results were actually critical theory. The second result is an analysis of the Harry Potter franchise. Otherwise the results were from non-scholarly periodicals.

As noted, the currency of the GS™ results is poor except for the citations for books in the Harry Potter series. Because of the nature of the study, the librarians could not know the source of the results. Therefore, they could not see that those that were full text records were questionable. Not only is copyright a problem, but questionable editing or optical character recognition software are even more important issues for evaluating reliability and relevance. Six of these received a 5 for reliability and relevance. Two were duplicates and were not counted in the average. With these scores removed the average for reliability and relevance is 1.85

The results in Summon™ were moderately current; in fact, it has the second highest average of currency in Summon™ for the study. Fourteen were graded 1 for reliability, and 17 for relevance. These were largely the news show transcripts, popular magazines, and the *Headache* letters. The only records the librarians did grade highly were the critical books. Limiting results to scholarly publications only helps marginally, but the three good results, the books, are then excluded.

4. (John Dewey Inquiry)

Table A-4. Librarian panel evaluation of (John Dewey inquiry)

Score	GS Currency	Summon Currency	GS Reliability	Summon Reliability	GS Relevance	Summon Relevance
1	1	0	0	0	1	0
2	1	0	0	3	4	3
3	5	11	6	11	6	9
4	5	5	5	6	1	7
5	11	6	12	2	11	3
Average	3.72	3.32	3.92	2.92	3.44	3.04

GS™ returned 59,400 results for John Dewey inquiry. Seventeen results in GS™ were books, of which 11 were editions of Dewey's work ranging from 1938 to 2006. Many of the earlier editions were scanned and available full text. Seven were from refereed publications. Dewey was the author of one of these. The two remaining records were written by Dewey for The Cornell Law Review in 1914 and The Elementary School Teacher in 1903.

Summon™ returned 17,901 results. The set presented is quite different from Google Scholar: 7 books, 11 dissertations, 5 scholarly journal articles, and 1 newsletter article. None of these were penned by Dewey. These results included some of the older records returned by Summon™ in this study, but this does not matter as much with such a topic.

Though many of the results are somewhat old, this is highest currency grade GS™ receives. The librarian panel noted this was "a reasonable list overall." This is one of the more positive evaluations they gave to a set in the study.

At an average of 3.77, this ranked the third highest for currency in Summon™. These are the second highest scores for Summon™ in reliability and relevance. Four of the articles from scholarly publications scored 3 or higher in all areas. One was a book review from 1955. The dissertations all received a 3 for reliability except for two duplicates that were not counted in the average. Five of the dissertations were given a 4 for relevance.

5. (Database Design)

Table A-5. Librarian panel evaluation of (database design)

Score	GS Currency	Summon Currency	GS Reliability	Summon Reliability	GS Relevance	Summon Relevance
1	6	3	0	2	9	3
2	13	0	1	0	5	3
3	3	5	13	9	8	3
4	3	7	10	6	3	7
5	0	2	1	0	0	1
Average	2.12	3.29	3.44	3.12	2.2	3

Google Scholar™ returned about 3,200,000 records for this search. GS™ results included 15 books and 7 articles from scholarly journals. Results include 5 records published in the 1990's and 13 from the 1980's. The first two records, books from 1992 and 1989 (a text book), deal with entity relationship modeling. Though this is a concept that has not changed much over time, the tools available for developing these models have changed considerably. The next record was published in 1999 and covers database management systems, which have advanced a great deal of the last decade. The most current title is a book published in 2006 that discusses refactoring databases. This is not design per se. It is more of a redesign concept based on existing tables. The next most recent publication is a 2004 text on IBM BD2 8.2 design, which has not been supported since 2009. Of the articles from scholarly publications, one is from 1995 and the others are from the 1980's.

Summon™ returned 600,933 results. Though Summon™ had many better results, it still returned some items of questionable merit. Twenty one of the results were books, but this included seven duplicates. The only article from a scholarly journal was from a 1991 issue of *Studies in Geophysics*, which was the oldest result. One of the non-scholarly publications was from *SQL Server Magazine*. The other two were presentations from the Missouri Spatial Information Service from 1999.

About the GS™ results, the librarians wrote "currency was particularly hard to judge" and that they "had to make a lot of assumptions regarding conceptual approaches vs. currently used tools." They considered the sources moderately reliable. Of the 11 scoring over a 3, 5 were from scholarly journals published between 1984 and 1995. The only result to score a 4 of better in all areas was a general/introductory text published in 2002 by Prentice Hall.

Summon™ presented far more current records. The reliability scores were rather average. The three that were given a 1 were specific to geospatial data. Two books were considered too specific and given a 2. Those that were graded well were from scientific and computer science industry publishers. With eight duplicate records in the results, the average scores are somewhat less reliable. Limiting to scholarly articles in Summon™ would not help find a general work, but the results are indeed largely scholarly journals. They are mainly specific to applications or types of data. Many of the articles are rather dated, though.

6. (Richard Florida)

Table A-6. Librarian panel evaluation of (Richard Florida)

Score	GS Currency	Summon Currency	GS Reliability	Summon Reliability	GS Relevance	Summon Relevance
1	0	5	0	5	1	13
2	0	0	0	10	0	2
3	13	7	1	7	4	3
4	9	10	5	1	0	2
5	1	1	17	0	18	3
Average	3.48	3.09	4.70	2.17	4.48	2.13

GS™ returned about 1,130,000 records for Richard Florida. The urban studies writer, Richard Florida, was the author of, co-author, or contributor to every record in the top twenty five results. Exclusion of results about the state of Florida or anyone else named Richard is a good demonstration of GS™ doing what Google often does well. Fifteen records were articles by Florida of which one was not from a scholarly publication. The other 10 were books.

Summon™ gave 141,695 results and had a much more difficult time returning useful results. The first result is a 2006 article in Business Week about Richard Florida. The second, third, and fifth results were reviews of performances of composer Richard Meale's work *Incredible Floridas* from the 1970's and 1980's in *Musical Times*. The fourth result is an article from a Croatian sociology journal about Richard Florida. Result 6 is an article about a 2003 visit by Richard Florida in a Phoenix, AZ culture magazine published by Village Voice Media. The seventh result is a paragraph long entry on Florida species in a list of noteworthy collections from a botanical journal. The eighth is a brief announcement in a newsletter that Richard Florida will be the keynote speaker at a conference. Only after these articles did the results improve, though only marginally. Only one book and one article were penned by Richard Florida.

The average difference for all searches in the study was 0.87. At 1.75, these results averaged the greatest difference. The GS™ results might have been given better numbers for relevance, but Richard Florida's contributions to some of the results was somewhat obscured by the citations and lack of access at Olin library. Otherwise the grading quite accurately reflects that someone searching for work by Richard Florida in GS™ will find them.

Brought down largely by the *Musical Times* entries, the currency average was the lowest for Summon™ in the study. This is the second worse score for Summon™ reliability. Only six results score a 3 or better in all three areas.

7. (Kuleshov Effect)

Table A-7. Librarian panel evaluation of (Kuleshov effect)

Score	GS Currency	Summon Currency	GS Reliability	Summon Reliability	GS Relevance	Summon Relevance
1	3	0	0	2	13	12
2	0	0	0	1	3	0
3	10	5	17	12	2	4
4	11	16	5	3	0	1
5	1	0	3	3	7	4
Average	3.28	3.76	3.44	3.19	2.4	2.29

GS™ returned about 5,510 for Kuleshov effect. All top 25 results in GS™ dealt specifically with the Kuleshov effect or were scientific works authored or co-authored by someone with the name Kuleshov. Though the combination of Kuleshov and effect did not limit results to the filmmaker and the experiment, currency and reliability were reasonable. Eighteen were from scholarly periodicals. Six were books. All of these related to the filmmaker or film. Eleven total results deal directly with the filmmaker. Six deal with film more generally including references to Kuleshov. Those that were not about film were about effects of sundry variables on results of scientific experiments. Most of these had over 50 or 100 authors with only one named Kuleshov.

The first 25 results of the Summon™ 1,069 results were not too dissimilar. Thirteen results were directly related to Kuleshov the filmmaker. Nine of these were from scholarly journals of which two were duplicates. One was a book, and one was a dissertation. Two were in Japanese. Fourteen records were scholarly articles. Five were books. The first eight results dealt with Kuleshov with one duplicate. The articles that were not related to Kuleshov the filmmaker were authored by someone else with the name Kuleshov and were largely scientific. The other Kuleshovs were the primary authors of most of these articles.

This search in the two interfaces returned the closest average difference between GS™ and Summon™, 0.28. They returned similar kinds of results. The biggest difference was distribution of the better records. The results in GS™ are not weighted for the works on the Kuleshov effect occurring first. As mentioned before, the Summon™ results are weighted.

8. (Gone with the Wind)

Table A-8. Librarian panel evaluation of (gone with the wind)

Score	GS Currency	Summon Currency	GS Reliability	Summon Reliability	GS Relevance	Summon Relevance
1	4	1	5	1	13	21
2	0	0	2	14	1	1
3	7	1	7	7	0	2
4	9	15	7	2	7	0
5	5	8	4	1	4	1
Average	3.44	4.16	3.12	2.52	2.52	1.36

Twenty four of the works in the GS™ results include the phrase, though only 12 actually refer to the book entitled *Gone with the Wind*, and related works. Four of these were the book or the film. Three were book reviews from 1936 and 1937. Two books dealt with the novel and the film. Two were books on the making of the film. One book was about the making of film adaptations of novels. In total eight records are books, nine are from scholarly journals, and two are the motion picture in different formats. A couple of results were from non-scholarly publications. Some were not easily identified by the brief citations. The records that were not Mitchell's book or did not deal directly with this work covered a wide range of topics from rental law in California to the violent interaction between galaxies.

Summon™ returned a total 153,353 records. The top results were not impressive. Similar to Google Scholar, all 25 of the results had the phase "gone with the wind" in the title. Only four dealt with Mitchell's work. Two of these were about a stage musical adaptation. Among the remaining were five articles on wind power, one review of turbo-charged motorcycles from *Cycle World*, one on improving fuel economy of semi tractors with wheel covers in *Fleet Owner*, and one on dish cleaning systems for caterers. One 2006 article regards labor talks between Delta and their pilots. Others included astronomy, finance, and sailing. Two of the results were from newspapers, which were supposed to be excluded.

This was the second worst reliability score for Google Scholar™. Still, eighteen results are given a grade of 3 or better. Most of the low reliability scores were from unclear citations. Average relevance is not great, but it is just below the median (2.6). As they thought contemporary responses to Mitchell's work interesting, the librarian panel gave a relatively high score of 4 to the three book reviews. They gave a 5 only to the book and film.

Summon™ received its highest average score for currency, but reliability and relevance did not match. Fifteen results were given a 2 or less for reliability. Twenty one were given a 1 for relevance. The first record to receive over a 2 for relevance was an article about a musical adaptation in Variety, the 11th result. This was the lowest average score of both tools for any area in the study.

9. (Linguistics Branding)

Table A-9. Librarian panel evaluation of (linguistics branding)

Score	GS Currency	Summon Currency	GS Reliability	Summon Reliability	GS Relevance	Summon Relevance
1	0	0	0	0	18	8
2	8	0	2	2	0	7
3	8	1	13	5	1	1
4	4	21	7	12	0	2
5	5	2	3	5	6	6
Average	3.24	4.04	3.44	3.83	2.04	2.63

GS™ returned about 9,710 results. The top results tended to be about linguistics, but few contained any synthesis of linguistics and branding. Ten were books, and nine were articles from scholarly journals. Three records were from the 1980's and one each from the 1960's and 1970's. Five results were from the 1950's. All six of the results that dealt with linguistics and branding were from the last decade.

Summon™ performed somewhat better with this search. Only 2,672 records were returned. All of the first 25 results were from the last decade. Sixteen records were from scholarly journals, and six were non-scholarly. Only one was a book. The last two were dissertations. Publications tended towards marketing and branding instead of linguistics. Only five results were not from marketing or business journals.

Summon's currency and reliability averages were close to overall averages for Google Scholar™, but this was the second lowest relevance score. The sixth record was the first to score of a 1. The next was the thirteenth. Only the Summon™ results for gone with the wind has more results graded 1.

This is the only search in which Summon™ scores higher than GS™ in all three categories, yet a 2.63 average for relevance, the third highest, is not too spectacular. With almost twice as many results scoring below 3 as above, this set of results is still only of limited value. It is also worth noting that both Summon™ and GS™ had six results that received a 5.

10. (Art Education)

Table A-10. Librarian panel evaluation of (art education)

Score	GS Currency	Summon Currency	GS Reliability	Summon Reliability	GS Relevance	Summon Relevance
1	1	4	0	11	4	16
2	5	0	0	2	0	5
3	14	2	10	6	6	3
4	5	16	15	6	12	1
5	0	3	0	0	3	0
Average	2.92	3.56	3.6	2.28	3.4	1.56

Google returned about 2,470,000 records for art education. Twenty one of the results were related to art education. Fifteen records were from the journal *Art Education*. Two records were about education but not art. Five results we from the 1980's. Five more were published before 1980.

Summon™ had 954,268 results. Though all twenty five records examined had the phrase art education in the title, very few were useful. The first result was a citation for the Journal *Art Education*. Six of the first eleven were articles from *Education Week*. Three more were from newsletters. Three of the next four results were LibGuides from Temple University, Montana State University, and Bowling Green State University. The sixteenth is a curriculum for elementary school art education for a county board of education from 1983. The eighteenth result is a 1997 radio news story from *All Things Considered*.

Again, currency was Google Scholar's™ biggest problem. The second record, which was published in 1962, was given a 1. Though no records were given a 5, having 15 graded at 4 helps the average reliability. The librarians considered these results quite relevant. Over half were given a score over 3. In addition, the average for the first 10 records was 4.

Currency was also not a problem for Summon™. With over half of the results scoring below 3, reliability was. This was the second lowest score for Summon™ and in the entire study. The relevance average for the first 10 Summon™ results is 1.1. Only one article scored a 4. The three records given a 3 were the LibGuides. When limiting results to scholarly articles, Summon™ results improved significantly.

APPENDIX B: SAMPLE TABLE AS PRESENTED TO LIBRARIANS

1A Rank	(venice and diplomacy) Citation	Abstract	Type	Cur	Rib	Rlv	Notes
1	Fubini R (2000) Diplomacy and government in the Italian city-states of the fifteenth century (Florence and Venice). In: Frigo D (ed) Politics and diplomacy in early modern Italy. Cambridge University Press, Cambridge, pp 25–48		B				
2	Osborne, J. (1999). Politics, diplomacy and the cult of relics in Venice and the northern Adriatic in the first half of the ninth century. *Early Medieval Europe*, 8(3), 369.	In early medieval Europe the cult of the saints emerged as a prominent focus for the construction of political identity. Corporeal relics became objects of importance, conferring status on their possessor; and, like other precious commodities, they frequently served as prestigious …	B				
3	Mattingly, G. (1988). *Renaissance diplomacy*. New York: Dover Publications.	…MEDIEVAL DIPLOMACY, FIFTEENTH CENTURY ranking diplomats in Christendom, the papal legates a latere about whom he was writing, under a definition…And it was beginning to be recognized that while Florence and Venice, Genoa and even Lubeck might play in such a …	B				
4	M. Mallett, 'Diplomacy and war in later fifteenth-century Italy', Proceedings of the British Academy 67 (1981), 267-88		N				
5	Frigo, D. (2000). Politics and diplomacy in early modern Italy: The structure of diplomatic practice, 1450-1800. Cambridge, UK: Cambridge University Press.	This volume is the first attempt at a comparative reconstruction of the foreign policy and diplomacy of the major Italian states in the early modern period.	B				

Section 4

The User Experience Part Two:
User Testing and User–Centered Design in Implementing Discovery Solutions

David Dahl
Towson University, USA

OVERVIEW

While user testing seems to indicate that it is the user of an interface that is being tested, the exact opposite is actually true. The purpose of this type of testing is to evaluate the tool's ability to effectively and efficiently satisfy the needs of the user. The philosophy behind user testing, or usability testing, is that it is the tool's responsibility to meet the needs of the user an intuitive manner rather than the user's responsibility to adapt to the tool. With the variety of search tools and online resources available to information seekers, libraries must ensure that their search tools help patrons rather than push them to use other methods of finding information.

Testing the usability of research tools has been and continues to be an important practice for libraries that strive to provide the best possible experience for their users. While discovery tool vendors sing the praises of their clean, easy-to-use interfaces, librarians understand that a discovery tool is only as good as their users' abilities to use it. Claims of being Google-like are not quite so easy given the complex information ecosystem that libraries embrace.

As the authors of these chapters exemplify, usability testing should play a key role in several stages of the discovery tool implementation process: user testing can justify the need to move away from federated searching towards discovery; it informs the evaluation and selection process, giving libraries insight into which tool will work best for their users; and it assesses the integration of the discovery tool within the library's Web presence.

While usability testing can be done on a single interface, these chapters show a variety of ways to increase the meaningfulness of results. Holman et al. test the usability of several discovery tools in order to compare and contrast the features and flows of each. Freund, Poehlmann, and Seale test existing systems to determine in which areas their users' experiences can improve. Palsson and O'Hara, Nichols, and Keiller test the usability of their Web site before and after implementing a discovery tool to assess its effectiveness. Kerico, Anthony, Bulock, and Fields support the pre- and post-test method, suggesting ongoing, iterative testing practices and a change in Web design philosophy to "perpetual beta."

User testing removes the speculation from the evaluation of resource discovery tools, leaving libraries with a realistic picture of the progress made and the work that remains.

Chapter 14
How Users Approach Discovery Tools

Lucy Holman
University of Baltimore, USA

Alice Hom
University of Baltimore, USA

Elias Darraj
University of Baltimore, USA

Heather Mathieson
University of Baltimore, USA

Jonathan Glaser
University of Baltimore, USA

Deane Nettles
University of Baltimore, USA

Aronya Waller
University of Baltimore, USA

ABSTRACT

Researchers observed 21 participants (undergraduates, graduate students, and faculty) conduct known item and topic searches using EBSCO Discovery Service (EDS)™[1], Ex Libris' Primo®[2], and Serials Solutions '®[3] Summon™[4] discovery tools to compare users' reaction to their interface design and evaluate each tool's functionality. Participants generally liked the tools' simple interfaces but had difficulty identifying material formats and faceted search features and were often confused by advanced search limiters and other features. Most demonstrated right-side blindness, failing to notice features or options on the right side of the screen. Participants expressed frustration with what they perceived as less than relevant results in many of their searches.

INTRODUCTION

Today's college students have grown up with the simple interfaces and natural language of search engines; they often turn to Google and other search engines for their academic research and

shy away from library tools that require more skill and expertise to use. Numerous national studies (Jones, 2002; OCLC, 2002; DeRosa, Cantrell, Hawk, & Wilson, 2006; Head & Eisenberg, 2009) have found that the majority of college students use search engines more than library resources for academic research. These studies point to user difficulty with navigating through library sites

DOI: 10.4018/978-1-4666-1821-3.ch014

and searching library databases (OCLC, 2002). Students are often confused about which databases to use, and they are often unsuccessful at cross-searching in the databases (Stein, Bright, George, Hurlbert, Linke & St. Clair, 2006). Users expect the simplicity of a single search box to search across sources and platforms (Stein, et al, 2006). They rarely use the advanced features in either search engines or databases, expecting the tool itself to know what they need (Williams, 1999).

Most information professionals realize that students will neither learn the more complex search strategies required by many commercial article databases nor search multiple databases to find different types of sources. Therefore, libraries face the challenge of meeting users' research needs with new search tools that have more robust algorithms and search capabilities across multiple data warehouses and formats. As more products, both commercial and open source, emerge in the marketplace, libraries must identify which tool offers both the most intuitive, user-friendly interface and the most robust search capabilities to effectively meet users' needs.

The leading discovery services offer similar features and can harvest items from subscription databases, local catalogs and digital collections. Therefore, comparisons among interfaces and general functionality are important for libraries in their decision-making. Task-based usability testing is a useful method for libraries to evaluate and compare discovery tools. Unlike other research methodologies that require large numbers of participants, usability testing can reveal common user problems with a small number of participants. Jakob Nielsen (2000, Nielsen & Landauer, 1993), a leading researcher and practitioner in usability testing suggests that as few as five users can identify 85% of usability concerns through task-based testing. Libraries may choose to use this methodology to study their own users in order to make an informed choice of a discovery service.

LITERATURE REVIEW AND BACKGROUND

In the mid-2000s, developers of integrated library systems and indexing and abstracting services began to create a next-generation system that would provide an alternative to the Z39.50 federated search process. Web-scale discovery harvests metadata and often full-text content from a variety of information sources, such as library catalogs, commercial databases, and local library digital repositories. This technology offers users a simple search interface and single (and, in most cases, faceted) results lists. What sets discovery services apart from federated search is in their creation of a centralized index of content across sources and platforms, which allows for a faster retrieval process (Vaughan, 2011e). Discovery tools can offer the "Google generation" an experience similar to a Google search with a broad range of academic sources. In recent years, several products, both proprietary and open-source, have emerged, including the four studied here: EBSCO Discovery Service (EDS)™, Innovative Interface's Encore™, Ex Libris' Primo®, and Serials Solutions®' Summon™.

EDS™ first appeared on the general market in early 2010 (Vaughan, 2011b). EDS™ contains content from almost 50,000 periodicals from more than 20,000 providers. It also includes metadata for almost 6 million books; 825,000 CDs and DVDs; and 20,000 conference proceedings (EBSCO Publishing, 2011). EDS™ offers a single search box with the option for additional search features as well as an advanced search, incorporating Boolean operators and select limiters. EDS™ offers faceted navigation including limiters such as source type/format, author, publication, subject (EBSCO subject headings), and publication date; these facets dynamically present themselves based on the nature of the search. EDS™ also employs a SmartText feature that interprets strings of user input into search terms that the system runs and offers a "Did you mean?" spelling suggestions for misspelled terms. Results appear with visual icons representing format, citation, abstract and subject headings. EDS™ also supports an API (Application Programming Interface) that allows libraries to embed the EDS™ discovery tool in many other areas of their Web sites, such as learning management systems and research guides as well as a number of export options including saving, emailing, or exporting to citation management software and provides persistent URLs so that libraries may embed these links in their own resources (Vaughan, 2011b).

Innovative Interfaces made its Encore™ discovery tool available in 2007 (Breeding, 2007). Encore™ employs federated search to retrieve items from a library's subscription databases; libraries can incorporate local digital content or holdings from other collections into Encore's search engine. Encore features a single search box with the option for advanced search; its facets include format, year, and language among others. Additionally, Encore offers "Did you mean?" spelling suggestions, relevancy rankings and Web 2.0 options to rate and review items (Innovative Interfaces, 2011).

Serials Solutions®' Summon™ discovery service was released in July 2009 (Vaughan, 2011d); it currently contains more than 500 million items from more than 94,000 periodicals (Serials Solutions®, 2011). Summon™ provides a single search box and an advanced search option, as well as a robust API (Application Programming Interface) that allows libraries to embed such a resource tool in many other areas of the library and university Web sites. Results are ranked by relevancy and can be sorted by date as well. The tool allows for refinements by facets such as format, author, publication date, subject terms, language, and region; the categories change as appropriate to the particular search results. Summon™ also features spelling suggestions, much like Google's "Did you mean?" and supports a number of export/save options and RSS feeds and employs persistent

URLs for embedding in other library materials (Vaughan, 2011d).

Ex Libris launched its Primo® discovery service in 2007 (Vaughan, 2011c). Primo Central™[5], Primo's® knowledge base or centralized index, contains 300 million items, including e-books and periodical articles from aggregators, publishers, and open repositories (Ex Libris, 2011; Vaughan, 2011c). Primo's® interface is customizable; libraries may select from a set of templates, design the interface, or use Ex Libris' application programming interface (API) to integrate Primo® into a local library interface. Brief results include visual icon for format, citation, and links to full text if available. Primo® offers a "Did you mean?" spelling suggestion feature; the service also supports a variety of export options and RSS feeds and offers persistent links for embedding as well as an API to embed a Primo® search box into learning management systems (Vaughan, 2011c).

Several recent articles and reports (Yang & Wagner, 2010; Emanuel, 2011; Allison, 2010; Vaughan, 2011a) have evaluated or compared several commercial and open-source discovery tools including Encore™, VuFind, Summon™, Primo, and OCLC's WorldCat Local. Most of these, however, compare the tools in terms of the features they offer and not in terms of usability or ease of use. Vaughan (2011a), for example, evaluated EDS™, Primo, and Summon™, along with OCLC's WorldCat Local. He compared content (the aggregators and serial titles included in each index) and interface features. Emanuel (2011) did test the usability of the University of Illinois at Urbana-Champaign's (UIUC) implementation of VuFind; however, that usability was in comparison to UIUC's WebVoyage OPAC. Her study did uncover user confusion over formats, particularly multimedia materials. Yang and Wagner (2010) evaluated 47 implementations at both public and academic libraries of 20 discovery tools (seven open source and 13 commercial) against a checklist of 13 features, such as simple search, faceted navigation, spelling correction/recommendation, relevancy, and persistent links. Their study found that Primo offered the most features (8 of the 13 listed), followed closely by Encore (7.5) and Summon™ (7) (Yang & Wagner, 2010). EDS™ was not included in their research.

While these services provide a simple interface and a number of enhanced features, such as faceted navigation, automated spelling correction, relevancy ranking, and enriched content, they do presume a level of expertise or familiarity of various information resources on the part of users. They expect users to be able in distinguish between online versions of books, journal articles, reports, primary documents and other materials. Unfortunately, users do not often distinguish between such sources, considering all online material to be similar (Whitlock & Kiel, 2011).

METHODOLOGY

The University System of Maryland and Affiliated Institutions (USMAI) is a statewide consortium comprised of 16 libraries in 13 institutions, including four-year liberal arts colleges and comprehensive universities, law schools, medical and allied health graduate schools. The consortium shares a single integrated library system and catalog and works collaboratively to purchase databases and other electronic materials. Currently, the consortium is preparing to purchase one or more discovery tools. The consortium has several established working groups, with representatives from libraries across the system, to address common issues and research new products and services in functional areas such as electronic resources, cataloging, resource sharing and user interface design to address consortial issues and research new products and services.

In the spring of 2011, the User Interface Task Group (UITG) from USMAI contracted with graduate students in the Interaction Design and Information Architecture program at the University of Baltimore to conduct task-based usability studies on four major discovery tools: EBSCO Discovery Service (EDS)™, Encore, Primo, and Summon™. In consultation with UITG, six teams of graduate researchers developed a set of tasks of both known-item and topic searches for users to complete during the testing. The researchers recruited participants from the University of Baltimore and other University System of Maryland campuses through campus announcements, flyers and through contacts at member universities. The researchers met with 21 participants, including eight undergraduates, seven graduate students, and six faculty members as they conducted topic and known-item searches using each of the four discovery tools. The research focused on participants' general search behaviors as well as their use of and preferences for specific features in each tool. Each participant worked with two systems; the researchers distributed specific tools across user types so that the overall project had multiple comparisons of each tool. In all, ten or eleven users examined each discovery service, which exceeds standard expectations concerning the number of participants required to identify a majority of issues. Participant tasks, which were determined with the assistance of information specialists from USMAI, included searching the discovery tools for known items, such as a specific book and journal article, conducting relative narrow topical searches for particular formats and types of sources, and employing specific limiters and faceted searches to narrow results.

The observations occurred in April 2011 using the University of Baltimore's state-of-the-art usability lab. Researchers used TechSmith's Morae video and screen capture software as well as Tobii eye-tracking software to compare participants' use of the four discovery tools. The nature or volume of content made available by each of these tools was not compared; researchers selected known items that were common to all four services and did not analyze the number of items retrieved. The focus of this research was strictly on discovery layer functionality and the ease in which participants learned and employed the tools to search for items.

In order to conduct task based tests, the researchers acquired access to campuses currently using each of the discovery services or were given access to a trial database. Ebsco and Encore provided access to a generic trial access, while Ex Libris provided temporary access to Boston College's Primo tool, and Serials Solutions® suggested the use of Arizona State University's Summon™ search. To ensure comparable results across tools, the researchers verified that the items used in the known item search tasks were available in all four products. Certain access problems arose in the discovery services' test environments; for example, Encore required a separate search in WorldCat Local for all books. This confused many of the participants who did not see the link to WorldCat Local and assumed that no book records were available; as a result the researchers decided not to discuss Encore in this comparison of discovery systems.

RESULTS

The results of this study focused on four main properties of the tool: interface design, search, faceted search features, and the ability to save articles for future retrieval. Additional results are shared when deemed appropriate.

EBSCO Discovery Service (EDS)

Interface

Participants found the main search interface to be very intuitive and minimalist in its approach. The results page presented a numbered list of search results, with an easily identifiable icon indicating the format. Participants clearly saw items with full text PDFs. The majority of the participants immediately noticed and used the facets available on the left side of the page. When a participant

clicked on an item on the search results page, the detailed record information was consistent for all participants and tasks. The interface design was uniform throughout the site, which helped reduce confusion. Participants overlooked available tools, such as Add to Folder, Print, and Email because they were located on the far right side of the page.

Search

When participants searched for known items with an exact full title, they obtained results quickly, and the desired text material appeared in the first few results. However, when a participant only used a partial title, the results were broad. Some participants were confused as they attempted to narrow down their results. Although the item was in the catalog, search terms had to be "just right" to get the results. By trying several keyword queries and selecting the keyword, title, or author radio buttons, the majority of participants were able to find the selections. Furthermore, additional search options including an advanced search and a visual search were completely ignored by the participants.

Participants search terms contained many spelling errors; however many did not yield any suggestions from the system. One participant typed "Medernism and the Harlem Renissance" while another typed "artificial intelegence" and a "Did you mean?" suggestion provided correct spelling. When the participants noticed the suggestion and clicked on the alternative search, more accurate results were presented. Yet, there were some basic searches such as "beginner Portuguese" that yielded no spelling suggestions.

A majority of participants experienced difficulty with topic searches. Generally, results were not related to the materials needed. A better term recognition algorithm and enhanced facets for other materials, such as audiovisual materials, would greatly assist users seeking those materials.

EDS™ uses inconsistent terminology in the tool. On the main search page, a Search Options link is provided. This is a basic search with built-in faceted information. The same functionality is labeled as Refine Search on the search result page. Many users confused the two labels and did not realize that neither option was in fact the advanced search. Advanced Search and Visual Search are options under search options interface but are not clearly highlighted.

Faceted Search

During testing, participants used the filtering capabilities, which are available on the left-hand side of the results page. EDS'™ facets are contextual; they vary based on the search query and the returned results. When participants made a selection using any of the facets, the entire page grayed out except for the facet window. Participants were then required to click Update once they selected their filters. Some participants expressed their annoyance about manually clicking an update button to display results.

Furthermore, many participants stated that they expected more faceted options such as language and audiovisual materials.

Once a participant made a selection in the facets, the selection made was noted on the top of the left column showing the expanders and limiters. However, none of the participants seemed to notice this visual cue. Instead of clicking the "X" to remove the selections, the participants continuously re-selected the All Results check box when they intended to expand the search and selected other options as needed.

Save

Very few participants identified ways to save the information they found. While an Add to Folder button is on the right hand side main results page, few participants drew the connection between the folder button and the save functionality. Furthermore, most participants did not identify and use the multiple options to save that are available on the detailed result page. This may have been due to right-side blindness, as about one third of participants never noticed the functionality on the right side. The few that used the feature were confident that the item was added once they identified the Add to Folder functionality. However, using the Save functionality led to confusing instructions that only worked depending on the browser and version used by the participant. If used, the majority of participants were able to retrieve items added to the Save Folder.

PRIMO®

Interface

Participants found the interface clean and easy to use. Participants noted that the results page was easy to browse and distinguish, with highlighted search criteria to aid in judging relevancy. The record detail pages were consistent and kept the participant within the Primo® interface.

Participants noted confusion when they unknowingly left the discovery tool. One participant clicked on the school's logo and was taken to the library's home page, which looked different from the Primo® home page. And when three professors abandoned Primo® and entered the databases directly, the look and feel of the site changed, which confused them, and the navigation did not then make it clear to them how to return to Primo®.

Search

Search functions for Primo® include a Basic Search similar to the Google search bar, an Advanced Search with limited filters for multiple content searches, publication date, material type, and language. Participants were successful with Basic Search and found it easy to narrow using both Advanced Search and Faceted Search filters. Unfortunately, the basic search terms entered by participants did not transfer to the Advanced Search page. "I would have liked it for the fields

I had already started to have remained," one said. In tasks involving known items, participants easily found a specific book using Basic Search, although participants sometimes confused citations for books and articles, overlooking the icons indicating the difference.

Two participants found the Material Type filter in the Advanced Search options limiting, as this option only allowed them to select one content type per search and they were interested in both books and journal articles. One user said "Here what's going through my mind is, is there a way of finding in the same place, both books and articles or do I have to do two separate searches?" Some participants expressed frustration with the designated publication date ranges; they preferred to limit through faceted search for more control. One participant said, "I wanted to use Article Finder, but I would need to know the exact issue and page number, etcetera…," and abandoned that feature.

Primo® continued to provide quick searches with relevant results. Search functions included spelling/alternate suggestions ("Did you mean?") which were often helpful. Yet, one participant followed a suggested alternative with zero results, lost his original results, and had to re-enter them. Search terms were highlighted in yellow in the search results, making it easy to determine relevance. Search terms from the last search are retained until the user clears them, though switching from Basic Search to Advanced Search cleared the search terms. One feature participants were impressed with was the ability to search individual libraries and have a map show where the book was located in the stacks.

Faceted Search

Once results have been found using Basic or Advanced Search, additional Faceted Search filters are available in a bar to the left of the results to further refine the search. Most Faceted Search options are shown by default; finding the cor-

rect filter often required scrolling through a long list that was difficult to scan quickly. In Faceted Search, the user can only select one filtering option at a time in each category. For example, searching for books and multimedia has to be done in two separate searches. Participants experienced in library searches began with the Advanced Search interface, where they were able to limit their searches to material from the last five years, but were unable to limit the articles to peer-reviewed from the Advanced Search options. On the results page, participants were often unable to locate the Peer-reviewed Journals filter located under the Availability heading, several headings down the page. Refining results to a custom date range through faceted search was made difficult by the seemingly arbitrary grouping of fixed dates.

Save

One undergraduate and one professor used Primo's® eShelf system to save their articles, but all but two of participants bookmarked their links using methods that did not involve Primo®.

SUMMON™

Interface

The Summon™ discovery service interface consists of a single search box, an advanced search page, and a comprehensive results page with an interactive left sidebar containing faceted filtering criteria. Anchored to the bottom of the browser is a bar containing the Saved Items folder. Dynamic features to refine, save, and export results were overlooked by many participants due to their subtle integration into the layout. The results appear as an unnumbered list of items in which a record preview appears when a user hovers over an item title or clicks a magnifying glass icon. Summon™ does not offer detailed record pages for the items in the search results; instead, item titles link directly to the detailed record in the source library catalog or database, an interface change that caused much confusion for participants.

Participants found the graphical layout implemented by Arizona State University Libraries too subtle; elements appear flat, lacking graphical hierarchy. Participants had trouble distinguishing item titles from bold search terms. Long headings appear as a mix of bold and normal type, leading to an uneven appearance that decreases readability. In addition, headings are set far left of the item description text block, breaking the vertical flow of browsing the text.

Even with visual cues indicating content type with an icon and a text field, some participants could not discern differences between listings. When asked to find a specific translation of the book Beowulf, multiple participants indiscriminately selected the first items without noticing they were peer-reviewed articles instead of a book. At a glance, the icons appeared similar in shape and coloring, without enough variation in the graphic photo to indicate different content types. In addition, full-text items are identified with a bright yellow sunburst on top of the icon, making the shapes more similar and calling more attention to the full text than the content type.

Search

Participants usually started at the Basic Search on the library homepage. Participants were overwhelmed with the library's multiple options; one participant expressed uncertainty, asking, "where do I start?" Those who wanted more control did not find a direct link to the advanced search options on the library's main search page; instead, they tried links to the native library catalogs and databases, which were not part of the discovery tool. Many participants perceived the library's diverse resources as a single entity, which led to confusion when they encountered inconsistent interfaces between Summon™ and the search pages of other databases. The advanced search

link only appears after an initial search has been conducted from the basic search box.

Often, Summon™ did not match the participants' keywords with their intended results. Many undergraduate participants entered full phrases from the prompt, which returned irrelevant results. This behavior is encouraged by popular internet search engines that incorporate algorithms to parse search terms based on natural language patterns. The basic search interface offers an auto-complete list of suggested terms, though it is not available on the library home page, where most initial search entry errors occur. "Did you mean?" misspelling corrections were relevant and helpful, but many participants did not notice them because they were not highlighted separately from the results list. The logic behind the relevancy ranking is not transparent in the list of results, and the interface does not support easy scanning of results.

Faceted Search

After an initial basic search, users are presented with a results page headed by a search box and options for advanced search. A few participants went directly to advanced search for subsequent search tasks and were successful in using the comprehensive options to complete tasks. Users transferred previously-entered search terms from the basic search to the advanced search form for convenience, which minimized entry errors that were observed when participants had to retype them. Although the search criteria were saved, the results page did not indicate which specific criteria or limiters users had employed.

Half of the participants did not engage deeply with Summon™'s interactive multi-faceted filters. Eye- and mouse-tracking patterns indicated that participants focused mainly on the listings section when scrolling through the results and may not have noticed options such as the graphical custom date slider located further down the page. Participants who tried the facets were reassured when options remained in place even as the results changed. One participant said, "Oh it keeps all my things here still." However, another participant had a black screen for about a second as the results were updated to reflect facet changes and led to the comment, "Again, oh I don't like that one." Except for dates, the filtered results are updated automatically after selecting checkboxes, but the update buffering page and sometimes blackout background can be a little jarring.

Save

Very few participants clicked on the folder icon within the item record to store the record in a temporary folder; those who did were very impressed with the export options. Many preferred to bookmark links in their browser.

Table 1 summarizes users' experiences with each tool.

DISCUSSION

This research revealed some similarities in the participants' approach to search. Users – faculty,

undergraduate students, and graduate students – almost instinctively began their first task by clicking on the search box and submitting their first query. This is remarkable because it demonstrates the pervasiveness of the simple search functionality. The participants across the various user groups trusted that the system would display appropriate results to their search. When users did not find the appropriate result, the similarities between and within user-groups became less evident in their advanced search approach and frustration threshold. Some users tried to anticipate what keywords the system would understand, while others tried to understand why the system did not understand their keywords. Another similarity between users was lack of knowledge of library jargon. Many users, including faculty, did not understand the Boolean search concept. Users were frustrated when they did not understand certain labels for functionality, like Boolean search. As users progressed through the tasks, several commented that they would have contacted a librarian to complete the task. Users seeking answers outside of the system is not a good indication of a tool's usability.

Table 1. Summary of discovery tool findings

Tool	Interface	Search	Faceted Search	Save Features
EDS	• Users recognized format icons and noticed limiting facets	• Topic searches yielded unrelated results • System did not offer suggestions for some misspellings • Users did not use advanced or visual search	• Users took advantage of facets • Users suggested additional facets • Users failed to notice which facets were being used	• Users failed to notice Add to Folder or Email options
Primo	• Users found interface easy to use • Icons and layout were consistent • Users were unaware when they left the tool.	• Users successful with basic search • Search string did not transfer from basic to advanced search	• Users found facet list too long • Users wanted to limit by multiple facets simultaneously	• Few users saved items using Primo's eShelf
Summon	• Users failed to visual cues such as format icons or full-text availability	• Users could not navigate directly to advanced search • Search terms yielded unrelated results • Some users failed to see suggested spellings	• Half of users did not engage with facets • Users appreciated that options remained when results changed	• Few used folder feature

Many of the tools display simple search functionality, challenging the algorithm to understand what knowledge the user is seeking. Most of the participants within the study preferred a clean, simple interface, even if it did not produce the "correct" results. However, an interface can be visually appealing and still have usability issues, as was the case with EDS™. While EDS™ is designed with a simple search interface, several participants expressed frustration due to inconsistent search results. Designers of discovery tools need to find the fine balance between simple interface design and powerful search and filtering capabilities.

The discovery tools' features confused many of the participants, particularly when the participants used the faceted search. For example, the way Primo's® filter list was displayed was so long that options at the bottom of the page were overlooked. Illogically, there were more filtering options available in the results sidebar than in the advanced search form. This may indicate the developer's expectation that users prefer to begin with a broad search, then narrow the results contextually rather than enter specific criteria through advanced search. In EDS™, the limiters change once a selection is made under the Show More link. This caused confusion among the participants. All the discovery tools still need to properly customize and test their search filters. Generally, participants succeeded in their search by starting from the simple search interface and then utilizing the advanced search functionality.

The most consistent issue among all the tools was the search for non-scholarly materials, such as textbooks and audiovisual materials. Participants appeared confused and became frustrated during this task. The inability to query based on audiovisual materials of some tools, and the user's tendencies to ignore visual cues for material type in other tools, made this task especially frustrating. Querying multiple academic databases does not prove effective in finding these materials, as the participants became inundated with scholarly articles.

Another consistent user problem throughout the tools is the inability of the user to distinguish the types of materials from the results. For example, participants often could not make a distinction between a book and an article. Additionally, problems arose with the publication name filtering capabilities within EDS™. The publication could not be filtered by publication name, *American Quarterly*, only by publication type, American Literature. Those participants ultimately had to include additional words to find the correct results. While EDS™ did have search filter to search by journal name, the majority of participants did not find it.

In testing, the user groups varied in their approach to completing their search. Undergraduate students seemed more willing to reenter keywords in the simple search repeatedly, while faculty were quicker to search using the advanced search capabilities. Discovery tools must retrieve the desired results or face the risk of losing the user to either a librarian or a different search system. Overall, these tools frustrated many of the users; however, some advanced users were excited about the potential of the technology.

It appears that the producers of discovery services considered the needs of the user. They realized that users need search tools with robust algorithms and the ability to search across multiple databases. They realized that these discovery tools must be intuitive and user-friendly. Yet, those considerations were not always successful. The research here discovered that it can be difficult to create one tool that addresses the needs of multiple types of users in a clean interface. If faceted search options and limiters are provided, vendors should use a minimalist approach. Companies should consider right-side blindness and information that is put "below-the-fold." The most important features of the discovery tool should be highlighted at the top of the screen or in the left column. Providing relevant spelling corrections and suggestions within the discovery tool may assist a user in finding the desired information, but the suggestions need to stand out to be noticed.

CONCLUSION

The three discovery tools examined here each have certain advantages and disadvantages over their competitors. However, the greatest problem found across all tools was retrieving meaningful and relevant results from a given keyword search. This should be a major concern for all companies since these are systems designed to search. Companies can provide a robust advanced search menu system, but they must also ensure that users will have frequent success within a simple search interface. In this age of technology, users have been trained to expect quick and easy results through Google. While librarians may be looking for the most sophisticated tools with the highest standards, companies should design discovery tools that work for the lowest common denominator. Let it be noted that this level is not based on role of undergraduate, graduate, or faculty; degree program; or institution. These results have proven that there were marked issues in locating even basic types of information. A discovery tool should be designed so that users do not need to locate help or "Frequently Asked Questions" before use.

The attempt to simplify a search across multiple databases and from a variety of sources is difficult to achieve. The potential is tremendous, but the execution must be flawless. In this research, the tools did not deliver such an execution, and as a result, many participants were frustrated with the tools. In order for discovery tools to succeed, users must find the information for which they are searching on the first page of the results. In 2009, Google had over 7,000 employees working on research and development and spent $2.8 billion dollars on Research and Development (Google, 2009). In copying the minimalistic user interface design of Google, users expect the system to operate with the same success. If the system is not perceived to work as efficiently, users will abandon the system. During this testing, many of the participants became frustrated, stating, "this is where I would go to Google" or "this is where I would go to Google Scholar;" some did abandon the systems tested. While discovery services offer library users an opportunity to quickly search multiple collections through a single interface, they still must provide more relevant results with more intuitive search features to compete successfully with search engines.

The research here yielded useful findings for libraries considering any of these discovery services and for the developers themselves; however, continued user testing is required. The producers frequently modify the interface, design and search features and should test with end-users with each modification. These results do not include Innovative Interfaces' Encore product, OCLC WorldCat Local or other open source discovery tools; further study with a wider selection of tools is warranted.

Lastly, product developers should observe user behavior in dealing with limitations in each of the discovery services. This study employed materials that researchers knew were available in all the products' knowledge bases. Unfortunately, no service fully integrates all of a library's resources; some content lives outside the tools' indexes and must be retrieved through federated search. It would be useful to examine how users respond to links outside the discovery service and then return to it; the research here observed some difficulty and confusion when users left the discovery tool and tried to return.

While discovery tools have offered libraries and their users a great service in gathering a myriad of library resources into one knowledge base with a single interface, searchers still face challenges with each of the products. In this age of Google, producers and librarians alike must continue to develop and support systems that provide robust search with simple, intuitive interfaces that serve meaningful, relevant results for simple (and often problematic) search strings in order for us to compete with public search engines.

FUTURE RESEARCH DIRECTIONS

The research here begins a process of observing actual end users in their search of library materials using discovery tools. Much more research needs to be done to explore the ways in which students generally approach the search process, the decisions they make about where to search and what criteria to use to measure items they find and success in their information seeking. Using methodologies such as contextual inquiry or ethnographic interviews, researchers can both observe student information seeking behaviors and question students on their thought processes and decision making. Many students seemed quite unaware of when they left one particular tool and entered another (for example leaving the discovery layer and entering a library catalog or particular database) and then had difficulty navigating back to where they began. While discovery tools' interfaces may be simplistic, the list of results and number of formats may still be daunting to students of the Google generation. More research is needed to understand how students formulate search queries, the way they combine terms and phrases so that discovery tools make strengthen and fine tune their algorithms. Developers must also observe students to recognize their thought processes in distinguishing between types of content and format and evaluating resources in terms of topical relevance, academic quality and appropriateness. Secondly, continued research is required to identify user frustrations in the discovery tools themselves. Studies must identify underutilized or undiscovered features and confusing labels or directions. Designers need to establish which facets users expect and they combinations and interaction of facets or limiters they most desire. As they recognize common behaviors

and mistakes developers can build more effective discovery services that can provide relevant, useful materials for the most novice of users.

REFERENCES

Allison, D. (2010). Information portals: The next generation catalog. *Journal of Web Librarianship, 4*(4), 375–389. doi:10.1080/19322909.2010.507972

Breeding, M. (2007). Encore. *Library Technology Reports, 43*(4), 23–27.

DeRosa, C., Cantrell, J., Hawk, J., & Wilson, A. (2006). *College students' perceptions of libraries and information resources: A report to the OCLC membership.* Dublin, OH: OCLC. Retrieved from http://www.oclc.org/reports/pdfs/studentperceptions.pdf

EBSCO Publishing. (2011). *EBSCO discovery service content.* Retrieved June 17, 2011, from http://www.ebscohost.com/discovery/eds-content

Emanuel, J. (2011). Usability of the VuFind next-generation online catalog. *Information Technologies and Libraries, 30*(1), 44–52.

Ex Libris. (2011). *Primo Central Index: An upgraded search experience.* Retrieved June 18, 2011, from http://www.exlibrisgroup.com/category/PrimoCentral

Google. (2009). Google Form 10-K. Retrieved June 18, 2011, from http://investor.google.com/documents/2009_google_annual_report.html

Head, A. J., & Eisenberg, M. B. (2009). *Finding context: What today's college students say about conducting research in the digital age.* Project Information Literacy Progress Report, Information School. University of Washington. Retrieved from http://projectinfolit.org/pdfs/PIL_Progress-Report_2_2009.pdf

Innovative Interfaces. (2011). *Encore products: Encore discovery*. Retrieved November 11, 2011, from http://encoreforlibraries.com/products/#ed

Jones, S. (2002). *The Internet goes to college: How students are living in the future with today's technology*. Washington, DC: Pew Internet and American Life Project. Retrieved from http://www.pewinternet.org/pdfs/PIP_College_Report.pdf

Nielsen, J. (2000). *Why you only need to test with five users*. Retrieved November 11, 2011, from http://www.useit.com/alertbox/20000319.html

Nielsen, J., & Landauer, T. K. (1993). A mathematical model of the finding of usability problems. *Proceedings of INTERCHI 1993*. New York, NY: ACM Press.

Online Computer Library Center. (2002). *OCLC white paper on the information habits of college students: How academic librarians can influence students' web-based information choices*. Retrieved from http://www.aect.org/publications/whitepapers/2010/informationhabits.pdf

Serials Solutions. (2011). *Summon content and coverage*. Retrieved June 17, 2011, from http://www.serialsolutions.com/summon-content-and-coverage

Stein, J., Bright, A., George, C., Hurlbert, T., Linke, E., & St. Clair, G. (2006). In their own words: A preliminary report on the value of the Internet and library in graduate student research. *Performance Measurement and Metrics, 7*(2), 117–115. doi:10.1108/14678040610679506

Vaughan, J. (2011a). Differentiators and a final note. *Library Technology Reports, 47*(1), 48–53.

Vaughan, J. (2011b). Ebsco Discovery Services. *Library Technology Reports, 47*(1), 30–38.

Vaughan, J. (2011c). Ex Libris Primo Central. *Library Technology Reports, 47*(1), 39–47.

Vaughan, J. (2011d). Serials Solutions Summon. *Library Technology Reports, 47*(1), 22–29.

Vaughan, J. (2011e). Web scale discovery: What and why? *Library Technology Reports, 47*(1), 5–11, 21.

Whitlock, B., & Kiel, S. (2011). *What I learned from teaching a for-credit information literacy class*. Presentation at the Maryland Library Association Annual Conference, *May 6, 2011*.

Williams, P. (1999). The Net generation: The experiences, attitudes and behavior of children using the Internet for their own purposes. *Aslib Proceedings, 51*(9), 315–322. doi:10.1108/EUM0000000006991

Yang, S. Q., & Wagner, K. (2010). Evaluating and comparing discovery tools: How close are we towards next generation catalog? *Library Hi Tech, 28*(4), 690–709. doi:10.1108/07378831011096312

ADDITIONAL READING

Alshamari, M., & Mayhew, P. (2009). Technical review: Current issues of usability testing. *IETE Technical Review, 26*(6), 402–406. doi:10.4103/0256-4602.57825

Anandhan, A., Dhandapani, S., Reza, H., & Namasivayam, K. (2006). Web usability testing: CARE methodology. *Proceedings of the Third International Conference on Information Technology, New Generations*. Los Alamitos, CA: IEEE Computer Society

Barnum, C. (2002). *Usability testing and research*. New York, NY: Longman.

Becher, M., & Schmidt, K. (2011). Taking discovery systems for a test drive. *Journal of Web Librarianship, 5*(3), 199–219. doi:10.1080/19322909.2011.583134

Christian Bastien, J. M. (2010). Usability testing: A review of some methodological and technical aspects of the method. *International Journal of Medical Informatics*, *79*(4). doi:doi:10.1016/j.ijmedinf.2008.12.004

Connaway, L. S., & Dickey, T. J. (2010). *Towards a profile of the researcher of today: What can we learn from JISC Projects? Common themes identified in an analysis of JISC virtual environment and digital repository projects.* Retrieved from http://ie-repository.jisc.ac.uk/418/2/VirtualScholar_themesFromProjects_revised.pdf

Connaway, L. S., Dickey, T. J., & Radford, M. L. (2011). "If it is too inconvenient I'm not going after it:" Convenience as a critical factor in information-seeking behaviors. *Library & Information Science Research*, *33*(3), 179–190. doi:10.1016/j.lisr.2010.12.002

Denton, W., & Coysh, S. J. (2011). Usability testing of VuFind at an academic library. *Library Hi Tech*, *29*(2), 301–319. doi:10.1108/07378831111138189

Dixon, L., Duncan, C., Fagan, J. C., Mandernach, M., & Warlick, S. E. (2010). Finding articles and journals via Google Scholar, journal portals, and link resolvers: Usability study results. *Reference and User Services Quarterly*, *50*(2), 170–181.

Duchowski, A. (2007). *Eye tracking methodology: Theory and practice* (2nd ed.). London, UK: Springer.

Gross, J., & Sheridan, L. (2011). Web-scale discovery: The user experience. *New Library World*, *112*(5/6), 236–247. doi:10.1108/03074801111136275

Hackos, J. T., & Redish, J. C. (1998). *User and task analysis for interface design.* New York, NY: Wiley.

Hornbæk, K. (2010). Dogmas in the assessment of usability evaluation methods. *Behaviour & Information Technology*, *29*(1), 97–111. doi:10.1080/01449290801939400

James, D., Garrett, M., & Krevit, L. (2009). Discovering discovery tools: Evaluating vendors and implementing Web 2.0 environments. *Library Hi Tech*, *27*(2), 268–276. doi:10.1108/07378830910968218

Jones, R., Milic-Frayling, N., Rodden, K., & Blackwell, A. (2007). Contextual method for the redesign of existing software products. *International Journal of Human-Computer Interaction*, *22*(1/2), 81–101.

Kuniavsky, M. (2003). *Observing the user experience: A practitioner's guide to user research.* San Francisco, CA: Morgan Kaufmann Publishers.

Lazar, J., Feng, J. H., & Hochheiser, H. (2010). *Research methods in human-computer interaction.* Chichester, UK: Wiley.

Leventhal, L. (2008). *Usability engineering: Process, products, and examples.* Upper Saddle River, NJ: Pearson/Prentice Hall.

Lindgaard, G., & Chattratichart, J. (2007). *Usability testing: what have we overlooked? Proceedings of the SIGCHI Conference on Human Factors in Computing Systems.* New York, NY: ACM Press.

Luther, J. J., & Kelly, M. C. (2011). The next generation of discovery. *Library Journal*, *136*(5), 66–71.

Nielsen, J., & Pernice, K. (2010). *Eyetracking web usability.* Berkeley, CA: New Riders.

Prasse, M. J., & Connaway, L. S. (2008). Usability testing: Method and research . In Radford, M. L., & Snelson, P. (Eds.), *Academic library research: Perspectives and current trends* (pp. 214–252). Chicago, IL: Association of College and Research Libraries.

Prescott, L., & Erway, R. (2011). *Single search: The quest for the Holy Grail*. Dublin, OH: OCLC Research. Retrieved from http://www.oclc.org/research/publications/library/2011/2011-17.pdf

Rubin, J. (2008). *Handbook of usability testing: How to plan, design, and conduct effective tests* (2nd ed.). Indianapolis, IN: Wiley.

U.S. Department of Health and Human Services. (2011). *Usability.gov*. Retrieved from http://www.usability.gov/

Vaughan, J. (2011). *Web scale discovery services*. Chicago, IL: ALA TechSource.

Williams, S. C., & Foster, A. K. (2011). Promise fulfilled? An EBSCO Discovery Service usability study. *Journal of Web Librarianship, 5*(3), 179–198. doi:10.1080/19322909.2011.597590

KEY TERMS AND DEFINITIONS

Application Programming Interface (API): A standard set of rules and tools used to build new programs or facilitate communication between programs. They can be considered building blocks developing new applications.

Below-the-Fold: Content on a Web site that requires scrolling in order to view it.

Eye-Tracking: A method of recording user eye movements and focal attention while he/she is viewing particular screen in order to identify areas of the screen the user views quickly and where focal attention lingers. These recorded saccadic movements and focal attention can be evaluated and compared to users' information processing to inform Web site visual design and usability.

Eye-Tracking Software: Computer program that monitors and records eye movements and creates images (see heat map) illustrating user visual paths and areas of the screen where users' focal attention concentrates.

Faceted Navigation: Movement on and through a Web site through the use of topical or format categories and subcategories

Graphical Hierarchy: A visual representation of hierarchical structure, offering a clear explanation of relative importance, size or differentiation.

Heat Map: A visual representation of the areas of a screen where a user's gaze is fixated.

Interface: The means through which a user interacts with a computer application/program. The interface includes a means by which a user offers input and a display of the application's response.

Interface Design: The development and implementation of an application's interface with a focus on the user's needs and desires. Many interface designs strive for simplicity and intuitiveness for ease of use.

Mouse-Tracking: A method of recording computer mouse cursor movements and clicks to determine user paths and patterns of mouse behaviors.

Right-Side Blindness (sometimes known as "Ad" Blindness): The inability to see items or features on the right side of a Web site; researchers find that users have unconsciously trained themselves not to look at areas of Web sites where advertisements are generally placed.

Task-Based Usability Study: A methodology whereby study participants are given a set of tasks to complete. Researchers measure rate and time of task completion and observe users' approaches to completing the tasks as well as observe users' reactions to the task. This method is typically preferable to interviewing users about their experiences with a particular interface; researchers can see what users actually do as opposed to what they think they would do or remember what they did.

ENDNOTES

[1] EBSCO Discovery Service is owned by EBSCO Publishing Industries

[2] Primo is a registered trademark of Ex Libris Ltd. or its affiliates

[3] Serials Solution is a registered trademark of Serials Solutions

[4] Summons is owned by ProQuest LLC

[5] Primo Central is owned by Ex Libris Ltd. or its affiliates

Chapter 15

Search Success at the University of Manitoba Libraries Pre- and Post-Summon Implementation

Lisa O'Hara
University of Manitoba Libraries, Canada

Pat Nicholls
University of Manitoba Libraries, Canada

Karen Keiller
University of New Brunswick Saint John Campus, Canada

ABSTRACT

The University of Manitoba Libraries (UML) hired an external company to perform usability testing on its website in 2008 and 2009. A component of the website testing required test participants to find particular books and articles and to identify materials on a particular specific topic using the UML's search tools. The need for a resource discovery tool was made clear when participants were not generally successful in completing these tasks. The UML released Request for Proposals (RFP) for a resource discovery tool in 2010 and shortly afterward acquired Summon™ as the successful tool. Usability testing was performed on the Summon™ resource discovery tool while it was still in beta development at UML to see if there was an improvement in search success for students. The results of the two usability studies are described in this chapter, with an emphasis on the Summon™ usability testing and suggestions for further research.

DOI: 10.4018/978-1-4666-1821-3.ch015

INTRODUCTION

In 2008, as a result of both anecdotal evidence and more formal feedback from the LibQual®2 survey in which the University of Manitoba Libraries (UML) participated in 2003, 2006 and 2007, a Website Usability Team was created to look critically at the website to improve clients' experience. In order to perform this task as objectively as possible, the team contracted with an external company, NeoInsight, which conducted usability tests on UML's website for two short time periods in 2008 and 2009. The external consultant was selected through a Request for Proposals (RFP) process and the UML became their first library client. The Website Usability Team was pleased to have a consultant that specialized in usability rather than libraries since the Team would provide the library expertise. Results from the testing showed that students were not only having trouble locating information on the UML's website, but they were also unsuccessful in locating library materials using the UML's array of tools including the library catalogue and various subject-specific and more general databases. In identifying this problem, the company recommended a single search tool that would incorporate all of the UML's search tools. The timing of this recommendation was fortuitous in that resource discovery tools were coming to the market. A Resource Discovery Layer Task Force was formed and after an RFP process and Summon™ was acquired and implemented in the late fall of 2009 for staff use. Usability testing was performed on the Summon™ search engine during the beta phase to test that it would improve the search experience of UML's clients. Summon™ was made available to students in May 2010 as "One Stop Search" with a search box directly on the UML's homepage, although there had been a link to One Stop Search since February. This chapter will discuss the results of both the external consultant's testing and the Summon™ usability testing.

BACKGROUND

The University of Manitoba Libraries is a doctoral-level university serving over 25,000 students and the UML's collections number over 1.8 million titles in 19 libraries including eight hospital libraries. For both the external consultants' testing and the Summon™ testing, the UML was using Sirsi-Dynix®3 Symphony®4 version 3.2 and Web2 was the web catalogue interface. The UML also uses SFX®5 as its OpenURL resolver which is called "GetIt@UML" on the UML site. The Libraries provide access to over 300 separate databases in a variety of subjects which support its programs and at the time of website testing databases were made available using a home-grown system. This system provided alphabetic and subject lists and also provided information about the database including a summary, number of concurrent users, whether it was SFX®-compliant and more. During the Summon™ testing, the Libraries had migrated the home grown system to a Drupal system which gave the same information as the home-grown system but in a different format. Although none of these Libraries' systems were looked at comprehensively in either test, the systems and their abilities were certainly factors in the usability testing of the Libraries' website and of Summon™.

As part of the usability testing process and investigation into resource discovery tools the Website Usability Team and then the Resource Discovery Layer Task Force examined the literature available in the area. Since the focus of this chapter is usability testing, only the relevant literature on usability testing will be discussed. Most definitions of usability are based on either the International Organization for Standardization definition or Nielson (Bevan, 2006; Nielsen, 1993, 2000; Y. Chen, Germain, & Rorissa, 2009). Usability is often associated with five dimensions: learnability, efficiency, memorability, errors, and satisfaction (Nielsen, 1993). The best definition of usability for our purposes was found in a 2001 article by McGillis and Toms as "the extent to which a product can be used by specified users to achieve designated goals with effectiveness, efficiency, and satisfaction in a specified context of use" (McGillis & Toms, 2001). Convenience is also an important factor in usability in the library context and has been found to be "the primary criteria used for making choices during the information-seeking process" (Connaway, Dickey, & Radford, 2011, p. 188).

Although a great deal has been written about usability testing on academic library websites, there is little that has been written about usability testing on search tools for academic libraries, and very little about resource discovery tools (Y.-H. Chen, Germain, & Yang, 2009, p. 954; Y. Chen, Germain, et al., 2009; Nathan & Yeow, 2008; Somerville & Brar, 2009; Teague-Rector, Ballard, & Pauley, 2011). There is a small body of literature about usability testing on metasearch engines which offered a basis for Summon™ usability testing at UML. A study at Hunter College Libraries was interested in determining how well gateway pages helped students at a number of information seeking tasks and found that there were a number of recommendations that could be implemented (Finder, Dent, & Lym, 2006). At the Oregon State University Libraries, Jung et al. compared a metasearch engine, LibraryFind, to Google Scholar and found that:

Our study reinforced that college undergraduates use what is familiar. Consequently, a new academic metasearch system needs to meld familiarity while capitalizing on the varying experience levels of users; however, if the metasearch interface is as familiar as that of a Web search engine, undergraduates expect it to deliver Web search engine performance and features, especially speed and relevance ranking... Participants' prior experience using an academic search system affects their expectations for and satisfaction with using a new system. (Jung et al., 2008, p. 388).

Another study completed at Texas A&M University found that, when prompted, users were quick to pick up on new navigation features and began to incorporate them into their search strategies (Ponsford & vanDuinkerken, 2007, p. 176). From the available literature, it appears that although users prefer to use familiar tools and have expectations of the tools based on whether they are similar to other tools, they will learn and adapt to new tools when the features of the tools are pointed out to them.

The most similar tool available to Summon™ at the time UML performed usability testing was WorldCat®6 Local. At the time, only one article was written about usability testing on WorldCat® Local from the University of Washington Libraries. The authors found that users "were generally successful finding materials" (Ward, Shadle, & Mofield, 2008, p. 18). However, problems were identified with book reviews appearing higher in the results than the book itself and with detailed record screens which were confusing to users. A second round of testing was underway with some of the problems identified in the first round addressed, but results were still being analyzed at the time of writing (Ward et al., 2008). Usability testing of MetaLib®7 using a think out-loud protocol was useful in providing recommendations to designers, including improving login, navigation and terminology (George, 2008). Usability testing for e-resource discovery at both Memorial University Libraries and Bowling Green State University conclude that well-designed pages are not enough and implementing a one search box for all of the library's content is crucial to helping students (Gibson, Goddard, & Gordon, 2009; Fry & Rich, 2011). This conclusion is not universal, after usability testing at Moraine Valley Community College librarians have decided against the "googlization" of the library's web site (Swanson & Green, 2011). Most library usability testing is done in-house, although there are advantages to consulting usability experts since most librarians are still gaining expertise in the area of usability

Figure 1. UML home page, pre-testing

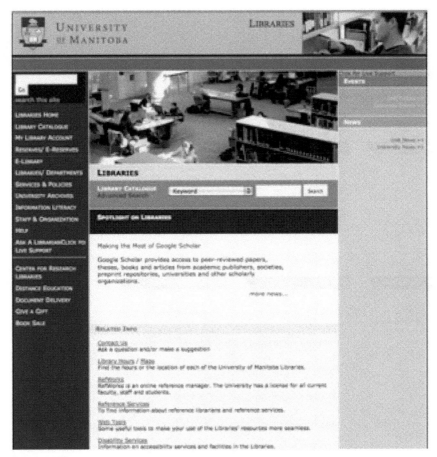

testing and an external expert may provide an unbiased viewpoint (Tolliver et al., 2005).

EXTERNAL CONSULTANT'S TESTING

Test Methodology

As a result of an RFP process in 2007, the external consultancy firm was hired to examine and test the University of Manitoba Libraries website. The initial contract was extended for a second year and eventually encompassed an expert review, a comparative analysis and four rounds of usability testing. In total 36 participants were recruited and asked to undertake a series of tasks using various features of our website.

The participants were recruited through campus-wide advertising to reflect a variety of disciplines; various experiences using the Libraries' website, from daily to never; and a balance of gender. Six participants were faculty, all others were students, two of the students used screen readers and two were distance education students. The various aspects of the website were modified for each round of testing with participants rating both the before and after versions. Although the changes were incremental and included changes throughout the website, as an example of the level of change, the initial and final versions of the UML homepage are shown in Figure 1 and 2.

Figure 2. UML home page, post-testing

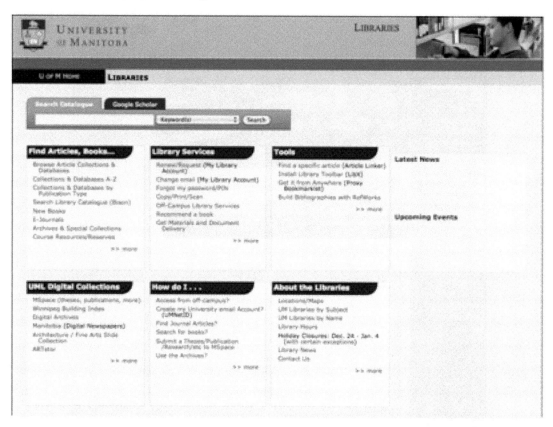

Each participant was given six tasks. The first task was the user's own task based on current research or an assignment. There were three research tasks, an administrative task, and a skills development task. (See Appendix 1 for the complete list of tasks). The one hour sessions were conducted by the external consultants working with the participants remotely using Morae®[8] (Techsmith®[9]) software to observe and record their actions. Participants used their own computer or a university computer. Some members of the Web Usability Team and other UML staff were able to observe the sessions. As well, the sessions were recorded for future analysis and summaries were created for staff discussion.

After each task, participants were asked for feedback and ratings, and for ideas on improvements. In addition:

Task performance was measured;

Task completion was recorded, including whether or not hints were given (which varied with the task and the participant) and time on task;

Participants rated how satisfied they were with how the website supported each task;

Participants rated the site overall, the current site and the modified site.

Test Results

Participants ranked their success as satisfactory. As seen in Figure 3, overall satisfaction and satisfaction in all but two of the tasks was above 50%.

Between the initial round of testing and the final round in the first year, task completion (see Figures 4 and 5) was made easier for some specific tasks (e.g. the Admin task) and completing a specific task was usually successful. Finding a

Figure 3. Task satisfaction

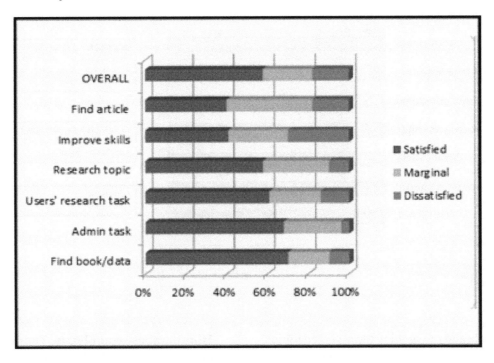

Figure 4. Task completion, round 1

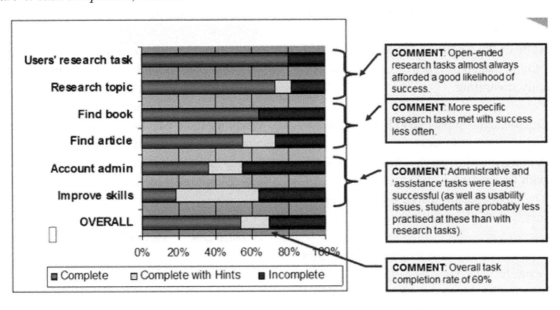

Figure 5. Task completion, round 3

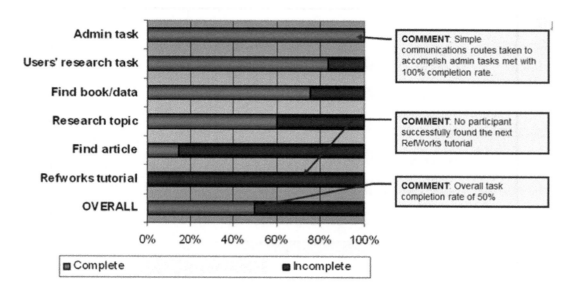

journal article and researching the assigned topic, however, remained difficult and frustrating.

Discussion of Results

Overall, participants ranked their success much better than observations by the testers and librarians would have ranked it.

In spite of the perceived success, the investigators found that some types of search task were especially frustrating:

- Open-ended 'topic' search tasks always met with some success
- A more specific search – find a book – met with less success
- The most specific search – for an article – met with the least success

Participants were most frustrated where they knew *exactly* what they were looking for, but could not find it because they did not know which database it would be found in.

A primary recommendation of the consultant's final report was:

Hide database complexity: The proliferation of resources is increasingly becoming a barrier to successful search and the adoption of sophisticated research strategies

We highly recommend hiding as much as possible of the database complexity behind a simple, Google-like search box. Provide a 'meta-search' that allows people to specify what they are looking for, without having to specify where it is.

Other recommendations are continuing to be implemented at UML but the truth of this recommendation was painfully obvious to the Website Usability Team who had observed the testing. The NeoInsight report was followed up with a search for and implementation of our choice of discovery tool: Summon™ by Serials Solutions®.

SUMMON™ TESTING

Test Methodology

Summon™ is a resource discovery tool which incorporates metadata from the Library catalogue, locally produced databases, free digital repositories and the Libraries' subscription databases (when available). Using a single, unified index, metadata is searchable through a single search box returning a quick browse list. Library clients can browse the list or narrow their results through facets available on the left-hand side of the screen. Facets include content type, subject terms, publication date, and library. The UML acquired Summon™ based on an RFP process where Summon™ was the only product that was ready for market and which met the Libraries' criteria. The primary criteria included a unified search index, faceted browsing, de-duplication, relevancy ranking and other sort options, the ability to refine by full-text only and peer-review, alternative word suggestions and spell-checking and known-item searching.

After Summon™ was implemented and ready for beta-testing at UML, staff partnered with Summon™ to carry out the usability testing on the UML's beta Summon™ site. Summon™ supplied funding for a research assistant, Morae software and Amazon gift certificates for test participants. The research assistant organized the participants and was a silent observer to all of the testing that took place.

Recruitment occurred through advertising on the UML's website, mentions by librarians in any instruction classes they were teaching and in-person recruitment at the coffee shop located in the main Arts & Humanities library at UML. Recruitment was not statistically reflective of the student body of the University of Manitoba Libraries. The aim was to perform informal testing by gathering a number of undergraduate students with a research assignment from a class they were currently taking who were willing to test the new Libraries' search tool. Each of the nine students completed research for an assignment for their class, so each session's participant had different objectives when using Summon™ (Appendix 3). Because the testing took place at the end of term, recruitment was not easy and the nine students who took part were from a larger group who initially expressed interest.

The students who took part in the testing had assignments to research in Music, Sociology, Management, Microbiology, Psychology, Political Science, English Literature, and Architecture. Four of the students were doing research for first-year level courses, one for a second-year level course, two for third-year level courses and two for fourth-year level courses. The student's years of university were not part of the information gathered; rather, the focus was on the research they were doing for a specific course which may or may not have been part of their major area of study. The search experience of the students was also not determined ahead of time. However, through conversations during the testing it was determined that it varied and included one student who worked in the libraries and claimed a good knowledge of searching and a first year student who had very little experience with the UML and its search tools.

Testing itself took place in one hour sessions with the student using his or her own computer or a computer in the University or the Library. The researcher and the research assistant viewed the search remotely at separate locations through the Morae® software which allowed them to view the participant's computer screen and actions on the screen (typing, mousing, etc.). The research assistant, the researcher and the participant all used computers in their own locations. The researcher and the participant communicated through a telephone and the sessions were recorded through Morae® which captured the participant's screen and actions and the conversation between the researcher and the participant. Each participant had previously completed a background questionnaire including information on their research assignments and each session began with a reiteration of the parameters of the study and the student's agreement to take part in it. Permission to carry out this research was obtained from the University of Manitoba's Research Ethics Board before testing took place as it was for the website usability.

Because each of the participants was researching a different topic, the sessions were not conducted in exactly the same way. Sessions were all begun the same way and a series of questions were asked each participant at the end of the session (available in Appendix 4), but the sessions themselves were not uniform and the researcher did offer the participants some help with their topic or with their search when they were stymied by the topic. Although this was mainly outside the parameters of the usability study, participants were occasionally prompted to look in a particular place when they were attempting to do something that could be done quite easily with Summon™ or when they were simply missing a piece of information that could help them. For example, a participant wondering how he could exclude book reviews from his results might be prompted "What is all that information on the left-hand side of the screen?" Whenever this was done, it was noted and will be commented upon in the results.

Test Results

Data for the tests was recorded through the Morae® software, in notes taken when viewing the sessions and collected in a spreadsheet.

Interface Design

Eight of the participants liked the design of the Summon™ interface with one describing it as "nice and clean (Figure 6 shows the interface at the time of testing). Only one participant commented that she didn't really like the colors and how the page looked. Two participants pointed out that something needs to be done to make the facets and choices for refining clearer, either by bolding or making the colors brighter. One participant commented that he thought that the single search box was a little too simple but that he ended up impressed with the product.

Figure 6. Summon™ results screen

Facets and Sorting

Only one of the participants found the facets available on the left-hand side of the screen without being prompted by the researcher. None of the participants clicked on the "more options" link at the bottom of the facets, even when this would have made their search more successful. When prompted, one participant commented in the post-search interview that "all the useful stuff is under more options! I can't say that I would have ever, ever clicked on that!"

Once participants were prompted by the researcher to look at the facets on the left-hand side of the screen, they readily narrowed the search by choosing one of the options at the top (limit to fulltext online, limit to scholarly articles, exclude newspapers). Two of the participants did not look any further down the left-hand side than that, although one of them was prompted four times by the researcher. Others went on to limit by content type, but only four participants went on to limit by subject, and only two used the date facet. One of the participants looked at the subject facet and instead of clicking on it to include or exclude it from the search results, went and added the term they wanted to the search box.

All of the participants found the sorting option at the right-hand side of the screen and only one had to be prompted to look there. Three of the participants immediately noticed the sorting option and were able to sort by the most recent materials, but one who was trying to find recent articles needed to be prompted to see it.

The search participants who came across book reviews had difficulties with them as did the participants in the University of Washington usability tests. One participant felt that the icon should be different for book reviews than for journal articles so that it would be easy to pick them out of the search results. The researcher pointed out to the participants who commented on book reviews that they could exclude them on the Advanced search screen.

Save Search Refinements

Three of the test participants used the facets and search refinements but also used different terms in their research and had problems because whenever they entered a new search, they lost their search refinements. Although there is a radio button right underneath the search box (see figure 6) which allows a user to keep their search refinements, none of the participants noticed this option on their own, and all three were confused by some of the results that were returned on the results screens. One participant suggested that once a search has been refined, this radio button should automatically be checked so that all subsequent searches will be refined in the same way however this also poses problems if users are searching for more than one assignment or research project.

Saving and Exporting

Because the testing occurred when Summon™ was still in beta at UML, not all features worked for all of the participants. For example, the fulltext linking was not working properly for half of the participants and the links to the UML's catalogue didn't work for any of them either. These problems were explained as being a result of the system still being in beta test mode to the participants and the researcher suggested that they add the items they were interested in to their folder and email the results to be located at a later time. This option was entirely acceptable to the majority of the participants although two repeatedly clicked on links and tried to link from Summon™ to the Libraries' resources although the linking was not functional. These features were mentioned as very valuable to the test participants in the post-search interview, but it is unclear whether participants would have discovered them on their own.

Figure 7. Summon™ advanced search screen

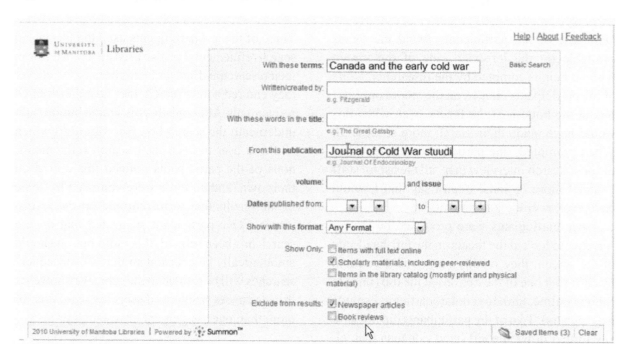

Advanced Search

Four participants clicked on the Advanced search screen including one participant who began her search on the Advanced search screen. Two of the participants chose the advanced search screen when looking for a specific item, and one commented that it looked very different from what he was used to seeing, with different terms instead of Author, etc. (see figure 7). The participant who began her search on the Advanced search screen was used to starting her research with books, and then examining the bibliographies of those books for more materials, so generally started any research in the library catalogue. Participants who used the advanced search screen tended to read the entire screen and try to enter as much information in as possible, including choosing the limits available at the bottom of the screen.

Post-Search Interview

In response to a post-search interview all of the participants rated their search experience as successful. All of the participants located material that was useful to the assignment they had brought to the search session and two commented that they had found material that they hadn't been able to find before using the "old" search tools. When asked what they found most useful, most mentioned the ability to put materials in a folder and email them to themselves at the end of the search, and the ability to view the abstract right in the resource discovery tool itself. Participants also discussed the fact that it consolidated searching and one found the inclusion of newspaper articles very useful.

Discussion of Results

The major problem encountered during Summon™ testing was the participants' failure to notice the facets on the left-hand side of the search screen. In fact, two participants commented that something needs to be done to make the facets and choices for refining clearer, either by bolding or making the colors brighter. The placement of the facets on the left-hand side of the screen seems to have misled students into thinking that the information found there isn't important. The participants search behavior tended to be similar to what was experienced during the original website testing, although because most of the UML's materials are included in Summon™ the search was more successful. Students tended to enter general terms and then refine their searches by adding new terms or similar terms to the search box. Their focus was entirely on the search results and anything else on the screen, including the facets on the left-hand side, was ignored. In order to narrow the search, the participants uniformly returned to the search box and added more keywords to the search in order to narrow it and would then return to scrolling through search results, with one participant willing to scroll through up to five pages before trying to redefine the search. Interestingly, the most inexperienced searcher was the one that went directly to the facets to narrow his search, which suggests that perhaps the participants ignored the left hand facets based on their experiences with UML's previous systems, again reinforcing the observations made by the researchers at Oregon State University Libraries. Further testing at UML and in other institutions would determine whether this was a result of UML clients' expectations of our locally implemented systems or a more general misconception.

It was also surprising to note that during the actual search process, none of the participants commented on the fact that they were able to search for more than one type of material, and it appeared that all of them took it for granted that many content types were included. This reinforces the findings at Oregon State University Libraries that researchers have expectations of search based on how the search engine appears: if it looks like a web search engine, they expect it to perform like a web search engine.

In response to the question posed during the post-search interview "Were you able to find the types of materials you wanted?" all of the participants replied "yes". During their searching, most of the participants needed to be prompted to limit by the content type facet, yet the ability to limit to one type of material or to exclude a type of material was something that was mentioned by four participants as one of the most valuable features of Summon™.

On the whole, the response to the Summon™ resource discovery tool was very positive. Out of the nine participants, seven were very enthusiastic about different features of Summon™. The two remaining participants were more reticent and compared it to other search engines that they were obviously very familiar with, perhaps indicating that for students who are more advanced in their studies and familiar with subject-specific databases, Summon™ is superfluous, but again reinforcing the findings from Oregon State University.

For the participants who were very positive about Summon™, comments included:

"That is classy! That right there... the smartest thing I've ever seen!"

"It's clearer than the normal library search thing."

"I was kind of skeptical because you open the page and it's only one line [the search box] but it's nice and simple... it worked really well, I'm impressed!"

"Very helpful, I found exactly what I needed and didn't have to go to outside sources except to get full text."

Findings

The website usability testing determined that the Libraries' clients were not able to find the materials they needed and resulted in the purchase of Summon™. The Summon™ testing determined that students' abilities to find materials improved but there were problems with Summon's™ usability at UML:

- Facets need to be made more prominent;
- The fact that articles were book reviews need to be made more obvious, whether through the use of an icon or bolder text;
- The means of saving of search refinements for subsequent searches needs to be clearer.

There were also some implications for liaison librarians in showing UML clients the Summon™ search interface, which was called One Stop Search at UML:

- Facets would need to be pointed out, along with a description of how the facets would work;
- Students using Advanced Search should learn to only enter information that would be important in the search.

The results of the Summon™ testing were shared directly with Summon™ who were partners in the testing. Results were also shared with the One Stop Search Rollout Task Force which was charged with promoting One Stop Search and ensuring that both staff and students understood its advantages and limitations. The Task Force used the information to ensure that liaison librarians would know that identifying the facets on the left-hand side of the screen was an issue for students and could use that information when showing Summon™ to students and faculty.

Other libraries implementing a resource discovery tool would be wise to wait until the tool is working fully with the library catalogue and other systems before testing. Since the full text linking and linking to the catalogue were not working for many of the participants, the researcher could not determine how students would react when Summon™ returned them to the catalogue or to the full text.

The use of Morae® and recording the sessions was extremely useful. It allowed UML staff to go back over the sessions and find where problems occurred and to really look at what the participants were doing rather than trying to capture everything during the session itself. Having the researcher and participant in remote locations was also beneficial since the participant was in a place he or she felt comfortable and could use the system the way they normally would without someone in the room. The researcher and observer felt that they were getting a very true picture of the participant's use of the system and this is born out in the Morae® recordings.

FUTURE RESEARCH DIRECTIONS

The first year student who was the least experienced searcher was the one who found the facet searching on his own and seemed to adapt fastest to using the features available in Summon™. Because the other participants have been accustomed to certain search strategies and results (although these varied widely between the participants) they were less likely to look at the whole screen and focused mainly on the results of the search, supporting the Oregon State researchers' findings that searchers bring to a new search tool expectations based on their past experiences. It would be beneficial to perform further testing with students who did not have pre-conceived notions of how to do research at the UML, and one area for further research would be to continue the usability testing with first year students who have no experience of the "old" systems, second year students who began their University careers when Summon™ was the main search engine on the UML's webpage, and "older" students who were initially trained on the "old" systems.

Another area of research would be to see how search behavior changes with clients of different library systems who are used to different "old" systems; the UML uses SirsiDynix®; determining how clients from libraries with different ILS systems search Summon™. Since Summon™ is not highly customizable, the search experience across Summon™ libraries should be fairly homogenous, but further research would determine if this was true, or if the results varied in different types of institutions and with different types of students.

Based on the UML experience of usability testing using both consultants and in-house expertise, the consultants were very helpful in convincing librarians that a radical change in our approach to web-site design and information discovery was necessary. A further area of research is determining whether using external usability consultants provides different conclusions than in-house usability testing.

CONCLUSION

Although search success is not yet perfected at UML, Summon™ has at least resulted in more successful searches for UML's clients based on these usability results. In contrast to the original testing which found that only 60% of participants found research materials they were looking for, all of the participants in the Summon™ searching found materials that they could use in their research.

The finding by the external consultant that UML's clients expect to find all materials by performing a single search in one database was confirmed by the assumption that participants in the Summon™ testing made that all content types were included in the search. Librarians have long believed that Google is changing students' search expectations and the UML's experience testing Summon™ supports this belief. The emergence

of many resource discovery tools to the library market and the uptake on these tools by libraries also shows that this belief is also supported in many libraries. As library clients become more accustomed to these tools and as the vendors continue to improve the relevance and recall of these tools, they may provide the search solution libraries have been searching for.

Serials Solutions® has continued to develop their product and has added features like referrer databases and the ability for libraries to choose colors and layouts which complement their library website design. Although some of the features that users in the UML usability study suggested have not been implemented, it is hoped that some of these might incorporated into the Summon™ services as the system becomes more sophisticated. It can also be hoped that the metadata that vendors and publishers submit to Summon™ will become more accurate and sophisticated allowing greater user satisfaction and search recall and relevancy.

REFERENCES

Bevan, N. (2006). International standards for HCI. In Ghaoui, C. (Ed.), *Encyclopedia of human computer interaction*.

Chen, Y., Germain, C. A., & Rorissa, A. (2009). An analysis of formally published usability and Web usability definitions. *Proceedings of the American Society for Information Science and Technology*, *46*(1), 1–18. doi:10.1002/meet.2009.1450460213

Chen, Y.-H., Germain, C. A., & Yang, H. (2009). An exploration into the practices of library Web usability in ARL academic libraries. *Journal of the American Society for Information Science and Technology*, *60*(5), 953–968. doi:10.1002/asi.21032

Connaway, L. S., Dickey, T. J., & Radford, M. L. (2011). "If it is too inconvenient I'm not going after it:" Convenience as a critical factor in information-seeking behaviors. *Library & Information Science Research*, *33*(3), 179–190. doi:10.1016/j.lisr.2010.12.002

Finder, L., Dent, V. F., & Lym, B. (2006). How the presentation of electronic gateway pages affects research behavior. *The Electronic Library*, *24*(6), 804–819. doi:10.1108/02640470610714233

Fry, A., & Rich, L. (2011). Usability testing for e-resource discovery: How students find and choose e-Resources using library web sites. *Journal of Academic Librarianship*, *37*(5), 386–401. doi:10.1016/j.acalib.2011.06.003

George, C. A. (2008). Lessons learned: usability testing a federated search product. *The Electronic Library*, *26*(1), 5–20. doi:10.1108/02640470810851707

Gibson, I., Goddard, L., & Gordon, S. (2009). One box to search them all: Implementing federated search at an academic library. *Library Hi Tech*, *27*(1), 118–133. doi:10.1108/07378830910942973

Jung, S., Herlocker, J. L., Webster, J., Mellinger, M., & Frumkin, J. (2008). LibraryFind: System design and usability testing of academic metasearch system. *Journal of the American Society for Information Science and Technology*, *59*(3), 375–389. doi:10.1002/asi.20749

McGillis, L., & Toms, E. G. (2001). Usability of the academic library web site: Implications for design. *College & Research Libraries*, *62*(4), 355–367.

Nathan, R. J., & Yeow, P. H. P. (2008). An empirical study of factors affecting the perceived usability of websites for student Internet users. *Universal Access in the Information Society*, *8*(3), 165–184. doi:10.1007/s10209-008-0138-8

Nielsen, J. (1993). *Usability engineering*. Boston, MA: Academic Press.

Nielsen, J. (2000). *Designing Web usability*. Indianapolis, IN: New Riders.

Ponsford, B. C., & vanDuinkerken, W. (2007). User expectations in the time of Google: Usability testing of federated searching. *Internet Reference Services Quarterly*, *12*(1/2), 159–178. doi:10.1300/J136v12n01_08

Somerville, M. M., & Brar, N. (2009). A user-centered and evidence-based approach for digital library projects. *The Electronic Library*, *27*(3), 409–425. doi:10.1108/02640470910966862

Swanson, T. A., & Green, J. (2011). Why we are not Google: Lessons from a library web site usability study. *Journal of Academic Librarianship*, *37*(3), 222–229. doi:10.1016/j.acalib.2011.02.014

Teague-Rector, S., Ballard, A., & Pauley, S. K. (2011). The North Carolina State University libraries search experience: Usability testing tabbed search interfaces for academic libraries. *Journal of Web Librarianship*, *5*(2), 80–95. doi:10.1080/19322909.2011.568822

Tolliver, R. L., Carter, D. S., Chapman, S. E., Edwards, P. M., Fisher, J. E., & Haines, A. L. (2005). Website redesign and testing with a usability consultant: Lessons learned. *OCLC Systems & Services*, *21*(3), 156–166. doi:10.1108/10650750510612362

Ward, J. L., Shadle, S., & Mofield, P. (2008). User experience, feedback, and testing. *Library Technology Reports*, *44*(6), 17–23.

ADDITIONAL READING

Avery, S., Ward, D., & Hinchcliffe, L. J. (2007). Planning and implementing a federated searching system: An examination of the crucial roles of technical, functional and usability testing. *Internet Reference Services Quarterly*, *12*(1), 179–194. doi:10.1300/J136v12n01_09

Caswell, J., & Wynsta, J. D. (2010). Improving the search experience: federated search and the library gateway. *Library Hi Tech, 28*(3), 391–401. doi:10.1108/07378831011076648

Cervone, F. (2005). Usability testing on OpenURL resolvers and federated searching. *Computers in Libraries, 5*(25), 11–14.

Fagan, J. C. (2006). Usability testing of a large, multidisciplinary library database: Basic search and visual search. *Information Technology & Libraries, 25*(3), 140–150.

Fang, W., & Crawford, M. (2008). Measuring law library catalog web site usability: A web analytic approach. *Journal of Web Librarianship, 2*(2-3), 287–306. doi:10.1080/19322900802190894

George, C. A. (2008). Lessons learned: Usability testing a federated search product. *The Electronic Library, 26*(1), 5–20. doi:10.1108/02640470810851707

Munger, H. L. (2003). Testing the database of international rehabilitation research: Using rehabilitation researchers to determine the usability of a bibliographic database. *Journal of the Medical Library Association, 91*(4), 478–483.

Ochoa, M., Jesano, R., Nemmers, J. R., Newsom, C., O'Brien, M., & Victor, P. Jr. (2007). Testing the federated searching waters: A usability study of MetaLib. *Journal of Web Librarianship, 1*(3), 47–66. doi:10.1300/J502v01n03_04

Pu, H. (2010). User evaluation of textual results clustering for web search. *Online Information Review, 34*(6), 855–874. doi:10.1108/14684521011099379

Randall, S. (2006). Federated searching and usability testing: Building the perfect beast. *Serials Review, 32*(3), 181–182. doi:10.1016/j.serrev.2006.06.003

Warraich, N., Ameen, K., & Tahira, M. (2009). Usability study of a federated search product at Punjab University. *Library Hi Tech News, 26*(9), 14–15. doi:10.1108/07419050911010750

Wrubel, L., & Schmidt, K. (2007). Usability testing of a metasearch Interface: A case study. *College & Research Libraries, 68*(4), 292–311.

KEY TERMS AND DEFINITIONS

ARL: Association of Research Libraries. ARL supplies a survey tool for its member libraries to track user satisfaction with library services called LibQual.

Beta-Testing: Final testing before a product is released to the public.

Expert Review: A review by website usability experts intended to identify likely problems users will encounter without having to go to the expense of involving users in testing.

Facet: A component of the search which can be used to narrow the search.

Morae (Techsmith) Software: Software for web user experience testing that records conversation and screen activity.

Recall/Search Recall: The fraction of the total available documents that are relevant to the search and are successfully retrieved.

RFP/Request for Proposal: A set of requirements for a product or service submitted to vendors asking for proposals for products or services that will fulfill those requirements.

Search Success: The degree to which a search of a particular product is successful in terms of usefulness to the searcher.

Summon: A resource discovery tool made available through Serials Solutions.

Task Performance: A measure of how effective test participants were in performing the task assigned.

ENDNOTES

[1]   Summon is owned by ProQuest LLC.

[2]   LibQual is a registered trademark of Association of Research Libraries.

[3]   SirsiDynix is a registered trademark of SirsiDynix Corporations.

[4]   Symphony is a registered trademark of SirsiDynix Corporations.

[5]   SFX is a registered trademark of ExLibris Ltd.

[6]   WorldCat is a registered trademark of OCLC.

[7]   MetaLib is a registered trademark of Ex Libris Ltd.

[8]   Morae is a registered trademark of TechSmith Corporations.

[9]   TechSmith is a registered trademark of TechSmith Corporations.

APPENDIX A. TASKS & POST-INTERVIEW QUESTIONS (EXTERNAL CONSULTANT TESTING)

A. Tasks

Each participant brought a research assignment to the session which he or she was working on for a course. This was always the first task to be carried out.

Other tasks included:

1. Find a specific book and request it be delivered to a library near them or find data on a topic (e.g. how many MRI scanners are there in Canada?)
2. Find an article given the reference to the article
3. Finding research material on a specific topic
4. Determining when and where a tutorial on RefWorks was being offered
5. Recommend to the libraries that they purchase a specific book

The research tasks were tailored to the discipline of the participants.

B. Post-Interview Questions

1. Given your experiences today, could you tell me how easy or difficult to use you think the website we've been looking at is? I'll send the response scale to your chat window.
2. Based on the information you've seen today, what were the two things you like most about the website?
3. What were the two things you like least about the website?
4. Are there any other suggestions you would like to make which would help the UML website better support your needs?

APPENDIX B. BACKGROUND QUESTIONNAIRE FOR EXTERNAL CONSULTANT TESTING

A. Confirm:

1. 1st year undergrad, 2nd or 3rd year undergrad, post-graduate, faculty
2. Arts, Sciences, Medicine
3. Library website usage approximate: once a week, once a day, more than once a day
4. Can you tell me where you usually access the University of Manitoba Libraries website from?
   a. From a library computer
   b. From Residence
   c. From home
   d. From a laptop connected to the wireless network

e.   Other

5.   Could you tell me how easy or difficult to use you think the current UML website is?

a.   Very easy to use
b.   Easy to use
c.   Neither easy nor difficult to use
d.   Difficult to use
e.   Very difficult to use

APPENDIX C. TASKS & POST-INTERVIEW QUESTIONS (SUMMON™ TESTING)

A. Tasks

Each participant brought a research assignment to the session which he or she was working on for a course. Other tasks included:

1.   Find articles on Canada's role in the early part of the Cold War
2.   Find resources on midwifery in Canada
3.   Find an article on physical activity, health or wellness
4.   Find articles on microbiological research
5.   Find information on reunification of Germany
6.   Find journal articles on architecture of the Pantheon
7.   Find information on variations of the Ellesmere and Hengwert manuscripts
8.   Find peer-reviewed articles on aggression
9.   Find information on Pakistan and India and the Non-Proliferation Treaty

B. Post-Interview Questions

1.   Did you feel that your search was successful?
2.   What would make you more successful?
3.   What was the most valuable part of the search tool?
4.   Were you able to locate the right types of information?
5.   What was your general impression?
6.   Was there something you really liked?
7.   Was there something you really disliked?
8.   Is there anything else you'd like to tell me?

APPENDIX D. BACKGROUND QUESTIONNAIRE FOR SUMMON™ TESTING PARTICIPANTS

A. Please give us some information about you:

1. Your name
2. Your telephone number
3. Your email address

B. Please pick a course for which you have a research assignment due:

1. What is the area of study for the course?
2. What level is the course?
3. What is the assignment and the research required (give topic as provided by professor if possible)?
4. At what point in the research process are you?
5. When is your project due

Chapter 16
Fostering Discovery through Web Interface Design:
Perpetual Beta as the New Norm

Juliet Kerico
Southern Illinois University Edwardsville, USA

Paul Anthony
Southern Illinois University Edwardsville, USA

Chris Bulock
Southern Illinois University Edwardsville, USA

Lynn Fields
Southern Illinois University Edwardsville, USA

ABSTRACT

In 2009, the Library & Information Services (LIS) Web Task Force of Southern Illinois University Edwardsville (SIUE) was charged with improving its website in light of the increasing challenges presented by organizing, maintaining, and promoting its rapidly expanding selection of electronic resources. Due to budgetary constraints, a commercial tool for improving resource discovery was not an option. The Task Force chose to consider improved Web design as a solution to the problem. The resulting process of ongoing library Web site redesign, fueled by extensive user feedback at multiple stages, is discussed. In addition, the progression from a paper-based survey to an observation study of users is outlined and analyzed. Such activities inform the user experience and provide an opportunity to use improved design to reinforce principles of library instruction.

DOI: 10.4018/978-1-4666-1821-3.ch016

INTRODUCTION

New resource discovery tools continue to enter the market in an attempt to answer the call for more user-friendly and efficient searching capability. However, many smaller libraries are finding it difficult to afford the cost of these new commercial tools, and despite the best efforts of their developers, no one tool seems capable of perfectly meeting all the needs of a library or its users. Whether or not cutting-edge discovery software is purchased and utilized, consideration of user expectations in web design remains a key factor in ensuring user satisfaction and research success. This chapter focuses on the efforts of a newly formed Web Task Force within Library & Information Services (LIS) at Southern Illinois University Edwardsville (SIUE). This small group of library faculty and staff members, charged with assessing and redesigning the Library webpage, began what is now an ongoing process of library Web site redesign, fueled by user feedback at multiple stages. The process of survey development and administration that was used by the Web Task Force, as well as the progression from a paper-based survey to an observational study of users will be described. Additionally, the philosophy of "perpetual beta" in web design as an alternative to, or enhancement of, commercial Web-scale discovery tools will be discussed, with a focus on how this methodology presents low-cost opportunities for significant improvement of information-seeking behavior through periodic user observation and redesign.

BACKGROUND

Library & Information Services (LIS) of Southern Illinois University Edwardsville (SIUE) serves approximately 14,000 students. Undergraduate enrollment numbers about 11,300, while graduate and professional schools account for another 3,300 students. In 2010, the Library's Web site had 359,563 visits. LIS electronic resources recorded 571,544 full text downloads, and the link resolver recorded 150,918 click-throughs. Although the library currently has access to WorldCat®[1] Local Quick Start, a version of the service free to all institutions that subscribe to WorldCat® on First-Search, it offers the ability to search only OCLC databases, and users cannot connect directly to external full text. In addition, WorldCat® Local Quick Start provides no method for customizing holdings display, thus severely limiting the integrated resource discovery experience an institution is able to present to its users.

When an institution is unable to implement a commercial Web-scale discovery tool, it must rely on other methods for improving resource discovery, namely improved web design and user education. Whether serving patrons at the Research & Information Desk, through formal bibliographic instruction, or in the design of the library Web site, all libraries aim to adhere to a coherent philosophy of library instruction. The accepted current framework for academic library instruction, the *Information Literacy Competency Standards for Higher Education* developed by the Association of College and Research Libraries, also forms the basis of library instruction activities at LIS. The library's mission is accomplished by:

1) fostering information literacy skills; 2) supporting faculty by providing their students with research skills needed to successfully complete specific assignments and coursework; and 3) fostering campus productivity by making faculty and staff aware of information resources and providing information literacy sessions in the use of those resources. (Library Instruction & Information Literacy Program Web site, LIS, SIUE, http://siue.libguides.com/content.php?pid=132799&sid=1138682)

In addition to making improved resource discovery more affordable, the decision to embark upon a Web site redesign project involving user input is, in its most basic and classical sense, an extension of the above LIS goals regarding library instruction. In order to best educate and serve users, an online environment that facilitates learning by intuitively leading users to the appropriate discovery tools needs to be created. This important step in the information-seeking process, which is a necessary precursor to information fluency at all academic levels, must be met first at the level of design rather than relying on one tool to solve all resource discovery problems.

LITERATURE REVIEW

Library Web Sites and Resource Discovery

As academic library Web sites continue to add large amounts of information, such as catalogs, indexes, collection information, and electronic resources, in addition to the services they provide, it becomes increasingly important that information is arranged in a way that is meaningful for the user (Liu, 2004). McMullen points out that an important design principle that supports resource discovery is to make the content as easy to understand as possible with clear and consistent navigation (2001). Consistent navigation is a theme that runs through the literature. According to Croft, resource discovery is increased when a Web site is logically laid out, but not overwhelming. It's important that the site be sophisticated enough for the experienced user, but simple enough for the inexperienced user (2001). Emde, Morris, and Claasen-Wilson agree that ease of use is crucial, and add that clear navigational features such as font size, unambiguous links and understandable terminology greatly enhance the usability of the library Web site (2009). Paying close attention to the structural order of headings and consistent navigation also increases a Web site's usability. (Dougan, Fulton, 2009).

Usability Testing of Library Web Sites

Usability plays a greater role as library Web sites continue to gain importance in academic libraries. King and Jannik (2005) state "In many ways a library's Web site is the library. It used to be that library Web sites contained information about resources, not the resources themselves, but that's all changed" (p. 235).

A trend toward fewer patrons coming to the Research & Information Desk for help indicates that individuals are attempting to use library Web sites on their own. To quote Jakob Nielsen, an expert in web usability, "Usability rules the Web. Simply stated, if the customer can't find a product, then he or she will not buy it" (Nielsen, 2000, p. 9). This maxim also holds true for libraries. If users cannot find what they are looking for on library Web sites, they will turn to commercial search engines.

Krug outlined two types of website usability testing: "get it" and "key tasks". "Get it" testing shows users the site to see if they understand the purpose of the website, how it's organized, how it works, etc. "Key tasks" testing gives the user a task and then watches how well they do it (Krug, 2000, p. 153). The trend in library Web site usability tests seems to be toward "key tasks."

Library Web Site Redesign and Iterative Development

Abels, White and Hahn argue that in a "user-based design process" the library Web site is never finished because feedback and suggestions occur continually (Abels, White, and Hahn, 1999). Librarians at Hunter College involved in the Hunter Library Web Study found that "As user needs change, so must the site. Thus, it is a work in progress subject to ongoing reiterative testing and modification" (Cobus, Dent, and Ondrusek, 2005, p. 232). This was echoed by UCLA librarians engaged in usability testing for a web redesign, "Web site design is an ongoing process that requires continuous usability testing as the institution it represents and the information it provides evolve and change" (Turnbow, Kasianovitz, Snyder, Gilbert, and Yamamoto, 2005, p. 234). There is a substantial body of literature on library Web site redesign and library Web site usability studies, but little has been written on small-scale, iterative changes, the path chosen for this redesign process.

Even though libraries know that their Web sites may not be achieving the desired results, Aaron Schmidt advises against attempting a total redesign. He notes that some of the most successful commercial Web sites like Amazon, Google and Netflix have never done major redesigns, but have made gradual improvements. Web site redesign projects are costly, time consuming, and require maintaining the current site while working on the new site. Schmidt recommends concentrating on the existing site to make it as good as it can be (Schmidt, 2011).

WEB SITE REDESIGN

Making Sense of Many Choices

In 2009, the LIS Web Task Force was formed and charged with considering the future of its Web site in light of the increasing challenges presented by organizing, maintaining, and promoting the library's rapidly expanding selection of electronic resources. Like many academic and public libraries over the past decade, the library's electronic holdings have significantly increased, with the majority of patron traffic occurring online. This traffic, along with current advances in database interface searching capability, required the task force to re-think the library's approach to reaching users in a digital environment.

The task force began to understand what was previously noted by King and Jannik (2005) in that it could no longer be assumed that each patron

would contact the library directly for clarification and instruction on accessing online resources. Realizing instead that students might rely entirely on freely available search engines such as Google Scholar, the task force sought to improve users' resource discovery process through a more intuitive Web site design. The current generation of Web-scale discovery tools was (and remains) out of the library's reach due to budgetary constraints. Instead, the task force embarked on a substantial and ongoing Web site redesign to highlight and enhance existing resource discovery tools, enlisting users in the process. Due to the large undergraduate population, it was concluded that any reorganization of the webpage would need to be considered in terms of the beginning users' needs and expectations, rather than the preferences of advanced users.

The main LIS webpage that existed prior to this redesign contained many direct links to various tools, resources, and auxiliary services (See Figure 1). These resource-specific links were centered on the page and organized under five main categories: Find Articles, Find Books and More, Research Help, Library Services, and About Library & Information Services. In addition to this central section of the page, there were also a series of links available in columns on the right and left-hand sides of the page, many of which duplicated the central links. Based on the high number of navigational questions the library received in-person, and via email and chat reference, in addition to a growing number of suggestions submitted via an anonymous online form, it became clear that an increasing number of patrons were having difficulty finding the electronic resources they needed. While the existing method of organization allowed for easy access to resources for those users who were already familiar with the site and library research, it seemed to create confusion for many, particularly those who had limited knowledge of academic research practices, and this webpage specifically.

Figure 1. Lovejoy Library main webpage prior to assessment and redesign (© 2009, Southern Illinois University Edwardsville; used with permission)

With the needs of undergraduate users at the forefront of their minds, the task force began a project that approached Web site redesign from the bottom up, enlisting user input to determine what site design would best highlight and intuitively funnel users toward appropriate discovery tools such as LIS's local and universal catalogs, the e-journal list (SFX®²), and the general and subject-specific databases lists. The task force conducted four user studies of the library's Web site, with a redesign taking place between each study. The details of those studies are outlined in the following sections.

PAPER STUDY ONE

Methods

The task force developed a paper worksheet that simulated navigating the library Web site. This initial survey centered around seven navigational questions of varying complexity. Of those seven, two dealt with crucial discovery issues and were retained for all four studies:

1. Where would you click on this page to find *The American Journal of Legal History* online?
2. Where would you click on this page to find journal and magazine articles on a specific topic?

For task 1, participants were expected to select the link to the SFX® journal list, as it is the only comprehensive list of the library's online full text journals. For task 2, participants were expected to click on the "Databases by Subject" link, as the most efficient way of finding articles by topic. The worksheet also prompted participants to indicate how confident they were in their choice (not confident, somewhat confident, not sure, confident, or very confident).

Included in this survey packet were two additional questionnaires. The first asked respondents to indicate their institutional status (undergraduate, graduate, faculty, staff, or other) and levels of experience with the library and its Web site. Experience was determined by three questions:

Figure 2. Institutional status of participants

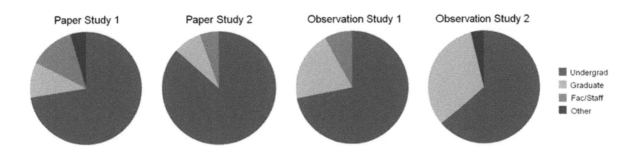

1. How do you rate your level of experience with using Lovejoy Library?
2. (not at all, somewhat experienced, not sure, experienced, or very experienced)
3. How do you rate your level of experience with using this library Web site?
4. (not at all, somewhat experienced, not sure, experienced, or very experienced)
5. Approximately how often do you use Lovejoy Library's services including walk-in visits to the library, use of the library Web site, telephone calls, chat reference, etc?
6. (less than once per month, 1-2 times per month, 3-5 times per month, 6-10 times per month, or more than 10 times per month)

The wrap-up questionnaire sought additional comments about ways to improve the site.

Participants were solicited at the Morris University Center and offered $5 gift certificates good at the university center. Participants were given verbal instructions for completing the form and either filled it out at the table with the experimenters or elsewhere in the university center.

Results

The study included 105 participants, the majority of which (79) were undergraduates (See Figure 2). The sample was rounded out by 11 graduate students, 14 faculty members and staff, and 5 participants who answered "other." These were typi-

cally alumni or visitors. Most of the participants were somewhat experienced (47) or experienced (33) with library use. Fewer reported they were very experienced (11), not at all experienced (9) or not sure (5). Library Web site experience levels were similar: 8 very experienced, 29 experienced, 42 somewhat experienced, 17 not at all, 9 not sure. Library visit frequency was fairly evenly distributed, ranging from 17 participants visiting less than once per month to 24 visiting 3-5 times per month.

For task 1, a minority (48) of participants selected the correct answer (See Figure 3). Others indicated they would try the alphabetical or subject lists of databases, or the catalog. Participants were slightly overconfident in their choices, with 57 confident or very confident, 28 somewhat or not confident, and 18 indicating they weren't sure of their confidence rating.

Participants fared somewhat better on task 2, selecting the appropriate answer in 62 cases (see Figure 4). Once again, participants were confident more often than they were correct, with 77 reporting they were confident or very confident, 17 somewhat confident or not confident, and 8 not sure.

The comments from the wrap-up questionnaire confirmed librarians' suspicions. One undergraduate stated, "It seems like the large amount of links on the front page may discourage casual users from using the Web site for trying to perform basic functions of library services," while an-

Figure 3. Correct and incorrect answers to task 1, "Where would you click on this page to find The American Journal of Legal History online?"

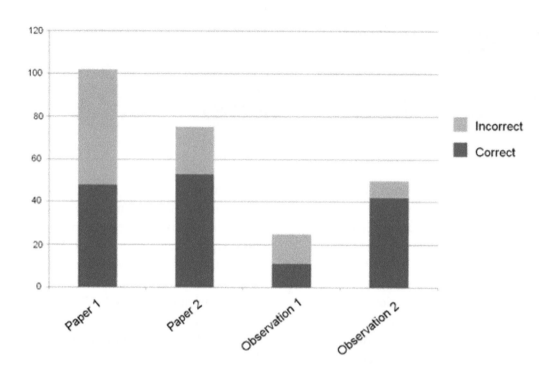

other said more succinctly, "Too many links." Other participants commented on the terminology used: "Not meaningful. Find better labels for sections."

Discussion

The data, along with many participants' comments, revealed a prevalence of confusion regarding the webpage, both in terms of its organization and use of library jargon. The findings mirrored those identified by Callicott (2002) who noted that "Rather than help a wide array of users find library resources that they needed, redundant links only serve to confuse users" (p. 13). Additionally, user feedback also helped support a rationale for designing what Callicott refers to as a "simpler and starker" interface (p. 14), leading to a more streamlined webpage for the library. As such, the

task force's first redesign goal became a focus on consistent, action-based natural language, organized by task and resource format rather than an extended listing of specific tools.

As a result, the central section of the webpage was reduced to three broad sections: Find, Help, and Services and About Us (See Figure 5). Under each of these sections were placed no more than four links of a directional nature, leading users to a secondary page with links to specific resource discovery tools by type. The left column of the page became reserved for quick links to high-use services, a widget enabling quick catalog searching, and a clear posting of the Library's address, main phone number, and operational hours. The right column links became the location for public relations items such as New Books, Featured Resources and Trials, Library News, and Suggestions. Additionally, the redesign utilized the space in

Figure 4. Correct and incorrect answers to task 2, "Where would you click on this page to find journal and magazine articles on a specific topic?"

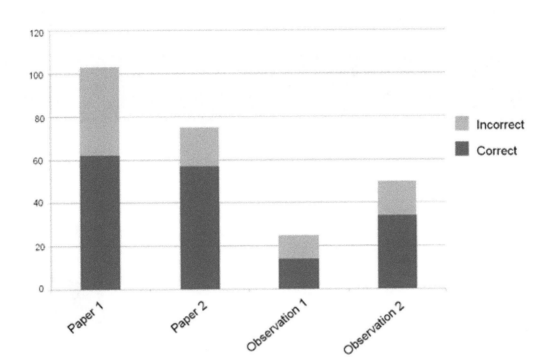

the lower right corner to highlight Digital Special Collections with a link featuring rotating images taken directly from those various collections.

Following this redesign, the web task force carried out a second study using a similar worksheet to determine whether the redesign met its goals. The web task force also sought to determine how the new design could be further fine-tuned to meet users' discovery needs.

PAPER SURVEY TWO

Methods

The survey instrument used for this study was identical to the first, except that the images of the previous webpage were replaced with current images. Task force members and other volunteers set up a table in the university center to solicit participants. Potential participants were told about the goals and procedures of the study and offered candy as compensation.

Due to the new Web site's organization, there were new correct answers for the two tasks. For both tasks on the new webpage, participants were expected to choose the "Find Journals, Magazines and More" link.

Results

The second study had 75 participants. Of those, 65 were undergraduates, 6 graduates, and 4 faculty or staff. Experience levels were similar to the previous study, with 7 very experienced, 22 experienced, 32 somewhat experienced, 8 not at all experienced, and 6 not sure. Library Web site experience followed the same pattern with 7

Figure 5. Redesigned Lovejoy Library main webpage (2010, Southern Illinois University Edwardsville; used with permission)

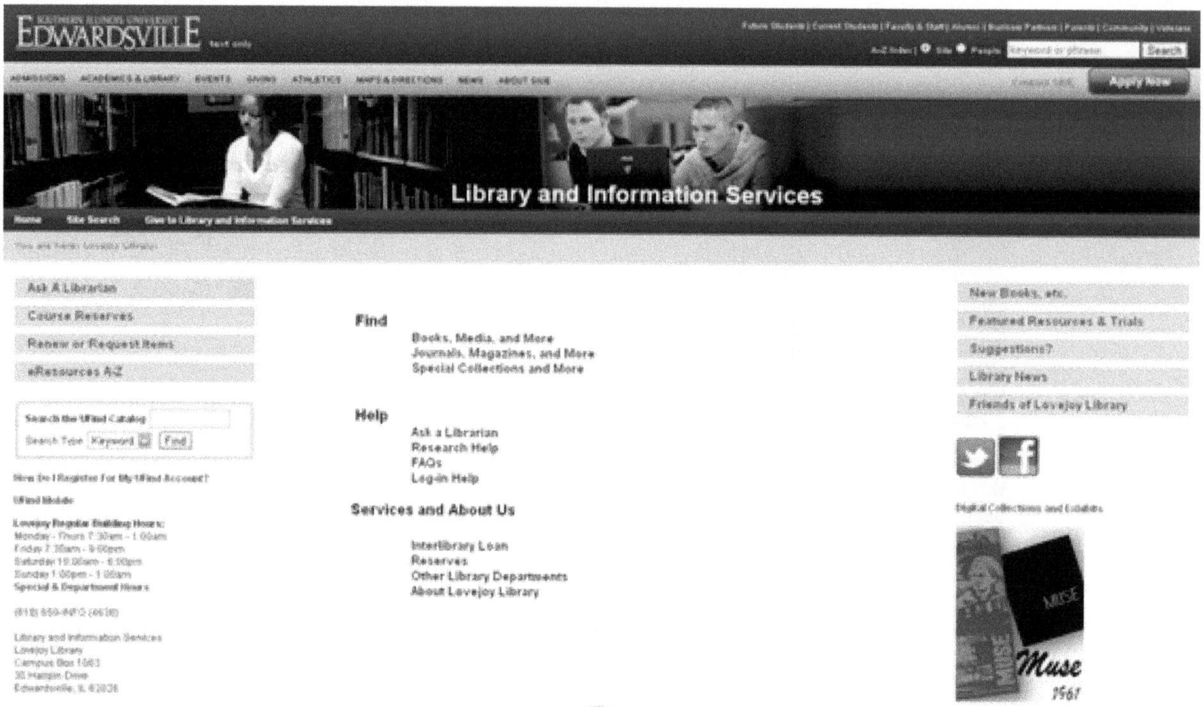

very experienced, 24 experienced, 35 somewhat experienced, 7 not at all experienced, and 2 not sure. Visit frequency was again fairly evenly distributed ranging from 11 participants visiting 6-10 times per month to 21 participants visiting 3-5 times monthly.

This time around, 53 participants selected the correct answer on task 1, while 22 selected other answers. Confidence levels were quite high, with 63 subjects confident or very confident, 5 somewhat or not confident, and 6 not sure.

Participants selected the correct link for task 2 in 57 cases, and were incorrect in 18. The participants were again quite confident, with 64 very confident or confident, 5 not sure, and 5 somewhat or not confident.

Comments in this survey confirmed the task force's design choices. One student said, "The division of links into concise sections (Find, Help, About Us) was helpful." Another expressed

gratitude for the change: "I like the new layout, thanks for your dedication." However, some participants indicated confusion regarding possible overlap between links, possibly stemming from unclear terminology.

Discussion

The results from this second study were encouraging. Participants were able to complete the discovery tasks correctly, and comments were generally more positive. However, the task force noted the need for more robust data to provide a clearer picture of the actual user experience with regard to the secondary pages. Because the library's main webpage had been simplified, the navigation of secondary pages had become more important to the discovery experience. Even if users linked successfully from the homepage, it was not clear if they would select the correct link on the secondary page, so the higher success rate this time around might have been artificial. Fichter and Wisniewski (2010) argue that "librarians need to care more about what people do than what they think,' and propose observational "task-based testing" as a key method for "discovering what people actually do" (p. 56).

To help fill in this gap in understanding of users' information-seeking behavior, and to fully study the effectiveness of the redesign, the task force set up an observational study that would provide richer data.

OBSERVATION STUDY ONE

Methods

The investigators recruited participants in the library, offering $5 gift cards to the university center. Participants were then directed to a library computer lab where they were given written copies of instructions that were also repeated verbally. Participants were asked to complete the same tasks as in the paper studies, but this time using the live Web site. Investigators observed participants as they completed the task, noting each link that was clicked and the time taken to complete the task. If participants felt they could not determine the answer, time was stopped at that point. Participants also completed the demographic and wrap-up surveys used previously. However, the demographic survey had two questions added asking whether they had received library instruction in either a class or a one-on-one setting.

Now that users were expected to move beyond the main webpage in completion of the discovery tasks, the criteria for success were a little different. While participants were still expected to click the "Find Journals, Magazines and More" link for each task, correct answers diverged from there. For task 1, participants were expected to choose the "By Title" link, which would take them to the library's e-journal list. For task 2, users were

expected to choose the "By Subject" link, which brings up a page directing users to database lists organized by subject.

Results

The investigators sought a smaller sample size for this new methodology, so recruitment was ended after 25 subjects had participated. Of those, 18 were undergraduates, 5 were graduates and 2 were faculty or staff. Most (13) were somewhat experienced using the library, with 2 very experienced, 6 experienced and 4 not at all. Library Web site experience was similar, with 2 very experienced, 6 experienced, 9 somewhat experienced, 5 not at all, and 3 not sure. The most common category for library visit frequency was 3-5 times per month, with 9 respondents. Four visited less than once per month, 4 visited 1-2 times per month, 2 visited 6-10 times per month, and 6 visited more than 10 times per month. Only 9 participants had received any kind of library instruction, and none had received one-on-one instruction.

As the investigators had anticipated, success rates in the observation study were lower than the paper study, due to confusion on secondary library web pages. On task 1, only 11 participants successfully completed the task, with 14 either unable to complete it, or choosing an incorrect link. The median number of links clicked was 4, and the median time taken to complete the task was 1 minute, 25 seconds. Results were only slightly better for task 2, with 14 participants successfully completing it. The median number of links clicked was 2, and the median time was 15 seconds.

Comments from the wrap-up survey were generally quite positive. However, several participants included qualifying statements indicating some hesitation. Several participants noted that the Web site would be very clear and easy to use once they had some more experience using it. Others noted that instruction would be helpful.

Figure 6. Secondary webpage menu for journals, magazines, and more (2010, Southern Illinois University Edwardsville; used with permission)

Discussion

The results of this study revealed that about half of all participants were unsuccessful in completing the discovery tasks, providing clear evidence that the new site design was not optimally serving users. While the homepage was now performing much better, it seemed necessary to modify the order of links and the language used on the secondary page for **Journals Magazines & More** (see Figure 6). The goal was to help clarify the difference between the journal list, the list of all e-resources (databases), and those e-resources (databases) organized by subject. Additionally, there was some concern that including a direct link to all **E-resources A to Z** in the left column on the main page was also confusing users.

After making those minor changes, a fourth iteration of testing was implemented in the form of an observation that focused on the two discovery tasks.

OBSERVATION STUDY TWO

Methods

Investigators once again set up in a library computer lab and solicited participants on the main floor of the library. The same demographic and wrap-up surveys previously used were given to all participants. They were asked to complete the two discovery tasks using the library Web site, while investigators timed and wrote notes regarding. To determine whether the eResources A to Z link on the main page was confusing users, participants were placed in one of two groups: one navigating the main webpage with the e-Resources A to Z link removed, and one where the link remained. Additionally, both groups navigated to the revised secondary page for Journals, Magazines & More. The decision to set up what Fichter and Weisniewski (2010) refer to as "A/B testing" helped establish a comparison point that tested for the users' comprehension of the more simplified language now employed, and the potential negative impact of having a redundant link placed directly on the main page (p. 58).

Results

The study included 50 participants, with 32 undergraduates, 16 graduates, and 2 other. Most (30) were somewhat experienced using the library, with 3 very experienced, 11 experienced, 2 not at all, and 3 not sure. Library Web site experience was similar, with 2 very experienced, 11 experienced, 18 somewhat experienced, 13 not at all, and 5 not sure. The most common category for library visit frequency was 1-2 times per month, with 14 respondents. Six visited less than once per month, 12 visited 3-5 times per month, 9 visited 6-10 times per month, and 8 visited more than 10 times per month. About a third (17) of participants had received group library instruction, and 5 had received one-on-one instruction.

Participants were much more successful with both tasks than in the previous observation study. On task 1, 42 selected the appropriate link, with a median of 3 steps in their process, taking 60 seconds. For task 2, 34 selected to correct link, with a median of 2 steps and 16.5 seconds taken to complete the task. The inclusion or exclusion of the eResources A to Z link did not appear to have an effect on performance. Only one participant clicked the link at all, indicating this did not distract users from discovery tasks.

Comments were again mostly positive. One participant described the site as "very easy to navigate." Some indicated that they still needed some time to get used to the new layout: "Once you know where everything is, it is easy." The most commonly expressed frustration was not with the library site at all, but with the university Web site's organization.

Discussion

Academic research is a complicated activity, particularly for students new to academic information seeking. Library users face many obstacles in the discovery process, particularly on the library Web site. Poor navigation, complicated web pages and unfamiliar vocabulary can present challenges to users, even at those libraries that do employ Web-scale discovery solutions.

Through these four studies, the investigators were able to greatly improve their understanding of users' interactions with the library Web site as well as users' experience with the site. The early studies indicated that users were often unable to successfully complete simple discovery tasks. Those that were able to find what they needed often took circuitous routes, or only learned the shortest path after months or years of experience. While the members of the web task force might have been able to engineer a better experience based on their own guesses, this injection of user input almost certainly improved the usability of the site.

User input did not just guide the initial redesign, but subsequent adjustments as well. Real life use is the best test of the library Web site's usability. Indeed, the results of the second observation study show that more improvements are still needed. Tasks as common as finding an online journal and looking for articles on a topic are still not entirely transparent. The task force will continue to make improvements and gauge their effect, trying to make discovery as quick and intuitive as possible.

FUTURE RESEARCH DIRECTIONS

At SIUE, the authors plan to continue redesigning and studying the usability of the library's Web site. Similar methods of usability testing could also be applied to specific discovery tools and other library web services (including link resolvers and catalogs).

Libraries implementing Web-scale discovery tools could use observation studies to refine the user experience and also to compare discovery with and without the new tool. Much has been promised with this new generation of products, and libraries must determine whether these tools are improving user success, and how Web site design can further support these improvements.

Another potential area for further study would be the appropriateness of tasks selected for usability testing. Alshamari and Mayhew (2009) discuss the merits of open-ended tasks compared to structured tasks. Because library Web sites and discovery tools serve diverse groups of users with many needs, developing appropriate tasks is not easy. Future studies could focus on the effect of different kinds of tasks and task wording on end results.

CONCLUSION

When applied to library Web site redesign projects, the philosophy of "perpetual beta" establishes a continuing, iterative process that is both informative and encouraging. The Task Force learned from the process that it is necessary to embrace a state of "perpetual beta" by regularly surveying and adjusting the design of the library's webpage to match user expectations for resource discovery. Originating first with software and system development, perpetual beta is becoming a necessary mindset for libraries seeking to keep up with rapid changes in resource discovery and information delivery. By surveying users, the authors found that efforts toward improved web design and resource discovery, paired with periodic assessment, worked in tandem to advance the goals of library instruction. This ongoing process supports the rapidly evolving process of establishing a more consistent, simplified vocabulary, and educating users regarding information fluency. Future research directions include applying similar usability testing methods to specific discovery tools or other library web services (including link resolvers and catalogs), as well as studying the appropriateness of tasks selected for usability testing.

The authors learned from this process that when it comes to users' navigational experience for resource discovery, it's important to regularly survey and adjust the design of the library's webpage to match user expectations for library Web sites and finding tools. Such activities enhance the user experience and provide an opportunity to used improved design to reinforce principle of library instruction. Without this input, librarians cannot adequately anticipate the needs of the beginning user, and instead, design pages that are more often geared toward the needs of the advanced user, or even those preferences of professional librarians and staff. Embracing a state of perpetual beta enables librarians to keep their assumptions and preferences in check, and to embrace change. Although this openness to regular review might challenge a traditional sense of completion, this research indicates that the increasing complexity of information needs and resources requires a progressive streamlining for simplicity in web design.

REFERENCES

Abels, E. G., White, M. D., & Hahn, K. (1999). A user-based design process for web sites. *OCLC Systems & Services, 15*(1), 35–44. doi:10.1108/10650759910257850

Alshamari, M., & Mayhew, P. (2009). Technical review: Current issues of usability testing. *IETE Technical Review, 26*(6), 402–406. doi:10.4103/0256-4602.57825

Callicott, B. (2002). Library website user testing. *College & Undergraduate Libraries, 9*(1), 1–17. doi:10.1300/J106v09n01_01

Cobus, L., Dent, V. F., & Ondrusek, A. (2005). How twenty-eight users helped redesign an academic library Web site: A usability study. *Reference and User Services Quarterly, 44*(3), 232–246.

Croft, J. B. (2001). Changing research patterns and implications for web page design: Ranganathan revisited. *College & Undergraduate Libraries, 8*(1), 75–84. doi:10.1300/J106v08n01_06

Dougan, K., & Fulton, C. (2009). Side by side: what a comparative usability study told us about a Web site redesign. *Journal of Web Librarianship, 3*(3), 217–237. doi:10.1080/19322900903113407

Emde, J., Morris, S., & Claassen-Wilson, M. (2009). Testing an academic library website for usability with faculty and graduate students. *Evidence Based Library and Information Practice, 4*(4), 24–36.

Fichter, D., & Wisniewski, J. (2010). Practical website improvement face-off. *Online, 34*(2), 55–57.

King, H. J., & Jannik, C. (2005). Redesigning for usability: Information architecture and usability testing for Georgia Tech library's website. *OCLC Systems & Services, 21*(3), 235–243. doi:10.1108/10650750510612425

Krug, S. (2000). *Don't make me think: A common sense approach to web usability*. Indianapolis, IN: New Riders Publishing.

Liu, H. (2004). Meeting user needs: A library website design. *Louisiana Libraries, 67*(1), 25-31.

McMullen, S. (2001). Usability testing in a library Web site redesign project. *RSR. Reference Services Review, 29*(1), 7–18. doi:10.1108/00907320110366732

Nielsen, J. (2000). *Designing web usability*. Indianapolis, IN: New Riders Publishing.

Schmidt, A. (2011). The user experience: resist that redesign. *Library Journal, 36*(4), 21.

Turnbow, D., Kasianovitz, K., Snyder, L., Gilbert, D., & Yamamoto, D. (2005). Usability testing for web redesign: A UCLA case study. *OCLC Systems & Services, 21*(3), 226–234. doi:10.1108/10650750510612416

ADDITIONAL READING

Battleson, B., Booth, A., & Weintrop, J. (2001). Usability testing of an academic library website: A case study. *Journal of Academic Librarianship, 27*(3), 188–198. doi:10.1016/S0099-1333(01)00180-X

Becker, D. (2011). Usability testing on a shoestring: Test-driving your website. *Online, 35*(3), 38–41.

Davidsen, S., & Yankee, E. (2004). *Web site design with the patron in mind: A step-by-step guide for libraries*. Chicago, IL: American Library Association.

Garlock, K. L., & Piontek, S. (1996). *Building the service-based library Web site: A step-by-step guide to design and options*. Chicago, IL: American Library Association.

George, C. A. (2005). Usability testing and design of a library website: An iterative approach. *OCLC Systems & Services, 21*(3), 167–180. doi:10.1108/10650750510612371

Holland, D. (2005). Practical experiences of using formal usability testing as a tool to support website redesign. *SCONUL Focus, 3*(6), 31–35.

Ipri, T., Yunkin, M., & Brown, J. M. (2009). Usability as a method for assessing discovery. *Information Technology and Libraries, 28*(4), 181–183.

Kaner, C., & Fieldler, R. (2005). Testing library Web sites for usability. *Knowledge Quest, 33*(3), 29–31.

Manzari, L., & Trinidad-Christensen, J. (2006). User-centered design of a Web site for library and information science students: Heuristic evaluation and usability testing. *Information Technology and Libraries*, *25*(3), 163–169.

Mariner, V. (2002). Logging usability. *NetConnect, Winter*, 30-31.

Norlin, E., & Winters, C. (2002). *Usability testing for library websites: A hands-on guide*. Chicago, IL: American Library Association.

Rogers, R., & Preston, H. (2009). Usability analysis for redesign of a Caribbean academic library Web site: A case study. *OCLC Systems & Services*, *25*(3), 200–211. doi:10.1108/10650750910982584

Shelstad, M. (2005). Content matters: Analysis of a website redesign. *OCLC Systems & Services*, *21*(3), 209–225. doi:10.1108/10650750510612407

Tolliver, R. L., Carter, D. S., Chapman, S. E., Edwards, P. M., Fisher, J. E., & Haines, A. L. (2005). Website redesign and testing with a usability consultant: lessons learned. *OCLC Systems & Services*, *21*(3), 156–166. doi:10.1108/10650750510612362

VandeCreek, L. M. (2005). Usability analysis of Northern Illinois University Libraries' website: A case study. *OCLC Systems & Services*, *21*(3), 181–192. doi:10.1108/10650750510612380

Ward, J. L. (2006). Web site redesign: The University of Washington Libraries' experience. *OCLC Systems & Services*, *22*(3), 207–216. doi:10.1108/10650750610686252

KEY TERMS AND DEFINITIONS

A/B Testing Protocol: A usability testing protocol in which investigators divide the subjects into two groups, each of which views a different version of the web page or site being tested. This method can be used to assess the impact of a change or alternative option.

Action-Based Natural Language: Language used for website links that indicates the action a user would like to initiate rather than a description of the tool or resource itself. Example: Find Books vs. Library Catalog

Click-Through: The number of times in a specified period that users click on a specified hyperlink. In the context of link resolvers, it is a count of the number of times users click links to full text articles, or other services such as ILL requests and catalog searches.

Intuitive web design: Attempting to design webpages based on the study of user tendencies, and in a manner that best anticipates the average user's expectations regarding where certain items will be located.

Perpetual Beta: The philosophy of continual revision and improvement as a necessary and integral part of improved interface design in digital environments. This concept recognizes that digital environments and interfaces are constantly in flux and, therefore, it is not possible for websites and software to be "perfected" prior to being made available for public use.

Observation Study: A method of collecting data regarding user navigational behavior by an organized, unobtrusive observation of certain navigational tasks in a live setting.

Usability: A term used to refer to the relative ease with which the average user can approach and navigate information within a digital environment.

ENDNOTES

[1]   Worldcat is a registered trademark of OCLC
[2]   SFX Link Resolver is a registered trademark of ExLibris

Chapter 17
Usability Testing Summon on the USC Libraries Home Page

Felicia Palsson
Sonoma State University, USA

ABSTRACT

This chapter describes the situational context and strategic goals at the University of Southern California (USC) Libraries that led to implementation of a discovery layer interface on the home page. User testing of the library website pointed to the need for unified and intuitive access to library holdings. Summon™ was introduced as a single access point, and usability testing was conducted on the website both pre- and post-Summon™ implementation. Results indicated that success rates for basic tasks improved after Summon™ became the default search box on the library home page. The objectives of the testing, methodology, demographics of test subjects, findings, and test instruments are described and shared.

INTRODUCTION

By the end of the first decade of the twenty-first century, user testing of academic library Websites was becoming common practice. At the Libraries of the University of Southern California, the Web developer and a few strong-willed librarians were part of the growing movement. The USC Libraries gathered together to conduct usability testing of their Website beginning in early 2008. The first

DOI: 10.4018/978-1-4666-1821-3.ch017

usability test spawned an agenda of redesign and iterative user testing. Happily, the multiple tests resulted in a much-improved Website, where research tools took priority on the home page, (over news, announcements, and other miscellany), and access to electronic journals was easier than ever before. This was made possible by the inclusion of a discovery layer interface. This chapter will outline the methods of usability testing and the process of decision-making that led to the Summon™ implementation.

BACKGROUND

Literature Review

Usability testing evolved as a subset of the field of Human-Computer Interaction. It gained traction in the late 1980s-early 1990s as a key element of product design focusing on the "work context in creating usable and functional products to improve productivity" (Dumas, 2007, p. 55). Following the growth of the World Wide Web, in 1999 one of the pre-eminent texts on Website usability, *Designing Web Usability*, was published by Jakob Nielsen, whose credentials are well documented (see his Website, useit.com). As Nielsen points out, "If a Website is difficult to use, people leave. If the homepage fails to clearly state what a company offers and what users can do on the site, people leave. If users get lost on a Website, they leave" (Nielsen, 2000, Why Usability is Important). Academic libraries were quick to adopt the practice of conducting usability tests on their Websites. Detailed case studies began to appear (see for example, Battleson et al., 2001; Cockrell & Jayne, 2002; Dickstein & Mills, 2000). Battleson et al. (2001), noted what is unique to usability testing a library Website: although it could potentially serve multiple functions, ranging from reference to materials renewal, "to ensure a user-centered approach, site functionality was defined in terms of what the *user* needed to do, rather than all of the possible tasks the site could support" (p. 190).

Libraries wanting to engage in usability testing faced several limitations. The typical library Web search may involve one or more systems, products and interfaces. VandeCreek (2005) noted that "the [usability] Committee was careful to include tasks that tested only Website content and structure that were within its control and could be modified in response" (p. 184). Within five years of the initial ramp-up of user-centric testing, libraries were beginning to find themselves in competition with Google and the phenomenon of its single search box. A large scale study by De Rosa et al. (2006)

revealed that only 2% of students used the library Website as a starting point for search. As well, 87% found Web search engines easier to use than the library. Sadeh (2007) concisely summarized the conditions necessitating major changes in library Web interfaces, specifically, changes in users' information seeking behavior and the search environments they are accustomed to. Summing up the problem, Sadeh writes, "One of the main challenges in offering any kind of scholarly search interface is to make it as familiar and intuitive as the one used by Web search engines and other internet tools but to guarantee that it yields better results" (p. 311).

After this point libraries began to examine the potential for discovery-layer interfaces, products that would streamline the user experience on their Website and provide access to the catalog as well as article indexes. Also known as "next-generation catalogs," these products began to gain popular standing around 2007; some early reviews were documented by Marshall Breeding in *Library Technology Reports*.

USC Libraries: Strategic Goals and the Need for Unified Access

The University of Southern California (USC) is a research-intensive, doctoral-granting university. During the period described in this chapter (2008-2010), the approximate number of full time enrolled undergraduates was 17,000 and the approximate number of graduate students was 18,000. USC's Graduate School offers about 300 graduate programs and seventeen professional schools. Accordingly, the university has a large and complex library system with a very diverse patron population that ranges from the traditional-age eighteen-year-old freshman to the middle-aged re-entry graduate student enrolled in an online program. The USC Libraries, as they are collectively known, comprise twenty-three libraries and information centers as well as the USC Digital Library. In the fall of 2008, the Dean of the Libraries implemented a strategic plan with directives in three categories: collections, public services, and technology-and-access. Committees were tasked with developing and delivering the improvements outlined in each area of the strategic plan. For the purposes of this chapter, the focus will be on two of the technology-and-access committees, for shorthand hereafter referred to as "T1" and "T2". The T1 committee was charged to "Create an intuitive, unified, electronic interface to library holdings" and the T2 committee was charged to "Improve accessibility and usability of e-resources in all languages and scripts."

As the underlying issues were identified, it became clear that the T1 charge had mostly to do with improving the Website architecture and T2 with the lack of Unicode functionality in the Libraries' ILS. The T2 committee addressed problems users encountered searching the library catalog in some foreign languages and non-Latin scripts (such as Chinese, Japanese and Korean – with a large East Asian Library this was a high priority). This group found a simple solution by upgrading the version of SirsiDynix®[1] ILS that was in place at that time, to provide Unicode functionality. That was simply a cost issue for the upgrade, and did not necessitate a move to an entirely new system.

Therefore the T1 goal presented the larger challenge. There were multiple search tools in place (as of early 2008), including the main library catalog, two additional catalogs (for the law and medical schools), the electronic resources management system (ERMS), a federated search tool on a dedicated e-resources Web page, and especially confusing to patrons, a legacy home-grown database of electronic holdings that was still being used to provide subject-based access to e-resources. The T1 goal of creating a unified interface was written largely in response to the results of an initial round of usability testing that had been done on the e-resources page in early 2008. Students were unable to locate information needed using the existing search tools, in particular, the federated search.

Comments by participants in the usability test of federated search were blunt and revealing. One aspect of the user experience with federated search was particularly enlightening: patrons strongly disliked the categorization of results according to database, rather than relevance. One user commented, "If I could turn off Engineering, I would." Another said she chose the first result with false expectations: "It was number one so I thought it would be the most relevant but I'm not sure what the order has to do with anything." Several participants felt the list of results was "way too long," "too numerous," or there was "too much to scroll through." Additionally, it was revealed that users desired customization features; search limiters were underutilized (because they were buried behind a link to advanced search); delays in the load time for results created impatience. All of these factors informed the process of redesigning the Website and choosing new search tools.

The first decision was to remove the separate, dedicated e-resources page (which was dedicated mostly to an ill-performing federated search). It was decided to re-design the Website so the home page would provide access to all the library holdings and allow users to search the catalog, the Digital Library, and e-resources from the front page. The second decision that needed to be made was whether to provide a single search box. The committee conducted an environmental scan of available discovery-layer products currently on the market. A list of desired features was compiled after interviewing various parties on campus on an informal basis, and used this preliminary list as an evaluative tool to compare discovery-layer products. The products reviewed in 2008 included well-known products from large entities, such as Innovative Interfaces' Encore and SirsiDynix's® Enterprise, as well as lesser-known or open-source alternatives such as VTLS'®[2] Virtualizer. At that time, the Summon™ product was not yet available. The USC Libraries were collectively dissatisfied with the options, concluding that the best tools were cost-prohibitive. The Libraries temporarily

Figure 1. Tabbed interface on the USC homepage without Summon™ tab

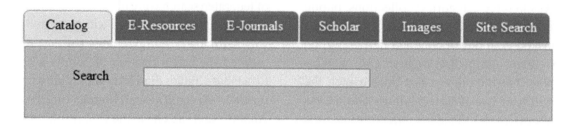

Figure 2. Tabbed interface on the USC homepage with Summon™ tab

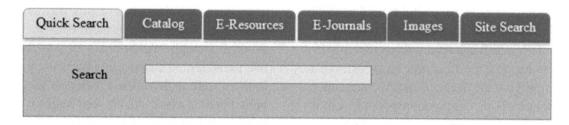

opted to achieve a unified interface by providing a tabbed search box on the home page. It took several months to complete the redesign, and by the time it was completed, Summon™ was available, which seemed like a perfect solution, pending user testing.

USABILITY TESTING BEFORE AND AFTER INCLUSION OF SUMMON™

Test Objectives

It's important to note that the Library was testing the usability of the home page. The objectives were designed to test core tasks that users wanted to be able to complete on the Website. It was not, strictly speaking, testing the interface of the Summon™ product, although many interesting things were learned. The Libraries were more interested in how successfully users completed tasks on the home page, and comparing their success "before" implementing Summon™ with "after." The Libraries wanted to know whether adding Summon™ as a

"Quick Search" as the default tab (open upon initial page load) would create problems for users and/ or what benefits it would provide to have it in the default position. In order to meet these objectives and compare user success rates on a version that included Summon™ to a version that did not, the existing page was tested and then a beta page was tested with "Quick Search" as the default tab. The beta page was live, and fully functional, but on a private URL (i.e. nothing linked to it), so it was not yet public, and only available in the testing room. Figures 1 and 2 depict the tabbed interface on the home page without and with Summon™, respectively (author's rendering).

The primary goal of user-centered design is to bring results to the user in as few clicks as possible, using the most convenient tools possible. For a general review of usability principles, The Libraries referred frequently to well-known authorities (see for instance Krug, 2006; Nielsen, 2000, March 19th; Nielsen, 2001; Rubin & Chisnell, 2008; Shneiderman, 2001). It was decided to use the scenario-based observation method. In this method, participants are given the opportunity to interact with a live Website, and asked to complete a series of tasks, mirroring as closely as possible a real-life scenario. The list of core tasks that users should be able to complete was as follows:

Users should be able (easily, quickly) to find:

- a book
- articles on a topic
- a (named) database
- a (named) e-journal
- the research guide for a named discipline

This task list was, with minor changes, the same one that had been in use for the past two years of user testing. (Note: At one point the visibility of links to the catalogs for medical and law schools was tested. For the actual instrument used in the Summon™ testing, see Appendix A.)

Methodology

The USC Libraries wanted to recruit approximately seven students for each round of usability testing. Their experience had proven that this was an adequate number. In usability testing, the difficulties that users encounter become obvious almost immediately. Also, Jakob Nielsen's research has shown that the probability of discovering new, unique problems on your Website decreases with increasing numbers of users. He states, "As you add more and more users, you learn less and less because you will keep seeing the same things again and again" (Why You Only Need to Test with Five Users, 2000). Another of the lessons learned from previous attempts at user testing was not to recruit from known groups. In 2008, participants were primarily recruited from a freshman writing course where there was plenty of interaction with students due to regularly scheduled library instruction sessions. That choice proved to be too narrow a demographic (and they were also familiar with library jargon, having received library instruction). In order to increase randomness further recruit-

ing using flyers on campus was employed and a feasible incentive was established (this hadn't been an option previously when recruiting from the freshman instruction sessions). Participants were offered a copy/print card in the amount of $10.00. It was assumed that this would be popular because of the extensive use of printers in the library. It was also an expenditure that, for the most part, would be returned to us. The goal was to recruit about ten students initially for each round, in the hopes that seven of the ten would be error-free. (Note: it is essential to recruit more people than you really need in terms of analyzing the results, partly due to the possibility of errors and partly the possibility of participants failing to appear, dropping out, or not completing the tests.) Then flyers advertising the usability test and the incentive were posted in various locations throughout campus, including the two main libraries' circulation desks, bulletin boards near large and/or popular classrooms, dining locations, and a few other highly-frequented venues.

Participants responded to the flyers by email and set up an appointment time. The test room was located in an empty office, in a quieter part of the library, and to prevent distraction the setup in the office included one Windows computer with a microphone, and nothing else. In a typical scenario-based observation test, the participant's clicks, mouse movements and interaction with the Website are observed, scored and when possible, recorded. We'd decided to use the Morae®[3] software by TechSmith®[4] so that participants could be observed and recorded remotely from another location. This method allowed participants much more freedom to "think aloud" while attempting to complete the tasks. Each participant was provided with an entrance interview and an instruction sheet (see Appendix B). When s/he arrived, the test administrator reviewed the instructions, encouraged the person to "think aloud" and not to hold anything back. This methodology was based in part by exemplary models of tests done at the libraries of North Carolina State University,

Table 1. Demographic data for usability test "after Summon™" (beta website)

	Q1: Class Level	Q2: Frequency of use (website)	Q3: Ever employed by a library?
Summon_user1	Undergraduate	A lot	No
Summon_user2	Undergraduate	Sometimes	No
Summon_user3	Graduate	A lot	No
Summon_user4	Graduate	Sometimes	No
Summon_user5	Graduate	Sometimes	No
Summon_user7*	Graduate	A lot	No

*User 7 was effectively User 6; due to error the data for User 6 had to be discarded.

University of Texas at Austin, and University of Washington (see complete references below). The test was completely anonymous, because the software did not record anything but the screen, mouse movements, clicks, and the recording of the user speaking aloud into the microphone. The test administrators demonstrated to each participant the guarantee of anonymity by pointing to the titled entry for his or her recording, designated "User 1" or "User 2," for example, and noted that the Webcam was disabled. It was also explained that although the participant was alone in the office, the test administrator would be sitting right outside the door in case anything was needed, or a computer error occurred. (See the Instruction Sheet, Appendix B.)

The participants completed the series of tasks without intervention, and with complete anonymity, and this resulted in a successful scenario for "thinking aloud." All but one of the students spoke out loud freely, providing helpful information that could be used to complement interpretation of the data. The software includes a built-in tool to direct the user from one task to the next. Meanwhile, it was possible to observe from another computer in the adjacent room, either during or subsequent to the actual student appointment.

Demographics

We inserted a short demographic survey at the very beginning of the test (see Appendix C). Predictably, faculty members were not recruited. In fact only students were recruited, though the possibility that staff or alumni might have responded to the flyer was taken into consideration. The first group of students, who took the "Before Summon™" test, was made up only of undergraduates. The second group of students, who took the "After Summon™" test, was made up mostly of graduate students (see Table 1). This represented one of the biggest challenges in interpreting the results. In an effort to broaden the participant demographic, the earlier practice of targeted recruitment was abandoned. However, attracting parallel demographics for the parallel usability test iterations was not accomplished (see more on this topic in the conclusions, below). Unfortunately, due to an error in data collection, a part of the survey data in the first round of testing that indicated frequency of use with the Website and knowledge of library operations was lost. This information was available only for the second round of participants.

Results and Analysis

Looking at the overall success rate (see Figure 3), participants performed much better with the new interface using Summon™, aka "Quick Search,"

Figure 3. Comparison of success distribution. Note: For each task, the first column is the "Before Summon™" test and the second column represents the test including Summon™ in the default tab position.

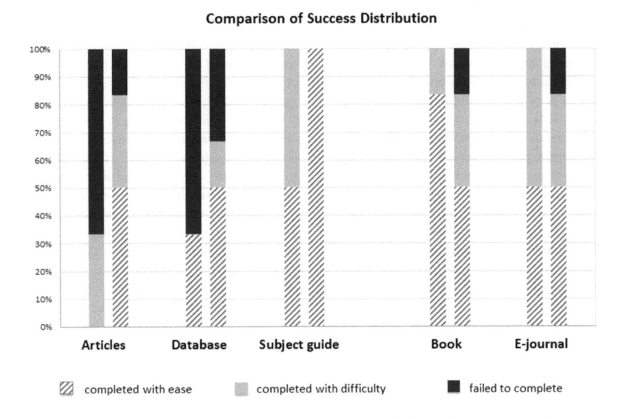

especially in the top "problem areas" of finding articles and finding a named database. Ironically, in finding a database, the e-resources tab was used more successfully. The same was true with finding an e-journal. This may be due to the sophistication of this particular group of participants. All participants showed advanced search skills and familiarity with the Website (see Table 1). Also, four out of six were graduate students. While this fact was taken into consideration, it was ultimately unclear to what degree their sophistication influenced the results, because in some areas they performed less successfully than the undergraduate group.

In finding articles, the overall success rate went from 34% to 83%. This was the biggest problem area when "Catalog" was the default tab (see Figures 1 and 2). Notably the inclusion of

"Quick Search" as a default made it much easier for users to locate articles just as quickly as they could locate books. Also, the 34% who succeeded before Summon™ did so with some difficulty. In finding a named database, the overall rate of success went from 34% to 67%. These were the biggest gains and these were the biggest problem areas in four previous usability tests over two years. Although the success rate in finding a book dropped a little, this was not a surprise given that the catalog had previously been the default tab.

In the first round of testing, all users tried to find articles in the catalog. Most users (five out of six) believed they could find articles in the catalog by clicking a radio button for "magazines, journals, and newspapers" (which was in fact a limiter intended for a periodical search in the catalog). Significantly, all participants used whatever search tab was open by default. It was observed that is not instinctive to users to scan through the whole screen and choose the best option before beginning search. This theme recurred across users, across questions. Whatever search tab was already open was the one they used. This had also been a consistent pattern in previous usability tests. Therefore it was a concern that, in implementing Summon™ as the default tab, users might experience greater difficulty in other areas, such as finding books or journals, which appeared to be easy using the catalog. In fact, only one user failed to locate a book in the Summon™ test. More significantly, only two out of six users in the Summon™ test actually limited themselves to the default tab. The others had no hesitations about exploring other tabs' search functions.

The other problem area was finding a named database. In the first round of testing, only two out of six participants were successful. Intriguingly, in the Summon™ test the success rate went up substantially. This was because more users were inclined to use the e-resources tab. The primary reason for difficulty with finding a database in the "Quick Search" iteration was that at that time, it was impossible to find a database using Summon™. Indeed, two users attempted to use facets to narrow by content type/database. One user commented, while scrolling through the "content type" options, "What are we looking for... we're looking for a *database*..." After she didn't find it listed as a content type, she said to herself, "This is wrong. Let's go back." (Note: Since the time this testing occurred, Summon™ has implemented a database recommendation tool that probably would have an impact on the usability with regard to locating a named database).

We were curious to analyze what problems occurred, in the cases where users had difficulty or failed to complete a task. One common problem was that a user would misspell a word and the systems did not have any kind of correction. In the case of the Library ERMS, participants would often encounter a blank screen, rather than suggestions such as "Did you mean?" or "Were you searching for...." Summon™ handled these kinds of issues much more effectively, offering suggestions for almost all the misspellings that were attempted (or witnessed). For an example of an analysis completed for each task in the task list, see Table 2, which discusses e-journals.

Another point of interest, in comparing the results before and after inclusion of Summon™ on the home page, was the use of facets. The USC Libraries were very interested in learning how faceted search results improved the user experience. Several participants commented on them, indicating generally that they liked having the facets, and that this made searching easier. One participant asked, "Why didn't you guys have this on the Website before?" (referring to the facets, specifically). Three out of the six participants used the facets specifically to achieve success in the designated tasks.

CONCLUSIONS ABOUT SUMMON™

The Summon™ product aligned nicely with the USC Libraries goals. In addition to supporting Unicode and working with the existing ILS, it also provided aggregated as opposed to federated search functionality. The use of an underlying index was significant to us, given the problems with federated search. The load time was much faster, and relevance ranking was crucial to meeting users' concerns. Faceted search results, as discussed, were a vast improvement and user comments indicated an overwhelmingly positive response. In addition to usability concerns, it was discovered that there were other benefits to choosing Summon™. For instance, The Libraries were able to implement Summon™ right "out of the box," with minimal customization needed. Also, Summon™ worked well with the mobile version of the Website. Most important, however, user testing indicated that the interface was less

Table 2. Methods of locating a named e-journal

Before Summon™	With Summon™
How did they find it? • E-resources/E-journals: 3 • Catalog: 2 • Site search: 1	How did they find it? • E-journals: 4 • Catalog: 1 • One never found it, though she came close, but could not read the E-journals page
Why did 3 out of 6 have difficulty? • Misspelling/typos (E-journals portal has no *"did you mean?"* feature) • System errors (e.g. Biography database not linked to individual journals)	Why did 3 out of 6 have difficulty? • Misspelling/typos (E-journals portal has no *"did you mean?"* feature) • System errors (e.g. One database does not work well with our link resolver – cookies error) • Inability to read the E-journals portal page (journal is there, but user does not see it) • Inability to interpret results in Summon interface

confusing, more intuitive, and provided the ability to use limiters up front to make finding relevant results extremely efficient.

Unfortunately, the reception by library faculty and staff was not immediately positive. Once user testing was complete and the home page was ready for launch, the Libraries began a program to train faculty and staff throughout the USC Libraries. One of the greatest difficulties of implementation was not technical, but a communication issue. The Libraries learned that, generally speaking, internal users were more attached to the catalog than external users. The goal of a unified access point to library holdings had been achieved. However, the idea of an aggregated search based on an underlying index of holdings was not altogether clear to many people. Librarians wanted to know "where the search results are coming from," an oft-repeated question that was not entirely easy to answer, given that it's not possible to provide a list of exactly which holdings were in the Summon™ index and which were not. It was not possible to claim that 100% were indexed, due to obstacles with mapping and metadata. It was estimated that

it was about 75% of holdings (at that time). When asked "which ones make up the 75%" or "which resources are missing" it was only possible to reiterate that Summon™ functions via aggregation and uses its own index. This created a great deal of confusion. In order to address many of the recurring questions, an FAQ document was created that was posted in various places on the Website and distributed during trainings. For an excerpt of this document, see Appendix D.

FUTURE RESEARCH DIRECTIONS

The Summon™ product has been tested and developed in accordance with usability principles. The USC Libraries local tests proved that it was a success with users. However, the usability testing process began in 2008 and it was apparent from the start that patrons did not understand many aspects of the library Website, beyond those encountered in a flawed federated search product. The USC Libraries faced challenges in the effort to consolidate access and streamline search tools.

It took a few years to accomplish the task, a strategic planning process, various committees and projects including a major Website redesign, and then, even after an appropriate search tool was implemented in response to users' needs, there was still resistance from librarians and library staff.

Further research must be done on the overall design of library Websites, including the use of tabbed pages. This was an area of testing that could have been explored with additional user interviews. Also, there remains the question of multiple search tools. The necessity for tabs arises from the variety of tools and electronic resources. There is an area as yet largely unexplored: what are librarians' real attitudes about multiple search tools? Does library instruction in a variety of databases take the user experience into account? Much has been written about the feeling by librarians that they are in competition with Google, and that students need to be compelled to use a myriad of other search tools with more sophisticated features. While there are benefits to library search tools, the primary challenge faced is integrating these multiple access points on a single library Website. It is unclear from the USC Libraries results whether the tabbed interface helped to resolve this conflict, since usage of the tabs was not a primary point of attention.

There is also room for research on recruitment methods, and in particular what constitutes an "ideal" demographic in usability testing. WHielt he USC Libraries attempted to run parallel tests based on a highly randomized recruitment method, the results indicated that the pre-Summon™ test demographic was undergraduate while the post-Summon™ test demographic was predominantly graduates. Was this affected by the timing of recruitment, or was this coincidental? More importantly, to what extent did it impact the results? As stated above, the graduates showed sophistication in some tasks, but not consistently. Because of the lack of an apparent consistent performance, the Libraries were inclined to conclude that the age or class level of the student participants did not impact the results. However, an entire study could be performed on this topic alone.

Finally, it is an open question how graduate programs in library science and professional library educators are integrating the concepts of usability, user experience, and user-centered design into the curriculum.

REFERENCES

Battleson, B., Booth, A., & Weintrop, J. (2001). Usability testing of an academic library website: A case study. *Journal of Academic Librarianship*, *27*(3), 188–198. doi:10.1016/S0099-1333(01)00180-X

Cockrell, B., & Jayne, E. A. (2002). How do I find an article? Insights from a web usability study. *Journal of Academic Librarianship*, *28*(3), 122–132. doi:10.1016/S0099-1333(02)00279-3

De Rosa, C., Cantrell, J., Hawk, J., & Wilson, A. (2006). *College students' perceptions of libraries and information resources: A report to the OCLC membership*. Retrieved from http://www.oclc.org/reports/perceptionscollege.htm

Dickstein, R., & Mills, V. A. (2000). Usability testing at the University of Arizona library: How to let the users in on the design. *Information Technology and Libraries*, *19*(3), 144–151.

Dumas, J. (2007). The great leap forward: The birth of the usability profession (1988-1993). *Journal of Usability Studies*, *2*(2), 54–60.

Krug, S. (2006). *Don't make me think: A common sense approach to web usability*. Berkeley, CA: New Riders.

Nielsen, J. (2000). *Designing web usability*. Indianapolis, IN: New Riders.

Nielsen, J. (2000, March 19). *Why you only need to test with five users*. Retrieved from http://www.useit.com/alertbox/20000319.html

Nielsen, J. (2001). *Usability metrics*. Retrieved from http://www.useit.com/alertbox/20010121.html

North Carolina State University. (2011). *User studies at NCSU libraries*. Retrieved from http://www.lib.ncsu.edu/userstudies/

Rubin, J., & Chisnell, D. (2008). *Handbook of usability testing: How to plan, design, and conduct effective tests*. Indianapolis, IN: Wiley.

Sadeh, T. (2007). Time for a change: New approaches for a new generation of library users. *New Library World, 108*(7/8), 307–316. doi:10.1108/03074800710763608

Shneiderman, B. (2011). *Research-based web design and usability guidelines*. Retrieved from http://www.usability.gov/guidelines/guidelines_book.pdf

University of Texas at Austin. (2009). *Develop the usability test documents*. Retrieved from http://www.utexas.edu/learn/usability/test.html

University of Washington. (2011). *Guide to planning and conducting usability tests*. Retrieved from http://www.lib.washington.edu/usability/resources/guides/tests

VandeCreek, L. M. (2005). Usability analysis of Northern Illinois' University libraries' website: A case study. *OCLC Systems & Services, 21*(3), 181–192. doi:10.1108/10650750510612380

ADDITIONAL READING

Campbell, N., & Library and Information Technology Association. (2001). *Usability assessment of library-related websites: Methods and case studies*. Chicago, IL: Library and Information Technology Association.

Cervone, F. (2005). What we've learned from doing usability testing on OpenURL resolvers and federated search engines. *Computers in Libraries, 25*(9), 10–14.

Chen, Y., Germain, C. A., & Yang, H. (2009). An exploration into the practices of library web usability in ARL academic libraries. *Journal of the American Society for Information Science and Technology, 60*(5), 953–968. doi:10.1002/asi.21032

Dixon, L., Duncan, C., Fagan, J. C., Mandernach, M., & Warlick, S. E. (2010). Finding articles and journals via Google Scholar, journal portals, and link resolvers: Usability study results. *Reference and User Services Quarterly, 50*(2), 170–181.

Dougherty, W. (2009). Integrated library systems: Where are they going? Where are we going? *Journal of Academic Librarianship, 35*(5), 482–485. doi:10.1016/j.acalib.2009.06.007

Dumas, J., & Loring, B. (2008). *Moderating usability tests: Principles and practice for interacting*. Amsterdam, The Netherlands: Morgan Kaufmann/Elsevier.

Fagan, J. C. (2010). Usability studies of faceted browsing: A literature review. *Information Technology and Libraries, 29*(2), 58–66.

Hertzum, M., & Clemmensen, T. (2012). How do usability professionals construe usability? *International Journal of Human-Computer Studies, 70*(1), 26–42. doi:10.1016/j.ijhcs.2011.08.001

Hom, J. (1998). *The usability methods toolbox*. Retrieved from http://usability.jameshom.com/

Jaworski, S., & Sullivan, R. (2011). Google's evolution leads to library revolution. *Journal of Educational Technology Systems, 39*(2), 107–118. doi:10.2190/ET.39.2.b

Kupersmith, J. (2011). *Library terms that users understand*. Retrieved from http://www.jkup.net/terms.html

Lehman, T., & Nikkel, T. (2008). *Making library Websites usable: A LITA guide*. New York, NY: Neal-Schuman Publishers.

Nichols, J., Bobal, A., & McEvoy, S. (2009). Using a permanent usability team to advance user-centered design in libraries. *Electronic Journal of Academic and Special Librarianship, 10*(2). Retrieved from http://southernlibrarianship.icaap. org/content/v10n02/nichols_j01.html

Norlin, E., & Winters, C. (2002). *Usability testing for library websites: A hands-on guide*. Chicago, IL: American Library Association.

Nuschke, P. (2008). *Quick turnaround usability testing* [Blog post]. Retrieved from http://www. boxesandarrows.com/view/quick-turnaround

Sadeh, T. (2008). User experience in the library: A case study. *New Library World, 109*(1), 7–24. doi:10.1108/03074800810845976

Society for Technical Communication. (n.d.). *Usability toolkit*. Retrieved from http://www.stcsig. org/usability/resources/toolkit/toolkit.html

Spivey, M. A. (2000). The vocabulary of library home pages: An influence on diverse and remote end-users. *Information Technology and Libraries, 19*(3), 151–156.

Ward, J. L., Shadle, S., & Mofield, P. (2008). User experience, feedback, and testing. *Library Technology Reports, 44*(6), 17–23.

Wrubel, L., & Schmidt, K. (2007). Usability testing of a metasearch interface: A case study. *College & Research Libraries, 68*(4), 292–311.

KEY TERMS AND DEFINITIONS

Aggregated Search: The search query is performed on a pre-existing index of compiled (aggregated) resources. The time it takes to load and display the results is faster because the possible results have been aggregated ahead of the search being performed. (Summon™ works this way, and so does Google.)

Federated Search: The search query is performed in multiple databases at the time the user sends the command. The time it takes to load and display the results depends upon the speed of retrieval from the various databases that are being searched.

Scenario-Based Observation (also known as Task-Based): A type of usability test where the participant is observed while attempting to complete specific tasks. It attempts to mimic as closely as possible a real-life scenario the user might find herself in (such as, trying to locate a book on the library Website). Instructions are presented in natural language.

Unicode: An international standard for metadata that is inclusive of all languages and scripts.

Usability: The quality of being easy to use.

Usability Test: An inquiry to determine the usability of a Website or piece of software. There are many different methods and kinds of usability tests.

User Experience (often shortened to UX): A speciality area within graphical or Web design, similar to the field of human-computer interaction (HCI), that asks questions about the human experience with software, equipment, or Website. Usability is one core value of UX design.

ENDNOTES

[1] SirsiDynix is a registered trademark of SirsiDynix Corporation.

[2] VTLS is a registered trademark of VTLS, Inc.

[3] Morae is a registered trademark of Techsmith Corporation.

[4] Techsmith is a registered trademark of Techsmith Corporation.

APPENDIX A

Final Usability Test Instrument for Summon™ on the Home Page

1. Please find a book about the Iraq war. Tell us any thoughts that come to your mind while you are looking. Make sure you can find the library location and call number for the book.
2. Imagine . . . your professor says you need to "find 3 articles on childhood obesity written in the last year." What steps would you take? Please try to find at least one relevant article now, and talk about your steps as you go.
3. Find the database called "America: History & Life." Again, talk about your steps as you do the search.
4. You want to read the American Economic Review online. Show us how you would do it.
5. Find the subject guide for Engineering. Please tell us any thoughts that come to your mind while you are looking.
6. Find Helix, the Health Sciences Library Catalog. Use Helix to search for information on childhood obesity.

APPENDIX B

Participant Instruction Sheet

Welcome to the USC Libraries Website usability study!
   Things to remember:

1. This is not a test of your abilities! We're testing out the Website, to see if it works. If it doesn't, that's something we need to know. There are no right or wrong answers.
2. Take your time. Read the instructions carefully and do your best. You will have approximately one hour to complete this usability test.
3. If you've tried and you still can't complete one of the questions, that's OK. You should spend no more than five minutes on each question. After that, it's time to move on.
4. Please read the questions out loud. We ask you to "think out loud" while you're using the Website. Reading the question to yourself is a good way to get comfortable thinking out loud. It may feel unnatural at first, but you'll get used to it. Your reactions to how the Website works (or doesn't!) will be the most helpful part of the whole study.
5. Thank you! We appreciate your help. When you have completed the 6 questions and answered the closing survey, we'll give you a $10.00 copy/print card.

   IMPORTANT! Please start each new task by clicking the Home icon in the browser.

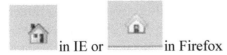 in IE or ——— in Firefox

APPENDIX C

Demographic Survey Instrument for Summon™ on the Home Page

1. Which of the following best describes you?
   a. USC graduate
   b. USC undergraduate
   c. USC faculty
   d. USC staff
   e. USC alumnus
2. Before today, how often have you used the library Website?
   a. Never
   b. Sometimes
   c. I use the Website a lot
3. Have you ever worked as a library employee?
   a. Yes
   b. No

APPENDIX D

Excerpt of Document Created for Training Purposes at USC Libraries

Summon™ (Quick Search) FAQ

SECTION ONE (Copied from Summon™ Website FAQs)

Where do the records in Summon™ come from? We cannot report on where citations come from because of our de-duplication system. When duplicate records occur, we combine them together into a Summon™ record and lose the origination details. The only way to determine where the content comes from is from your link resolver. It will tell you which providers (to which your institution subscribes) provide the article or citation in question. Also, keep in mind that we may have acquired the content from a different source than where you subscribe to for access to the content.

Are there any stop words in Summon™ and, if so, can we get a list of them? We don't use a stop-word list in the traditional sense, which is a list of words that are dropped from the index and not used for searching. We index *all* words in Summon™, even "the." For example, if you do a search for "the office" (without the quotation marks), Summon™ finds appropriate documents, not just passing references to the term "office."

What is included in your index and what is searched? Does this depend on publisher? We gather metadata for article-level information from multiple sources, including full-text sources and abstracting and indexing (A&I) sources. If we have multiple sources of information for a single article, we de-duplicate the information and create a single record that included subject headings, abstracts, citation information, unique identifiers, full-text, etc. Whatever we have for that article -- from any source -- is all indexed and searchable.

What is provided by full-text publishers versus those that include A&I services? A&I services provide specialized information that full-text publishers don't provide. We take advantage of both types of information in the Summon™ index. Publishers and A&I companies do not necessarily provide standard sets of data. So, it can really depend on the company/service. We take information from any source that will provide table of contents, subject headings, full text, etc.:

- Table-of-contents information comes primarily from publishers, but some might come from A&I or other sources.
- Subject headings can come from any source: A&I, full-text providers, etc.
- Full text comes from full-text providers, including Open Access databases.

Our list of both A&I and full-text providers is quite substantial. Because article information comes from multiple sources, which we de-duplicate, we find it more useful to provide lists of full-text eJournals covered in Summon™, and we can do a coverage analysis of a library's collection. We have had enthusiastic participation from providers of all types.

SECTION TWO (Local USC Libraries FAQ)

How does the relevancy ranking work? We don't know the exact formula. To help illustrate how it works, and build our collective understanding, we will list examples of relevancy-related questions in this section of the FAQ document.

Relevancy Question & Answer Example 1. Why doesn't "sound and the fury" bring up William Faulkner's work first? It's about the frequency of the words both together and separately in the text that's indexed by the search engine. In this case it is doing a straight phrase search. If you search "sound and the fury" in any system, except the Faulkner archives, it's possible you may not get the book. It's a phrase that's used in many contexts and often quoted. Originally it came from Shakespeare, "out out brief candle, life's but a walking shadow....It is a tale told by an idiot full of sound and fury, signifying nothing."

Why can't we know which 25% of our e-resources are excluded if we know that 75% are included (approximately)? This is only an estimate. What we can do is take their list of what they've got indexed and compare it with what we've got.

How should we explain in instruction classes what is included and what is not? For instruction classes we can say: It contains over 1/2 billion citations most of which have content available online. It's good for finding current information to which the library subscribes as well as other online scholarly information. It's not as good at finding highly specialized content, content available in print only and historical information.

How is the subject term list created? The subject terms that come up on the left side of the screen are coming from all USC resources searched. The subject terms are the terms that appear in those bibliographic records (depending on how they're indexed). They may include keyword field results and not only controlled vocabulary.

How does the language refinement work? Why when I limit to Armenian do I also get English language materials? It will bring back Armenian-language-only results if you go to "more options" and ALSO EXCLUDE English. Otherwise Summon™ retrieves all English translations. Look at the list in both Summon™ and Homer. Some of the works are important historical Armenian texts in a book with critical discussions in English about those texts, or with English translations in the document. If you did this in the classics, then Latin and Greek works with English translations wouldn't appear, nor would critical works in English that contain the Greek and Latin texts.

Also, the use of the language filter and expectations will be different for people in different fields. Examples: "I can read science articles in English or Spanish or French or Russian"; "I only want Italian translations of Macbeth"; "I was looking for Don Quixote in Spanish and was happy to find that it came with an English translation and commentary."

For languages, the facets broaden the search and act like "OR" if you select something other than "ANY". It's English OR French when they are both selected. It's easy to exclude English (or any other language and by extension multilingual works) after selecting a language.

Section 5
Implementation

Kristine R. Brancolini
Loyola Marymount University, USA

OVERVIEW

Once a library selects a discovery platform, the librarians and other staff turn their attention to implementation of the discovery service. The authors of the "Implementation" section approach their topics from different perspectives, but many common themes emerge related to the organizational, technical, and cultural challenges associated with implementation. In addition to implementation, these authors address marketing, assessment, and the impact of discovery services on the work of librarians. Advance planning is essential to implementation, but no guarantee that unforeseen obstacles will not arise. Each of these authors builds upon the experiences of other librarians while analyzing their own experiences, urging us to focus on the factors we can control, while we prepare as best we can for the unexpected. Discovery services are new but share many characteristics with previous technology implementations. In many ways, it's business as usual for academic libraries. These authors help smooth the way for their colleagues just embarking upon the adventure of discovery service implementation.

Andrew Welch describes the implementation of EBSCO Discovery Service (EDS) at Drake University's Cowle Library in the summer of 2010. He notes that resource and content provider issues persist and must be addressed during implementation. Ironically, one of the most challenging problems relates to the resources that have been excluded from the discovery services; Welch offers suggestions for promoting these resources, along with the newly-implemented discovery service. He also highlights concerns related to display and interface choices, emphasizing usability over cosmetic customization. Drake University's made a conscious decision to address the needs of "power users" within the discovery service, rather than assuming that they would be served best by accessing resources directly.

Amy Jackson *et al.* from the University New Mexico University Libraries, describe their experiences creating a Content Management System by implementing a commercial federated search for licensed content in conjunction with an open-source Drupal-based federated search for bibliographic data and digital content. The University of New Mexico used Drupal to gather records and digital content from all major libraries and special collections across the state to create a centennial portal, *Celebrating New Mexico Statehood (CNMS,* with interesting results.

Nina Exner *et al.* describe the transition from federated search to discovery service at North Carolina Agricultural and Technical State University. Contrary to some libraries that engaged in a lengthy period of evaluation and review, librarians at the F.D. Bluford Library found themselves pressured to make a quick decision regarding the identification of an appropriate discovery service and the rapid implementation of the new tool due to university holiday scheduling and budget availability.

David Dahl and Patricia MacDonald explore the complexities of implementing a discovery service in a consortial environment. The University of Maryland and Affiliated Institutions (USMAI) implemented WorldCat Local in 2009, encountering resistance on the part of librarians. Their chapter reports the results of a study they conducted, using a survey and interviews, to uncover the sources of this resistance, as well as broader librarian concerns regarding implementation and use of a discovery service. The authors use their results to make recommendations on planning an effective discovery service implementation.

Scott Garrison *et al.* advocate the embedding of discovery services within a user's academic context in order to maximize the probability that users and find and use our new tool. In addition to careful placement on the library's Web site, the authors argue for embedding the discovery service in campus systems, such as the enterprise portal and the learning management system. They offer concrete practical advice on the organizational and technical challenges related to embedding. However, the authors also note the difficulty of evaluating the effectiveness embedding and pose useful questions for further investigation.

Mark Christel *et al.* offer another look at implementation in a consortial environment, The Five Colleges of Ohio (Ohio5), comprised of liberal arts colleges. Their experience highlights the challenges related to implementing a discovery services, in this case Serials Solutions' Summon, across multiples institutions, given that not all share an OPAC or license the same resources. The authors offer a candid assessment of the organizational and technical obstacles that Ohio5 faced, emphasizing the need for clear objectives and flexibility.

Meris A. Mandernach and Jody Condit Fagan address internal library attitudes and the critical organizational issue of buy-in with regard to successfully implementing a discovery service. The authors identify and explore three important areas for buy-in: the anticipated impact of the discovery service on key library departments, training for library staff and users, and monitoring and assessing performance and impact. They emphasize the importance of clearly written goals and measurable objectives.

Mary Mintz from American University focuses on marketing their library's new discovery service and provides valuable feedback from users regarding their experiences. The marketing plan for their Summon implementation in August 2010 featured three components: branding; Web publicity; and viral marketing, including a coffee sleeve placed on the coffee cups in a popular campus café. Mintz offers a series of recommendation on marketing a new discovery service. She emphasizes that marketing the service and assessing its effectiveness should be considered separately, but both should be assessed.

Jan Kemp from the University of Texas at San Antonio continues the theme of assessment, focusing on changes in collection use following implementation of Summon in January 2010. During the first full year of implementation, Kemp's study revealed a dramatic increase in use of electronic resources. Kemp considered a number of possible plausible explanations and concluded that Summons deserves the credit for the increased use.

Pamela Harpel-Burke surveyed librarians at 275 libraries that have implemented a discovery service in order to explore the impact of these services on catalog maintenance and authority control activities.

Respondents were asked to provide data on the same activities before and after implementation of the discovery service. Harpel-Burke also documented potential changes in workflows and compared catalog librarian use of the traditional OPAC and the public interface of the discovery service.

Chapter 18
Implementing Library Discovery:
A Balancing Act

Andrew J. Welch
Drake University, USA

ABSTRACT

In the summer of 2010, Drake University's Cowles Library implemented EBSCO Discovery Service™ (EDS). During the implementation and throughout the first year of use, the library faced challenging decisions regarding resource selection, how to present resources in a way that maximized their utility, and configuring the public interface to appeal to both first-time users and experienced researchers. This chapter provides libraries considering or having purchased a Web-scale discovery tool a look at the various issues and potential solutions they may face when implementing a discovery service. It will specifically target those aspects of implementation that concern resource selection and configuration of the public interface. Issues and examples discussed refer to EDS™, but many of the issues are common to all discovery solutions.

INTRODUCTION

The theory of Web-scale discovery—harvesting many discrete metadata and content silos and indexing them in a single, searchable layer—has generated much interest from the library community in recent years (Breeding, 2010). The discovery solutions themselves, however, are not a panacea. After evaluating the available products and deciding to purchase, libraries will continue to find themselves facing challenging decisions. In the summer of 2010, Cowles Library found itself in such a position: energized by the prospect of gathering its disparate collections under a single, simplified, searchable interface in EBSCO Discovery Service™ (EDS), while at the same time tasked with configuring a fledgling product that seemed to mature and evolve daily. This chapter

DOI: 10.4018/978-1-4666-1821-3.ch018

will provide libraries that are considering or have purchased a Web-scale discovery product a look at the various issues, potential solutions and outcomes libraries may face when implementing a discovery service. It will specifically focus on resource selection and configuration of the public interface. While the issues and examples in this chapter reflect Cowles Library's experience with EDS™, many of the issues discussed are common to all Web-scale discovery products.

LITERATURE REVIEW

In early 2010, when Cowles Library began searching for a discovery solution, very little had been written in the library literature about Web-scale discovery products. Perhaps the first mention of this kind of tool was made by Marshall Breeding shortly after Google Scholar™[2] was introduced (Breeding, 2005). Breeding made a distinction between the many limitations of on-the-fly federated searching and what he termed "centralized search" (p. 27) approaches; namely, scalable systems that are able to store and search harvested content in a central index. Prior to 2010, the only other significant examination of this category of tools was a discussion of a prototype library discovery system developed by the University of Nevada Las Vegas Libraries (Dolski, 2009).

Since early 2010, Rowe (2010) and Vaughan (2011) have reviewed the major Web-scale discovery products. Rowe examined Serials Solutions'[®3] Summon™[4], EDS™ and OCLC's WorldCat[®5] Local, scoring each on content, user interface/searchability, pricing and contract options. Vaughan took an extensive look at those three products, as well as Primo Central™[6] from Ex Libris™[7], and pointed out several important realities to keep in mind when evaluating discovery services: 1) Web-scale discovery tools do not provide access to a library's complete collection; 2) libraries will need to maintain some separate data silos and interfaces; 3) existing discovery services

cannot anticipate the researcher's exact needs, but progress continues to be made on relevancy ranking and resource recommender features; and 4) Google and Wikipedia will continue to be popular destinations for researchers, and libraries must continue to develop strategies for connecting users with library resources.

Julia Gross and Lutie Sheridan (2011) conducted usability testing on Edith Cowan University Library's implementation of Summon™ and found that, while users were able to quickly and easily find large amounts of information with Summon™, they remained confused about result formats and usefulness of the information. Sarah Williams and Anita Foster (2011) carried out a usability study of EDS™ on a small sample of six participants at Illinois State University's Milner Library. While engaging in five research scenarios, participants in this study had little trouble identifying and applying both pre- and post-search limits, but all were confused about the role of federated search results in EDS™. One of the discoveries made by Williams and Foster is that, while participants generally found it easy to retrieve relevant results using EDS™, they still require (and desire) some kind of instruction to fully utilize the capabilities of a powerful discovery tool (Williams and Foster, 2011).

Doug Way (2010) conducted an analysis of database usage at Grand Valley State University both before and after implementation of Summon™. After Summon™, Way discovered both a decrease in the direct use of databases and a dramatic increase in full-text downloads, indicating that Summon™ was perhaps more successful than individual databases at directing users to full-text content.

BACKGROUND

Drake University, located in Des Moines, Iowa, offers more than seventy programs of study, including graduate programs in Business & Public

Table 1. Type and growth of electronic records held by Cowles Library

Type of electronic resource	2006	2010
Subscription databases	61	143
E-Journal titles	26,000	92,450
E-Book titles	41,000	145,490
Other electronic documents	0	580,000

Administration, Education, Journalism & Mass Communication, Pharmacy & Health Sciences, and Law. Cowles Library serves as the main University library, while Opperman Law Library serves the Drake Law program. The university enrolls just over 4,600 FTE students, 3,200 (71%) of which are undergraduates.

Cowles Library uses SirsiDynix[8] Symphony[9] for its integrated library system (ILS) and has a variety of digital collections in addition to a growing institutional repository of more than 1,300 titles.

At the beginning of 2010, Cowles Library faced a number of realities:

- Between 2006 and 2010, the library saw a marked increase in the number and variety of purchased and subscribed electronic resources (Table 1).
- The percentage of the library's acquisitions budget devoted to electronic resources increased from 35% in 2006 to nearly 60% in 2010.
- The number of physical volumes in the library's collection decreased from just over 427,000 in 2006 to 362,600 in 2010, a 15% decrease.
- Of the 143 subscribed databases, three packages—EBSCO Academic Search™[10], EBSCO Business Source®[11] and PsycARTICLES®[12]—accounted for 70% of the library's total full-text retrievals in 2010.
- The library was dissatisfied with its ILS-delivered OPAC; the navigation was clunky and unintuitive and, while the library could customize the display, the learning curve for making even small changes was quite steep.

The library needed a new way to meet the challenge of delivering useful results from an increasing number of disparate, valuable resources—including its physical collection—in a way that did not force users to consult dozens of separate databases and navigate vastly different, often complex interfaces.

RESOURCE AND CONTENT PROVIDER ISSUES

The concept and ultimate goal of a discovery service is to amass the library's disparate collections and resources into a unified, searchable index. In practice, however, discovery systems are unable to harvest content from every possible library resource, and the library must make a series of decisions regarding which resources make sense—logistically, financially and pedagogically—to include in the discovery index. The library may discover that there are reasons not to include certain resources, and factors beyond the library's control may determine the fate of still other resources. After deciding what content will be included in the discovery index, the library will likely face its most challenging task: developing strategies for promoting the continued use of resources that are *not* included in discovery.

Demand-Driven and Open Access Resources

Patron-Driven Acquisition (PDA) is becoming an increasingly attractive collection development method, and research indicates that materials acquired through PDA tend to have higher circulation than those purchased via traditional acquisition methods (Nixon & Saunders, 2010). In one PDA model, book purchases are driven by interlibrary loan (ILL) requests; when a patron requests a book via ILL, the library purchases the book rather than requesting it from another library (Nixon & Saunders, 2010). Another model involves loading vendor-provided "placeholder" records into the discovery index as part of the library's local catalog, allowing users to view these records alongside "owned" records. The library might then generate a purchase as soon as a user requests an item. The benefit of including placeholder records in the discovery index is that library users are more apt to find and request items of interest to them, thereby increasing the library's perceived value. Due to increased exposure, however, the library should be prepared to receive and manage a noticeable increase in the number of demand-driven requests once PDA records are included in discovery. Also, because pricing models for some discovery systems may factor in the number of local bibliographic records, the library should establish with discovery vendors whether PDA records will be included in the calculation.

Several discovery tools allow the inclusion of open access (OA) journal repositories like OAIster®[13], Arxiv and HathiTrust, and libraries must decide whether or not these resources add sufficient value to be worth inclusion. The author is not implying that open access content is not valuable; rather, that the inclusion of open access resources in the discovery process has the potential to detract from the user's discovery experience. It can be very tempting to augment the discovery index with thousands of free scholarly works. However, the heterogeneity of OA target records

means their URLs require a great deal of maintenance, and it is not uncommon for OA content to cease to exist (Crawford, 2011). Furthermore, issues of incomplete or inferior metadata in OA records (Beall, 2009) have implications for relevancy ranking. Such records have less chance of matching a user's search terms, thereby achieving a lower relevancy ranking, even though they may be more suitable than records with rich metadata.

Factors beyond the Library's Control

There are—and will likely continue to be—publishers and aggregators of electronic content who are unwilling to partner with a particular discovery vendor. The reasons behind their reluctance may be because they have a competing discovery product or a competing resource, or perhaps because no fair trade exists for their product.

Libraries should also be aware that a resource may not be perpetually available via their discovery vendor. As electronic resources undergo ownership changes, the dynamic of the discovery partnership may also change, resulting in the removal of subscribed resources from the discovery index. Libraries should find out from their discovery vendors what, if any, compensation will be offered in these situations (e.g., provide a prorated credit or refund, or add another subscribed resource at no charge).

Some resources may be available in the discovery index, but the library's subscription to those resources may limit the number of allowed simultaneous users. Because each discovery search occupies a connection to each resource it searches, the library's limit is quickly reached, effectively blocking the resource from additional users until a connection can be freed. Such was the case with ABC-CLIO's *America: History & Life* and *Historical Abstracts*. Cowles Library had user-limited subscriptions for each database and had decided not to include them in the EDS™ index; when EBSCO obtained the databases and offered unlimited use subscriptions for only a few hundred dollars more, the library considered it a worthwhile upgrade and added them to the discovery index.

Regardless of simultaneous user restrictions, other resources may not be good candidates for discovery. For example, the detailed parameters and calculations available in a statistical resource such as ProQuest®[14] Statistical DataSets cannot possibly be replicated in a discovery environment.

Promoting Excluded Resources

Though the reasons for exclusion may vary, the consequence remains the same: resources excluded from discovery are at risk of becoming "orphans," particularly if the library promotes the discovery service as the primary method of accessing its collections. The extent to which usage of these resources might decline may depend on the resource's usage level or prominence prior to discovery implementation. Library users who have had success using a particular resource are likely to continue using that resource, but it must remain easily accessible. By excluding resources from discovery, the library is forced to assign abstract, unintuitive "partner" or "non-partner" designations to its collection.

To address the issue of publishers unwilling to become discovery partners, libraries can contact their representatives at such publishers and let them know that it is very important to the library that the publisher become a discovery partner. Discovery vendors may even be willing to draft a generic letter for the library that outlines the advantages of such a partnership. Perhaps the most persuasive evidence the library can include in these letters are usage statistics. Aggregators want their products to be used and publishers want their content to be valued. As discovery systems become more prevalent, usage statistics will become increasingly important, not only for individual libraries to make collection development decisions, but also for the discovery community as a whole. Likewise, libraries should let

their discovery vendors know which publishers are most important to them. While any discovery vendor likely has a prioritized list of publishers and aggregators with whom the vendor wants to partner, customer input can only help a vendor refine its priorities.

Another option is to ensure that excluded resources are included in a subject guide or research guide that can be easily accessed from within the discovery interface. Most libraries have as a component of their Web sites a list of resources organized by subject area. At minimum, the library could provide a static link to its research guide from the discovery menu. Some discovery products allow libraries to create widgets that can be embedded into the search result and/or individual record displays, and research guides can be good candidates for such a feature.

The library could also offer a link to its complete list of databases and online resources from within the discovery interface. These "A to Z" lists can be cumbersome and somewhat impractical for beginning users who are unfamiliar with which resources might be most appropriate, but experienced searchers and users looking for a specific database may find them quite valuable. The method Cowles Library uses to generate this list is discussed in the Display & Interface Issues section of this chapter.

Serials Solutions® provides a feature in Summon™ that helps emphasize excluded resources that may be appropriate to a particular search. Summon's™ Database Recommender uses keyword triggers and analyzes current search results to "[point] users to specialized resources that can assist their research, whether they're indexed by Summon™ or not" (Serials Solutions®, 2010). A similar feature is being considered for future inclusion in EDS™ (Vaughan, 2011). This type of feature is valuable to the user because it is contextually appropriate, presenting specialized resources at the user's point of need. At the same time, it provides value to libraries by highlighting essential resources that might otherwise go unnoticed and unused.

At the heart of any promotion of library resources is user education, and this is especially appropriate for resources excluded from discovery. Cowles Library uses its liaison program to notify university faculty of new and important resources in their academic disciplines. In addition, when librarians schedule information literacy sessions with classes, they cover not only the discovery service but also the individual resources—which may or may not be included in the discovery index—that will be most appropriate and useful for the course's topic.

The limitations of federated searching have been documented (Herrera, 2007; Warren, 2007), and while a complete examination of federated search integration is outside the scope of this chapter, libraries should consider what role—if any—federated searching will play in their discovery implementation. The desire to provide access to as many resources as possible must be weighed against a number of issues, which are briefly discussed below:

- Latency and response time issues typically preclude federated search results from being included with results from the unified index; discovery tools must provide better ways of integrating federated resources.
- While latency issues are not as obvious in an asynchronous implementation (where federated search continues to establish connections and retrieve results after indexed results have already appeared), broken and dropped connections to federated resources are common. This leads to inconsistent results from one search to the next, which can be frustrating for users.
- Resources with simultaneous use restrictions should be avoided as federated search targets, for reasons outlined in the previous section of this chapter.

- Less commonly, some content providers are unable to handle federated search traffic. Providers accustomed to a certain level of server requests may find themselves overwhelmed by the exponentially higher number of requests generated by discovery services. Cowles Library has had at least one content provider ask to be excluded from its EDS™/EBSCOhost® Integrated Search implementation for this reason.
- In the case of EDS™, each federated resource—or "connector"—incurs an extra cost. The library must pay close attention to usage statistics of these resources via EDS™ to determine whether the added cost is justified.

Federated search issues presented the greatest challenge during Cowles Library's EDS™ implementation, and the library will be carefully evaluating its approach to this feature with the help of usage statistics and usability testing. For example, preliminary data from a click-tracking utility, which the library implemented on the EDS™ results page, indicates that users are not taking advantage of the displayed federated resources. Out of more than 23,000 visits over a one-month period, users clicked on federated resources a total of 112 times. Usability testing will help the library ascertain whether this behavior is due to lack of visibility, lack of interest, lack of understanding, or some combination of these.

Ongoing Evaluation of Resources

At Cowles Library, the evaluation of resources already included in the discovery index will continue as before; whether the library cancels a database subscription will depend on overall usage and pedagogical needs, not on its performance in EDS™. The library wants to maximize exposure to these expensive and valuable resources, and removing them from the discovery index contradicts that goal. Federated search resources are a different story, however. Because the library is paying to connect to each resource, and because of the way EDS™ presents those resources to the user, their usage level within EDS™ may not justify the expense. The library may need to set minimum "cost-per-EDS™-use" expectations to each resource.

Summary of Resource and Content Provider Issues

The goal of placing all possible library resources into a searchable, unified index is not yet feasible. Libraries must evaluate which resources are available from a given discovery vendor, determine whether the indexed content is full text or only metadata, and decide whether to include federated search in the library's overall discovery strategy. Perhaps the most challenging decision involves strategies to encourage continued use of resources that have been excluded from the discovery implementation. A combination of approaches can be used, from user education to federated search. Depending on the discovery tool, solutions may also be found within the discovery interface itself.

DISPLAY AND INTERFACE ISSUES

If the purpose of Web-scale discovery services is to provide faster, easier access to relevant content, a major factor in discovery's success is the user interface. User-friendly features like faceted browsing, "Did You Mean?" suggestions and citation exporting are important to the user experience, but there are underlying aspects of the discovery interface that force the library to make choices about the role the discovery product will play and how effective it will be in the user's discovery process.

Discovery Tool vs. Traditional Catalog

An important decision the library must make is whether or not the discovery interface will replace the library's current online catalog. If not, it will be important for the library to reconcile the two points of access in a way that minimizes user confusion. A common method libraries use to address the difference is to apply "beta" and "classic" labels to the discovery and traditional interfaces, respectively. After a period of time, the library may drop the "beta" designation but keep "classic" indefinitely. If the library has branded the existing catalog in some way, it may help users distinguish it from the discovery tool, but simply applying a clever or catchy name to the library catalog does not guarantee that users will know what the catalog is or does (Majors, 2011).

Cowles Library chose not to change its existing online catalog interface upon implementing EDS™. Users can access the traditional interface as they always have, and the catalog's name remains unchanged. Instead, the library chose a strong brand for the discovery interface, renaming it SuperSearch and creating a distinctive logo. A help icon next to the search box links to a brief description and instructional video. In addition, the library waged a campus-wide library-user-as-superhero marketing campaign prior to launching SuperSearch that included bookmarks, posters, banners and t-shirt giveaways. The library's approach in information literacy and instruction sessions was to promote SuperSearch as the primary—but certainly not only—method of discovery. Within SuperSearch, users are able to select a "Cowles Catalog Only" limiter to restrict their search results to records from the traditional catalog.

If a library chooses to replace its existing online catalog with the discovery interface, there are a number of factors to consider.

- **Guest Access** – Most discovery services allow guest access at some level. Typically, this means that non-authenticated users will be able to perform searches and view a limited amount of search result metadata. The amount of unrestricted metadata available depends upon individual publisher agreements with the discovery vendor, and might include only citation information. An authentication prompt will only be presented to the user when he or she attempts to view or access licensed content.

- **Item Types, Collection Locations and other "cat" codes** – Libraries rely on these codes to accurately represent and limit searches in their existing online catalogs. However, discovery vendors may be unable to map to these codes, or mapping may be incomplete. For example, a library may have painstakingly separated its collection of videos into VHS and DVD, and created separate item type codes for each, but the discovery system may only able to represent items as "Videos." Likewise with distinguishing music CDs from audiobooks on CD. Discovery products offered by the same vendor as the library's ILS may have an advantage here, as the product may have been optimized to map to ILS field codes. Cowles Library observed that early versions of EDS™ fell short of the need to recognize the diverse material types represented in the local catalog. For example, EDS collectively classified eBooks, audiobooks, audio CDs and various video formats as "non-print resources." Recent enhancements to EDS™ have added "Audio" and "Video" as material types.

- **Traditional searches (Author/Title, Series, Journal Title) may not exist** – Many search indexes in the traditional online catalog are not available in discovery systems. In many ways, this is desirable; to search for an ISBN, for example, the user can simply enter the number and need not select the ISBN index. Other searches, like Series or Periodical Title, become multi-step processes in discovery. Libraries must evaluate the importance and utility of such searches to their users, and whether the loss of those searches will negatively impact users' ability to find materials.

- **Links to "other" electronic records (e.g., e-books, digital collections)** – Libraries have traditionally relied on the MARC 856 field to provide full-text links to materials in, for example, digital collections. However, these links may not display the same way as full text links from discovery resources, creating inconsistent user experience. For example, the discovery interface may only offer default link text, such as "Online version," rather than utilizing the more descriptive MARC 856 subfields (3, y, z).

Customizing the Display

Whether or not the discovery tool replaces a library's online catalog, the library will likely want to put its own brand on the interface. All discovery services allow some level of customization, from basic color scheme changes to APIs, widgets and other open Web technologies (Vaughan, 2011). While custom names, colors, logos and CSS styles are important, they are primarily cosmetic. This section will instead focus on customizations that impact the user's ability to more effectively use the discovery tool.

- **Labels and terminology** – Different vendors use different terminology to describe various features (e.g., EDS uses "Content Provider" instead of "Database"). It is well known that library users often do not understand library jargon (Kupersmith, 2011), so the ability for libraries to assign labels that make the most sense to their users is essential. The ability to display labels in multiple languages might be important as well.

- **Adding or removing facets** – Different resources offer different facets, but those facets might not be necessary for general or interdisciplinary searches. For example, MEDLINE®[15] offers Age and Gender facets, which are applied to participants of research studies and clinical trials. The consequence for the user is that, although the vast majority of discovery resources do not utilize facets for Age or Gender, he will be presented with those facets if his search results include just one result from MEDLINE®. Cowles library looked at each facet available in EDS™ and made a decision whether it would be useful to the *majority* of users; if not, it was suppressed.

- **Subject-specific "profiles"** – EDS™ offers the ability to create subject-specific versions of the interface, which retrieve results from a library-selected subset of resources. The *Accommodating Power Users* section of this chapter contains a more complete description of this feature.

- **APIs and widgets** – Many discovery products can be extended by integrating third-party services via widgets, or by enabling discovery features to be incorporated elsewhere online via an application programming interface (API). For example, Summon™ offers an API suite for functions such as real-time availability checking, displaying cover images and searching the Summon™ index (Serials Solutions, 2009). The University of Michigan Library used the Summon™ API to build a Drupal module that conducts article searches in Summon™. (Varnum, 2011). EDS™ provides widgets for bringing content from other library service providers, such as ChiliFresh, Goodreads and LibGuides, into search result and detailed record displays.

There are some interesting customer-driven EDS™ widget projects that inject more dynamic content, such as context-sensitive subject guide recommendations, into the EDS™ interface (Frierson, 2011).

EBSCO designed the EDS™ interface to closely resemble that of its EBSCO*host*® database products, presumably so that users already familiar with the appearance and features of those databases will be immediately familiar with the discovery interface. However, this similarity has the potential to cause confusion for such users, who may equate "EBSCO" with only database content and assume that they still need to search elsewhere for the library's print or media collections. This is another reason Cowles Library chose to brand EDS™ as "SuperSearch."

The technical staff at Cowles Library believes that an interface—particularly one that is so integral to information access and delivery—should offer as much customizability as possible. In fact, this author would argue that there is no such thing as "too customizable," provided that the interface is delivered with an acceptable default configuration.

Mobile Interface

It is increasingly important that services offered by libraries have either a mobile interface or a mobile component. At the time Cowles Library implemented EDS™, the web-based mobile interface was based on the existing EBSCOhost® mobile platform. It had enough limitations that the library chose not to promote it in conjunction with its main EDS™ rollout in September 2010. EBSCO has since made improvements to EDS™ mobile, including applications for iPhone and Android platforms, and the library began promoting it at the start of the 2011-2012 academic year.

All of the major discovery products offer a mobile-optimized version of their interface, and some also offer device-specific mobile applications. Summon™, for example, will automatically recognize a user's mobile device and present a mobile interface. It appears to work well on iPhone and Android devices, but Blackberry and Palm users may experience difficulty performing an advanced search or viewing full-text content. OCLC moved its WorldCat® Local mobile-optimized views from beta to production in June 2011, and WorldCat® Local libraries can direct mobile users to a mobile view with a URL in the format http://[institution].worldcat.org/m (Online Computer Library Center [OCLC], 2011).

Accommodating Power Users

A discovery interface is an access tool. It is not intended to replace the resources that comprise it. Experienced researchers, sometimes called power users, may prefer searching individual, discipline-specific databases that return sets of more focused results (Luther & Kelly, 2011). Rather than send these users to a separate area of the library website, Cowles Library wanted to meet the needs of experienced users from within the discovery interface. There are at least two ways of accomplishing this:

1. Easily allow searching individual databases (or subsets of databases) using the discovery interface. This can be achieved by using a Database facet to limit results to one or more resources, but it requires the user to first perform a search and then apply the limiter. In many discovery interfaces, if the user modifies the search terms, the limiter is lost. Alternatively, EDS™ allows libraries to create multiple subject-specific profiles as a way of presenting users with a subset of resources pertinent to their particular discipline. Cowles Library realized early in the planning phase that these specialized profiles would be of major interest to faculty and experienced researchers. So, for example, the library offers Pharmacy SuperSearch, which is used by Drake University's College of Pharmacy and Health Sciences and includes im-

portant resources such as AccessPharmacy™[16], MEDLINE® and ScienceDirect.

2. Provide links to individual databases from within the discovery interface. Cowles Library was able to leverage the ability to insert custom JavaScript, along with a combination of EBSCO's existing modal window styles and a snippet of PHP, to provide a "Go to a database" link under the search field. The resulting window displays a list of database links (including those that are not part of the discovery index), which minimizes the necessary amount of screen "real estate" while providing the desired result. It would not have been possible without the ability to modify the interface by inserting custom code.

One of the hallmarks of discovery search interfaces is a Google-like search box, which most users appreciate for its simplicity. However, many power users have also become accustomed to using Boolean operators and constructing advanced search queries, so it is important that a discovery tool provide an advanced search interface. If libraries have a choice of which interface to offer as the default, they must decide which would be most useful for their users. EDS™ offers an advanced search, with multiple input fields and field types, as well as the ability to limit results to, for example, one or more locations, languages or publication dates. Interestingly, in the process of creating the specialized instances mentioned above, SuperSearch Pharmacy users indicated that they preferred to have Advanced Search be the default search interface, which EDS™ profiles accommodate. Other discovery tools also offer advanced search capability. For example, Primo Central™ provides an Advanced Search link next to the main search field, which allows users to pre-limit searches by search field, publication date, material type and scope. Encore's advanced search presents users with multiple search fields arranged in Boolean fashion, with options to limit by material type, location, publication date and language.

Interlibrary loan is a critical component of the discovery interface; experienced researchers know—and beginners quickly discover—that when all else fails in their quest for full text, they can request ILL delivery. However, each request made for an item the library already owns or can access increases the workload and decreases the efficiency of the ILL department. Discovery tools should include logic that recognizes when full text is unavailable (whether from the unified index or via link resolver) and presents the user with a link to the library's ILL form or service.

Summary of Display and Interface Issues

Every library's user group is unique. Libraries will need to find ways of tailoring the discovery interface to strike a balance that satisfies the majority of their users while at the same time meeting the often more demanding needs of experienced researchers. The chosen role of the discovery product in relation to the traditional catalog, as well as how well the product represents traditional catalog metadata, affects that balance. Discovery products must also allow libraries to make functional, not just cosmetic, customizations.

ENHANCEMENTS AND ISSUE TRACKING

At the time of this writing, discovery systems are still in their infancy; each is striving to become the market leader and actively developing enhancements to that end. Discovery vendors rely on their library customers to a certain degree to generate, evaluate and prioritize enhancements. An important consideration, however, is whether the vendor has a formal mechanism in place for continued customer-driven enhancements. If such a mechanism exists, how transparent is it? Can customers track their requests, or view and support requests submitted by other customers? It

is important for vendors for provide a dedicated enhancement process for their discovery products, as the development cycle for discovery typically outpaces the cycle of the vendor's other core products.

An established enhancements process is particularly useful as libraries begin the initial implementation of a discovery product. Regardless of a library's diligent product testing and inquiries about features and functionality, unanticipated issues will always arise during implementation for which the only remedy is a product enhancement. When Cowles Library started implementing EDS™, EBSCO had no official (public-facing) enhancements process. The library addressed concerns and made requests through its Customer Account Specialist, who assigned case tracking numbers and facilitated communication between the library and EDS™ developers. Because no customer interface existed for monitoring the library's increasing number of cases, the library established its own in-house process using a rudimentary issue-tracking product. Such a process is inefficient, of course, because it duplicates the vendor's own internal procedures. By contrast, Encore customers go through a formal enhancements submission and voting process that is managed by the Innovative Users Group. At any time, customers can search for, view, and add their support to enhancements submitted by other Encore customers. When voting concludes, all enhancements—with ballot winners marked as such—are forwarded to the Encore product development team for consideration.

FUTURE RESEARCH DIRECTIONS

Cowles Library is in the second year of its discovery implementation, at the time of this writing. The library intends to spend much of the next year conducting various usability tests in an attempt to further improve not only its own implementation of EDS™, but also the product as a whole. In addition, the library will continue to evaluate resources it has included in EDS™ by examining usage statistics, paying particular attention to federated resources that are included in the central index.

As publishers and aggregators decide how best to deal with this new type of library service, Web-scale discovery will continue to experience growing pains, even as it defines how library collections are searched. In addition, the rapid growth of the Web-scale *management* market will likely have a direct effect on the success of individual discovery services; vendors who can offer a fully functional discovery service that is seamlessly integrated into a comprehensive Web-scale management service will hold an advantage. It would be particularly useful for the library community to see studies that directly compare multiple Web-scale discovery products using the same, "real-world" collection (as opposed to an individual vendor's "test" collection). Acknowledging that discovery vendors each have different partnerships with content providers, such studies would not only identify those partnerships, but also provide an essential comparison of relevancy ranking among discovery products. As the amount of content available from the library search box continues to grow, a discovery tool's relevancy ranking performance will become increasingly important.

CONCLUSION

As Cowles Library put Web-scale discovery theory into practice with EDS™, it faced challenging decisions regarding which resources should be included in discovery and how best to promote those that were not. While creating a unique look and feel for the user interface was an important implementation step, the library also wanted to focus on those aspects of the interface that could be customized to improve functionality for the user. The EDS™ implementation process provided a

more complete understanding of the capabilities and limitations of discovery, and the library has learned that implementing a discovery product involves making some compromises and continually balancing new and old, cost and utility, and intuition and experience.

REFERENCES

Beall, J. (2009). Free books: Loading brief MARC records for open-access books in an academic library catalog. *Cataloging & Classification Quarterly*, *47*(5), 452–463. doi:10.1080/01639370902870215

Breeding, M. (2005). Plotting a new course for metasearch. *Computers in Libraries*, *25*(2), 27–30.

Breeding, M. (2010). The state of the art in library discovery 2010. *Computers in Libraries*, *30*(1), 31–35.

Crawford, W. (2011). *Open access: What you need to know now*. Chicago, IL: American Library Association.

Dolski, A. A. (2009). Information discovery insights gained from MultiPAC, a prototype library discovery system. *Information Technology & Libraries*, *28*(4), 172–180.

Frierson, E. (2011, July 18). *Research guide recommendations*. [Web log post]. Retrieved from http://thirdpartylibrarian.wordpress.com/2011/07/18/research-guide-recommendations/

Gross, J., & Sheridan, L. (2011). Web scale discovery: The user experience. *New Library World*, *112*(5), 236–247. doi:10.1108/03074801111136275

Herrera, G. (2007). Meta searching and beyond: Implementation experiences and advice from an academic library. *Information Technology & Libraries*, *26*(2), 44–52.

Kupersmith, J. (2011). *Library terms that users understand.* Retrieved from http://www.jkup.net/terms.html

Luther, J., & Kelly, M. C. (2011). The next generation of discovery. *Library Journal, 136*(5), 66–71.

Majors, R. (2011, June). *Usability of next-gen interfaces & discovery tools.* Presented at the Annual Conference of the American Library Association, New Orleans, LA.

Nixon, J. M., & Saunders, E. (2010). A study of circulation statistics of books on demand: A decade of patron-driven collection development, part 3. *Collection Management, 35*(3/4), 151–161. doi:10.1080/01462679.2010.486963

Online Computer Library Center. (2011). *WorldCat Local Mobile enhanced, moves into production.* Retrieved from http://www.oclc.org/news/announcements/2011/announcement46.htm

Rowe, R. (2010). Web-scale discovery: A review of Summon, EBSCO Discovery Service, and WorldCat Local. *Charleston Advisor, 12*(1), 5–10. doi:10.5260/chara.12.1.5

Serials Solutions. (2009). *API documentation center.* Retrieved from http://api.summon.serialssolutions.com/help/api/

Serials Solutions. (2010). *Summon service debuts Database Recommender* [Press release]. Retrieved from http://www.serialssolutions.com/news-detail/summon-service-debuts-database-recommender/

Varnum, K. (2011). *Announcing a Drupal module for searching Summon via API* [Blog post]. Retrieved from http://mblog.lib.umich.edu/blt/archives/2011/06/announcing_a_dr.html

Vaughan, J. (2011). *Web scale discovery services: A library technology report.* Chicago, IL: ALA Editions.

Warren, D. (2007). Lost in translation: The reality of federated searching. *Australian Academic & Research Libraries, 38*(4), 258–269.

Way, D. (2010). The impact of web-scale discovery on the use of a library collection. *Serials Review, 36*(4), 214–220. doi:10.1016/j.serrev.2010.07.002

Williams, S. C., & Foster, A. K. (2011). Promise fulfilled? An EBSCO Discovery Service usability study. *Journal of Web Librarianship, 5*(3), 179–198. doi:10.1080/19322909.2011.597590

ADDITIONAL READING

Adamich, T. (2010). Metadata and the next generation library catalog: Will the catalog become a true discovery system? *Technicalities, 30*(3), 12–14.

Allison, D. (2010). Information portals: The next generation catalog. *Journal of Web Librarianship, 4*(4), 375–389. doi:10.1080/19322909.2010.507972

Antelman, K., Lynema, E., & Pace, A. K. (2006). Toward a twenty-first century library catalog. *Information Technology & Libraries, 25*(3), 128–139.

Biddix, J. P., Chung, J. C., & Han, W. P. (2011). Convenience or credibility? A study of college student online research behaviors. *The Internet and Higher Education, 14*(3), 175–182. doi:10.1016/j.iheduc.2011.01.003

Boss, S. C., & Nelson, M. L. (2005). Federated search tools: The next step in the quest for one-stop-shopping. *The Reference Librarian, 44*(91), 139–160. doi:10.1300/J120v44n91_10

Bowen, J. (2008). Metadata to support next-generation library resource discovery: Lessons from the eXtensible catalog, phase 1. *Information Technology & Libraries, 27*(2), 5–19.

Braunstein, L., Cocklin, J., DeFelice, B., Hall, L., Holt, J., & Lowenstein, N. …Wheelock, C. (2009). *An evaluation of Serials Solutions Summon as a discovery service for the Dartmouth College Library.* Retrieved from http://www.dartmouth. edu/~library/admin/docs/Summon_Report.pdf

Breeding, M. (2008). Beyond the current generation of next-generation library interfaces: Deeper search. *Computers in Libraries, 28*(5), 39–40.

Breeding, M. (2011). The new frontier. *Library Journal, 136*(6), 24–34.

Calhoun, K. (2006). *The changing nature of the catalog and its integration with other discovery tools: Final report.* Washington, DC: Library of Congress. Retrieved from http://www.loc.gov/ catdir/calhoun-report-final.pdf

Calhoun, K., & Cellentani, D. (2009). *Online catalogs: What users and librarians want: An OCLC report.* Dublin, OH: OCLC.

Carter, J. (2009). Discovery: What do you mean by that? *Information Technology & Libraries, 28*(4), 161–163.

Fagan, J. (2010). Usability studies of faceted browsing: A literature review. *Information Technology & Libraries, 29*(2), 58–66.

Fry, A., & Rich, L. (2011). Usability testing for e-resource discovery: How students find and choose e-resources using library Web sites. *Journal of Academic Librarianship, 37*(5), 386–401. doi:10.1016/j.acalib.2011.06.003

Gibson, I., Goddard, L., & Gordon, S. (2009). One box to search them all: Implementing federated search at an academic library. *Library Hi Tech, 27*(1), 118–133. doi:10.1108/07378830910942973

Horava, T. (2010). Challenges and possibilities for collection management in a digital age. *Library Resources & Technical Services, 54*(3), 142–152.

Jung, S., Herlocker, J. L., Webster, J., Mellinger, M., & Frumkin, J. (2008). LibraryFind: System design and usability testing of academic metasearch system. *Journal of the American Society for Information Science and Technology, 59*(3), 375–389. doi:10.1002/asi.20749

Korah, A., & Cassidy, E. (2010). Students and federated searching: A survey of use and satisfaction. *Reference and User Services Quarterly, 49*(4), 325–332.

Luther, J. (2003). Trumping Google: Metasearching's promise. *Library Journal, 128*(16), 36–39.

Majors, R., & Mantz, S. L. (2011). Moving to the patron's beat. *OCLC Systems & Services, 27*(4), 275–283. doi:10.1108/10650751111182588

Merčun, T., & Žumer, M. (2008). New generation of catalogues for the new generation of users: A comparison of six library catalogues. *Program: Electronic Library & Information Systems, 42*(3), 243–261. doi:10.1108/00330330810892668

Newcomer, N. L. (2011). The detail behind web-scale: Selecting and configuring web-scale discovery tools to meet music information retrieval needs. *Music Reference Services Quarterly, 14*(3), 131–145. doi:10.1080/10588167.2011.596098

Safley, E., Montgomery, D., & Gardner, S. (2011). Oasis or quicksand: Implementing a catalog discovery layer to maximize access to electronic resources. *The Serials Librarian, 60*(1-4), 164–168. doi:10.1080/0361526X.2011.556028

Stone, G. (2009). Resource discovery . In Woodward, H. M., & Estelle, L. (Eds.), *Digital information: Order or anarchy?* (pp. 133–164). London, UK: Facet Publishing.

Stone, G. (2010). Searching life, the universe and everything? The implementation of Summon at the University of Huddersfield. *Liber Quarterly: The Journal of European Research Libraries, 20*(1), 25–42.

Varnum, K. (2010). Project lefty: More bang for the search query. *Computers in Libraries, 30*(3), 20–23.

Yang, S. Q., & Wagner, K. (2010). Evaluating and comparing discovery tools: How close are we towards next generation catalog? *Library Hi Tech, 28*(4), 690–709. doi:10.1108/07378831011096312

Zylstra, R. (2011). A mobile application for discovery. *Computers in Libraries, 31*(2), 11–14.

KEY TERMS AND DEFINITIONS

Application Programming Interface (API): A standardized method for a software program, like a Web application, to request information from the underlying operating system or from another software program.

Faceted Browsing: Also called faceted navigation or faceted search, a method of dynamically grouping search results into categories (facets), allowing users to narrow the focus of their search by selecting and deselecting various facets.

Federated Searching: Retrieving a small subset of on-the-fly results directly from multiple heterogeneous resources and combining those results into a single result list.

Integrated Library System (ILS): A suite of software modules (e.g., Circulation, Acquisitions, Cataloging, OPAC) that manages inventory control and circulation of library materials.

Item Type: Also called Format or Material Type, a description of the physical or electronic item (e.g., Book, DVD, Magazine). In integrated library systems, this information is usually stored as a fixed-length code and displayed to the user as descriptive text.

Latency: In the context of federated search, the amount of time it takes for results to be retrieved from an external resource and displayed to the user.

Patron-Driven Acquisitions (PDA): Also known as Demand-Driven Acquisitions (DDA),

a method of just-in-time collection development whereby the library purchases materials at the time a patron requests them. Requests could be placed via interlibrary loan, a placeholder record in discovery, a purchase suggestion form on the library's Web site, or any combination of these.

Web-Scale Discovery: A method for pre-harvesting and pre-indexing metadata and full text content from multiple discrete online resources; this unified index can be accessed from a single search box and can display results in a single ranked list.

Web-Scale Management: A cloud-based service that replaces traditional integrated library system software with Web services that interact, usually via open API calls, with third party services and the library database.

Widget: A snippet of HTML markup and/or JavaScript code that can be inserted into a Web page to provide additional functionality from a third-party resource. For example, a custom search box widget.

ENDNOTES

[1] EBSCO Discovery Services is a trademark of EBSCO Publishing Industries.
[2] Google Scholar is a trademark of Google, Inc.
[3] Serial Solutions is a registered trademark of Serial Solutions.
[4] Summon is a trademark of Serial Solutions
[5] WorldCat is a registered trademark of OCLC
[6] Primo Central is a trademark of Ex Libris Ltd.
[7] ExLibris is a trademark of Ex Libris Ltd.
[8] SirsiDynix is a registered trademark of SirsiDynix Corporation
[9] Symphony is a registered trademark of SirsiDynix Corporation
[10] EBSCO Academic Search is a trademark of EBSCO Publishing Industries

[11] EBSCO Business Source is a registered trademark of EBSCO Publishing Industries

[12] EBSCO PsycARTICLES is a registered trademark of EBSCO Publishing Industries

[13] OAIster is a registered trademark of OCLC

[14] ProQuest® is a registered trademark of Pro-Quest LLC

[15] Medline is a registered trademark of US National Library of Medicine

[16] AccessPharmacy is a trademark of McGraw-Hill Companies.

Chapter 19
Discovering Our Library's Resources:
Vendor Tools Versus In-House Tools

Amy S. Jackson
University of New Mexico, University Libraries, USA

Kevin Comerford
University of New Mexico, University Libraries, USA

Suzanne M. Schadl
University of New Mexico, University Libraries, USA

Rebecca Lubas
University of New Mexico, University Libraries, USA

ABSTRACT

The University Libraries (UL) at the University of New Mexico has experience implementing both a resource discovery tool from a standard library vendor and an in-house, custom built federated search using Drupal® as a Content Management System. The standard vendor-based resource discovery tool was the library's first attempt at a federated search, and feedback from librarians and users was not always positive, largely because results seemed inconsistent and lacking clear relevance to the terms searched. The Drupal® approach proved to be straightforward to implement, very flexible, and customizable, but the project team determined it would not be scalable as a solution for searching the library's entire collection. This chapter describes the UL's experience with both tools, and provides best practices and recommendations for libraries considering either type of approach.

DOI: 10.4018/978-1-4666-1821-3.ch019

INTRODUCTION

Like most other academic libraries, the University Libraries (UL) at the University of New Mexico (UNM) pursues resource discovery tools that facilitate positive user experiences. However, the UL has struggled to identify a one-size-fits-all, one-stop shop that can efficiently lead new users and seasoned researchers to resources on multiple heterogeneous platforms. These platforms include standard library subscription databases, digital images and other media housed in ContentDM, an institutional repository built on DSpace, a custom-built data warehouse of Encoded Archival Description (EAD) finding aids, and the Innovative Interfaces Millennium Online Public Access Catalog (OPAC). The UL also understands that many library users are more accustomed to Internet discovery services than library catalogs and they find legitimate sources in web-born data. For this reason, the UL seeks to incorporate homegrown platforms into Internet discovery services while also using social networking and open source content management for acquisitions.

Experimentation with commercial and open source discovery tools reveals that each tool has advantages and disadvantages, depending on the varying needs of user communities. The availability of staff and financial resources impacts the depth and granularity reflected in these discovery tools. This chapter compares the UL's implementation of Serials Solutions'[®1] commercial 360 Search to the execution of an in-house open source Content Management System (CMS) facilitating federated search across records from multiple platforms. The in-house project, Celebrating New Mexico Statehood (CNMS) (http://digitalnm.unm.edu/), customizes Drupal[®] nodes to facilitate broad access to diverse resources.

The types of users these tools serve vary. The federated search helps UNM students, faculty, and staff find books in the catalog and articles in select subscription databases. It does not lead them to special collections. CNMS enables community members from across the state, including students and instructors from eighth grade through college, to interact with special collections. This tool does not incorporate subscription databases.

BACKGROUND

Content Management Systems (CMSs) have evolved significantly over the past 10 years (Souer et al., 2008) and as a result have become extremely popular alternatives for building sophisticated content-driven websites, particularly in the academic library community (Coombs, 2009). The advantage of CMS systems such as Drupal[®2], Joomla[®3], WordPress[™4] and others is that they bundle together many prebuilt website components. These components include full-text searching, text and image formatting and display functions, system administration tools, and desirable end-user features, such as social media communication, commenting and collaboration tools. These features previously required a substantial amount of system administration and/or development time to implement on a standard website. With a good CMS package, it is now possible to set up and configure a full-featured website in several hours, without weeks or months of development time. In addition to effectively lowering development and implementation costs, many CMS systems are also freely available as open source software, making them extremely attractive solutions for library project needs.

Discussions of resource discovery tools in libraries are recent, and include descriptive reviews of commercial tools (Rowe, 2010) as well as white papers (Clarke, 2006; Uzwyshyn, 2007; Burrows et al., 2007), conference documentation (http://twapperkeeper.com/hashtag/ucryh), web pages, and blogs. Paul Stainthorp's blog (2011), for example, informs of an event in which librarians from four universities in the United Kingdom shared notes on next-generation resource-discovery tool implementation. Librarians have also engaged in discussions of Internet resource discovery and social tagging tools. Karen Calhoun (2006) notes that rapid growth and usability in web generated data and pervasive computer access make it easier for students to bypass library catalogs for Internet discovery tools. Mark Dahl (2009) explains that libraries acquiring and organizing newly accessible full text e-articles leave Google to perfect on-line searches with page rank algorithms for massive web and network scale searching. George Macgregor and Emma McCulloch (2006) suggest that tagging in library catalogs could emulate these page-ranking algorithms for greater effectiveness.

Much discussion in academic journals regarding implementation of resource discovery tools focuses on user studies and implementation challenges. User studies have found "serial failure" (Bowen et al., 2004, p.48) in academic libraries, a failure common to all academic libraries of not helping students easily locate journal articles. Addressing this failure is a major challenge in keeping libraries relevant to users. In addition to electronic journal literature, libraries also need to integrate access to the online public access catalog (OPAC), local digital collections, and relevant information on the open web in order to meet patron needs. Preliminary feedback suggests that users value portals that provide integrated access to all of these materials from one location (Norman et al., 2006). Implementation challenges include cross-departmental coordination between library Information Technology (IT) departments, digital librarians, and reference librarians (Lockwood and MacDonald, 2007). Keeping these challenges in mind, the UL attempted to meet patron's needs through a vendor-based metasearch tool, and an in-house federated search tool.

The UL serves nearly 29,000 students pursing over 100 baccalaureate degrees, 70 master's degrees, and 46 doctoral or professional degree programs. A Tier I Research and a designated Hispanic and Native American Serving Institution, UNM attracts a culturally diverse student population and serves as the largest academic library system in the state of New Mexico. Throughout the past decade, the UL has engaged other state institutions in a large scale effort to digitize unique collections in order to make them more widely available throughout the state and beyond. This project, named "Celebrating New Mexico Statehood," has bolstered strong academic and research programs associated with the Southwest, including New Mexico and Native American Pueblo history as well as Spanish American chronicles and antiquities, with over 290,000 titles in Spanish. Efforts to support student success have also prompted the UL to make all library resources, including three million cataloged volumes, 348,149 e-books and some 58,000 electronic journals with 2,000 additional print journals, more discoverable for students across disciplines.

VENDOR-BASED METASEARCH TOOL

Work began at the UL in 2008 to implement a vendor's metasearch tool for access to the library's licensed electronic content and traditional catalog holdings. More experienced users, especially graduate students and new faculty, had exposure to discovery tools at other institutions and demanded that the UL provide a more universal search. Less sophisticated users, such as new undergraduates with limited library and technology experience, expected simple answers to their information needs. The UL tried to address both of these needs swiftly and selected 360 Search from Serials Solutions®, from which the UL previously used the Electronic Resource Management System (ERM). Personnel assigned to implementation were the Electronic Resources Team, a work group that resided within the Collections and Acquisitions Services department. This group managed electronic resources, especially development and maintenance of the UL's ERM and e-journal finder. Subject specialists and other front-line public services personnel provided input while the UL's

Figure 1. Tabbed search box on the UL's webpage. "Quick Search" searches the library's federated search product (Pronto or WorldCat®5 Local).

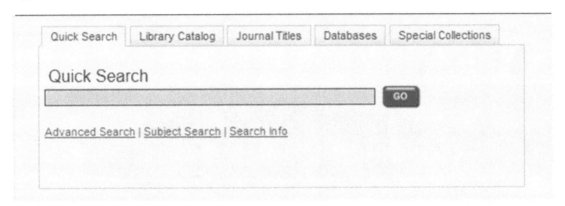

web committee worked on integrating the service within the library's web presence.

The spring 2009 public implementation came in two parts, coordinated with a web site redesign. A tab on the UL's web site labeled "Quick Search" provided the 360 Search box, locally named "Pronto," which became the default search on the UL's webpage (see Figure 1). This search pulled results from broad-subject databases plus the Libraries' catalog. The idea was to provide fast results for the user in the beginning stages of more complex research while also meeting the needs of those seeking specific relevant resources. The second phase manifested in the Pronto Subject Search, which appeared in the Databases tab on the webpage and provided a drop-down menu of subjects (see Figure 2). This search narrowed the returned results to a selection of databases specific to the subject indicated. The Library Catalog tab provided access to the Web OPAC, and additional tabs provided access to the "Journal One" search, and Special Collections. The special collections tab provided links to the institutional repository, finding aids, and other special collection information. The UL advertised the new Pronto service widely in Fall 2009, inserting it in library instruction and promoting it with flyers, bookmarks, and notepads.

Response to the tool was mixed. The default confused users who had been used to the Librar-

ies' OPAC being the default link. Some also felt that the search was too slow because it included too many databases, and the number of records overwhelmed users. Often the quickest returns in the search were not the most relevant. Additionally, integration with the OPAC resulted in its records receiving less relevance and falling to the bottom of the list. The Subject Search was better received because time spent selecting the databases paid off in satisfied searchers. After roughly eighteen months, and input from subject specialists, reference staff, and instruction staff, the Quick Search tab was changed from Pronto to an implementation of the free version of OCLC's WorldCat® Local. Users familiar with OCLC's open access public interface, WorldCat.org recognized the interface and a fair mix of the UL's holdings were available through the search, including books as well as some full-text articles. The free version of WorldCat® Local, although limited in terms of customization, was a quick, easy solution to the dissatisfaction with Pronto. This implementation was intended to be a stopgap solution until the 360 Search license expired and a decision about future investment in search tools could be made. WorldCat® had name recognition among more experienced library users such as graduate students, and in general the implementation was well received by public service and

Figure 2. The "subject search" option provides a federated search across databases relevent to specific disciplines

reference librarians, despite limits in special collections records and serials holdings. The UL retained the Pronto Subject Search alongside WorldCat® Local, understanding that a single discovery tool would likely not meet all user needs, especially not those seeking specialized content.

IN-HOUSE FEDERATED SEARCH TOOL

New Mexico celebrates its 100th year of statehood in 2012, and the UL is creating a commemora-

tive website, *Celebrating New Mexico Statehood* (CNMS) (http://digitalnm.unm.edu). This site brings together catalog records, documents, and images from all major library and special collections across New Mexico. In effect, CNMS serves as an electronic gateway to New Mexico's cultural heritage. The concept for this project came from the Center for Southwest Research (CSWR), the special collections division of the UL, and was funded by the Center for Regional Studies (CRS), also a division of the UL. While there are many cultural and educational institutions housing important individual collections across the state, and there have been piecemeal efforts between institutions to increase access to resources, there is not a single resource in print or online where a teacher, student, or interested public user can obtain universal access to all New Mexico library, archives and museum collections. CNMS provides a centralized online search interface to remedy this problem.

CNMS provides federated search capabilities and historical background materials on issues surrounding New Mexico's statehood. The design also includes social media features enabling users to leave comments, contribute their own content, and host online Centennial-related activities for students and teachers from the public school system (particularly grades 8-12), through community college and university freshmen and sophomores. This project is recognized as an official project of the New Mexico State Centennial (see http://nmcentennial.org/2011/03/celebrating-new-mexico-statehood/) because of its focus and versatility.

This project evolved in two phases. In the first phase of the project, which began in 2009, the primary function was to provide users several methods of access to UNM's ContentDM digital image collections. ContentDM is a digital collection management software product from OCLC, and the UL uses this software to provide access to images, texts, and other multi-media, primarily from the library's special collections. The second phase of development was substantially more complicated, and involved both expanding the searchable content available and making a number of major changes to the site infrastructure. Major changes included moving the site to Drupal®, an open source CMS, implementing new navigational, search and social media features, and expanding on the breadth and depth of the information resources offered. In addition to the UL's ContentDM holdings, the Phase II site incorporated holdings from the statewide LIBROS consortium online catalog (library OPAC), electronic EAD finding aids from New Mexico institutions published in the Rocky Mountain Online Archive (RMOA), and UNM's DSpace repository. The

inclusion of these records transforms CNMS into a centralized repository of collection information about New Mexico and the Southwest. The site provides access to content for users through a cross-collection, cross-institutional search engine that enables users to simultaneously scan collections of books, images, archival material, and documents from the many different institutions across the region. The CNMS Drupal® application provides a shell, or framework around which the website is created.

The cross-institutional, cross-collection search tool within Drupal® is by far the most significant new enhancement to the second phase of the project. This capability creates a database within CNMS of collection records from four statewide repository systems. The most important part of the configuration process is the preparation of the CNMS Drupal® installation to receive the collection records and ensure that the Drupal® search engine is set to index appropriate fields across all of the record types. Drupal® organizes different classes of data records into categories called Content Types. A Content Type is essentially a formatted record template that contains its own set of customized fields. Table 1 shows the relationship between the record sources, their specialized types of content, and the Drupal® Content Types and Fields. The Drupal® Custom Fields are fields specific to each content type within CNMS.

In CNMS, each record includes a hyperlink pointing the user to the original record on its parent system. For example, a user searching for a book in CNMS sees the basic bibliographic information and a hyperlink to that record in the OPAC. This feature enables users to easily search across repositories, but also makes use of specialized features available only in the parent repository system. Bulk loading records into the CNMS database involves extracting raw collection data from separate repositories like the OPAC, mapping metadata to be compatible in both structure and content format, and processing the finished

Table 1. Relationship of content collections to Drupal® content types

Content Source	Content Description	Drupal Content Type	Drupal Custom Fields (Sample)
ContentDM	Digital Images	Image	Caption
LIBROS Library Catalog Records	Library Catalog Records	Book	Publisher Library (Owner)
Rocky Mountain Online Archive	EAD-Encoded Finding Aids	Finding Aid	Collection Identifier Access Terms
LoboVault (UNM DSpace Repository)	Electronic Theses & Dissertations	ETD	Document Type

data into Structured Query Language (SQL) scripts.

The CNMS implementation team has selected a set of 18,000 records related to New Mexico and Southwest culture and history from across the OPAC. These works consist primarily of books and print materials. Extraction of the OPAC data is remarkably easy. A cataloger selects records and fields to be indexed, and pulls the data into a tab-delimited text file. This file is then imported into Microsoft Excel and processed with several pre-defined macros (abbreviated rules for specific outputs).

UNM's institutional repository, a DSpace server that has been locally branded as "LoboVault" (http://repository.unm.edu/), contains over 7,500 open access documents, including over 620 electronic theses and dissertations slated for inclusion in the CNMS database. Fortunately, DSpace (an open-source institutional repository software product) runs on top of a standard SQL-compliant database, and extracting all of the LoboVault record data as a SQL script requires only minor modifications for direct importation into CNMS, making it as simple as importing the OPAC records.

The same ease was also found in extracting records from New Mexico's Digital Collections (http://econtent.unm.edu/), built on a ContentDM server, although it required a slightly different process. New Mexico's Digital Collections contains over 67,000 digital images, as well as audio and video resources. ContentDM has an easy to use export utility on its site administration page. The metadata records are exported directly into tab-delimited format files, which are then imported into a custom Microsoft Excel template file, which converts the data into SQL database scripts. The scripts are then inserted into the CNMS SQL database using an open source database administration tool called MySQL Workbench. Additionally, each ContentDM metadata record in CNMS requires a corresponding thumbnail image. A copy of all ContentDM image files are reformatted to 30% of their original size and attached to the metadata records in the CNMS database.

Rocky Mountain Online Archive (RMOA) (http://www.rmoa.unm.edu) is an online repository of Encoded Archival Description (EAD) archival finding aids used by the UL's special collections department and a consortium of 26 other archives and special collections in the Rocky Mountain States. The UL has contributed 1,265 full-length EAD records to RMOA, documenting thousands of individual pieces from the special collections. CNMS offers a condensed EAD record from RMOA. This record provides enough descriptive information about each collection to be discoverable by users. As with all of the content records imported in to CNMS, these records include a hyperlink to the full-length finding aid in RMOA.

The process of converting the EAD-encoded finding aids and processing them into condensed records is technically the most complex of the CNMS project's data handling tasks. To accomplish it, an XML Editor and Parser creates an XML Extensible Stylesheet Language Transformation (XSLT) template, through which the EAD data records are processed. This transforms the records into a formatted plain text file, which can then be manipulated using Microsoft Excel and a series of macros into SQL scripts. The end result of the conversion process yields an easily readable summary of the full length EAD records.

In addition to importing records, the CNMS Phase II implementation team identified end-user features and capabilities necessary to make the website fulfill the original objectives of the project. They discovered that the depth and breadth of new functionality precluded the development of a completely custom-built website from scratch. The team evaluated existing types of web publishing solutions and decided on Drupal®, a freely available open source Content Management System (CMS), known for its wide acceptance and overall maturity.

In Drupal®, site administrators can configure and customize most aspects of a site, such as its menu structure and visual theme, without writing program code. Additional features and functionality can be added to Drupal® though the installation of custom software modules, hundreds of which are available to extend a website's capabilities, ranging from fairly simple visual enhancements to highly sophisticated applications which add significant features, such as digital image galleries or integration with external web services. Drupal® modules are generally written and maintained by a volunteer developer or development team, which pledges to provide ongoing support for the modules for a specified period of time. Interestingly, each piece of content on a Drupal® website, regardless of whether it is a web page, blog posting, document, or image, is managed individually as a node. Drupal® has proven generally unproblematic to install and maintain, and straightforward to work with, especially with regard to bulk loading of data records, images, and document files.

Once the team installed the Drupal® core components on the CNMS Phase II server, they added a number of Drupal® modules to provide specific features and data handling capabilities. The most important modules included Biblio, Content Construction Kit (CCK), Faceted Search, Image and Image_Assist, Fivestar, and Views. The Biblio module is designed to manage bibliographic records. It works extremely well in handling library catalog and holdings data. The CCK module enables the creation of a variety of custom fields for specialized data management needs. Faceted Search creates subject or data type facets, such as author, genre, media type, etc., from records, enabling users to conduct searches with the Drupal® Advanced Search tool. Image and Image_Assist enable digital images and accompanying metadata to be imported into Drupal® as searchable records. Fivestar allows users to rate content discovered on a Drupal® site with one to five stars, while the Views module creates multiple data displays for content hosted on a Drupal® website, allowing for context-sensitive record displays in CNMS.

After installing the required software modules, the team combined a variety of elements to create the site organization and menu structure required for users to navigate content collections. They enabled social media features, such as user-contributed comments and ratings, and loaded online help and information content for teachers and students.

A variety of online, print, and traditional advertising accompanies the CNMS Phase II launch. The primary logistical challenge with the CNMS implementation is moderating the user-contributed comments and uploaded files. User content must be reviewed and approved, requiring staff time as well as diplomatic balm toward enthusiastic user-contributors.

Pros and Cons

The 360 Search vendor tool and in-house tool implemented by the UL both had positive and negative points. The vendor tool had several strengths, including low overhead (compared to the in-house tool) and functionality. It was easy to implement without serious time commitment from the library's IT department. Additionally, it was generally inclusive of most subscription databases, particularly in the subject search option. This allowed for databases strong in a particular subject to be targeted during the search, yielding highly relevant results with minimal effort for users. However, drawbacks of the tool included a lack of customization, particularly in the simple search box for the basic user, lack of contextual information, and the default search returned large sets of irrelevant results. Additionally, the slowness of some result returns was frustrating to users. While the free version of WorldCat® Local was perceived as an improvement, the restrictions on customization were also an issue. There was more tolerance for this limitation by library personnel as it was understood that it was a free, quick-fix resource.

The custom-built tool had many strong points, including flexibility and customizability. Due to the specific subject coverage, all results were relevant to a general user. Additionally, due to the use of the Drupal® platform, social networking tools, such as commenting, polling, voting and tagging

were available. It also integrated well into the web environment with which users were already familiar, including Facebook™[6], Twitter™[7] and Flickr®[8]. However, the cons of this approach were a high overhead with lots of support needed from the IT department, and lots of staff time needed to pull records into the project database. In an IT department that already has a full workload maintaining library resources and platforms, the addition of maintaining this type of platform may be out of reach. Additionally, as special departments across campus feel the impact of hard economic times, staff time may be reallocated to more pressing projects. The Drupal® approach also leaves many questions about scalability. The size and scale of the current project is only a fraction of the entire UL's holdings' records. If a metasearch were implemented, it could be difficult to visually present both metasearch records and back-end database records simultaneously.

Best Practices and Recommendations

If the local library system has expertise in using open source tools, as well as IT resources to support these tools, a custom built, open source CMS tool may be a good approach for searching across multiple digital platforms hosted by the library. Most digital library software supports standard metadata schemas, such as Dublin Core, and standard protocols, such as the Open Archives Initiative Protocol for Metadata Harvesting (OAI-PMH). Although the UNM local project did not use these standards, they create an easy environment for accessing metadata records created locally, and importing them into a single database for searching and retrieval. Additionally, most databases supporting these digital library applications are easy to access, and it may be possible to collect records directly from a database dump.

Although metadata from local digital collections are easy to access, OPACs are generally closed, and the metadata records are not easy to fully harvest without additional plug-ins or added cost. Even though the CNMS project was able to harvest records from the OPAC, these records were not the full MARC records. Additionally, this approach was appropriate to a limited number of records, but would not be scalable to all records in the OPAC. Another problem is that most metadata records from subscription databases are not available for harvesting and integrating into local databases. The records must be searched live using metasearch protocols. If this type of search is performed on a custom built federated search tool, it is difficult to integrate these results with results from the local digital collections. Because of these reasons, the UL recommends locally built tools for smaller, subject-based projects integrating and searching the library's collections' strengths.

The UL's experience with vendor tools suggests that these tools need to be flexible and customizable. They should include searches across local digital collections, and these searches should be gathered into broad subject-based areas. Patrons' understandings of results will vary based on their experiences with library resources. Contextualization needs to be provided to help inexperienced users understand result sets. These inexperienced users need to understand that there are significant resources available that are not being searched with the federated tool, such as the local digital collections.

FUTURE RESEARCH DIRECTIONS

Enhancing discovery tools to make library resources findable for patrons is a significant task for all academic libraries. The UL is continuing in its quest to find a one-stop shop that provides easy access to all relevant resources for patrons by experimenting with metasearch products from other vendors, including a recent implementation of EBSCO Discovery Service™[9]. Further research about ways users interact with one-stop

tools will be important to libraries implementing discovery products.

An additional area of interest is the use of federated search or discovery tools to select, organize, manage, and make discoverable free web resources related to collection strengths and vetted by librarians. An important goal for libraries is to provide seamless access to all resources, including physical and digital holdings, resources subscribed to by the library, and freely available resources on the Internet.

Additionally, to further understand patrons' use of library resources within social networking contexts, the Celebrating New Mexico Statehood project is monitoring patron use of the CNMS site and interactions with the social networking tools in Drupal®. The UL intends for this project to connect people with similar interests and provide seamless access to New Mexico history resources.

CONCLUSION

Federated search tools can be very helpful to library patrons. However, in order to be most helpful, a patron needs to understand what is being searched, if the results are thorough and comprehensive, and how to interpret these results. Although advanced library users may understand the complexities of a federated search tool, inexperienced users will need more contextual clues in order to fully understand the results. Systems that provide a more comprehensive search of available materials, including the local library OPAC, local digital collections, and subscription databases, will help ensure that relevant items are available to the users, especially inexperienced users who may not be aware that their search is not comprehensive. Additionally, federated search tools that can limit results to specific subjects are successful. At the UL, the most successful tools were database searches limited to specific topics/subjects, and a home grown federated search tool targeting resources about the state's history. The least successful tool was a general search across all subscription databases without contextualization, problematic integration of the library's OPAC, and no integration of local digital collections. The authors hope that the "new" next generation of discovery tools will remedy these shortcomings, and provide comprehensive searches that can be customized to specific subject areas.

REFERENCES

Bowen, J., Briden, J., Burns, V., Lindahl, D., Reeb, B., Stowe, M., & Wilder, S. (2004). Serial failure. *Charleston Advisor, 5*(3), 48–50.

Burrows, T., Croker, K., Kiel, R., & Nicholls, S. (2007). *Resource discovery – Issues for the UWA Library*. Retrieved from http://www.uwa.edu.au/__data/assets/pdf_file/0011/524864/Resource_Discovery_Webversion.pdf

Calhoun, K. (2006). *The changing nature of the library catalog and its integration with other discovery systems*. Retrieved from http://www.loc.gov/catdir/calhoun-report-final.pdf

Clarke, E. (2006). *DICE project final report: Resource discovery tools evaluation and integration*. Retrieved from http://www.staffs.ac.uk/COSE/DICE/DICEfinal.pdf

Coombs, K. (2009). Drupal done right: Libraries using this open source content management system pioneer new tools and services. *Library Journal, 134*(19), 30–32.

Dahl, M. (2009). Evolution of library-discovery systems in the web environment. *Oregon Library Association Quarterly, 15*(1), 5–9.

Lockwood, C., & MacDonald, P. (2007). Implementation of a federated search system in the academic library: Lessons learned. *Internet Reference Services Quarterly, 12*(1), 73–91. doi:10.1300/J136v12n01_04

Macgregor, G., & McCulloch, E. (2006). Collaborative tagging as a knowledge organisation and resource discovery tool. *Library Review, 55*(5), 291–300. doi:10.1108/00242530610667558

Norman, M. A., Schlembach, M. C., Shelburne, W. A., & Mischo, W. H. (2006). *Journal and article locator (JAL): Federated access to electronic/ print journals and article full-text, 2006*. In 26th Annual Charleston Conference, Charleston (US), 8-11 November 2006. Libraries Unlimited.

Rowe, R. (2010). Web-scale discovery: A review of Summon, EBSCO Discovery Service, and WorldCat Local. *Charleston Advisor, 12*(1), 5–10. doi:10.5260/chara.12.1.5

Sally, D., & Uzwyshyn, R. (2007). New information discovery tools environmental scan: Executive summary and web addresses. Retrieved from http://rayuzwyshyn.net/20072008PDF/NewInformationDiscoveryTools.pdf

Souer, J., Honders, P., Versendall, J., & Brinkkemper, S. (2008). A framework for web content management system operations and maintenance. *Journal of Digital Information Management, 6*(4), 324–331.

Stainthorp, P. (2011, May 17). *How commercial next-generation library discovery tools have *nearly* got it right* [Blog Post]. Retrieved July 28, 2011, from http://jerome.blogs.lincoln.ac.uk/2011/05/17/how-commercial-next-generation-library-discovery-tools-have-nearly-got-it-right/

ADDITIONAL READING

Aksulu, A., & Wade, M. (2010). A comprehensive review and synthesis of open source research. *Journal of the Association for Information Systems, 11*(12), 576–656.

Antelman, K., Lynema, E., & Pace, A. K. (2006). Toward a twenty-first century library catalog. *Information Technology and Libraries, 25*(3), 128–139.

Benlian, A. (2011). Is traditional, open-source, or on-demand first choice? Developing an AHP-based framework for the comparison of different software models in office suites selection. *European Journal of Information Systems, 20*(5), 542–559. doi:10.1057/ejis.2011.14

Bothmann, R. L., & Clink, K. (2011). "Free puppies": Integrating web resources into online catalogs . In Woodsworth, A. (Ed.), *Librarianship in times of crisis* (pp. 159–181). Bingley, UK: Emerald. doi:10.1108/S0065-2830(2011)0000034011

Bowen, J. (2008). Metadata to support next-generation library resource discovery: Lessons from the eXtensible catalog, phase 1. *Information Technology and Libraries, 27*(2), 5–19.

Breeding, M. (2009). Library automation in a difficult economy. *Computers in Libraries, 29*(3), 22–24.

de Jager, K. (2007). Opening the library catalogue up to the web: A view from South Africa. *Information Development February, 23*(1), 48-54.

Engard, N. C. (2010). *Practical open source software for libraries*. Cambridge, UK: Chandos Publishing. doi:10.1533/9781780630434

Garza, A. (2009). From OPAC to CMS: Drupal as an extensible library platform. *Library Hi Tech, 27*(2),252–267.doi:10.1108/07378830910968209

Gulli, A., & Signorini. (2005). Building an open source meta-search engine. *Special interest tracks and Posters of the 14th International Conference on World Wide Web*, Chiba, Japan, 5, May 2005, (pp. 1004-1005).

Huttenlock, T. L., & Beaird, J. W. (2006). Untangling a tangled web: A case study in choosing and implementing a CMS. *Library Hi Tech, 24*(1), 61–68. doi:10.1108/07378830610652112

Joint, N. (2010). The one-stop shop search engine: A transformational library technology?: ANTAEUS. *Library Review, 59*(4), 240–248. doi:10.1108/00242531011038550

Kim, Y., & Abbas, J. (2010). Adoption of library 2.0 functionalities by academic libraries and users: A knowledge management perspective. *Journal of Academic Librarianship, 36*(3), 211–218. doi:10.1016/j.acalib.2010.03.003

Mi, J., & Nesta, F. (2006). Marketing library services to the Net generation. *Library Management, 27*(6/7), 411–422. doi:10.1108/01435120610702404

Morrissey, S. (2010). The economy of free and open source software in the preservation of digital artefacts. *Library Hi Tech, 28*(2), 211–223. doi:10.1108/07378831011047622

Murrain, M., Quinn, L., & Starvish, M. (2009). Comparing open source content management systems: WordPress, Joomla, Drupal and Plone. *Idealware Consumer Reports, 2009*, 60.

Neves, B., & Pinheiro, D. (2011). *Os Sistemas de Gestão de Conteúdos aplicados à gestão da informação em bibliotecas universitárias* [em linha]. Retrieved from http://hdl.handle.net/10316/14462

Olson, T. A. (2007). Utility of a faceted catalog for scholarly research. *Library Hi Tech, 25*(4), 550–561. doi:10.1108/07378830710840509

Payne, A., & Singh, V. (2010). Open source software use in libraries. *Library Review, 29*(9), 708–717. doi:10.1108/00242531011087033

Ponsford, B. C., & van Duinkerken, W. (2007). User expectations in the time of Google: Usability testing of federated searching Internet. *Reference Services Quarterly, 12*(1-2), 159–178.

Poulter, A. (2010). Open source in libraries: An introduction and overview. *Library Review, 59*(9), 655–661. doi:10.1108/00242531011086971

Russo-Gallo, P. (2009). Nuevas tecnologías en abierto para bibliotecas. *Boletín de la Asociación Andaluza de Bibliotecarios, 2009*(94-95), 11-26.

Sadeh, T. (2007). Time for a change: New approaches for the new generation of library users. *New Library World, 108*(7/8), 307–316. doi:10.1108/03074800710763608

Seadle, M. (2008). The digital library in 100 years: Damage control. *Library Hi Tech, 26*(1), 5–10. doi:10.1108/07378830810857744

Tonta, Y. (2008). Libraries and museums in the flat world: Are they becoming virtual destinations? *Library Collections, Acquisitions & Technical Services, 32*(1), 1–9. doi:10.1016/j.lcats.2008.05.002

Way, D. (2010). The impact of web-scale discovery on the use of a library collection. *Serials Review, 36*(4), 214–220. doi:10.1016/j.serrev.2010.07.002

Yu, H., & Young, M. (2004). The impact of web search engines on subject searching in OPAC. *Information Technology and Libraries, 23*(4), 168–180.

KEY TERMS AND DEFINITIONS

Content Management System (CMS): A computer application designed to manage web content (images, multi-media, texts, etc.), website authoring, workflows, and administration tasks with little or no expectation of additional software development.

Drupal: An open-source content management system written in PHP, which is a popular scripting language used to create web applications. Due to Drupal®'s popularity and the ease of creating additional addons, the user community has contributed thousands of modules expanding on and enhancing Drupal®'s core capabilities.

Drupal® Nodes: In Drupal®, each piece of content (web page, blog posting, document, image etc.), is referred to and managed individually as a node.

Encoded Archival Description (EAD): An XML standard maintained by the Library of Congress for encoding archival finding aids.

Federated Search: A generic term for any product providing search results from multiple databases, by searching these databases directly.

Finding Aid: A document created to help describe an archival collection and provide an inventory of the items in the collection.

Institutional Repository: A service generally offered by a library to a community for archiving and distribution of electronic scholarly output.

Metadata: Information about a resource.

Metasearch: A specific type of federated search that sends requests to multiple databases simultaneously. Results are returned to the users as the metasearch tool receives them.

SQL Compliant Database: A relational database that can be managed using SQL (Structured Query Language).

SQL Script: A set of commands written in SQL used to manipulate data in a relational database.

ENDNOTES

[1] Serials Solution is a registered trademark of Serials Solutions

[2] Drupal is a registered trademark of Dries Buytaert.

[3] Joomla is a registered trademark of Open Source Matters, Inc.

[4] Wordpress is a trademark of the Wordpress Foundation.

[5] WorldCat is a registered trademark of OCLC.

[6] Facebook is a trademark of Facebook Inc.

[7] Twitter is a trademark of Twitter, Inc.

[8] Flickr is a registered trademark of Yahoo! Inc.

[9] EBSCO Discovery Service is a trademark of EBSCO Publishing Industries.

Chapter 20
Discovery in a Hurry:
Fast Transitions from Federated Search to Article Discovery

Nina Exner
North Carolina Agricultural and Technical State University, USA

Stephen Bollinger
North Carolina Agricultural and Technical State University, USA

Iyanna Sims
North Carolina Agricultural and Technical State University, USA

ABSTRACT

F.D. Bluford Library is a mid-sized library serving over 10,000 undergraduate and graduate students. In 2010, the Library began to transition from federated search technology to Web-scale discovery to meet user expectations. Users expected to have quick access to the library resources. The promise of discovery was an idealized solution for all stakeholders. Discovery platform vendors touted quick access to multiple resources using centralized indexing or highly-efficient database connectors. In the selection process, however, it became evident that there are no easy choices. Each platform currently on the market had advantages and disadvantages. The library's task force therefore defined priorities and environmental factors to select the optimum solution while meeting an aggressive deadline for selection. This chapter discusses the particular needs of mid-size libraries and makes suggestions for an evaluation process.

INTRODUCTION

The fourth law of Ranganathan's Five Laws of Library Science states "[s]ave the time of the reader" (Ranganathan, 1957, p. 287). Librarians continue to adapt this law to new technological environments and develop new approaches. Michael Gorman's addition to Ranganathan's five laws in *Future Libraries: Dreams, Madness and Realities* is an appropriate example of this – "use technology intelligently to enhance service." (Crawford & Gorman, 1995, p. 7-8). Libraries have historically used technologies as they became available to facilitate timely discovery of

DOI: 10.4018/978-1-4666-1821-3.ch020

information. These tools initially were print-based, such as card catalogs and print indexes, but have evolved to adapt to new technologies (Vaughan, 2011). The promise of contemporary Internet technologies, to allow libraries to provide the right information to the right person at the right time without the time limitations and physical barriers of traditional print media, is mired in the reality of our society's current struggle over intellectual content ownership and distribution in a virtual environment. Content owners store information in discrete repositories, metaphorically known as "silos," with various limits to access. Discovery platforms are the latest promising attempt to balance the rights of content owners to control their information with the needs of librarians, students, faculty and researchers needing to readily find information across those multiple silos (Breeding, 2010; Breeding, 2011a).

BACKGROUND

Literature Review

Single-box searching--the ideal of being able to type a search string into one single search box to retrieve results from all relevant sources --is not new. In the early 2000s, federated search promised to simplify the search process for users by offering a single search box that searched across multiple database platforms at once (Tennant, 2003). The single-box interface that searchers prefer has consistently presented both technological and user behavior concerns (Boyd, Hampton, Morrison, Pugh, & Cervone, 2006). While academic library users enjoy the simplicity of the interface, they also expect familiar, easy usability; advanced users may also require fast options to refine and revisit searches beyond what federated search tools have offered (Gibson, Goddard, & Gordon, 2009). The federated search technology has also proven to have some limitations: the technology is slow, search results are not comprehensive, and

users perceive them to be poorly organized and not always relevant (Korah & Cassidy, 2010; Luther & Kelly, 2011; Williams, Bonnell, & Stoffel, 2009). Despite these issues, single-box searching also offers advantages both in user satisfaction and Web site design flexibility, enabling libraries to offer the most user-friendly interface designs and generally to boost user satisfaction (Caswell & Wynstra, 2010).

Almost a decade after the federated search debut, libraries may now have available the best generalized information retrieval platform yet, the discovery platform (Vaughan, 2011). Older federated tools often lack integration with Library 2.0 tools, interaction with personal information management tools, and "next generation" options such as faceting and advanced relevancy options (Gibson, Goddard, & Gordon, 2009). Article discovery on the "Web-scale" offers cross-platform article retrieval much faster than federated search typically does, incorporating a simple interface and many of the advanced information seeking tools that users desire (Gross & Sheridan, 2011; Keene, 2011). These discovery tools should be a large step forward for academic searchers. Discovery tools' breadth of options offer promise for smaller and mid-sized libraries which need flexible and varied solutions.

Mid-sized libraries offer their own unique technological issues. Faculty expectations at mid-sized institutions are robust (Weber & Flatley, 2006) as are student needs, but these libraries lack the systems development resources and personnel of larger institutions. Fiscal and personnel realities affect a variety of systems projects in smaller and medium-sized libraries. Mid-sized libraries may have issues in systems projects such as electronic resource management (Condic, 2008; Milczarski & Garofalo, 2011) and institutional repository development (Oguz & Davis, 2011). Many Webmasters at mid-sized academic libraries do not describe Web development as their primary task and are rarely highly experienced in advanced programming languages (Kneip, 2007). A Web/

software development team is beyond the means of many of these institutions.

The Bluford Library Case

The F.D. Bluford Library is located on the campus of North Carolina A&T State University, a land-grant, historically black, doctoral degree-granting university focusing on science and technology disciplines. A staff of fifty serves approximately 10,000 undergraduate and graduate students. As of 2012, the Library has over 700,000 books; 150,000 electronic books; 160,000 print, electronic journals, and serials; and 300 databases. In addition, a digital collection and institutional repository are being built. The library strives to provide easy access to all of its resources and to take advantage of technology that fosters this type of interaction. As of 2012, a full-time systems staff of three librarians and one professional staff member supports this mission, an increase from one librarian and one professional in 2005.

In 2005 the Library implemented a federated search tool. At that time, the federated search technology provided the best means of searching information indexed in multiple databases at once. Unfortunately, the technology was not as user-friendly as anticipated. Users expected an experience similar to that of a standard Web search engine and considered federated searching to be slow and inefficient regardless of the complex technical accomplishments it represented. Ultimately, whatever its problems, the tool was underutilized.

Two years later, another federated search product was selected to replace the first, and by 2007, federated search technology had improved. The needs of the users were better met by the tool, which included an improved user interface, facile navigation, and organized search results with relevancy. The federated tool, with numerous connectors, appeared to have finally satisfied the need of providing seamless access to multiple electronic resources and the library catalog. How-

ever, there was a new configuration introduced by the vendor in 2009 that was incompatible with the library's off-campus user authentication infrastructure. Remote users were asked to authenticate every time a destination database from the search result set was accessed and sometimes queries failed entirely. As a solution, the vendor offered migration to a new federated search platform that handled authentication differently.

During the migration process, federated search was unavailable and the resulting outcry from large numbers of users further confirmed that a simple search interface was a necessity for the university. A largely unexpected finding from the feedback was that federated search was popular among graduate students and faculty, a reality not anticipated by faculty at the library and a contradiction to research findings that have indicated that federated tools are not much used or liked by graduate students (Korah & Cassidy, 2010). Although it was assumed that federated search is a simplified tool for Internet-generation undergraduates, it was used by a much broader campus constituency with widely differing levels of research skills.

Despite an emergency migration to the alternative platform over the summer of 2010 in hopes of meeting users' needs and expectations, the third instance of federated search only amplified the shortcomings of that technology. While the tool indeed allowed multiple resources to be searched from one interface, users and librarians alike noted slowness and sometimes-incomprehensible search results. Search results could not be grouped by relevance across database providers, another crucial user expectation. Unfortunately even mature federated search technology was not meeting the needs and expectations of the library and its users. It was obvious that a new approach was needed. With emerging discovery platforms touting faster, easier, more user-friendly search, it was time to investigate the new approach.

A library task force, expanded from a standing Technology Committee, composed of Public

Service, Technical Services, and Systems staff, was convened to investigate and make recommendations for the adoption of a discovery tool. The task force was charged to identify a tool or make an alternate recommendation if discovery was not the right approach. The discovery tool had to meet the needs of a diverse user group; provide coverage for both specialized collections and the majority of databases relevant to the university's science, technology, and engineering disciplines; integrate with the university's and library's current technological infrastructure; and harvest metadata from the forthcoming institutional repository and an ever-expanding collection of LibGuides. The charge had to be completed within six to eight weeks due to university holiday scheduling and budget availability.

The aforementioned factors were not as challenging as the impending question --what exactly is a discovery tool?

DISCOVERY IN FIVE MINUTES OR LESS

Issues, Controversies, and Problems

Emerging technologies have often been difficult to immediately define and discovery is no different (Carter, 2009; Notess, 2011). While the literature does provide some guidance, a closer examination shows there are three practical ways to look at discovery as a tool. These categories are not mutually exclusive, nor are they a firm model of discovery design. They are merely used here to explain the broad types of theoretically and practically available functionality. They also demonstrate the breadth of results that a search for discovery tools may find in the literature. Pragmatically, one might define discovery in the following broad categories:

Category One:

Catalog discovery: an interface primarily aimed at catalog records. Depending on what resources are extant in the catalog, this may be print-oriented or may extend further.

Category Two:

Article discovery: an interface primarily aimed at retrieving individual articles across many database and e-resource subscriptions.

Category Three:

Generalized discovery interfaces: a separate "user interface" layer that can be applied over an infinitely variable number of back-end information sources, content non-specific.

The earliest discovery products in implementation were in Category One, catalog discovery. As the main repository for records of library information and an information store that is clearly locally owned, the catalog is a sensible starting place. The catalog discovery product range is moderately sizable and has been around for a few years now. In fact, many of the Web sites and articles discussing library discovery are specifically talking about catalog discovery (Adamich, 2010; Bowen, 2008; Dolski, 2009; Matthews, 2009; McCullough, 2010; Yang & Wagner, 2010; Zeigen & Crum, 2009); catalog discovery is the main area that is mature enough to have had time for research to be developed and to enter into the literature. It is also the only area where open source products -- such as Scriblio, SOPAC, VuFind, and Blacklight -- have been developed. Unsurprisingly, this category includes the commercial offerings from the traditional ILS (Integrated Library System) vendors, whereas article discovery corresponds with the platforms offered by longtime content vendors.

Article discovery tools are those products that are mainly created for the retrieval of smaller information objects in full: mainly full text articles but also book chapters, conference proceedings, statistical charts, and related parts of online works. This model angles towards the same niche that many libraries seek to fill with federated search tools. These are often products that are also "Library 2.0" types of interfaces. Open source platforms for article discovery are not available, possibly because open-source developers cannot negotiate rights for pre-indexing or database connectors with vendors.

Category Three might be the ideal solution; it would be a user interface only, adapted to an array of information sources. Discovery developers could then concentrate on the user experience foremost. Although this is perhaps the ideal–and many vendors talk about their discovery products like an "experience" beyond mere tools– here does not appear to be any such product yet. It may be a purely theoretical construct, useful for discussion but not for application. In the pursuit of the "Google-like" ideal, many products in categories one and two are trying to converge on a generalized discovery interface. Some very large libraries have developed their own discovery "layers" to create a unified user experience across all back-end data sources, but this is a specialized process beyond the scope of a mid-sized library.

It is notable that the phrase "W-scale discovery" is becoming prominent, confusing the matter even more. Generally, W-scale discovery seems to be used as a way to refer to article discovery products that incorporate catalog and other resources in pursuit of becoming generalized discovery interfaces. This is the "Google-like" ideal. As discovery technologies mature, perhaps catalog and journal discovery will merge into a true all-purpose discovery interface that can incorporate all tools. Some products approach this to some extent. For example, both catalog-oriented and article-oriented products often include the ability to incorporate institutional repositories. Some can also include locally generated Website materials, LibGuides pages, and a wide variety of other

electronic materials. It is hoped these evolutions will remove the relatively artificial division between the ideal generalized discovery and the more pragmatic catalog and journal discovery.

Understanding the functionality being described in each tool is important in identifying a tool that meets a library's specific needs. Vendor descriptions often use broad phrases claiming that resources will be easily found by users, without specifying which resources. The process of finding this can be awkward, as the Bluford Library found out. Learning that not all discovery tools are the same, it becomes necessary to examine which ones perform the needed functions. In the Bluford case, transitioning from federated search, the critical function was article discovery. Once the tools were examined and tested for focus on that functionality, it became possible to enter the selection process.

Bluford's Discoveries

Based on the decision that article discovery was critical to Bluford users, the task force focused on this functionality. Researching available formal peer-reviewed library journals was much more complicated than imagined. As already mentioned, the literature did not fully explore each category of discovery. Subsequently, vendor product information was researched but was difficult to synthesize as well. Vendors often provide limited details regarding system integration and detailed technical specifications. Others focus on user studies without much product detail.

Practical application of discovery proved to be a valuable source of information. Informal sites such as the Unified Resource Discovery Wiki[1] were more helpful than the literature. More critically, independent exploration was a must. A particularly useful site, Library Technology Guides Discovery Interfaces page[2] provided an excellent source of links to see which tools were being implemented with which integrated library systems. This provided an invaluable opportunity to see the results of real-world efforts to use a given technology stack. Task force members were able to survey libraries' instances of discovery products, confirm article level results, and demonstrate the speed of result retrieval. This was critical to determine which tools felt comparable to the federated tools being replaced and to form a value-neutral sense of the tools before listening to the marketing presentations the vendors would bring.

From the literature research, product information, and a scan of library implementations, there were five discovery tools at that time that addressed article discovery in a way suitable to Bluford Library needs:

- EBSCO Discovery Service™[3]
- ExLibris Primo Central™[4]
- III Encore Synergy™[5]
- OCLC WorldCat®[6] Local
- Serials Solutions®[7] Summon™[8]

Priority-Driven Selection

Establishing priorities is a must for libraries choosing a discovery platform. A widely accepted homily is the importance of "knowing oneself" and it is apt one for any library team considering discovery options. Like other libraries, the task force prioritized user needs foremost (Ruddock & Hartley, 2010). While other factors were important, including the technology stack, concerns and avoiding incurred costs, product selection was driven by public service need. This was an explicit choice adopted by the task force after discussion.

The most critical point was that the discovery platform needed to be usable without training or library intervention. It must serve as an easy point of entry to library resources for distance learning students, users who may never set foot in the library, or those who never receive library instruction. Another priority was robust searching features to serve graduate students, researchers, and faculty users. The chosen discovery platform also had to cover a comprehensive set of the da-

tabases that are most relevant to the disciplines studied at the university and include features such as EndNote® exporting. An evaluation method was developed on these basic criteria and each of the five platforms was ranked accordingly.

A survey of all interested librarians and staff, especially those in public service, was performed asking them to rank their views of the five platforms based on vendor training materials and testing implementations at other libraries. Feedback from this process determined which vendors to invite for a demonstration. In early discussions, many of the staff believed WorldCat® Local was a good product but had a strong focus on physical holdings. In evaluating what the library wanted and needed, the task force identified that article discovery was more important than catalog discovery. This realization occurred well into the process, after the distinctions between catalog and article discovery began to emerge. Library expenditures for electronic resources dwarfed those for physical collections and that investment could not be fully realized without effective article discovery. It became evident to the task force that while the catalog and its resources must be represented in the discovery tool's search results, effective article discovery was crucial to success of the project. This will obviously be different for each library and must be carefully considered.

With no consensus on the remaining four products, vendors were invited for live demonstrations of their products. The task force members created a master list of questions reflective of broader staff interest and concerns. Though some questions could not be answered without a full implementation of each product in Bluford Library's environment, it was advantageous to have vendors be cognizant of expectations during the presentation. Technical questions were often deferred to the vendors' technical staff for later clarification but it was beneficial for the task force to have an accurate list of technological concerns to ensure compatibility.

There were similarities among each vendor visit. Every vendor touted usage and access increases, though the methodology for determining these increases was usually inscrutable. All visiting vendors boasted large lists of partnerships. However, with large numbers of e-journal and database subscriptions both directly through the library and statewide via (North Carolina's state wide online library, NCLive, it was imperative to see a master list of relevant publisher relationships and specific database coverage to do a meaningful comparison among vendors. Since none could share a master list, each vendor offered to perform a coverage analysis. The coverage report was necessary to accurately compare which vendor had the highest proportion of locally subscribed e-journals and databases available via connector or included in their central index. In the interest of time, each vendor was asked to generate coverage analyses, as well as price quotes, promptly after each vendor visit.

While each visit provided some insight and vendor representatives were amendable to requests, the presentations would have proved to be more helpful for an audience still deciding *whether* to implement rather than *which* product to implement. The bulk of each presentation was irrelevant to clear product comparison, focusing on the case for discovery instead of the case for the vendor's product over competitors' products. Librarians who are already knowledgeable about discovery, as the task force in its entirety was by this step in the process, may find these presentations tedious, repetitive, and fairly unhelpful to a comparison-oriented selection process. Documenting an accurate list of technical questions and the evaluation criteria developed earlier in the task force's progress were critical to keeping the team focused throughout the vendor demonstrations.

After each demonstration a "first impressions" discussion was held to compare initial thoughts, suggestions, and concerns. The immediate debriefings became increasingly important as selection progressed and the details between the vendors began to blur. It helped to share and note immediate impressions before they were forgotten. After the task force saw all the vendor demonstrations, links to demonstration and example sites were sent to all librarians and staff to evaluate and to share with subject liaisons in the university's schools and departments if possible. Notes from those who responded were taken for discussion and a chart of pros and cons was (see Table 1) developed for each product.

Solutions and Recommendations

No universal solution for discovery has been created and there is no evidence at the moment that a universal discovery solution will be created in the near future. Any solution must therefore be tailored to the needs and environment of the institution during their selection process. A similar process to the one described above, tailored to local needs, may be a good starting place. The finding at Bluford, which is likely to be similar at other libraries, was that each product had strengths and weaknesses. The unique character of each product makes it hard to compare on any true one-to-one basis. Unique strengths and weaknesses were often the items most focused-on during discussion. A critical selection point must be which weaknesses are least problematic and which strengths are most advantageous based on each library's individual needs.

Different libraries will find some strengths or weaknesses to be more critical than others; some strengths that were barely noticed by this assessment team might override another library's considerations.

Since Discovery is a relatively new and extremely fast-evolving technology, many of the above-listed strengths and weaknesses were already being addressed in different ways. It is certain that by the time this book is published, platforms will already have shifted and new weaknesses and strengths will likely have evolved.

Table 1. Discovery task force reactions by platform

Perceived Strengths and Advantages	
EBSCO Discovery Service™	EDS™ emphasized human-mediated indexing and deep metadata, for better quality results. It also leveraged abstracting databases better than others (some other products ignored abstracting products). EDS™ had a familiar interface for library users because the local collection includes many EBSCO products.
ExLibris™ Primo Central™	ExLibris™ is reminiscent of an Amazon-like interface including an excellent "readers who viewed this also liked..." function. It clearly had the most precise control of the article-to-book mix, the best statistics module and an easily accessible "crowdsourced" development community.
III Encore Synergy™	Results are accurate with the most recent, up-to-the-minute updates. A current III customer, Bluford would have a familiar support team and administrative modules. A good catalog discovery layer and integration would be an added bonus.
Serials Solutions® Summon™	A Google-like interface that creates a simple and familiar feel. Summon™ is probably the best-established of the products, with more research about library and end-user outcomes.
Perceived Weaknesses and Concerns	
EBSCO Discovery Service™	Authentication was clunky. Coverage concerns existed for the particular local collection holdings.
ExLibris™ Primo Central™	The navigation was awkward for some features. The vendor displayed no interest in presenting non-full-text holdings at all.
III Encore Synergy™	Subject faceting was nonexistent at the time of review; there was no way to narrow results by topic, which was locally considered an essential discovery/2.0 feature. (This will likely have changed by the date of publication of this chapter.)
Serials Solutions® Summon™	Absolutely geared towards the novice searcher, Summon™ had little advanced search functionality for serious researchers. Print holdings were overwhelmed and aesthetic customizations were limited.

Table 1. Discovery Task Force Reactions by Platform

Some items may be neutral to some libraries and not to others. For example, Encore Synergy™ and Primo Central™ both have the advantage of being relatively content-provider-neutral, whereas Summon™ and EBSCO Discovery Service™ show an unmistakable bias towards ProQuest®[9] and EBSCO resources respectively, although each has methods to ensure coverage was still possible. Some libraries may prefer provider-neutrality but some collections may not foster a concern.

It is also worth mentioning that some of these products had traits that could be considered positives or negatives, depending on the view of the library considering them. For example, one trait worth mentioning is Encore Synergy's™ use of WebConnect technology rather than a pre-indexing technology. This concept makes implementation somewhat structurally similar to setting up federated search connections but operates faster than federated search technology. In this model, the library chooses databases or database sets to be included rather than content being provided from a large predetermined data pool. This means the library is not restricted to preset groups of data. However, it also means that the implementation team must prioritize databases and not all of the available full-text articles can be leveraged unless the budget allows for a connector to be built for every database. Live connecting also means results come back in real time from the provider; the results are the most up-to-date as possible.

For larger academic libraries with a robust development team expected to heavily integrate or customize it, Summon's™ API product may be an advantage. For smaller libraries, APIs may be luxuries, aspirant in nature, and not a priority for a discovery tool. Customizations without APIs may be of importance for most libraries and the Bluford task force felt that, despite branding and customization options, EBSCO Discovery Service™ had an unmistakably EBSCO-platform feel to it, too closely resembling EBSCOhost. Whether that is a concern depends on the library but this trait certainly was prominent.

With the variety of different strengths and weaknesses it was hard to say that any one product really transcended the others. How does one compare dynamic, real-time facet generation and regeneration versus human-mediated indexing? Both have advantages, but if they cannot be found together robustly in one product it becomes hard to determine which should get the greater emphasis. Similarly, comparing a familiar Google-like interface versus a familiar Amazon-like one, both are associated among users with different aspects of the information-seeking process. Each has its own advantages and disadvantages. Even when the library evaluation team looked at products with comparable outcomes, the products still had such different appeals it was difficult to compare. The ideal situation will include more end-user comparisons and user behavior studies, but practical considerations often preclude robust investigations.

As a result of the disparate nature of comparison, the final decision was driven by a factor having less to do with the product. As discussed, the task force created an evaluation method to make a decision based on meeting user needs and expectations but a strict timeline had a strong impact on the final decision. One vendor, possibly delayed by holiday scheduling, did not provide a coverage report by the recommendation deadline. Understandably, the task force was unable to recommend a product without knowing the coverage.

Another vendor, whose product was well liked by the task force, was eliminated because of probable delays expected with the contract review by the university's legal department. Of the two choices remaining, task force members were strongly partisan towards each. Practical considerations and majority preference of non-task-force librarians were the resolving factors to choose Summon.

FUTURE RESEARCH DIRECTIONS

The field of research for discovery tools of all kinds is wide open. User-oriented information retrieval issues abound in all search platforms and discovery has not solved them.

Issues that should be considered by future researchers include interface design concerns and usability issues, ways to make faceting simpler and more intuitive, and ontological metadata issues to help translate between what the user types and what the user means. As the Bluford experience shows, speed is a definite issue as well. Retrieval speed is a technological challenge that needs to be constantly addressed as users' expectations for fast results grow.

The overuse of the term "discovery" for all manner of tools is perhaps not a research issue but it is an industry concern nonetheless. Until it becomes easier to identify what libraries desire among unrelated offerings, many libraries simply will not have the time or inclination to explore.

Federated search technology is not inherently inferior; there are advantages. The WConnect approach that Encore Synergy™ takes is an interesting version of this approach, combining some pre-harvested and some live-retrieved data (Luther & Kelly, 2011). Federated search technologies are worthy of continued development until they can be blended with discovery approaches to make a product that combines the advantages of speed and timeliness.

CONCLUSION

Non-ARL and mid-sized libraries can benefit from discovery tools. Though able to countenance the costs and commitments to deploy a discovery product, with fewer resources, smaller staffs, and less opportunity to dedicate committee members' time to in-depth analyses of products, the mid-sized library has unique challenges.

A good approach is to begin with an overview of the library's goals. Identify the users, the main points of concern (speed, comprehensiveness, ease of use, marketing, or other issues) and priorities, and time frame. If possible, attempt to allow plenty of time not only for the library assessment but for campus-level processes that may slow down final purchasing. As was found in this case, contract negotiation issues with new vendors can narrow the field of options considerably.

Implicit in the priorities is a consideration of systems expertise and availability. Implementation and maintenance of any discovery tool will require the dedicated time of someone willing and able to engage with the technical details. The best discovery platform is useless if it cannot be successfully implemented. One important reason for the failure of early federated search efforts at Bluford Library was an over-committed and understaffed Systems department.

After the time frame and priorities are identified, compose a task force that is truly representative of all of the departments of the library. Remain cognizant that departments such as cataloging and archives must be involved for components such as loading MARC records and integrating an institutional repository. Try to involve every department if at all possible; broad participation can garner unexpected insights.

Plan for personnel to examine the candidate products in advance of the vendor presentations and create lists of questions for everyone to consider. At the vendors' visits assume that they will not be able to answer every question and allot time for an immediate debriefing after the presenta-tion to share fresh reactions. It is easy to forget important questions and first impressions. This may lead to long meetings but can be exceedingly helpful in the process when distinctions began to blur between the products.

Have staff reconsider products after the vendor presentations. A re-examination provides a wider view of the products and a vendor's showcase of libraries will often show the best each tool has to offer, while those found independently may better illustrate troubled implementations.

Finally, recognize that complications are a normal part of any project. Campus legal or budgetary issues may trump library issues, despite careful planning and consideration. Vendors' coverage analyses are critical; it may be that coverage of the particular library's holdings must outweigh interface issues. Warn committee members that ranking is more important than agreement on one key item; commitment to a team favorite may only end in disaster when the real world intrudes.

REFERENCES

Adamich, T. (2010). Metadata and the next generation library catalog: Will the catalog become a true discovery system? *Technicalities*, *30*(3), 12–15.

Bowen, J. (2008). Metadata to support next generation library resource discovery: Lessons from eXtensible catalog, phase 1. *Information Technology & Libraries*, *27*(2), 5–19.

Boyd, J., Hampton, M., Morrison, P., Pugh, P., & Cervone, F. (2006). The one-box challenge: Providing a federated search that benefits the research process. *Serials Review*, *32*(4), 247–254. doi:10.1016/j.serrev.2006.08.005

Breeding, M. (2010). The state of the art in library discovery 2010. *Computers in Libraries*, *30*(1), 31–34.

Breeding, M. (2011a). Building comprehensive resource discovery platforms. *Smart Libraries Newsletter, 31*(3).

Breeding, M. (2011b). *Discovery layer interfaces.* Retrieved from http://www.librarytechnology.org/discovery.pl

Carter, J. (2009). Discovery: What do you mean by that? *Information Technology & Libraries, 28*(4), 161–163.

Caswell, J. V., & Wynstra, J. D. (2010). Improving the search experience: federated search and the library gateway. *Library Hi Tech, 28*(3), 391–401. doi:10.1108/07378831011076648

Condic, K. (2008). Uncharted waters: ERM implementation in a medium-sized academic library. *Internet Reference Services Quarterly, 13*(2/3), 133–145. doi:10.1080/10875300802103643

Crawford, W., & Gorman, M. (1995). *Future libraries: Dreams, madness & reality.* Chicago, IL: American Library Association.

Dolski, A. A. (2009). Information discovery insights gained from MulitPAC, a prototype library discovery system. *Information Technology & Libraries, 28*(4), 172–180.

Gibson, I., Goddard, L., & Gordon, S. (2009). One box to search them all: Implementing federated search at an academic library: Implementing federated search at an academic library. *Library Hi Tech, 27*(1), 118–133. doi:10.1108/07378830910942973

Gross, J., & Sheridan, L. (2011). W-scale discovery: the user experience. *New Library World, 112*(5/6), 236–247. doi:10.1108/03074801111136275

Hadra, J. (2009). Discovery marketplace is red hot at ALA. *Library Journal, 134*(13), 13–14.

Keene, C. (2011). Discovery services: Next generations of searching scholarly information. *Serials, 24*(2), 193–196. doi:10.1629/24193

Kneip, J. (2007). Library Webmasters in medium-sized academic libraries. *Journal of Web Librarianship, 1*(3), 3–23. doi:10.1300/J502v01n03_02

Korah, A., & Cassidy, E. D. (2010). Students and federated searching: A survey of use and satisfaction. *Reference and User Services Quarterly, 49*(4), 325–332.

Luther, J., & Kelly, M. C. (2011). The next generation of discovery. *Library Journal, 136*(5), 66–71.

Matthews, J. G. (2009). We never have to say goodbye: Finding a place for OPACS in discovery environments. *Public Services Quarterly, 5*(1), 55–58. doi:10.1080/15228950802629162

McCullough, J. (2010). Adapting to change in Encore Synergy: New directions in discovery. *Computers in Libraries, 30*(8), 10–11.

Milczarski, V., & Garofalo, D. A. (2011). True serials: A true solution for electronic resource management needs in a medium-size academic library. *Journal of Electronic Resources Librarianship, 23*(3), 242–258. doi:10.1080/1941126X.2011.601228

Notess, G. R. (2011). Deciphering discovery. *Online, 35*(1), 45–47.

Oguz, F., & Davis, D. (2011). Developing an institutional repository at a medium-sized university: Getting started and going forward. *Georgia Library Quarterly, 48*(4), 13–16.

Ranganathan, S. R. (1957). *The five laws of library science* (2nd ed.). Madras, India: The Madras Library Association.

Ruddock, B., & Hartley, D. (2010). How UK academic libraries choose metasearch systems. *Aslib Proceedings, 62*(1), 85–105. doi:10.1108/00012531011015226

Tennant, R. (2003). The right solution: Federated search tools. *Library Journal, 128*(11), 28–29.

Unified Resource Discovery Comparison Wiki. (2011). *Unified resources discovery comparison.* Retrieved April 14, 2012, from https://sites.google.com/site/urd2comparison/

Vaughan, J. (2011). Chapter 1: W-scale discovery what and why? *Library Technology Reports, 47*(1), 5–11.

Wer, M. A., & Flatley, R. (2006). What do faculty what?: A focus group study of faculty at a mid-sized public university. *Library Philosophy & Practice, 9*(1), 1–8.

Williams, S. C., Bonnell, A., & Stoffel, B. (2009). Student feedback on federated search use, satisfaction, and Webpresence: Qualitative findings of focus groups. *Reference and User Services Quarterly, 49*(2), 131–139.

Yang, S. Q., & Wagner, K. (2010). Evaluating and comparing discovery tools: How close are we towards next generation catalog? *Library Hi Tech, 28*(4), 690–709. doi:10.1108/07378831011096312

Zeigen, L., & Crum, J. (2009). Library catalogs and other discovery tools. *OLA Quarterly, 15*(1), 1.

ADDITIONAL READING

Best, R. D. (2009). Is the "big deal" dead? *The Serials Librarian, 57*(4), 353–363. doi:10.1080/03615260903203702

Bogstad, J. M. (2010). Federated search: Solution or setback for online library services. *Library Collections, Acquisitions & Technical Services, 34*(1), 43. doi:10.1016/j.lcats.2009.08.002

Boock, M., Jeppesen, B., & Barrow, W. (2003). Getting digitization projects done in a medium-sized academic library: A collaborative effort between technical services, systems, special collections, and collection management. *Technical Services Quarterly, 20*(3), 19–31. doi:10.1300/J124v20n03_02

Brown-Sica, M., Beall, J., & McHale, N. (2010). Next-generation library catalogs and the problem of slow response time. *Information Technology and Libraries, 29*(4), 214–223.

Chen, X. (2006). MetaLib, WFeat, and Google: The strengths and weaknesses of federated search engines compared with Google. *Online Information Review, 30*(4), 413–427. doi:10.1108/14684520610686300

Conrad, J. G. (2010). E-Discovery revisited: The need for artificial intelligence beyond information retrieval. *Artificial Intelligence and Law, 18*(4), 321–345. doi:10.1007/s10506-010-9096-6

Cox, C. (2006). An analysis of the impact of federated search products on library instruction using the ACRL standards. *portal . Libraries and the Academy, 6*(3), 253–267. doi:10.1353/pla.2006.0035

Fagan, J. C. (2010). Usability studies of faceted browsing: a literature review. *Information Technology and Libraries, 29*(2), 58–66.

Fahey, S. (2007). F******ED searchers? The debate about federated search engines. *Feliciter, 53*(2), 62–63.

Gail, H. (2007). MetaSearching and beyond: Implementation experiences and advice from an academic library. *Information Technology and Libraries, 26*(2), 44–52.

Grefenstette, G., & Wilber, L. (2010). Search-based applications: At the confluence of search and database technologies. *Synthesis Lectures on Information Concepts, Retrieval, and Services, 2*(1), 1–141. doi:10.2200/S00320ED1V01Y-201012ICR017

Hyland, A. M. (2004). Providing access to atypical items in an academic library. *Collection Management, 29*(1), 57–72. doi:10.1300/J105v29n01_06

Ipri, T., Yunkin, M., & Brown, J. M. (2009). Usability as a method for assessing discovery. *Information Technology & Libraries*, *28*(4), 181–183.

Joint, N. (2009). Managing the implementation of a federated search tool in an academic library. *Library Review*, *58*(1), 11–16. doi:10.1108/00242530910928898

Kress, N., Bosque, D., & Ipri, T. (2011). User failure to find known library items. *New Library World*, *112*(3/4), 150–170. doi:10.1108/03074801111117050

Lamothe, A. (2008). Electronic serials usage patterns as observed at a medium-sized university: Searches and full-text downloads. *Partnership: The Canadian Journal of Library & Information Practice & Research*, *3*(1), 1–22.

Menasce, D. A. (2004). Response-time analysis of composite Web services. *IEEE Internet Computing*, *8*(1), 90–92. doi:10.1109/MIC.2004.1260710

Meng, W., & Yu, C. T. (2010). Advanced metasearch engine technology. *Synthesis Lectures on Data Management*, *2*(1), 1–129. doi:10.2200/S00307ED1V01Y201011DTM011

Morris, M. R., & Teevan, J. (2009). Collaborative Web search: Who, what, where, when, and why. *Synthesis Lectures on Information Concepts, Retrieval, and Services*, *1*(1), 1–99. doi:10.2200/S00230ED1V01Y200912ICR014

Moulaison, H. L. (2008). OPAC queries at a medium-sized academic library: A transaction log analysis. *Library Resources & Technical Services*, *52*(4), 230–237.

Nagy, A. (2011). *Analyzing the next-generation catalog*. Chicago, IL: ALA TechSource.

Stern, D. (2009). Harvesting: power and opportunities beyond federated search. *Online*, *33*(4), 35–37.

Tolppanen, B. P., Miller, J., Wooden, M. H., & Tolppanen, L. M. (2005). Library World Wide Web sites at medium-sized universities: A re-examination. *Internet Reference Services Quarterly*, *10*(2), 7–18. doi:10.1300/J136v10n02_02

Tunkelang, D. (2009). Faceted search. *Synthesis Lectures on Information Concepts, Retrieval, and Services*, *1*(1), 1–80. doi:10.2200/S00190ED-1V01Y200904ICR005

Turner, R. (2009). The future of federated search, or what will the world look like in 10 years. *Computers in Libraries*, *29*(4), 39–41.

White, R. W., & Roth, R. A. (2009). Exploratory search: Beyond the query-response paradigm. *Synthesis Lectures on Information Concepts, Retrieval, and Services*, *1*(1), 1–98. doi:10.2200/S00174ED1V01Y200901ICR003

Xu, F. (2009). Implementation of a federated search system: Resource accessibility issues. *Serials Review*, *35*(4), 235–241. doi:10.1016/j.serrev.2009.08.019

Yeh, S., & Liu, Y. (2011). Integrated faceted browser and direct search to enhance information retrieval in text-based digital libraries. *International Journal of Human-Computer Interaction*, *27*(4), 364–382. doi:10.1080/10447318.2011.540492

KEYTERMS AND DEFINITIONS

API (Application Programming Interface): A specification in software source code that allows programs to communicate with each other. The API usually includes the necessary specifications for a programmer to combine it with other programs. This is critical for harnessing data from one source to use in a different interface, or for deep customization of search interfaces. Programmers at Oregon State University and the University of

Michigan have used the API program to create a locally customized view of Summon.

Coverage Analysis: A report provided by a discovery vendor, presenting the percentage of the library's full-text online holdings is represented in the discovery tool's database. This shows how much of the digital collection can be accessed through the discovery tool.

Discovery: Currently in libraries, discovery is the key term indicating the latest generation of software tools to allow searching across multiple databases simultaneously, although the term itself is loosely defined.

Faceting: The practice of grouping the properties of a set of results in order to allow a user to expand, refine or narrow his or her search using the grouped property information. Common facets a user might use to refine a search include author, medium, publication date, and subject keywords. Note that some search interfaces limit faceting to only one of these behaviors, such as facets only narrowing a search; it is important to know how faceting works in a product.

Federated search/metasearch: An approach to searching across multiple, discrete databases that relies on sending user search queries out to them individually and then aggregating the results as they are returned.

ILS: Integrated Library System, the core library operations software most commonly encompassing acquisitions, cataloging, circulation, online catalog, and resource management.

Library 2.0: A loosely-defined attempt to apply Web 2.0 technologies in the library environment primarily focused on improved online services and often incorporating social media, sometimes including mash-ups (see below).

Mash-Up: In the broader Internet vernacular, software development that combines disparate information or features from other resources or tools that allows interactions in new or novel ways, often connoting a rough and unfinished nature. Specifically to discovery, Innovative Interfaces Incorporated uses the term to denote clusters of

XML database connectors that can be aggregated in their Encore Synergy product.

NC Live Service: A statewide collection of library resources including article databases and eBooks, provided to all libraries in North Carolina through the State Library.

Open Source: Freely-available computer software source code, distributed under a specific legal license allowing for modification and reuse, often requiring that enhancements to the code be similarly distributed.

Pre-Indexing: The technological method of compiling a central index of metadata provided or harvested from discrete repositories of content, sometimes with human mediation to improve indexing quality, and often with the express cooperation of the repositories' owners. Key to the effectiveness of this approach, the index needs to be promptly updated as each of the discrete repositories changes. The primary benefit of this approach is the speed of searching against this central index and the ability to readily relevance rank the results.

Social Media: Broadly defined, Web and software tools to enable sharing and communication between networks of social contacts. Often shorthand for Facebook and Twitter, the term also includes Flickr, Yelp!, YouTube, and even mobile applications like Instagram.

Technology Stack: The existing, configured library systems in place, such as a link resolver, Integrated Library System, and authentication proxy. A discovery platform that requires a change in a library's existing technology stack to work effectively will increase indirect costs, implementation complexity, and project difficulty.

Web 2.0: A broad movement to embrace technologies enabling the Web to provide features and functionality previously limited to software applications on a user's local computer. Social media integration and mash-ups (see above) often form an integral part of these efforts.

WebConnect Technology: Innovative Interfaces Incorporated's cross-platform search XML connector technology, which they describe as being superior in speed and responsiveness to federated search connectors.

ENDNOTES

1. The Unified Resource Discovery Wiki is a useful Web site of practical information on discovery, at https://sites.google.com/site/urdcomparison/
2. The Library Technology Guides Discovery Interfaces page is a list of libraries with specific ILS/Discovery combinations, at http://www.librarytechnology.org/discovery.pl
3. EBSCO Discovery Service is owned by EBSCO Publishing Industries
4. Primo Central is owned by Ex Libris Ltd. or its affiliates.
5. Encore Synergy™ is a trademark of Innovative Interfaces
6. Worldcat is a registered trademark of OCLC
7. Serials Solution is a registered trademark of Serials Solutions
8. Summons is owned by ProQuest LLC
9. ProQuest® is a registered trademark of ProQuest LLC

Chapter 21
Implementation and Acceptance of a Discovery Tool:
Lessons Learned

David Dahl
Towson University, USA

Patricia MacDonald
Towson University, USA

ABSTRACT

Discovery tools have the potential to disrupt the workflows and established practices of libraries, which can lead to resistance in their use. In 2009, the University System of Maryland and Affiliated Institutions (USMAI) consortium acquired WorldCat Local (WCL). Survey and interview instruments were developed to examine staff's reasons for resisting and motivations for accepting discovery tools. All librarians and staff at USMAI libraries were invited to participate in a Web survey and interviews were arranged with key individuals who were involved with the implementation of WCL at their respective institutions. Results indicate that technical issues are the most common reason for resistance, but other factors have an impact as well. The state of "perpetual beta" in which most discovery tool applications are developed requires continued attention and dedicated staffing and resources to ensure acceptance.

INTRODUCTION

New technologies have the potential to disrupt the workflows and established practices of an organization. As complex organizations in an evolving information technology environment, libraries are subject to these disruptions as well. Discovery tools represent a new type of disruptive technology in the library environment. Because discovery tools can create significant interruptions in the practices of library staff and librarians, organizations should expect a degree of resistance from staff.

DOI: 10.4018/978-1-4666-1821-3.ch021

The University System of Maryland and Affiliated Institutions (USMAI) consortium was an early adopter of the WorldCat® Local discovery tool. The adoption across the majority of institutions in the consortium created an ideal test case for understanding the implementation, use, and resistance of a discovery tool in an academic library environment. A survey of library staff at thirteen of the institutions in the USMAI consortium was conducted, as well as interviews with ten library staff involved in the implementation at their institutions.

The purpose of the present study is to examine staff's reasons for resisting and motivations for accepting the use of discovery tools in order to improve internal acceptance of these and perhaps other new search technologies. The results are used to establish best practices for libraries to follow when implementing a discovery tool, as well as identifying types of adoption issues of which libraries should be aware.

BACKGROUND

Evaluation & Acquisition of Worldcat Local by USMAI

USMAI is a consortium of libraries that serves sixteen public universities and colleges in Maryland. The University System of Maryland includes a range of universities, law schools, a medical school, and professional and health schools as listed in Table 1, along with two affiliated institutions. Thus, the libraries in the consortium also vary from a large research library at the College Park campus to several libraries that serve a mix of undergraduate and graduate programs, special libraries, and a library that provides primarily online resources for distance education. While these libraries operate independently as part of their respective institutions, they also have a long history of collaboration in order to collectively acquire and share information resources, including a shared library catalog, link resolver, and many electronic databases.

The consortium is governed by the Council of Library Directors (CLD), which consists of the director from each library. Technical support for shared systems is provided by the University of Maryland Libraries Information Technology Division, located at College Park. A number of task groups that deal with concerns related to shared resources, such as cataloging, electronic resources, and user interface issues, also exist.

In an initiative to transition to a next generation catalog and discovery tool, CLD began communication with OCLC regarding WorldCat® Local in late 2007. In 2008 OCLC developed a test database using selected USMAI holdings for a trial of WorldCat® Local, and CLD called for USMAI librarians to serve on a WorldCat® Local Review Group in order to evaluate this new discovery tool. The group gathered feedback from their respective libraries and submitted a report to CLD on the strengths and weaknesses of WorldCat® Local. Although the Review Group had some reservations about the viability of WorldCat® Local, CLD decided to fund a one year subscription beginning in April 2009 as the library directors considered WorldCat® Local an opportunity to introduce a discovery tool without a long-term commitment. An implementation support group was formed at College Park to continue working with OCLC on functional problems and to provide information on the configuration and branding of WorldCat® Local to other USMAI libraries. Each library made its own decision on the implementation and use of the new discovery tool. The degree of interest in WorldCat® Local varied greatly among the institutions: College Park provided sustained support for implementation; other institutions added a link to WorldCat® Local but did not actively promote it; and some libraries that served special populations such as the health professions or distance education students, decided that WorldCat® Local had little value for its community and did not implement it. The adoption across the majority of institutions

Table 1. Institutions in the USMAI consortium

Institution	Type	Headcount
Bowie State University	Master's	5578
Coppin State University	Master's	3800
Frostburg State University	Master's	5470
Salisbury University	Master's	8397
Towson University	Master's	21840
University of Baltimore (UB)	Master's; Law School	6501
University of Maryland, Baltimore	Law School, Medical & Health Schools	6349
University of Maryland, Baltimore County (UMBC)	Doctoral/Research	12888
University of Maryland, College Park	Doctoral/Research	37641
University of Maryland Eastern Shore (UMES)	Master's	4540
University of Maryland University College (UMUC)	Master's/Distance Education	58587
University of Maryland Center for Environmental Science	Laboratories	100
Affiliated Institutions		
Morgan State University	Master's	7226
St. Mary's College of Maryland	Liberal Arts/ Baccalaureate	2060

in the consortium, however, created an ideal test case for understanding the implementation and acceptance of a discovery tool in an academic library environment.

LITERATURE REVIEW

The literature on disruptive technologies, resistance to change, and change management is reviewed in order to gain a broader perspective about the impact of technological change in libraries and to consider strategies to facilitate acceptance of new technologies.

Disruptive Technologies

Lewis (2004) refers to Christensen's *The Innovator's Dilemma*, which distinguishes disruptive from sustaining technologies. Sustaining technologies are improvements to current products or processes, while disruptive technologies introduce an innovation that is fundamentally different and

so interrupts the current market or established systems. This new development may start at the fringe and be problematic; but it offers advantages that, as it improves, soon outstrip established models or competitors (Lewis, 2004, p.69). Disruptive technologies, however, involve a high risk of failure due to the potential for resistance from customers (Walsh, 2004, p. 166). In the case of discovery tools, libraries must not only consider the risk of resistance by external customers but also by their own staff, making the implementation process extremely important to the success of these tools.

Technology Implementation in Libraries

Case studies on the implementation of new search tools demonstrate typical issues that arise with the use of disruptive technologies. Herrera (2007) discusses the tension that new search tools can cause due to differing attitudes of staff. In her study of the University of Mississippi's implementation of a metasearch tool, some instructional librarians had an underlying fear that their jobs would no longer be necessary. Expert searchers questioned the usefulness of a "dumbed-down interface" (Herrera, 2007, p. 44) while staff responsible for electronic databases management looked on the new search tool as an opportunity to make users more aware of these resources. Herrera recommends including reference, collection, and systems staff in the implementation team and giving librarians the ability to choose metasearch customization options that best suit their needs in order to increase their support (Herrera, 2007, p. 49). In the implementation of a new federated search tool, the Loyola Notre Dame Library learned that it is necessary to have IT and reference staff work together in the development and implementation of new research tools (Lockwood and MacDonald, 2007). University of Washington's case study of WorldCat® Local underlines the importance of a comprehensive plan and the involvement of numerous staff and departments during implementation. Although UW prepared for the project with a detailed plan in mind, staff also worked with OCLC to solve problems as they arose (Ward, Shadle, & Mofield, 2008). Madison and Hyland-Carver (2005) stress that "perfection [is] not required" in the implementation of new library technologies (Madison & Hyland-Carver, 2005, p.113).

Change Management

Implementation of disruptive technologies often results in change within the organization. Benemati and Lederer (2010) consider the relevance of seminal theories of organizational change by Lewin and Orlikowski in today's technological environment. Lewin proposed that organizational processes operate in a quasi-equilibrium of social forces for or against change which results in a three-stage process of organizational change. These stages include *unfreezing*, when the readiness to change the status quo increases; *moving*,

i.e., the shift to a different process; and *refreezing*, or establishing a new state of equilibrium (Benemati & Lederer, 2010, p.2)

Orlikowski and Hofman (1997), on the other hand, suggest that organizations use an improvisational model of change when implementing new information technologies, particularly those that are customizable and have an unknown impact on the organization. The authors refer to the work of Suchman who uses navigational metaphors to describe approaches to technology: the European who charts and adheres to a course during a voyage and the Trukese who begins with a destination and adjusts to weather conditions to reach it (Orlikowski & Hofman, 1997, p.2). While organizations may plan for the former approach, frequently they need to improvise Trukese-style to handle unforeseen developments according to Orlikowski's model.

The distinction between linear and fluid frameworks for change management are well-documented. In his well-known eight-stage model for achieving change, Kotter emphasizes the importance of the linear sequence of steps within the process (Smith, 2010, p. 119). A newer modified version of this model was developed by Doppelt whose research demonstrated that change can occur in a variety of sequences, based on environmental factors or interventions. Thus, Doppelt proposed a wheel of change that, while cyclical, shares common elements with Kotter's model, including the importance of creating a sense of urgency to disrupt an organization's established mind-set, communicating the change vision throughout the organization, and enabling feedback loops (Smith, 2010, p. 119).

Factors affecting Acceptance

Regardless of the approach, the final stage of any planned change activity is the institutionalization of the change within the organization (Lippert & Davis, 2006, p. 436). The institutionalization of new technologies, such as discovery tools, is reached when the new technology is widely accepted throughout the organization. Numerous factors affect a user's acceptance of a new technology, and several frameworks exist to help understand the influence that these factors have on technology acceptance.

TAM

Among the earliest attempts to validate factors affecting technology acceptance is the Technology Acceptance Model (TAM) (Davis, Bagozzi, Warshaw, 1989, p. 985). Based on research from several disciplines, Davis (1989) measured perceived ease of use and perceived usefulness as variables in the likelihood of acceptance of new technologies. These variables typically account for about 40% of the variance in individual's usage intentions and behaviors (Venkatesh & Davis, 2000, p. 186).

TAM2

Venkatesh and Davis (2000) later extended the original TAM model, creating TAM2. This theoretical model accounts for social and cognitive variables believed to affect the perceived usefulness of new technologies (Venkatesh & Davis, 2000, p.187). The model's social variables include subjective norm, voluntariness, and image. Subjective norm accounts for the pressure an individual feels to "perform the behavior in question" based on whether that person believes others think they should or should not perform the action (Venkatesh & Davis, 2000, p.187). Voluntariness describes the degree to which the action of acceptance is based on compliance or user choice (Venkatesh & Davis, 2000, p.188). Image is "the degree to which use of an innovation is perceived to enhance one's...status in one's social system" (Venkatesh & Davis, 2000, p.189). As a user's experience with the technology increased the impact of these social influences diminished (Venkatesh & Davis, 2000, p.199). Contrarily, cognitive variables that

impact the perceived usefulness of new technologies were not affected by a user's increasing experience with the technology (Venkatesh & Davis, 2000, p.199). Variables in the Cognitive Influence Process include job relevance, output quality, and result demonstrability. Output quality accounts for how well the technology performs its relevant tasks (Venkatesh & Davis, 2000, p.191). Result demonstrability encompasses the ability for users to observe the benefits of using the technology (Venkatesh & Davis, 2000, p.192). Job relevance is the degree to which the technology is "applicable to his or her job" (Venkatesh & Davis, 2000, p.191).

Other Factors

Lippert and Davis (2006) study the effect that trust has on planned change activities: "Understanding how trust influences an individual's willingness to change may increase the rate at which a new technology is introduced and ultimately internalized" (Lippert & Davis, 2006, p.444). Powerlessness, resulting from the limiting of information to employees, has a negative impact on any organizational change (Kanter, 2010). Craine (2007) focuses on the importance of the individual's emotional response to the acceptance of technological change. His change cycle includes four emotional zones: The Comfort Zone, The "No" Zone, The Chasm, and The "Go" Zone (Craine, 2007, p.45). The author states that "change affects people's ability to feel comfortable, capable, and confident because it means that they must learn new systems, work in new ways, and accept new responsibilities" (Craine, 2007, p.44). In their theory of competing commitments, Kegan and Lahey (2001) state that underlying assumptions and hidden issues can make it difficult for people to change their behavior (Kegan & Lahey, 2001).

Strategies to Counter Resistance

Resistance should be anticipated whenever disruptive technologies are implemented in an organization. However, careful planning and strategy can reduce and even eliminate individuals' resistant behavior. Strategies to overcome resistance can be classified into two categories: *participative* and *directive*, according to Jiang, Muhanna, & Klein (Jiang, Muhanna, & Klein, 2000, p. 27). Their study determined that participative strategies were preferred by participants. Directive strategies, such as role modification, job reassignment, and power redistribution, were viewed negatively by study participants (Jiang, Muhanna, & Klein, 2000, p. 33). Benamati and Lederer (2010) identify five coping mechanisms for addressing problem types caused by IT change, including *education and training, endurance, internal procedures,* and *vendor/consultant support* (Benemati & Lederer, 2010, p. ?).

To address Kegan and Lahey's theory of competing commitments, Cervone (2007) recommends a three-stage process for overcoming the problem of competing commitments and underlying assumptions: (1) a series of questions to help people become aware of their competing commitments, (2) a method for finding and evaluating their core beliefs, and (3) a process for altering their behavior. Though this process is highly personal, Cervone believes that dealing with competing commitments can increase empathy and spur creativity within project teams (Cervone, 2007, p. 253).

METHODOLOGY

Two instruments, a Web survey and interview questions, were created in order to examine staff's reasons for resisting and motivations for accepting the use of a discovery tool in light of variations in implementation processes in their respective libraries. The authors knew that three schools had made a conscious decision not to implement WorldCat® Local after evaluating it. These institutions were not included in this study. A total of thirteen USMAI libraries were invited to participate in the study.

Survey

An anonymous survey instrument was created (Appendix A), consisting of thirteen questions. This survey was emailed in June 2011 to all library employees who were listed in the institution's staff directory for each of the 13 participating institutions. Participants had two weeks to respond to the survey with reminder emails sent periodically.

Interviews

Interviews were sought with a key person involved in the implementation of WorldCat® Local at each institution in order to gain a better understanding of the implementation process at that institution. Directors at each USMAI library were contacted in order to identify key individuals, and these potential interviewees were emailed in June 2011 to schedule the interviews. Interviews consisted of eight pre-determined questions (Appendix B).

Institutional Characteristics

Two characteristics of each institution were also collected: (1) size and (2) prominence of WorldCat® Local. Size was measured according to the number of library staff employed at the institution (as indicated on each institution's online staff directory). Institutions were subsequently grouped into categories of Large (50 or more employees), Medium (21-49 employees), and Small (20 or less employees). The prominence of WorldCat Local on each library's website was also determined using a 1 to 5 rating scale, with 1 being the least prominent and 5 being the most. Both authors evaluated the prominence characteristic for each

Figure 1. Completed surveys compared to staff size at individual USMAI libraries

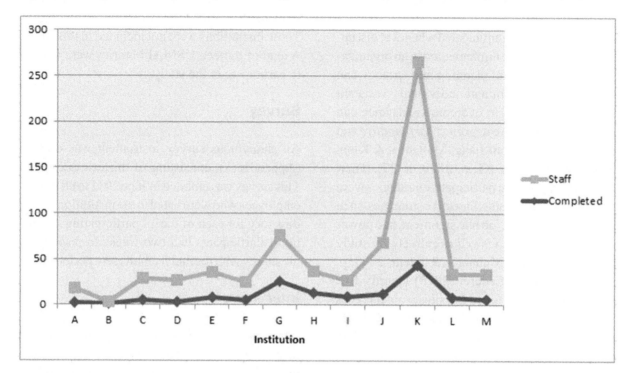

institution and an average was taken to determine the final level of prominence.

RESULTS

Response Rate

The survey was sent to 537 librarians and library staff at the thirteen participating USMAI libraries. A total of 131 participants completed the survey resulting in a 24.4% response rate. The distribution of responses among the USMAI libraries is generally proportional to the staff size of each institution as shown in Figure 1. Interviews were conducted with a key staff member responsible for WorldCat® Local's implementation at 10 of the 13 participating institutions. Other institutions did not respond to the authors' invitations.)

Demographics

Survey participants' employment length at their current USMAI library ranged from less than one year to 42 years. Those employed one or fewer years and those employed for three years were the most represented age groups with fourteen survey participants each. On average, representation decreased as length of employment increased. However, the median employment length was ten years. For further analysis, length of employment was divided into five groups as represented in Figure 2.

Institutional Characteristics

Size

Table 2 summarizes the characteristics of individual libraries. Libraries were grouped into three categories (Small, Medium, and Large) to indicate

Figure 2. Distribution of survey participants' length of employment (in years) at their current institution

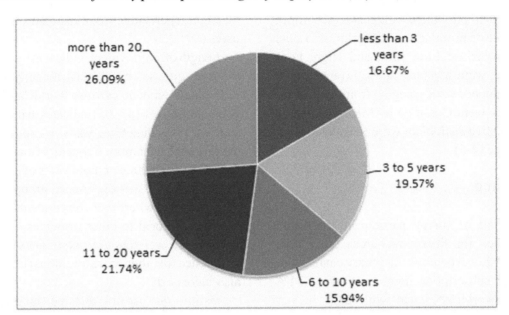

Table 2. Organizational characteristics of each USMAI library

Institutional Code	Staff size	Size category	WCL Prominence (1=least; 5=most)	Prominence category
A	16	Small	3.5	Mid
B	2	Small	3	Mid
C	24	Medium	2.5	Low
D	24	Medium	2	Low
E	28	Medium	1.5	Low
F	20	Small	2	Low
G	50	Large	5	High
H	24	Medium	3.5	Mid
I	18	Small	4	High
J	56	Large	3.5	Mid
K	222	Large	4	High
L	26	Medium	4	High
M	28	Medium	5	High

size. Four institutions are included in Small, six in Medium, and three in Large libraries. Variance in size was substantially greater among Large libraries than either Small or Medium libraries.

WorldCat® Local Prominence

USMAI Libraries demonstrate a broad range of WorldCat® Local integration into their websites with mean scores ranging from 1.5 to 5. Website integration ranged from prominent search boxes on the library's home page to difficult-to-find links on secondary library pages. Institutions were divided into three categories according to the level of prominence of WorldCat® Local on their websites: Low, Mid, and High. Four institutions were included in the Low category with prominence scores ranging from 1.5-2. Four institutions were classified as Mid prominence (3-3.5) and five institutions were considered High prominence (4-5).

Preference

Overall, half of survey participants indicated a preference for library resources other than WorldCat® Local (such as the library catalog and individual subscription databases). Over 21% preferred WorldCat® Local while 28% did not have a preference. Most users who did not have a preference concluded that different resources were better for different types of tasks. Several factors were determined to have had an impact on participants' preferences for either WorldCat® Local or other library resources, namely use, involvement, and colleagues' opinions.

Use

Survey question #3 directly addresses staff use of WorldCat® Local. Responses were coded one through four, with one equalling frequent use and four equalling no use. Sixty-nine percent of participants reported using WorldCat® Local occasionally or more often. Fifteen participants reported that they had never used WorldCat® Local. A single factor ANOVA indicates that the prominence of WorldCat® Local on each institution's website significantly impacted use. At institutions in the Low prominence category, nearly 67% of participants rarely or never used WorldCat® Local. Use at Mid (mean=1.79) and High (mean=2.09) prominence institutions was significantly higher ($p < .05$) than use at Low (mean=3.00) prominence institutions. While the majority of frequent users came from institutions in the High prominence category, users at institutions with Mid prominence accounted for the highest percentage of occasional and frequent users (89%).

Length of employment, indicated by responses to survey question #2, also significantly impacted individuals' tendencies to use WorldCat® Local. A two-sample t-test ($p < .05$) indicates that individual staff with less than three years of experience use WorldCat® Local more frequently (mean = 1.78) than those with three or more years of experience (mean = 2.22). This experience group was also the only group where more respondents preferred WorldCat® Local to other resources or to those not having a preference. As experience increased, preference for other, more traditional library tools also increased

Institutional use also differed significantly as demonstrated by a single factor ANOVA analyzing use broken down by institution. Institution H reported the highest mean use (mean = 1.46) of all institutions. This mean falls in between frequent and occasional use of WorldCat® Local. Incidentally, Institution H also has one of the lowest average lengths of employment across employees who participated in the survey (mean=9.08 years).

A two-sample t-test reveals that frequency of use is highly correlated to users' preferences ($p < .05$). Sixty-four percent of participants who preferred WorldCat® Local reported using it frequently (mean = 1.48) compared to only 11% of those who preferred other library resources, as indicated in Table 4. Average use score for those preferring other library resources was 2.48.

Involvement

The majority of respondents (56%) disagreed when asked if they were involved in the implementation of WorldCat® Local. However, only 17% felt that the implementation of WorldCat® Local was not a collaborative process. Institution size did not impact participants' feelings about whether the process was collaborative, though reports of involvement did decrease as institutional size

Table 4. Resource preference was affected by use

		Preference							
		WCL		Other Resources		No preference		Total	
		Count	Percent	Count	Percent	Count	Percent	Count	Percent
Use	Yes, frequently	16	64.00%	7	11.48%	13	38.24%	36	30.00%
	Yes, occasionally	6	24.00%	27	44.26%	17	50.00%	50	41.67%
	No, rarely	3	12.00%	18	29.51%	2	5.88%	23	19.17%
	No, never	0	0.00%	9	14.75%	2	5.88%	11	9.17%
	Total	**5**	100.00%	61	100.00%	34	100.00%	120	100.00%

Figure 3. Mean scores for collaboration distributed by individuals' levels of involvement with the implementation

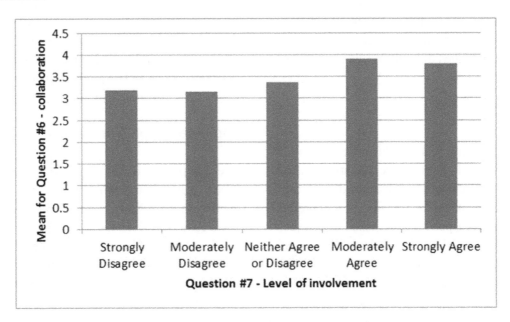

increased. Individuals who were involved in the implementation were more likely (p < .05) to describe the implementation as collaborative (Figure 3), those who preferred WorldCat® Local felt the implementation was more collaborative. A single factor ANOVA indicates that respondents' opinions of the collaborative nature of the implementation varied significantly across institutions. Respondents at institutions C and K reported significantly higher scores (mean = 4.4 and 3.675,

respectively) when asked if the implementation was collaborative.

Colleagues' Opinions

Co-workers' attitudes toward WorldCat® Local also appear to influence participants' preferences. Over 50% of respondents agreed that others at their institution consider WorldCat® Local a useful resource. Approximately 25% disagreed with this statement. Of those who preferred WorldCat®

Table 5. Number of issues per category

Issue Type (acceptance factor)	Number of Issues Reported
Technical (output quality)	24
Patron confusion (result demonstrability)	13
Usefulness (perceived usefulness)	13
Usability (perceived ease of use)	11
Organizational (subjective norm)	7
User uncertainty (trust)	6
Unused (experience)	6

Local, 75% felt that others considered WorldCat® Local useful. Only three respondents in this category disagreed with this statement while 20 respondents who preferred other resources felt that their colleagues did not find WorldCat® Local useful.

Issues

Survey participants recorded 60 issues relating to WorldCat® Local and its implementation at their institution. These issues were extracted from comments participants left related to their tool preference and direct responses when asked what issues had arisen from the implementation of WorldCat® Local. Issues were grouped into categories with some reported issues matching more than one category. Each category was matched to a factor affecting adoption mentioned earlier (indicated in parentheses in Table 5). Categories and the number of issues reported per category are shown in Table 5. Technical issues, which were matched to output quality from the TAM2 model, were the most prevalent type of issue reported, followed by patron confusion (result demonstrability), and usefulness (perceived usefulness).

Interviews

Of the 10 interviews conducted, four interviewees held positions dealing primarily with information technology and systems, two were directors, two were in technical services, and two held positions that included both IT and a public service function. Interviewees represented institutions from all three size and prominence categories. Only one interviewee had responsibility for WorldCat® Local as their primary job function.

Implementation Concept

The complexity of the implementation process varied greatly between interviewees. The implementation processes ranged from doing a few basic customizations to the interface and putting a link on the website to more in-depth evaluations of the tool and its interface, including ensuring the integration of its functions with existing workflows. Neither institution size nor the prominence of WorldCat® Local affected the complexity significantly. Rather, the position of the individual charged with handling the implementation of WorldCat® Local was the most significant factor in the complexity of the implementation. Potential reasons for this are discussed later.

Plans for future developments also varied greatly, with some interviewees reporting that they simply need to check and make sure links are working occasionally, while others indicated ongoing maintenance and updating of WorldCat® Local. Several indicated that they are continuing to interact with OCLC to offer suggestions for improving the tool and fixing technical issues. Generally, interviewees who reported some level of issue with WorldCat® Local also indicated that regular maintenance was ongoing.

Issues

Interviewees reported a range of issues, which coincided with many of the issues reported by survey participants. Issues ranged from technical problems with holdings information and resource sharing functions to members of the organization resisting use of WorldCat® Local. Several interviewees reported that many librarians were unsatisfied with the discovery tool's ability to make searching more effective and efficient for their patrons.

DISCUSSION

In many ways, discovery tool implementation in libraries resembles other planned change activities, especially those involving new information technologies. Survey results make clear that a split exists between those who prefer the new resource discovery tools and those who prefer more traditional research tools, such as library catalogs and databases. Additionally, a significant portion of survey participants expressed no preference, perhaps signaling uncertainty about the direction their libraries, or the profession in general, will take in the future. Due to the disruptive nature of these search tools, special attention should be given to the careful management of the organizational transition to a resource discovery environment. Those involved in discovery tool implementation should prepare for the issues that will arise from the use of discovery tools, account for the factors that can affect adoption, and allocate sufficient resources and staffing to allow for the successful institutionalization of the discovery tool.

Discovery Tool Issues

Several types of issues arise during the transition to a discovery tool. The most frequent type of issue reported by survey respondents were technical problems. Interview results suggest that many flaws were fixed early in the implementation process through collaboration with the vendor. Several interviewees also indicated vendor interest in their feedback in order to help improve the product. This suggests that the vendor considers their product to be in a state of "perpetual beta" - a state of regular change and improvement. But, if users, or in this study librarians, initially determine the system to be of little use, they may not return to it even if improvements are made. One interviewee accurately described this changing trend from the release of finished products to the acquisition of products in "beta mode", adding that staff need to "be responsive to whatever comes up" and value responsiveness to these types of issues as part of their work environment.

The lack of a polished product can leave library staff feeling unsure about their ability to deliver consistent, stable services to users. Patron confusion accounted for the second highest number of issues with WorldCat® Local. While library staff has become accustomed to overcoming patron confusion through training and instruction, this effort becomes less effective as interface changes are continually made. Participants noted that patrons were confused by both the number and types of results provided in WorldCat® Local, an issue that is likely to be prevalent amongst all discovery tool platforms. Library staff also expressed confusion and uncertainty over what materials they are searching. One participant stated that they avoided using WorldCat® Local for finding articles because they are "unclear on exactly what it indexes". With increasingly complex licensing agreements between vendors and publishers, this will most likely continue to be an issue in the future.

Factors affecting Adoption

Issue types reported in the survey match the factors found in Venkatesh and Davis' (2000) TAM2, as well as those factors identified in other frameworks (Lippert & Davis, 2006; Craine, 2007; Kegan &Lahey, 2001), that affect adoption of new technologies. The uncertainty of library staff corresponds directly to Lippert and Davis' (2006) discussion of technology trust as a vital component "necessary to effectively manage IT-directed change initiatives (Lippert & Davis, 2006, p. 444). Result demonstrability is directly related to the issue of patron confusion. As one of the major selling points of a discovery tool is simplification of the research process for users, this reported confusion contradicts one of the proposed benefits of these search tools.

Additionally, Venkatesh and Davis (2000) show that gains in experience can lessen the impact of perceived usefulness and perceived ease of use (Venkatesh & Davis, 2000, p.199). This finding held true in the current study with the majority of those who use WorldCat® Local frequently preferring it over other library tools. However, it is also observable that length of employment within a particular work environment, which implies more experience with established technologies, makes it more unlikely that staff will adopt a new technology. Frequency of use can be improved by giving the discovery tool more prominent real estate within the library's Web presence, as users from institutions where WorldCat® Local was highly prominent used WorldCat® Local at a far greater frequency than other institutions (Table 3).

Though the present study was not designed to directly measure participants' emotional responses to WorldCat® Local, some strong emotional responses were detectable through survey participants' comments. Words like 'hate' and 'disdain', as well as sarcasm and the use of capitalization for emphasis, indicate that many library staff are experiencing the emotions found in the Change Cycle (Craine, 2007, p. 45).

Resources and Staffing

Those involved in the implementation of World-Cat® Local represented a variety of job titles and responsibilities. Most were either self-selected because of an interest in WorldCat® Local and technology initiatives, though a few were assigned in a more formal manner. No conclusion can be drawn as to whether self-selection or assignment is more likely to lead to a successful implementation. However, a few conclusions can be drawn about the role of staff in the implementation process. First, as one interviewee observed, discovery tool implementation is a "different type of beast" from other technology implementation projects. The implementation may involve, but does not necessarily require, the skills of a systems or Web person, though this was often the staff member who ended up with responsibilities for the implementation. Implementation processes that were the most iterative and collaborative were the responsibility of individuals who split their job responsibilities between an IT function and public services. This is most likely due to the individual's position within the organization, serving as a boundary spanner between multiple departments. Many implementation processes resulted in responsibility being passed along to individuals in different departments as certain steps in the process were completed. For instance, a cataloger might initially hold responsibility for checking the accuracy of the library's holdings, who then passes responsibility to an IT person to customize the interface, who then passes it along to someone in public services to test it with both internal users and library patrons. This type of process takes advantage of individual skill sets throughout the implementation process. However, since implementation is often an iterative process, communication needs to remain open among

Table 3. Frequency of use by prominence of WorldCat® Local on libraries' websites

Use	Low	Mid	High	Total
Frequently (1)	1	9	26	**36**
Occasionally (2)	6	16	40	**62**
Rarely (3)	6	3	20	**29**
Never (4)	8	0	7	**15**
Total	**21**	**28**	**93**	**142**

these different personnel in order to add or change features, correct errors, or discuss other issues.

As one interviewee noted, it is also important to recognize that no matter who holds primary responsibility for the implementation and maintenance of the discovery tool, this responsibility will require a significant portion of their workload. The majority of interviewees indicated a low level of ongoing maintenance and development after the initial implementation of WorldCat® Local. While technical maintenance may be minimal, the issues reported in the survey data indicate a need for ongoing training and communication about product updates in order to increase awareness of improvements and to encourage staff to continue using the discovery tool. Although many interviewees indicated some plans for training and updating staff about WorldCat® Local, only one addressed it in a significant and concrete manner. This librarian was also officially designated as the WorldCat® Local staff member and had overall responsibility for communication and ongoing training as well as implementation. At other US-MAI institutions, the lack of initiative for ongoing work with WorldCat® Local is probably due to the fact that responsibility for the discovery tool takes time away from other established job duties. While the University of Washington Library administration specified that staff responsible for WorldCat® Local would have a reduced workload for other duties (Ward et al., 2008, p.26), only one USMAI institution indicated a decrease in

other work responsibilities for staff involved with WorldCat® Local.

Implications for Practice

Because of the perpetual beta status of discovery tools and their substantial impact on the organization, libraries should adopt Orlikowski's (1997) improvisational model of change. Those institutions who requested frequent feedback from library staff and made changes iteratively, created a more collaborative atmosphere, which ultimately lead to more use and greater acceptance of the discovery tool. Institution H exemplified a collaborative, improvisational process of implementation. The systems librarian at this medium-sized institution was also a member of the reference department and acted as a boundary spanner, in the manner previously stated, by providing both IT support and public service. This interviewee worked closely with other reference librarians to make iterative changes to the configuration of WorldCat® Local based on their feedback. An unexpected outcome was that the systems librarian was eventually able to merge the WorldCat® Local configuration for this library with that of another branch library in order to improve access to both library collections. This unplanned outcome aligns with Orlikowski's (1997) theory of improvisational change as staff were able to take advantage of an unforeseen opportunity in developing a new technology. The success of this implementation relied on the initiative and technical skills of the systems librarian as well as the collaborative efforts to make ongoing improvements to the discovery tool. The librarians at this institution also seemed more open to change as most were dissatisfied with the existing catalog while librarians at other institutions expressed a preference for the catalog, especially its authority records. Considering Lewin's theory of the stages of organizational change, Institution H began the implementation in the unfreezing stage due to their dissatisfaction with the current library catalog. Other libraries, on the other hand, were more satisfied with the established search tools and were less motivated to make this transition. The lower mean employment length at Institution H factored into the library's wilingness to make this change.

Brown et al. (2007) also support this iterative implementation process. Furthermore, they suggest that different phases of the implementation process require different skill sets and solutions. For instance, knowledge, which can be acquired through training, is most important during the initial stages of the implementation process while communication is more important during the adoption stage (Brown, Chervany, & Reinicke, 2007, p.94). This concept is especially important for libraries in determining how to allocate staff and resources in order to lessen resistance to a discovery tool after its initial implementation.

Institutions should utilize participative strategies for encouraging adoption of discovery tools. This may include offering regular training, creating systems for open communication about news and updates related to the product, and rewarding behaviors and ideas that support the successful integration of the discovery tool into the library environment. Institution K, the library that formed a WorldCat® Local support group to lead customization efforts and work on technical issues, established a listserv and Facebook page to provide multiple channels of communication to library staff. The implemented discovery tool should also maintain medium to high prominence within the library's Web presence in order to en-

courage use. Lack of prominence will negatively impact use by staff, which will adversely affect the adoption of this technology.

An important participative strategy that cannot be emphasized enough is the wide dissemination of information regarding the plans for the discovery tool. Information about product updates, as well as institutional plans for developing and integrating the tool into the library's workflow should be communicated to all staff. As Kanter (2010) notes, lack of information leads to feelings of powerlessness that can cause resistance. Survey results demonstrate that this is true, as most respondents who were kept informed about the implementation of WorldCat® Local also felt that it was a collaborative process.

Finally, libraries should recognize the emotional responses that technological change can cause in individuals. Patience is necessary in dealing with resistant staff. Open, empathetic discussion of competing commitments as recommended by Cervone (2007) is important as staff may fear loss of their jobs or specific roles and responsibilities. For instance, librarians may believe discovery tools will make library instruction unnecessary, but they can be encouraged to see the opportunities that the new technology can provide. Understanding that a high percentage of resistance has positive intentions and using those intentions appropriately will ultimately improve the discovery tool and its integration into the library's workflows.

FUTURE DIRECTIONS

USMAI's acquisition and implementation of WorldCat® Local provided an opportunity to gain insight into the organizational issues that arise from the implementation of discovery tools, namely their acceptance among library staff. While the present study avoided analysis of features specific to WorldCat® Local, similar studies should be conducted with other discovery tools to validate results. This study identified several factors that played a significant role in the acceptance of disruptive technologies like discovery tools. Future studies could investigate individual factors, such as trust, perceived usefulness, and subjective norm, in order to more fully understand these factors and identify appropriate means to address them. Various change management strategies could be compared to determine the effectiveness of each strategy at overcoming resistance. Finally, this study focused on discovery tool acceptance by an internal audience. Similar studies could consider the effects of this type of disruptive technological change on library patrons.

CONCLUSION

While discovery tools are promoted as simple solutions to address the search needs of patrons, this study demonstrates that there are many organizational issues that can arise from the implementation of a discovery tool, affecting its adoption and use by library staff. Technical issues represented the greatest number of issues leading staff to prefer other search solutions over WorldCat® Local, but other factors, such as trust, perceived usefulness, and subjective norm, also affected staff's adoption. As indicated in interviews with key individuals involved in the implementation of WorldCat® Local at USMAI libraries, these issues coincide with a new paradigm in library technology - the concept of perpetual beta. This approach to developing library technology relies on incremental, continuous revisions to the original application, fixing errors and adding features throughout the application's life cycle. Extended beta development is mostly unfamiliar to libraries that traditionally provide consistent, stable tools and services for their patrons. However, this trend is not likely to change as more library technology tools and services become web-based.

In order to achieve the institutionalization of disruptive technologies like discovery tools,

libraries must assess the capability of their organizational culture to accommodate tools that exist in perpetual beta. Libraries will need to adopt change management strategies that rely on improvisation and iteration rather than planned, linear processes. The goal of libraries' efforts should not be to simply motivate users to adopt their current discovery tool, but to create a culture that is prepared to adapt to new developments in library technology.

REFERENCES

Benemati, J., & Lederer, A. L. (2010). Managing the impact of rapid IT change. *Resources Management Journal*, *23*(1), 1–16. doi:10.4018/irmj.2010102601

Brown, S. A., Chervany, N. L., & Reinicke, B. A. (2007). What matters when introducing new information technology. *Communications of the ACM*, *50*(9), 91–96. doi:10.1145/1284621.1284625

Cervone, H. F. (2007). Working through resistance to change by using the "competing commitments model". *OCLC Systems & Services*, *23*(3), 250–253. doi:10.1108/10650750710776378

Craine, K. (2007). Managing the cycle of change. *The Information Management Journal*, *41*(5), 44–50.

Davis, F. D. (1989). Perceived usefulness, perceived ease of use, and user acceptance of information technology. *Management Information Systems Quarterly*, *13*(3), 319–340. doi:10.2307/249008

Davis, F. D., Bagozzi, R. P., & Warshaw, P. R. (1989). User acceptance of computer technology: A comparison of two theoretical models. *Management Science*, *35*(8), 982–1003. doi:10.1287/mnsc.35.8.982

Herrera, G. (2007). MetaSearching and beyond: Implementation experiences and advice from an academic library. *Information Technology and Libraries, 26*(2), 44–52.

Jiang, J. J., Muhanna, W. A., & Klein, G. (2000). User resistance and strategies for promoting acceptance across system types. *Information & Management, 37*(1), 25–36. doi:10.1016/S0378-7206(99)00032-4

Kanter, R. M. (2010). Powerlessness corrupts. *Harvard Business Review, 88*(7), 36.

Kegan, R., & Lahey, L. (2001). The real reason people won't change. *Harvard Business Review, 79*(10), 85–92.

Lewis, D. W. (2004). The innovator's dilemma: Disruptive change and academic libraries. *Library Administration & Management, 18*(2), 68–74.

Lippert, S. K., & Davis, M. (2006). A conceptual model integrating trust into planned change activities to enhance technology adoption behavior. *Journal of Information Science, 32*(5), 434–448. doi:10.1177/0165551506066042

Lockwood, C., & MacDonald, P. (2007). Implementation of a federated search system in the academic library: Lessons learned. *Internet Reference Services Quarterly, 12*(1/2), 73–91. doi:10.1300/J136v12n01_04

Madison, O. M. A., & Hyland-Carver, M. (2005). Issues in planning for portal implementation: Perfection not required. *Journal of Library Administration, 43*(1/2), 113–134. doi:10.1300/J111v43n01_08

Orlikowski, W. J., & Hofman, J. D. (1997). An improvisational model of change management: The case of groupware technologies. *Sloan Management Review, 38*(2), 11–21.

Smith, I. (2010). Organisational quality and organisational change: Interconnecting paths to effectiveness. *Library Management, 32*(1/2), 111–128. doi:10.1108/01435121111102629

Venkatesh, V., & Davis, F. D. (2000). A theoretical extension of the technology acceptance model: Four longitudinal field studies. *Management Science, 46*(2), 186–204. doi:10.1287/mnsc.46.2.186.11926

Walsh, S. T. (2004). Roadmapping a disruptive technology: A case study: The emerging microsystems and top-down nanosystems industry. *Technological Forecasting and Social Change, 71*(1/2), 161–185. doi:10.1016/j.techfore.2003.10.003

Ward, J. L., Shadle, S., & Mofield, P. (2008). Planning and implementation. *Library Technology Reports, 44*(6), 26–36.

ADDITIONAL READING

Boston, MA: Harvard Business School Press.

Bowe, C., Lahey, L., Armstrong, E., & Kegan, R. (2003). Questioning the 'big assumptions'. Part I: Addressing personal contradictions that impede professional development. *Medical Education, 37*(8), 715–722. doi:10.1046/j.1365-2923.2003.01579.x

Bowe, C., Lahey, L., Kegan, R., & Armstrong, E. (2003). Questioning the 'big assumptions'. Part II: Recognizing organizational contradictions that impede institutional change. *Medical Education, 37*(8), 723–733. doi:10.1046/j.1365-2923.2003.01580.x

Christensen, C. M. (1997). *The innovator's dilemma: When new technologies cause great firms to fail.*

Doppelt, B. (2010). *Leading change toward sustainability: A change-management guide for business, government and civil society*. Sheffield, UK: Greenleaf.

Ferneley, E. H., & Sobreperez, P. (2006). Resist, comply or workaround? An examination of different facets of user engagement with information systems. *European Journal of Information Systems*, *15*(4), 345–356. doi:10.1057/palgrave. ejis.3000629

Greenwood, R., & Hinings, C. R. (1996). Understanding radical organizational change: Bringing together the old and the new institutionalism. *Academy of Management Review*, *21*(4), 1022–1054. doi:doi:10.5465/AMR.1996.9704071862

Kanter, R. M. (2001). *Evolve! Succeeding in the digital culture of tomorrow*. Boston, MA: Harvard Business School Press.

Kotter, J. P. (1996). *Leading change*. Boston, MA: Harvard Business School Press.

Kotter, J. P. (2008). *A sense of urgency*. Boston, MA: Harvard Business Press.

Kotter, J. P., & Cohen, D. S. (2002). *The heart of change: Real-life stories of how people change their organizations*. Boston, Mass: Harvard Business School Press.

Lewin, K. (1947). Frontiers in group dynamics: Concept, method, and reality in social science, social equilibria, and social change. *Human Relations*, *1*(2), 143–153. doi:10.1177/001872674700100201

McLaughlin, J. (2002). *Valuing technology: Organisations, culture, and change*. London: Routledge.

National Academy of Engineering Staff & National Research Council Staff. (1991). *People and technology in the workplace*. Washington, DC: National Academies Press.

Nov, O., & Chen, Y. (2009). Resistance to change and the adoption of digital libraries: An integrative model. *Journal of the American Society for Information Science and Technology*, *60*(8), 1702–1708. doi:10.1002/asi.21068

Orlikowski, W. J. (1996). Improvising organizational transformation over time: A situated change perspective. *Information Systems Research*, *7*(1), 63–92. doi:10.1287/isre.7.1.63

Ward, J. L., Shadle, S., & Mofield, P. (2008). WorldCat Local at the University of Washington Libraries. *Library Technology Reports*, *44*(8), 5–42.

Wenger, E. (2000). Communities of practice and social learning systems. *Organization*, *7*(2), 225–246. doi:10.1177/135050840072002

Wenger, E. C., & Snyder, W. M. (2000, January 01). Communities of practice: The organizational frontier. *Harvard Business Review*, *78*(1), 139–145.

KEY TERMS AND DEFINITIONS

Change Management: The strategic method of creating and managing organizational change.

Competing Commitments: Underlying, often subconscious, assumptions, that thwart a person's ability to change.

Discovery Tool: A search engine that combines multiple library resources, including the library catalog, database subscriptions, and additional resources into a single, centrally indexed search interface.

Disruptive Technologies: Any technology that, when implemented, interrupts the existing practices, processes, and workflows of an organization.

Implementation: The integration of a new product or service into an organization.

Organizational Change: The transition from the current state within an organization to a new state.

Participative Strategies: Strategies that promote the inclusion of individuals in decision-making processes within an organization. Resistance: a behavior resulting in the lack of adoption of a new technology.

Technology Acceptance: The adoption and integration of a new technology into an individual's or organization's work environment.

WorldCat Local: A subscription-based, locally branded version of WorldCat which includes and highlights the collection of a specific library or association of libraries.

APPENDIX A

WorldCat Local Implementation Survey

1. For which institution do you work? (radio buttons with each institution listed)
2. How many years have you been employed at this institution? (drop-down number range (1-50) or text field that only accepts integer values)
3. Do you use WorldCat Local in your work?
    Yes, frequently
    Yes, occasionally
    No, rarely
    No, never

Please indicate your level of agreement with the following statements.

4. I am comfortable promoting the use of WorldCat Local as a research tool at my institution.
    Strongly disagree
    Moderately disagree
    Neither agree nor disagree
    Moderately agree
    Strongly agree
5. Librarians and library staff at my institution consider WorldCat Local a useful resource.
    Strongly disagree
    Moderately disagree
    Neither agree nor disagree
    Moderately agree
    Strongly agree
6. Implementing WorldCat Local was a collaborative effort at my library
    Strongly disagree
    Moderately disagree
    Neither agree nor disagree
    Moderately agree
    Strongly agree
7. I was involved in the implementation of WorldCat Local
    Strongly disagree
    Moderately disagree
    Neither agree nor disagree
    Moderately agree
    Strongly agree
8. Were you provided with information about WorldCat Local when it became available at your institution?
    Yes
    No

Don't remember
9. My feedback regarding WorldCat Local has been encouraged by my institution.
    Strongly disagree
    Moderately disagree
    Neither agree nor disagree
    Moderately agree
    Strongly agree
10. I have been kept informed about my institution's future plans for WorldCat Local.
    Strongly disagree
    Moderately disagree
    Neither agree nor disagree
    Moderately agree
    Strongly agree
11. Will you use WorldCat Local in the future?
    Yes, definitely
    Yes, probably
    No, probably not
    No, definitely not

Please respond to the questions below in the space provided:

12. Do you prefer to use WorldCat Local or other library resources such as the Aleph catalog and specific databases?
    WCL, please explain
    Other library resources - Why? (free text)
    No preference, please explain
13. What issues have arisen from the implementation of WorldCat Local at your institution? (free text)

APPENDIX B

WorldCat Local Interview Instrument

Purpose of the Study

This study is designed to investigate the implementation of WorldCat Local at institutions within the University System of Maryland and Affiliated Institutions (USMAI). In combination with a Web survey sent to all employees of USMAI libraries, this research will explore best practices for implementing resource discovery tools and issues that may arise from their implementation. The Principal Investigators hope that this research will prove useful to other institutions planning to implement a resource discovery tool.

Procedures

Participants will be asked to respond verbally to questions given by the interviewee. The interviewee will take notes during the participant's responses. The interview session will be recorded and, later, transcribed. The interview will take no more than one hour.

Questions

At which USMAI institution are you employed?

Did you participate in the evaluation and selection of WCL by either the USMAI consortium or your own institution? How?

Describe the process of implementing WCL at your institution. What was your role in this process?

How did you become involved in its implementation?

Approximately how many people were involved in the implementation? (i.e. was it a team process or individual?) What were their roles? What departments were involved?

Were any issues encountered along the way? How were they addressed?

What is the current state of development for WCL at your institution? Are any future developments planned?

How will your experience implementing WCL affect future implementations of new technologies?

Chapter 22
Putting Library Discovery Where Users Are

Scott Garrison
Ferris State University, USA

Anne Prestamo
Oklahoma State University, USA

Juan Carlos Rodriguez
Grand Valley State University, USA

ABSTRACT

A number of studies have shown that people start research with Google and other easy, convenient tools. Though they recognize the value of library content, users prefer unmediated, intuitive searching, and consult libraries less than before alternatives existed. To "bring users back," libraries began adopting discovery systems more like Google in the late 2000s. While these systems, especially good for beginning research, are proving popular, libraries must ask how many users are finding them given how few begin research at the library. This chapter describes why and how to place library discovery systems within the user's academic context and what tools may facilitate the process, and suggests how libraries may determine how well discovery systems are working, within and beyond this context.

INTRODUCTION

Libraries have traditionally been one of few places to find quality information for work and everyday life. While print sources moved to the Web, online search tools coalesced around librarians' goal of helping users find and evaluate, rather than on users' own expectations for self-sufficiency that Google and others had engendered. Library-provided tools featured inconsistent interfaces and features, and formed content "silos" that became increasingly difficult for users to distinguish between and use as they proliferated. By the early 2000s, libraries had lost many users to Google due to its simplicity, ease of use, and increasingly large single index. Though users' trust in libraries for the content and services they offer has remained, convenience has emerged for many as the most important factor in finding information (Connaway et al., 2011). One example of how

DOI: 10.4018/978-1-4666-1821-3.ch022

Google and other search tools offer ultimate convenience is that they have become directly embedded in the very Web browser software that users use every day.

Libraries have increasingly responded to the loss of users by offering federated search, next-generation catalogs, and Web-scale discovery systems. These three types of products have progressively helped libraries' efforts and made the process of starting research easier, but each has the same set of problems. For example, many librarians are less comfortable using and recommending these tools because they are built to meet user, rather than librarian, expectations. However, the chief problem is arguably that most libraries have expected users to find these tools at their own websites, which is not where most users start research (DeRosa et al., 2010).

It is incumbent on libraries to offer discovery tools in contexts and systems where all users need to carry out learning-related and business functions (Gibbons, 2005). As a Web browser is required to use the Web, enterprise software such as portals and learning management systems (LMS) are increasingly required for academic users to function. In many cases, students use a portal to register, check schedules and grades, and pay tuition and other bills. More and more courses have some component in the LMS, whether simply a syllabus and grades, or extending to online readings, assignments and quizzes, discussion and other group work, and more. Libraries have begun to embed discipline-specific resources, and now discovery tools, directly into these environments.

This chapter will frame why it is important to put discovery tools where users are. It will detail approaches to embedding discovery tools into enterprise portals and LMSs as two examples (though others are suggested in the conclusion). It will close by suggesting how libraries may determine how well discovery tool placement is working to connect users with the vast, valuable content that these tools expose.

BACKGROUND: WHERE TO EMBED DISCOVERY AND WHY

The tradition of libraries as research mediators has clearly given way to a new reality of easy, convenient direct user searching. A 2002 report from the Pew Charitable Trust's Pew Internet & American Life Project found that 73 percent of college students use the Internet more than their library when searching for information, while only nine percent use the library more than the Internet (Jones & Madden, 2002).

OCLC[®1]'s 2005 *Perceptions of Librarians and Information Resources* study reported that 89 percent of undergraduate and graduate students use Web search engines to begin research, while only two percent of users began research on a library website (DeRosa et al., 2005). OCLC[®]'s 2010 *Perceptions* study reported that 83 percent of college students use search engines to begin information searches, and that zero percent begin searches at the library website. Further, the study found that "the number of college students using the library Web site declined" from 61 percent in 2005 to 57 percent in 2010 (DeRosa et al., 2010, p. 52), and that "college students feel that search engines trump libraries for speed, convenience, reliability and ease of use" (though "libraries trump search engines for trustworthiness and accuracy;" DeRosa et al., 2010, p. 54).

The 2010 Project Information Literacy progress report entitled "Truth Be Told" found that the number of survey respondents who used scholarly research databases for course-related research dropped from 94 percent in 2009 to 88 percent in 2010 (along with a remarkable drop for everyday life research from 66 to 40 percent), compared to a smaller drop in respondents who used search engines including Google (96 percent in 2009 to 92 percent in 2010 for course-related research, and 99 to 95 percent for everyday life research). Arguably of greatest concern to libraries is the Project Information Literacy finding that 84 percent of respondents' most difficult step in course-related research is getting started (Head & Eisenberg, 2010).

Libraries have also used LibQUAL+®2 (Association of Research Libraries, 2011) and other means to gauge user satisfaction over time. LibQUAL+® Information Control questions ask users to rate their experience using the library to find information. Western Michigan University Libraries and their peer libraries have found greater than minimum, but less than desired undergraduate student satisfaction for questions IC-6 and IC-7 (defined in Key Terms and Definitions below) in several LibQUAL+® iterations, and Greenwood, Watson and Dennis (2011) document a relatively flat overall adequacy gap in Information Control questions for the University of Mississippi's 2005, 2007, and 2009 LibQUAL+® iterations, even as online content increased.

Libraries have moved from federated search and next-generation catalogs to Web-scale catalog and article discovery systems with a single index. For example, according to SerialsSolutions®3' Andrew Nagy, the Summon™4 service was launched in 2009 with fewer than ten subscribing libraries, and had over 270 subscribing libraries by July 2011 (A. Nagy, personal communication, August 2, 2011). The most common way to find these tools is to consult the library website. However, given the aforementioned decline in library website users, Connaway, Dickey and Radford (2011) suggest that

Librarians are finding that they must compete with other, often more convenient, familiar and easy-to-use information sources. The user once built workflows around the library systems and services, but now, increasingly, the library must build its services around user workflows. (Connaway, Dickey & Radford, 2011, p. 179)

Librarians recognize that is important to tie research instruction to a point of need in order to assess instruction effectiveness. Similarly, when determining where to embed discovery systems, point of need should be a major consideration. While Google became the norm, colleges and universities were also applying other technologies that began to change how users worked and became new points of need. The enterprise portal and learning management system (LMS; or course management system) are two examples.

Enterprise Portals

Institutions using enterprise portals as a way of interacting with constituents have increased significantly in the past ten years (Kendall 2005; Whitehouse 2006). Portals are designed as a one-stop site providing role-based, secure, customizable and personalized academic and business services and internal institutional marketing to students, faculty, and staff. Some of the most common portal functions include brokering access to information stored in student information, human resources, and other enterprise systems, such as course registration and schedules, grade submission and lookup, financial aid and payroll transactions, library services, and campus news and events, and seamless access to email and the LMS.

Common portal products include Sungard®5 Luminis, PeopleSoft®6 Application Portal and the open source Jasig uPortal. Portals typically offer sets of links to various functions in "blocks" within a browser window. These links most commonly broker access through enterprise single sign-on or other identity management solutions or XML-based Web services.

The portal's convenient, often seamless access to multiple authenticated functions makes it a logical place in which to embed discovery systems that expose content restricted to an institutional community. The ability to embed depends on several factors, including the level of interoperability between the portal and other systems, the layout and space devoted to external application interfaces and data (e.g. tabs and blocks), and how authentication and authorization may be handled (e.g. in conjunction with other enterprise systems).

Little (2001) predicted that enterprise portals would present customized information to users based on their organizational role such as current or prospective students, alumni, faculty and staff, and that "the enterprise portal can provide content from various parts of the university and promote resource discovery" (p. 53). Little cites Lynch's idea that libraries may contribute channel-oriented data in ways that are interoperable with other campus data providers "to expose their metadata and use it as input to value-added services" using such means as XML and OAI (Little, 2001, p. 54). Though focused on embedding tools such as subject guides in portals, Little's viewpoint is as valid regarding more modern general-purpose discovery systems as it is regarding the more specialized guides that libraries have maintained for years. Stoffel and Cunningham investigated library participation in campus portals and the trend during the 2000s in which libraries created their own portals, in order to allow users to personalize their experience with discipline-specific information. Due to user desire for fewer portals and greater convenience, this trend has waned in favor of libraries participating in enterprise portals as Little had suggested (Stoffel & Cunningham, 2004).

Learning Management Systems

One of a library's main objectives should be to provide seamless resource access to support and enhance the learning process. While an instructor typically controls the information in a particular course, librarians should offer links to full text articles, search boxes (whether generic or customized for particular courses), and other tools that allow students to discover relevant resources easily and support their learning.

The LMS has become a major tool for containing, organizing, and transacting course content and function. Kim posits that "the growth and entrenchment of the [LMS] is arguably the most important campus trend since 2004 because it plays such a large role in the central mission of instruction" (Kim, 2010, p. 20). Greater than 90 percent of respondents in the 2009 EDUCAUSE Core Data Service Report reported having at least one commercial or homegrown LMS (Arroway et al., 2009). The 2010 ECAR Study of Undergraduate Students and Information Technology found that 80 percent of student respondents reported using an LMS at least weekly in their courses, with 33 percent using an LMS daily (Kim, 2010).

Lawrence (2006) and Gibbons (2005) advocate connecting library resources to online course technology. Gibbons states that "if the library can push relevant resources into the course sites, those resources gain importance [to the students] because of their presence within the course sites" (p. 22). Lawrence views integration as not only beneficial to student learning, but also vital to the future of libraries: "Libraries must also insert themselves into the [LMS] to preserve and/or reinvent their symbolic place in the institution" (p. 248). Lawrence further suggests that "[r]ather than establishing a desired level of deep course integration with only one or two courses, it can be argued that a generic, global link to the library will better serve all students by increasing the ease of access to library resources" (p. 246), and that "macro-level approaches make the provision of library services a scalable endeavor while working to increase the ease of access for students and faculty" (p. 257). An important feature to a top-down approach is making the libraries' resources an expected and predictable portion of a course's online presence. Every effort should be made to proactively embed discovery systems into all courses in an LMS as the default in order to bring consistent access to library resources directly into the student and instructor workflows, as Lawrence (2006) advocates. Gulbahar and Yildirim (2006) also cite consistency as very important to students in Web-based online courses.

The most common LMSs in higher education are Blackboard®[7], Moodle, Desire2Learn®[8] and Sakai, with 71, 16, 10, and 5 percent market share respectively (Green, 2010). Like the portals through which they are frequently accessed, LMSs typically offer sets of links to various resources that are displayed either in the LMS browser window or a separate window. Integrating discovery systems into LMSs typically involves embedding HTML and JavaScript containing search boxes and logic within blocks or "widgets" in the LMS browser window.

HOW TO APPROACH EMBEDDING DISCOVERY

Library and Institutional Context

Beginning from the premise that embedding library discovery systems within a user's academic context is a primary objective, it is useful to conduct an environmental scan to determine and prioritize the logical and possible places to integrate an entry point for the library's discovery system. Such an environmental scan should include, at a minimum:

1. Undertake efforts to understand students' information seeking behavior
2. Analyze usage of the library's existing website to determine pages and resources of high use
3. Survey the campus Web environment to identify potential opportunities (e.g. portal and LMS)
4. Once potential targets are identified in steps 2) and 3), become well educated on what unit(s) control those resources and seek to understand the underlying software capabilities of each

Perhaps the most far-reaching effort to understand students' information seeking behavior is the two-year project documented in the University of Rochester *Studying Students* report (Gibbons & Foster, 2007). The project involved approximately

one-third of the River Campus Libraries staff using anthropological and ethnographic methods to learn more about undergraduate students and how they work. Such an ambitious project may be well beyond the means of many libraries, but the published outcomes yield many valuable insights.

Library website use analysis can guide where to place discovery search boxes. Usability testing has increasingly been used in academic libraries to better understand how students navigate existing library resources, as well as to inform redesign efforts (documented by over 200 articles published since 2000 indexed in *Library, Information Science & Technology Abstracts*™ as of July 2011). Reeb (2008) presents an excellent overview of testing methods, and connects usability practice to Web design. Fagan (2010) recommends a standard approach to faceted discovery system usability testing. Web analytics are also increasingly used to better understand how users use a website (Marek, 2011), and discovery systems such as SerialsSolutions®' Summon™ offer usage and analytic data.

The final step in the environmental scan should be to examine the compiled list of desirable targets in light of three criteria:

1. What unit or units control desired target access and customization?
2. What is the underlying software and code base?
3. How much customization flexibility exists?

Web pages and applications under direct library staff control will present the fewest challenges. Decisions about placing a discovery system search point within existing library resources will likely center much more around theoretical and content discussions than technical considerations. Potential targets outside the library generally fall into one of three categories: commercial, licensed products; open source products; or locally developed and maintained resources. Whether licensed and open source products are locally or remotely hosted is also key, since that may influence customization options. In general, locally developed and open source products will offer the most customization flexibility, provided staff with the necessary coding skills are available to work on such a project. If these resources are controlled and maintained outside the library, this may present challenges. Commercial licensed products may carry restrictions that limit what is possible from both technological and contractual standpoints. In addition, embedding discovery systems into what may be a long-standing layout, and/or long-established set of enhancement project priorities managed by a change management group or systems integration team may be difficult, depending on the approach the library proposes.

To illustrate some of the potential hurdles in placing discovery systems into individual courses within an institution's LMS, consider the following scenario from Oklahoma State University (OSU).

OSU hosts Desire2Learn® (D2L). Maintenance and development within D2L® is divided between two campus units. Campus IT staff have responsibility for access control, as well as server and software administration. A unit of Academic Affairs responsible for faculty technology support and development handles course template design and customization.

A library proposal to embed a "MyLibrary" course-by-course customized library presence (including discovery system search functions) involved the following steps. D2L® does not provide any pre-configured options for this purpose.

1. A librarian with extensive coding experience in multiple languages invested significant time in researching the underlying D2L® software code to determine customization possibilities.

2. The library sought Associate Vice President for Academic Affairs and OSU Instruction Council approval for D2L® course access for the librarian.

3. A lengthy negotiation process with campus IT administrators determined access rights and testing parameters. Ultimately, the library installed an offline D2L® test server to facilitate development and testing, as campus IT was unwilling to allow the librarian to test on their servers. The library also built an SQL database on their existing SQL server to feed customized data elements into each D2L® course's MyLibrary module.

4. The library negotiated further with personnel in the faculty technology support and development unit to determine MyLibrary module placement and appearance within the course template.

5. Any MyLibrary enhancements must be developed and tested on the library's server, and moving updates to production is entirely at the discretion of campus IT staff.

This scenario may paint a daunting picture, and is only provided to illustrate some issues a library might encounter.

In 2009, California State University (CSU), Sacramento IT and library staff created a "library tab" integrating "channels" of library resources into the university's enterprise uPortal-based portal. One of the channels contained an embedded search box for CSU's open source Xerxes application, which facilitates customizable interfaces to Ex Libris®'[9] MetaLib™[10] federated search product (Walker, 2011). CSU Sacramento has achieved seamless library searching and access through integrating MetaLib™ through Xerxes, and the library's proxy server, into the portal using its single sign-on environment. Figure 1 shows an early beta version of how the library tab was implemented. Later enhancements included a simplified search box and allowing users to manage their saved searches and citations from within the library tab. CSU is currently enhancing Xerxes to be used with discovery systems such as Primo Central™[11], Summon™, EBSCO® Discovery Service™[12], and WorldCat Local™[13].

Figure 1. An early beta of CSU Sacramento's library portal tab

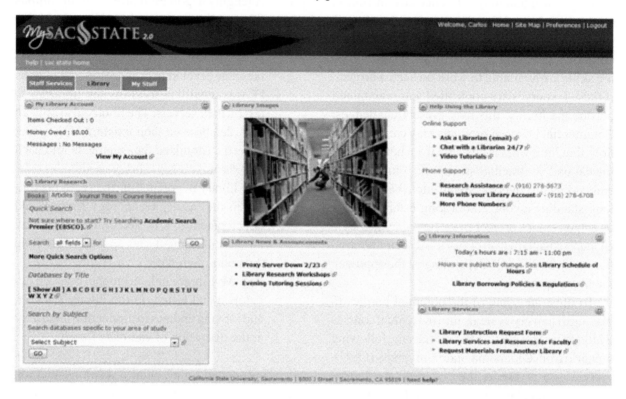

Placing Summon™ within Arizona State University (ASU)'s portal and Blackboard® LMS also required a months-long negotiation and development process involving library Web and marketing personnel and ASU technology and provost office staff (T. Allgood, personal communication, December 13, 2011). Figure 2 shows ASU's Library OneSearch in the MyASU portal.

Western Michigan University (WMU) Libraries had an associate dean on the Faculty Senate Academic and Information Technology Council who joined WMU's Elearning Transition Team following a decision to migrate from Blackboard® Vista™ to D2L®. Though individual team members expressed concern over setting precedent through which other WMU units might expect default widgets, the associate dean convinced the team (including faculty, IT, Extended University Programs, instructional designers, and Office of Faculty Development personnel) that WMU Libraries should have a D2L® widget featuring a

Summon™ search box available in both the user "home" view, and in all courses by default. Libraries staff decided which functions and links the widget would offer, and instructional designers and D2L® administrators placed the widget in production in December, 2011 when cutting over from Blackboard® Vista™ to D2L®. Figure 3 shows WMU's widget in WMU Elearning.

The authors recommend careful strategic thought to realistically prioritize potential target feasibility.

LEVELS OF EMBEDDING

As discussed in the portal and LMS sections above (see Background), there are several ways to embed discovery tools. The most common way is to place an HTML and/or JavaScript-driven search box in a block inside a portal or LMS browser window. Other key considerations are how to handle needed

Figure 2. ASU's Library OneSearch in the MyASU portal

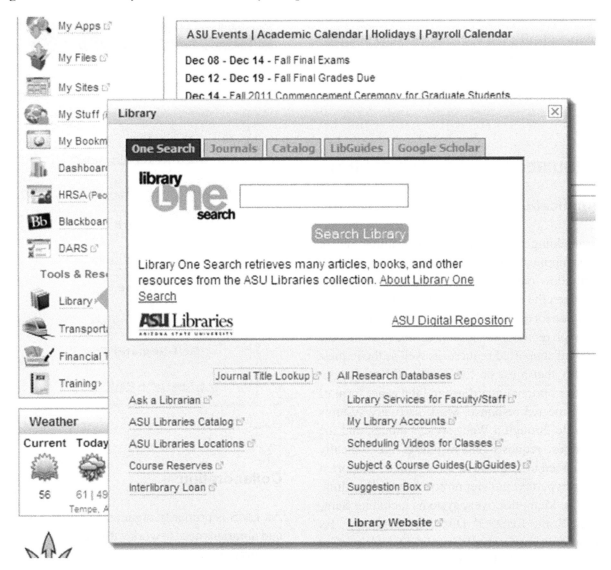

authentication, and display results. "Complete" embedding may consist of search, authentication, and results display and access all directly within the portal or LMS. "Partial" embedding may consist of only search within the portal or LMS, and authentication, display and access in one or more separate browser windows. The best approach at a particular institution will depend on local parameters like authentication (e.g. whether single sign-on is available, and includes proxy access).

While complete embedding may seem more ideal, browser window space constraints can greatly limit display and access options, especially for mobile devices. In addition, though many institutions have single sign-on, true complete integration is not necessarily realistic, as demonstrated by some portal functions such as payroll that require the user to click to view a paystub in the portal, but view it in a separate window using a human resources system's Web interface or a PDF reader.

Partial embedding is typically the simplest approach, and the best way to start. Especially users with off-campus portal, LMS and/or library research experience should already be accustomed to less convenient multiple windows and separate proxy authentication that partial embedding can require.

REQUIREMENTS FOR EMBEDDING

Application Programming Interfaces

Embedding discovery systems requires one or more application programming interfaces (APIs) that allow one-way or two-way communication between the discovery system and its embedded location for query and results display. APIs operate through requests and responses, and must include a set of supported requests as well as the request syntax that must be followed, and any mandatory or optional qualifiers and the exact form of the expected response. Most discovery systems operate through a Web services model, and the services, requests and responses are typically expressed in some variation of XML, transported over hypertext transfer protocol (http; Breeding, 2009). Many discovery systems including Summon™, the EBSCO® Discovery Service™, Ex Libris®' Primo Central™, and OCLC®'s WorldCat Local™ offer APIs. Talsky (2008) explains how to use a link resolver's API to auto-populate an interlibrary loan form, and Klein (2010) describes using Summon™'s APIs to modify results display according to local preferences.

Leveraging APIs is one of many potential technical skillsets needed in order to embed discovery systems. Other skills such as system administration, data manipulation and other programming, interface design, and usability testing may be required, depending on a library's approach.

Figure 3. WMU libraries' e-learning widget

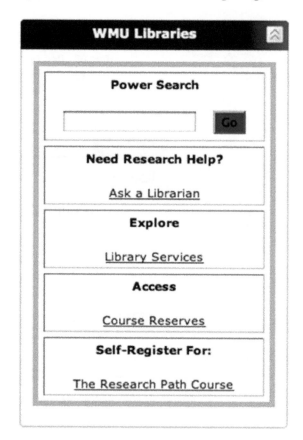

Collaboration

An LMS is primarily organized around courses, and librarians need to work with faculty to identify resources for courses as they have done for years. Jackson (2007) surveyed 171 librarians throughout the California State University system with the objective of assessing librarians' understanding of how to use the Blackboard® LMS as a teaching and learning tool for information literacy. The study's results revealed several barriers to collaboration and integration. Respondents indicated that faculty buy-in, cooperation, time, staffing, funding, and the technology learning curve contributed to a lack of librarian involvement in online courses. Surprisingly, 47 of 56 (83.9 percent) respondents who completed LMS training reported infrequently or never collaborating with faculty to include information literacy (Jackson, 2007, p. 456). In another study by Hightower, Rawl and Schutt (2008), faculty also argued that "the librarians must be proactive in their efforts to encourage and educate faculty about their library and the ways in which the library's resources and services can be integrated into WebCT courses" (Hightower, et al., 2007, p. 550). Given discovery systems' easy search through simple embeddable search boxes, discovery systems can clearly bridge some of these gaps.

Successful discovery system integration requires library, information technology (IT), online learning, faculty development and/or teaching and learning organizations to collaborate closely and articulate a shared vision of the future built around how students learn. Depending on the relationships between the library and other campus units, it may take considerable time to arrive at a shared vision and plan of action. It is best to cultivate positive working relationships with other campus units, in order to find opportune moments to integrate, such as when an institution prepares inevitable transitions between portals, LMSs, discovery and other systems. Some suggestions on how to build strong collaborative relationships with other stakeholders include:

- becoming familiar with campus portal and LMS functionality, and getting to know system and functional administrators, and their own and faculty change management priorities;
- encouraging or requiring liaison librarians to become as embedded as possible in courses (e.g. from guides and basic contact information to helping grade assignments with information literacy components);
- participating in discussions focused on the development/enhancement of campus systems;
- having an open mind and being willing to compromise (e.g. what is "good enough"

to start with, and which improvements can wait for later?);
- publishing and presenting with other stakeholders at workshops and conferences on the value and experience of integrating the library into the larger campus environment;
- developing a sense of mutual understanding and respect between stakeholders by addressing technical and non-technical issues together;
- being involved in the planning stages for new portals and LMSs to ensure that these systems allow embedding, but also that other stakeholders recognize the ability to embed as important;
- and considering the institutional context when selecting discovery and other systems (e.g. what APIs and other tools does a discovery vendor offer, do they participate in groups such as InCommon®[14] for federated identity management, and how have other customers already integrated into common enterprise systems?).

Identity Management

Like previous library search systems, discovery systems can require off-campus authentication in different ways and at different times, whether prior to searching, or in order to access (or request) results. Ideally, seamless integration from a portal or LMS to discovery system would include brokering credentials in the background where possible so that users need only sign in once. Various institutions have implemented varying levels of single sign-on that extends to library access. As some have seen increases in traffic to traditional library databases following discovery system implementations (Way, 2010), discovery renders even more acute the need to simplify remote access to more library resources. It is ideal for institutions, their libraries, and portal, LMS and discovery vendors to have federated identity management solutions such as Shibboleth

Table 1. Authentication methods for Web-scale discovery systems

Product	Point of Authentication (Prior to Initial search or at full-text request)	Type of Authentication	User Account
Encore Synergy™	Allows for both methods	Proxy & Single Sign-On (SSO)	Yes - Optional. Session-based save and export functions available.
Primo Central™	Allows for both methods	Proxy Server & Single Sign-On (SSO)	Yes - Optional. Session-based save and export functions available.
WorldCat Local™	Allows for both methods	Proxy Server & Single Sign-On (SSO)	Yes - Optional
EBSCO® Discovery Service™	Allows for both methods.	Proxy Server & Single Sign-On (SSO)	Yes - Optional
Summon™	At the time of full-text resource request	Proxy Server & Single Sign-On (SSO)	None. However session-based save and export functions available

(InCommon® Federation, 2011). Table 1 below shows how several discovery systems handle authentication and/or offer accounts for users to manage information.

Simple versus Customized Discovery

Portals and LMSs are organized around the individual user's role in an institution or course, providing some level of personalization that libraries may wish to exploit. For example, a student enrolled in a molecular biology course using the portal or LMS may wish to see only molecular biology resources, and possibly a pre-scoped discovery search for only biology and other appropriate resources. In the portal, this sort of functionality requires knowing which courses a particular student is taking, from the student information system. The librarian can work with faculty to identify key words for course-based discovery pre-scoping. Though faculty know discipline-specific databases and journals, discovery

systems can also work well for interdisciplinary research. Student information systems may also provide lists of courses taught that would allow discipline-appropriate resources to be pre-scoped for particular faculty. Combined with information about their research interests, libraries could also generate RSS feeds for faculty.

Some libraries have embedded pre-scoped discovery search on websites and in guides. Grand Valley State University (GVSU) created a tool written in HTML 5 and Javascript that allows librarians and faculty to easily generate easily embeddable HTML code for a custom pre-scoped Summon™ search (Reidsma, 2011). The HTML code is generated by entering one or more search terms and selecting search limits (e.g. content type, publication date, language, availability of full text and peer-reviewed articles) as shown in Figure 4. This is a simple example of how to use an API to embed discovery.

While some libraries have a history of operating library portals, and leverage institutional information to offer their own integrated views of

Figure 4. GVSU's Summon™ create custom search tool

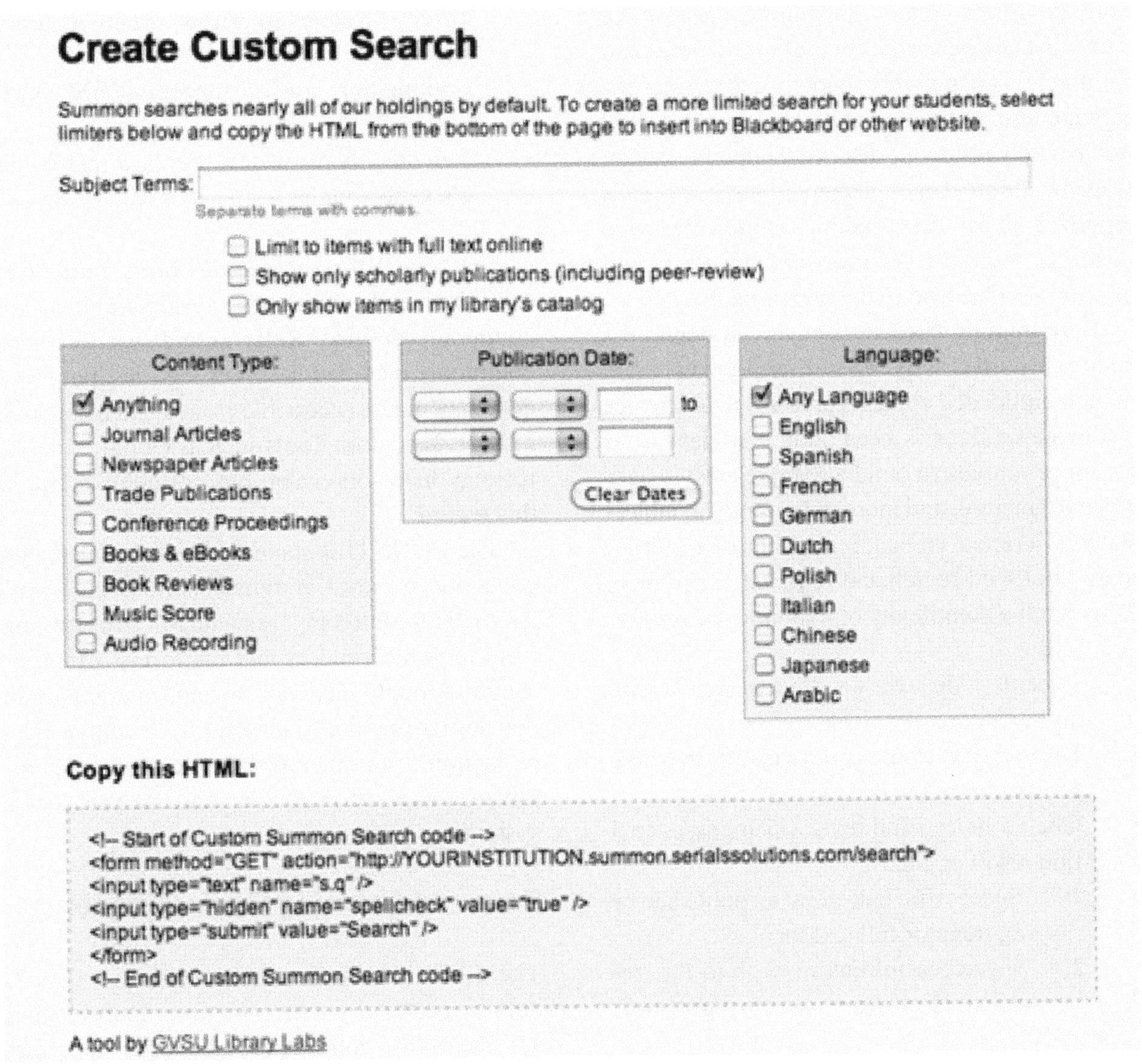

Create Custom Search

Summon searches nearly all of our holdings by default. To create a more limited search for your students, select limiters below and copy the HTML from the bottom of the page to insert into Blackboard or other website.

Subject Terms: [   ]
Separate terms with commas.

☐ Limit to items with full text online
☐ Show only scholarly publications (including peer-review)
☐ Only show items in my library's catalog

Content Type:
☑ Anything
☐ Journal Articles
☐ Newspaper Articles
☐ Trade Publications
☐ Conference Proceedings
☐ Books & eBooks
☐ Book Reviews
☐ Music Score
☐ Audio Recording

Publication Date:
[ ] [ ] [   ] to
[ ] [ ] [   ]
(Clear Dates)

Language:
☑ Any Language
☐ English
☐ Spanish
☐ French
☐ German
☐ Dutch
☐ Polish
☐ Italian
☐ Chinese
☐ Japanese
☐ Arabic

Copy this HTML:

```
<!-- Start of Custom Summon Search code -->
<form method="GET" action="http://YOURINSTITUTION.summon.serialssolutions.com/search">
<input type="text" name="s.q" />
<input type="hidden" name="spellcheck" value="true" />
<input type="submit" value="Search" />
</form>
<!-- End of Custom Summon Search code -->
```

A tool by GVSU Library Labs

liaison-selected discipline-specific resources for courses (Casden, 2009), the authors have observed that students tend to identify one or more search tools of choice that they use throughout college. Given the Project Information Literacy data cited above, an unscoped, broad discovery search is the single best thing for students to find and use as a general-purpose tool during and beyond college.

FUTURE RESEARCH DIRECTIONS

Data Analysis

Determining whether embedding discovery systems in users' environments has been successful presents some significant challenges. Studies on discovery system impact on full text resource use have begun to appear in the literature. Way (2010) reports significant increases in full text downloads/page views following GVSU's Summon™ implementation. Way points out that compiling and analyzing these data is challenging, because the data must be gathered from multiple sources and vendors. It is plausible to conclude that a significant increase in full text downloads in the period immediately following discovery implementation is attributable to that implementation. COUNTER reports from full text vendors can indicate usage increases, but there is no way to know the origin of searches that lead to the increased use.

Determining whether discovery systems embedded in portals and LMSs are used and valuable in their embedded contexts presents even greater challenges. Libraries need additional data from yet more sources to build a comprehensive user behavior picture, and more importantly to understand if libraries' embedding efforts are resulting in an improved search and retrieval experience. Consider the complexity of a sample user query:

- Execute a discovery system search within an LMS course widget
- Discovery system displays results in a new browser window outside the LMS
- Click a link to full text, which passes to a link resolver, then
    1. Successful link goes to publisher or aggregator full text, or
    2. Unsuccessful link may go to ILL request. How many users just give up?

Given the interconnectivity between discrete systems and services this chapter describes, and considering that many of these are not under direct library control, consider the following questions:

- Are exit link data available from the portal or LMS to indicate how often discovery is used there?
- Are referral link reports available from the discovery system to know where users came from?

- Are exit link data available from the discovery system to know whether users linked to full text?
- Can the link resolver report inbound links' sources?
- Can the link resolver report how many link clicks to content were successful?

In each of these cases, a library must also ask whether the data these systems collect are commonly defined. Referral and exit links are commonly recorded in server log files, but these data may not be accessible from systems outside a library's control. Tools such as Google Analytics may help somewhat, but not completely, in this regard.

The COUNTER standard has facilitated data collection, retrieval, and analysis, allowing libraries to analyze and compare standardized usage data from multiple vendors and platforms. Libraries should strongly advocate for and participate in developing similar standards to facilitate data extraction from other Web-based systems to allow user interaction tracking and analysis across systems.

Personal Learning Environments

The EDUCAUSE Learning Initiative (2009) defines personal learning environments (PLEs) as "the tools, communities, and services that constitute the individual educational platforms learners use to direct their own learning and pursue educational goals" (p. 1). While LMSs are more course-centric, PLEs are learner-centric. They may not typically be based on one institutional application, but rather a collection of interoperating Web applications that allow users to organize how they discover, generate, and interact with one another about information. Involving blogs and other Web 2.0 information sharing tools, PLEs are designed to be flexible and allow individuals to control their own learning environment. Unlike an LMS, where every learner experiences content in much the same way, PLEs would allow learners to manage and share content meaningful to them, with both formal and informal networks of peer learners, for their own learning goals within and beyond a particular course. Sclater (2008) suggests three distinct perspectives on what PLEs should encompass and how they should function. First, a PLE should mediate between the learner and online learning and scholarly resources. Second, a PLE should be a Web-based portal rather than specific software. Third (though still somewhat amorphous as of 2011), PLEs already exist and many online learners are already customizing and using them effectively. Examples of Web-based tools with PLE characteristics include Netvibes, PageFlakes, Elgg and iGoogle. Discovery tool search functionality could be integrated into these sites through apps, plugins, "gadgets" or widgets that libraries could create using aforementioned tools such as HTML/JavaScript and pre-scoping.

Users may discover information through their libraries, and wish to share it with others in PLE-supported networks that may extend outside their own institutions. While license restrictions may make this difficult or impossible for publisher-owned content, the shift toward open access will increase sharable content. Seamless federated authentication mechanisms between "trusting" institutions may also facilitate sharing between individuals.

There are a number of technologies and initiatives that may impact PLE development and implementation. Libraries should follow these and become actively involved. See for example:

- the e-Framework for Education and Research, an attempt to create interoperability standards for LMSs, PLEs and related tools;
- Google's Open Social, a set of common APIs for building social applications across many websites;
- the Open ID project, a shared identity project that allows Internet users to sign on to many different websites using a single username and password;
- and the Open Courseware Consortium, a collaboration of over 250 institutions sharing open learning resources.

Mobile Environment

A growing number of library search systems, including discovery, already offer mobile interfaces. Kim (2010) points out that though mobile device usage continues to rise, "It is not clear, however, how many college- or education-related tasks are being done on these mobile [W]eb devices" (p. 22). Libraries need to study how much their mobile apps and websites are actually being used, and for what purposes. Agent logs and analytics can reveal the proportion of mobile browsers accessing discovery systems. While it is straightforward to embed existing mobile discovery interfaces into library and campus apps and mobile-enabled sites, the authors' suggestions regarding portal and LMS collaboration above also apply to the mobile environment.

CONCLUSION

Given that the majority of the research literature this chapter cites predates the aforementioned existing library discovery systems, and that the number of libraries implementing these products continues to grow, libraries are clearly working to "catch up" with users' expectations for simpler and more convenient searching. If users can use discovery where they work, it will be easier for them to begin research, and spend less time finding and more time evaluating what they find (an important tenet of information literacy).

The enterprise portal and learning management system are not the only environments where students are expected to be. Kim (2010) suggests that some students and faculty have begun using social and popular media sites such as Facebook and YouTube for course-related purposes. Libraries have also begun using such sites to expand their reach, but should ask whether they are catching up with one set of expectations as other sets such as social and mobile are taking hold. Enterprise and discovery vendors have begun to recognize the need to integrate social and mobile-friendly functions, and libraries must also be ready to adapt. Do users really need detailed lists of resources and finely-tuned pre-scoped searching and results, displayed in a library-hosted, library-centric interface? Is a wide-open simple search box to the vast majority of library content, with results containing suggestions to specific databases, links to subject guides, and the like, "good enough?"

It is important to keep in mind that indirect assessments such as surveys may be of limited value in answering questions libraries must ask, due to the self-selected nature of respondents. Studying students as the University of Rochester has done, and robust usage data and analytics yield much greater food for thought.

The biggest challenges to becoming embedded are quite likely political rather than technological. Gaining agreement within a library and across a campus on what goes where, how it should function, and what is "good enough" at what point in time, is arguably the greatest challenge of all.

REFERENCES

Arroway, P., Davenport, E., Xu, G., & Updegrove, D. (2009). *EDUCAUSE core data service fiscal year 2009 summary report*. Retrieved from http://net.educause.edu/ir/library/pdf/PUB8007.pdf

Association of Research Libraries. (2011). *LibQUAL+®*. Retrieved from http://www.libqual.org/about/about_survey

Breeding, M. (2009). Opening up library systems through web services and SOA: Hype, or reality? *Library Technology Reports, 45*(8), 1.

Casden, J., Duckett, K., Sierra, T., & Ryan, J. (2009). Course views: A scalable approach to providing course-based access to library resources. *Code4Lib Journal, 6*. Retrieved from http://journal.code4lib.org/articles/1218

Connaway, L., Dickey, T., & Radford, M. (2011). "If it is too inconvenient I'm not going after it": Convenience as a critical factor in information-seeking behaviors. *Library & Information Science Research, 33*(3), 179–190. doi:10.1016/j.lisr.2010.12.002

DeRosa, C., Cantrell, J., Carlson, M., Gallagher, P., Hawk, J., & Sturtz, C. (2010). *Perceptions of libraries, 2010: Context and community*. Dublin, OH: OCLC®. Retrieved from http://www.oclc.org/reports/2010perceptions.htm

DeRosa, C., Cantrell, J., Cellentani, D., Hawk, J., Jenkings, L., & Wilson, A. (2005). *Perceptions of libraries and information resources*. Dublin, OH: OCLC®. Retrieved from http://www.oclc.org/reports/2005perceptions.htm

EDUCAUSE Learning Initiative. (2009). 7 things you should know about personal learning environments. *EDUCAUSE*. Retrieved from http://net.educause.edu/ir/library/pdf/ELI7049.pdf

Fagan, J. (2010). Usability studies of faceted browsing: A literature review. *Information Technology and Libraries, 29*(2), 58–66.

Gibbons, S. (2005). Who should care and why. *Library Technology Reports, 41*(3), 21–23.

Gibbons, S., & Foster, N. F. (Eds.). (2007). *Studying students: The undergraduate research project at the University of Rochester*. Chicago, IL: Association of College and Research Libraries.

Green, K. C. (2010, October). *Campus comput-ing 2010: The 21st national survey of computing and information technology in US higher educa-tion.* Paper presented the Annual Conference of EDUCAUSE, Anaheim, CA. Retrieved from http://www.campuscomputing.net/sites/www.campuscomputing.net/files/Green-CampusComputing2010.pdf

Greenwood, J. T., Watson, A. P., & Dennis, M. (2011). Ten years of LibQual: A study of qualitative and quantitative survey results at the University of Mississippi 2001-2010. *Journal of Academic Librarianship, 37*(4), 312–318. doi:10.1016/j.acalib.2011.04.005

Gulbahar, Y., & Yildirim, S. (2006). Assessment of web-based courses: A discussion and analysis of learners' individual differences and teaching-learning process. *International Journal of Instructional Media, 33*(4), 367–378.

Head, A. J., & Eisenberg, M. B. (2010). *Truth be told: How college students evaluate and use information in the digital age.* Seattle, WA: Project Information Literacy/University of Washington Information School. Retrieved from http://projectinfolit.org/pdfs/PIL_Fall2010_Survey_Full-Report1.pdf

Hightower, B., Rawl, C., & Schutt, M. (2008). Collaborations for delivering the library to students through WebCT™. *RSR. Reference Services Review, 35*(4), 541–551. doi:10.1108/00907320710838363

InCommon® Federation. (2011). *InCommon® identity and access management.* Retrieved August 22, 2011, from http://www.incommon.org/

Jackson, P. A. (2007). Integrating information literacy into Blackboard®: Building campus partnerships for successful student learning. *Journal of Academic Librarianship, 33*(4), 454–461. doi:10.1016/j.acalib.2007.03.010

Jones, S., & Madden, M. (2002). *The Internet goes to college: How students are living in the future with today's technology.* Washington, DC: Pew Internet and American Life Project. Retrieved from http://www.pewinternet.org/~/media//Files/Reports/2002/PIP_College_Report.pdf.pdf

Kendall, J. R. (2005). Implementing the web of student services. *New Directions for Student Services, 112*, 55–68. doi:10.1002/ss.184

Kim, J. (2010). Following their lead: An introduction . In Smith, S. D., & Caruso, J. B. (Eds.), *The ECAR study of undergraduate students and information technology* (pp. 19–25). Boulder, CO: EDUCAUSE Center for Applied Research.

Klein, M. (2010). Hacking Summon™. *Code4Lib Journal, 11.* Retrieved from http://journal.code4lib.org/articles/3655

Lawrence, D. H. (2006). Blackboard® on a shoe-string: Tying courses to sources. *Journal of Library Administration, 45*(1/2), 245–265. doi:10.1300/J111v45n01_14

Little, J. R. (2001). A librarian's perspective on portals. *EDUCAUSE Quarterly, 24*(2), 52–54.

Marek, K. (2011). Getting to know web analytics. *Library Technology Reports, 47*(5), 11–16.

Reeb, B. (2008). *Design talk: Understanding the roles of usability practitioners, web designers, and web developers in user-centered web design.* Chicago, IL: Association of College and Research Libraries.

Reidsma, M. (2011). *Custom Summon™ searches* [Software]. Retrieved from http://gvsulib.com/labs/custom_summon/

Sclater, N. (2008). Web 2.0, personal learning environments, and the future of learning management systems. *Research Bulletin, 13.* Boulder, CO: EDUCAUSE Center for Applied Research. Retrieved from http://net.educause.edu/ir/library/pdf/ERB0813.pdf

Stoffel, B., & Cunningham, J. (2005). Library participation in campus web portals: An initial survey. *Reference Services Review, 33*(2), 144-160. doi: 10. 1108/00907320510597354

Talsky, D. (2008). Auto-populating an ILL form with the Serial Solutions link resolver API. *Code4Lib Journal, 4.* Retrieved from http:// journal.code4lib.org/articles/108

Walker, D. (2011). *Xerxes* (Version 1.8) [Software]. Retrieved from http://code.google.com/p/ xerxes-portal/

Way, D. (2010). The impact of web-scale discovery on the use of a library collection. *Serials Review, 36*(4), 214–220. doi:10.1016/j.serrev.2010.07.002

Whitehouse, K. (2006). Cutting through the clutter: What makes an intranet successful? *EDUCAUSE Quarterly, 29*(1), 65–69.

ADDITIONAL READING

Abuhamdieh, A. H., & Sehwail, L. (2007). A comparative study of campus portal user acceptance: Student and faculty perspectives. *Journal of STEM Education: Innovations and Research, 8*(3/4), 40–49.

Bell, S. J., & Shank, J. D. (2004). Linking the library to courseware: A strategic alliance to improve learning outcomes. *Library Issues, 25*(2), 1–4.

Bielema, C., Crocker, D., Miller, J., Reynolds-Moehrle, J., & Shaw, H. (2005). Faculty and librarian collaborations: A case study and proposal for online learning environments. *Research Strategies, 20*(4), 334–345. doi:10.1016/j. resstr.2006.12.008

Black, E. L. (2008). Toolkit approach to integrating library resources into the learning management system. *Journal of Academic Librarianship, 34*(6), 496–501. doi:10.1016/j.acalib.2008.09.018

Buehler, M. A. (2004). Where is the library in course management software? *Journal of Library Administration, 41*(1/2), 5-84. doi: 10.1300/Jl 11 v41 nO1_07

Cohen, D. (2002). Course-management software: Where's the library? *EDUCAUSE Review, 37*(3), 12–13.

Collard, S., & Tempelman-Kluit, N. (2006). The other way in: Goal-based library content through CMS. *Internet Reference Services Quarterly, 11*(4), 55–68. doi:10.1300/J136v11n04_04

Davies, R. (2007). Library and institutional portals: A case study. *The Electronic Library, 25*(6), 641–647. doi:10.1108/02640470710837083

Flecker, D., & McLean, N. (2004). *Digital library content and course management systems: Issues of interoperation.* Retrieved from http://old.diglib. org/pubs/dlf100/cmsdl0407.pdf

George, J., & Martin, K. (2004). Forging the library courseware link: Providing library support to students in an online classroom environment. *College & Research Libraries News, 65*(10), 594–613.

Hanson, C., Nackerud, S., & Jensen, K. (2008). Affinity strings: Enterprise data for resource recommendations. *Code4Lib Journal, 5.* Retrieved from http://journal.code4lib.org/articles/501

Kesselman, M. A., & Watstein, S. (2009). Creating opportunities: Embedded librarians. *Journal of Library Administration, 49*(4), 383–400. doi:10.1080/01930820902832538

McLean, N., & Lynch, C. (2004). *Interoperability between library information services and learning environments-bridging the gap: A joint white paper on behalf of the IMS Global Learning Consortium and the Coalition for Networked Information.* Retrieved from http://www.immagic. com/eLibrary/ARCHIVES/GENERAL/CNI_US/ C040510M.pdf

Nichols, J., & Mellinger, M. (2007). Portals for undergraduate subject searching: Are they worth it? *portal . Libraries and the Academy, 7*(4), 481–490. doi:10.1353/pla.2007.0052

Presley, A., & Presley, T. (2009). Factors influencing student acceptance and use of academic portals. *Journal of Computing in Higher Education, 21*(3), 167–182. doi:10.1007/s12528-009-9022-7

Sabharwal, A. (2005). Vision and strategy towards the course-embedded library: New possibilities for a "virtual carrel" initiative. *MLA Forum, 4*(1). Retrieved from http://www.mlaforum.org/volumeIV/issue2/article3.html

Shank, J., & Bell, S. (2006). A FLIP to courseware: A strategic alliance for improving student learning outcomes. *Innovate: Journal of Online Education, 2*(4). Retrieved from http://www.innovateonline.info/pdf/vol2_issue4/A_FLIP_to_Courseware-__A_Strategic_Alliance_for_Improving_Student_Learning_Outcomes.pdf

Solis, J., & Hampton, E. M. (2009). Promoting a comprehensive view of library resources in a course management system. *New Library World, 110*(1/2), 81–91. doi:10.1108/03074800910928603

Washburn, A. (2008). Finding the library in Blackboard®: An assessment of library integration. *Journal of Online Learning and Teaching, 4*(3), 301–316. Retrieved from http://jolt.merlot.org/vol4no3/washburn_0908.pdf

York, A. C., & Vance, J. M. (2009). Taking library instruction into the online classroom: Best practices for embedded librarians. *Journal of Library Administration, 49*(1/2), 197–209. doi:10.1080/01930820802312995

KEY TERMS AND DEFINITIONS

Application Programming Interface (API): A code-based specification used as an interface by software components to communicate with each other.

Authentication: Confirming the identity of a person within an organization, e.g. through username and password credentials.

Authorization: Allowing an authenticated person access to information or functionality based on their role as defined within a system.

COUNTER: A standard for Counting Online Usage of NeTworked Electronic Resources that libraries offer.

Discovery System (or Web-Scale Discovery System): A system allowing searching across a vast range of preharvested and indexed content quickly and seamlessly.

Enterprise Portal: A framework for integrating "channels" of information, people and processes across organizational boundaries, through a secure unified Web interface.

Identity Management: Identifying individuals in a system and controlling access to the resources in that system by placing restrictions on the established identities of the individuals.

InCommon®: A federation of institutions, societies, publishers and other companies who agree to adhere to standard federated identity management approaches including Shibboleth.

Learning Management System (LMS): A software application for administrating, documentating, tracking, and reporting on hybrid and fully online courses, training content, and other organized activity between teachers and learners.

LibQUAL+® Information Control Question 6: Measures user perception of whether a library offers "Easy to-use access tools that allow me to find things on my own."

LibQUAL+® Information Control Question 7: Measures user perception of whether a library is "Making information easily accessible for independent use."

OpenURL: A standardized format of Uniform Resource Locator (URL) intended to enable Internet users to more easily find a copy of a resource that they are authorized to access.

Shibboleth: Identity management software that allows users to securely send trusted information about themselves to remote resources in order to authenticate, without having to send their credentials over the Web; can facilitate single sign-on.

Single Sign-On: A means of controlling access to multiple related, but independent, software systems, i.e. in one user-facing authentication step, and passing credentials between systems in the background.

ENDNOTES

[1] OCLC is a registered trademark of OCLC.

[2] LibQUAL+ is a registered trademark of Association of Research Libraries

[3] SerialsSolutions is a registered trademark of SerialsSolutions

[4] Summon is owned by ProQuest LLC

[5] Sungard is a registered trademark of Sungard Corporation

[6] PeopleSoft is a registered trademark of PeopleSoft, Inc.

[7] Blackboard is a registered trademark of Blackboard Solutions

[8] Desire2Learn is a registered trademark of Desire2Learn, Inc.

[9] ExLibris is a trademark of Ex Libris Ltd.

[10] MetaLib is a trademark of Ex Libris Ltd.

[11] Primo Central is owned by Ex Libris Ltd. or its affiliates.

[12] EBSCO Discovery Service is owned by EBSCO Publishing Industries

[13] WorldCat is a registered trademark of OCLC.

[14] InCommon is a registered trademark of InCommon, LLC.

Chapter 23
Implementing a Discovery Layer in a Consortial Environment

Mark Christel
The College of Wooster Libraries, USA

Jacob Koehler
The College of Wooster Libraries, USA

Michael Upfold
The Five Colleges of Ohio, USA

ABSTRACT

A consortium of five liberal arts colleges (Denison, Kenyon, Oberlin, Wooster, and Ohio Wesleyan), decided to investigate discovery tools, established a process for reviewing and selecting a product, and worked through the delicate implementation decisions of a shared resource. Consortial cooperative efforts between libraries have very deep roots in Ohio, where OhioLINK has established an enviable record of success. This effort of The Five Colleges of Ohio marks one of the first forays into consortial discovery layer implementation. Selection criteria for use in a consortial environment and best practices for implementation are included in the chapter. Throughout the selection and implementation process, local preferences and considerations were continually balanced against the needs of the consortium

INTRODUCTION

One of the big challenges presented by significant innovations, especially processes, products, and approaches that require a paradigm shift, is the timing. It is easy to recognize the bleeding edge of an innovation, when investments of time and money are so prohibitively high that the great majority of libraries cannot consider early adop-

tion, even should they be willing to work through the inevitable bumps of beta. It is much harder to identify that perfect moment in time when yesterday's cutting edge becomes today's best practice. Timing has always been difficult, even when most libraries operated relatively independently and each could make decisions based largely upon local circumstances and resources. In today's "flat world," most libraries have become involved in, perhaps even entangled by, partnerships, coalitions, and consortia. Those multiple relationships,

DOI: 10.4018/978-1-4666-1821-3.ch023

for all their wonders, bring with them an infinitely more complex decision-making process even as the pace of change continues to accelerate.

For academic libraries, one of the innovations du jour is, of course, the discovery layer or service. Although this new service is appealing to many libraries, it is relatively expensive in terms of both purchase/subscription costs and staff time for implementation. Consortial purchase and implementation of a discovery layer, which can offer significant financial savings and leverage the shared expertise of multiple institutions, may be a very practical approach for many libraries to consider. Careful planning, pre-defined evaluation criteria, and equal participation and contributions by all members throughout the selection and implementation processes will help minimize the potential risks of multi-institutional collaborations.

BACKGROUND

Cooperative efforts among libraries in the United States have a long and vibrant history. Melvil Dewey himself authored, "Library Co-operation" in an 1886 issue of *Library Journal* and the American Library Association included a Co-operation Committee as early as the 1880's (Kopp, 1998). Indeed, library consortia, "which involve groups of libraries cooperating for mutual benefit, are a natural outgrowth of a spirit of sharing that lies at the foundation of all libraries" (Alberico, 2002, p. 63). In her article, "The History and Development of Academic Library Consortia in the United States: An Overview," Sharon L. Bostick identifies resource sharing, lending privileges, book purchasing and cataloging, automation of library systems, staff development, and cost savings through group purchasing power as goals of early library cooperative efforts (Bostick, 2001).

Studies looking at more contemporary roles of consortia naturally begin to focus on the impact of new technologies and highlight the importance

of a unified search platform. In 2002, Jackson and Preece discuss broad interest in creating portals to unify the myriad online resources available and suggest that consortia might, "serve as a sounding board for new initiatives and may represent a safe haven for experimentation...[and] allow libraries to experiment collectively with innovative ways to provide information" (Jackson & Preece, 2002, p.160). The successes of consortia in the 1990's to purchase content helped create a recognized need for better discovery tools: "More recently, as the corpus of on-line information offered by consortia has grown, now including millions of journal articles available from some consortia, concerns about enabling resource discovery and promoting information literacy have come to the forefront" (Alberico, 2002, p. 64). Nfila and Darko-Ampem, in their overview about consortia from the 1960s through 2000, end their article with a similar conclusion: "Academic libraries are fast shifting from sharing bibliographic information to sharing technology for bibliographic control. This trend is bound to continue" (Nfila & Darko-Ampem, 2002, p.211).

At this time, however, very little on consortial implementations of discovery tools has made its way into the professional literature. Digby and Elfstrand's article on MnPALS Plus (Digby, 2011), a VuFind-based discovery tool developed for PALS, a consortium of Minnesota colleges and universities, is one of the few examples. However, many of the challenges and obstacles identified and best practices suggested about other consortial efforts with shared systems remain very pertinent to discovery layer implementations. Recent literature on institutional repository software includes two very useful articles on consortial instances, one at the Washington Research Library Consortium (Hulse, 2007) and the other for SHERPA-LEAP, a consortium of seven academic institutions in the UK (Moyle, 2007). Many articles are also available that discuss consortial library automation and shared ILS systems, but one of the most helpful for considering consortial efforts is Vaughan and

Costello's, "Management and Support of Shared Integrated Library Systems," (Vaughan, 2011). The authors, involved in a multi-institutional ILS system in Nevada using Innovative Interfaces' platform, conducted a survey of libraries involved in consortial systems using the Innovative User's Group's listserv. Their survey focuses on four areas: background information, funding, support and training/professional development.

Several foundational readings are particularly helpful in considering potential implications and advantages of consortial discovery layer implementations. G. Edward Evans identifies five benefits of collaboration and six areas for possible conflict in his excellent article, "Management Issues of Co-operative Ventures and Consortia in the USA. Part One" (Evans, 2002). Thomas A. Peters, in a somewhat similar exercise, defines twelve "inherent consortial discontents" and then offers suggestions for minimizing those potential obstacles (Peters, 2003, p.111). In an article in *The Harvard Business Review*, "Collaborative Advantage: The Art of Alliances," Rosabeth Moss Kanter provides key insights about successful collaborations she gained after interviewing over 500 individuals at 37 companies that were involved in "successful" partnerships (Kanter, 1994). One of her contributions is a hierarchy of collaborative relationships, running from "mutual service consortial" at the weakest end up to "value-chain partnerships" as the strongest and most productive collaborations (Kanter, 1994, p.98). Kanter downplays the financial and stereotypical business aspects of collaboration, highlighting instead the "partnership in human terms" (Kanter, 1994, p. 96).

CONTEXT

The College of Wooster, Denison University, Kenyon College, Oberlin College, and Ohio Wesleyan University are largely residential colleges, with student bodies ranging from 1,600 to 2,800. In 1995, with support from The Andrew W. Mellon

Foundation, the group formed The Five Colleges of Ohio consortium, or the Ohio5. Their libraries have a long history of working together collaboratively on various initiatives, from information literacy to cooperative collection development efforts (Curl, 2004). Four of the institutions, all of the members except Oberlin, have a shared catalog. More recent and ambitious consortial projects include a plan for a shared, distributed depository library collection and a merged technical services operation between two of its members: Kenyon and Denison. The Ohio5 colleges are also members of OhioLINK, one of the world's pre-eminent, innovative, and productive library networks (Kohl & Sanville, 2006 and Sanville, 2007). As the individual schools considered discovery layers, each had the option of proceeding independently, seeking a cooperative solution with the other Ohio5 members, or awaiting a state-wide effort by OhioLINK.

OhioLINK was early in recognizing the need for a search tool to integrate and deliver all of its content. An ambitious plan to develop its own state-of-the-art discovery tool that would become freely available to all OhioLINK members stalled due to the economic meltdown of 2008, consolidation efforts within various state agencies, and the departure of Tom Sanville, OhioLINK's long-term Executive Director (Oder, 2010), and other key OhioLINK staff. While the five private colleges had awaited the development of an OhioLINK product, commercial discovery tools had quickly matured and were now largely recognized as a desirable, if not standard, product for academic libraries. To borrow Malcolm Gladwell's entirely apt phrase, the tipping point had come and gone and the five small colleges now found themselves playing catch up.

On April 7, 2010, the library directors of the Ohio5 colleges met at Oberlin College and discussed the situation and how each planned to proceed. While OhioLINK's project had lost its momentum, the directors were still convinced that a collaborative approach could offer the most efficient option for their schools. Several key considerations informed the decision to proceed with an Ohio5 approach to implementing a discovery system:

- All were using the same ILS and four of the colleges shared an OPAC, so each needed to work through many of the same issues and could do so more effectively working together.
- All needed to develop solutions for incorporating the substantial OhioLINK resources into their discovery systems.
- The smaller size of the consortium and relatively equal standing of the individual members meant that the colleges could draw on the collective expertise and financial assets of the group without sacrificing undue levels of control over the process.
- The Ohio5 consortium employs a central systems librarian who would be essential in assisting the colleges as they implemented discovery products. If each selected a different system, inevitable delays would occur as he needed to work with the different vendors.
- Collectively, they had a large staff with deep expertise in systems, technical services, and public services/instruction who could effectively troubleshoot issues and develop implementation plans. Individually, their staffs would be stretched by a rapid implementation of a discovery layer.
- The five libraries could move quickly because they had a long history of successful collaborations and had established a culture of trust.

While consortial ties, or other less formal interdependent relationships, can sometimes complicate decision making processes (Peters, 2003), in this case each of the consortial members realized they needed to move as quickly as possible to implement a discovery system and it was clear that the consortium was the ideal means of

facilitating a rapid deployment. By the end of the April meeting, the directors had set an ambitious timeline for selecting an Ohio5 discovery layer:

1. April 15, 2010 – Each college would identify a staff member to serve on an Ohio5 Discovery Layer Task Force.
2. May 1, 2010 – The task force would begin meeting.
3. October 15, 2010 – The task force would issue a recommendation on a discovery layer product to the Ohio5 directors.
4. January 1, 2011 – The colleges would begin a soft launch of their discovery layer system for the Spring 2011 semester.

The Discovery Layer Task Force was charged with investigating available discovery layer options and completing its evaluations in time to make a recommendation before mid-October of 2010. Since the group was fully conscious of OhioLINK's ongoing work toward implementing a statewide discovery system and remained committed to that broader effort, an important parameter for the task force was that potential candidates must have an annual licensing option, rather than a significant up-front cost that would lock the Ohio5 colleges into a long-term product. If/when the OhioLINK product became available, the Ohio5 wanted an option to adopt that solution and transition away from any discovery layer implemented in the interim.

REVIEW AND SELECTION

Any library in the process of large-scale purchasing is faced with the daunting task of deciding how to find products that will best serve the needs of local patrons. In the consortial purchasing and decision making model, local needs are balanced against the needs of the consortium as a whole (Kinner, 2009). The Ohio5 library directors, understanding these challenges inherent to consortial purchasing, formed a task force consisting of one member from each library and led by the Ohio5 system librarian. The discovery layer selection and purchasing process requires more complex and nuanced investigation than what is needed in normal "big-ticket" purchasing, and the charge of this committee was rather encompassing: learn as much as possible about discovery layer technology, determine the strengths and weaknesses of available commercial and open-source discovery layer products, and make a recommendation of which product to select.

The initial work of the task force focused solely on information gathering. As discovery layers were still a relatively new technology, the members of the committee needed to look into not only the products themselves, but also the terminology associated with the products. The members may have had some familiarity with topics such as "link resolvers" and "faceted searching," but it was quickly apparent that a thorough understanding of these (and other topics) was integral to understanding discovery layer technology. Along with the larger question of how discovery layers work, the group also focused their time during this period identifying discovery layers to investigate further.

Early task force discussions raised the possibility of an open-source option. These were quickly ruled out, however, due to several reasons: existing open-source options at the time were mainly designed to meet the needs of one library and would not easily transfer to a consortial setup; commercial counterparts were more robust; and local technical expertise required to customize the products was a concern.

Taking out the open-source options still left the committee with an array of commercial discovery layer options. Most were eliminated as too immature in their development at that time. The three final competitors were OCLC's WorldCat®[1] Local, Serials Solutions®[2] Summon™[3], and Ex Libris™[4] Primo Central™[5]. In August of 2010, the three vendors were invited to present their products to a group of assembled staff from the Ohio5. Staff feedback from these presentations led to a quick decision to remove WorldCat® Local from the running. The reasons that WorldCat® Local was eliminated included a requirement that each resource in our local catalog have an OCLC number; most Ohio5 electronic resources are either lacking any number or, more commonly, have some other identifier.. Also, the presentation focused primarily on discovery of physical library resources rather than electronic ones (leading to the conclusion that Primo Central™ and Summon™ could provide a more direct and transparent route for Ohio5 patrons to all material, though several attendees commented that WorldCat® Local had desirable features for OPAC data).

Both Primo Central™ and Summon™ had strong support among members of the Ohio5 task force and consortium staff. At the time, the committee felt that both products had the major functionality required by the consortium. The remaining discussions focused on those aspects of each that were felt to best meet the consortium needs and expectations. Primo Central™, while seemingly much more locally configurable, was felt to have weaker search functions, and relied too heavily on federated search. Summon™, though customizable, was viewed as a having more searching capabilities.

In consideration of the remaining differences in the two top discovery layer options, the committee ultimately decided to recommend Serials Solutions®' Summon™ product to the Ohio5 directors. While the committee was somewhat split on a few small differences in preference, the decision was unanimous, and the ordering process began in earnest October of 2010.

IMPLEMENTATION

Serials Solutions® proposed that there be five separate instances of Summon™: one for each school in the consortium. It had always been difficult to imagine a single discovery layer configuration that

Figure 1. An example of an item with unique institutional URLs

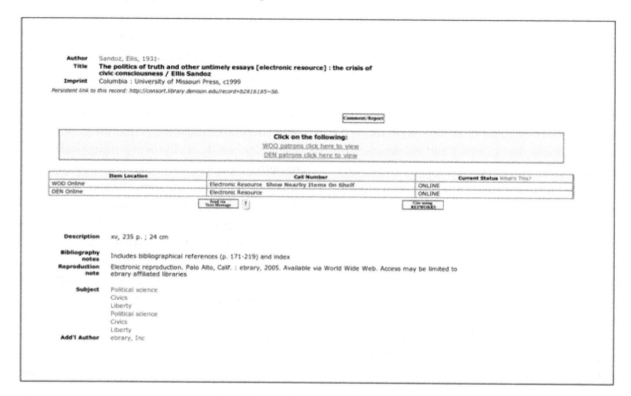

would work for a consortium of five schools, two online catalogs, and some shared and other unique electronic resources, so this proposal seemed the best way to address that challenge. None of the vendors was able to offer a proposal for a unified approach that would truly work for the entire consortium, so they all essentially proposed a multiple-instance solution that mirrored, in many ways, a more typical installation.

One unintended consequence of this approach was a dilution of the group's consortial philosophy. Procedures for sharing physical resources, in terms of both purchasing and circulating material among the member libraries, had been developed over several years. Patrons at any of the CONSORT schools can by default see and borrow materials from each library. In addition, all of the members of the Ohio5 consortium contribute their records to the central OhioLINK database, and so can see and borrow materials from virtually any academic library in Ohio. This had been much more problematic for electronic resources, and one of the identified weaknesses of the shared OPAC had been the difficulty of presenting those resources to users in an understandable, straightforward way. The Ohio5 has struggled with this for some years without finding a 'consortial' solution that satisfied any constituency, and had hoped a collaborative discovery layer would open up new options for us.

Figure 1 is an image from the OPAC shared by four of the colleges. This image displays the problem experienced with electronic resources. It shows a resource that is available at some, but not all of the schools, and lists unique URLs for each subscriber.

As illustrated, patrons from the other schools in the consortium that do not subscribe are asked for a username/password if they click on either

URL. In addition, patrons from the subscribing schools must click on the correct URL for access.

At the start of the Summon™ implementation process, each school was assigned an implementation coordinator; though the end result was that the same coordinator worked with all five of the colleges. One of the initial hurdles was the complexity of our consortial arrangement. The Summon™ implementation department was not used to working with individual libraries that were also part of a consortium. It has taken many lengthy explanations on both sides to be able to reach a comfortable level of mutual understanding. Having multiple contacts at five institutions involved in creating five linked, but independent discovery layers was not an ideal scenario for either consortial libraries or vendors.

As mentioned earlier, four of the five members of the Ohio5 share a single Millennium ILS named CONSORT. The other member, Oberlin College, has its own stand-alone Millennium ILS named OBIS. The Ohio5 systems manager is only responsible for the CONSORT system; OBIS is a separate, independent system, maintained and managed at Oberlin. Although information was shared among all of the members of the consortium, including Oberlin College, the Summon™ system at Oberlin was implemented independently. The comments that follow concerning implementation, are restricted to implementation within the CONSORT shared ILS.

Serials Solutions® training on Summon™ consisted of two separate phases. There was a brief introduction to the Client Center, which is used to build the knowledge base of journal subscriptions, and then training on the actual implementation of the individual Summon™ instance. The introductory overview was done jointly for the consortium, and then the actual implementation training was done separately for each library.

The first issue encountered was that consortium members had markedly different levels of familiarity with Serials Solutions®' products. Two of the members already used Serials Solutions®' A to Z lists of journals; for them, the Client Center interface was familiar, but the other two had no one on staff that had previously seen the interface. For those libraries especially, the conceptual and practical bar was markedly higher, and it took somewhat longer for them to be able to start moving forward on implementation.

We also quickly discovered that the timeframe Serials Solutions® proposed (a fairly short implementation time of approximately 6-8 weeks, dependent on the library's ability to accomplish specific goals), was not one that any of the libraries, for multiple reasons, was able to meet. All of the libraries in the consortium are small, with staff members who each wear multiple "hats," so the amount of time that could be devoted to Summon™ implementation was limited. Also, length of time to reach consensus varied directly with the size of the local committees: some libraries had small committees, others were not so small.

In addition to the local implementation committees at each school, there was also a consortial committee, consisting of one representative from each school (a person also serving on the local committee) and the Ohio5 systems librarian. The consortial committee primarily served to share common information/difficulties and remove redundancy from the process. For example, because the libraries share catalog records, it made sense to approach the mapping of content types consortially.

It took some time for the consortial committee to find an optimal way to share information. Meetings were held virtually and infrequently, presenting some challenges for effective communication. The group eventually began using Google Sites and Google Documents to share information more effectively, as illustrated in figure 2.

Although one of the primary reasons for launching this project was to make our growing collection of electronic resources easily "discoverable," the most familiar context for many library staff was the existing public catalog and the underlying catalog records. Interestingly, both Serials Solu-

Figure 2. The Ohio5 Summon™ implementation group Google site

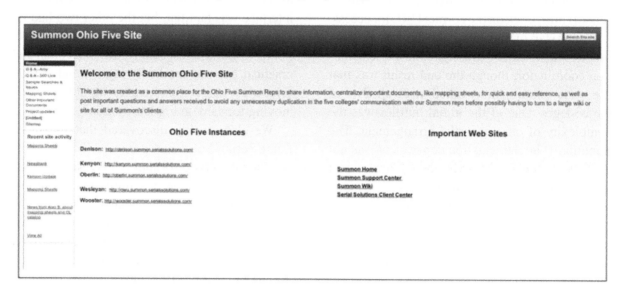

tions® implementation documentation and much of the training focused on those catalog records. As a result, a preponderance of our collective time and effort was concentrated on what is fast becoming a small minority of the library's available resources. Again, this was familiar territory for the libraries, but did have a negative impact on implementation due to the fact that relatively minor points of display could be debated at great length.

For the bulk of the records in Summon™ (i.e. electronic journal articles, eBooks, etc., which were not being pulled from catalog records in the ILS), there were few decisions to make beyond their inclusion in or exclusion from the discovery layer.

For both philosophical and practical reasons, it was decided to upload the full consortial database for all items representing physical materials, as well as all electronic resources shared by the full group. In addition, each school's unique electronic resources were uploaded to its instance. Subsequent updates would also use the same parameters. For each instance of Summon™, the display would then by default include records available to all patrons in the consortium, plus those additional

electronic resources only available on a particular campus. This was a significant reason for implementing separate discovery layer instances.

The Ohio5 systems librarian had responsibility for sending records from the catalog to Serials Solutions®. Because of the complexity of the ongoing requirement for sending regular updates and deletes, he decided to automate the task, using a combination of Expect and perl scripts (all edited from the work of others) and the use of crontab on a Linux desktop. As individual libraries often purchased electronic titles with accompanying MARC records which were loaded into the ILS database, these updates varied between several dozen and several thousand titles per day.

From the beginning of the process, the Five Colleges had planned to use the "OLinks" OpenURL resolver developed by OhioLINK. The resolver had been in use for electronic journals within the consortium for some years and it was assumed that it would work in this context as well. Links from Summon™ to electronic journal entries did re-direct correctly, but records for any other online resources (eBooks, newspaper articles, etc.) did not. It was later found that the OhioLINK OpenURL resolver was developed initially to handle linking to electronic journal articles only, and by design did not resolve any other request. Not determining this at the beginning of the project was a significant oversight by both the consortium and the Serials Solutions® sales team. Once it was confirmed that the OhioLINK OpenURL resolver would not work, the consortium and Serials Solutions® were able to implement linking via their own resolver, 360 Link.

The implementation of a discovery layer itself brought a number of technical and conceptual hurdles for the libraries, and having to learn the details of a new OpenURL resolver meant there was now an additional layer of complexity added to the project. In most cases, these products were sold and implemented separately, so that there were normally multiple learning curves rather than a single steep one. There were also several occasions when it would have been more efficient to immediately refer questions to the Serials Solutions® implementation specialist, rather than to speculate on a particular result.

LOOKING FORWARD

A first version of Summon™ was introduced on the Ohio5 campuses in late summer, 2011, before the beginning of the fall semester; although additional tweaking of parameters has continued. Having a discovery layer presents a new situation for the consortium, and raises several related issues for both teaching librarians and technical services staff. So far, it is unknown what kind and how much ongoing maintenance will be required, as well as who will be responsible for various aspects of the new products. As noted above, the consortium has a single systems librarian, and although that has worked well for the shared ILS, which primarily focuses on physical resources, it is less likely to work in an environment of locally licensed electronic resources, where local practices and procedures take precedence. Over the past months, several consortial workshops

have touched on these issues, and the libraries are currently discussing how best to teach Summon™ in the Consortium.

FOR FURTHER RESEARCH

Throughout the selection and implementation process, there was some concern among the schools about using a discovery layer in our consortial environment. In many ways, we were to be the test case to see if this process could work well with multiple institutions and multiple needs. From this standpoint, the Ohio5 libraries have identified several lingering questions that will require further research and assessment. The consortium is interested in investigating the following: how use of a discovery layer will impact cooperative collection development, the advantages of our smaller consortial discovery layer implementation against the potential benefits of an OhioLINK state-wide discovery layer, best practices for library instruction in a post-discovery layer environment, and coordinating protocols for effective management of the discovery layer.

PLANNING FOR DISCOVERY IN A CONSORTIUM: ADVICE AND SUGGESTIONS

As institutions are deciding whether or not a consortial approach is most appropriate for them, there are several initial factors that might be particularly useful to consider. Do some consortial members already have discovery layer products, are they using the same one, and under what conditions would they be open to migrating to another product if the full consortium preferred one? Are there any baseline requirements that a commercial product would need to accommodate to be considered (e.g. the ability to include a central catalog)? If the group were to select a product, would each institution get an equal vote in the final decision or would some member(s) have a greater voice due to their size, budgetary contribution, staff expertise, or other factor? If the consortia were to proceed, what contribution would each member make in the selection process, implementation, and ongoing maintenance of the discovery layer? Finally, is there an existing consortial committee with established working relationships that could be assigned some of the work relating to the discovery layer? Such a group, even if it needs to be slightly augmented to bring in additional expertise, might be a very efficient team to consider discovery tools.

In order to facilitate a smooth consortial implementation process, the following unique concerns should be addressed at the outset:

- The integrity of individual or shared catalogs is important. Cataloging and other metadata will need to be easily combined if multiple schools' holdings are to be displayed in the chosen discovery layer.
- Schools will need to investigate how an implemented discovery layer will work with other individually or consortially-owned, related products (A-Z lists, ERMs, etc.).
- Discovery layer customization must be considered. This may happen through either combined or individual decisions, depending on whether the consortium decides on one or multiple instances.
- A consortial working group must be established (or co-opted) to work on new workflows required by the discovery layer.

CONCLUSION

The experiences of the Five Colleges of Ohio throughout this process have shown that a consortial approach to both purchasing and implementing a discovery layer is possible. However, a project of this size requires both a clear need for this type of service at all partnering institutions and similar programmatic and instruction goals. It also does not hurt to have an existing network of trust and a history of successful collaborations. Throughout the process, the Five Colleges collaborated well in understanding the needs of the consortium, as well each individual school's needs. The selection committee was able to agree on a product, and the implementation, though not without challenges, was successful. The group continues to work together to ensure that our discovery layer is well-maintained.

REFERENCES

Alberico, R. (2002). Academic library consortia in transition. *New Directions for Higher Education*, (120): 63–72. doi:10.1002/he.90

Bostick, S. L. (2001). The history and development of academic library consortia in the United States: An overview. *Journal of Academic Librarianship*, *27*(2), 128–130. doi:10.1016/S0099-1333(00)00185-3

Curl, M. W., & Zeoli, M. (2004). Developing a consortial shared approval plan for monographs. *Collection Building*, *23*(3), 122–128. doi:10.1108/01604950410544656

Digby, T., & Elfstrand, S. (2011). Discovering open source discovery: Using VuFind to create MnPALS plus. *Computers in Libraries*, *31*(2), 6–10.

Evans, G. E. (2002). Management issues of cooperative ventures and consortia in the USA: part One. *Library Management*, *23*(4/5), 213–226. doi:10.1108/01435120210429943

Hulse, B., Cheverie, J. F., & Dygert, C. T. (2007). ALADIN research commons: A consortial institutional repository. *OCLC Systems & Services: International Digital Library Perspectives*, *23*(2), 158–169. doi:10.1108/10650750710748469

Jackson, M. E., & Preece, B. G. (2002). Consortia and the portal challenge. *Journal of Academic Librarianship*, *28*(3), 160–162. doi:10.1016/S0099-1333(02)00306-3

Kanter, R. M. (1994). Collaborative advantage: The art of alliances. *Harvard Business Review*, *72*(4), 96–108.

Kinner, L., & Crosetto, A. (2009). Balancing act for the future: How the academic library engages in collection development at the local and consortial levels. *Journal of Library Administration*, *49*(4), 419–437. doi:10.1080/01930820902832561

Kohl, D. F., & Sanville, T. (2006). More bang for the buck: Increasing the effectiveness of library expenditures through cooperation. *Library Trends*, *54*(3), 394–410. doi:10.1353/lib.2006.0022

Kopp, J. J. (1998). Library consortia and information technology: The past, the present, the promise. *Information Technology and Libraries*, *17*(1), 7–12.

Moyle, M., Stockley, R., & Tonkin, S. (2007). SHERPA-LEAP: A consortial model for the creation and support of academic institutional repositories. *OCLC Systems & Services*, *23*(2), 125–132. doi:10.1108/10650750710748423

Nfila, R. B., & Darko-Ampem, K. (2002). Developments in academic library consortia from the 1960s through to 2000: A review of the literature. *Library Management*, *23*(4/5), 203–212. doi:10.1108/01435120210429934

Oder, N. (2010, Jan. 14). After 17 years heading OhioLINK, Sanville leaves for LYRASIS job. *Library Journal Academic Newswire*. Retrieved from http://www.libraryjournal.com/article/CA6714727.html

Peters, T. (2003). Consortia and their discontents. *Journal of Academic Librarianship*, *29*(2), 111–114. doi:10.1016/S0099-1333(02)00421-4

Sanville, T. (2007). OhioLINK: A US resource sharing facility – Issues and developments. *Interlending & Document Supply*, *35*(1), 31–37. doi:10.1108/02641610710728177

Vaughan, J., & Costello, K. (2011). Management and support of shared integrated library systems. *Information Technology and Libraries*, *30*(2), 62–70.

ADDITIONAL READING

Allen, B. M., & Hirshon, A. (1998). Hanging together to avoid hanging separately: Opportunities for academic libraries and consortia. *Information Technology and Libraries*, *17*(1), 36–44.

Breeding, M. (2004). The trend toward outsourcing the ILS: Recognizing the benefits of shared systems. *Computers in Libraries*, *24*(5), 36–38.

Brooks, S., & Dorst, T. J. (2002). Issues facing academic library consortia and perceptions of members of the Illinois digital academic library. *Portal-Libraries and the Academy*, *2*(1), 43–57. doi:10.1353/pla.2002.0005

Evans, G. E. (2002). Management issues of consortia, part two. *Library Management*, *23*(6/7), 275–286. doi:10.1108/01435120210432246

Hirshon, A. (1999). Libraries, consortia, and change management. *Journal of Academic Librarianship*, *25*(2), 124–126. doi:10.1016/S0099-1333(99)80011-1

Hormia-Poutanen, K., Xenidou-Dervou, C., Kupryte, R., Stange, K., Kuznetsov, A., & Woodward, H. (2006). Consortia in Europe: Describing the various solutions through four country examples. *Library Trends*, *54*(3), 359–381. doi:10.1353/lib.2006.0026

Jin, X., & Maurer, M. B. (2007). Managing the advantages and challenges of multiple library consortia: The view from within the library. *Journal of Access Services*, *4*(1-2), 41–58. doi:10.1300/J204v04n01_03

Mestre, L. S., Turner, C., Lang, B., & Morgan, B. (2007). Do we step together, in the same direction, at the same time? How a consortium approached a federated search implementation. *Internet Reference Services Quarterly*, *12*(1/2), 111–132. doi:10.1300/J136v12n01_06

Potter, W. (1997). Recent trends in statewide academic library consortia. *Library Trends*, *45*(3), 416–434.

Pritchard, S. (2009). Crises and opportunities. *portal. Libraries and the Academy*, *9*(4), 437–440. doi:10.1353/pla.0.0074

Webster, P. (2006). Interconnected and innovative libraries: Factors tying libraries more closely together. *Library Trends*, *54*(3), 382–393. doi:10.1353/lib.2006.0030

Wright, D. A. (2005). Library consortia: Do the models always work? *Resource Sharing & Information Networks*, *18*(1), 49–60. doi:10.1300/J121v18n01_05

KEY TERMS AND DEFINITIONS

CONSORT: Name of the Millennium ILS shared by Denison University, Kenyon College, Ohio Wesleyan University, and The College of Wooster.

Consortium: Among libraries, this term denotes a group of libraries that works together to achieve common goals.

Expect: A Unix automation and testing tool.

Faceted Searching (also called Faceted Navigation or Faceted Browsing): In information resources, a facet is an attribute (for example, format) that can be used to refine or filter a set of search results. Use of one or multiple facets can enable a user to pinpoint information that more closely matches his/her information need.

Link Resolver: A service that direct users from a public online link to content that the user has a right to read, normally by virtue of institutionally subscribed resources.

OBIS: Name of the Millennium ILS used exclusively at Oberlin College.

Ohio5 (also called The Five Colleges of Ohio): Consortium for Denison University, Kenyon College, Oberlin College, Ohio Wesleyan University, and The College of Wooster.

OhioLINK: Consortium of a large number of Ohio's public and private colleges and universities.

OpenURL: A standardized format of Uniform Resource Locator (URL) intended to enable Internet users to more easily find a copy of a resource that they are allowed to access. Although OpenURL can be used with any kind of resource on the Internet, it is most heavily used by libraries to help connect patrons to subscription content.

ENDNOTES

[1]   Worldcat is a registered trademark of OCLC.
[2]   Serials Solution is a registered trademark of Serials Solutions
[3]   Summon is owned by ProQuest LLC
[4]   ExLibris is a trademark of Ex Libris Ltd.
[5]   Primo Central is owned by Ex Libris Ltd. or its affiliates.

Chapter 24

Creating Organizational Buy-in:
Overcoming Challenges to a Library-Wide Discovery Tool Implementation

Meris A. Mandernach
James Madison University, USA

Jody Condit Fagan
James Madison University, USA

ABSTRACT

While launching a discovery tool can be technically easy, establishing a process that will result in organizational buy-in for the tool is an exceptionally important first step for a successful implementation. Many lessons about creating organizational buy-in can be learned from experiences with federated search software and next-generation catalogs. Libraries must grapple with three critical areas before discovery tool implementation. First, the library will need to consider how the discovery tool will affect key library departments and create a plan for addressing their concerns. Second, training will need to be developed for staff as well as end users. Finally, monitoring and assessing the discovery tool's performance and impact will inform future decision-making related to the tool's integration with the library's other systems and services. Each of these areas will be explored in the context of existing library research, with illustrations from James Madison University's discovery tool implementation.

DOI: 10.4018/978-1-4666-1821-3.ch024

INTRODUCTION

Discovery tool implementations should be carefully planned and executed in order to improve organizational buy-in and enhance the resulting user experience. Many of the issues and concerns libraries face related to discovery tools have broad implications and need to be approached with perspectives from multiple stakeholders. This chapter will explore several critical areas using research from the literature and examples from James Madison University (JMU). JMU is a predominantly undergraduate institution of approximately 19,000 students in the commonwealth of Virginia. Some of JMU's programs of strength include communication sciences and disorders, music, psychology, nursing, business, and education. The libraries have a strong instructional program, and have been successful at partnering with other departments on campus to implement a required information literacy test for all students entering their sophomore year. Over twenty liaison librarians provide subject-specific library instruction. Additionally, a general education librarian has recently begun working with the campus general education committee to increase the libraries' connections to lower-division students. Because of this strong commitment to student instruction, implementing a discovery tool at JMU necessitated involving numerous internal stakeholders in the process.

Discovery tools bring profound changes to the nature of searching that affect staff and patrons in different ways. While many library systems, such as the catalog and traditional article indexes, were initially designed for librarians and scholars, discovery tools were designed for library patrons. Discovery tools eliminate the need for users to choose among library tools before beginning a search. With a discovery tool, a patron has to learn only one interface; the user can gather books, articles, and other types of items into one folder; and can limit effectively to full-text online without reducing result sets. However, library staff will need to illustrate to patrons that there are additional choices beyond the discovery tool that could be valuable for specialized searching.

While discovery makes search more manageable for patrons, it can be disruptive for librarians. Librarians do not need the library catalog to be combined with article indexes; in fact, it is more comfortable for most library staff to search such tools separately. When searching separate tools, characteristics such as authority and consistency are crucial. Discovery tools, on the other hand, compromise in these areas in order to be current, relevant, and provide as much content as possible. Whereas patrons need to think like librarians in order to use the catalog and article indexes, librarians may need to start to think more like patrons in order to understand discovery tools.

This chapter will begin with lessons gleaned from the literature relating to the advent of federated search, next-generation catalogs, and discovery tools. It will then examine three key areas for organizational buy-in related to the implementation of discovery tools: how the discovery tool will affect key library departments, developing training materials for staff and end users, and monitoring and assessing the discovery tool's performance and impact.

BACKGROUND

The vision for discovery software as a unified search of library collections has its origins in federated search, which combined library catalogs, databases, and journals in one search interface, providing a similar search to Google and other search engines (Cervone, 2005; Miller, 2004). This desire was based on knowledge of users' expectations to simply search, not to choose among various databases (Alling & Naismith, 2007, p. 195; Cervone, 2005, p. 10; Randall, 2006, pp. 181-182; Tallent, 2004, p. 69-75). However, the performance of federated search software disappointed many libraries, with problems related to uncertainty about their precision and recall (Lampert & Dabbour, 2007; Tang, Hsieh-Yee, & Zhang, 2007; Williams & Foster, 2011).

The next development in discovery-style searching was the advent of next-generation catalog interfaces, which featured faceted browsing and an up-to-date look and feel for traditional library catalogs (Fagan, 2010). Studies of these interfaces found increased use of article databases as well as an increased use of narrowing facets such as format, media type, and library location (Allison, 2010; Ballard & Blaire, 2011).

Discovery tools are the newest technology in the marketplace of library search (Brunning & Machovec, 2010a; Brunning & Machovec, 2010b). In this chapter, the term "discovery tool" will be defined as software that includes both a library catalog and article indexes in a unified index and search interface. This approach differs from federated search software, which searches multiple databases separately and aggregates the results post-search. Early investigations of discovery included reviews of content (Rowe, 2010; Stevenson et al., 2009) and explanations of selection decisions (Vaughan, 2011; Webb & Nero, 2009; Koch & Davis, 2011). Usability studies have been suggesting that discovery tools offer an improved experience for users over federated search (Williams & Foster, 2011). Findings seem to support the overall idea of discovery while offering a list of issues for vendors to address (Ward, Shadle, & Mofield, 2008; Boock, Chadwell, & Reese, 2011; Thomas & Buck, 2010; OCLC, 2009; NCSU 2011; Fagan, Mandernach, Nelson, Paulo, & Saunders, 2012). No single product seems to have a significant advantage over the others in terms of usability, perhaps because vendors are so fiercely competitive in terms of discovery tool interface features.

One of the major differences between the library environment and the corporate sector is the need to achieve organizational buy-in for technological change (Fagan & Keach, 2009, p.

39). Libraries are beginning to realize that careful planning for the introduction of new technologies can result in wider adoption, reduced stress, and more efficient implementation (Ballard & Teague-Rector, 2011; Sharpe & Vacek, 2011). With broad and deep organizational implications, discovery tools pose a significant change for libraries and therefore selection and/or implementation teams should be formed. Libraries also need to determine which departments will have a stake in the tool's success, and plan to involve them in the process.

DEVELOPING A SHARED VISION FOR DISCOVERY

When implementing a discovery tool, one of the first discussions within the library should be related to the tool's vision and mission. By having these discussions early in the implementation process, there will be established mutually agreed upon definitions and priorities related to this technology. While details may vary by institution, clarifying the tool's purpose will inform numerous future discussions and smooth technical implementation.

In 2010, JMU launched EBSCO Discovery Service™[1] (EDS), participating as a beta development partner. A selection team recommended the tool after reviewing the major next-generation catalogs and discovery tools on the market. A separate implementation team provided guidance for customization decisions, integration of the tool into the library Web site, and numerous other questions that arose during discovery (Fagan & Mandernach, 2011b). At JMU, a formal mission statement was written and approved by a council of approximately 20 unit managers:

JMU Libraries' discovery tool provides frontline access to physical and virtual library collections, including books and articles. Its purpose is to support users' most common information needs, such as:

- Finding a selection of relevant sources about a topic
- Determining whether JMU libraries owns / has access to a specific item
- Getting online full text or items-in-hand.

By offering a tool to search library/subscription resources that is similar to Google, we intend to expand our presence in users' virtual worlds, and raise the library's stature in their research context. Such a tool also offers a first tier of search to complement our learning commons service model.

Because such statements have wide-reaching implications, the process for creating them should be open and transparent. Discovery selection teams or project leaders should explicitly present underlying assumptions and premises of the discovery tool and facilitate conceptual conversations about discovery tool software, integration, the tool's purpose, and how it supports the library's larger mandate of connecting users with resources. Settling on a working mission and vision document can be challenging; therefore, library leadership will need to be prepared to arbitrate disagreements as they arise. Depending on an institution's culture, such a mission statement may be written before, during, or after implementation. Libraries with high-vision leadership may be able to tolerate a mission statement written by one or a few people in advance (Wallace, 2004, p. 19). Libraries with a highly participative culture may need to wait until during or after implementation before settling on a mission statement in order for sufficient stakeholders to obtain experience working with the tool.

Regardless of institutional culture, all libraries have multiple internal stakeholder groups who will have strong opinions about the tool and how it is presented. The reference department will face front-line questions about using the search tool and working with the large results sets. Instruction staff will need to decide whether and how to incorporate discovery into classes. The cataloging department may feel threatened and/or empowered by the fact that the library catalog will be imported into a new interface. Access services and interlibrary loan may have questions about patron account integration and whether requests for materials will rise due to the discovery tool's broad scope.

After preparing these key departments for impact, the organization will need to consider training for staff as well as users. One might consider it presumptuous to think that librarians would need to be taught about a search tool, but discovery software has some unusual technical aspects that are not initially apparent. Because of the nature of discovery, it would be useful for staff to understand that various decisions made during implementation may affect the tool's performance and results sets. For example, the catalog's material types may need to be mapped to the discovery tool's source types; understanding how that mapping works is necessary to understand how to use the resulting source type facets effectively. An informed staff will be better equipped to participate in the discussions and decision-making processes necessary for buy-in. Library users, while caring less about behind-the-scenes details, will want to know how to search effectively and improve their results sets.

Preparing departments for the discovery tool and developing training for staff and users will set the tool up for success, but monitoring and assessing the software is necessary for tracking the numerous issues that will inevitably arise. Institutions will need to know how well the tool is fulfilling its purpose. Objective information such as usage statistics will provide one view of the tool's impact, while qualitative inquiry can provide insight into the user experience.

CREATING ORGANIZATIONAL BUY-IN

Impact of a Discovery Tool on Library Units

Discovery tool implementation will affect most areas in the library, but reference, instruction, and cataloging may find their work relates most directly to the discovery tool. Interlibrary loan and access services should also be prepared to adapt to changes to workflow due to implementation of the discovery tool.

Reference and Instruction

Many of the concerns over discovery tools in the areas of reference and instruction are linked to fundamental values these areas share, such as information literacy and quality of service. First, there is the issue of *whether* to incorporate discovery tools into instruction and at the reference desk. One might think that spending thousands of dollars on a new search tool would obligate librarians to use it, but similarly to federated search tools and Google Scholar, librarians may have serious questions about these products (Lampert & Dabbour, 2007; Tang, Hsieh-Yee, & Zhang 2007). One concern with federated search was the lack of users' interest in determining the sources behind their searches (Curtis & Dorner, 2005). This led librarians to question whether these products, like discovery tools and Google Scholar, made research "too easy" for users, seducing them into inferior research habits (Frost, 2004; Lampert & Dabbour, 2007; York, 2005; Koch & Davis, 2011). Finally, even librarians who were interested in overcoming these challenges had problems finding time to demonstrate an additional system in a 50-minute instruction class and adapt existing pedagogies (Lampert & Dabbour, 2007; Koch & Davis, 2011).

Discovery software has overcome many of the technical barriers presented by federated search tools, but questions related to values remain. Reference and instruction departments should hold fora about questions and concerns surrounding implementation. Librarians and support staff should discuss their convictions about how to uphold information literacy ideals while avoiding "broccoli librarianship" (Vaughn & Callicott, 2003, p. 2), or the idea that libraries should impose the information librarians perceive as necessary rather than providing the quickest and most direct path (Benjes & Brown, 2000, p. 38). Reference staff may also wish to have conversations related to the scenario where a patron wants to use the discovery tool even when it is not the best tool to use. How heavily should the staff persuade users to consider other tools versus honoring the user's choice? Such discussions should draw from recent research about user behavior, to avoid relying solely on anecdotal experiences. For example, in a study of the next-generation catalog Encore™[2], Ballard and Blaine (2011) found that users were 15 times more likely to refine a search if they were using Encore™ instead of the New York Law School's classic catalog interface (p. 111). In a user study of the next-generation interface Aquabrowser®[3], Tod Olson found that doctoral students were able to find additional resources for their dissertations despite having already done thorough literature reviews (2007). Mississippi State University found that faculty and doctoral students welcomed the serendipity of discovery's cross-disciplinary search, especially with extremely narrow topics (Powers, 2011).

Staff working at public service desks will face the challenge of determining how the discovery tool will fit into the service desk mission, training, or core competencies. At JMU, the discovery tool mission statement itself specified that the tool would offer a first tier of search to complement the JMU learning commons service model. Library assistants and student workers were specifically encouraged to use the discovery tool with patrons, because it was well suited for general, exploratory topics. If the question seemed to go beyond discovery, desk workers were instructed to refer the patron to a subject specialist. All desk staff were expected to be able to locate and explain what types of information could be found using the discovery tool as well other specified library systems. As the library gains more experience with the chosen tool, follow-up training and discussions may further direct when the discovery tool is to be used.

To inform their thinking and planning, instruction librarians may wish to review how others have suggested that federated search, and now discovery, fit within the ACRL Information Literacy Competency Standards (Labelle, 2007; Fagan, 2011). Other questions they should discuss include: Should the discovery tool be a one-stop shop or merely the first of many steps in the research process? Is the discovery tool serving a particular type of user? Practically, instruction librarians also need to know the timeline for the discovery tool implementation and be updated about releases of new content into the discovery tool to ensure that they and their course materials are prepared for instruction sessions.

Cataloging

In discovery tools, the success of results sets will directly reflect the work of the cataloger, especially subject headings and local notes for records from the library catalog. With catalog records more visible, the cataloging department may get an increased number of questions and requests for changes in practice (Wynne & Hanscom, 2011). This presents both challenges and opportunities. Without attention during implementation, a cataloging department may feel left behind, overworked, and undervalued as the "classic" catalog takes a back seat to the discovery tool. If the discovery tool implementation uses the expertise of catalogers and involves this unit in discussions, the department's work can instead be seen as instrumental to the success of this new type of software.

One major contribution of catalogers to implementation of discovery tools is to evaluate search results and catalog displays. Wynne and Hanscom noted several areas in which catalogers have provided input to vendors on system-level issues, including which MARC fields to include in which facets and search indexes; the order of MARC fields; the display of notes; and hyperlinking fields such as earlier / later titles of serials (2011, p. 192). At JMU, the cataloging department played an instrumental role by comparing search records and result sets between the "classic" catalog and the discovery tool and evaluating how well the catalog records were represented within the discovery tool result sets. Yang and Wagner compiled a twelve-point checklist of common features in discovery tools and next-generation catalogs in order to review and evaluate both open source and proprietary interfaces (2010). Checklist items related to catalog display included a single point of entry for all library information, faceted navigation, and relevancy ranking (Yang & Wagner, 2010).

The metadata that catalogers have added over the years will help catalog records compete for relevance in discovery tool results sets and form the substance of discovery tool facets, which allow overviews of the collection using metadata such as subject, author, and geographic location. However, Naun (2010) noted that facets bring their own challenges; while they work well for categories such as format and location, "where the number of possible values is usually relatively small and easily accommodated in the limited screen area given to each facet," the large number of subject terms retrieved can be very large, limiting the ability for the interface to display them (p. 336). Specific tests used at JMU related to cataloging are described in the "Monitoring and Assessment" section of this chapter.

It is clear that catalogers should be involved in the organization-wide discussions about the discovery tool. Wynne and Hanscom noted that cataloging departments should be involved with both selection and implementation of new tools related to or making use of catalog records, and have often served in leadership roles during such processes (2011). Still, among Wynne and Hanscom's survey respondents, only 45% of libraries had catalogers on implementation committees, and 35% on next-generation catalog selection committees. Some institutions they surveyed noted that catalogers had negative perceptions of next-generation catalogs, which may be one reason for exclusion. Recommendations from respondents suggested that catalogers need to be open to learning as much as possible during the process, and to be willing to speak from existing knowledge. Cataloging and/or technical services leaders may need to offer staff a positive vision of discovery tool implementation and be prepared to offer lists of benefits and opportunities offered by the tool (Wynne & Hanscom, 2011, p. 197).

Another challenge for cataloging departments preparing for a discovery tool is the impact on cataloging workflows. In a report on the implications of next-generation catalogs, Karen Calhoun noted several steps catalogers could take to streamline workflows, increase linkages in and out of the catalog, and to innovate and reduce costs (Calhoun, 2006, p. 17-18). Wynne & Hanscom (2011) noted specific ways that cataloging practices affect next-generation catalogs (p. 187-190).

Access Services / Interlibrary Loan (ILL)

For Interlibrary Loan and Access Services departments, questions about patron accounts and course reserves are common queries. Pathways to these services may not be obvious (or possible) in the discovery tool. Given the change in the discovery environment, access services should adapt and change with the technology in order to provide service consistent with user expectations. Users should be able to "focus their attention on information content, not the process we have in place for housing the material" (Chang & Davis, 2010, p. 113-114). Therefore, these departments will

need to develop clear pathways to these materials (in and out of the discovery tool) and be ready to offer answers to patrons' questions. Tutorials, Web page instructions, or FAQs may need to be developed to answer these queries. Chang and Davis advocate for staff development activities, networking with users, and cross-training within the library as a means of staying current in the face of technological change (2010). Since standards and technologies within the discovery tool are always changing, staff should monitor developments related to opportunities to provide clear pathways to library services.

Another potential impact of the discovery tool on interlibrary loan is increased borrowing due to the discovery of material outside the library's local collections. While discovery tools highlight materials available locally to patrons, they also highlight materials that can be requested through ILL. Frank and Bothmann (2007) noted that students initiated interlibrary loan request three times more frequently using an OpenURL resolver than from another starting point. However, in cases where auto-fill features from OpenURL resolvers fail, ILL staff should be prepared to troubleshoot issues from the discovery tool. Additionally, ILL and access services should also be prepared to examine circulation reports and ILL usage reports since the discovery tool has the opportunity to highlight resources that users previously had to work to uncover.

With some discovery tools, the implementation team may be able to customize the content searched by default. At some institutions, such as the University of Washington, the default search might be as comprehensive as possible. At institutions with more limited loan resources, the initial search might limit results to locally held materials. A compromise is to provide limiters based on ease of access. At JMU, the discovery tool's "Full Text (online)" limiter limits to catalog records with a URL in the 856 field in the MARC record that provides the electronic location, EBSCO records with attached full text, and any records for items that show full-text holdings in JMU's e-resource knowledge base from Serials Solutions®[4].

TRAINING / LIBRARY INSTRUCTION

Training and instruction will provide support for discovery tool implementation and adoption by helping staff understand how the tool works, as well as its strengths and weaknesses. Understanding the training and instruction needs of both internal and external users will help the implementation team and other library staff develop workshops and materials for both audiences. This section will outline the needs for staff and end-user training related to discovery.

Training for Public Services Staff

Staff who are unfamiliar with the discovery tool will be hesitant to use it at the service desk. With little or no training, reference services may be inconsistent, with some staff frequently recommending the tool, and others avoiding it. Instead, reference staff should discuss the discovery tool mission and purpose and how that translates to reference interactions.

In order to have informed opinions about *when* to use discovery, reference and instruction librarians and staff will need training in how the discovery tool software works (Koch & Davis, 2011, slide 17). Given that they will commonly be the front-line staff for patrons, they should be familiar with the content and interface features, including strengths and weaknesses of the discovery tool. Because local customizations and implementation decisions greatly affect the user experience, the implementation team should not assume librarians will automatically understand the content and features of the discovery tool.

Vendors' aggressive development of the software may also mean changes due to product enhancement. Although initial experiences with searching for known items from JMU's catalog records within the discovery tool were problematic, the vendor made significant improvements. A recent comparison study at JMU of known-item searching in the classic catalog interface and the discovery tool showed at least equal performance when searching for books. It is important to share this type of information with public services staff so their understanding grows with the tool's development.

Staff training at JMU began with a collaborative process to create a series of videos that were used to train staff and student workers (http://www.lib.jmu.edu/eds). The process used to create the videos was to draft an outline, which was reviewed with service desk supervisors and the director of instruction; conduct a presentation for librarians and public services staff that followed the outline, and invite feedback; and finally to record the videos, which were modified to respond to feedback received from the presentations. This process supported staff participation in creating the videos, as well as initial training for staff. Additionally, the JMU implementation team wrote FAQs for the public Web site with answers to common questions about the discovery tool (http://www.lib.jmu.edu/info/faqscategory.aspx?id=102). Initially, many of these were intended for staff, who had plenty of questions during initial implementation, such as the difference between "academic journals" and "scholarly journals" limiters. Based on the FAQs' popularity, it is clear that patrons are finding these useful as well.

Instructional Materials for End Users

End users will also need training in using the discovery tool. With federated search, students and librarians agreed that information literacy programs should include knowledge and skills to use these tools (Tang, Hsieh-Yee, & Zhang, 2007). Likewise, libraries should not expect users to immediately grasp how to use a discovery tool, but should provide direct training and support. This can occur in workshops focusing directly on the tool, during library instruction sessions, and through online tutorials.

At JMU, a series of library workshops for freshmen included two sessions featuring the discovery tool. The first, "Library Research Boot Camp," covered the scope of the tool and contrasted it with the library's other research databases; topic development and basic Boolean searching; discovery tool limiters and facets; and linking to full text. The second, "Procrastinators Anonymous," included a shorter version of this material. Since users were now able to search books and articles concurrently, it was found to be especially important to explain how to identify information source types and narrow topics.

Since it is likely the discovery tool will be prominently featured on the library home page, instruction librarians should plan to cover it in every class, however briefly. For general education classes, spending significant time teaching the discovery tool can provide a bridge between Google and library databases and introduce academic source types (K.E. Clarke, personal communication, 2011). One study of federated search suggested that equal promotion of single database and federated searching was needed for such students (Armstrong, 2009). For classes within an academic major, librarians must balance discovery tool instruction with subject-specific resources. One biology librarian at JMU handled this challenge by spending five minutes discussing the discovery tool, and then explained why instead the class would focus on biology databases and their unique features. (D. Y. Jones, personal communication, 2011)

Online tutorials for discovery can support a variety of end-user needs, depending on their composition. Longer tutorials can provide comparable instruction for distance learners, but should still be kept modular and succinct. JMU chose to create a short, one-minute tutorial in order to provide a quick overview of the tool's most helpful features: using AND and OR to work with topics; the source type facets; and the scholarly article limiter (http://www.lib.jmu.edu/resources/connect.aspx?id=3306&s=219). Drake University created a "Basic SuperSearch" video (http://library.drake.edu/pages/about-supersearch).

Although there may be different opinions about a discovery tool, library staff should develop clear, consistent, and accurate messages for handouts, online tutorials, and other instructional materials. In a review of library Web guides related to Google, York found inconsistent and often negative messages as librarians struggled to defend subscription resources (2005). While instructional messages should be informed by discussions about the purpose of the discovery tool within the context of instruction, they should be positive, or at least neutral, in tone. At a minimum, they should cover what the discovery tool searches as well as what resources or types of materials are not covered in the tool. For example, Drake University created a draft e-mail message library liaisons could send to faculty in their departments (Koch & Davis, 2011, slide 19).

MONITORING AND ASSESSMENT OF THE DISCOVERY TOOL

Discovery tools are new, large, and complex; therefore, another challenge is whether the software and customizations are working as intended. Additionally, vendors will continue to add and change features. This section reviews some of the specific needs related to monitoring and assessing discovery tools.

Allocating Staff Resources

Although responsibilities relating to monitoring and assessing discovery will likely be distributed to current staff as opposed to new hires, this should be done as carefully as if new position descriptions were being written. One of the most critical roles is that of project manager. A project manager oversees projects that cross library departments

Figure 1. Recommended documentation for discovery tool implementation

- Issue list: *Use this to track issues reported to vendors and follow up with patrons and staff.*
- Documents that supported selection / decision-making related to the tool: *When software is ready to be renewed, similar criteria or processes can be used if documented. These documents can also be useful for reminding stakeholders who made decisions.*
- Evaluation results: *Showcasing user tests, survey data, usage statistics, and reports helps the organization connect decisions to user needs.*
- Metadata chart(s): *Show how metadata is mapped from the catalog to the discovery tool.*
- Screenshots of the discovery tool interface: *These help track what customizations were made, and when.*
- Training materials: *share handouts, video tutorials, etc. in an easily accessible, central location.*

and oversees organization-wide discussions. At JMU, the work of the project manager was supplemented with the creation of an advisory committee, constituted of representatives from public services, technical services, and instructional technology. Due to its diversity, this group was able to advise the project manager on how to best communicate with stakeholders, provide quick feedback on customization decisions, and brainstorm solutions to complex problems.

While the project manager does not need to do all the project-related communication, he/she needs to ensure strong involvement for both internal and external stakeholders, and track project accomplishments. Figure 1 shows some of the documentation compiled on JMU's intranet to support monitoring and assessment of the discovery tool. Drake University used a wiki to organize several sub-groups and their work (http://supersearch-implementation.drake. wikispaces.net/). By making documents easily available to the library staff, those who might miss a workshop or presentation can remain up-to-date. It will also provide more transparency into the decision-making processes.

Another of the project manager's or project team's challenges will be to identify who will fill additional roles and complete needed tasks related to monitoring and assessment, including: initial technical testing, documenting errors and reporting these to vendors, reviewing product

improvements and enhancements, and conducting user evaluation and assessment of the discovery tool following implementation. These tasks may fit neatly into existing job descriptions; for example, at JMU, cataloging, e-resources, and research databases specialists were able to perform technical testing in their areas. However, a portion of a new, part-time position was allocated to review discovery product improvements and enhancements, including content releases and new features specific to the discovery tool.

Initial Technical Testing

Initially the discovery tool should be tested to ensure that the search functions are meeting library expectations. It is likely that these will be tested during the selection phase of a discovery tool. This testing can be done by a single individual within the library, or a library could create a group whose members could each test one area of the system (basic search, advanced search, limiters, etc.).

Libraries have experience testing and evaluating database interfaces, but discovery tools have a few new concepts that will benefit from focused testing. It is essential that library catalog records integrate into the discovery tool results lists. Therefore, it will be critical to examine how catalog data is displayed in the discovery tool. The discovery tool may not include all of the fields from the MARC record commonly displayed through an online catalog. Libraries can ask vendors to provide a list or chart of how the MARC fields map to the discovery tool's fields as well as which discovery tool fields are searchable by the different types of searches. For example, libraries will want to know whether the discovery tool title list includes both main title and alternate title. After libraries gain an understanding of the display, a list of test searches for items and topics known to be covered in the catalog should be created. Library staff should execute these searches in both the discovery tool and the catalog to determine whether the relevance ranking is working effectively. If results are less than satisfactory, the vendor may be able to adjust the relevance ranking to boost catalog records.

Many library assignments ask students to locate both books and articles; historically, this was a challenge for users because it required them to choose different search tools for these materials. Therefore it will be necessary to test the discovery tool's balance between material types, especially books and articles. Testers should perform searches on topics appropriate for book-length and article-length treatment, and review result sets to determine if relevant results are returned. General topics should produce results sets with at least some books, while specific topics should contain mostly articles. At JMU, public services librarians who were learning about discovery tools used their expertise to identify relevancy issues with results sets and they gained an increased understanding of how the tool could be used during library instruction and in reference interactions.

A variety of methods can be employed when performing technical tests including checklists or testing scripts. Checklists can be useful when first evaluating software, to ensure all of the required conditions are being examined, and when evaluating software after changes have been implemented (Ebenau & Strauss, 1994, p .86). Regardless of which method(s) are employed for technical testing, successfully testing for errors requires simulating the search environment of the user

(Whittaker, 2000). At JMU, a testing script was created and staff were allocated to troubleshoot each feature of the discovery tool. Step-by-step testing scripts may seem time consuming to create, but will save time and increase testing consistency (Fagan & Keach, 2009). While it may seem beyond the library's scope of responsibility to do this, it will save the time of the users who would otherwise be the first to encounter any bugs. Additionally, if front-line library staff are the first to encounter bugs, this will foster a poor impression of the software.

Documenting Bugs and Reporting These to Vendors

Regardless of how good the initial testing is, new errors and issues will be uncovered. It will be important for libraries to provide a method for both users and staff to report issues with discovery tool functionality. Particularly when the discovery tool is new, patrons and staff will encounter numerous technical issues. The implementation team will likely anticipate the need to troubleshoot and report issues, but it can also be a challenge to get users and staff to submit trouble reports. The solution to this is twofold: first, provide an easy way for users and staff to submit issues; second, implement a tracking system for technical issues to help back-end staff stay organized and follow up. In addition to resolving technical issues, these activities are critical for increasing organizational buy-in and communicating efficiently and effectively with the vendor. Libraries will need to create workflow procedures for adding issues to the list and determine how responses will be communicated back to contributors. By tracking issues as they are found, the project manager and other team members will stay coordinated. An example of the JMU "issue list," created with spreadsheet software, is shown in figure 2.

Figure 2. An example bug list

Description	Who Reported	Where Reported	Date Reported	Date Initial Response	Date Resolved	Date Status Last Checked	Current Status	Current Status Date	Current Status Source	Notes	Related Files
Publication Type/Source type need to be collapsed into one category	JCF	Vendor Webinar	4/22/11	4/22/2011		6/12/11	OPEN - Service Issue	5/18/11	EDS Webinar & Jane Doe	If you do a search on aliens, then limit to journal Discourse Processes, all facets disappear and only images are found.	File1.xls
Search / browse call numbers, preferably as part of interface	JCF	Jim Doe	6/22/11			7/3/11	OPEN – Should be in September Release	6/22/11	Jane Doe	Call numbers not searchable	
Show ebook icon for ebooks / show text labels for icons	JCF	Bob Smith	6/30/11	7/2/2011	7/9/11		RESOLVED	7/9/10	Jim Doe		Icon.jpg

Figure 3. Example goals, objectives, and measures for a discovery tool

> ***Example Goal***: Users who currently rely on Google / Google Scholar as their first point of research will instead use the discovery tool to find books, articles, and other materials for relevant assignments.
>
> *Objective*: Users are satisfied with the discovery tool's ease of use.
> *Measure:* High user satisfaction ratings after completing a usability test.
>
> *Objective*: Increase discovery of the library physical collection.
> Measure: Circulation numbers increase.
>
> *Objective:* Increase discovery in the library's online collections.
> *Measure:* Total electronic resource queries increase.
>
> *Objective*: Increase use of full-text articles.
> *Measure:* Total full-text article requests for the library increase.

Reviewing Product Improvements and Enhancements

Vendors will identify some of the issues that will be uncovered as "product enhancements." Many vendors release software in beta form before all of the features are fully functional. Vendors are in a highly competitive, fast-paced market and may roll out features before they are properly tested. Therefore, this list can serve multiple purposes and can be used to track promised / potential new features. Since software testing is an iterative process, the tester should contact the vendor with each software update for a list of changes to the system and use the testing script to target those areas, revising the testing script if new features are added.

Assessment and User Evaluation

Each library needs to identify what measures and evaluation activities might be useful based on the tool's local mission and goals. For any evaluation project, identifying what to measure will be the most time-intensive part of the process. Most libraries will use a combination of quantitative and qualitative information, including usability test results (Koch & Davis, 2011). At JMU, an examination is currently underway to determine

what impact the discovery tool has on the usage of databases within and outside of the discovery tool. Figure 3 shows a sample goal, objectives, and measures.

Libraries will need to identify which person or people will conduct the evaluation, gather data, analyze findings, report results, and store assessment data, reports, and presentations. In order to manage the incredible amount of data that the discovery tool can report, libraries will need to ensure systems are set up to collect data. For example, at JMU, programmers set the library home page search box to anonymously log user queries and chosen limiters so librarians can observe how the tool is being used. Likewise, when the library's chat widget was placed in the discovery tool, a specific "queue" was chosen so it would be easy to determine what types of questions were coming from the discovery tool. Vendors may also be able to provide information related to how searches within the discovery tool affect the overall database statistical reports for databases included in the discovery tool.

FUTURE RESEARCH DIRECTIONS

Libraries' systems, services, and collections will continue to change, meaning that successful integration of discovery software into the library organization will require ongoing research and experimentation. One area open to exploration is whether subject-specific discovery tools remain of interest and utility. Preliminary usage information shows discovery increases full-text downloads and subject database use, but use of some native interfaces to subject-specific databases remains steady (Fagan & Mandernach, 2011a). Many libraries set up subject profiles for federated search software, and others are trying this with discovery. Drake University has created several subject-specific variants of EBSCO Discovery Service™, with marketing messages specifically targeted toward these disciplines (Koch & Davis, 2011, slide 9).

Cataloging workflows will also continue to evolve. For large record sets such as e-book collections, some cataloging departments have already begun to shift to bulk import procedures. An obvious consideration is whether discovery tool vendors can "turn on" such record sets for their customers, potentially removing the need to add those records to the traditional library catalog. At JMU, while records for print government documents are still added to the library catalog, records for electronic government documents are now imported only to the discovery tool.

Research into the effects of discovery on interlibrary loan patterns will also be needed. Additionally, vendors may add technical capabilities for more direct pathways to interlibrary loan. The relationship of interlibrary loan and the inclusion of consortial or world-wide catalogs within the discovery tool will also be important for libraries to review carefully in the light of local user expectations and desires.

As libraries develop staff and end-user training, the instruction community will gain increased insight into how the pedagogy of teaching search has changed and needs to change further in order to keep up with the user's context. How do information literacy skills need to evolve in order to support lifelong learning as well as college assignments? Research into users' mental models

about discovery tools, other library databases, and Web search engines will be useful for illuminating this area.

Libraries have long been aware of technical issues related to vendor usage statistics. With discovery tools, libraries are finding themselves re-examining which types of statistics are most useful, not only for measuring discovery tool impact, but also overall collection use. Searches and sessions were once of great interest; now, record views and full-text downloads seem to be increasing in prominence. Research will be needed to develop new key performance indicators related to library collection discovery and use, and to connect those indicators to strategic planning.

Finally, the big commercial search engine companies could dramatically change the discovery landscape. Microsoft has renewed its development of Academic Search (http://academic.research.microsoft.com/), and Google Scholar recently expanded its Scholar Citations service (Cordell, 2011). With just a little attention to some key features, these commercial products could become more central to libraries (Fagan, 2012). Alternatively, discovery tool vendors, publishers, and/or libraries might explore exposing more metadata to public search engines, expanding an additional avenue of discovery.

CONCLUSION

While discovery tool implementation is a time-consuming project involving numerous library departments, the investment of staff time and energy will pay off in a thoughtful, well-planned launch of the discovery tool. This can result in greater buy-in, better staff morale, and less disruption to users. Because of the new possibilities offered by discovery tools, this is also an opportune time to review other library systems, the library Web presence, and library marketing efforts. Ensuring that all areas of the library are prepared for a discovery tool implementation will allow for the maximum integration and adoption of the discovery tool into the modern library organization.

REFERENCES

Alling, E., & Naismith, R. (2007). Protocol analysis of a federated search tool: Designing for users. *Internet Reference Services Quarterly*, *12*(1/2), 195–210. doi:10.1300/J136v12n01_10

Allison, D. A. (2010). Information portals: The next generation catalog. *Journal of Web Librarianship*, *4*(1), 375–389. doi:10.1080/19322909.2010.507972

Armstrong, A. R. (2009). Student perceptions of federated searching vs single database searching. *RSR. Reference Services Review*, *37*(3), 291–303. doi:10.1108/00907320910982785

Ballard, A., & Teague-Rector, S. (2011). Building a library Web site: Strategies for success. *College & Research Libraries News*, *72*(3), 132–135.

Ballard, T., & Blaine, A. (2011). User search-limiting behavior in online catalogs: Comparing classic catalog use to search behavior in next-generation catalogs. *New Library World*, *112*(5/6), 261–273. doi:10.1108/03074801111136293

Benjes, C., & Brown, J. F. (2000). Test, revise, retest: Usability testing and library Web sites. *Internet Reference Services Quarterly*, *5*(4), 37–54. doi:10.1300/J136v05n04_08

Boock, M., Chadwell, F., & Reese, T. (2009, April 2). *WorldCat Local task force report to LAMP*. Corvallis, OR: Oregon State University. Retrieved from http://hdl.handle.net/1957/11167

Brunning, D., & Machovec, G. (2010a). Interview about Summon with Jane Burke, vice president of Serials Solutions. *The Charleston Advisor*, *11*(4), 60–62.

Brunning, D., & Machovec, G. (2010b). An interview with Sam Brooks and Michael Gorrell on the EBSCOhost Integrated Search and EBSCO Discovery Service. *The Charleston Advisor*, *11*(3), 62–65.

Calhoun, K. (2006). *The changing nature of the catalog and its integration with other discovery tools: Final report*. Prepared for the Library of Congress. Retrieved from http://www.loc.gov/catdir/calhoun-report-final.pdf

Cervone, F. (2005). What we've learned from doing usability testing on OpenURL resolvers and federated search engines. *Computers in Libraries*, *25*(9), 10–14.

Chang, A., & Davis, D. (2010). Transformation of access services in the new era. *Journal of Access Services*, *7*(2), 109–120. doi:10.1080/15367961003608369

Cordell, R. (2011). *Google Scholar citations now open to all* [Web log post]. Retrieved from http://chronicle.com/blogs/profhacker/google-scholar-citations-now-open-to-all/37372

Curtis, A., & Dorner, D. G. (2005). Why federated search? *Knowledge Quest: Journal of the American Association of School Librarians*, *33*(3), 35–37.

Ebenau, R. G., & Strauss, S. H. (1994). *Software inspection process*. New York, NY: McGraw-Hill.

Fagan, J. C. (2010). Usability studies of faceted browsing: A literature review. *Information Technology & Libraries*, *29*(2), 58–66.

Fagan, J. C. (2011). Discovery tools and information literacy. *Journal of Web Librarianship*, *5*(3), 171–178. doi:10.1080/19322909.2011.598332

Fagan, J. C. (2012). Search engines for tomorrow's scholars, part two. *Journal of Web Librarianship*, *6*(1), 69–76. doi:10.1080/19322909.2012.650897

Fagan, J. C., & Keach, J. A. (2009). *Web project management in academic libraries.* Oxford, UK: Chandos. doi:10.1533/9781780630199

Fagan, J. C., & Mandernach, M. A. (2011a). Discovery by the numbers: An examination of the impact of a discovery tool through usage statistics. *Charleston Conference Proceedings 2011.* Santa Barbara, CA: Libraries Unlimited.

Fagan, J. C., & Mandernach, M. A. (2011b). A roadmap for discovery service implementation at an academic library. Poster presented at the Meeting of the Association of College and Research Libraries, Philadelphia, PA. Retrieved from http://www.lib.jmu.edu/documents/discovery/roadmap.aspx

Fagan, J. C., Mandernach, M. A., Nelson, C. S., Paulo, J. R., & Saunders, G. (2012). Usability test results for a discovery tool in an academic library. *Information Technology and Libraries.* 31(1), 83-112. Retrieved from http://ejournals.bc.edu/ojs/index.php/ital/article/view/1855/1745

Frank, P. P., & Bothmann, R. L. (2007). Assessing undergraduate interlibrary loan use. *Journal of Interlibrary Loan . Document Delivery & Electronic Reserve, 18*(1), 33–48. doi:10.1300/J474v18n01_05

Frost, W. J. (2004). Do we want or need metasearching? *Library Journal, 129*(6), 68.

Koch, T., & Davis, M. (2011). *A discovery case study: EBSCO Discovery Service at Cowles Library, Drake University* [PowerPoint slides]. Retrieved from http://www.slideshare.net/marc_davis/a-discovery-case-study

Labelle, P. R. (2007). Initiating the learning process: A model for federated searching and information literacy. *Internet Reference Services Quarterly, 12*(3/4), 237–252. doi:10.1300/J136v12n03_01

Lampert, L. D., & Dabbour, K. S. (2007). Librarian perspectives on teaching metasearch and federated search technologies. *Internet Reference Services Quarterly, 12*(3/4), 253–278. doi:10.1300/J136v12n03_02

Miller, T. (2004). Federated searching: Put it in its place. *Library Journal, 129*, 32.

MoreBetterLabs, Inc. (2010). *Final Summon user research report.* Prepared for the NCSU Libraries. Retrieved from http://www.lib.ncsu.edu/userstudies/studies/2010_summon/

Naun, C. C. (2010). Next generation OPACs: A cataloging viewpoint. *Cataloging & Classification Quarterly, 48*(4), 330–342. doi:10.1080/01639370903437709

OCLC. (2009). *Some findings from WorldCat Local usability tests prepared for ALA Annual.* Dublin, OH: OCLC. Retrieved from http://www.oclc.org/worldcatlocal/about/213941usf_some_findings_about_worldcat_local.pdf

Olson, T. A. (2007). Utility of a faceted catalog for scholarly research. *Library Hi Tech, 25*(4), 550–561. doi:10.1108/07378830710840509

Powers, A. C. (2011, December 7). Discovering what works: Librarians compare discovery interface experiences. *Library Journal Reviews.* Retrieved from http://reviews.libraryjournal.com/2011/12/reference/discovering-what-works-librarians-compare-discovery-interface-experiences/

Randall, S. (2006). Federated searching and usability testing: Building the perfect beast. *Serials Review, 32*(3), 181–182. doi:10.1016/j.serrev.2006.06.003

Rowe, R. (2010). Web-scale discovery: A review of Summon, EBSCO Discovery Service, and WorldCat Local. *The Charleston Advisor, 12*(1), 5–10. doi:10.5260/chara.12.1.5

Sharpe, P. A., & Vacek, R. E. (2010). Intranet 2.0 from a project management perspective. *Journal of Web Librarianship, 4*(2/3), 239–249. doi:10.1080/19322909.2010.500860

Stevenson, K. K., Elsegood, S. S., Seaman, D. D., Pawlek, C. C., & Nielsen, M. P. (2009). Next-generation library catalogues: Reviews of Encore, Primo, Summon and Summa. *SERIALS, 22*(1), 68–78. doi:10.1629/2268

Tallent, E. (2004). Metasearching in Boston College Libraries: A case study of user reactions. *New Library World, 105*(1/2), 69–75. doi:10.1108/03074800410515282

Tang, R., Hsieh-Yee, I., & Zhang, S. (2007). User perceptions of MetaLib combined search: An investigation of how users make sense of federated searching. *Internet Reference Services Quarterly, 12*(1/2), 211–236. doi:10.1300/J136v12n01_11

Thomas, B., & Buck, S. (2010). OCLC's WorldCat Local versus III's WebPAC: Which interface is better at supporting common user tasks? *Library Hi Tech, 28*(4), 648–671. doi:10.1108/07378831011096295

Vaughan, J. (2011). Questions to consider. *Library Technology Reports, 47*(1), 54–59.

Vaughn, D., & Callicott, B. (2003). Broccoli librarianship and Google-bred patrons, or what's wrong with usability testing? *College & Undergraduate Libraries, 10*(2), 1–18. doi:10.1300/J106v10n02_01

Wallace, L. K. (2004). *Libraries, mission, & marketing: Writing mission statements that work.* Chicago, IL: American Library Association.

Ward, J. L., Shadle, S., & Mofield, P. (2008). User experience, feedback, and testing. *Library Technology Reports, 44*(6), 17–23.

Webb, P. L., & Nero, M. D. (2009). OPACs in the clouds. *Computers in Libraries, 29*(9), 18–22.

Whittaker, J. (2000). What is software testing? And why is it so hard? *IEEE Software, 17*(1), 70–79. doi:10.1109/52.819971

Williams, S. C., & Foster, A. K. (2011). Promise fulfilled? An EBSCO Discovery Service usability study. *Journal of Web Librarianship, 5*(3), 179–198. doi:10.1080/19322909.2011.597590

Wynne, S. C., & Hanscom, M. J. (2011). The effect of next-generation catalogs on catalogers and cataloging functions in academic libraries. *Cataloging & Classification Quarterly, 49*(3), 179–207. doi:10.1080/01639374.2011.559899

Yang, S. Q., & Wagner, K. (2010). Evaluating and comparing discovery tools: How close are we towards a next generation catalog? *Library Hi Tech, 28*(4), 690–709. doi:10.1108/07378831011096312

York, M. C. (2005). Calling the scholars home: Google Scholar as a tool for rediscovering the academic library. *Internet Reference Services Quarterly, 10*(3/4), 117–133. doi:10.1300/J136v10n03_11

ADDITIONAL READING

Bhatnagar, G., Dennis, S., Duque, G., Henry, S., & MacEachern, M. … Varnum, K. (2010). *Article Discovery Group: Final report.* Retrieved from http://www.lib.umich.edu/files/adwg/final-report.pdf

Centre for Information Behaviour and Evaluation of Research. (2008). *Information behaviour of the researcher of the future: A CIBER briefing paper.* London, UK: University College London, CIBER. Retrieved from http://www.jisc.ac.uk/media/documents/programmes/reppres/gg_final_keynote_11012008.pdf

Connaway, L. S., & Dickey, T. (2010). *The digital information seeker: Report on findings from selected OCLC, RIN and JISC user behaviour projects*. Retrieved from http://www.jisc.ac.uk/media/documents/publications/reports/2010/digitalinformationseekerreport.pdf

Connaway, L. S., Dickey, T. J., & Radford, M. L. (2011). "If it is too inconvenient I'm not going after it": Convenience as a critical factor in information-seeking behaviors. *Library & Information Science Research, 33*(3), 179–190. doi:10.1016/j.lisr.2010.12.002

Cox, C. (2006). An analysis of the impact of federated search products on library instruction using the ACRL standards. *Portal: Libraries & the Academy, 6*(3), 253–267. doi:10.1353/pla.2006.0035

ERIAL. (2012). *Conference presentations*. Retrieved from http://www.erialproject.org/publications/presentations/

Hargittai, E. (2007). The social, political, economic, and cultural dimensions of search engines: An introduction. *Journal of Computer-Mediated Communication, 12*(3), 769–777. doi:10.1111/j.1083-6101.2007.00349.x

Nagra, K. A., & Coiffe, D. J. (2010). Management of online tutorials: A model for a step-by-step approach. *Journal of the Library Administration & Management Section, 7*(1), 4–17.

Revels, I. (2012). *Managing digital projects*. Chicago, IL: ALA Editions.

Tervonen, I., & Kerola, P. (1998). Towards deeper co-understanding of software quality. *Information and Software Technology, 39*(14/15), 995–1003. doi:10.1016/S0950-5849(97)00060-8

Webster, P. (2004). Metasearching in an academic environment. *Online, 28*(2), 20–23.

KEY TERMS AND DEFINITIONS

Discovery Tool: Software that includes both a library catalog and article indexes in a unified index and search interface; this approach differs from federated search software, which searches multiple databases and aggregates the results.

Federated Search: Software that searches multiple information sources simultaneously, but separately, combining results post-search into a unified results list.

Issue Tracking: The process of monitoring a list of known issues of a software system. This will include dates when the issue was first reported, who reported it, when the vendor was notified, name of the representative from the vendor who responded, action the vendor took, verification locally that the issue was resolved.

MARC: A format for bibliographic records containing a physical description of the item, subject headings, and classification or call number of the item. MARC stands for MAchine-Readable Cataloging.

Precision: A measure of an information system's ability to return only relevant items.

Project Management: The process of directing the execution of an initiative through its lifecycle, including defining the project, collaborating with stakeholders, leading project team members, monitoring timeline and deadlines, overseeing organizational communication, and bringing the project to conclusion.

Recall: A measure of an information retrieval system's ability to return all objects relevant to a given query.

Stakeholders: Individuals within an organization who have an interest in a process or product.

Search Box Widgets: Homegrown or vendor-provided code (usually in HTML, CSS, and JavaScript) for one or more input boxes that a library can embed into a Web page.

Technical Testing: The process of examining software using a checklist or with a script in order to simulate user behavior and ensure that the software is behaving as expected.

ENDNOTES

[1]   EBSCO Discovery Service is owned by EBSCO Publishing Industries

[2]   Encore is a trademark of Innovative Interfaces

[3]   AquaBrowser is a registered trademark of Serials Solutions

[4]   Serials Solutions is a registered trademark of Serials Solutions

Chapter 25
Introducing Discovery Systems to Academic User Communities:
A Case Study with Recommendations

Mary Mintz
American University, USA

ABSTRACT

This chapter provides information about why marketing a new discovery system is important both for libraries and for users. It also presents a case study of the American University Library experience in marketing a new discovery system, including an innovative technique for viral marketing. Results of the marketing program probably contributed to overall use of the discovery system, but did not guarantee system success as reflected in user responses to the system. Recommendations based on lessons learned from the American University Library experience and from marketing best practices that can be applied to planning, branding, publicity venues, language, and assessment are presented to assist other libraries.

INTRODUCTION

Implementing a discovery system for an academic library is a process largely invisible to users. The end result of the process, however, should be highly visible. If the discovery tool itself is not "discoverable," a significant library investment is diminished and more importantly, users miss

a potential opportunity to enhance their research. According to a recent study (University College London, CIBER Group, 2008):

Younger scholars especially have only a very limited knowledge of the many library sponsored services that are on offer to them. The problem is one of both raising awareness of this expensive

DOI: 10.4018/978-1-4666-1821-3.ch025

and valuable content and making the interfaces much more standard and easier to use. (p. 30)

As one commentator sums up this challenge common to many academic libraries: "More often than not . . . students use what they can find and professors use what they are accustomed to. Libraries pay thousands of dollars a year for digital resources they carefully select. . . . " He also asks, "How is it that faculty and student use of quality digital resources remains so chancy?" (Menchaca, 2008, p. 111).

Proactive promotion of a discovery system can leave less to chance. Academic libraries, concerned about expensive yet underutilized electronic resources/services and about remaining relevant in the Google age, should accompany implementation with promotion. Generating awareness and use is not simply directed at realizing the potential of a library/university investment, but primarily at improving research for students and faculty who may benefit from the availability of a powerful discovery tool. By promoting a discovery system, a library may be able to reverse a national trend at the local level. According to a recent study (De Rosa et al., 2011), for college and university students, "search engines continue to dominate, topping the list of electronic sources most used to find online content (93%), followed closely by Wikipedia (88%). . . . Results show a decline in use of library Web sites, e-journals and online databases since 2005." (p. 52).

Evidence that the trend can be reversed, however, is noted in the same study which found that "While the number of college students using the library Web site declined (61% to 57%), those who do so are using it more frequently—22% use it at least weekly, up from 15% in 2005," (De Rosa et al., 2011, p. 52). This finding strongly suggests that informed users are repeat users. Thus, the process of introducing users to a beneficial new discovery tool is an important area that requires focus and coordination among library person-

nel associated with implementation, individual instruction at service points, group instruction in classrooms, and outreach or marketing. A strategic planning process for outreach, marketing, or publicity can be almost as essential as selection and implementation. In fact, the introduction of a new discovery tool represents an opportunity for a library to brand (or re-brand) an important user service and to establish a significant new information technology presence in its user community.

BACKGROUND

In this paper the terms, *marketing*, *outreach*, *promotion*, and *publicity* are interchangeable and self-explanatory as they often are in libraries and library literature. These terms refer to communication directed at current and potential users with the goal of promoting awareness of library services or resources. A "discovery system" in this context is a service that provides users with the capability of simultaneous searches across multiple electronic resources through one access point with the goal of "revitaliz[ing] the stodgy online catalogs of the past to deliver to library patrons an experience of the collections and services of the library more in tune with the expectations set by the mainstream Web" (Breeding, 2011, p. 21).

Recently, interest in marketing for academic libraries has increased. The Association of College and Research Libraries (ACRL) established its first Best Practices in Marketing Academic and Research Libraries @Your Library award in 2005. In 2009, a poll administered by ACRL's University Libraries section revealed that "Academic Outreach" would be the most desirable new committee for that organization (Leeder, 2009), and it was subsequently established. An expanded interest in marketing is reflected in the large number of books published during the past decade, most of them applicable to all types of libraries. Among those publications, Matthews

(2009) is the rare monograph focusing exclusively on academic library marketing, and Dowd (2010) is almost unique in including electronic resources. The "Tech Set" series from the Library and Information Technology Association (LITA) covers a variety of marketing-related topics such as microblogging and lifestreaming (Hastings, 2010), videos and Webcasts (Robinson, 2010), and blogging (Crosby, 2010). Woods's article (2008) provides a general overview of marketing electronic resources, especially databases; Fagan's (2009) is about marketing of the "virtual library." Golderman (2007) takes an "infiltration" approach similar in philosophy to Matthews'. Sachs (2011) discusses Facebook™[1] as a marketing tool. Dubicki (2007) edited a themed journal issue on marketing electronic resources which was subsequently republished as a book (2008). Petruzelli (2005) also edited a book which covers a variety of academic marketing issues and simultaneously appeared as a special journal issue.

While discovery systems themselves are a relatively new phenomenon with virtually no coverage in the library marketing literature, federated search services and "next generation" catalogs, predecessors of the newer discovery platforms, are the focus of helpful case studies by Cox (2007) and Wisniewski (2007). Boock (2006), Gerrity (2002), Gibson (2009), King (2008), Madison (2005), Herrera (2007), and Rainwater (2007) also look briefly at marketing in the same context. Because promoting virtual reference is somewhat analogous to promoting a discovery system, Vilelle's (2005) excellent compilation is useful. On the Web, library marketing sites tend to be general and non-specific for library types or electronic services. The second edition of the Reference and User Services Association (RUSA)'s *Guidelines for the Introduction of Electronic Information Resources to Users* (Reference, 2006), is an exception with a general checklist and a separate section on "Publicity."

Context

The American University Library (AU Library) recently implemented and marketed a new discovery system. American University (AU) is a private, medium-sized research university located in Washington, D. C. The student body of approximately 10,000 is divided almost equally between undergraduate and graduate students. Most undergraduates are residential students who live on or near campus. Many graduate students hold full-time jobs and live off-campus. About 500 full-time faculty and a slightly lesser number of adjunct faculty drawn from government and various professions provide instruction. Among its other distinctions, AU requires equally outstanding teaching and research for tenure-line faculty seeking tenure and promotion. AU also places a great deal of emphasis on experiential learning for students who can earn credit for internships on Capitol Hill, in research institutes, and in national and international organizations. Many curricular areas are multi- or inter-disciplinary. For instance, in addition to diplomacy, the largest school, International Service, has programs in comparative politics, economic development, and communication that could easily be housed elsewhere in the university if not for their international emphases. The activist student body often ranks first or near the top nationwide for engagement in politics and social causes. While the overall percentage of international students is not as high as that for many other institutions, AU usually has the highest number of different countries represented in its student body. In turn, AU students who are U.S. citizens often study abroad. Together, AU faculty and students are highly engaged in local, national, and international teaching, learning, and research experiences and potentially benefit from a time-saving discovery system.

AU has a separately-administered law school library and a branch performing arts library. All

Figure 1. SearchBox logo by Jonathan Silberman, AU library designer (Used with permission of American University)

other programs in the liberal arts curriculum as well as the professional programs such as public administration, communication, international service, and business are supported by the main library. The library, which is a member of the Washington Research Library Consortium (WRLC) with a shared catalog and other services, has approximately 1.2 million volumes and expends more than half of its collection budget on electronic resources, including e-books and several hundred subscription databases. The library is staffed with a relatively small number of about twenty professional library faculty and about sixty full-time staff, some with library science degrees, and many part-time students.

Implementation

AU Library selected and then to the fullest extent possible at the time, implemented Summon™² from Serials Solutions®³ as its first discovery system in August, 2010. Ninety percent of the library's database subscriptions were included; the omissions were primarily statistical databases that could not interface with Summon™. The WRLC catalog was also included to the extent possible at launch; for technical reasons two member library catalogs had to be incorporated late in the fall semester, several months after implementation. For the libraries that were included in the initial implementation, local holding information could not be displayed on search results pages. An AU student had to click through up to five records to determine if AU library owned a title. Faceted

library location searching was subsequently implemented when it became available in March, 2011.

THE AMERICAN UNIVERSITY LIBRARY EXPERIENCE

Marketing

The library's Public and University Relations (PUR) division developed a marketing plan for Summon™ implementation with three major components: branding, Web publicity, and viral marketing. After the name "SearchBox" was chosen by the library's administrative council from a list generated through an open invitation to all library staff, the PUR library designer developed a "look" or logo (Figure 1) to brand SearchBox for a prominent position on the library home page. The look includes a design element for the letter "o" in SearchBox that simultaneously echoes both a compass and a lodestar (guide star) and subtly suggests that SearchBox helps users navigate through many resources.

The Web-based promotion for SearchBox included a news story (Appendix A) placed in the most prominent news area on the library home page. The library also used Facebook™ and Twitter™⁴ to announce the arrival of SearchBox. Faculty received an announcement about SearchBox in their annual library fall updates email. Additional awareness of the new SearchBox was generated through demonstrations in many of the 434 library instruction sessions provided for 8,887

Figure 2. Illustration for coffee sleeve by Jonathan Silberman, AU library designer (used with permission of American University)

I need more information on...

users during the 2010/2011 academic year. At the discretion of individual reference librarians and staff, some of the year's nearly 20,000 transactions (desk, online chat, email) and 247 individual appointments incorporated SearchBox.

AU Library also promoted SearchBox through a subtle form of viral marketing. The most popular campus coffee cafe, "Davenport," or "The Dav," agreed to use a specially designed coffee cup sleeve to promote the new SearchBox. Sleeves were chosen because they have become ubiquitous and essential to many coffee drinkers, but as accessories, they do not have the same storage or cost challenges as cups. Coffee sleeves also travel well; their messages can spread virally but innocuously into classrooms, faculty offices, and residence halls. For the AU sleeve, the designer used the new SearchBox logo and filled in the "search box" with a phrase, "Fair Trade Coffee," as a reference to the cup contents (Figure 2). This phrase has special resonance among the politically aware AU students who had previously negotiated with university administration to ensure that all campus vendors served "fair trade" coffee.

Though only intended as an example, not an inspiration for users to take action, it is interesting to note that since the implementation of Summon,

the words in the phrase, "fair trade coffee" have been used in some combination twenty-four times in SearchBox, most likely for actual student research. A QR code was also added to the coffee sleeve design to pique further interest. The QR code which led to a Web page with SearchBox received only thirty-five views. This low figure does not necessarily mean that the library's message was not delivered because the main message was intact on the sleeve itself, only that the students did not pro-actively respond to it. QR code "fatigue" has also been widely reported in the media.

User Responses to SearchBox

The goal of the marketing plan was to build awareness of SearchBox and to encourage its use by the entire campus community. Though no formal assessment of the AU marketing plan was conducted, statistics for SearchBox use suggest that the marketing likely had some impact because the service was ranked second behind JSTOR and ahead of Academic Search Premier (Figure 3) in terms of platform use. Some of that use can probably be attributed to the three promotional marketing components as well as to

Figure 3. Summon™ Use compared to other platforms, August 2010-November 2011 (Reeves, 2011)

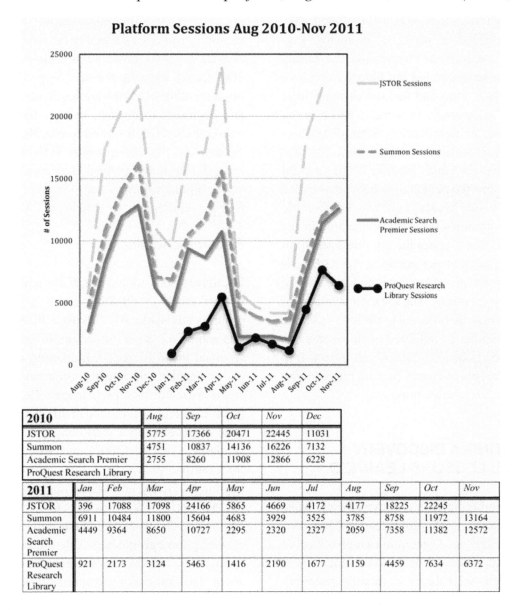

2010	Aug	Sep	Oct	Nov	Dec
JSTOR	5775	17366	20471	22445	11031
Summon	4751	10837	14136	16226	7132
Academic Search Premier	2755	8260	11908	12866	6228
ProQuest Research Library					

2011	Jan	Feb	Mar	Apr	May	Jun	Jul	Aug	Sep	Oct	Nov
JSTOR	396	17088	17098	24166	5865	4669	4172	4177	18225	22245	
Summon	6911	10484	11800	15604	4683	3929	3525	3785	8758	11972	13164
Academic Search Premier	4449	9364	8650	10727	2295	2320	2327	2059	7358	11382	12572
ProQuest Research Library	921	2173	3124	5463	1416	2190	1677	1159	4459	7634	6372

library instruction and other exposure, including prominent placement on the library home page.

The marketing plan seemed to be at least partially successful in promoting SearchBox use. However, user response to SearchBox was not always favorable. Initial feedback for SearchBox arrived in direct comments to librarians and in the library's online suggestion box (Appendix B),

a PUR responsibility. Some comments reflected the inability to display individual consortium library ownership for books on a search results page. User dissatisfaction of various kinds became more apparent in a spring LibQual+ assessment that followed fall implementation (Appendix B). Undergraduates tended to view SearchBox more favorably than graduate students and faculty, but even their comments were mixed (Appendix B).

User response in personal comments, suggestion box entries, and especially the formal LibQual+ assessment led the library to remove the SearchBox logo and the search itself from the library's top page. In summer 2011, about one year after implementation, SearchBox/Summon™ was relocated to two less-prominent tabs labeled "Articles" and "Ebooks." The original catalog became the default search for tabs labeled "Books," "Visual Media," and "Music." Because only two comments have since appeared in the Suggestion Box (Appendix B), one each from faculty and student perspectives, SearchBox is either not much missed or users may be satisfied with its new locations. The location changes for SearchBox may be reflected in the lower use rate when the number of fall 2010 platform sessions is compared to fall 2011 data (Figure 3); the drop is only in the fifteen-twenty percent range for the less-visible SearchBox, however.

MARKETING A DISCOVERY SYSTEM: LESSONS LEARNED

It was not marketing's role to convince users to *like* the new discovery system, only to try it. Marketing probably did succeed generating a higher level of awareness about SearchBox, but subsequent user feedback led AU Library to modify discovery location and default discovery scope.

Planning

AU Library used the existing PUR division to plan marketing for the discovery tool. AU's implementation coordinator regularly provided progress reports and other information so that PUR could plan ahead. This cooperative relationship ensured that PUR was prepared to market

at time of implementation. With hindsight, AU might have delayed implementation until library location display functionality became available. Herrera suggests, however, in a similar context, "Do not try to make the service perfect before implementing it. Most libraries do not have time and resources to do this. Instead find ways to gain continual feedback and constantly adjust and develop" (p. 51). Ultimately an individual library must decide how "perfect" a system should be before implementation and what the impact on user perception may be (Madison, 2008).

Recommendations

If a library does not have staff already dedicated to marketing, establishing an ad hoc working group is advisable. AU Library's PUR included this author and other library employees who had received the 2005 ACRL marketing award and had engaged in subsequent continuous marketing and outreach efforts, experience reflected in the recommendations provided in this chapter. Guidance in developing a marketing plan is widely available. Dubicki (2007) and Woods, (2008), for example, provide excellent information for beginners. Hiring an outside marketing firm is another option (Wisniewski, 2007, p. 348). In addition to the usual best management practices of setting strategic goals, establishing a budget (if applicable), and anticipating assessment, clarity about decision-making responsibilities such as final name selection, is essential. Staff involved in implementation must keep the library marketing group adequately informed for planning purposes. Marketing groups should also have an advisory role on the timing of a discovery tool launch. Previous experience with marketing a federated search (Cox, 2007), indicates that a "soft" or preliminary campaign may be desirable to gauge user reception. A mid-semester launch can provide an opportunity "to market the product as widely as possible," (Gibson, 2009) though some libraries may prefer to have a new service available at the beginning of a new semester or year.

Branding

While AU's chosen SearchBox name has the advantage of describing the most obvious visual feature of a discovery system, librarians often have to use both the generic phrase, "search box," and the new proper name, SearchBox with some frequency within the same reference transactions and instruction sessions. Ultimately the logo and look of SearchBox probably helped distinguish between the two at AU.

Recommendations

A specific design or logo can reinforce branding. A look without a name is not recommended because it is difficult to reference in publicity and instruction. Libraries should engage in broad consultation prior to finalizing the brand or name of a discovery tool. In the best possible outcome, the name will become synonymous with effective research. As Dempsey (2004) has observed, "Life used to be so simple: A brand was a name, like Coke or IBM. But the science of brand management [has become] . . . a process for owning a space in the psyche of the customer" (p. 34). Naming a discovery system can have a lasting impact as evidenced by the number of online catalog names that remain in use, some for decades. "Trendy" names should be avoided since any branded discovery system may become a durable library feature, even if the underlying software changes. Options for branding include university themes such as sports mascots like GamecockPowerSearch (King, 2008), library buildings, or campus traditions. A focus on the research function of the tool or emphasis on its broad discovery powers is another option, but it must not be too bland or meaningless, as some libraries discovered when naming federated search

products with MetaFind (Boock, 2006) or "Find-It!" (Cox, 2007). It also should not raise unrealistic expectations as "Zoom!" did about search speed (Wisniewski, 2007). An internal or external prize contest for naming a discovery tool can bring many creative minds to bear on the challenge. A student contest can also build anticipation for the service and present naming or branding possibilities with greater multi-generational appeal.

Publicity Venues

AU Library used Web venues and coffee cup sleeves as its primary marketing venues for SearchBox. These particular venues were probably more effective at reaching undergraduates. Had the library been able to anticipate concerns about SearchBox, a different marketing strategy targeted to teaching faculty probably could have focused on the merits of a discovery system for particular kinds of research, such as multi-disciplinary research. A series of departmental meetings with subject librarians might have proved to be effective as it has elsewhere (Cox, 2007).

Recommendations

Clearly marketing venues should appeal to all targeted user groups. Undergraduates may prefer social media contacts and coffee. Some libraries have experienced dramatic increases with traditional media such as campus newspapers and newsletters (Boock, 2006), but as Matthews (2009, p. 2) says, "The guiding principle [is] that library advertising should focus on the lifestyle of the user." Effective media used in AU Library promotions have included Web videos, campus bus posters, and electronic display slides. A well-designed poster or slide incorporating the unexpected can help generate effective student peer-to-peer conversation. While libraries may have been hesitant in the past to market overtly to faculty, at least one institution has discovered that faculty themselves may find marketing desirable when it relates to electronic resources (Herrera, 2007). A top ten list (Gerrity, 2002) may provide useful talking points for faculty & librarians alike.

Language

Avoiding library jargon may seem like an obvious point, but it is worth noting here. AU Library successfully avoided all references to commercial names (Summon™ and Serials Solutions®, for instance) and even library jargon such as "discovery system" or "discovery tool" when promoting the new SearchBox (Appendix A). This decision is supported by Cervone's (2005, p. 12) conclusion that metasearch "means absolutely nothing" to typical faculty and students.

Recommendations

Google may actually be an apt comparison for describing a discovery system though care should be taken to explain the content covered by the discovery system to avoid any confusion with site searches. The Google analogy may also offer a library an opportunity to educate users about the distinctions between Google, Google Scholar™[5], and a discovery system and the advantages of using the latter, but brevity should prevail in marketing. Content for any articles does not have to be complicated because, "Making the description connect to your audience doesn't have be time consuming. Just write it as a benefit statement. The trick to writing the benefit statement is answering the question, "Why would your customer use this?" (Dowd, 2010, p. 39).

Assessment

Making a distinction between assessment of marketing efforts and assessment of the discovery tool itself is important. AU Library did not plan any formal assessment of the SearchBox marketing and instead, invested in assessment of the discovery system and related resources through LibQUAL+®[6]. In the past, however, AU Library has found that marketing, formal assessment, and subsequent planning can be successfully tied together (Becher, 2006).

Cox (2007) is correct, however, in his assertion, "Always build in assessment" (p. 160) for marketing even on a campus like that of AU where concern about assessment fatigue is ongoing. A survey with questions as simple as, "Where is SearchBox?" or "Have you heard of SearchBox? If yes, how?" accompanied by multiple choice responses may be helpful. Assessment for marketing of a discovery tool can also become part of a wider assessment of overall marketing efforts. In addition to formal assessments, feedback that arrives less formally but continually through library instruction, reference services, and social media should be considered. A significant implementation can have an equally significant impact on the users' overall perception of the library; therefore, any marketing group must maintain an awareness of both formal and informal feedback. A library should be ready to acknowledge limitations in newly implemented systems. Receiving and responding to negative as well as positive feedback may present an opportunity to educate users and to encourage additional feedback.

FUTURE RESEARCH DIRECTIONS

As discovery systems are implemented and enhanced in academic libraries, it will be helpful for those libraries to share their marketing experiences and their users' reactions both to the marketing and to the systems themselves. In the AU Library experience, having aware users meant that the library was able to acquire informed feedback about SearchBox. This user feedback has already led the library to re-position SearchBox and will inform future local implementations both of discovery systems and other electronic resources and services.

The collective experiences of libraries shared throughout these pages and in future studies can assist libraries in becoming more effective at serving their users during the marketing, implementation, and refinement of discovery systems. Future studies could also usefully explore the complex area of faculty attitudes toward discovery systems and how those attitudes affect librarians and students. For instance, anecdotal information suggests that AU librarians were initially positive in their reception of the discovery system, but further study would have to be conducted to determine to what extent faculty attitudes impacted librarian and student perceptions.

CONCLUSION

Strategic marketing is comprised of two essential parts. First, there needs to be a tool or product that meets a demand or need. Secondly, communication about the product generates awareness. Communication about a discovery system is most appropriately conducted through a marketing strategy that includes considerations of branding, venues, language, and assessment. Libraries must ensure that their users discover the discovery system in order to realize their investment and more importantly, to enhance the user research experience. As Balas (2011, p. 32) has noted, "'I didn't know the library had that,' are words that make librarians cringe." Even faculty want to be better informed in this critical area according to one study. They believe that "The marketing of library e-resources should be a critical component of academic libraries' activities." (Jankowska, 2004, p.63). If discovery systems have any chance of becoming truly useful and truly tested by users, communication to and from those users is

essential. As the American University Library experience indicates, feedback can inform the library about users' preferences and establish the library's service priorities.

REFERENCES

Balas, J. (2011). Online treasures: Can QR codes be used to deliver library services. *Computers in Libraries, 31*(2), 32.

Becher, M., & Flug, J. (2006). Using student focus groups to inform library planning and marketing. *College & Undergraduate Libraries, 12*(1), 1–18. doi:10.1300/J106v12n01_01

Boock, M., Nichols, J., & Kristick, L. (2006). Continuing the quest for the quick search holy grail: Oregon State University Libraries' federated search implementation. *Internet Reference Services Quarterly, 11*(4), 139–153. doi:10.1300/J136v11n04_09

Breeding, M. (2011). Discovering Harry Pottery barn. *Computers in Libraries, 31*(2), 21–23.

Centre for Information Behaviour and Evaluation of Research. (2008). *Information behaviour of the researcher of the future: A CIBER briefing paper.* London, UK: University College London, CIBER. Retrieved from http://www.jisc.ac.uk/media/documents/programmes/reppres/gg_final_keynote_11012008.pdf

Centre for Information Behaviour and Evaluation of Research. (2008). *Information behaviour of the researcher of the future.* London, UK: University College London. Retrieved from http://www.jisc.ac.uk/media/documents/programmes/reppres/gg_final_keynote_11012008.pdf

Cervone, F. (2005). What we've learned from doing usability testing on OpenURL resolvers and federated search engines. *Computers in Libraries, 25*(9), 10–14.

Cox, C. (2007). Hitting the spot: Marketing federated searching tools to students and faculty. *The Serials Librarian, 53*(3), 147–164. doi:10.1300/J123v53n03_10

Crosby, C. (2010). *Effective blogging for libraries*. New York, NY: Neal-Schuman Publishers.

De Rosa, C., Cantrell, J., Carlson, M., Gallagher, P., Hawk, J., Sturtz, C., et al. (2011). *Perceptions of libraries, 2010: Context and community*. Retrieved from http://www.oclc.org/reports/2010perceptions.htm

Dempsey, B. (2004). Target your brand. *Library Journal, 129*(13), 32–35.

Dowd, N., Evangeliste, M., & Silberman, J. (2010). *Bite-sized marketing: Realistic solutions for the overworked librarian*. Chicago, IL: American Library Association.

Dubicki, E. (2007). Basic marketing and promotion concepts. *The Serials Librarian, 53*(3), 1–25. doi:10.1300/J123v53n03_02

Dubicki, E. (2008). *Marketing and promoting electronic resources: Creating the e-buzz!* Abingdon, NY: Routledge.

Fagan, J. C. (2009). Marketing the virtual library. *Computers in Libraries, 29*(7), 25–30.

Gerrity, B., Lyman, T., & Tallent, E. (2002). Blurring services and resources: Boston College's implementation of MetaLib and SFX. *RSR. Reference Services Review, 30*(3), 229–241. doi:10.1108/00907320210435491

Gibson, I., Goddard, L., & Gordon, S. (2009). One box to search them all: Implementing federated search at an academic library. *Library Hi Tech, 27*(1), 118–133. doi:10.1108/07378830910942973

Golderman, M., & Connolly, B. (2007). Infiltrating net gen cyberculture: Strategies for engaging and educating students on their own terms. *The Serials Librarian, 53*(3), 165–182. doi:10.1300/J123v53n03_11

Hastings, R. (2010). *Microblogging and lifestreaming in libraries*. New York, NY: Neal-Schuman Publishers.

Herrera, G. (2007). Meta searching and beyond: Implementation experiences and advice from an academic library. *Information Technology and Libraries, 26*(2), 44–52.

Jankowska, M. (2004). Identifying university professors' information needs in the challenging environment of information and communication technologies. *Journal of Academic Librarianship, 30*(1), 51–66. doi:10.1016/j.jal.2003.11.007

King, D. (2008). Many libraries have gone to federated searching to win users back from Google. Is it working? *Journal of Electronic Resources Librarianship, 20*(4), 213–227. doi:10.1080/19411260802554520

Leeder, K. (2009). *The new committees you asked for* [Web log post]. Retrieved from http://www.acrl.ala.org/ULS/?p=55

Madison, O., & Hyland-Carver, M. (2005). Issues in planning for portal implementation: Perfection not required. *Journal of Library Administration, 43*(1-2), 113–134. doi:10.1300/J111v43n01_08

Matthews, B. (2009). *Marketing today's academic library: A bold new approach to communicating with students*. Chicago, IL: American Library Association.

McHale, N. (2007). Accidental federated searching: Implementing federated searching in the smaller academic library. *Internet Reference Services Quarterly, 12*(1), 93–110. doi:10.1300/J136v12n01_05

Menchaca, F. (2008). Funes and the search engine. *Journal of Library Administration, 48*(1), 107–119. doi:10.1080/01930820802035224

Petruzzelli, B. (2005). Real-life marketing and promotion strategies in college libraries: Connecting with campus and community. *College & Undergraduate Libraries, 12*(1-2).

Rainwater, J. (2007). Maintaining a federated search service: Issues and solutions. *Internet Reference Services Quarterly, 12*(3), 309–323. doi:10.1300/J136v12n03_05

Reference and User Services Association. (2006). *Guidelines for the introduction of electronic information resources to users.* Retrieved from http://www.ala.org/ala/mgrps/divs/rusa/resources/guidelines/guidelinesintroduction.cfm

Robinson, T. (2010). *Library videos and Webcasts.* New York, NY: Neal-Schuman Publishers.

Sachs, D., Eckel, E., & Langan, K. (2011). Striking a balance: Effective use of Facebook in an academic library. *Internet Reference Services Quarterly, 16*(1-2), 35–54. doi:10.1080/10875301.2011.572457

Vilelle, L. (2005). Marketing virtual reference: What academic libraries have done. *College & Undergraduate Libraries, 12*(1-2), 65–79. doi:10.1300/J106v12n01_05

Wisniewski, J. (2007). Build it (and customize and market it) and they will come. *Internet Reference Services Quarterly, 12*(3-4), 341–355. doi:10.1300/J136v12n03_07

Woods, L. (2007). A three-step approach to marketing electronic resources at Brock University. *The Serials Librarian, 53*(3), 107–124. doi:10.1300/J123v53n03_08

ADDITIONAL READING

Association of College & Research Libraries. (2005). *Marketing @ your library.* Retrieved from http://www.ala.org/acrl/issues/marketing

Baer, W. (2004). Federated searching: Friend or foe? *College & Research Libraries News, 65*(9), 518–519.

Breeding, M. (2007). The birth of a new generation of library interfaces. *Computers in Libraries, 10*(9), 34–37.

Coffman, S. (2003). Marketing virtual reference services . In *Going live: Starting & running a virtual reference service* (pp. 73–89). Chicago, IL: American Library Association.

Cole, K., Graves, T., & Cipkowski, P. (2010). Marketing the library in a digital world. *The Serials Librarian, 58*(1-4), 182–187. doi:10.1080/03615261003625729

Dempsey, K. (2009). *The accidental library marketer.* Medford, NJ: Information Today.

Elder, J. J., Forrest, C., & Thomas, S. (2005). Students are users, too: A research library reaches out to the "undergraduate market" at Emory University. *College & Research Libraries News, 66*(3), 214–215.

Fisher, P., Pride, M., & Miller, E. (2006). *Blueprint for your library marketing plan: A guide to help you survive and thrive.* Chicago, IL: American Library Association.

Frumkin, J. (2005). The wiki and the digital library. *OCLC Systems & Services, 21*(1), 18–22. doi:10.1108/10650750510578109

Germain, C. (2000). 99 ways to get those feet in the door: How to develop a public relations campaign. *College & Research Libraries News, 61*(2), 93–96.

Gould, M. R. (2009). *The library PR handbook: High-impact communications*. Chicago, IL: American Library Association.

Gupta, D. K. (2006). *Marketing library and information services: International perspectives*. München, Germany: K. G. Saur.

Hall, P. (2002). Not all sources are created equal: Student research, source equivalence. *Internet Reference Services Quarterly, 7*(4), 13-21. doi: 10.1300/ J136v07n04_02

Harley, D. (2006). *Use and users of digital resources: A focus on undergraduate education in the humanities and social sciences*. Berkeley, CA: Center for Studies in Higher Education. Retrieved from http://cshe.berkeley.edu/research/digitalresourcestudy/report/digitalresourcestudy_final_report.pdf

Janson, B., Zhang, M., & Schultz, C. (2009). Brand and its effect on user perception of search engine performance. *Journal of the American Society for Information Science and Technology, 60*(8), 1572–1595. doi:10.1002/asi.21081

Johnson, P. (2004). Marketing, liaison, and outreach activities . In *Fundamentals of collection development & management* (pp. 172–198). Chicago, IL: American Library Assocation.

Karp, R. S., & Library Administration and Management Association. (2002). *Powerful public relations: A how-to guide for libraries*. Chicago, IL: American Library Association.

Lee, D. (2005). Can you hear me now? Using focus groups to enhance marketing research. *Library Administration & Management, 19*(2), 100–101.

Lindsay, A. (2004). *Marketing and public relations practices in college libraries*. Chicago, IL: College Library Information Packet Committee, Association of College and Research Libraries.

Siess, J. A. (2003). *The visible librarian: Asserting your value with marketing and advocacy*. Chicago, IL: American Library Association.

Sodt, J., & Summey, T. (2009). Beyond the library. *Journal of Library Administration, 49*(1-2), 97–109. doi:10.1080/01930820802312854

Tebbutt, D. (2004). Beware the march of the Googlistas! *Information World Review, 199*, 13.

Woodward, J. A. (2009). *Creating the customer-driven academic library*. Chicago, IL: American Library Association.

Zeigen, L., & Crum, J. (2009). Library catalogs and other discovery tools. *OLA Quarterly, 15*(1), Retrieved from http://data.memberclicks.com/site/ola/olaq_15no1.pdf

KEY TERMS AND DEFINITIONS

Assessment: Assessment is the process of evaluating a product or service and its effectiveness.

Branding: Branding is the provision of a specific name or distinctive identity for a product or service.

Discovery System/Discovery Tool: A discovery system is electronic, Web-based software that provides users with the capability of simultaneous searches across multiple electronic resources through one access point.

Marketing: Marketing and its related activities of promotion, publicity, and outreach, consists of communication to an audience or potential audience to inform them about a service that offers potential benefits. Promotion implies encouragement to use a product. Publicity emphasizes generating awareness. Outreach suggests efforts to reach specific audiences in their specific environments.

Search Box: A search box is the physical representation of a box where a user enters search terms.

ENDNOTES

1   Facebook is a trademark of Facebook, Inc.

2   Summon is a trademark of Serials Solutions.

3   Serials Solution is a registered trademark of Serials Solutions

4   Twitter is a trademark of Twitter, Inc.

5   Google Scholar is a trademark of Google, Inc.

6   LibQUAL+ is a registered trademark of Association of Research Libraries

APPENDIX A

Web News Story on the Introduction of SearchBox, AU Library's Implementation of Summon™, August 2, 2010

AU Library Unveils New Unified Search

Have you ever wanted to search the library's Web resources all at once? Find both books and articles with just one search engine? Your dream is very near reality because AU Library has added SearchBox. With SearchBox, library researchers can search simultaneously the ALADIN Catalog and approximately ninety percent (yes, 90%!) of the library's electronic resources, including journal, magazine, and newspaper articles in databases. "SearchBox is the most revolutionary and amazing new development since the library went online two decades ago," says one longtime AU librarian.

For students and faculty, research will be much faster and easier because they can conduct Google-style searches of the library's vast array of electronic resources. These resources are not available through a regular public Google search because the resources are privately paid for by the library through subscription fees. SearchBox also covers the consortium-wide holdings of the ALADIN Catalog and the digital repository, American University Research Commons. The only resources that the SearchBox engine cannot currently search are some statistical and financial databases. Those databases can still be searched individually. In fact, all databases can still be searched individually, which is particularly important to researchers who want to execute more sophisticated or complex searches that take advantage of specific database features.

SearchBox is supported with material from 6,800 publishers, 94,000 journal titles, and 550 million indexed items—numbers that increase daily. It has many powerful features that will help researchers. For instance, researchers can limit search results to full text or to peer-reviewed/scholarly journals or both. The default for displaying search results is relevancy ranking, but the results can also be displayed in ascending or descending order by date of publication. Other limits include subject, content type, and language. Individual items can be saved and displayed in selected citation formats. Results can also be exported to citation management software such as EndNote. Unlike the ALADIN Catalog or most current databases, SearchBox can also correct for spelling. For instance, if a researcher mistakenly types "Humon rights," SearchBox will query, "Did you mean human rights?"

Using SearchBox is easy and highly intuitive, but as always, researchers may wish to contact a reference librarian if questions arise.

APPENDIX B

Fall Semester, 2010 --Comments and Responses About AU Library's SearchBox, AU Library's Implementation of Summon™

August 27, 2010
  Comment:
  SearchBox is amazing!!! Thank you so much for adding this much needed and very useful tool!

October 5, 2010

Comment 1 on SearchBox

The new search box is awesome. It's so much easier to search online articles. However, can you add a side box to limit searches by location? When I'm searching for a book, it's really annoying that I cannot just click a box for "American."

Comment 2 on SearchBox

I hate the new library "Search Box". I did a search for What Is Happening to News by Jack Fuller and found that I had to click on the availability of each book and had to go 4 options down to see that we even own it. Just for kicks, I then searched for All the President's Men, sorted by book (when the book by this title should just show up first anyway, along with showing that the library owns it as it's a classic) and had to click through 5 links to see that the library's copy is on reserves. I appreciate the library's effort to improve the catalog, but I think this new version is less intuitive and cumbersome than the old one.

October 29, 2010

Comment:

SEARCH BOX NEVER WORKS. PLEASE FIX IT.

Spring Semester 2011 -- LibQual+ Comments on AU Library's Implementation of Summon™

Faculty

I find the AU Library portal's search capability to be somewhat cumbersome to use and slow. Since that's the primary interface that I have with the library, improvement to its abilities would be very beneficial to me.

The main problem with the online library Web site is the difficulty in finding AU - as opposed to GWU or Catholic or Univ-DC or Gallaudet etc. - pages that take you to journals where you can see and download PDF files of major journals....There ought to be a simple route to these journal subscriptions and not all this confusion about e- journals available through another university in the consortium...

I've been unable to navigate, activate, figure out the current search system (Search Box?) and am greatly frustrated by that. I should make the time to go in an ask someone to explain it but it seems to me that I should be able follow instructions on screen - they should be there and not so arcane that I am lost. That is the one weakness I have found - clear instructions one can go back to and figure out.

The search box is so clumsy, I pretty much always start with Google Scholar™. But I am happy with the range of materials available, and with the service provided by staff.

I like the SearchBox function

I am impressed with the way the library addresses current opportunities, including streaming video, IM for Ask a Librarian, and SearchBox.

I find the new "SearchBox" engine to be very unsatisfactory - a basic search rarely turns up the most relevant or most applicable results, especially when it comes to major topics in international relations and major journals/authors.

The new search procedures are good...

New SearchBox is junk - it deludes student into thinking they have strategically searched for quality materials. Bring back a way to store a(n) (individualize) commonly used database lists. Students need to understand how to use the best possible databases for their research, not keep stock in a crappy global search devise that returns far too much useless information and junk.

I like the online interface with the exception of the SearchBox (it never retrieves the right stuff) and the duplicate records for the same book at different libraries (makes it hard to sift through records quickly-and I tend to use Amazon to search because it lists related books and offers reviews.)

I like using the multiple options on the library Web page, especially the SearchBox.

I'm becoming more familiar with the new SearchBox, though (perhaps out of familiarity) I preferred the old search function.

Graduate Students

Searchbox was good idea, but doesn't actually work too well. If it could be integrated with all of the online journals AU has access to, that would be helpful.

The library Web site search system needs improvement - it is very hard to find good materials, and it is annoying to have to sift through all the book reviews and newspaper articles every time, and constantly make custom selections... I have found other library search sites easier to use.

The Web site, although much better, still needs a lot of improvement, especially when it comes to searching information. Certainly, Google Scholar™ search helps. But why not have that very same search box, for all the materials available through our library, on the Web site itself, instead of the confusing and unhelpful current one?

Undergraduate Students

I love SearchBox!

The new SearchBox is very useful.

I love all the new innovations, but SearchBox, I think, needs some real work. It's hard to find articles and books! It would be nice if the books and articles were listed by title, and after clicking on one, a list of locations (ranked by proximity) were offered. Right now we're offered ten different links at separate locations right from the beginning and it's hard to find the one you need.

Fall Semester 2011 -- Comments Concerning AU Library's Implementation of Summon™, with Library Response

Comment from Professor on How Students Use SearchBox:

Thanks for taking Search Box off of the front page of your site. I noticed that last year my students were using almost exclusively non-scholarly resources in their research papers, and I couldn't understand the change. From what I could tell, Search Box was the culprit. The students thought that if they found the item through the AU library, it was scholarly. (Love Search Box, btw. Use it all the time.)

Reply:

Thanks for sharing your observations about removing SearchBox from the home page with us. We are very pleased to get this kind of comment from a faculty member and wish we could have more! Thank you also for giving us the opportunity to share more information with blog readers about SearchBox.

Sometimes improvements in library research services have unintended consequences as you observed from your students' work last year. Researchers have long requested–literally almost from the inception of online databases–the ability to simultaneously search multiple databases. Database vendors have recognized this need for several years and have provided cross-searching for their proprietary databases.

For instance, if you open a single ProQuest database, you have the option to select our other ProQuest database subscriptions and search all of them simultaneously.

To resolve the greater challenge of searching many different databases simultaneously from different vendors, academic libraries have begun to acquire these new "google-like" tools, commonly called "discovery systems" in our profession. AU Library carefully selected one of these products actually named "Summon," implemented it, and renamed it "SearchBox." It searches about ninety percent of our databases; the exceptions are the databases which are primarily statistical. After we placed it on the library home page last year, it received lots of use and lots of comment, though as always, we would like to hear more.

In the case of your students, SearchBox may indeed have been the unintentional and unwitting culprit as you indicate. We can take a further educated guess and say that the students may have used SearchBox without taking an important extra step to use an important additional feature–the ability to "Limit to articles from scholarly publications, including peer-review," an option which appears on the top left side of the screen under "Refine your search," after the initial search is completed. For example, as of this moment, if we search Gunter Grass in SearchBox, we receive 2,198 articles from all sources except newspapers which we have by default exempted. If we take the extra step of applying the limit to scholarly materials, then the number of articles drops to 1,484. (That number is of course still way too high for a reasonable search, and other search modifications would be needed if this search were for actual research).

We try to communicate with students in as many ways as possible, through reference services, our Web site and social media, and particularly library instruction about the most appropriate ways to use the library resources. But to some extent we have to rely on having "out-of-the-box" intuitive interfaces from the vendors and hope that researchers who do not interact directly with us will find the "faceted" search features on their own. Of course we work closely with the vendors to share the kind of genuinely valuable comment you are making and to the extent possible, we customize the user interface within the limitations introduced by the vendors to help researchers make more informed choices.

Given the experience you had last year, we would welcome the opportunity to meet with the students in your courses for group library instruction to talk with them about the differences between scholarly and non-scholarly publications and how to make distinctions on their own and also about when it is appropriate to use SearchBox and when it is appropriate to use individual databases within the discipline. We can reserve a library classroom or visit your regular classroom and make a brief or longer presentation as you wish.

Thank you again for your comment and also for telling us that you love SearchBox and use it frequently. I hope you have found it since we have placed it under a new tab that is simply labeled "Articles." With or without library instruction sessions since you may prefer to alert your students yourself, we hope you will stay in touch with us and send us further comments about SearchBox or any library resources.

Comment:

What happened to the Search Box?!

Reply:

It's now just one click away under the black and white tab near the top left side of your screen under "Articles." Based on feedback we have received in the past year about SearchBox, we decided this arrangement might be more useful for your searching. Glad to hear you cared enough to ask!

Chapter 26
Does Web–Scale Discovery Make a Difference?
Changes in Collections Use after Implementing Summon

Jan Kemp
University of Texas at San Antonio, USA

ABSTRACT

The University of Texas at San Antonio Libraries implemented the Summon™[1] Discovery Service in January 2010 to provide a convenient starting point for library research, particularly for undergraduate students who are less experienced in library research. Librarians thought Summon™ would help users find and use materials more effectively; therefore, implementation of the discovery tool was expected to positively influence collections use. At the end of the first year following Summon™ implementation, statistics on the use of collections showed significant increases in the use of electronic resources: link resolver use increased 84%, and full-text article downloads increased 23%. During the same period, use of the online catalog decreased 13.7%, and use of traditional indexing and abstracting database searches decreased by 5%. The author concludes that the increases in collections use are related to adoption of a Web-scale discovery service.

DOI: 10.4018/978-1-4666-1821-3.ch026

INTRODUCTION

In 2010, the University of Texas at San Antonio (UTSA) Libraries implemented Serials Solutions'® Summon™ Web-scale discovery service. This study reports on the increases in the use of collections following the implementation. Summon™, like other discovery services, provides streamlined access to a wide range of library resources, both physical and electronic, including printed books, DVDs, e-books, online journal content and metadata from thousands of database producers and publishers, and local digital content such as image collections. Having a single search box interface and quick access to full-text material across databases and formats would presumably serve a range of users; however, it appeared to hold particular promise for undergraduate students.

As Web-scale discovery services began to appear over the past several years, the tools clearly had the potential to address the need for a student-friendly search option that would not require specialized instruction. With over 7,000 incoming freshmen each year and a student body of over 31,000, offering a more intuitive means of accessing collections would enable UTSA undergraduate students to be more self-sufficient and to connect with information resources easily—in effect, lowering the barrier to successful library research. The library assumed that following Summon™ implementation most graduate student and faculty research would continue to be conducted in subject-specific databases. The new discovery tool would serve as a safety net for undergraduates, providing 24/7 research support whether or not a student understood the difference between the catalog and a database, whether or not they knew how to select an appropriate database for their topic, and whether or not they understood the search process from the library perspective.

As one means of evaluating the effectiveness of Summon™, librarians planned to monitor collection use and compare post-Summon™ use with previous use. If a discovery tool can lower the barrier to effective library research, then the number of downloads of journal articles, for example, would be expected to rise as students made increased use of available resources. The purpose of a discovery tool is to help users successfully find and access library materials; examining changes in collection use would be one indication of the value of the service. The chapter discusses changes in the use of physical materials and electronic collections following Summon™ implementation, as well as marketing approaches the library employed to encourage Summon™ use. The discovery service has been in use since January 2010, and statistics for the first year of use demonstrate both the acceptance of Summon™ as a discovery tool and accompanying growth in the use of collections.

BACKGROUND: WEB-SCALE DISCOVERY SERVICES ENTER THE MARKET

One of the fastest-growing educational institutions in Texas, UTSA enrolls over 31,000 students in 64 undergraduate, 48 masters, and 22 doctoral programs. The university began offering classes in 1970, and its goals include expansion of the graduate programs and eventual status as a Tier One university. The library maintains four facilities on three campuses: the John Peace Library on the main campus; the Downtown Campus Library; the Applied Engineering and Technology (AET) Library, a 2,200 square-foot bookless satellite library on the main campus; and the Special Collections Manuscripts Unit at the HemisFair Park Campus. The library's collection includes 1,747,000 volumes (809,644 e-books), 3.2 million microform items, 68,866 current serial titles, and 375 electronic reference sources and aggregation services. In 2010, the library spent approximately 68% of its 5.6 million dollar collections budget on e-resources. The library has a staff of 105 full-time librarians and classified staff.

As the library's collections have expanded, particularly in electronic format, librarians were concerned that many students struggled to find appropriate research materials. UTSA librarians thought a Web-scale discovery service had the potential to improve students' access to materials, and they believed that improved access would likely result in increased use of the collections. Once implemented, librarians would need to determine whether the discovery service was usable and effective, and use of the collections would be one measure of success.

The UTSA Libraries had not offered a federated search engine before implementing a Web-scale discovery service. Without a federated search product, the library relied on its database list and e-journal locator to provide access to electronic resources, which were available from the library home page along with the link to the online catalog. Brief online instructional modules were created to help students find relevant books and articles and to help them identify and use appropriate databases for certain disciplines. The modules can be viewed at http://lib.utsa.edu/Research/tutorials.html. The modules were linked from within Blackboard, the course management system in use at UTSA; from many of the online LibGuides subject guides; and from the library home page. Although UTSA's databases and full-text e-journals offered a wealth of information, interactions with students indicated that the means of accessing the resources was confusing. At a previous institution where this author worked, even after a federated search product had been implemented, the goal of patron self-sufficiency was not achieved. During one reference interaction, an undergraduate business student listened patiently while the access path was explained to her, and she then inquired, "How would I have known that?"

In discussing this challenge for patrons, Doug Way noted, "In contrast to Google, the nature of library research with its silos of content spread among hundreds of databases with dozens of different interfaces seems both antiquated and daunting" (Way, 2010, p. 214). Way explained that federated searching was intended to enable students to perform library research "without having to select a specific database or the library catalog" (Way, 2010, p. 214). However, he noted that libraries experienced various problems with federated searching: it could be difficult to implement, provided slow response time, and limited the number of resources that could be simultaneously searched (2010). Marshall Breeding agreed that the goal of libraries should be to enable users to be self-sufficient and noted, "The complexities of the tools that libraries use to manage content and the bundles in which we acquire resources should be transparent to users" (Breeding, 2010, p. 32). He continued, "I think that users might be better served through a more unified approach in the way that it delivers access to all these different areas of content" (Breeding, 2010, p. 33).

Web-scale discovery services have been on the market for a relatively brief time, and for the most part, published information about the tools has discussed the rationale for implementing a discovery service, has listed methodologies for selection of a discovery service, or has enumerated features of the various services. Discovery service rationale, functionality, features, and content options have been described by various authors in the past few years (OCLC, 2009; Stevenson, 2009; Breeding, 2010; Brubaker, Leach-Murray, & Parker, 2011; Luther & Kelly, 2011; Notess, 2011; Vaughan, 2011).

Increased Use of Collections Noted With Discovery Services

Several authors have stated that the use of library collections can be an important indicator of the effectiveness of Web-scale discovery service, because usage provides evidence that patrons are more successfully finding and accessing research materials. In his 2011 *Library Technology Report* on Web-scale discovery services, Jason Vaughan noted, "Extensive research into whether these

Web-scale discovery services increase discovery and usage of publisher and aggregator content does not yet exist, though it seems reasonable to assume that if materials are more easily discoverable, they will be used more heavily and access statistics will increase" (Vaughan, 2011, p. 8). Luther and Kelly agreed, stating that "Early results indicate that while searches in the separate databases have declined, downloads of content from them have increased when discovery tools are used" (Luther & Kelley, 2011, p. 70).

In one of the few published studies discussing changes in collections use following discovery service implementation, Doug Way reported increased use of electronic collections after one semester of Summon™ use at Grand Valley State University. Following implementation, GVSU experienced a "sharp decline in database use combined with a steep increase in full-text downloads and link resolver click-throughs" which Way believed "suggests Summon™ had a dramatic impact on user behavior and the use of library collections during this time" (Way, 2010, p. 219). Similarly, in a presentation at the 2011 American Library Association annual conference, Rachel Vacek reported dramatic growth in the use of e-journal content from several major publishers following the Summon™ implementation at the University of Houston. The usage growth for a group of four selected publishers' journals ranged from approximately 30% to over 200% (2011). Tony Greiner, reporting one year after a World-Cat®2 Local implementation at three institutions, reported that Willamette University experienced a 54% increase in link resolver hits and Willamette and Portland Community College saw 29% and 24% increases respectively in full-text downloads. The schools also all experienced a decline in the use of the local physical collections along with a rise in interlibrary loan borrowing (2011). Luther and Kelly noted in their survey of the discovery service market, "Early results show increased usage of library databases" (Luther & Kelley, 2011, p. 70).

IMPLEMENTATION AND MARKETING SET THE STAGE

Implementation

While some writers recommend a deliberate review of the merits of discovery tools prior to purchase, Marshall Breeding has argued that time is of the essence for libraries in implementing discovery tools. "These strides in innovation on the resource discovery front will be made in vain unless libraries implement them expeditiously. I continue to observe sluggish adoption cycles despite the availability of many compelling products in both commercial and open source flavors" (Breeding, 2010, p. 34). The discovery service selection process at the UTSA Libraries could not have been described as sluggish. Following the library's review of discovery services options in late summer 2009, library administrators finalized the selection decision, and by the end of September the items necessary for implementation had been submitted. Among the factors influencing the selection of Summon™ was the fact that UTSA was already using Serials Solutions'® suite of services. The Summon™ implementation project required making modifications to over 1.3 million bibliographic records, preparation of a MARC mapping spreadsheet, and updating information about electronic resources content, among other efforts. In late November 2009, a task force initiated testing and provided feedback on UTSA's instance of the Summon™ service. Summon™ was made available to the public in January 2010.

Marketing and the Growth of Summon Use

For the first three months after implementation in January 2010, the library offered access to Summon™ via a link in the "Find Information" menu on the library home page, and use was quite low. During that time, the number of searches was fewer than 1,000 per month. In April 2010, a large

Figure 1. Library home page with Summon search box and Summon Mobile advertisement

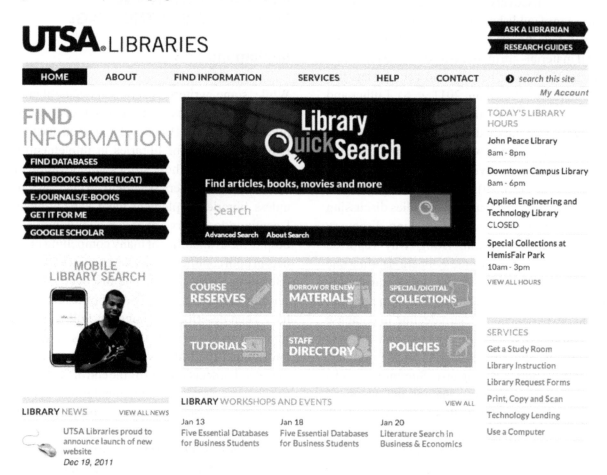

single search box was placed prominently on the library home page, as shown in Figure 1. In that month, searches jumped to more than 18,000. The library subsequently renamed the service "Library Quick Search," a name that was selected to communicate the purpose of the search tool to users.

Figure 2 shows the number of monthly searches conducted in Summon. Use grew quickly in the fall 2010 semester. 39,017 searches were logged in September, and Summon™ searching reached a semester high of 44,081 in November 2010. During this time, library staff explained the use of Summon™ in instruction sessions, at the information desk, and during individual consultations, as well as adding links to

LibGuides. Summon™ searches subsequently peaked at 46,085 in April 2011.

Summon Mobile Service

Marshall Breeding addressed the importance of delivering content and services to mobile users, stating, "The increasing preference to access resources by small mobile devices ranks as one of those trends that libraries cannot afford to ignore (Breeding, 2010, p. 33). Aware that undergraduate students particularly were mobile users, the library implemented Summon™ Mobile in Summer 2010 and created a 42-second video to promote the service (Williams & Peters, 2012). The video featured a charismatic library student

Figure 2. Monthly Summon™ searches, January 2010 – May 2011

assistant in the role of a Summon™ Mobile user and was intended to answer the question, "Why would I want to search library resources on my phone?" The Association of College and Research Libraries' (ACRL) Peer-Reviewed Instructional Materials Online Database (PRIMO) selected the Summon™ Mobile video for inclusion, and it can be viewed at http://lib.utsa.edu/Help/Summon/mobile.html. An advertisement for Summon™ Mobile with a link to the promotional video has been featured on the library home page in a rotating display since the service was implemented, and it continues to raise user awareness of the service (Figure 1).

Link Resolver Project Facilitates Full-Text Access

A 2009 report from OCLC discussed the results of a study to determine what end users want. The findings revealed that access to full-text is very important to users. "Discovery is important, but delivery is as important if not more important, than discovery. The findings suggest that a seamless, easy flow from discovery through delivery is critical to end users" (Calhoun, Cantrell, Gal-

lagher, Hawk & Cellentani, 2009, p. 20). Luther and Kelly agree, noting, "While link resolvers appear to be compatible, data management may be required to address holdings or other factors that receive new visibility" (Luther & Kelly, 2011, p. 68). This was the case with the UTSA Libraries' link resolver, and following Summon™ implementation the library undertook a project to improve the effectiveness of the link resolver to help make full-text retrieval more reliable. Previously some system-generated messages had been ambiguous or superfluous, and multiple links to resources sometimes resulted in a confusing set of options. A task force led by the electronic resources librarian improved the functionality of the link resolver by taking several actions.

The first step was to reprioritize the list of databases from which the link resolver retrieved full-text, to ensure that the most reliable resources were displayed at the top of the list. This step immediately improved the delivery of full-text, providing more consistent results. The group worked with the library's communications specialist to reword and reposition the messages displaying options and information to achieve greater clarity for the user. This included deleting unnecessary

Figure 3. Circulation and link resolver usage

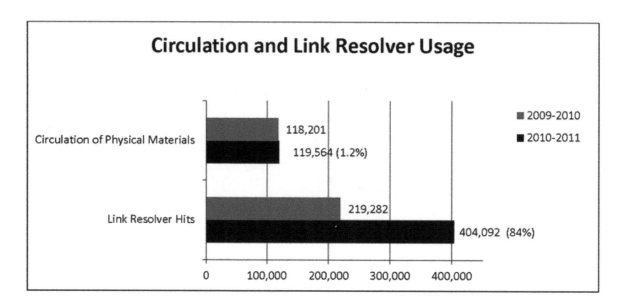

information (for example, the display of interlibrary loan as a default option, even when library owned an item) and adding other information that was missing (for example, a message asking the patron to please wait while the file loaded). Other changes included ensuring that the UTSA Libraries information would be present on intermediate pages, so users wouldn't feel lost when going from one resource to another. The "Ask-a-librarian" link was also added to the intermediate frame to provide user support.

CHANGES IN THE USE OF COLLECTIONS

Use of Physical Collections

The time periods for the statistics in this report are June 1, 2009 – May 31, 2010 and June 1, 2010 – May 31, 2011. The June – May period is used throughout the University for the annual strategic goals review process.

As illustrated in Figure 3, in the first full year of Summon™ use, initial circulations of printed books, DVDs, and other physical materials increased by 1.2% over the previous year. In effect, this was a slight drop in use, because enrollment increased by 4.5% from Fall 2009 to Fall 2010.

It should be mentioned that reserve materials were excluded from this circulation figure. In this particular year, most of UTSA's reserve circulation resulted from the use of high-demand undergraduate textbooks that were purchased for a textbook reserve lending project (Chang & Garrison, 2011). The reserve textbooks circulated very heavily, and if these materials had been included in the statistics, this use would have accounted for practically the entire increase in physical collections use. In fact, when reserve transactions are added to the circulation total, the library had a 32% increase in the use of physical collections, with a 30% increase in circulation by undergraduates. As encouraging as those figures appear, this usage is unrelated to the effect of a discovery service on the use of collections.

Figure 4. Database searches decrease / full-text accesses increase

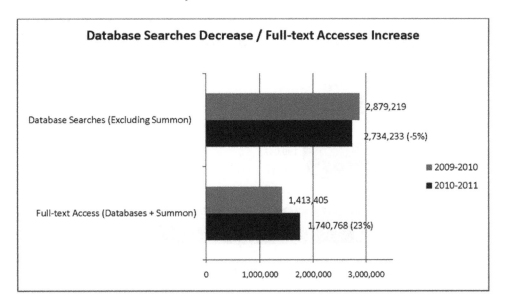

Increase in Link Resolver Use

Figure 3 also shows the number of click-throughs or hits to *360 Link* the library's link resolver. Since Summon™ functions only as an index, the link resolver is used each time a patron clicks on a link to view full-text material. From June 2010 through May 2011, the number of link resolver hits increased dramatically over the previous year from 219,282 to 404,092, an increase of 84%. The count reflects both Summon™ and individual database links. As Doug Way explains (2010), link resolver statistics indicate where the user of the link resolver is going (the source of the full-text), but unfortunately do not provide information on where the user was coming from—whether from Summon™ or another searching tool.

Summon™ does appear to be largely responsible for the increase in link resolver activity, since the number of searches in individual databases decreased by 5% during this time period (Figure 4). Statistics for the number of database searches were taken from the COUNTER Database Report 1 or Database Report 3. This count of database searches does not include Summon™ searches, because Summon™ does not actually search the databases in the traditional sense. Summon™ searches are executed in the massive single index developed and continuously updated by Serials Solutions which contains the metadata for articles, chapters, and other items in the commercial databases to which the library subscribes. Summon™ then uses the library's link resolver to connect to the full-text material from the subscribed database. Figure 5 also shows that use of the library's e-journal locator declined by 5% during this period. Meanwhile the number of Summon™ searches reached 347,548 in the first full year of use, an increase of 1,160% over the previous year (which included the first five months of Summon™ use, when use was quite low).

Database Searching Decreases while Full-Text Accesses Increase

As mentioned previously, database searching decreased slightly from the previous year; however, during this time, not only did link resolver hits increase, but full-text accesses (downloads) increased by 23%, as shown in Figure 4. As with

Figure 5. Summon™, e-journal locator, and OPAC searches

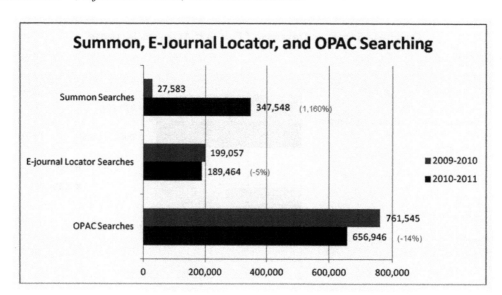

the link resolver statistics, the count of full-text accesses reflects the use of both Summon™ and the databases. Doug Way provides detailed statistics on the use of specific databases and journal collections in his one-semester study of Summon™ use, noting that some resources saw increases in use while others declined or stayed the same—a pattern (or an apparent lack of pattern) that also held true at UTSA. Way's analysis of the five thousand journal titles with the highest use in 2008 showed that "On average, these journals saw their use increase by sixty-six per cent, totaling an additional 81,371 click-throughs" (Way, 2010, p. 218). The 66% increase in click-throughs at GVSU is interesting to compare with UTSA's increase of 84%; the increases in use of electronic resources are of similar magnitude at the two institutions. Note that a decreasing number of database searches would not be likely to cause a library to consider canceling database subscriptions, since Summon™ itself does not include the full-text content from the databases. The databases would still be needed to provide the library with access to the full-text content. The Summon™ model has been described as a Google for the library's academic content—an index that helps people discover information.

Decreases in E-Journal Locator Use and OPAC Searches

Figure 5 compares Summon™ use with decreases in the use of two other search tools, the e-journal locator and the online catalog. From the standpoint of user self-sufficiency, these decreases can be seen as positive changes. Users searched the e-journal locator 5% less frequently, and OPAC searches declined by 14% after Summon™ implementation. While the e-journal locator has been a necessary tool in libraries, lower use may indicate that fewer users now need to employ this approach to accessing journal content. The decline in OPAC searches may indicate that the single search box now serves in place of the catalog for some patrons. Particularly for undergraduates, using a single search box for a range of types of library materials may free them from the need to have specialized information on finding and accessing library resources. It has the potential to save the time of the user and to save less experienced users from frustration and abandoned searches.

Discussion

An obvious question to ask is how much credit Summon™ deserves for the increase in the use of electronic materials. The precept that the library is a living organism remains true, and in fact, a number of other changes took place during the year that may have affected collection use. Enrollment increased from 28,955 in Fall 2009 to 30,258 in Fall 2010, a 4.5% increase. The main campus library reopened several new spaces following a renovation project that extended the Information Commons, added a large quiet study room, and created space for the university tutoring and writing center programs. The library gate count increased by 49% over the previous year. These facts notwithstanding, 347,000 Summon™ searches were logged during the year, and usage of the link resolver increased by 84%, paired with a 23% increase in full-text accesses. At the same time, use of the library's other search tools for electronic resources decreased: e-journal locator and database searches both declined by 5%.

The use of the library's physical collections did not increase following implementation. However, the use of these materials remained relatively steady at a time when "the use of academic libraries' physical collections—especially of printed books—is dropping" (Anderson, 2011, p. 38). A related point to consider is that the library's expenditures for physical materials represent a smaller percentage of the collections budget each year, and in many disciplines, electronic has been designated as the preferred format for purchase. Given these facts, the use of printed materials by faculty and graduates students would naturally be expected to trend downward in those disciplines where a growing percentage of new scholarly books are acquired in digital form. In the past year, over 350,000 Electronic Book Library (EBL) titles were loaded into the UTSA online catalog (and thus into Summon™) as part of a patron-driven acquisitions plan. This approach extends the user's access to research materials in electronic format.

Although the physical collection also grows, it does not grow at a comparable rate.

Although librarians thought the principal users of the discovery tool would be the undergraduates who wanted a familiar Google-like interface and immediate full-text results, the tool has proven valuable to more advanced researchers as well. Information about these successes is anecdotal, but it shows the discovery tool in a good light from an academic standpoint. One situation involved a doctoral student in the counseling field who was having difficulty finding material on a relatively new topic related to community counseling. She asked her subject librarian for assistance, since the subject-specific databases had not been helpful. A Summon™ search yielded good results—perhaps indicating that in some cases the discovery tool's indexing responds more nimbly to searches for very new topics than the previous generation of search tools could. In another case, an administrator was surprised to find material she had never come across before in her field of research when she used Summon™ for the first time. As Vaughan has noted, discovery services are continually adding new features and attempting to optimize their search strategies (2011). The next year the discovery service may provide options that will further increase its effectiveness.

FUTURE RESEARCH DIRECTIONS

The Web-scale discovery environment is evolving continuously, and options for further research will be extensive. At a minimum, libraries may want to compare the statistics for discovery tools from year-to-year to determine if there is a correlation between the growth of searches and the use of electronic materials. Libraries will undoubtedly monitor the number of discovery searches to learn whether the use continues to increase, flattens, or decreases over time, and to determine whether marketing affects use. Libraries may want to conduct focus groups and usability testing to learn whether aspects of the user interface should be changed, to determine if patrons are satisfied with the search results, and to learn whether the tool enables students to be self-sufficient searchers. Subject librarians can compare search results from subject-specific databases with discovery tool searches to learn about the strengths of various searching options. For example, libraries could investigate anecdotal reports that discovery tools are especially useful for interdisciplinary research by testing it against the results from several subject-specific databases. A wide range of discovery topics related to instruction could be undertaken; for example, bibliographies from student research papers using a discovery tool as a primary searching tool could be compared with bibliographies for the same assignment from a traditional interdisciplinary database.

CONCLUSION

Statistics indicate that UTSA library users have accepted the Summon™ discovery tool and are using it in increasing numbers. Librarians expected Summon™ to help users find materials more effectively due to its intuitive interface and cross-platform searching capabilities, and in the first year after implementing Summon™, the library experienced a marked increased in the use of electronic resources. Given Summon™'s simple interface paired with improved access to high quality, full-text academic content; perhaps the discovery tool's great strength will be its ability to lower the bar of inquiry for students. With discovery, students do not need to know which database to select before they start their research, and they do not need to know what an OPAC is. Students can easily search at will, and this affords them a better environment in which to develop ownership of their own learning, to develop the habit of inquiry.

REFERENCES

Anderson, R. (2011). Print on the margins. *Library Journal, 136*(11), 38–39.

Breeding, M. (2010). The state of the art in library discovery. *Computers in Libraries, 30*(1), 31–35.

Brubaker, N., Leach-Murray, S., & Parker, S. (2011). Shapes in the cloud: Finding the right discovery layer. *Online, 35*(2), 20–26.

Calhoun, K. Cantrell, J., Gallagher, P., Hawk, J., & Cellentani, D. (2009). *Online catalogs: What users and librarians want: An OCLC report.* Dublin, OH: OCLC Online Computer Library Center, Inc. Retrieved from http://www.oclc.org/us/en/reports/onlinecatalogs/fullreport.pdf

Chang, A., & Garrison, J. (2011). Textbook lending service: Providing a service students need when they need it. *College & Research Libraries News, 72*(9), 527–530.

Greiner, T. (2011, March). *How does switching to a discovery tool affect circulation?* Paper presented at the conference of the Association of College and Research Libraries, Philadelphia, PA. Retrieved July 26th, 2011, from http://www.ala.org/ala/mgrps/divs/acrl/events/national/2011/papers/how_does_switching.pdf

Luther, J., & Kelly, M. (2011). The next generation of discovery: The stage is set for a simpler search for users, but choosing a product is much more complex. *Library Journal, 136*(5), 66–71.

Notess, G. R. (2011). Deciphering discovery. *Online, 35*(1), 45–47.

Stevenson, K. (2009). Next-generation library catalogues: Reviews of Encore, Primo, Summon, and Summa. *Serials, 22*(1), 68–82. doi:10.1629/2268

Vacek, R. (2011, June). *Discovery @ the University of Houston Libraries.* Presentation at the Conference of the American Library Association, New Orleans, LA. Retrieved July 27th, 2011, from http://www.slideshare.net/vacekrae/discovery-at-the-university-of-houston-libraries

Vaughan, J. (2011). Web scale discovery services. *Library Technology Reports, 47*(1), 1–62.

Way, D. (2010). The impact of Web-scale discovery on the use of a library collection. *Serials Review, 36*(4), 214–220. doi:10.1016/j.serrev.2010.07.002

Williams, H., & Peters, A. (2012). (forthcoming). And that's how I connect to my library: How a 42-second promotional video helped to launch the UTSA Libraries' new Summon Mobile application. *The Reference Librarian, 53*(3).

ADDITIONAL READING

Ballard, T. (2011). Comparison of user search behaviors with classic online catalogs and discovery platforms. *Charleston Advisor, 12*(3), 65–66. doi:10.5260/chara.12.3.65

Breeding, M. (2011). Discovering Harry Pottery barn. *Computers in Libraries, 31*(2), 21–23.

Connaway, L., Dickey, T., & Radford, M. (2011). "If it is too inconvenient, I'm not going after it:" Convenience as a critical factor in information-seeking behaviors. *Library & Information Science Research, 33*(3), 179–190. doi:10.1016/j.lisr.2010.12.002

Gross, J., & Sheridan, L. (2011). Web scale discovery: The user experience. *New Library World, 112*(5/6), 236–247. doi:10.1108/03074801111136275

Hanson, C., Hessel, H., Barneson, J., Boudewyns, D., Fransen, J., & Friedman-Shedlov, L. ... Traill, S. (2009). *Discoverability phase 1 final report.* University of Minnesota Libraries. Retrieved from http://purl.umn.edu/48258

Hanson, C., Hessel, H., Barneson, J., Boudewyns, D., Fransen, J., & Friedman-Shedlov, L. ... Traill, S. (2011). *Discoverability phase 2 final report.* University of Minnesota Libraries. Retrieved from http://purl.umn.edu/99734

Newcomer, N. (2011). Summon. *Music Reference Services Quarterly, 14*(1/2), 59–62. doi:10.1080/10588167.2011.571502

Rowe, R. (2010). Web-scale discovery: A review of Summon, EBSCO Discovery Service, and WorldCat Local. *Charleston Advisor, 12*(1), 5–10. doi:10.5260/chara.12.1.5

Schonfeld, R., & Housewright, R. (2010). Discovery and the evolving role of the library. In *Faculty Survey 2009: Key Strategic Insights for Libraries, Publishers, and Societies* (pp. 1-13). New York, NY: Ithaka S+R. http://www.ithaka.org/ithaka-s-r/research/faculty-surveys-2000-2009/Faculty%20Study%202009.pdf.

Stone, G. (2010). Searching life, the universe, and everything? The implementation of Summon at the University of Huddersfield. *The Library Quarterly, 20*(1), 25–52.

Timpson, H., & Sansom, G. (2011). A student perspective on e-resource discovery: Has the Google factor changed publisher platform searching forever? *The Serials Librarian, 61*(2), 253–266. doi:10.1080/0361526X.2011.592115

Yang, S., & Wagner, K. (2010). Evaluating and comparing discovery tools: How close are we toward the next generation catalog? *Library Hi Tech, 28*(4), 690–709. doi:10.1108/07378831011096312

KEY TERMS AND DEFINITIONS

COUNTER (Counting Online Usage of Networked Electronic Resources): An organization of libraries: vendors and content aggregators who have developed and maintained an international set of standards for the recording and reporting of electronic collections usage data.

Discovery tool: See "Web-scale discovery service" above.

Full-Text Accesses Or Downloads: A full-text access occurs and is counted each time a user downloads the full-text of an item.

General Collection: For the purposes of this discussion, physical materials in the library collection excluding special collections and materials in electronic format.

Link Resolver: A product that provides users with access to the library's full-text resources by linking from the citation to the full-text of an item. In some cases, a library has access to a full-text item from multiple resource aggregators, and the link-resolver can be configured to retrieve the full-text from the aggregator that provides the most reliable service.

Link Resolver Hits or Click-Throughs: A hit or click-through occurs and is counted each time a user clicks on a citation for an item, and the link resolver retrieves the full-text.

Physical Materials: For the purpose of this discussion, physical materials includes printed books, bound journals, DVDs, videocassettes, and other library collections items owned in physical format, as opposed to electronic format. This term excludes equipment and group study room (facilities) items that may be circulated, but are not part of the research collections.

Web-Scale Discovery Service: A service that searches pre-harvested remote full-text and indexed content (e-journals, databases, e-books, etc.) simultaneously with a library's local holdings to provide the user with relevancy-ranked results across all types of materials and formats. The service provides a simple, single search box as a starting point for research, freeing users from the need to identify the appropriate database or search tool.

ENDNOTES

[1] Summons is owned by ProQuest LLC

[2] Worldcat is a registered trademark of OCLC

Chapter 27
Catalog Maintenance and Authority Control in Discovery Systems:
A Survey of Early Adopters

Pamela Harpel-Burke
Hofstra University, USA

ABSTRACT

With the implementation of discovery systems, cataloging maintenance and authority control activities need to be re-evaluated. The online survey product Qualtrics™[1] was used to solicit completion of only one survey per library (275) who has adopted a discovery system. Questions about changes in tasks and staffing before and after implementation of commercial discovery systems (AquaBrowser®[2], EBSCO Discovery Services™[3], Encore™[4], Primo®[5], Summon™[6], and WorldCat®[7] Local) were central to the survey. Ninety-eight libraries responded with usable surveys (36% response rate). Results indicated that there were no significant differences between maintenance and authority control tasks before and after discovery implementation. Although the length of time since implementation compared to workflow changes indicates that change decreases over time, effects of the discovery system may not yet have reached maintenance and authority control staff. Cataloging staff were also surveyed to measure their awareness on how local holdings in the new discovery environment are presented to the public. Results also indicate that significantly more survey respondents anticipate that their legacy OPAC will persist alongside their discovery system.

DOI: 10.4018/978-1-4666-1821-3.ch027

INTRODUCTION

Web-scale discovery systems are the most recent configuration in the evolution of library collection finding tools. Originally, the online public access catalog (OPAC) searched and retrieved results only for locally-held materials, providing local information such as shelving location and circulation status. As libraries began to provide materials outside of the OPAC, such as electronic databases and full-text journal articles, separate indexes were mounted on their Web sites. In order to complete a search of the library's resources beyond the OPAC, users were compelled to consult several disparate silos of information on the library's Web site. In an attempt to address this disjointed approach to information and service delivery, federated search or metasearch products such as, WebFeat[8] and MetaLib[9], became available.

Federated search takes real-time queries and broadcasts them to multiple information targets, such as the integrated library system (ILS), digital collections, proprietary databases, i.e., ProQuest[10], EBSCOhost[11], etc. (Breeding, 2010). Although this approach addressed the problem of users being forced to consult several separate indexes and catalogs, additional problems arose. With no centralized indexes, results of the search were scattered and often only a limited number of results from each database were retrieved. All of these factors combined to make it tedious to determine relevancy rankings for results.

The next stage in the OPAC's evolution was the next-generation discovery interface. The simple vision was to provide a single point of entry to both remote and local content and services offered by the library (Breeding, 2010). In addition to a single search box, the next-generation discovery interface offers faceted navigation, search aids (i.e., did you mean?), relevance ranked results, and displays such as book covers and summaries. Initial products focused on technology and locally-installed software. This approach was based more on products that were locally installed. In this study, AquaBrowser[®], Ex-Libris' Primo[®] and Innovative Interfaces'[®12] Encore™ are examples of these interfaces.

The current phase of discovery systems focuses on pre-populated indexes that strive to provide Web-scale discovery (Breeding, 2010). These indexes generally include harvested local content (ILS, digital collections) and harvested vendor-supplied indexes of library content (electronic journals, research databases, and full-text of articles). Along with other amenities from the discovery interface, the single search box remains. Searches now successfully reach outside of the local library's collection. In this study, Web-scale discovery services include EBSCO Discovery Services™ (EDS™), Serials Solutions' Summon™, OCLC's WorldCat[®] Local, Ex-Libris' Primo Central™, and Innovative Interfaces'[®] Encore Synergy™.

Cataloging within the Discovery System[13]

How will the current role of the cataloging department adapt to include oversight of the local collection within the discovery system? The discovery service shifts the focus from the catalog of hundreds of thousands of items to "the *hundreds of millions* of items not present in the ILS —the massive, current, growing body of journal articles, newspaper articles, conference proceedings" (Vaughan, 2011, p. 50). Traditional OPAC functions (i.e., holds, requests) may be fully integrated into the discovery system or require the library to continue its legacy OPAC for real-time information. As Vaughan (2011) emphasizes, "the pool of traditional library holdings- physical items cataloged into the ILS- is not the shining star and chief selling point for Web-scale discovery" (Vaughan, 2011, p.50).

Although other search options are available, the discovery services rely heavily on faceted navigation and keyword searching. Systems with an article focus (such as in EDS™ and Summon™)

may also use indexes specific to the database being searched. Within the ILS, however, the cataloging department generally provides Library of Congress Subject Headings. Will these records become lost in the sea of records from the discovery service?

According to research on OPAC transactions, catalog users generally avoid subject searching already (Moulaison, 2008; Antell & Huang, 2008). However, Gross and Taylor (2005) underscore the importance of a controlled vocabulary in generating useful keyword searches. Subject headings may also be a factor in relevancy ranking, as in EDS™. Nevertheless, the ongoing debate concerning keyword vs. controlled vocabulary searching will continue and is not the focus of this study.

In-house procedures and workflows will need to be adjusted so that newly cataloged items are integrated into this single unified index of library content. Even if the legacy OPAC is still presented separately to users, decisions about ongoing quality control must be considered. With discovery systems, "the portion for which a local library … may have been responsible is small and getting smaller" (Hill, 2008, p. 20). After implementation, decisions made for the previous local environment may be inconsistent with the discovery system environment and the reality of following them may become irrational.

Authority control and cross-referencing practices may also be in place for authors, subjects and uniform titles. Catalog departments may rely on in-house personnel or outsource authority work to a vendor (Wolverton, 2005). In addition to the ongoing authority control for newly-acquired materials, older items in the catalog are affected by updates to the Library of Congress subject headings and changes made for authors whose authority records have been updated to reflect their death. Libraries today rely on various sources for bibliographic and authority records that follow national standards. Therefore, consistency of these records cannot be ignored. Decisions regarding authority control vary by library.

Survey of Early Adopters

The central focus of the survey was catalog maintenance and authority control activities in relation to discovery systems. Catalog maintenance focuses on "the quality of individual records … and the quality (accuracy, extent, and usability) of the overall catalog structure" (Hill, 2008, p. 12). Authority control attempts to collocate and maintain consistency of name, subject, series and uniform titles. In the ILS, these two components of the cataloging workflow are intertwined in their focus on database integrity. Modifications are constantly made to provide better access for catalog users. Other maintenance activities may include resolving system-generated errors (i.e., MARC tags, filing indicators, etc.), correction of spelling errors and responding to problems reported by catalog users. Catalog records may also be upgraded to reflect current cataloging changes.

Does the implementation of a discovery system affect catalog maintenance and authority control activities in academic libraries? Are there changes in tasks and staffing after implementation? In addition, how are local holdings presented to the public? Are they intermingled with the other resources or presented separately from the discovery system? Are the cataloging staff aware of how their maintenance and authority control efforts display in the public interface?

To answer these questions, a target group of academic libraries with discovery systems were surveyed on their catalog maintenance and authority activities. The libraries were at various stages of implementation. Six commercial products were examined: EBSCO Discovery Service™, Encore™, Primo®, Serials Solutions'® products Summon™ and AquaBrowser® and OCLC World-Cat® Local. Insight from early adopters of these discovery systems can guide libraries in their transition. There was no intention of endorsing or censuring any of these discovery products. The primary focus was to examine post-implementation effects of discovery systems in general on catalog maintenance and authority control.

Because it is a major player in the discovery landscape WorldCat® Local was included in the survey even though its structure for local materials differs considerably from the other products. With WorldCat® Local, local bibliographic data is drawn directly from the master record in WorldCat®. All WorldCat® Local users see the same bibliographic record; holdings information is culled from each library's ILS. Cataloging emphasis is at the network level; the catalog maintenance and authority work is not reflected locally.

LITERATURE REVIEW

Due to their recent evolution from next-generation catalogs to Web-scale discovery systems, little has been published on the impacts of discovery systems to cataloging departments. Early implementation of WorldCat® Local was covered extensively by Ward, Shadle and Mofjeld (2008). Zhu has provided insights on the catalog department's part in Washington State University's implementation of-WorldCat® Local (2009 & 2010). Presentations at American Library Association conferences by early adopters (Gowing, 2008; Lasater, 2008; Pennell, 2007; Pennell, 2008) and experts (Breeding, 2008) on these evolving interfaces were essential in identifying how MARC cataloging data would be translated and viewed in these new interfaces. Pennell (2008) specifically stressed the importance of data cleanup for faceted navigation. Subject headings would need to be regularized for form of material (subfields v and x), time period (subfield y) and geography (subfield z) (Pennell, 2008).

Nuan (2010) looks at these new interfaces in conjunction with how "established cataloging practices are coming under increased scrutiny" (p. 331). Existing catalog data from the traditional ILS is manipulated and repackaged for use in these new systems. Wynne and Hanscom (2011) seriously examine how these systems may affect catalogers and cataloging functions. With a survey posted on Autocat (an international discussion list for catalogers), they took the first major step toward understanding how these systems affect cataloging functions after implementation. They surveyed the involvement of catalogers from the implementation stage through to changes in procedures, workflow and personnel in cataloging after implementation. In their limitations section, they note that they "did not attempt to gather a representative sample of institutions of individuals" (Wynne & Hanscom, 2011, p. 184). They also pointed out the possibility that there was more than one respondent per institution since they did not gather identifying information about the respondent's institution. This factor led to the targeted survey of those libraries who had implemented a discovery system.

However, the aspect of quality control in the discovery environment has not been sufficiently addressed. Hill (2008) provides an excellent overview by providing a descriptive timeline of the decisions that have been involved with database quality. She begins with the one user/independent library scenario and guides readers through the advent of shared cataloging via multiple sources. Now that libraries are moving away from the local catalog toward discovery systems she points out that "the old decisions may at the very least appear to be inconsistent, and adherence to them may no longer be realistic" (Hill, 2008, p. 11). Thus, catalog maintenance and its close associate authority control are ripe for exploration within the discovery environment.

SURVEY METHODOLOGY

Targeting Libraries

In April 2011, the advanced options mode at Marshall Breeding's *lib-web-cats* on the Library Technology Guides Web site (www.librarytechnology.org) was used to identify the target sample of libraries for the survey. Searches were limited to academic libraries in the United States. Additional limits were by "discovery interface": AquaBrowser®, EDS™, Encore™, Primo®, Summon™, and WorldCat® Local. Results often included a main library and its branches. For example, the University of New Hampshire was identified as an Encore™ user along with these four libraries: Biological Sciences, Chemistry, Engineering, Math and Computer Science, and Physics. In such cases, links were verified to ensure that the affiliated libraries led to the same Web site. Law and medical libraries were excluded from the sample.

Vendors were also contacted for a client list to supplement the sample pool. Vendors were informed of this upcoming IGI book, the sample from *lib-web-cats*, and the nature of the survey. They were also assured that their clients' responses would be anonymous and not tied to specific libraries. Two vendors supplied lists of clients who had given permission for the release of their names. There was no response from the other vendors.

Identifying Contact Persons

Each library's Web site was consulted to determine a specific contact person, using the link supplied by *lib-web-cats*. Generally, the "about us" link or tab was initially followed. The staff directory section was explored for the name, title and email of the contact. If there was no clear link to a staff directory or departmental functions, the 2011 edition of the *American Library Directory* was used for clues. The person closest to workflow was contacted for catalog maintenance and/or authority control. In general, librarians and administrators were favored as contact persons. However, for smaller universities, information often led to support staff so the contact may have been as high as the library director. In situations where it was unclear which person was responsible for these tasks, information was collected for two people who may have been able to answer the survey.

Generally, catalog librarians or technical services librarians were contacted.

Emails via Qualtrics

Qualtrics (an online survey and analysis product) was used to build email lists and the actual survey. The author's email address was used to avoid spam filters. Each email contained a unique URL for the survey and the closing date of July 15, 2011. The contact's name, university, and position title were pulled from embedded data for a more personalized email. Contacts were asked to forward the message to another representative of their library if someone else was better able to answer the survey. The messages assured anonymity of responses and that only summary data would be reported in the results. A link to opt out of the survey was also included; two people took this option.

In early June 2011, 275 emails were sent out via Qualtrics to users of AquaBrowser® (62), EDS™ (14), Encore™ (107), Primo® (29), Summon™ (27), and WorldCat® Local (36) via Qualtrics. Follow-up reminder emails (211) were sent to non-respondents in three weeks and the last week of the survey (191). In the final reminder, a second contact was used when available.

QUESTIONS ASKED

The author drew from 23 years experience as a cataloger and database manager at several libraries to construct the catalog maintenance and authority control questions for the survey. She also relied on her committee involvement and participation in American Library Association conferences, a review of technical services Web sites, and the listserv Autocat. Research by Wynne and Hanscom (2011) was particularly useful in identifying catalog maintenance issues that are exposed with discovery systems. The effect that the discovery system had on these activities was of particular interest. The aim was to determine if some of the tasks were abandoned after the discovery system was in place, and whether staffing had shifted to deal with more problems.

The survey has not been reproduced in its entirety here because data analysis is ongoing. Only questions discussed in this paper are included in the Appendix (see Appendix: *Survey of Discovery systems and catalog maintenance*).

After identifying their institution, the first question on the survey asked the name of the discovery system. Product names were included with their parent company. Options included: AquaBrowser®, EBSCO Discovery Service™, Encore™ or Encore Synergy™, Primo® or Primo Central™, Summon™ and WorldCat® Local. Two products by the same company were paired with their earliest and latest iteration of their discovery tool and will be referred to as Encore™ and Primo® throughout the chapter.

General demographic questions were also asked: ILS, highest degree offered at the institution, size of the student body in FTEs (full-time equivalent) and the respondent's position in the library. Libraries that were not in charge of their own cataloging were weeded out. If the library is not responsible for its cataloging, authority control or maintenance tasks are rarely included in the workflow.

Authority Control and Catalog Maintenance Tasks

Specific authority control and catalog maintenance tasks were presented in matrices with categories for staff (support staff, cataloger, vendor) and "before and after" implementation. Qualtrics calls this question type "side by side"; this presentation has questions in a grid with questions next to each other in a column format with rows of questions for each column. There was also an option to indicate if these tasks were "Not Done" pre- and post-implementation. In each matrix, participants were also given the opportunity to write in tasks not given in the survey.

Specific authority control tasks (question 7) performed at many libraries were listed in the matrix: authority control of subject headings, name headings, and series and/or uniform titles. Also included was "periodic review of LC subject heading updates (via weekly lists or *Cataloging Service Bulletin-CSB*)". Cataloging departments rely on regular updates to LC subject headings which are posted on the LC Web site. The *CSB*, a quarterly publication, was also used for new and changed subject headings until the title ceased in late 2010. Another task "periodic review of death dates to name headings" refers to name authority records that have been modified with that author's death date.

This matrix did not address at what point in the workflow authority work was done or how it was accomplished. A library may have several workflows for authorities. In some libraries, heading verification is addressed at the point of cataloging by various levels of staff, or there may be a specific unit or staff member who is primarily responsible for these tasks. Libraries may also rely heavily on reports generated by the library's integrated library system (ILS). When a vendor is used, authority control may be initially addressed by their automated systems but flagged headings may still be examined by staff.

Tasks included in the catalog maintenance (question 8) grid were duplicate detection and merging of bibliographic records, MARC indicator corrections that affect access (i.e., "the"), spelling/typographical error corrections, upgrading of bibliographic records to reflect current cataloging practices, diacritics and punctuation. One task that was given, "modifications to the gmd (245 $h)", refers to the general material designation, the medium for non-print materials which is in the title field surrounded by brackets. Diacritics are the marks that appear above or below an alphabetic character, such as the tilde in "señor". They often cause display and retrieval problems in OPACs. Two other tasks are particularly relevant in the discovery environment are coding in the 008/fixed fields and MARC tag corrections (i.e., obsolete coding). The fixed fields contain codes of a predetermined length which represent information on the material type, language, and several other factors. MARC fields with obsolete coding, specifically subject headings with form subdivisions which tell the user that the item being described is in that format are (i.e., biography) *not* about it. Correct fixed field coding and coding in MARC tags are necessary for faceted navigation in discovery systems.

The final "before and after" category addressed the number of full-time equivalents (FTE) that were dedicated strictly to authority control or catalog maintenance activities (question 10). Respondents were given four options and were asked to exclude student workers and to check each box that was applicable to them.

Respondents evaluated the changes to their catalog maintenance activities to get a better sense of how they were affected by the discovery systems. They were asked to exclude one-time clean-up projects in their assessment (question 9).

Public Interface of Local Holdings

Familiarity with the public catalog is essential to good cataloging, and, hence, good catalog maintenance. As a cataloger, the author often views the MARC record in the public display to see it as the user sees it. Changes made to records in the back office may not display in the OPAC because of system settings, or the changes that looked good to the cataloger may not make sense to the user. With the discovery system, the cataloger needs to know how the data displays in both the legacy OPAC and the public interface of their new system. There were two questions designed to address these points.

In one question, cataloger familiarity through frequency of use with the public catalog interface of their discovery system (question 5) was assessed. Respondents were able to categorize their answers into always, sometimes and never

categories. They were asked if they had used the interface, if they used it for their own needs (i.e., research, reading), and if they provide reference services. More specifically, they were asked if catalog records were viewed during cataloging or maintenance.

In addition to this question about the public interface of their discovery system, they were asked if the traditional OPAC was still in use (question 6). The four options included: No, we do not use it; I don't know; Yes we have not made plans to abandon it; and Yes and we plan to abandon it.

RESULTS

Surveys Completed

Of the 275 surveys mailed, 118 surveys were started (=43% initial response rate). Some of these were not useful for data manipulation; ten were incomplete with insufficient data, eight of those contacted had no system; and two institutions answered in duplicate (see Figure 1.) Thus, 98 surveys provided at least some viable data for analysis in this study, bringing the actual response rate to 36%. Encore™/Encore Synergy™ was the most widely used system overall, thirty-one survey respondents choosing this option; eighteen used Summon™; eighteen used WorldCat® Local; Primo®/Primo Central™ was used by fourteen respondents; eight used AquaBrowser®; EBSCO Discovery Systems was used by only five. Four users indicated 'Other' and two were using a combination of discovery interfaces: Primo® with Summon™ and WorldCat® Local with EDS™. OCLC WMS (OCLC Web-scale Management) and "transitioning from WorldCat® Local to Summon™" were the other responses. For the purposes of this survey, all four of these answers were tabulated in the 'Other' category of discovery system.

Depending on the question, some of the 98 surveys could not be included in the data tabula-

Figure 1. Received surveys: by discovery system & viability

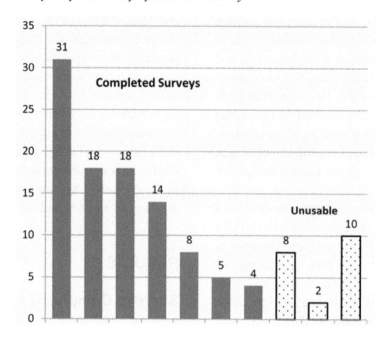

tions that follow. From these 98 usable surveys, five were unfinished but were used when they had the data supplied. Three libraries indicated that it was too early to give valid answers on the "after" portions of the matrices questions. Five libraries outsourced their cataloging and were unable to complete the survey. Thus, the sample size varies for each data tabulation following.

Before-After Data Pairs Tests

In several of the questions, participants were asked to provide before and after implementation assessments of their activities. These will be referred to as before-after data pairs throughout the paper. Five sets of before-after data pairs were examined. Significant differences between before-after pairs where the value of either cell <5 occurrences were not tested because these sample sizes are too small for accurate X^2 tests. Other before-after data pairs were tested for significant differences using two-tailed X^2 tests and $\alpha = 0.05$. There was no significant difference found for these pairs (all $p > 0.5$),.

In the first set, the examination sought to ascertain if the discovery system itself had any effect on the authority control tasks performed. Within this group, changes in levels of staff who perform these authority tasks were also analyzed (see Table 1). Catalog maintenance tasks were also looked at for staff and discovery system changes (see Table 2). The number of FTEs dedicated to catalog or authority control tasks before and after implementation was also examined.

Authority Control and Catalog Maintenance Tasks

The final "before and after" category dealt exclusively with the number of FTE staff for catalog maintenance and authority control (question 10). Overall there was a negligible amount of change. For catalog maintenance, there was only a slight change in the "1 to 1.9" group; there were 17 FTE before and 14 after. For both authority control and catalog maintenance, the other groups changed by + or − 1. The largest group for both was "up to .9" with respondents totaling 33 FTE before

Table 1. Authority control tasks by staff and tasks: responses

	Support		Cataloger		Vendor		Not Done	
	Before	**After**	**Before**	**After**	**Before**	**After**	**Before**	**After**
LCSH	38	38	68	64	42	40	11	10
LCSH Review	19	20	38	32	16	14	28	30
Name	44	42	63	62	41	38	8	9
Death Dates	23	20	38	32	42	40	31	29
Uniform Titles	36	32	57	54	32	31	17	18

Note: There were no significant differences between any sufficiently large (n≥5) before-after data pairs (all p>0.5).

Table 2. Catalog maintenance tasks by staff and tasks: responses

	Support		Cataloger		Vendor		Not Done	
	Before	**After**	**Before**	**After**	**Before**	**After**	**Before**	**After**
MARC	56	53	60	59	18	18	11	9
Indicators	62	57	61	56	16	18	4	4
Ffields	45	42	56	53	12	13	8	7
Duplicate records	50	48	48	50	7	7	9	10
Spelling	67	68	63	60	3	3	3	4
Upgrade	43	40	46	43	5	6	20	20
Diacritics	39	34	43	42	11	11	16	15
GMD	42	38	50	46	7	8	16	17
Punctuation	49	46	46	42	9	9	22	22

Note: There were no significant differences between any sufficiently large (n≥5) before-after data pairs (all p>0.5).

and 32 after for catalog maintenance. Authority control responses totaled 35 FTE before and 36 after implementation.

In the authority control tasks matrix, there were no significant differences between any sufficiently large (n≥5) before-after data pairs (all p>0.5). One problem with the format of the question for both the authority control and catalog maintenance tasks was the "Other" category. Respondents were expected to supply information that was not supplied in the survey in both of these

areas. Unfortunately, results in this category were confusing in several ways. This was not the best way to solicit this information. Respondents did not always choose a staff level or a before and/or after category. In addition, Qualtrics included the text given under 'Other' under each staff level. It was difficult to manipulate the answers and determine their accurate category. The number of written responses did not equal what the Qualtrics software had calculated for either matrix. After considering all of these difficulties, the results

Table 3. Discovery systems and workflow changes

System	Yes	No	Don't Know	Totals
EDS™	1	1	3	5
Encore™	3	22	4	29
Primo®	2	7	3	12
Summon™	1	12	3	16
WorldCat® Local	7	6	4	17
Other	2	1	1	4
AquaBrowser®	0	6	1	7
	16	55	19	**90**

of the "Other" category was also discarded from analysis for both of these matrices.

Most of the fourteen "Other" responses in the authority matrix addressed the varied ways that each cataloging department deals with authority control. Most of the answers (seven) dealt with interactions between the vendor and the cataloging department. One respondent answered: "Authority work performed by vendor, based on records submitted during our implementation of Voyager, not all records in our database are processed by that vendor". The rest of the responses involved either consortial authority control or how ILS system supplied reports were used.

In the catalog maintenance tasks matrix, there were no significant differences between any sufficiently large (n≥5) before-after data pairs (all p>0.5). As discussed in the previous section, the "Other" category was not included in any analysis. Eight respondents filled in this category. One response was intriguing and needed more explanation: "none of the above are done because of the discovery system".

Discovery Systems and Workflow Changes

Since the focus of this study is on workflow changes overall, this question was tested against several variables: "Aside from one time clean-up projects, have you changed (or are you changing) your catalog maintenance activities as a direct result of the implementation of the discovery system? (question 9)".

In this test, the effect of the discovery system on changes in the overall workflow was examined (see Table 3). There were no significant differences between any sufficiently large (n≥5) yes-no data pairs (all p>0.5). With all systems combined, there were significantly more "no" than "yes" (X^2=21.42, d.f.=1, P<0.0001). Thus, in this sample, the discovery system had no effect on changes in the overall workflow. WorldCat® Local had the largest number of respondents (seven) indicating changes in workflow. This can most likely be directly attributed to WorldCat® Local's master record approach which emphasizes cataloging at the network level.

Implementation Time and Workflow Changes

In this test, the length of time since system implementation was compared with the likelihood that respondents answered "No" to the question about workflow changes (Table 4). Data on length of time since implementation was collected categorically ("in process", "0-6 months", "6-12 months", "1-2 yrs", and "2 or more yrs"). Standard regression analysis could not be used because the independent variable is ordinal, not cardinal, so I $\log_{10}$

Table 4. Implementation time and workflow changes

Since implemented	Yes	No	Don't Know	Totals
In process	2	7	11	20
0-6 mos	1	1	1	3
6-12 mos	3	7	2	12
1-2 yrs	8	27	2	37
2 or more	3	13	3	19
	17	55	19	**91**

transformed the dependent data and performed an ordinal regression.

With all time periods combined, there were significantly more "no" than "yes" (X^2=20.06, d.f.=1, P<0.0001). The relationship between length of time since the system was implemented with the likelihood that respondents answered "No" was significant using ordinal regression ($F_{1,3}$=40.024, p=0.024). The longer since the system was implemented, the more likely respondents were to answer "No". Basically, the test indicates that initially the respondents thought they might have to change maintenance activities. But the longer that the respondents have the discovery system, the less likely they are to change these activities.

In their survey Wynne and Hanscom (2011) did a similar comparison between workflow and implementation time. They asked: "If you have made changes to regular cataloging workflow, policies, or procedures, please explain briefly if desired" (Wynne & Hanscom, 2011, p. 206). An ordinal regression was also performed on their data as presented. When the author's data set and the Wynn & Hanscom data set were compared the data included 91 responses in each. The raw number of responses from both data sets in the "No" and "Don't know" categories was quite different. Wynne and Hanscom (2011) recorded 37 "No" and 38 "Don't know"; this survey had 55 and 19 respectively. With less "Don't know" in the data set and more "No", the comparison tests indicate a greater level of certainty in this

survey than in Wynne and Hanscom (2011) that workflow changes are less likely to occur overall.

Use of OPAC and Changes in Workflow

Familiarity with the library's public interface of local holdings was examined here. This is a comparison between the workflow question (question 9) with the continuation of the use of the traditional OPAC alongside the discovery system (see Table 5). Here the majority of survey respondents are continuing to use their legacy OPAC alongside their discovery platform with no plans to abandon its use. As for workflow changes, there were significantly more "No" than "Yes" (X^2=21.73, d.f.=1, P<0.0001). The libraries who are continuing to use their OPAC have not indicated changes in catalog maintenance activities. If they are not relying on the discovery system for the identification of local items, this makes sense that they would not abandon it or see a reason to change their workflow.

Comparison between the Use of the Traditional OPAC and the Public Interface of the Discovery System

The respondents' familiarity with the public catalog interface of their discovery system was examined in relation to their libraries' continuation of the legacy OPAC (see Table 6). Most of the groups were too small for statistical comparison

Table 5. Use of OPAC and changes in workflow

OPAC w/ discovery	Changes in workflow			
	Yes	No	Don't know	Totals
NO	1	0	0	1
Yes & keeping	13	50	11	74
Yes & abandoning	2	5	4	11
Don't know	1	0	4	5
	17	55	19	**91**

Note: All yes-no groups were too small for statistical comparison except for the "Yes & keeping". In this group there were significantly more No than Yes (X2=21.73, d.f.=1, P<0.0001).

with five exceptions. For respondents who said that they "Used the public interface" always* or sometimes**, significantly more said that they were going to keep their traditional OPAC (X^2=12.50, d.f.=1, P=0.0004 and (X^2=35.28, d.f.=1, P=0.0001, respectively). For respondents who said that they "Viewed catalog records during cataloging and/or maintenance" always***, significantly more said that they were going to keep their traditional OPAC (X^2=32.96, d.f.=1, P<0.0004). For respondents who said that they "Use the OPAC for their own needs" always [t], significantly more said that they were going to keep their traditional OPAC (X^2=10.00, d.f.=1, P=0.0016). For respondents who said that they "Provide references duties[tt], significantly more said that they were going to keep their traditional OPAC (X^2=21.43, d.f.=1, P,0.0001). Therefore in all cases where samples sizes permitted statistical tests, tests showed that significantly more people expected to keep their OPAC. The general trends were the same when there was significance, suggesting that all of the data point in the same direction. A larger sample size would most likely have the same trend also.

Solutions and Recommendations

There was a good response rate (36%) for this survey on catalog maintenance and discovery systems. The follow-up reminder emails were helpful in engendering more responses. However, the response rate could have been much better if the survey had not been sent out in the summer. Many academic librarians may be off campus, on vacation, or conducting research.

A weakness with the survey can be attributed specifically to the Qualtrics® product. For the crucial questions (i.e., discovery system name), the software allowed a response to be "forced" before the respondent continued with the survey. With most of the other questions, a "response requested" trigger was used to alert the survey taker that a question had been skipped. However, this function could not be used for the side-by-side matrices where a considerable amount of data were collected. Perhaps these questions should have been separated more instead of asked in a matrix format.

This survey's aim was to look at the aspect of the local holdings as they were included within the greater infrastructure of the index of articles, full-text, and research databases. In addition, this sample may not have been a good representation of "true" discovery systems. AquaBrowser® was included and the Primo® and Encore™ products were grouped. However, Primo Central™ and Encore Synergy™ are Web-scale discovery systems while their predecessors were not. Thus, it was not possible to identify if these users had transitioned to a Web-scale discovery system. Also, because

Table 6. Comparison between the use of the traditional OPAC and public interface of discovery system

		NO OPAC	Don't Know	Yes, Keep	Yes, Abandon	
Used the public interface	Always	1	2	26*	6*	35
	Sometimes	0	2	46**	4**	52
	Never	0	1	1	1	3
Catalog records viewed during cataloging and/or maintenance	Always	1	2	22***	3***	28
	Sometimes	0	2	46	5	53
	Never	0	1	4	3	8
Use it for my own needs	Always	0	1	23 ᵗ	6 ᵗ	30
	Sometimes	1	3	36	4	44
	Never	0	0	11	1	12
Provide reference duties	Always	1	1	12	2	16
	Sometimes	0	1	24	3	28
	Never	0	3	36 ᵗᵗ	6 ᵗᵗ	45
		4	19	287	44	354

they were still using their legacy OPAC and planning to keep it, this may not give an accurate picture of how the catalog maintenance activities are affected in the context of discovery systems.

FUTURE RESEARCH DIRECTIONS

For future research, the importance of "clean" data in the context of the discovery system as perceived by those involved with catalog maintenance and authority control is planned. . One established viewpoint is that "[to] maximize the effectiveness of a discovery interface, all efforts must be made to ensure accurate and clean metadata" (Breeding, 2010, p. 111). Discovery systems may expose more errors and problems in the database than did the traditional OPAC, whereas, catalog data may become buried or diminished within the context of the discovery system.

Another issue is the market for discovery systems is expanding rapidly. When research began for this survey, EDS™ and Summon™ were fairly new systems. The initial searches performed on lib-web-cats for all of the discovery systems were also recreated. From searches in late March 2011, 275 libraries were surveyed; in December 2011, the search yielded 363 libraries. By adding other commercial systems, the sample size would certainly increase. In a few years, if Web-scale discovery systems have become more commonplace in academic libraries, a similar survey with the limitations addressed should be replicated. In addition, this survey is only from the back office viewpoint of catalog maintenance and authority control tasks. Public services staff who have more interaction with users may have interesting and valuable input.

However, the overall context of quality control for the public catalog needs to be researched more fully. Hill (2008) comments on this much more eloquently:

Some actions may be taken so much for granted that they are continued without question far past the time that they have any utility, while others may be airily jettisoned only to give rise to unfortunate consequences because the reasons behind them were not fully understood (p. 6).

The workflow and decisions made in this area are not always backed by supported data. She notes that there is "a lack of serious research into user needs and benefits, and the actual impact on users of database quality decisions" (Hill, 2008, p. 5).

CONCLUSION

Revisiting the questions asked at the beginning of this study provides a good framework for discussion of the results. *Does the implementation of a discovery system affect catalog maintenance and authority control activities in academic libraries? Are there changes in tasks and staffing after implementation?* Results of this study do not indicate major changes in these activities. For authority and catalog maintenance tasks, there were no significant differences between sufficiently large (n≥5) before-after pairs (all p>0.5). The FTEs dedicated to these catalog maintenance and authority control tasks had a negligible change. In addition, there were no significant differences in the comparison of discovery systems and workflow changes; the discovery system has no effect on the changes in the overall workflow. This lack of difference in behavior and planning is in itself an important trend, even though the results are not statistically significant.

The lack of differences found in the study may be attributed to several other factors. Due to quick turnaround times necessary for new materials, quality of the records may be considered secondary to the cataloging department's function. The literature tends to focus on the cost and value of actual cataloging activities (Stahlberg & Cronin, 2011; McCain & Shorten, 2002; Morris, Hobert, Osmus, & Wool, 2000) while maintenance tasks are only briefly mentioned in these studies. Thus, the effects of the discovery systems may not yet have trickled down to these maintenance functions and maintenance staff.

However, survey respondents had anticipated workflow changes with the discovery system. In comparing implementation times with workflow changes, the test indicates that initially the libraries thought that they might have to change maintenance activities. But the longer that they have the discovery system, the less likely they are to change these activities. A comparison with Wynne and Hanscom's (2011) data validates this.

Questions about the public interface were also addressed. *In addition, how are local holdings presented to the public? Are they intermingled with the other resources or presented separately from the discovery system?* In examining the effect of the public interface, the majority of survey respondents who are continuing to use their legacy OPAC have not indicated changes to catalog maintenance workflows. When comparing the use of the traditional OPAC with the public interface of the discovery system, tests showed that significantly more people expected to keep their legacy OPAC. Thus, at this point, few discovery systems are replacing the traditional OPAC, but rather co-exist with the catalog.

In a general sense, this question was answered. *Are the cataloging staff aware of how their maintenance and authority control efforts display in the public interface?* The underlying theme of this question was to determine if catalog staff look at their work in the public interface and if they know whether their catalog records are intermingled with records from article databases (i.e., EDS™, Summon™). However, a broader interpretation of this question could lead to research on the overall context of quality control for the OPAC.

In conclusion, with the adoption of the upcoming catalog code *RDA: Resource, Description & Access*, libraries will need to consider how these changes will affect catalog maintenance. For example, *RDA* will make the gmd (general material designation) obsolete. Should bibliographic records be upgraded to reflect *RDA* changes? Coupled with the advent of discovery systems, the lack of research in catalog maintenance is much more obvious. Hill (2008) notes that:

[L]ibraries can no longer neglect serious research into the characteristics and needs of all users. They must come to a better understanding of the impact of current and proposed practices on the quality and capabilities of the new discovery tools, including the catalog. (p. 23)

Some catalog departments have been dedicated to the Sisyphean task of the pristine catalog with no empirical data to support that these efforts are beneficial to OPAC users.

REFERENCES

American library directory, 2010-2011 (64th ed.). (2011). Medford, NJ: Information Today.

Antell, K., & Huang, J. (2008). Subject searching success: Transaction logs, patron perceptions, and implications for library instruction. *Reference and User Services Quarterly, 48*(1), 68–76.

Breeding, M. (2008, June 30). *Cataloging for the new generation of library interfaces.* Presented at American Library Association Conference, ALCTS, Copy Cataloging Discussion Group, Annaheim: CA [PowerPoint slides]. Retrieved from http://www.librarytechnology.org/ltg-displaytext.pl?RC=13385

Breeding, M. (2010, May 6). *Understanding the discovery landscape: Federated search, web-scale discovery, next-generation catalog and the rest.* Presented for Library Journal webcast [PowerPoint slides] Retrieved from http://www.librarytechnology.org/ltg-displaytext.pl?RC=14728

Breeding, M. (2010). *Next-gen library catalogs.* New York, NY: Neal-Schuman Publishers.

Breeding, M. (2011). *Library technology guides: Discovery layer interfaces.* Retrieved from http://www.librarytechnology.org/discovery.pl

Gowing, C. (2008). *III's ENCORE: Old records, new records, new interfaces.* Presented at American Library Association Conference, ALCTS, Catalog Form & Function Interest Group, Anaheim, CA [PowerPoint slides]. Retrieved from http://alcts.ala.org/cffigwiki/index.php?title=ALA_Annual_2008_report

Gross, T., & Taylor, A. G. (2005). What have we got to lose?: The effect of controlled vocabulary on keyword searching results. *College & Research Libraries, 66*(3), 212–230.

Hill, J. S. (2008). Is it worth it? Management issues related to database quality. *Cataloging & Classification Quarterly, 46*(1), 5–26. doi:10.1080/01639370802182885

Lasater, M. C. (2008. June 28). *Old records, new records, new interfaces: Primo at Vanderbilt University.* Presented at American Library Association Conference, Annaheim: CA. [PowerPoint slides] Retrieved from http://alcts.ala.org/cffigwiki/index.php?title=ALA_Annual_2008_report

McCain, C., & Shorten, J. (2002). Cataloging efficiency and effectiveness. *Library Resources & Technical Services, 46*(1), 23–31.

Morris, D. E., Hobert, C. B., Osmus, L., & Wool, G. (2000). Cataloging staff costs revisited. *Library Resources & Technical Services, 44*(2), 70–83.

Moulaison, H. L. (2008). OPAC queries at a medium-sized academic library: A transaction log analysis. *Library Resources & Technical Services, 52*(4), 230–237.

Nuan, C. C. (2010). Next generation OPACs: A cataloging viewpoint. *Cataloging & Classification Quarterly, 48*(4), 3330–3342. doi:doi:10.1080/01639370903437709

Pennell, C. (2007, June). *Presentation: Forward to the past: resurrecting faceted search @NCSU libraries.* Presented at American Library Association Conference, ALCTS Authority Control Interest Group, Washington, D.C. [PowerPoint slides]. Retrieved from http://www.lib.ncsu.edu/endeca/presentations.html

Pennell, C. (2008 June). *Presentation: NCSU Endeca 2 1/2 years on: from Next Gen to normalcy.* American Library Association, Anaheim, CA [PowerPoint slides]. Retrieved from http://www.lib.ncsu.edu/endeca/presentations.html

Stahlberg, E., & Cronin, C. (2011). Assessing the cost and value of bibliographic control. *Library Resources & Technical Services, 55*(3), 124–137.

Vaughan, J. (2011). Differentiators and a final note. *Library Technology Reports, 47*(1), 48–53.

Ward, J. L., Shadle, S., & Mofjeld, P. (2008). Planning and implementation. *Library Technology Reports, 44*(6), 26–36.

Wolverton, R. E. Jr. (2005). Authority control in academic libraries in the United States: A survey. *Cataloging & Classification Quarterly, 41*(1), 111–131. doi:10.1300/J104v41n01_06

Wynne, S. C., & Hanscom, M. J. (2011). The effect of next-generation catalogs on catalogers and cataloging functions in academic libraries. *Cataloging & Classification Quarterly, 49*(3), 179–207. doi:10.1080/01639374.2011.559899

Zhu, L. (2009). Single-record versus separate-record approaches for cataloging e-serials in the OCLC WorldCat Local environment. *Cataloging & Classification Quarterly, 47*(2), 161–170. doi:10.1080/01639370802575583

Zhu, L. (2010). The role of the cataloging department in the implementation of OCLC WorldCat Local. *Library Collections, Acquisitions & Technical Services, 34*(4), 123–129. doi:10.1016/j.lcats.2010.06.001

ADDITIONAL READING

Bogan, R. A. (2004). Redesign of database management at Rutgers University Libraries. In Eden, B. L. (Ed.), *Innovative redesign and reorganization of library technical services: Paths for the future and case studies* (pp. 161–177). Westport, CT: Libraries Unlimited.

Bolin, M. K. (2000). Catalog design, catalog maintenance, catalog governance. *Library Collections, Acquisitions & Technical Services, 24*(1), 53–63. doi:10.1016/S1464-9055(99)00097-4

Calhoun, K. (2006). *The changing nature of the catalog and its integration with other discovery tools: Final report March 17, 2006: Prepared for the Library of Congress.* Washington, DC: Library of Congress. Retrieved from http://www.loc.gov/catdir/calhoun-report-final.pdf

Calhoun, K. Cantrell, J., Gallagher, P., Hawk, J., & Cellentani, D. (2009). *Online catalogs: What users and librarians want: An OCLC report.* Dublin, OH: OCLC Online Computer Library Center, Inc. Retrieved from http://www.oclc.org/us/en/reports/onlinecatalogs/fullreport.pdf

Campbell, D. G., & Fast, K. V. (2004). Panizzi, Lubetzky and Google: How the modern web environment is reinventing the theory of cataloguing. *Canadian Journal of Information and Library Science, 28*(3), 25–38.

Carlyle, A., Ranger, S., & Summerlin, J. (2008). Making the pieces fit: Little Women, works and the pursuit of quality. *Cataloging & Classification Quarterly*, *46*(1), 35–63. doi:10.1080/01639370802182992

DeRosa, C., Cantrell, J., Carlson, M., & Gallagher, P. Hawk, J. & Sturtz, C. (2011). *Perceptions of libraries, 2010: Context and community: A report to the OCLC membership*. Dublin, OH: OCLC Online Computer Library Center, Inc. Retrieved from http://www.oclc.org/us/en/reports/2010per ceptions/2010perceptions_all.pdf

DeRosa, C., Cantrell, J., Cellentani, D., Hawk, J., Jenkins, L., & Wilson, A. (2005). *Perceptions of libraries and information resources: A report to the OCLC membership*. Dublin, OH: OCLC Online Computer Library Center, Inc. Retrieved from http://www.oclc.org/reports/pdfs/Percept_all.pdf

Hanson, H., & Schalow, J. (1999). Two aspects of quality in technical services: Automating for quick availability, and identifying problems, effecting solutions. *Library Collections, Acquisitions & Technical Services*, *23*(4), 433–441. doi:10.1016/S1464-9055(99)00085-8

Mercun, T., & Zumer, M. (2008). New generation of catalogues for the new generation of users: A comparison of six library catalogues. *Program*, *42*(3), 243–261. doi:10.1108/00330330810892668

Paiste, M. S. (2003). Defining an achieving quality in cataloging in academic libraries: A literature review. *Library Collections, Acquisitions & Technical Services*, *27*(3), 327–338. doi:10.1016/S1464-9055(03)00069-1

Smith, V. T. (2009). Staffing trends in academic library technical services: A qualitative analysis . In Eden, B. L. (Ed.), *More innovative redesign and reorganization of library technical services* (pp. 95–105). Westport, CT: Libraries Unlimited.

Warren, J. (2007). Directors' views of the future of cataloguing in Australia and New Zealand: A survey. *Australian Academic & Research Libraries*, *38*(4), 239–251.

KEY TERMS AND DEFINITIONS

008/Fixed Fields: Contain codes of a predetermined length in the MARC bibliographic record. Some Integrated Library Systems display the fixed fields with mnemonics for each code; some display the coding in the 008 field. Codes represent information on publication dates, material types, language, and several other factors useful for faceted navigation in discovery systems.

Authority Control: The process of maintaining consistency in the way that an access point is used in the catalog. Entries are matched to the established form of the name, subject, series or uniform title and collocated accordingly. Authority records also provide cross references to other entries.

Catalog Maintenance: Addresses quality control issues involved with cataloging, classification, and authority control after the initial cataloging has been performed.

CSB (*Cataloging Service Bulletin*): A publication of the Library of Congress which included information about changed subject headings and LC cataloging policies and procedures. Last issue published in Fall 2010; archives are available online (http://www.loc.gov/cds/PDFdownloads/csb/index.html)

Death Dates: In 2006, LC policy changed and closed dates (death dates) were now added regularly to personal name headings. Weekly updates and archives are posted on the OCLC web site (http://www.oclc.org/us/en/rss/feeds/authorityrecords/default.htm)

Diacritics: Marks appearing above or below an alphabetic character, such as the tilde in "señor". Often cause display problems in OPACs

Faceted Navigation: Allows users to narrow searches by various facets, particularly given as a visual display in discovery interfaces. Facets may include: formats (book, journal, image, etc.); authors; topics (subject headings, geographical settings, etc.); locations (branch, collection, department); language and date of publication.

GMD (General Material Designation): Indicates the medium for non-print materials. Appears in variable field 245 in subfield h and is surrounded by brackets.

Indicator: A one character field associated with a variable field in the MARC record. Indicators supply information about the field for indexing or other system functions.

Library of Congress Subject Headings (LCSH): Standardized descriptive words or phrases that characterize the content of the work. New and changed subject headings are posted regularly on the Library of Congress' Cataloging and Acquisitions web page. http://www.loc.gov/aba/cataloging/subject/weeklylists/

MARC: (Machine Readable Cataloging) The bibliographic format is an international standard for the representation and exchange of bibliographic data in machine-readable form. Contains tags, fixed fields, variable fields, indicators, subfield codes, and other coded values.

Material Type: Coding in the fixed fields of the MARC record that indicates the format of material, such as, printed materials, printed music, maps, projected medium, sound recording, or spoken recording. Useful in searching legacy catalogs and discovery interfaces.

Tag: A three digit number used in the MARC format to signal the beginning of a variable field.

ENDNOTES

[1] Qualtrics is a registered trademark of www.qualtrics.com, Inc.

[2] Aquabrowser is registered trademark of Serial Solutions.

[3] EBSCO Discovery Service is owned by EBSCO Publishing Industries

[4] Encore is a registered trademark of Innovative Interfaces

[5] Primo is owned by Ex Libris Ltd. or its affiliates.

[6] Summons is owned by ProQuest LLC

[7] Worldcat is a registered trademark of OCLC

[8] WebFeat is owned by Serial Solutions.

[9] MetaLib is owned by Ex Libris Ltd.

[10] ProQuest is a registered trademark of ProQuest LLC

[11] EBSCOhost is a registered trademark of EBSCO Publishing Industries

[12] Innovative Interfaces is a registered trademark of Innovative Interfaces, Inc.

[13] In this study, "discovery system" or "discovery tool" will be used when referring to the discovery and next-generation catalog products surveyed. The term "catalog" conveys the concept of the siloed approach for information discovery. When it is necessary to refer to the traditional catalog, "catalog" or "online public access catalog" (OPAC) is preferred.

Section 6
Discovery in the Wild:
Representative Examples of Discovery Tools in Use

Shane Nackerud
University of Minnesota, USA

OVERVIEW

As is suggested by the publishing of this collection, we are at the edge of a new discovery landscape, one that promises to consolidate library resources, create simplified and faster user interfaces, and better reveal our libraries' rich collections and resources to our users. Like explorers during the original Age of Discovery, a number of libraries have already ventured forward, blazing a trail "into the wild" by being some of the first libraries to implement these new discovery systems. In this section, several of these intrepid libraries share what they have learned in the course of implementing various Web-scale discovery solutions, detailing weaknesses, pitfalls, and, of course, the benefits and overall impact on their users, libraries, and collections.

The chapters in this section are case studies and give representative examples of libraries that have implemented Web-scale discovery tools. Each chapter attempts to cover the implementation process including selection, configuration of the tool, presentation to users, user reactions, and impact on the library. Various Web-scale discovery products are represented: Primo is discussed by librarians and archivists from Notre Dame and the Center for Jewish History; WorldCat Local is covered by librarians from Macalester College and the University of Louisville; EBSCO Discovery Service is discussed by librarians from Illinois State University and Indiana University; Summon is discussed by librarians from Montana State University and Huddersfield and Northumbria Universities; and Encore Synergy is covered by representatives of the University of Nebraska at Omaha.

Again, these libraries recognized early on the power of these new Web-scale discovery tools and have already implemented a solution with varying degrees of success. Each of these libraries has a unique story to tell, but almost all of them report interesting and useful responses from their users, and a significant overall impact on their libraries. The lessons learned and shared in these chapters should be instructive for all librarian readers, especially those who have decided to venture forward themselves "into the wild" of this new discovery system frontier.

Chapter 28
Early Adoption:
EBSCO Discovery Service at Illinois State University

Anita K. Foster
Illinois State University, USA

Sarah C. Williams
University of Illinois at Urbana-Champaign, USA

ABSTRACT

This chapter provides a case study of EBSCO Discovery Service™ at Illinois State University's Milner Library. After a formal selection process, Milner chose EBSCO Discovery Service™ to replace its federated search engine. The implementation team considered what local collections to include, ways to present catalog data, and the customizations to make. EBSCO Discovery Service™, locally called Search It, was implemented in August 2010. During the Fall, six informal usability sessions were conducted to determine Search It's ease of use for students. Since Milner's initial implementation, several changes have been made to Search It locally and by EBSCO. The presentation of Search It on Milner's website also changed and became more prominent, due to a Web site redesign and user feedback. Statistics indicate that EBSCO Discovery Service™ has resulted in a significant increase in Milner's database usage.

INTRODUCTION

Illinois State University is a Carnegie Doctoral/ Research University located in Normal, Illinois. Named for an early university librarian, Milner Library is the only library at Illinois State University. It has more than 1.6 million items in its collection, including approximately 70,000 electronic journals and 200 databases.

Milner Library, an active member in CARLI (Consortium for Academic and Research Libraries in Illinois), first offered a federated search system to the university community in 2006. WebFeat®[2], fully subsidized by CARLI, was the system used.

DOI: 10.4018/978-1-4666-1821-3.ch028

In 2009, CARLI did not renew WebFeat® for its member libraries and the WebFeat® vendor announced an end of life date for the product and plans to merge it with another system. These events spurred Milner Library to investigate new federated search products. Shortly after the search began, resource discovery tools became available. Milner Library's federated search task force found the discovery concept intriguing, with a potential to overcome problems of traditional federated search products. The task force decided to evaluate the new discovery products along with federated search systems.

SELECTION

The process of selecting a resource discovery tool for Milner Library began in October 2009. The Dean's Technology Advisory Committee (DTAC), which shepherds Milner's technology initiatives, created a federated search task force with representatives from the Public Services, Systems and Electronic Resources units. The task force had two goals: find a replacement for WebFeat® and improve cross-database searching for end users.

The task force began the selection process by researching existing federated search products and identifying vendors to contact for additional information. During this initial phase, resource discovery tools were released and included in the discussion. However, since the technology was very new and funding for a new product was uncertain, the task force focused on traditional federated search products.

By January 2010, the task force had identified three vendors to invite for on-campus demonstrations. Each of the vendors had a federated search product, and their resource discovery tools were available or would be available soon. The vendors were asked to demonstrate both the federated search and resource discovery tools. The task force invited all Milner Library faculty and staff

to attend the demonstrations and provide feedback on the systems.

Following the demonstrations, the task force realized that the search technology advancement displayed by resource discovery tools was an opportunity for Milner Library to provide users with a better search experience. Since there were indications that resource discovery tools were significantly more expensive than federated search products, the task force consulted with DTAC and the library Dean about funding. Enough funding was available to pursue a resource discovery tool, but a Request for Proposal (RFP) was needed, since the cost of a resource discovery tool could potentially exceed the university's purchasing threshold that triggers a RFP.

The RFP was written in such a way that a vendor could respond with information on a federated search system, a resource discovery tool, or both products. Some of the specific questions listed in the RFP included the process for incorporating catalog data into the system, interoperability with other systems, and customization options. The university posted the RFP in March 2010, and it ran for four weeks. Three vendor responses were received.

The task force considered a variety of information to help reach a final decision. In addition to the RFP responses, the group utilized insights gained from Milner's WebFeat® experience. Another factor was the expectations and information-seeking behaviors of students. Studies have indicated that convenience and speed are important to users (Connaway, Dickey, & Radford, 2011; De Rosa, 2006). The task force also had feedback from the library faculty and staff who attended the vendor demonstrations in January. Based on all of this information, the task force chose EBSCO Discovery Service™ (EDS) as the best product to replace WebFeat®. Recognizing a need to continue federating some resources, the task force recommended that EBSCOhost®[3] Integrated Search™[4] be purchased to provide cross-platform searching for nearly all online

Figure 1. Timeline for selection, purchase, and implementation

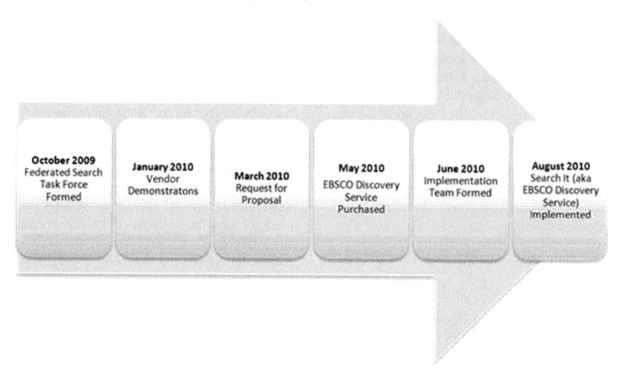

resources. EBSCOhost®[5] Integrated Search™[6] allows users to do a metasearch across databases and other electronic resources. The task force leader presented a report detailing the strengths and weakness of each system to DTAC and the library Dean. The library Dean agreed with the task force's recommendation and authorized the purchase of both EBSCO Discovery Service™ and EBSCOhost® Integrated Search™. The implementation of EBSCO Discovery Service™ began with the formation of an implementation team in June 2010 and by August 2010 EDS™ was in production.

PLANNING AND IMPLEMENTATION

Planning

A feature of resource discovery tools is the ability to incorporate local data into the system's unified index. Milner Library's implementation team discussed which local collections should be included. It was critical to include catalog data in EDS™ from the beginning. Inclusion of Milner's digital collections was less time-sensitive. They were added to EDS™ in January 2011. Milner Library's users and staff also frequently utilize the consortial catalog (I-Share) when looking for resources so it was vital that I-Share was accessible via EDS™.

The implementation team also discussed the databases and other resources to incorporate into the EDS™ index and those to configure in EBSCOhost® Integrated Search™. One area of concern was whether to include databases with limited simultaneous users. The team decided to include all databases, regardless of limitations and observe the impact on end users.

Figure 2. Sample of the location linking file

LOCATION_CODE	Copy_Display	Facet_Display	Limiter_Display
2circ	Circulation Desk: 1 Hour Building Use Only	Milner Library	Circulation Desk
2desknc	Reference Desk: Building Use Only	Milner Library	Milner Reference
2mform	Microform Area: Building Use Only	Milner Library	Microforms
2newshelf	New Books Shelves	Milner Library	Milner Library New Books
2per	Current Periodicals: Building Use Only	Milner Library	Current Periodicals
2pernp	Current Newspaper Area: Building Use Only	Milner Library	Current Newspapers
2refmfinc	Reference, Microform Indexes: Building Use Only	Milner Library	Milner Reference Microform Indexes
2refnc	Reference: Building Use Only	Milner Library	Milner Reference
2res	Course Reserve Desk: Building Use Only	Milner Library	Course Reserves
2shelfnc	Microform Area: Building Use Only	Milner Library	Microforms
3shelf	Floor 3 Shelves	Milner Library	Milner Library
3shelfnc	Floor 3 Shelves: Building Use Only	Milner Library	Milner Library
4ovshelf	Floor 4 Oversize Materials	Milner Library	Milner Library
4ovshelfnc	Floor 4 Oversize Materials: Building Use Only	Milner Library	Milner Library
4shelf	Floor 4 Shelves	Milner Library	Milner Library
4shelfnc	Floor 4 Shelves: Building Use Only	Milner Library	Milner Library
5ovshelf	Floor 5 Oversize Materials	Milner Library	Milner Library
5ovshelfnc	Floor 5 Oversize Materials: Building Use Only	Milner Library	Milner Library
5shelf	Floor 5 Shelves	Milner Library	Milner Library
5shelfnc	Floor 5 Shelves: Building Use Only	Milner Library	Milner Library
6miniscore	Floor 6 Miniature Score Shelves	Milner Library	Milner Library Miniature Scores
6ovshelf	Floor 6 Oversize Materials	Milner Library	Milner Library
6ovshelfnc	Floor 6 Oversize Materials: Building Use Only	Milner Library	Milner Library
6shelf	Floor 6 Shelves	Milner Library	Milner Library
6shelfnc	Floor 6 Shelves: Building Use Only	Milner Library	Milner Library
archivnc	Univ. Archives--Warehouse Road: Building Use Only	Illinois State University Archives	Illinois State University Archives
archivrfnc	Univ. Archives Reference--Warehouse Road: Building Use Only	Illinois State University Archives	Illinois State University Archives
browsing	Floor 2 Browsing Area	Milner Library	Milner Library Browsing Books
docmfidx	Floor 2 Documents Microform Index Area	Federal Government Resources	Federal Government Resources Microforms
docmformnc	Floor 2 Documents Microforms: Building Use Only	Federal Government Resources	Federal Government Resources Microforms
docpam	Floor 2 Documents Pamphlets	Federal Government Resources	Federal Government Resources Pamphlets
docper	Floor 2 Federal Documents Periodicals: Building Use Only	Federal Government Resources	Federal Government Resources Periodicals
docrefnc	Floor 2 Documents Reference: Building Use Only	Federal Government Resources	Federal Government Resources Reference
docshelf	Floor 4 Federal Documents	Federal Government Resources	Federal Government Resources
docshelfnc	Floor 4 Federal Documents: Building Use Only	Federal Government Resources	Federal Government Resources

Catalog Data

Milner Library uses Voyager®[7] for its integrated library system. As part of the initial EDS™ set up, EBSCO sent a questionnaire with catalog related questions. Questions dealt with catalog record structure, frequency of data updates, Z39.50 connection information for activation of the real time availability feature, and link resolver information. In addition to the questionnaire, EBSCO also asked that a linking table be created to match catalog location codes to display names used within EDS™ for limiters, expanders and real time catalog information.

EDS™ provides the ability to filter results sets based on library locations. Milner Library has nearly 90 location codes configured for its catalog, far too many to display effectively. It was decided that only truly unique collections or locations would be included in the facet and limiter display names. Locations that are more general would be combined into one facet. For example, location designations indicate the floor on which materials are shelved. All of the location codes with such designations received the same facet display name – Milner Library. The floor designation is still available for users as it is included in the real time availability data that is displayed. Some of the unique display names retained for the facet display were the Teaching Materials Center collection, Government Documents and the holdings of the University's two laboratory schools.

Catalog data can be sent to EBSCO as frequently as an individual library wishes. At Milner Library, CARLI, the library's consortium, hosts the Voyager® system for member libraries. CARLI, not Milner Library, is responsible for sending the data extracts to EBSCO for inclusion in the unified index. For this to happen, Milner had to send a work request to CARLI detailing the requirements of the data extract. A decision was made to include only records not hidden from public viewing and that had unsuppressed holding records. The implementation team felt it was important to send data extracts to EBSCO that were as clean as possible. The work request also specified which holdings data MARC fields needed to be included with the extracted records. At the implementation stage, CARLI extracted all the library catalog data and loaded the files on an EBSCO server. Subsequent data loads happen weekly. When the catalog data was first loaded into EDS™, EBSCO reported that only 15,000 records (from over 1.3 million) were rejected with errors. When the records were investigated, it was determined that the problem was likely due to bad data in records that had transitioned from library systems used prior to Voyager®. Due to the age of the titles and the difficulty involved in identifying the records, no attempt was made to correct the errors and reload that set of titles.

Customization

EBSCO Discovery Service™ includes a number of customization options. The Milner implementation team discussed the customizations would benefit users. It was decided that colors in EDS™ should be different from those used in Milner's other EBSCOhost® databases to give a visual cue to users that EDS™ was a different kind of resource. Milner Library includes a chat widget in all EBSCOhost® database interfaces and this practice was continued with EDS™. The EBSCOhost® Integrated Search™ widget label was changed to "Additional Results," which the team hoped would be more intuitive to end users. The team also discussed what to call EDS™. The team decided to provide continuity between the WebFeat® implementation and EDS™ by using the same name, Search It. A new logo, utilizing the university's mascot, was developed and was located near the search boxes in EDS™.

EBSCOhost Integrated Search

Although many Milner Library electronic resource subscriptions are available via the EDS™ unified index, some frequently used resources such as the I-Share library catalog are not included. EBSCOhost® Integrated Search™, EBSCO's federated search product, provided an opportunity to include that resource in a more flexible way than had been possible in the past. Databases and other electronic resources are searched via connectors, which are configured by EBSCO on request of customers. Connectors in EBSCOhost® Integrated Search™ can include free and subscription based resources. There is a charge for connectors and some resources are not available for inclusion in EBSCOhost® Integrated Search™.

When determining which resources to include in EBSCOhost® Integrated Search™, the implementation team decided to include all the resources that had been available in WebFeat®, plus resources with limited simultaneous users. After EBSCO Discovery Service™ and EBSCOhost® Integrated Search™ were implemented, the EDS™ administrator discovered that inclusion in EBSCOhost® Integrated Search™ adversely affected the accessibility of the limited user databases via their native interfaces. Many of the limited user databases were removed from EBSCOhost® Integrated Search™ during the first year and all were eventually deleted from Milner's EBSCOhost® Integrated Search™ account when it was renewed for a second year.

USABILITY FEEDBACK

From mid-October to early November 2010, informal testing was conducted to determine the usability of *Search It* for students (Williams & Foster, 2011). The study involved two juniors, two seniors, and two graduate students from a variety of disciplines. At the sessions, the participants spent two to three minutes exploring *Search It* on their own, worked through five research scenarios, and completed a brief, written questionnaire. The research scenarios were based on common student tasks - (1) find and email records for a book and a peer-reviewed article, (2) open a full-text article published since 2005, (3) determine whether the library has an available copy of a poem published in a book, (4) find an article on a complex topic and decide how to share it with group members, and (5) identify a relevant citation from a specific database in the Additional Results. Several highlights emerged from the usability testing observations and analysis.

The participants frequently used limiters and refinements, both pre-search and post-search. The most frequently used limiters and refinements were peer-reviewed journals, format, location, publication date, library catalog, full text, and available in library collection. Of the six participants, five used the peer-reviewed limiter, and four used the publication date, library catalog, and full text limiters and refinements.

Other *Search It* features and widgets were not heavily used. On the results page, *Search It* displays a number of facets (e.g., source type, subject, content provider), but most participants only explored these facets if they were struggling with a scenario. One usability scenario asked participants to decide how they would share an article record with group members. *Search It* provides at least four ways to share records and full text, but all six participants chose email, although one participant mentioned that she might have used texting, if it had been an option. In *Search It*, library catalog holdings information displays on the brief results page, but only one participant commented on this feature and only after she had already clicked on the book's detailed record link. Milner's EDS™ implementation includes EBSCOhost® Integrated Search™ as a custom widget labeled Additional Results. Although the widget was available for all scenarios, the participants did not use it until it was required for the last scenario. Even the participants who commented on the Additional Results during the exploration time did not use the widget again until the last scenario.

The participants recorded similar responses on the written post-test questionnaire. A majority agreed or strongly agreed that they were able to easily find relevant results with *Search It* and that they liked the interface. All participants indicated that they would be likely or very likely to use *Search It* again and to recommend it to friends for their research. All participants also indicated that they felt *Search It* was a useful tool for their actual research or coursework. Notably, all participants agreed or strongly agreed that instruction would be helpful for *Search It*. Several comments and suggestions related to instruction were also recorded in the open-ended questions. The feedback suggested that the students felt comfortable with *Search It*'s basic functionality but they would like instruction or help with more advanced features.

CHANGES SINCE INITIAL IMPLEMENTATION

Since Milner's initial implementation, several changes were made to *Search It* locally and by EBSCO. The *Search It* implementation on Milner's Web site has also changed, due to a Web site redesign.

Local EDS™ Changes

Several of the local *Search It* changes resulted from Milner's usability testing. On the search page, some of the participants were confused by

Figure 3. Placement of EDS™ on Milner Library's homepage following implementation, August 2010

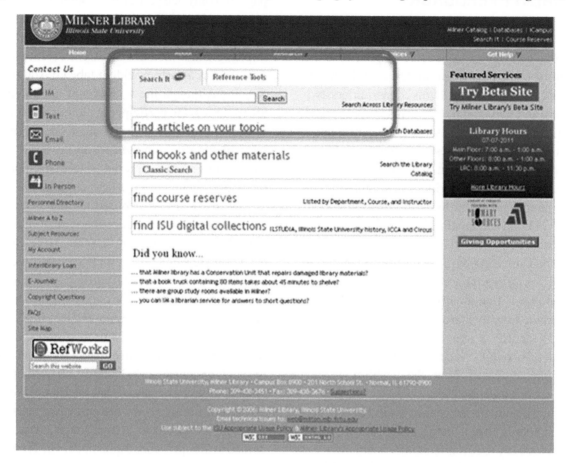

the Source, Author and Title search boxes, which can only be used in conjunction with terms in the primary search box. Therefore, the Source, Author and Title boxes were removed. After the usability study was completed, EBSCO added Keyword, Title, and Author radio buttons under the basic search box, which may have resolved some of this confusion. Another participant did not understand the purpose of the Location box on the search page. To help clarify this limiter the label was changed to "Location in Milner." During the usability testing, the authors noticed that the Basic and Advanced search pages provided different limiter options, so the options were made consistent on the two search pages. Since

exploration of the less prominent results page facets happened only when participants were struggling, two additional facets – Subject and Subject: Major Heading – were opened by default to make them more prominent.

Other changes and enhancements were based on input from library staff. Milner worked with EBSCO to implement the harvesting of metadata from two digital collections – International Collection of Child Art and Passion for Circus, and Milner will continue to add collections. Milner catalog data was initially included in *Search It*, but as library staff gained more experience with *Search It*, they provided suggestions for refining the display of catalog data. Milner collaborated

Figure 4. Placement of EDS™ following Milner Library homepage redesign, January 2011

with EBSCO to display temporary locations (e.g., course reserves) of catalog items, and the display of call numbers was refined to improve DVD and CD searching and retrieving. An additional widget containing call number location maps was also added.

Vendor EDS™ Changes

Since Milner implemented *Search It*, EBSCO has released some enhancements to the EDS™. Several new content providers have added their metadata to the EDS™ index (e.g., Web of Science[8], JSTOR[9], and Elsevier ScienceDirect[10]). EBSCO also made enhancements related to catalog data. EBSCO added additional formats, such as audio and video, for limiting catalog results. In the detailed record of catalog items, EDS™ now offers lists of books on a similar subject, books by the same author, and reviews of that title.

Placement on the Milner Library Website

Although it is possible to search EDS™ directly, Milner Library also integrated a search box into the library Web site. With WebFeat®, Milner Library used a search box placed in the center of its homepage (http://library.illinoisstate.edu). For EDS™, the implementation team decided to continue that practice but wanted to highlight the service. The revised search box was placed higher on the page to increase its visibility and provide another cue that this was a new service (Figure 3).

In January 2011, Milner Library went live with a redesigned Web site (see Figure 4). Based on the recommendation of the campus Web group working on the redesign project, the name *Search It* was replaced by the phrase Search Anything. The new site featured a larger Search Anything box. The previous site had a tabbed search box, with the *Search It* tab using EDS™ and a Reference Tools tab utilizing EBSCOhost® Integrated Search™. The new Web site had only the single

Figure 5. Change in usage for selected databases

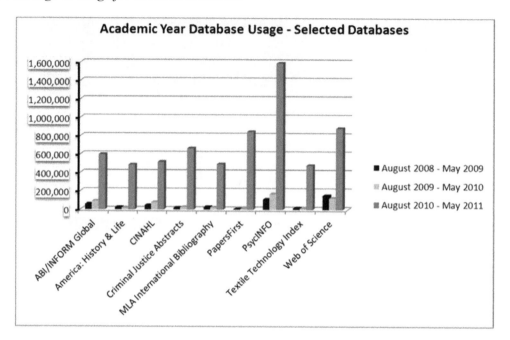

Search Anything box, but a frequent comment from users was a desire for a more prominent search box for the library catalog. In March 2011, the homepage search box was modified to have three tabs – a "Search Anything" tab, a "Books and Media" tab for the library catalog data (run by EDS™), and a "This Website" tab.

IMPACT ON RESOURCES

With WebFeat®, only 12 databases were included in the Quick Search box located on Milner Library's homepage. Due to faster results retrieval, a majority of Milner Library's databases can be included in an initial EDS™ search. Usage for all the library databases skyrocketed following the EDS™ implementation. Between the 2010 and 2011 academic years, database usage increased 1910%. Some of the increase was due to the addition of more full text databases but the growth in usage due to EDS™ is evident when looking

at specific databases. The selected databases in Figure 4 were available on the same platform and in the same configuration before and after EDS™ was implemented. Although some change in use may be due to varying curricular needs, the leap in the post implementation numbers suggests that EDS™ has a significant impact on the use of library databases.

CONCLUSION

When starting the implementation process for EDS™, the Milner Library team approached it much like previous federated search products. As EDS™ evolved and familiarity with it grew, library users and staff embraced the strengths of the resource discovery tool on its own merits. The flexibility of the system provides opportunities for EDS™ to meet current user needs and to adapt to future needs.

Implementing EDS™ at Milner Library has been a positive experience. End users have adjusted well to the new opportunities provided by the resource discovery tool. The changes to the system incorporated from user and library staff feedback helped hone the system into an indispensable tool for satisfying the information needs of the Illinois State University community.

REFERENCES

Connaway, L., Dickey, T., & Radford, M. (2011). "If it is too inconvenient, I'm not going after it:" Convenience as a critical factor in information-seeking behaviors. *Library & Information Science Research, 33*(3), 179–190. doi:10.1016/j.lisr.2010.12.002

De Rosa, C. (2006). *College students' perceptions of libraries and information resources: A report to the OCLC membership.* Dublin, OH: OCLC Online Computer Library Center. Retrieved from http://www.oclc.org/reports/pdfs/studentperceptions.pdf

Williams, S., & Foster, A. (2011). Promise fulfilled? An EBSCO Discovery Service usability study. *Journal of Web Librarianship, 5*(3), 179–198. doi:10.1080/19322909.2011.597590

KEY TERMS AND DEFINITIONS

CARLI: Consortium of Academic and Research Libraries in Illinois, based in Champaign, IL, consisting of 153 member libraries of all sizes, ranging from community colleges to special libraries to research universities.

Content Provider: Resource, publisher or database from which content included in EBSCO Discovery Service originates.

Facet: Classification of information by attributes. In EBSCO Discovery Service™, facets are used to narrow search results by attributes such as subject, publication title, location and more.

Federated Search: Searching multiple databases simultaneously in a single interface or by connecting to the native database interface to search. Also known as cross-database searching.

I-Share: Name of the Voyager integrated library system online catalog utilized by many CARLI member libraries.

Real Time Availability Checking (RTAC): Process that queries a library's Z39.50 catalog server to retrieve real-time holdings information such as charge status, call number and item location.

Search It: Local name of the EBSCO Discovery Service™ implementation at Milner Library.

Widget: A small piece of computer code that can be placed on a web page or screen to provide a graphical interface to complete a particular task. In discovery tools, this might be a text box that allows a reference question to be asked via instant messaging.

Z39.50: This standard - ANSI/NISO Z39.50 Information Retrieval (Z39.50) Application Service Definition and Protocol Specification - defines a protocol for search and retrieval of information from databases.

ENDNOTES

[1] EBSCO Discovery Service is owned by EBSCO Publishing Industries

[2] WebFeat is a registered trademark of ProQuest LLC

[3] EBSCOhost is a registered trademark of EBSCO Publishing Industries

[4] Integrated Search is owned by Ebsco Publishing Industries

[5] EBSCOhost is a registered trademark of EBSCO Publishing Industries

[6] Integrated Search is owned by Ebsco Publishing Industries

[7] Voyager is a registered trademark to ExLibris Ltd.

[8] Web of Science is a registered trademark of Thompson Reuters

[9] JSTOR is a registered trademark of ITHAKA

[10] Science Direct is a registered trademark of Elsevier B.V.

Chapter 29
The Long and Winding Road:
Implementing Discovery at Indiana University Bloomington Libraries

Courtney Greene
Indiana University, USA

ABSTRACT

In early 2010, Indiana University Bloomington Libraries became a beta tester for the EBSCO Discovery Service (EDS)™[1] product, and subsequently selected it in September of that year. After working through various issues with library content and staff expectations, the IUB Libraries launched EDS™ - branded as OneSearch@IU, in August 2011. This case study provides an overview of the decision-making process and challenges encountered in the process of implementation of a Web-scale discovery tool. Specific topics such as working with a vendor Application Program Interface (API) to integrate a discovery tool within a library website, formulating an effective extract of library catalog records to import into a discovery tool, customizing a vendor discovery interface, and assessing use and user satisfaction with a discovery system are described. Broad concepts addressed in this chapter include information technology project implementation and library information systems.

DOI: 10.4018/978-1-4666-1821-3.ch029

INTRODUCTION

As an institution, the Indiana University Libraries are committed to the idea of facilitating discovery, and as a Web-scale discovery tool, EBSCO Discovery Service (EDS)™ is one part of an overall effort to unify the Library Web presence and present the Libraries' collections, services and resources in a way that enables a more holistic approach to supporting teaching, learning and research in the Indiana University community.

In an article, published in 2006, Dempsey describes a leveraged discovery environment (a vended solution, one outside the library's control) – a concept quite familiar to us now – and cites as its primary goal to bring users back into the local library catalog. For library users, the gap between any library collection that is findable (cataloged) and the portion of the collection that is available or obtainable in a networked environment is "the difference between discovery (identifying resources of interest) and location (identifying where those resources of interest are actually available)." (Dempsey, 2006)

In recent years, the IUB Libraries have prioritized providing broader access to catalog data through new discovery tools with powerful, user-friendly interfaces. In early 2010, Indiana University Bloomington Libraries became a beta tester for EDS™; it was selected in September of that year and launched in August 2011, branded as OneSearch@IU. A related project in the works is the implementation of an open-source discovery layer (Blacklight) as the primary OPAC interface overlaid on the existing SIRSIDynix®2 ILS system. Scheduled for a summer 2012 launch, the transition to a new public interface will be followed by a complete migration from SIRSIDynix® to the community-sourced Kuali®3 Online Library Environment infrastructure (currently in development) sometime in the following year. (Kuali Foundation, 2010)

While the ability to integrate catalog results in EDS™ provides one more means to lead users back to IUCAT, the IU Libraries' shared catalog, at this time there is no single tool with an interface that simultaneously meets existing needs relating to discovery to the Libraries' satisfaction. Indiana University Libraries feel strongly that discovery is a key area for investment of library resources; the library catalog and a Web-scale discovery system, such as EBSCO Discovery Service™, Summon™4, for example, or discovery interface (such as Blacklight or VuFind), are seen as complementary tools that work together to better meet the needs of the broadly diverse user group – undergraduates (primarily novice users), scholars & faculty (discipline experts who also typically have more expertise in research), graduate students & interdisciplinary researchers (somewhere in between the other two groups).

As with any new endeavor, there are competing priorities and areas of uncertainty: how to display data that is meaningful and helpful to users in a number of different systems and interfaces; how to balance the needs for attention to detail and to the user experience with the realities of constrained resources & staff time, while scaling up to deliver data to multiple systems; and, how much can be accomplished through post-processing catalog extracts, and in which areas must local practices be carefully re-examined?

This case study provides an overview of the decision-making process that led to the selection of EBSCO Discovery Service™ by the IU Bloomington Libraries, and its subsequent implementation, focusing on the integration of EDS™ into the library Website, and the challenges encountered in working to optimize display and search of catalog data.

When embarking on a project of this kind, goals exist at different levels: first, and most simple to define and later assess, is the goal of successful implementation – that is, to complete the steps necessary to select a product, load the data, customize the interface, then make the product available to end-users. Despite this seemingly straightforward process, numerous unforeseen complications and difficulties inevitably arise throughout the project lifespan. In an environment where so much is new, in which the environment (locally and within the marketplace) is constantly evolving, it can be difficult to set long-term goals with much specificity. Indeed, throughout the course of this implementation, changes both to the product itself and to local circumstances have required numerous course corrections. In the end, a series of short-term goals, together with a philosophy that embraces this kind of fluidity and views frequent iteration as success, proved most effective. Throughout, both positive and negative outcomes were valued as providing data leading to better decision-making in future.

The goals for the implementation were also influenced by the vision for change for the library's Web presence, one that conceptualizes not simply a migration and redesign, but a re-envisioning of the methods by which information, services, and resources are seamlessly delivered to users in a variety of venues with a high degree of personalization: directly via the Website, via the campus portal, using mobile devices, on- or off-campus, etc. With an emphasis on flexibility, this vision relies on the ability to reuse and re-mix content to be provided at the time and place of need and provide scaffolding to lead to other resources and services as appropriate. The implementation of EDS™ is a crucial part of this strategy to deliver library services and resources as effectively and efficiently as possible in as many venues as possible.

BACKGROUND

The IU Bloomington Libraries serve a population of almost 3000 faculty and over 40,000 students in a wide range of undergraduate, masters, doctoral and post-doctoral programs. Named the top university library by the Association of College and Research Libraries in 2010, the IUB Libraries hold extensive print and electronic collections: well over seven million books, journals, maps, films, and audio/visual materials in over 900 languages; access to more than 600 databases, and many thousands of e-journals, and e-books; and locally developed digital content (Indiana University Bloomington Libraries, 2010). Statewide, Indiana University has eight campuses, with a total enrollment of nearly 110,000 students in fall 2010. (University Institutional Research and Reporting, 2010a) The Indiana University Libraries system includes libraries at each campus location.

Known for its natural and architectural beauty, the Bloomington campus is the largest within the statewide system, both in size (approximately 2000 acres) and in enrollment, accounting for nearly forty percent of total system enrollment. (University Institutional Research and Reporting, 2010b) Founded in 1820, its status as the flagship campus results in a history rich with tradition paired with a commitment to research, teaching and scholarship, which earned it a designation as a Carnegie Research I University. Graduate and undergraduate programs in a variety of disciplines are highly ranked, including the well-known Jacobs School of Music, Kelley School of Business, and Maurer School of Law; and in 2006, IUB placed third on PC Magazine's Top 20 Wired Colleges, the highest ranked public university on that list. (IU News Room, 2011; Jacobowitz, 2006)

The culture of the Bloomington campus balances between a conscious preservation of the traditional and an emphasis on innovation, experimentation and the interest in breaking new ground. These factors are combined with some sense of responsibility to lead, technologically and in other areas, both for the benefit of other campuses in the IU system, and amongst peers nationally and globally. This culture also manifests in the goals and direction of the Libraries, and has influenced decision-making in embracing new approaches, actively contributing to open-source communities such as Kuali®, the Sakai Project, and Blacklight, and moving forward to implement technologies as they develop – such as within the emerging discovery marketplace.

IMPLEMENTING DISCOVERY AT IUB LIBRARIES

Initial Efforts

Like scores of other libraries, IU implemented federated search technology branded as One-Search@IU in 2005. For its many flaws, federated search was an important step forward on the road to discovery, but was not the solution either users or librarians had hoped it might be. (Fagan, 2011) In 2008, IUB Libraries went live with WorldCat Local®⁵ (WCL); the primary motivator for this decision was user dissatisfaction with the library catalog interface. The dissatisfaction had manifested itself through feedback collected in several ways: focus groups, the LIBQUAL study completed earlier that year, and in regular, annual surveys administered by University Information Technology Services (UITS), the unit overseeing all campus computing services. Some specific examples of desired functionality which WCL® successfully provided include: search and display of results in non-Roman alphabets (e.g., Cyrillic, Arabic, Hebrew, East Asian languages); improving users' ability to find a known item; allowing the easy creation of lists of items that could then be publicly shared; and achieving better response times on searches. Unfortunately, despite improvements in the user experience overall, some specific needs of the libraries' constituency were still going unmet – namely, since WCL® does not allow the inclusion of electronic journal, title records from sources such as Serials Solutions®⁶, nor e-books from aggregators, a significant portion of Library content was inaccessible to users. Further, patrons struggled with the interface, finding it difficult to interpret the way that WCL® combined records in a version of FRBR.

While in many ways quite successful, WCL® ultimately proved not to be the right fit for this organization. The previously mentioned issue related to display and search of non-Roman characters was resolved by undertaking a major software upgrade to enable support for Unicode in the SIRSIDynix® catalog in December 2010. Over time, staff support for WCL® waned, as did its usage, resulting in the eventual termination of the subscription in March 2011.

Enter EBSCO

In early 2010, EBSCO approached the IU Bloomington Libraries with an invitation to be a beta partner in testing EBSCO Discovery Service™. Students, faculty and staff responded favorably to the product and to the interface. The timing of this event coincided with a point in the WCL® project where it had become clear that it would be necessary to reconsider the options available in the market, rather than being able to meet the need for a discovery tool within the context of the evolution of a product (that is, WorldCat Local®) selected to fulfill a different purpose.

EDS™ was particularly attractive for several reasons. First, the state of Indiana has an ongoing contract with EBSCO to provide a number of databases that, together with Gale®⁷ databases, make up INSPIRE, Indiana's Virtual Library, freely available to anyone with an IP address within Indiana. (Indiana State Library, n.d.) This promotes heavy usage of EBSCO resources at every grade level and by the general public, and results in a high level of familiarity with the EBSCOHost interface and recognition for the EBSCO brand with a large proportion of the University constituency. Secondly, EBSCO's implementation process, which was not technically intensive, and their high-touch customer support were especially appealing given the constraints on staff availability. The IU Bloomington Libraries had recently reorganized and created a new department responsible for the Libraries' Website and for related services such as a discovery tool. At that time, the department numbered only two: a search was still underway for a department head to lead the new unit, and all development resources were managed by working in coordination with

Figure 1. IU Bloomington Libraries home page, http://www.libraries.iub.edu

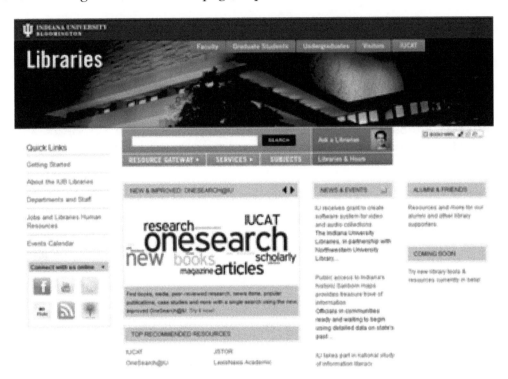

another department outside the library. Finally, in contrast to WorldCat Local®, EDS™ provides direct links to catalog records, giving access to both e-journals and e-books and to local notes for archival and rare book material.

These and other reasons led to the selection of EDS™ as a Web-scale discovery solution in September 2010. (McEvoy, 2010)

Creating an Integrated Discovery Experience

As mentioned in the introduction, it has always been a goal to integrate EDS™ into the Libraries' Web presence to the fullest degree possible. Furthermore, setting any loftier goals aside for a moment, a discovery tool is no small investment, and prioritizing this resource contributes toward making the best use of the funds dedicated. The public launch, which took place in August 2011, included the following components:

Branding: Not only are branded services easier to publicize, they are also easier to talk about. The already existing OneSearch@IU brand, previously associated with a federated search product, was co-opted for use with EDS™. EDS™ could then be promoted and publicized at the Bloomington campus as "an all new, improved OneSearch@ IU" – a logical next step in the process of better enabling discovery across all Library collections.

API/Web Service: A major goal of the implementation was to use the EBSCOHost Integration Toolkit (EIT) Web service, or API, to present results from EDS™ within the Library's Website search results. (EBSCOHost, n.d.) It also provided a way to address requests from the student body to integrate more visual cues into search results – format icons, book covers, etc.

The Libraries Website presents users with a single search box (sometimes called the "resource discovery search," or in other cases more simply "the orange box") that retrieves results from a

Figure 2. IUB Libraries site search results, showing OneSearch@IU results provided via EIT Web service

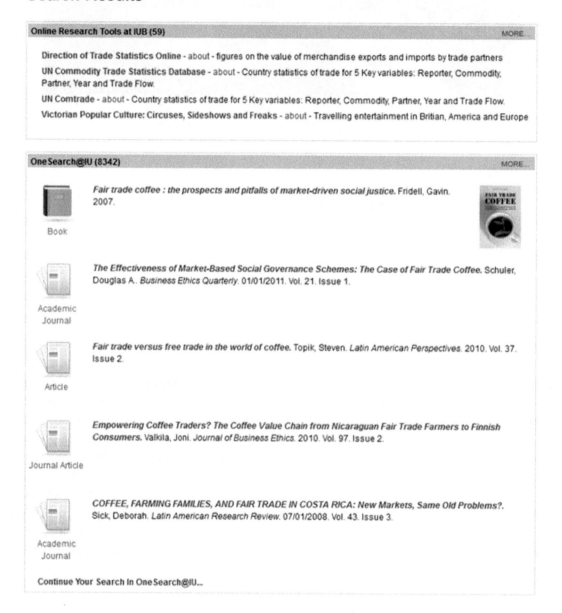

variety of sources, including resource information (databases), Serials Solutions® e-journal list, and Website search. [Figure 1] These results from diverse sources are then assembled on a single page. Previously, results from the federated search product were also returned; at launch, the page

was updated to instead display results from EDS™ provided via the EIT Web service. [Figure 2]

Subject pages The EDS™ search box was made available within the Libraries' research guides as a separate tab, in lieu of the federated search option that had previously appeared there. (Figure 3) The intention was to provide easy ac-

Figure 3. African Studies subject research guide, showing OneSearch@IU tab

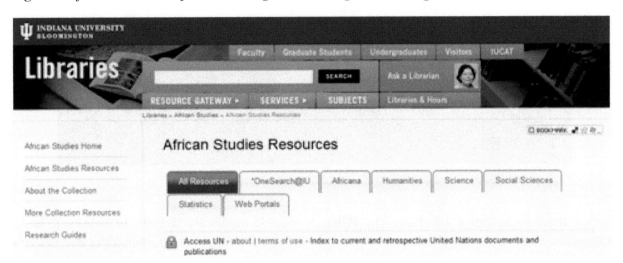

cess to this resource for all users while retaining the carefully constructed resource listings maintained by collection managers. This is viewed as an intermediate step, and with the intention of exploring more active integration in this area.

"Find Information" page The "Find Information" page has historically served as the page to which databases refer users upon ending or exiting a session. While many vendors have moved away from this behavior, the page still sees reasonably heavy use: it indexes high in Google search results for IUB Libraries, and is also the target of a library link appearing within the course management system for a small number of courses not associated with specific departments or programs. This page provided an opportunity to begin testing the integration of search behaviors, such as tabbed search boxes, planned to be integrated throughout the Website in future. (Figure 4)

Implementation: A Moving Target

Like other discovery solutions available on the market, EDS™ includes information from multiple sources pulled together into a larger data set that is then indexed as a whole: the base index,

content from subscribed databases (EBSCO and others), and the catalog extract. The base index, common to all EDS™ customers, includes citation and abstract data from approximately 20,000 providers (at the time of writing). (EBSCO Publishing, 2011) To this is added metadata from other sources to which the customer subscribes, both EBSCO databases (enabling full-text linking) and other providers with whom EBSCO has negotiated agreements (enabling direct linking to full text in those sources, called "custom links"). Finally, each customer provides an extract of their catalog data – a snapshot, if you will, of the bibliographic records and holdings information – which is also included in that customer's EDS™ dataset. EBSCO then indexes all this data together and results are returned based on their proprietary relevancy ranking algorithm.

Some adjustments can be made to the relevancy ranking by the vendor. For example, early in the IUB beta period, results from a specific content source were drowning out results from nearly all other sources, including the catalog, and EBSCO was able to make adjustments to correct this.

Customers cannot alter the contents of the base index, but specific subscribed databases can be included or removed from EDS™ content from

Figure 4. "Find information" page tabbed search box

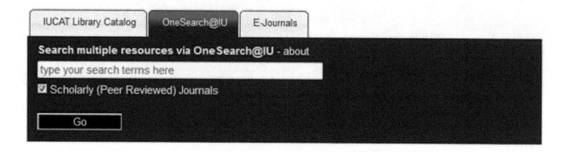

within the administrative interface. The IUB Libraries opted to remove several sources in this way, either because the content was felt to be unnecessary within the specific context of EDS™ (e.g., Funk and Wagnall's New World Encyclopedia), or the content was useful or usable only to a very narrow set of users (e.g., KISS: Korean Studies International, from which results display in Korean). In one case, content from OAIster (The Open Archives Initiative metadata harvesting protocol) was added and then removed, as results proved to be duplicative with high levels of variance in metadata quality.

Integrated Search

EDS™ includes "Integrated Search" as a means of including content from data not currently available either through the base index or as additional subscription-based sources. This federated search functionality can be enabled or disabled. Despite reservations about federated search generally, IU Bloomington opted to include a small number of sources (primarily ProQuest® products) at launch. User testing will be conducted in early 2012 to assess its efficacy and the importance of continuing with this feature.

API

Through the use of the EIT Web service, results from EDS™ are returned within the search results page in the library Website. In addition to basic citation information (author, title, date), icons indicating item type, and when available, book covers, are presented as part of the results.

Upon querying the EDS™ partners listserv, an active community for discussion and support, regarding issues relating to the API, it seemed that the primary interest of that group at that time was in integrating search-box code provided by the vendor rather than in working with the API. Happily, Hassan Sheikh, Head of Systems Development for The Open University in the United Kingdom responded with information about similar integrations within their Website, and he was extremely helpful in answering questions. (Sheikh, personal communication, June 17, 2011) The most pressing of the issues encountered was slow response times for results which initially might take as long as twenty seconds to return. EBSCO also proved very responsive and made changes which resulted in a huge improvement in result times, with results in just two or three seconds.

Staff reactions to the integration of EDS™ API results on the search results data have been varied, from the very positive to the extremely negative. In some cases it has been unclear whether the dissatisfaction felt centers specifically on the API data, or whether it is more generally related to the overall design of the search results page. To date, no negative comments on the change have been received from users, however; extensive user testing focusing on the search results page and specifically on the API results is planned in the near future.

Catalog Extract

Catalog data is extracted from the SIRSIDynix® integrated library system and provided to EBSCO in a machine-readable file, which includes the bibliographic record and holdings data for each item. At IUB, updates are provided and loaded weekly. As previously noted, IUCAT is a shared online catalog for the entire Indiana University system, and IU Kokomo, which implemented EDS™ in summer 2010, shares this same catalog extract. While there has been some discussion of the possibilities of generating multiple extracts and thus enabling individual campuses to load only their holdings, there are no plans to proceed in that manner at this time.

Once the catalog extract is uploaded as part of the EDS™ dataset, EBSCO provides real-time availability checking of location, call number, and status (including due date, if appropriate) for items by communicating with the institution's Z39.50 server. If the Z39.50 server cannot be reached to display the most current data, the holdings data from the extract will be displayed.

Often, it has been in working with the catalog extract that the most interesting challenges have arisen, and these have accounted for the bulk of the time elapsed in the period spanning from adoption to public launch.

A great deal of time has been invested in customizations to the interface of the SIRSIDynix® OPAC, smoothing out rough places, introducing improvements where possible, and generally tidying up. After such careful consideration of how the catalog data and the interface of the ILS work together – making countless adjustments, both to highlight and to obscure various characteristics of the system (SIRSIDynix's® double tab) or pieces of information (system-generated call numbers) – viewing the data in a new interface was a real eye-opener.

Over seven million records representing a wide array of formats provided plenty of opportunity for detecting anomalies, or sub-optimum data display (that is to say, records that looked just plain ugly, wherever they were viewed). Testing identified a few classes of records that were duplicative, unhelpful, or problematic (for example, stub records provided by vendors). Early in the process, the decision was made to remove title-level electronic journal records provided by Serials Solutions® from the extract with the rationale that these records did not add value for users within the context of searching EDS™. E-book records obtained from Serials Solutions® have been retained since it is judged that these do increase access for users.

In some cases, records from specific locations have been filtered. Many libraries in the IU system share records in IUCAT. Other libraries do not, for specific reasons: The Lilly Library and Music Library each have their own records because they add extra information to the record that is appropriate for their specialized collections; and the professional health schools (Medicine and Dentistry) share a record. In other cases, separate records are created for specific collections or locations: the Archives of Traditional Music, Kinsey Institute Library, Bloomington Law Library, and the Bloomington Residential Programs and Services Libraries are extra-systems libraries and their materials are not owned by the IU Bloomington Libraries. Specifically, in Kinsey records, additional data such as donor information is often added; because those items do not circulate, and because that private donor information is part of a notes field that cannot be suppressed from display for all records, Kinsey records have been filtered out of the catalog extract provided to EBSCO.

As these and other classes of records have been filtered out of the extract, new sources of clutter have been revealed. Over the long term, as the venues in which IUCAT data can be discoverable are further expanded, local cataloging practices will need to be carefully considered to enable consistency across discovery interfaces.

EBSCO enables customization of display of catalog records both within the result list and for the detailed bibliographic record. Significant improvements were achieved by working with them to suppress certain fields or specific data. For example, fields that were suppressed following launch were the 050 (call number; this often differs from the local call number, stored in the 999), the 024 (other standard number, such as UPC if included), and the 074 (Government Printing Office item number) field. It is also possible to suppress only certain data from a given field – system-generated call numbers, for example. All of this data is available in the IUCAT full display, easily accessible in just one click; within EDS™, this information was confusing to users and so it was eliminated.

In many cases, records downloaded from OCLC® include additional information that is not useful locally. While in some cases the record is edited prior to inclusion in the local database, in some cases data is simply suppressed from display in the OPAC – foreign language subject headings, as one example. However, because this data remained in the record, it was visible within OneSearch@IU, so that Steve Krug's book *Rocket Surgery Made Easy* showed subject headings of not just "Web-based user interfaces – Evaluation," but also for "Benutzeroberfläche," the German heading. This was corrected by requesting that EBSCO suppress all values of 65x (subject heading) fields with indicator 7 (denoting foreign language).

In some cases, where multiple records existed for the same item (for the reasons mentioned above), the holdings would simply … "jump." An example – there are two records for *The Catcher in the Rye*: copy 1 shows holdings for IUB, IUPUI, and IU East; copy 2 shows a single holding for Residential Programs and Services. Sometimes, copy 1 would show all 4 holdings records while copy 2 showed none; other times, it might be the reverse. (*Figure 1, 2*) It was this very changeable-

ness that slowed resolution, because results could not always be reliably replicated.

After a period of extensive testing, it was determined that the problem arose from multiple records with the same value in the 001 field. The 001 field is generally used as a unique identifier for records; because in these cases, multiple records were assigned the same value in the 001, there was no way to use the 001 to re-assemble them properly, or consistently, when loaded into OneSearch@IU. In SIRSIDynix®, the system-assigned unique record ID number is the "ckey" (catalog key) number. This was already being used within EDS™ to point to the appropriate record in IUCAT, both from the search results list and the full bibliographic record. When viewing a catalog record within EDS™, the "retrieve catalog item" link from the search results list or the record itself links with the catalog key to the specific record in IUCAT. (For example, the OneSearch@IU record *Rocket Surgery Made Easy* [Figure 5] takes the user to the IUCAT record as '1 of 1 for search " 9536208{ckey}."' [*Figure 6*]) The solution, then, was to provide EBSCO with a catalog extract in which the ckey values appeared in the 001 field.

Assessment: User Feedback and Evaluation

In early 2010, a representative from EBSCO Publishing conducted on-campus testing of a beta version of EDS™ at multiple locations nationwide, including the Herman B Wells Library on the Bloomington campus. At IUB, a total of seven participants (4 undergraduates, 2 graduate students, and one library staff member) each completed at least two scenario-based tasks using the beta version of EDS™, and each was also asked to test upcoming features using a prototype. Generally, participants reacted favorably, specifically mentioning that EDS™ was easy to use and that they were pleased by the ability to search a large proportion of the Libraries' content through a single search box. Undergraduates rated their

Figure 5. OneSearch@IU record, Rocket Surgery Made Easy

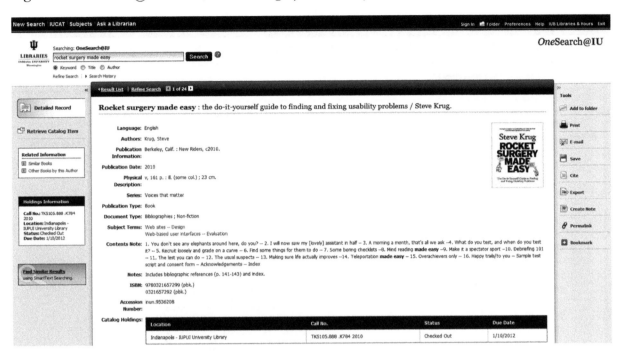

overall experience in using EDS™ as a 4.25 (on a scale of 1 to 5, with five being 'very usable'). Interestingly, when asked how likely they might be to use EDS™ again, graduate students' rating was highest – a 5 (on a scale of 1 to 5, 5 being 'very likely'), with undergraduates' rating being a 4.25. These positive results were influential in IUB Libraries' decision to subscribe to EDS™.

OneSearch@IU launched in late August 2011, immediately previous to the start of the fall semester. Marketing and promotion was limited to a feature on the home page of the library Website, fliers (distributed to all campus libraries including those located in the Halls of Residence) and a display in the main lobby of the Herman B Wells Library. Usage has climbed throughout the fall semester, although it is still considerably less than combined usage of all other EBSCO databases. It is hoped that continued promotion in a number of venues, including demonstrating the resource in library instruction sessions, will result in a continued increase in usage.

Internally, amongst library staff, reactions to EDS™ have been mixed. Initially there was considerable concern of a general nature: what impact a discovery tool might have on user behavior, and whether usage of more specialized databases might be negatively affected; whether a discovery tool adequately served all populations, specifically advanced researchers; and whether it might be incorrectly inferred by users that all library content was available through the discovery tool. While these are certainly worthy questions, they relate more to the overall concept of discovery itself, rather than to any specific tool such as EDS™, and as such are common to any implementation. In early stages of the beta release, some of the data and display issues detailed in the previous section were also causes of concern to staff. As those have been resolved, most staff have become more positive about OneSearch@IU, with the Reference and Teaching & Learning departments showing support throughout the implementation process. One specific area in which OneSearch@IU has been useful in providing reference service

Figure 6. IUCAT record, Rocket Surgery Made Easy

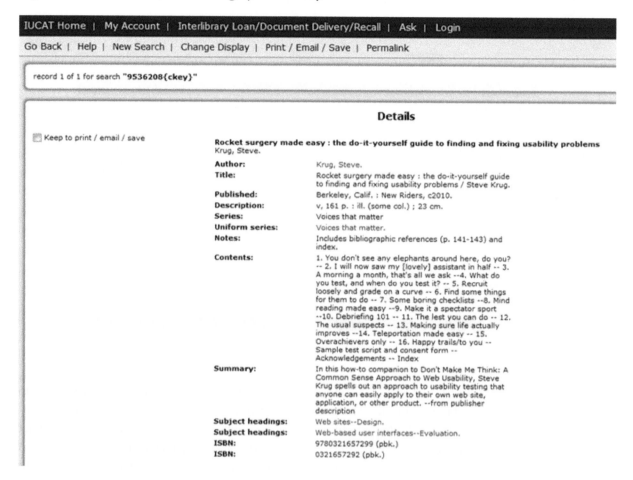

is the ease of providing patrons with permalinks to results sets that include both journal literature and items from IUCAT, the shared catalog – particularly helpful within instant message reference transactions. Undoubtedly, however, the most enthusiastic internal adopters of OneSearch@ IU have been the reference assistants – graduate students from the Indiana University School of Library and Information Science who staff the reference desks at the Wells Library. That group has also been quite helpful in troubleshooting and reporting problem records.

In July 2011, Sarah Williams and Anita Foster published the results of a usability study of the Illinois State University implementation of EDS™, called SearchIt; the first round of usability testing

of OneSearch@IU, planned for early 2012, will build off of their work, using many of the same tasks. (Williams & Foster, 2011) This initial testing will focus on what changes or improvements can be made to the local configuration options available within EDS™ itself.

Within the EDS™ partner community, EBSCO has announced plans to continue development of the API/EIT Web Service, and IUB Libraries will participate as a beta tester in that project. Given that the integration of API results into the Library Website has been an important part of the implementation project, and that there is interest in identifying additional for integration of EDS™ results within the Web presence, the second phase of user testing will focus on the Libraries' search results page and the presentation of EDS™ results via the API.

FUTURE RESEARCH DIRECTIONS

Additional areas of interest for future user testing include more in-depth research into use of facets; gauging user awareness of, and perceived value for, the integrated search (federated search) functionality; testing of the mobile application slated to be released by EBSCO sometime in 2012; and, of course, ongoing testing as EBSCO continues to release changes or add features to the product.

On a larger scale, further investigation is needed to begin to assess the impact of discovery tools on user behavior, in general and within specific populations (undergraduates, graduates, faculty, researchers, and for each of those groups within different disciplines). What impact does a discovery tool have on the usage of other databases and of the library catalog? Will discovery tools have the hoped-for impact – that is, increased usage of library resources?

CONCLUSION

Following the user testing planned for early 2012, several areas of concentration in the medium-term include pursuing more in-depth user feedback through focus groups to investigate how One-Search@IU might be best marketed to various audiences, and which improvements should be prioritized; and investigating opportunities for campus-level integration of OneSearch@ IU into venues such as OnCourse, the Indiana University course management system (part of the Sakai Project). Efforts are now in progress at other institutions (the University of Michigan [US] and the University of Oxford [UK]) to enable the integration of discovery products from Serials Solutions® and ExLibris™[8] into Sakai,

and there is local interest in doing so at IUB with EDS™ in 2012.

Looking to the future, however, there are larger questions that must be considered: What is the role of a research library as related to discovery? While the capacity for discovery, such as that delivered by a Web-scale discovery tool, does not increase the size of the information universe. It increases the proportion discoverable to any individual patron; conversely, this sense of expanded capacity further isolates those items and collections not included in the discovery environment. The primary target audience for many discovery solutions – the undergraduate – will feel no lack, either in quantity of results, or in the quality of the user experience through which they are accessed. This is not to say that discovery holds nothing for the graduate student, the faculty member, and the scholar, but simply that those groups tend to have already identified at least a reasonable proportion of the information universe that is likely to be relevant to their research. Discovery in its present incarnation both helps and hinders research libraries in the Libraries' role as information curators, which up to this time has consisted primarily of carefully and thoughtfully selecting, compiling and preserving materials, and of presenting various content silos, both internally and externally created, to their best advantage - which is as they intersect with the needs of the user population. It helps in that silos are reduced, and content is more widely accessible; and it hinders in that now more than ever, what is not explicitly included is implicitly obscured. Doubtless as Web-scale discovery platforms evolve, improvements will be achieved that will mitigate some of the concerns about completeness.

Lorcan Dempsey's assertion that discovery systems exist as a means of directing users back to the library catalog is arguable, not in terms of what it intends to achieve (ultimately, broader usage of library collections), but in terms of how it may best be achieved. Is the user best served by remaining within the local catalog, or can better success be achieved by focusing more on integrating catalog data within other systems, such as OneSearch@IU? In 2007, prior to the advent of Web-scale discovery products, Marshall Breeding stated that that any next-generation catalog (NGC) that did not include information from article databases stood incomplete as a service to users. (Breeding, 2007, p. 35) Andrew Nagy in his 2011 Library Technology Reports issue "Analyzing the Next-Generation Catalog," states, "The NGC is a stepping-stone technology, preparing libraries for the migration to Web-scale services … [it] does not meet user expectations: … it does not search everything." (Nagy, 2011, pp. 11, 26) At this stage, neither the NGC nor the Web-scale discovery platforms can claim to contain everything. Most importantly, even if at some point they should, enabling the fullest degree of discovery for users relies entirely on the quality, completeness, and consistency of Library data, whether the source is the library catalog or a licensed index.

Locally, the parallel efforts both to implement EBSCO Discovery Service™ and to adopt a new discovery interface for IUCAT, followed by the planned migration to the Kuali® OLE system, underscore the belief that at this time, a Web-scale discovery service and a next-generation library catalog are complementary tools that work together to better meet the needs of diverse user communities.

REFERENCES

Breeding, M. (2007). The birth of a new generation of library interfaces. *Computers in Libraries*, *27*(9), 34–37.

Dempsey, L. (2006). *The library catalogue in the new discovery environment: Some thoughts.* Retrieved from http://www.ariadne.ac.uk/issue48/dempsey/

EBSCO Publishing. (2010). *EDS usability test report.* Unpublished report.

EBSCO Publishing. (2011). *EDS content.* Retrieved December 28, 2011, from http://www.ebscohost.com/discovery/eds-content

EBSCOHost. (n.d.). *EBSCOhost integration toolkit.* Retrieved July 31, 2011, from http://eit.ebscohost.com/

Fagan, J. C. (2011). Federated search is dead – And good riddance! *Journal of Web Librarianship*, *5*(2), 77–79. doi:10.1080/19322909.2011.573533

Indiana State Library. (n.d.). *Frequently asked questions.* INSPIRE Indiana's Virtual Library. Retrieved July 31, 2011, from http://www.in.gov/library/inspire/faq.html

Indiana University Bloomington Libraries. (2010). *IUB libraries: Fact sheet.* Retrieved July 31, 2011, from http://www.libraries.iub.edu/index.php?pageId=5430

IU News Room. (2011, March 15). *"U.S. News" gives high marks to IU programs in nursing, law, business, education, medicine.* Retrieved from http://newsinfo.iu.edu/news/page/normal/17756.html

Jacobowitz, P. (2006, December 20). #3 Indiana University Bloomington – Top 20 wired colleges. *PCMag.com.* Retrieved from http://www.pcmag.com/article2/0,2817,2073461,00.asp

Kuali Foundation. (2010). *Kuali OLE.* Kuali Foundation. Retrieved July 31, 2011, from http://www.kuali.org/ole

McEvoy, K. (2010, June 7). *Indiana University selects EBSCO Discovery Service™ to give users what they expect online.* EBSCO Publishing. Retrieved from http://www.ebscohost.com/discovery/view-news/indiana-university-selects-EDS

Nagy, A. (2011). Analyzing the next-generation catalog. *Library Technology Reports*, *47*(7), 1–27.

University Institutional Research and Reporting. (2010a). *IU fact book 2010: Bloomington.* Retrieved from http://www.iu.edu/~uirr/reports/standard/factbook/campus_fb/2010-11/Bloomington/FactBook1011_BL.pdf

University Institutional Research and Reporting. (2010b). *IU fact book 2010-11: University.* Retrieved from http://www.iu.edu/~uirr/reports/standard/factbook/campus_fb/2010-11/University/FactBook1011_Web.pdf

Williams, S., & Foster, A. (2011). Promise fulfilled? An EBSCO Discovery Service usability study. *Journal of Web Librarianship, 5*(3), 179–198. doi:10.1080/19322909.2011.597590

ADDITIONAL READING

Briceño-Rosales, Z. C. (2011). OCLC WorldCat: Interactivity and mobility create a winning combo. *Library Journal, 136*(Reference Supplement), 15-16.

Coyle, K. (2010). FRBR, the domain model. RDA vocabularies for a twenty-first-century data environment [Special issue]. *Library Technology Reports, 46*(2), 20.

Fernandez, R. (2011). Ex Libris's Primo: Easy to implement, intuitive to use. *Library Journal, 136*(Reference Supplement), 17.

Hanson, C., Hessel, H., Barneson, J., Boudewyns, D., Fransen, J., & Friedman-Shedlov, L. … Traill, S. (2009). *Discoverability phase 1 final report.* University of Minnesota Libraries. Retrieved from http://purl.umn.edu/48258

Hanson, C., Hessel, H., Barneson, J., Boudewyns, D., Fransen, J., & Friedman-Shedlov, L. … West, A. (2011). *Discoverability phase 2 final report.* University of Minnesota Libraries. Retrieved from http://purl.umn.edu/99734

Luther, J., & Kelly, M. C. (2011). The next generation of discovery. *Library Journal, 136*(5), 66–71.

Newcomer, N. L. (2011). The detail behind Web-scale: Selecting and configuring Web-scale discovery tools to meet music information retrieval needs. *Music Reference Services Quarterly, 14*(3), 131–145. doi:10.1080/10588167.2011.596098

Powers, A. C. (2011). EBSCO's EDS: Relying on patron data to show the way. *Library Journal, 136*(Reference Supplement), 14-15.

Thornton-Verma, H. (2011). Discovering what works: Librarians compare discovery interface experiences. *Library Journal, 136*(Reference Supplement), 14.

Varnum, K. (2011). Serials Solutions' Summon: Familiarity breeds success. *Library Journal, 136*(Reference Supplement), 18.

Vaughan, J. (2011). Web scale discovery services. *Library Technology Reports, 47*(1), 5–29.

KEY TERMS AND DEFINITIONS

API (Application Programming Interface): Sometimes used interchangeably with "Web service," an API provides a way for applications to communicate and share data. In other words, by using certain protocols or standards, data can be retrieved, processed, and displayed by other applications and in other contexts than the originating data source. Examples of well-known APIs are the Google Maps API, or the WorldCat® API. One example of the use of an API would be many popular third party Twitter applications (e.g. TweetDeck); these applications query the Twitter API to bring back the data within their own interface.

Community Source: Community source refers to a specific type of open source project in that a specific community entity, often comprised of representatives from supporting institutions or organizations, has committed ongoing funding, support and other resources to the project. Examples of well-known community source entities are the Sakai Project (http://sakaiproject.org/) and the Kuali Foundation (http://kuali.org/).

Discovery Tool: A platform featuring a unified index created by bringing together data from a wide array of publishers, vendors and other sources (including library catalog records), resulting in improved relevancy ranking across the entire set. This allows users to simultaneously broaden the scope of their search and to increase the precision of the results returned, and the discovery tool typically presents an attractive interface designed to meet user expectations for ease-of-use, sharing, and other functions common to commercial Websites such as Amazon or Google.

Federated Search: Sometimes referred to as "metasearch" tools, federated search tools allow a single query to be simultaneously delivered to multiple information resources, and then to collect those results and display them as a single set. To accomplish this, the tool must generally rely on "translators" which enable communication with the varied sources.

FRBR (Functional Requirements for Bibliographic Records): For more detailed information, see http://www.ifla.org/publications/functional-requirements-for-bibliographic-records.

Kuali Online Library Environment: A community sourced initiative to develop and release a product that meets the needs of academic and research libraries to acquire, describe, circulate, and provide access to their collections.

Unicode: A standard that allows for the consistent searching, rendering and display of text across the majority of the world's written languages.

Web Service: A Web service is more or less an API that uses certain Web protocols to communicate. A concrete example of this might be a Web service that maintains information about library hours; information about hours is loaded into a database, which can be communicated with via the Web service; that Web service could then be queried by code placed in a variety of places on the library Website, and this would result in dynamic display of the hours information, always direct from the authoritative source (the database). A helpful analogy for the less technical might be an RSS feed: by subscribing to that RSS feed, its information is delivered to you – the underlying concept of data sharing is the key idea.

ENDNOTES

[1] EBSCO Discovery Service is owned by EBSCO Publishing Industries

[2] SIRSIDynix is a registered trademark of SIRSIDynix Corporation.

[3] Kuali is an open source administrative software.

[4] Summons is owned by ProQuest LLC

[5] Worldcat is a registered trademark of OCLC.

[6] Serials Solutions is a registered trademark of Serials Solutions

[7] Gale is a registered trademark Gof Cengage Learning

[8] ExLibris is a trademark of Ex Libris Ltd.

Chapter 30

Encore Synergy Implementation at a Medium–Sized University Library:
Unforeseen Challenges and Opportunities

Rachel A. Erb
Colorado State University, USA[1]

ABSTRACT

Implementing Web-scale discovery at the University of Nebraska at Omaha's (UNO) Criss Library presented some unexpected challenges. The UNO library selected Encore Synergy from Innovative Interfaces, Vendor homogeneity between Innovative Interfaces' Integrated Library System (ILS), and the discovery tool did not prevent problems regarding ILS module interoperability. This chapter describes the solutions found. Web-scale discovery via Encore also did not include all of the library's electronic resources, but only a few aggregator databases. A representative sample of approximately thirty resources, however, was accessible via pass-through search from Encore to Innovative's federated search tool, Research Pro. An initial examination of database usage indicates a decline in the use of databases not directly searchable in Encore.

DOI: 10.4018/978-1-4666-1821-3.ch030

INTRODUCTION

The University of Nebraska at Omaha (UNO) currently has a population of approximately 14,000 total undergraduate and graduate students and has experienced exponential growth during the past several years. Part of this growth can be attributed to UNO's new classification as a doctoral/research university according to the Carnegie Foundation. Several years prior to this designation, the Library had lagged behind its peer institutions in offering search technologies that provide seamless delivery of full-text resources. Specifically, the Library lacked an OpenURL link resolution system and a federated search product. However, in 2007, under new leadership, the Library added OpenURL link resolving (Serial Solutions[®2] Article Linker) as well as federated searching (Serial Solutions® 360 Search). Although not formally surveyed, many students and faculty expressed concern with 360 Search's speed and retrieval of relevant results. Librarians at UNO were also not satisfied with 360 Search and eschewed including it in bibliographic instruction. The Library worked with Serials Solutions® to troubleshoot the product's slowness in yielding search results. Serials Solutions® recommended the Library reduce some of the database clusters because many of them had more than twenty databases per subject category. After the Library streamlined the number of databases per category to no more than ten, 360 Search's speed did improve, but the retrieved results were still problematic. General dissatisfaction with 360 Search led to its discontinuation prior to the end of the three-year contract, but no alternative federated search product was considered. Despite overt criticism of 360 Search, the discontinuation of federated search altogether generated many inquiries from faculty and students. Many of them suggested that the Library offer something akin to 360 Search. As expected, neither faculty nor students offered any federated search product examples that they may have encountered at other libraries.

The feedback from faculty and students convinced the Library it was important to offer a searching experience reminiscent of Google that would allow users to search the local catalog and a selection of full-text sources from a single interface. The Library determined that discovery tools eclipsed federated search utilities in meeting the objective of searching the library's local and electronic collections, and decided to implement Innovative Interfaces' Encore Synergy™. Interestingly, the Library also implemented another federated search product, Innovative Interfaces' Research Pro because it integrates with Encore.

While other institutions are able to incorporate digital collections, locally developed collections, and institutional repositories, these collections are still in their infancy at the Library. Because of these limitations, the Library's search tool is not quite the "the foundation for portal development" that may currently exist at other institutions (Allison, 2010, p. 13). However, the tool for ensuing portal development, Encore Synergy™, is now present in the Library. While many accounts of discovery tool implementation discuss the inclusion of digital collections and localized search interface customizations, this account focuses on some fundamental issues encountered while implementing the Web-scale discovery tool, Encore Synergy™. In addition, Web-scale discovery's impact on the use of library resources which indicates that Encore Synergy™ is well-positioned to serve as a portal will be explored.

SELECTION

Having identified the need for a discovery tool, the Criss Library sought quick implementation because two other universities in Nebraska, the University of Nebraska-Lincoln and the University of Nebraska-Kearney, already offered Encore Synergy™. In the interest of rapidly selecting and deploying a discovery tool for the upcoming 2010-2011 academic year, the Library did not have a formal selection process that involved a cross-departmental library committee in order to review discovery systems from a variety of vendors. Instead, the Library's Administration tasked the Virtual Services Department with reviewing a few products for selection and recommending at least one. Neither the Virtual Services department nor the Library's Administration insisted on a specific set of evaluation criteria to establish a framework for requirements before undertaking the review and selection process. The only requirement explicitly expressed by both groups was that the selected discovery tool system must provide an architecture that is compatible with the existing Innovative ILS (Integrated Library System). This requirement coupled with the fact that two other libraries in the NU system implemented Encore Synergy™, pointed to the likelihood that UNO would follow suit. Nonetheless, the Virtual Services department reviewed two Web-scale discovery services; Serial Solutions®' Summon™ and Innovative's Encore Synergy™ (Encore). While the Virtual Services Department unanimously preferred Summon™ to Encore, the cost of the latter was prohibitive for investing in the still evolving environment of Web-scale discovery. The Virtual Services Department deemed Summon™ a superior discovery tool because it pre-harvests the library's local content and electronic content from over 6,000 providers in a single index. As a result, searching via a pre-coordinated search index expedites search results and does not rely on a federated search utility to access the content, producing results presented in a single set, unfettered by potentially biased relevancy ranking technology. The Library was very satisfied with the quality and performance of the Serial Solutions® knowledge base, 360 Core, and this knowledge base integrates with Summon™ to indicate even more full-text availability than does Encore as it does not integrate with any knowledge base. As a Library that has explored mobile technology and conducted usability studies regarding mobile

interfaces, the Virtual Services Department appreciated the mobile interface Summon™ offered.

ENCORE SYNERGY (ENCORE) AT THE UNIVERSITY OF NEBRASKA AT OMAHA

After comparing Summon™ and Encore, the Library ultimately chose Encore for several key reasons. Because the Library administration was uncertain there would be a return on investment with Web-scale discovery, they opted for the more conservative approach and selected the less costly Encore. In addition, the Library has employed Innovative's Integrated Library System (ILS) since the early 1990's, and therefore, opted for Encore because there would be no potential system interoperability issues. Innovative offered a hosted leasing option that allows the Library to subscribe for three years while determining how Web-scale discovery is used by the UNO community without a substantial long-term financial investment. Upon expiration of the lease, the Library will have the freedom to investigate and consider other discovery tools that might better fit UNO's needs. Innovative also included their federated searching utility, Research Pro, which is fully integrated with Encore, at a discounted price. It should be noted that Encore does not require Research Pro in order to function, but the Library decided to purchase Research Pro because Encore did not search all of the library's electronic resources.

RESEARCH PRO

A significant part of the Encore implementation was configuring Research Pro. The Virtual Services Department selected thirty resources to be added to Research Pro. All of the resources, with a few exceptions that included some subscription cancellations, were previously included in 360

Table 1. Research Pro: subject categories with respective databases

Art & Humanities	Business & Economics	Education	Engineering &Technology	Government & Law	History
MLA	ABI Global	ERIC	IEE Xplore	Lexis Nexis	JSTOR
JSTOR	ABI Trade & Industry	PsycInfo	Google Schoar	CQ Researcher	Project Muse
ArtStor	ABI Dateline	Physical Education Index	JSTOR	Criminal Justice Abstracts	NYT Historical
Academic Search Premier	Google Scholar	Academic Search Premier	Wiley Interscience	Google Scholar	Google Scholar
Communication & Mass Media Complete		Readers Guide Retro			
Google Scholar		Google Scholar			
		JSTOR			
		Project Muse			

Search's database profile. This original list was compiled by the Research Services Department. The final list of thirty resources was submitted to Innovative along with a list of subject categories for all the databases that will display the end-user interface. The subject categories are as follows in Table 1.

After the preliminary work was completed, Innovative's technical support expediently configured Research Pro according to the resources the Library selected. This does not mean, however, that the configuration work was completed. The Systems Librarian had to code the HTML files and the CSS style sheets in order to reflect the Library's branding and color scheme. Innovative's default category label for popular aggregator databases is "Best Bets." The Library changed this to "Top 10" to reflect the Top Ten dropdown menu on the Library's homepage.

The Library's Top Ten databases are as follows:

1. Academic Search Premier
2. Business Source Premier
3. Cambridge Scientific Abstracts
4. CQ Researcher
5. ERIC (Cambridge Scientific Abstracts)
6. JSTOR
7. LexisNexis Academic
8. MLA International Bibliography
9. PsycInfo
10. WilsonOmniFile Full Text

The Library also decided the name Research Pro did not reflect an adequate description that was intuitive to users. Instead, the Library opted to change the name in the public interface to "Multi-Search."

Table 2. Research Pro: subject categories with respective databases (continued)

Image & Media	News & Current Events	Science & Medicine	Social Sciences & Statistics	General Reference
ArtStor	NYT Historical	PubMed	Criminal Justice Abstracts	Gale Virtual Reference Library
JSTOR	Lexis Nexis Academic Universe	Wiley Interscience	PsycInfo	Funk and Wagnall's New World Encyclopedia
Google Images	Academic Search Premier	BioOne	Communication & Mass Media	Books in Print
Artcyclopedia	Google Scholar	BioMed Central	Google Scholar	
		Google Scholar	JSTOR	
		CSA: Biological Sciences	Project Muse	

The Systems Librarian was then able to test how well Research Pro integrates with Encore. A search initiated in Encore will automatically incorporate the search results of all the databases as it would in Research Pro. Integration with Encore means that there is a pass-through search in Research Pro. After a keyword search is performed in Encore, the end-user will have the option to select the link, "More Resources," which will populate the search terms in Research Pro's search window, but the user must select the relevant cluster or clusters of databases and then initiate the search. Because this can be potentially confusing to the Library's users, the Director of the Virtual Services Department created a tutorial including a comprehensive demonstration of the Library's version of Research (http://youtube/eLzjBf8jMkE).

ELECTRONIC RESOURCES AND ENCORE

After the Research Pro configuration and testing were complete, the next step was to determine which electronic resources should be added to Encore. At the time of implementation, Encore searched up to five databases in real-time direct from the resources. For these, there would be no pass-through search to Research Pro as the search results from these resources will be displayed in Encore. The Research Services Department decided that the five databases to be included were: EBSCO (Premier Sources), ArtSTOR™[3], LexisNexis®[4] Academic, JSTOR™[5], and Wilson OmniFile. The most popularly searched databases were added to Encore. There was, however, one exception; ArtSTOR™, was included in order to offer a searchable digital collection that has grown so much in scope during the past several years, and as a result, has uses in many other disciplines besides art and art history. ArtSTOR™ was the only digital collection the library could offer at the time because the Library was just beginning to work on creating local digital collections. Only for the purposes of selection, Innovative counted both EBSCO's Academic Search Premier and Business Source Premier as one resource. In the search results, however, each citation clearly indicates the specific Premier Source database in which the citation is stored.

In addition to Encore not searching all of the Library's databases, Encore is not compatible with Serial Solutions® knowledge base, Core 360. As a result, not all of the Library's e-journals can be retrieved in Encore. The Library subscribes to Serial Solutions® MARC 360 service with MARC record delivery for most electronic resources in the knowledge base, but not all of them because the Library did not include Serial Solutions®' brief records as part of the service profile.

Another limitation regarding searching electronic resources involves journal title keyword searching. Because the Library does not subscribe to Innovative's Open URL link resolver, WebBridge, a title keyword search for a journal title does not include articles from a particular journal in the search results. While the Library subscribes to Serial Solutions® Article Linker 360, this product does not integrate with Encore. Encore's inability to integrate with other vendor products circumvents the Library from offering Web-scale discovery similar to those libraries that either subscribe to all Innovative electronic resource management tools or use Summon™ for Web-scale discovery.

Encore assists users with differentiating between print and online items by offering the ability to refine their searches according to the preferred format. Specifically, Encore offers an "Availability" facet which allows users to refine between items that are "Online" or items that are "At the Library." In order to enable this feature, Encore's technical support was provided with a comprehensive list of material type codes which are used to designate as online items. Those ma-

terial types excluded from this designation are considered "At the Library."

INTEGRATION WITH INNOVATIVE MODULES

Prior to implementing Encore, the Library did not consider the possibility that not all of Innovative's ILS modules would be interoperable with the discovery tool. It was assumed that all other Innovative Modules fully integrated with Encore. The Library also expected that all legacy catalog enhancements would be reproducible in the Encore interface. The internal launch, however, proved that these mistaken assumptions needed to be immediately addressed with workaround solutions whenever possible.

One might expect that a vendor's ILS modules would seamlessly integrate with the same vendor's discovery tool, but there are a few Innovative modules that currently do not integrate with Encore. For example, the Library purchased Material Bookings in 2009 in order to offer self-booking of study rooms, laptops, Kindles, cameras, etc., only to discover a year later that self-booking can only be performed in the legacy catalog. This lack of module interoperability is particularly problematic because one of the most frequent keyword searches in both the legacy catalog and Encore is "group study room." In general, study rooms are very popular at the Library and it is important that users can reserve rooms in either the legacy catalog or Encore. The Systems Librarian devised a solution that would allow patrons to be redirected to self-bookable items in the legacy catalog. She edited every bibliographic record that indicated an item was bookable and added a link in each record to redirect the patron to the corresponding bibliographic display in the classic catalog where the patron can book the item.

Encore also lacks interoperability with Innovative's RSS (Really Simple Syndication) Feed Builder module. Feed Builder allows libraries to create custom RSS feeds using data from records such as bibliographic records, and resource records (Electronic Resource Management (ERM)) stored in the ILS. Feed Builder allowed the Library to meet a long-standing demand of faculty who frequently requested the Library offer new material RSS feeds. Shortly after purchasing Feed Builder in 2009, the Library began to offer many RSS feeds of new materials in various subject areas and formats. The RSS feeds are hosted on the legacy catalog's server for viewing and are also available for subscription via RSS feed reader. The Library's investment in RSS technology was not realized in Encore. Encore's customization restrictions only permitted three custom links and the Library needed to use the three available to link to essential services. Thus, the Library was unable to include a link to its 34 RSS feeds. A keyword search in Encore also did not retrieve any relevant RSS feeds. Considering the efforts made to offer RSS feeds, it was disappointing that these feeds did not integrate with Encore. Discovery tools such as Encore should leverage RSS technology for preferred search queries, new material lists, most circulated item lists, etc. (Yang & Wagner, 2010).

ENCORE CUSTOMIZATION

In addition to Innovative modules that cannot integrate with Encore, there are also several locally developed legacy catalog enhancements, mostly coded in JavaScript, which cannot be replicated in Encore. Encore's software is hosted on a separate server off-site, and therefore, the Systems Librarian did not have access to the HTML Encore screens and Web server for scripting. One such popular enhancement is a call number text message service the Library offers in the legacy catalog. The popularity of this feature reflects the increasing use of mobile technology and the inflexibility of Encore in this instance counters

the whole idea of a Next-Generation catalog's compatibility with emerging technologies.

In 2008, the Library subscribed to the LibraryThing For Libraries (LTFL) tag-based discovery feature as an enhancement to the legacy catalog. Installing the LTFL widget involves coding the bibliographic display HTML page of the classic catalog in order for the tags to display in the fully bibliographic catalog display entry. From a given bibliographic record, a patron can click on LTFL tags and view the Library's holdings that have the same tag as the viewed bibliographic record. LFTL requires a user to create a personal account to be able to assign tags. Tags are not automatically added to the bibliographic record, but the Library's LTFL account is updated monthly with a batch load of new ISBNs. The tags that will ultimately display in the bibliographic record are the top twenty assigned tags in LTFL for a given title. LibraryThing's developers routinely perform quality control for all assigned tags.

LTFL tags cannot be imported into Encore. While Encore generates tags from existing metadata in bibliographic records and allows users to create and add their own tags, the LTFL tags provide a well-established, and purely user-created source of metadata that is currently absent in Encore.

There were, however, a few modifications Encore's technical support were able to accomplish to suit the Library's needs. The Library uses Meebo for chat reference service and this mode of communication has become very popular at the Library. The Research Services Department wanted to have this widget embedded in Encore in order to offer user assistance. The Systems Librarian sent Encore's technical support the coding for the Meebo widget and it was quickly installed and available after updating the server overnight.

After Encore was installed for the Library, the Metadata Librarian noticed that it was not possible to perform number searches in Encore such as ISSN, ISBN, and call numbers. Technical support ran a process to index those three fields and the capability was ready the next day after the overnight server update.

Encore also offers a simultaneous search in WorldCat Local that is not interfiled with the search results, but is offered as a link in the right hand container labeled "More Resources." The link indicates the number of relevant keyword searches found in WorldCat Local. For example, a keyword search of "worms" generated "Show 58,320" beneath the WorldCat Local icon; there are 58,320 items in WorldCat Local that have the keyword "worms" in their metadata. Once the user clicks on this link, the WorldCat Local interface opens in another window with the search results displayed. WorldCat, and more recently World-Cat Local, have been a core element in library instruction for many years and it was imperative to include this feature.

RefWorks is an online bibliographic research management tool that allows users to store bibliographic information and generate citations according to numerous citation style manuals. RefWorks is another core element of bibliographic instruction at the Library and is widely used by faculty and students. In addition to incorporating RefWorks into bibliographic instruction, the Library created and maintains a very detailed LibGuide explaining how to use this research tool. Encore offers the ability to directly export bibliographic records into RefWorks; this feature was lacking in the legacy catalog and RefWorks exports required many steps by the user. Encore enabled network functionality for RefWorks and the export process is not cumbersome as it is with the legacy catalog.

There was, however, one enhancement the Library avoided—the ability for the location code in item records to link to a Google Map display of the item's location. This feature is based on the 'branch address" associated with the location code. The Library does not have any branches, so this feature was not useful to the user community.

Encore also had one default feature installed that was not of use to the Library--a link to

PathfinderPro, a product the Library does not offer. Pathfinder Pro associates user searches and search results and dynamically generates links to databases, Web sites, book reviews, full-text journals, e-books, and other resources. Encore's technical support promptly removed the link to PathfinderPro, but it is worth noting that this product enhances Web-scale discovery.

METADATA ERRORS, INCONSISTENCIES, AND ENSUING RECORD CLEAN-UP

While there are many enhancements in the legacy catalog that the Library could not include in Encore, the Library can employ metadata to have some control over the order and display of retrieved search results. There is a direct relationship between the metadata quality and the accuracy of retrieved search results. All discovery tools rely on accurate metadata to create facets, to rank results by relevance, and to enhance results in "many other ways not exploited in traditional catalogs" (Breeding, 2004, p 79). These interfaces now employ metadata to group and organize records as detailed in the Functional Requirements for Bibliographic Records (FRBR). The Library quickly discovered that Web-scale discovery disclosed problems that were not apparent in the legacy catalog.

Cataloging Hardware: Kindle Reader and Laptop Records

Kindle readers and laptops can be easily found in the legacy catalog, but this was not the case in Encore. Access issues for Kindles and laptops are due largely to the way they are cataloged. Specifically, there are bibliographic records for eight Kindle readers and, as titles are downloaded to these devices, the titles are included in the Kindle record as added author/title (MARC 700) entries. This policy allows circulation staff to quickly add

Figure 1. Example of a keyword search in Encore with separate search results from WorldCat Local

a book to the record without the assistance of the cataloging department, but this local cataloging practice ultimately makes finding titles available on a Kindle reader more difficult for patrons who use Encore. For example, if a patron searches for the title "Mockingjay" the Kindle's added title does not display; instead the patron sees a title entry for "Kindle." If the patron enters the keywords "Mockingjay" and "Susanne Collins," the Kindle format for this title is listed in the results as "Kindle." The patron would have to select the entry for "Kindle" in order to view the record, and hopefully, notice the added entry.

Another problem with Kindles is that they are inconsistently cataloged. The Library circulates twelve Kindles, but not all of them readily display in Encore's keyword search results using the keyword "Kindle." Some are fully cataloged and those items display in the beginning of the search results. The others with minimal cataloging are not visible in the first page of retrieved results. Books and articles about Kindles are interfiled with those complete records. As a result, it is almost impossible to generate a cohesive list from Encore of all Kindles available in the Library.

The completeness of bibliographic records also affects the search results of circulating laptop computers in Encore. Again, those that are fully cataloged according to current standards are easily retrievable in Encore. Laptop computers with minimal records do not appear on the first page of the listed results. Complete records and e-books about laptops are ranked higher than minimal bibliographic records of laptops in the search results.

Unfortunately, the Library is neither able to request that Innovative accommodate the Library by altering the search results algorithm nor does the Library have direct control over search results algorithm in order to resolve this problem. The only means of control the Library has is to ensure all bibliographic records are complete. Thus, metadata policies and procedures for media equipment need immediate revision when such problems are detected.

Encoding Issues: Fixed Fields in the MARC Record

In addition to revealing that local cataloging procedures need some modification, Encore also exposed cataloging errors and inconsistencies that were not detectable in the legacy catalog owing to differences between the legacy catalog's and Encore's search algorithm. Innovative recommends that ILS managers perform several field statistics reports using Millennium's Statistics Module. These field statistics reports detect invalid and missing codes in the fixed fields of bibliographic, item, order, patron, and resource (ERM) records. Innovative recommends these reports be generated and reviewed on an annual basis. ILS record maintenance projects were not routinely performed because there was frequent employee turnover in the position responsible for this task. Once these reports were generated, numerous errors found in the statistics report needed immediate correction. The Systems Librarian decided to embark on a wide-scale data correction project before unveiling Encore to the public.

An example of a significant cataloging error that would adversely impact an Encore results list was that approximately 27,000 bibliographic records lacked a code in the fixed field for language (Lang) of the MARC record. Approximately 3,700 of these records were from the newly cataloged music collection and all had *n/a* in the Lang fixed field. Despite the invalidity of this code, *n/a* was used for items with no linguistic content. All of these records had to be individually checked in order to verify there was no linguistic content and were assigned their proper code, *zxx*. In addition, there were 17 records that had outdated language codes and were appropriately updated. There were also many records that did not have the correct language designation. For example, there were items coded as Russian when the materials were actually in the Tajik language, which is an Eastern dialect of Persian called Dari, written and printed using the Cyrillic alphabet. This error is, perhaps, more significant at the Library because it houses the Arthur Paul Afghanistan collection which is recognized as one of the largest collections of its kind in the world. Materials printed in languages of the region, Dari, Persian, and Pashto, represent a significant portion of the collection.

Lastly, there were several hundred records that were incorrectly designated "undetermined," *und*. Many of these items were multi-language and were assigned the correct code *mul*. Approximately 100 records for English language materials were coded for language with *und* and these were corrected with *eng*. It was difficult to globally update many of these corrections because many of these problems required close inspection of the bibliographic records. All of these errors will greatly impact the search results in Encore because they will not be filed into the proper language facet, and therefore, many potentially relevant records would have been either excluded from the search or filed in the incorrect facet.

In addition to language (Lang) fixed field errors, 1654 format codes (BCODE1) needed manual correction. The most common problem encountered with format (BCODE1) fields was that they were left blank. Most of the records with blank format fields were United States Federal Documents in microfiche. Again, these format codes needed correction so these records would be properly filed in the format facet "Microform."

Presentation of URLs (MARC 856)

There was one noticeable MARC tag that required modification--the URL (856) field. The HTML coding "target="_blank was not functional in Encore. Specifically, the Library's bibliographic load tables had this coding in the proxy string so the link can be opened in a new window. For example, the previous coding for this resource, Credo Reference, allows the resource to open in a new window so the user can still readily access the catalog if necessary:

856 41 |u http://leo.lib.unomaha.edu/ login?url=http://www.credoreference.com " target="_blank |z Access to Credo Reference

The Library's Encore representative indicated this HTML code deprecates in Encore and approximately 80,000 bibliographic records were globally updated to remove "target="_blank from the 856 field. The 856 field now displays as follows:

856 41 |u http://leo.lib.unomaha.edu/ login?url=http://www.credoreference.com|z Access to Credo Reference

In addition to globally updating bibliographic records that had an 856 field, the load tables with the proxy string coding also had "target="_blank and were modified to ensure future records would be loaded without the deprecated code in the Encore environment.

Future Bibliographic Record Maintenance

One area that still needs thorough review is the geographical subdivisions of the Library of Congress Subject Headings (LCSH) for all bibliographic records. These geographical subdivisions are mapped to Encore as geographical location, known as the "Place" facet in Encore. Without correct geographical designations, the "Place" facet will not be accurate. This project could take several months, but it is worth the effort.

The quantity of errors indicates that overlooking data review is no longer acceptable in the new discovery environment where the unique discovery tool search algorithm might make formerly innocuous errors relevant in search results. As records are loaded from different vendors with varying record quality, this issue becomes more crucial. For any discovery tool to be successfully employed, cataloging policies and procedures should be carefully reviewed and amended as necessary.

LAUNCHING ENCORE

To permit the Library's faculty and staff to become accustomed to using a Web-scale discovery system, the Library decided to test Encore internally throughout the spring of 2010. This also gave the Systems Librarian ample time to resolve access and display issues that would inevitably arise and

Figure 2. The Library's home page: Encore's search window embedded in the tabbed menu

to spend the rest of the term configuring Research Pro. The internal launch of Encore officially began when the Library's sales representative and Encore representative led a promotional event at the Library referred to as the "Encore Kickoff." During this event, promotional materials were distributed and the Innovative team unveiled Encore and was on hand to answer questions.

In the fall of 2010, Encore was made available to the public as the main search box for materials on the Library's website, with a link to the legacy catalog beneath Encore's search box. It is located on the right side of website, underneath the tab labeled "Books & More" without any reference to the name of the Web-scale discovery platform.

With no library-wide promotional strategy for Encore in place, the publicity for Encore was uneven. Some reference librarians included a search box in their subject guides created with LibGuides and the Systems Librarian created guides specifically for Encore and Research Pro detailing their features. There was also an article in the Library's newsletter introducing Encore.

Encore was further publicized by the Acting Dean who demonstrated Encore at a campus-wide Dean's meeting and received a favorable response. During this time, the Reference Librarians incorporated Encore into lower-level bibliographic instruction classes. The students, overall, seemed to prefer Encore to the classic catalog. While there has been no formal survey to this date, this anecdotal feedback correlates with the usage data of Encore compared with the legacy catalog presented later in this study.

USER PARTICIPATION: TAGGING

Since patrons are not able to either view or add LibraryThing For Libraries (LTFL) tags in Encore, rendering this feature in the legacy catalog completely inoperable, the Library wanted to offer Encore's tagging feature to anyone with a current library account. Restricting patron types such as students and faculty from adding user tags in Encore will circumvent the ongoing service learning children's literature genre tagging project and other similar projects in the future. Encore's administrative interface allows the Library to monitor and delete inappropriate tags. Fortunately,

Figure 3. Tagging activity among patron types at UNO

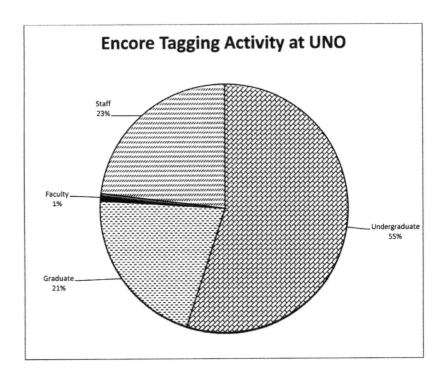

the Library's patrons demonstrate responsible use of Encore's tagging feature, and therefore, no tags have needed to be deleted.

The administrative interface also stores tagging activity statistics according to patron type. The Library's current statistics are rather compelling--tagging is most popular with undergraduate students who are currently responsible for 55% of assigned tags out of 18,735 total (as of June 30, 2011). Here is the tag assignation distribution among patron types:

Tagging activity among patron types at Nebraska's flagship institution, the University of Nebraska—Lincoln (UNL) is rather different than at UNO--library faculty assign the majority of tags in Encore (Allison, 2010). UNL's librarians are proactively adding tags to expand on existing metadata in bibliographic records. The UNO Library should consider enhancing records with tagging.

USAGE DATA

Google Analytics and Encore

Usage metrics are essential for assessing the impact of a library's Web-scale discovery tool. Encore's administrative interface does not provide usage reports and the Library must rely on Google Analytics in obtaining useful metrics. The Library previously installed and employed Google Analytics as an adjunct to the readily available metrics from the Innovative system for the classic catalog. Google Analytics can neither be installed in Encore by the Library nor is automatically installed. Encore's service team installed this application in Encore on December 9, 2010, which was around the time Innovative publicized this feature. The metrics indicated the number of site visits to the legacy catalog dropped precipitously with the presence of Encore:

Figure 4. Visits to Encore vs. visits to the legacy catalog

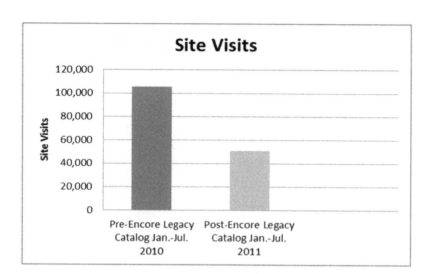

In addition to the greater number of visits to Encore compared to legacy catalog visits, from the time Google Analytics was added to May 31, 2011, 70% of all visitors had at least one previous session using Encore. There were 45,572 returning visitors out of a total of 65,848 visitors. Only 7,685 of returning visitors were accessing Encore from the Library's domain name that is linked to its Internet service provider (ISP). The other ISPs were from local Internet providers in the Omaha metropolitan area. This correlates with the fact that 40,575 (89%) returning visitors are from Omaha. The remaining 5,003 repeat visitors are from various towns in Nebraska.

Another aspect of Google Analytics is ability to analyze the extent to which users refine searches in Encore after initiating a keyword search. There were approximately 122,125 keyword searches in Encore and only 11,216 were further refined using at least one facet, but about a third were refined with two or three facets. Media type was the most common facet refinement with 3,962 instances. Availability, whether online or in the library, was another frequent facet selection that was present in 3,361 search strings. Other facets such as language, location, place, and publication

date were less commonly employed as they were each selected less than 1,000 times.

It is also instructive to examine how the legacy catalog was used during this time period. Users searched the legacy catalog quite differently than Encore. Out of 83,300 searches in the legacy catalog, 23,368 of them involved searching for an electronic resource or database. While very few patrons log into Encore, 17,103 logged into the classic catalog in order to view and manage their patron accounts. Format and language searches were scant in this environment, but there were still a substantial number of title (2,690), subject (2,643), and author (1,095) searches in the classic catalog. RSS feeds are also important to the Library's users because there were 1,016 site views on the RSS feed page that is hosted on the same server as the legacy catalog and linked throughout the search and display screens.

The results of data obtained from Google Analytics for Encore and the legacy catalog indicate that while overall use of the legacy catalog has sharply declined, there are still preferences for certain features in the legacy catalog. The usage data from both Encore and the legacy catalog need further analysis to determine whether there have been any changes in searching behavior since June 1, 2011. The Library should also consider negotiating with Innovative to include a link to RSS feeds. Another possible solution is to create bibliographic records and enhance the metadata with tags to ensure RSS feeds are accessible in Encore.

Research Pro

Google Analytics was installed in Research Pro in September 2010. Because Research Pro is integrated with Encore, the usage data offers valuable insight regarding its impact. During the time period from September 1, 2010 through May 31, 2011, Research Pro had 2,082 site visits. The majority of visitors were new (66%); only 34% returned to search Research Pro. In essence, even though Research Pro has thirty databases, including many subject-specific resources, the pass-through search feature clearly did not influence the majority of users to search beyond the few databases offered in Encore.

The number of page views indicates pages viewed within Research Pro. This number is greater than the number of site visits because it takes in to account pages of actual search results. Out of 3,648 page views, 1,344 views of the search interface were counted in this total. The majority of page views (2,002), as indicated by search query in the URL, were pass-through searches via Encore. Therefore, the majority of searches in Research Pro were conducted after a search in Encore. The remaining 302 searches were from users directly accessing Research Pro. Research Pro is also offered by the Library as a federated search product and is linked on the Library's website with the Library's local name for Research Pro, "Multi-Search." The low usage is rather compelling because Research Pro is consistently taught in bibliographic instruction classes and there are supplemental tutorials presented using LibGuides and screen cast software.

Research Pro's usage data from Google Analytics disclose that its presence may have enhanced Encore for only a small fraction of users, at least during this time period. Because Research Pro was also a new resource at the time, usage may have changed over time. The Library should continue to monitor the use of Research Pro and consider conducting a user study to gauge the user experience of using both Encore and Research Pro in tandem.

Library Thing for Libraries

In addition to the presence of Encore affecting legacy catalog usage, LibraryThing for Libraries (LFTL) usage data indicated a decline in the number of tags clicked, since LFTL is inoperative in Encore.

Now that users can assign tags after logging into Encore, the process is more streamlined than in LTFL. Because tags in LTFL have to be added to the LibraryThing interface as previously described, the user would have to work within two interfaces in order to accomplish this and not immediately see his or her tagging efforts rendered in the legacy catalog's bibliographic display. This is not the case with Encore and it is no wonder that tag creation and usage in the Encore environment is more popular among the Library's patrons.

Impact on Electronic Resource Usage

An examination of the impact of Encore on the use of aggregator and subject databases is particularly illuminating (Way, 2010). Databases designated and displayed on a dropdown menu labeled as the "Top 10" on the Library's Web site were examined for the period of September through November during the years 2009 and 2010 ascertain any changes during the initial months of Encore implementation. Usage statistics for the entire years of 2009 and 2010 were also analyzed to further determine the impact of

Figure 5. Number of tags clicked in LTFL

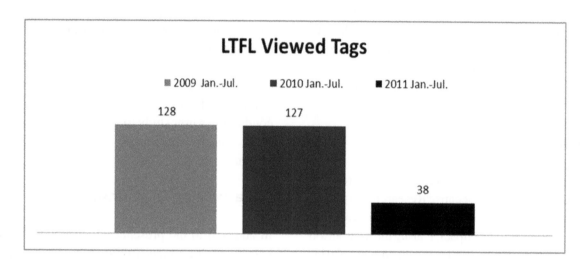

Encore on these most popularly used electronic resources. All the of databases integrated with Encore that offer usage data based on the total number of searches (COUNTER DB 1 or DB 3) were included in this analysis; both of these reports have the total number of searches within a resource. Interestingly, all of databases that are searchable in Encore show an increase in usage, but the remaining five not integrated with Encore, despite their availability in Research Pro, show a marked decrease in use (Table 3).

Even though ArtSTOR's™ usage data is non-COUNTER compliant, it is still relevant to note that overall use increased more than the other resources integrated with Encore. There are probably several reasons for ArtSTOR's™ sharp increase in use. ArtSTOR™ is the Library's sole digital collection incorporated in Encore. It has also become more visible as a resource in the web scale discovery environment as a facet listed in the container "Articles and More."

Abstracting and indexing (A&I) databases such as ERIC and MLA have clearly decreased in use and this is similar to the results of Way's comprehensive study that included an analysis of his library's A&I database collection (Way, 2010). In addition, other full-text databases not integrated with Encore, but available in Research Pro, with the exception of PsycInfo, have also declined in use (Table 4). The usage data reveals that aggregate use of electronic resources only increased when the resource was fully integrated with Encore and its integration with Research Pro was negligible. This is consistent with the prior discussion of the Research Pro's low use according to data obtained from Google Analytics.

It is also possible to obtain metrics regarding full-text downloads for resources that report JR 1 COUNTER reports. One resource, IEEE XPLORE® is not integrated with Encore, but is one of the databases configured for Research Pro.

Most of the resources included in Encore show an increase in the number of full-text articles downloaded; the only anomaly is JSTOR™ and it is difficult to conclude why there has been a decrease in full-text articles downloaded (Table 5). Even more compelling is the precipitous decline (65%) in full-text article downloads for IEEE XPLORE®[8], despite the growth of engineering and computer science programs at the university. Even though IEEE XPLORE® is available as a pass-through search from Encore to Research Pro, it is possible that users are satisfied with Encore's search results. The only way to know

Table 3. Comparison of database searching in pre-Encore and Encore environments

Integrated With Encore	Pre-Encore, Sep.-Nov. 2009	Encore, Sep.-Nov. 2010	Percent Change	2009 Total Pre-Encore	2010 Total Post-Encore	Percent Change
Academic Search Premier	111070	111293	.2	205719	216482	5
ArtStor	3539	7490	111	11014	17382	57
Business Source Premier	19167	27052	41	37761	43140	14
Lexis Nexis[6]	37736	18907	-49	92695	106015	14
Wilson Omnifile	11716	13890	19	31868	38251	20

Table 4. Comparison of database searches: remainder of the top 10 not integrated with Encore

Remainder of Top 10, included in Research Pro	Total Searches Pre-Encore Sep.-Nov. 2009	Total Searches Post-Encore Sep.-Nov. 2010	Percent Change	2009 Total Pre-Encore	2010 Post Encore	Percent Change
CQ Researcher	10256	9126	-11	21500	18002	-16
CSA	100250	72140	-28	307496	230694	-25
ERIC (CSA)	12043	12457	3	39407	33864	-14
MLA	10799	9213	-15	31204	27267	-13
PsycInfo	30281	24996	-17	82553	85266	3

for certain is to determine whether engineering and computer science students and researchers prefer Encore's results and do not need to search IEEE XPLORE® or are retrieving articles from another source.

FUTURE RESEARCH DIRECTIONS

Web-scale discovery profoundly impacts legacy catalog and database usage. Encore should be compared to other discovery tools in order to determine if electronic resource usage is dependent on their inclusion in the discovery tool. Furthermore, while this case study points to the hypothesis that Encore's pass-through search to Research Pro is an obstacle to retrieving additional resources, it is essential to conduct a usability study to find out why the pass-through search feature is not widely used.

Another area needing further study is the use of Google Analytics for obtaining usage data for discovery tools. Google Analytics was developed in order to assist commercial organizations assess the return on investment (ROI) for their Web sites. How effective is Google Analytics in collecting usage data for web-scale discovery? What are the data's limitations compared to legacy catalog usage data available from the ILS?

CONCLUSION

On the surface, implementing a Web-scale discovery tool at a mid-sized university might appear to be a one-sided project, with the vendor entirely responsible for configuring and installing the product. After all, mid-sized university libraries tend to either not have a high volume of locally digitized collections or may even lack them altogether. Ad-

Table 5. Database full-text downloads before and after Encore implementation.[7]

Integrated With Encore	2009 Total Pre-Encore	2010 Total Post-Encore	Percent Change
Academic Search Premier	161878	166316	2.7
Business Source Premier	37895	43140	13.8
JSTOR	101957	85593	-16
Wilson Omni-file	39478	41256	4.5
Not Integrated With Encore			
IEEE Xplore	16178	5625	-65
CQ Researcher	21,869	18,163	-17
BioOne	822	328	

ditionally, in many cases, these university libraries also subscribe to fewer electronic resources than larger university libraries, easing implementation. Prior to subscribing to Encore, it was not surprising that many library faculty and staff assumed the launch of Web-scale discovery would be seamless. Compounding this assumption was the fact that Encore was developed by the same vendor as the Library's ILS, Innovative Interfaces Inc., implying that all of the Innovative modules would completely integrate with Encore. In reality, the size of a library's collection has relatively little relationship with the complexity of discovery tool implementation. Vendor homogeneity of the ILS and discovery tool is also no guarantee of module compatibility with Web-scale discovery.

Confronting these realities enables a library to become proactive in offering a more effective discovery tool. Metadata maintenance projects are at the core of ensuring a quality Web-scale discovery user experience. In order to effectively address metadata issues, it is necessary to revisit local cataloging standards and practices in light of the discovery environment.

Once the Library revises current practices, staff should focus on the concept of Web-scale discovery and whether Encore truly allows users to access all of the library's collections. The onus is on both the Library and the vendor. The Library should prioritize digitizing local collections to be included in Web-scale discovery. Conversely, Encore must be re-engineered by Innovative to facilitate searching of a library's entire electronic resource collection. The pass-through search in Encore to Research Pro is woefully inadequate in comparison with other discovery tools that allow more comprehensive searching. This observation is further supported by the precipitous decline in the use of electronic resources that are not integrated with Encore. A more comprehensive study is essential for the Library to determine if Encore hinders a return on investment of subject specific electronic resources.

ACKNOWLEDGMENT

I would like to thank Beth Oehlerts, DebbieMc-Clelland, and Lynda Hoffmann for their assistance and suggestions regarding the images included in this chapter. The author would also like to thank Daniel Draper for reviewing the Metadata section and providing additional insights that helped strengthen this section.

REFERENCES

Allison, D. (2010). Information portals: The next generation catalog. *Journal of Web Librarianship*, *4*(4), 375–389. doi:10.1080/19322909.2010.507972

Breeding, M. (2004). *Next-Gen library catalogs*. New York, NY: Neil Schuman Publishers.

Way, D. (2010). The impact of Web-scale discovery on the use of a library collection. *Serials Review*, *36*(4), 214–220. doi:10.1016/j.serrev.2010.07.002

Yang, S., & Wagner, K. (2010). Evaluating and comparing discovery tools: How close are we towards next generation catalog? *Library Hi Tech*, *28*(4), 690–693. doi:10.1108/07378831011096312

ADDITIONAL READING

Ballard, T. (2011). Comparison of user search behaviors with classic online catalogs and discovery platforms. *The Charleston Advisor*, *12*(3), 65–66. doi:10.5260/chara.12.3.65

Breeding, M. (2007). Encore. *Library Technology Reports*, *43*(4), 23–27.

Fifarek, A. (2007). The birth of catalog 2.0: Innovative Interfaces' Encore Discovery Platform. *Library Hi Tech News*, *24*(5), 13–15. doi:10.1108/07419050710780353

Griffis, P., & Ford, C. (2009). Enhancing OPAC records for discovery. *Information Technology & Libraries*, *28*(4), 191–193.

Majors, R. (2009). Local tagging for local collections. *Computers in Libraries*, *29*(9), 11.

Rowe, R. (2011). Encore Synergy, Primo Central. *The Charleston Advisor*, *12*(4), 11–15. doi:10.5260/chara.12.4.11

KEY TERMS AND DEFINITIONS

A&I Databases: Abstracting and indexing databases containing journal article citations.

COUNTER (Counting Online Usage of NeTworked Resources): An international initiative for the consistent reporting of usage data for electronic resources to facilitate meaningful comparative analyses of data.

Fixed Fields: Items from the leader fields coded in a predetermined position and order.

FRBR (Functional Requirements for Bibliographic Records): First created by the International Federation of Library Associations (IFLA), the FRBR standard creates relationships among data in catalog and other bibliographic databases to reflect the conceptual structure of information and to relate these data to user research needs. The relationships can be equivalent (resources in different formats, derivative (including abstracts, chapters, editions, and translations), or descriptive (book reviews, commentaries and critiques).

Leader Fields: Located at the beginning of the MARC record, there are 24 positions comprising the leader. Of particular interest for discovery tools is the fact that granular format information is included.

Metadata: Descriptive data created by humans to represent attributes of an item.

Open URL Resolver: The actual tool that functions according to the Open URL standard that enables linking A&I database citations to full-text articles.

RSS Feeds: (RDF Site Summary--often referred to as Really Simple Syndication) Web feed formats providing updated information that is accessible with an RSS feed reader.

Tags/Tagging: User-generated keywords that are not dependent on a controlled vocabulary and are assigned to Web content. Tagging is the act of assigning tags.

Web-Scale Discovery: A Web searching experience that allows users to search all of the library's resources. The pre-harvested indexes germane to

Web-scale discovery allow the expedient retrieval of relevant results.

ENDNOTES

[1]   Formerly Systems Librarian at the University of Omaha

[2]   Serials Solution is a registered trademark of Serials Solutions

[3]   ARTStor is trademarked by ARTStor Inc.

[4]   LexisNexis is a registered trademark of LexisNexis

[5]   JSTOR is a registered trademark of ITHAKA

[6]   Lexis-Nexis was not added to Encore until mid-October, 2010

[7]   Due to the author's change in employment accessing usage data for other relevant databases was not feasible.

[8]   XPLORE is a registered trademark of IEEE

Chapter 31
Primo Central:
A Step Closer to Library Electronic Resource Discovery

Dale Poulter
Vanderbilt University, USA

ABSTRACT

Vanderbilt University implemented Primo Central™ in early 2010. Although several factors went into the decision to adopt Primo Central™ early in its development, this chapter focuses on the initial reasons that Vanderbilt considered using Primo Central™, methods used to determine if the service was being used, and challenges encountered, both during implementation and ongoing. The chapter also discusses items that should be considered when subscribing to and implementing the Primo Central™ Index. The last portion of the chapter discusses possible ways Primo Central™ content can be leveraged for future services.

INTRODUCTION

Vanderbilt University was founded in 1873 by Commodore Cornelius Vanderbilt when the Commodore gave $1 million to endow the building of the University. This was the Commodore's only major philanthropy. The Peabody College for Teachers, founded in 1875, merged with Vanderbilt in 1979.

The University currently offers undergraduate degrees in the liberal arts and sciences as well as education and human development, engineering, and music. In addition to undergraduate degrees, Vanderbilt offers graduate degrees in medicine, religion, law, and management, as well as many other areas. The Library employs 210 library staff and 160 student assistants in ten different libraries and two offsite storage locations. During the 2010/2011 school year, enrollment included a

DOI: 10.4018/978-1-4666-1821-3.ch031

total of 12,714 students including 5,835 graduate and professional students. In 2011 the Vanderbilt Graduate School of Education was ranked 1st by the US News and World Report, and Vanderbilt University was ranked as the 17th best national undergraduate university.

In order to serve the needs of a diverse student body, the library provides access to an increasing number of electronic materials from a wide array of sources. In addition to subscription materials, the Vanderbilt University Library continues to increase the number of unique collections that can be accessed online. As a result of the significant investment in materials, the library consistently works to increase awareness of the materials available to users in their academic pursuits. When Vanderbilt was first considering Primo Central™, it was already providing several tools to users to access both physical and electronic collections. These tools included SirsiDynix Symphony®2 ILS, SFX®3 Openurl resolver, Metalib, Primo®4, and Verde®5 from ExLibris™6. In addition to these commercial packages, the library also has a locally-developed database of databases and utilizes Umlaut, the open source front-end for SFX® developed by Ross Singer at Georgia Tech University and currently maintained by Jonathan Rochkind of Johns Hopkins University.

Vanderbilt implemented Primo Central™ as another tool to enhance the user experience and increase visibility of some resources that the library selected. While the implementation of Primo Central™ has provided many challenges, the most significant as of this writing has been communication about what the Primo Central™ index is in the context of Primo®.

BACKGROUND

Vanderbilt was a Primo® development partner with ExLibris™. During many of the early discussions of Primo, one goal was to provide a single search method for accessing the quality material that the Library licenses and owns. The first attempt to search journal articles was made using Metalib, a federated search tool. The results were disappointing due to both slow search speed and the results returned; only a limited number of results were returned for each selected database, with no sense of ranking by relevance overall. Vanderbilt attempted to combine the federated search and the local search, but the performance and consistency were ultimately unacceptable for the desired application. This was not much of a surprise since the Z39.50 protocol used by Metalib was developed in the age of dial-up internet access and was intended as a way to search MARC resources and not full-text resources. The protocol has been enhanced over the years and federated search tools have continued to develop new methods (such as xml gateways) for searching, but the fact that each database is indexed using a ExLibris different set of rules and results are returned using different algorithms continues to be a barrier to fast and consistent search results. As a result of these limitations, Vanderbilt implemented a two-tab interface for searching. The first tab included the library catalog, several locally created database resources, and the U.S. Congressional Serial Set, while the second included federated searching using Metalib. Even after implementing this solution, ExLibris™, Vanderbilt and other institutions continued to discuss the ultimate goal of quick and universal access. The ExLibris™' response to these discussions is Primo Central™.

CONCEPT OF PRIMO CENTRAL IN CONTEXT WITH PRIMO

The first issue encountered, and an ongoing challenge even now, is expressing the difference between Primo®, Primo Central™, and federated searching. Defining the difference between these items is easy technically but difficult conceptually. Primo® is the search interface and allows a user to input a search term and search multiple resources (including, for example, the library catalog, local databases, Primo® Central™ Index, and Metalib resources). It provides a way of searching multiple indexes and resources at the same time. Primo Central™ is an aggregated index of many resources from many different free and subscription services. Lastly, Primo® passes search terms to a federated search tool (Metalib in this case) which then sends a translated search to each individual resource selected, and integrates the results returned from the federated search tool. Conceptually the definitions can seem much more complicated. One way to think of Primo®, Primo Central™, the local index and a federated search tool is a library system. Each library branch contains resources that are included only in that branch, but also some items duplicated elsewhere in the system. Primo® is a tool, similar to a traditional catalog, which allows a user to find and obtain an item from any of the branches, i.e., the local resources or Primo Central™. Due to the speed of obtaining search results from a federated search tool, the federated search tool is analogous to a library system annex.

Primo Central™ is a scoped index of many resources. The concept allows the library to automatically filter the incoming results to materials that are selected by the library. This method provides several advantages over a federated search tool. One of the largest advantages is that this pulls all of the resources together and indexes them using the same rules. This allows for consistent searching across all of the resources. Since Primo Central™ is a single index, it is easier to configure. Primo Central™ also returns all of the results of a search, a large improvement to most federated search tools which limited the number of results returned in order to improve performance.

When Vanderbilt was approached about Primo Central™, several questions were raised, including whether it would work in out Primo® environment, if it offered information that the library users would find helpful and whether it would be better than Metalib. The decision to test Primo

Central™ was discussed by the Dean's group during the fourth quarter of 2009. The decision was to move forward with exploring the service. At that point a call went out to Vanderbilt staff in each of the libraries for a list of databases that would be good to have in the index. ExLibris™ provided an initial list but ExLibris™ wanted to understand which would be the most useful to help set priorities. ExLibris™ continues to request content suggestions for Primo Central™. Although everything in Vanderbilt's initial list is still not available, ExLibris™ continues to increase the amount of information provided via Primo Central™ regularly. Primo Central™ was activated January 6, 2010 on Vanderbilt's test server and a group of people made up of reference, technical services, and library technology were asked to test the system. The group identified several issues including full text availability, sorting, and relevance challenges. The group also commented that the system would be better if specific resources were included. This provided additional resources for Vanderbilt to send to ExLibris™ as suggestions. The introduction of Primo Central™ seemed to open the idea of a blended search, a search that allows searches content in the library catalog as well as in remote databases. Since the speed was very different than Metalib many staff perceived this as good opportunity for users, but they also realized that all of the resources were not available.

As Vanderbilt continued to test Primo Central™ they encountered a basic problem with any new service for users. How can a system for users be tested without getting users to do some of the testing? Staff tested the search functionality as described above and with ExLibris™ worked out many of the issues. Vanderbilt decided to move the Primo Central™ search option into production but as a separate search option. Once it was seen that several users were using the new search option with positive results, the Vanderbilt Dean's group recommended adding Primo Central™ to the default search option. This move received a

Figure 1. Example activation screen for Primo Central

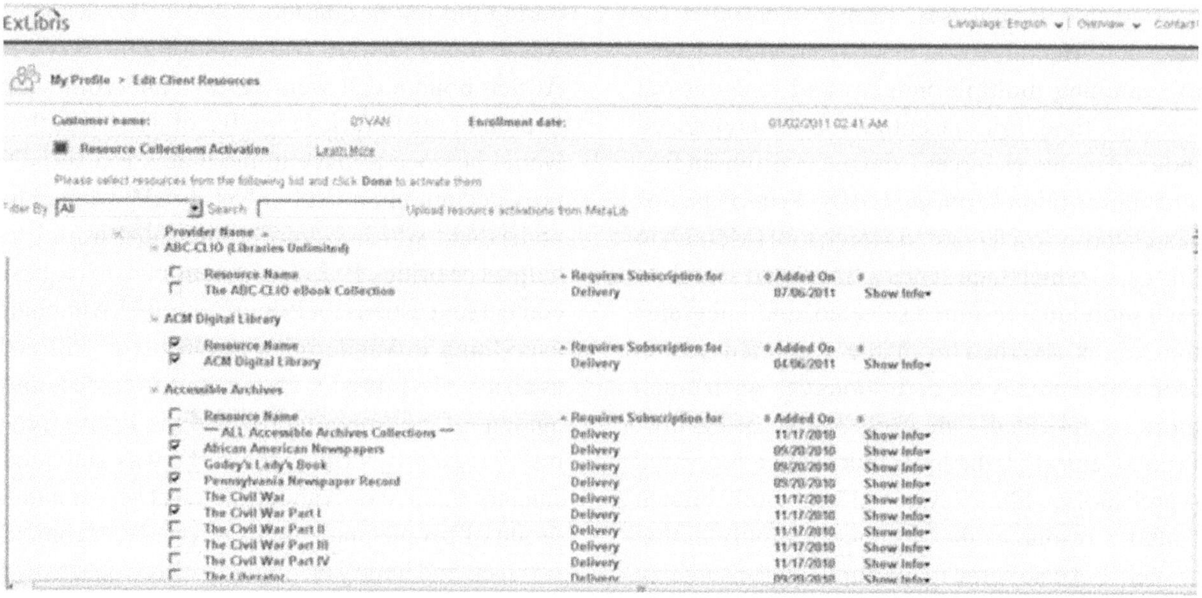

mixed reception since it seemed to amplify the next issue.

It's All about the Data

One of the goals of Primo Central™ is to bring many resources together. The achievement of this goal is dependent on ExLibris™ and the various database vendors reaching agreements to allow content to be placed in Primo Central™. As a result of these continuing negotiations, it was almost impossible to know what was included in Primo Central™ early on in its development. A related issue is that when a new collection was available, the library could not activate the resource themselves but had to send an email to ExLibris™ to request activation. ExLibris™ addressed these issues by creating a portal for libraries to activate and review available targets at any time (see Figure 1). ExLibris™ also provides a list of journals that are available. Although this does assist the library in knowing what is available to be searched and how often it is updated, it still leaves several other questions outstanding

including what are the coverage dates of the various journals being searched and which resources index the full text of the resource as opposed to only abstract and citation.

Since multiple vendors may provide data for the same journal were encountered two additional challenges; how to handle duplicate articles and how to communicate with staff about accessing articles for one database from metadata provided from another vendor. An example is that vendor A may only have a record with basic information and an abstract, but vendor B may have the full text without an abstract. The information that Primo Central™ will search consists of the combined information.

Most of the duplicated articles were corrected with a recent patch which combined the metadata from the various sources. The upside to this is that the resulting metadata is often better than any of the individual records. Some of the duplicate articles do persist but the problem is caused by inconsistent metadata, including articles. Primo Central™, as well as any aggregate index, emphasizes the fact that data providers lack consistency in the metadata that they utilize for building individual indexes. Since it is doubtful that data entry will ever be perfect, this is an issue that will persist into the future.

Although Primo Central™ contains a growing collection of resources, it does not contain all of the resources that Vanderbilt would like to provide to users. Early on one resource was initially provided to ExLibris™ but was then withdrawn. As is often the case the reason for this move was kept internal to both companies, but the end result is that libraries and users paid the price with decreased access to the information. Although ExLibris™ provided a work around for this loss of data, the result was still a decrease in functionality.

Primo Central™ does continue to add resources from various sources as well as updating currently available resources, and the richness of the metadata continues to improve. In many, but not all, cases journals from one resource may also be available from another source. Primo Central™ allows the library to pull these resources together to provide a better experience for users. Most of the collections available through Primo Central™ allow anyone to search the metadata, even institutions that do not currently have a subscription. However, some of the collections that are free to search require a subscription to deliver the material to the user. This provides a great tool for the library, since it is possible to mix and match the resources and increase the value of Primo Central™ to our users. This also allows libraries to provide search access to larger collections.

The access to larger collections does not come without a tradeoff. In most libraries, when a user searches for an item, they expect to have access to that material – even if they need to wait because the item is on loan. However, in the case of Primo Central™ increasing the search scope to include materials not owned, the library increases the chance of the user finding an item that is not immediately accessible. When Vanderbilt initially activated some of the targets that were only partially owned, it increased the numbers questions

from users about why so many of the results were unavailable. This issue was caused by Primo Central™ not accessing current library holdings. This is similar to what happens when searching a remote database except in most cases the remote database only displays a link the openurl resolver and does not indicate availability. The solution that Vanderbilt applied was to allow Primo Central™ to access the holdings and show the availability of the item. In addition, the library limited the initial results returned to items that the user could gain immediate access (see Figure 2).

Another concern that some library professionals have expressed is that this "dumbs down" the search experience. Although the method for searching within Primo Central™ is extremely easy and quick, it does not require the searcher to understand what the results actually mean. The searcher does not have to understand what a peer reviewed journal is, only that they need to select the peer review facet.

SOLUTIONS

Most library professionals and students have utilized Google or Google Scholar at some point in their careers with mixed results. Often results from Primo Central™ are compared to the results received from Google. Is this the case though? Are the results a library user gets at a bookstore the same as what they get in the library? I would suggest absolutely not. Like library physical collections, libraries carefully select the electronic resources to make available to their users. In the same way, it is important for databases that are selected to be searched within Primo Central™ for a specific library to be based on the collection development policy for the library.

So what has been learned from the experience at Vanderbilt? I would suggest that the correct question is what is Vanderbilt learning from Primo Central™? First, no system is perfect. The fact that much of the metadata is computer-generated

Figure 2. Search results screen indicating availability of Primo Central resources

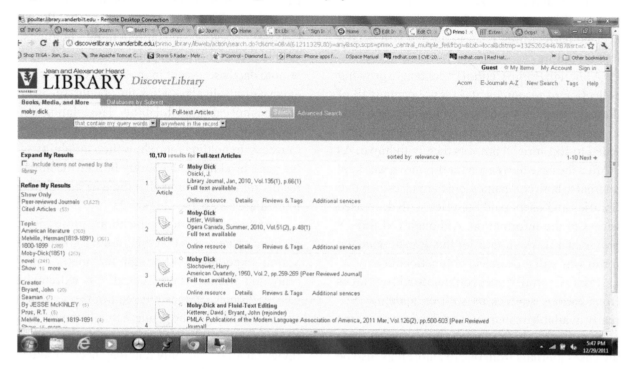

means that some errors are introduced. Some errors are introduced even when the metadata is created by librarians. It is impossible to clean up all of the duplicate records. Since libraries pay a great deal of money to various vendors for the metadata Libraries need to continue to press vendors that provide the metadata to the aggregate indexes to improve the consistency of the metadata.

No system exists that contains all of the metadata a library desires. This is true due to a resource being provided by a niche publisher or not being provided due to licensing issues.

The decision to obtain Primo Central™ should be tied to the information it provides for a library's user population. In other cases Primo Central™ is an invaluable asset, but in some it would be an inappropriate use of library funds. In the case of Vanderbilt, it is a great resource and allows many of our users to quickly start their research tasks. It does not allow this to occur for all of the users though. Due to contractual issues, some core religious resources are not currently avail-

able within Primo Central™. As a result of these missing resources, Primo Central™ has limited the use in our School of Divinity. ExLibris™ has provided a work around for some of these resources but performance and functionality are not the same. Hopefully these issues will be resolved in the future. Even with these resources missing, Primo Central™ has been well received by users at Vanderbilt.

RECOMMENDATIONS

First, aggregate index providers such as Primo Central™ provide a service that libraries have wanted for many years. However, the service is not perfect and can only be improved by libraries actively engaging with publishers and vendors.

Second, it is extremely important to engage library staff at all levels early in the process. Extra communication and time spent on the front-end of the project will pay large dividends on the back-end of the process. It is too easy for staff and users to misunderstand what the Primo Central™ index actually contains and what it can do. This is especially true when the search is done within a system such as Primo® that searches multiple indexes simultaneously.

Third, when selecting resources to be activated in the Primo Central™ index it is important to engage the collection development librarians. The resources available are after all a collection development decision. Systems departments are already understaffed and this is an opportunity to empower staff in other areas of the library. Primo Central™ is a great opportunity for different areas of the library to work together and increase understanding on both sides. Libraries can no longer work in silos with Collection Development, Reference, Order Services, Cataloging and Systems all working separately for the same goal. This process may have worked well in the past with Collection Development providing an overall goal for the collection, Reference staff interfacing with users and often selecting materials, Order Services placing the orders and Cataloging making the materials findable in the ILS that the Systems department keeps running. The lines between these areas are increasingly blurred. All library staff have a need to know more about the technology and how it interacts with all areas of the library. Likewise, Systems departments now have the opportunity to interface more with end users and need to continually update their understanding of what the goals and processes are in other parts of the library. Primo Central™ is a good example of this new paradigm in that Systems will better understand what is being searched and how it is being searched but Reference will have a better idea as to what resources are being used outside of Primo Central™, Collection Development will have a better idea as to what portion of Primo Central™ is actually within the library's collection scope and Order Services will have the best idea as to what has been ordered and from which vendor.

Fourth, ensure that staff understands that the source of the metadata does not make a difference as far as linking to resources for users. It is, of course, important to maintain the access to the best metadata possible.

Fifth, Primo Central™ does provide a Google-like simple search but unlike Google which includes a wide variety of resources, Primo Central™ is scoped to your users, not to the world. The scoping that is done within Primo Central™ is comparable to any other collection development decision in the library.

Sixth, Vanderbilt did see an increase in Interlibrary Loan requests once Primo Central™ was implemented. Although it is difficult to be sure that all of the increase was due to Primo Central™, it is reasonable to believe that at least a portion of the increase was directly due to implementing Primo Central™.

Lastly, it is important for any site considering an aggregate index such as Primo Central™ to understand that while making the process of searching easier for users, the library needs to determine better ways of teaching information literacy. Libraries are given fewer one-on-one opportunities for teaching information literacy. Users are becoming increasingly dependent on facets or other ways to limit searches to retrieve a manageable and useful set of results. The introduction of Primo Central™ may increase the difficulty of traditional teaching of information literacy since users often find what they desire with little assistance.

NEXT STEPS

Primo Central™ has a rich API that will allow many additional services to be offered. One service that could be of use to users is a "universal" alert for specific journals. Multiple different locations currently offer tables of contents for journals. This combined with Primo Central™ and an Openurl resolver could provide a RSS feed to users in other systems such as a course management system.

Given the flexibility of the API it could be interesting to explore the usability of scoped searches for targeted groups of users. This could be as a simple as providing a search in context tool or it could be much more elaborate.

CONCLUSION

Primo Central™ provides an easy way for libraries to offer a quality single search interface to a large array of journal indexes. Although many people compare a Primo Central™ search to a Google search, it is important to remember that the resources available in Primo Central™ are the same resources librarians actively select and are generally more reliable. Vanderbilt's experience has been positive but not without challenges. Users quickly began to utilize resources provided by Primo Central™ once it was introduced. The information available in Primo Central™ continues to increase but libraries need to examine the information indexed within Primo Central™ the same way they would examine any other database. Primo Central™ gives an excellent way to provide a quick integrated search to users and to make that information available to them where they need it.

In additional to providing a great resource to users, Primo Central™ presents a great opportunity for various areas in a library to increase understanding of what each other actually do in the library and for the users. In order for Primo Central™ to truly shine as a service for users, all areas of the library need to be involved. If only systems or collection development are involved in the process, Primo Central™ will not reach its potential. Just as it takes a village to raise a child, it takes the entire library to provide an excellent service such as Primo Central™ to the user.

ADDITIONAL READING

Joint, N. (2010). The one-stop shop search engine: A transformational library technology? ANTAEUS. *Library Review, 59*(4), 240–248. doi:10.1108/00242531011038550

Way, D. (2010). The impact of Web-scale discovery on the use of a library collection. *Serials Review, 36*(4), 214–220. doi:10.1016/j.serrev.2010.07.002

Wisniewski, J. (2010). Web scale discovery: The future's so bright I gotta wear shades. *Online, 34*(4), 55–58.

KEY TERMS AND DEFINITIONS

Aggregate Index (Mega-Index): An aggregate index, or mega-index, is created by combining data from multiple indexing services. Primo Central™ is an example of an aggregate index.

API: (Application Programing Interface): The API is a specification that provides a method of accessing features and information from one software program to be included in another program, without utilizing the interface provided by the program vendor.

Federated Search: A method to search different resources simultaneously to bring information directly from each resource. Initially, federated searching was performed using the Z39.50 protocol designed for bibliographic databases. The methods have expanded to include XML Gateways but this method is still considered slower than searching a local resource.

Local Index: In the context of Primo®, the local index is a collection of local resources that are indexed together. Vanderbilt's local index includes information from the catalog, institutional repository, and other local databases.

Metadata: In this context, metadata is descriptive information (title, author, abstract, summary, etc.) about a larger piece of information.

Scoped Index: A filtered search within a larger index. For instance, an index may include 30 resources but allow a user to only search 15 of the resources. This is similar to limiting a catalog search to only one library branch.

Search Scope: The information being searched at a given time. In many cases this does not include all available information but only information that the searcher has access.

ENDNOTES

[1]   Primo Central is owned by ExLibris Ltd. or its affiliates.

[2]   SirsiDynix Symphony is a registered trademark of SirsiDynix Corporation.

[3]   SFX OpenURL link resolver is a registered trademark of ExLibris Ltd

[4]   Primo is a registered trademark of ExLibris Ltd

[5]   Verde is a registered trademark of ExLibris Ltd

[6]   ExLibris is a trademark of ExLibris Ltd.

Chapter 32
The Single–Search Project:
Selecting and Implementing Primo at a Research and Cultural Heritage Institution

Jennifer Palmisano
Center for Jewish History, USA

ABSTRACT

The mission of this chapter is to demonstrate one research/cultural institution's discovery solution journey. This includes information about the Center for Jewish History, its history and development as an organization, how these factors affect implementation at the Center, and the Center's selection and implementation of Primo. This chapter delves into the challenges faced by smaller cultural and research institutions with special collections that wish to stay ahead of the curve in what some consider a "library-centric" environment and the challenges inherent in the search and implementation process. It discusses how digital, archival, and museum data, in conjunction with library data, shaped the development and needs of this project from its inception. Other topics described include phased implementation, authentication, customization of data sources, and evaluating impact of a discovery tool. Most importantly, this chapter shows how usability concerns have been resolved for the Center's researchers and staff alike.

INTRODUCTION

The Center for Jewish History and its Data Landscape before Discovery

The Center for Jewish History is a research and cultural heritage institution dedicated to the pres-ervation of and access to Jewish history. It was created by the union of five partner institutions, with that union necessitating the creation of new systems to facilitate greater access to the partner collections. However, over the years the global online environment has become fragmented, a situation that is magnified the more complex data becomes. Affected by this fragmentation, the Center chose to combat its sprawling online

DOI: 10.4018/978-1-4666-1821-3.ch032

presence through implementation of a discovery solution that serves as both an index to all its content (library, archival, digital, electronic, and museum) and a unified user interface to ease the researcher's online experience at the Center.

The Center supports three OPACs (Online Public Access Catalogs) – Library/Archives (ExLibris'™[1] Aleph®[2] ILS), Digital (ExLibris'™ DigiTool®[3]), and Museum (KE's Electronic Museum system). The purpose of the Single-Search project was to incorporate all of these resources into the Single-Search interface or portal. For the majority of their research, patrons used the Aleph catalog from ExLibris™. In Aleph®, data is in MARC format, with capability to covert to MARC XML. The Center's data can be found in a number of different languages, including German, Hebrew, Yiddish, and Russian. DigiTool®, the ExLibris™ digital asset management system, is used to search and manage digital content. Items in DigiTool® generally have an equivalent record in Aleph®, so there is some duplication between the two systems. Like most digital asset management systems, DigiTool® is Dublin Core and MARC XML compliant, but the Center generally uses MARC XML. DigiTool® also houses the Center's collection of over 7,000 finding aids. For museum materials, one partner organization chose to use the Aleph database, but most of the museum and cultural artifact records are held in KE's Electronic Museum System (Emu). This system does not use MARC. However, its data can be converted to Dublin Core. Many of the more granular fields are missing after this conversion to Dublin Core, but it provides a good option for sharing metadata. In addition to these OPACs, the Center also uses Metalib®[4] and SFX®[5] for e-resource management and access, and numerous project Websites. While it was not a high priority to include these last systems in the final product, their inclusion and thus higher visibility was desired.

In summary, the average researcher faces a very tumultuous online environment at the Center. Failing to use any specific search tool could lead to fragmented research and a less than comprehensive picture of the Center's collections. Yet the likelihood that the average researcher looks in all these search environments is minimal, even with staff intervention.

Does Special Library Equal Special Needs?

While limited literature is available on creating discovery interfaces for library, archive, and museum institutions, there is a wealth of knowledge about collaborative projects that mirror the mission of the Single-Search project. Most of these projects refer to multiple institutions with separate databases and different organizational culture.

Many of these projects mirror the objectives of the Single-Search Project, but most of them vary greatly in levels of scope, audience, and funding. The breadth of the Center project was consistent with that of the Smithsonian and Europeana, but there is considerable disparity in the number of resources and funding available (Edson, 2010; Angelaki, 2010).

Through a project review, one finds that there are similarities between the challenges that are faced in these cultural heritage projects. Data differences are one of the most challenging aspects of these projects and work at the Center in general. "Good quality metadata aids discoverability of content. And good quality metadata is not just about structure, but also about shared approaches to data values in dates, subject terms, and so on" (Gow, 2010, p.12). In the Center's data, a user could interact with a number of non-Roman language scripts, international cataloging practices, archival, museum, or other types of format, and any number of other oddities.

Other institutions have struggled with the same metadata challenges in similar projects, particularly with facets. The "big three" as Nate Solas (2010) refers to them – "Creator, Medium, and Culture" – are very similar to challenges that libraries and archives face with author, form/

genre, and subject (p.4). So much authority control is necessary in these types of resources, and yet it is almost never available. Form and genre terms are particularly important to the successful development of a discovery interface for museums and archives, and each data source requires considerable mapping.

THE SEARCH FOR A DISCOVERY SYSTEM

Filling a Need and Acknowledging Unique Challenges

Identifying data issues early can lead to better questions and analysis of discovery systems. The Center has a unique need set. The Center's high content of non-Roman languages (more than a third of the Center's collections) stands them apart from most American libraries. The Center's archival content commands more flexibility than most software systems offer, because most library-related software systems assume the data is not unique and that most libraries follow the same or similar workflows. For archives, neither is the case. Additionally, the Center's partner make-up requires something close to a consortium-like network of resources and products. As a result, any software chosen for the Center needs to be highly flexible and customizable, as well as abide by international standards for data presentation and content encoding.

Three vendors were consulted for an in-depth comparison: ExLibris™ (Primo®), EBSCO (Discovery Service)™, and Serials Solutions®[6] (Aquabrowser®[7] and Summon™[8]). At this point open source options were considered, but only as a last option. The Center staff is limited, and while open source options offer the highest level of flexibility, it would be impractical to manage such hands-on software for this project and in the future.

Since the Center decided proprietary options would best suit the needs of the Center, each of the products that were evaluated came from industry leaders in library services and publishing. Each product was evaluated by three members of the Center staff, and the final recommendation was made by the project leader and Associate Director of Library Systems (the author). The implementation process would need to be methodical and thoughtful, taking into consideration all of the Center resources already available on-site and in the general online environment.

Key Discussion Points

- Site-maps to Google and other search engines: Can the resource be made visible to search engines, like Google?
- Social networking tools: Can users create a unique experience and save information key to their research? Can this information be made available to other users?
- Single sign-on for patron authentication: Do users need authentication for each source, like Aleph® and DigiTool®? Or can they use one sign-on and continuously retain authentication in each system?
- Real time Aleph® item and patron information: Can users check an item's availability? Can users create hold requests? Can users review their past loan transactions?
- Incorporation of Metalib's® federated search for access to all the Center's electronic resources: Do users have access to electronic resources? If so, how much of the Metalib® functionality is incorporated? And if not, do they have to go directly to the Metalib® interface to access those resources? Is there another option for access to electronic resource content?
- WARC harvesting for the Center community and project Website: Can users search all of the Center's online content? Or are

data sources limited to library systems and databases?

- Multiple interface languages: How many interface languages come 'out of the box'? How many of those are non-Roman languages? How much configuration is required to make customizations?
- Aleph® via The Open Archives Initiative Protocol for Metadata Harvesting (OAI-PMH): Can Aleph® data be harvested with OAI-PMH? Can Aleph® data be updated continuously, throughout the day? Do we have to set up Aleph® data exports? How automatic is data exchange between this resource and other systems?
- Extremely flexible and open architecture for customizations: Is this open software? Are systems staff members allowed to make customizations? Does systems staff have access to general configurations? Or are all customizations and configuration changes completed by vendor staff? What kinds of customizations can systems staff complete - simple interface colors and icon changes, or more complex processing configurations?
- Strong support community: Is there an email listserv or forum for customers to discuss troubleshooting techniques and configuration changes? If so, how many customers participate in such a group? Is it vibrant? Is there vendor support? Can the vendor provide references to their support? Does the vendor provide documentation?

Authentication

EBSCO Discovery Service (EDS)™⁹, Aquabrowser®, and Summon™ do not allow users to reserve materials from Aleph. Instead, the user views the record in the native Aleph OPAC interface, logs in, and then creates the reservation. Users can create profiles in Aquabrowser and EDS™, but that username is system specific and cannot be used in Aleph® or DigiTool®. The converse is also true; Aleph® and DigiTool® usernames cannot be used in Aquabrowser® or EDS™. This would most likely cause confusion for the Center's patrons and staff. Primo® was the only product reviewed that had a single sign-on option.

Customization and Additional Data Sources

For each of the products a few of the content features, like book covers, are only accessible with a subscription to Syndetics™¹⁰. Both EDS and Aquabrowser® had very limited ability to customize the interface, aside from changing background colors and icons. Additionally, Aquabrowser® was not yet Unicode compliant. Even though Serials Solutions® assured the Center that compliancy would be attained within the year 2011, it did not bode well for the Center's plethora of records in non-Roman scripts like Hebrew and Russian. There are several interface languages for all three options; however, Aquabrowser® did not include any non-Roman scripts.

Primo® has the capability to add Google sitemaps (tool that generates lists of links organized by navigation for a Website), as well as harvesting the Center's homepages and project Website by harvesting WARC files (Web ARChive file format), thus creating a real 'one-stop-shop' for any online content provided by the Center or the Center's partner institutions. Neither of the other vendors provided similar options without significant cost increase.

Additional Costs: Metalib and Local Hosting

At the time of the Center's search, only Primo® was able to work with Metalib®. Thus, including any electronic resources would require a subscription to 360 Search (bundled for the Aquabrowser® quote), or in the EDS case, create custom connectors for each resource not available. In Primo® a subscription to Primo Central™ permitted access to the index's publisher-provided metadata. In addition to Primo Central®, Primo® incorporates Metalib® into the user interface, allowing users to access federated search or direct links to databases whenever content was not available in the Primo Central™ Index.

Primo® was also the only option (aside from open source) to offer local hosting. While the other hosting options from ExLibris™ and the other vendors were of interest, the Center hosts all of its systems on-site. The Center has considered moving some systems to a hosted environment, but relinquishing complete control of these systems has never been an option. With the infrastructure already in place to host the Single-Search project locally, an in-depth cost analysis revealed that the cost of local hosting may initially be higher than the other options during implementation, but in the long run the cost will decrease with each year that the Center retains Primo® as its discovery system.

Final Decision

With serious consideration of each product and the criteria listed above, the Center chose to implement Primo® with Primo Central™. Primo Central™ serves as another avenue of electronic resource access, and the Center retained Metalib to preserve access to electronic resources not yet available in the Primo Central Index™. Primo® is highly flexible and customizable. As current customers of ExLibris™, the Center has firsthand knowledge of the ExLibris™ support practices and the expertise yielded through customer email discussion lists. Primo® may not have all of the functionality desired 'out of the box', but with time the Center (with help from the customer community and Primo support) can complete all the project goals.

IMPLEMENTATION IN PHASES

It's an ExLibris World

The first and easiest phase of implementation was integrating the ExLibris™ products into Primo®. This included Aleph®, DigiTool®, Metalib®, and SFX®. Metalib required some additional work, caused by the Center's general under-use of Metalib® in the past. Most of this ExLibris™ product work was completed by the ExLibris™ Implementation Manager. The most challenging areas of this phase were related to mapping resource types and form/genre for DigiTool® and single sign-on using PDS.

Integrating Museum Systems

This is an issue with which the Center is still grappling. Primo® is Dublin Core compatible, but the transition of converting EMu data to Dublin Core, and then Dublin Core to Primo®, has not been an easy one. Since there are not many (if any) other ExLibris™ customers using EMu data in Primo®, there is little to no support from the user community or ExLibris™ staff. The Center has been able to successfully harvest and display some of the fields, but the customization process has been slow and this is in no way close to completion. The data is available in Primo®, but the Center plans to continue develop these mapping tables.

Websites, Websites, Websites

The Center's Websites are rich with data and information for the Center's users, both about the Center and partners themselves as well as the collections housed within. The ability to integrate these resources was a major plus in Primo's® selection. Websites are harvested using Heritrix software and converted into WARC format files, which are then harvested by Primo®. While this did not pose any expected challenges, the Center found that once the files were in Primo®, configuration and normalization of the data was more difficult. It is the Center's impression that while this was a celebrated feature during the selection of Primo®, the Primo® support team has little experience implementing such data sources. The Center looks forward to advancing the customizations of these types of data sources in the future, and perhaps becoming a voice of experience for the Primo® customer community.

Training and Internal Development: Looking for More than "Out-of-the-Box"

A question asked in any process like this is, "Does one ever receive as much training as one thinks is needed?" The Center found that training during implementation and with each customization was fragmented. Basic training did help fit all the pieces together, but as usual, and particularly in a project of this scope, troubleshooting is best learned on the job. Training cannot anticipate all the challenges one might face, especially when it comes to LAM data. The Center continues to monitor the Primo discussion lists to look for more configuration recommendations by the user group and take every challenge as a learning opportunity.

MEASURING SUCCESS AND TANGIBLE RESULTS

After the soft roll-out of Primo®, the Center created a survey to facilitate discussions with staff and advanced users about their expectations and impressions of the new Single-Search interface, in order to examine the usability and shortfalls of the new Single-Search interface. The survey was created as a form in Google Documents. The survey is listed under Appendix A. The Center plans to release new surveys designed specifically for staff and new users in the coming year to continue evaluating user perceptions and expectations of Primo®.

A direct link to the Advanced User Survey was distributed to a selected group of participants. There were 12 responses. Most of the participants were research fellows, regular researchers at the Center, and genealogists. There is a noted difference in opinion between the researchers (regulars and fellows) and genealogists. The factors that influence the differences are most likely type of research, general resistance to change, and age of survey participant. The opinions of the genealogists particularly cause concern in regards to usability for older users. Regardless of general opinion, the survey results showed either maintained or significantly increased ease of use when the users compared Primo® with the other Center OPACs, like Aleph® and DigiTool®.

Addressing Survey Results

Creating multiple 'views' (or additional search interfaces) in Primo will help the Center identify some key groups of researchers at the Center with special research needs, such as genealogists. Primo® is exemplary for this type of flexibility and the Center plans to use this in the future for any number of projects, including separate customizable views for each partner institution.

The Center also convened the Single-Search Subcommittee to discuss the features, language, and general functionality of the Single-Search interface. This group of peers has representatives from each of the partner organizations who will review the results of the aforementioned survey and offer feedback on how the user experience might be improved.

FUTURE RESEARCH DIRECTIONS

…Museums, libraries, and archives are bursting with rich content, but they have difficulty in either reaching the public or in maximizing the public's use of their content. (Pijeaux, 2007, p.58)

In the future, the Center looks forward to seeing how other special libraries and cultural heritage institutions interact with software like Primo®. Below is a list of challenges that the Center has faced during implementation and hopes to learn more about in the future.

Authority Control in the Discovery Environment

Are library systems developers looking into harvesting authority data for application across data sources in discovery systems? For example, will Aleph® authority data ever be able to be applied to other data sources in Primo®?

Use of Social Networking Features at Research Institutions

The Center has found little patron interest in user created content, like writing reviews and tagging. Are these features as useful for research institutions as public libraries?

Usability Concerns for Different Types of Research Users

How do discovery systems interact with different types of users? Do older users find the features of discovery systems as approachable and helpful as younger users? Are these systems actually more intuitive for first time users? Are search results more overwhelming for users? Do users narrow results with refine options, like facets? Or do they simply look at the first page of results?

Intersection of Special Collections, Archives, and Museums Encoding

Do discovery systems serve as a new way for different systems to communicate with each other? How do discovery systems affect the development of special collections, archives, and museum software?

Use of Discovery Solution APIs to Re-Purpose Data

How are cultural institutions repurposing data from discovery systems? What kind of interesting projects are being made possible because of discovery systems like Primo®?

CONCLUSION

For the Center, discovery is the beginning of a new way to look at systems and online presence in general. It is time for the Center to think of online space less like an access point and more like a virtual community center (Solas, 2010). The added benefit of multiple views, social media features, and general ease of use will contribute to easing patron difficulties when accessing Center resources and community information. The Center will then be one step closer to creating a friendly online environment for the community.

REFERENCES

Angelaki, G., Caffo, R., Hagedorn-Saupe, M., & Hazan, S. (2010). ATHENA: A mechanism for harvesting Europe's museum holdings into Europeana. In J. Trant & D. Bearman (Eds.), Museums and the Web 2010: Proceedings. Toronto, Canada: Archives & Museum Informatics. Retrieved July 8, 2011, from http://www.museumsandtheweb.com/mw2010/papers/angelaki/angelaki.html

Edson, M., & Cherry, R. (2010). Museum commons: Tragedy or enlightened self-interest? In J. Trant & D. Bearman (Eds.), Museums and the Web 2010: Proceedings. Toronto, Canada: Archives & Museum Informatics. Retrieved July 15, 2011, from http://www.archimuse.com/mw2010/papers/edson-cherry/edson-cherry.html

Gow, V., Brown, L., Johnston, C., Neale, A., Paynter, G., & Rigby, F. (2010). Making New Zealand content easier to find, share and use. In J. Trant & D. Bearman (Eds.), Museums and the Web 2010: Proceedings. Toronto, Canada: Archives & Museum Informatics. Retrieved July 15, 2011, from http://www.museumsandtheweb.com/mw2009/papers/gow/gow.html

Pijeaux, L. J., Jr. (2007). The Birmingham Civil Rights Institute: A case study in library, archives, and museum collaboration. RBM: A Journal of Rare Books, Manuscripts, and Cultural Heritage, 8(1), 56-60. Retrieved from http://rbm.acrl.org/content/8/1/56.full.pdf

Solas, N. (2010). Hiding our collections in plain site: Interface strategies for "findability." In J. Trant & D. Bearman (Eds.), Museums and the Web 2010: Proceedings. Toronto, Canada: Archives & Museum Informatics. Retrieved July 15, 2011, from http://www.archimuse.com/mw2010/papers/solas/solas.html

ADDITIONAL READING

ARLIS/NA. (2008). Next generation OPACs: Bibliography [Blog post]. From http://arlisnamw.wordpress.com/virtual-poster-sessions/whats-hot-whats-not-trends-in-technologies-and-services-in-libraries/next-generation-opacs-current-practices-future-opportunities-for-art-libraries/next-generation-opacs-bibliography/

Barry, A. (2010). NaturePlus – Developing a personalized visitor experience across the museum's virtual and physical environments. In J. Trant & D. Bearman (Eds.), Museums and the Web 2010: Proceedings. Toronto, Canada: Archives & Museum Informatics. Retrieved from http://www.archimuse.com/mw2010/papers/barry/barry.html

Calhoun, K. (2006). The changing nature of the catalog and its integration with other discovery tools. Washington, DC: Library of Congress. Retrieved from http://www.loc.gov/catdir/calhoun-report-final.pdf

Cameron, F., & Kenderdine, S. (Eds.). (2010). *Theorizing digital cultural heritage*. Cambridge, MA: MIT Press.

Christenson, H., & Tennant, R. (2005). Integrating information resources: Principles, technologies, and approaches. Retrieved from http://www.cdlib.org/inside/projects/metasearch/nsdl/nsdl_report2.pdf

De Caro, S., Di Blas, N., & Spagnolo, L. (2010), In search of novel ways to design large cultural websites. In J. Trant & D. Bearman (Eds.), Museums and the Web 2010: Proceedings. Toronto, Canada: Archives & Museum Informatics Retrieved from http://www.archimuse.com/mw2010/papers/decaro/decaro.html

Durbin, G. (2010). More than the sum of its parts: Pulling together user involvement in a museum website. In J. Trant & D. Bearman (Eds.), Museums and the Web 2010: Proceedings. Toronto, Canada: Archives & Museum Informatics. Retrieved from http://www.archimuse.com/mw2010/papers/durbin/durbin.html

Eklund, P., Goodall, P., Lawson, A., & Wray, T. (2010). CollectionWeb digital ecosystems: A semantic Web and Web 2.0 framework for generating museum Websites. In J. Trant & D. Bearman (Eds.), Museums and the Web 2010: Proceedings. Toronto, Canada: Archives & Museum Informatics. Retrieved from http://www.archimuse.com/mw2010/papers/eklund/eklund.html

Elings, M., & Waibel, G. (2007). Metadata for all: Descriptive standards and metadata sharing across libraries, archives, and museums. *First Monday, 12*(3). Retrieved from http://firstmonday.org/htbin/cgiwrap/bin/ojs/index.php/fm/article/view/1628/1543

Ellis, M., & Zambonini, D. (2010). Hoard it: Aggregating, displaying and mining object-data without consent (or: Big, hairy, audacious goals for museum collections on-line). In J. Trant & D. Bearman (Eds.), Museums and the Web 2010: Proceedings. Toronto, Canada: Archives & Museum Informatics. Retrieved from http://www.museumsandtheweb.com/mw2009/papers/ellis/ellis.html

Falk, J. H., & Sheppard, B. K. (2006). *Thriving in the knowledge age: new business models for museums and other cultural institutions.* Lanham, MD: Altamira Press.

Foster, N. F., Clark, K., Tancheva, K., & Kilzer, R. (Eds.). (2011). *Scholarly practice, participatory design and the eXtensible catalog.* Chicago, IL: American Library Association.

Hedstrom, M., King, J. L., & School of Information University of Michigan. (n.d.). On the LAM: Library, archive, and museum collections in the creation and maintenance of knowledge communities. Retrieved from http://www.oecd.org/dataoecd/59/63/32126054.pdf

Jastram, I. (2011). Heads they win, tails we lose: Discovery tools will never deliver their promise. Pegasus Librarian. Retrieved from http://pegasuslibrarian.com/2011/01/heads-they-win-tales-we-lose-discovery-tools-will-never-deliver-on-their-promise.html

Jones-Garmil, K. (Ed.). (1997). *The wired museum: Emerging technology and changing paradigms.* Washington, DC: American Association of Museums.

Keene, S. (1998). *Digital collections: Museums and the information age.* Boston, MA: Butterworth-Heinemann.

La Barre, K. (2007). Faceted navigation and browsing features in new OPACs: Robust support for scholarly information seeking? *Knowledge Organization, 34*(2), 28–90.

Lang, J. (2007). "Have you searched Google yet?" Using Google as a discovery tool for cataloging. Library Philosophy and Practice 2007, LPP Special Issue on Libraries and Google (June). Retrieved from http://unllib.unl.edu/LPP/lang.htm

Rowley, S., Schaepe, D., Sparrow, L., Sanborn, A., Radermacher, U., & Wallace, R. … Goffman, T. (2010), Building an on-line research community: The reciprocal research network. In J. Trant & D. Bearman (Eds.), Museums and the Web 2010: Proceedings. Toronto, Canada: Archives & Museum Informatics. Retrieved from http://www.archimuse.com/mw2010/papers/rowley/rowley.html

Royston, C. (2009). A guide to managing a large multi-institutional project in the cultural sector. In J. Trant & D. Bearman (Eds.), Museums and the Web 2009: Proceedings. Toronto, Canada: Archives & Museum Informatics. Retrieved from http://www.museumsandtheweb.com/mw2009/papers/royston/royston.html

Seeger, A., & Chaudhuri, S. (2004). *Archives for the future: Global perspectives on audiovisual archives in the 21st century.* Calcutta, India: Seagull Books.

Stille, A. (2002). *The future of the past.* New York, NY: Farrar, Straus, and Giroux.

Tarulli, L. (2009). Choosing a discovery tool [Blog post]. The Cataloguing Librarian. Retrieved from http://laureltarulli.wordpress.com/2009/02/05/choosing-a-discovery-tool/

Tennant, R. (2009). 21st century description and access. In Biblioteconomia i Documentacio, 22. Retrieved from http://www.ub.edu/bid/22/tennant2.htm

Tonta, Y. (2008). Libraries and museums in the flat world: Are they becoming virtual destinations? *Library Collections, Acquisitions & Technical Services, 32*(1), 1–9. doi:10.1016/j.lcats.2008.05.002

Van Camp, A. (2003). RLG, where museums, libraries, and archives intersect. *LIBER Quarterly, 13*(3/4), 312–318.

Wilde, E., & Mann, L. (2010), Open source collaboration: New models for technology development in the museum community. In J. Trant & D. Bearman (Eds.), Museums and the Web 2010: Proceedings. Toronto, Canada: Archives & Museum Informatics. Retrieved from http://www.archimuse.com/mw2010/papers/wilde/wilde.html

Yarrow, A., Clubb, B., & Draper, J. L. (2008). Public libraries, archives, and museums: Trends in collaboration and cooperation. International Federation of Library Associations and Institutions, IFLA Professional Reports (p. 108). Retrieved from http://archive.ifla.org/VII/s8/pub/Profrep108.pdf

Zorich, D. M., Waibel, G., & Erway, R. (2008). Beyond the silos of the LAMS: Collaboration among libraries, archives, and museums. Report produced by OCLC Research. Dublin, OH: OCLC Research. Retrieved from http://www.oclc.org/research/publications/library/2008/2008-05.pdf

KEY TERMS AND DEFINITIONS

360 Search: Serial Solutions; metasearch option that aggregates electronic resources.

Aleph: Software from ExLibris ILS. The Center uses Aleph for library and archival management and OPAC.

Aquabrowser: One of Serials Solutions' discovery systems. This system was evaluated by the Center and considered for purchase.

The Center: Center for Jewish History.

Cultural Heritage Institutions: Institutions or organizations that house art or cultural artifacts in addition to archives and library materials.

Data: Records or other descriptive content that come from a data source.

Data Set or Data Source: Set of data from a particular source, like an Integrated Library System.

DigiTool: ExLibris digital assets management system. The Center uses DigiTool for management of digital collections and online access to those collections.

Discovery Solution or System: Proprietary or open source system that integrates data from multiple data sources into a single index that searches all sources simultaneously.

Dublin Core: Encoding standard that uses a set of metadata elements. It is not defined as a set of numerical codes like MARC, but rather uses the actual terms for syntax, like Title, Creator, and Subject. Dublin Core is often used for descriptive cataloging of objects and digital objects.

EBSCO Discovery Solution (EDS): EBSCO's discovery system. This system was evaluated by the Center and considered for purchase.

EMu: KE's museum system. The Center uses EMu for museum collections management and online access to those collections.

Harvest: Means of extracting data from one data source to be integrated into another. OAI-PMH is a popular way to harvest data.

Heritrix: software used to harvest usable metadata from Websites to create WARC files (which are later harvested by Primo).

ILS: Acronym used to describe Integrated Library System, also referred to as OPACs. These systems are used by libraries to manage collections.

LAM: Acronym used to describe partnerships of Libraries, Archives, and Museums or institutions that are all three.

MARC: Acronym used to describe Machine Readable Cataloging. This encoding format is used by most ILS and OPACs to store bibliographic data.

MARC XML: Acronym used to describe Machine-Readable Cataloging in Extensible Markup Language (XML). XML stands for eXtensible Markup Language. XML allows creation of a customized markup language to define data elements on a Web page. MARC 21 is an encoding standard maintained by the Library of Congress that uses numerical codes to identify fields for content. MARC XML is an encoding standard that uses the MARC 21 standard with XML coding.

Metadata: Commonly defined as 'data about data'. For the purposes of this chapter, however, this term is used to describe data content or descriptive data used within an encoded record. For instance, the data used to describe an object or book in a MARC XML, MARC, or Dublin Core record is referred to as metadata.

Metalib: ExLibris metasearch product. The Center uses Metalib to assist in management and access of subscription electronic resources and free scholarly resources available online.

OAI-PMH: acronym used to describe Open Archives Initiative Protocol for Metadata Harvesting. This protocol is used to pass data from one system to another. This allows for greater interoperability between systems. There is also less need for human intervention after the initial connection and coding has been built.

OPAC: Online Public Access Catalog or online catalog.

PDS: Acronym used to describe Patron Directory Services. PDS is a component of ExLibris systems that allows users to have one login for all the ExLibris products held by an institution, instead of multiple logins (one for each product).

This also allows users to pass more freely from one product to another without logging in multiple times. One product must be chosen as the PDS database of record, and for CJH purposes the Aleph ILS was chosen.

Primo: ExLibris discovery solution. This system was evaluated by the Center and eventually purchased.

Primo Central: ExLibris index of aggregated electronically published content. This index was evaluated as part of Primo functionality and eventually purchased with the Center's subscription to Primo. In the Center's implementation, this index is used in conjunction with Metalib to give access to the Center's subscription electronic resource content.

SFX: ExLibris link resolver. The Center uses SFX for access to e-journals provided through the Center's subscription electronic resources.

Single-Search: The Center project name for implementing a discovery system.

Summon: One of Serials Solutions' discovery systems. This system was evaluated by the Center and considered for purchase.

WARC: Acronym used to describe Web ARChive file format. This file format is used to harvest Website metadata for inclusion in (for instance) a discovery product, like Primo.

ENDNOTES

[1] Ex Libris is a trademark of Ex Libris Ltd.

[2] Aleph is a registered trademark of Ex Libris Ltd.

[3] Digitool is a registered trademark of Ex Libris Ltd.

[4] MetaLib is a registered trademark of Ex Libris Ltd.

[5] SFX OpenURL link resolver is a registered trademark of Ex Libris Ltd

6   Serials Solution is a registered trademark of Serials Solutions

7   AquaBrowser is a registered trademark of Serials Solutions

8   Summon is owned by ProQuest LLC

9   EBSCO Discovery Services is owned by EBSCO Publishing Industries.

10   Syndetics is a trademark of Serials Solutions.

APPENDIX

Single Search at CJH: Advanced User Survey

In early April CJH released the beta version of our new single search site - http://search.cjh.org. This site integrates all of our OPACs (Online Public Access Catalog) into a single search interface. This includes our Library/Archives Catalog, Digital Collections, and Museum Collections. This site also offers a new way to access our electronic resources. As our development of this site continues, we would like to hear from you about your experience with the site and what you think it should do better. Please fill out the following survey and feel free to add any other comments in the open text box at the bottom. Thank you very much for your time and input. Sincerely, CJH Library Systems Department

* Required

Tell us about your research and interaction with CJH online content

Before the introduction of the single search site, which catalogs did you use the most frequently? * Check all that apply.

- ☐ Library/Archives Catalog (Aleph system)
- ☐ Digital Collections (DigiTool system)
- ☐ Museum Collections (EMu system)
- ☐ Electronic resources (Metalib system)
- ☐ E-Journals (SFX system)
- ☐ Partner Websites (ajhs.org, lbi.org, etc)
- ☐ Partner Project Websites (YIVO encyclopedia, DigiBaeck, etc)
- ☐ Other: [＿＿＿＿＿]

How did you access these resources? * Check all that apply.

- ☐ CJH Website (cjh.org)
- ☐ Partner Website
- ☐ Google
- ☐ Bookmarked catalog Websites (navigate directly to site)
- ☐ Flickr
- ☐ WorldCat.org
- ☐ Facebook
- ☐ Recommended (please specify in other)
- ☐ Other: [＿＿＿＿＿]

Please describe the type of research that you do at CJH. * Choose only one.

- ☐ Family history, genealogy
- ☐ Undergraduate research
- ☐ Graduate research
- ☐ Doctoral research
- ☐ Research Fellowship
- ☐ Personal research
- ☐ Other: [＿＿＿＿]

Tell us about this site and visiting CJH

Please tell us a little bit about where you use our online content. * Check all that apply.

- ☐ On-site, at CJH
- ☐ From home
- ☐ From work
- ☐ From school
- ☐ Other: [＿＿＿＿]

How likely are you to visit CJH? * Choose number in scale.

	1	2	3	4	5	
Not likely to visit in person	☐	☐	☐	☐	☐	Will definitely visit CJH in person

Did this site make it easier for you to determine whether you need to visit CJH in-person or not? * Choose only one.

- ☐ Yes
- ☐ No
- ☐ Other: [＿＿＿＿]

Please explain why. Free text.

[text box]

Tell us about the general navigation and efficiency

Did you find the site easy to use? * Choose number in scale.

        1   2   3   4   5

Very difficult ☐   ☐   ☐   ☐   ☐   Very easy

Has the new single search aided your research at CJH? * Choose number in scale.

        1   2   3   4   5

Has not aided the ease of your research at CJH.	☐	☐	☐	☐	☐	Has revolutionized the ease of your research at CJH.

Where you able to find the items you were looking for? * Choose number in scale.

        1   2   3   4   5

I wasn't able to find what I wanted ☐   ☐   ☐   ☐   ☐   I was able to find everything

Did the single search site make it easier for you to navigate the CJH Collections? * Choose number in scale.

        1   2   3   4   5

Significantly harder to navigate ☐   ☐   ☐   ☐   ☐   Significantly easier to navigate

If it was easier to navigate, please specify which features made it easier to navigate (if any). Choose all that apply.

   ☐ All resources in single interface

   ☐ Facets (refine my results)

   ☐ Sorting

   ☐ General look and feel of the site

   ☐ None of the above

   ☐ Other: [   ]

If it was NOT easier to navigate, please specify which features made it more difficult to navigate (if any). Choose all that apply.

   ☐ All resources in single interface

   ☐ Facets (refine my results)

   ☐ Sorting

   ☐ General look and feel of the site

   ☐ None of the above

   ☐ Other: [   ]

Compared to the other CJH catalogs, would you say that the single search site has increased your efficiency in researching at CJH? * Choose number in scale.

	1	2	3	4	5	
Significantly decreased your efficiency	▢	▢	▢	▢	▢	Significantly increased your efficiency

Do you think you spend more or less time doing online research now at CJH? * Choose number in scale.

	1	2	3	4	5	
Considerably more time	▢	▢	▢	▢	▢	Considerably less time

Please explain. Free text.

```

```

Tell us about the special features

Was the information provided in the result tabs intuitive (like Location, Details, etc.)? * Choose one.

▢ Yes, I was able to find what I needed.

▢ No, I was unable to find the information I needed.

▢ Other:

Were you able to identify the call number easily? * Choose one.

▢ Yes

▢ No

▢ Other:

Did you utilize the 'Refine your results' facets on the left side of the screen? * This feature allows you to limit your search by subject, creator, years, collections, format, etc. Choose only one.

▢ Yes

▢ No

If yes, please describe the facets that you used and whether this aided your search. Free text.

Please describe other facets that you think might be helpful for narrowing search results. Free text.

Please check all other features that you used on the site. * Check all that apply.

☐ Alternate search scopes

☐ Find databases

☐ e-Journals A-Z

☐ Advanced search

☐ Suggested new searches

☐ RSS Feed

☐ e-shelf

☐ None of the above

☐ Other: [   ]

Tell us about your interaction with cultural artifacts

Before we introduced the single search site, had you ever accessed the Museum Collections? * Choose only one.

○ Yes

○ No

○ Not sure

In your experience with the single search site, did you encounter cultural, art, or religious objects? * Choose only one.

- ☐ Yes
- ☐ No
- ☐ Not sure

If yes, did you find these items helpful to your research? Choose only one.

- ☐ Yes
- ☐ No
- ☐ Other: [   ]

Tell us about overall ease of use

Do you think the site was easier to use than our other catalogs? * Choose number in scale.

	1	2	3	4	5	
Not easier to use	☐	☐	☐	☐	☐	Significantly easier to use

Please explain. Free text.

Additional comments?

Do you have any other comments to share with us? If yes, please enter them below. Free text.

Chapter 33

Implementing Primo for the Michiana Academic Library Consortium (MALC)

Aaron B. Bales
University of Notre Dame, USA

Mark Dehmlow
University of Notre Dame, USA

ABSTRACT

The University of Notre Dame and the Michiana Academic Library Consortium (MALC) have implemented Ex Libris'™ Primo®2 as its next generation discovery system. The consortium initially implemented the system in public beta and transitioned Primo® to the default discovery system for the Libraries in the Spring of 2011. This chapter discusses the rationale for acquiring Primo®, the implementation and customization, user response, and long term hopes for the system. It also touches on the early evaluation and implementation steps for the Primo Centralized Index.

INTRODUCTION

The University of Notre Dame and the Michiana Academic Library Consortium (MALC) selected Ex Libris'™ Primo® as its next generation discovery system in the fall of 2008. The consortium chose Primo® from a slate of over 10 systems because of its modularity, extensibility, and customizability. Primo® is robust, both in its ability to make adjustments to the interface through its default wizards, but also in its system architecture which facilitates customization for organizations that would like to create a beyond out-of-the-box experience. Primo® is also a full-featured discovery system with its native configuration. The libraries initially implemented Primo® in public beta, branded as CatalogPlus, and made it available in parallel with the classic Online Public Access Catalog (OPAC) – Ex Libris'™ Aleph Integrated Library System.

DOI: 10.4018/978-1-4666-1821-3.ch033

Primo® was released as the default search for library collections in January 2011, after two years of public beta. The libraries also kept the classic OPAC available as an alternative, and plan to keep it available indefinitely. Early feedback has helped guide the development of locally programmed customizations that have significantly enhanced the Primo® interface, especially in the areas of locations for physical materials and extended services. This chapter discusses how Primo® is designed to work, implementation and customization choices for the system, early response from users, work with their feedback, and how the University of Notre Dame hopes to extend the system in the future. While this chapter discusses Primo® in the context of the consortium, the perspective represented is that of the system managers at the University of Notre Dame Hesburgh Libraries, hitherto referred to as Hesburgh Libraries.

BACKGROUND

The University of Notre Dame is a member of a the Michiana Academic Library Consortium (MALC), a small local consortium comprising the University of Notre Dame, Saint Mary's College, Bethel College and Holy Cross College. This consortium was originally formed in 1990 to support the Northwestern Online Total Integrated System (NOTIS) as a shared library resource. Notre Dame had already implemented NOTIS in 1986 and provided hosting and technical support services for the consortium.

MALC libraries migrated from NOTIS to Aleph 500 in 1998/99. The Kresge Law Library at Notre Dame was not part of this migration; they had previously switched to Innovative Interfaces Incorporated's Integrated Library System (III). From 1992-1996 the law library used NOTIS for cataloging, and INNOVAC (Innovative Interfaces) for acquisitions and serials. In 1996, they migrated to III's INNOPAC for all modules and upgraded to Millennium in 2001.

DECIDING, ACQUIRING, AND IMPLEMENTING EX LIBRIS' PRIMO

Assessing What Was Needed in a Next Generation Discovery System

In 2008, the libraries formed a Resource Discovery Assessment Working Group to assess options for a new discovery system in the wake of the emerging "next generation" OPAC landscape. The group included 10 members, from various areas in the libraries.

The group hoped to address a number of issues as it considered options for Resource Discovery Systems. One was the desire to provide a Union Catalog search for the consortium. Even though the libraries were on a shared system, each MALC member had a separate catalog database and it was not easy to cross-search them. There was a Union Catalog option available for the Aleph system, but the consortium had not implemented it. The law library's records were not in the Aleph system at all. A union search would be a convenience to users, rather than conducting multiple searches to find out what they had easy access to use. It is worth noting that MALC patrons have cross borrowing privileges and a shared catalog would address the directors' goal toward inter-institutional resource sharing and promotion of the consortium.

Another major issue was the changing nature of library collections. The biggest change at the time was the introduction of electronic resources. At the time of the assessment, the libraries were already subscribing to the majority of their journals in electronic format and anticipated increasing collections of electronic books in the future. In the vast majority of cases, there were separate records in the Integrated Library System (ILS) for the print and electronic copies. While this had advantages for managing the collection, it was confusing for users.

There were also library collections that were not in the catalogs at all. For example, the Architecture Library at Notre Dame has a collection of lanternslides that they have digitized and would like to make available to their users. While the slides can be searched separately, users may not be aware that they need to use another system. The Hesburgh Libraries would also like to include manuscripts and archival collections in the discovery system.

Finally, MALC wanted to provide an improved user experience, ideally balancing the needs of experienced and novice users. Library staff had worked to make the OPAC as good as it could be, and had even been cited as a best practices example (Mi & Weng, 2008). However, it did not have advanced features that were becoming commonplace to users. Most of the article indexes had already introduced faceted browsing, which was also common on many Web sites, bookstores, and other commercial retail stores.

The Assessment Team devised a list of 47 criteria, in seven categories, for evaluating the candidate systems:

- Search functionality
  ○ Indexing improvements
  ○ Simplified search & browse
  ○ Spelling correction/suggestions
- User experience
- Integrability
  ○ Index capability
  ○ Record enrichment
  ○ Supported data formats/sources
  ○ ILS integration
- Web 2.0 functionality
  ○ Social computing
  ○ Enhanced services
- System and personnel requirements
- Extensibility
- Support options

In addition to this checklist, the group considered some scope issues. The solution should focus on resource discovery, and act as a supplement to, rather than a replacement for, the ILS. Additionally, the group wanted to recommend systems

that were complete, and could be implemented without requiring extensive local development. At the same time, the group wanted a system that was flexible and allowed for local customizations and extension. The group was open to both commercial and open source solutions.

Some of the initial candidates were assessed as out of scope as being too broad, having been designed as an ILS. At the other end, some of the initial candidates were tools or components that could have been used to develop a solution, but were not complete solutions in themselves.

Using these criteria, the Assessment Group narrowed the list to three finalists, which appeared to best meet the needs of the consortium. These included two commercial solutions (Primo® and Aquabrowser®[3]) and one open source solution (VuFind). These three solutions were recommended to the directors of the member libraries, who selected Primo®.

About a year later, Ex Libris™ announced a companion product to Primo® called Primo Central™[4] Index. Together, these two products form a full Web-scale discovery environment, which provides targeted access to local collections while simultaneously providing search services against hundreds of millions of scholarly works, articles, books, etc.

Primo and Primo Central Index

Primo® is the "next generation" discovery system developed by Ex Libris™ Group, the company that developed the Aleph 500 integrated library system, currently in production at Notre Dame. In most configurations, Primo® is a decoupled front end for older integrated library systems, a trend that emerged five or six years ago. It was initially designed to work with bibliographic data, starting with MARC and Dublin Core formats. In its current iteration, Primo® is capable of handling almost any metadata format, empowering organizations to provide aggregated discovery services over most of the resources they feel are relevant to their users.

Currently, Notre Dame's implementation focuses on the catalogs of the MALC institutions, but the Libraries are in discussions to include Encoded Archival Descriptions of resources from various University archives and even brief descriptive records of library services like Interlibrary Loan and Document Delivery.

Primo® itself is available in one of three configurations depending on the needs of an organization:

1. It can be hosted and managed locally, giving the organization full control over system implementation and configuration including access to the UNIX environment.
2. It can be hosted by Ex Libris™ while allowing the organization to have access to most of the back end files for configuration.
3. It can be implemented by Ex Libris'™ Total Care program, where Ex Libris™ does most of the system implementation and configuration based on the organization's preferences; this option includes only limited access to configuration tools.

At the time MALC acquired Primo®, it had already been adopted by some of their peer institutions, such as the University of Iowa, Boston College, and Vanderbilt, but is now in use at more than 700 institutions globally (Ex Libris Group, 2011). MALC chose to implement Primo® using the first option, to host and manage the system locally because of the desire for a high level of customization.

Primo Central™ Index (PCI) is a "cloud" based, mega index of aggregated scholarly materials. It is similar in concept to Google Scholar™, but has a few added benefits. First, it is focused on data from scholarly resources that libraries select for their users. Second, it not only aggregates openly available metadata from journal publishers and other open metadata sources, but also from many additional data sources available only in the deep Web, including resources that libraries can access only through subscriptions, e.g., full text collections, digital reference collections, and abstracting and indexing resources. PCI™ tightly integrates into an organization's localized instance of Primo®.

Priming the Engine: Normalization, De-duplication, FRBRization, and Enhancement

To implement Primo®, data first needs to be extracted from a source and ingested into Primo®. MALC's starting point was to focus on Aleph based MARC data, with the intent to integrate the Law Library's III MARC data shortly after, and then look at alternative data sources that would be important in a localized, but extended, scholarly discovery system. The Aleph publishing process enhances bibliographic data with holdings and availability information for optimal display in Primo®. Once the data is extracted, it is loaded into the Primo® system through tools that normalize, deduplicate, FRBRize, and enhance the data. The normalization process prepares the data to be consumed by the front end user interface vis-à-vis the search engine, facets, indexes and Primo® records.

The normalization process converts the source data into a proprietary XML format that Primo® uses to store the data. One of the main advantages of converting the incoming data to XML is that it allows the library to combine data from a variety of sources. It does not matter whether the original data is MARC, Dublin Core, various forms of XML, or any other format. Currently, Primo® is able to handle MARC21, Dublin Core, and a few source specific data formats out of the box, but it also has the ability to convert almost any metadata format with the use of a special plug-in that requires some Java programming.

Primo® comes with an out-of-the-box set of normalization rules for converting source data to XML. The normalization process is powerful, and is not limited to simply copying data from the

MARC record. It has the ability to extract data conditionally, modify the data in a variety of ways (including the use of Regular Expressions), and map data to locally defined values.

The next step is to deduplicate the XML records. Each incoming record is checked against the existing database to determine matching records. The Primo® de-duplication algorithm is based on the one used for the Aleph Union Catalog, which Ex Libris™ developed in cooperation with the California Digital Library (G. Gal, personal communication, August 22, 2011).

When matches are identified, a merged record is derived by combining matching records and although the individual records are retained, they become invisible to the end user. The merged records are indexed and included in search results. There are two main cases where duplicate records are merged. One is that many titles have duplicates across libraries. The other is that the same title may have multiple records for different formats. The library generally has separate records for multiple formats, especially print and online, in the ILS. (This is a practice; it is not constrained by the ILS.) Those records are also merged in Primo®, so that the user sees a single record for each title.

Following de-duplication, the records are checked against the database to identify FRBR groups. These records represent various editions of the same title and are grouped rather than merged. When the search results include FRBRized records, a representative record is chosen to display in the brief search results, along with a link to the full group that reads "There are n versions of this item."

The final step in the process is enhancement. This is where Primo® can interact with a supplementary data source to add data to the search or display elements of the record. Some possible sources that could be of interest would be services like Syndetic Solutions, Table of Contents from Blackwell or another vendor, or data from social networking sites like LibraryThing. Primo®'s system architecture allows customers to define

plug-ins for the enhancement step. If an institution has a data source it would like to exploit, and some knowledge of Java, it can interject its data of interest into Primo® records.

Integrating non-Aleph ILS data: Law III

One of the goals of the project was to integrate the Kresge Law Library's collection. As mentioned above, the Law Library has a separate ILS, III Millennium. Although Aleph has specific publishing functions intended to work with Primo®, that does not mean that Primo® is unable to use data from other systems. MARC data is regularly extracted from the law library catalog for loading into Primo®. One issue is that the export of the Bibliographic data from the Law Library does not include holdings information. The holdings records are exported from Millennium separately, in a spreadsheet format. A Perl script is used to add the data from the holdings file to the appropriate MARC records prior to loading them into Primo®.

The other main difficulty with the Law Library export is that it does not include any availability information. As a result, Primo® is unable to indicate whether items at the Law Library are currently available. It is possible to export availability information separately, and then programmatically merge it with the bibliographic information and this approach for record loading is being investigated. Virginia Tech has also developed a JavaScript Object Notation (JSON) based tool for providing real time availability from III systems that is compatible with Primo®, it is called majax2 (Back & Baily, 2010) and the code is available at http://code.google.com/p/majax2/. Implementation of this script is anticipated in 2012.

Custom Normalization Rules

In Primo®, libraries also have the ability to customize the normalization rules that map incoming data (MARC or other formats) to Primo®'s record structure. This includes the ability to redefine and alter existing Primo® record fields, or even to define new ones. One case was to add the relator fields that are present in some MARC records, particularly for music, to the author headings in Primo®. Relator terms may indicate, for example, that a particular individual was the composer, conductor, or performer of a musical work. One record in the Hesburgh Libraries' catalog contains a number of headings, including these fields:

7001 |a Mahler, Gustav, |d 1860-1911. |4 cnd
7001 |a Abendroth, Irene. |4 prf
7001 |a Bahr-Mildenburg, Anna, |d 1872-1947. |4 prf

A custom normalization rule looks up subfield |4 in a table of relator codes from the Library of Congress (which was locally loaded into Primo® for this purpose). It then adds the corresponding term to the Primo® record contributor field. As a result, in the Primo® display the user sees:

Gustav Mahler 1860-1911. [Conductor] ;
Irene Abendroth [Performer] ;
Anna Bahr-Mildenburg 1872-1947. [Performer] ;

The Hesburgh Libraries made similar updates to include the relator terms for both display and search. These fields are linked in the Primo® display, so that the user can easily find just the 36 records for which Gustav Mahler was the conductor.

Normalization rules can also be used to control the matching fields used in the de-duplication and FRBR algorithms. The Hesburgh Libraries has made a few changes to these rules, in order to tweak the outcome of these procedures. For example, some online serials did not initially merge as desired with their print counterparts. Those records that failed to merge often included online-specific LCCN (Library of Congress Card Number) numbers. Excluding the LCCNs for online (but not print) serials from the matching fields

Figure 1. Sample section of a record

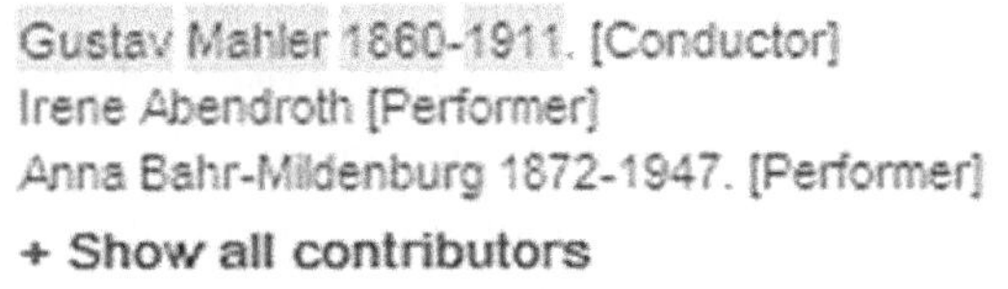

Gustav Mahler 1860-1911. [Conductor]
Irene Abendroth [Performer]
Anna Bahr-Mildenburg 1872-1947. [Performer]
+ Show all contributors

fixed the problem. Secondly, as a general rule, FRBR grouping was not helpful for musical scores or for works of art due to the heavy use of generic titles, such as sonatas, or using the artist's name as the title for art collections. To avoid poor groupings for these items, the normalization rules were set to exclude them from the FRBR process altogether, based on material type and call number.

Creating the User Interface: Out of the Box Configuration

Primo® has many options for institutions to tailor the Primo® user interface toward their collections and customer base. Customization focuses on three broad areas: search, services, and interface. Together, the interplay between these three areas ultimately becomes the user experience for the system.

In the area of search, Primo® indexes many fields into the broad keyword index, but allows organizations with access to the configuration system – a Web based set of wizards and tables – the ability to add, subtract, or modify what goes into existing fields or to create new ones. The customization tools allow authorized staff to do a great deal of the configuration work without having to access the UNIX part of the server through an SSH (Secure Shell) client. Out of the box, Primo® comes with many search options, such as keyword, title, author, subject, ISSN, and ISBN fielded searches. It also allows for the addition of many customer-defined fields. The Hesburgh Libraries have already added custom fields for uniform title, series, call number, and publisher.

Primo® allows the ability to give ranking boost to specific records should an institution want certain resources/items to always rise to the top. The Hesburgh Libraries have been giving some thought to adding common services from the Web site like Interlibrary Loan, Document Delivery, Approval Forms, and the like to the search index. Boosting these resources would ensure that when a user enters Interlibrary Loan into the search box, the first record they see is for that service.

Along with fielded searches, one of the core search concepts in Primo® is the notion of "scoping," putting records together within a specific context, such as a collection. Local scopes have been defined for each of the MALC libraries, the branch libraries, special collections, and institutes separately. Scope limiters manifest themselves in the front user interface as tabs and dropdown options available to users at the time of search.

Primo® also allows for the addition of customer-defined sort fields, but comes pre-configured with sort by relevancy, title, author, and popularity, which is based on user clicks in the system.

For services, Primo® has a handful of links it provides out of the box, including links to an OpenURL link resolver, Amazon, Google Book, back to a source ILS, and WorldCat®[5], just to name a few. Utilizing the configuration tool, it is relatively easy to add custom links that follow a specific URL pattern and utilize data from the source system records. In addition to building links, Primo® is now equipped to provide OPAC functionality such as recalls and holds directly in its interface; Ex Libris™ calls this feature OPAC via Primo® (OVP). OVP is implemented using the Digital Library Federation (DLF) defined standard for ILS interaction with external discovery applications and allows for OPAC services to be provided in the Primo® interface instead of sending users in and out of the old OPAC interfaces (Ockerbloom et al., 2008). Primo® is able to do this with Aleph, but could theoretically be extended to interact with any OPAC that follows the DLF specification.

Primo® wraps all of these configuration options into the interface through different instances of the front end. The editor for creating front ends allows organizations to create custom user experiences and locally branded interfaces. Primo® allows for as many custom front ends as an organization would like to create. MALC has created a separate view for each of the member libraries. Within the view editor, organizations choose the out-of-the-box features they would like to display in the user interface and set parameters to define how they function. In the front end editor, a library can determine the facets to display, how many terms display within a facet by default, the search scopes to associate with a front end, whether to use tabs or not, set or "skin" the look and feel to match an organization's Web site, determine which fields display in an advanced search dropdown, and many more options. The front end editor even allows users to reorder HTML page elements or use custom created Java Server Pages through the customized layout editor.

Customizing the User Interface

Primo® is highly configurable, which is beneficial for sites which like to have a lot of control over how their systems behave and perform. Of course, sites can always just accept the out-of-the-box configuration should they not want to invest time in heavy customization. The scope of this chapter only allows exploration of some of the more significant configuration options. Organizations interested in what Primo® is capable of should be aware there is more to discover.

There are several levels at which a library can customize the user interface (UI). At the first level, a great deal of the configuration work for Primo® is done in the Web based configuration tools mentioned before. With the front end editor, mentioned above, the library can set search options for the basic and advanced search. It can configure what fields are included in the record display, for both the results list and the full record view. Other configuration options control the text that appears in the UI (field labels, headings for limits, etc.). If the library wishes to provide a multilingual UI, the tools also provide a mechanism to set equivalent text for each language.

Secondly, the library can use cascading style sheets (CSS) to modify the appearance of the UI. The system comes with an out-of-the-box CSS file that provides the default appearance for the UI. But the library can add its own CSS files, and specify which file(s) the UI will use for each institution. MALC uses three files for each of its institutions: 1) the original default file, which provides the base appearance, 2) a local file that applies to the whole consortium and overrides settings from the default file, and 3) a unique file, for decision elements limited to that institution.

The next level of modification that MALC has used is JavaScript. JavaScript allows modification of elements that are out of the reach of CSS, such as transporting HTML elements to radically different regions of the results screen. JavaScript can also provide more customized interactivity. Primo® includes the jQuery JavaScript library, a powerful JavaScript library that makes it possible to perform complex JavaScript tasks with terse code. In Primo®, it is not practical to edit the HTML for the UI, as it is generally generated by the software. The primary advantage of jQuery in this context is that it is "unobtrusive;" it can be implemented without using any inline JavaScript, and does not require editing any of the HTML. It works similarly to CSS. All of the functions can be handled in separate JavaScript files, which are called from the page header.

The jQuery functions are executed in response to various page events. Many jQuery actions are called by the "document.ready" event, a special JavaScript event that indicates the core HTML is loaded, but that does not wait for images and supplementary files to load, so that they execute early in the page loading process. Other functions are triggered by user events, such as mouse clicks or hovers. HTML elements in the page can be referenced in jQuery by their tags, IDs, or classes. These can be used both to identify events associated with the element, and to manipulate the content of the elements. Some of the effects that MALC uses are to insert new elements, show and hide elements, or to clone elements and place them elsewhere on the page.

The "Show all contributors" link in figure 2 was inserted using jQuery with a function that counts the number of contributors in a record. If there are more than 3 contributors, they are hidden and the link is inserted in the page. The link is bound to a function that displays the remaining contributors. A companion link is also displayed at that time that allows the user to hide them again.

One of the more significant local changes was to recreate the "Locations" tab, an actionable window that gives details about where copies of a title are. The MALC libraries wanted to simplify the look and feel of the tabbed window, add functionality such as their maps links, and give more information about why something is not available while provisioning some alternative services for the user. Many of these features were implemented as specific responses to early user feedback. The pieces on the Primo® side that invoke this new tab are reasonably simple from a programming standpoint – it is primarily Asynchronous JavaScript and XML (AJAX), a JavaScript technique that allows webpages to feel particularly interactive, and a Java Server Page (JSP) on the Primo® server that acts as a proxy Web-service to a script on a local Web server, which in turn creates the contents of the tab. The JavaScript code was provided by Ex Libris™ as an interface Application Programmer Interface (API) for adding tabs into the Primo® UI. The JSP was written locally, but is fairly straightforward and passes a couple of variables to a local script. The local script does all of the work, interacting with the Primo® WebService/XML based API to get source system record numbers, do look-ups in Aleph, retrieve URLs for maps pertaining to specific locations, and then uses the metadata

Figure 2. Example of search scopes expressed in the tabs as well as the dropdown menu

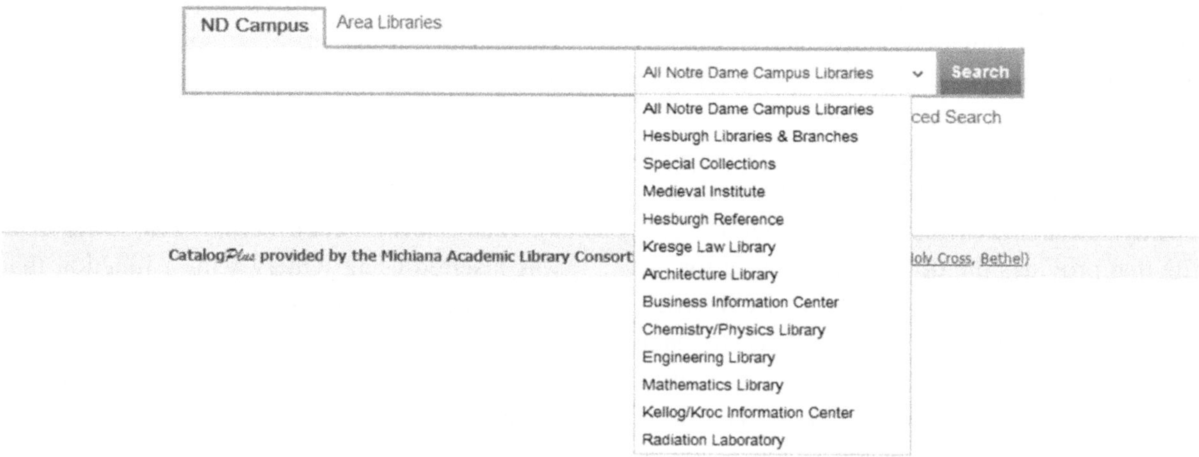

Figure 3. The out of the box implementation of the Primo® interface

from all of those sources to create the final product.

It is notable that while these two implementations contain much of the same information, creating a local version of the tab allowed the addition of custom services and links.

Another area for local improvement had to do with request functionality. There is an out of the box 'request' function which relays circulation requests for holds or recalls to the ILS. The main difficulty with this function was that Primo® displays a request function on all records, but the majority of titles are not eligible for circulation requests. To compound the problem, the error messages for ineligible items were too generic and confusing to users. Combining jQuery with

a separate behind the scenes lookup suppressed the request link except for those titles which actually have requestable items. Additionally, the Hesburgh Libraries used jQuery to add links to a "Deliver" service that is restricted to faculty and graduate students. Again, behind the scenes lookups are used to limit the links to requestable titles. (Since the MALC Libraries do not require user login at the search stage, the links appear to all users, but the intended audience is indicated in the link text.)

The Primo® system architecture also supports a concept called tiling, which allows for different sections of the results screens to be componentized. A tile could be simply a piece of HTML, but it could be more complex, such as a JSP. When

Figure 4. Includes new locations tab as well as other added features

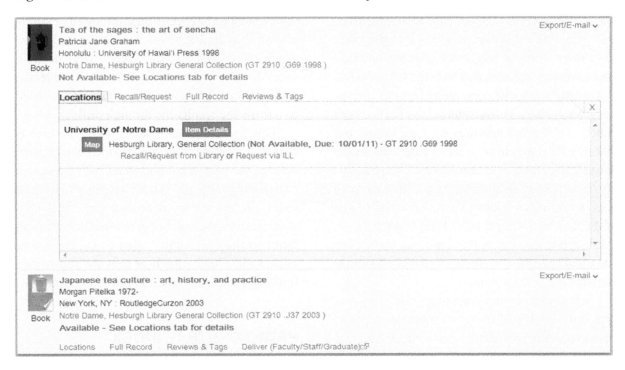

combined with the custom view editor, in which a staff member can invoke new tiles and reorder existing ones, this gives customer sites the ability to significantly alter the Primo® interface without necessarily having to create a full new "skin" using the APIs and a series of programs. MALC does not currently use custom tiles in their implementation, but tiles offer a significant opportunity for altering the user interface in small chunks that are sewn together, making the task of creating components and maintenance simpler.

Application Programming Interfaces (APIs)

Primo® has a number of APIs and Software Development Kits (SDKs) for extension of both the UI and the code in the configuration tools that manages the data Primo® consumes. An SDK is different from an API in that the SDK provides a mechanism for customers to write plug-ins for Primo® using the native language, Java. It can be a powerful tool for sites with advanced skills to extend the system at a foundational level. This is a feature often found in most enterprise grade software. While there are too many to mention in this chapter, the Primo® APIs include XML based Web-services to retrieve results and records in a computer readable way for which the data can be easily repurposed in various scripts the customer chooses to create. Primo® SDKs include adaptors for merging searches from external systems, adapters for ingesting data in formats that Primo® doesn't come configured for out of the box, and more.

The User Experience

Primo®'s user interface includes many standard options users have come to expect in a catalog interface. Examples include the ability to select records and store them in a basket like queue, the ability to email or export records individually or in aggregate, and the ability to store queries – even have them run periodically and have the system notify you when there are new records in the result set. It also features many of the characteristics of next generation discovery systems including facets, did a user mean, suggested searches, and tags and reviews. Currently, the Hesburgh Libraries has not pushed the social networking features such as reviews and tags. Those features have not had very much use, not because they are hard to use, but because they are not necessarily core features for the user base in an academic library. One possibility to explore is seeding the tags with data from a system such as LibraryThing4Libraries to see if the data encouraged more local contributions. Although not essential, these are nice features to have and open the door for doing more with social networking in the future.

At the center of implementing a discovery system is the quality of the user experience. Primo® end-users are presented with a much cleaner, simpler interface with many expanded options and services than traditional OPACs. Although it is not quite one-box/one-button, there is not an overwhelming number of search options. For example, MALC has not opted to provide any search limits (format, etc.) on the basic search screen. In the traditional OPAC, in order to arrive at the desired results, users were expected to set limits at the beginning of the search. Someone who is interested in Mark Twain is expected to indicate at the beginning whether they are interested in Mark Twain as an author, or as a topic. Of course, it helps if they know to type "Twain, Mark" instead of "Mark Twain." In addition, to limit the results to, say, electronic resources, users must indicate that before they click "Go." Otherwise, they are likely to find themselves retyping the search.

The traditional OPAC may have a mechanism to narrow results after searching, but, in this case, users had to go to a separate "modify" screen to do so. The modify screen has a fixed set of options, whether they apply to that particular search or not. The user had to select limits with no idea whether they would return results (or how many), and wait for the search to re-execute.

In most discovery systems, including Primo®, this orientation has been turned around. The search engine is geared towards the simple, unlimited 1-3 keyword searches that most users actually use. Along with the results, the user is presented with a list of facets and terms that can be used to narrow the results list through drilling down.

This has a few advantages. One, the user is only given options that apply to the actual results set, e.g. the user is not presented with the option of limiting the results to Irish language materials, unless, in fact, the set includes them. The system also indicates the number of results for each facet term, so the user knows what to expect before clicking it. Finally, the user sees the results and limiting options together on the same screen.

PRIMO CENTRAL INDEX

As noted before, the Primo Central™ Index is a mega aggregated index add-on to the Primo® system. Primo®'s configuration provides enough flexibility to integrate other Web-scale discovery solutions into the Primo® interface. Some sites such as the Claremont College Consortium and Princeton University have experimented with an approach to blend both Primo® and Summon, for instance. Considerations for a site looking to do this would be to review the quality of the result blending and pricing. It is very likely that implementing two solutions from different vendors is going to have cost implications in both time and dollars. Sites might also wish to consult with vendors about their relevancy strategies. With hundreds of thousands or hundreds of millions of results, relevancy needs to be more than a simple word match algorithm. Issues of terminology used in the query, knowledge of who the user is, e.g. undergraduate or faculty, etc., and what their research context is could play in an important role in delivering a better experience. One of the features that makes Google's ranking relatively effective is the impact of the Web as a social publication medium, where resources that are cited on more webpages often have a heftier ranking than others.

Currently, the Primo® Central Index activation process involves the customer site selecting from a list of resources that exist in the index. The selection is based on site preference and for some resources, particularly those where the data is the value of the resource, on current subscription status. A benefit to this approach is that there is a level of transparency around what exactly is indexed in PCI. It also gives the customer site some flexibility to tune the user experience by selecting which resources are included in their view of the index. Primo® has a handful of configuration options so that organizations can tune Primo Central™ behavior in their Primo® instance, for example, sites can tweak how results from both systems blend together and are presented to the user.

To get a sense of user satisfaction with Primo Central™ Index, readers may wish to contact institutions such as Boston College, Vanderbilt, or BYU who were early implementers of PCI. MALC is currently engaged in discussions about how to best implement a Web-scale scholarly discovery system. Notre Dame in particular has spent considerable energy in optimizing the configuration of metasearch, for example, metasearches at Notre Dame are organized within a subject context to provide users with the most relevant results based on their research perspective. Notre Dame also uses the Xerxes front end to Metalib, which provides a clean and optimal user experience. Notre Dame has a heavily customized discovery environment. In implementing an aggregated Web-scale discovery tool, the goal is to keep as much functionality as possible that users have become comfortable with, and while the technology staff at Notre Dame acknowledge that aggregation is by far a better approach to information retrieval systems, there are still many questions about how to best provide a quality user experience within the users' search context. In some cases this could be

a very wide search across all resources, but then what does a user do with hundreds of thousands or millions of results? Search context matters. The Hesburgh Libraries are working on an evaluation strategy for implementation of a Web-scale tool. Introducing yet another discovery layer in addition to all of the rest needs to be handled carefully to minimize confusion for users. At this time, Notre Dame is also evaluating the content, functionality, and features of the Primo Central™ Index with the goal of assessing overall strengths and weaknesses. Once these are understood, the Hesburgh Libraries can best equip employees to answer questions about what the system is, how it works, and for what subject areas it is strong. System opacity is often a frustration for internal stakeholders, and this evaluation will help ease anxieties about new approaches to discovery tools.

In the end, the Hesburgh Libraries sees significant value in implementing a Web-scale aggregated discovery tool, the goal is do so thoughtfully to provide an optimized experience for users.

Responses and Reactions

Responses to the Notre Dame Primo® implementation have been mixed depending on the community of users. The Libraries conducted usability tests and focus groups with students and faculty both during the beta phase and following the production release. The overall response was positive, and the undergraduates in particular found the system easy to use and liked many of the features. Most of the faculty users and many of the graduate students gravitated to the advanced search features, but still had an overall positive response.

Even though the system was in live beta for more than 18 months, the implementation caused some concern for library staff. Many of the Hesburgh Libraries' librarians and some faculty found the new interface to be different enough from the classic OPAC that they were a bit disoriented by it. Some reported problems – either features that were missing or features that were unclear, some just had trouble re-orienting themselves to a new search interface even though they could find similar results, and some didn't trust the new system because it displayed results in a different order and merged some records. Some of this response is due in part to a kind of OPACHölm Syndrome, where users were captive to learned, complicated methods of searching the classic OPAC and began to see that strategy as the credible way to find information. In part, the Hesburgh Libraries technical staff knew there would be an adjustment period which is what prompted them to keep the classic OPAC around indefinitely while users adjust to the new search interface.

In aggregate, Primo® has provided some significant improvements as a discovery system for MALC collections and beyond. On a fundamental level, it is a modern platform that will provide a foundation for extending the existing discovery environment for the next 5 to 7 years. The architecture alone will enable MALC to address user needs and concerns more agilely. For patrons, the user experience in Primo® compared to the classic OPAC is a much closer match to the way most discovery systems work on the commercial internet. Results come back quickly, usually within a second or two, and features such as facets, a construct Karen Schnieder once called "MARC made useful," create a powerful, yet easy way to navigate the library collection (Schnieder, 2007). Relevance ranking is much better in Primo® than in the OPAC. This is particularly striking for known item searches. Possibly the worst example from the classic OPAC is *Nature*. As a single term key-word search, this returns 24,521 records. Relevancy did not work at all for over 5000 hits, and so the results were presented in random order. In Primo®, the journal *Nature* is the top result, followed by three monographs also titled, simply, *Nature*. Even in cases where the OPAC is not overwhelmed by sheer numbers, relevance still does not work well. A search for *Journal of education and teaching* returns the desired result

as number 12 of 144 in the OPAC, but as number 1 of 329 in Primo®.

For the MALC libraries, Primo® has two main shortcomings. First, the way it manages dates in the search context does not align with how researchers use dates. In the facets, Primo® chunks dates in odd record number groups, so date ranges often begin and end with strange years, for example before 1958, 1958 – 1971, etc. instead of being chunked into decades, the organization strategy that best fits the researcher mental model. It would also be helpful to have the ability to specify year ranges in the advanced search, so researchers could hone in easily on time frames they are specifically interested in. As it is currently implemented, Primo® only provides ranges to filter for, for example, the most recent n years where n could be 1, 2, 5, 10, and 20. Many researchers are interested in a specific past period, rather than recent publications.

The main missing feature in Primo® is a true browse search. In the traditional OPAC, the user can search an author, title, subject or call number, and browse the headings alphabetically. Once in the browse list, the user can page forward or backward through the entire catalog. Once a heading is selected, the user is presented with the matching records. Browse can be helpful in a couple of ways, first it exposes different ways a name might be cataloged which in turn lets the user find all of the held materials for a particular author despite cataloging inconsistencies. For call numbers and subjects, browse is a powerful tool for seeing an overview of subject areas in the collection, leveraging the most useful aspect of classification schemes – collocation. Utilizing browse lets users narrow and widen their interaction with library collections in an interactive way, exposing materials that meet their interest, but may not have been found with a simple keyword search.

Traditional browse does not exist, as such, in Primo®, though it is generally not found in article indexes or other similar Web sites either. The closest feature that is available in Primo® is a

Figure 5. Aleph title browse and Primo® title starts with search

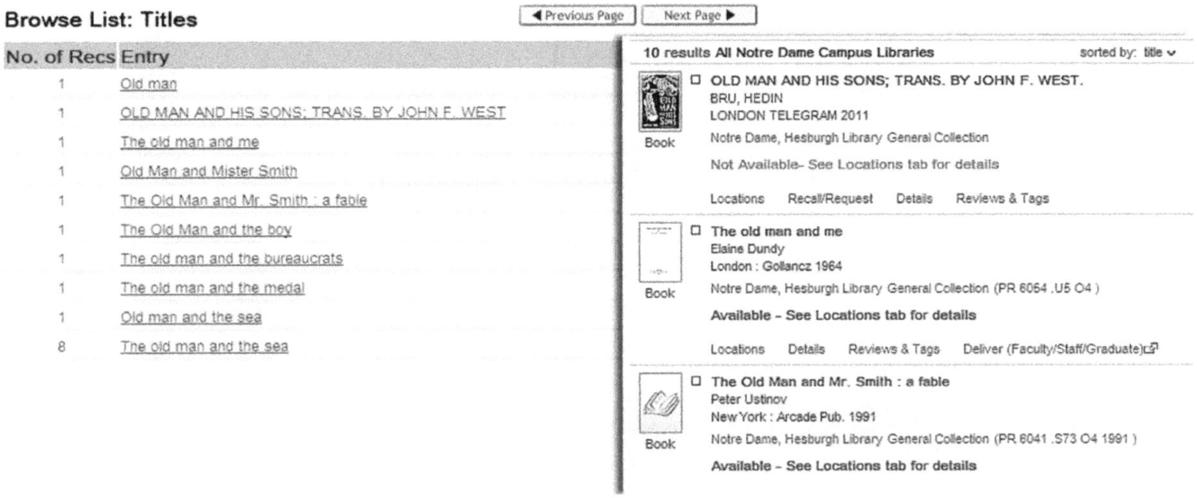

left-anchored title "starts with" search option. The title "starts with" search returns matching records based on the beginning of the title.

The main difference between title starts with in Primo® and an OPAC browse search is that the Primo® search returns the matching records directly, rather than a list of headings. The matching records are not separated by heading, and the user cannot page forward or backward beyond that set. Here is a comparison of a title browse search and title "starts with" search for "old man and" in the OPAC and Primo®.

Although the searches do not function the same way, they do allow the user to accomplish similar goals. MALC hopes to see further development to see additional "starts with" options for other search types, especially author, subject, and call number.

LESSONS LEARNED AND NEXT STEPS

The toughest lesson the Hesburgh Libraries technology staff learned with implementing Primo® was the degree to which some users, particularly library staff, struggled with the transition from the traditional OPAC to a next generation discovery tool. The Hesburgh Libraries technology staff strongly recommend that regardless of the tool being implemented, libraries must consider a significant corresponding marketing/training campaign to prepare their organizations and public service teams for the changes. Many users will have no difficulty understanding these new systems, but those with a more traditional orientation to library research will need help with the transition. This was a tough lesson to learn on the implementation side, but technology staff have spent the better part of a summer organizing trainings and Q&A sessions with library staff to build their expertise with Primo®. These sessions have bought quite a bit of good will, empowered staff to build expertise with the system, and even uncovered some complex techniques for searching Primo® for library staff who may want advanced capabilities for finding research materials.

To date, MALC has focused energies on migrating and merging the library catalogs for the four institutions. While this has been a long desired outcome, one of the Hesburgh Libraries' staff asked the question, "I see all of the catalog information, now where is the plus?" From the beginning of the implementation, it has long been

Figure 6. The different content intended for integration with Primo®

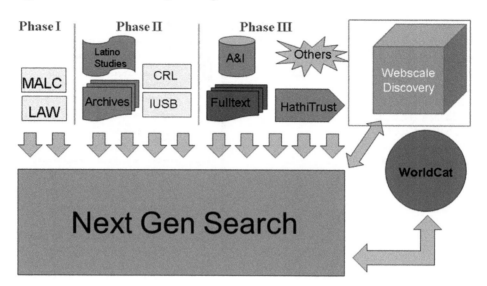

the intent to broaden Primo® as a discovery system. In fact, Primo®'s extensibility was a core factor in the decision to select Primo® as a discovery system.

In line with Phase II of the diagram above, the Hesburgh Libraries have begun working on integrating non-MARC based resources such as Encoded Archival Description records from Special Collections and Archives. This was possible, but somewhat complicated in Primo® version 2. It is now easier to do in Primo® version 3, and Notre Dame Libraries will be working this next year to make those resources and the full descriptions discoverable in Primo®. Additionally, the Hesburgh Libraries have ramped up their local Institutional Digital Repository activities and have a locally implemented IDR based on Fedora Commons and Blacklight. These resources are also low hanging fruit to integrate into Primo®.

Simultaneously, the Hesburgh Libraries are also beginning work in parallel on Phase III which represents scholarly information not locally held. This stage has three main objectives – integrate an aggregated Web-scale solution such as Primo Central™ Index, explore building a search adapter for the WorldCat API that would allow WorldCat results to display within the native Primo® in-

terface, and investigate the integration of other external scholarly resources that are appropriate for inclusion in the discovery environment. As mentioned before, the Hesburgh Libraries is taking a phased approach to implementing an aggregated discovery element to Primo®. Taking time will not only give the Libraries the ability to be thoughtful about its approach, but it will also give them a chance to market the service to users and to prepare library staff for a significant change in the way they provision discovery. While this approach is appropriate for Notre Dame, other organizations such as Vanderbilt University and Brigham Young University have had success with early implementations of the Primo Central™ Index (Poulter et al., 2010).

The Primo Central™ Index integrates seamlessly with local instances of Primo®, be they locally hosted or hosted by Ex Libris™. Primo® from the beginning was designed to connect with other Primo® implementations at a foundational level. For all intents and purposes, the integration of Primo Central™ into Primo® is invisible to the end user. Results are retrieved and merged as quickly as Primo® as a standalone, and there is little problem with the local catalog records not living within the Primo Central™ Index itself. Some critics like to make a big deal about this distinction, but the experience at Notre Dame so far is that it really is not that important because the Primo® architecture accommodates the Primo®/ Primo Central™ blend. One feature of Primo®/ Primo Central™ is that the Primo® configuration tool allows the organization to tune how their collections merge with Primo Central™ results. One common complaint about Web-scale discovery services is that local library collections, because of their relatively small size compared to the hundreds of millions of records in Web-scale systems, are often entirely lost. Primo® allows institutions to bump relevant local resource to the top. The configuration allows the user to adjust for the location (top, bottom, etc.) and number of local results to promote.

Outside of this 3 phased content approach, Notre Dame is also looking at implementing a feature of Primo® that publishes the local index to a format that Google can easily harvest, thereby extending the footprint and accessibility of library collections out into the commercial internet.

CONCLUSION

Implementing a next generation discovery tool is about creating a better overall search experience for users, while providing a robust platform for the library to build its discovery and service environment on. Primo® is a feature rich and customizable next generation discovery system – this was the primary reason MALC selected it out of the field of existing systems, both commercial and open source. Primo® is fairly robust out of the box, which gives flexibility to organizations regarding time and effort investments needed to customize the system.

Primo® is a major component of the future strategy for providing discovery for local collections as well as to the larger domain of scholarly materials. Notre Dame expects in 2012 to launch

an aggregated index component of Primo® to the user community. One of the most important lessons learned from this experience is to consider more deeply the potential impact on the organization before implementing new systems. Initially, technology staff thought implementing Primo® represented a small change given that people had exposure to the system for over two years, but in reality, people often do not invest a lot of time in interfaces that don't have immediate impact on their work flow. The experience is starting to shape strategies for future technology implementation, particularly for systems that are as core to the organization like the catalog is. Ultimately, the technology staff hope to improve communication, give a couple of months' lead time to try out new fully production ready systems, proactively interact with affected parties (as opposed to only a lot of email announcements), and provide some formal and informal training before production launch dates. It will require participation from library staff as well, but hopefully rethinking implementation strategies will ease future anxieties and create a general sense of good will.

Many in the library profession have been eagerly awaiting the day when the technology would facilitate the ability to provide a search across many, or even most, relevant scholarly resources. There is much more to explore including how to build the searchers context into the process of discovery so that the undergraduate looking for a quick article for a composition course is presented with different results than the scientific researcher looking for deeply scholarly materials relevant to their research. There will be questions about how to serve relevant results to interdisciplinary research as well.

What is remarkable is the opportunity to begin simplifying the process for novice users, extend the possibilities for sophisticated users, and extend the ease and reach of core library services. The Primo® platform has already opened a lot of doors to create a better overall search experience for users and to deliver services at the point of need instead of requiring users to magically know about all of the services the Hesburgh Libraries can provide them (and then go looking for them on the library Web site). It will take some time and patience to bring everyone in the organization along – research practices are almost like muscle memory, they are habitual and ingrained, and even if a process is complex, once it is learned, it takes effort to learn something different. It will be important to have a well-defined strategy for bringing the organization into the next generation of research tools, but it is great to know that the technology is becoming less of a barrier to realizing a long awaited future vision.

REFERENCES

Back, G., & Bailey, A. (2010). Web services and widgets for library information systems. *Information Technology & Libraries*, *29*(2), 76–86.

Ex Libris Group. (2011). *Ex Libris Primo reaches a major milestone as its customer base exceeds 750 institutions.* Retrieved August 14, 2011, from http://www.exlibrisgroup. com/default.asp?catid={45B7B8F9-C9B2-4C1F-AFCE-CCD62D4950D7}&details_ type=1&itemid={238A3327-04DF-4388-A44B-BD7EC0B4FE9C}

Mi, J., & Weng, C. (2008). Revitalizing the library OPAC: Interlace, searching, and display challenges. *Information Technology & Libraries*, *27*(1), 5–22.

Ockerbloom, J., Reese, T., Martin, P., Lynema, E., Grappone, T., Kennedy, D., et al. (2008). *DLF ILS discovery interface task group (ILS-DI) technical recommendation.* Retrieved from https://confluence.ucop.edu/download/attachments/34668692/ DLF_ILS_Discovery_1.0.doc?version=1&modi ficationDate=1275674626000

Poulter, D., Thacker, C., & Sadeh (Panelists), & Kaplan, M. (Moderator). (2010). Primo Central: The ultimate in next-gen discovery: Raising research to a new level. [Video webcast]. *Library Journal.* Retrieved from http://www. libraryjournal.com/lj/tools/webcast/883876-388/ webcast_primo_central_the_ultimate.html.csp

Schnieder, K. (2007, September). *The OPAC sucks.* In the Symposium on the Future of Integrated Library Systems. Champaign, IL.

KEY TERMS AND DEFINITIONS

API (Application Programmer Interface): An interface to a system that sends data in a format that programs can reuse, often times in XML or JSON.

Browse: A search method in which the user enters a headings index alphabetically, and can page forwards and backwards from that point.

De-Duplication: A matching procedure run on new and updated records to indentify and merge matching records.

FRBR (Functional Requirements for Bibliographic Records): In the context of Primo, this is primarily a function to group editions of the same work.

jQuery: A JavaScript library that allows the programmer to use unobtrusive scripts that run in response to a variety of events.

Normalization: The process of converting incoming records to different format.

OPAC via Primo: Providing OPAC functionality (such as requests or renewing loans) within the Primo discovery interface, so that the user does not need to link to the OPAC.

Relevance: Sorting records by how closely they match the search, with higher weight given to more important fields.

Scope: A subset of the database that can be searched separately.

ENDNOTES

1   ExLibris is a trademark of Ex Libris Ltd.

2   Primo is a registered trademark of Ex Libris Ltd

3   AquaBrowser is a registered trademark of Serials Solutions

4   Primo Central is owned by Ex Libris Ltd. or its affiliates.

5   Worldcat is a registered trademark of OCLC.

Chapter 34
Simplifying Resource Discovery and Access in Academic Libraries:
Implementing and Evaluating Summon at Huddersfield and Northumbria Universities

June Thoburn
Northumbria University, UK

Annette Coates
Northumbria University, UK

Graham Stone
University of Huddersfield, UK

ABSTRACT

The University of Huddersfield and Northumbria University were two of the first adopters of the Summon™ Web-scale commercial discovery system in Europe. Both universities were moved to implement a discovery tool because they had encountered issues with their existing federated searching products, with students and staff expressing dissatisfaction. This chapter describes the selection, implementation, and testing of Summon™ at both universities drawing out common themes and differences, with suggestions for those intending to implement Summon™ and some ideas for future development. User feedback from surveys, focus groups, and user testing is described, and instruments are appended. User testing evaluated user search refinement, satisfaction with relevancy ranking, comprehension of results presentation, and feature approval responses. The perceived success rate in comparison with Google search results is briefly described. Other concepts described include launching new functionality, key points for effective implementation, MARC mapping, staff training, and marketing a discovery tool.

DOI: 10.4018/978-1-4666-1821-3.ch034

INTRODUCTION

At an online conference in 2009, John Shipp, the University Librarian at the University of Sydney, commented that facilitating information discovery and maximising value for money from library materials is a key driver for academic libraries. Users are confused by the complexity of our collections and are often reluctant to spend time learning how to use individual databases - comparing them unfavourably to intuitive search engines like Google (Duddy, 2009). As a consequence, the library may be seen as too complicated and time consuming and many valuable resources remain undiscovered or underused. Federated search tools were the first commercial products to focus on this problem. While going some way to address this issue, users complained that they were clunky and complicated to use (Stone, 2009). In 2007, Tenopir (2007) commented that "The jury is still out on federated search systems, even though more libraries now have them. There are murmurings that federated search has lower-than-expected use and may not be the magic search bullet we were led to believe" (p. 30)

The development of web-scale discovery services promised to improve the search experience by harvesting and indexing metadata direct from publishers and local library collections into a single index, making searching simple and fast. (Gibson, et. al. 2009)

The Universities of Huddersfield and Northumbria are similar institutions: both are large UK 'post-1992' universities (23,000 and 24,000 FTE students respectively) with specialist and increasing areas of research excellence. At Huddersfield the Library is part of a converged Computing and Library Service while Northumbria Library and Learning Services is separate from the University IT department. While both University Libraries have been successful in delivering innovative and user centric services, Huddersfield have a dedicated Library Systems Manager with the technical expertise to customise systems to local

requirements. At Northumbria, the policy has been to outsource and develop computer systems with third party suppliers rather than in house.

In 2009 both Huddersfield and Northumbria Universities purchased Serials Solutions®[1] Summon™ to replace existing federated search products. This case study describes the selection, implementation and testing of Summon™ at both universities drawing out common themes and differences, with suggestions for those intending to implement Summon™ and some ideas for future development.

SELECTION

Huddersfield

At Huddersfield a project group was established to examine the existing arrangements for the provision of e-resources and suggest recommendations for the future. One of the tasks of the project team was to invite suppliers in to discuss products in order to understand the different offerings within the market place. A 'clean sheet of paper' approach was used, with the project team identifying four main 'vision objectives' for the future system.

- First class search engine
- Provide a 'one stop shop' for all electronic resources
- Greater interoperability and flexibility
- More efficient management and administration

These criteria were used to evaluate supplier offerings from a range of suppliers of discovery solutions including Ex-Libris™[2], EBSCO and Serials Solutions® as part of the review. As a result it was agreed to conduct a restricted European Union (EU) tender for a provider of a library discovery service of pre-harvested content. The contract was awarded to Serials Solutions®.

Table 1. Implementation milestones at Huddersfield (Stone, 2010)

Milestones	Estimated implementation Date	Actual implementation Date
Contract signed	Aug 2009	Aug 2009
Implementation starts	Sep 2009	Sep 2009
Summon™ instance delivered	Oct 2009	Oct 2009
Beta launch	Jan 2010	Mar 2010
360 Link to replace SFX	Aug 2010	Feb 2010
E-resources wiki to go live	Aug 2010	Mar 2010
Summon™ to replace MetaLib	Aug 2010	Aug 2010

Northumbria

Northumbria had been using WebFeat®[3] federated search alongside Serials Solutions® electronic resources management products (360 Core KnowledgeBase, 360 Link -OpenURL link resolver and 360 Resource Manager) since 2006. In February 2008 WebFeat® was purchased by Proquest / Serials Solutions® whose stated intention was to migrate WebFeat® and Serials Solutions® 360 Search to a single federated search product. Northumbria therefore had to make the decision to either migrate to the new Serials Solutions® federated search or look for an alternative search and discovery solution.

With the emergence of web-scale discovery services, suppliers were invited to demonstrate their systems during early 2009. In addition to Summon™, Primo®[4] from Ex Libris™ and EBSCO Discovery Service™[5] were considered. After analysing each of these Northumbria selected Serials Solutions® Summon™ for four main reasons:

- Breadth of content
- Ease of use and the subsequent improvement to the student search experience
- Hosted solution operated and fully supported by 3rd party supplier

- Integration with existing Serials Solutions® products
- Value for money pricing - Serials Solutions® were keen to get some early adopters in the UK and offered an attractive upgrade path from WebFeat® federated search to Summon™.

IMPLEMENTATION

Serials Solutions® aim to have each Library's instance of Summon™ configured within six weeks once configuration information and local data have been supplied to them. Table 1 shows the estimated and actual implementation times at Huddersfield and Table 2 those at Northumbria.

The main steps are described below.

Supply of a Full Export of Local Catalogue Metadata in MARC21 Format

At Northumbria the work to extract the catalogue records was done by the ILS supplier (Capita, formerly Talis[6]). Since Northumbria were the first Talis library to implement Summon™, this did take longer than anticipated, but once Serials

Table 2. Implementation milestones at Northumbria

Milestones	Estimated implementation Date	Actual implementation Date
Contract signed	Oct / Nov 2009	Oct / Nov 2009
Implementation starts	Nov 2009	Dec 2009
Summon™ instance delivered	Jan 2010	March 2010
Beta launch	May 2010	June 2010
LibGuides implemented	July / Aug 2010	Aug 2010
Exports from Library catalogue set up	April / May 2010	July 2010
Summon™ to replace WebFeat	Sep 2010	Aug 2010

Solutions® received the data Summon™ was delivered within the six week timescale as promised.

At Huddersfield it was necessary to review some cataloguing practices. Print and e-book records, which had previously been catalogued under a single record had to be separated out before loading into Summon™. Major inconsistencies in cataloguing practices also became apparent, e.g. music scores failed to show in Summon™ and DVDs showed as books. These errors in the MARC header fields were fixed by global edits to the records.

MARC Mapping

Serials Solutions® supply a MARC mapping spreadsheet so that each Library can decide how the library catalogue data is indexed and displayed in Summon™. Huddersfield used the default mappings but Northumbria wanted to apply more customisation. As early adopters, it would have been helpful to experiment with different mapping configurations on a test site, but in the end default mapping was used. With hindsight, it is worth spending some time getting this right because the time it can take to rectify MARC mapping errors can be quite substantial and until it is corrected the catalogue data may look odd.

Supply of Configuration Data

The data supplied was

- Library web site URL
- OPAC Record URL - the base URL for a direct link to a record page in the OPAC
- Summon™ URL Codename - based on the institution domain name
- Summon™ Web Site Title
- Details of Link Resolver and Base URL
- Authentication EZProxy®[7] URL
- IP Range
- Feedback email address – the address to which feedback is delivered through the link on the Summon™ interface
- Image files (institutional logos)

Setting up a Process to Send Regular Exports of Record Updates from the ILS to the Serials Solutions Summon Server

At Huddersfield all print books and journal records were exported into Summon™ fairly easily. In-house scripts were developed to upload deletions, changed records and new records on a daily basis. The process did not run as smoothly as planned; there were initial communication issues with deletions, which took some time to be processed, although this is now working well. E-books, e-journals, "fast adds", temporary Inter-Library Loan records and records that were on order or unavailable in the upload were not included in the upload.

At Northumbria the implementation of a new version of the library catalogue (Talis Prism3) provided the facility for setting up a regular export of catalogue record updates to the Summon™ server. Talis used the existing functionality within the ILS that generates new, edited and deleted files for the OPAC, to do the same for export to the Summon™ server.

Updating Local Electronic Resource Holdings

As existing Serials Solutions® customers Northumbria's full-text e-resources were already included in the knowledge base; abstracting and indexing databases were also added. At Huddersfield the migration of data from SFX®[8] to 360 Link went very smoothly and the majority of changes were completed quickly, in fact the implementation of 360 Link was brought forward significantly (see Table 1).

Including Other Library Resources

The initial six week configuration includes MARC mapping and knowledge base set-up only. Libraries then have the option of adding further in-house resources, institutional research repositories were the priority here for both universities. The process for including the data depends on whether the repository supports the OAI-PMH protocol, if so, data can be automatically harvested and this was the case with Northumbria's D Space based repository. At Huddersfield loading data from the EPrints repository into Summon™ was straightforward, but there are ongoing issues with the display because metadata only records are treated as though they are full text records, which

can be frustrating for users. A further advantage of adding Institutional Repositories are that all Summon™ customers can also add them to their own knowledge base.

Huddersfield's digital off-air recordings database was also included; this is password protected and not available to other Summon™ customers. It is hoped to add streaming videos of lectures in the near future.

Access to Native Databases and Subject Collections

Summon's™ coverage of publisher and aggregated content is extremely comprehensive and new content is added regularly[9], in fact on implementation Summon™ covered 94% of all journals that Huddersfield subscribed to and 87% of titles for Northumbria.

However, some resources are not (and may never be) included, for example law and chemistry resources, while other abstract and indexing resources such as Medline®[10], Web of Knowledge[SM11] and Scopus offer specialist searching, e.g. MESH headings and citation searching and therefore need to remain as standalone resources in their own right. Hence it is still necessary to provide direct links to native databases and to group these into subject collections. Both Universities intended to do this regardless, recognising that Summon™ is an alternative not a substitute means of resource discovery.

At Huddersfield a wiki was used to generate alphabetical and subject lists[12] and 'dummy' MARC records for databases were created to enable users to find database titles on Summon™ (see figure 1). Northumbria implemented Springshare's web-based LibGuides[13] service to generate alphabetical and subject lists. This solution was relatively inexpensive and easy to customise. SpringShare work in partnership with Serials Solutions® to facilitate the creation of an A to Z list of resources via the automatic export of the knowledgebase

Figure 1. Database recommender service and dummy MARC record for CINAHL

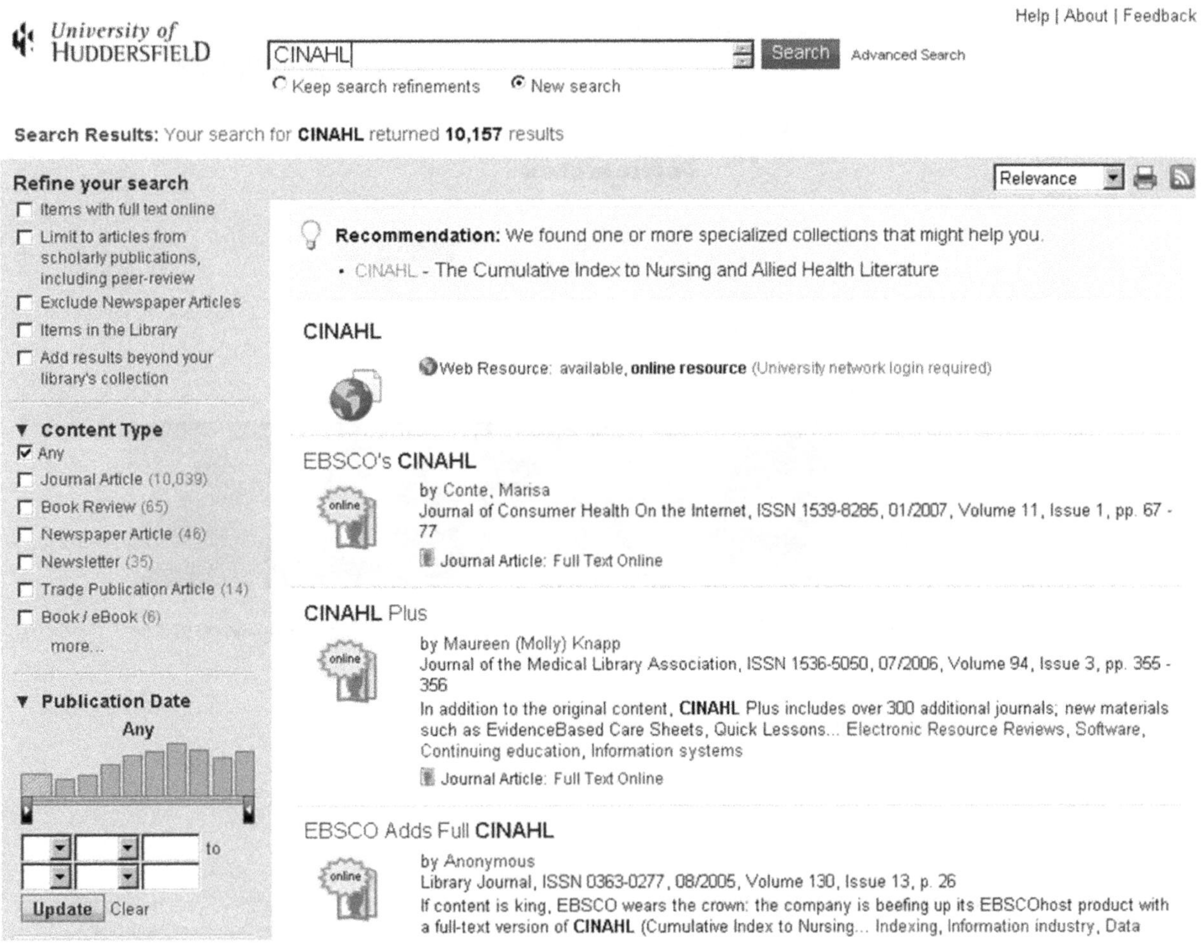

into the service. These links to native resources can then be reused within the subject collections.

Additionally, figure 1 shows a Database Recommender service that Summon™ has included to point users to subject specific databases based on their search terms and results.

Customisation

Customisation of the interface itself is limited. Adding institutional logos is the only element that can be changed on the main search pages. Therefore, both Huddersfield and Northumbria have developed their own Summon™ web pages which are hosted on institutional servers.

However, both the 360 and Summon™ APIs[5] allow for a certain amount of customisation, for example at Huddersfield, Summon™ has been linked to the in house MyReading project[14]. A tab is available on Summon™ to allow academics to add content to reading lists, thus automatically adding URLs, subject terms etc. (see Figure 3)

Authentication

No login or authentication is required to search Summon™ so anyone can use the system and find references and results that reflect the holdings in Huddersfield or Northumbria collections. Users cannot access full text until they have been

Figure 2. Northumbria University's NORA web page incorporating Summon™ search box

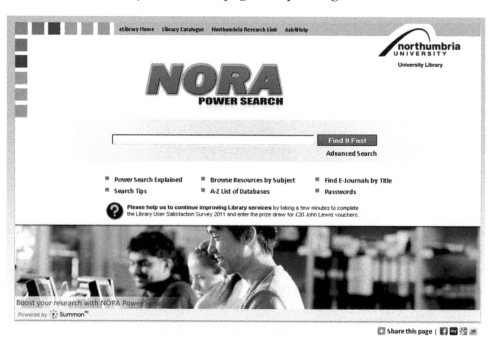

Figure 3. Beta test of a MyReading tab using the Summon™ API

Alfred Hitchcock's "Rear window" as Critical Allegory

by TOLES, GEORGE E
Boundary 2, ISSN 0190-3659, 1989, Volume 16, Issue 2, pp. 225 - 245
Alfred Hitchcock's "Rear Window" is examined for evidence of a critical allegory. The relationship
between the photo-journalist/lead character and the audience... Motion picture criticism, Allegory

Journal Article: Full Text Online

item options: add to MyReading

authenticated and abstracting and indexing database metadata is only available to the subscribing Library. This approach was favoured by Serials Solutions® and acts as a 'shop window' for potential customers. At Huddersfield authentication is via EZProxy® where possible; at Northumbria access is either via Shibboleth or through IP address recognition via the University's desktop virtualisation service.

Serials Solutions® have also developed an 'authentication banner'. This appears at the top of the Summon™ search screen and allows institutions with a proxy server to login at the start of their search rather than at the point of accessing full text; however this is not compatible with Shibboleth or Northumbria's desktop virtualisation service. Serials Solutions® have recommended that Northumbria pursue the possibility of a proxy server in order to streamline authentication for users.

Support and Documentation

The support from Serials Solutions® during the initial set up period was good, especially as they

Table 3. Breakdown of respondents to online surveys

Type of respondent	Huddersfield	Northumbria
Undergraduate	63%	55%
Taught postgraduate	19%	26%
Research postgraduates	9%	7%
Other (including academic staff, support staff, visitors etc)	6%	5%

were setting up a significant number of new 'early adopters' at the same time and had to deliver these according to the stated time period of six weeks from receipt of configuration data. They were fast to respond to questions although sometimes more detailed guidance and documentation would have been helpful, e.g. in relation to the MARC mapping process.

After initial concerns excellent communication channels were established via the Summon™ user group, listserv and Serials Solutions®. There is also a Summon™ wiki which is hosted by the Summon™ User Group[5].

FEEDBACK AND USABILITY TESTING

Summon™ was piloted at both Universities prior to its official launch, with federated search continuing to run in parallel. This allowed us to gather feedback and make further refinements before withdrawing federated search and formally launching Summon™ at the beginning of the new academic year in September 2010.

Feedback was gathered in a number of ways from staff and students through formal training sessions, demos and anecdotal feedback. Both Universities worked together to devise a similar online survey and a common approach to running focus group sessions. These are analysed in detail below.

Online Survey Results

There were 102 responses to the Huddersfield survey and 523 to Northumbria's. At Huddersfield the survey ran from March to July 2010, whilst the survey at Northumbria ran from June 2010 until the end of October 2010. The difference in response rate was probably due to the length of time the surveys were open. However the percentage breakdown of respondents by type and School were very similar, as was the feedback on the service.

Respondents

At both institutions shown in table 3, over half of the respondents were undergraduates followed by graduate students and a small percentage of academic and support staff.

Responses

Table 4 shows the broad responses received to the main areas of the questionnaire for both institutions.

Ease of Use

Respondents reported that the Summon™ screens were easy to understand, they also found the icons easy to use. At Northumbria there were many comments about preferring Summon™ to the previous federated search for its speed and ease

Table 4. Response breakdown by institution

Online survey questions	Huddersfield response	Northumbria response
Easy to use	90% agreed	100% agreed
No help needed to use	63% agreed	76% agreed
Icons clear	88% agreed	93% agreed
Refined their search	44% did so	65% did so
Clear layout of results	89% agreed	88% agreed
Used advanced search	32% had used	42% had used
Did not use advanced search	68% had not used	58% had not used
Found what they wanted	77% agreed	85% agreed
Relevant results	82% agreed	88% agreed

of use. The majority of those who commented on ease of use felt that they would not require any help in using Summon™. Other comments indicated that only a brief run-through was needed. Of the low percentage of people who would have liked more help, the majority asked for help screens or online user guides.

Some library users wanted to know which databases the results were from:

"I wasn't sure what databases I was searching in, but after completing a search I realised it showed anything relevant'. (Huddersfield)

"couldn't see how to access Westlaw, Nexis, etc" (Northumbria)

On some occasions users at both universities have struggled with the concept of Summon™ as a 'one stop shop' approach compared to the use

of 'traditional' online databases, which are still very relevant for specific disciplines and complex searches. Both universities added alphabetical lists and subject guides on web pages at the front end of Summon™ but this approach may lack clarity. Northumbria are currently reviewing the layout of their initial NORA web page in order to try to make the distinction more obvious for users, by possibly placing less emphasis on the Summon™ search box on the page and improving the guidance provided about accessing resources.

In a recent thread on the ILI-L Discussion List, Pete Coco of Grand Valley State University (Coco, 2011) outlines exactly what the advantages of Summon™ are in relation to information literacy and ease of use,

'What Summon™ frees me to do… …particularly in freshman courses, is to focus more on the concepts of information literacy that this system so

elegantly demonstrates. What is peer-review? Why does it matter? What is the difference between Google and the library? How does Google decide what to show you? Summon™? Why isn't the stuff in Summon™ in Google?'

However, Coco does note that the trade-off between Summon™ and other specialist or research based online databases, such as Web of Science™[5], is noticeable in terms of 'narrowing a search for your needle to its haystacks', but that this can be alleviated by an effective search strategy.

Refining Searches

Users who refined their search did so by using the facet options. The comments imply that those that did, found it an easy process; one user commented that they used '+' and '-' as they did on Google, while others used Boolean operators to refine the search. Most of those who did not choose to refine their search in this way said it was because they had found what they wanted without having to do so; there were one or two comments where users did not know that they could do this.

"I had 7,000 results that I couldn't narrow down which I found quite annoying" (Huddersfield).

Success in Finding References

Most respondents at both institutions said they were successful in finding what they wanted; some comments indicated that they found more than they expected:

"I looked at an area I am working on for my MSc so I already had an idea what I might find based on previous research. I was very impressed that Summon™ found some relevant articles from the last few years that I had not seen before. "
(Northumbria)

Some were more pragmatic:

"some useful, some not so useful ....it's the same with any search. The more you refine it, the more relevant your results will be" (Huddersfield)

Different users had different expectations and some were confused by the one stop search concept:

"it seems rather odd to request "limit to articles from scholarly publications" ... if something has a non-scholarly source we can use other tools (e.g. Google, newspaper CDROMs) to find them"
(Northumbria).

Layout of Results

The majority of respondents at both institutions stated the layout of results were clear, citing the facets and the ability to preview the abstract as particularly useful. Negative comments related to too many results and not being able to distinguish between different types of results e.g. article, book, review article, newspaper article. Some found it hard to identify the source of the material. These comments related both to not knowing which specific databases were being searched or the clarity of the journal title / citation display on the Summon™ page.

Relevance of Results

Over 80% at both institutions agreed that results were relevant to their research topic and that they had found what they were looking for. There were many positive comments about relevance, with an acknowledgement that the search strategy had to be good to begin with and that results could be refined using the facets and filters provided.

Comparison with Usual Search Starting Point

At both institutions in around 50% of cases this was Google, but a minority of users cited specific subject or A & I databases. Over 80% at Northumbria found Summon™ better than their usual normal starting point:

"While Google Scholar™[16] is sometimes useful you don't have the option to refine your search often bringing up results from just the US ... Nora brings up more relevant information and even spell checks your searches" (Northumbria).

Advanced Search

Those who used the advanced search at both institutions found it easy to use with the right amount of options available. However, over half did not use the Advanced search at all; it is not clear whether this is because they felt it was unnecessary to do so or if they did not realise this feature was available.

Features Users Would Like to See

Many of the responses to this question from both institutions referred to options that were already available, which clearly has implications for training and refining help pages, e.g. reducing or increasing the number of references displayed on a page; saving the references; Boolean searching (though this is currently not available in Advanced Search); limiting the search to full text resources.

Other suggestions included facility to search within the results to further refine a subset of references; 'back button'; a list of the most popular resources accessed; subject tab. The request for a 'subject tab' so that users could specify a subject area before beginning their search was quite common, and somewhat ironic given that this was regarded as a weakness of federated search as users were not sure which subject they should choose

- or wanted to search more than one subject area at a time. It is likely that people saw this as a way of limiting their search results rather than using the filters and facets within Summon™ to do so.

Features Users Liked Best

"Ease of use" and "simplicity" ranked highly as the best features at Huddersfield and Northumbria. One user found Summon™ "incredibly simple to use, seems much faster to access journals / articles", while another liked "the fact that it brings all the different parts of the library into a Google-like search option". (Huddersfield). The full text icon was also popular:

"...the pictures of FULL TEXT were great as I knew which ones to use." (Northumbria)

Features Users Liked Least

About 25% of respondents at both institutions stated that there was nothing that they did not like. Different users demonstrated different perspectives e.g. one commented that "it's still not a Google box", while another disliked it because of "its Google-like operationality" (Huddersfield). Some comments were also received about the order of results and that Summon™ did not list the results on the initial screen by type, e.g. article, book, book review etc.

Some users did not like having to wait for filters to take effect one by one – they wanted to be able to select all the relevant filters at once to obtain a smaller more relevant results set more quickly; and also to save the same preferences for all their searches (e.g. scholarly and peer reviewed material only, full text only). Although it is possible to keep the same search refinements in one search session, users would like to save these preferences for future search sessions.

In conclusion, the survey feedback on Summon™ was very positive, particularly in relation to speed and ease of searching. Some of the frustrations relate to either the need to improve search strategies or difficulties linking to full text. There was a common theme of wanting to search a specific database or pre selecting a subject area before searching. However, it is interesting to note that attitudes to a service like Summon™ can differ as the two directly opposite comments reveal:

"... I think it would have a very negative effect on students' ability to access electronic and other library resources. Students need to be made aware that certain resources are appropriate for certain tasks; this mode of presentation presents book reviews on the same level as books, ... newspaper articles on the same level as current scholarly articles. This will tend to direct students towards the wrong kinds of resources ... (Northumbria)

"A powerful but easy-to-use and above all fast search engine for peer-reviewed work is exactly what I want. I really have no desire to be an expert on a dozen different ... database interfaces as I currently have to be. I love the Summon™ single search box as I can feel confident in asking "Give me some good and recent suggestions for this subject" and know I will get a good result. However underneath it there's still the ability to refine and rework the search as I need to ... - " (Northumbria)

Focus Groups with Students

Small groups of students were invited to focus groups and were given sheets with screen shots and thought bubbles on which to record their opinions as they used Summon™ without any assistance. Staff observed and recorded how they used the service. After thirty minutes staff then questioned users, recording this as an MP3 file. The questions echoed the online survey, and focussed on ease of use, relevance of results, most and least popular features and how they thought Summon™ compared to other search engines. Again the response

was very positive and students generally found it very easy to use without instruction.

Features students liked were:

- Facility to see immediately which articles are available in full text
- Preview of abstract before linking to full text
- Speed of returning results
- Facility to refine searches easily
- Ease of saving and exporting references to Endnote
- 'Did you mean' function to correct spelling mistakes
- Layout and appearance

The queries and suggestions for improvement were: wanting to know which database results came from, how to access individual databases and confusion over multiple pages opening when linking to full text.

Staff observing focus groups noted that some students took a while to notice and use the facets to refine their search; and the standard message from 360 Link about what to do about missing content prompted some users to close down the window instead of waiting for the information to load. This message was subsequently amended.

Feedback from Library Staff

Feedback from Library staff was obtained through focus groups and training. The positive comments were largely the same as those with students, i.e. ease of use, speed of searching, clear identification of full-text material, and easy refinement of results using the facets, simple layout and links to the library catalogue.

However, Library staff wanted to know more about how the service actually worked, e.g. how subject terms are generated, Boolean searching, and limiting search to the abstract field. Linking and coverage were also concerns and are discussed below.

MARKETING AND TRAINING

At Huddersfield, the Serials Solutions® Summon™ branding and name was retained and the service was marketed as a new kind of search. At Northumbria, the internally well-known NORA (broadly Northumbria Online Resource Access) brand was retained and called NORA Power Search, and the new system was marketed as an upgrade to the existing service, albeit a 'next generation' search. A comprehensive marketing campaign (see Figures 4 and 5), with posters, flyers, emails, Library and University bulletins, press releases, twitter feeds and drop in training sessions was organised by both Libraries.

Although Summon™ is intuitive to first-time users, significant time was invested in creating introductory guides and leaflets to ensure that staff and students could use it to best effect and user guides and flyers continue to be updated as new functionality is developed.

KEY POINTS FOR EFFECTIVE PRACTICE

The following are some key points and lessons learned to consider when planning the implementation of Summon™ and which may impact on project planning and timescales for implementation.

Catalogue Records

Records not created to standard cataloguing rules may cause problems so these may need work beforehand and editing these may impact significantly on project timescales.

Ingesting Data from Local Sources

If you are the first library using your ILS to implement Summon™ build into your schedule time for slippage in this area in case things take longer than anticipated. The Summon™ listserv

and wiki[17] are valuable tools for contacting other institutions and sharing expertise.

Linking to Full Text and Indexing Issues

Much of the success of Summon™ relies upon how effectively you can link from it to the full-text material to which you subscribe. Summon™ does a great job finding results but if users are unable to connect to these smoothly then one of the main frustrations of federated searching is replicated. Take time to ensure the setup of your link resolver is as good as it can be. Serials Solutions® have themselves recognised this and have worked with publishers to set up direct links into their content rather than relying on OpenURL technology.

Indexing problems may be caused by incorrect or misleading data supplied by publishers being ingested into Summon™ index which then causes problems when trying to connect to full-text. These queries can be time-consuming and complex to unpick and involve contacting Serials Solutions® and often the publisher and provider of the metadata, but seem to be an inevitable consequence of this work.

De-Duplication of References

Although Serials Solutions® normalise the content they ingest to avoid duplication of records there are still some issues that require further refinements. Duplication can cause some confusion for users and library staff e.g. duplication of records included in a research repository with subscribed journal articles.

"Discovery Service" Concept

The concept of the product as a discovery service was difficult to convey to some users, including Library staff. Although content coverage may not be comprehensive in some areas Summon™ helps users find content that they may not have

Figure 4. NORA Power Search poster

previously discovered precisely because there is no pre-selection of subject area or databases. Summon™ is one element of a search strategy that should also include searching individual subject databases where appropriate. Nonetheless some Library staff, notably in Law, saw the potential of Summon™ for supplementing the information that users would find in specialist databases.

Concern about Loss of Subject Databases

Some Library staff were also concerned about users not being aware of the high quality databases and journal articles which were not indexed in Summon™; and also the sophisticated interfaces supplied by some specialist databases and journals. There were also worries that the use of these would fall dramatically and eventually be cancelled because of low usage statistics. In fact this has not been the case and there have been large increases in the use of full-text sources as

Summon™ makes more material more easily discoverable.

Coverage

Coverage is a major concern for subject librarians. They want to be very certain about which subject material is included in the Summon™ index. Although Serials Solutions® provided an analysis of journal title coverage and estimated that over 85% of subscribed journal content was being indexed, subject librarians want to know what percentage of databases in their subject area is indexed and what gaps there are. This has recently been acknowledged by Serials Solutions® who now make this information freely available from their website[2].

Launch of new developments and functionality

During the implementation period and immediately afterwards many new developments and

Figure 5. Summon™ banners at Huddersfield

functionality were implemented, most of which were well received. However, they were sometimes rolled out very quickly without much notice to customers who had no opportunity to try them in a non-public test environment or to update colleagues and documentation. In some cases the developments were inappropriate to some institutions – e.g. the authentication banner– but were switched on regardless and had to be hastily removed to avoid confusing users. This has now been addressed by Serials Solutions® through a regular fortnightly updating schedule, for which a few days notice is given, allowing at least some time for customers to inform Serials Solutions® of their wish to opt out of developments if required.

Summon Listserv and Wiki

There is a very useful and active Summon™ listserv. As well as raising queries or suggestions directly through the Serials Solutions® Client Centre, this is an excellent facility for communicating and exchanging experience with other customers (or even just lurking). It is actively monitored by Serials Solutions® staff who also contribute to discussions or give general advice. A wiki has also been developed by the User Group where customers share information and practice.

Training

Summon™ is a deceptively easy to use product and most people can use it without any training. However, it also has rich functionality that may not evident from using the single search box so there is still a need to educate both users and Library staff to make the most effective use of it. This has issues for training both staff and users. For example, Advanced search can be used in a quite sophisticated way to specify search criteria, whether looking for a specific article in a specific journal.

RECOMMENDATIONS FOR FUTURE DEVELOPMENTS

Personalisation

Users can save results into a temporary folder in order to export, e-mail or print them. These are cleared when the user leaves the Summon™ search session. In common with other electronic resources it would be good to be able to personalise Summon™ so that these search strategies (including preferred filters for full text or scholarly resources only), results and alerts could be saved more permanently. Due to the fact that no login is required to search Summon™ this is not currently possible. The use of scoped searches is an alternative whereby users can search a limited subject set if preferred.

Timeliness of Adding New Content

Serials Solutions® are constantly acquiring new content for Summon™. However, there can be a significant delay between acquiring the content and making it available to customers via the 360 KnowledgeBase. Whilst this is understandable given the vast amount of content to be added, there is a lack of clarity about the planned availability date of this content. This may of course depend on the complexity of the data acquired and the time needed to process it; however, a degree of transparency in this matter would help customers manage user expectations.

Likewise, it is essential that new issues of journal content are added as quickly as possible, and customers advised of any significant delay. Users expect new content to be available immediately and to keep pace with native interfaces.

Development of a Non-Public Test Environment

We have alluded above to the frequent development of new functionality in Summon™, which while mostly very welcome may not always be appropriate for all customers. It would be useful for customers to have their own private test environment to try out new functionality. There is a central Serials Solutions® test area that customers can look at but this is not the same as testing with your own local data.

CONCLUSION

Testing and feedback to date tells us there is no doubt that Summon™ has been well received at both Universities and as a way of simplifying access to information resources and it goes a long way to addressing the Google challenge. Most users appreciate the speed and simplicity of searching, which brings together both print and electronic materials in a single search and many also found that by using Summon™ they could get results from sources they had not previously considered using. Early indications show that COUNTER[18] JR1 and JR1a reports show a rise of as much as 400% for many journal subscriptions since the launch of Summon™, conversely, DB1 reports show a major drop for online A&I databases.

Summon™ is an addition, not a substitute, for access to native resources. As Summon™ continues to mature a number of similar competitor products have also been developed. It will be interesting to see how these products compare when both Universities come to the end of their current contracts in 2012.

REFERENCES

Coco, P. (2011). *RE: Teaching discovery* [LIST-SERV Message]. ILI-L Discussion List - ALA Mailing List Service - American Library Association. Retrieved December 11, 2011, from http://lists.ala.org/sympa/arc/ili-l/2011-11/msg00174.html

Duddy, C. (2009). A personal perspective on accessing academic information in the Google era, or 'How I learned to stop worrying and love Google'. *Serials, 22*(2), 131–135. doi:10.1629/22131

Gibson, I., Goddard, L., & Gordon, S. (2009). One box to search them all: Implementing federated search at an academic library. *Library Hi Tech, 27*(1), 118-133. Retrieved December 11, 2011, from http://dx.doi.org/10.1108/07378830910942973

Stone, G. (2009). Resource discovery. In H. Woodward & L. Estelle (Eds.), *Digital information: Order or anarchy?* (pp. 133-164). London, UK: Facet. Retrieved December 11, 2011, from http://eprints.hud.ac.uk/5882/

Stone, G. (2010), Searching life, the universe and everything? The implementation of Summon at the University of Huddersfield. *LIBER Quarterly, 20*(1), 25-42. Retrieved December 11, 2011, from http://liber.library.uu.nl/publish/issues/2010-1/index.html?000489

Tenopir, C. (2007), Online databases: Can Johnny search? *Library Journal, 132*(2), 30. Retrieved December 11, 2011, from http://www.libraryjournal.com/article/CA6407784.html?industryid=47130

ENDNOTES

1. Serials Solution is a registered trademark of Serials Solutions
2. ExLibris is a trademark of Ex Libris Ltd.
3. WebFeat is a registered trademark of Serial Solutions.
4. Primo is a registered trademark of Ex Libris Ltd.
5. EBSCO Discovery Service is owned by EBSCO Publishing Industries
6. Capita Libraries: http://www.capita-software.co.uk/software/pages/libraries.aspx
7. EZProxy is a registered trademark of OCLC
8. SFX is a registered trademark of Ex Libris Ltd.
9. Summon: content and coverage: http://www.serialssolutions.com/discovery/summon/content-and-coverage/
10. Medline is a registered trademark of US National Library of Medicine
11. Web of Knowledge is a service mark of Thomson Reuters.
12. Electronic Resources List: http://library.hud.ac.uk/wiki/Main_Page
13. A-Z list of databases at Northumbria University Library: http://northumbria.libguides.com/start
14. University of Huddersfield MyReading Project blog: http://library.hud.ac.uk/blogs/projects/myreading/
15. Web of Science is a trademark of Thomson Reuters.

16   Google Scholar is a trademark of Google, Inc.

17   Summon Community Wiki. Widgets and API gallery: http://community.summon. serialssolutions.com/index.php/Main_Page#Widgets_and_API_Gallery

18   COUNTER: http://www.projectcounter.org/

Chapter 35
Implementation of Resource Discovery:
Lessons Learned

Elizabeth P. Babbitt
Massachusetts Board of Library Commissioners, USA

Amy Foster
Montana State University, USA

Doralyn Rossmann
Montana State University, USA

ABSTRACT

Academic libraries have a myriad of information sources for their communities, yet meeting users at their point of need can be a daunting task. Web-scale discovery tools offer a way to pull together many library resources for retrieval through a single search interface. The lessons learned in this case study at Montana State University include challenges with implementation, troubleshooting, collection development, and user education. Strategies and solutions to problems such as "full-text red herrings" (broken links to articles from aggregated databases) as well as techniques for prioritizing search results are described. Incorporating locally digitized collections in the discovery tool is also explained. The impact of discovery on collection development can take many forms and this case study details three issues that this implementation caused to emerge. The examples described in this chapter serve as helpful considerations for other academic libraries in their Web-scale discovery product exploration, implementation, and analysis.

DOI: 10.4018/978-1-4666-1821-3.ch035

BACKGROUND OF THE CASE: TESTING WORLDCAT LOCAL, IMPLEMENTING SUMMON

Montana State University (MSU) in Bozeman decided to enter the Web-scale discovery service market in January 2010. Following a trial of WorldCat[1] Local from OCLC and an examination of alternative tools, MSU chose to subscribe to Summon,[2] a Serials Solutions[3] product. This chapter describes the decision to use Summon™, the implementation process, and lessons learned since rolling out this search platform in August 2010.

MSU is the land-grant institution for Montana -- a state which has a small population (fewer than one million people), a large geographical area (fourth largest in the United States), and low personal income (43rd lowest household income) (U.S. Census Bureau, 2010). Located in Bozeman, it serves over 14,000 students, 2,400 employees, and the citizens of the state (Montana State University Office of Planning and Analysis, 2011). It is one of 108 schools on the Carnegie Foundation's list of top research institutions (Carnegie Foundation for the Advancement of Teaching, 2011). The MSU Library has over 775,000 book volumes and subscribes to more than 15,000 serials and databases. Its employee base includes seventeen librarian faculty members, two professional staff, thirty-three classified staff, and twenty-five student assistants; it operates on a total budget of approximately seven million dollars (Montana State University Library, 2011).

Along with MSU, nine other libraries share the SirsiDynix integrated library system (ILS), Symphony[4] which serves as a searchable inventory control database of all of the physical items held in the libraries' collections. These libraries coordinate cataloging practices and share one record for all formats, except for e-books. In 2006, an MSU Library taskforce looked into employing federated searching, but concluded that it was not developed enough at the time. Meanwhile, Web-scale discovery technologies emerged. In January 2010, MSU began participation in a WorldCat[®] Local pilot project with the Montana State Library and a large public library. The biggest challenge encountered was related to OCLC accession numbers, which is how WorldCat[®] Local matches records between WorldCat[®] and local catalogs. MSU was a member of the Western Library Network prior to its merger with OCLC in 1999. The pre-1999 records in the catalog (approximately two-thirds of the catalog records) do not contain OCLC accession numbers. This situation caused search results to be confusing to library patrons. When a locally-owned title was searched in WorldCat[®] Local, the brief title list would indicate that MSU held the item. When a patron clicked on the link to view the full record, and the record was one without the OCLC accession number the following message would appear, "We were unable to get availability information for this item. Please check at the circulation desk for assistance." A patron would then have to search for the title again in the local catalog to see if MSU did, in fact, own the title.

Another challenge in the pilot project was that MSU uses one record for all formats (excluding e-books). However, MSU marks holdings in OCLC on all appropriate records. In order for WorldCat[®] Local to display correct results, MSU would need to have OCLC accession numbers for all the corresponding format records in the one local record. The final challenge was that MSU does not mark holdings in OCLC for everything owned, such as: United Stated Federal government documents, e-journals, e-books, and select other materials. If any of these materials were searched in WorldCat[®] Local, the message, "No results match your search for ..(the title searched)..when limited to MSU-Bozeman libraries" would appear.

It would be possible to have the OCLC accession numbers added to the local bibliographic records, but to do so would be a large scale project entailing an extensive clean up. The pilot allowed for the opportunity to test WorldCat[®] Local to see if such a large project would be worth the effort. In the end it was determined, because of these challenges, that WorldCat® Local was not the best resource discovery tool for the institution's needs.

Following the WorldCat® Local trial, the Dean of the MSU Library made inquiries into other Web-scale discovery tools, discussed experiences with colleagues at peer institutions already implementing such tools, and ultimately selected Summon™. By committing to a three-year contract and signing on as early adopters of the software, MSU hoped to shape the product in ways which would benefit its users. MSU already had its data in Serials Solutions'® 360 Resource Manager, their electronic resources management tool. Because MSU uses this product to manage its e-journals and some e-books, it was anticipated that Summon™ implementation could be swiftly accomplished.

SUMMON IMPLEMENTATION: GETTING STARTED

There were approximately eight weeks from the time the contract was signed until completed implementation. It was decided, based on experiences with WorldCat® Local, that a cross-team implementation approach would work best for utilizing expertise throughout the library. The work group consisted of the Associate Dean, the team leaders for Reference and Systems, the Electronic Resources Librarian and the Web Services Librarian. Librarians from Cataloging and Processing, Collection Development, and Digital Access were brought in as needed, such as when catalog mapping and local collections were discussed. A first task was to determine how information in the ILS would be mapped to display in Summon™ properly. This catalog mapping process entailed determining which MARC fields were to be used in the brief title list. For example, the subjects displayed would come from the 650, 651, and 690 fields. Systems and Cataloging worked together

through this process. This situation was challenging since it was not clear how things would appear in the Summon™ results list until the data was indexed and searchable, eight weeks later.

A good deal of time was spent on branding and naming Summon™. Staff members suggested potential names and MSU's mascot, the Bobcats, served as inspiration for several suggestions: Cat Prowler, Cat Quest, Cat Box. Other ideas included: Search it all, All in One, and One Search. The latter set was rejected because it implied to users that Summon™ is comprehensive in its coverage of the library's resources, when, in fact, it is not. In the end the decision was made to go with Cat Search and an accompanying cat eye logo was designed.

Testing was limited prior to roll out in late August of 2010, just in time for the fall semester. Cat Search sat front and center on the library's Web site, replacing the catalog search box (see Figure 1). One concern that was quickly discovered was that local call numbers sometimes displayed incorrectly. As previously mentioned, MSU shares bibliographic records and uses one record for all formats (with the exception of e-books). In the shared ILS, several class schemes are used, including Library of Congress (LC), Dewey for juvenile materials, SuDoc (for U.S. government documents, from the U.S. Superintendent of Documents), and even local schemes for microforms and maps. This information is part of what in SirsiDynix's Symphony® system is known as the item record, storing the local item ID number, item type, class scheme, location, and the call number that is displayed to patrons. Because Summon™ pulls the call number from the MARC record and not from the ILS item level record, results did not always display the correct call number. At times, Summon™ would show an LC number for maps which actually had a locally created scheme, or one of the other libraries' call numbers would appear. Because there was no way to determine a way for the appropriate call number to appear in every circumstance, there was no way to resolve

Figure 1. Montana State University Library's website (www.lib.montana.edu)

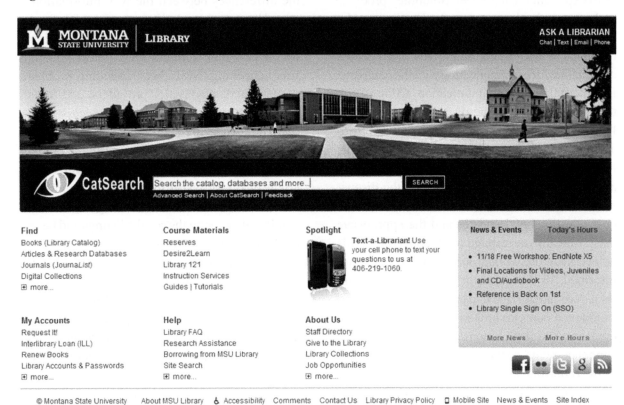

this issue. In the end, it was decided to remove the call number from the initial search results. In order for patrons to find the location and call number they must click on the correct title in the brief title list, which is a link into the ILS.

At this time, MSU is the only library within their shared catalog group using Summon™. Each library is its own unit with no centralization of operations or budgets. It is unknown how results would appear if other units also purchased Summon™ and unlikely that all ten units will purchase Summon™ individually or as a group.

SUMMON IMPLEMENTATION: LESSONS LEARNED

Staffing and Workflows

As discussed previously, a cross-team approach was used for implementation. Early on responsibility was divided up between groups and individuals for specific parts of the implementation. It soon became clear that although ownership of specific parts by individuals or groups was an advantage in distributing workload, lines of communication needed to be clarified. At the beginning of the process, conversations with Serials Solutions® were dispersed between Systems, Collection Development and Administration, depending on the issue. This caused confusion because sometimes issues were reported to Serials Solutions® twice or not at all. Since Collection Development had the most experience using Serials Solutions® products and communications centers (both online and by telephone) and had formed solid working relationships with sales representatives, they became responsible for communicating with the company. For internal library communication, a Summon™ thread was added to the discussion area on the library's intranet to reduce duplication of effort. The intranet is a Web site which is specific to the internal-functions of the MSU library and is only available to its employees. Through the discussion forum on this site, all staff members could post questions and updates and the appropriate party was able to respond to all concerned. This helped keep the work group and the Dean better informed. In the Summon™ discussion forum, issues are categorized into topics, or threads, such as indexed content, broken links, slow response time, and Serials Solutions® Summon™ upgrade announcements, so that there is less confusion for those reporting and troubleshooting problems. MSU uses discussion forum software from discusware.com, but a Google search of "discussion forum" reveals that there are many such products and providers of this type of solution. Another important part of communication was subscribing to the listserv: Summon™ Clients, where institutions using Summon™ share observations, problems, and solutions with other libraries and Serials Solutions.

Troubleshooting

Broken links were common, especially from aggregated sources like EBSCO, Lexis/Nexis®[5] or Gale/Cengage®[6]. These links are often referred to on the Summon™ clients listserv as "full-text red herrings." MSU started reporting them to Serials Solutions® shortly after roll out and for a long time was under the impression that these issues were due to the way MSU had implemented the product. Only after several months did it become clear that other libraries were having many of the same problems. The main problem stems from the differences between the way information is stored in aggregator databases and the data format which the publisher gives to Serials Solutions® for indexing in Summon™. Unclear why this was happening, MSU began sending problems to publishers, aggregator providers, and Serials Solutions® so each was aware of access issues. Most publishers are keen to make sure that their content is being found in Summon™. To reduce user frustration, MSU changed its settings in its article linker software (360Link) and renumbered the order of the databases so that aggregated ones would fall lower on the results listings and be less likely to be chosen by users.

Another problem encountered was the removal of deleted ILS records from the Summon™ index. Primary challenges included the MSU Library and Serials Solutions® developing mutually agreed upon naming conventions and locations for files and timing of updates in the Summon™ index. For several months, deleted records in the ILS were not removed from the Summon™ index because there was not a common understanding of how this process would work. These problems were eventually resolved after several attempts at routinizing and documenting processes with Serials Solutions®.

Deciding on appropriate indexing and access points for e-books proved a significant challenge. E-books were displaying from both the ILS and the vendor's platform, therefore appearing multiple times in the Cat Search results. While the library promotes Summon™ as its front-and-center search point, users still turn to the catalog to search for books, regardless of their format. Serials Solutions® does have some e-books in its resource manager, but this data seems to lag behind when the books are published. Given these factors, MSU decided to continue loading MARC records for e-books into its catalog, knowing that they would be picked up by the Summon™ index faster. As the e-book market grows and evolves however, this may not be a sustainable approach with regard to staff time.

Some problems were brought about by Serials Solutions® releasing enhancements like the Database Recommender without notice or thorough testing. This added to the confusion and frustration of MSU librarians and users. More recently though, Serials Solutions® sends notification of enhancement dates and features ahead of their arrival, with new updates occurring at regular intervals.

Searching

Since the library features Cat Search on its main Web page, users quickly uncovered its successes and challenges. Successes include interdisciplinary and cross-disciplinary subject searching and finding information on current events. Challenges range from the dominance of certain item types in search results, subjects with more robust coverage than others, and interface technologies not ideally suited to the Summon™ search environment.

Book reviews and newspaper articles dominate the item types retrieved. Although Summon™ includes library catalog data, the sheer number of book reviews causes confusion for users in search of an actual title. Newspaper articles are numerous and published frequently, thus they rank highly in search results. As a result, researchers seeking information in formats other than newspaper articles have to limit search results to exclude newspaper articles or they have to sift through many irrelevant results. Robust with limiters and other features, Summon™ retrievals can be narrowed down to more pertinent items but users must be willing to take the time to do so.

For users not familiar with specialized databases, or for even the most highly trained librarian, Summon™ can be a good starting place for interdisciplinary and cross-disciplinary topics. The Database Recommender points users to selected databases which produce high numbers of results. For example, a search on global warming might point users to databases focused on ecology, biology, political science, or geology. A football player searching for information on helmets, concussions, and player safety might find information in databases covering athletics, the sporting goods industry, or in popular magazines. Users may stay within Summon™ for their search or may leave Summon™ to go to the recommended database.

Other areas, however, are less well-suited to Summon™. Some business resources, data-driven in their native interface (such as Mergent Online™[7]), may not have search features that include the proper limiters to retrieve information in Summon™. Other databases, like ProQuest®[8] Statistical Datasets, are not ideally suited for the Summon™ environment since their searches are driven by choosing from multiple data points to generate tables and graphs. Likewise, PsycInfo®[9] and Medline®[10] do not have the same searchable sub-sets of indexes and limiters in Summon™ as they do in their native interfaces. It is important to be aware of all of these strengths and weaknesses in Summon™ when communicating preferences for future product development or in working with users searching for information.

Web Page and Digital Services

While some libraries may consider creating a home-grown or locally-housed indexing solution, this can require much more staff and resource time for development and production than going with a system developed by an outside vendor. By choosing to use a third party product such as Summon™, libraries save time and money in system production and maintenance. In exchange, understanding how the product works in the local environment is fundamental in making resources accessible.

The Summon™ index includes MSU's local, digitized collections. Initially, collections are included by providing the Summon™ metadata librarian at Serials Solutions a link to the library's Open Archives Initiative (OAI) endpoint. OAI "develops and promotes interoperability standards that aim to facilitate the efficient dissemination of content" (Open Archives Initiative, n.d., Standards for Web Content Interoperability). Although Summon™ harvests the OAI metadata and "ingests" it into the index, there are no specific search limiters to hone in on these collections. Searching by the collection name or description in combination with the item types of 'archival material' and 'photograph' brings some of these items to the top of the search results. Common item types like books and journals that reside in these local collections are not easily sorted from other search results. Consequently, the specificity and quality of the OAI metadata becomes important for findability, particularly with the data description and subjects used.

A somewhat new feature to Summon™ is the ability to analyze search logs of Summon™ via the Summon™ administration Web site. These statistics, provided in daily increments, reflect search terms in the exact order entered by users. Local analysis reveals that some users understand the general purpose of Summon™, while others do not. For those who misunderstand Summon™, terms employed include a blank search, Google-like searches for domains (e.g. facebook.com, amazon.com, etc.) and the phrase "Search the catalog, databases, and more...". "Search the catalog..." is what appears in the Summon™ search box before users type in their own text. Some users seem to regard the search box on the library's main Web page as a site search for things like library hours, or circulation policies. In more successful endeavors, users employed single-words, Boolean operators, natural-language queries, and truncation in their searches. While a cursory review of the search terms used in Summon™ is revealing, more robust analysis is needed.

Another challenge is displaying CatSearch results within an overall mobile Web design for the library. Summon™ provides a mobile site, but, unfortunately, MSU's catalog is not as friendly in a mobile environment without purchasing an additional ILS module. Therefore, Summon™

mobile in MSU's implementation, takes users directly into a non-mobile version of the catalog.

Collection Development

Three broad issues related to collection development emerge with Summon™. First, the content coverage was an important factor in deciding to subscribe to Summon™ as MSU wanted to be sure that users could access as much of its materials as possible. When considering a new purchase or subscription, MSU takes into account if the resource is indexed in Summon™ and encourages vendors which do not have their content indexed there to do so. MSU reminds vendors that this coverage or lack thereof may influence purchase and subscription decisions. As MSU completes its first year of Summon™ implementation, it will consider database and journal usage before and after implementation to understand more how users are finding information.

The second issue concerns coverage of e-journal holdings. For example, a journal might have coverage for certain dates in Summon™ while the library actually has access to additional years through the publisher but that content is not indexed in Summon™. Ideally, users would get complete access to library content via Summon™.

A third challenge is effectively measuring and assessing Summon™ usage and its return on investment (ROI). With Web-scale discovery, investments would include subscription costs, staff maintenance time, and user search time. Returns would include increased use of library resources, improved findability of information, savings in user time, and more thorough literature reviews (thus more informed research). Since Summon™ is primarily a gateway to access, it is difficult to determine if resources are used because of discovery through Summon™ because they may or may not have been found without it. Also, users may be sent to less helpful resources than they might have used otherwise, by using a subject specific database, resulting a net loss of time. Benchmarks such as database usage statistics, quality of search terms and strategies (as reflected in the Summon™ usage data) and citation analysis of users' research for measuring Web-scale discovery tools ROI may be useful as MSU continues to evaluate Summon™ and its value.

Reference and Library Instruction

How is Summon™ being taught at the reference desk and in instruction sessions? Is it being bypassed in favor of other resource platforms? A focus group meeting of MSU Library Faculty revealed that, after initially using Summon™, librarians gave up and reverted to the resources that were in place prior to implementation. This was mostly due to the prevalence of "full-text red herrings." Instruction levels varied depending on the librarian teaching, the classroom instructor's request, and the level of student concerned-- lower-division undergraduate vs. upper-division. Lower-division student needs are better suited to Summon™ than upper-division students who benefit more by knowing the databases and journals in their field of study. One librarian however, has been using Summon™ as a teaching tool, showing ways to narrow searches starting with Google, then Summon™, and ending with subject specific databases.

REFLECTIONS AND IMPLICATIONS FOR OTHER LIBRARIES

Looking back over MSU's implementation, several themes emerge for libraries wanting to use Web-scale discovery. Some complications were caused by having multiple formats cataloged on one bibliographic record in the ILS. The decision to catalog materials this way was made in the mid-1980's when MSU first migrated to an online catalog. Non-standard cataloging practices complicate the use of discovery tools such as Summon™.

The MSU Library put Summon™ in a prominent location on its Web site. In doing so, it sent a message of the importance of Cat Search as a discovery tool. Libraries will want to consider what the library hopes to achieve in implementing a resource discovery tool. Is it intended to be a comprehensive search of the library's ILS, journals, and digital collections? Or, is meant to be a place to search as many of the library's journal holdings as possible? At MSU, there is still not a consensus of what the primary purpose of Cat Search is intended to be.

As was discovered at MSU, there needs to be a balance between the time allotted in testing the product and putting it into production. Testing before roll out may ultimately limit the frustration of users and librarians as broken links and incorrectly indexed resources can be fixed. But, working to achieve perfection may prevent users from ever having access to Summon™. Additionally, libraries have a specific contract length and will want to see real-life use of the product in a timely fashion.

In the experience at MSU, it can be challenging to keep librarians engaged enough in Summon™ to realize when it is a tool that truly satisfies their desired needs. Because Summon™ does not index every library resource, it is viewed by some as inadequate. The biggest issue with lack of librarian buy-in is a result of the "full-text red herrings", discussed earlier. Questions linger about when the product will round the corner of usability that will satisfy librarians? Also, will there ever be a time when every librarian will be willing to use, and even promote, the product?

With the addition of Summon™ at MSU, librarians adjusted some of their instruction and reference approaches. Usage statistics indicate that some users turn to online help as they search Summon™ on their own. As a result, librarians made sure that there were guides and tutorials at the point of need to benefit these users and that links to chat, email, and telephone reference were clearly visible from the Cat Search site. For classroom-based instruction, librarians use Cat Search when demonstrating basic features of a database and when searching cross-disciplinary topics. In other library instruction, Cat Search is not covered because specialized databases are a more appropriate search tool.

FUTURE RESEARCH DIRECTIONS

MSU's experiences highlight two important areas for research as more libraries implement discovery tools. What is the impact of past cataloging practices on the ability of the discovery tool to find resources in the library collection? Are there changes that can be made prior to implementation? What kinds of data cleanup are the most useful? Are the cleanup costs of worth the benefits? Several libraries have implemented only an article search in their discovery tool implementations. What is the impact of that decision on the ability of their users to find information?

Second, acceptance and promotion by librarians is crucial to the effectiveness of the discovery tool and its use by students, faculty and staff. Librarians must be knowledgeable about the tool and its strengths as well as its weaknesses and they must be willing to promote the tool at the reference desk and in the classroom. Best practices for involvement of library stakeholders need to be discovered and shared.

CONCLUSION

While each library will tailor its choices to what is most appropriate to the local environment, the lessons learned at MSU demonstrate some challenges to consider with the implementation and use of a Web-scale discovery tool.

REFERENCES

Carnegie Foundation for the Advancement of Teaching. (2011). *The Carnegie classification of institutions of higher education.* Retrieved from http://classifications.carnegiefoundation.org/lookup_listings/institution.php

Montana State University Library. (2011). *Statistical profile.* Retrieved from http://www.lib.montana.edu/about/statprofile.php

Montana State University Office of Planning and Analysis. (2011). *Quick facts.* Retrieved from http://www.montana.edu/opa/quickfactsindex.html

Open Archives Initiative. (2011). *Open archives initiative.* Retrieved from http://www.openarchives.org

U.S. Census Bureau. (2010). *2010 census data.* Retrieved from http://2010.census.gov/2010census

KEY TERMS AND DEFNITIONS

Catalog Mapping: The process which entails determining which MARC field(s) are used in the brief title list in Summon. Other vendors also include options for mapping facets.

Database Recommender: A Summon-feature which recommends library databases for users based on an algorithm from the search terms used and the primary sources of the search results

Discussion Forum: A Web site which provides basic framework to post, search, and receive e-mail notification of postings.

Intranet: A Web site which is specific to the internal-functions of an organization and is only available to its employees.

Integrated Library System (ILS): A searchable inventory control database of all of the physical items held in the libraries' collections. The ILS encompasses the "back room" processes such as acquisitions, cataloging, and circulation. The software that runs the public catalog can be included or an open source next generation resource can be used to supply a patron interface.

Item level Record: The record in the ILS which is for individual copies of a title and includes information such as item circulation statistics, cost, holds, date added to the system, etc.

Return on Investment (ROI): A comparison of the amount of resources invested (staff time, money) to benefit received (time saved, knowledge gained).

Thread: A posting on a discussion forum on a particular topic which has subsequent postings on related topics

ENDNOTES

1   Worldcat is a registered trademark of OCLC
2   Summons is owned by ProQuest LLC
3   Serials Solution is a registered trademark of Serials Solutions
4   SirsiDynix Symphony is a registered trademark of SirsiDynix Corporation
5   LexisNexis is a registered trademark of Lexis Nexis
6   Gale/Cenage is a registered trademark of Cenage Learning
7   Mergent Online is owned by Mergent, Inc.
8   ProQuest® is a registered trademark of Pro-Quest LLC
9   PsychInfo is a registered trademark of the American Psychological Association
10 Medline is a registered trademark of the U.S. National Library of Medicine

Chapter 36
WorldCat Local:
A Transformative Solution

Angi Faiks
Macalester College, USA

Johan Oberg
Macalester College, USA

Katy Gabrio
Macalester College, USA

ABSTRACT

OCLC's WorldCat[®1] Local has offered users at Macalester College information discovery and retrieval experiences well beyond what was provided by traditional library catalogs. WorldCat[®] Local has seamlessly exposed campus users to a range of resources including institutional repository items, vendor-based database content, digital collections, traditional local collections, and library holdings worldwide. In this new information environment, the ability to search only one library's traditional collection is fast becoming an outdated notion, especially in the age of Google. This chapter describes how the library at Macalester College has harnessed the power of a new form of discovery system and transformed the user experience for staff, faculty, and students.

INTRODUCTION

Libraries continue to search for a discovery system that offers users a powerful, productive, and interactive information retrieval experience well beyond what is offered by traditional local catalogs. OCLC's WorldCat[®] Local product provides a unique means of meeting this goal. This chapter will describe the vision, architecture, and functionality of WorldCat[®] Local and the implications for libraries and users. The chapter will discuss how these offer significant opportunity to think seriously and creatively about a discovery system that may render obsolete the library's traditional discovery tool, the local online catalog, and the typical user experience with such systems. Through Macalester's DeWitt Wallace Library experience, data collected, user observations, and future plans, the chapter will also illuminate how

DOI: 10.4018/978-1-4666-1821-3.ch036

the implementation of WorldCat® Local can be transformational for a library.

BACKGROUND

A library discovery layer is defined by Lorcan Dempsey (2010) as "a single point of access to the full library collection across bought, licensed and digital materials." In addition, a discovery layer "[…] provide[s] more functionality, such as federated searching, faceted browsing, spell checking and more." (Yang & Hofmann, 2011, p. 268). While WorldCat® Local meets these definitions; it goes beyond them in several ways. Most significantly, users of WorldCat® Local are automatically exposed, in every search, to resources in libraries worldwide, resulting in a unique and powerful search experience. Ultimately, this is a critical distinction. A user interacting with World-Cat® Local versus a more traditional catalog or traditional discovery layer is exposed to the wide breadth of information available on a topic, as opposed to what their local library, or at best their local library consortium, happens to own.

Macalester College is a small, internationally focused, liberal arts institution located in Saint Paul, Minnesota. In 2011, the student population was 1,987. Opportunities to expose users to a wider set of information than what has traditionally been possible for smaller institutions, is perhaps more significant for a smaller library such as the Macalester College library. When WorldCat® Local became available, staff at the Macalester library saw it as an opportunity to ensure that students, faculty, and staff are exposed to and have access to the best possible and widest range of information from around the world.

The Macalester library, as part of a consortium of local college libraries, has for many years used the III Millennium integrated library system. The library has also experimented with using ExLibris'™² MetaLib®³ federated search product, but discontinued the subscription of this product in 2009. WorldCat® Local is the only resource the library currently uses to offer a federated search experience for its patrons. The library continues to use ExLibris'™ SFX®⁴ link resolver product; however, it is currently evaluating the WorldCat® Local link resolver which is included with a WorldCat® Local subscription.

Using the term "discovery layer" to define WorldCat® Local is somewhat limiting. Initially, discovery layers were intended to overlay a catalog and to offer a more sophisticated and pleasing user interface. Over time, and it became possible to point to or incorporate records from resources beyond the catalog, such as subscription databases or open-access repositories. WorldCat® Local is quite different in its development, architecture, and many of its available features. This chapter will highlight the areas where WorldCat® Local is distinct from other discovery layers, what challenges it presents, and what has changed in the library since adopting this product. This will be followed by a discussion of the community's experience of using WorldCat® Local at Macalester College.

MAIN FOCUS OF THE CHAPTER

Design and Development

A significant aspect of WorldCat® Local is that it has not been built for librarians but for users, and there is a recurring theme of "design for users, not librarians." As a result of a strong focus on the user, there are no longer MARC record views or the ability to search in every possible way on terms that only library staff understand. This has caused consternation among some staff, requiring them to find ways to work around this limitation. OCLC has considered adding more staff-focused functionality but not at the expense of the general user.

The development of this product follows a more Google-like pattern in that it undergoes constant updates and improvements. Currently, new features and fixes are added quarterly, or more frequently if the change is critical. While customers are alerted to the changes, they are not presented for approval or adoption. Instead, the product continues to evolve and library staff and patrons alike become accustomed to the ongoing changes. In this environment, and by design, significant local customization is not possible. In many ways this eliminates what could have amounted to extra work for both OCLC and for the local library, as time and resources do not have to be devoted to customized solutions and minuscule tweaks. Furthermore, all updates and improvements are rolled out to all customers without additional costs. This model of development contrasts greatly with traditional catalog vendors, where, in many cases, new features are suggested, voted upon, developed, added in time, and where significant functionality comes with a price tag.

Active Support Community

WorldCat® Local customers are invited to participate in a user support community. The support community is a highly active place where library staff share ideas, report issues, and work together on solutions. OCLC staff regularly participate in conversations and debates and use discussions to inform product development. As part of this community, small groups may be pulled together to propose solutions to issues or product weaknesses, user studies may be conducted at sites to inform development, and Web meetings and training webinars are held regularly. In this way, many voices are heard and ideas that come out of these conversations impact development. Macalester has been an active participant in providing feedback and several of the improvements suggested by staff have been implemented. This positive outcome leads library staff to continue to share experiences and examples that will improve the system.

Architecture

The WorldCat® Local solution breaks apart the traditional catalog architecture such that the bibliographic data and interface are in the cloud, entirely separate from the local library holdings and status information. It was designed to be catalog vendor-neutral such that it can overlay and interact with most traditional library systems. Local holdings and other local data such as local notes are matched to OCLC's bibliographic data on-the-fly and integrated with the OCLC records as they are accessed. This design requires that everything a WorldCat® Local library wants to provide access via the "catalog" must be reflected in OCLC. Additionally, everything that any library shows as held in OCLC can be searched and retrieved.

Default search results are returned to the user using a ranking called *Library and Relevance* that includes search term relevancy combined with holding library location. Materials most accessible to the user are ranked higher than those held at locations further away. Customers have up to four levels of locations that they can set. In Macalester's case, the college's holdings are ranked first, followed by holdings of the local consortium. Next are the holdings of the group of libraries in Minnesota with which Macalester most efficiently shares materials via inter-library loan, and the remainder is worldwide holdings. Users have the option of changing the results-sorting scheme to *Relevance, Author,* or *Date*. There is also a *Top 5* search results option, which, when enabled, displays the five most relevant items first, regardless of location, followed by the rest of the results displayed using the default sort method.

In addition to items that are findable due to being held in OCLC, WorldCat® Local is also a discovery tool for article and e-book content through central indexing as well as the WorldCat® Local Knowledge Base (KB). WorldCat® Local is one of several tools the library offers to locate and access article and e-book content. More advanced patrons will utilize the library's Journal

Finder driven by the SFX® Knowledge Base as well as the native interface of any of the library's numerous online databases and electronic collections. A library can be selective in the databases that they have included in the WorldCat® Local central index. It is possible that a library may have access to resources that have proprietary records and are not included in WorldCat® Local, and their exclusion is a concern for many libraries. Additionally, there are still several resources that are not yet available for central indexing in WorldCat® Local. In those situations, the library again directs patrons to a Journal Finder or into the native interface of the resource in question. OCLC is working with publishers and vendors to obtain permission to make proprietary records available in WorldCat® Local. This has already happened for two resources to which Macalester subscribes. Availability of MARC records in OCLC is often a top criterion for WorldCat® Local libraries when evaluating whether or not to add a new resource. Macalester continues to bring this important issue to the attention of all current and potential vendors.

Overall, the strength of WorldCat® Local is largely the ability to search the world's knowledge as defined by library holdings including articles, institutional repositories, and digital collections, and to make connections to available content. It is perhaps closer to searching a library version of Google than perhaps any other system or vendor has yet been able to provide. After implementing WorldCat® Local, the idea of "searching what you happen to own" becomes rather arbitrary and quaint. Macalester has shifted to thinking that their collection consists of "what we can get" versus "what we own" and the library has even considered combining inter-library loan statistics with circulation statistics to reflect patrons' broader use of the library.

Article/Database Content

Discovery layers have become more complex over time and have incorporated technologies that allow users to search not only their physical holdings, but electronic holdings as well. Initially this type of search was accomplished using federated search technology. More recently, some discovery layers have begun centrally indexing licensed content to streamline the search and retrieval process. Central indexing has resulted in a shorter retrieval time for search results, fixing a common complaint about federated search products. WorldCat® Local utilizes both central indexing and federated search technologies. OCLC has continued to seek permissions from publishers to make content available through central indexing in World Cat® Local. For those publishers with which OCLC does not have a central indexing agreement, there is often still an option to configure the resource for federated searching.

Central indexing also plays a role in the use of proprietary MARC records. When subscribing to or purchasing digital collections, libraries are frequently offered the option to purchase a MARC record set for the new collection. In some cases these are proprietary MARC records that cannot be loaded into OCLC. Some vendors have chosen to make the metadata for their collections available in WorldCat® Local through central indexing. This allows their customers' patrons to locate their content in the WorldCat® Local environment even though the MARC records are not in OCLC.

A WorldCat® Local Knowledge Base (KB) that is freely available to WorldCat® Local subscribers can be used to track electronic holdings, facilitate the implementation of the "View Now" feature in WorldCat® Local, and also serve as the KB for those using the WorldCat® Local link resolver. The "View Now" link allows users to access full-text content right from the brief results list. While the KB and the link resolver are included in a WorldCat® Local subscription, each library can choose whether or not to populate and implement these features. Additionally, the KB will also be replacing OCLC's e-Serials Holdings program as the method for libraries to reflect their electronic holdings in WorldCat®. The KB can also be used to track inter-library loan license restrictions for e-resources, a feature that can help facilitate direct requesting for articles.

Adding data to a knowledge base can require a substantial effort. OCLC is interested in helping libraries with this work by streamlining work flows and by offering additional means of populating the KB. Besides the typical options of populating the KB by either uploading or manually entering holdings, OCLC has been working with PubGet, a private company focused on delivering search and content in the life sciences area, to provide a third option for getting data into the KB. This service is included with a WorldCat® Local subscription. As part of this third option, a library identifies the resources they have access to and enters their login credentials in PubGet. PubGet can then routinely go to each of the publisher vendor sites, collect their holdings information and then update the WorldCat® KB for the library. Once a library has set its publisher vendor information in PubGet, the amount of time needed to populate and maintain holdings in the WorldCat® KB can be greatly reduced. This reduction of time is especially helpful for those libraries that also maintain a separate KB for their library's link resolver. Macalester implemented the WorldCat® Local KB to reduce the number of clicks it takes to connect our patrons to the content they need. To achieve this, they use both PubGet and manual updates to maintain the accuracy of the KB. PubGet reduces the amount of time needed to maintain holdings for many resources, and any publishers and platforms that are not currently represented in PubGet are added into the KB manually by library staff.

In addition to the streamlining efforts mentioned above, OCLC's quarterly updates also support the tracking of electronic resources. Tracking and linking to a library's electronic collections are large and fairly complex tasks.

And the larger and more complex the task, the more probable technical problems such as linking errors may arise. These types of errors happen in all such systems, including WorldCat® Local. The key is making sure that WorldCat® Local customers report the problems to OCLC staff. A problem that goes unreported is not likely to be resolved. OCLC, however, is able to make efforts to resolve problems on a regular basis through the quarterly updates.

Course Reserves

WorldCat® Local recently implemented a Course Reserves feature. Through this feature, libraries can create "courses" in WorldCat® Local and link to the appropriate bibliographic record for the items that are on reserve. Once implemented, patrons can conduct course reserve searches in WorldCat® Local, an interface with which they are familiar. Macalester's library has tested this new feature, and while staff liked the integration of reserves into WorldCat® Local and the attractiveness of the display page for each course, there is room for improvement. The search box is fairly general-looking without any indication that you will only be searching professor and course name fields. This could be frustrating for some patrons who may start the search with an author or title. In addition, while the display page for each course is very attractive, it currently lacks availability information. Patrons need to click into each item's individual record to obtain the availability status. Improvement of this module is ongoing.

POST-IMPLEMENTATION EXPERIENCE

User Perceptions

Since employing WorldCat® Local, system and collection usage data, resource-sharing statistics, and anecdotal feedback indicate success. Overall, users' reception of WorldCat® Local has been overwhelmingly positive, which is evidenced both in user surveys and in interactions with faculty, staff and students. A major change has happened on a conceptual level in terms of how users refer to the system. The word "*catalog*" is now rarely used either by staff or by patrons, and it is now rarely used in library instruction sessions. Instead, library staff tend to use the phrase *Macalester WorldCat®*, as in "*Let's check Macalester World-Cat®.*" In meetings, library staff often refer to it as WorldCat® Local. Students, on the other hand, tend to call it simply "*the library search.*"

The majority of campus users do not seem to miss "the catalog" concept. In campus-wide surveys conducted in 2010, a clear majority of the respondents indicated that they were satisfied or very satisfied with both WorldCat® Local and the Macalester's library Web site. Initially, some users did look for the previous, traditional catalog system because they were used to it. Once they had been shown WorldCat® Local, they were generally impressed and the number of inquiries about the traditional catalog is now low. This is also confirmed in statistics from the old OPAC: Searches in traditional OPAC dropped by 50 percent in the year that WorldCat® Local was implemented.

One comment from a Macalester College librarian was that it was easy to teach: "Students like the Google-like search, and getting good, ranked results. Students initially did not want to try it, but once I showed them, they were hooked on WorldCat® Local. I'm hooked on WorldCat® Local."

In addition, the following are some comments from faculty members, also from the 2010 campus survey:

- "It's amazing what students are able to access."
- "Love that students are searching WorldCat® automatically and I don't have to force them. This is so much better."

- "Wow. This is terrific! Makes my job much easier--and gives me faster access to more knowledge, and an easier way to distribute it to students. Thanks."

Analytics and Usage Statistics

Following the implementation of WorldCat® Local, Macalester saw significant increases in WorldCat® Local Web site visits. During the first year after implementation, visits to WorldCat® Local increased significantly and have continued to increase albeit at a slower pace in the second year of implementation. The Web site visits data is provided via a system called Adobe®[5] SiteCatalyst®[6], a product similar to Google Analytics™[7] that is available to all WorldCat® Local customers. The Web site visits data is not fully reliable because of the way the system tracks visits. According to OCLC (2011), a Web site visit recorded in Adobe® SiteCatalyst® is any activity within a session of at least 30 minutes. In a multi-user setting such as a library computer lab, where multiple users may use a computer within a 30-minute time span, it is possible that there were more visits in reality. Regardless of the exact numbers, what has been most interesting to us is to see steadily increasing usage.

Perhaps the most significant indication of positive user reception, however, is the impact on circulation statistics. Alongside the increase in WorldCat® Local Web site visits, Macalester library's circulation numbers increased from an average of about 57,000 in the three years immediately prior to the year of implementation, to over 62,000 in the year of implementation. This upward trend has continued steadily after the implementation with roughly 69,000 (2008/2009), 73,000 (2009/2010), and 75,000 (2010/2011) circulations post-implementation. On average, numbers for Macalester's library have increased about 8% per year since 2006/2007 or a total of about 24%.

Figure 1. Web visits to Macalester library's WorldCat Local following the implementation in 2008

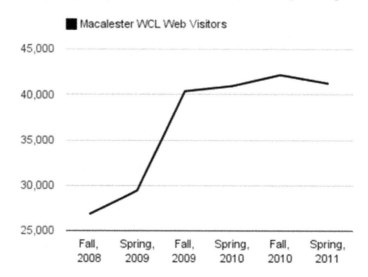

■ Macalester WCL Web Visitors

Figure 2. Changes in circulation statistics for the Macalester College library, 2004-2011

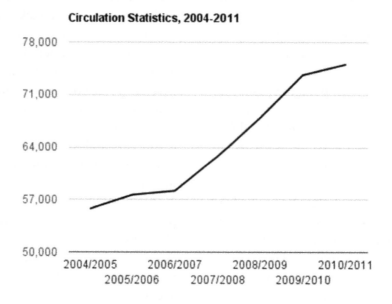

Circulation Statistics, 2004-2011

Since searching the holdings of the world's libraries is one of the key features of WorldCat® Local, it should come as no surprise that inter-library loan (ILL) transactions increased after we implemented WorldCat® Local. Prior to the implementation, from 2005 to 2007, Macalester's library experienced an average of 2,090 fulfilled requests per year. Immediately after implementation, Macalester's library noticed a sharp increase in inter-library loan requests, both for non-returnables (e.g. articles & chapters) and returnable items (e.g. books & DVDs), but especially for returnable items. Overall, Macalester sees this increase in fulfilling ILL as a good and positive use of resources.

Figure 3. Changes in inter-library loan usage at Macalester College. Non-returnable items, 2005-2011.

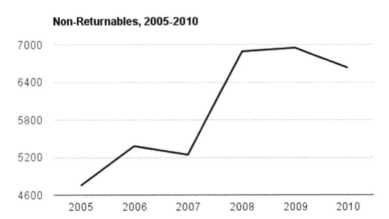

At the same time, the number of inter-library loan requests requiring cancellation has quadrupled, while remaining proportional to the total number of cancellations. In 2005 through 2007, cancellations were at an average of 22.02% of total ILL requests. In 2008-2011, cancellations were at an average of 24.20% of the total ILL requests. Although the proportions of cancellations are similar before and after the launch of World-Cat® Local, the library did notice a spike in 2009 with the cancellations at 27%. To counter this, the library changed a WorldCat® Local setting which brought Macalester holdings first in a search, then holdings from the consortium of local libraries, followed by regional ILL partners, and then the remaining worldwide holdings last. Among the common reasons for cancellation are the requested item was out of the immediate borrowing region, holdings records may not have been clear or detailed enough, or that link resolver settings were not accurately reflecting the library's holdings. In some cases, the requested material is held by one of the local consortium libraries, which results in a request separate from ILL. Finally, in some cases the library does have the material and it is simply an opportunity to educate users on how to best make use of the library.

In addition to acquiring WorldCat® Local, other factors may have contributed to the increased

circulation statistics. In 2009, the library launched a more user-friendly Web site designed to give users an overall improved user experience. One notable change on the new Web site was the placement of a search box. The new Web site featured the WorldCat® Local search box prominently both on the homepage and at the top of the every page. When WorldCat® Local was initially deployed at Macalester, the WorldCat® Local search box was only featured on the homepage. In years prior, a search box for the traditional catalog had appeared, disappeared, and re-appeared several times in slightly different locations on the homepage.

Realizing the full potential of a library discovery system is highly dependent upon the prominence of its search box as well as integration throughout virtual spaces. In 2009, OCLC shared statistics with Macalester library's staff to illustrate this point. From February to August 2009, Macalester had 24,154 visits to WorldCat® Local by Macalester's 2,000 FTE students. It should be noted that Macalester does not have any classes in the summer so the months of June, July and August produce little scholarly activity. In comparison, a 45,000 FTE university had a total of 3,348 visits over the same period of time. Although there is not enough data to draw any conclusions as to why there is such a significant difference between Macalester and the larger research institution, it

Figure 4. Changes in inter-library loan usage at Macalester College. Returnable items, 2005-2011.

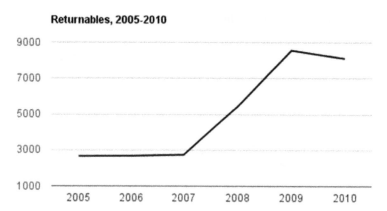

Figure 5. Returnables cancellations at Macalester College, 2005-2011

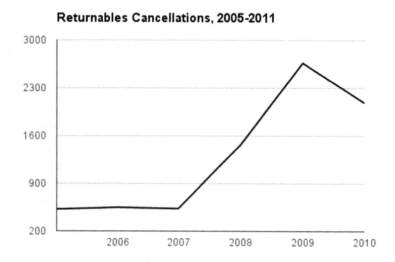

is interesting to note that the Macalester library chose a primary placement for their WorldCat® Local search on their homepage, and the other institution chose to put it on a secondary page.

Overall, Macalester's library staff put a great deal of thought into increasing the prominence and power of WorldCat® Local via the library's Web site and beyond. The library aims to integrate library resources into all relevant virtual spaces on campus such as the learning management system, the campus Web content management system, and throughout library's Web site.

Solutions and Recommendations

As mentioned throughout this chapter, there are some areas of WorldCat® Local that could benefit from further development. Some libraries have completed extensive user studies to evaluate user experiences with WorldCat® Local (Thomas & Buck, 2010; Ward J., et al, 2008). While the Macalester library has not performed in-depth user studies, it has found some common issues in using the system. Specifically, these issues include: known-item searching, facet displays, link resolver functionality, and course reserves.

Figure 6. WorldCat® Local results screen with the top 5 relevancy ranking turned on (© 2001-2011, OCLC; used with permission)

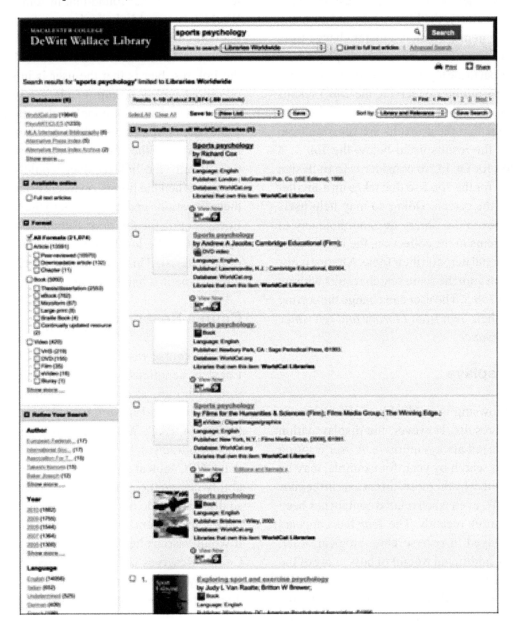

Known-Item Searching

Known-item searching has been problematic from WorldCat® Local's inception. WorldCat® Local users made their concerns known to OCLC, and OCLC responded by pulling together a small group of users to identify ways to improve known-item searching. This effort produced the *Top 5 Relevancy* search results that libraries could choose to turn on. While *Top 5* does improve known-item searching, there are some concerns that it causes confusion for users and may lead them to assume the library does not have anything on their topic in the collection. In particular, library staff's concerns are: the display takes up a great deal of screen space on the search results screen (see image below); the library may not own any of the *Top 5* items, which is a major change from the library's current default results display where holdings float to the top; and, depending on the size of the user's monitor or screen, the *Top 5* results may not be visually highlighted enough for users to recognize that these results are separate from the rest of the results listed below the *Top 5*. A suggestion for OCLC to consider is to re-design the display for the *Top 5* so that takes up a smaller portion of the screen. Doing so may help users to see that even if a library does not hold any of the *Top 5* items in the collection, the library does hold additional items on their topic. Alternatively, a library can gain the same search results without turning on *Top 5*. The user can change the sorting option on their own from *Library and relevance* to just *Relevance*.

Facet Displays

Faceted browsing is a valuable tool for narrowing search results. However, the display within the facets is not always intuitive. A user wanting to narrow a search by year, for example, may be confused as to why the most current date in the *Year* facet is 2007, even when related content has been published more recently. The *Year* facet appears to be displayed in reverse chronological order, but with an additional weight of how many of the search results are associated with that particular year. The user needs to click on "Show More" in order to see a full list of dates to choose from, including more current content.

Link Resolver Functionality

The launching of the link resolver has the potential to streamline work flow for WorldCat® Local libraries that are currently using the WorldCat® KB and have also had to populate a separate KB for their library's current link resolver. In testing, Macalester found that in some cases the WorldCat® Local link resolver performed better than the current link resolver (e.g. deeper linking into LexisNexis®[8] Academic). One challenge with the link resolver is that the user is immediately presented with a prompt to place a request for any articles that are not included in the library's electronic holdings, regardless of whether or not the library has the content in their print collection. Ideally the link resolver would be able to identify when the library owns the print format in these situations and offer a link to the WorldCat® Local record for the print format so the patron can identify the location and availability of the print material. This issue has been reported and improvement is anticipated.

Course Reserves

Making course reserves findable in WorldCat® Local is beneficial to Macalester's library patrons, who are already more familiar with the WorldCat® Local environment than they are with the local OPAC. While the course page display may be attractive, the suggestion has been made that OCLC look at adding call number and availability information in the course page results list so that patrons do not have to make an additional click into the item's record for that information. It would also be helpful to include a note on the Course Reserves search page directing users to search by professor or course names as the search does not include the title or author fields.

FUTURE RESEARCH DIRECTIONS

The Macalester library proposes that OCLC and WorldCat® Local customers would benefit from additional research around the driving factors in their system design and the resulting outcomes. Some questions that remain to be addressed are as follows: how FRBR benefits users; how OCLC's relevance ranking hinders more predictable results; about the complexities of connecting to electronic full text in this environment; about the ever-challenging nature of cross-database searching. OCLC often refers to user studies being done on behalf of customers as they develop their product and not only would it be useful to actually see these studies but to have additional studies carried out by libraries.

CONCLUSION

WorldCat® Local has transformed Macalester's library, the user experience, and the library's services. Perhaps most significantly, because patrons have been largely successful in using the new discovery system, it has helped library staff loosen their control over the catalog. Furthermore, library staff members do not have to be as concerned with continued updates to the product, and that, while it is not a perfect product; it is certainly better than the library catalog that Macalester patrons had been using previously. Patrons for the most part are unaware of and unhindered by any imperfection that trained library staff may see, and therefore library staff have become less concerned with perfection. This shift has helped library staff to better trust the system and the user, and to trust that the library can be as effective, if not more effective, with less control. At the same time library staff members are more engaged in product improvement discussions with the vendor and WorldCat® Local community than before and are generally satisfied with the responsiveness of the vendor. Overall, this results in a more positive organizational outlook, a better use of library resources, and improved service to the campus community.

Macalester's DeWitt Wallace Library is not alone in remaining optimistic about the future of WorldCat® Local and OCLC's plans for developing the product. Many libraries are also encouraged by OCLC's development of an entirely new library system infrastructure, Worldshare Management® Services, which would include a comprehensive back-end library management system for World-Cat® Local. This cloud-based system is made up of an entirely new library system architecture and per the vendor would free libraries from maintaining local data and systems and instead allow customers to "manage their library, not their technology." For example, the long-held practice of downloading bibliographic records to a local catalog and updating holdings at OCLC is rendered unnecessary in this environment. The ability to use, share, and reuse data among other member libraries becomes feasible in ways not previously possible. OCLC is in a unique position to radically change the work of libraries and many libraries are ready for and energized by this level of potential change.

REFERENCES

Dempsey, L. (2010). Discovery layers - Top tech trends 2 [Blog post]. Retrieved August 16, 2010, from http://orweblog.oclc.org/archives/002116.html

Thomas, B., & Buck, S. (2010). OCLC's WorldCat local versus III's WebPAC: Which interface is better at supporting common user tasks? *Library Hi Tech*, *28*(4), 648–671. doi:10.1108/07378831011096295

Ward, J., Shadle, S., & Mofjeld, P. (2008). User experience, feedback, and testing. *Library Technology Reports*, *44*(6), 17–23.

Yang, S. Q., & Hofmann, M. A. (2011, June 14). Next generation or current generation? A study of the OPACs of 260 academic libraries in the USA and Canada. *Library Hi Tech*, *29*(2), 266–300. doi:10.1108/07378831111138170

ADDITIONAL READING

Ballard, T., & Blaine, A. (2011). User search-limiting behavior in online catalogs: Comparing classic catalog use to search behavior in next-generation catalogs. *New Library World, 112*(5/6), 261–273. doi:10.1108/03074801111136293

Becher, M., & Schmidt, K. (2011, July 01). Taking discovery systems for a test drive. *Journal of Web Librarianship, 5*(3), 199–219. doi:10.10 80/19322909.2011.583134

Breeding, M. (2007). *Next-generation library catalogs.* Chicago, IL: ALA TechSource.

Breeding, M. (2010, May). OCLC reshapes its content strategy as it expands WorldCat Local discovery. *Smart Libraries, 30*(5), 3.

Collins, M., & Rathemacher, A. J. (2010). Open forum: The future of library systems. *The Serials Librarian, 58*(1-4), 167–173. doi:10.1080/03615261003625703

Deardorff, T., & Nance, H. (2009). WorldCat local implementation: The impact on interlibrary loan. *Interlending and Document Supply, 37*(4), 177–180. doi:10.1108/02641610911006265

Eden, B. L. (2010). The new user environment: The end of technical services? *Information Technology & Libraries, 29*(2), 93–100.

Garcia, M. M., Boyd, M., Hartel, L., Kilzer, R., & Kuehn, J. (2008). Search OSU and beyond . In *The impact of WorldCat Local at OSU.* Columbus, OH: Ohio State University.

OCLC. (2010). Some findings from WorldCat Local usability tests prepared for ALA Annual, July 2009. Retrieved December 19, 2011, from http://www.oclc.org/worldcatlocal/about/213941usf_some_findings_about_worldcat_local.pdf

OCLC. (2011). Findings from WorldCat Local usability tests, July, 2009 - September 2010. Retrieved December 19, 2011, from http://www.oclc.org/worldcatlocal/about/213941usf_some_findings_about_worldcat_local_2011.pdf

Rowe, R. (2010). Web-scale discovery: A review of Summon, EBSCO Discovery Service, and WorldCat Local. *The Charleston Advisor, 12*(1), 5–10. doi:10.5260/chara.12.1.5

Shadle, S. (2009). Electronic resources in a next-generation catalog: The case of WorldCat Local. *Journal of Electronic Resources Librarianship, 21*(3/4), 192–199. doi:10.1080/19411260903446006

Singer, R. (2008). In search of a really "next generation" catalog. *Journal of Electronic Resources Librarianship, 20*(3), 139–142. doi:10.1080/19411260802412752

Tamar, S. (2007). Time for a change: New approaches for a new generation of library users. *New Library World, 108*(7/8), 307–316. doi:10.1108/03074800710763608

Ward, J. L., Shadle, S., & Mofjeld, P. (2008). WorldCat Local at the University of Washington Libraries. *Library Technology Reports, 44*(6), 41.

Yang, S. Q., & Wagner, K. (2010). Evaluating and comparing discovery tools: How close are we towards next generation catalog? *Library Hi Tech, 28*(4), 690–709. doi:10.1108/07378831011096312

Zhu, L. (2010). The role of the cataloging department in the implementation of OCLC WorldCat local. *Library Collections, Acquisitions & Technical Services, 34*(4), 123–129. doi:10.1016/j.lcats.2010.06.001

KEY TERMS AND DEFINITIONS

Central Index/Central Indexing: Index of metadata stored within one database.

Cloud-Based: Applications and services offered over the Internet.

E-Serials Holdings Program: A free service offered by OCLC to indicate a library's electronic serials holdings in WorldCat.

Federated Search: A search sent out to several databases that results in a single results list.

Knowledge Base: A database used for tracking a library's electronic holdings. This data is the backbone of a link resolver and is also used to create an a-z list of journal holdings.

Link Resolver: Software that connects a user from a citation to the actual article/chapter/book. Examples include: ExLibris' SFX, Serials Solutions' 360 Link, and EBSCO's LinkSource.

ENDNOTES

[1]   Worldcat is a registered trademark of OCLC.

[2]   ExLibris is a trademark of Ex Libris Ltd.

[3]   MetaLib is a registered trademark of Ex Libris Ltd.

[4]   SFX is a registered trademark of Ex Libris Ltd.

[5]   Adobe is a registered trademark of Adobe Systems Inc.

[6]   SiteCatalyst is a registered trademark of Adobe Systems Inc.

[7]   Google Analytics is owned by Google Inc.

[8]   LexisNexis is a registered trademark of LexisNexis

Chapter 37
Tiptoeing Forward:
Implementing and Integrating WorldCat Local as a Discovery Tool

Tyler Goldberg
University of Louisville, USA

Anna Marie Johnson
University of Louisville, USA

Randy Kuehn
Eastern Illinois University, USA

ABSTRACT

This chapter describes the implementation of the WorldCat[®1] Local discovery tool in a multiple-library system at a mid-sized university. The catalog data preparation required for implementation is a key focus, including discussion of the use of the OCLC holdings reclamation process. Special circumstances and limitations regarding government documents records are described. The challenge that WorldCat® Local's architecture presents for a library system with multiple processing units is explained. Additional concepts discussed are the decisions regarding configuration and presentation on the Library's Web interface, the challenges faced by librarians and staff, and the impact on instruction and reference. Comparisons between the number of searches in the traditional library catalog and WorldCat® Local are presented as well as interlibrary loan requests statistics pre and post implementation. Various difficulties encountered and the applied solutions are explained and discussed as well as ongoing challenges and issues.

DOI: 10.4018/978-1-4666-1821-3.ch037

INTRODUCTION

Once upon a time Online Public Access Catalogs (OPAC) resembled tools of the future. The ability to do keyword searching of records and to not be restrained by officially-approved subject headings was a revelation in information retrieval. Today, OPACs represent the dinosaurs of the information retrieval world, headed for slow, albeit sure, extinction among rapidly evolving metasearch, discovery tools, and of course, Google. The culture of libraries is a strange one. Librarians work hard to preserve information, mostly in a 500 year old format, but also have one foot in the future and are often trying out new technologies, just to see if they will work. The University of Louisville (UofL) Libraries are no different. As the Libraries have implemented the WorldCat® Local discovery tool, it has been a journey of excitement and trepidation, and it is one that is not over yet.

BACKGROUND

The University of Louisville is a metropolitan university offering master, doctoral, and professional degrees. In fall 2010 there were 18,295 FTE students. The UofL Libraries consist of the Art Library, Music Library, Health Sciences Library, Law Library, University Archives, and the Ekstrom (main) Library. The Libraries use Ex Libris' Voyager®2 integrated library system (ILS), as well as SFX®3 (OpenURL link-resolver).

The UofL Libraries conducted a trial of World-Cat® Local as part of a consortial offer to the libraries in Kentucky's state supported institutions. Following this successful trial, WorldCat® Local seemed a logical choice for UofL's discovery tool for several reasons. The Libraries had been contributing cataloging records to the OCLC WorldCat® database since 1975. Another attractive feature was that in addition to the 194 million records created by libraries globally for the materials they hold, WorldCat® Local also has 501 million citations to articles from several databases, including Article-First®4, ERIC, MEDLINE®5, GPO, and JSTOR®6. OCLC as a vendor was a known quantity, even if this was a new product for them. Furthermore, OCLC offered the UofL Libraries the means to make sure that the Libraries' data in OCLC was accurate through OCLC's reclamation process. OCLC had adopted FRBR (Functional Requirements for Bibliographic Records), which would provide users with a single result by grouping different editions or formats together. Users have the option of viewing all the editions and formats that have been FRBR-ized, but it was thought that most users were not searching for a specific book, and any edition would be sufficient. WorldCat® was always one of the most heavily used databases at UofL, so the "brand" of WorldCat® was already a familiar one to many of the libraries' users. The idea of including local content, such as UofL Libraries' digital special collections via CONTENTdm was also exciting. Since OCLC had also discussed creating an integrated library system at some point in the future, this seemed like a good opportunity to get in on the "ground floor" of that effort and perhaps have a voice in the creation process. Last but not least, the cost of WorldCat® Local was reasonable at that time. While there were some drawbacks, overall, WorldCat® Local-represented a solid choice for UofL's library system.

PREPARATION OF CATALOGING RECORDS AND CONFIGURATION

WorldCat® Local gives users the ability to discover from a single search box all items from the Libraries' catalog and the collections made available through OCLC, including books, databases, articles, and digital materials. A library generally configures WorldCat® Local so that users retrieve search results that display items from the library's local collection first. In its implementation of FRBR, WorldCat® Local uses the record with the

Figure 1. WorldCat® Local: Sample search. (© 2011 OCLC. Used with permission. WorldCat® and the WorldCat® logo are registered trademarks/service marks of OCLC.).

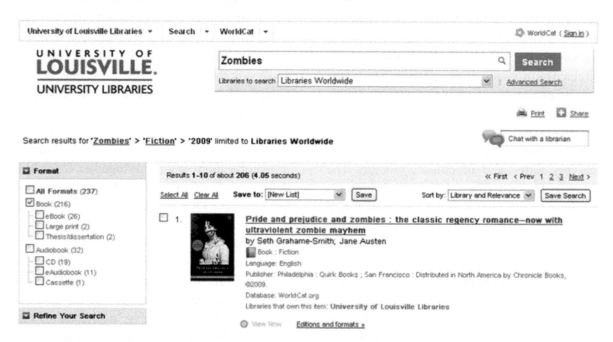

library's OCLC holdings symbol to tie the records for similar works together. Items are identified as belonging to a library because a library's holdings symbol has been attached to a specific OCLC record (see figure 1).

From the "search results" screen a user retrieves an item record in WorldCat® Local, which provides basic bibliographic information. Additional bibliographic information from the OCLC master record is available at the bottom of the screen, including the collation, subject headings, contents, and the OCLC record number. All of this information comes from the OCLC master bibliographic record to which the library's holdings symbol is attached. This record can be different from the same record in a library's local catalog if editing is done only to the local record. In addition to the item record, WorldCat® Local also provides information about an item's location and availability, as well as other libraries nearby that also own the item.

Of the six libraries at the UofL, four of these libraries (Ekstrom, Kornhauser, Law, and Music Libraries) have separate processing units, each with its own OCLC symbol. The extent of the editing of records varies between processing units. All libraries use AACR2. All libraries, except Kornhauser, use Library of Congress subject headings (LCSH) and Library of Congress (LC) classification. Kornhauser Library uses MeSh (Medical Subject Headings) and both National Library of Medicine (NLM) and Library of Congress classifications. Historically, duplication of holdings is common among the UofL Libraries, and the same OCLC record is used by each processing unit when adding duplicate copies. In the Libraries' Voyager® catalog, duplication of OCLC records has been the practice and the Voyager® OPAC clearly indicates each individual library that owns the title when multiple libraries own the same title.

Reclamation

An important first step in implementing World-Cat® Local was the reclamation process, which is a batch load project designed to make sure one's holdings are correct in OCLC. A library sends its records to OCLC who processes the records to ensure that a library's holdings are on the records sent and are removed from OCLC records that were not received. During this time, a period of just over a month, all UofL Libraries could not withdraw any items because deleting any holdings from OCLC would cause errors in reclamation. Adding holdings was not a problem, so cataloging went on as usual. In July 2010, the libraries pulled 1,106,170 records from three processing units to send to OCLC (one library felt that its holdings were correct). Records were pulled using the OCLC number. While this doesn't appear to be a complicated process, the OCLC number resides in the 035 field of the Voyager® record, and over the years this field not only had OCLC numbers, but also had other numbers, primarily from authority projects and government documents processing. In addition, the OCLC number could have multiple prefixes (ocm or ocn) or no prefix. Early on in the process it appeared that multiple prefixes might create insurmountable issues, but OCLC resolved this issue before the project started. Records with no OCLC numbers were automatically excluded, e.g. records for archival materials, AV equipment, and provisional records for items awaiting cataloging. Any problems reported by OCLC were examined and fixed manually after reclamation was completed.

The government documents records were particularly problematic. Government documents records had been added to Voyager® as part of retrospective conversion project done by Marcive. Many had been examined over the years, reclassified to use Library of Congress classification (LC) numbers, and holdings added to the correct OCLC record. However, approximately 50,000 documents records remained that it was anticipated might need manual correction before submitting to OCLC for reclamation. Preprocessing these records was a necessary step that required the Libraries' to think creatively in order to meet reclamation requirements. In-house programming by the Libraries' systems personnel using Java and MARC4J (http://marc4j.tigris.org/), an open source Java library used for processing MARC records, took care of most of these records. Each record was first examined for the number of 035 fields, with the assumption that each record should have only two 035 fields, one for GPO and a second for the OCLC number. A stepped approach was developed to filter and modify the records. Assuming a record contained only two instances of the specified field, the content of each instance was then inspected. If the first contained "(GPO)" followed by a numeric value in subfield "a" and the second only contained a numeric value, the record met the criteria necessary. The prefix "(OCoLC)" was then appended to the second numeric value. Records that did not meet the criteria were simply noted for manual correction. In the end, 47,865 records were corrected using this process, leaving a much more manageable number of records for manual correction.

Configuration Decisions

Following reclamation, configuration of the Libraries' customized WorldCat® Local was the next step following the very detailed instructions in the manual (http://www.oclc.org/support/documentation/worldcatlocal/ServiceConfigurationGuide.pdf). Besides "branding" the catalog, there are decisions that need to be made in order to display local holdings information in WorldCat® Local. One of two options can be applied for managing basic holdings configuration, the Z39.50 protocol or screen scraping. The Libraries chose to implement the latter method to access item information from the OPAC. The display of the holdings in WorldCat® Local is contingent upon the configuration determined by the combination of item status, location, various fulfillment options, and direct linking options (see figure 2). Distinctive selections can also be made for different item types, namely monographs, serials, articles, e-serials, digitized items, and other e-content. Items from any OPAC location can be assigned a "status treatment" message to be displayed in WorldCat® Local in relation to the availability of an item. With over 400 locations in the UofL Libraries' collections and 25 status options this could have been an arduous task, but an exclusionary technique was used to provide a manageable configuration solution for holdings. In other words, only circulating locations were individually configured, while for non-circulating locations, such as microforms, a single display option was applied.

Unforeseen Challenges Encountered

Since the impetus for using WorldCat® Local was to improve the user's search and retrieval experience, UofL Libraries have been hampered by several challenges that are the result of WorldCat® Local's architecture and the Libraries' infrastructure and processes. The biggest challenge is the fact that WorldCat® Local's architecture does not work with a library system having multiple processing units with duplicate OCLC records in the same ILS. Therefore, if two or more processing units at UofL use the same OCLC record, WorldCat® Local can't display them correctly. For example, three University of Louisville libraries own the *Encyclopedia of Louisville*, and all three processing units use the same OCLC record for cataloging. When a user retrieves the item record, no location or availability information is retrieved for any of the University Libraries. Instead, all the UofL libraries that own the title are listed under "Worldwide libraries own this item." This issue has been reported but has been unresolved to this point.

Another display issue concerns FRBR. The data structure that FRBR provides is specifically based on relationships built between bibliographic elements. It is this structure that can provide a more streamlined discovery experience for users by grouping related items, thus condensing search results into a more manageable display combining multiple formats, multiple editions and the like into one entry. The application of FRBR within WorldCat® Local can be somewhat confusing to users because not all related items are necessarily combined according to standard FRBR logic. While some systems allow librarians to define FRBR rules, "WorldCat Local does not offer any control options for its FRBR-ized content" (Brubaker, Leach-Murray, & Parker, 2011, p. 3). While the Libraries have options related to relevancy, it would be nice to control how FRBR is defined, or to allow users to opt out of FRBR-izing records in a particular search.

Implementation of WorldCat® Local has made UofL Libraries more aware of the need to make sure that the Libraries' record does not deviate substantially from the OCLC master record since this is what the patron sees in WorldCat® Local. As Zhu (2010) noted, "Since only OCLC WorldCat® master bibliographic records display in WSU [Washington State University] WorldCat®, WSU Cataloging Department needs to catalog at the network level (OCLC WorldCat-level) (p. 125). Since the Libraries continue to maintain two catalogs, it is clear that the UofL Libraries have not yet embraced this concept fully but have tried to enhance OCLC records on a regular basis to more closely match the records in the Voyager® catalog. Finally, the display for serial holdings and their call numbers is misleading. WorldCat® Local interprets a multi-volume serial or monograph as one item (see figure 3). If one volume of the serial is checked out, the system displays no volumes as available. In the future, more options for configurations would be welcomed.

Figure 2. WorldCat® Local: Sample configuration. (© 2011 OCLC. Used with permission. WorldCat® and the WorldCat® logo are registered trademarks/service marks of OCLC.).

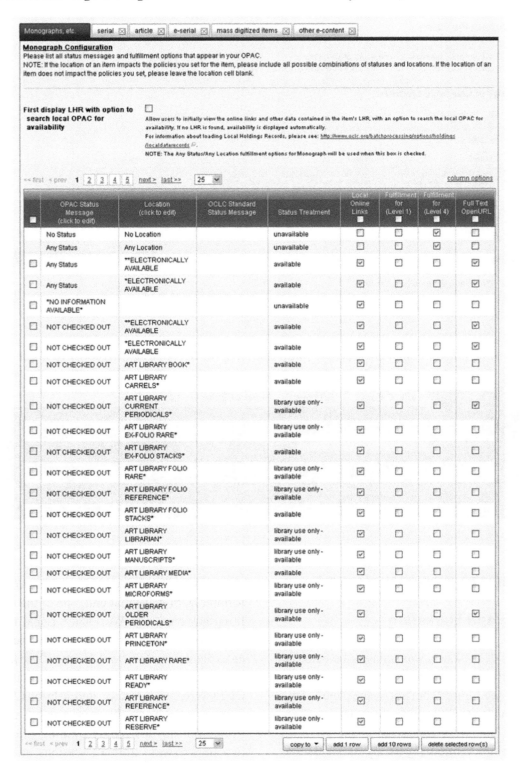

Figure 3. WorldCat® Local: Multi-volume display. (© 2011 OCLC. Used with permission. WorldCat® and the WorldCat® logo are registered trademarks/service marks of OCLC.).

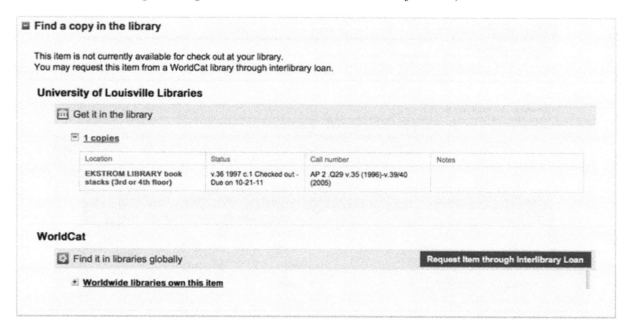

Figure 4. University of Louisville Library: Main search options. (© 2011 University of Louisville)

WORLDCAT LOCAL AND USERS

Training and Marketing

Since WorldCat® Local was going to be featured prominently on the main University Libraries webpage (see figure 4) but not on the pages of the professional school libraries, the training efforts originated and were conducted at the Ekstrom (main) Library. While many library staff had some familiarity with WorldCat®, WorldCat® Local was new to them, and everyone needed to be comfortable with it. To that end, one of the reference librarians created a WorldCat® Local LibGuide for both staff and patrons. This LibGuide contains an explanation of the tool, frequently asked questions, help and tip sheets in PDF format, links to OCLC-created tutorials, and a brief (2 minute) video created by the librarian using Camtasia®[7]. In addition to this online training information, two library-wide training sessions attended by approximately 40 staff and a training session

Table 1. ILL requests over the past 5 years (WCL implementation 2010-2011)

Interlibrary Loan Requests

□Books ■Articles

specifically for student assistants were conducted by members of the reference department.

Marketing efforts consisted of a formal press release, announcements in campus news outlets such as a faculty/staff daily e-mail campus-wide newsletter, a student news announcement, announcements on the library main webpage and the library Facebook page, digital sign slides, and a reception. Despite the campus-wide marketing efforts, WorldCat® Local is seen primarily as a tool for arts and sciences faculty, staff, and students.

Meeting a Variety of Users' Needs

WorldCat® Local is the primary search box on the main Libraries' webpage. For undergraduate students, it provides a one-search box solution to finding many kinds of materials for their papers and projects. For graduate students and faculty, WorldCat® Local provides a world of resources both popular and obscure at their fingertips. Anecdotal comments from both of these groups indicate they very much appreciate the ease with which they can find the materials they need. This anecdotal evidence is reinforced by interlibrary

loan (ILL) data which is similar to other-WorldCat® Local sites in that the implementation resulted in more requests for book borrowing. Users seem to be finding items that they want (see Table 1).

WorldCat® Local does not figure prominently in most of the library instruction sessions taught at Ekstrom Library. One reason for this is that much of the instruction is not focused on a particular tool but rather on concepts such as evaluation of information or the differences between search engines and library databases. Another reason reflects concerns found in the literature as to how to best teach a discovery tool or federated search. (Lampert & Dabbour, 2007) There are so many layers or aspects to these tools, which while relatively easy to use, require a depth of understanding of library databases to interpret that most students do not have and are unable to get from a 50 minute session.

Ironically, library staff members are the ones who seem to have had the most difficulty making the transition to using WorldCat® Local, and many feel that it is problematic for their daily use in a way that the traditional OPAC and the WorldCat® database are not; consequently, the traditional OPAC, called "UofL catalog" or "Minerva" is still

Table 2. Comparison of the number of searches in the traditional OPAC and WCL during the first year with WCL

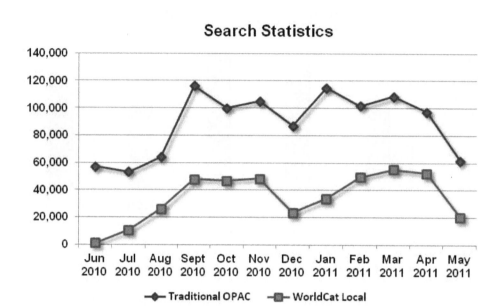

Not explicitly teaching WorldCat® Local, the professional schools not displaying it on their webpage, staff preference for the traditional catalog as well as other yet unknown factors may be affecting the usage of WorldCat® Local as shown by the greater number of searches in the traditional OPAC, despite its prominent placement on the main Webpage (see Table 2).

Web analytics for WorldCat® Local are provided using Adobe®[8] SiteCatalyst®[9] (http://www.omniture.com/en/products/analytics/sitecatalyst), which offers a wide variety of usage statistics and reporting options. All of the standard statistics one might expect can be produced in great detail, such as the number of visits, searches, and search terms used. Looking at the top search terms, there was a discernible correlation between classes that have utilized WorldCat® Local as part of library

instruction; clearly teaching it has an effect on its use. It may also be noteworthy that the name of the traditional OPAC ("Minerva") and the name of one of the most heavily used databases (EBSCO Academic Search™[10] Premier) were also two of the top search terms. Assessing WorldCat® Local with all users would be the next step in determining what various groups of users need and prefer.

Today's Issues/Continuing Challenges

For Ekstrom Library, the implementation of WorldCat® Local has provided good publicity and provoked interesting discussions. As with any system that a library implements, there are always elements that are made more complicated by an institution's unique workflows and procedures. While the Libraries participated in a trial of WorldCat® Local, some of the issues that arose during implementation were not evident during the initial trial. A major issue that remains for the proper implementation of WorldCat® Local is the fact that records can't be accurately harvested due to the UofL Libraries use of the same OCLC record by multiple processing units. At the current time, there are no plans to reduce the number of processing units, though this seems to be an issue worth considering.

Another issue that prevents WorldCat® Local from being used as a full-fledged discovery tool is the way aggregator databases are searched. To include them in the default search seems to slow down the entire system dramatically. It is unclear whether this is due to UofL's implementation or if this is a deficit of the product. E-books also continue to be problematic because of the decision at UofL to use the print record for both print and electronic books. This results in UofL's symbol not being included on the electronic book record in WorldCat® Local which means that patrons do not realize that UofL owns the item electronically.

A less problematic but still important issue is OPAC records not yet in OCLC. While reclamation has made the Libraries' catalog cleaner, and UofL Libraries' data in OCLC more accurate, there are still records in the local Voyager® catalog that are not in OCLC. While some are not appropriate for OCLC, others may need to be converted to OCLC in order to more fully implement WorldCat® Local. The concept of cataloging at the network level is one that must be more fully explored. As Goldner & Calhoun noted, it is time to rethink the idea of each individual library taking network level records and making local enhancements and changes. (Goldner & Calhoun, 2008) WorldCat® Local has created an opportunity for the UofL Libraries to have a discussion about the importance of the role of the traditional catalog versus the discovery tool and whether and how to maintain data in what are essentially two library catalogs.

Configuration is the key to WorldCat® Local. However, it was not as simple as it initially appeared. Interoperability with other products, such as SFX®, required the examination of the configuration of associated products, in order to make sure

WorldCat® Local was working optimally. Book cover displays and Web 2.0 features are intended to meet users' expectations of a current, typical website experience, and WorldCat® Local provides this; however users are most impressed when they can get seamlessly to the journal article they want and this is currently not always the case with this implementation for reasons the Libraries are still investigating. OCLC continues to enhance the system, making configuration of the system an ongoing process.

CONCLUSION

While WorldCat® Local represents a step forward for UofL Libraries, there is still a long way to go in order to implement the system to its full potential. This includes internal challenges that must be resolved within the libraries, as well as issues with WorldCat® Local itself that must be addressed by OCLC. WorldCat® Local's greatest strength, its wide-ranging but structured database is also in some ways its greatest weakness. Unlike other discovery tools, a library is not limited to its own OPAC holdings, but the structured nature of the database does seem to limit the customization that is possible in UofL's experience. Regular, responsive communication between the library and OCLC is imperative. Still OCLC's discovery tool represents the future direction of the OPAC, and it is progress in the right direction for library patrons.

REFERENCES

Brubaker, N., Leach-Murray, S., & Parker, S. (2011). Shapes in the cloud: Finding the right discovery layer. *Online*, *35*(2), 20–26.

Goldner, M., & Calhoun, K. (2008). *Web-Scale cataloging and metadata management*. Paper presented at the ALA Midwinter Meeting ALCTS Forum 'Moving Library Services to the Network Level', Philadelphia, PA. Retrieved from http://www.oclc.org/news/events/presentations/2008/Goldner-Calhoun_ALCTS_Forum_200801.pdf

Lampert, L. D., & Dabbour, K. S. (2007). Librarian perspectives on teaching metasearch and federated search technologies. *Internet Reference Services Quarterly*, *12*(3/4), 253–278. doi:10.1300/J136v12n03_02

OCLC. (n.d.). *FRBR work-set algorithm*. Retrieved from http://www.oclc.org/research/activities/past/orprojects/frbralgorithm/default.htm

Reitz, J. M. (2010). *ODLIS: Online dictionary for library and information science*. Santa Barbara, CA: ABC-CLIO. Retrieved from http://www.abc-clio.com/ODLIS/about.aspx

Zhu, L. (2010). The role of the Cataloging Department in the implementation of OCLC WorldCat Local. *Library Collections, Acquisitions & Technical Services*, *34*(4), 123–129. doi:10.1016/j.lcats.2010.06.001

ADDITIONAL READING

HathiTrust, OCLC introduce WorldCat local prototype. (2011). *Advanced Technology Libraries, 40*(2), 5.

Maxwell, R. L. (2008). *FRBR: A guide for the perplexed*. Chicago, IL: American Library Association.

Rapp, D., & Hadro, J. (2010). OCLC's cloud-based ILS enters next phase. *Library Journal, 135*(13), 16–18.

Rowe, R. (2010). Web-Scale discovery: A review of Summon, EBSCO Discovery Service, and WorldCat Local. *The Charleston Advisor, 12*(1), 5–10. doi:10.5260/chara.12.1.5

Rowe, R. (2011). Encore Synergy, Primo Central. *The Charleston Advisor*, *12*(4), 11–15. doi:10.5260/chara.12.4.11

Sellberg, R. (2010). Cooperative cataloging in a post-OPAC world. *Cataloging & Classification Quarterly*, *48*(2/3), 237–246. doi:10.1080/01639370903535734

Thomas, B., & Buck, S. (2010). OCLC's WorldCat Local versus III's WebPAC: Which interface is better at supporting common user tasks? *Library Hi Tech*, *28*(4), 648–671. doi:10.1108/07378831011096295

Vaughan, J. (2011). Web-scale discovery: What and why? *Library Technology Reports*, *47*(1), 5–11.

Ward, J. L., Shadle, S., & Mofjeld, P. (2008). Worldcat Local at the University of Washington Libraries. *Library Technology Reports, 44*(6), 41.

Wolverton, R. E., & Burke, J. (2009). The OPAC is dead: Managing the virtual library. *The Serials Librarian*, *57*(3), 247–252. doi:10.1080/03615260902877019

KEY TERMS AND DEFINITIONS

FRBR (Functional Requirements for Bibliographic Records): "The FRBR model brings together bibliographic records that are intellectually related as "works". Having resources brought together under the "works" umbrella enables users to sift through the myriad resources available digitally. It will help them acquire the work, or content, that they are looking for, irrespective of the specific "container" or item the content is carried in".(OCLC, n.d).

GPO: "The U.S. Government Printing Office, the government agency responsible for collecting, publishing, and distributing federal government information" (Reitz, 2010, http://www.abc-clio.com/ODLIS/odlis_G.aspx?#gpo).

Holdings symbol (OCLC): Libraries that are members of OCLC are assigned a symbol composed of letters and numbers. These symbols are input into catalog records in the OCLC WorldCat® database to allow the database to display the fact that the library owns a title or volume.

ILS (Integrated Library System) or LMS (Library Management System): "In automated systems, an integrated set of applications designed to perform the business and technical functions of a library, including acquisitions, cataloging, circulation, and the provision of public access" (Reitz, 2010, http://www.abc-clio.com/ODLIS/odlis_I.aspx#libms).

Item Type: A code in the item record for a bibliographic item in a library collection that, in conjunction with patron type, determines the loan rule applied when the item is checked out by a specific borrower.

MARC4J: An open source Java programming language library used to handle the processing and manipulation of MARC records.

Marcive: "A commercial service providing catalog records for U.S. government publications (retrospective and current) that can be loaded into a library's local online catalog, and a Shipping List Service that provides SuDocs labels, brief MARC records, smart barcode labels, and shelflist cards" (Reitz, 2010, http://www.abc-clio.com/ODLIS/odlis_M.aspx?#marcive).

OCLC: OCLC is a membership group of libraries from around the world. Members build and use a worldwide database of library records, make their library collections available through reference, document delivery and other services, and share the work to reduce processing costs.

OPAC (Online Public Access Catalog): "An acronym for online public access catalog, a database composed of bibliographic records describing the books and other materials owned by a library or library system, accessible via public" computers (Reitz, 2010, http://www.abc-clio.com/ODLIS/odlis_O.aspx?#opac).

Reclamation: Process used by OCLC in which a library sends all records from its local system to OCLC where holdings are set or canceled.

Screen Scraping: A programming method used to collect data from one webpage in order to repurpose the data and incorporate it into another webpage.

Z39.50 Protocol: A client-server protocol established as a NISO standard that allows the computer user to query a remote information retrieval system using the software of the local system and receive results in the format of the local system, often used in portal and gateway products to search several sources simultaneously and integrate the results" (Reitz, 2010, http://www.abc-clio.com/ODLIS/odlis_XYZ.aspx?#z3950).

ENDNOTES

[1] Worldcat is a registered trademark of OCLC.

[2] WorldCat® Local

[3] SFX OpenURL link resolver is a registered trademark of Ex Libris Ltd

[4] ArticleFirst is a registered trademark of OCLC.

[5] Medline is a registered trademark of US National Library of Medicine

[6] JSTOR is a registered trademark of ITHAKA

[7] Camtasia Studio is a registered trademark of TechSmith Corporation

[8] Adobe is a registered trademark of Adobe Systems Incorporated

[9] SiteCatalyst is a registered trademark of Adobe Systems Incorporated

[10] EBSCO Academic Search Premier owned by EBSCO Publishing Industries

Section 7
Critique of Discovery

Scott Walter
DePaul University, USA

OVERVIEW

Throughout this collection, the question of Web-Scale Discovery Systems (WSDS) has been pursued as if their adoption was (almost) unquestionably to the good. Indeed, even in this brief section dedicated to "critique," readers find one author taking as a given that "There is broad agreement that a single place to search for, and to immediately access, materials is what information users are looking for." While this may be true, and certainly there is evidence to suggest that a "pragmatic" approach to search and discovery is precisely what many desire (Kolowich, 2011), readers should note both the promise and the limitations of WSDS as librarians enter an era in library technology where it appears their adoption may become the norm. More to the point, one must ask what may be lost when the single search box is gained?

What may be gained has been the subject of much of this collection, e.g., greater convenience to library users, greater opportunities for collaboration among libraries, and greater potential for discovery of materials that might have otherwise remained "hidden" in traditional library systems. Guldi (2007) provided an early (and enthusiastic) example of the manner in which easy access to the full text of scholarly materials through Google Books promised to "transform the academic profession" through enhanced opportunities for discovery and greatly increased ease of delivery. For anyone who has employed Web-scale discovery, whether through the library or through Google, what one may gain through their use is obvious; the question of what may be lost is more complex.

Some years ago, this author touted the transition to electronic journals to a colleague in the English Department. Promising access to scholarly content not limited either by the physical location of libraries or by their hours of service, and allowing even the simplest search to retrieve articles of interest, the rise of the electronic journal appeared to be (almost) unquestionably to the good. But, as he explained, it was not so simple. Article-level access to the literature took materials from their intended context, especially in the "theme issues" of literary journals that are an important part of scholarship in his field.

Access was increased, but context was lost, and that context is an important facet of scholarly communication in the field of literary research. Even "access" was limited in his field, for, while many major journals were available electronically, a critical set of materials was not – the literary journals which have long served as the first site of publication for a variety of creative works and critical essays. For his field, electronic access was less than complete, and, even when complete, less than conducive to the promotion of important conventions of scholarly communication. Electronic access eased discovery for those experienced with literary research, but did not support the introduction of students to the scholarly conventions of the field in the way that older models for access did. Bransford, Brown, and Cocking (2000) have noted that the way in which an expert thinks about a field differs from the way in which a novice thinks, and the question was whether a library's commitment to ease of access as the impetus for change might compromise its ability to maintain a commitment to other scholarly goals. By easing access for the novice, did librarians compromise the development of the expert? These issues, not yet even fully addressed in regard to digital content, are raised again in regard to this next generation of discovery systems.

In the chapters to follow, readers will find questions of pragmatism and purpose. Webster, for example, enumerates the many limitations to the data currently available to serve as the foundation for Web-Scale discovery systems, including less than complete access to important pools of content, as well as diverse approaches to the construction of metadata governing access to available pools. Breitbach, by contrast, asks more fundamental questions along the lines of those suggested by my colleague years ago, e.g., what academic goals are less likely to be supported by library systems for which simple access is the sole criterion for success? Webster invites us to explore the technical solutions that may allow us to improve on the first generation of Web-scale discovery systems, while Breitbach encourages us to consider what complementary systems – whether related to access services, information services, or instructional services – librarians may need to maintain, improve, and promote in order to address more fundamental limitations of these systems.

In a recent essay published in The New York Times, Pamela Ban, a Harvard undergraduate, argued for the continued relevance of the research paper as an academic requirement; as she wrote: "The Internet makes it easy to treat the research paper as a Google exercise. However, any perceived 'failure' of the research paper isn't in the medium itself or the use of the Internet, but in the way we are tempted to approach it" (Ban, 2011). A research paper, she concluded, should not be a simple exercise in discovery, but an exercise in synthesis and critical thinking. As the essays in this section suggest, there is much work to be done in terms of improving the mechanics of discovery, but also in ensuring that discovery systems are designed to complement other systems – both technological and human – that promote a full range of academic goals.

REFERENCES

Ban, P. (2011, August 29). A learning experience. *The New York Times*. Retrieved from http://www.nytimes.com/roomfordebate/2011/08/28/are-research-papers-a-waste-of-time/a-learning-experience

Bransford, J. D., Brown, A. L., & Cocking, R. R. (Eds.). (2000). *How people learn: Brain, mind, experience, and school*. Washington, DC: National Academic Press. Retrieved from http://www.nap.edu/catalog.php?record_id=9853

Guldi, J. (2007, March 14). *How Google Books is changing academic history* [Blog post]. Retrieved from http://landscape.blogspot.com/2007/03/how-google-books-is-changing-academic.html

Kolowich, S. (2011, August 22). What students don't know. *Inside Higher Education*. Retrieved from http://www.insidehighered.com/news/2011/08/22/erial_study_of_student_research_habits_at_illinois_ university_libraries_reveals_alarmingly_poor_information_literacy_and_skills

Chapter 38
Web-Scale Discovery:
A Library of Babel?

William Breitbach
California State University, USA

ABSTRACT

With significant developments in library discovery systems, many libraries are exploring options for improving access to content. Although these new systems appear to be better than what has come before (federated searching), many problems remain. Libraries therefore should consider a number of inter-related issues/challenges before investing. These challenges include: an information glut, devaluation of metadata, disconnection of content from discourse communities, the notion that libraries compete with Google, and the creation of false expectations for users searching for scholarly content.

INTRODUCTION

When it was first proclaimed that the Library contained all books, the first impression was one of extravagant happiness (Borges, 1962, p. 55).

In Jorge Luis Borges' famous short story *The Library of Babel*, a universal library exists where every possible book is located. However, its vastness and lack of organization make the library es-sentially useless. Because of the continued failure of users to understand the library's organization, many go mad, commit suicide or become para-noid. Although the author of this chapter does not anticipate such calamity as libraries adopt Web-scale discovery systems (WSDS), there are a wide range of potential problems libraries need to consider before we reach the stage of "extrava-gant happiness."

There have been significant developments in WSDS over the past few years. Many libraries have adopted or are considering the adoption of such services. WSDS have great potential, but

DOI: 10.4018/978-1-4666-1821-3.ch038

readers should pursue their adoption with a critical eye. Before investing in these expensive systems, libraries should consider the problems they are trying to solve and whether these systems will solve them. To assist in the evaluation of these systems, a discussion of the following interrelated issues/challenges govern the body of this essay: an information glut, devaluation of metadata, disconnection of content from discourse communities, the notion that libraries compete with Google, and the creation of false expectations for users searching for scholarly content.

BACKGROUND

The goal of a single search for all library resources has been around for some time. The first glimpse of the presumed future came with federated searching. However, the poor search performance and poorly designed user interfaces left much to be desired. Moreover, most of the studies on federated searching focused on user satisfaction and perception (for examples, see Armstrong, 2009; Williams, Bonnell, & Stoffel, 2009) rather than student outcomes or performance measures of the systems. A few studies of federated searching did indeed attempt to tackle the more essential issue of task performance. These studies used research scenarios to assess user outcomes by counting the number of documents saved, time saved with federated search, and quality of results (Haya, Nygren, & Widmark, 2006; Belliston, Howland, & Roberts, 2007). However, these studies did not show better task performance with federated searching, begging the question of why libraries would invest in systems that make little to no difference in learning/discovery outcomes?

A new wave of discovery services has arrived. WSDS offer many of the same promises of federated search but differ in some very important ways. Federated search engines search and retrieve records from multiple databases from multiple hosts simultaneously. WSDS are different in that they use a single centralized and pre-aggregated index. This offers opportunity for improving performance (speed), relevance, and normalization of data. Jason Vaughan's much discussed issue of *Library Technology Reports* (2011) gives a substantive description of the promises of Web-scale discovery, but does not adequately address the associated challenges. Some of the early studies of WSDS show increases in the use of content by measuring SFX®[1] click-throughs (Garrison, Boston, & Bair, 2011; Way, 2010). Although these studies are certainly interesting, welcome, and even promising, additional information on how users interact with the information beyond simply clicking is warranted. That said, a recent task-oriented usability study shows some evidence that EBSCO Discovery Service™[2] performs better than federated searching in terms of finding relevant content and in ease of use (Williams & Foster, 2011). Williams & Foster (2011) created task oriented scenarios to test different parts of EBSCO Discovery™. These tasks were based on research scenarios such as finding an article on a complex topic, finding and emailing records, accessing full text, and discovering books in a local collection. In the author's view, the type of task-oriented research in the Williams and Foster (2011) study offers a good start, but comparative research where students solve common task-oriented problems in both WSDS and traditional databases is warranted.

Issues, Controversies, Problems

The notion of a single discovery interface for all available resources has great surface appeal. A beautiful and elegant search box that alleviates the need to navigate complex Web sites, learn multiple information systems, and which streamlines access to content has been a dream for at least a decade. Moreover, the vision of delivering high quality content within an interface that is somewhat familiar to novice users sounds compelling. This is essentially the promise of WSDS.

On the surface, this vision is indeed a beautiful one; however, before adopting a WSDS, attention should be paid to a number of factors including: information overload, their impact on subject specific metadata, aspects of information literacy and discourse communities, and whether or not we really want to or should compete with Google.

Information Overload

Much has been written about information overload (see Eppler & Mengis, 2004 for a summary). Although there are some minor differences in definitions, information overload can generally be described as the point at which the amount of information exceeds the cognitive processing capacity of an individual. The argument here is that the sheer volume of search results when using WSDS will lead to some level of information overload. The causes of information overload are multifaceted, as they not only depend on the information system being used but also the tasks being performed, complexity of the information itself, and the novelty of the situation. For many undergraduates, all three of these factors may play a role. When one combines these factors with thousands of search results (of which only a handful are likely germane to the initial query), discovery of high quality and appropriate subject level content may be hindered. In the author's experience, users do not necessarily need more citations, they need to search mindfully and they need to read and reflect on the works they discover. Subject databases help users survive the information glut because they deliver subject level content. Using subject databases, searchers will get fewer, more relevant results making the selection of appropriate content simpler. Moreover, some scholars have shown that users are less satisfied with large search results lists and more choices can lead to decision paralysis, poor choices, and decreased satisfaction (Oulasvirta, Hukkinen,& Schwartz, 2009). That said, the information architecture of such systems is rapidly

changing and advanced filtering features, system design (including the library Website from which these systems are accessed), and improvements in search algorithms can help reduce the cognitive load. More research is needed to determine how these systems affect cognitive load during the information discovery process.

Metadata and Discourse Communities

Libraries considering subscriptions to WSDS may also want to be concerned about the impact such systems have on information literacy. Although some have suggested that WSDS may lead to positive outcomes in some of the ACRL information literacy standards (Fagan, 2011), there are problems that arise from merging content from multiple disciplines together. As Condit-Fagan (2011) points out, "discovery tools combine thesauri together, blend collections of journals, and can offer effective limiters only where metadata is shared among resources" (p. 172). Since subject specific metadata varies between disciplines, the semantic meaning of the search terms may be lost. For example, Summon has a match and merge process that corrects, de-duplicates, and normalizes metadata (Serial Solutions, n.d.). This process will devalue subject specific metadata because the same metadata terminology can have different meanings in different disciplines. The problem is that conceptual boundaries of subject disciplines in such systems are broken.

Moreover, subject specific metadata elements provide clues or "information scents" to assist users with the search process. Information scents provide proximate clues (metadata, citation, and abstract) to the value of the distal information (full text of the source) (Pirolli & Card, 1999). Merging numerous disciplines together in systems that do not highlight subject specific content and metadata may throw users off the "scent trail" because the context and meaning of metadata will differ between disciplines. This begs the question:

how will users pick up on the appropriate context clues to distinguish what is important and what is unimportant within large results lists that merge multiple discourses?

The concern is that merging all scholarly content together de-contextualizes information from the subject discipline. As university students study a particular discipline, they are learning about and interacting with discourse communities that have "domain specific rhetorical processes." (Simmons, 2005, p. 298). These discourses represent "normal" ways of communicating within a particular community. Through the assignments that students complete using subject specific resources, they are learning conventions and communication practices. Discourse communities have "unique research methodologies, accept different kinds of proof, and prefer different kinds of writing" (Elmborg, 2003, p. 73). WSDS may not be designed to efficiently facilitate this critical component of information seeking and information literacy. This problem is especially significant for novice scholars who are just learning about their subject discipline. Developing an understanding of these rules and codes is part of the experience of earning a university degree in a particular discipline. Unfortunately, the notion of participation in a discourse community is often not made explicit to students and WSDS may make understanding these communities more difficult since they merge multiple discourses.

As professional educators, librarians should help users understand that they are interacting within a discourse community when they search for and select content for their assignments (Simmons, 2005). In this context, how does putting everything together help users distinguish content for quality and relevance? And how is the library's role in information literacy hindered? In a recent editorial, Fagan (2011), concurs that discovery systems may mask how they differ from subject databases. WSDS may actually undermine the library's role in helping the user locate texts within a discourse community. Additional research is needed comparing WSDS and traditional databases in finding subject specific relevant content.

EBSCO Discovery Service™, Primo®[3], and Summon™[4] provide what appear to be good subject facets on the surface. However, it is unclear how the normalization of this data will help in the discovery of discipline specific content. Summon™ helps alleviate this problem (in some implementations) by referring users directly to subject specific resources on the search results page. In any case, users will need to be educated on the use of these features because this is where WSDS depart from Google-like searching.

Competing with Google and User Expectation

The development of WSDS is partially driven by user expectations to have systems that work like Google. This notion is problematic on several levels. Google is an advertising company whose objective is to sell products and services. The more people search and click, the greater the opportunity Google has to make money. Google's market imperative is fundamentally different than the scholarly imperative of libraries. That said, the challenge of getting students to use high quality sources is certainly real and in that sense, one might say libraries "compete" with Google for attention. A recent study from OCLC shows that 83% of college students do indeed start their research with search engines (De Rosa, et al., 2011). Starting with search engines is not inappropriate and is sometimes sufficient. However, libraries should continue to distinguish themselves from Google because the library's purpose is different. Being overly concerned about competing with Google does not advance our efforts as professional educators.

According to recent research (De Rosa, et al., 2011; Connaway, Dickey, & Radford, 2011), students are drawn to Google and other search engines because of perceptions of speed, ease and convenience. Libraries should certainly seek easy discovery solutions for users, but this does not negate the need to help them understand the difference between quick information searching and scholarship. Users should not expect scholarship to mimic the quick information searching one typically uses with Google.

Scholarship requires linkages, connections, contexts, and overviews of relationships; quick information seeking is largely satisfied by discrete information or facts without the need to also establish the contexts and relationships surrounding them. Scholarship is judged by the range, extent, and depth of elements it integrates into a whole; quick information seeking is largely judged by whether it provides a "right" answer or puts out an immediate informational "brush fire" (Mann, 2008, p. 5).

The Connaway et al. (2011) study gives cause for concern, as scholarly work is not supposed to be "convenient." It should be engaging, reflective, and thoughtful. Users should not expect the information needed to solve complex problems to be as easily discovered as a movie review via a Google search. Moreover, the perceived inconvenience may not involve overcoming substantial hurdles, but may simply mean one or two extra clicks, reading and reflecting on the results of a query, or slightly more thoughtful searching. The apparent indifference to thoughtful, substantive and scholarly work suggested by the results of the OCLC report (De Rosa, et al., 2011) and Connaway et al. (2011) may reflect a major cultural and literacy problem. The information needed for exploring complex problems usually takes effort to discover and students should expect it to. It is interesting to note that the OCLC report found that overall favorable impression of all information resources (search engines, libraries, and bookstores) has declined since 2005 (De Rosa, et al., 2011, p.35-36). It is not known why favorability has declined or how users expect to find information to solve complex problems.

On a related note, promoting a single search as an all-in-one solution also makes the search for information appear easy and masks the complexity of the information discovery process. Students may therefore never know what they have missed and will make decisions about content selection without complete knowledge. In fact, the single search could dramatically influence discovery path choices and the execution of alternate and future search strategies. Rather than allowing users some agency in discovery by showing options of subject-specific resources, we are bounding their decision-making processes. We may in effect be hiding the existence of content not included in these systems (Mann, 2008) and alternative ways of searching. The author's concern here is that novice information seeking will be reduced to a "random and contingent selection of sources" (Bawden & Robinson, 2009, p.185) because the "scent trail" is distorted. In addition, a single search interface may encourage students to treat the search process as a purely instrumental practice rather than a reflective and iterative one. If the expectation for quick and easy solutions to complex and multifaceted problems is indeed a cultural and literacy problem, new discovery systems are not going to solve it no matter how much they look and work like Google.

SOLUTIONS AND RECOMMENDATIONS

Whether libraries move forward aggressively or develop a wait and see strategy in the allocation of new discovery platforms will depend on a variety of internal factors. The adoption of WSDS requires yearly subscriptions which can range from $9,000 to $100,000 per year depending on a variety of factors (Rowe, 2010). Considering the current budgetary situation in which many libraries find themselves and the absence of research showing significant learning/discovery outcomes, suggestions for a cautious approach follow.

Libraries with a desire to experiment with new forms of discovery should first consider whether they have adequately harnessed or can harness resources they already have at their disposal. The simplest way to begin using WSDS that work like Google is to use Google Scholar. Linking to library subscription content via Google Scholar can happen in a variety of ways. Most libraries will be able to create this link via the administrative interface of their link resolver. Also, libraries without link resolvers can provide access to both EBSCOhost®[5] and ProQuest®[6] content via Google Scholar by selecting the appropriate local administrator settings. Some research even shows that Google Scholar out-performs many subscription databases in terms of precision for some research topics (Walters, 2009).

In addition, libraries may also be able to leverage other systems that they currently have to improve or experiment with new models of discovery. Libraries that have a significant portion of their content supplied by EBSCOhost® can create a lite version of WSDS by using the EBSCOhost® Integration Toolkit's XML gateway. This will allow libraries to search all EBSCOhost® resources at once and display results outside the EBSCOhost® interface. Some libraries are using this option along with an open search platform called Solr (http://lucene.apache.org/solr) to improve library catalog display and show results for both articles and books in a tabbed interface (as an example, see Cal State Monterey Bay Library http://library.csumb.edu). This option requires libraries to have computer programmers on staff. They also have many of the same potential problems mentioned with subscription-based WSDS discussed in this chapter; these are worth noting so libraries can make informed decisions. Libraries that prefer to have a full-scale WSDS, and have the budget for one of the subscription services, should read through this volume and the literature cited here to help in the selection of the most appropriate option. However, decision-makers may want to await additional research about outcomes beyond clicks and user affect. Otherwise, libraries may make significant investments in tools that do not

improve learning and educational outcomes for users. Also, libraries adopting such systems will want to think about how these systems fit into the big picture of library resources and services. With the adoption of such systems, libraries may want to think and plan for their impact on Web site design, library instruction, reference work, and possibly some aspects of collection development.

FUTURE RESEARCH DIRECTIONS

Although WSDS appear to be better than federated search in terms of speed and access to content, they should also be expected to perform well in terms of finding relevant subject-level content. Thus far, there is a single usability study and a few studies measuring the number of clicks as a result of implementing these new services. The usability study (Williams & Foster, 2011) provides useful and promising information (although the sample size is very small). This research is a good start and we should welcome further studies that assess task performance outcomes on the types of assignments that are frequently required of college students. Scenario-based performance assessments similar to the one conducted by Williams & Foster (2011) will be an important way forward, but should have larger sample sizes and compare multiple systems. Additional research could involve qualitative citation analysis of bibliographies where separate groups of students use WSDS and subject-specific databases and results are compared. Using scenarios that reflect the complexity of real-world scholarly information queries, this research might compare different systems based on the citing of key research, journals, theories, and authors in the discipline. Researchers will also want to compare WSDS against subject databases in terms of precision and recall.

Although not discussed in the current essay, the impact such systems have on acquisitions and collection development should be studied. Since WSDS will expose users to a great deal of content not locally available, use of interlibrary loan and demand-driven acquisitions could increase substantially. On the other hand, WSDS may also provide the opportunity to explore the cancelation of some indexes and full text services in favor of acquiring items discovered through such systems just-in-time rather than having them just-in-case.

CONCLUSION

References to Jorge Luis Borges' *Library of Babel* may seem a bit polemic. However, they are meant to introduce a breadth of skepticism into discussions surrounding WSDS. The need remains for conceptually organized information and user education and initial discussions of WSDS appear to be overly exuberant. Although these systems likely have a place in the future of libraries, they do have implications that should be carefully considered. The problems outlined here are certainly not new, but they are significant as they may challenge our traditional practices and values. As information professionals, we need to remain critical of these systems as the critiques will drive us to make better decisions with implementation (or not) and will alert us to the potential for needed changes that may follow in user education, Web site design, reference work, and even collection development.

REFERENCES

Armstrong, A. R. (2009). Student perceptions of federated searching vs single database searching. *RSR. Reference Services Review, 37*(3), 291–303. doi:10.1108/00907320910982785

Bawden, D., & Robinson, L. (2009). The dark side of information: Overload, anxiety and other paradoxes and pathologies. *Journal of Information Science, 35*(2), 180–191. doi:10.1177/0165551508095781

Belliston, C. J., Howland, J. L., & Roberts, B. C. (2007). Undergraduate use of federated searching: A survey of preferences and perceptions of value-added functionality. *College & Research Libraries, 68*(6), 472–486.

Borges, J. L., Irby, J. E., & Yates, D. A. (1962). *Labyrinths: Selected stories and other writings* [translated from Spanish]. New York, NY: New Directions.

Connaway, L. S., Dickey, T. J., & Radford, M. L. (2011). "If it is too inconvenient I'm not going after it:" Convenience as a critical factor in information-seeking behaviors. *Library & Information Science Research, 33*(3), 179–190. doi:10.1016/j.lisr.2010.12.002

De Rosa, C., Cantrell, J., Carlson, M., Gallagher, P., Hawk, J., & Sturtz, C. … Dalrymple, T. (2011). *Perceptions of libraries, 2010: Context and community.* Dublin, OH: OCLC. Retrieved from http://www.oclc.org/reports/2010perceptions.htm

Elmborg, J. K. (2003). Information literacy and writing across the curriculum: Sharing the vision. *RSR. Reference Services Review, 31*(1), 68–80. doi:10.1108/00907320310460933

Eppler, M., & Mengis, J. (2004). The concept of information overload: A review of literature from organization science, accounting, marketing, MIS, and related disciplines. *The Information Society, 20*(5), 325–344. doi:10.1080/01972240490507974

Fagan, J. C. (2011). Discovery tools and information literacy. *Journal of Web Librarianship, 5*(3), 171–178. doi:10.1080/19322909.2011.598332

Garrison, S., Boston, G., & Bair, S. (2011, April). *Taming lightning in more than one bottle: Implementing a local next-generation catalog versus a hosted web-scale discovery service.* Paper presented at the Association of College and Research Libraries Annual Conference, Philadelphia.

Haya, G., Nygren, E., & Widmark, W. (2007). Metalib and Google Scholar: A user study. *Online Information Review, 31*(3), 365–375. doi:10.1108/14684520710764122

Mann, T. (2008). The Peloponnesian War and the future of reference, cataloging, and scholarship in research libraries. *Journal of Library Metadata, 8*(1), 53–100. doi:10.1300/J517v08n01_06

Oulasvirta, A., Hukkinen, J. P., & Schwartz, B. (2009). When more is less: The paradox of choice in search engine use. *Proceedings of the 32nd International ACM SIGIR Conference on Research and Development in Information Retrieval*, (pp. 516–523). doi:10.1145/1571941.1572030

Pirolli, P., & Card, S. (1999). Information foraging. *Psychological Review, 106*(4), 643–675. doi:10.1037/0033-295X.106.4.643

Rowe, R. (2010). Web-scale discovery: A review of Summon, EBSCO Discovery Service, and WorldCat Local. *Charleston Advisor, 12*(1), 5–10. doi:10.5260/chara.12.1.5

Serial Solutions. (n.d.). *Summon key database and packages – A&I*. Retrieved from http://www.serialssolutions.com/resources/detail/summon-key-databases-and-packages-ai

Simmons, M. H. (2005). Librarians as disciplinary discourse mediators: Using genre theory to move toward critical information literacy. *portal . Libraries & the Academy, 5*(3), 297–311. doi:10.1353/pla.2005.0041

Vaughan, J. (2011). Web scale discovery what and why? *Library Technology Reports, 47*(1), 5–11.

Way, D. (2010). The impact of web-scale discovery on the use of a library collection. *Serials Review, 36*(4), 214–220. doi:10.1016/j.serrev.2010.07.002

Williams, S. C., Bonnell, A., & Stoffel, B. (2009). Student feedback on federated search use, satisfaction, and web presence: Qualitative findings of focus groups. *Reference and User Services Quarterly, 49*(2), 131–139.

Williams, S. C., & Foster, A. K. (2011). Promise fulfilled? An EBSCO Discovery Service usability study. *Journal of Web Librarianship, 5*(3), 179–198. doi:10.1080/19322909.2011.597590

ADDITIONAL READING

Brabazon, T. (2002). *Digital hemlock: Internet education and the poisoning of teaching*. Sydney, Australia: UNSW Press.

Brabazon, T. (2007). *The university of Google: Education in the (post) information age*. Hampshire, UK: Ashgate.

Carr, N. G. (2010). *The shallows: What the Internet is doing to our brains*. New York: W.W. Norton.

Jeanneney, J. N. (2007). *Google and the myth of universal knowledge: A view from Europe*. Chicago, IL: University of Chicago Press.

Pariser, E. (2011). *The filter bubble: What the Internet is hiding from you*. New York, NY: Penguin Press.

Sundar, S. S., Knobloch-Westerwick, S., & Hastall, M. R. (2007). News cues: Information scent and cognitive heuristics. *Journal of the American Society for Information Science and Technology, 58*(3), 366–378. doi:10.1002/asi.20511

KEY TERMS AND DEFINITIONS

Discourse Community/Communities of Discourse: A community of individuals who have common language conventions, research methodologies, and types of evidence.

Facets: Subject specific descriptors that link content within an information system

Federated Search: The ability to search multiple databases at a time and display results in a single interface

Information Scent: Proximate information (title, abstract, and metadata) that help users decide whether or not to pursue the distal source (full text).

Normalize: The merging and de-duplicating of metadata from different subject level databases

WebScale Discovery Service: Discovery tools that use a massive single centralized and preaggregated index of articles, books, multimedia and other content

ENDNOTES

[1]   SFX OpenURL link resolver is a registered trademark of Ex Libris Ltd

[2]   EBSCO Discovery Service is owned by EBSCO Publishing Industries

[3]   Primo is a registered trademark of Ex Libris Ltd

[4]   Summons is owned by ProQuest LLC

[5]   EBSCOhost is a registered trademark of EBSCO Publishing Industries

[6]   ProQuest® is a registered trademark of Pro-Quest LLC

Chapter 39
The Web–Scale Discovery Environment and Changing Library Services and Processes

Peter Webster
Saint Mary's University, Canada

ABSTRACT

Discovery services, such as Serials Solutions Summon, OCLC Local WorldCat, ExLibris Primo, and EBSCO Discovery Service, are built around increasingly comprehensive indexes to books, articles, and other materials. Discovery services and the global bodies of metadata which support them make up an online discovery environment. This chapter outlines the current makeup of this metadata environment. It explores the possibilities and the challenges this environment presents for libraries. It addresses discovery services' central role in reducing the fragmentation of library resources. The chapter looks at the areas where discovery services can provide access to expanded and more comprehensive collections of materials. It discusses discovery services' role as central hubs, seamlessly linking library access and delivery services together. The chapter addresses opportunities for more centralized and cooperative management of library metadata, and the need for less reliance on duplication of MARC format metadata.

DOI: 10.4018/978-1-4666-1821-3.ch039

INTRODUCTION

Much of the recent discussion about library discovery services has focused on major improvements to the library search experience and on integrating local library collection search with online journal article search. But discovery search is about more than just improved new interfaces for existing library catlogs and resources. Discovery services are built around large, often Internet wide, centralized indexes to material, which use powerful and standardized Solr and Lucene Web indexing technology. So the term "Web-scale discovery" has come into use to describe them.

A new Web-scale library environment has emerged, which is centered on global index repositories and shared access to pools of metadata, rather than on independent management of local library collections.

This chapter will explore the current makeup of this discovery environment, which elements are most fully developed, and the areas where it is still becoming coherent.

Discovery services provide the tools for using the new environment to bring together a wide variety of materials from diverse sources. They encourage searching of regional, or global library collections in addition to local collections. They challenge libraries to offer greatly expanded bodies of materials integrated with new and better services. Discovery services accessing the new metadata environment offer an alternative to repetitive management of MARC and other metadata in individual local library databases.

Discovery services are one element of an information environment where libraries are being transformed from being providers of limited local collections to being partners in providing comprehensive search and access to global collections through centralized management of library materials' metadata.

This chapter will consider the potential benefits of the discovery environment. It will examine how well these benefits are being realized so far, and will consider several of the challenges to be resolved before the Web-scale discovery environment is fully developed. It will look at the important opportunity libraries now have to set the direction of this new environment as it grows and evolves.

BACKGROUND

The Current Shape of the Discovery Environment

Jason Vaughan recently provided one of the most complete summaries of the key discovery products in his Library Technology Reports issue "Web-scale Discovery Services". Vaughan (2011) provides a valuable look at the resources currently covered by the different discovery products. It is estimated that there are half a billion individual documents indexed by both Serials Solutions and OCLC. Though Vaughan still largely focuses on implementation concerns related to the specific discovery products, he provides a good overview of the discovery environment.

The elements currently central to the discovery environment are well known. They include the following pools of metadata.

Link resolver services which offer a common pool of metadata on the e-journal holdings of online article databases. This common data pool is approaching comprehensiveness, though it is very far from authoritative.

Metadata describing e-journal articles: This body of metadata encompasses information from the large inventory databases of serials subscription agents, and table of contents services like Ingenta and the British Library Document Supply Centre. Sources like the Database of Open Access Journals DOAJ also contribute to this pool. Discovery services' e-journal indexes are being built upon this pool of e-journal metadata. Serials Solutions and EBSCO have had something of an advantage in building these indexes, since EBSCO is a major serials subscription agent, while Serials Solutions has access to the large serials information resources of its affiliated companies - Proquest, Bowker and Ulrich's.

Library union catalogs of MARC records: OCLC's WorldCat has been the foundation upon which most central discovery indexes have been built. Other discovery service providers, particularly the library system companies, such as Ex Libris are also developing repositories of bibliographic metadata independently, since they have access to large amounts of metadata through their client libraries. The major e-book publishers and aggregators such as Baker and Taylor, EBL and Ebsco are also making available catalogs of MARC records describing their fast growing collections.

Metadata from Online archival collections and institutional repositories: The OAIster database is a freely available central index to digital materials held by thousands of institution repositories and digital archives around the world. It is the most prominent of many repositories harvesting metadata using the Open Archives Initiative Protocol for Metadata Harvesting (OAI-PMH) standard.

The body of material which is currently accessible from discovery services is quite large. However, there are also many other important pools of metadata which are not yet fully accounted for in discovery services. We must consider the following additional bodies of materials when considering the full scope of the Web-scale discovery environment.

Online book sellers epitomized by Amazon have offered highly developed centralized Web accessible indexes to their products. The book trade uses the standard Onix format to maintain metadata, as well as standardized processes for metadata created by publishers to be incorporated by online bookstores.

Many important institutional and subject specific repositories wait to be centrally indexed and centrally searched. Hirwade and Bherwani (2009, pp. 140-265) surveyed 60 OAI-PMH indexing re-

positories around the world. This network indexes over 6000 source archives, while OAIster currently holds information from only 1600 organizations. Though Dspace is the most common repository software used, PKP and CDSware are also common. The Dublin Core, Metadata Encoding and Transmission Standard (METS), and Metadata Object Description Schema (MODS) description standards are most common, but Encoded Archival Description (EAD), Darwin Core for biological science materials, and ONIX from the publishing industry, are also prevalent.

There remain many institutional repositories which have not been made available to OAI-PMH harvesting. There are also large bodies of digital material that are not in digital repositories, but have been added to library catalogs, which are for the most part, not harvested by OAI-PMH centralized harvesters.

E-book collections are developing rapidly. These are available from companies like Taylor and Francis, Ingram, EBL and Overdrive, as well as from book sellers like Amazon or Barnes and Noble. There are several million commercial e-books currently available. Through innovative patron directed purchasing programs, libraries can allow their users to select from very large numbers of e-books not yet purchased by the library. Most recently vendors are developing rental or pay per use options for e-books as well (Rapp, 2011).

There are also large collections of public domain e-books such as the more than 1.6 million e-books available from the Open Content Alliance. Many individual and regional library consortiums are scanning materials and making them available in e-book form. In the Canadian province of Ontario, the Scholars Portal consortium of academic libraries has made 350,000 Canadian e-books available.

As of February 2010, Google Books is reported to have scanned over 12 million books (Oder, 2010b). The HathiTrust consortium of academic libraries offers over 4.5 million e-books (Christenson, 2010). There are many issues still to be worked out before full text of all this material becomes widely available - still, a very large body of searchable material is already available.

Early in 2011, it was announced that the full text of the HathiTrust materials will be searchable via the Serial Solutions Summon discovery service (Quint, 2011). The catalog records from these resources have been searchable in discovery services for some time, particularly from OCLC. But including full text book search in discovery, and seamlessly integrating with links to library holdings, fundamentally changes what discovery can achieve.

Government documents were formerly an important part of library collections. Through library deposit programs, governments relied on libraries to manage and provide access. Government agencies are now publishing directly to the World Wide Web in most cases. Huge bodies of important materials are available.

Some of this material is already available in discovery services. But a great deal of material still remains to be added. Overall the potential body of metadata is very great.

Discovering the Body of Freely Available Online Materials

Several libraries have investigated the benefits of adding very large accounts of freely available Web accessible material to library catalogs. Acquiring or creating MARC records for various online collections and batch loading these into the local library catalog has become a common means of expanding library collections. These new catalog records then become part of the normal process of indexed library holdings by whatever discovery service a library is using. There continues to be debate about the value of adding large batches of MARC records for electronic materials to library catalogs. URLs for such materials can change frequently and must be kept up to date, so the ongoing maintenance effort for such materials can be substantial. But many libraries are finding that

merging selected, relevant, quality, online material with available library collections is a useful addition and well used by library users.

Meagher and Brown (2010) have described the University of Denver's work adding over 180,000 internet records to their catalog. The records came from 20 agencies including the American Museum of Natural History, the Academy of Natural Science, the Brookings Institute, the United Nations and the World Bank.

Many government publishing agencies including the Canadian Government and U.S. Government Printing Office, as well as state and provincial agencies provide freely available MARC records for their print and publicly available online publications. A number of libraries have created MARC records of their books scanned by the Google Books project. The University of Michigan's Mbooks project made available in 2006 was an early example (Kelleher Powell, 2008) There are a host of other subject specific or location specific online resources where high quality materials are freely available. Many organizations offering online content, including museums, think tanks, and large nonprofit organizations, make MARC records of their materials freely available. In cases where MARC records are not available, it is often possible to access metadata via an application programming interface (API).

Other means can be devised for harvesting metadata from such resources and making it available as part of library search. Terry Reese (2009) has reported on work by Oregon State University and others to convert OAI harvested metadata from online archives to MARC for inclusion in library catalogs. The process for using XML as a tool for doing this is well established. A number of libraries are automating processes for moving records into their discovery services. Several of the discovery services provide APIs for this purpose. In other cases libraries are simply adding useful online resources into their library catalogs one record at a time.

The Rationale for Discovery Services and the Web-Scale Discovery Environment

In 2006, Lorcan Dempsey discussed the need to aggregate library service and resources in new ways in the article "The Library Catalog in the New Discovery Environment: Some Thoughts". Dempsey noted that large Web presences like Google and Amazon "provide a unified discovery experience and work hard to reduce transaction costs." They allow the user to search many resources at once, and they seamlessly link resources together behind the scenes so that users will not have to (Dempsey, 2006, para. 8). He also states that "they aggregate demand by mobilizing large network audiences for resources." In contrast "the fragmentation of library resources reduces the gravitational pull of any one resource on the network" (Dempsey, 2006, para. 8).

Dempsey highlighted the importance of libraries aggregating supply of their services as well as aggregating demand by developing shared global services (Dempsey, 2006, para. 9). Dempsey states that "much of what I have said supports consolidation into general network level services. The unified discovery experience of the search engines, Amazon, iTunes, and so on, has been a very powerful example. And we will certainly see greater consolidation of discovery opportunities in the library space" (Dempsey, 2006, para. 29). In this brief but influential article, Dempsey outlined many of the concerns which have directed the development of the discovery environment since then. These include the problems of bringing together "article level" and book level information in a common search (Dempsey, 2006, para. 32). They also include the need to tie discovery services closely with the "apparatus of delivery"(Dempsey, 2006, para. 37). Dempsey's thinking has influenced OCLC's development decisions with its WorldCat Local discovery tools.

In the last few years, several prominent library agencies have produced reports which explore the shortcomings of library cataloging, and the future of library search. The United States Library of Congress has produced several key studies including *The Changing Nature of the Catalog and its Integration with Other Discovery Tools* (Calhoun, 2006), and *On the Record: A Report of the Library of Congress Working Group on the Future of Bibliographic Control*" (On the Record, 2008). The Research Information Network (RIN) in the U.K produced *Creating Catalogues: Bibliographic Records in the Networked World* (Creating Catalogues, 2009).

OCLC has published a number of reports related to the future of the library catalog. These have included *Environmental Scan: Pattern Recognition* (De Rosa 2003), *Online Catalogs: What users want and librarians want*" (Calhoun, 2009). The National Library of Australia produced the report *Rethinking the Catalogue* (Dellit & Fitch, 2007).

These reports broadly support the view expressed by Calhoun (2006, p. 5) that "The catalog is in decline, its processes and structures are unsustainable, and change needs to be swift". They have recognized that library resources in general – and the library catalog in particular - are declining in importance to information seekers. The fragmented nature of library resources is one of a number of important issues which need to be addressed. They also recognize that traditional cataloging practices do not meet the growing challenges of the networked information world.

Martin Flynn (2010) published a very useful commentary on the results of four of these important reports; RIN in the U.K., the National Library of Australia, the U.S. Library of Congress, and OCLC. Flynn notes that "these reports produced by some of the leading organizations in the library sector have a remarkable degree of unanimity in their conclusions" (Flynn, 2010, p. 3). He states that

There are convincing arguments in the reports for abandoning local catalogs in favor of unified catalogs based on sectoral, national, trans-

national or subject parameters which would contain significant enhancements, have greater visibility in popular networked environments and eliminate inefficient duplication of effort" (Flynn, 2010, p. 3).

Different agencies have come to many similar conclusions. They have a common understanding that a library search must be able to accommodate multiple kinds of material, therefore multiple kinds of metadata. They agree that much more centralized metadata management is needed, to broaden user access, aggregate the supply of information for users, and aggregate user demand, as Lorcan Dempsey put it, to achieve economies of scale, and reduce costly duplication of effort.

There is broad agreement that a single place to search for and access materials is the user experience that library users are looking for. In a networked world they will move to other resources if their needs are not being met. The fragmentation of library resources needs to be addressed. More unified discovery services which are well integrated with available materials are more than a desirable service enhancement; they are a survival strategy for libraries. Directly and indirectly, the discovery services which have been developed in the last few years have been created to address these key concerns.

FOCUS ON THE ISSUES

As the discovery environment develops there are a number of important issues which must be addressed. It is often useful to consider the purposes for which discovery services were created, and the benefits they can potentially provide, in looking at the present circumstances.

Comprehensiveness

The completeness of the various bodies of metadata which make up the discovery environment is one of the issues where libraries need to remain focused. The full benefits of the discovery environment will not be realized until discovery services can be relied upon to search complete and comprehensive bodies of materials, all books, all journal articles, etc. This is no small task. In some cases, there are materials for which good metadata is not yet readily available. This is particularly true for journal articles and for archival collections of many types, both produced by libraries and by other agencies.

Link resolver metadata is perhaps the closest to being comprehensive, though the inaccuracies and shortcomings of this information are well known. The complete body of bibliographic metadata is also close to being comprehensive. However, often the problem is not that complete metadata does not exist. The problem is that the metadata is held by many agencies in different repositories, and is not commonly accessible and shared between them. Therefore, no single discovery service or individual library has complete and comprehensive access to the whole body of material.

Fragmentation

Reducing the fragmentation of library resources has been one of the critical issues libraries have sought to address with discovery services. Unfortunately, so far the current array of discovery search products has not really addressed this issue. Although each individual discovery tool centralizes access to a group of resources, they are not committed to unified access to metadata; in fact, they are increasingly dividing and segregating it, perpetuating fragmentation of library resources.

There are several reasons for this fragmentation, but one important cause is the highly competitive, proprietary economic model of the for profit e-materials, e-journal and library services marketplace.

Discovery service companies are not primarily focused on building common bodies of metadata; instead, they are working to keep their indexing content separate and distinct from the content of others. Each service has developed separate index repositories. They are not working to develop the common bodies of metadata; instead they are competitive commercial products. Each company's effort is to make their own index repository as comprehensive as possible, while preventing their competitors from being so.

In the e-serials market place, the pursuit of exclusive rights to key content is a growing issue. There was considerable concern recently as EBSCO announced exclusive contracts for serial content (Oder, 2010a). In the discovery services market, companies like EBSCO, Ex Libris and Serials Solutions are pursuing the same goal of exclusivity, offering unique materials and withholding their indexing from others. EBSCO has recently removed its indexing content from the Ex Libris Primo discovery index (Breeding, 2011, para. 3).

In a recent editorial, Marshal Breeding (2011) joined a growing call by libraries to make access to metadata more open. He noted that libraries "have an interest in the highest level of cooperation between the publishers and providers from which they license content and the organizations that offer discovery systems. Marshal Breeding" (2011). Comprehensive bodies of metadata, the open exchange of basic indexing information and a fair market for metadata, should be major goals for every library and every library organization. Such an open market is in the interests of all e-content vendors, discovery services, and libraries. If users can easily discover the complete worldwide bodies of materials, this must draw more users to the library discovery tools, and drive increasing traffic to sources of content. Aggregating library resources to provide users with a unified search has been one of the key rationales for libraries moving to Web-scale discovery services. This unified search is essential to libraries success. By extension, it is essential to the success of publishers and content vendors who have libraries as their primary customers.

This is another area where link resolver knowledge bases are something of a model. Link resolver companies basically offer a common body of metadata. They compete on many attributes including software features and service, but they do not compete by offering differing bodies of metadata. It is not in the interests of any content publisher or vendor to withhold metadata about their content from any link resolver company.

Cooperative and Centralized Metadata Management

The discovery environment also presents the library community with some large and important challenges in working together more cooperatively. The ability of Web-scale discovery indexes to provide common access to many different library catalogs is one of its key benefits. The indexes make it simpler than ever before to provide library union catalogs, for communities, regions, or groups of libraries. All that is needed is for each library in an area to allow their catalog to be harvested and indexed by a central repository. Many of the common cataloging practices and procedures which are required for a shared integrated library system are no longer needed.

We can see from the availability and use of OCLC WorldCat searching that it is now possible for users to discover all the libraries in their community from a single WorldCat search, without the libraries even having any formal consortium or union cataloging arrangements. All that is necessary is for each library to contribute their metadata to OCLC.

For libraries using other discovery services there is considerably more work, harvesting holdings from other libraries. Still, discovery services make this a far easier process than ever before and a feature that library users are coming to expect. So the emergence of discovery tools should be a new impetus for libraries to provide merged search services for all the libraries, at least in their local area. One of the purposes for the development of discovery services has been the need to reduce the costly and unsustainable redundancy of individual libraries parsing the same metadata records into thousands of individual library catalogs, by sharing and centralized management of metadata.

Library catalogers have made a long standing effort to have metadata produced as close to the creation of the content as possible, and then to avoid recreating or duplicating metadata as much as possible. Discovery services should be able to further develop this effort. Metadata should be created and made accessible by the publishers of works and then disseminated to centralized index repositories from there.

As in several other areas, journal article link resolvers provide something of a model for the level of centralization that can be achieved. Link Resolver companies take on the ongoing responsibility of maintaining up-to-date title list metadata. Each library simply must mark the database packages they subscribe to in order to have a complete database of all the serials they have available and their dates of coverage. Metadata about what journals and article coverage are available from each database product are maintained in one central repository. All the many hundreds of libraries which make use of Ex Libris SFX or Ebsco Link Manager, or Serials Solutions 360 benefit from the same repository of information. Metadata is provided once, directly by the publishers or content vendors. Individual libraries do not make duplicate copies of the metadata, or move it from place to place. They can access the metadata from a central location. They have tools to add to and amend their metadata as needed, but the work is not duplicated many times by many different libraries. The metadata does not need to be stored in a library integrated management system (ILS) or any other repository.

Anyone who has worked with a link resolver is aware that in practice libraries devote a great deal of time to correcting and supplementing the metadata in their link resolver knowledgebase. Data inaccuracies and errors are a major ongoing problem. A close partnership between a library and its link resolver company, and shared responsibility for data management, is needed to ensure link resolver effectiveness. Full descriptive metadata is more complex than link resolver title list information, but discovery services have the potential to provide the same shared centralized management.

Link between Discovery and Access (Finding and Getting)

Using a discovery service involves searching an index of materials from different sources. One is not searching the source database, such as a library's management system, or an e-content database, directly. The ability to search global indexes is of limited value without tools to rapidly connect the user with the discovered materials. Discovery services have been devised to move beyond former, poorly integrated, search services which only locate available resources, but then leave searchers on their own to pursue access.

The OCLC 2009 report *Online Catalogs: What Users and Librarians Want* pointed out that "The end user's experience of the delivery of wanted items is as important if not more important than his or her discovery experience" (Calhoun, 2009, p. *v*.). The link between discovery, the finding of existing materials, getting access and obtaining available material is critical to the success of discovery services.

Identifying what online full text is available, what local hardcopy is available, and where to find it, are critical steps. It is also critical to provide additional steps to pursue material which is not immediately available. The success of a discovery tool often hinges on how well it interconnects with other services. Since users do not ultimately distinguish any element of the supply chain, the success of the whole process hinges on how directly and seamlessly users are linked to needed information. Call numbers, shelf availability, in addition to hold and check out information are critical for hard copy materials. Direct and reliable linking to full text is critical for online materials. So interconnection with the link resolving, document delivery and citation management software is another measure of a discovery services' success. The ease of known copy look up and filtering to just immediately accessible content are key tests. More than simply a search tool, a discovery service must be a reliable central interface which seamlessly connects to a large range of information, access, and delivery services.

More Shared Metadata Management: Less Reliance on Loading MARC

The movement of batches of MARC records and the creation of MARC records from other formats has become one of the main ways new materials are entering discovery indexes. In this way, libraries become conduits for many online resources, and form partnerships with the organizations, such as museums and subject specific archives, which produce them. These are exciting developments, but so far libraries are expanding the reach of discovery services through a great deal of duplicated work carried out by each individual library.

One of the expected advantages of Web-scale discovery is the efficient shared management of metadata. Centralized management of metadata holds the promise to reduce the costly redundancy of parsing the same metadata records into thousands of library catalogs. For journal article and link resolver metadata, discovery tools do provide central management. But for bibliographic materials, including the latest collections of e-books, a wide array of freely available electronic collections, consortium holdings, and many other collections, the repetitive loading of MARC records is the default method. Local MARC records are input into the ILS of each local library. In a separate process, records are then harvested by the discovery index. It is common for each library to duplicate metadata in several library systems. Many libraries pay link resolver

companies to provide MARC records of their serial holdings which are batch loaded into their ILS systems, only to be reported to or harvested by their discovery service, on a regular basis. Dublin Core metadata in institutional repositories can be centrally harvested by OUI repositories, and moved directly into discovery services from there, as is done with OAIster. But records are often converted to MARC and then batch loaded to library catalogs as well.

Each of the major discovery services are providing centralized access to records of the institutional digital repositories which report to OAIster or they are indexing many individual institutional repositories. Large collections of metadata from major e-book companies are also now being added to their central repositories of MARC records. This is in addition to article level metadata for tens of thousands of electronic journals.

However, there are many collections of local importance to individual libraries which are not yet indexed by discovery services. Even if needed collections are indexed in a discovery service, individual libraries often have no way of directing their users to particular subsets of e-books, or repository collections which they have access to. They also often have no way of linking to the collections of other nearby libraries.

So, although a great deal of material is already available in central repositories, there are many situations in which a library must input additional collections, most often by creating MARC records. Both Ex Libris and OCLC are developing ILS systems which allow libraries to interact with shared repositories of MARC and other metadata, as well as managing a local database. This will be an important direction for the future. But at present, there are too few tools for libraries to interact directly with metadata records stored in central repositories, or for merging different bodies of metadata into common indexes. The current discovery process still relies too heavily on the movement of MARC records by individual libraries.

Solutions and Recommendations

The metadata used in discovery services is maintained by different providers; it comes from different sources, and was created for different purposes. The separate bodies of metadata, which describe books, journal articles, and online repository materials, are not cohesively centralized in one repository. We have tended to think in terms of individual products. Each of these bodies of metadata provides valuable descriptive information about materials that libraries steward. In order to make discovery services more effective, libraries should be approaching these bodies of metadata as a common unified environment. We can then seek comprehensiveness of coverage, quality, uniformity, standardization, and other issues in a systematic way.

A great deal of metadata both currently in discovery services and not yet added, is readily accessible and often freely available. What is still needed is the additional effort to make this material uniformly and commonly available. This does not mean that there should not be multiple discovery service providers, or that there should be no cost for metadata. But libraries must be seeking fair and common access, so that discovery services move toward comprehensiveness, and that both for-profit, open source, and not-for- profit discovery services can develop on an equal footing. Libraries must be working collectively to encourage publishers and content suppliers, large and small, to make their metadata available. They must be working actively to encourage companies to make their index information available. Libraries must also be working to ensure that metadata created by libraries are shared.

The proprietary, highly competitive information services marketplace is not new. The competitive market helped to foster much of the innovation that is beneficial to libraries. Libraries accept the need for companies to seek to differentiate themselves from their competitors. Libraries must be encouraging vendors to seek economic models that allow them to be fairly compensated for their products without fragmenting and restricting the information environment.

Libraries should be looking for better tools for managing metadata in an efficient and shared manner. Libraries should be looking to discovery services to intake records in other formats as well as MARC. They should also be expecting discovery services to directly collect and manage metadata from a far wider array of content sources than they currently do. Libraries and discovery service providers should be working rapidly toward duplicating the success of link resolvers in providing openness, uniformity, and interoperability from their vendors.

When libraries have come to consensus in the past, they have had considerable success advocating for improved services. Examples include the COUNTER code of practice for database statistics, wide availability of application programming interfaces (API), and the development of standards for materials handling and transmission such as NCIP and Open URL.

From the library side, what is now needed is more emphasis on sharing batches of records to build on already strong processes for sharing individual MARC records. If one library is creating MARC records from an online archive, these should be widely shared, rather than repeatedly recreated. This approach will be needed until discovery services provide better central management tools, and until ILS systems that provide for shared centralized management of metadata, come into common use. Libraries should also be extending their partnerships with online content providers, such as museums, archives and other memory institutions to encourage them to provide MARC and other metadata, and to work with discovery service providers to have content from these sources indexed directly.

Discovery services must be seen as central hubs that are linked to by other systems and services, including supplemental information, enriched content, cover images, reviews and readers' comments, as well as document delivery and pay per use services. Libraries must be looking to their discovery service, and other service providers for improved connections between their services. Libraries themselves must work to develop all their services to work seamlessly together.

FUTURE RESEARCH DIRECTIONS

There are many interesting areas of research which will have an impact on the development of the discovery environment. The following are just a few examples.

More work is needed on processes for making make metadata more interoperable. A good deal of work has been done on the manual conversion of batches of metadata from archival formats to MARC and vice versa. The use of XML as a common vehicle for conversion is promising. More work on automating the processes of conversion is still needed.

Standardized methods for sharing and merging of Solr/Lucene Indexes are well documented in the computing literature. But more work is needed on the combining and exchange of Lucene indexes in library applications.

HathiTrust and Google Books have been available as independent tools for full text searching for materials in library collections. But integrating this full text searching into library search tools has just begun to be explored. Many other library collections are being scanned. The potential for incorporating full text searching into discovery is great and needs to be explored.

The possibilities for sharing metadata between libraries, and between libraries and online content producers are great. More exploration is needed of both formal and informal arrangements for sharing batches of metadata.

CONCLUSION

Discovery Search services connect each library and its local collection with a worldwide information environment. In this new environment libraries can offer shared and aggregated access to greatly expanded book, journal and online materials collections. The discovery environment is fundamentally changing how libraries think about their collections. It is also profoundly changing many library processes and services.

Discovery services have provided libraries with great advances in search and access. But there is much further to go to extend the range of content they index, and move toward more comprehensive coverage. Discovery services also have some way to go before libraries can achieve the full benefits of centralized management of metadata, where index information is stored globally and accessed as needed without being duplicated, reloaded or reformatted.

Libraries must do everything possible to ensure that the emerging discovery environment is made up of commonly available pools of metadata, fairly shared between all service providers, so that full information is available to all libraries regardless of which discovery services they choose to use.

The considerable potential of the Web-scale discovery environment will be most quickly realized if libraries come to a clear set of priorities for the environment and improvements needed for discovery services, and then to act collectively on those priorities.

REFERENCES

Breeding, M. (2011). Building comprehensive resource discovery platforms. *ALA Techsource*. Retrieved November 30, 2011, from http://www. alatechsource.org/blog/2011/03/building-comprehensive-resource-discovery-platforms.html

Calhoun, K. (2006). *The changing nature of the catalog and its integration with other discovery tools. Library of Congress*. Ithaca, NY: Cornell University Press.

Calhoun, K., Cantrell, J., Gallagher, P., Hawk, J., & Cellentaini, D. (2009). *Online catalogs: What users and librarians want: A report to the OCLC membership*. Retrieved November 30, 2011, from http://www.oclc.org/us/en/reports/onlinecatalogs/fullreport.pdf

Christenson, H. (2010). HathiTrust: A research library at web scale. *LRTS, 55*(2), 93–101.

De Rosa, C., Dempsey, L., & Wilson, A. (2003). *OCLC environmental scan pattern recognition: A report to the OCLC membership*. Retrieved December 8, 2011from http://www.oclc.org/us/en/reports/escan/

Dellit, A., & Fitch, K. (2007). *Rethinking the catalogue*. Paper presented at the Innovative Ideas Forum, National Library of Australia, Canberra, New South Wales.

Dempsey, L. (2006). The library catalogue in the new discovery environment: Some thoughts. *Ariadne, 48*. Retrieved December 8, 2011 from http://www.ariadne.ac.uk/issue48/dempsey/

Flynn, M. (2010). *From dominance to decline? The future of bibliographic discovery, access and delivery*. Paper presented at the World Library and Information Congress: 76th IFLA General Conference and Assembly, Gothenburg, Sweden. Retrieved December 8, 2011 from http://www.ifla.org/files/hq/papers/ifla76/71-flynn-en.pdf

Hadro, J. (2010). Patron-driven ebook model simmers as Ebrary joins ranks. *Library Journal.com*. Retrieved from http://www.libraryjournal.com/lj/communityacademiclibraries/887246-419/patron-driven_ebook_model_simmers_as.html.csp

Hirwade, M. A., & Bherwani, M. T. (2009). Facilitating searches in multiple bibliographical databases: Metadata harvesting service providers. *Liber Quarterly, 19*(2), 140-265. Retrieved December 8, 2011 from http://liber.library.uu.nl/publish/issues/2009-2/index.html?000474

Jackson, M. (2008). Using metadata to discover the buried treasure in Google book search. *Journal of Library Administration, 47*(1-2), 165–173. doi:10.1080/01930820802111108

Kelleher Powell, C. (2008). OPAC integration in the era of mass digitization: The MBooks experience. *Library Hi Tech, 26*(1), 24–32. doi:10.1108/07378830810857771

Meagher, E., & Brown, C. (2008). Turned loose in the OPAC: URL selection, addition, and management process. *Library Hi Tech, 28*(3), 360–376. doi:10.1108/07378831011076620

Oder, N. (2010). Google book search by the numbers: Affidavit says 12 million books digitized, $2.5 million a year spent on metadata. *Library Journal.com*. Retrieved November 30, 2011, from http://www.libraryjournal.com/article/CA6718929.html

Oder, N. (2011). Popular magazines from Time, Inc., Forbes, others, involved. *Library Journal.com*. Retrieved November 30, 2011, from www.libraryjournal.com/article/CA6716017.html

On the record: Report of the Library of Congress working group on the future of bibliographic Control. (2008).Washington, DC: Library of Congress. Retrieved December 8, 2011, from http://www.loc.gov/bibliographic-future/news/lcwg-ontherecord-jan08-final.pdf

Quint, B. (2011, April 7). HathiTrust discovers Serials Solutions' Summon and vice versa. *Information Today, Newsbreaks*. Retrieved on April 7, 2011, from http://newsbreaks.infotoday.com/NewsBreaks/HathiTrust-Discovers-Serials-Solutions-Summon-and-Vice-Versa-74825.asp

Rapp, D. (2011). Ingram announces new library ebook access model and audiobook shift. *Library Journal.com*. Retrieved November 30, 2011, from http://www.libraryjournal.com/lj/home/890315-264/ingram_announces_new_library_ebook.html.csp

Reese, T. (2009). Automated metadata harvesting: Low-barrier MARC record generation from OAI-PMH repository stores using MarcEdit. *Library Resources & Technical Services, 53*(2), 121–132.

Research Information Network (RIN). (2009). *Creating catalogues: Bibliographic records in a networked world: A Research Information Network report*. Retrieved August 10, 2010, from http://www.rin.ac.uk/files/Creating_catalogues_REPORT_June09.pdf

Vaughan, J. (2011). Web Scale Discovery Services. *Library Technology Reports, 47*(1).

ADDITIONAL READING

Banusha, D. (2010). Cooperative cataloging at the intersection of tradition and transformation: Possible futures for the program for cooperative cataloging. *Cataloging & Classification Quarterly, 48*(2-3), 247–257. doi:10.1080/01639370903535742

Bowen, J. (2008). Metadata to support next-generation library resource discovery: Lessons from the eXtensible catalog, phase 1. *Information Technology & Libraries, 27*(2), 5–19.

Breeding, M. (2010). The state of the art in library discovery 2010. *Computers in Libraries, 30*(1), 31–35.

Breeding, M. (2011). The special challenges for national libraries. *Computers in Libraries, 31*(6), 21–25.

Cathro, W., & Collier, S. (2010). *Developing trove: The policy and technical challenges*. Staff paper, National Library of Australia. Retrieved November 30, 2011, from http://www.vala.org.au/vala2010/papers2010/VALA2010_127_Cathro_Final.pdf

Colati, G. C., Crowe, K. M., & Meagher, E. S. (2009). Better, faster, stronger: Integrating archives processing and technical services. *Library Resources & Technical Services, 53*(4), 261–270.

Connaway, L. S., Dickey, T. J., & Radford, M. L. (2011). "If it is too inconvenient I'm not going after it:" Convenience as a critical factor in information-seeking behaviors. *Library & Information Science Research, 33*(3), 179–190. doi:10.1016/j.lisr.2010.12.002

Dempsey, L. (2008). Reconfiguring the library systems environment. *portal . Libraries & the Academy, 8*(2), 111–120. doi:10.1353/pla.2008.0016

Frick, R. L. (2011). Enabling noncompetitive collaboration at web scale. *Educause Review, 46*(3). Retrieved August 10, 2010, from http://www.educause.edu/EDUCAUSE+Review/EDUCAUSEReviewMagazineVolume46/EnablingNoncompetitiveCollabor/228661

Gartner, R. (2008). Metadata for digital libraries: State of the art and future directions. *JISC Technology and Standards Watch*. Bristol, UK: JISC. Retrieved November 30, 2011, from http://www.jisc.ac.uk/media/documents/techwatch/tsw_0801pdf.pdf

Godby, C. J. (2010). From records to streams: Merging library and publisher metadata. In D. I. Hillman & M. Lauruhn (Eds.), *DC-2010: Proceedings of the International Conference on Dublin Core and Metadata Applications*, (pp. 138-149). Dublin Core Metadata Initiative. Retrieved from http://dcpapers.dublincore.org/ojs/pubs/article/view/1033

Hanson, C., Hessel, H., Barneson, J., Boudewyns, D., Fransen, J., & Friedman-Shedlov, L. … Traill, S. (2009). *Discoverability phase 1 final report.* University of Minnesota Libraries. Retrieved from http://purl.umn.edu/48258

Hanson, C., Hessel, H., Barneson, J., Boudewyns, D., Fransen, J., & Friedman-Shedlov, L. … Traill, S. (2011). *Discoverability phase 2 final report.* University of Minnesota Libraries. Retrieved from http://purl.umn.edu/99734

JISC. (2009). *JISC user behaviour observational study: User behaviour in resource discovery: Final report.* Retrieved November 30, 2011, from http://www.jisc.ac.uk/media/documents/publications/programme/2010/ubirdfinalreport.pdf

Klein, M. B. (2010). Hacking Summon. *Code{4} lib, 11.* Retrieved December 9th, 2011, from http://journal.code4lib.org/articles/3655

Lavoie, B., & Dempsey, L. (2010). Rethinking the boundaries of the academic library. *NextSpace, 17,* 16–17.

Losoff, B. (2009). Electronic scientific data and literature aggregation: A review for librarians. *Issues in Science and Technology Librarianship, 59.* Retrieved December 9, 2011 from http://www.istl.org/09-fall/refereed2.html

Meagher, E., & Brown, C. (2008). Cataloging free e-resources: Is it worth the investment? *Interlending and Document Supply, 36*(2), 135–141. doi:doi:10.1108/02641610810897845

Pal, J. K. (2010). Metadata initiatives and emerging technologies to improve resource discovery. *Annals of Library and Information Studies, 57*(1), 44–53.

Pearson, S., & Biedenbach, A. (2011). Making content discoverable through collaboration. *Against the Grain, 23*(1), 22.

Reese, T. Jr, & Banerjee, K. (2007). *Building digital libraries.* New York, NY: Neal-Schuman.

Sellberg, R. (2010). Cooperative cataloging in a post-OPAC world. *Cataloging & Classification Quarterly, 48*(2-3), 237–246. doi:10.1080/01639370903535734

Silipigni Connaway, L., & Dickey, T. J. (2010). *The digital information seeker: Report of the findings from selected OCLC, RIN, and JISC user behaviour projects.* OCLC. Retrieved December 9, 2011, from http://www.jisc.ac.uk/media/documents/publications/reports/2010/digitalinformationseekerreport.pdf

Timms, K. (2009). New partnerships for old sibling rivals: The development of integrated access systems for the holdings of archives, libraries, and museums. *Archivaria, 68,* 67–95.

Wakimoto, J. C. (2009). Scope of the library catalog in times of transition. *Cataloging & Classification Quarterly, 47*(5), 409–426. doi:10.1080/01639370902865371

Ward, J., Mofjeld, P., & Shadle, S. (2008). WorldCat Local at the University of Washington Libraries. *Library Technology Reports, 44*(6).

Webster, P. (2008). *Managing electronic resources: New and changing roles for libraries.* Oxford, UK: Chandos Publishing.

KEY TERMS AND DEFINITIONS

Aggregated Library Resources: These are Web-scale library resource which bring together and centralize management of resources formerly offered by individual libraries. OCLC WorldCat and OAIster are examples of aggregated library services.

Applications Programming Interface (API): API's are Web accessible interfaces made available by many online databases and other systems. Requests are sent to the internet address of a particular system's API, in a standardized format, often a simple text string. An online system responds by returning a particular set of data elements, often in XML format, or by performing a requested action such as a database search and returning the results. API's allow automated systems to interact and share information with one another over the internet. They are an important tool for creating customized software to interact with online systems and services.

Discovery Environment: All of the metadata and software components which go into providing library discovery services. This includes the bodies of metadata for different kinds of materials and different metadata formats. Book type materials in MARC format are included. Also included are serials database title and coverage metadata in link resolver knowledge bases, and serials article metadata, from basic table of contents information to enhanced indexing. Additional metadata comes from diverse online archival sources, often in Dublin Core metadata format, but also in a host of other formats.

Extensible Markup Language (XML): Is a standardized format for coding text based information to be transported over the internet. XML is a markup language like HTML. Where HTML is a standard means of tagging text based information to be formatted and displayed by Web browsers, XML is a standard means of tagging text to be transported over the internet and processed by computer systems. XML provide a common format for exchanging data between online systems.

Fragmentation: The many individual resources which libraries offer are often described as silos. The complete body of journal literature, for example, cannot be searched from any one source, it is fragmented, and hundreds of individual sources must be searched to fully explore it.

Integrated Library Systems (ILS): Are also known as Library Management Systems (LMS). These server based online software applications provide each library with a database for library holdings stored in MARC bibliographic format. They integrate this database with library lending services, materials acquisitions functions, as well

as cataloging and metadata management functions. Major vendors of ILS systems include SirsiDynix, Innovative Interfaces, and ExLibris Group.

Lucene: Is high speed Web indexing software, which can be used to create online text search applications. Lucene is one of the software projects of the Apache Open Software Foundation, which is responsible for popular Apache and Tomcat Web server software. This software is open source, freely available to all users, developed and maintained by its user community. More information about Lucene can be found at http://lucene.apache.org/.

Metadata: Is descriptive information about any collection of objects. Many different metadata systems provide standardized elements to describe different materials, from paper publications, to digital media files, to plant and animal species. Libraries commonly describe books and other materials using the MARC metadata standard, with elements such as author, title, and publisher. Digital archival collections are often described using the Dublin Core metadata standard, using simple elements such as title, creator, resource type, which can be applied to a broad range of materials from print documents, to images to audio files.

Online Archival Collections: A growing array of formerly paper materials is now freely available on the Web. These materials may be accessible via search engine, but often they are relatively hidden in individual repositories or databases. Government agencies, museums and archives, as well as many special topic organizations have such collections available. The formats of such material include MARC, many types of archival metadata, geographical materials, and growing bodies of scientific data.

Open Archives Initiative: Protocol for Metadata Harvesting (OAI PMH), is a standardized method for digital archive servers to exchange information about their holdings. OAI metadata is transferred over the internet in XML format. Most institutional repositories using popular software such as Dspace, ContentDM, or Fedora, are OAI PMH compliant. An OAI PMH compliant server offers its metadata, on request in a standardized form. Any OAI PMH harvesting server can contact one or many OAI PMH compliant servers, and request standardized metadata describing the digital resources held by that server. An OAI PMH harvester creates a searchable index to the holdings of many different institutional repositories. The digital resources themselves are not centrally stored. A metadata description of each digital item is stored in a common index with URL links to the digital items themselves, stored in many different repository servers. An OAI harvester thus provides a Web searchable interface to digital content stored in many locations. More information about OAI PMH can be found at http://www.openarchives.org/

Open URL: Is a standardized method for passing detailed information about documents between systems over the internet. An open URL request is simple an http: style Web address which contains descriptive information such as author, title, journal title, volume, issue and page number, in a standard form. Library link resolver software works by locating information about a particular journal article, and passing this information as an open URL request to the appropriate e-journal database. The e-journal database responds by returning the full text of the requested article. More information about the Open URL standard can be found at http://www.niso.org/apps/group_public/project/details.php?project_id=82 .

Seamless Linking: A search of any library discovery service involves interacting with a number of different online systems. Search results are retrieved from the discovery index. Location information is then retrieved from a separate local library catalog system. Serials availability and access information is provided by a link resolver system. Supplemental material such as cover images is often supplied by a separate system. If materials are not available, the user is often passed to a document deliver or pay per use system. A search and access transaction can involve interaction with more than a dozen separate online services, potentially from different providers. To be most useful, all of this interaction must be invisible (seamless) to the library user, who should see the search process as one continuous, uninterrupted transaction.

Shared Metadata Management: Current library practice is for each individual library to manage its own database(s) of metadata. Much of this information is shared and duplicated, but it is ultimately managed in separate library systems. Some library system and discovery system vendors are moving to systems which allow metadata to be stored in a common database. Libraries share the work of maintaining and adding to this repository, and link local amending information as needed. But they do not maintain complete separate copies of most metadata.

Solr: is open source, text indexing and full text search software which is built on top of Lucene indexing functionality. Solr offers important search functionality like relevancy ranging, and search result faceting. It is very fast and powerful, and can be used on any size of database. This software is maintained by the Apache Open Software foundation. More information about Solr can be found at http://lucene.apache.org/solr/ .

Web-Scale: Refers to Web accessible resources which offer services to everyone on the World Wide Web and seek to address the comprehensive needs of a global audience. Though the challenges of offering Web-scale resources are great, the benefits of economy of scale are also high, with many contributors sharing the work and cost of developing and maintaining central resources. Amazon and Wikipedia are examples of Web-scale resources.

Chapter 40
The Trial of Searching for Musical Works Using Resource Discovery Tools

Anita Breckbill
University of Nebraska-Lincoln, USA

ABSTRACT

It is not possible to perform a complete or efficient search for musical works using current resource discovery tools. Using examples from Encore, EBSCO Discovery Service™¹, Primo®², and WorldCat®³ Local, the author shows the limitations inherent in using the latest generation of discovery tools for music searches. Music searching is problematic in these tools for three reasons: inadequate use of authority information, displays which do not use uniform titles, and systems that do not recognize that results appearing in a single field have a higher relevancy. They cannot fulfill a basic catalog objective of finding and displaying what works a library has by a composer. Music librarians must band together to tell vendors the needs for music searching. Librarians must be vigilant to present catalogs and discovery tools in the most useful way to patrons.

INTRODUCTION

The recent advent of discovery tools as an adjunct to classic catalogs in libraries is an attempt to simplify and broaden the search process. In providing a search experience that is more Google-like, the goal is to be all things for all people. But, just as the laws of Newtonian physics fail at the edges of time and space, so the discovery tool fails at the edges of searching. Music is one such edge.

A straightforward catalog objective, suggested by Ralph Papakhian in the article "Music Librarianship at the Turn of the Century: Cataloging" (Papakhian, 2000, p. 587), is to be able to find

DOI: 10.4018/978-1-4666-1821-3.ch040

and clearly display what works a library has by a composer. Are discovery tools able to fulfill this objective? Using four discovery tools, Encore, EBSCO Discovery Service™ (EDS), Primo®, and WorldCat® Local, the present chapter explores why music is challenging to search and what kind of searching will make the process most efficient and complete. It finds that discovery tool interfaces are not able to find and clearly display what works a library has by a composer.

Discovery tools make searching and finding music problematic for three major reasons:

1. An incomplete or nonexistent use of the authority file
2. A display by the title published on the item, not by the uniform title
3. Search results that connect information from different fields when the patron needed the information to appear in one field

BACKGROUND

For the present topic it is important to understand both the theoretical basis for the uniform title and, more pragmatically, how the uniform title has been used by music cataloging librarians over time. Sherry Vellucci and Richard Smiraglia address these areas in a number of publications. Vellucci has focused on relationships in music catalogs and on the future of music metadata, though she was writing before the advent of discovery tools. In 2001 she noted:

Research has shown that because of the complex nature of music and the documents in which music is represented, there is a high proportion of relatedness among musical bibliographic entities, and the bibliographic families created by this relatedness are complex. Authority control is needed, therefore, in order to help users understand the relationships among musical works and their many instantiations and to facilitate *the discovery and retrieval of related items and works. (Vellucci, 2001, p. 551)*

Vellucci continues "With the traditional success factors now mitigating against successful authority control in the global metadata environment, the collective information organization communities must work together to develop new methods to ensure the success of authority control" [(Vellucci, 2001, p. 553)].

Smiraglia taught a generation of music catalogers with his book, the most recent edition of which is entitled *Describing music materials: a manual for descriptive cataloging of printed and recorded music, music videos, and archival music collections: for use with AACR2 and APPM* (1997). A recent book, *Bibliographic control of music, 1897-2000* (2006) gives a bibliographic overview and an essay on more than a century of music cataloging. Earlier Smiraglia (1989) noted that "The history of music cataloging is essentially the story of the search for solutions to the problems of identifying, collocating and distinguishing musical works" (Smiraglia, 1989, p.98). In this article, he counted the multiple manifestations of musical works in a sample (over 80% had multiple manifestations) and the variation of titles in the sample. "Works with distinctive titles averaged 15 manifestations that carried 3 different titles proper. Works with generic titles averaged 35 manifestations on which 11 different titles proper were found" (Smiraglia, 1989, p.106). He concluded that "an authority-controlled collocating device is necessary for musical works" (Smiraglia, 1989, p.97).

In an article in *Notes* entitled "Music Librarianship at the Turn of the Century: Cataloging," Ralph Papakhian wrote, "the music library community has been unsuccessful in communicating the difficulties or requirements of music cataloging relative to books or periodicals" (Papakhian, 2000, p. 584). Looking to the future, he said "I predict that this new Babel of metadatabases and ILSs will eventually lead to a renewed call for simplification and standardization" (Papakhian, 2000, p. 588)

Music librarians have begun to write about music searching in relation to discovery tools only in the past year. An optimistic view of the subject is written by an information technology director and a music cataloger in "Moving to the patron's beat." Majors and Mantz found that "Discovery tools are particularly well suited to searching for music materials"… "Library users are often looking for just enough information rather than conducting an exhaustive research exercise" (Majors & Mantz, 2011, p. 275). Their findings contradict this author's thesis, that discovery tools are not well-suited to searching for music materials, partially because the patrons they envision are casual users rather than serious researchers.

Finally, a subgroup of the Music Library Association's (MLA) Emerging Technologies Committee published "Music Discovery Requirements: Draft". They note that "As libraries and vendors develop and implement … changes, the specialized discovery needs arising from music materials are often lost in the shuffle" (MLA Emerging Technologies Committee, 2011, p. 3). The document is a detailed field-by-field guide to aid vendors and librarians who are developing or implementing discovery tools. The chair of the subgroup, Nara Newcomer, also wrote an article to help vendors. Newcomer looks at local catalog content, local and public domain repository content and article-level content and makes suggestions on indexing and displaying the data, noting that "indexing and display of catalog data can make or break a discovery tool's success in locating music materials" (Newcomer, 2011, p. 135).

SEARCHING FOR MUSIC

In music more than any other discipline, the title is not the title. That is, the title printed on the piece of music or on the recording playlist may not be the title under which the work was originally published, or may differ from how the work is known in an English-speaking country. Establishing a uniform title for a work bridges this gap, so that a piece of music, in whatever format, edition, medium of performance, or language, can reliably be found under one title in the catalog, in addition to the one that is actually on the item being cataloged. In the catalog the uniform title unites different manifestations of the work and is more important for identifying the work than is the title on the piece.

Searching for music in catalogs differs from searching for music using discovery tools, as will be demonstrated below.

Searching for Music Using Catalogs

When searching for musical works by composer using most catalogs, a patron encounters an alphabetical list that includes uniform titles of the composer's works and cross-references to uniform titles. It is clear to the patron that they are searching information that has been carefully organized and systematized.

Part of a music cataloger's job is to create the authority records for uniform titles. The resulting cross-references in the catalog enable users to find the piece they are seeking. As an example, if a patron is looking for a recording of Haydn's *Surprise Symphony*, he may search "Haydn, Joseph" as an author, then select "Surprise" in the resulting alphabetical list of titles. In many catalogs a patron would see a cross reference to the uniform title in the search results list that would look something like this: *Surprise symphony -- See Haydn Joseph 1732-1809 Symphonies, H. I, 94, G major*. Clicking on the uniform title will bring up a list of the items (scores, recordings, etc.) that contain this symphony. Vellucci (1997) found that 73.9% of a sample of 329 scores from the Sibley Music Library at the Eastman School of Music had a cross-reference for a name/title entry (p. 79). It is clear that the cross-referencing system is important in music catalogs.

The uniform title and cross-reference conventions facilitate comprehensive search results in first- and second-generation online library catalogs. In the University of Nebraska—Lincoln (UNL) catalog, which uses Innovative Interfaces software, a patron searching for a specific piece of music searches by the author and is shown an alphabetical list of uniform titles and of cross references which lead to proper uniform titles. A music patron who does not know the uniform title for the desired work can be led to the correct place in the catalog by cross references or by simply seeing what appears in the list. If a patron is looking for a Mozart piano sonata, he sees the other uniform titles under "Sonatas" and notes that the uniform title will be under "Sonatas" (plural), and that one needs a medium of performance (piano), a Köchel number (Mozart's thematic index number) and a key to go to the right place in the catalog. What the patron sees in the list leads him in the right direction. Up until now, music patrons have learned to depend on the alphabetical layout of uniform titles in their results to guide them to the correct uniform title for a work.

Another publication reality that tends to put music on the edge of the bibliographic universe is that recordings and scores are often published with multiple works per item. The sample of music scores at the Sibley Music Library mentioned above showed that 42.9% of the sample "does not fall into the common structure of one work: one item" (Vellucci, 1997, p. 46). Recordings even more frequently have multiple tracks, each of which is a distinct manifestation of a work and needs its own entry in the catalog. For successful searching, the title on the recording is usually not as important as the name-title added entries on each bibliographic record. Consider, for example, a CD entitled simply "Choral music." The title is neither very meaningful nor memorable. The name-title added entries of the twelve individual works on the recording are what make the bibliographic record useful.

Searching for Music Using Discovery Tools

With discovery tools, the search is by keyword and the display is by title on the item, not by uniform title. The search and display mechanism throws the music patron into a results list that appears to be in no particular order, leaving the patron to pick through the random-looking results. Organization of the results list in a discovery tool is by relevancy rankings. The patron does not usually know how these relevancy rankings are determined, or whether they take into account what is really relevant for music. According to a recent OCLC report the "state of relevance ranking in library catalogs does not appear to meet the expectations of today's end users. It is somewhat surprising that more has not been accomplished". (Calhoun, K., Cantrell, J., Gallagher, P., Hawk, H., & Cellentani, D., 2009, p. 54). Truly relevant results are often not the first listed in a search for a musical work, and each of the results must be individually studied to see if it contains the piece sought.

There are many kinds of music searches and there are many kinds of results, but let us consider a typical example: a search for a violin sonata by Gabriel Pierné. At UNL, a patron who is searching in the catalog for this piece might search by the author "Pierné, Gabriel," then jump or scroll to "Sonata," where he would quickly see two uniform titles neatly laid out on the screen: "Sonatas, violin, piano, op. 36" for the original and "Sonatas, violin, piano, op. 36; arr." for an arrangement. Note that the uniform title includes the word "Sonatas" in the plural, because Pierné wrote more than one sonata. Our patron would find one recording and one score of the original composition and three recordings of the arrangement for flute and piano of Pierné's sonata. These are the complete holdings at the UNL Libraries for this work.

By contrast, if the patron does a search in UNL's discovery catalog, Encore, for "Pierné sonata" (a common way to format the search in this instance), he will retrieve bibliographic records for seven items. Three are for recordings of the work, which are the arrangements for flute and piano that we previously found in the catalog, and four are results for items that include works by Pierné and sonatas written by other people, but do not include a Pierné sonata. The patron would retrieve neither the violin/piano score nor the recording for the original work, because it happens that the word "Sonata" does not appear in either of the records. The word appears in French, *sonate*, but that does not help the patron. It is likely that the patron would mistakenly but justifiably assume that the library did not own the original violin/piano score or recording of the Pierné sonata. This is worth pondering. Neither of the two items one would most expect to retrieve with a basic Google-like search actually appears.

The Pierné search illustrates a basic difference between catalogs and discovery tools—the objective of finding everything versus that of finding merely something. In an academic setting, the goal is to find all the scores and sound recordings of a particular work. When a student has some experience in searching, a catalog can often fill that goal, and students can choose what they need from a complete overview of what is available. Discovery tools are meant to be what their name implies—a way to discover things that will be of use. They are a monument to serendipity. A search using a discovery tool, though, might retrieve only a partial list of what is available for a specific musical work, and it might retrieve a massive list of items, only a few of which are pertinent to the patron. It may be that finding one recording of a work or one score is good enough for the patron and all that is needed. Unfortunately, the sample patron looking for a Pierné sonata using the discovery tool left the library feeling that he had done an adequate search, but he did not actually find the score or recording of the violin sonata that the library owned.

How Discovery Tools Treat Music Searches

The discovery tool interface makes searching and finding music problematic for three major reasons:

1. An incomplete or nonexistent use of the authority file
2. A display by the title published on the item, not by the uniform title
3. Search results that connect information from different fields when the patron wanted them in the same fields (e.g. searching "Mozart Divertimento" could pull up a sound recording containing a concerto by Mozart and a divertimento by another composer but not a divertimento by Mozart.)

Vendors address the problems in music searching in a variety of ways. Vendors try to be as flexible as possible in the implementation process of their tools, so each library has multiple decisions to make. Any individual discovery tool may be different, both in appearance and in searching capability, from one institution to another. Since it is not feasible to look at every manifestation of every discovery tool, the following section will discuss how the three major problems are addressed in discovery tools as they are implemented at four different institutions.

1. Encore—through Innovative Interfaces (as seen at the University of Nebraska—Lincoln: http://libraries.unl.edu/)
2. Primo®—through Ex Libris (as seen at Northwestern University: http://www.library.northwestern.edu/)
3. EBSCO Discovery Service™ (EDS)--through EBSCO (as seen at Indiana University: http://www.libraries.iub.edu/index.php) Note: a password is needed to enter fully into the utility.

Table 1. Use of authority information in discovery tools

Encore	EDS	Primo	WorldCat Local
Presents uniform title information as an "established term"	N/A	Shows other "versions" of work using uniform title	N/A

4. WorldCat® Local—through OCLC (as used at the University of Southern California in fall 2011)

Authorities

The search in a discovery tool is by keyword only. How can information from an authority file work in this environment? If information from the authority file is retrieved by a keyword search, how would it be presented to the patrons? Does it make sense to do so? The four evaluated discovery tool vendors have recognized the problems and have chosen not to provide information to the patron directly from the authority file. Several of them have approaches which allow them to use authority or uniform title information, with mixed results. Table 1 summarizes the approach to information in the authority file used by each of the discovery tools, and examples and discussion follow. The examples will be of two varieties: a distinctive title search, Stravinsky's *Rite of Spring*, and a generic title search, a Mozart piano sonata.

Encore

Encore presents an "established term" that can sometimes, but not always, lead the patron through a uniform title to a list of hits. If a patron does a search on "rite of spring," for example, he will find at the bottom left side of the results page a link called "Established term" as illustrated below.

Established Terms

♦Stravinsky, Igor, 1882-1971. Vesna sviashchennaia.

Encore arrived at this term by using information from the authority file that leads from the title "Rite of spring" to the uniform title "Vesna sviashchennaia." Clicking on the link will lead the patron to a complete list of items that contain Stravinsky's *Rite of Spring*.

Unfortunately the ability of the system to recognize an appropriate "established term" is spotty, leading to a music searching tool that is both incomplete and inadequate while giving the impression of completeness. As an example, a generic title search, "Mozart piano sonata," generates a display of three "established terms" as shown:

Established Terms

Mozart, Wolfgang Amadeus, 1756-1791. Allegro und minuet, piano, K. 498a, Bb major

Mozart, Wolfgang Amadeus, 1756-1791. Allegros, piano, K. 400, Bb major

Mozart, Wolfgang Amadeus, 1756-1791. Sonatas, violin, piano, K. 304, E minor

One can understand how the computer arrived at these established terms. One of the cross-references in each authority record used the three terms of our search, "Mozart piano sonata," and the established terms in the list are from the first three authority records that the computer found alphabetically. But none of these "established terms" is for a work that is actually a piano sonata. The usefulness of established terms in this instance is minimal and will probably confuse the patron instead of leading him to find what he is seeking.

This feature in Encore is more likely to work with distinctively-named musical works or with nicknamed or translated titles of musical works like Stravinsky's *Rite of Spring*. It is less likely to work with musical works that have generic titles.

EBSCO Discovery Services (EDS)

When patrons perform searches in EDS™, no information at all is culled from authority records. A representative from EBSCO reports that "The Custom Catalog cannot load MARC authority files. It will attempt to load them as actual bibliographic records. Authority Files are available through the EBSCO*host*®⁴ interface; however, they are not available through *EBSCO Discovery Service™* interface at this time." (A. Chute, personal communication, June 16, 2011)

Primo

Primo® approaches the problem of authority control differently than either Encore or EDS™. When a search in Primo® returns a result with a uniform title (MARC 240 field), it will find other similar uniform titles and display the direction: "Click to view [number] versions." The computer will take the first item in the MARC record (from the 100/240 fields) and find others in the system that match. For example, when a patron looking for a score or recording of Stravinsky's *Rite of Spring* searches "rite of spring" in Primo®, the second result is a score, which displays as below.

[Petrushka; arr.]. Petrushka ; and, The rite of spring: for piano four hands or two pianos / Igor Stravinsky.

Igor Stravinsky 1882-1971.

Click here to view 5 versions

This is a potentially helpful way to pull uniform titles together. In this case, though, the five versions correspond to the uniform title *Petrushka*, the first musical work in the score, not to the *Rite of Spring*, which is what the patron searched. The patron must go to the third item on the browsing screen to find other versions of the *Rite of Spring*. Here eleven versions are listed. If the patron wanted to listen to one of these recordings, or all eleven, the search would be considered successful. But the patron might think that he did a complete search. If we search the corresponding catalog at Northwestern University, we find that Northwestern owns thirty-four versions of the *Rite of Spring*, not just eleven, and twenty-three of the results are recordings. The eleven versions listed in this Primo® search are only the items that have the *Rite of Spring* as the first item on the recording or score. Primo® is apparently not searching an authority file. Using a keyword search, it finds a hit with the first uniform title in the record (a 240 field), and then finds other matching 240 fields.⁵

Doing the generic title search in Primo® for "Mozart piano sonata" yields 4515 results, and the second item on the list links to two versions of the collective uniform title for Mozart, "Piano music. Selections." The sixth item links to six versions of the uniform title for Mozart, "Sonatas, piano. Selections." For this result, though, one has to click through to the catalog to find out what information Primo® is using for the link. For some reason the uniform title is not displayed, even when clicking on the detailed Primo® record, and the patron is left to puzzle out the relationships between the "versions."

The patron was able to find some Mozart piano sonatas on the first page of the result list with this search, but to be more complete the patron would have to look at each of the 4515 hits or find other ways to narrow his search. Even then the search might not be complete. There is nothing that leads the patron to a list of Mozart piano sonatas or gives a clue about how to find such a list, which a well-run catalog would do.

WorldCat Local

WorldCat® Local, like EDS™, has no special way of mining the authority file or the uniform titles even in the "Editions and formats" display.

Of the four discovery tools tested, two of them, Encore and Primo®, make an attempt to use authority information. Encore pulls information from the authority file and Primo® pulls information from the uniform title (240 field only) in such a way that will be occasionally helpful for

Table 2. Display of item from brief display in four discovery tools

Discovery Tool	A *Rite of Spring* Citation from Brief Display
Encore	Firebird [electronic resource] ; The rite of spring / Stravinsky Stravinsky, Igor, 1882-1971 Zhar-ptitsa. Suite (1919)
EDS	**Firebird** [electronic resource] ; The **rite** of **spring** / Stravinsky. By: Stravinsky, Igor. [Hong Kong]: Naxos Music Library, [2004] 01/01/2004 Language: No linguistic content Subjects: Suites (Orchestra); Ballets
Primo	**Firebird [electronic resource] ; The rite of spring / Stravinsky.** **Igor Stravinsky 1882-1971.** **Hong Kong: Naxos Music Library 2004** *Online access* Click here to view 5 versions
WorldCat Local	Firebird [electronic resource] ; The rite of spring Stravinsky, Igor, 1882-1971. Zhar-ptitsa. Suite (1919)

the patron. The inability of these discovery tools to use the authority information consistently, however, means that the tools cannot be efficient or dependable when doing a basic search for a musical work. Given the importance of authorities to music searching, it seems to be a significant oversight not to use authority information at all, but one ponders the relative value of having a solution that sometimes works, as do Encore and Primo®, versus not entering the ring at all, as do EDS™ and WorldCat® Local.

Displays

Returning to the simple catalog objective noted at the beginning of this chapter—to be able to find and clearly display what works a library has by a composer—we have seen that discovery tools with their keyword search cannot consistently find all manifestations of a given work by a composer. How do they do with display?

The first thing to note is that most catalogs are able to display a list of works by a composer when a patron does a composer search. Such a listing by composer is not possible using a keyword search, because keyword searches pull information from any part of the cataloged record. The result cannot be limited to a specific name in an author field.

Discovery tools therefore fail the first test—clearly displaying the works by a composer.

Given that discovery tools cannot fulfill the first need of display for musical works, what do they display? When searching for a musical work, the most pertinent information for display is composer/uniform title.[6] Do discovery tools display the composer/uniform title information in a useful way? Note that options for display in each discovery tool are somewhat flexible. A representative from Primo® says the system affords "100% control of what metadata is harvested and how it is displayed" (G. Gosselin, personal communication, June 2011). In this section we will discuss the displays used in the specific version of the discovery tool at the universities we have chosen.

Table 2 shows a display for the same item in each of our discovery tool examples. Each display is a hit for a recording retrieved when "rite of spring" is searched. In Encore, Primo® and WorldCat® Local the item appeared on the first screen in the browsing display. In EDS™ the item appeared later on the list.

The brief displays are similar in the four discovery tools, but not identical. There are elements of these displays that are good or neutral:

1. The title on the piece is included.
2. All four displays list the composer.
3. Two of the discovery tools, Encore and WorldCat® Local, display the uniform title (from the 240 field).
4. Other information is included in EDS™ (publisher and subject information) and in Primo® (a link to other versions).

There are also elements of these displays that do not work well for music.

1. The composer/uniform title is the most important information to display for music items. Only two discovery tools display the uniform title. In each case, the uniform title is for the first work in the item, the *Firebird Suite* (the uniform title is Zhar-ptifsa. Suite (1919)), not for the work the patron sought, the *Rite of Spring* (the uniform title is Vesna svi͡a͡shchennai͡a͡).
2. The five other versions displayed in Primo® are other versions of the first work on the item, the *Firebird Suite*, not the work the patron sought, the *Rite of Spring*.
3. The composer displayed comes from the main entry or 100 field. If there were more composers represented on this item, the other composers would not be listed in any of these four discovery tools.

A chapter like this does not permit space to comment on all the possible permutations of a display, but there is one glaring fault in all of the displays. Going back to Papakhian's (2000) objective of finding and clearly displaying the works a library has by a composer, one can see that for an item with multiple works, there would need to be multiple entries. For the CD "Choral works" mentioned earlier, there would need to be 12 entries in the discovery tool as there are in a catalog; one for each work on the CD. For this Stravinsky item, two entries in the discovery tool would be needed, one for the *Firebird Suite* (using

its uniform title) and one for the *Rite of Spring* (using its uniform title). Having only one entry, and a display that shows only the first work of the item, requires the patron to do the hard work of picking through the results.

Music patrons need to be able to see uniform titles and name/title added entries in the browsing displays and the more detailed displays. Ideally these would be linked to enable the patron to go to other records with the same musical work. None of the four systems fulfills this need fully, although Encore, EDS™, and WorldCat® Local do have linked added entries in the detailed displays. Encore currently does not link to the 240 field, but this may be temporary.

Search Terms in Same Field

Usually in a music search the patron would like the terms he searches to appear in the same field[7] in the results list (that is, the 700 |t, or the 100/240 treated as one field). But keyword searching pulls results from the whole record, not individual fields. Could vendors use relevancy rankings to help, raising items in the ranking if the terms searched appear in the same field? Then, in a search for "Brahms Quartets," the top items would actually contain a Brahms Quartet, instead of, say, a Schubert quartet and a Brahms quintet. Such an approach to relevancy rankings would be an improvement over what happens now when searching Encore, EDS™, Primo®, and WorldCat® Local, which is a strict keyword search that pulls keywords from any field.

In sum, Encore, EDS™, Primo®, and World-Cat Local do not adequately address the three major issues that make music hard to find using discovery tools: they do not use authority information usefully or at all, they do not consistently display uniform titles and added entries, and they do not provide results that recognize the value of having the search terms appear in the same field. Searching for musical works using discovery tools is inefficient, and such a search will yield incomplete results.

What Discovery Tools do to Fill in the Gap

We have shown that the keyword searches in discovery tools are not able to give music patrons results in a form, or with a consistency, that is needed. Vendors, though, have found useful ways of limiting results lists in discovery tools--so useful that one article can say the following: "Discovery tools are particularly well suited to searching for music materials. They empower the user by providing effective tools such as facets and tags to manipulate the large, varied search results users encounter when searching for music materials" (Majors & Mantz, 2011, p. 275). This optimism, however, is only justified in cases where an institution's catalog does not display a list of uniform titles alphabetically when doing a composer search. In such cases, the difference in functionality between the catalog and the discovery tool when searching musical works is less obvious, and the music librarian will embrace a discovery tool more readily.

A patron can use facets and tags to quickly narrow search results when using a discovery tool. Four facets are especially useful for narrowing a result in a music search: author, format (scores or recordings), subject heading (often called "tag"), and publication date.

All four of the discovery tools enable limiting by these four facets and others. All use post-search limiting except WorldCat® Local which enables pre-search limiting by author and subject heading. Encore, Primo®, and EDS™ enable limiting by subject heading terms that are suggested by the system, and EDS™ enables limiting by author terms suggested by the system. Encore and Primo® show the numbers of results for some of their facets, giving the searcher more information as he continues to narrow his search. All of these options for limiting by facet are useful and efficient, and

they make the problems of searching for music in the discovery tool less conspicuous. If a patron does not need to do a complete search and is not overly concerned about missing an item, searching in a discovery tool and limiting by facets and tags can enable a patron to find something quickly.

Discovery tools can also find musical works that are indexed outside of the library catalog. As an example, UNL has a database, indexed in ContentDM, of recitals and concerts given in the School of Music. These records are indexed but not cataloged fully, and the works are not given uniform titles. Records are "harvested" from this collection and can be searched by keyword using Encore, though they do not appear in UNL's catalog. The information provided makes finding these records in Encore somewhat arbitrary and gives results that are less systematized than in the catalog, but the discovery tool does allow for searching a collection such as this.

SOLUTIONS, RECOMMENDATIONS, AND FUTURE RESEARCH DIRECTIONS

Much laudable creative thinking has gone into creating the latest discovery tools, but this work, while it sometimes helps in searching for music, is not sufficient. In the case of searching for a musical work, a functional catalog works most efficiently and completely. As library catalogs have moved from card catalog to text-based online catalog to Web catalog, each new search medium is fueled by what vendors think libraries want. Sensitivity to individual disciplines, like music, is low on the priority list. In many cases, each new utility never quite reached the level of functionality of the previous one for music searching before the next catalog came into being. Then discovery tools were created without taking into account the structure that music cataloging requires. If attention were given to the needs of patrons searching for music, music patrons could benefit from the new technology, but such attention has been only partial to this point and is generally low on a vendor's list.

It is the task of music librarians to help vendors find ways to serve them in the complicated world of music searching. Laura Snyder, music librarian at the University of Alberta, said it more provocatively: We need to "articulate what we need and why and to band together to foment rebellion" (L. Snyder, personal communication, June 14, 2011). In an individual library, the voice of the music librarian is one small voice, crying in the wilderness. Only by joining forces can music librarians establish enough clout to have an effect on how discovery tools work.

There are a few recommendations we can make to vendors of discovery tools that will improve music searching. These include:

- Use information in authority records. Continue to work to find the most helpful way to use this information. We have seen how Encore uses authority information and presents it as "established terms" and Primo® uses authority information to give access to "other versions," both with mixed results. Another approach might be to expand the results to retrieve records that contain the authorized form of the title, even if the records do not contain the variant title used in the search. Thus, users would not miss relevant results simply because they did not enter the uniform title. For example, if a user were to perform a search for "Pictures at an exhibition," the results would be preceded by the message, "Your query has been expanded with these terms: Kartinki s vystavki" (Snyder, 2010, p. 82). This approach would work more consistently with distinctive title searches than with generic title searches. More thinking needs to be done to determine what would be really useful for music patrons, or whether discovery tools can ever

deliver the authority information necessary to search for music.

- Display uniform titles together with their corresponding authors on browsing displays and in detailed displays. Link them, so that they can be used to execute a new search for other manifestations of the same work. Recognize that the author main entry and uniform title added entry (the 100 and the 240 fields) and the name-title analytical added entry (7xx 1x |t) give information equivalent in function and importance.
- Remember that information in each name/title added entry is valuable by itself distinct from other added entries. Recognize this in a patron's search, and bring pertinent items up in the relevancy rankings.
- Recognize how complicated this topic is. Use a group of music librarians as consultants.

There are also some cautions to give to library deans and directors and to those who are making the decisions to use discovery tools in our library Web sites. At this point the catalog remains the best way to search for music. Do not hide the catalog. Place it front and center on your main page. Think of a way to make clear to patrons that a search for a musical work (and, arguably, any known-item search) is best approached via the catalog.[8]

Finally, music librarians should be vigilant about how their search tools work. Make certain your catalog is working as well as it can by displaying uniform titles in an alphabetical list under the composer's name. Verify that your discovery tool is working as well as possible for music, using the list above. Find ways to lead your patrons to the catalog for music searches and provide music-specific bibliographic instruction that will teach the use of uniform titles. Talk with other music librarians and lobby for your needs with vendors. Look for allies in other fields, such as literature or law. Consider doing a music user study to help with decision-making.

CONCLUSION

Vendors claim that discovery tools are the wave of the future. They "deliver the library of the future today" (Encore, 2011); they are a "one-stop discovery and delivery solution" (ExLibris, 2011); they provide a "complete discovery solution" (EBSCO, 2011); they get "users the results they're looking for" (WorldCat Local, 2011). For the present, however, they are inadequate in searching for musical works. Until the discovery systems harvest relevant information from authorized headings, display uniform titles in search results, and recognize that results that appear in a single field have a higher relevancy, they will continue to be inefficient and to generate incomplete search results for musical works.

REFERENCES

Calhoun, K., Cantrell, J., Gallagher, P., Hawk, H., & Cellentani, D. (2009). *Online catalogs: What users and librarians want.* Dublin, OH: OCLC Online Computer Library Center, Inc. Retrieved from http://www.oclc.org/reports/onlinecatalogs/fullreport.pdf

EBSCO. (2011). *EBSCO Discovery.* Retrieved July 22, 2011 from http://www.ebscohost.com/discovery

Encore. (n.d.). *Overview.* Retrieved July 22, 2011 from http://encoreforlibraries.com/overview/

ExLibris. (2011). *ExLibris: Primo.* Retrieved July 22, 2011 from http://www.exlibrisgroup.com/

King, D. M. (2005). Catalog user search strategies in finding music materials. *Music Reference Services Quarterly, 9*(4), 1–24. doi:10.1300/J116v09n04_01

Majors, R., & Mantz, S. L. (2011). Moving to the patron's beat. *OCLC Systems & Services: International Digital Library Perspectives, 27*(4), 275–283. doi:10.1108/10650751111182588

Music Library Association Emerging Technologies Committee. Music Discovery Requirements Document Subgroup. (2011). *Music discovery requirements: Draft.* Retrieved February 21, 2012, from personal.ecu.edu/newcomern/musicdiscoveryrequirements.pdf

Newcomer, N. (2011). The detail behind Webscale: Selecting and configuring Web-scale discovery tools to meet music information retrieval needs. *Music Reference Services Quarterly, 14*(3), 131–145. doi:10.1080/10588167.2011.596098

OCLC. (2011). *OCLC: WorldCat Local.* Retrieved December 19, 2011, from http://www.oclc.org/worldcatlocal/

Papakhian, A. (2000). Cataloging: Music librarianship at the turn of the century [Special issue]. *Notes, 56*(3), 581–590.

Smiraglia, R. P. (1989). Uniform titles for music: An exercise in collocating works. *Cataloging & Classification Quarterly, 9*(3), 97–114. doi:10.1300/J104v09n03_06

Smiraglia, R. P., & Pavlovsky, T. (1997). *Describing music materials: A manual for descriptive cataloging of printed and recorded music, music videos, and archival music collections for use with AACR2 and APPM* (3rd ed. rev. and enl.). Lake Crystal, MN: Soldier Creek Press.

Smiraglia, R. P., & Young, J. B. (Eds.). (2006). *Bibliographic control of music, 1897-2000.* Lanham, MD: Scarecrow Press

Snyder, T. (2010). Music materials in a faceted catalog: Interviews with faculty and graduate students. *Music Reference Services Quarterly, 13*(3/4), 66–95. doi:10.1080/10588167.2010.528746

Vellucci, S. L. (1997). *Bibliographic relationships in music catalogs*. Lanham, MD: Scarecrow Press.

Vellucci, S. L. (2001). Music metadata and authority control in an international context. *Notes, 57*(3), 541–554. doi:10.1353/not.2001.0063

ADDITIONAL READING

Anglo-American cataloguing rules (2nd ed., 2002 rev.). (2002). Chicago, IL: American Library Association.

Bade, D. (2009). *Irresponsible librarianship: A critique of the report of the Library of Congress Working Group on the Future of Bibliographic Control and thoughts on how to proceed*. Paper presented at the 2009 Music OCLC Users' Group meeting. Retrieved from http://eprints.rclis.org/bitstream/10760/12804/1/MOUG_2009.pdf

Ballard, T. (2011). Comparison of user search behaviors with classic online catalogs and discovery platforms. *Charleston Advisor, 12*(3), 65–66. doi:10.5260/chara.12.3.65

Caldwell, A., Earnest, J., Gullickson, L., & Koth, M. (2002). *Types of compositions for use in music uniform titles: A manual for use with AACR2, Chapter 25: Final report of the MLA Working Group on Types of Compositions* (2nd updated ed., 1997; rev., 2002; with updates to 2011). Retrieved from http://www.library.yale.edu/cataloging/music/types.htm

Cary, P., & Sampsel, L. J. (2006). Information literacy instructional objectives for undergraduate music students: A project of the Music Library Association, Bibliographic Instruction Subcommittee. *Notes, 62*(3), 663–679. doi:10.1353/not.2006.0008

Dunn, J. W., Byrd, D., Notess, M., Riley, J., & Scherle, R. (2006). Variations2: Retrieving and using music in an academic setting. *Communications of the ACM, 49*(8), 53–58. doi:10.1145/1145287.1145314

Fling, R. M. (1993). Music bibliographic instruction on microcomputers: Part 1 . In Green, R. D. (Ed.), *Foundations in music bibliography* (pp. 157–163). New York, NY: Haworth Press.

Flury, R. (2010). The enemy within the gates or the future of music libraries. *Music Reference Services Quarterly, 13*(3/4), 59–65. doi:10.1080/10588167.2010.528718

IFLA Study Group on the Functional Requirements for Bibliographic Records. (1998). *Functional requirements for bibliographic records: Final report*. München, Germany: K.G. Saur.

Leazer, G. H. (1992). The effectiveness of keyword searching in the retrieval of musical works on sound recordings. *Cataloging & Classification Quarterly, 15*(3), 15–55. doi:10.1300/J104v15n03_03

Matthews, J. G. (2009). We never have to say goodbye: Finding a place for OPACS in discovery environments. *Public Services Quarterly, 5*(1), 55–58. doi:10.1080/15228950802629162

Minibayeva, N., & Dunn, J. W. (2002). A digital library data model for music. In G. Marchionini & W. Hersh (Eds.), *Proceedings of the Second ACM/IEEE-CS Joint Conference on Digital Libraries, July 14-18, 2002, Portland, Oregon* (pp. 154-155). New York, NY: ACM Press.

Music Library Association, Bibliographic Control Committee, Metadata Working Group. (2008). *Musical attributes, refinements, and recommendations for their use*. Retrieved from http://bcc.musiclibraryassoc.org/BCC-Historical/BCC2008/BCC2008MSWG2.html

Music Library Association Statement on Authority Control. (2009). *The Music Library Association statement on authority control.* Retrieved from http://bcc.musiclibraryassoc.org/PositionPapers/Authority_Control_Statement_2009.pdf

Notess, M., Riley, J., & Hemmasi, H. (2004). From abstract to virtual entities: Implementation of work-based searching in a multimedia digital library. In R. Heery & L. Lyon (Eds.), *Research and Advanced Technology for Digital Libraries: 8th European Conference,* ECDL 2004, Bath, UK, September 12-17, 2004 (pp. 157-167). Berlin, Germany: Springer.

Olson, T. A. (2007). Utility of a faceted catalog for scholarly research. *Library Hi Tech, 25*(4), 550–561. doi:10.1108/07378830710840509

Rowe, R. (2010). Web-scale discovery: A review of Summon, EBSCO Discovery Service, and WorldCat Local. *Charleston Advisor, 12*(1), 5–10. doi:10.5260/chara.12.1.5

Smiraglia, R. P. (1989). *Music cataloging: The bibliographic control of printed and recorded music in libraries.* Englewood, CO: Libraries Unlimited.

Troutman, L. (2000). User education: Music librarianship at the turn of the century [Special issue]. *Notes, 56*(3), 620–627.

Vellucci, S. L. (1990). Uniform titles as linking devices. *Cataloging & Classification Quarterly, 12*(1), 35–62. doi:10.1300/J104v12n01_03

Vellucci, S. L. (1998). Bibliographic relationships and the future of music catalogues. *Fontes Artis Musicae, 45*(3/4), 213–226.

Vellucci, S. L. (1999). Metadata for music: issues and directions. *Fontes Artis Musicae, 46*(3/4), 205–217.

Vellucci, S. L. (2000). Metadata and authority control. *Library Resources & Technical Services, 44*(1), 33–43.

Yang, S. Q., & Wagner, K. (2010). Evaluating and comparing discovery tools: How close are we towards next generation catalog? *Library Hi Tech, 28*(4), 690–709. doi:10.1108/07378831011096312

Yee, M. M. (2001). Musical works on OCLC, or, what if OCLC were actually to become a catalog? *Music Reference Services Quarterly, 8*(1), 1–26. doi:10.1300/J116v08n01_01

KEY TERMS AND DEFINITIONS

100/240: MARC fields consisting of a name (100) and a uniform title (240).

700 |t: A MARC field that is an added entry consisting of a name and a uniform title.

Authority File: A separate index of records that provide authoritative information about the form of a name or subject which governs the headings used in a library catalog.

Brief Title Display: A hit list of bibliographic records displayed in brief format for ease of browsing.

Cross Reference: A direction from one entry not used in the catalog to another that is used in the catalog.

Distinctive Title: A title for a musical work that does not consist of the name of a type of composition.

Generic Title: A title for a musical work that contains the name of one or more types of composition (e.g., sonata, symphony, quartet, etc.).

MARC Record: Machine-readable cataloging record. MARC is a standard format for bibliographic records.

Music Searching: Searching for musical works (scores, recordings, audio-visual materials) in a library's catalog or discovery tool.

Name-Title Added Entry: An entry, additional to the main entry, consisting of the name of a person and the uniform title of a work.

Uniform Title: A specific title that uniquely identifies a work and collocates similar printed and recorded works within a catalog.

ENDNOTES

[1]   EBSCO Discovery Service is owned by EBSCO Publishing Industries

[2]   Primo is a registered trademark of Ex Libris Ltd

[3]   Worldcat is a registered trademark of OCLC.

[4]   EBSCOhost is a registered trademark of EBSCO Industries Inc.

[5]   Nara Newcomer (2011) notes that "The mere presence of an autocomplete or autosuggest feature is no guarantee it is utilizing data from the LC/NAF. There are numerous sources of data for such features, and determining what is powering the feature can require direct questions to vendors in combination with hands-on testing of the feature" (p. 136). The same is true here for Primo's use of "versions." It appears not to be using information from the authority file.

[6]   The composer/uniform title information in a MARC record appears in the 100 and 240 fields and the 700 |t fields. The title actually on the piece, as entered in the 245 field, is of secondary importance.

[7]   The AACR2 decision to have author/uniform title information in two separate fields, 100/240, at the top of the record but in the same field, 700, at the bottom of the record, has caused lots of confusion. Ideally the 100/240 fields would be treated together in a link.

[8]   "Known item searching is more common in the search for music materials than in looking for a book. ... Users in the two music studies were seeking out known musical materials approximately 90% of the time" (King, 2005, p. 7).

Compilation of References

Abels, E. G., White, M. D., & Hahn, K. (1999). A user-based design process for web sites. *OCLC Systems & Services, 15*(1), 35–44. doi:10.1108/10650759910257850

Adamich, T. (2010). Metadata and the next generation library catalog: Will the catalog become a true discovery system? *Technicalities, 30*(3), 12–15.

Agosto, D. E. (2002). Bounded rationality and satisficing in young people's Web-based decision making. *Journal of the American Society for Information Science and Technology, 53*(1), 16–27. doi:10.1002/asi.10024

Alberico, R. (2002). Academic library consortia in transition. *New Directions for Higher Education,* (120): 63–72. doi:10.1002/he.90

Albert, B., Tullis, T., & Tedesco, D. (2010). *Beyond the usability lab: Conducting large-scale online user experience studies.* Amsterdam, The Netherlands: Morgan Kaufmann/Elsevier.

Allgood, T. (2010, October). *Library one search: implementing Web-scale discovery in an academic research library.* Paper presented at the Library and Information Technology National Forum, Atlanta, GA. Retrieved from http://connect.ala.org/files/90278/library_one_search_lita2010_pdf_12610.pdf

Alling, E., & Naismith, R. (2007). Protocol analysis of a federated search tool: Designing for users. *Internet Reference Services Quarterly, 12*(1/2), 195–210. doi:10.1300/J136v12n01_10

Allison, D. (2010). Information portals: The next generation catalog. *Journal of Web Librarianship, 4*(4), 375–389. doi:10.1080/19322909.2010.507972

Alshamari, M., & Mayhew, P. (2009). Technical review: Current issues of usability testing. *IETE Technical Review, 26*(6), 402–406. doi:10.4103/0256-4602.57825

American library directory, 2010-2011 (64th ed.). (2011). Medford, NJ: Information Today.

Anderson, T. D. (2010). Kickstarting creativity: Supporting the productive faces of uncertainty in information practice. *Information Research, 15*(4). Retrieved from http://www.eric.ed.gov/PDFS/EJ912765.pdf

Anderson, R. (2011). Print on the margins. *Library Journal, 136*(11), 38–39.

Angelaki, G., Caffo, R., Hagedorn-Saupe, M., & Hazan, S. (2010). ATHENA: A mechanism for harvesting Europe's museum holdings into Europeana. In J. Trant & D. Bearman (Eds.), Museums and the Web 2010: Proceedings. Toronto, Canada: Archives & Museum Informatics. Retrieved July 8, 2011, from http://www.museumsandtheweb.com/mw2010/papers/angelaki/angelaki.html

Antell, K., & Huang, J. (2008). Subject searching success: Transaction logs, patron perceptions, and implications for library instruction. *Reference and User Services Quarterly, 48*(1), 68–76.

Antelman, K., Lynema, E., & Pace, A. K. (2006). Toward a twenty-first century library catalog. *Information Technology & Libraries, 25*(3), 128–139.

ARL Scholars Portal Working Group. (2002). *ARL scholars portal working group final report.* Washington, DC: Association of Research Libraries. Retrieved from http://www.arl.org/resources/pubs/portals/report-may-2002.shtml

Armstrong, A. R. (2009). Student perceptions of federated searching vs single database searching. *RSR. Reference Services Review*, *37*(3), 291–303. doi:10.1108/00907320910982785

Arroway, P., Davenport, E., Xu, G., & Updegrove, D. (2009). *EDUCAUSE core data service fiscal year 2009 summary report*. Retrieved from http://net.educause.edu/ir/library/pdf/PUB8007.pdf

Association of Research Libraries. (2011). *LibQUAL+®*. Retrieved from http://www.libqual.org/about/about_survey

Avery, S., Ward, D., & Hinchliffe, L. J. (2007). Planning and implementing a federated searching system: An examination of the crucial roles of technical, functional, and usability testing. *Internet Reference Services Quarterly*, *12*(1), 179–194. doi:10.1300/J136v12n01_09

Axia Consulting. (2010). *RFP scoring guidelines, 15 key guidelines for scoring IT software proposals / RFP's*. Retrieved from http://www.axia-consulting.co.uk/html/rfp_scoring_guidelines.html

Back, G., & Bailey, A. (2010). Web services and widgets for library information systems. *Information Technology & Libraries*, *29*(2), 76–86.

Baer, W. (2004). Federated searching: Friend of foe? *College & Research Libraries News*, *65*(9), 518–519.

Balas, J. (2011). Online treasures: Can QR codes be used to deliver library services. *Computers in Libraries*, *31*(2), 32.

Ballard, A., & Teague-Rector, S. (2011). Building a library Web site: Strategies for success. *College & Research Libraries News*, *72*(3), 132–135.

Ballard, T. (2011). Comparison of user search behaviors with classic online catalogs and discovery platforms. *The Charleston Advisor*, *12*(3), 65–66. doi:10.5260/chara.12.3.65

Ballard, T., & Blaine, A. (2011). User search-limiting behavior in online catalogs: Comparing classic catalog use to search behavior in next-generation catalogs. *New Library World*, *112*(5/6), 261–273. doi:10.1108/03074801111136293

Baro, E. E., Onyenania, G. O., & Osaheni, O. (2010). Information seeking behaviour of undergraduate students in the humanities in three universities in Nigeria. *South African Journal of Library & Information Science*, *76*(2), 109–117.

Barrett, A. (2005). The information-seeking habits of graduate student researchers in the humanities. *Journal of Academic Librarianship*, *31*(4), 324–331. doi:10.1016/j.acalib.2005.04.005

Bates, M. (2003). *Task force recommendation 2.3 research and design review: Improving user access to library catalog and portal information, final report, version 3* (pp. 1-58). Retrieved from http://www.loc.gov/catdir/bibcontrol/2.3BatesReport6-03.doc.pdf

Bates, M. J. (1989). The design of browsing and berrypicking techniques for the online search interface. *Online Review*, *13*(5), 407–424. doi:10.1108/eb024320

Battleson, B., Booth, A., & Weintrop, J. (2001). Usability testing of an academic library website: A case study. *Journal of Academic Librarianship*, *27*(3), 188–198. doi:10.1016/S0099-1333(01)00180-X

Bawden, D., & Robinson, L. (2009). The dark side of information: Overload, anxiety and other paradoxes and pathologies. *Journal of Information Science*, *35*(2), 180–191. doi:10.1177/0165551508095781

Beale, J. (2008). The weaknesses of full-text searching. *Journal of Academic Librarianship*, *34*(5), 438–444. doi:10.1016/j.acalib.2008.06.007

Beale, R. (2007). Supporting serendipity: Using ambient intelligence to augment user exploration for data mining and web browsing. *International Journal of Human-Computer Studies*, *65*(5), 421–433. doi:10.1016/j.ijhcs.2006.11.012

Beall, J. (2009). Free books: Loading brief MARC records for open-access books in an academic library catalog. *Cataloging & Classification Quarterly*, *47*(5), 452–463. doi:10.1080/01639370902870215

Beccaria, M., & Scott, D. (2007). Fac-back-OPAC: An open source interface to your library system. *Computers in Libraries*, *27*(9), 6–56.

Becher, M., & Flug, J. (2006). Using student focus groups to inform library planning and marketing. *College & Undergraduate Libraries*, *12*(1), 1–18. doi:10.1300/J106v12n01_01

Becher, M., & Schmidt, K. (2011). Taking discovery systems for a test drive. *Journal of Web Librarianship*, *5*(3), 199–219. doi:10.1080/19322909.2011.583134

Belliston, C. J., Howland, J. L., & Roberts, B. C. (2007). Undergraduate use of federated searching: A survey of preferences and perceptions of value-added functionality. *College & Research Libraries*, *68*(6), 472–486.

Benemati, J., & Lederer, A. L. (2010). Managing the impact of rapid IT change. *Resources Management Journal*, *23*(1), 1–16. doi:10.4018/irmj.2010102601

Benjes, C., & Brown, J. F. (2000). Test, revise, retest: Usability testing and library Web sites. *Internet Reference Services Quarterly*, *5*(4), 37–54. doi:10.1300/J136v05n04_08

Bent, M., Gannon-Leary, P., & Webb, J. (2007). Information literacy in a researcher's learning life: The seven ages of research. *New Review of Information Networking*, *13*(2), 81–99. doi:10.1080/13614570801899983

Berry, M. W., & Browne, M. (2005). *Understanding search engines: Mathematical modeling and text retrieval*. Philadelphia, PA: SIAM, Society for Industrial and Applied Mathematics. doi:10.1137/1.9780898718164

Bevan, N. (2006). International standards for HCI. In Ghaoui, C. (Ed.), *Encyclopedia of human computer interaction*.

Bhatnagar, G., Dennis, S., Duque, G., Henry, S., MacEachern, M., Teasley, S., & Varnum, K. (2009). *University of Michigan Library Article Discovery Working Group final report*. Retrieved from http://www.lib.umich.edu/files/adwg/final-report.pdf

Bhatnagar, G., Dennis, S., Duque, G., Henry, S., MacEachern, M., Teasley, S., & Varnum, K. (2010). *University of Michigan library article discovery working group final report*. Retrieved from http://www.lib.umich.edu/files/adwg/final-report.pdf

Bhatnagar, G., Dennis, S., Duque, G., Henry, S., MacEachern, M., Teasley, S., & Varnum, K. (2010). *University of Michigan Library Article Discovery Working Group final report*. University of Michigan Library. 1-15. Retrieved from http://www.lib.umich.edu/files/adwg/final-report.pdf

Bhatnagar, G., Dennis, S., Duque, G., Henry, S., MacEachern, M., Teasley, S., & Varum, K. (2010). *Article discovery working group final report*. University of Michigan Library. Retrieved from http://www.lib.umich.edu/files/adwg/final-report.pdf

Biddix, J. P., Chung, C. J., & Park, H. W. (2011). Convenience or credibility? A study of college student online research behaviors. *The Internet and Higher Education*, *14*(3), 175–182. doi:10.1016/j.iheduc.2011.01.003

Björneborn, L. (2008). Serendipity dimensions and users' information behavior in the physical library interface. *Information Research*, *13*(4). Retrieved from http://InformationR.net/ir/13-4/paper370.html

Bolt, N., & Tulathimutte, T. (2010). *Remote research: Real users, real time, real research*. Brooklyn, NY: Rosenfeld Media.

Boock, M., Buck, S., Chadwell, F., Nichols, J., & Reese, T. (2009). *Discovery services task force recommendation to university librarian* (pp. 1-8). Retrieved from http://ir.library.oregonstate.edu/xmlui/bitstream/handle/1957/13817/discovery%20search%20task%20force%20recommendations%20-%20redacted%20version.pdf

Boock, M., Chadwell, F., & Reese, T. (2009). *WorldCat local task force report to LAMP* (pp. 1-15). Retrieved from http://ir.library.oregonstate.edu/xmlui/bitstream/handle/1957/11167/WorldCat%20local%20task%20force%20report_cost%20redacted.pdf;jsessionid=4C7ED6F788688C5C307B9C2601B2C4BB?sequence=1

Boock, M., Chadwell, F., & Reese, T. (2009, April 2). *WorldCat Local task force report to LAMP*. Corvallis, OR: Oregon State University. Retrieved from http://hdl.handle.net/1957/11167

Boock, M., Nichols, J., & Kristick, L. (2006). Continuing the quest for the quick search holy grail: Oregon State University Libraries' federated search implementation. *Internet Reference Services Quarterly, 11*(4), 139–153. doi:10.1300/J136v11n04_09

Borges, J. L., Irby, J. E., & Yates, D. A. (1962). *Labyrinths: Selected stories and other writings* [translated from Spanish]. New York, NY: New Directions.

Borgman, C. L. (1986). Why are online catalogs hard to use? Lessons learned from information-retrieval studies. *Journal of the American Society for Information Science American Society for Information Science, 37*(6), 387–400.

Borgman, C. L. (1996). Why are online catalogs still hard to use? *Journal of the American Society for Information Science American Society for Information Science, 47*(7), 493–503. doi:10.1002/(SICI)1097-4571(199607)47:7<493::AID-ASI3>3.0.CO;2-P

Borgman, C. L., Moghdam, D., & Corbett, P. K. (1984). *Effective online searching: A basic text.* New York, NY: M. Dekker.

Boss, R. (2002). *Library technology reports: How to plan and implement a library portal.* Chicago, IL: American Library Association.

Boss, S. C., & Nelson, M. L. (2005). Federated search tools: The next step in the quest for one-stop-shopping. *The Reference Librarian, 44*(91/92), 139–160. doi:10.1300/J120v44n91_10

Bostick, S. L. (2001). The history and development of academic library consortia in the United States: An overview. *Journal of Academic Librarianship, 27*(2), 128–130. doi:10.1016/S0099-1333(00)00185-3

Bowen, J. (2008). Metadata to support next-generation library resource discovery: Lessons from the eXtensible catalog, phase 1. *Information Technology & Libraries, 27*(2), 5–19.

Bowen, J., Briden, J., Burns, V., Lindahl, D., Reeb, B., Stowe, M., & Wilder, S. (2004). Serial failure. *Charleston Advisor, 5*(3), 48–50.

Boyd, J., Hampton, M., Morrison, P., Pugh, P., & Cervone, F. (2006). The one-box challenge: Providing a federated search that benefits the research process. *Serials Review, 32*(4), 247–254. doi:10.1016/j.serrev.2006.08.005

Boyd, J., Hampton, M., Morrison, P., Pugh, P., Cervone, F., & Scherlen, A. (2006). The one-box challenge: Providing a federated search that benefits the research process. *Serials Review, 32*(4), 247–254. doi:10.1016/j.serrev.2006.08.005

Brajnik, G., Mizzaro, S., Tasso, C., & Venuti, F. (2002). Strategic help in user interfaces for information retrieval. *Journal of the American Society for Information Science and Technology, 53*(5), 343–358. doi:10.1002/asi.10035

Braunstein, L., Cocklin, J., DeFelice, B., Hall, L., Holt, J., & Lowenstein, N. …Wheelock, C. (2009). *An evaluation of Serials Solutions Summon as a discovery service for the Dartmouth College Library.* Retrieved from http://www.dartmouth.edu/~library/admin/docs/Summon_Report.pdf

Breeding, M. (2008, June 30). *Cataloging for the new generation of library interfaces.* Presented at American Library Association Conference, ALCTS, Copy Cataloging Discussion Group, Annaheim: CA [PowerPoint slides]. Retrieved from http://www.librarytechnology.org/ltg-displaytext.pl?RC=13385

Breeding, M. (2010). State of the art in library discovery 2010. *Computers in Libraries,* January-February. Retrieved from http://www.librarytechnology.org/ltg-displaytext.pl?RC=14574

Breeding, M. (2010, May 6). *Understanding the discovery landscape: Federated search, web-scale discovery, next-generation catalog and the rest.* Presented for Library Journal webcast [PowerPoint slides] Retrieved from http://www.librarytechnology.org/ltg-displaytext.pl?RC=14728

Breeding, M. (2011). Building comprehensive resource discovery platforms. *ALA Techsource.* Retrieved November 30, 2011, from http://www.alatechsource.org/blog/2011/03/building-comprehensive-resource-discovery-platforms.html

Breeding, M. (2011). *Library technology guides: Discovery layer interfaces.* Retrieved from http://www.librarytechnology.org/discovery.pl

Breeding, M. (2011a). Building comprehensive resource discovery platforms. *Smart Libraries Newsletter, 31*(3).

Breeding, M. (2011b). *Discovery layer interfaces.* Retrieved from http://www.librarytechnology.org/discovery.pl

Breeding, M. (2004). *Next-Gen library catalogs*. New York, NY: Neil Schuman Publishers.

Breeding, M. (2005). Plotting a new course for metasearch. *Computers in Libraries, 25*(2), 27–30.

Breeding, M. (2007). Encore. *Library Technology Reports, 43*(4), 23–27.

Breeding, M. (2007). Introduction. *Library Technology Reports, 43*(4), 5–14.

Breeding, M. (2007). Primo. *Library Technology Reports, 43*(4), 28–32.

Breeding, M. (2007). The birth of a new generation of library interfaces. *Computers in Libraries, 27*(9), 34–37.

Breeding, M. (2009). Opening up library systems through web services and SOA: Hype, or reality? *Library Technology Reports, 45*(8), 1.

Breeding, M. (2010). *Next-gen library catalogs*. New York, NY: Neal-Schuman Publishers.

Breeding, M. (2010). The state of the art in library discovery 2010. *Computers in Libraries, 30*(1), 31–35.

Breeding, M. (2011). Discovering Harry Pottery barn. *Computers in Libraries, 31*(2), 21–23.

Broadbent, E. (1986). A study of humanities faculty library information seeking behavior. *Cataloging & Classification Quarterly, 6*, 23–37. doi:10.1300/J104v06n03_03

Brown, M. E. (1991). A general model of information-seeking behavior. Proceedings of the 54th ASIS Annual Meeting, 28, (pp. 9-14).

Brown, S. A., Chervany, N. L., & Reinicke, B. A. (2007). What matters when introducing new information technology. *Communications of the ACM, 50*(9), 91–96. doi:10.1145/1284621.1284625

Brubaker, N., Leach-Murray, S., & Parker, S. (2011). Shapes in the cloud: Finding the right discovery layer. *Online, 35*(2), 20–26.

Brunning, D., & Machovec, G. (2010). An interview with Nancy Dushkin, VP discovery and delivery solutions at Ex Libris, regarding Primo Central. *The Charleston Advisor, 12*(2), 58–59. doi:10.5260/chara.12.2.58

Brunning, D., & Machovec, G. (2010). An interview with Sam Brooks and Michael Gorrell on the EBSCOhost integrated search and EBSCO Discovery Service. *The Charleston Advisor, 11*(3), 62–65.

Brunning, D., & Machovec, G. (2010). Interview about Summon with Jane Burke, vice president of Serials Solutions. *The Charleston Advisor, 11*(4), 60–62.

Buchanan, G., Cunningham, S. J., Blandford, A., Rimmer, J., & Warwick, C. (2005). Information seeking by humanities scholars. *Lecture Notes in Computer Science, 3652*, 218–229. doi:10.1007/11551362_20

Burrows, T., Croker, K., Kiel, R., & Nicholls, S. (2007). *Resource discovery – Issues for the UWA Library*. Retrieved from http://www.uwa.edu.au/__data/assets/pdf_file/0011/524864/Resource_Discovery_Webversion.pdf

Calhoun, K. (2006). *The changing nature of the library catalog and its integration with other discovery systems*. Retrieved from http://www.loc.gov/catdir/calhoun-report-final.pdf

Calhoun, K., Cantrell, J., Gallagher, P., Hawk, J., & Cellentaini, D. (2009). *Online catalogs: What users and librarians want: A report to the OCLC membership*. Retrieved November 30, 2011, from http://www.oclc.org/us/en/reports/onlinecatalogs/fullreport.pdf

California Digital Library. (August 25, 2005). *SearchLight: Lights out!* Retrieved from http://www.cdlib.org/cdlinfo/2005/08/25/searchlight-lights-out/

Callicott, B. (2002). Library website user testing. *College & Undergraduate Libraries, 9*(1), 1–17. doi:10.1300/J106v09n01_01

Calvert, P., & Read, M. (2006). RFPs: A necessary evil or indispensable tool? *The Electronic Library, 24*(5), 649–661. doi:10.1108/02640470610707259

Campbell, J. D. (2000). The case for creating a scholars portal to the web: A white paper. *ARL: A Bimonthly Report on Research Library Issues and Actions from ARL, CNI, and SPARC, 211*. Retrieved from http://www.arl.org/resources/pubs/portals/case-whitepaper.shtml

Campos, J., & de Figueiredo, A. D. (2001). Searching the unsearchable: Inducing serendipitous insights. In R. Weber & C. Gresse (Eds.), *Proceedings of the Workshop Program at the Fourth International Conference on Case-Based Reasoning, ICCBR 2001, Technical Note AIC-01-003* (pp. 159-164). Washington, DC: Naval Research Laboratory, Navy Center for Applied Research in Artificial Intelligence.

Carnegie Foundation for the Advancement of Teaching. (2011). *The Carnegie classification of institutions of higher education.* Retrieved from http://classifications. carnegiefoundation.org/lookup_listings/institution.php

Carter, J. (2009). Discovery: What do you mean by that? *Information Technology & Libraries, 28*(4), 161–163.

Casden, J., Duckett, K., Sierra, T., & Ryan, J. (2009). Course views: A scalable approach to providing course-based access to library resources. *Code4Lib Journal, 6.* Retrieved from http://journal.code4lib.org/articles/1218

Case, D. O. (2008). *Looking for information: A survey of research on information seeking, needs, and behavior.* Bingley, U.K: Emerald.

Caswell, J. V., & Wynstra, J. (2007). Developing the right RFP for selecting your federated search product: Lessons learned and tips from recent experience. *Internet Reference Services Quarterly, 12*(1/2), 49–71. doi:10.1300/J136v12n01_03

Caswell, J. V., & Wynstra, J. D. (2010). Improving the search experience: Federated search and the library gateway. *Library Hi Tech, 28*(3), 391–401. doi:10.1108/07378831011076648

Caswell, J., & Wynstra, J. (2007). Developing the right RFP for selecting your federated search product: Lessons learned and tips from recent experience. *Internet Reference Services Quarterly, 12*(1-2), 49–71. doi:10.1300/J136v12n01_03

Centre for Information Behaviour and Evaluation of Research. (2008). *Information behaviour of the researcher of the future: A CIBER briefing paper.* London, UK: University College London, CIBER. Retrieved from http://www.jisc.ac.uk/media/documents/programmes/reppres/gg_final_keynote_11012008.pdf

Cervone, F. (2005). What we've learned from doing usability testing on openURL resolvers and federated search engines. *Computers in Libraries, 25*(9), 10–14.

Cervone, H. F. (2007). Working through resistance to change by using the "competing commitments model". *OCLC Systems & Services, 23*(3), 250–253. doi:10.1108/10650750710776378

Chang, A., & Davis, D. (2010). Transformation of access services in the new era. *Journal of Access Services, 7*(2), 109–120. doi:10.1080/15367961003608369

Chang, A., & Garrison, J. (2011). Textbook lending service: Providing a service students need when they need it. *College & Research Libraries News, 72*(9), 527–530.

Chapman, S. (2011). *ArticlesPlus launch survey report.* Retrieved from http://www.lib.umich.edu/usability-report/articlesplus-launch-survey

Chapman, A. (2007). Resource discovery: Catalogs, cataloging, and the user. *Library Trends, 55*(4), 917–931.

Chen, Y., Germain, C. A., & Rorissa, A. (2009). An analysis of formally published usability and Web usability definitions. *Proceedings of the American Society for Information Science and Technology, 46*(1), 1–18. doi:10.1002/meet.2009.1450460213

Chen, Y.-H., Germain, C. A., & Yang, H. (2009). An exploration into the practices of library Web usability in ARL academic libraries. *Journal of the American Society for Information Science and Technology, 60*(5), 953–968. doi:10.1002/asi.21032

Chew, C., Fransen, J., Gangl, S., Hendrickson, L., Hessel, H., Mastel, K., & Nelsen, A. … Peterson, J. (2010). *MNCAT Plus and MNCAT classic survey: Results and analysis.* Retrieved from http://purl.umn.edu/92473

Chew, C. (2010). Next generation OPACs: A cataloging viewpoint. *Cataloging & Classification Quarterly, 48*(4), 330–342. doi:10.1080/01639370903437709

Christenson, H., & Tennant, R. (2005). *Integrating information resources: Principles, technologies, and approaches* (pp. 1-16). Retrieved from http://www.cdlib.org/inside/projects/metasearch/nsdl/nsdl_report2.pdf

Christenson, H. (2010). HathiTrust: A research library at web scale. *LRTS, 55*(2), 93–101.

Clarke, E. (2006). *DICE project final report: Resource discovery tools evaluation and integration.* Retrieved from http://www.staffs.ac.uk/COSE/DICE/DICEfinal.pdf

Clarke, C. L. A., Cormack, G. V., & Tudhope, E. A. (2000). Relevance ranking for one to three term queries. *Information Processing & Management, 36*(2), 291–311. doi:10.1016/S0306-4573(99)00017-5

Clegg, H., & Montgomery, S. (2006). How to write an RFP for information products. *Information Outlook, 10*(6), 23–31.

Cobus, L., Dent, V. F., & Ondrusek, A. (2005). How twenty-eight users helped redesign an academic library Web site: A usability study. *Reference and User Services Quarterly, 44*(3), 232–246.

Cockrell, B., & Jayne, E. A. (2002). How do I find an article? Insights from a web usability study. *Journal of Academic Librarianship, 28*(3), 122–132. doi:10.1016/S0099-1333(02)00279-3

Coco, P. (2011). *RE: Teaching discovery* [LISTSERV Message]. ILI-L Discussion List - ALA Mailing List Service - American Library Association. Retrieved December 11, 2011, from http://lists.ala.org/sympa/arc/ili-l/2011-11/msg00174.html

Collins, M., & Rathemacher, A. J. (2010). Open forum: The future of library systems. *The Serials Librarian, 58*(1-4), 167–173. doi:10.1080/03615261003625703

Colorado State University Libraries. (2009). *Library/IT task force final report.* Retrieved from http://lib.colostate.edu/images/about/goals/it/LibraryTFreportFINAL.docx

Condic, K. (2008). Uncharted waters: ERM implementation in a medium-sized academic library. *Internet Reference Services Quarterly, 13*(2/3), 133–145. doi:10.1080/10875300802103643

Connaway, L. S., & Dickey, T. J. (2010). *The digital information seeker: Report of findings from selected OCLC, RIN and JISC user behaviour projects.* London, UK: HEFCE on behalf of the JISC.

Connaway, L. S. (2007). Mountains, valleys, and pathways: Serials users' needs and steps to meet them; Part I: Identifying serials users' needs: Preliminary analysis of focus group and semi-structured interviews at colleges and universities. *The Serials Librarian, 52*(1-2), 223–236. doi:10.1300/J123v52n01_18

Connaway, L. S., Dickey, T. J., & Radford, M. L. (2011). "If it is too inconvenient, I'm not going after it": Convenience as a critical factor in information-seeking behaviors. *Library & Information Science Research, 33*(3), 179–190. doi:10.1016/j.lisr.2010.12.002

Cook, C., Heath, F., & Thompson, B. MaShana, D., Kyrillidou, M., & Webster, D. (2007). *LibQUAL+®2007 survey: University of Chicago Library.* Washington, DC: Association of Research Libraries. Retrieved from http://www.lib.uchicago.edu/e/surveys/2007/UofCLibQUAL-2007DataNotebook.pdf

Coombs, K. (2009). Drupal done right: Libraries using this open source content management system pioneer new tools and services. *Library Journal, 134*(19), 30–32.

Cooper, A. (1999). *The inmates are running the asylum.* Indianapolis, IN: Sams.

Cooper, M. D. (2001). Usage pattern of a Web-based library catalog. *Journal of the American Society for Information Science and Technology, 52*(2), 137–148. doi:10.1002/1097-4571(2000)9999:9999<::AID-ASI1547>3.0.CO;2-E

Cooper, M. D., & Chen, H. (2001). Predicting the relevance of a library catalog search. *Journal of the American Society for Information Science and Technology, 52*(10), 813–827. doi:10.1002/asi.1140

Cordell, R. (2011). *Google Scholar citations now open to all* [Web log post]. Retrieved from http://chronicle.com/blogs/profhacker/google-scholar-citations-now-open-to-all/37372

Cosijn, E. E., & Bothma, T. T. (2006). Contexts of relevance for information retrieval system design. *South African Journal of Library and Information Science, 72*(1), 27–34.

Cox, C. (2007). *Federated search: Solution or setback for online library services.* Binghamton, NY: The Haworth Information Press.

Cox, C. (2007). Hitting the spot: Marketing federated searching tools to students and faculty. *The Serials Librarian, 53*(3), 147–164. doi:10.1300/J123v53n03_10

Craine, K. (2007). Managing the cycle of change. *The Information Management Journal, 41*(5), 44–50.

Crawford, W. (2011). *Open access: What you need to know now*. Chicago, IL: American Library Association.

Crawford, W., & Gorman, M. (1995). *Future libraries: Dreams, madness & reality*. Chicago, IL: American Library Association.

Croft, J. B. (2001). Changing research patterns and implications for web page design: Ranganathan revisited. *College & Undergraduate Libraries, 8*(1), 75–84. doi:10.1300/J106v08n01_06

Cromley, J. G., & Azevedo, R. (2009). Locating information within extended hypermedia. *Educational Technology Research and Development, 57*(3), 287–313. doi:10.1007/s11423-008-9106-5

Crosby, C. (2010). *Effective blogging for libraries*. New York, NY: Neal-Schuman Publishers.

Curl, M. W., & Zeoli, M. (2004). Developing a consortial shared approval plan for monographs. *Collection Building, 23*(3), 122–128. doi:10.1108/01604950410544656

Curtis, A., & Dorner, D. G. (2005). Why federated search? *Knowledge Quest: Journal of the American Association of School Librarians, 33*(3), 35–37.

Dahl, M. (2009). Evolution of library-discovery systems in the web environment. *Oregon Library Association Quarterly, 15*(1), 5–9.

Dartmouth College Library. (2009). *An evaluation of serials solutions summon as a discovery service for the Dartmouth College Library*. Retrieved December 9, 2011, from http://www.dartmouth.edu/~library/admin/docs/Summon_Report.pdf

Davis, F. D. (1989). Perceived usefulness, perceived ease of use, and user acceptance of information technology. *Management Information Systems Quarterly, 13*(3), 319–340. doi:10.2307/249008

Davis, F. D., Bagozzi, R. P., & Warshaw, P. R. (1989). User acceptance of computer technology: A comparison of two theoretical models. *Management Science, 35*(8), 982–1003. doi:10.1287/mnsc.35.8.982

De Rosa, C. (2006). *College students' perceptions of libraries and information resources: A report to the OCLC membership*. Dublin, OH: OCLC Online Computer Library Center. Retrieved from http://www.oclc.org/reports/pdfs/studentperceptions.pdf

De Rosa, C., Cantrell, J., Carlson, M., Gallagher, P., Hawk, J., Sturtz, C., et al. (2011). *Perceptions of libraries, 2010: Context and community*. Retrieved from http://www.oclc.org/reports/2010perceptions.htm

De Rosa, C., Cantrell, J., Cellentani, D., Hawk, J., Jenkins, L., & Wilson, A. (2005). *Perceptions of libraries and information resources. A report to the OCLC membership*. Dublin, OH: OCLC Online Computer Library Center. Retrieved from http://www.oclc.org/reports/pdfs/Percept_all.pdf

De Rosa, C., Cantrell, J., Hawk, J., & Wilson, A. (2006). *College students' perceptions of libraries and information resources* (pp. 1-100). Dublin, OH: OCLC Online Computer Library Center, Inc. Retrieved from http://www.oclc.org/reports/pdfs/studentperceptions.pdf

De Rosa, C., Dempsey, L., & Wilson, A. (2003). *OCLC environmental scan pattern recognition: A report to the OCLC membership*. Retrieved December 8, 2011 from http://www.oclc.org/us/en/reports/escan/

Deardorff, T., & Nance, H. (2009). WorldCat Local implementation: The impact on interlibrary loan. *Interlending & Document Supply, 37*(4), 177–180. doi:10.1108/02641610911006265

DeFelice, B., Kortfelt, J., et al. (2009). *An evaluation of serial solutions summon as a discovery service for the Dartmouth College Library*. Retrieved from http://www.dartmouth.edu/~library/admin/docs/Summon_Report.pdf

DeFelice, B., Kortfelt, J., Mead, J., Mounts, M., Pawlek, C., & Seaman, D. …Wheelock, C. (2009). *An evaluation of Serials Solutions Summon as a discovery service for the Dartmouth College Library*. Retrieved from http://www.dartmouth.edu/~library/admin/docs/Summon_Report.pdf

Delgadillo, R., & Lynch, B. P. (1999). Future historians: Their quest for information. *College & Research Libraries, 60*(3), 245–259.

Dellit, A., & Fitch, K. (2007). *Rethinking the catalogue.* Paper presented at the Innovative Ideas Forum, National Library of Australia, Canberra, New South Wales.

Dempsey, L. (2006). The library catalogue in the new discovery environment: Some thoughts. *Ariadne, 48.* Retrieved December 8, 2011 from http://www.ariadne.ac.uk/issue48/dempsey/

Dempsey, L. (2010). Discovery layers - Top tech trends 2 [Blog post]. Retrieved August 16, 2010, from http://orweblog.oclc.org/archives/002116.html

Dempsey, B. (2004). Target your brand. *Library Journal, 129*(13), 32–35.

Dempsey, L. (2006). The library catalogue in the new discovery environment: Some thoughts. *Ariadne, 48,* 1.

Dennis, S., Duque, G., MacEachern, M., Samuel, S., & Varnum, K. (2010). *University of Michigan Library Article Discovery Working Group supplementary report.* Retrieved from http://www.lib.umich.edu/files/adwg/supplemental-report.pdf

Dentinger, S., Keclik, K., Barclay, A., Bruns, T., Larson, E., Quattrucci, K., et al. (2008). *Resource discovery exploratory task force final report.* Retrieved May 24, 2011, from http://staff.library.wisc.edu/rdetf/RDETF-final-report.pdf

DeRosa, C., Cantrell, J., Carlson, M., Gallagher, P., Hawk, J., & Sturtz, C. (2010). *Perceptions of libraries, 2010: Context and community.* Dublin, OH: OCLC®. Retrieved from http://www.oclc.org/reports/2010perceptions.htm

DeRosa, C., Cantrell, J., Cellentani, D., Hawk, J., Jenkings, L., & Wilson, A. (2005). *Perceptions of libraries and information resources.* Dublin, OH: OCLC®. Retrieved from http://www.oclc.org/reports/2005perceptions.htm

DeRosa, C., Cantrell, J., Hawk, J., & Wilson, A. (2006). *College students' perceptions of libraries and information resources: A report to the OCLC membership.* Dublin, OH: OCLC. Retrieved from http://www.oclc.org/reports/pdfs/studentperceptions.pdf

Dervin, B., & Nilan, M. (1986). Information needs and uses. *Annual Review of Information Science & Technology, 21,* 3–33.

Detinger, S., Keclik, K., Barclay, A., Bruns, T., Larson, E., Quattrucci, A., et al. (2008). *Resource discovery exploratory task force final report.* Retrieved from http://staff.library.wisc.edu/rdetf/RDETF-final-report.pdf

deVoe, K. (2007). Innovations affecting us—Open source in the library: An alternative to the commercial ILS? *Against The Grain, 19*(2), 88-89.

Dickstein, R., & Mills, V. A. (2000). Usability testing at the University of Arizona library: How to let the users in on the design. *Information Technology and Libraries, 19*(3), 144–151.

Digby, T., & Elfstrand, S. (2011). Discovering open source discovery: Using VuFind to create MnPALS plus. *Computers in Libraries, 31*(2), 6–10.

Dolski, A. A. (2009). Information discovery insights gained from MultiPAC, a prototype library discovery system. *Information Technology & Libraries, 28*(4), 172–180.

Dorner, D. G., & Curtis, A. (2004). A comparative review of common user interface products. *Library Hi Tech, 22*(2), 182–197. doi:10.1108/07378830410543502

Dorner, D., & Curtis, A. (2004). A comparative review of the common user interface products. *Library Hi Tech, 22*(2), 182–197. doi:10.1108/07378830410543502

Dougan, K., & Fulton, C. (2009). Side by side: what a comparative usability study told us about a Web site redesign. *Journal of Web Librarianship, 3*(3), 217–237. doi:10.1080/19322900903113407

Dowd, N., Evangeliste, M., & Silberman, J. (2010). *Bite-sized marketing: Realistic solutions for the overworked librarian.* Chicago, IL: American Library Association.

Dubicki, E. (2007). Basic marketing and promotion concepts. *The Serials Librarian, 53*(3), 1–25. doi:10.1300/J123v53n03_02

Dubicki, E. (2008). *Marketing and promoting electronic resources: Creating the e-buzz!* Abingdon, NY: Routledge.

Duddy, C. (2009). A personal perspective on accessing academic information in the Google era, or 'How I learned to stop worrying and love Google'. *Serials, 22*(2), 131–135. doi:10.1629/22131

Dumas, J. (2007). The great leap forward: The birth of the usability profession (1988-1993). *Journal of Usability Studies, 2*(2), 54–60.

East, J. (2003). Z39.50 and personal bibliographic software. *Library Hi Tech Journal, 21*(1), 34–43. doi:10.1108/07378830310467382

Ebenau, R. G., & Strauss, S. H. (1994). *Software inspection process*. New York, NY: McGraw-Hill.

EBSCO Publishing. (2010). *EDS usability test report*. Unpublished report.

EBSCO Publishing. (2011). *EBSCO discovery service content*. Retrieved June 17, 2011, from http://www.ebscohost.com/discovery/eds-content

EBSCO Publishing. (2011). *EDS content*. Retrieved December 28, 2011, from http://www.ebscohost.com/discovery/eds-content

EBSCO. (2011). *EBSCO Discovery*. Retrieved July 22, 2011 from http://www.ebscohost.com/discovery

EBSCOHost. (n.d.). *EBSCOhost integration toolkit*. Retrieved July 31, 2011, from http://eit.ebscohost.com/

Edmunds, A., & Morris, A. (2000). The problem of information overload in business organizations: A review of the literature. *International Journal of Information Management, 20*(1), 17–28. doi:10.1016/S0268-4012(99)00051-1

Edson, M., & Cherry, R. (2010). Museum commons: Tragedy or enlightened self-interest? In J. Trant & D. Bearman (Eds.), Museums and the Web 2010: Proceedings. Toronto, Canada: Archives & Museum Informatics. Retrieved July 15, 2011, from http://www.archimuse.com/mw2010/papers/edson-cherry/edson-cherry.html

EDUCAUSE Learning Initiative. (2009). 7 things you should know about personal learning environments. *EDUCAUSE*. Retrieved from http://net.educause.edu/ir/library/pdf/ELI7049.pdf

Elliot, S. A. (2004). *Metasearch and usability: Towards a seamless interface to library resources*. White paper, Consortium Library, University of Alaska Anchorage. Retrieved from http:www.lib.uaa.alaska.edu/tundra/msuse1.pdf

Ellis, D. (1989). A behavioural approach to information retrieval system design. *The Journal of Documentation, 45*(3), 171–212. doi:10.1108/eb026843

Ellis, D. (1993). Modeling the information-seeking patterns of academic researchers: A grounded theory approach. *The Library Quarterly, 63*(4), 469–486. doi:10.1086/602622

Elmborg, J. K. (2003). Information literacy and writing across the curriculum: Sharing the vision. *RSR. Reference Services Review, 31*(1), 68–80. doi:10.1108/00907320310460933

Emanuel, J. (2011). Usability of the VuFind next-generation online catalog. *Information Technologies and Libraries, 30*(1), 44–52.

Emde, J., Morris, S., & Claassen-Wilson, M. (2009). Testing an academic library website for usability with faculty and graduate students. *Evidence Based Library and Information Practice, 4*(4), 24–36.

Encore. (n.d.). *Overview*. Retrieved July 22, 2011 from http://encoreforlibraries.com/overview/

Eppler, M., & Mengis, J. (2004). The concept of information overload: A review of literature from organization science, accounting, marketing, MIS, and related disciplines. *The Information Society, 20*(5), 325–344. doi:10.1080/01972240490507974

Erdelez, S., & Makri, S. (2011). Introduction to the thematic issue on opportunistic discovery of information. *Information Research, 16*(3). Retrieved from http://informationr.net/ir/16-3/odiintro.html

Erdelez, S. (1999). Information encountering: It's more than just bumping into information. *Bulletin of the American Society for Information Science, 25*(3). Retrieved from http://www.asis.org/Bulletin/Feb-99/erdelez.html

Evans, G. E. (2002). Management issues of co-operative ventures and consortia in the USA: part One. *Library Management, 23*(4/5), 213–226. doi:10.1108/01435120210429943

Ex Libris Group. (2011). *Ex Libris Primo reaches a major milestone as its customer base exceeds 750 institutions.* Retrieved August 14, 2011, from http://www.exlibrisgroup.com/default.asp?catid={45B7B8F9-C9B2-4C1F-AFCE-CCD62D4950D7}&details_type=1&itemid={238A3327-04DF-4388-A44B-BD7EC0B4FE9C}

Ex Libris. (2011). *Primo Central Index: An upgraded search experience.* Retrieved June 18, 2011, from http://www.exlibrisgroup.com/category/PrimoCentral

ExLibris. (2011). *ExLibris: Primo.* Retrieved July 22, 2011 from http://www.exlibrisgroup.com/

Fagan, J. C., & Mandernach, M. A. (2011a). Discovery by the numbers: An examination of the impact of a discovery tool through usage statistics. *Charleston Conference Proceedings 2011.* Santa Barbara, CA: Libraries Unlimited.

Fagan, J. C., & Mandernach, M. A. (2011b). A roadmap for discovery service implementation at an academic library. Poster presented at the Meeting of the Association of College and Research Libraries, Philadelphia, PA. Retrieved from http://www.lib.jmu.edu/documents/discovery/roadmap.aspx

Fagan, J. C., Mandernach, M. A., Nelson, C. S., Paulo, J. R., & Saunders, G. (2012). Usability test results for a discovery tool in an academic library. *Information Technology and Libraries.* 31(1), 83-112. Retrieved from http://ejournals.bc.edu/ojs/index.php/ital/article/view/1855/1745

Fagan, J. (2010). Usability studies of faceted browsing: A literature review. *Information Technology and Libraries, 29*(2), 58–66.

Fagan, J. (2011). Federated search is dead-And good riddance! *Journal of Web Librarianship, 5*(2), 77–79. doi:10.1080/19322909.2011.573533

Fagan, J. C. (2009). Marketing the virtual library. *Computers in Libraries, 29*(7), 25–30.

Fagan, J. C. (2010). Usability studies of faceted browsing: A literature review. *Information Technology & Libraries, 29*(2), 58–66.

Fagan, J. C. (2011). Discovery tools and information literacy. *Journal of Web Librarianship, 5*(3), 171–178. doi:10.1080/19322909.2011.598332

Fagan, J. C. (2011). Federated search is dead -- And good riddance. *Journal of Web Librarianship, 5*(2), 77–79. doi:10.1080/19322909.2011.573533

Fagan, J. C. (2012). Search engines for tomorrow's scholars, part two. *Journal of Web Librarianship, 6*(1), 69–76. doi:10.1080/19322909.2012.650897

Fagan, J. C., & Keach, J. A. (2009). *Web project management in academic libraries.* Oxford, UK: Chandos. doi:10.1533/9781780630199

Fast, K. V., & Campbell, D. G. (2004). "I still like Google": University student perceptions of searching OPACs and the Web. *Proceedings of the 67th ASIS&T Annual Meeting, 41,* (pp. 138-146).

Fei, X. (2009). Implementation of a federated search system: Resource accessibility issues. *Serials Review, 35*(4), 235–241. doi:10.1016/j.serrev.2009.08.019

Fichter, D., & Wisniewski, J. (2010). Practical website improvement face-off. *Online, 34*(2), 55–57.

Finder, L., Dent, V. F., & Lym, B. (2006). How the presentation of electronic gateway pages affects research behavior. *The Electronic Library, 24*(6), 804–819. doi:10.1108/02640470610714233

Fisher, K. E., & Julien, H. (2009). Information behavior. *Annual Review of Information Science & Technology, 43*(1), 1–73. doi:10.1002/aris.2009.1440430114

Fister, B. (1992). The research processes of undergraduate students. *Journal of Academic Librarianship, 18*(3), 163–169.

Fleming-May, R., & Yuro, L. (2009). From student to scholar: The academic library and social sciences PhD students' transformation. portal. *Libraries and the Academy, 9*(2), 199–221. doi:10.1353/pla.0.0040

Flynn, M. (2010). *From dominance to decline? The future of bibliographic discovery, access and delivery.* Paper presented at the World Library and Information Congress: 76th IFLA General Conference and Assembly, Gothenburg, Sweden. Retrieved December 8, 2011 from http://www.ifla.org/files/hq/papers/ifla76/71-flynn-en.pdf

Ford, L., O'Hara, L. H., & Whiklo, J. (2009). Shelflessness as a virtue: Preserving serendipity in an electronic reference collection. *Journal of Electronic Resources Librarianship, 21*(3/4), 251–262. doi:10.1080/19411260903466558

Foster, A. (2006). A non-linear perspective on information seeking. In A. Spink & C. Cole (Eds.), *New directions in human information behavior* (155-170). Dordrecht, The Netherlands: Springer.

Foster, A., & Ford, N. (2003). Serendipity and information seeking: An empirical study. *The Journal of Documentation, 59*(3), 321–340. doi:10.1108/00220410310472518

Frank, P. P., & Bothmann, R. L. (2007). Assessing undergraduate interlibrary loan use. *Journal of Interlibrary Loan. Document Delivery & Electronic Reserve, 18*(1), 33–48. doi:10.1300/J474v18n01_05

Friedel, R. (2001). Serendipity is no accident. *The Kenyon Review, 23*(2), 36–46.

Frierson, E. (2011, July 18). *Research guide recommendations.* [Web log post]. Retrieved from http://thirdpartylibrarian.wordpress.com/2011/07/18/research-guide-recommendations/

Froehlich, T. J. (1994). Relevance reconsidered—Towards an agenda for the 21st century: Introduction to special topic issue on relevance research. *Journal of the American Society for Information Science American Society for Information Science, 45*(3), 124–134. doi:10.1002/(SICI)1097-4571(199404)45:3<124::AID-ASI2>3.0.CO;2-8

Frost, W. J. (2004). Do we want or need metasearching? *Library Journal, 129*(6), 68.

Fry, A., & Rich, L. (2011). Usability testing for e-resource discovery: How students find and choose e-Resources using library web sites. *Journal of Academic Librarianship, 37*(5), 386–401. doi:10.1016/j.acalib.2011.06.003

Garrison, S., Boston, G., & Bair, S. (2011, April). *Taming lightning in more than one bottle: Implementing a local next-generation catalog versus a hosted web-scale discovery service.* Paper presented at the Association of College and Research Libraries Annual Conference, Philadelphia.

George, J. (2005). Socratic inquiry and the pedagogy of reference: Serendipity in information seeking. In *ACRL Twelfth National Conference: Currents and convergence: Navigating the rivers of change* (pp. 380-387). Chicago, IL: American Library Association. Retrieved from http://www.ala.org/ala/mgrps/divs/acrl/conferences/pdf/george05.pdf

George, C. A. (2008). Lessons learned: usability testing a federated search product. *The Electronic Library, 26*(1), 5–20. doi:10.1108/02640470810851707

Gerrity, B., Lyman, T., & Tallent, E. (2002). Blurring services and resources: Boston College's implementation of MetaLib and SFX. *RSR. Reference Services Review, 30*(3), 229–241. doi:10.1108/00907320210435491

Gest, H. (1997). Serendipity in scientific discovery: A closer look. *Perspectives in Biology and Medicine, 41*(1), 21–28.

Ge, X. (2010). Information-seeking behavior in the digital age: A multidisciplinary study of academic researchers. *College & Research Libraries, 71*(5), 435–455.

Gibbons, S. (2005). Who should care and why. *Library Technology Reports, 41*(3), 21–23.

Gibbons, S., & Foster, N. F. (Eds.). (2007). *Studying students: The undergraduate research project at the University of Rochester.* Chicago, IL: Association of College and Research Libraries.

Gibson, I., Goddard, L., & Gordon, S. (2009). One box to search them all: Implementing federated search at an academic library. *Library Hi Tech, 27*(1), 118-133. Retrieved December 11, 2011, from http://dx.doi.org/10.1108/07378830910942973

Gibson, I., Goddard, L., & Gordon, S. (2009). One box to search them all: Implementing federated search at an academic library. *Library Hi Tech, 27*(1), 118–133. doi:10.1108/07378830910942973

Given, L. M. (2002). The academic and the everyday: Investigating the overlap in mature undergraduates' information-seeking behaviors. *Library & Information Science Research, 24*(1), 17–29. doi:10.1016/S0740-8188(01)00102-5

Golderman, M., & Connolly, B. (2007). Infiltrating net gen cyberculture: Strategies for engaging and educating students on their own terms. *The Serials Librarian, 53*(3), 165–182. doi:10.1300/J123v53n03_11

Goldner, M., & Calhoun, K. (2008). *Web-Scale cataloging and metadata management.* Paper presented at the ALA Midwinter Meeting ALCTS Forum 'Moving Library Services to the Network Level', Philadelphia, PA. Retrieved from http://www.oclc.org/news/events/presentations/2008/Goldner-Calhoun_ALCTS_Forum_200801.pdf

Google Timeline. (n.d.). *Website.* Retrieved from http://www.google.com/corporate/timeline/#1997

Google. (2009). Google Form 10-K. Retrieved June 18, 2011, from http://investor.google.com/documents/2009_google_annual_report.html

Google. (2011). *About Google Scholar.* Retrieved from http://www.scolar.google.com/intl/en/scholar/about.html

Gow, V., Brown, L., Johnston, C., Neale, A., Paynter, G., & Rigby, F. (2010). Making New Zealand content easier to find, share and use. In J. Trant & D. Bearman (Eds.), Museums and the Web 2010: Proceedings. Toronto, Canada: Archives & Museum Informatics. Retrieved July 15, 2011, from http://www.museumsandtheweb.com/mw2009/papers/gow/gow.html

Gowing, C. (2008). *III's ENCORE: Old records, new records, new interfaces.* Presented at American Library Association Conference, ALCTS, Catalog Form & Function Interest Group, Anaheim, CA [PowerPoint slides]. Retrieved from http://alcts.ala.org/cffigwiki/index.php?title=ALA_Annual_2008_report

Graham, R. Y. (2004). Subject no-hits searches in an academic library online catalog: An exploration of two potential ameliorations. *College & Research Libraries, 65*(1), 36–54.

Green, K. C. (2010, October). *Campus computing 2010: The 21ˢᵗ national survey of computing and information technology in US higher education.* Paper presented the Annual Conference of EDUCAUSE, Anaheim, CA. Retrieved from http://www.campuscomputing.net/sites/www.campuscomputing.net/files/Green-CampusComputing2010.pdf

Greenwood, J. T., Watson, A. P., & Dennis, M. (2011). Ten years of LibQual: A study of qualitative and quantitative survey results at the University of Mississippi 2001-2010. *Journal of Academic Librarianship, 37*(4), 312–318. doi:10.1016/j.acalib.2011.04.005

Greiner, T. (2011, March). *How does switching to a discovery tool affect circulation?* Paper presented at the conference of the Association of College and Research Libraries, Philadelphia, PA. Retrieved July 26ᵗʰ, 2011, from http://www.ala.org/ala/mgrps/divs/acrl/events/national/2011/papers/how_does_switching.pdf

Griffiths, J. R., & Brophy, P. (2005). Student searching behavior and the Web: Use of academic resources and Google. *Library Trends, 53*(4), 539–554.

Gross, J., & Sheridan, L. (2011). Web scale discovery: The user experience. *New Library World, 112*(5), 236–247. doi:10.1108/03074801111136275

Gross, T., & Taylor, A. G. (2005). What have we got to lose?: The effect of controlled vocabulary on keyword searching results. *College & Research Libraries, 66*(3), 212–230.

Guenther, K. (2006). Developing personas to understand user needs. *Online, 30*(5), 49–51.

Guha, M. (2009). Serendipity versus the superorganism. *Journal of Mental Health (Abingdon, England), 18*(4), 277–279. doi:10.1080/09638230903078669

Gulbahar, Y., & Yildirim, S. (2006). Assessment of web-based courses: A discussion and analysis of learners' individual differences and teaching-learning process. *International Journal of Instructional Media, 33*(4), 367–378.

Gup, T. (1997, November 21). The end of serendipity. *The Chronicle of Higher Education, 44*(13), A52.

Hadra, J. (2009). Discovery marketplace is red hot at ALA. *Library Journal, 134*(13), 13–14.

Hadro, J. (2010). Patron-driven ebook model simmers as Ebrary joins ranks. *Library Journal.com.* Retrieved from http://www.libraryjournal.com/lj/communityacademiclibraries/887246-419/patron-driven_ebook_model_simmers_as.html.csp

Hannan, P. J. (2006). *Serendipity, luck and wisdom in research*. Lincoln, NE: iUniverse, Inc.

Hanson, C., Hessel, H., Barneson, J., Boudewyns, D., Fransen, J., & Friedman-Shedlov, L. ... Traill, S. (2009). *Discoverability phase 1 final report*. University of Minnesota Libraries. Retrieved from http://purl.umn.edu/48258

Hanson, C., Hessel, H., Barneson, J., Boudewyns, D., Fransen, J., & Friedman-Shedlov, L. ... West, A. (2011). *Discoverability phase 2 final report*. University of Minnesota Libraries. Retrieved from http://purl.umn.edu/99734

Hanson, C., Nackerud, S., & Jensen, K. (2008). Affinity strings: Enterprise data for resource recommendations. *Code4Lib*, (5). Retrieved from http://journal.code4lib.org/articles/501

Hartman, K. A., & Mullen, L. B. (2008). Google scholar and academic libraries: An update. *New Library World*, *109*(5/6), 211–222. doi:10.1108/03074800810873560

Hastings, R. (2010). *Microblogging and lifestreaming in libraries*. New York, NY: Neal-Schuman Publishers.

Haya, G., Nygren, E., & Widmark, W. (2007). Metalib and Google Scholar: A user study. *Online Information Review*, *31*(3), 365–375. doi:10.1108/14684520710764122

Head, A. J., & Eisenberg, M. B. (2009). Finding context: What today's college students say about conducting research in the digital age. Project Information Literacy Progress Report, Information School. University of Washington. Retrieved from http://projectinfolit.org/pdfs/PIL_ProgressReport_2_2009.pdf

Head, A. J., & Eisenberg, M. B. (2010). *Truth be told: How college students evaluate and use information in the digital age*. Seattle, WA: Project Information Literacy/University of Washington Information School. Retrieved from http://projectinfolit.org/pdfs/PIL_Fall2010_Survey_FullReport1.pdf

Hearst, M. (2009). *Search user interfaces*. Cambridge, UK: Cambridge University Press.

Hepworth, M. (2007). Knowledge of information behaviour and its relevance to the design of people-centred information products and services. *The Journal of Documentation*, *63*(1), 33–56. doi:10.1108/00220410710723876

Herrera, G. (2007). MetaSearching and beyond: Implementation experiences and advice from an academic library. *Information Technology and Libraries*, *26*(2), 44–52.

Herskovic, J. R., Tanaka, L. Y., Hersh, W., & Bernstam, E. (2007). A day in the life of PubMed: Analysis of a typical day's query log. *Journal of the American Medical Informatics Association*, *14*(2), 212–220. doi:10.1197/jamia.M2191

Hightower, B., Rawl, C., & Schutt, M. (2008). Collaborations for delivering the library to students through WebCT™. *RSR. Reference Services Review*, *35*(4), 541–551. doi:10.1108/00907320710838363

Hill, J. S. (2008). Is it worth it? Management issues related to database quality. *Cataloging & Classification Quarterly*, *46*(1), 5–26. doi:10.1080/01639370802182885

Hirwade, M. A., & Bherwani, M. T. (2009). Facilitating searches in multiple bibliographical databases: Metadata harvesting service providers. *Liber Quarterly*, *19*(2), 140-265. Retrieved December 8, 2011 from http://liber.library.uu.nl/publish/issues/2009-2/index.html?000474

Hoeflich, M. H. (2007). Serendipity in the stacks, fortuity in the archives. *Law Library Journal*, *99*(4), 813–827.

Hoffman, R. (2005). Serendipity, the grace of discovery. *Innovation (Abingdon)*, *5*(2), 68–69.

Howard, D., & Wiebrands, C. (2011). *Culture shock: Librarians' response to Web scale search*. Paper presented at the 2011 ALIA Information Online Conference, Sydney, N.S.W. Retrieved from http://ro.ecu.edu.au/cgi/viewcontent.cgi?article=7208&context=ecuworks

Howland, J. L., Wright, T. C., Boughan, R. A., & Roberts, B. C. (2009). How scholarly is Google Scholar? A comparison to library databases. *College & Research Libraries*, *70*(3), 227–234.

Hsieh-Yee, I. (1993). Effects of search experience and subject knowledge on the search tactics of novice and experienced searchers. *Journal of the American Society for Information Science American Society for Information Science*, *44*(3), 161–174. doi:10.1002/(SICI)1097-4571(199304)44:3<161::AID-ASI5>3.0.CO;2-8

Hulse, B., Cheverie, J. F., & Dygert, C. T. (2007). ALADIN research commons: A consortial institutional repository. *OCLC Systems & Services: International Digital Library Perspectives, 23*(2), 158–169. doi:10.1108/10650750710748469

InCommon® Federation. (2011). *InCommon® identity and access management.* Retrieved August 22, 2011, from http://www.incommon.org/

Indiana State Library. (n.d.). *Frequently asked questions.* INSPIRE Indiana's Virtual Library. Retrieved July 31, 2011, from http://www.in.gov/library/inspire/faq.html

Indiana University Bloomington Libraries. (2010). *IUB libraries: Fact sheet.* Retrieved July 31, 2011, from http://www.libraries.iub.edu/index.php?pageId=5430

Innovative Interfaces. (2011). *Encore products: Encore discovery.* Retrieved November 11, 2011, from http://encoreforlibraries.com/products/#ed

IU News Room. (2011, March 15). *"U.S. News" gives high marks to IU programs in nursing, law, business, education, medicine.* Retrieved from http://newsinfo.iu.edu/news/page/normal/17756.html

Jackson, M. (2008). Using metadata to discover the buried treasure in Google book search. *Journal of Library Administration, 47*(1-2), 165–173. doi:10.1080/01930820802111108

Jackson, M. E., & Preece, B. G. (2002). Consortia and the portal challenge. *Journal of Academic Librarianship, 28*(3), 160–162. doi:10.1016/S0099-1333(02)00306-3

Jackson, P. A. (2007). Integrating information literacy into Blackboard®: Building campus partnerships for successful student learning. *Journal of Academic Librarianship, 33*(4), 454–461. doi:10.1016/j.acalib.2007.03.010

Jacobowitz, P. (2006, December 20). #3 Indiana University Bloomington – Top 20 wired colleges. *PCMag.com.* Retrieved from http://www.pcmag.com/article2/0,2817,2073461,00.asp

Jacsó, P. (2008). Google Scholar revisited. *Online Information Review, 32*(1), 102–114. doi:10.1108/14684520810866010

Jacsó, P. (2009). Google Scholar's ghost authors. *Library Journal, 134*(18), 26–27.

Jankowska, M. (2004). Identifying university professors' information needs in the challenging environment of information and communication technologies. *Journal of Academic Librarianship, 30*(1), 51–66. doi:10.1016/j.jal.2003.11.007

Jansen, B. J. (2006b). Using temporal patterns of interactions to design effective automated searching assistance. *Communications of the ACM, 49*(4), 72-73-74.

Jansen, B. J., & Spink, A. (2003). An analysis of Web documents retrieved and viewed. In *Proceedings of the 4th International Conference on Internet Computing,* Las Vegas, Nevada, 23-26 June (pp. 65-69).

Jansen, B. J. (2005). Seeking and implementing automated assistance during the search process. *Information Processing & Management, 41,* 909–928. doi:10.1016/j.ipm.2004.04.017

Jansen, B. J. (2006a). Search log analysis: What it is, what's been done, how to do it. *Library & Information Science Research, 28,* 407–432. doi:10.1016/j.lisr.2006.06.005

Jansen, B. J., Booth, D. L., & Spink, A. (2009). Patterns of query reformulation during Web searching. *Journal of the American Society for Information Science and Technology, 60*(7), 1358–1371. doi:10.1002/asi.21071

Jansen, B. J., & Spink, A. (2006). How are we searching the World Wide Web? A comparison of nine search engine transaction logs. *Information Processing & Management, 42*(1), 248–263. doi:10.1016/j.ipm.2004.10.007

Jansen, B. J., Spink, A., & Saracevic, T. (2000). Real life, real users, and real needs: A study and analysis of user queries on the Web. *Information Processing & Management, 36*(2), 207–227. doi:10.1016/S0306-4573(99)00056-4

Jansen, B., & Spink, A. (2006). How are we searching the World Wide Web? A comparison of nine search engine transaction logs. *Information Processing & Management, 42*(1), 248–263. doi:10.1016/j.ipm.2004.10.007

Jansen, B., Zhang, M., & Schultz, C. (2009). Brand and its effect on user perception of search engine performance. *Journal of the American Society for Information Science and Technology, 60*(8), 1572–1595. doi:10.1002/asi.21081

Jiang, J. J., Muhanna, W. A., & Klein, G. (2000). User resistance and strategies for promoting acceptance across system types. *Information & Management, 37*(1), 25–36. doi:10.1016/S0378-7206(99)00032-4

Johnson, I. M. (2010). Supporting serendipity? *Information Development, 26*(3), 202–203. doi:10.1177/0266666910376211

Joint, N. (2010). The one-stop shop search engine: A transformational library technology? ANTAEUS. *Library Review, 59*(4), 240–248. doi:10.1108/00242531011038550

Jones, S. (2002). The Internet goes to college: How students are living in the future with today's technology. Washington, DC: Pew Internet and American Life Project. Retrieved from http://www.pewinternet.org/pdfs/PIP_College_Report.pdf

Jones, S., & Madden, M. (2002). *The Internet goes to college: How students are living in the future with today's technology.* Washington, DC: Pew Internet and American Life Project. Retrieved from http://www.pewinternet.org/~/media//Files/Reports/2002/PIP_College_Report.pdf.pdf

Jung, S., Herlocker, J. L., Webster, J., Mellinger, M., & Frumkin, J. (2008). LibraryFind: System design and usability testing of academic metasearch system. *Journal of the American Society for Information Science and Technology, 59*(3), 375–389. doi:10.1002/asi.20749

Kakai, M., Ikoja-Odongo, R., & Kigongo-Bukenya, I. M. N. (2004). A study of the information-seeking behavior of undergraduate students of Makerere University, Uganda. *World Libraries, 14*(1), 14–26.

Kanter, R. M. (1994). Collaborative advantage: The art of alliances. *Harvard Business Review, 72*(4), 96–108.

Kanter, R. M. (2010). Powerlessness corrupts. *Harvard Business Review, 88*(7), 36.

Karamouzis, F., & Longwood, J. (2007). *Guidelines of an RFP process for standardized IT service provider selections.* Gartner Research Group.

Keene, C. (2011). Discovery services: Next generations of searching scholarly information. *Serials, 24*(2), 193–196. doi:10.1629/24193

Kegan, R., & Lahey, L. (2001). The real reason people won't change. *Harvard Business Review, 79*(10), 85–92.

Kelleher Powell, C. (2008). OPAC integration in the era of mass digitization: The MBooks experience. *Library Hi Tech, 26*(1), 24–32. doi:10.1108/07378830810857771

Kendall, J. R. (2005). Implementing the web of student services. *New Directions for Student Services, 112*, 55–68. doi:10.1002/ss.184

Kennedy, L., Cole, C., & Carter, S. (1999). The false focus in inline searching: The particular case of undergraduates seeking information for course assignments in the Humanities and Social Sciences. *Reference and User Services Quarterly, 38*(3), 267–273.

Kenney, B. (2011). Liverpool's discovery. *Library Journal, 136*(3), 24–27.

Kent, A., Berry, M., Leuhrs, F. U., & Perry, J. W. (1955). Machine literature searching VIII. Operational criteria for designing information retrieval systems. *American Documentation, 6*(2), 93–101. doi:10.1002/asi.5090060209

Kim, J. (2010). Following their lead: An introduction. In Smith, S. D., & Caruso, J. B. (Eds.), *The ECAR study of undergraduate students and information technology* (pp. 19–25). Boulder, CO: EDUCAUSE Center for Applied Research.

Kim, K. (2001). Information seeking on the Web: Effects of user and task variables. *Library & Information Science Research, 23*(3), 233–255. doi:10.1016/S0740-8188(01)00081-0

King, D. (2008). Many libraries have gone to federated searching to win users back from Google. Is it working? *Journal of Electronic Resources Librarianship, 20*(4), 213–227. doi:10.1080/19411260802554520

King, D. M. (2005). Catalog user search strategies in finding music materials. *Music Reference Services Quarterly, 9*(4), 1–24. doi:10.1300/J116v09n04_01

King, H. J., & Jannik, C. (2005). Redesigning for usability: Information architecture and usabilaity testing for Georgia Tech library's website. *OCLC Systems & Services, 21*(3), 235–243. doi:10.1108/10650750510612425

Kinner, L., & Crosetto, A. (2009). Balancing act for the future: How the academic library engages in collection development at the local and consortial levels. *Journal of Library Administration, 49*(4), 419–437. doi:10.1080/01930820902832561

Klein, M. (2010). Hacking Summon™. *Code4Lib Journal, 11*. Retrieved from http://journal.code4lib.org/articles/3655

Kneip, J. (2007). Library Webmasters in medium-sized academic libraries. *Journal of Web Librarianship, 1*(3), 3–23. doi:10.1300/J502v01n03_02

Knievel, J. E., Wakimoto, J. C., & Holladay, S. (2009). Does interface design influence catalog use? A case study. *College & Research Libraries, 70*(5), 446–458.

Knight, S. A., & Spink, A. (2008). Toward a Web search information behavior model. In Spink, A., & Zimmer, M. (Eds.), *Web search: Multidisciplinary perspectives* (pp. 209–234). Berlin, Germany: Springer. doi:10.1007/978-3-540-75829-7_12

Koch, T., & Davis, M. (2011). *A discovery case study: EBSCO Discovery Service at Cowles Library, Drake University* [PowerPoint slides]. Retrieved from http://www.slideshare.net/marc_davis/a-discovery-case-study

Kohl, D. F., & Sanville, T. (2006). More bang for the buck: Increasing the effectiveness of library expenditures through cooperation. *Library Trends, 54*(3), 394–410. doi:10.1353/lib.2006.0022

Koltay, Z., & Tancheva, K. (2010). Personas and a user-centered visioning process. *Performance Measurement and Metrics, 11*(2), 172–183. doi:10.1108/14678041011064089

Kopp, J. J. (1998). Library consortia and information technology: The past, the present, the promise. *Information Technology and Libraries, 17*(1), 7–12.

Korah, A., & Cassidy, E. D. (2010). Students and federated searching: A survey of use and satisfaction. *Reference and User Services Quarterly, 49*(4), 325–332.

Korobili, S., Malliari, A., & Zapounidou, S. (2011). Factors that influence information-seeking behavior: The case of Greek graduate students. *Journal of Academic Librarianship, 37*(2), 155–165. doi:10.1016/j.acalib.2011.02.008

Kraft, D., & Lee, T. (1979). Stopping rules and their effect on expected search length. *Information Processing & Management, 15*(1), 47–58. doi:10.1016/0306-4573(79)90007-4

Kriewel, S., & Fuhr, N. (2007). Adaptive search suggestions for digital libraries. *Lecture Notes in Computer Science, 4822*, 220–229. doi:10.1007/978-3-540-77094-7_31

Krikelas, J. (1983). Information-seeking behavior: Patterns and concepts. *Drexel Library Quarterly, 19*(2), 5–20.

Krug, S. (2000). *Don't make me think: A common sense approach to web usability*. Indianapolis, IN: New Riders Publishing.

Krug, S. (2006). *Don't make me think: A common sense approach to web usability*. Berkeley, CA: New Riders.

Krug, S. (2010). *Rocket surgery made easy: The do-it-yourself guide to finding and fixing usability problems*. Berkeley, CA: New Riders.

Kuali Foundation. (2010). *Kuali OLE*. Kuali Foundation. Retrieved July 31, 2011, from http://www.kuali.org/ole

Kuhlthau, C. C. (1985). A process approach to library skills instruction. *School Library Media Quarterly, 13*(1), 35–40.

Kuhlthau, C. C. (1988a). Developing a model of the library search process: Cognitive and affective aspects. *Research Quarterly, 28*(2), 232–242.

Kuhlthau, C. C. (1988b). Perceptions of the information search process in libraries: A study of changes from high school through college. *Information Processing & Management, 24*(4), 419–427. doi:10.1016/0306-4573(88)90045-3

Kuhlthau, C. C. (2004). *Seeking meaning: A process approach to library and information services* (2nd ed.). Westport, CT: Libraries Unlimited.

Kupersmith, J. (2011). *Library terms that users understand*. Retrieved from http://www.jkup.net/terms.html

Kyrillidou, M. (2011). *Library investment index 2002-03 through 2009-10*. Retrieved from http://www.arl.org/bm~doc/index10.xls

Labelle, P. R. (2007). Initiating the learning process: A model for federated searching and information literacy. *Internet Reference Services Quarterly, 12*(3/4), 237–252. doi:10.1300/J136v12n03_01

Lampert, L. D., & Dabbour, K. S. (2007). Librarian perspectives on teaching metasearch and federated search technologies. *Internet Reference Services Quarterly, 12*(3/4), 253–278. doi:10.1300/J136v12n03_02

Larson, R. R. (1991). The decline of subject searching: Long-term trends and patterns of index use in an online catalog. *Journal of the American Society for Information Science and Technology, 42*(3), 197–215. doi:10.1002/(SICI)1097-4571(199104)42:3<197::AID-ASI6>3.0.CO;2-T

Lasater, M. C. (2008. June 28). *Old records, new records, new interfaces: Primo at Vanderbilt University.* Presented at American Library Association Conference, Annaheim: CA. [PowerPoint slides] Retrieved from http://alcts.ala.org/cffigwiki/index.php?title=ALA_Annual_2008_report

Lau, E. P., & Goh, D. H. (2006). In search of query patterns: A case study of a university OPAC. *Information Processing & Management, 42*(5), 1316–1329. doi:10.1016/j.ipm.2006.02.003

Lawrence, D. H. (2006). Blackboard® on a shoestring: Tying courses to sources. *Journal of Library Administration, 45*(1/2), 245–265. doi:10.1300/J111v45n01_14

Leckie, G. J. (1996). Desperately seeking citations: Uncovering faculty assumptions about the undergraduate research process. *Journal of Academic Librarianship, 22*(3), 201–208. doi:10.1016/S0099-1333(96)90059-2

Leeder, K. (2009). *The new committees you asked for* [Web log post]. Retrieved from http://www.acrl.ala.org/ULS/?p=55

Lee, H. (2008). Information structures and undergraduate students. *Journal of Academic Librarianship, 34*(3), 211–219. doi:10.1016/j.acalib.2008.03.004

Lewis, D. W. (2004). The innovator's dilemma: Disruptive change and academic libraries. *Library Administration & Management, 18*(2), 68–74.

Liao, Y., Finn, M., & Lu, J. (2007). Information-seeking behavior of international graduate students vs. American graduate students: A user study at Virginia Tech 2005. *College & Research Libraries, 68*(1), 5–25.

Libraries, U. W. (n.d.). *Personas development.* Retrieved from http://kwhitenton.com/libraries_personas/index.html

Library Journal Reviews. (2011, December 7). *Discovering what works: Librarians compare discovery interface experiences.* Retrieved from http://reviews.libraryjournal.com/2011/12/reference/discovering-what-works-librarians-compare-discovery-interface-experiences/

Liestman, D. (1992). Chance in the midst of design: approaches to library research serendipity. *Research Quarterly, 31*(4), 524–532.

Lightman, A. (2006). Wheels of fortune. *Science & Spirit, 17*(3), 28–33. doi:10.3200/SSPT.17.3.28-33

Lindahl, D. (2007). Metasearch in the users' context. *Serials Librarian, 51*(3/4), 215-216-234.

Lippert, S. K., & Davis, M. (2006). A conceptual model integrating trust into planned change activities to enhance technology adoption behavior. *Journal of Information Science, 32*(5), 434–448. doi:10.1177/0165551506066042

Little, J. R. (2001). A librarian's perspective on portals. *EDUCAUSE Quarterly, 24*(2), 52–54.

Liu, H. (2004). Meeting user needs: A library website design. *Louisiana Libraries, 67*(1), 25-31.

Liu, W. (2010). Remote users' OPAC searching habits: A comparative case study through Web transaction log analysis. *Kentucky Libraries, 74*(3), 6–13.

Lockwood, C., & MacDonald, P. (2007). Implementation of a federated search system in the academic library: Lessons learned. *Internet Reference Services Quarterly, 12*(1), 73–91. doi:10.1300/J136v12n01_04

Lombardo, S. V., & Condic, K. S. (2001). Convenience or content: A study of undergraduate periodical use. *RSR. Reference Services Review, 29*(4), 327–337. doi:10.1108/EUM0000000006494

Lown, C., & Hemminger, B. (2009). Extracting user interaction information from the transaction logs of a faceted navigation OPAC. *The Code4Lib Journal, 7*, 1-1.

Lucas, W., & Topi, H. (2005). Learning and training to search. In A. Spink, & C. Cole (Eds.), *New directions in cognitive information retrieval* (pp. 209-210-226). Netherlands: Springer.

Luther, J. (2003). Trumping Google? Metasearching's promise. *Library Journal, 128*(16), 36–39.

Luther, J., & Kelly, M. C. (2011). The next generation of discovery. *Library Journal, 136*(5), 66–71.

Lu, Z., Kim, W., & Wilbur, W. J. (2009). Evaluating relevance ranking strategies for MEDLINE retrieval. *Journal of the American Medical Informatics Association, 16*(1), 32–36. doi:10.1197/jamia.M2935

Macgregor, G., & McCulloch, E. (2006). Collaborative tagging as a knowledge organisation and resource discovery tool. *Library Review, 55*(5), 291–300. doi:10.1108/00242530610667558

Madison, O., & Hyland-Carver, M. (2005). Issues in planning for portal implementation: Perfection not required. *Journal of Library Administration, 43*(1-2), 113–134. doi:10.1300/J111v43n01_08

Magazine, P. C. (1999). *Top 100 websites*. Retrieved from http://web.archive.org/web/19990508042436/www.zdnet.com/pcmag/special/web100/search2.html

Majors, R. (2011, June). *Usability of next-gen interfaces & discovery tools*. Presented at the Annual Conference of the American Library Association, New Orleans, LA.

Majors, R., & Mantz, S. L. (2011). Moving to the patron's beat. *OCLC Systems & Services: International Digital Library Perspectives, 27*(4), 275–283. doi:10.1108/10650751111182588

Malliari, A., Korobili, S., & Zapounidou, S. (2011). Exploring the information seeking behavior of Greek graduate students: A case study set in the University of Macedonia. *The International Information & Library Review, 43*(2), 79–91. doi:10.1016/j.iilr.2011.04.006

Malliari, A., & Kyriaki-Manessi, D. (2007). Users' behaviour patterns in academic libraries' OPACs: A multivariate statistical analysis. *New Library World, 108*(3/4), 107–122. doi:10.1108/03074800710735311

Maness, J., Miaskiewicz, T., & Sumner, T. (2008). Using personas to understand the needs and goals of institutional repository users. *D-Lib Magazine, 14*(9/10). doi:10.1045/september2008-maness

Mann, T. (1993). *Library research models: A guide to classification, cataloging, and computers*. New York, NY: Oxford University Press.

Mann, T. (2008). The Peloponnesian War and the future of reference, cataloging, and scholarship in research libraries. *Journal of Library Metadata, 8*(1), 53–100. doi:10.1300/J517v08n01_06

Marcin, S., & Morris, P. (2008). OPAC: The next generation. *Computers in Libraries, 28*(5), 6–64. doi:doi:10.1108/07378831111138170

Marek, K. (2011). Getting to know web analytics. *Library Technology Reports, 47*(5), 11–16.

Markey, K. (2007a). Twenty-five years of end-user searching, part 1: Research findings. *Journal of the American Society for Information Science and Technology, 58*(8), 1071–1081. doi:10.1002/asi.20462

Markey, K. (2007b). Twenty-five years of end-user searching, part 2: Future research directions. *Journal of the American Society for Information Science and Technology, 58*(8), 1123–1130. doi:10.1002/asi.20601

Marshall, P., Herman, S., & Rajan, S. (2006). In search of more meaningful search. *Serials Review, 32*(3), 172–180. doi:10.1016/j.serrev.2006.06.001

Matthews, B. (2009). *Marketing today's academic library: A bold new approach to communicating with students*. Chicago, IL: American Library Association.

Matthews, J. G. (2009). We never have to say goodbye: Finding a place for OPACS in discovery environments. *Public Services Quarterly, 5*(1), 55–58. doi:10.1080/15228950802629162

Matthews, J. R., & Lawrence, G. S. (1984). Further analysis of the CLR online catalog project. *Information Technology and Libraries, 3*, 354–376.

Mayr, P., & Walter, A. (2007). An exploratory study of Google Scholar. *Online Information Review, 31*(6), 814–830. doi:10.1108/14684520710841784

McBirnie, A. (2008). Seeking serendipity: The paradox of control. *Aslib Proceedings: New Information Perspectives, 60*(6), 600–618. doi:doi:10.1108/00012530810924294

McCain, C., & Shorten, J. (2002). Cataloging efficiency and effectiveness. *Library Resources & Technical Services, 46*(1), 23–31.

McCay-Peet, L., & Toms, E. (2011). Measuring the dimensions of serendipity in digital environments. *Information Research, 16*(3), 1-6. Retrieved from http://www.eric.ed.gov/PDFS/EJ946482.pdf

McCullough, J. (2010). Adapting to change in Encore Synergy: New directions in discovery. *Computers in Libraries, 30*(8), 10–11.

McEvoy, K. (2010, June 7). *Indiana University selects EBSCO Discovery Service™ to give users what they expect online*. EBSCO Publishing. Retrieved from http://www.ebscohost.com/discovery/view-news/indiana-university-selects-EDS

McGillis, L., & Toms, E. G. (2001). Usability of the academic library web site: Implications for design. *College & Research Libraries, 62*(4), 355–367.

McHale, N. (2007). Accidental federated searching: Implementing federated searching in the smaller academic library. *Internet Reference Services Quarterly, 12*(1), 93–110. doi:10.1300/J136v12n01_05

McMullen, S. (2001). Usability testing in a library Web site redesign project. *RSR. Reference Services Review, 29*(1), 7–18. doi:10.1108/00907320110366732

Meagher, E., & Brown, C. (2008). Turned loose in the OPAC: URL selection, addition, and management process. *Library Hi Tech, 28*(3), 360–376. doi:10.1108/07378831011076620

Medeiros, N. (2009). Researching the research process: Information-seeking behavior, Summon, and Google Books. *OCLC Systems & Services, 25*(3), 153–155. doi:10.1108/10650750910982520

Meho, L. I., & Tibbo, H. R. (2003). Modeling the information-seeking behavior of social scientists: Ellis's study revisited. *Journal of the American Society for Information Science and Technology, 54*(6), 570–587. doi:10.1002/asi.10244

Mellon, C. A. (1986). Library anxiety: A grounded theory and its development. *College & Research Libraries, 47*(2), 160–165.

Menchaca, F. (2008). Funes and the search engine. *Journal of Library Administration, 48*(1), 107–119. doi:10.1080/01930820802035224

Merton, R. K., & Barber, E. (2004). *The travels and adventures of serendipity: A study in sociological semantics and the sociology of science*. Princeton, NJ: Princeton University Press.

Mi, J., & Weng, C. (2008). Revitalizing the library OPAC: Interlace, searching, and display challenges. *Information Technology & Libraries, 27*(1), 5–22.

Milczarski, V., & Garofalo, D. A. (2011). True serials: A true solution for electronic resource management needs in a medium-size academic library. *Journal of Electronic Resources Librarianship, 23*(3), 242–258. doi:10.1080/1941126X.2011.601228

Miller, T. (2004). Federated searching: Put it in its place. *Library Journal, 129*, 32.

Mishra, S. (2011). *The making of the HathiTrust personas*. Retrieved from http://www.hathitrust.org/documents/HathiTrust_Personas_Report.pdf

Montana State University Library. (2011). *Statistical profile*. Retrieved from http://www.lib.montana.edu/about/statprofile.php

Montana State University Office of Planning and Analysis. (2011). *Quick facts*. Retrieved from http://www.montana.edu/opa/quickfactsindex.html

MoreBetterLabs, Inc. (2010). *Final Summon user research report*. Prepared for the NCSU Libraries. Retrieved from http://www.lib.ncsu.edu/userstudies/studies/2010_summon/

Morris, D. E., Hobert, C. B., Osmus, L., & Wool, G. (2000). Cataloging staff costs revisited. *Library Resources & Technical Services, 44*(2), 70–83.

Moukdad, H., & Large, A. (2001). Users' perceptions of the Web as revealed by transaction log analysis. *Online Information Review, 25*(6), 349–359. doi:10.1108/EUM0000000006534

Moulaison, H. L. (2008). OPAC queries at a medium-sized academic library: A transaction log analysis. *Library Resources & Technical Services, 52*(4), 230–237.

Moyle, M., Stockley, R., & Tonkin, S. (2007). SHERPA-LEAP: A consortial model for the creation and support of academic institutional repositories. *OCLC Systems & Services, 23*(2), 125–132. doi:10.1108/10650750710748423

Music Library Association Emerging Technologies Committee. Music Discovery Requirements Document Subgroup. (2011). *Music discovery requirements: Draft.* Retrieved February 21, 2012, from personal.ecu.edu/newcomern/musicdiscoveryrequirements.pdf

Nagy, A. (2011). Analyzing the next-generation catalog. *Library Technology Reports, 47*(7), 1–27.

Nathan, R. J., & Yeow, P. H. P. (2008). An empirical study of factors affecting the perceived usability of websites for student Internet users. *Universal Access in the Information Society, 8*(3), 165–184. doi:10.1007/s10209-008-0138-8

National Information Standards Organization. (2011). *NISO launches new open discovery initiative to develop standards and recommended practices for library discovery services based on indexed search.* Retrieved from http://www.niso.org/news/pr/view?item_key=21d5364c586575fd5d4dd408f17c5dc062b1ef5f

Naun, C. C. (2010). Next generation OPACs: A cataloging viewpoint. *Cataloging & Classification Quarterly, 48*(4), 330–342. doi:10.1080/01639370903437709

Nazim, M. (2008). Information searching behavior in the Internet age: A users' study of Aligarh Muslim University. *The International Information & Library Review, 40*(1), 73–81. doi:10.1016/j.iilr.2007.11.001

Neuhaus, C., Neuhaus, E., & Asher, A. (2008). Google scholar goes to school: The presence of Google scholar on college and university Web sites. *Journal of Academic Librarianship, 34*(1), 39–51. doi:10.1016/j.acalib.2007.11.009

Neuhaus, C., Neuhaus, E., Asher, A., & Wrede, C. (2006). The depth and breadth of Google scholar: An empirical study. *Portal: Libraries and the Academy, 6*(2), 127–141. doi:10.1353/pla.2006.0026

Newcomer, N. (2011). The detail behind Web-scale: Selecting and configuring Web-scale discovery tools to meet music information retrieval needs. *Music Reference Services Quarterly, 14*(3), 131–145. doi:10.1080/10588167.2011.596098

Nfila, R. B., & Darko-Ampem, K. (2002). Developments in academic library consortia from the 1960s through to 2000: A review of the literature. *Library Management, 23*(4/5), 203–212. doi:10.1108/01435120210429934

Nicholas, D., Clark, D., Rowlands, I., & Jamali, H. R. (2009). Online use and information seeking behaviour: Institutional and subject comparisons of UK researchers. *Journal of Information Science, 35*(6), 660–676. doi:10.1177/0165551509338341

Nicholas, D., Williams, P., Rowlands, I., & Jamali, H. R. (2010). Researchers' e-journal use and information seeking behaviour. *Journal of Information Science, 36*(4), 494–516. doi:10.1177/0165551510371883

Nielsen, J. (2000). *Why you only need to test with five users.* Retrieved November 11, 2011, from http://www.useit.com/alertbox/20000319.html

Nielsen, J. (2001). *Usability metrics.* Retrieved from http://www.useit.com/alertbox/20010121.html

Nielsen, J. (2003). *Usability 101: Introduction to usability.* Retrieved from www.useit.com/alertbox/20030825.html

Nielsen, J., & Landauer, T. K. (1993). A mathematical model of the finding of usability problems. Proceedings of INTERCHI 1993. New York, NY: ACM Press.

Nielsen, J. (1993). *Usability engineering.* Boston, MA: Academic Press.

Nielsen, J. (2000). *Designing web usability.* Indianapolis, IN: New Riders Publishing.

NISO (National Information Standards Organization). (n.d.). *NISO metasearch initiative.* Retrieved from http://www.niso.org/workrooms/mi/#background

Niu, X., Hemminger, B. M., Lown, C., Adams, S., Brown, C., & Level, A. (2010). National study of information seeking behavior of academic researchers in the United States. *Journal of the American Society for Information Science and Technology, 61*(5), 869–890. doi:10.1002/asi.21307

Nixon, J. M., & Saunders, E. (2010). A study of circulation statistics of books on demand: A decade of patron-driven collection development, part 3. *Collection Management, 35*(3/4), 151–161. doi:10.1080/01462679.2010.486963

Norman, M. A., Schlembach, M. C., Shelburne, W. A., & Mischo, W. H. (2006). *Journal and article locator (JAL): Federated access to electronic/print journals and article full-text, 2006.* In 26th Annual Charleston Conference, Charleston (US), 8-11 November 2006. Libraries Unlimited.

North Carolina State University. (2011). *User studies at NCSU libraries.* Retrieved from http://www.lib.ncsu.edu/userstudies/

Notess, G. R. (2011). Deciphering discovery. *Online, 35*(1), 45–47.

Novotny, E. (2004). I don't think I click: A protocol analysis study of use of a library online catalog in the internet age. *College & Research Libraries, 65*(6), 525–537.

Nuan, C. C. (2010). Next generation OPACs: A cataloging viewpoint. *Cataloging & Classification Quarterly, 48*(4), 3330–3342. doi:doi:10.1080/01639370903437709

Nutefall, J., & Ryder, P. M. (2010). The serendipitous research process. *Journal of Academic Librarianship, 36*(3), 228–234. doi:10.1016/j.acalib.2010.03.005

O'Connor, B. (1988). Fostering creativity: Enhancing the browsing environment. *International Journal of Information Management, 8*(3), 203–210. doi:10.1016/0268-4012(88)90063-1

Ochoa, M., Jesano, R., Nemmers, J., Newsom, C., O'Brien, M., & Victor, P. (2007). Testing the federated searching waters. *Journal of Web Librarianship, 1*(3), 47–66. doi:10.1300/J502v01n03_04

Ockerbloom, J., Reese, T., Martin, P., Lynema, E., Grappone, T., Kennedy, D., et al. (2008). *DLF ILS discovery interface task group (ILS-DI) technical recommendation.* Retrieved from https://confluence.ucop.edu/download/attachments/34668692/DLF_ILS_Discovery_1.0.doc?version=1&modificationDate=1275674626000

OCLC. (2009). *Some findings from WorldCat Local usability tests prepared for ALA Annual.* Dublin, OH: OCLC. Retrieved from http://www.oclc.org/worldcatlocal/about/213941usf_some_findings_about_worldcat_local.pdf

OCLC. (2010). *Findings from WorldCat Local usability tests.* Retrieved from http://www.oclc.org/worldcatlocal/about/213941usf_some_findings_about_worldcat_local_2011.pdf

OCLC. (2011). *OCLC: WorldCat Local.* Retrieved December 19, 2011, from http://www.oclc.org/worldcatlocal/

OCLC. (n.d.). *FRBR work-set algorithm.* Retrieved from http://www.oclc.org/research/activities/past/orprojects/frbralgorithm/default.htm

O'Connor, L., & Lundstrom, K. (2011). The impact of social marketing strategies on the information seeking behaviors of college students. *Reference and User Services Quarterly, 50*(40351), 352–365.

Oder, N. (2010). Google book search by the numbers: Affidavit says 12 million books digitized, $2.5 million a year spent on metadata. *Library Journal.com.* Retrieved November 30, 2011, from http://www.libraryjournal.com/article/CA6718929.html

Oder, N. (2010, Jan. 14). After 17 years heading OhioLINK, Sanville leaves for LYRASIS job. *Library Journal Academic Newswire.* Retrieved from http://www.libraryjournal.com/article/CA6714727.html

Oder, N. (2011). Popular magazines from Time, Inc., Forbes, others, involved. *Library Journal.com.* Retrieved November 30, 2011, from www.libraryjournal.com/article/CA6716017.html

Oguz, F., & Davis, D. (2011). Developing an institutional repository at a medium-sized university: Getting started and going forward. *Georgia Library Quarterly, 48*(4), 13–16.

Olson, T. A. (2007). Utility of a faceted catalog for scholarly research. *Library Hi Tech*, *25*(4), 550–561. doi:10.1108/07378830710840509

On the record: Report of the Library of Congress working group on the future of bibliographic Control. (2008). Washington, DC: Library of Congress. Retrieved December 8, 2011, from http://www.loc.gov/bibliographic-future/news/lcwg-ontherecord-jan08-final.pdf

Online Computer Library Center. (2002). OCLC white paper on the information habits of college students: How academic librarians can influence student's web-based information choices. Retrieved from http://www.aect.org/publications/whitepapers/2010/informationhabits.pdf

Online Computer Library Center. (2011). *WorldCat Local Mobile enhanced, moves into production*. Retrieved from http://www.oclc.org/news/announcements/2011/announcement46.htm

Open Archives Initiative. (2011). *Open archives initiative*. Retrieved from http://www.openarchives.org

Orlikowski, W. J., & Hofman, J. D. (1997). An improvisational model of change management: The case of groupware technologies. *Sloan Management Review*, *38*(2), 11–21.

Oulasvirta, A., Hukkinen, J. P., & Schwartz, B. (2009). When more is less: The paradox of choice in search engine use. *Proceedings of the 32nd International ACM SIGIR Conference on Research and Development in Information Retrieval*, (pp. 516–523). doi:10.1145/1571941.1572030

Ozmutlu, S., Spink, A., & Ozmutlu, H. C. (2004). A day in the life of Web searching: An exploratory study. *Information Processing & Management*, *40*(2), 319–345. doi:10.1016/S0306-4573(03)00044-X

Papakhian, A. (2000). Cataloging: Music librarianship at the turn of the century [Special issue]. *Notes*, *56*(3), 581–590.

Pennanen, M., & Vakkari, P. (2003). Students' conceptual structure, search process, and outcome while preparing a research proposal: A longitudinal case study. *Journal of the American Society for Information Science and Technology*, *54*(8), 759–770. doi:10.1002/asi.10273

Pennell, C. (2007, June). *Presentation: Forward to the past: resurrecting faceted search @NCSU libraries.* Presented at American Library Association Conference, ALCTS Authority Control Interest Group, Washington, D.C. [PowerPoint slides]. Retrieved from http://www.lib.ncsu.edu/endeca/presentations.html

Pennell, C. (2008 June). *Presentation: NCSU Endeca 2 1/2 years on: from Next Gen to normalcy.* American Library Association, Anaheim, CA [PowerPoint slides]. Retrieved from http://www.lib.ncsu.edu/endeca/presentations.html

Peters, C. (2011). *An overview of the RFP process for nonprofits and libraries.* Retrieved from http://www.techsoup.org/learningcenter/techplan/page5507.cfm

Peters, T. (2003). Consortia and their discontents. *Journal of Academic Librarianship*, *29*(2), 111–114. doi:10.1016/S0099-1333(02)00421-4

Peters, T. A. (1993). The history and development of transaction log analysis. *Library Hi Tech*, *11*(2), 41–66. doi:10.1108/eb047884

Petruzzelli, B. (2005). Real-life marketing and promotion strategies in college libraries: Connecting with campus and community. *College & Undergraduate Libraries*, *12*(1-2).

Pijeaux, L. J., Jr. (2007). The Birmingham Civil Rights Institute: A case study in library, archives, and museum collaboration. RBM: A Journal of Rare Books, Manuscripts, and Cultural Heritage, 8(1), 56-60. Retrieved from http://rbm.acrl.org/content/8/1/56.full.pdf

Pirolli, P., & Card, S. (1999). Information foraging. *Psychological Review*, *106*(4), 643–675. doi:10.1037/0033-295X.106.4.643

Ponsford, B. C., & vanDuinkerken, W. (2007). User expectations in the time of Google: Usability testing of federated searching. *Internet Reference Services Quarterly*, *12*(1/2), 159–178. doi:10.1300/J136v12n01_08

Poulter, D., Thacker, C., & Sadeh (Panelists), & Kaplan, M. (Moderator). (2010). Primo Central: The ultimate in next-gen discovery: Raising research to a new level. [Video webcast]. *Library Journal.* Retrieved from http://www.libraryjournal.com/lj/tools/webcast/883876-388/webcast_primo_central_the_ultimate.html.csp

Powers, A. C. (2011, December 7). Discovering what works: Librarians compare discovery interface experiences. *Library Journal Reviews.* Retrieved from http://reviews.libraryjournal.com/2011/12/reference/discovering-what-works-librarians-compare-discovery-interface-experiences/

Prabha, C., Connaway, L. S., Olszewski, L., & Jenkins, L. R. (2007). What is enough? Satisficing information needs. *The Journal of Documentation, 63*(1), 74–89. doi:10.1108/00220410710723894

Pradhan, D. R., Trivedi, K., & Arora, J. (2011). *Searching online resources in new discovery environment: A state-of-the-art review.* Retrieved from http://ir.inflibnet.ac.in/dxml/bitstream/handle/1944/1623/14.pdf?sequence=1

Prescott, L., & Erway, R. (2011). *Single search: The quest for the holy grail. OCLC research.* Retrieved from http://www.oclc.org/research/publications/library/2011/2011-17.pdf

Prescott, M., & Veldof, J. (2010). A process approach to defining services for undergraduates. *portal. Libraries and the Academy, 10*(1), 29–56. doi:10.1353/pla.0.0085

Queens University. Kingston, Ontario, Canada. (2010). *Summon frequently asked questions.* Retrieved December 9, 2011, from http://library.queensu.ca/summon/faq

Quint, B. (2011, April 7). HathiTrust discovers Serials Solutions' Summon and vice versa. *Information Today, Newsbreaks.* Retrieved on April 7, 2011, from http://newsbreaks.infotoday.com/NewsBreaks/HathiTrust-Discovers-Serials-Solutions-Summon-and-Vice-Versa-74825.asp

Rainwater, J. (2007). Maintaining a federated search service: Issues and solutions. *Internet Reference Services Quarterly, 12*(3), 309–323. doi:10.1300/J136v12n03_05

Randall, S. (2006). Federated searching and usability testing: Building the perfect beast. *Serials Review, 32*(3), 181–182. doi:10.1016/j.serrev.2006.06.003

Ranganathan, S. R. (1957). *The five laws of library science* (2nd ed.). Madras, India: The Madras Library Association.

Rapp, D. (2011). Ingram announces new library ebook access model and audiobook shift. *Library Journal. com.* Retrieved November 30, 2011, from http://www.libraryjournal.com/lj/home/890315-264/ingram_announces_new_library_ebook.html.csp

Reeb, B. (2008). *Design talk: Understanding the roles of usability practitioners, web designers, and web developers in user-centered web design.* Chicago, IL: Association of College and Research Libraries.

Reese, T. (2009). Automated metadata harvesting: Low-barrier MARC record generation from OAI-PMH repository stores using MarcEdit. *Library Resources & Technical Services, 53*(2), 121–132.

Reference and User Services Association. (2006). *Guidelines for the introduction of electronic information resources to users.* Retrieved from http://www.ala.org/ala/mgrps/divs/rusa/resources/guidelines/guidelinesintroduction.cfm

Reidsma, M. (2011). *Custom Summon™ searches* [Software]. Retrieved from http://gvsulib.com/labs/custom_summon/

Reitz, J. M. (2010). *ODLIS: Online dictionary for library and information science.* Santa Barbara, CA: ABC-CLIO. Retrieved from http://www.abc-clio.com/ODLIS/about.aspx

Research Information Network (RIN). (2009). *Creating catalogues: Bibliographic records in a networked world: A Research Information Network report.* Retrieved August 10, 2010, from http://www.rin.ac.uk/files/Creating_catalogues_REPORT_June09.pdf

Research Libraries Group. (2005). *Metasearch survey among RLG members.* Retrieved from http://www.oclc.org/research/activities/past/rlg/metasearch.htm

Rice, J. (1988). Serendipity and holism: The beauty of OPACs. *Library Journal, 113*(3), 138–141.

Robinson, T. (2010). *Library videos and Webcasts.* New York, NY: Neal-Schuman Publishers.

Rochkind, J. (2011). *Article search, and catalog search.* Bibliographic Wilderness Blog. [Web log comment]. Retrieved from http://bibwild.wordpress.com/2011/08/08/article-search-and-catalog-search/#comment-9644

Roe, S. (1999). Online subject access. *Journal of Internet Cataloging, 2*(1), 69–78. doi:10.1300/J141v02n01_07

Rowe, R. (2010). Web-Scale discovery: A review of Summon, EBSCO Discovery Service, and WorldCat Local. *The Charleston Advisor, 12*(1), 5–10. doi:10.5260/chara.12.1.5

Rowe, R. (2011). Encore Synergy and Primo Central: Web-scale discovery: A review of two products on the market. *The Charleston Advisor, 12*(4), 11–15. doi:10.5260/chara.12.4.11

Rubin, V. L., Burkell, J., & Quan-Haase, A. (2011). Facets of serendipity in everyday chance encounters: A grounded theory approach to blog analysis. *Information Research, 16*(3). Retrieved from http://informationr.net/ir/16-3/paper488.html

Rubin, J., & Chisnell, D. (2008). *Handbook of usability testing: How to plan, design, and conduct effective tests.* Indianapolis, IN: Wiley.

Ruddock, B., & Hartley, D. (2010). How UK academic libraries choose metasearch systems. *Aslib Proceedings, 62*(1), 85–105. doi:10.1108/00012531011015226

Russell, D. M. (2007). *Keynote address: What are they thinking? Searching for the mind of the searcher.* Vancouver, Canada: Joint Conference on Digital Libraries.

Ruthven, I. (2008). Interactive information retrieval. *Annual Review of Information Science & Technology, 42,* 43–91. doi:10.1002/aris.2008.1440420109

Ryan, T. (2004). Turning patrons into partners when choosing an integrated library system. *Computers in Libraries, 24*(3), 6–56.

Sachs, D., Eckel, E., & Langan, K. (2011). Striking a balance: Effective use of Facebook in an academic library. *Internet Reference Services Quarterly, 16*(1-2), 35–54. doi:10.1080/10875301.2011.572457

Sadeh, T. (2007). Time for a change: New approaches for a new generation of library users. *New Library World, 108*(7/8), 307–316. doi:10.1108/03074800710763608

Sally, D., & Uzwyshyn, R. (2007). New information discovery tools environmental scan: Executive summary and web addresses. Retrieved from http://rayuzwyshyn.net/20072008PDF/NewInformationDiscoveryTools.pdf

Sanville, T. (2007). OhioLINK: A US resource sharing facility – Issues and developments. *Interlending & Document Supply, 35*(1), 31–37. doi:10.1108/02641610710728177

Saracevic, T. (1987). *Experiments on the cognitive aspects of information seeking and information retrieving (NSF Research Project IST-850 5411).* Cleveland, OH: Case Western Reserve University.

Saracevic, T., & Kantor, P. (1988a). A study of information seeking and retrieving, II: Users, questions, and effectiveness. Journal of the American Society for Information Science, 39(3), 177-196. doi:0.1002/(SICI)1097-4571(198805)39:3<177::AID-ASI3>3.0.CO;2-F

Saracevic, T. (1975). Relevance: A review of and a framework for the thinking on the notion in information science. *Journal of the American Society for Information Science American Society for Information Science, 26*(6), 321–343. doi:10.1002/asi.4630260604

Saracevic, T. (2007a). Relevance: A review of the literature and a framework for thinking on the notion in information science. Part II: Nature and manifestations of relevance. *Journal of the American Society for Information Science and Technology, 58*(13), 1915–1933. doi:10.1002/asi.20682

Saracevic, T. (2007b). Relevance: A review of the literature and a framework for thinking on the notion in information science. Part III: Behavior and effects of relevance. *Journal of the American Society for Information Science and Technology, 58*(13), 2126–2144. doi:10.1002/asi.20681

Saracevic, T., & Kantor, P. (1988b). A study of information seeking and retrieving, III: Searchers, searches, and overlap. *Journal of the American Society for Information Science American Society for Information Science, 39*(3), 197–216. doi:10.1002/(SICI)1097-4571(198805)39:3<197::AID-ASI4>3.0.CO;2-A

Saracevic, T., Kantor, P., Chamis, A. Y., & Trivison, D. (1988). A study of information seeking and retrieving, I: Background and methodology. *Journal of the American Society for Information Science American Society for Information Science, 39*(3), 161–176. doi:10.1002/(SICI)1097-4571(198805)39:3<161::AID-ASI2>3.0.CO;2-0

Savolainen, R. (2006). Time as a context of information seeking. *Library & Information Science Research, 28*(1), 110–127. doi:10.1016/j.lisr.2005.11.001

Savolainen, R. (2007). Filtering and withdrawing: Strategies for coping with information overload in everyday contexts. *Journal of Information Science, 33*(5), 611–621. doi:10.1177/0165551506077418

Schachter, D. (2004). How to manage the RFP process. *Information Outlook, 8*(11), 10–12.

Schamber, L. (1994). Relevance and information behavior. *Annual Review of Information Science & Technology, 29,* 3–48.

Schamber, L., Eisenberg, M. B., & Nilan, M. S. (1990). A re-examination of relevance: Toward a dynamic, situational definition. *Information Processing & Management, 26*(6), 755–776. doi:10.1016/0306-4573(90)90050-C

Schmidt, A. (2011). The user experience: resist that redesign. *Library Journal, 36*(4), 21.

Schnieder, K. (2007, September). *The OPAC sucks.* In the Symposium on the Future of Integrated Library Systems. Champaign, IL.

Schonfeld, R., & Housewright, R. (2010). *Faculty survey 2009: Key strategic insights for libraries, publishers, and societies* (pp. 1-35). Retrieved from http://www.ithaka.org/ithaka-s-r/research/faculty-surveys-2000–2009/Faculty%20Study%202009.pdf

Schrage, M. (1996). RFPs: May they rest in peace. *Computerworld, 30*(14), 37.

Sclater, N. (2008). Web 2.0, personal learning environments, and the future of learning management systems. *Research Bulletin, 13.* Boulder, CO: EDUCAUSE Center for Applied Research. Retrieved from http://net.educause.edu/ir/library/pdf/ERB0813.pdf

Serial Solutions. (n.d.). *Summon key database and packages – A&I.* Retrieved from http://www.serialssolutions.com/resources/detail/summon-key-databases-and-packages-ai

Serials Solutions. (2009). *API documentation center.* Retrieved from http://api.summon.serialssolutions.com/help/api/

Serials Solutions. (2010). *Summon service debuts Database Recommender* [Press release]. Retrieved from http://www.serialssolutions.com/news-detail/summon-service-debuts-database-recommender/

Serials Solutions. (2011). Summon content and coverage. Retrieved June 17, 2011, from http://www.serialsolutions.com/summon-content-and-coverage

Shadle, S. (2009). Electronic resources in a next-generation catalog: The case of Worldcat Local. *Journal of Electronic Resources Librarianship, 21*(3/4), 192–199. doi:10.1080/19411260903446006

Sharpe, P. A., & Vacek, R. E. (2010). Intranet 2.0 from a project management perspective. *Journal of Web Librarianship, 4*(2/3), 239–249. doi:10.1080/19322909.2010.500860

Shen, Y. (2007). Information seeking in academic research: A study of the Sociology faculty at the University of Wisconsin-Madison. *Information Technology and Libraries, 26*(1), 4–13.

Shneiderman, B. (2011). *Research-based web design and usability guidelines.* Retrieved from http://www.usability.gov/guidelines/guidelines_book.pdf

Shumaker, D., & Strand, J. (2009). Changing your game through alignment. *Information Outlook, 13*(7), 41–44.

Simmons, M. H. (2005). Librarians as disciplinary discourse mediators: Using genre theory to move toward critical information literacy. *portal. Libraries & the Academy, 5*(3), 297–311. doi:10.1353/pla.2005.0041

Singer, R. (2008). In search of a really "next generation" catalog. *Journal of Electronic Resources Librarianship, 20*(3), 139–142. doi:10.1080/19411260802412752

Smiraglia, R. P., & Pavlovsky, T. (1997). *Describing music materials: A manual for descriptive cataloging of printed and recorded music, music videos, and archival music collections for use with AACR2 and APPM* (3rd ed. rev. and enl.). Lake Crystal, MN: Soldier Creek Press.

Smiraglia, R. P., & Young, J. B. (Eds.). (2006). *Bibliographic control of music, 1897-2000.* Lanham, MD: Scarecrow Press

Smiraglia, R. P. (1989). Uniform titles for music: An exercise in collocating works. *Cataloging & Classification Quarterly, 9*(3), 97–114. doi:10.1300/J104v09n03_06

Smith, I. (2010). Organisational quality and organisational change: Interconnecting paths to effectiveness. *Library Management, 32*(1/2), 111–128. doi:10.1108/01435121111102629

Snyder, T. (2010). Music materials in a faceted catalog: Interviews with faculty and graduate students. *Music Reference Services Quarterly, 13*(3/4), 66–95. doi:10.1080/10588167.2010.528746

Solas, N. (2010). Hiding our collections in plain site: Interface strategies for "findability." In J. Trant & D. Bearman (Eds.), Museums and the Web 2010: Proceedings. Toronto, Canada: Archives & Museum Informatics. Retrieved July 15, 2011, from http://www.archimuse.com/mw2010/papers/solas/solas.html

Solomon, P. (2002). Discovering information in context. *Annual Review of Information Science & Technology, 36*(1), 229–264. doi:10.1002/aris.1440360106

Somerville, M. M., & Brar, N. (2009). A user-centered and evidence-based approach for digital library projects. *The Electronic Library, 27*(3), 409–425. doi:10.1108/02640470910966862

Souer, J., Honders, P., Versendall, J., & Brinkkemper, S. (2008). A framework for web content management system operations and maintenance. *Journal of Digital Information Management, 6*(4), 324–331.

Spink, A. (2010). *Information behavior: An evolutionary instinct*. Berlin, Germany: Springer.

Spink, A., Jansen, B. J., & Ozmultu, H. C. (2000). Use of query reformulation and relevance feedback by Excite users. *Internet Research: Electronic Networking Applications and Policy, 10*(4), 317–328. doi:10.1108/10662240010342621

Spink, A., Wolfram, D., Jansen, B. J., & Saracevic, T. (2001). Searching the Web: The public and their queries. *Journal of the American Society for Information Science and Technology, 52*(3), 226–234. doi:10.1002/1097-4571(2000)9999:9999<::AID-ASI1591>3.0.CO;2-R

Stahlberg, E., & Cronin, C. (2011). Assessing the cost and value of bibliographic control. *Library Resources & Technical Services, 55*(3), 124–137.

Stainthorp, P. (2011, May 17). *How commercial next-generation library discovery tools have *nearly* got it right* [Blog Post]. Retrieved July 28, 2011, from http://jerome.blogs.lincoln.ac.uk/2011/05/17/how-commercial-next-generation-library-discovery-tools-have-nearly-got-it-right/

Stein, J., Bright, A., George, C., Hurlbert, T., Linke, E., & St. Clair, G. (2006). In their own words: A preliminary report on the value of the Internet and library in graduate student research. *Performance Measurement and Metrics, 7*(2), 117–115. doi:10.1108/14678040610679506

Steinrová, J. (2007). Relevance assessment for digital libraries. *Mousaion, 25*(2), 37–57.

Stevenson, A. (Ed.). (2010). *Serendipity. Oxford Dictionary of English*. Oxford Reference Online.

Stevenson, A., Tuohy, C., & Norrish, J. (2008). Ambient findability and structured serendipity: Enhanced resources discovery for full text collections. *IATUL Proceedings, 2008*, 1–10.

Stevenson, K. (2009). Next-generation library catalogues: Reviews of Encore, Primo, Summon, and Summa. *Serials, 22*(1), 68–82. doi:10.1629/2268

Stevenson, K. K., Elsegood, S. S., Seaman, D. D., Pawlek, C. C., & Nielsen, M. P. (2009). Next-generation library catalogues: Reviews of Encore, Primo, Summon and Summa. *SERIALS, 22*(1), 68–78. doi:10.1629/2268

Stoffel, B., & Cunningham, J. (2005). Library participation in campus web portals: An initial survey. *Reference Services Review, 33*(2), 144-160. doi: 10.1108/00907320510597354

Stoffle, C. J., & Cuillier, C. (2011). From surviving to thriving. *Journal of Library Administration, 51*(1), 130–155. doi:10.1080/01930826.2011.531645

Stone, G. (2009). Resource discovery. In H. Woodward & L. Estelle (Eds.), *Digital information: Order or anarchy?* (pp. 133-164). London, UK: Facet. Retrieved December 11, 2011, from http://eprints.hud.ac.uk/5882/

Stone, G. (2010), Searching life, the universe and everything? The implementation of Summon at the University of Huddersfield. *LIBER Quarterly, 20*(1), 25-42. Retrieved December 11, 2011, from http://liber.library.uu.nl/publish/issues/2010-1/index.html?000489

Stone, S. (1982). Humanities scholars: Information needs and uses. *The Journal of Documentation, 38*(4), 292–313. doi:10.1108/eb026734

Swain, D. E. (1996). Information search process model: How freshmen begin research. Proceedings of the ASIS Annual Meeting, 33, (pp. 95-99).

Swanson, D. R. (1986). Undiscovered public knowledge. *The Library Quarterly, 56*(2), 103–118. doi:10.1086/601720

Swanson, T. A., & Green, J. (2011). Why we are not Google: Lessons from a library web site usability study. *Journal of Academic Librarianship, 37*(3), 222–229. doi:10.1016/j.acalib.2011.02.014

Tallent, E. (2004). Metasearching in Boston College libraries – A case study of user reactions. *New Library World, 105*(1), 69–75. doi:10.1108/03074800410515282

Tallent, E. (2010). Where are we going? Are we there yet? *Internet Reference Services Quarterly, 15*(1), 3–10. doi:10.1080/10875300903543770

Talsky, D. (2008). Auto-populating an ILL form with the Serial Solutions link resolver API. *Code4Lib Journal, 4.* Retrieved from http://journal.code4lib.org/articles/108

Tang, R., Hsieh-Yee, I., & Zhang, S. (2007). User perceptions of MetaLib combined search: An investigation of how users make sense of federated searching. *Internet Reference Services Quarterly, 12*(1/2), 211–236. doi:10.1300/J136v12n01_11

Tarulli, L. (2009). *Choosing a discovery tool* [Blog post]. Retrieved December 9, 2011, from http://laureltarulli.wordpress.com/2009/02/05/choosing-a-discovery-tool/

Tatarka, A. (2007). *LibQUAL+ survey 2007 results.* Retrieved from http://www.lib.uchicago.edu/e/surveys/2007/UofCLQSummary.pdf

Tatarka, A., Larsen, D., Olson, T., Schilt, M., & Twiss-Brooks, A. (2010). *Library survey 2010: Graduate and professional students.* Retrieved from http://www.lib.uchicago.edu/e/surveys/2010/Lbrary%20Survey%202010%20Full%20Report.pdf

Teague-Rector, S., Ballard, A., & Pauley, S. K. (2011). The North Carolina State University libraries search experience: Usability testing tabbed search interfaces for academic libraries. *Journal of Web Librarianship, 5*(2), 80–95. doi:10.1080/19322909.2011.568822

Tennant, R. (2003). The right solution: Federated search tools. *Library Journal, 128*(11), 28–30.

Tenopir, C. (2007), Online databases: Can Johnny search? *Library Journal, 132*(2), 30. Retrieved December 11, 2011, from http://www.libraryjournal.com/article/CA6407784.html?industryid=47130

Thomas, B., & Buck, S. (2010). OCLC's WorldCat Local versus III's WebPAC: Which interface is better at supporting common user tasks? *Library Hi Tech, 28*(4), 648–671. doi:10.1108/07378831011096295

Tolliver, R. L., Carter, D. S., Chapman, S. E., Edwards, P. M., Fisher, J. E., & Haines, A. L. (2005). Website redesign and testing with a usability consultant: Lessons learned. *OCLC Systems & Services, 21*(3), 156–166. doi:10.1108/10650750510612362

Toms, E. G. (2000). Serendipitous information retrieval. *Proceedings of the First DELOS Network of Excellence Workshop on Information Seeking, Searching and Querying in Digital Libraries* (pp. 11-12). Sophia Antipolis, France: European Research Consortium for Informatics and Mathematics.

Topi, H., & Lucas, W. (2005a). Mix and match: Combining terms and operators for successful Web searches. *Information Processing & Management, 41*, 801–817. doi:10.1016/j.ipm.2004.03.007

Topi, H., & Lucas, W. (2005b). Searching the Web: Operator assistance required. *Information Processing & Management, 41*(2), 383–403. doi:10.1016/S0306-4573(02)00092-4

Tunkelang, D. (2009). *Faceted search.* San Rafael, CA: Morgan & Claypool Publishers.

Turnbow, D., Kasianovitz, K., Snyder, L., Gilbert, D., & Yamamoto, D. (2005). Usability testing for web redesign: A UCLA case study. *OCLC Systems & Services*, *21*(3), 226–234. doi:10.1108/10650750510612416

Turner, S. (2004). Resource integration in the library: Link-Resolvers and federated searching. *Mississippi Libraries*, *68*(3), 63–66.

Twait, M. (2005). Undergraduate students' source selection criteria: A qualitative study. *Journal of Academic Librarianship*, *31*(6), 567–573. doi:10.1016/j.acalib.2005.08.008

U.S. Census Bureau. (2010). *2010 census data*. Retrieved from http://2010.census.gov/2010census

U.S. National Library of Medicine. (March 15, 2010). *NLM gateway fact sheet*. Retrieved from http://www.nlm.nih.gov/pubs/factsheets/gateway.html

Unified Resource Discovery Comparison Wiki. (2011). *Unified resources discovery comparison*. Retrieved April 14, 2012, from https://sites.google.com/site/urd-2comparison/

University Institutional Research and Reporting. (2010a). *IU fact book 2010: Bloomington*. Retrieved from http://www.iu.edu/~uirr/reports/standard/factbook/campus_fb/2010-11/Bloomington/FactBook1011_BL.pdf

University Institutional Research and Reporting. (2010b). *IU fact book 2010-11: University*. Retrieved from http://www.iu.edu/~uirr/reports/standard/factbook/campus_fb/2010-11/University/FactBook1011_Web.pdf

University of California Libraries Bibliographic Services Task Force. (2005). *Rethinking how we provide bibliographic services for the University of California: Final report*. University of California Libraries. Retrieved from http://libraries.universityofcalifornia.edu/sopag/BSTF/Final.pdf

University of Chicago Library. (2010). *Survey 2010 comments: E-resources*. Retrieved from http://www.lib.uchicago.edu/e/surveys/2010/comments/2010eresources.html

University of Minnesota Libraries. (2006). *A multidimensional framework for academic support: Final report*. University of Minnesota Libraries. Retrieved from http://purl.umn.edu/5540

University of Minnesota Libraries. (2010). *Library user communities*. University of Minnesota Libraries. Retrieved from http://purl.umn.edu/99734

University of Nevada Las Vegas University Libraries. (2009). *UNLV libraries strategic plan 2009-2011*. Retrieved from http://library.nevada.edu/about/strategic_plan09-11.pdf

University of Texas at Austin. (2009). *Develop the usability test documents*. Retrieved from http://www.utexas.edu/learn/usability/test.html

University of Washington. (2011). *Guide to planning and conducting usability tests*. Retrieved from http://www.lib.washington.edu/usability/resources/guides/tests

Uzelac, E. (2009). *Creating data-driven personas to aid selection and implementation of a next-generation discovery interface*. Poster presented at the Fourteenth National Conference of the Association of College & Research Libraries, Seattle, WA. Retrieved from http://bit.ly/2waVux

Uzelac, E., Conaway, A., & Palmer, L. A. (2008). *Using data-driven personas to guide discovery tool selection and implementation*. Paper presented to the Post-Horizon Working Group at the Sheridan Libraries, Johns Hopkins University, Baltimore, MD. Retrieved July 24, 2011, from https://wiki.library.jhu.edu/download/attachments/30752/UNAPersonasCompressed.pdf

Vacek, R. (2011, June). *Discovery @ the University of Houston Libraries*. Presentation at the Conference of the American Library Association, New Orleans, LA. Retrieved July 27th, 2011, from http://www.slideshare.net/vacekrae/discovery-at-the-university-of-houston-libraries

Valentine, B. (1993). Undergraduate research behavior: Using focus groups to generate theory. *Journal of Academic Librarianship*, *19*(5), 300–304. doi:10.1016/0099-1333(93)90026-2

VandeCreek, L. M. (2005). Usability analysis of Northern Illinois' University libraries' website: A case study. *OCLC Systems & Services*, *21*(3), 181–192. doi:10.1108/10650750510612380

Varnum, K. (2011). *Announcing a Drupal module for searching Summon via API* [Blog post]. Retrieved from http://mblog.lib.umich.edu/blt/archives/2011/06/announcing_a_dr.html

Vaughan, J. (2011). Investigations into library Web scale discovery services. *Information Technology and Libraries, 125*(1), 669-678. Retrieved from http://www.ala.org/lita/ital/

Vaughan, J., & ALA TechSource. (2011). *Web scale discovery services.* Chicago, IL: ALA TechSource.

Vaughan, J., & Hanken, T. (2011). *Evaluating and implementing Web-scale discovery services in your library.* Retrieved from http://www.alatechsource.org/blog/2011/07/continuing-the-conversation-evaluating-and-implementing-web-scale-discovery-services--0

Vaughan, V., & Hanken, T. (2011c) *Continuing the conversation: Evaluating and implementing web-scale discovery services in your library* [PowerPoint Presentation]. Retrieved from http://www.alatechsource.org/blog/2011/07/continuing-the-conversation-evaluating-and-implementing-web-scale-discovery-services-in.

Vaughan, V., & Hanken, T. (2011d) *Continuing the conversation: Evaluating and implementing Web-scale discovery services in your library (Part 2)* [PowerPoint Presentation]. Retrieved from http://www.alatechsource.org/blog/2011/07/continuing-the-conversation-evaluating-and-implementing-web-scale-discovery-services--0

Vaughan, J. (2011). Chapter 1: W-scale discovery what and why? *Library Technology Reports, 47*(1), 5–11.

Vaughan, J. (2011). Differentiators and a final note. *Library Technology Reports, 47*(1), 48–53.

Vaughan, J. (2011). Ebsco Discovery services. *Library Technology Reports, 47*(1), 30–38.

Vaughan, J. (2011). Ex Libris Primo Central. *Library Technology Reports, 47*(1), 39–47.

Vaughan, J. (2011). *Library technology reports: Library-Web scale discovery services.* Chicago, IL: American Library Association.

Vaughan, J. (2011). OCLC WorldCat Local. *Library Technology Reports, 47*(1), 12–21.

Vaughan, J. (2011). Questions to consider. *Library Technology Reports, 47*(1), 54–59.

Vaughan, J. (2011). Serials Solutions Summon. *Library Technology Reports, 47*(1), 22–29.

Vaughan, J. (2011). Web scale discovery services. *Library Technology Reports, 47*(1), 1–62.

Vaughan, J. (2011). Web scale discovery: What and why? *Library Technology Reports, 47*(1), 5–11.

Vaughan, J. (2011a). Differentiators and a final note. *Library Technology Reports, 47*(1), 48–53.

Vaughan, J. (2012). Investigations into library Web-scale discovery services. *Information Technology and Libraries, 31*(1), 32–82. doi:10.6017/ital.v31i1.1916

Vaughan, J., & Costello, K. (2011). Management and support of shared integrated library systems. *Information Technology and Libraries, 30*(2), 62–70.

Vaughn, D., & Callicott, B. (2003). Broccoli librarianship and Google-bred patrons, or what's wrong with usability testing? *College & Undergraduate Libraries, 10*(2), 1–18. doi:10.1300/J106v10n02_01

Vellucci, S. L. (1997). *Bibliographic relationships in music catalogs.* Lanham, MD: Scarecrow Press.

Vellucci, S. L. (2001). Music metadata and authority control in an international context. *Notes, 57*(3), 541–554. doi:10.1353/not.2001.0063

Venkatesh, V., & Davis, F. D. (2000). A theoretical extension of the technology acceptance model: Four longitudinal field studies. *Management Science, 46*(2), 186–204. doi:10.1287/mnsc.46.2.186.11926

Vilelle, L. (2005). Marketing virtual reference: What academic libraries have done. *College & Undergraduate Libraries, 12*(1-2), 65–79. doi:10.1300/J106v12n01_05

Villen-Rueda, L., Senso, J. A., & de Moya-Anegon, F. (2007). The use of OPAC in a large academic library: A transactional log analysis study of subject searching. *Journal of Academic Librarianship, 33*(3), 327–337. doi:10.1016/j.acalib.2007.01.018

Walker, D. (2011). *Xerxes* (Version 1.8) [Software]. Retrieved from http://code.google.com/p/xerxes-portal/

Wallace, L. K. (2004). *Libraries, mission, & marketing: Writing mission statements that work*. Chicago, IL: American Library Association.

Walsh, S. T. (2004). Roadmapping a disruptive technology: A case study: The emerging microsystems and top-down nanosystems industry. *Technological Forecasting and Social Change, 71*(1/2), 161–185. doi:10.1016/j.techfore.2003.10.003

Walters, W. H. (2009). Google scholar search performance: Comparative recall and precision. *Portal: Libraries and the Academy, 9*(1), 5–24. doi:10.1353/pla.0.0034

Ward, J. L., Shadle, S., & Mofield, P. (2008). Planning and implementation. *Library Technology Reports, 44*(6), 26–36.

Ward, J. L., Shadle, S., & Mofield, P. (2008). User experience, feedback, and testing. *Library Technology Reports, 44*(6), 17–23.

Ward, J. L., Shadle, S., & Mofield, P. (2008). WorldCat Local impact summary at the University of Washington. *Library Technology Reports, 44*(6), 41.

Ward, J. L., Shadle, S., & Mofjeld, P. (2008). Planning and implementation. *Library Technology Reports, 44*(6), 26–36.

Ward, J., Shadle, S., & Mofjeld, P. (2008). User experience, feedback, and testing. *Library Technology Reports, 44*(6), 17–23.

Warren, D. (2007). Lost in translation: The reality of federated searching. *Australian Academic & Research Libraries, 38*(4), 258–269.

Warwick, C., Rimmer, J., Blandford, A., Gow, J., & Buchanan, G. (2009). Cognitive economy and satisficing in information seeking: A longitudinal study of undergraduate information behavior. *Journal of the American Society for Information Science and Technology, 60*(12), 2402–2415. doi:10.1002/asi.21179

Watson-Boone, R. (1994). The information needs and habits of humanities scholars. *Research Quarterly, 34*(2), 203–216.

Way, D. (2010). The impact of Web-scale discovery on the use of a library collection. *Serials Review, 36*(4), 214–220. doi:10.1016/j.serrev.2010.07.002

Webb, P. L., & Nero, M. D. (2009). OPACs in the clouds. *Computers in Libraries, 29*(9), 18–22.

Wer, M. A., & Flatley, R. (2006). What do faculty what?: A focus group study of faculty at a mid-sized public university. *Library Philosophy & Practice, 9*(1), 1–8.

Westfall, M. (2011). Using a request for proposal (RFP) to select a serials vendor: The University of Tennessee experience. *Serials Review, 37*(2), 87–92. doi:10.1016/j.serrev.2011.01.005

Whitehouse, K. (2006). Cutting through the clutter: What makes an intranet successful? *EDUCAUSE Quarterly, 29*(1), 65–69.

Whitlock, B., & Kiel, S. (2011). What I learned from teaching a for-credit information literacy class. Presentation at the Maryland Library Association Annual Conference, *May 6, 2011.*

Whitmire, E. (2002). Disciplinary differences in undergraduates' information-seeking behavior. *Journal of the American Society for Information Science and Technology, 53*(8), 631–638. doi:10.1002/asi.10123

Whitmire, E. (2003). Epistemological beliefs and the information-seeking behavior of undergraduates. *Library & Information Science Research, 25*(2), 127–142. doi:10.1016/S0740-8188(03)00003-3

Whitmire, E. (2004). The relationship between undergraduates' epistemological beliefs, reflective judgment, and their information-seeking behavior. *Information Processing & Management, 40*(1), 97–111. doi:10.1016/S0306-4573(02)00099-7

Whittaker, J. (2000). What is software testing? And why is it so hard? *IEEE Software, 17*(1), 70–79. doi:10.1109/52.819971

Wildemuth, B. M., & O'Neill, A. L. (1995). The "known" in known-item searches: Empirical support for user-centered design. *College & Research Libraries, 56*(3), 265–281.

Williams, S. C., & Foster, A. K. (2011). Promise fulfilled? An EBSCO discovery service usability study. *Journal of Web Librarianship, 5*(3), 179-180-198. doi:10.1080/19322909.2011.597590

Williams, H., & Peters, A. (2012). (forthcoming). And that's how I connect to my library: How a 42-second promotional video helped to launch the UTSA Libraries' new Summon Mobile application. *The Reference Librarian, 53*(3).

Williams, P. (1999). The Net generation: The experiences, attitudes and behavior of children using the Internet for their own purposes. *Aslib Proceedings, 51*(9), 315–322. doi:10.1108/EUM0000000006991

Williams, S. C., Bonnell, A., & Stoffel, B. (2009). Student feedback on federated search use, satisfaction, and web presence: Qualitative findings of focus groups. *Reference and User Services Quarterly, 49*(2), 131–139.

Williams, S. C., & Foster, A. K. (2011). Promise fulfilled? An EBSCO Discovery Service usability study. *Journal of Web Librarianship, 5*(3), 179–198. doi:10.1080/1932 2909.2011.597590

Williams, S., & Foster, A. (2011). Promise fulfilled? An EBSCO Discovery Service usability study. *Journal of Web Librarianship, 5*(3), 179–198. doi:10.1080/19322 909.2011.597590

Wilson, T. D. (1981). On user studies and information needs. *The Journal of Documentation, 37*(1), 3–15. doi:10.1108/eb026702

Wilson, T. D. (1997). Information behaviour: An interdisciplinary perspective. *Information Processing & Management, 33*(4), 551–572. doi:10.1016/S0306-4573(97)00028-9

Wilson, T. D. (1999). Exploring models of information behaviour: The 'uncertainty' project. *Information Processing & Management, 35*(6), 839–849. doi:10.1016/S0306-4573(99)00029-1

Wilson, T. D., Ford, N., Ellis, D., Foster, A., & Spink, A. (2002). Information seeking and mediated search, Part 2: Uncertainty and its correlates. *Journal of the American Society for Information Science and Technology, 53*(9), 704–715. doi:10.1002/asi.10082

Wisniewski, J. (2007). Build it (and customize and market it) and they will come. *Internet Reference Services Quarterly, 12*(3-4), 341–355. doi:10.1300/J136v12n03_07

Wisniewski, J. (2009). Next-gen OPACs: No time like the present. *Online, 33*(5), 54–57.

Wisniewski, J. (2010). Web scale discovery: The future's so bright, I gotta wear shades. *Online, 34*(4), 55–58.

Wolverton, R. E. Jr. (2005). Authority control in academic libraries in the United States: A survey. *Cataloging & Classification Quarterly, 41*(1), 111–131. doi:10.1300/J104v41n01_06

Woods, L. (2007). A three-step approach to marketing electronic resources at Brock University. *The Serials Librarian, 53*(3), 107–124. doi:10.1300/J123v53n03_08

Wrubel, L., & Schmidt, K. (2007). Usability testing of a metasearch interface: A case study. *College & Research Libraries, 68*(4), 292–311.

Wynne, S. C., & Hanscom, M. J. (2011). The effect of next-generation catalogs on catalogers and cataloging functions in academic libraries. *Cataloging & Classification Quarterly, 49*(3), 179–207. doi:10.1080/016393 74.2011.559899

Yang, K. (2005). Information retrieval on the web. *Annual Review of Information Science & Technology, 39*, 33–80. doi:10.1002/aris.1440390109

Yang, S. Q., & Hofmann, M. A. (2011, June 14). Next generation or current generation? A study of the OPACs of 260 academic libraries in the USA and Canada. *Library Hi Tech, 29*(2), 266–300. doi:10.1108/07378831111138170

Yang, S. Q., & Wagner, K. (2010). Evaluating and comparing discovery tools: How close are we towards the next generation catalog? *Library Hi Tech, 28*(4), 690–709. doi:10.1108/07378831011096312

Yi, K., Beheshti, J., Cole, C., Leide, J. E., & Large, A. (2006). User search behavior of domain-specific information retrieval systems: An analysis of the query logs from PsycINFO and ABC-clio's historical abstracts/America: History and life. *Journal of the American Society for Information Science and Technology, 57*(9), 1208–1220. doi:10.1002/asi.20401

York, M. C. (2005). Calling the scholars home: Google Scholar as a tool for rediscovering the academic library. *Internet Reference Services Quarterly, 10*(3/4), 117–133. doi:10.1300/J136v10n03_11

Yuan, X., & Belkin, N. (2010). Evaluating an integrated system supporting multiple information-seeking strategies. *Journal of the American Society for Information Science and Technology, 61*(10), 1987–2010. doi:10.1002/asi.21352

Yu, H., & Young, M. (2004). The impact of Web search engines on subject searching in OPAC. *Information Technology and Libraries, 23*(4), 168–180.

Zach, L. (2005). When is "enough" enough? Modeling the information-seeking and stopping behavior of senior arts administrators. *Journal of the American Society for Information Science and Technology, 56*(1), 23–35. doi:10.1002/asi.20092

Zeigen, L., & Crum, J. (2009). Library catalogs and other discovery tools. *OLA Quarterly, 15*(1), 1.

Zhu, L. (2009). Single-record versus separate-record approaches for cataloging e-serials in the OCLC WorldCat Local environment. *Cataloging & Classification Quarterly, 47*(2), 161–170. doi:10.1080/01639370802575583

Zhu, L. (2010). The role of the cataloging department in the implementation of OCLC WorldCat Local. *Library Collections, Acquisitions & Technical Services, 34*(4), 123–129. doi:10.1016/j.lcats.2010.06.001

About the Contributors

Mary Pagliero Popp is the Resource and Discovery Services Librarian at Indiana University (IU) Bloomington and has been with the University in various capacities for nearly 40 years. She has been involved with IU's IUCAT Web catalog and works with the team developing the Blacklight next generation catalog for all IU campuses. Mary has also worked on IU Bloomington's implementations of both WorldCat Local (2009-2011) and EBSCO Discovery Service (2010 to the present). She holds an MLS and an M.S. in Adult Education. Active in the American Library Association, she has served as President of the Library Instruction Round Table and will serve as President, Reference and User Services Association (RUSA) in 2012-2013. Her research interests include discovery systems, characteristics of library users, usability testing of library resources, and active learning techniques.

Diane Dallis is the Associate Dean for Library Academic Services at Indiana University Bloomington Libraries. In this role she oversees library public service departments including Access Services, Area Studies, Arts and Humanities, Digital User Experience, Government Information Services, Reference Services, Sciences, Social Sciences, and Teaching and Learning. From 2004-2009 she was Head of the Information Commons, from 2003-2004 she was the Instructional Services Librarian, and from 1998 to 2003 she was the Instructional Design Librarian at the Indiana University Bloomington Libraries. She received her B.S. in Education in 1994 and she earned her M.L.S. in 1998 from Indiana University Bloomington.

* * *

Paul Anthony has been employed in various professional librarian positions at Southern Illinois University Edwardsville since 1988, beginning as Head of Circulation, then as a Technical Services Librarian, and since 1997 as Business & Engineering Librarian. He is currently serving as Director of Access Services. Previously he was the Director of Instructional Resources for Parks College of St. Louis University, 1985-88; Market & Product Analyst for OCLC, 1984-85; College Librarian, Cardinal Newman College, 1978-84; and Original Catalog Librarian, Louisiana State University, 1977-78. He received his BA in History from the University of Notre Dame, 1972, MLS from Indiana University, 1977, and an MBA from the University of Missouri, 1983.

Elizabeth (Liz) Babbitt is the State Aid Specialist at the Massachusetts Board of Library Commissioners where she works to certify public libraries to receive state aid. Previously, Liz was Assistant Professor/Electronic Resources Librarian at Montana State University. At MSU, Liz was involved with implementation of a WorldCat Local trial and then Summon, which is currently being used on that campus. Since July 2010, she has served as vice chair then chair of the American Library Association - Association of Cataloging and Technical Services Electronic Resources Interest Group. Liz has a BLA in Humanities from Harvard University and a MLib from the University of Washington Graduate School of Library and Information Science.

Aaron Bales is the Systems Librarian at the Hesburgh Libraries of Notre Dame. He has an MLS from Indiana University and a Bachelor's degree in Philosophy from Harvard University. Prior to systems, Aaron worked in both public and technical service areas, beginning with Government Documents and Catalog/Database Maintenance. He also worked in the Engineering Library as Branch Supervisor and Assistant Engineering Librarian. Aaron's professional interests are focused on library technology, including search systems, library data management, and process improvement.

David Bietila seeks to provide tools that are helpful to library patrons. He has worked in library technology since 2000. He's currently Web Program Director at University of Chicago, but started out as a student staffer doing desktop maintenance at University of Wisconsin Libraries. His works interests include interface design, information architecture, and learning about user behavior through qualitative and ethnographic research. He has an MA in LIS from University of Wisconsin, and an MA in American Studies from George Washington University.

Stephen Bollinger is an Assistant Professor and Web Services Librarian at the F.D. Bluford Library of the North Carolina Agricultural & Technical State University. He received his MS in information from the School of Information at the University of Michigan in 2000 and his BA in U.S. History and Visual Design from Michigan State University in 1996. He is currently inquiring into the deployment and use of tablets in library instruction, for delivering library services, and for general student use in higher education.

Carol Ann Borchert has been the Coordinator for Serials at the University of South Florida (USF) since 2004. Previously, she was in the Reference and Government Documents departments at USF, and in the Cataloging, Serials, Reference, and Government Documents departments at Furman University's James B. Duke Library. She holds an MLS from the University of Kentucky and an M.A. in Spanish from USF.

Deborah K Boudewyns is the Arts, Architecture & Landscape Architecture Librarian at the University of Minnesota. As part of the University Libraries' initiatives she serves on the Digital Arts & Humanities Group and the Scholarly Communications Collaborative. She has been an active member of the Art Libraries Society of North America and served on the ARLIS/NA Executive Board from 2006-2009. Deborah received her Master's in Library and Information Studies from Syracuse University with a focus on arts librarianship. She has been involved with the evolution of arts technology since 1998, and co-organized the Minnesota Electronic Resources in the Visual Arts (MINERVA) symposia from 2001-2004. Deborah's focus on Discovery systems considers the representation and accessibility of visual information and media.

Chris Bulock has been the Electronic Resources Librarian at Southern Illinois University Edwardsville since December 2009. Prior to that, he held positions at the William Andrews Clark Memorial Library and at Occidental College in Los Angeles, California. Chris received his Master of Library and Information Science from the University of California Los Angeles in 2009. He received a Bachelor of Arts with a major in Cognitive Science from Occidental College. His research interests include library Web site and catalog user studies, discovery systems, and perpetual access to electronic resources.

Kristine Brancolini is the Dean of University Libraries at Loyola Marymount University (LMU) in Los Angeles. Prior to her arrival at LMU in July 2006, she had been a librarian at Indiana University in Bloomington for more than twenty years, where she held a number of positions, including Director of the Digital Library Program, 1998-2006. Her first major project was the design and construction of the new William H. Hannon Library, which opened in 2009. Since that time, Dean Brancolini has focused on creating a learning environment within the library, with an emphasis upon evidence-based decision making. Her research interests include digital library development, inclusive excellence in libraries, and research methods for librarians. Following a systematic process, the William H. Hannon Library selected Ebsco Discovery Services (EDS) as its discovery platform. The library's project team will be implementing EDS in 2012.

Anita Breckbill is head of the Music Library at the University of Nebraska—Lincoln. She is a member of the Music Library Association and is currently chair of the regional chapter, Mountain Plains Music Library Association. She has worked for years on the issue of online catalogs and their practical use for music materials. Her research interests include music publishing and distribution in nineteenth-century France.

William Breitbach is Instruction & Information Services Unit Head at the Pollak Library, California State University, Fullerton. He holds a BA in Physical Anthropology from University of California Santa Barbara, an MA in Political Science from California State University, Los Angeles, and an MLIS from University of California, Los Angeles. He currently oversees a variety of services at the Pollak Library and serves as liaison to the Departments of Nursing, Social Work, and Political Science. His research interests include emerging technologies in libraries and psychological barriers to help seeking. He has published articles and presented on these topics at a number of professional conferences.

David P. Brennan is Assistant Librarian, Collection Development/Digital Resources Management at the George T. Harrell Health Sciences Library, Penn State College of Medicine, Hershey, PA. He has over 20 years experience in academic libraries both as a systems librarian (Clifford E. Barbour Library, Pittsburgh Theological Seminary) and as a library director (St. Francis Health System, Pittsburgh, PA). He has presented at MLA and PaLA conferences and published numerous articles on technology topics.

Suzanne Chapman has an undergraduate degree in Fine Arts from Ohio University and a Master of Science in Information from the University of Michigan's School of Information. Suzanne is currently the head of the University of Michigan's User Experience (UX) Department. The UX Department supports the interface design, user research, usability, Web use analysis, and accessibility needs for the University of Michigan Library's primary interfaces and HathiTrust Digital Library. She specializes in user-centered design and budget usability techniques and writes about these on her blog www.userslib.com.

Mark Christel is the Director of Libraries at the College of Wooster.

Annette Coates (BA (Hons), MA, MCLIP) has 13 years of experience of working in academic libraries. She is currently Service Manager of the Digital Library Services team at Northumbria University Library. Her responsibilities there include the management and development of the library's core online services - the Web site, ILS and discovery service - as well as the acquisition and management of print journals and electronic resources. She previously worked for Manchester Metropolitan University Library in a variety of roles, the last of which was as Library Service Manager of the Electronic Services Development team.

Kevin J. Comerford is currently an Assistant Professor of Librarianship and Digital Initiatives Librarian at the University of New Mexico. He holds a Master of Information Science degree from the University of North Texas and a Master of Fine Arts degree from Texas Christian University. From 1990-1995 he was the Visual Resources Manager for the Dallas Museum of Art, and a Technology Consultant for the Sixth Floor Museum in Dallas. From 1995-2008 he served as Group Manager for Media Content Management at Microsoft Corporation in Redmond, Washington. Professor Comerford has designed and implemented numerous digital content management systems and most recently completed a major upgrade of the Celebrating New Mexico Statehood Web site (nmstatehood.unm.edu). He serves as the chair of the University Libraries research data archives initiative and is also developing several electronic and open access journals at UNM.

Jody Condit Fagan currently serves as Director of Scholarly Content Systems and Associate Professor in Libraries & Educational Technologies at James Madison University. She led project teams to select and implement JMU's first discovery tool, EBSCO Discovery Service, and now coordinates discovery software and library systems. She is also a PhD candidate in JMU's School of Strategic Leadership Studies. She is a proud graduate of the College of Information Studies at the University of Maryland, College Park. Jody is currently the editor of the *Journal of Web Librarianship* and has recently published two books, *Comic Book Collections for Libraries*, with Bryan D. Fagan (Libraries Unlimited, 2011), and *Web Project Management for Academic Libraries* (Chandos, 2009), with Jennifer A. Keach.

David Dahl is Information Technology Librarian at Towson University where he provides leadership in the Library's evaluation, selection, and implementation of new technologies, Web services, and research tools. He has assumed primary responsibility for maintaining Towson's instance of WorldCat Local and evaluating the ever-changing discovery tool landscape. David holds Master's degrees in Library Science and Information Science from Indiana University and Bachelor's degrees in Music Composition and Comparative Literature. His research interests range from creativity to organizational informatics to mobile technologies. His main interest is improving organizational processes and workflows through the use of technology and common sense. David is currently Vice President/President-Elect of the Maryland Chapter of ACRL.

Elias Darraj is a Senior Content Manager at CareFirst in Baltimore Maryland.

Mark Dehmlow is the Head of the Web and Information Technology Systems Department at the Hesburgh Libraries at the University of Notre Dame. He is responsible for the overall Web presence, the integrated library system, and ancillary productivity tools, as well as the server, programming, and technology infrastructure that supports most of the forward facing and internal productivity tools for the Hesburgh Libraries. Prior to his current position, Mark also held the positions of Digital Initiatives Librarian and Electronic Services Librarian, positions in which he created and maintained Web based discovery tools and services including Notre Dame's locally developed eReserves system. Mark's professional interests are in Web based discovery and services, library management systems, open source software development in libraries, system infrastructure, and user engagement. Mark has a Master of Science in Library and Information Science from the University of Illinois.

Scott Dennis is Humanities Librarian and Coordinator of Core Electronic Resources at the University of Michigan Library. He has been a reference librarian with collection development and management responsibilities for over 20 years, first at Marquette University in Milwaukee, Wisconsin and since 1997 at U-M Ann Arbor, where has contributed to the development and implementation of new methods to present and interconnect electronic resources in more user-friendly ways, via browse lists, next-generation online catalogs, cross-search engines, OpenURL linking, search facets, and "web-scale" discovery environments. He lectures regularly at the University of Michigan School of Information and is the 2011 recipient of U-M's University Librarian Achievement Award. He received his BA in Philosophy from the University of Chicago, his MA in English from the University of California-Berkeley, and his MILS from the University of Michigan.

Rachel A. Erb is the Electronic Resources Management Librarian at Colorado State University. Professor Erb earned her M.S. in Library Science at Florida State University, an M.A. in Slavic Languages and Literatures at Ohio State University, and a B.A. with distinction at Dickinson College. Professor Erb has taught undergraduate classes in Technical Services and in 19th Century Russian Literature. She has worked for over a decade in technical services with the last several focusing on ILS management and emerging technologies. She was the former Systems/Virtual Services Librarian at the University of Nebraska at Omaha.

Nina Exner is the Evening Services Librarian (Assistant Professor) at the F. D. Bluford Library at North Carolina Agricultural and Technical State University. She is a member of the steering committee of the Distance Learning Interest Group of the North Carolina Library Association and the social media project coordinator for BLINC: Business Librarianship in North Carolina. She received her MLS from North Carolina Central University and an MA from the University of North Carolina at Greensboro. Nina is currently a part-time Doctoral student at the University of North Carolina. Her research interests include issues in user information seeking experiences as well as administrative strategies for encouraging scholarly productivity among academic librarians.

Angi Herold Faiks is Associate Library Director for Collection Development and Discovery at Macalester College's DeWitt Wallace Library. She is a graduate of the University of Illinois' School of Library and Information Science. Angi oversees the implementation and related development of

WorldCat Local. In her 15 years in librarianship, Angi has been deeply involved in the implementation and development of systems that enhance user access to rich library collections.

Nancy Falciani-White is leader of the Teaching and Outreach Group at Buswell Memorial Library, Wheaton College (IL). In this role she oversees the areas of instruction, outreach, reference, educational technology, and assessment. She is in the process of completing her Ed.D. in Instructional Technology at Northern Illinois University. Current research interests include the many components of the activity of research, including reading, information seeking, information processing, and information organization and management. She is also interested in the ways in which those components interact and how they are affected by technological developments. Other research interests include the role of academic libraries in higher education and library science curriculum and education.

Lynnette Fields is the Director of Technical Services at Southern Illinois University Edwardsville. Prior to her appointment as Director she was a Catalog and Metadata Librarian. Lynnette has also been a Cataloging Trainer for The MARC of Quality, the Database Consultant for the Lewis and Clark Library System, and a Catalog Librarian for St. Louis Public Library. Lynnette is an SCCTP trainer and has been an adjunct instructor for the University of Missouri, School of Information Science & Learning Technologies. She holds an M.A. in Library Science from the University of Missouri.

Kathleen Folger is Electronic Resources Officer at the University of Michigan Library. She has more than a decade of experience in negotiating and licensing electronic resources for the campus and has participated in multiple library projects and initiatives designed to facilitate and enhance access to those resources. Kathleen currently chairs the NISO Business Information Topic Committee and serves as a member of the NISO Architecture Committee. Kathleen received her Master of Library Science degree from North Carolina Central University in Durham, NC and her Bachelor of Arts degree from Meredith College in Raleigh, NC. She has worked at the University of Michigan Library since 1995 in a variety of public service and collection development positions.

Amy Foster is an Associate Professor and the Team Leader for Cataloging & Processing at Montana State University. Amy had a lead role in the WorldCat Local trial for MSU, and was involved in the early stages of implementing Summon. She received her MS in Library Science from the University of North Texas, and has a BS in Sociology from Montana State University.

Anita Foster is the Electronic Resources Librarian at Illinois State University's Milner Library. She has worked with library systems and technologies for 16 years. She has extensive experience in implementing new systems, including electronic resource management systems, federated search, and resource discovery systems. She led task forces that chose and implemented one of the first resource discovery systems in the state of Illinois. Anita's interests include end user experiences and the impact of changes in information seeking behavior on electronic resource usage.

Janet (Jan) Fransen is a liaison librarian at the University of Minnesota, working primarily with students and faculty in the Aerospace Engineering, Computer Science, Electrical Engineering, and History of Science and Technology fields. Jan was a member of all three Discoverability groups, acting as a voice for the needs of different user communities. Her interests include analyzing the types of literature used by researchers in engineering and computer science, and finding ways to educate new researchers on the breadth of material that will be useful to them.

Dace Freivalds is Associate Librarian and Head, Department for Information Technologies at the Pennsylvania State University Libraries in University Park, PA. She has over 25 years of experience in library information technology, and has been involved in the design and implementation of both locally developed and commercial library management systems at Penn State. Over the years, Dace's main interest has been in making the Libraries' resources accessible by users, and most recently she co-chaired the teams that selected and implemented Penn State University Libraries' discovery system. Dace is also the sponsor of the Libraries' newly formed Discovery and Access Steering Team that is responsible for ensuring a cohesive and integrated search experience across all of the Libraries' discovery and access products.

LeiLani Freund is currently a reference librarian and the linguistics selector and subject specialist at the University of Florida's Library West Humanities and Social Sciences (HSS) Branch Library. She served in 2010 as the Interim Chair of Library West following two years as Associate Chair. Other assignments have included the Chair of the HSS Reference Services Department, Electronic Resources Coordinator, and Head of Interlibrary Loan. As the co-chair of the Resource Navigation Group, LeiLani played a leading role in the 2006 evaluation and implementation of MetaLib at the University of Florida and is now part of the task group evaluating the UF pilot implementation of the Summon OneSearch product. Her research focus is on reference models, development and evolution of information commons, and the user experience.

Lara Friedman-Shedlov is Description and Access Archivist for the Kautz Family YMCA Archives, a unit of the Department of Archives and Special Collections at the University of Minnesota Libraries. She previously worked as an archivist for the Minnesota Historical Society. For the past 15+ years, her work has focused primarily on the challenges of making archival material discoverable, a perspective she brought to the table as a member of all three of the Libraries' Discoverability groups. Other interests include the uses of social media in libraries/archives and information technology in general. She has been an active member of the Midwest Archives Conference and the Rare Books and Manuscripts Section (RBMS) of the Association of College and Research Libraries (ACRL).

Katy Gabrio is the Electronic Resources & Serials librarian at Macalester College in St. Paul, MN. Katy received her MLIS from University of Wisconsin - Madison. During her career she has been involved in the selection, implementation, and management of ILS', federated search products, and the WorldCat Local discovery system.

Scott Garrison is Dean of the Ferris Library for Information, Technology and Education at Ferris State University. He received his undergraduate degree from UC San Diego, and his MLS from UCLA. His focus is to leverage the flux, uncertainty and disruption libraries face, existing and new tools and user behavior, and key relationships across campuses and regions to foster greater user, library, and institutional success. In his former role as Associate Dean for Public Services and Technology at Western

Michigan University (WMU) Libraries, he led the first Summon implementation in Michigan as the final Summon beta partner, and successfully advocated for including a Summon search box in WMU's e-earning and portal systems.

Jonathan (Yoni) Glaser is a Senior Business Analyst at a Fortune 500 company based in Baltimore, Maryland. He has worked on several large projects that range from a customer acquisition portal to a large-scale internal application. Yoni has extensive experience in prototyping IT solutions that are user-friendly. He graduated from the University of Massachusetts-Amherst with a Bachelor's degree in Finance, and is currently completing a Graduate Certificate in Interaction Design and Information Architecture from the University of Baltimore.

Tyler Goldberg is Head of Technical Services at Ekstrom Library at the University of Louisville. She has had several positions over the last 32 years at the University of Louisville, including Principal Cataloger and Head, Serials Cataloging. She has published articles and given presentations on a variety of technical services subjects, including serials management and metadata for stereographs. She has been actively involved in the implementation of several different integrated library systems over the years, and was instrumental in the realization of the University Libraries' first discovery tool.

Courtney Greene is Head of the Digital User Experience department at Indiana University Bloomington Libraries. Her professional interests are focused on the intersection of emerging technologies and library public services, and on implementing user-centered design methods and philosophies in libraries. She has presented and written on a variety of topics, most recently on the selection and implementation of discovery tools and on mobile services for libraries, including co-authoring a book, *The Anywhere Library: A Primer for the Mobile Web*. She earned her Master of Library Science degree, as well as a BA in English and Journalism, from Indiana University Bloomington, and holds a Master of Science in Human-Computer Interaction from DePaul University in Chicago.

Melanie Griffin is an Assistant Librarian in Special & Digital Collections at the University of South Florida, where she recently served as the Special Collections representative to the USF Libraries task force charged with selecting a discovery tool. She holds a MLIS and an MA in English literature, both from the University of South Carolina. Her research interests include resource description and access in special collections and archival repositories.

Pamela (Pam) Harpel-Burke is catalog librarian at Hofstra University in Hempstead, NY. In her 23 years in systems and cataloging at academic, public and special libraries, her emphasis was not on following rules but on making information available to library users. She believes that discovery systems are the greatest step towards ease of access to all the library's resources. She served for Association for Library Collections & Technical Services, Cataloging and Classification Section as Vice-Chair/Chair for the Cataloging Management Discussion Group (2003/2004 term) and the Copy Cataloging Discussion Group(2004/2005 term). She also served two terms on the Catalog Use Committee (2004-2006; 2006-2008) for Reference and User Services Association, Reference Services Section.

Deborah Henry is a librarian with over 20 years' experience in research, reference and instruction at Poynter Library, University of South Florida St. Petersburg. She has held memberships and leadership roles in library associations and is particularly active in the Florida Library Association. Mrs. Henry served on a USF system-wide committee exploring and evaluating discovery service products. Her research and publications focus on academic librarianship, tenure and promotion issues, and reference services. Along with co-authors Tina Neville and Bruce Neville, she published the book "Science & Technology Research: Writing Strategies for Students" (Scarecrow Press, 2002).

Lucy Holman is currently the Director of Langsdale Library and Associate Professor in the Division of Science Information Arts and Technologies at the University of Baltimore, where she teaches graduate courses in information architecture and user research methods. She received her MSLS from the University of North Carolina at Chapel Hill, with a focus on academic librarianship and user education/information literacy, and her doctorate in Communications Design from the University of Baltimore. Her Doctoral dissertation research explored college students' mental models of information retrieval and her subsequent work examines how students approach research tools. Prior to her current position at the University of Baltimore, she served as Dean of Library and Instructional Resources at Harford Community College in Bel Air, MD; Associate Director and Head of Reference at Langsdale Library; and reference librarian at the University of Maryland Baltimore County.

Alice Hom is a graphic designer and database consultant at the Easter Island Statue Project. She has participated in five survey seasons and uses insights on the usage of data in the field to design an online archaeological inventory database enabling data sharing between researchers. She is interested in experience design, visualization, and education: using design as a means to inform and instruct. She has a BFA in Design from the University of California, Los Angeles and is a MFA candidate in Graphic Design at Maryland Institute College of Art.

Amy Hoseth is an Assistant Professor at Colorado State University's Morgan Library in Fort Collins, where she serves as liaison to the School of Education and the Departments of Psychology and Philosophy. Prior to joining CSU, Amy was the communications coordinator for the LibQUAL+ survey program at the Association of Research Libraries (ARL) in Washington, DC. She holds an MLS degree from the University of Maryland at College Park and a BA degree from Drake University in Des Moines, Iowa. Amy's research interests include discovery services, users' interactions with and perceptions of e-books, and the impact of patron-driven acquisitions on library collections.

Amy S. Jackson is an Assistant Professor and Digital Initiatives Librarian at the University of New Mexico (UNM) Libraries. In this position, she works with digital projects, the institutional repository, and scholarly communications. Prior to moving to New Mexico, Amy was the project coordinator for the IMLS-funded Digital Collections and Content project at the University of Illinois at Urbana-Champaign, a project focused on harvesting metadata from OAI-PMH compliant data providers. Amy received her MLIS from Simmons College in Boston and also holds a Master of Music degree from the Peabody Institute of the Johns Hopkins University. Her research interests include metadata interoperability and enhancing discoverability of electronic resources.

Anna Marie Johnson is Head of Reference and Information Literacy at Ekstrom Library, University of Louisville. Before stepping into the role of department head, she worked as Coordinator of Information Literacy for 13 years. Since 2001, she has compiled the annual bibliography for library instruction and information literacy published in *Reference Services Review* and has published on a variety of user instruction issues in several other venues including *Research Strategies, Journal of Education in Library and Information Science*, and *portal: Libraries and the Academy*. Her interest in discovery tools comes out of this work in IL and also from serving as co-chair of the OPAC workgroup at her institution.

Karen Keiller is the Director of Information Services and System at the University of New Brunswick Saint John, which includes library and student technology services in the Hans W. Klohn Commons, information technology and networking, and educational and classroom technology. She received her Master of Library and Information Science from the University of Western Ontario and her BA (honours) in Geography from the University of Winnipeg. Prior to joining UNB Saint John in 2010 she headed up library technology at the University of Manitoba, was the acting University Librarian at University of Winnipeg and has held positions as information literacy coordinator, access and collection development coordinator, and reference librarian at Red River College and the University of Winnipeg. Karen is frequent speaker at library conferences on topics usually related to new technology in libraries and teaching and learning. As chair of the Student Technology Fee Committee she championed the iPad Pilot Project and the UNBSJ Mobile App.

Jan Kemp is Assistant Dean for Public Services at the University of Texas at San Antonio Libraries. She received her MLS from the University of Texas at Austin and the MS in Management Information Systems from Texas Tech University. Her 30 years of experience in academic libraries includes both technical and public services positions. She has been active in the Association of College and Research Libraries and currently serves on the University Libraries Section Executive Board as an At Large Member, and as the leader of the ACRL Heads of Public Services Discussion Group. Her experience implementing discovery tools includes participating in the evaluation of discovery service options at the UTSA Libraries and coordinating public services staff input for UTSA's Summon implementation. Her interests include new models for public services, the effects of discovery services on use of collections, and change management in academic libraries.

Juliet Kerico holds an MLS from the University of Illinois at Champaign-Urbana and an MA in Literature from Case Western Reserve University. She held the diverse positions of Humanities Librarian, Acting Head of Reference & Instruction, and Electronic Resources Librarian while working at Indiana State University. At Southern Illinois University—Edwardsville, she served as the Science and Health Sciences Librarian. Ms. Kerico's research interests include user behavior and Web usability.

Jacob Koehler is the Collection Management and Discovery Services Librarian at The College of Wooster, where he oversees both traditional and more modern technical services functions. He received an MLIS from Kent State University in 2008. His current research interests are: The discovery layer user experience, management issues in libraries, and collaboration among library technical services departments.

Randy Kuehn is the Systems Librarian and the University of Louisville.

Rebecca L. Lubas is currently Director of cataloging and discovery services at the University of New Mexico Libraries. Before coming to New Mexico in 2008, she was at the Massachusetts Institute of Technology (MIT) Libraries as head of cataloging and metadata services and special formats cataloger. She was a founding member of MIT Libraries' Metadata Services Unit. Prior to her time at MIT, she was serials cataloger and audiovisual cataloger at Ball State University. She was President of the Online Audiovisual Catalogers in 2005 and a featured speaker at Library Week in Kosovo in 2006. She has an MA in English literature from Ball State University and an MLIS from Louisiana State University.

Binky Lush is a Programmer/Analyst in the Department for Information Technologies at the Pennsylvania State University Libraries in University Park, PA. She co-chaired the teams that led to the selection and implementation of the Penn State University Libraries' discovery system and currently co-chairs the Libraries' newly formed Discovery and Access Steering Team charged with ensuring a cohesive and integrated search experience across all of the Libraries' discovery and access products. Binky's research interests include emerging technologies, discovery and access of Libraries' resources, and Web accessibility.

Patricia MacDonald is Associate University Librarian for Administrative Services at Towson University, where she manages assessment, human resources, staff development, budgeting, security, and facilities activities; oversees marketing initiatives; and participates in strategic planning and decision-making for the library. Prior to Towson, she has 15 years of experience as the head of research and instruction at both an academic and a public library. Her research interests focus on user-centered access to library services and resources, as well as organizational development. Patricia completed work for a graduate certificate in Information Design from the University of Baltimore School of Information Architecture and Interaction Design. She also has an M.L.S. from the University of Maryland, College Park; an M.A.T. degree from Duke University; and a B.A. in English from the University of California, Berkeley. She is the outgoing Convener of the ACRL Residency Interest Group and served as the President of the Maryland Chapter of ACRL.

Heather Mathieson was a graduate student at the University of Baltimore.

Meris Mandernach is the Collection Management Librarian and Associate Professor in Libraries & Educational Technologies at James Madison University. She's participated on project teams to implement and evaluate JMU's discovery tool, EBSCO Discovery Service, and examines access to resources not covered through discovery. She graduated from the GSLIS program at the University of Illinois at Urbana-Champaign. Her other research interests are varied and include library collection analysis, librarian training, embedding information literacy into the chemistry curriculum, and mentoring and recruitment in libraries.

Monica Metz-Wiseman is the Coordinator for Electronic Collections at the University of South Florida (USF). She headed the USF Libraries Discovery Services Task Force in the selection as well as the implementation of USF's discovery tool, EBSCO's EDS. Monica also served as chair for the implementation of OCLC's WorldCat Local and has responsibilities for the continued development of this tool at USF. She was Project Coordinator for the USF Virtual Library Project for five years preceded by her tenure as Head of Reference, USF Tampa Library. Her research area is online resources and services in academic libraries. Monica holds a M.L.S. from the University of Pittsburgh.

Mary Mintz is Associate Director for Outreach at American University in Washington, D.C. She is also the Senior Reference and Instruction Librarian at American. Prior to her current positions she was Head of Reference at American for nine years and had also previously served as Coordinator of Library Instruction. She earned her undergraduate degree in English at Davidson College and received her Master of Science in Library Science from the University of North Carolina at Chapel Hill. She also holds a Master's degree in English from North Carolina State University. Ms. Mintz was part of the American University Library team that received ACRL's first Best Practices in Marketing Academic and Research Libraries @your library Award.

Shane Nackerud (MLS, Indiana University 1996) is the Director of Web Development for the University of Minnesota Libraries. In this role, Shane manages the University Libraries' web presence and web application development. Shane's research interests include library use assessment, resource integration, and web design.

Deane Nettles is a Freelance Art Director in Baltimore, Maryland. He is committed to clearly communicating for his clients, which have included National Geographic, the International Monetary Fund and the U.S. Postal Service. He has a BA in News Journalism from Kent State University and is an MFA candidate in Integrated Design at the University of Baltimore. In addition, he teaches graphic design at area colleges and is a past president and Life Member of the Art Directors Club of Metropolitan Washington.

Pat Nicholls is the Coordinator of Libraries Systems at the University of Manitoba. Libraries Systems includes the ILS (SirsiDynix' Symphony), link resolver and ERM (ExLibris SFX and Verde), and discovery tool (SerialsSolutions Summon). Two other academic libraries in the province, Collège Universitaire de Saint-Boniface and University College of the North also use the ILS. Pat Nicholls has been responsible for implementing 3 integrated library systems as well as Summon. She received her Master of Library and Information Science and her MA in History from the University of Western Ontario and her BA from Waterloo Lutheran University. Research and presentations have included "Keyword Searching and Subject Headings at the University of Manitoba Libraries" and "Making our Catalogue Usable," a presentation at the 2011 COSUGI Conference in Phoenix, Arizona.

David Noe is an Assistant Professor and the Digital Services Librarian for the Olin Library at Rollins. He has been working in library systems for six years. His main interests are unified discovery layers, data migration, open/community source library software, and open access publishing and institutional repositories. He received his MLIS from the University of Alabama in 2005.

Johan Oberg is a graduate of the University of Michigan's School of Information, with a focus on Human-Computer Interaction; Johan is responsible for the Macalester College Library's Web presence. As part of this responsibility, he works to create effective user experiences that efficiently connect users to the digital content and services provided by the Library. Johan is experienced with usability and user interface design and has broad experience with library services. He is the former chair of the American Library Association's Video Round Table, and the former chair of the Association of Colleges and Research Libraries' Media Resources Discussion Group.

Lisa O'Hara is the Head, Discovery and Delivery Services at the University of Manitoba Libraries where she is responsible for the Technical Services, Libraries Systems, Digital Initiatives, Web Usability and Document Delivery departments. Lisa graduated with a MLS from the University of Toronto and has worked in technical services in academic, special and public libraries during her career. She has written on numerous topics and been a frequent speaker at conferences including Electronic Resources and Libraries, COSUGI, ELUNA, and the Charleston Conference and is a member of the OCLC Global Council as well as the Pan-Canadian Working Group on Cataloguing with RDA.

Tod A. Olson helps scholars find the materials they need. He has worked in library computing for over two decades, making software work in ways the library and its patrons' desire. This includes working with and customizing Greenstone, a few generations of catalogs, and federated search systems. Tod has done usability work on these interfaces and has been involved in other assessment activities, trying to remove obstacles from the paths of library users. He also serves as a local expert on identity management and Shibboleth. In 2005, Tod received his MSLIS from the University of Illinois at Urbana-Champaign. He is currently employed as a Systems Librarian in the Integrated Library Systems group at the University of Chicago.

Jennifer Palmisano is Senior Manager for Library Systems at the Center for Jewish History in New York City. She received her Master's degree in Library and Information Science from Pratt Institute in 2007. She has four years' experience managing library systems and her interests range from library systems and cataloging to electronic resources and Web reporting. Jennifer is dedicated to making library, archives, and museums more accessible to the public through her work with library systems and professional associations. She was the Center for Jewish History's project manager for implementing ExLibris' Primo and continues to lead other projects to forward the Center's mission and facilitate greater access to their collections.

Felicia Palsson is the Library Instruction Coordinator at Sonoma State University. She previously held the position of Distance Learning and Outreach Librarian at the University of Southern California. Felicia earned her MLIS from San Jose State University and a BA in Philosophy from UC Berkeley. Felicia teaches information literacy, media literacy, and critical thinking skills to undergraduates, both in the classroom and online using a variety of e-learning technologies. In addition to teaching, her interests include student learning assessment, user experience and user-centered design. She was the lead usability librarian at the University of Southern California for three years. Now at Sonoma State, she is integrating her knowledge of user-centered design into e-learning tools and instructional design using Moodle.

Billie Peterson-Lugo is the Director for Resources and Collection Management Services and Associate Professor in the Electronic Library at Baylor University. She oversees the Baylor University Libraries' digitization initiatives, online systems and also works with electronic resources, scholarly communication, and copyright. She co-chairs the libraries' Scholarly Communication Task Force, presents information on copyright to faculty, students, and staff, works to increase campus awareness of scholar communication issues, and assists in the investigation and implementation of new initiatives, such as web scale discovery services. Since 1993, she has written a quarterly column, "Tech Talk," for the American Library Association *Library Instruction Round Table Newsletter.* Additionally, she has served in a number of volunteer capacities for the American Library Association, including the ALA Web Advisory Committee, ALA Sage New Media Scholarship Committee, Carroll Preston Baber Research Grant Committee, and the LIRT Electronic Resources Manager.

Christian Poehlmann has extensive experience as a Business Librarian. He is currently the Bibliographer for Business and Economics at University at Albany, SUNY, where he is responsible for collecting materials in these disciplines as well as teaching Information Literacy to undergraduate and graduate students. He has held this position since March of 2012. He was also a Business Librarian at the University of Notre Dame and University of Washington. Additionally, he was the Electronic Resources Librarian, and head of the Electronic Resources Unit at the University of Florida from 2008 to 2012. In this role, he was responsible for the acquisition and access for all electronic resources. Additionally, he was responsible for the selection, implementation, and maintenance of a discovery solution.

Dale Poulter received a Bachelor's degree in Chemical Engineering in 1987 from Texas Tech University and a Master's in library science in 1996 from University of North Texas. He worked at Texas Tech as a systems manager before coming to Vanderbilt University to work with the IRIS and ATHENA virtual catalogs. He then began working with the SirsiDynix ILS and was a member of the team from Vanderbilt during the development partnership for the Primo discovery system. In 2011 Dale was name the Coordinator of Search and Core Services. In this role he is responsible for administration and development coordination of the search products used by Vanderbilt as well as coordinating the team that maintains desktop and server support.

Anne Prestamo is Associate Dean for Collection & Technology Services and the Claud D. Kniffin Professor of Library Service and Education at the Oklahoma State University Libraries. She received her undergraduate degree from Kent State University, her MLIS from the University of Wisconsin–Milwaukee, and Doctorate from Oklahoma State University. Her responsibilities focus on evaluation and implementation of electronic services and resources. She has garnered a reputation for thoughtful and creative risk-taking as she works diligently to deploy emerging technologies to enhance the user experience. The value of the relationships that she has built has been evidenced by numerous invitations to participate in focus groups and beta tests for new products and platforms. Oklahoma State University, along with Dartmouth College, served as the beta development partners for Serials Solutions Web-scale discovery service, Summon.

Tammera Race is an Assistant Professor and Science & Technology Catalog Librarian at Western Kentucky University. She holds a MLIS from the School of Information Studies, University of Wisconsin-Milwaukee, an MS in Horticultural Science from the University of Florida, and a BA in Environmental Studies from New College of Florida. Combining her conservation and environmental education experience with her library work, Tammera's research interests include the history of women in botany, providing access to scientific gray literature, and the importance of accident in the discovery of new information.

Juan Carlos Rodríguez is the Associate Dean of Technology & Information Services at Grand Valley State University where he leads the library technology and systems department, the technical services and e-resources management department and the access services department. He has over 20 years' experience working with information technologies in academic libraries. Mr. Rodríguez's interests include: integrating emerging technologies into libraries and the development of new and innovative learning environments. He is also dedicated to the recruitment and mentoring of minority students into higher education and the library profession. Mr. Rodríguez currently serves on the Board of Directors of REFORMA (The National Association to Promote Library & Information Services to Latinos and the Spanish-Speaking) and has been an active member of LITA and EDUCAUSE. He is a 2008 fellow of the Frye Leadership Institute and a 2012 UCLA Senior Fellow. He holds an M.L.I.S. from UCLA and a B.A. from UC Riverside.

Doralyn Rossmann has served as Collection Development Librarian at the Montana State University (MSU) Library since 2008. She has an MSLS and a Bachelor of Arts in Political Science and English from the University of North Carolina at Chapel Hill and has a Master's in Public Administration from MSU. Her previous positions at the University of Wyoming, Rice University, and the University of Illinois at Chicago include Reference, Systems, Multimedia Projects, and GIS/Data Librarianship. Her current research focuses on public budgeting, Web-scale discovery tools, and managing e-book collections. In 2012, she is chairing a committee assessing MSU's Summon implementation. She has presented in many venues including the Electronic Resources & Libraries conference, the ACRL National Conference, the Charleston Conference, and the Qualitative and Quantitative Methods in Libraries conference. Her most recent articles appear in *Serials* and *Public Administration Review.*

Suzanne M. Schadl is an Assistant Professor and Curator of Latino and Latin American Collections at the University of New Mexico (UNM) Libraries. She manages the University Libraries' extensive Spanish and Portuguese language collections, administering budgets, purchases and major gifts for print and electronic collections in library circulation and special collections. Dr. Schadl also engages cross-departmentally and cross-institutionally in outreach initiatives which promote these collections locally, nationally and internationally. A strong advocate for the maintenance of significant print collections, particularly in underrepresented languages and cultures, Dr. Schadl also supports innovative Web collection development and management.

Colleen Seale currently serves as the Collection Manager for Humanities & Social Sciences Reference and Women's and Gender Studies at the George A. Smathers Libraries, University of Florida. She has worked at the University of Florida for over twenty years and has published on various topics related to the academic library environment. She recently co-authored a technology fee proposal to implement a next-generation search and discovery service at the University of Florida which was funded in 2011. She now serves on a task group to evaluate the selection and pilot implementation of the Summon Web-Scale Discovery Service.

Iyanna Sims is currently the Systems Librarian at North Carolina Agricultural and Technical State University. She received her Master of Library Science degree from Clark Atlanta University. She has experience working in special and academic libraries. Iyanna's professional interests include library technology and a budding interest in recruitment.

Graham Stone (BSc (Hons), DipILS, MCLIP, FHEA) is Information Resources Manager at the University of Huddersfield and has 17 years' experience in working in academic libraries. He is responsible for the library information resources budget, the management and operation of the Acquisitions and Journals and E-Resources Teams and University Repository. He is also leading the University of Huddersfield Press initiative. Graham has managed a number of JISC funded projects including the Library Impact Data Project and the Huddersfield Open Access Publishing project. He is UKSG Publications Officer and a member of the Electronic Information Resources Working Group (EIRWG), the PALS metadata and interoperability working group, and chair of the JISC Collections Journal Archives Advisory Board.

Nicole Theis-Mahon is the Head of Collection Development and Acquisitions for the Health Sciences Libraries at the University of Minnesota. She has been a member of the University of Minnesota's Discoverability 2 work group where her work focused on a vision for discoverability and the different needs of the various user communities at the University of Minnesota. She is also a member of the Discoverability 3 group, which is investigating Web-scale discovery tools.

Stacie Traill is the Cartographic and Electronic Resources Cataloging Coordinator at the University of Minnesota. She received her MLIS from the University of Wisconsin-Milwaukee in 2003. She was a member of the working groups for the first and second phases of the University of Minnesota's Discoverability project, and has contributed to implementation efforts for a number of Libraries-wide systems for metadata management and discovery. She has been involved in standards and best practices development for cataloging non-book resources through OLAC's Cataloging Policy Committee. Her research is focused on the quality issues and management challenges surrounding metadata for electronic resources.

June Thoburn is Head of Content Services and Library Systems at Northumbria University Library (UK), a role which encompasses resource acquisition, metadata, access, library computer systems and compliance. She has been responsible for the development of resource discovery systems at Northumbria from early OPACs through federated search to the current generation of Web-scale discovery services like Summon. She is also actively involved in library procurement issues and is Chair of the North Eastern and Yorkshire Academic Libraries Purchasing Consortium Books Group (UK) which manages monograph / e-book supply contracts for 22 academic libraries in the region, and is a member of the national Joint Consortia Group which negotiated a UK wide national monographs supply contract.

Michael Upfold is the CONSORT Library System Manager for the Five Colleges of Ohio. He has been in this position for over eleven years, and in that time has been involved in numerous projects with the consortium. He was the coordinator of the search committee that investigated various discovery layer products, and once the consortium chose to implement Summon, was primarily responsible for retrieving relevant records from the shared catalog and delivering them to Serials Solutions.

Ken Varnum is Web Systems Manager at the University of Michigan Library. He has almost 20 years of experience developing patron-focused Web-based information services. At U-M, Ken has focused on knocking down information silos and building a user-focused discovery tools. In 2009, he led a U-M project to integrate Summon into its Drupal Web site with a Drupal module that has since been made public. He is a member of the 2013 LITA National Forum planning committee and serves on the NISO Open Discovery Initiative workgroup. Ken received his MA in Information & Library Science from the University of Michigan and his Bachelor of Arts from Grinnell College. He writes and speaks about libraries and technology. His first book, "Drupal in Libraries," was published in spring 2012.

Jason Vaughan is Director of Library Technologies and full professor at the University of Nevada, Las Vegas. In this capacity he serves as a senior administrator and provides overall leadership for three departments within the UNLV Libraries: Digital Collections, Library Systems, and Web and Application Development Services. Vaughan holds an MLS from the University of North Carolina, Chapel Hill, and has published and presented extensively on library and library technology topics, including library automation, discovery services, digitization, planning, and policy. He is the author of the January 2011 "Library Technology Reports" on Web-scale Discovery Services. To date Vaughan has served as co-PI on multiple federal grants totaling nearly a half million dollars.

Aronya Waller is employed as a course developer for Laureate Education, Inc. and is responsible for creating and developing curriculums for online graduate programs. She is adept in integrating media and technology components in classroom lessons and teaching environments to promote and enhance the student learning experience. Aronya has a Bachelor of Arts in Journalism and a Master of Arts in Producing for Film and Video from American University located in Washington, D.C. Aronya received a Graduate Certificate in Information Design from the University of Baltimore. She is a member of Sigma Gamma Rho Sorority, Inc. and the Emerging Leaders United of the United Way of Central Maryland.

Scott Walter is the University Librarian at DePaul University. Previously, Scott was the Associate University Librarian for Services and Associate Dean of Libraries at the University of Illinois at Urbana-Champaign. He has also served as Assistant Dean of Libraries for Information & Instructional Services at the University of Kansas, Interim Assistant Director of Libraries for Public Services & Outreach at Washington State University, Collection Manager for Education at The Ohio State University Libraries, and as Humanities and Education Reference Librarian at the University of Missouri-Kansas City. Scott received his M.A. in Russian Area Studies from Georgetown University, his M.A. in Education from American University, and his M.L.S. and M.S. in History & Philosophy of Education from Indiana University. Scott completed his Ph.D. in Higher Education Administration at Washington State University in 2005.

Peter Webster is Associate University Librarian, Information Technology Services at the Patrick Power Library, Saint Mary's University, where he has worked since 1993. He holds an MLS from Dalhousie University. He has served on management and technical committees for the NOVANET academic library consortium and the Council of Atlantic University Libraries / Le Conseil des bibliothèques universitaires de l'Atlantique" (CAUL-CBUA). His current work includes development of the OCLC

WorldCat Local discovery service among NOVANET and CAUL-CBUA member libraries. Peter's recent publications include *The Development of Electronic Journal Infrastructure* in "The Handbook of Public Information Systems," 3rd edition, 2010. "Managing Electronic Resources, Changing Roles for Libraries," Chandos, Oxford, 2008, and "Challenges for Federated Searching" (Internet Reference Services Quarterly, 12(3/4), 2007). He has presented at conferences including Computers in Libraries, Library and Information Technology (LITA) National Forum, ACCESS, The American Library Association (ALA), and The Canadian Library Association (CLA).

Andrew Welch is the Librarian for Discovery Services & Technology at Drake University's Cowles Library. In addition to coordinating the Library's discovery efforts, he manages the Library's integrated library system. He has 12 years of experience working with library technology and received his Master of Arts in Library and Information Science from the University of Iowa in 2003. He has served as an Innovative Users Group Functional Expert for Patron Functions in the Web OPAC, and his current research interests include discovery tool usability, integrating third-party services into library discovery and implementing patron-driven acquisitions services in library discovery.

Sarah C. Williams is the Life Sciences Data Services Librarian at University of Illinois at Urbana-Champaign. She is a member of the Library's Web-scale discovery implementation team, which will be implementing Primo. Previously, Sarah was at Illinois State University's Milner Library, where she chaired the committee that planned for and implemented Milner's federated search engine and served on the committee that selected EBSCO Discovery Service as its replacement. Sarah's research interests include user-centered approaches to implementing federated search and Web-scale discovery systems. She has a Bachelor's degree in Soil and Crop Science from Purdue University, a MLS from Indiana University, and a Master's degree in Information Systems from Illinois State University.

728

Index